TENTH EDITION

PUBLIC
BUDGETING SYSTEMS

Robert D. Lee, Jr.
The Pennsylvania State
University
Professor Emeritus

Ronald W. Johnson
RTI International, Retired

Philip G. Joyce
University of Maryland
School of Public Policy

JONES & BARTLETT
LEARNING

World Headquarters
Jones & Bartlett Learning
5 Wall Street
Burlington, MA 01803
978-443-5000
info@jblearning.com
www.jblearning.com

Jones & Bartlett Learning books and products are available through most bookstores and online booksellers. To contact Jones & Bartlett Learning directly, call 800-832-0034, fax 978-443-8000, or visit our website, www.jblearning.com.

Production Credits
VP, Product Management: Amanda Martin
Director of Product Management: Laura Pagluica
Product Manager: Sophie Fleck Teague
Product Specialist: Sara Bempkins
Manager, Project Management: Lori Mortimer
Project Specialist: John Coakley
Senior Digital Project Specialist: Angela Dooley
Cover Design: Michael O'Donnell
Media Development Editor: Faith Brosnan

Rights Specialist: James Fortney
Senior Marketing Manager: Susanne Walker
Production Services Manager: Colleen Lamy
VP, Manufacturing and Inventory Control: Therese Connell
Composition: Exela Technologies
Printing and Binding: LSC Communications
Cover Image (Title Page, Chapter Opener):
   © Mihai_Andritoiu/Shutterstock

Library of Congress Cataloging-in-Publication Data
Names: Lee, Robert D. | Johnson, Ronald Wayne, 1942- | Joyce, Philip G., 1956-
Title: Public budgeting systems / Robert D. Lee, Jr., Ronald W. Johnson, Phillip G. Joyce.
Description: 10th Edition. | Burlington : Jones & Bartlett Learning, 2021. | Revised edition of the authors' Public budgeting systems, c2013. | Includes bibliographical references and index. | Summary: "This book, which has been in continuous use through 9 editions since it was first published in 1973, is a general text on public budgeting in the United States. Its intent is to provide an overview of the complex environment of budgeting in the public sector. It focuses on all three levels of government (federal, state and local) and on the various systems, processes and rules that affect the collection of revenues and the allocation and management of resources. The book is the most comprehensive and current treatment of what is the crucial topic that dictates the success or failure of governments at all levels. Current and prospective public managers, accordingly, often succeed or fail in their careers based in large part on whether they are intelligent consumers of financial data and have an adequate understanding of the budget process. By providing a detailed overview of all aspects of budgeting and financial management, the book enables students to gain an appropriate understanding of a complex topic"– Provided by publisher.
Identifiers: LCCN 2020018963 | ISBN 9781284198980 (paperback)
Subjects: LCSH: Budget–United States. | Budget process–United States. | Program budgeting–United States.
Classification: LCC HJ2051 .L4 2020 | DDC 352.4/80973–dc23
LC record available at https://lccn.loc.gov/20200189636048

Printed in the United States of America
24 23 22 21 20   10 9 8 7 6 5 4 3 2

Dedicated to

Ann, Rob, Tatiana, Craig, Dan, Cameron, and Bob

and to

Sally, Ron and Amber, Jennifer and Scott, Zac, Landen, Lucas, and Abi

and to

Rita, Christopher, Mariah, and Samuel

In addition, the authors dedicate this new edition to the thousands of students, colleagues, and practitioners with whom we have associated throughout our professional careers.

Brief Contents

Contents

Preface

This is a general book on public budgeting. Its purpose is to survey the current state of the art of budgeting among all levels of government in the United States. Where their inclusion is illustrative, examples from other countries and from some nongovernmental organizations are used. In addition, we emphasize methods by which financial decisions are reached within a system and ways in which different types of information are used in budgetary decision making. We stress the use of program information in a political system because budget reforms for decades have sought to introduce greater program considerations into financial decisions made in an inherently political process.

Budgeting is considered within the context of a system containing numerous components and relationships. A problem of such an approach is that because all things within a system are related, it is difficult to find an appropriate place to begin. Although we have divided the text into chapters, the reader should recognize that no single chapter can stand alone. Every chapter mentions some topics and issues that are treated elsewhere in the book.

A discussion of budgeting may be organized in various ways. Historical or chronological sequence is one possible method of organization, although this approach would require discussing every relevant topic for each time period. Another strategy is to arrange topics by level of government, with separate sections for local, state, and federal budgeting. Such an approach again would involve extensive rehashing of arguments and information. Yet another approach is to focus on phases of the budget cycle from preparation of the budget through auditing of past activities and expenditures. Rigid adherence to this approach

would be inappropriate because the budget cycle is not precisely defined and many issues cut across several phases of the cycle. Another approach would be to organize the discussion around the contrast between the technical and political problems of budgetary decision making.

The organization of this book is a combination of these approaches. Although we have not formally divided the book, readers will see that the chapters easily group into five sections plus an appendix discussing the beginning of the COVID-19 recession. The first four chapters lay out an overall framework for budgeting, budget decisions, and budgeting systems. The discussion is of U.S. budgeting, but the framework is applicable for the most part to any budgeting system whether national, state, or local, or whether it is in Europe or any other continent. Chapter 1, *Introduction*, begins with the concepts of budgets and budgeting systems. It provides a general discussion of the nature of budgetary decision making, including distinctions between private and public budgeting, the concepts of responsibility and accountability in budgeting, the possibility of rationality in decision making, and the nature of budgeting and budget systems. Chapter 2, *The Public Sector in Perspective*, addresses the issues of the size of the public sector and the arguments about what is appropriate for the public sector versus the private sector. It reviews the scope of the public sector, the magnitude of government, the sources of revenue, and the purposes of government expenditures.

Chapter 3, *Government, the Economy, and Economic Development* goes into detail, primarily for the United States, in discussing government's responsibilities for and impacts upon the overall health of the economy. Specific attention is given to the government's role in periods of economic recession, the two most recent recessions being the Great Recession of 2007–2009, the worst recession since the Great Depression, and the COVID-19 recession that may replace the Great Recession as the worst recession since the Depression. Because the book's manuscript was being finalized at the onset of COVID-19, most of the material on the COVID-19 recession is in a special appendix. Only the first two quarters of this recession are covered.

Budget cycles are the topic of Chapter 4, which summarizes the basic steps in budgeting: preparation and submission, approval, execution, and auditing. Chapter 4 forecasts the more detailed discussions in the following two groups of chapters. Together the first four chapters provide a basic framework for the remainder of the book.

The next six chapters are organized around budget decision-making processes and the principal actors involved from the initial steps of budget preparation through budget approval by legislative bodies. These chapters set up the subject of budget decisions for the annual, recurrent budget, also called the operating budget. The topics are revenues and expenditures; reform efforts that have focused on improving annual budget decisions; and detailed budget preparation and approval. A separate chapter is devoted to the U.S. congressional approval process and its outcomes. In these six chapters we treat budget decisions on both the preparation and approval sides, and on revenues and expenditures. We note that reform efforts have focused almost exclusively on the expenditure side.

The purpose of these six chapters is to provide the reader with an understanding of the types of deliberations involved in developing a proposed budget. Chapter 5, *Budgeting for Revenues: Income Taxes, Payroll Taxes, and Property Taxes*, considers the different sources from which governments obtain their funds, the criteria for evaluating revenue sources, and specific sources such as income, payroll, and property taxes. Chapter 6, *Budgeting for Revenues: Transaction-Based Revenue Sources*, continues the discussion of revenues by considering sales taxes, user fees, and the like. Chapter 7, *Budget Preparation: The Expenditure Side*, discusses early budget reform efforts and contemporary approaches to developing proposals for funding government programs, including the use of performance information to inform decision making. Chapter 8, *Budget Preparation: The Decision Process*, examines the process of putting together a budget proposal that includes recommended revenue and expenditure levels and then reviews the types of budget documents that are used in government.

Chapters 9 and 10 deal with the budget approval process. Chapter 9, *Budget Approval: The Role of the Legislature*, provides a general account of the processes used by legislative bodies. Chapter 10, *Budget Approval: The U.S. Congress*, separately treats the special factors and problems associated with congressional budgeting.

The third grouping contains two chapters that concentrate on the execution, audit, and evaluation phases of budgeting. Chapter 11, *Budget Execution*, considers the roles played by the chief executive, the budget office, and the line agencies. The chapter discusses the topics of tax administration, cash management, procurement, and risk management. Chapter 12, *Financial Management: Accounting, Reporting, and Auditing*, presents the basic features of accounting systems and processes, reviews the various types of reports that flow from accounting systems, and explains the types of audits that are conducted. These chapters provide considerable detail on how budgets actually are implemented once the formal decision cycle through approval is complete, and how honesty and integrity are attained, or at least sought, through the accounting, reporting, and auditing systems and processes.

The fourth group of chapters focuses entirely on systems for making long-term investment decisions and financing long-term capital assets, in contrast to the previous six chapters that focus mainly on the annual operating budget. Of course much of the political processes involved in decisions on the annual operating budget apply to capital budget decisions as well. However, Chapters 13 and 14 deal only with decisions to purchase assets or make investments that will not be consumed or exhausted in a single year and, in many cases at the state and local level, will be financed over a long time period, sometimes as much as 20 to 30 years.

Chapter 13, *Capital Assets: Planning and Budgeting, Analysis, and Management*, examines capital budgeting as a decision process. Decision processes that focus on long-term capital budgeting and methods for financing capital investments differ significantly from decision processes for the annual revenues and expenditures discussed in Chapters 5 through 10. Decisions about capital budgeting actually occur throughout the budget process, although capital programming occurs during budget execution. Chapter 14, *Capital Finance and Debt Management*, considers the financing of long-term capital investments through debt and equity instruments.

The final chapter is separate unto itself in that it is more about the interactions among levels of government—in the United States, federal, state, and local—and not on specific decision processes. Chapter 15, *Intergovernmental Relations*, examines the financial interactions among governments, the types of fiscal assistance in use, and possible means of restructuring intergovernmental relationships.

The book closes with some brief concluding remarks on themes that can be expected to receive considerable attention from budgeting practitioners and scholars in the next several years. The bibliographic note provides guidance on keeping informed about changes in the field of budgeting.

Overall, this edition retains much of the structure of the ninth edition. As with that edition, this *Tenth Edition* includes increased attention to some topics, such as the longer-term results of the massive fiscal and monetary programs that were put in place to combat the Great Recession's effects. Many chapters look at various aspects of the growth in size of the annual budget deficit and the overall national debt. In particular, the chapters on budgetary decision making and approval discuss the consequences of an increasingly partisan climate that has hampered the ability to complete budget approval on a timely basis. Various revenue sources, capital budgeting, and state and local debt management also receive additional attention. This text also reflects the continuing impact of the need to combat potential and actual acts of terrorism and of the large increase in the costs of natural disasters and their human and economic impacts. Text, tables, and exhibits have been completely updated.

Drs. Lee and Johnson began the first edition as faculty members in the Institute of Public Administration at The Pennsylvania State University. Ten editions later, Dr. Lee is Professor Emeritus of Public Administration and Professor Emeritus of Hotel, Restaurant, and Recreation Management at The Pennsylvania State University. Dr. Johnson has retired as Executive Vice President for International Development and Senior Policy Advisor at RTI International. This *Tenth Edition* is now the fourth edition in which Dr. Philip G. Joyce plays a key role as an integral member of our writing team. He is Professor of Public Policy and Senior Associate Dean at the University of Maryland's School of Public Policy. The COVID-19 pandemic affected the completion of the book in some ways. Drs. Lee and Johnson had more flexible schedules to incorporate early information on the COVID-19 recession into the book, including adding the appendix. Dr. Joyce, as a senior associate dean, experienced the challenges of keeping a major university functioning for students converting to online instruction midway through the semester, while still managing his roles in this new edition.

Our hope is that this new edition will be useful to readers from many backgrounds and with widely diverse purposes.

Acknowledgments

Having gone through nine previous editions, this *Tenth Edition* is the product of numerous individuals, not just its three authors. We are indebted to current and former colleagues at The Pennsylvania State University, RTI International, and the University of Maryland. Colleagues and students at other institutions, including a variety of colleges and universities, have provided valuable advice. Practitioners in the United States and many developing countries have helped refine our understanding with real-world situations. In preparing the book, we received considerable advice from expert practitioners in the executive and legislative branches of federal, state, and local governments and from their counterparts in nonprofit organizations. The responsibility for the final product, of course, belongs to us alone.

CHAPTER 1

Introduction

Budgeting involves the selection of ends and the means to reach those ends. That is true for public budgeting, family budgeting, and budgeting in all types of other organizations. This text is about complex governmental institutions that make decisions about the ends to be pursued and securing the means to achieve those ends while operating in a complex world economy and society. The book considers budgets, budgeting systems, and budgeting processes; the nature of the decisions that are made; and the processes by which those decisions are made. Budgeting has always been about information. In contemporary society, information is available to politicians, public servants, and the public in vast quantities. Sorting out what information is available, relevant, and necessary to making budgetary decisions, and then assessing the accuracy and even truthfulness of what is purported to be information, is not a simple task. It is easy to see why many have characterized the twentieth and twenty-first centuries as "the information age."[1] Budget systems are about gathering the best information available, whether that information be primarily of a technical nature or of a political nature, and bringing that information to bear on decisions about allocating resources to purposes.

A household budget in simpler times was a box with envelopes. Each envelope was labeled with the "purpose" (groceries, school lunches, clothing, gas for the car, etc.). In each envelope was cash, put in the envelope when a paycheck

was cashed or any other income came into the household. That was the budget, containing the ends, or purposes, and the means, cash. Budgeting was estimating what the income would be for the month or taking stock of the money already on hand after cashing the paycheck and deciding how much to place in each envelope.

Today, organizations, governments, and other institutions such as churches do the same thing, but with larger purposes and resources. Public budgeting involves the division of society's economic and financial resources between the public sector and the private sector, as well as the allocation of such resources among competing public sector needs. Public budgeting systems are systems for making choices of ends and means. These choices are guided by theory, by hunch, by partisan politics, by narrow self-interest, by altruism, and by many other sources of value judgment, including perceptions of the public interest and even avarice. It is not unusual for politicians to be accused of making public budget decisions because it will contribute to their private wealth.

Public budgeting systems work by channeling various types of information about societal conditions and the private and public values that guide resource allocation decision making. Complex channels for information exchange exist. Through these channels, people process information on what is desired, make assessments of what is or is not being achieved, and analyze what might or might not be achieved. Integral to budgeting systems are intricate processes that link both political and economic values. In making decisions that ultimately determine how resources are allocated, the political process uses sometimes bewildering and often conflicting information about values, actual conditions, and possible condition changes. This text analyzes procedures and methods—past, present, and prospective—used in the resource allocation process.

This chapter examines some basic features of decision-making and budgeting systems. First, some major characteristics of public budgeting are explained through comparing and contrasting with private forms of budgeting. Second, the development of budgeting as a means of holding government accountable for its use of society's resources is reviewed. Next, budgets and budgeting systems are defined. Finally, the role of information in budgetary decision making is considered.

Distinctions Regarding Public Budgeting

Budgeting is a common phenomenon that involves the allocation of what are invariably scarce resources. To some extent, everyone does it. People budget time, dollars, food—almost everything. The family hardware store budgets, Walmart budgets, and governments budget. Moreover, important similarities exist in the budgeting done by large public and private bureaucracies.[2]

Budgeting includes the following:

1. setting goals and objectives;
2. allocating the resources necessary to achieve those objectives;
3. monitoring the expenditure of those resources;
4. measuring progress in achieving objectives;
5. identifying weaknesses or inadequacies in organizations; and
6. controlling and integrating the diverse activities carried out by numerous subunits within large bureaucracies, both public and private.

Budgeting is the manifestation of an organization's strategies, whether those strategies are the result of thoughtful strategic planning processes, the inertia

of long years of doing approximately the same thing, or the competing political forces within the organization bargaining for shares of resources. Once resources are allocated through the budgetary process, the organization's strategies become apparent even if they have not been articulated as strategies. A citizen who wants to know the long-term goals and strategies of their local government can normally find it in two places. The first is the town's vision (goals) or strategies, usually found on the town's website (either on the home page or a linked page). The second place is the town's budget, very likely also on the town's website. The result may be surprising, as sometimes how the town spends its money, as made visible in the budget, does not always appear to match the priorities as stated in the town's vision. The link between how tax dollars will be spent and the vision may not be clear.

Budgeting means examining how the organization's resources have been used in the past, analyzing what has been accomplished and at what cost, and charting a course for the future by allocating resources for the coming budget period. Whether this process is done haphazardly or after exhaustive analyses, whether it is carried out by order of the chief executive officer or requires the extensive input of citizens, it is still budgeting.

Public budgeting is also about assigning responsibility for accomplishing the results intended by the executive and legislative actors that ultimately set the budget. The mayor and the council, the governor and the legislature, the president and the Congress do not actually perform the work required to achieve results. Budgets are generally executed by individuals in large bureaucracies. Budget allocations identify not only the amounts to be spent and the intended purposes of those expenditures, but also the unit within the bureaucracy—and by implication, the individuals managing that unit—responsible for achieving the intended results. In the contemporary age, in which much of the value in any process, whether producing a commercial good or producing a public service, is in the information or knowledge applied, responsibility for budget decisions and budget implementation is vastly more complicated. First, the information available to the decision makers, whether they choose to use it or not, is much more extensive. Second, decision-making processes are highly visible to citizens and other stakeholders. Thus, for practical reasons, and because strong central government controls are politically less feasible than in the past in most countries, budgetary decisions are more decentralized than ever.

Public and Private Sector Differences: Objectives

Resource Availability

Important differences exist between the private and public spheres. In the first place, the amount of resources available for allocation in the budget process varies greatly. Both family and corporate budgeting are constrained by a relatively fixed set of available resources, even if vastly different in size. Income is comparatively fixed, at least in the short run, and therefore outgo must be equal to or less than income. Of course, income can be expanded by increasing the level of production and work, such as a member of the family taking a second job, or temporarily by borrowing, but the opportunities for increasing income are limited.

Governments, in contrast, are bound by much higher limits. In the United States, at least, government does not use nearly all the possible resources available. Only in times of major crises, such as World War II and the Great Recession (2007–2009), has the government of the United States begun to approach upper limits on its resources. In 1943, the federal deficit was 27% of the economy's total production (gross domestic product or GDP); it exceeded 20% in the next 2 years as well. Much of the economy's total production was spent directly and indirectly on the war effort. Rationing, price controls, and other measures were imposed to severely limit private sector consumption and, in its place, to allocate most of society's resources to the government. In the Great Recession, the federal budget deficit was almost 10% of GDP in 2009 and exceeded 8% in both 2010 and 2011.[3] Total debt (also called gross

debt) outstanding is the cumulative debt owed by the government at any one time. During and immediately following the Great Recession, government borrowing, on top of decades of annual budget deficits, resulted in total government debt equal to or greater than total GDP. Borrowing during the recession had a different purpose, of course—to stimulate the economy and to put money in the hands of producers and consumers. (See the chapter on government and the economy for discussion of total or gross debt and debt held by the public, the latter being smaller than total debt, and the uses for each of the two concepts; the chapter on government and the economy and the chapter on budgeting for the U.S. Congress for a more detailed discussion of federal deficits and debt; and the chapter on capital finance and debt management for discussion of state and local government borrowing and debt.) The coronavirus pandemic, like the Great Recession, had major impacts on society's resources. The effects on public sector debt and the overall economy likely will last long after the health crisis ends.

During times not characterized by crisis, much of the total economy is left to the private sector, with government using only a fraction of society's workforce, goods, and services. In 2010, combined federal, state, and local government expenditures amounted to 36% of total GDP, with about three-fifths of that from the federal government. That percentage was several points higher, a result of government stimulus programs to combat the recession, than the 25% to 30% that was typical prior to that recession. Since 2010, all government spending in the United States has generally been about 32% to 33%.[4] That percentage is still on the lower end compared to most industrialized countries.[5] Government has the power to determine how much of society's total resources will be used for public purposes.

Profit Motive

Another major distinction between private and public budgeting is the motivation behind budget decisions. The private sector is characterized by the profit motive, whereas government undertakes many things that are financially unprofitable.

In the private sector, profit serves as a ready standard for evaluating previous decisions. Successful decisions are those that produce profits (as measured in dollars). Some companies, of course, focus on short-term profits, while others may take a longer-term view, but in the end, failure to achieve a profit or at least break even means the company goes out of business.

The concept of profit, however, can lead to gross oversimplifications about corporate decision making. Not every budget decision in a private firm is determined by the criterion of making an immediate profit. Corporations sometimes forgo profits in the short run. In the case of price wars, they attempt to increase their share of a given market even if it means selling temporarily at a loss. At other times, they incur large debts and take other, apparently unprofitable, actions to combat a hostile takeover, an attempt by an outsider to purchase enough stock to exercise control over a corporation's assets. Their major objectives are sometimes to produce a good product and to build public confidence; they have enough confidence in their pursuit of customer service that the result will be sustained, long-run profits.

At other times, corporations undertake actions for mainly social motives, wishing to make a contribution to the society that sustains their corporate existence, a concept known as corporate social responsibility.[6] Corporate social responsibility has grown in the decades since 2000 to be a significant motivation in many companies. Beyond the profit motive, many social objectives are important to employee retention and in positioning a company in the competitive market. Workforce diversity, equal opportunity, climate change, standards imposed on suppliers, customer data privacy, and many other issues affect corporate resource allocations and business practices now more than ever in history.[7] Still, in private sector firms, revenues must exceed costs over the long run.

Large firms also budget significant resources for research and development (R&D) activities, only a few of which will eventually lead to a product that generates large sales and profits. An R&D division can be evaluated over the long term by how many of its developments contribute to profits, but this kind of evaluation is difficult. Often, the results of R&D are subtle improvements in existing products, so measuring the amount of investment relative to the incremental profit gain is impossible. In this regard, private budgeting for R&D is no less difficult than the federal government's support of R&D. Overall, the evidence is that investing in R&D yields positive returns on that investment.[8]

Regardless of the role profit plays in the private sector, government decision making in general lacks even this standard for measuring activities. Exceptions to this generalization are government activities that yield revenues. State control and sale of alcoholic beverages, whether undertaken for profit or for regulation of public morals, can be evaluated, like any other business, in terms of profit and loss. Similarly, the operation of a water system, a public transit authority, or a public swimming pool can be evaluated in business profit-and-loss terms. This does not mean that each of these should turn a profit—after all, operating a public swimming pool may be the result of a decision to provide subsidized recreation to a low-income neighborhood whose residents cannot afford other private recreational alternatives. The budgeting process, however, can be used to assess the operation as a business to clarify the subsidy level and to aid decision makers in comparing costs with those for other public services provided free of direct charge. (See the chapter on capital assets.)

Nevertheless, most private sector budget decisions pertain to at least long-term profits, and most public sector budget decisions do not. Governments undertake some functions deliberately instead of leaving them to the private sector. Public budgetary decisions, for example, frequently involve allocation of resources among competing programs that are not readily susceptible to measurement in dollar costs and dollar returns. For example, there are no easy means of measuring the costs and benefits of a life saved through cancer research, although the value of future earnings is sometimes used as a surrogate measure of the value of life. The U.S. government undertakes large programs to control or eradicate malaria and other tropical diseases in Africa, based not on economic or financial returns, but on a broad concept of the public interest in eradicating diseases that affect low-income populations in developing countries. Addressing some diseases, such as Ebola and coronavirus that may have originated in other countries, serves not only a broad concept of the public interest but also to reduce the threat to the United States as the disease spreads. Nor is there a ready means of clearly separating private incentives from public incentives. For example, public budget spending on biomedical research in the United States has been just over 40% of total spending. Public sector spending, mainly through the various National Institutes of Health, is mainly for basic research and discovery; private sector spending is more concentrated on developing drug and other treatments and bringing them to market.[9]

Just because most public sector activities are not intended to be profitable does not mean that business-like measurement of results in relation to costs is useless. Although not susceptible to bottom-line or profit-and-loss measurement, many government programs are able to measure their results in terms of output (efficiency) and outcome (effectiveness). The disease eradication programs undertaken by the U.S. government in other countries, for example, can and are measured by the efficiency and effectiveness with which the programs are implemented. The chapter on the expenditure side of budget preparation includes an extensive discussion of the use of performance measures in federal-, state-. and local-level programs.

Public and Private Sector Differences: Services Provided

Public Goods

Some government services yield public or collective benefits that are of value to society as a whole, whereas corporate products are almost always consumed by individuals and specific organizations. When Ford Motor Company produces automobiles, people buying the automobiles use them to meet their own personal needs. When the Departments of Defense and Homeland Security produce a network for preventing nuclear devices from entering the nation's ports, that network benefits the public in general. Economists call these kinds of products and services *public goods*. They have two properties. The first is *nonexcludability*. Once the defense network is in place, no one can be excluded from its benefits, even if they are unwilling or unable to pay for them.[10] The second is *nonrivalness*. One person's use of the good or service does not diminish another person's use. For example, a second person can "consume" national defense without lessening the benefits that the first person gets from that public good. Of course, few public products and services qualify as pure public goods, and many goods and services produced by governments are also produced by the private sector. Police protection is a public service, but communities, companies, and individuals also purchase various forms of protection against crime from private security companies.

Externalities

Another class of government services consists of those from which individuals can be excluded but for which the benefits, or costs, extend beyond those who are the immediate targets of the service. When Ford Motor Company sells a car, its stockholders enjoy the benefits of the profits, but those profits do not spill over to society at large. However, when a child is educated through a school system, not only does the child benefit, but society's productive capacity is also enhanced. Many private schools educate children for a profit, and the owners of the schools enjoy the benefits of the profits in addition to the benefits experienced by children and society. However, it seems unlikely that these same for-profit schools would willingly provide equivalent education to all children who cannot make tuition payments. Economists label the benefits that spill over to the rest of society *externalities*. Governments provide at least some services that produce significant externalities because the private sector would provide these only to the extent that profit could be made. Education, if left entirely to the private sector, would presumably be available only to those who could pay or would be provided in insufficient quantity and quality for the needs of society. Government actions, or inactions, also may produce negative externalities. Reducing regulations requiring private companies to limit harmful releases into the air and water may save those companies money and increase their profits, but the health impacts from release of toxins are a negative externality, or cost, imposed on the population.

Pricing Public Services

Defining just what is clearly public in nature and determining what the private sector presumably cannot or will not provide is controversial. Notions of what are public services and what should be left to the private sector change over time. Many services, especially at the state and local level, once thought to be exclusively public were converted to private services or to public services provided by private firms on a contract basis when federal assistance dropped dramatically during the 1970s through the early 1980s.[11] That trend continued when state and local budgets shrank dramatically in the two recessions of the first two decades of the 2000s, though there is some evidence that smaller jurisdictions or smaller private contracting for public services has waned somewhat, while large contracts seem to be increasing.[12]

This trend advanced throughout many countries with public sectors even larger than in the United States. The Margaret Thatcher government (1979–1990), in privatizing many formerly public services, such as the water utilities, throughout the United Kingdom, served as a model for the early 1980s movement in the United States and around the world (See the chapter on capital finance for a discussion of various forms of privatization and private participation in public services.)

This type of conversion is not a new idea, but public sector budget pressures have changed the landscape to require those who benefit directly from a government service to pay for its cost. For example, in the 1990s, the U.S. Coast Guard stopped providing towing services to disabled boats unless a genuine emergency existed; it began notifying private operators, who charged the cost to the disabled boats' captains. That practice cut back significantly on calls for towing in general, with prices providing a rationing mechanism. What is private and what is public varies over time, and public budgeting is affected by those variations.

Other Public and Private Sector Differences

Whatever objectives, other than profit, that private corporations may have, to stay in business they must seek economic efficiency and obtain the greatest possible dollar return on investments. In contrast, governments may be intentionally inefficient in resource allocations, undertaking services that the private sector would be reluctant to provide at all. For example, government-financed medical care for the elderly may be inefficient in the sense that other government programs, such as education and infrastructure investments, provide greater economic returns to society, but it has been agreed that at least some support should be provided to the elderly. Governments are also charged with other unique responsibilities, such as intervention in the economy during periods of economic decline. (See the chapter on government and the economy.)

Another difference between private and public organizations lies in the clientele and the owners of the means of production. In theory, at least, both corporations and governments are answerable to their stockholders and clients. In the private sector, these individuals can disassociate themselves from firms by selling their stocks or not purchasing a company's products. Their counterparts in the public sector are denied this choice except through the extreme act of moving to another governmental jurisdiction. Private stockholders expect dollar returns on their investments, and if they are not satisfied, they sell their shares. Because government costs and returns are not so easily evaluated, the electorate has no simple measure for assessing the returns on the taxes they pay, and they have no means to sell their shares. Even so, many state and local governments provide annual reports to citizens that are similar in purpose to stockholder reports. These reports emphasize the investments government is making and the benefits citizens are receiving in lieu of profits. Of course, from time to time the stockholders of corporations and of governments force management to change, the latter through regular elections.

Corporate budgetary decision making is usually more centralized than government decision making. Corporations can stop production of economically unprofitable goods, such as a fast-food restaurant chain phasing out a nonprofitable menu item.

Given the nature of the public decision-making process, however, governments encounter more difficulty in making decisions both to inaugurate programs and to eliminate them. For example, though there was an apparent large majority consensus for more than two decades that the Medicare program that assists the elderly in financing health care should include some form of prescription drug coverage, it was not until 2006 that a program was finally implemented.

Responsible Government and Budgeting

The emergence and reform of formal government budgeting can be traced to a concern for holding public officials accountable for their actions.[13] The government performance monitoring movement represents the most recent manifestation of a rather ancient concern that public officials be held accountable for their actions. No matter the particular reform terminology in vogue, in a democracy, budgeting is a device for limiting the powers of government. Two issues recur in the evolution of modern public budgeting as an instrument of accountability: responsibility to whom and for what purposes.

Responsible to Whom?
Responsibility to Constituency

Basically, responsibility in a democratic society entails constituents holding their officials answerable, usually through elections. Elected executives and legislative representatives at all levels of government are, at least in theory, held accountable through the electoral process for their decisions on programs and budgets. In actuality, budget documents are not the main source of information for decisions by the electorate. Obviously, most voters do not diligently study the U.S. budget before casting their votes in presidential and congressional elections. However, when the government's share of the total economy grows, it is increasingly clear that voters do hold elected representatives responsible for the overall performance of the economy and often for the impact of a budget deficit, if any, on the economy. That the electorate holds presidents responsible for the economy was evidenced in 1992 by President George H. W. Bush's defeat in his bid for reelection. Eight years later, the 2000 election showed that even during a booming economy, many voters were more concerned about apparent ethical and moral lapses in the White House than their happiness with the economy. Not all elections turn on the state of the economy or the government budget. The rhetoric of Donald Trump's successful 2016 presidential campaign focused more on the concept of America's standing in the world and the concerns among disaffected blue-collar working-class families that the government did not care about them.

State and local governments have specific creditors: the purchasers of bonds issued to finance long-term capital improvements. The interest rates that state and local governments must pay on their bonds are affected by their ability to provide creditors with convincing evidence of their creditworthiness. Hence, financial institutions that purchase bonds and ratings institutions that rate state and local bonds are important constituents to whom these governments are accountable. (See the chapter on capital finance and debt management.)

The other accountability mechanisms are the concepts of *separation of powers* and *checks and balances* as means of providing for responsible government. Power is divided among the executive, legislative, and judicial branches, and each provides some checks on the others. Although the president is held responsible to Congress for preparation and submission of an executive budget, only Congress can pass the budget. Specifically, the U.S. Constitution, in Article 1, Section 9, states that "no money shall be drawn from the Treasury, but in consequence of appropriations made by law...."

Even that strong constitutional language is challenged from time to time. President Donald Trump reallocated funds appropriated to the Defense Department to the project to build a wall on the U.S. southern border, citing presidential emergency powers. A lower court ruled that this reallocation violated federal law. The Supreme Court in a 5-4 decision stayed the injunction issued by the lower court, on the technical grounds that the parties bringing the suit may not have been the proper plaintiffs.[14] In most states and many localities, the chief executive has a similar responsibility to recommend a plan for taxes and expenditures. The legislative body passes judgment on these recommendations and subsequently holds the executive branch responsible for carrying out the decisions. Local government practice varies more because some local governments do not have an elected chief executive.

Development of the Executive Budget System

The development of an executive budget system for holding government accountable was a long process that can be traced as far back as the Magna Carta in 1215. The main issue that resulted in this landmark document was the Crown's taxing powers. The Magna Carta did not produce a complete budget, but concentrated only on holding the Crown accountable to the nobility for its revenue actions.[15] At the time, the magnitude of public expenditures and the use of these funds for public services were of less concern than the power to levy and collect taxes. It was not until the English Consolidated Fund Act of 1787 that the rudiments of a complete system were established. A complete account of revenues and expenditures was presented to Parliament for the first time in 1822.[16]

The same concern in eighteenth-century England for executive accountability was exhibited

in other countries and carried over to the American experience even prior to the ratification of the Constitution in 1789. Fear of a strong executive branch was evidenced by the failure to provide for such a branch in the Articles of Confederation in 1781. Fear of "taxation without representation" probably explains why the Constitution is more explicit about taxing powers than the procedures to be followed in government spending.

Modern Executive Budgeting

By the beginning of the twentieth century, changing economic conditions stimulated the demand for more centralized and controlled forms of budgeting. E. E. Naylor wrote that before this time there was little "enthusiasm for action ... since federal taxes were usually indirect and not severely felt by any particular individual or group."[17] By 1900, however, existing revenue sources no longer consistently produced sufficient sums to cover the costs of government. At the federal level, the tariff could not be expected to produce a surplus of funds, as had been the case. Causes of this growing deficit were the expanded scope of government programs and, to a lesser extent, waste and corruption in government finance. The latter is often credited as a major political factor stimulating reform.

Local government led the way in the establishment of formal budget procedures. Municipal budget reform was closely associated with general reform of local government, especially the creation of the city manager form of government. In 1899, a model municipal corporation act, released by the National Municipal League, featured a model charter that provided for a budget system whose preparation phase was under the control of the mayor. In 1907, the New York Bureau of Municipal Research issued a study called Making a Municipal Budget that became the basis for establishing a budgetary system for New York City.[18] By the mid-1920s, most major U.S. cities had some form of budget system.

Substantial reform of state budgeting occurred between 1910 and 1920. This reform was closely associated with the overall drive to hold executives accountable by first giving them authority over the executive branch. The movement for the short ballot, aimed at eliminating many independently elected administrative officers, resulted in governors being granted greater control over their bureaucracies. Ohio, in 1910, was the first state to enact a law empowering the governor to prepare and submit a budget. A. E. Buck, in assessing the effort at the state level, suggested that 1913 marked "the beginning of practical action in the states."[19] By 1920, some budget reform had occurred in 44 states, and all states had a central budget office by 1929.[20]

Simultaneous action occurred at the federal level, and much of what took place there contributed to the reforms at the local and state levels. The Budget and Accounting Act, which established the new federal system, was passed in 1921.[21] In the interim, deficits were recorded every year between 1912 and 1919, except for 1916. The largest deficit occurred in 1919, when (largely because of the need to finance World War I) expenditures were three times greater than revenues ($18.5 billion in expenditures as compared with $5.1 billion in revenues). During this period, vigorous debate centered on the issue of whether budget reform would, in effect, establish a superordinate executive over the legislative branch. In 1920, President Wilson vetoed legislation that would have created a Bureau of the Budget and a General Accounting Office on the grounds that the latter, as an arm of Congress, would violate the president's authority over the executive branch. The following year, President Warren G. Harding signed virtually identical legislation, creating both agencies and imposing the requirement that an executive budget be presented to the Congress.

Thus, an executive budget system was established, despite a historical fear of a powerful chief executive. In 1939, as a result of recommendations made by President Franklin D. Roosevelt's Committee on Administrative Management (the Brownlow Committee), the Bureau of the Budget was removed from the Treasury Department and placed in the newly formed Executive Office of the President. This shift reflected the growing importance of the Bureau in assisting the president in managing the government. The Budget and Accounting Procedures Act of 1950 reinforced the trend of presidential control by explicitly granting the president control over the "form and detail" of the budget document.[22] The Second Hoover Commission in 1955 endorsed strengthening the president's power in budgeting as a means of restoring the "full control of the national purse to the Congress."[23] A president, who had full control of the bureaucracy, could be held accountable by Congress for action taken by the bureaucracy.

One of the stated goals of the reform movement was to bring the sound financial practices of business to the presumably disorganized public sector—a goal often expressed by current reformers. Available evidence, however, indicates that business practices were not particularly exemplary at the beginning of the twentieth century, suggesting that the reforms were largely invented in the public sector rather than being transferred into government from the outside.[24] It remains popular to advocate bringing good business practices to government, but the corporate accounting scandals at various periods in modern American history and the subprime mortgage investment practices of the major financial market institutions that led to the Great Recession suggest that private practices are not always exemplary.

Responsible for What?
Revenue Responsibility

The earliest concern for financial responsibility centered on taxes. As indicated earlier, the Magna Carta imposed limitations not on the nature of the Crown's expenditures, but on the procedures for raising revenue. The same concern for the revenue side of budgeting was characteristic of the early history of budgeting in this country. The Constitution is more explicit about the tax power of the government than about the nature or purposes of government expenditures.

Expenditure Control, Management, and Planning

The larger the budget has become, the more the concern has shifted to expenditures. Increasing emphasis has been placed on the accountability of government for what it spends and for how well it manages its overall finances. Expenditure accountability may take several different forms. Budgeting scholar Allen Schick described the focus on accountability in U.S. budgeting as having gone through three stages by the 1960s.[25]

The first stage he characterized as concern for tight control over government expenditures. The most prevalent means of exerting this type of expenditure control is to appropriate by line item and object of expenditure. Financial audits are then used to ensure that money is, in fact, spent for the items authorized for purchase. This information focuses budgetary decision making on the things government pays for, such as personnel, travel, and supplies—the objects of expenditure—rather than on the accomplishments of government activities. In other words, responsibility is achieved by controlling the resources or input side.

Schick's description of the second stage was that of a management orientation, with emphasis on the efficiency of ongoing activities. Historically, this orientation is associated with the New Deal (Franklin Roosevelt administration) through the First Hoover Commission (1949). The emphasis was on holding administrators accountable for the efficiency of their activities through methods such as work performance measurement. Budgeting by activity achieves accountability by measuring the activities carried out for the money expended.

The third stage of budget reform Schick identified was based on the post–Hoover Commission concern regarding the planning function served by budgets. The traditional goal of controlling resource inputs may be accommodated in the short time frame of the coming budget year. Managerial control over efficiency, although aided by a longer time perspective, also may be accommodated in a traditional budget-year presentation. The planning emphasis focuses on a longer time frame. Many objectives of government programs cannot be accomplished in one budget year; a multiyear presentation of the budget is thus necessary to indicate the long-range implications, both financial and program results, of current budget decisions.

The advent of program budgeting in the 1960s, with its focus on multiyear planning and the ultimate results of government programs, was the culmination of the planning focus on outcomes that must be measured outside the government itself. Control-oriented information like objects of expenditure and managerial-oriented information such as the outputs produced by government activities (and the costs to achieve those outputs) do not really require measurement outside the orbit of governmental agencies. A focus on outcomes requires much more extensive information that is not generated by the accounting system. Understanding outcomes requires information about what happens as a result of government expenditures. Typically, these outcomes are achieved only by commitment of resources over many budget years.

Some services provided by government lend themselves well to measures of accomplishment, and some do not. Federal responsibilities for defense and foreign policy certainly have visible consequences, but narrowing down to particular budget decisions on expenditures and defense or foreign policy outcomes is both conceptually and practically difficult at best. Local government services such as water, streets, solid waste collection and disposal, and so forth are much more susceptible to results measurement. The planning approach epitomized by program budgeting reforms stressed outcome measurement over a multiyear horizon. Are society's ends being achieved as a result of program expenditures? (See the chapter on the expenditure side of budget preparation for more extensive discussion of focusing on the results of government expenditures.)

Financial Management, Financial Condition, and Program Performance

Since those three stages were first characterized in the 1960s, additional improvements in using information to ensure responsible government budgeting have become standard practice. Some have suggested that these efforts since the 1960s constitute additional or new stages of budget reform. One author has offered up prioritization, characterized by budget cutbacks in both federal and state government budgeting in the 1980s, as a fourth stage, and accountability, emphasizing performance measurement, as a fifth stage.[26] Another has suggested a similar fourth stage, labeling it limitation, emphasizing the attempts in the 1980s to shrink the federal budget and state taxing and expenditure limitations.[27] (See the chapter on budgeting for revenues and taxes.)

While budgeting at the federal, state, and local levels continues to change in terms of emphasis and focus, the labeling of additional stages is somewhat in the eye of the beholder. It is difficult to discern a major difference between *limitation* and *control*, for example. It is also clear that some additional budgetary analysis and planning tools have become important in public budgeting systems since the three-stages description was first put forward. One of these is performance measurement and performance management, which enhances the ability to budget for the achievement of results. Another is financial management, which entails greater attention to the financial soundness of public sector institutions and new and enhanced tools to measure and report on financial soundness. Measuring financial health and increased use of business-like financial management tools enhances the ability of elected leaders to exert control over resources.

Performance Management

Performance measures associated with work activities and with long-term results are not new, as already noted. However, performance measurement has evolved and expanded since the 1980s. Program budgeting was much more an approach for the executive to gain greater understanding and control over spending by focusing on plans and results. Today, performance measurement and management have a strong emphasis on public reporting on progress and redefining programs based on citizen response to the measured progress. This emphasis on public reporting is a logical extension of the broader concept of *accountability for results* that characterizes budgeting systems

and reforms in budgeting. Newer information tools are focused on external communications. Local government budgeting increasingly focuses on performance budgeting as the major tool for communicating with the public and garnering public support for the budget.[28] With or without a complete budgetary system overhaul such as program budgeting entails, all levels of government in the United States, and especially state and local government, typically have extensive performance management systems.[29]

Performance management emphasizes setting objectives and then motivating managers to be entrepreneurial in their pursuit of those objectives. Of course, although managing growth and achieving efficiencies is such a strong focus in performance management, the tools also may be used in government to shrink programs for other than managerial reasons. Other countries also have given the same emphases to results-oriented or value-driven budgeting as a primary tool in increasing the efficiency and reducing the size of the public sector.[30]

Financial Management

Another feature that has seen heightened focus is the financial health of the governmental entity or the entire government. There are two facets to this: (1) improved public reporting on the financial condition of government, and (2) a significant focus on the value and condition of long-lived assets such as infrastructure systems. Publicly traded corporations have always had to answer to their stockholders for the financial condition of the corporation, and privately held companies, at a minimum, must demonstrate sound financial condition to secure debt financing from lenders. But the application of financial management concepts to focus on the financial condition of government agencies was new in the late 1980s. The emphasis has been on creating tools for measuring the financial condition of government, adapted from private financial and managerial accounting practices, and new mechanisms for ensuring that the government remains in a sound financial position.

One of the motivations behind the concern to hold government accountable for its long-run financial position was the New York City budget crisis of the mid-1970s. Following on the heels of that near-bankruptcy, both financial institutions that purchased municipal bonds and citizens who wondered about their own cities sought to improve the reporting of the long-term financial position of governments. (See the chapter on intergovernmental relations for discussion of managing financial crises at the local government level.) At the time, the general operating budget and related accounting reports often did not reveal the overall financial position of the government entity. Now, virtually every large local and state government in the United States, as well as the federal government, routinely produces reports, often with much public fanfare on their financial condition.[31] Despite major improvements in government financial analysis and reporting, massive catastrophes such as Detroit's declaration of bankruptcy in 2013 can and do occur.[32] (See the chapter on intergovernmental relations for discussion of managing financial crises at the local government level.)

Fixed Asset Management

Concern at the federal level has led to a much greater emphasis on fixed asset management and increased attention in the annual budget to investments in long-lasting assets. The Governmental Accounting Standards Board Statement No. 34 (GASB 34) requires state and local governments and other public entities to report on their fixed assets (see the chapters on financial management and capital assets). Some government expenditures are really investments in future economic productivity. Others primarily consume resources with little hope of any future payoff. Investment means creating additional productive capacity, such as improving transportation networks that reduce the cost of private sector economic activity through more efficient means of transportation and upgrading education systems that enhance the long-term intellectual ability of students to develop new products and new processes. (See the chapters on financial management and capital assets.)

All governments budget for these activities, but not all government budgeting systems make explicit the consumption-versus-investment tradeoffs in budget decisions. While most state and local governments employ formal capital budgeting techniques, federal agencies typically do not, although in specific types of investments, such as information technology, formalized capital investment planning and analysis are required.[33] (See the chapter on capital assets.)

Most of the emphasis in this text is on the budget as an instrument for financial and program decision making at all levels of government—federal, state, and local. The one responsibility that most sharply differentiates federal budget decisions from state and local decisions is the federal government's responsibility for the overall state of the economy. Not only does the federal budget allocate resources among competing programs, but it is also an instrument for achieving economic stability and growth (see the chapter on government and the economy). The responsibility to use the federal budget as an instrument of economic policy has been a part of the federal budgetary process since the Employment Act of 1946.[34] (See the chapter on government and the economy.)

Budgeting is an important process by which accountability or responsibility can be provided in a political system. As has been discussed, responsibility varies both in terms of the people to whom the system is accountable and in terms of its purposes. Given the various forms of accountability and the types of choices that decision makers have available to them, different meanings can be attached to the terms *budget* and *budgeting system*. Depending on the purposes of a budget, decision makers will need different kinds and amounts of information to aid them in making choices. The following sections focus on the kinds of information required for different budgetary choices and the kinds of procedures for generating the necessary information.

Budgets and Budgeting Systems

What Is a Budget?
Budget Documents

In its simplest form, a budget is a document or a collection of documents that refers to the financial condition and future plans of an organization (family, corporation, government), including information on revenues, expenditures, activities, and purposes or goals. In contrast to accounting statements, which are mainly retrospective in nature, referring to past conditions, a budget is prospective, referring to anticipated revenues, expenditures, and accomplishments. Of course, budgets always contain some information about past revenues and expenditures that is consistent with accounting records. Historically, the word *budget* referred to a leather pouch, wallet, bag, or purse. More particularly, "In Britain the term was used to describe the leather bag in which the Chancellor of the Exchequer carried to Parliament the statement of the Government's needs and resources."[35]

The status of budget documents is not consistent across political jurisdictions. In the federal government, the budget normally means the president's budget recommendation and, as such, has limited legal status. It is the official recommendation of the president to Congress, but it is not the official document under which the government operates. As discussed in the chapter on Congress and budget approval, the official operating budget of the United States consists of several documents—namely, appropriation acts and laws authorizing mandatory spending and revenues. In contrast, local budgets proposed by mayors may become official working budgets adopted in their entirety by the city councils.[36]

In still other instances, there may be a series of budget documents instead of one budget for any given government. These may include (1) an operating budget, which handles the bulk of ongoing operations; (2) a capital budget, which covers major new construction projects; and (3) a series of special fund budgets that cover programs funded by specific revenue sources (see the chapter on financial management). Special fund budgets commonly include those for highway programs financed through gasoline and tire sales taxes. In such cases, revenue from these sources is earmarked for highway construction, improvement, and maintenance. As another example, fishing and hunting license fees may constitute the revenue for a special fund devoted to the stocking of streams

and the provision of ample hunting opportunities. (See the chapter on financial management.)

The format of budget documents also varies. Overall, budget documents tend to provide greater information on expenditures than on revenues, which are usually treated in a brief section. On the expenditure side, budgets are multipurpose, in that no single document and no single definition can exhaust the functions budgets serve or the ways they are used. At the most general level, budgets can be conceived of as (1) descriptions, (2) explanations or causal assertions, and (3) statements of preferences or values.

Budgets as Descriptions

Budgets are first descriptions of the status of an organization, whether it is an agency, a ministry, or an entire government. The budget document may describe what the organization purchases, what it does, and what it accomplishes. Descriptions of organizational activity are also common in budget documents. Expenditures may be classified according to the activities they support. For example, a revenue department may be concerned with initial tax collection, taxpayer assistance, and audit/enforcement. Another type of description, organizational accomplishments, states the consequences of resource consumption and work activities for those outside the organization. For example, successful job placements for individuals finishing a vocational rehabilitation program constitute one type of outcome or consequence of a public expenditure. These statements require external verification of the effects of the organization on its environment.

As descriptions, budgets provide a discrete picture of an organization at a point or points in time, in terms of resources consumed, work performed, and external effects. The dollar (or euro or pound sterling) revenues and expenditures, according to these types of descriptions, may be the only quantitative information supplied. Alternatively, information may be supplied about the following:

1. the number and types of personnel;
2. the quantity and kinds of equipment purchased;

3. measures of performance, such as the number of buildings inspected, or the number of acres treated; and

4. measures of impact, such as the number of accidents prevented, the amount of crop yield increases, and so forth.

Generally, the more descriptive material supplied, the more the organization can be held accountable for the funds spent, the activities supported by those expenditures, and the external accomplishments produced by those activities. Much of the history of budget reform reflects attempts to increase the quantity and quality of descriptive material available both to decision makers and to the public.

Budgets as Explanations

When they describe organizations in terms of purchases, activities, and accomplishments, budgets also at least implicitly serve a second major function—explanation of causal relationships. The expenditure of a specific amount for the purchase of labor and materials that will be combined in particular work activities implies the presumed existence of a causal sequence that will produce desired results. Regardless of how explicit or how vague the budget document or the statements of officials may be, budgetary decisions always imply a causal process in which work activities → consume resources → to achieve goals. Some organizations may have little accurate information about accomplishments, especially public organizations whose accomplishments are not measured in terms of profit and loss. Governments may choose not to be explicit about particular results because they are difficult to measure, politically sensitive, or both. Regardless of the availability of information or the willingness of an organization to collect and use it, the budget is an expression of a set of causal relationships.

Budgets as Preferences

Budgets are statements of preferences. Whether intended or not, the allocation of resources among different agencies, among different activities, or among different accomplishments reveals the preferences of those making the allocations. These may be the actual preferences of a few decision makers, but more often they are best thought of as the collective preferences of many decision makers arrived at through complex bargaining. Preferences reflect, if not any one individual's values, an aggregate of choices that become the collective value judgment for the local government, state, or nation.

What Is a Budgeting System?

Systems

Budgeting can best be understood as a kind of system, which the Business Dictionary defines as:

> An organized, purposeful structure that consists of interrelated and interdependent elements (components, entities, factors, members, parts, etc.). These elements continually influence one another (directly or indirectly) to maintain their activity and the existence of the system, in order to achieve the goal of the system.[37]

Budgetary decision making consists of the actions of executive officials (both in a central organization such as the governor's office or the mayor's staff and in executive line agencies), legislative officials, organized interest groups, and perhaps unorganized interests that may be manifested in a generally felt public concern about public needs and taxes. All these actions are related, and understanding budgeting means understanding the interrelationships. Such understanding is best achieved by thinking in terms of complex systems.

A system may be thought of as a network typically consisting of many different parts with information flowing among the parts. The elements of systems interact with each other to produce system results, or consequences, and the network of interactions may produce the same set of results through several different paths, or the same path may from time to time produce different results.[38] Budgeting systems involve political actors, economic and social theories, numerous institutional structures, and competing norms and values, all of which produce outputs in patterns not immediately evident from studying only budget documents.

Budget System Outputs

In a budgetary system, the outputs flowing from the network of interactions are budget decisions, and these vary greatly in their overall significance. Not every unit of the system will have equal decisional authority or power. A manager of a field office for a state health department is likely to have less power to make major budgetary decisions than the administrative head of the department, the governor, or the members of the legislative appropriations committees. Yet each participant does contribute some input to the system. The field manager may alert others in the system to the emergence of a new health problem and, in doing so, may contribute greatly to the eventual establishment of a new health program to combat that problem. Modern information technology and the greater emphasis on responsibility at all levels of the organization for achieving results means the lower-level staff in an agency are much more influential than they have been in the past. Even actors not in the formal budgeting system may influence the decisions. For example, doctors and hospitals, who are part of surveillance for early detection of the latest flu, in effect are providing inputs to the budgeting system. When a crisis develops, the issue becomes one of who knew what and when and what was done. The Flint, Michigan, water crisis that developed in 2014 and continued into 2020 arose from an effort to reduce city water costs but resulted in contamination of the water distribution system and possibly the spread of Legionnaires' disease.[39]

Like the outputs of any other system or network, budget decisions are seldom final and more commonly are sequential. Decisions are tentative, in that each decision made is forwarded for action to another participant in the process. This does not mean that all decisions are reversible. Major breakthroughs, such as passage of the Elementary and Secondary Education Act of 1965, which provided substantial federal aid to education, are abandoned only in response to powerful political pressure.[40] The No Child Left Behind Act,[41] which reauthorized major elements of federal assistance to elementary and secondary education, continued most of the key elements of the original 1965 legislation, but the Every Student Succeeds Act of 2015 substantially reduced the federal role to funding support for state-controlled initiatives.[42] Likewise, the introduction of prescription drug care into Medicare in 2003 was only after years of debate and proposals.[43] Despite dissatisfaction, eliminating such hard-won programs once in place is nearly impossible. Subsequent budget decisions, therefore, are in large part bounded by previous decisions. The subsequent decisions tend to center on the question of changing the level of commitment—allocating more resources, fewer resources, or different kinds of resources—to achieve desired levels of impact or different types of impact.

System Interconnectedness

Another feature of a system is that a change in any part of it will alter other parts. Because all units are related, any change in the role or functioning of one unit necessarily affects other units. In some instances, changes may be of such a modest nature that their ramifications for other parts of the system are difficult to discern. However, when major budgetary reforms are instituted, they assuredly affect most participants. For example, if one unit in the system is granted greater authority, individuals and organizations having access to that unit have their decisional involvement enhanced, whereas those groups associated with other units have diminished roles.[44] Thus, each individual and institution evaluates budget reforms in terms of how political strengths will be realigned under the reforms.

Information and Decision Making

Types of Information

To serve the multiple functions described in the preceding section, budgeting systems must produce and process a variety of information.

Most of the major reforms, whether attempted or proposed, in public budget systems have been intended to reorganize existing information and to provide participants with new and greater quantities of information (see the chapter on the expenditure side of budget preparation). Basically, two types of information exist: program information and resource information. The latter is more traditional. People are accustomed to thinking of budgets in terms of resources, such as monetary units and personnel. A budget would not be a budget if it did not contain dollar, ruble, or other monetary figures. Similarly, budgets commonly contain data on employees or personnel. (See the chapter on the expenditure side of budget preparation.)

Conventional accounting systems provide much of the information that public organizations use for budgetary decisions. This type of information is limited to the internal aspects of organizations—for example, the location of organizational responsibility for expenditures and the resources purchased by those expenditures. When the decision-making system incorporates information about the results or implications of programs, one must leave the boundaries of the organization to examine consequences for those outside it. This step requires more extensive and more explicit clarification of governmental goals and objectives and increases the importance of analysis. These features of budget reforms, such as program budgeting, zero-base budgeting, managing for results, and performance budgeting, with their emphasis on program information and priority setting, have generated the most heat among critics of budget reform.[45]

Decision Making

Much of the criticism of reform has involved the arguments that reform of decision-making systems must take into account the limitations on human capabilities to use all the information that might be collected and analyzed and the strong influence of political considerations.[46] Although sometimes-subtle differences distinguish theories of how decisions are made, the various theories are often classified into three basic approaches: pure rationality, limited or bounded rationality, and incrementalism.[47] An early application of these notions to public sector decision making, still used in military leadership programs, is Graham Allison's study of the 1962 Cuban Missile Crisis, *The Essence of Decision*, in which he characterized three models as rational, organizational, and governmental/political.[48] These are descriptive theories as well as prescriptions for how decisions ought to be made.

Rational Decision Making

Decision making, according to the pure rationality approach, consists of a series of ordered, logical steps. First, an organization's or a society's numerous goals are ranked according to priority. Second, all possible alternatives are identified. The costs of each alternative are compared with anticipated benefits, and judgments are made as to which alternative comes closest to satisfying the relevant needs or desires. The alternative with the highest payoff and/or least cost is chosen. Pure rationality theories assume that complete and perfect information about all alternatives is both available and manageable. Decision making, therefore, is choosing among alternatives to maximize some objective function. The rational choice model is built on microeconomics and the notion of the individual actor making an optimal choice to maximize the decision maker's utility.

The applicability of the rationality model is limited, and few argue that it is a description of how ordinary human beings make most decisions. It is most consistent with notions of technical or economic rationality, where objectives can be stated with some precision and the range of feasible alternatives is finite.[49] Also, the model can be of use where accurate predictions of behavior are possible, such as in the private market, where assumptions regarding rational behavior can be used to predict future economic trends.[50]

As a description of how government budgeting works, the pure rationality model is obviously misleading. Meeting the complete requirements of even a few of the steps is impossible. It has been argued that the costs of information are so high as to make it rational to be ignorant—that is, to make decisions based on a limited search and limited information. Some attempts at budget reform have been criticized as attempts to impose an unworkable model, pure rationality, on government financial decision making. The use of program information has been a particular target for criticism.[51] However, this criticism is somewhat misdirected in that it is not the information search cost that is limiting. The widespread availability of electronic information searches and sophisticated software to analyze both quantitative and qualitative information make information search cost less of a limiting factor. The more limiting factor is the limited capacity of the decision-making system to process the information in a given budget cycle. Public budgeting decisions are made in a larger political context with numerous actors involved, each with their own perspectives. This is a much more complicated situation than the clear-sighted approach toward an agreed-upon objective that is the essence of the rational choice model.

Limited or Bounded Rationality

The second approach to decision making is called limited rationality, or sometimes bounded rationality. This model recognizes the inadequacies in the assumptions behind the pure rationality description of decision making as applied to complex problems. While acknowledging the inherent constraints of human cognitive and political processes, limited rationality does not suggest that a deliberate search for alternative approaches to goal achievement is of no avail. Searching for alternatives is used to find solutions that are satisfactory but not necessarily optimal.

Limited rationality suggests that large forces are marshalled at times for major change, and incremental adjustments are made at other times for issues that do not generate demand for substantial departure from the status quo. Decision theories do differ in how they view the values that decision making serves and the capacities of decision makers to serve those values. One model assumes virtually no limits on human capacities for processing information, another suggests that decision making should be sensitive only to partisan political interests, and still other attempts to strike a balance between the other models. The history of budgeting and budget reform, we argue, reflects the tensions among these approaches to decision making.

Incrementalism

The third approach to decision making, incrementalism, sometimes labeled muddling through, is more akin to the organizational and political processes of actual decision making identified by Allison. It has been advocated as more realistic by critics of pure rationality, such as Charles E. Lindblom, Aaron Wildavsky, and others.[52] According to this view, decision making involves a conflict of organizational and individual interests and a corresponding clash of information that results in the accommodation of diverse partisan interests through bargaining.

"Real" decision making is presumed to begin as issues are raised by significant interest groups that request or demand changes from the existing state. Decision making is not some conscious form of pure rationality, but a process of incrementally adjusting existing practices to establish or reestablish consensus among participants. Alternatives to the status quo are normally not considered unless partisan interests bring them to the attention of the participants in the decision-making process. There is only a marginal amount of planned search for alternatives to achieve desired ends. The decision process is structured so that partisan interests have the opportunity to press their desires at some point in the deliberations. Decisions represent a consensus on policy reached through a political, power-oriented bargaining process.

The most important characteristic of the muddling through, or incremental, approach is its emphasis on the proposition that budgetary decisions are necessarily political. Its descriptive appeal is that it more accurately depicts a process in which numerous actors, each with a different point of view, negotiate and bargain for a consensus. The larger the issue, the more difficult it is to achieve consensus for radical change, which results most often in incremental adjustments to the status quo. Whereas a purely rational approach might suggest that budgetary decisions are attempts to allocate resources according to economic or other "objective" criteria, the incremental view stresses the extent to which political considerations outweigh calculations of optimality. The strongest critics of many budget reforms have tended to equate those reforms with seeking to establish the pure rationality model or a solely economic model, a description rarely accepted by those proposing budget reforms. As will be seen throughout this text, any "real" budget reform is forced to accommodate the political nature of decision making. In reality, elements of rationalism and incrementalism pervade the budgetary process.[53]

It is evident that many decisions are indeed incremental, and clearly each budget decision does not require a thorough review of all options and careful calculations of the possible outcomes of each option. Yet major decisions that depart dramatically from the past are made from time to time in the budgetary process. Nonincremental change, especially at the macro level, addressing major deficits and surpluses, does occur.[54] And, of course, major events such as terrorist threats and creating a new agency such as the Department of Homeland Security cause nonincremental change, although the core of federal budgeting did not change significantly after September 11, 2001.[55] Furthermore, decision makers often do attempt to achieve public values and are motivated more by the social and economic problems their agencies must address than by bureaucratic budget maximizing and interest-group pressures.[56]

Summary

Public budgeting involves choices among ends and means. Public budgeting shares many characteristics with budgeting in the private sector, but it often requires the application of criteria different from those used by private organizations. Chief among these differences is that few public sector decisions can be assessed in terms of profit and loss. Private sector decisions, in contrast, ultimately must consider the long-run profit-or-loss condition of the firm.

Budgeting systems involve the organization of information for making choices and the structure of decision-making processes. Public budgeting systems have evolved as one means of holding government accountable for its actions. Budgetary procedures are developed to hold the government in general accountable to the public, the executive branch accountable to the legislature, and subordinates accountable to their managers. Budgetary procedures also are developed to specify what the executive is accountable for. Concern for the financial solvency of some city governments and the size of the federal budget deficit and total debt have led to reform proposals to use budgeting as a device for holding governments accountable for their long-term financial position. Renewed interest is evident in citizens demanding that governments report regularly on their performance.

Budgetary systems work through information flows. However, each participant in the budgetary process pays selective attention to information. The various theories of decision making differ in terms of how much information decision makers are willing and able to consider. The decision-making approach that seems best to characterize budgetary systems is the limited rationality approach. This approach underlies the discussions throughout this text.

Notes

1. Warsh, D. (2006). *Knowledge and the wealth of nations: a story of economic discovery*. New York, NY: W. W. Norton; Ferguson, N. (2011). Ferguson, N. (2012). *Civilization: the west and the rest*. London, UK: Penguin.
2. Downs, A. (1967). *Inside bureaucracy*. Boston, MA: Little, Brown; Wilson, J. (2000). Preface. In *Bureaucracy: what government agencies do and why they do it*. New York, NY: Basic Books.
3. Federal Reserve Bank of St. Louis (2019). *Federal surplus or deficit (–) as a percent of gross domestic product*. Federal Reserve Economic Data. Retrieved October 12, 2019, from https://fred.stlouisfed.org/series/FYFSGDA188S.
4. U.S. Department of Commerce, Bureau of Economic Analysis (2019). *Table B-49: Federal, state and local government current receipts and expenditures, 1968–2018*. Retrieved October 12, 2019, from https://www.govinfo.gov/app/collection/erp/2019.
5. Organization for Economic Cooperation and Development (2015). *General government spending: total, % GDP, 2015*. Retrieved October 12, 2019, from https://data.oecd.org/gga/general-government-spending.htm#indicator-chart.
6. Porter, M., & Kramer, M. (2006). Strategy and society: the link between competitive advantage and corporate social responsibility. *Harvard Business Review, 84*, 78–92.
7. McPherson, S. (2018). 8 Corporate responsibility (CSR) trends to look for in 2018. *Forbes.com*, January 12. Retrieved October 12, 2019, from https://www.forbes.com/sites/susanmcpherson/2018/01/12/8-corporate

-social-responsibility-csr-trends-to-look-for-in-2018/#799d0fb140ce.

8. Science: Business Network (2017). R&D pays: economists suggest 20% return on public investment for research and innovation. *Science: Business Network Newsletter*, June 27. Retrieved October 12, 2019, from https://sciencebusiness.net/news/80354/R%26D-pays%3A-Economists-suggest-20%25-return-on-public-investment-for-research-and-innovation.

9. Sampat, B. (2011). Appendix D: The impact of publicly funded biomedical and health research, a review, in *Measuring the impacts of federal investments in research: a workshop summary*. Washington, DC: National Academies Press. Also available at https://www.ncbi.nlm.nih.gov/books/NBK83123/.

10. Rosen, H., & Gayer, T. (2013). *Public finance* (10th ed.). New York, NY: McGraw-Hill/Irwin.

11. Office of Management and Budget (2020). Budget of the United States government, fiscal 2020, historical tables. *Table 12.1: summary comparison of total outlays for grants to state and local governments, 1940–2018*. Retrieved October 15, 2019, from https://www.govinfo.gov/app/collection/budget/2020/BUDGET-2020-TAB; Brooks, R. (2004). Privatization of government services: an overview and review of the literature. *Public Budgeting, Accounting and Financial Management, 16*, 467–491; Leavitt, W., & Morris, J. (2007). Public works services arrangements in the twenty-first century: the multiple sector partnership as an alternative to privatization. *Public Works Management Policy, 12*, 325–330.

12. Rubin, I. (2006). Budgeting for contracting in local government. *Public Budgeting & Finance, 26, Spring*, 1–13; Little, R. (2011). The emerging role of public-private-partnerships in mega-project delivery. *Public Works Management Policy, 16*, 240–249.

13. White, M. (1978). Budget policy: where does it begin and end? *Governmental Finance, 7*, 2–9. Credits W. F. Willoughby's *The problem of a national budget* (1919) with an early statement of budgeting as a process for holding government accountable.

14. Barnes, R. (2019). Supreme Court says Trump can proceed with plan to spend military funds for border wall construction. *The Washington Post*, July 26. Retrieved October 15, 2019, from https://www.washingtonpost.com/politics/courts_law/supreme-court-says-trump-can-proceed-with-plan-to-spend-military-funds-for-border-wall-construction/2019/07/26/f2a63d48-aa55-11e9-a3a6-ab670962db05_story.html.

15. Webber, C., & Wildavsky, A. (1986). *A history of taxation and expenditure in the western world*. New York, NY: Simon & Schuster.

16. Burkhead, J. (1956). *Government budgeting* (pp. 2–4). New York, NY: Wiley.

17. Naylor, E. (1941). *The federal budget system in operation* (pp. 22–23). Washington, DC: Author.

18. Burkhead, J. (1956). *Government budgeting*, 12–13.

19. Buck, A. (1919). *Public budgeting*, 14. New York: Harper.

20. Burkhead, J. (1956). *Government budgeting*, 23; Willbern, Y. (1967). Personnel and money. In J. Fesler (Ed.), *The 50 states and their local governments* (p. 391). New York, NY: Knopf.

21. Budget and Accounting Act of 1921. Ch. 18, 42 Stat. 20.

22. Budget and Accounting Procedures Act of 1950. Ch. 946, Title I, part I, 64 Stat. 832.

23. U.S. Commission on Organization of the Executive Branch of the Government (1955). *Budget and accounting* (p. ix). Washington, DC: U.S. Government Printing Office.

24. Rubin, I. (1993). Who invented budgeting in the United States? *Public Administration Review, 53*, 438–444.

25. Schick, A. (1966). The road to PPB: the stages of budget reform. *Public Administration Review, 26*, 243–258; Caiden, N. (2010). Challenges confronting contemporary public budgeting: retrospectives/prospectives from Allen Schick. *Public Administration Review, 70*, 203–210.

26. Tyer, C., & Willand, J. (1997). Public budgeting in America: a twentieth century retrospective. *Journal of Public Budgeting, Accounting and Financial Management, 9*, 189–219.

27. Bartle, J. (2001). Budgeting, policy, and administration: patterns and dynamics in the United States. *International Journal of Public Administration, 24*, 21–30.

28. Yang, K., & Holzer, M. (2006). The performance-trust link: implications for performance measurement. *Public Administration Review, 66*, 114–126; Berman, B. J. (2006). *Listening to the public: adding the voices of the people to government performance measurement and reporting*. New York, NY: Fund for the City of New York; Epstein, P. D., et al. (2006). *Results that matter: improving communities by engaging citizens, measuring performance, and getting things done*. Hoboken, NJ: Jossey-Bass.

29. Holzer, M., et al. (2009). *Literature review and analysis related to measuring local government efficiency*. Newark, NJ: Rutgers University School of Public Affairs and Administration.

30. McCormack, L. (2007). Performance budgeting in Canada. *OECD Journal on Budgeting, 7*(4), 1–18. See also, in the same journal issue, articles on performance budgeting in Denmark, Korea, and the Netherlands. The journal regularly publishes articles detailing performance budgeting in a large number of countries. Journal contents can be viewed online at https://www.oecd.org/canada/43411424.pdf.

31. A good example is Comptroller, State of New York (published annually since 2003; see most recent year). *State of New York financial condition report*. Albany, NY: Comptroller's Office of Public Information. Retrieved October 15, 2019, from https://www.osc.state.ny.us/finance/finreports/fcr/2018/fcrindex.htm.

32. Lambert, L., & Pierog, K. (2014). Detroit leads 2013 U.S. bond defaults: Moody's. *Reuter's Business News*, May 7. Retrieved January 12, 2020, from https://www.reuters.com/article/us-usa-municipals-defaults-idUSBREA4603920140507.

33. Office of Management and Budget (2019). *Circular A-11: Part 7, Principles of budgeting for capital asset acquisitions*. Retrieved October 15, 2019, from https://www.whitehouse.gov/wp-content/uploads/2018/06/a11_web_toc.pdf.

34. Employment Act of 1946. Ch. 33, 60 Stat. 23.
35. Burkhead, J. (1956). *Government budgeting*, 2.
36. Bland, R. (2013). *A budgeting guide for local government* (3rd ed.). Washington, DC: International City Management Association.
37. Businessdictionary.com. *System*. Retrieved October 15, 2019, from http://www.businessdictionary.com/definition/system.html.
38. Kendall, K., & Kendall, K. (2010). *Systems analysis and design* (8th ed.). New York, NY: Prentice-Hall.
39. Khan, N. (2019). Here's the latest on the officials facing charges for the Flint water crisis. *Michigan Radio NPR*, April 25. Retrieved January 12, 2020, from https://www.michiganradio.org/post/here-s-latest-officials-facing-charges-flint-water-crisis.
40. Elementary and Secondary Education Act of 1965 (P.L. 89-10).
41. No Child Left Behind Act of 2001 (P.L. 107-110).
42. Every Student Succeeds Act of 2015 (P.L. 114-95).
43. Medicare Prescription Drug, Improvement and Modernization Act (MMA) of 2003. Public Law 108-173.
44. Jones, L., & McCaffery, J. (1994). Budgeting according to Aaron Wildavsky: a bibliographic essay. *Public Budgeting & Finance, 14*, Spring, 16–43.
45. Wildavsky, A., & Caiden, N. (2000). *The new politics of the budgetary process* (4th ed.). New York, NY: Longman Press; Kelly, J. (2003). The long view: lasting (and fleeting) reforms in public budgeting in the twentieth century. *Public Budgeting, Accounting and Financial Management, 15*, 309–326; Kasdin, S. (2010). Reinventing reforms: how to improve program management using performance measures. Really. *Public Budgeting & Finance, 30*, Fall, 51–78.
46. Knoll, M. (2010). The role of behavioral economics and behavioral decision making in Americans' retirement savings decisions. *Social Security Bulletin, 70*(4). Retrieved December 5, 2011, from http:// www.ssa.gov/policy/docs/ssb/v70n4/v70n4p1.html.
47. Brewer, G., & de Leon, P. (1983). *The foundations of policy analysis*. Chicago, IL: Dorsey.
48. Allison, G., & Zelikow, P. (1999). *Essence of decision: explaining the Cuban missile crisis* (2nd ed.). New York, NY: Longman.
49. The terms *technical* and *economic rationality* are the names of two of five basic types of rationality identified by Diesing, P. (1962). *Reason and society*. Urbana, IL: University of Illinois Press.
50. Friedman, M. (1953). *Essays in positive economics*. Chicago, IL: University of Chicago Press.
51. Wildavsky, A. (1979). *Speaking truth to power: the art and craft of policy analysis*. Boston, MA: Little, Brown.
52. Lindblom, C. (1959). The science of "muddling through." *Public Administration Review, 19*, 79–88; Jones, L. (1997). Changing how we budget: Aaron Wildavsky's perspective. *Journal of Public Budgeting, Accounting and Financial Management, 9*, 46–71.
53. Reddick, C. (2002). Testing rival decision-making theories on budget outputs: theories and comparative evidence. *Public Budgeting & Finance, 22*, Fall, 1–25.
54. Reddick, C. (2003). Budgetary decision making in the twentieth century: theories and evidence. *Journal of Public Budgeting, Accounting and Financial Management, 15*, 251–274; Reddick, C. (2007). State resource allocation and budget formats: towards a hybrid model. *Journal of Public Budgeting, Accounting and Financial Management, 19*, 222–245; the Federal Reserve Board's history of the Great Recession is a good illustration of major directional changes in policy and action during the course of managing the biggest financial crisis in the U.S. since the Great Depression. *The Great Recession: December 2007 – June 2009*, retrieved October 15, 2019, from https://www.federalreservehistory.org/essays/great_recession_of_200709.
55. Joyce, P. (2005). Federal budgeting after September 11th: a whole new ballgame, or is it déjà vu all over again? *Public Budgeting & Finance, 25*, Spring, 15–31.
56. Reddick, C. (2004). Rational expectations theory and macro budgetary decision-making: comparative analysis of Canada, UK, and USA. *Journal of Public Budgeting, Accounting and Financial Management, 16*, 316–356.

CHAPTER 2

The Public Sector in Perspective

Depending on how we are affected personally by government and our general philosophical views about the roles of the public and private sectors, we have different and sometimes contradictory views about the public sector. Some may think it is too big; some may think it is too small. Often, we do not think of the government at all, except when government intrudes in obvious ways. Federal income tax filing time in the United States is one of those intrusions, and it often leads one to say: "Government is too big; I pay too much in taxes." The Great Recession and the coronavirus crisis were two dramatic events that led most people to demand faster and more massive responses from both federal and state governments.

One danger of generalizing about the size of the public sector of society is that any single generalization necessarily ignores important information. Although the statement "government is vast" may be valid, it fails to recognize the difficulties in determining what is and is not government or the fact that government is also small in some respects. The chapter explores three main topics. The first is the relative sizes of the private and public sectors of society and the reasons for the growth of government. The second is the magnitude of government and the historical growth of local, state, and federal finances. The third section contrasts the purposes of government expenditures with the sources of revenue used by the three main levels of government in the United States.

Relative Sizes of the Private and Public Sectors

Basic to all matters of public budgeting is the issue of the appropriate size of the public sector. This issue is inherently political, not only in the partisan sense but also in the sense that it involves fundamental policy questions about what government should and should not do, and what it can and cannot do. At stake are a congeries of competing public and private wants and needs and competing philosophies of the role of the public sector in society. Many of the framers of the Constitution wanted to keep the central government small to protect individual liberty. However, other early leaders, such as Alexander Hamilton, sought a more active role for the new government.[1]

Reasons for Growth
Value Questions

The issue of size relates to the values of freedom and social welfare. Keeping government small has been advocated as a means of protecting individuals from tyranny and stimulating individual independence and initiative. In contrast, critics charge that sometimes reliance on the private sector causes the underfinancing of public programs and the failure to confront major social problems.[2] Some people argue that the behavior of large mortgage lending institutions in the years immediately prior to the Great Recession was in part caused by placing too much faith in an unfettered—or more precisely, unregulated—private sector.

The U.S. political system, of course, is not structured in such a way that any single and overriding decision is made as to the size of this sector. The multiplicity of governments makes it virtually impossible to reach any single decision about overall governmental size. Decisions relevant to size are made in a political context within and between the executive and legislative branches and among the three major levels of government—local, state, and federal. Decisions by all these branches and levels of government contribute to an ultimate resolution of the question, but the resolution is really a result of tallying many individual choices. And any time we decide to measure the size of the public sector, we are only capturing a snapshot at that point in time. Significant changes in public sector size occur over time, sometimes quite rapidly.

Government Responses

Why government expands has been the subject of extended debate.[3] One of the two main reasons is that government is being "responsive" to the demands of society. Wagner's law of increasing public spending, originally proposed in the 1880s, holds that economic growth creates demands for new activities that government alone can perform.[4] The second reason is that government has a supposed propensity to grow. In this case, government grows as a result of empire building by government bureaucrats, supported by political leaders.[5] Among the numerous factors suggested as stimulating responses from government are the following:[6]

- *The need for collective goods.* Because defense, homeland security, disaster response, and some other programs benefit all citizens and cannot be handled readily by the private sector, the government becomes involved. When wars occur, governments grow; after the conflict, they tend to remain larger than during the prewar period. Education

is another important collective good. Educated people tend to be more productive and increase the total wealth of the society, and the private sector cannot be relied on to provide an appropriate level of public education.

- *Demographic changes.* Increases in total population and in the number of newborns and the elderly stimulate the creation and expansion of government programs.
- *Changes in living patterns.* As people move from rural to urban areas, and then from cities to suburbs, demands for government services follow them. Governments must then provide more schools, roads, public utilities, and public safety.
- *Externalities.* Industrial firms, which are concerned mainly with making a profit, may pollute the air and water. Government is expected to control the social costs arising from these private actions.
- *Economic hardships.* Depressions and other negative economic situations stimulate the growth of government.
- *High-risk situations.* When risks are high, the private sector is unlikely to invest large quantities of resources, so government is called upon to support programs. Examples include the development of nuclear energy as a source of electrical power, dealing with a worldwide pandemic, and the creation of the space program. Once the risks of certain aspects of space activity became manageable as a result of government intervention, commercial interests engaged in space research and moved into the launching of private vehicles and satellites.
- *Technological change.* With the advent of new technology, government has provided support, as in the case of roads and airports, to accommodate improved transportation modes and information highways, such as the Internet, and to regulate new industries, as in the case of railroads, radio, and television.

These reasons are helpful in explaining why government is necessary and why it has expanded over time, but they do not give a single answer to the question of whether the size of government at any one point in time is too large, too small, or just right. Proposals to expand or contract the scope of the public sector also reflect many political considerations. Principally, any proposal for the expansion of services that results in an increase in taxes is likely to have unfavorable political repercussions. Therefore, the size issue always relates to both government expenditures and revenues (taxes, user charges, and fees). Decision makers, no matter how crude or approximate their methods of calculating, attempt to weigh the merits of coping with the current situation with the available resources against the merits of recommending new programs that may alleviate problems but at the same time raise the ire of taxpayers. The appeal of Donald Trump in 2016 to reduce government's domestic and foreign commitments caught the imagination and matched the beliefs of many voters, enough perhaps to turn sufficient numbers of voters who normally voted for Democratic candidates to elect him the 45th President. Of course, campaign promises of presidential candidates to reduce the size of government, or to introduce new programs, are easier to promise than to achieve.

Private and Public Sector Boundaries

Major problems are encountered when attempts are made to gauge the sizes of the public and private sectors and to distinguish between one government and another. Government has become so deeply involved in society that one may frequently have difficulty discerning what is not at least quasi-public. Moreover, governments have extensive relationships with each other, to the point where a discussion of any single government becomes meaningless without a discussion of its relationships with other governments.

Statistical data on government revenues and expenditures fail to reflect adequately the size of government. For instance, the entire political campaign process is clearly governmental in that substantial sums of money are spent to elect people to political offices. These funds are not recorded as government expenditures, but nonetheless are "governmental" in nature.[7] Federal Election Commission statistics show that spending in the 2016 presidential election exceeded $1.8 billion, about the same as the last campaign with no incumbent running, and more than four times the amount spent in the 2000 election.[8] Also, the size of government tends to be understated in cases where government activities require relatively little money and personnel but have a substantial impact on the private sector or other governments. This is especially true with respect to regulatory activities, such as the federal government's control of interstate commerce, occupational safety, and environmental health.

Nonexhaustive Expenditures

It can be misleading to rely exclusively on revenue and expenditure data for measuring size for another reason. Sometimes the assumption is made that all government expenditures represent a drain on the private economy. In fact, government expenditures can be nonexhaustive as well as exhaustive. Exhaustive expenditures occur when government consumes resources, such as facilities and manpower, that might otherwise have been used by the private sector. Nonexhaustive expenditures occur when government redistributes or transfers resources to components of the society instead of consuming them. Interest payments on the national debt, unemployment compensation, aid to the indigent, and old-age and retirement benefits are major examples of nonexhaustive government expenditures. Nonexhaustive expenditures, while not consumed by government, generally are redistributive, namely moving money from one group of people to another.

Another form of nonexhaustive expenditures is investment for the future, whether for capital facilities (see the chapter on capital assets) or for services, as in education for children. Government aid to small businesses, support of research and development, and similar activities are forms of investment in future economic development. As a result of these kinds of expenditures, the cost of government is less than the total dollar figures reported in budgets. Some money that is spent by governments will generate future revenue for both society and its governments.

Effects on the Private Sector

Government expenditures have specific effects on industries, occupations, geographic regions, and subpopulations. These effects are especially evident in the field of defense. During the Cold War, clusters of firms and their employees became highly dependent upon defense outlays, resulting in what President Dwight Eisenhower in 1961 decried as the military-industrial complex. The role of defense contractors in the Iraq and Afghanistan wars, or more generally the war on terror, if anything has magnified Eisenhower's concern about the interdependency between the defense industry and military budgets. Over a decade after 9/11, disbursements to contractors comprised about 57% of total military spending.[9] The case could be made that a dangerous symbiotic relationship developed between the military, with its penchant for new weaponry, and corporations eager to supply such weaponry. Periodic scandals in defense contracting offer seeming confirmation of the fears expressed by President Eisenhower.

The effects of defense are particularly pronounced regarding employment, despite the downsizing that has occurred since the end of the Cold War. In 2019, civilian employment in the Department of Defense accounted for just over 0.4% of the private sector labor force. In addition, in 2019 the federal government employed more than 1.3 million active duty armed services personnel. Total military and civilian defense employment constituted 1.2% of total U.S. employment in 2019.[10] Those figures are almost unchanged over the past 15 years.

The effects of defense expenditures on the private economy also have been substantial. Defense expenditures account for a significant percentage of private sector jobs in various industries. The creation of defense-related jobs entices people into educational programs that help them develop the requisite skills. As a result, people are attracted to technical career fields that are dependent upon continued defense spending. These people suffer or flourish based on which policies prevail.

Geographic and Industry Effects

Military research, development, and procurement are of such great magnitude that many specific industries and corporations become quasi-public institutions. In 2017, the Department of Defense obligated $320 billion in total contracts. Of this amount, 93%, or $299 billion, was for work performed in the United States. These contract values were considerably down from 2008, which had $401 billion in contracts for work in the United States and $21 billion for work outside the United States.[11] Defense expenditures greatly influence the private sector—in firms that engage in shipbuilding, aircraft construction, and telecommunications, to name just three examples—and the importance of defense expenditures on the private sector increases in periods of defense buildup. Besides providers of military equipment, such as Boeing, General Dynamics, General Electric, and General Motors, numerous consulting and research and development firms are dependent on military expenditures. Nondefense contracting firms are similarly dependent, with 60% to 80% of their revenues coming from government contracts. The role of contractors in Iraq and Afghanistan in performing what had historically been military functions, and in the massive reconstruction programs, received special attention from government watchdog agencies, such as the Government Accountability Office, and the appointment of Special Inspector Generals for Iraq and Afghanistan in the face of charges of poor oversight, waste, fraud, and simply an excessive reliance on contractors mounted.[12]

Employees of these varied private sector firms, judging from their length of service on government projects, are doing work that otherwise would be done (and, in many cases, used to be done) by career civil servants. One difference between these contractors and the civil servants they supplant is that the pay of managerial staff in these firms is often higher than that of similarly trained government employees. Professional salaries, such as for engineers and scientists, tend to be relatively equal, because government must meet private sector salaries to recruit and retain professionals.

Another difference is that private sector employees do not necessarily constitute an ongoing expense to the government. These workers are not protected by civil service laws and are ineligible for government pension benefits. Furthermore, when these workers' services are not needed, government has no obligation to them as it would to its own employees. When partial government shutdowns occur, contractors possibly go without payments and in turn do not pay their employees who normally work on government contracts.

The geographic effects of defense expenditures are equally important because they are not uniformly distributed throughout the nation. In 2017, the Department of Defense spent $407 billion on payroll and contracts within the United States. Five states—California, Virginia, Texas, Maryland, and Florida—accounted for $173 billion, or about 43% of that total.[13]

Defense, while the most striking example of private dependence upon public outlays, is not the sole example. Highway construction also involves large sums of public money. The employees of construction firms specializing in bridge and highway construction are, in effect, government employees. The same is true for suppliers of road-building equipment. A related size measure is the role of contracted personnel producing public services in place of federal employees. In 2015, an estimated 4.3 million individuals worked for federal agencies and on federal programs as contract or grant employees.[14]

In some cases, the impact of government on an industry is greater as a result of what government does *not* do than what it *does* do. The federal government's choice not to tax interest paid on home mortgages (see the chapter on budgeting for revenues and taxes), for example, has a far greater effect on the housing industry than all federal expenditures for public housing and redevelopment.

The lack of clear-cut distinctions between the public and private sectors and between one government and another is evident in education. Elementary and secondary education are a function of local governments (cities, towns, counties, school districts), but about one-half of the funds used by these districts comes from state governments, with additional funds coming from local sources of revenue, primarily property taxes, and some funds from the federal government. The states have the primary role in funding public higher education, with important federal support, especially in the form of student aid and research financing. Governments also selectively subsidize private colleges and universities. Private corporations also make important contributions to both public and private schools. In 2002, the U.S. Supreme Court ruled that it is constitutional for governments to use public funds to provide vouchers to parents whose children attend private or parochial schools.[15] Since that ruling, some states have adopted statutes permitting school vouchers, but most have not.

In addition, the level of funding may understate the degree of federal involvement in elementary and secondary education. The federal government can, as a condition of the receipt of federal assistance, insist that state and local governments adopt policies they might otherwise have chosen not to adopt. The best recent example of this was the federal No Child Left Behind Act, which forced state and local governments to adopt specific accountability standards in the form of testing requirements in order to continue to receive federal funds.[16] Under the constitutionally provided federal system, the national government cannot directly compel states and localities to establish such standards, but the threat of the loss of federal funds is sufficient to encourage most to go along with the federal requirements. The Every Student Succeeds Act, replacing No Child Left Behind, substantially reduced the federally imposed testing requirements, providing funding for state-designed testing and other accountability programs.

Subpopulation Effects

Taxes and expenditures affect different subpopulations in different ways. In the example given earlier of the federal government allowing income tax deductions for interest paid on home mortgages, the middle and upper classes benefit far more than lower-income groups, who are typically renters rather than homeowners. This tax expenditure—namely, the government's not taxing something that could be taxed—has a redistributional effect in favor of the middle and upper classes (see the chapter on budgeting for revenues: income taxes, payroll taxes, and property taxes).

Government actions also have important effects on generations, including those yet to be born. Taxing and spending policies can help or harm children (born and unborn) through health and education programs, the working-age population through transportation programs, and the elderly through government-sponsored nursing care and the like. Future generations benefit from government programs that encourage investment in economic development, but excessive debts that governments may accumulate may harm these same people in the future.

The Magnitude and Growth of Government

There are many ways to measure the magnitude of government, but measurements of dollars and people are generally the easiest. By focusing on revenues, expenditures, and numbers of employees, we can use comparable standards in contrasting governments with each other and with private organizations. These measures, then, are the main ones used in this section. While care has been taken in making these comparisons to obtain the most recent and accurate data possible, some of the data here must be considered approximate.[17]

Revenues

One approach to assessing the size of government is to compare many governments with each other, as well as with large private sector organizations. **Table 2-1** makes such comparisons, using revenues or receipts, which allows comparisons among private and public organizations.[18] The table ranks the 25 largest governments and industrial corporations in the world, as measured by revenues. Eleven of the 25 are governments, with the U.S. federal government ranked first. Significantly, 14 of the world's 25 largest organizations are not governments at all, but are instead private

sector corporations (all multinational), with Walmart coming in as the eighth largest. No U.S. state governments make the list of 25; California is the closest, but 23 global corporations' revenues were higher than California's.

Figure 2-1 shows central government revenue as a percentage of gross domestic product (GDP) for 2017 for Organization for Economic Cooperation and Development (OECD) countries, excluding two countries with no data for 2017. On that list, the United States ranks sixth from the bottom, probably surprising to most U.S. citizens. Note, however, that the figures are for central government revenues only. Many OECD countries are unitary states, so that all government revenues are central, whereas government in the United States, as noted in this chapter, includes substantial financial roles for state and local governments. Thus, comparing the U.S. federal government only with countries that have no state and local governments is somewhat misleading. Adding state and local revenues to federal revenues and dividing by GDP moves the United States three more places up the list, but it is still near the bottom. One other observation is important, and that is that the revenue figures do not consider borrowing. U.S. expenditures as a percentage of GDP are considerably higher—37%—than U.S. revenues—16%—due to expenditures financed by borrowing (see the chapter on government and the economy for a discussion of deficits and debt).

A comparison of organizations in the United States only also demonstrates the significant size of the governmental sector, although in the past decade, the growth of U.S. corporations has pushed all but one state government out of the list of the 20 largest organizations in the United States (see **Table 2-2**). California ranks 15th. If we consider the top 50 U.S. organizations, New York State would be ranked 35th.[19]

These statistics dramatically underscore the need for caution in generalizing about governments or private corporations. It is necessary to recognize the important differences in the functions of government and industry and the methods by which these organizations make decisions (see the introductory chapter discussion of public

Table 2-1 Twenty-Five Largest Governments and Industrial Corporations in the World by Revenues, 2017

Rank	Governments	Revenues (Billions of Dollars)	Private Corporations
1	United States (Federal)	$3,316.2	
2	Japan	$1,516.2	
3	Germany	$1,387.0	
4	France	$1,194.3	
5	United Kingdom	$874.0	
6	Italy	$792.1	
7	Canada	$532.8	
8		$500.3	Walmart
9	Spain	$441.5	
10	Australia	$362.0	
11		$348.9	State Grid
12		$327.0	Sinopec Group
13		$326.0	China National Petroleum
14	Netherlands	$322.0	
15		$311.9	Royal Dutch Shell
16		$265.2	Toyota Motors
17		$260.0	Volkswagen
18		$244.6	BP
19		$244.4	Exxon Mobil
20		$242.1	Berkshire Hathaway
21	Sweden	$236.6	
22		$229.2	Apple
23		$211.9	Samsung
24		$205.5	Glencore
25		$201.2	United Health Group

Governments: Organization for Economic Cooperation and Development (2018). *Revenue statistics: 2018.* Retrieved May 5, 2019, from https://read.oecd-ilibrary.org/taxation/revenue-statistics-2018/total-tax-revenue-in-billions-of-us-dollars-at-market-exchange-rates_rev_stats-2018-table26-en#page1; U.S. Government U.S. Council of Economic Advisors (2019). *Economic report of the president.* Washington, DC: U.S. Government Printing Office, 552. Corporations: Global Finance (2019). *World's largest companies.* Retrieved May 5, 2019, from file:///C:/Users/rwjoh/Documents/PBS%2010/Info%20Resources%20multiple%20chapters/World's%20Largest%20Companies%202018%20_%20Global%20Finance%20Magazine.html

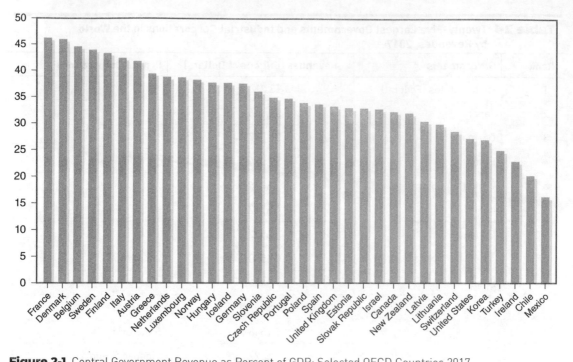

Figure 2-1 Central Government Revenue as Percent of GDP: Selected OECD Countries 2017.

Organization for Economic Cooperation and Development (2019). *Revenue statistics – OECD countries: comparative tables.* Retrieved May 5, 2019, from https://stats.oecd.org/Index.aspx?DataSetCode=REV#

versus private sector differences). Differences also abound within each of these types of organizations. The services provided and methods of decision making are not identical in the governments of Japan, Germany, and the United Kingdom, nor are they the same among such different private corporations as Walmart, United Health Group, and General Motors. In contrast, using the standard of revenue size may provide more insights into the operations of organizations than simply classifying organizations as public or private, national or local, and so forth. Revenue is a key measure of the economic impact of an organization—revenue collected from the private sector by governments or sales by private companies (see the chapter on government and the economy). Though not all industrial firms are like General Motors, nor are all state governments like California, all organizations of any given size, regardless of their private or public character, may exhibit some common traits, and all of a similar size represent similar proportions of the total economy. Many large private organizations in the United States, such as

General Motors, received massive bailout funds during the 2008–2010 recession, further blurring private versus public distinctions. More recently, some companies, and individuals such as farmers, have received federal assistance to help offset the loss of export sales as a result of tariffs imposed by other countries on U.S. goods sold to them, in retaliation for U.S. tariffs imposed on foreign goods entering the United States.[20]

Although total revenues or expenditures are useful as approximate guides in measuring the size of government, these data need to be assessed considering the varied capabilities of societies to support government. Unfortunately, reliable international data are often unavailable. Therefore, drawing useful comparisons among international organizations is difficult.

Even given these limitations, it is obvious that the U.S. economy is one of the most prosperous in the world. The high per capita GDP in the United States, $53,129 in 2018, has allowed for both big government and a large private sector.[21] The size of federal, state, and local government receipts as a

Table 2-2 Twenty Largest U.S. Organizations by Revenues, 2018 (in Millions of Dollars)

1	United States Federal	$3,340.4
2	Wal-Mart Stores	$500.3
3	Berkshire Hathaway	$242.1
4	Apple	$229.2
5	United Health Group	$201.2
6	McKesson	$198.5
7	CVS Health	$184.8
8	Amazon	$177.9
9	AT&T	$160.5
10	General Motors	$157.3
11	Ford Motor	$156.8
12	AmerisourceBergen	$153.1
13	Chevron	$134.5
14	Cardinal Health	$130.0
15	State of California	$129.8
16	Costco	$129.1
17	Verizon Communications	$126.0
18	Kroger	$122.7
19	General Electric	$122.3
20	Walgreens Boots Alliance	$118.2

U.S. Government: U.S. Council of Economic Advisors (2019). *Economic report of the president.* Washington, DC: U.S. Government Printing Office, 552. Corporations: Global Finance (2019). *World's largest companies.* Fortune (2019). *Fortune 500: who made the list?* Retrieved May 9, 2019, from http://fortune.com/fortune500/list/; California Legislative Analyst's Office (2018). *The 2018 budget: California spending plan.* Retrieved May 9, 2019, from https://lao.ca.gov/Publications/Report/3870

proportion of GDP has remained steady at around 31% since 2005, with the significant exception of the jump up to 36% in 2010 at the end of the recession, falling back down to 31% in 2016.[22] This figure, however, is misleading in regard to the size of the public sector in that only about one-half of federal receipts go toward the purchase of goods and services—the other half is used for transfer payments and interest payments on debt.

Expenditures

Because early records on state and local finance are spotty, federal expenditure data must be used to obtain some overall perspective on the growth of government since the eighteenth century. **Table 2-3** shows federal spending from 1789 through 2019. During this period, expenditures rose from only $4.3 million in the first few years to over $4.4 trillion annually in fiscal year 2019 (bear in mind that an important contributor to this difference is inflation).

The twentieth century saw important differences in the expenditure patterns of the federal government and those of state and local governments. Federal expenditures fluctuated most, primarily because of war-related activities. The first year in which federal expenditures exceeded $1 billion was 1865, the peak year of the Civil War. Later, in response to World War I, federal expenditures jumped from $0.7 billion in 1916 to $18.5 billion in 1919, then dropped to $6.4 billion the following year. They also increased from $13.3 billion in 1941, the year the United States entered World War II, to $92.7 billion in 1945, then declined just after the war. During the Korean War, expenditures rose from $42.6 billion in 1950 to $74.3 billion in 1953, and then dropped to $68.4 billion in 1955, after the war.[23]

In general, the past century has seen a pattern where federal expenditures rose during wartime and then declined, but not to prewar levels, resulting in a cumulative increase over time. The Vietnam War era, however, departed from this pattern: federal expenditures rose both during and after the war. One of the reasons for the continued high spending from the 1960s onward was the creation and growth of large entitlement programs, such as Social Security, Medicare, and Medicaid. More recently, the Afghanistan and Iraq wars and related conflicts in Syria and Yemen resulted in increases in federal spending as a proportion of GDP, and a substantial increase in federal debt (see the chapter on government and the economy).

Table 2-3 Federal Government Expenditures, Selected Years, 1789–2019 (Millions of Dollars)

Year	Amount	Year	Amount	Year	Amount
1789–91	4	1880	268	1965	118,228
1800	11	1885	260	1970	195,649
1805	11	1890	318	1975	332,332
1810	8	1895	356	1980	590,947
1815	33	1900	529	1985	946,423
1820	18	1905	567	1990	1,253,198
1825	16	1910	694	1995	1,515,837
1830	15	1915	746	2000	1,789,216
1835	18	1920	6,358	2005	2,472,205
1840	24	1925	2,924	2010	3,455,800
1845	23	1930	3,320	2011	3,603,100
1850	40	1935	6,412	2012	3,536,900
1855	60	1940	9,468	2013	3,454,600
1860	63	1945	92,712	2014	3,506,100
1865	1,298	1950	42,562	2015	3,688,400
1870	310	1955	68,444	2016	3,852,600
1875	275	1960	92,191	2017	3,981,600
				2018	4,109,042
				2019	4,412,000

Bureau of the Census, U.S. Department of Commerce (1975). *Historical statistics of the United States: colonial times to 1970*, part 2. Washington, DC: U.S. Government Printing Office, 1114; U.S. Office of Management and Budget (2007). *Historical tables, Budget of the United States Government: fiscal year 2007*. Washington, DC: U.S. Government Printing Office, 53–54. U.S. Congressional Budget Office (2019). *The budget and economic outlook: fiscal years 2019–2029*. Washington, DC: U.S. Government Printing Office, 154.

One might have expected a significant jump in federal outlays during and shortly after the recession of 2008–2010. The actual federal outlays shown in Table 2-3 do not confirm that expectation. There was a jump in outlays as a percentage of GDP from 20.2% in 2008 to 24.4% in 2008, but outlays fell off for 2010 and 2011 and then declined to around 21% of GDP.[24] Annual increases in outlays have generally been around $1.0 to $1.5 trillion annually, dropping to less than $0.5 trillion increase in 2018 over 2017. However, the amount of federal outlays financed by borrowing, rather than tax and other revenue sources, has steadily increased, contributing to large increases in the national debt (discussed in the chapter on government and the economy).

State and local expenditures, in contrast, have fluctuated less. In 1902, state and local expenditures were $1.1 billion, and they have continued to grow steadily over the past 110 years, to $2.8 trillion in 2018, with no significant reductions during any period.[25]

Important shifts have occurred in the extent to which the nation relies on different levels of government. At the turn of the century, local governments were by far the biggest spenders, followed by the federal government and then the states. During the Great Depression, federal spending spurted above local expenditures, and the gap has continued to widen. As of 2018, federal expenditures stood at $4.1 trillion,[26] compared with $2.8 trillion for state and local governments combined.[27] Caution should be exercised in interpreting these numbers, in that each includes intergovernmental transfers—namely, grants from one government to another. Of the $4.1 trillion in federal expenditures, an estimated $0.7 trillion was in federal grants to state and local governments (see the chapter on intergovernmental relations for more detailed discussion of intergovernmental transfers).[28] Though data for local governments distinct from state governments are not as readily available, in 2016, state and local government revenue included about the same $0.7 trillion in transfers from the federal government. It is good practice to net out spending from the source of an intergovernmental transfer ($0.7 trillion in federal in 2018) and assign it to the level(s) at which it is spent (state and local).

One means of looking at the growth of government over time, while controlling for price changes, is to consider government expenditures as a percentage of GDP. **Figure 2-2** shows

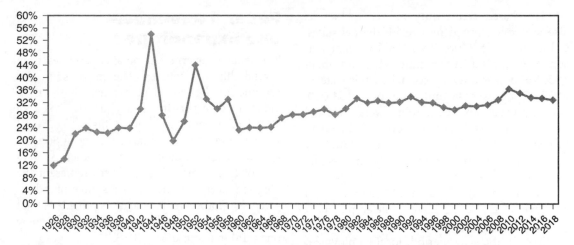

Figure 2-2 All Government Expenditures as a Percentage of Gross Domestic Product, 1926–2018.

Bureau of Census, U.S. Department of Commerce (1969). *Historical statistics on governmental finances and employment.* Washington, DC: U.S. government Printing Office, 1, 36–37; U.S. Department of Commerce, Bureau of Economic Analysis (2019). *Table B-49: Federal, state and local government current receipts and expenditures, 1968–2018,* Retrieved May 13, 2019, from https://www.govinfo.gov/app/collection/erp/2019

that, from 1926 to 2018, the cost of government rose from 12% to 33% of GDP. Increases first occurred in the 1930s due to the Great Depression, and World War II brought expenditures to an all-time high at about one-half of GDP. A sharp cutback followed in the postwar years, and expenditures dropped to a low of just under 20% by 1948. The Cold War and the Korean War occasioned another sharp increase in the early 1950s, and—after reductions in military spending in the late 1950s—the Great Society programs and the Vietnam War resulted in increased spending again during the 1960s; the spending has continued since that time. Although there has been some year-to-year fluctuation, the percentage of GDP devoted to government remained relatively stable between 28% and 34% since 1970, rising to 36% in 2010 as a result of economic stimulus programs and defense spending.

Public Employment

Another way to measure the size and growth of government is to examine trends in the number of government employees. In 1816, there were fewer than 5,000 full- and part-time civilian employees in the federal service. Much growth in public employment followed the Civil War.

In 1871, there were more than 50,000 federal employees, and this number doubled to 100,000 by 1881. The period of fastest growth was from the Great Depression through World War II. In 1931, there were still only 610,000 employees, but by 1945—the peak of the wartime economy—the federal civilian workforce had climbed to nearly 4 million. Within a year, however, it was reduced to fewer than 3 million employees, and since then, only once (in 1950) has the federal workforce dropped below 2 million. Federal civilian personnel averaged nearly 3 million between 1970 and 2000 but decreased to about 1.9 million by 2018.[29]

Although the size of the federal bureaucracy is extraordinarily large, the government's personnel are geographically dispersed. In 2017, California had 142,900 federal civilian employees, a figure equal to almost 20% of Alaska's population. Federal employees (excludes military personnel) are also numerous in other states, including Virginia, with 135,000; Maryland, with 130,000; and Texas, with 115,000.[30] States have become painfully aware of their dependence on federal employment during different periods of downsizing. California's federal civilian workforce was, in 2017, only about 75% of its size in 2010. Other states experienced similar decreases.

U.S.-based active duty military personnel also are concentrated in a relatively few states. California, in addition to federal civilian personnel employed in the state, also had about 185,000 active duty personnel in the state in 2017. Texas was second with over 164,000, and Virginia and North Carolina were third and fourth with just over 115,000 and 113,000, respectively.[31] Civilian employment and military employment also do not rise and fall necessarily in the same time periods.

At the state and local levels, the number of employees has also increased. State employment grew from 3.8 million in 1980 to 5.4 million in 2016. In the same period, local employment increased from 9.6 million to 14.0 million.[32] However, growth in both state and local employment had slowed in 2010 as a result of the recession and has remained steady since then. Significantly, the growth at the local level has been accompanied by a decline in the number of local governments. In 2017, there were more than 90,000 local governments, 30,000 fewer than five decades earlier. This decline is largely attributable to school district consolidation. Since 1972, the number of local governments has been increasing gradually, due mainly to increases in the number of special districts—that is, governments that typically provide a single service such as water provision or recreation services. There were almost 39,000 of these special district governments in 2017.[33]

Sources of Revenue and Purposes of Government Expenditures

In general, government does not simply get money and spend it. Rather, governments obtain revenue from specific sources and spend it on specific public goods and services. The following discussion considers the relationships between income and outgo—that is, the ways in which revenue is generated and the purposes of government expenditures.

Federal Revenues and Expenditures

The federal government obtains revenues from several different sources. The major source of revenue for the federal government is the individual income tax. In fiscal year 2018, 51% of all federal revenues came from this source. Social insurance taxes (payroll taxes for Social Security and Medicare) accounted for another 35% of the total. Corporate income taxes represent the biggest percentage change as a source of federal revenues: Corporate income taxes provided about 9% of federal revenues in 2010 and were down by one-third to about 6% in 2018.[34]

These three sources accounted for 92% of all federal revenues. This distribution represents a substantial shift from the early 1900s, when customs duties and excise taxes were the major revenue sources. Those sources now account for only 1% of total federal revenues. **Table 2-4** shows a summary of federal revenues and expenditures.

There are two main types of federal spending: discretionary spending, which is provided for through the annual appropriations process, and mandatory spending, which is provided for through "permanent" law. Discretionary appropriations provide for most of the core functions of government, including the operations of major federal departments. This category accounted for about 31% of all federal spending in 2018, and about one-half of this amount went for defense. This represents a substantial decline in the relative importance of discretionary spending from the 1970s. In 1973, 50% of expenditures were discretionary, and the figure was 65% in 1967.[35] Increased defense spending associated with military activities in Iraq and Afghanistan increased the percentage of the budget accounted for by discretionary spending. In more recent years, modernization of weapons systems and replacement of systems consumed in over a decade of war contributed to reversing the previous trend.

Mandatory spending (chiefly entitlements) accounted for about 61% of federal spending in 2018. This was a substantial increase in the proportion of the budget that went to mandatory spending since 1970, when the figure was 35%.

Table 2-4 Federal Revenues and Expenditures, 2018 (Billions of Dollars)

Revenues			Expenditures		
Source	Dollars (Billions)	Percent	Source	Dollars (Billions)	Percent
Individual Income Taxes	1,684	50.6	Social Security	982	23.9
Payroll Taxes[1]	1,171	35.2	Medicare	704	17.1
Corporate Income Taxes	205	6.2	Medicaid	389	9.5
Estate and Gift Taxes	23	0.7	Other Spending	703	17.1
Excise Taxes	95	2.9	Offsetting Receipts (3)	−259	−6.3
Total Taxes	**3,178**	**95.4**	**Total Mandatory**	**2,519**	**61.3**
Federal Reserve Remittances	71	2.1	Defense	622	15.1
Customs Duties	41	1.2	Nondefense	642	15.6
Miscellaneous Fees and Fines	40	1.2	**Total Discretionary**	**1,264**	**30.8**
Total Receipts	**3,330**	**100.0**	**Net Interest**	**325**	**7.9**
			Total Outlays	**4,108**	**100.0**

[1]Mainly Social Security and Medicare Part A.

U.S. Congressional Budget Office (2019). *The budget and economic outlook: fiscal years 2019–2029*. Washington, DC: U.S. Government Printing Office, 54, 91.

The major single entitlement—24% of total mandatory spending—is Social Security. The health entitlements (Medicare and Medicaid) together make up another 43% of all mandatory spending. The expansion of mandatory spending since the mid-1960s (fueled by the demographic shifts of an increasingly aging population and the economic shifts of increases in individuals at or near the poverty level) has increased the proportion of the federal budget devoted to mandatory spending.

The other category of federal spending is net interest. The federal government's spending on interest has increased and decreased, depending on the federal government's reliance on deficit financing and on interest rates. In 2010, it was 6% of the budget. In 1995, that figure was 15%. The reason for the much lower interest percentage in 2010, with a much larger debt, is historically low, near zero, interest rates. In 2018, net interest had grown to nearly 8%, largely as a result of deficits driven by stimulus programs and defense expenditures and expected interest rate increases.

Extreme partisan differences have made it extraordinarily difficult for the U.S. Congress to reach any compromise on a balance between expenditures and revenue.

State and Local Revenues and Expenditures

State and local revenues and expenditures are summarized in **Table 2-5**. The first thing to note about state revenues shown in the table is that 30% comes from other governments, mostly from the federal government. Of their own source revenues, taxes are the largest revenue source—43% in 2016. Sales and gross receipts taxes account for 21% of state government revenue. States obtain another 16% from individual income taxes, and 16% comes from user charges, such as utility charges. Not every state taps into each of the varied revenue sources that the states use. Some states have both a sales tax and an individual income tax. Others have only one or the other,

Table 2-5 State and Local Revenues and Expenditures, 2017 (in Millions of Dollars)

Source	State & Local	State	State Percent	Local	Local Percent
Total Revenue	3,401,687	2,136,454	100.0%	1,805,683	100.0%
General Revenue	3,008,262	1,909,322	89.4%	1,639,390	90.8%
General Revenue from Own Sources	2,318,053	1,272,154	59.5%	1,045,899	57.9%
Taxes	1,599,514	922,856	43.2%	676,658	37.5%
Property	503,262	15,945	0.7%	487,317	27.0%
Sales and Gross Receipts	558,871	441,124	20.6%	117,747	6.5%
Individual Income	376,297	343,621	16.1%	32,677	1.8%
Corporate Income	54,259	46,202	2.2%	8,057	0.4%
Motor Vehicle Licenses	27,504	25,566	1.2%	1,938	0.1%
Other Taxes	79,319	50,397	2.4%	28,922	1.6%
Charges and Miscellaneous General Revenue	718,539	349,298	16.3%	369,241	20.4%
Utility Revenue	164,127	13,824	0.6%	150,304	8.3%
Liquor Store Revenue	9,511	8,089	0.4%	1,422	0.1%
Insurance Trust Revenue	219,787	205,221	9.6%	14,567	0.8%
Intergovernmental Revenue	690,209	637,168	29.8%	593,491	32.9%
From Federal Government	690,209	621,509	29.1%	68,700	3.8%
From State Government		15,659	0.7%	524,791	29.1%
From Local Government					
Total Expenditures	3,517,971	2,225,107	100.0%	1,838,515	100.0%
Intergovernmental	3,388	532,699	23.9%	16,340	0.9%
Direct by Function	3,514,583	1,692,408	76.1%	1,822,175	99.1%
Direct General Expenditure	2,944,651	1,373,167	61.7%	1,571,484	85.5%
Capital Outlay	299,493	121,146	5.4%	178,346	9.7%
Other Direct General Expenditures	2,645,159	1,252,021	56.3%	1,393,138	75.8%
Education and Library Services	984,948	304,714	13.7%	680,234	37.0%
Public Welfare	637,644	581,912	26.2%	55,732	3.0%
Hospitals	183,141	79,102	3.6%	104,040	5.7%

Table 2-5 State and Local Revenues and Expenditures, 2017 (in Millions of Dollars)   *(continued)*

Source	State & Local	State	State Percent	Local	Local Percent
Health	96,611	44,165	2.0%	52,446	2.9%
Employment Security Administration	3,905	3,863	0.2%	41	0.0%
Veterans' Services	1,353	1,353	0.1%		0.0%
Highways	174,990	104,849	4.7%	70,140	3.8%
Other Transportation	31,837	3,914	0.2%	27,924	1.5%
Police Protection	109,210	15,003	0.7%	94,207	5.1%
Fire Protection	47,776		0.0%	47,776	2.6%
Corrections	78,017	49,040	2.2%	28,977	1.6%
Protective Inspection & Regulation	14,802	9,106	0.4%	5,696	0.3%
Natural Resources	30,805	21,508	1.0%	9,297	0.5%
Parks and Recreation	42,003	5,539	0.2%	36,463	2.0%
Housing & Community Development	50,173	8,676	0.4%	41,497	2.3%
Sewerage	55,613	1,246	0.1%	54,367	3.0%
Solid Waste Management	24,604	1,348	0.1%	23,256	1.3%
Governmental Administration	135,100	55,361	2.5%	79,739	4.3%
Interest on General Debt	104,572	44,624	2.0%	59,948	3.3%
Other General					
Utility Expenditures	224,247	27,246	1.2%	197,000	10.7%
Liquor Store	7,682	6,447	0.3%	1,235	0.1%
Insurance Trust	338,003	285,548	12.8%	52,455	2.9%
Misc., Other and Unallocable	137,548	37,544	1.7%	99,704	5.4%

Notes: (1) Duplicative intergovernmental transactions are excluded. (2) Authors/sum of state expenditures in table is $400 thousand off due to unexplained difference in source data.

Data from Bureau of the Census, U.S. Department of Commerce (2018). State and local government finances by level of government and by state: 2016. Retrieved May 19, 2019, from https://www.census.gov/data/datasets/2016/econ/local/public-use-datasets.html

and two states (Alaska and New Hampshire) have neither.

Local governments obtain about 33% of their money from other governments and the rest mainly from their own sources. Of all local revenue, 27% comes from property tax. A little over 20% is obtained from charges, miscellaneous general revenue, and utility fees. While some local governments have income and sales taxes, these sources contribute only about 8% of all local revenues in aggregate.

State and local expenditures also follow different patterns. Some expenditures that are important for the federal government are nonexistent in states and localities. For example, neither the states nor their local governments are responsible for defense, postal service, or space exploration. When looking at direct expenditures (that is, expenditures that are made directly by the government, as opposed to assistance provided to some other level), public welfare is the largest expense for states (about 26%), with education spending (primarily for higher education) ranked second. Other significant areas of state expenditure include highways and corrections.

Education spending is by far the largest category of local expenditures. The 37% spent on education is more than three times the percentage that is devoted to the second-ranked category, utility expenditure. Other significant areas of expenditure include public safety (police and fire), hospitals, and highways.

Summary

Government is indeed large. The growth pattern of the public sector has been upward and drawing a definitive line today between the public and private sectors is virtually impossible. If present trends continue, government can be expected to become even larger, albeit at a slower rate, providing more services directly or ensuring the provision of services by regulating the private sector.

Governments in the United States differ in the types of revenue sources used and main areas of expenditure. The federal government relies primarily on personal income taxes and social insurance taxes, while corporate income taxes play a decreasing role. Federal expenditures are concentrated in defense, medical entitlements, and social insurance. States obtain almost 30% of their revenue from the federal government, and the remainder largely from sales and individual income taxes. State expenditures are concentrated in education, social services, and welfare. Local governments, in contrast, receive one-third of their funds from other governments and one-fourth from property taxes, while their most expensive function is education.

Notes

1. Zuckert, M., & Webb, D. (Eds.). (2009). *The anti-federalists writing of the Melancton Smith circle.* Indianapolis, IN: Liberty Fund; Beer, S. H. (1993). *To make a nation: the rediscovery of American federalism.* Cambridge, MA: Belknap Press; White, L. D. (1948). *The federalists: a study in administrative history, 1789–1801.* New York, NY: Free Press.

2. Galbraith, J. K. (1973). *Economics and the public purpose.* Boston, MA: Houghton Mifflin.

3. Musgrave, R. A., & Musgrave, P. B. (1989). *Public finance in theory and practice* (5th ed.). New York, NY: McGraw-Hill; Hyman, D. N. (2010). *Public finance: A contemporary application of theory to policy* (10th ed. online). Florence, KY: Cengage Books; Rosen, H. S. (2005). *Public finance* (7th ed.). New York, NY: McGraw-Hill Irwin.

4. Lamartini, S., & Zaghini, A. (2008). *Increasing public expenditures: Wagner's law in OECD countries.* Frankfurt: Center for Financial Studies. Retrieved September 15, 2011, from http://www.ifk-cfs.de/fileadmin/downloads/publications/wp/08_13.pdf; Light, P. (2017). The true size of government: tracking Washington's blended workforce, 1984–2015. *The Volcker Alliance.* Retrieved May 5, 2019, from https://www.volckeralliance.org/sites/default/files/attachments/Issue%20Paper_True%20Size%20of%20Government.pdf.

5. Berry, W. D., & Lowery, D. (1987). Explaining the size of the public sector. *Journal of Politics, 49,* 401–440; Larkey, P. D., et al. (1981). Theorizing about the growth of government. *Journal of Public Policy, 1,* 157–220.

6. Beck, M. (1981). *Government spending: trends and issues.* New York, NY: Praeger; Lewis-Beck, M. S., & Rice, T. W. (1985). Government growth in the United States. *Journal of Politics, 47,* 2–30.

7. Polsby, N. W. (2004). *Presidential elections* (11th ed.). New York, NY: Chatham House.

8. Salant, J. D. (2008). Spending doubled as Obama led first billion dollar race in 2008. *Bloomberg News.* Retrieved September 25, 2011, from http://www.bloomberg.com/apps/news?pid=newsarchive&sid=aerix76GvmRM; Allison, B., Rojanasakul, M., Harris, B. & Sam, C. Tracking the 2016 presidential money race. *Bloomberg LP.* Retrieved May 4, 2019, from https://www.bloomberg.com/politics/graphics/2016-presidential-campaign-fundraising/.

9. Hartung, W. (2013). *The military-industrial complex revisited: shifting patterns of military contracting in the post-9/11 period.* Retrieved January 13, 2020, from https://watson.brown.edu/costsofwar/files/cow/imce/papers/2011/The%20Military-Industrial%20Complex%20Revisited.pdf.

10. Defense civilian employment from U.S. Department of Defense (2019). *Civilian Personnel in the DoD.* Retrieved May 4, 2019, from https://diversity.defense.gov/Portals/51/Documents/Resources/Docs/Civilian%20Employment/Civilian%20Employment.pdf; Defense Manpower Data Center (2019). *Total armed forces from U.S. Department of Defense.* Retrieved May 4, 2019, from https://www.dmdc.osd.mil/appj/dwp/dwp_reports.jsp; Statistica (2019). *Monthly civilian labor force in the United States from March 2018 to March 2019 (in millions, seasonally adjusted).* Retrieved from https://www.statista.com/statistics/193953/seasonally-adjusted-monthly-civilian-labor-force-in-the-us/.

11. Schwartz, M., et al. (2018). *Defense acquisitions: how and where DOD spends its contracting dollars* (pp. 10–11). Washington, DC: Congressional Research Service.

12. U.S. Government Accountability Office (2009). *Hard lessons: the Iraq reconstruction experience.* Washington, DC: Government Printing Office; Schwartz, M., & Church, J. (2013). *Department of Defense's use of contractors to support military operations; background, analysis and issues for Congress.* Washington, DC: Congressional Research Service. Retrieved May 5, 2019, from https://apps.dtic.mil/dtic/tr/fulltext/u2/a590715.pdf.

13. Vergun, D. (2019). Which state ranks highest in military spending? *U.S. Department of Defense.* Retrieved May 5, 2019, from https://www.defense.gov/explore/story/Article/1789129/which-state-ranks-highest-in-military-spending/.

14. Light, P. C. (2019). The true size of government: tracking Washington's blended workforce.

15. *Zelman v. Simmons–Harris* (2002). 536 U.S. 639.

16. U.S. Department of Education (2019). *Every Student Succeeds Act (ESSA).* Retrieved August 4, 2019, from https://www.ed.gov/essa; Smith, E. (2005). Raising standards in American schools: the case of No Child Left Behind. *Journal of Education Policy, 20*(4), 507–524.

17. All illustrations in the book were prepared using the most current data available. Federal statistical series and data collection has suffered significantly since the 1980s, resulting in fewer data collections, such as detailed information on state and local government finances. When comparing across levels of government, complete data for federal, state, and local vary in availability, so some tables and figures necessarily use the most common denominator—meaning if the most recent local government data available are from 2017, then all comparisons with state and federal also use 2017 data, even though more recent federal figures may be available. Another important note is that unlike governments that are generally stable, corporations can change dramatically in size, and consequently their rankings reflected in Tables 2-1 and 2-2 may go up or down sharply within the span of a few years. This can occur, for example, as the result of a major IPO (initial public offering). Changes in corporate rankings reflect their relative successes and failures in sales and also reflect various forms of corporate mergers.

18. The original idea of comparing private and public organizations was suggested by Robert J. Mowitz, then Director, Institute of Public Administration, The Pennsylvania State University, for the first edition of *Public Budgeting Systems.*

19. New York State, Division of the Budget (2018). *Mid-year financial plan update.* Retrieved May 9, 2019, from https://www.budget.ny.gov/pubs/archive/fy19/enac/fy19myfp.pdf.

20. Swanson, A. (2019). Trump gives farmers $16 billion in aid amid prolonged China trade war. *New York Times.* Retrieved January 13, 2020, from https://www.nytimes.com/2019/05/23/us/politics/farm-aid-package.html.

21. Trading Economics (2019). *United States GDP per capita.* Citing unpublished World Bank data. Retrieved May 12, 2019, from https://tradingeconomics.com/united-states/gdp-per-capita.

22. U.S. Council of Economic Advisers (2019). *Economic report of the president,* 552, 556.

23. Bureau of the Census, U.S. Department of Commerce (1975). *Historical statistics of the United States: colonial times to 1970* (part 2, p. 1114). Washington, DC: U.S. Government Printing Office.

24. Congressional Budget Office (2019). *Historical Budget Data: outlays by major category since 1965.* Retrieved January 13, 2020, from https://www.cbo.gov/about/products/budget-economic-data#2.

25. U.S. Council of Economic Advisers (2019). *Economic report of the president,* Table B-49.

26. U.S. Office of Management and Budget (2019). *Budget of the United States Government: fiscal year 2020, historical tables. Table 1.1. Summary of Receipts, Outlays, and Surpluses or Deficits (-): 1789–2024.* Retrieved May 23, 2019, from https://www.whitehouse.gov/omb/historical-tables/.

27. U.S. Council of Economic Advisers (2019). *Economic report of the president,* Table B-49.

28. U.S. Congressional Budget Office (2018). *Federal grants to state and local governments: a historical perspective on contemporary issue* (p. 4). Washington, DC: U.S. Government Printing Office.

29. Office of Personnel Management (2018). *Data, analysis & documentation: federal employment reports.* Retrieved January 13, 2020, from https://www.opm.gov/policy-data-oversight/data-analysis-documentation/federal-employment-reports/reports-publications/federal-civilian-employment/. Earlier years from ProQuest , LLC. (2019). *ProQuest statistical abstract of the United States,* 319 (Bethesda, MD: Rowman & Littlefield).

30. ProQuest, LLC. (2019). *ProQuest statistical abstract of the United States,* 340.

31. Governing (2019). Military active-duty personnel, civilians by state. *Governing the states and localities.* Retrieved March 12, 2020, from https://www.governing.com/gov-data/public-workforce-salaries/military-civilian-active-duty-employee-workforce-numbers-by-state.html.

32. Bureau of the Census, U.S. Department of Commerce (2001). *Statistical Abstract of the United States: 2001,* 294; ProQuest, LLC. (2019). *ProQuest statistical abstract of the United States,* 319.

33. Bureau of the Census, U.S. Department of Commerce (2017). *2017 Census of governments – organization: tables 1 and 8.* Retrieved January 13, 2020, from https://www.census.gov/data/tables/2017/econ/gus/2017-governments.html.

34. (2011). Source for 2010 data. U.S. Congressional Budget Office (2011). *The budget and economic outlook: fiscal years 2011–2021* (pp. 54, 87). Washington, DC: U.S. Government Printing Office.

35. U.S. Congressional Budget Office (2006). *The budget and economic outlook: fiscal years 2007–2016* (p. 144). Washington, DC: U.S. Government Printing Office.

CHAPTER 3

Government, the Economy, and Economic Development

The sheer size of the government sector in the U.S. economy guarantees that government action will have a major impact on overall economic performance. Total government expenditures as a percentage of gross domestic product (GDP)—a measure of the size of the economy—are more than 34%, and the federal share alone exceeds 22%.[1]

This chapter focuses on the impact of government budgets—primarily the federal government's budget—on the overall economy, and the impact of the overall economy on the federal budget. The first section introduces basic National Income Accounting concepts in measuring the economy. These concepts are used throughout the chapter. The second section considers the U.S. economy and its interdependence with the economies of other nations. Other governments and private individuals in other countries react to actions taken by the U.S. federal government, and actions taken by these external parties cause economic changes within the United States. To understand government and the economy, one first must understand the conditioning factors of the world economy.

The third section summarizes the major objectives sought by U.S. government economic policy. Included is a discussion of deficit control and management of the federal debt. In contrast to state and local borrowing, which is used mainly to finance capital investment, federal deficit spending and subsequent borrowing are the result of both macroeconomic policy reasons and the inability or unwillingness of the Congress and the White House to control federal spending.

The fourth section briefly discusses how governments and businesses attempt to forecast the economic future, and the fifth examines the principal tools used to influence the economy. For the federal government, these tools conventionally include fiscal and monetary policy. For state and local governments, tools to influence their economies include infrastructure investments and taxing or spending decisions that are intended to affect the local and state business climate. The final section focuses on the role of government in securing equity through influencing the distribution of income and other social goods in society.

Measuring the Size of the Economy

Economists measure the economy in many ways. Two basic concepts, production and income, characterize the economy in terms of the total value of goods and services produced and the income derived from the production of those goods and services. These two concepts are at the base of all the size measures discussed in this section. Production and income are the opposite sides of the coin. In principle, these two concepts are the same. The costs of goods and services sold (the value of the output) are equal to the receipts received by the producers (the value of the income). In practice, there are measurement imperfections. Precise measurement is complicated and beyond the scope of this book.

Gross Domestic Product

Gross domestic product (GDP) is the basic measure of economic output. It is the value of the total goods and services produced by the nation—the aggregate of personal consumption expenditures, gross private domestic investment, net exports of goods and services, and government purchases of goods and services.

Gross National Product

Gross national product (GNP), for many years, was the most common indicator of total production. In 1992, the federal government and most analysts switched to GDP for comparison purposes, because most other countries report production in terms of GDP. The main difference between the two measures is that GDP excludes the earnings of U.S. businesses and residents abroad and the earnings of foreign workers in the United States that are remitted abroad. Thus, GDP reflects production within the U.S. economy as opposed to production by U.S. economic entities wherever they may be.

For the United States, GDP and GNP typically do not differ much because income earned abroad and income remitted abroad tend to balance out. For some economies, especially developing economies, remittances from citizens working abroad are a significant source of national income. In 2018, remittances from the United States and many other economies to Latin American and Caribbean nations totaled more than $88 billion.

Net remittances for Haiti amounted to more than 30% of national income in 2018; in El Salvador, it was 21%, and for Egypt, 12%.[2]

Net National Product and National Income

Two related indicators, both derivatives of GDP, are net national product (NNP) and national income (NI). Gross domestic product includes all capital investment, some of which does not create new productive capacity but instead replaces capacity that has been used up, such as obsolete equipment no longer capable of producing. Net national product measures only capital investment net of depreciation. Capital replacement expenditures do not count in NNP. In 2018, the U.S. GDP was $20.6 trillion, while the U.S. NNP was $17.6 trillion, meaning that approximately $3 trillion of GDP did not represent new production capacity. Tracking NNP provides clues about future production because if the economy is using up capital stock and not replacing it, the production of goods and services that depend on that decreasing capital stock will decline or grow at a slower rate.

National income is derived from NNP by eliminating indirect business taxes included in the price of goods sold and business transfer payments. The table contained in **Exhibit 3-1** summarizes the relationships among GDP, GNP, NNP, and NI for the U.S. economy. Note that beginning in 2004, the statistical tables prepared by the Bureau of Economic Analysis lumped indirect business taxes, business transfer payments, and net surpluses of government enterprises into *statistical discrepancy*, masking somewhat the underlying differences among the measures. The text in the illustration assesses some of the underlying changes in the U.S. economy since 2000, revealed by evaluating GDP, GNP, NNP, and NI from 2000 to 2018.

There are other measures used to capture different aspects of a national economy that play lesser roles than the four primary measures discussed previously and in Exhibit 3-1. Some of these measures have been developed to make

Exhibit 3-1 Relationships among GDP, GNP, NNP and NI: 2000–2018

There are several measurements of the size of the economy. They are all based on the value of production in the economy, or the income derived from that production. Understanding how the different measures relate to each other is important because each basic measure of the size of the economy captures somewhat different concepts. The following table shows how each measure is derived from gross domestic product.

	2000	2010	2015	2016	2017	2018
Gross domestic product (GDP)	10,252	14,992	18,225	18,715	19,519	20,580
Plus: Income receipts from the rest of the world	381	715	838	862	958	1,106
Less: Income payments to the rest of the world	346	519	613	644	715	838
Equals: Gross national product (GNP)	10,287	15,188	18,449	18,933	19,763	20,848
Less: Consumption of fixed capital	1,511	2,391	2,917	2,992	3,121	3,291
Equals: Net National Product (NNP)	8,776	12,797	15,533	15,942	16,641	17,557
Less: Statistical discrepancy	−96	61	−255	−112	−68	11
Equals: National income (NI)	8,872	12,736	15,788	16,054	16,709	17,546

Extracted from Bureau of Economic Analysis (2019). *NIPA-AU19-summary of results tables only.* Retrieved August 26, 2019, from https://www.bea.gov/docs/gdp/summary-of-results-for-2014-2018-tables-only

The four measures reveal several changing characteristics of the U.S. economy. Beginning in the 1980s, GDP started rising from around 10% to the period covered in the table, where GDP is about 15% to 18% larger than NI. Gross national product and GDP are within 1% or 2% of each other for all the years in the table. Income earned abroad by U.S. concerns and income earned in the United States and remitted abroad by non-U.S. entities generally balance each other out. The increase in GDP relative to NI is caused by increases in the consumption of fixed capital by both the private sector and government, more than doubling from 2000 to 2018. Phrased differently, neither the private sector nor government is investing in fixed assets, meaning the kind of assets that will yield future production, at the same rate relative to the existing capital stock as in earlier years. Discussion of gross and net savings rate later in the chapter reveals that the United States, in recent decades, saves less from within the economy and relies more on investments in capital from abroad to finance private sector capital investment and the government budget deficit.

comparisons across countries more meaningful. For example, the concept of purchasing power parity (PPP) considers what it costs to purchase goods and services in an economy. For a high-income country compared with a low-income country, GDP may overstate the difference between the two countries because the cost of goods and services may be lower in the lower-income countries. Economists estimate the price of a basket of goods and use that to adjust for the difference between purchasing power. The World Bank, for example, includes GNI (gross national income) in both current U.S. dollars and in PPP. In 2018, Canada's GNI per capita was approximately $45,000; in per capita PPP, it was approximately $47,000.[3] The implication of the difference is that Canada enjoys a higher standard of living considering PPP than when not considering prices.

The United States and the World Economy

Cross-Border Economic Shocks

Most U.S. citizens after World War II thought of the United States as not only the most significant contributor to, but also the economic controller of, the world economy. The U.S. economy's dependence on imported oil was of little note until the Organization of Petroleum Exporting Countries (OPEC) curtailed oil production in 1973 and 1974, and U.S. citizens, for the first time in the postwar era, realized the significant effects on U.S. prices by other actors in the world economy. There were other oil shocks that affected the U.S. economy after that, but greater exploitation of shale oil and other energy sources in the United States have substantially reduced its dependency on imports. In 2018, only 11% of U.S. petroleum consumption was based on imported products, the lowest percentage since 1957.[4] Though not immune to disruptions in world oil production, the U.S. economy is less susceptible to shocks from sudden changes in worldwide production and/or trade patterns.

Similarly, economic growth in several nations with economies once considerably smaller than that of the United States, including China, Japan, and Germany, and others mean that the United States, although still a major component of the world economy, is merely one among several important national economies. The top 10 world economies also now include nations that once were low-income countries, such as Brazil and India.[5]

With the strengthening of other economies relative to our own, citizens are more attuned to how much U.S. economic well-being depends on the economic behavior of billions of individuals around the world and on the economic policy decisions of dozens of other governments. In addition, the economies of both underdeveloped and developing nations, not just those of industrialized nations, can have huge impacts on the United States and other industrialized economies,

and vice versa. The tsunami that hit Japan in 2011 had economic impacts felt particularly in Japan's European trading partners.[6] Impacts are not only based on imports and exports: The summer meeting in 2019 of the G7 economies (self-selected seven largest advanced economies) included as one major agenda item massive wildfires in the Brazilian Amazon region that threatened the rain forests that absorb an important share of the world's carbon dioxide emissions.[7]

Contributing to further intertwining among economies is investment across borders in productive assets, such as factories and retail establishments, and portfolio investments in stocks, bonds, and other financial instruments. Each category adds value to the recipient country, with investment in productive assets, classified as *foreign direct investment* (FDI), generally being the most desirable because it builds the assets for future economic growth. Direct investment in productive assets in a country represents a potentially longer-term commitment on the part of the investor. Building and owning an industrial facility repays the investor over the long term from sales of the products of the facility. FDI is usually highly sought after by countries where investment capital is less readily available, particularly less developed economies.

Portfolio investment means investing in stocks, bonds, and other financial instruments. These investments provide capital that may be used to build productive capacity, but the portfolio investor can more readily sell stocks, bonds, or other financial instruments. In a period of financial turmoil, such as the massive Asian financial crisis that started in 1997, investors selling their portfolio investments in those economies caused economies to tumble, first throughout Asia, then other emerging markets. Many of those investors reinvested in the U.S. and other Western industrial markets.

Advanced economies also are susceptible to rapid sales of portfolio investments. The financial collapse of Western industrial markets in 2007 made some newly strong economies, such as Brazil, Russia, India, and China, even more attractive as investors looked to alternatives to industrialized country investments. Both situations show that when investors quickly sell off their holdings if there is any hint that economic conditions are declining, markets in the affected countries can swing wildly. Pandemic diseases such as coronavirus can cause major market swings in most financial markets, sometimes well in excess of the prevalence of the disease.

Global direct investment flows have declined considerably even after the general recovery from the Great Recession. Foreign direct investment in developed economies in 2018 fell to their lowest point since 2004, declining by 27%. During the same period, FDI flows to developing economies were generally stable. Developing economies in 2018 were the recipients of a record 54% of total global foreign direct investment. The United States is, and generally has been, the largest source of FDI outflows to other countries.[8] Because FDI flows directly create productive assets, changes in FDI flows tend to reflect investors' predictions about long-term trends in the target economies.

Another economic variable linking national economies is the purchase of goods and services across borders. If you buy a vehicle with components mainly manufactured in another country, or if your business sells pumps to oil companies in other countries, the result is a cash flow inward or outward, to or from one's own economy. The value of international trade—exports plus imports—grew from 16% of U.S. GDP in 1975 to nearly 30% in 2008. Between 2008 and 2018, including the period of the Great Recession, exports plus imports varied from 25% to 30% of GDP.[9]

Other cross-border shocks can cause significant economic disruption, particularly when economic conditions are already fragile. As noted previously, the 2011 tsunami in Japan disrupted European markets. For the United States, the automobile industry, which was getting back on its feet after almost disappearing during the Great Recession, felt the effects for most of the remainder of 2011 as parts and other supplies from Japanese manufacturers were disrupted by the catastrophe, which slowed U.S. production.[10]

The notion that there is now a global economy, and that the United States is a part of that global economy but not the controlling agent, is accepted by most people, albeit for some quite uncomfortably. Of course, the United States is also vehemently criticized for its size and the influence of its economy in some countries.

The United States as a Debtor Nation

A second major factor influencing today's world economy involves the debt of U.S. individuals, corporations, and governments. Citizens notice price increases in gasoline and other products dependent on imports and dramatic political conditions such as terrorism; not as obvious are the credit flows among nations and how the United States is both actor and reactor to worldwide economic forces. In 1985, the United States became a net debtor nation for the first time. Formally, that meant that the value of foreign investments in the United States exceeded the value of U.S. investments abroad.

In 2018, the value (measured at current market price) of foreign investments in the United States was approximately $35.8 trillion, and U.S. investments abroad were valued at $25.4 trillion. Of that $36 trillion, 25% was direct investment and 54% was portfolio investment. Approximately 16% of the total investment was in U.S. treasury securities, both short and long term, reflecting official U.S. borrowing from abroad (discussed in more detail later in this chapter). These investments in U.S. government debt are counted in the portfolio investment total.[11] The net difference, about $10.4 trillion, reflects a long-term pattern.

Investments in the United States continue to be more attractive to foreign investors than investments abroad are to U.S. investors, although economic and stock market fluctuations affect the short term from time to time. Foreign asset holdings in the United States, in descending order, are in (1) debt and equity securities of U.S. companies through portfolio investment; (2) U.S. Treasury securities held by official governments and private investors; and (3) fixed assets, including resorts, factories, and even public utilities such as water companies through direct foreign investment.[12] Prior to the surge in U.S. government debt beginning in the early 2000s, an even higher percentage of foreign investments was going into the U.S. stock market and less into U.S. government securities such as Treasury bills (see the chapter on budget execution). The U.S. federal budget surplus of the late 1990s had substantially reduced federal borrowing needs. Rising federal budget deficits, of course, require federal borrowing, much of it from foreign investors, so the trend since 2001 has been for relative growth in foreign purchases of U.S. government debt. (See the chapter on budget execution.)

The inflow of foreign capital has helped keep U.S. interest rates low because it fills part of the demand for borrowing created by federal budget deficits and it finances high levels of consumption, including imported products, by U.S. households. In addition, foreign investment produces jobs in the United States. On the other hand, when the net inflow of foreign capital replaces domestic capital for investment, it makes the economy even more linked to the rest of the world's economies. The U.S. savings rate is too low to finance all the demand for investments, leaving the economy increasingly dependent on the confidence of foreign investors in the U.S. economy. U.S. households' high consumption patterns, which include huge purchases of imported goods, and government budget deficits require importing foreign capital to finance consumption and debt.

If foreign investors are confident in the U.S. economy, these patterns may not be a problem. Major threats to foreign confidence, such as the stock market drop in 2000–2002, the disasters of September 11, 2001, and ongoing problems with the wars in Afghanistan and Iraq, caused some concerns among foreign investors, but by comparison with other investment opportunities, the U.S. economy remained attractive. The 2007 financial market collapse had a temporary effect, but simultaneous debt crises in several European Union (EU) countries discouraged flight from the United States to other Western economies.[13] The international trade war, particularly with China, of the Trump administration shook the world investment community with the possibility of a new recession.[14] If confidence in the U.S. economy

were to wane significantly, then interest rates in the United States most likely would have to rise to attract investors. Such rates would be guided by monetary policy actions (discussed later in this chapter) taken by the Federal Reserve Board.

Value of the U.S. Dollar in the World Economy

The third phenomenon relates to changes in the value of the dollar in the world economy. When relatively few citizens traveled abroad, and trade accounted for less than 10% of the U.S. economy, most Americans never thought about the value of the dollar against foreign currencies.

Americans now travel extensively abroad and have for the last half century. Also, most Americans purchase imported goods. Likewise, citizens from countries around the world travel extensively in the United States and purchase U.S. products. Changes in the value of the dollar relative to other currencies now are quite visible to most consumers and travelers. Early in the 1970s, the dollar purchased a lot of goods and services in or from other countries, as the dollar value was high relative to most major currencies.

By 1987, the value of the dollar relative to other currencies had reversed. Since then, U.S. residents have watched the incoming flood of foreign visitors to the United States, while prices for comparable trips for U.S. residents abroad climbed. Imported cars, stereos, and televisions that had been bargains a year before became unaffordable for many. This reversal occurred for two reasons. First, per capita incomes grew faster in several other countries, which increased their purchasing power and drove up prices for goods produced in those economies. Second, the value of the U.S. dollar, except for a brief period during the budget surplus period of 1998 to 2001, fell relative to most other major world currencies. **Figure 3-1** shows the value of the dollar for the time period 1990 through 2018. The figure compares the U.S. dollar against an index of other major world currencies. The base year for the index value of 100 is 1973, when the value of the dollar against the index was 1.00. Changes up or down in the figure reflect increases or decreases in

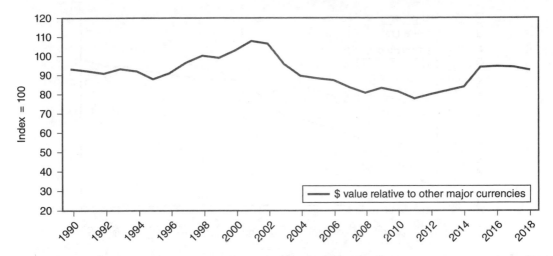

Figure 3-1 Value of the Dollar Relative to Other Major Currencies: 1990–2018.

Federal Reserve Bank of St. Louis (2019). *Economic research*. Retrieved August 27, 2019, from https://fred.stlouisfed.org/series/DTWCXM#0

the purchasing power of the dollar against other major currencies such as the British pound, the EU euro, and the Japanese yen.

One of the major factors affecting the value of the dollar has been the introduction, in 1999, of a common currency in most of Europe—the euro. Initially, the dollar and the euro were valued within about 10% of each other. The U.S. economy was booming and there were federal budget surpluses. Since the introduction of the single European currency, the value of the euro to the dollar has fluctuated widely, from a low of 0.85 in November 2000 to a high of 1.59 in July 2011. In practical terms, in July 2011, the euro could buy 59 cents more in goods and services than could a dollar.[15]

Economists now understand that the value of the dollar fluctuates with changes both within the influence range of the U.S. private economy and government action and with changes in other economies. Since the mid-1980s, the dollar no longer dominates world currencies, but is merely one of several dominant currencies.

Competitiveness of the U.S. Economy

A fourth key economic phenomenon is the competitiveness of the U.S. economy relative to that of other industrial powers. Though "cheap

foreign labor" is a periodic target for criticism by business leaders and politicians, historically the U.S. advantage in technological innovation made the economy competitive on the world market, although not in all industries. However, as early as the 1980s, the United States started encountering serious competition in computer design, electronics, and other high-technology areas. Some other countries began to produce not only cheaper but, in the minds of many consumers, better products. Countries such as China not only are competitive in producing sophisticated electronics, but also compete effectively in sophisticated electronics design, space technology, stem cell research, and other arenas, largely due to major research and development (R&D) investment growth, more than double the growth in the United States and Europe.[16] U.S. productivity, led by significant private sector restructuring and manifested in part by downsizing of the workforce in many industries, surged from the late 1990s, closing with the Euro area by end of the Great Recession. **Figure 3-2**, however, shows the United States again lagging from 2010 through 2017.

Another factor is the increasing competitiveness of emerging economies such as the BRIC nations (Brazil, Russia, India, and China), which have experienced GDP growth rates exceeding

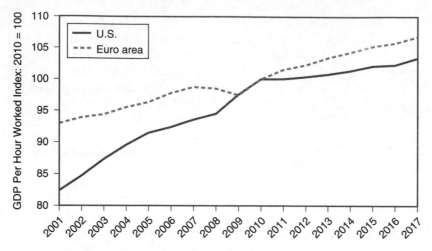

Figure 3-2 U.S. and Euro Area Labor Productivity: 2001–2017.

Organization for Economic Cooperation and Development (2019). *GDP per hour worked: 2001–2017.* Retrieved August 27, 2019, from https://data.oecd.org/lprdty/gdp-per-hour-worked.htm

those of the United States and Europe, though slowing somewhat since 2016, especially Russia.[17] These economies have enjoyed the contribution to production growth of expanding labor forces. In addition, with investments in industrial modernization, any labor-based economy will experience significant growth in production. The United States and other industrial economies, however, achieve productivity gains only through increasing the productivity of a labor force that grows in size slowly, if at all, and increasing the proportion of the labor force employed.[18] Russia is an exception in the emerging market powers in that its population is not growing. The role of productivity in achieving economic growth is discussed in detail in the next section.

The U.S. economy is so interdependent with those of other nations that no significant actions that the United States takes lack repercussions around the world. Likewise, no significant economic events in other major industrial nations or groups of developing nations fail to have repercussions in the United States. As populous countries like Brazil, China, and India continue to industrialize, demand for resources, especially oil, becomes a major variable in every economy in the world. Too much dependence on foreign sources for critical products and services also may have national security implications. The

U.S. dependence on China as the major source of pharmaceuticals was a matter of concern during the trade war between the United States and China during the Trump administration.[19] Understanding the role of the government in the U.S. economy thus means casting a wider net and considering the actions and reactions of the country's major trading partners and major creditors.

Objectives of Economic Policy

The role of the federal government in the economy consists of several interrelated functions. First, the government provides the legal framework in which economic transactions take place. Second, it directly produces services and some goods, and it regulates private production. Also, it purchases significant quantities of goods and services and redistributes income among individuals and groups. Some argue that governments should also promote their countries' economic competitiveness in the global marketplace. There is a major divide between those who argue that government should invest directly in economic promotion and those who argue that the more appropriate government role is creating the right economic climate for growth.[20]

One goal of the government's regulation of economic transactions through setting the legal framework is sometimes described as maintaining a "level playing field"—making sure that all economic actors play by the same rules and succeed or fail solely on the basis of their own strengths and weaknesses. The accounting scandals in which companies such as Enron (2001) and WorldCom (2002) apparently inflated earnings by using unacceptable accounting practices resulted in major civil and criminal prosecutions and significant federal legislation, notably Sarbanes-Oxley (see the chapter on financial management: accounting, auditing and reporting). Similarly, the financial crisis that started in 2007, set off by the weakly regulated use of esoteric derivatives in the U.S. mortgage market, created demands for increasing regulations in the securities market. Several years after the Great Recession, there was some rollback by the Trump administration in government regulations on the financial sector that were put in place to address the practices that contributed to the recession. Almost 200 regulations, most pertaining to regulation of industrial and business practices, were either repealed or in process of repeal, primarily by presidential executive orders, just over halfway through the administration's first term.[21] Setting the legal framework is the subject of texts on regulation, business, and constitutional law. This section focuses on the government's effects on the economy's overall performance.

In 1932, Franklin D. Roosevelt promised to involve the federal government in the solution to economic problems brought on by the Great Depression, but it was not until after World War II that the overall role of the government in stimulating the economy was formalized through legislation. The Employment Act of 1946, later amended by the Full Employment and Balanced Growth Act of 1978, set several macroeconomic policy objectives for the federal government.[22] Primary among these were full employment, price stability, and steady economic growth. Though not formalized in legislation, two additional objectives are accepted in policy now—equilibrium in the balance of transactions between the U.S. economy and other economies, and debt management.[23]

Most industrial nations share these objectives, whether they rely primarily on the private market, central planning, or a mix of central control and market activity to achieve them. Less-industrial, developing, and emerging market countries also share these objectives, but the most prominent economic policy objective for these nations is the promotion of economic development. The mood in most industrial economies has consistently favored a less activist role for government in economic promotion, although from time to time during periods of economic distress a more activist's role for government surfaces. Some tactics employed by government in combatting the Great Recession in the latter part of the (George W.) Bush administration and the Obama administration included stimulus grants for target industries, such as solar technology. Subsequent to that recession, the less activist role prevailed again.

The first three objectives of the federal government are primarily domestic in nature. In many respects, they can be summarized in a single prescription: achieve a level of economic growth that produces full employment without unacceptable inflation. Economic growth is the engine that drives demand for employees. However, running that engine too fast or with too rich a fuel mixture may cause prices to rise unacceptably. Reformulating these objectives into a single statement brings out the causal connection between economic growth and employment. It also brings into the discussion two key value-laden terms: full employment and unacceptable inflation.

Full Employment
Definition of Full Employment

As a measure of economic performance, employment is the number of civilians over age 16 outside of institutions who are working in formal income-producing jobs. About 60,000 households, consisting of about 110,000 individual eligible adults and statistically representative of the country, are surveyed each month in the Current Population Survey (CPS). The survey asks the respondent about his or her activities during the preceding week. If a person responds that he or she worked at a job for pay, worked in a family enterprise without being paid, or was on vacation or some other similar situations, the individual is employed. If a person did not work in any of these situations or is not temporarily ill, on vacation, and so forth, and is looking for a job, he or she is unemployed. All others are considered not in the labor force. To be considered unemployed, a person currently does not have a job, has actively looked for work in the prior 4 weeks, and is currently available for work. If a person is temporarily laid off and waiting to return to work, that person is considered unemployed.[24] Data from the CPS household survey are used to estimate the unemployment rate.

In addition to the monthly CPS, the Census Bureau surveys approximately 142,000 businesses and government agencies, representing 698,000 worksites. The Current Employment Statistics (CES) survey estimates the number of individuals employed. It is important to note that both are survey estimates, not actual counts of the number employed or the number of individuals active in the labor force. Annually, the CES compares its monthly estimates against the actual counts, for the month of March, derived from state unemployment insurance tax records. The number of individuals employed measure is then adjusted against this benchmark, usually amounting to +/− 0.2%. The March 2019 benchmark comparison resulted in a negative 0.3% adjustment, meaning 501,000 fewer individuals were employed than previously estimated.[25]

It is important to pay attention to possible differences between the initial release from the Bureau of Labor Statistics, labeled preliminary, and the final release. If the preliminary release reports "good numbers," then the current administration in the White House promotes that number. Politicians reacted loudly to the revised 2019 numbers: Democrats cited the statistics as showing that the tax cuts from the Tax Cut and Jobs Act had not contributed to increased employment, and the White House complained that the numbers were rigged.[26] Though political figures trumpet or criticize these revisions, which occur on a regular basis, the revisions rarely affect the business climate, as the stock market reactions to the August 2019 revision showed.[27] The explanation is that though the job creation numbers typically have the biggest political mileage, they usually do not alter the unemployment rate noticeably.

The most used measure of employment is the unemployment rate. The unemployment rate is the proportion of the workforce not employed at a given time. To be considered unemployed, one must be seeking employment as measured in the survey by such activities as sending out resumes, visiting unemployment offices, calling about employment, placing ads, conducting online job searches, and so forth. The definition of seeking employment excludes individuals who reported that they were discouraged by failure to find work, but who had not looked for work in the past 12 months. Merely looking at want ads or online employment opportunities does not count. Individuals who have taken no active steps during the 4 weeks prior to the interview are not counted in the labor force.

There is no legislated definition of full employment, although an unemployment rate of 3% to 4% was often cited as the criterion of full employment after the 1946 Employment Act. Until the 1980s, the thinking was that about 3% to 4% of the workforce at any given time will be between jobs or otherwise temporarily unemployed, and thus we can never achieve unemployment below that threshold. Some members of the workforce are considered at least temporarily unemployable because of changes in jobs and skill requirements. Some economists do not count these "structurally" unemployed as part of the base for calculating full employment. Homemakers returning to the workforce, young people voluntarily switching jobs, and fluctuations in demand in the global economy also make it difficult to achieve a 3% to 4% target. There also are concerns that developments in artificial intelligence combined with robotics may make some workers unemployable.[28] The unemployment rate was around 4% or below only 13 times in the 79 years from 1948 through 2018. It fell below 4% again, to 3.9%, in 2018.[29] Most in the United States have come to accept an unemployment rate higher than 4% as consistent with the term "full employment."

The acceptance of a higher unemployment rate as the criterion of full employment is connected to the fact that the U.S. economy is much more susceptible to external events than it once was. As external economic shocks occur and consumer tastes change more rapidly, U.S. businesses simply cannot react as quickly as they once could, leading at times to downturns and unemployment. Post–September 11, 2001, with wars in Afghanistan and Iraq and renewed, large federal budget deficits, unemployment rates returned to the 5% to 6% range except for 2006–2007. Even aside from the extremely high unemployment rates associated with the Great Recession, around 9% from 2009 through 2011, the patterns since the late 1990s reinforce the old notion of 3% to 4% as unsustainable.

Political Acceptability of Unemployment

The political system has a varying capacity to accept unemployment. A nationwide unemployment rate of 9% or 10%, a rate reached in the early 1980s and again after 2008, is clearly unacceptable by current standards, but it is substantially lower than the peaks during the Great Depression of the 1930s and the Coronvirus pandemic that started in 2020. As the rate declines toward 5%, acceptance increases. The extent to which society tolerates unemployment is partially dependent on who is unemployed. Although there may be a tendency to accept high unemployment among low-skilled, minority group, or younger workers, tolerance for unemployment quickly dissipates when it reaches middle-income, white-collar workers.

Politically, the unemployment rate is not the only important issue. Since the late 1980s, when the rate hovered around 5% or less, citizens have been more concerned with the types of new jobs that are being created and what these jobs pay in wages or salaries. The concern is that many new jobs have been either service jobs that pay only the minimum wage or part-time jobs that pay few or no benefits, especially health care and retirement benefits. That certainly was a criticism in the 1990s boom and was repeated in the middle of the first decade of 2000 and in the post–Great

Recession recovery. Of greater concern to some than job quality has been the concentration of wealth in the United States in the top 5%, top 2%, and top 1% of individuals. We discuss this issue in a section on equity and income inequality later in the chapter.

Another issue is the controversy over part-time work. Many people choose part-time work, but companies also have increased the number of workers they hire either as part-time workers or as temporary contract workers in order to reduce total wage costs by not paying fringe benefits. When companies downsize their workforces during downturns, an increasing percentage of the national labor force works part-time and in temporary activity. Although their total employment often amounts to full 40-hour or more weeks, these workers lack the job security of regular employment and the benefits of health insurance and retirement plans. A Gallup Poll found that more than one-third of the U.S. workforce is employed in what is called the gig economy, some as truly independent contractors and some as employees, but employees without traditional fringe benefits.[30]

Controlling Inflation
Relationship Between Unemployment and Inflation

The more the unemployment rate declines, the more difficult it becomes to find workers. As a result, wage rates may be bid up, creating inflationary pressures. That relationship held up for decades, with few exceptions, until a recession in the mid-1970s that saw both rising unemployment and rising prices. At the peak, 1974 prices rose 11% over those of the year before, and 1975 prices rose another 7%. During that time, unemployment peaked at more than 8%. Notably, the rapid price increase matched by an increase in unemployment was triggered mainly by the OPEC oil embargo discussed earlier in this chapter. Sharp drops in the oil supply triggered the rapid price increases, and simultaneously reduced production in major U.S. industries, leading, in turn, to workforce reductions. As noted earlier in the chapter, that marked the first dramatic demonstration that internal relationships in the U.S. economy may be substantially altered by external events.

Figure 3-3 illustrates that the expected relationship between the two measures continues to be somewhat more erratic than the historical pattern. The Great Recession caused a dramatic increase in unemployment, matched by a dramatic drop in consumer prices. As the economy recovered, there was a more extended decline in unemployment while changes in consumer prices year to year stayed around 2%, contrary to traditional theory. In the global economy, major sectors of the economy have choices about whether they employ American workers or move significant operations offshore. Wages since the Great Recession have not increased for most of the workforce at the same rate as the economy has grown. As a result, there has been less pressure on prices to go up. This is likely to be the new normal in the future.

A more refined notion of a "natural rate of employment" and the relationship between inflation and unemployment emphasizes monetary policy over fiscal policy (see discussion later in this chapter). Milton Friedman, in 1968, proposed to the American Economic Association that there is a natural rate of inflation on which the economy stabilizes for any given unemployment rate. The theory is that there is a natural rate of employment that does not put pressure on prices.[31] This *nonaccelerating inflation rate of unemployment* (NAIRU) concept particularly gained currency in the 1990s and is still used, for example, by the Congressional Budget Office in assessing the labor market's impact on demand and prices. If the labor market contains some slack, defined as unused productive labor, then employment can increase without putting pressure on wages, which in turn may put pressure on prices. "Potential employment is the number of people employed when unemployment is at its natural rate – the rate that arises from all sources except fluctuations in aggregate demand – and when labor force participation is at its potential rate."[32] The latter was proposed as the rate of unemployment below which excess demand for

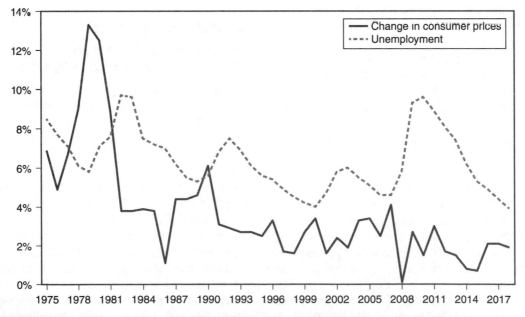

Figure 3-3 Changes in Consumer Prices and Unemployment: 1975–2018.

U.S. Council of Economic Advisers (2019). *Economic report of the president: 2019, Tables B-27 and B-38,* respectively. Retrieved from https://www.govinfo.gov/app/search/%7B%22query%22%3A%22economic%20report%20of%20 the%20president%20b-27%22%2C%22offset%22%3A0%7D and https://www.govinfo.gov/app/search/%7B"query"%3A"economic%20report%20of%20the%20president%20consumer%20prices"%2C"offset"%3A0%7D

labor is thought to set off wage and price inflation. Unemployment below this range presumably will set off wage-led inflation.

Figure 3-3 illustrates the occasions when the unemployment rate has dropped accompanied by, or shortly followed by, some increase in consumer prices: 1975–1979, 1990–1991, 1999–2000, and just prior to the onset of the Great Recession. In the decade since that recession, after the peak unemployment rate started falling in 2010–2011, consumer price rate increases have stayed between 1% and 2%. According to the theory of a nonaccelerating inflation rate, monetary policy actions to control inflation need be taken only when the actual unemployment rate falls below the NAIRU. That has not happened during the period covered by Figure 3-3 (within half a percent).[33]

The noninflationary rate can change over time for many reasons. For instance, severe drought conditions or a hard winter freeze in major citrus-growing regions can cause food prices to increase, contributing to overall higher consumer prices unrelated to wage pressures. Increased worker productivity can increase output without setting off price deflationary pressures, and more workers can be hired if the productivity rate remains constant or increases without putting pressure on wages. This balance is one of the explanations for the ability of the U.S. economy prior to and after the Great Recession to have low inflation and low unemployment. In addition, greater pressure on jobs from foreign competition holds wage rates down regardless of what is happening in the domestic economy. If wage demands grow too high too rapidly, companies may intensify their search for foreign production sources.

After the Great Recession, concern increased about structural unemployment. After the recession, it took much longer for the unemployment rate to fall than it took the stock market to recover. By early 2012, more than 40% of the 6 million unemployed Americans had been unemployed longer than 6 months, even though the financial markets had recovered most of their losses by mid-2011 and corporate profits were growing significantly. Unemployment in

excess of 9% gave rise to concerns about long-term unemployment.[34] The unemployment rate stayed above 5% until 2016, falling to near 4% only in 2018, before rising rapidly in the first quarter of 2020 due to the coronavirus crisis.[35]

Increased structural unemployment in the United States or any other country in the future may be the result of world economic conditions and greater fluidity across borders as companies choose where to produce their goods and services. In those circumstances, countries that can increase the productivity of their workforce through technology and infrastructure investments are more likely to both increase production and decrease unemployment.[36]

Economic Growth
Economic Productivity

Unemployment is not the only measure of the economy's health. Even if the rate of unemployment and the rate of inflation are both at acceptable levels, the overall productivity of the economy could be seriously declining. The change in GDP (growth or decline from one year to the next) is commonly used as an indicator of economic productivity. Heavily populated countries inevitably have a higher GDP than less populous countries. Therefore, when comparing countries in a single time period, the preferred measure is GDP per capita, which normalizes GDP for population differences. Year over year growth is calculated as the average annual growth rate. Because GDP will increase during inflationary periods, real or constant GDP is used to eliminate the effect of increase in prices. For the United States, the average annual GDP growth rate from 1997 through 2018 was 2.4%. For Japan, the comparable figure was 0.8%. For the Euro area (EU countries whose currency is the euro), the average annual growth rate in that period was 1.6%, and for the United Kingdom, it was 2.1%.[37]

Figure 3-4 compares the United States, Japan, the United Kingdom, and the countries of the Euro area for the period 1997–2018. The figure adjusts for inflation and population differences by displaying *real GDP per capita in constant*

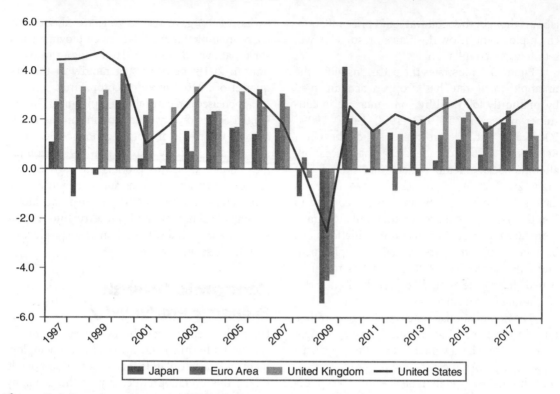

Figure 3-4 Percentage Change in GDP Per Capita: Selected Countries, 1997–2018.

Data from World Bank national accounts data and OECD national accounts data files. GDP growth (annual %). Retrieved August 30, 2019, from https://data.worldbank.org/indicator/NY.GDP.MKTP.KD.ZG? (downloaded data file all countries).

local currency. Japan had much higher growth rates from the 1960s through the 1980s, when its economic base was much smaller. By the 1990s, Japan's economy had reached mature status, yielding growth rates like those of the United States and other advanced economies. Through the period shown in Figure 3-4, Japan's changes in GDP growth generally followed the same patterns as the United States and the Euro area, with some exceptions, but the highs were not as high and the lows were lower, especially in the major drop during the Great Recession.

Since 1997, the U.S. and the U.K. economies generally have outperformed the economies of EU countries. Technological innovation is generally cited as explaining the U.S. and U.K. advantage, and, as Figure 3-2 showed earlier in the chapter, U.S. labor productivity moved ahead of the Euro area in 2010. More generally, labor shifting from low-productivity work to higher productivity work is the most compelling factor explaining overall economic growth, also explaining the patterns for the more recent countries that have moved into the classification of major economic powers, such as Brazil, Russia, India, China, and South Africa.[38]

Inflation varied in the countries illustrated during the period covered by Figure 3-4, but it does not affect the comparisons because the figure is based on *real GDP in constant local currency*. Japan experienced very little inflation during the time period covered by the figure, whereas the United States suffered from at least two inflationary periods. Using *nominal* (unadjusted for inflation) GDP, the United States would have been much higher in some periods, masking similarities and differences across countries. This demonstrates the importance of looking at real GDP for the measure not to appear larger than warranted.

Impact of Government on Productivity

Most economists think that the primary impact of the government on economic productivity and long-term growth is due to influences on knowledge development and investment in productive capacity. Recent presidents including William Clinton, George W. Bush, and Barack Obama all emphasized the importance of government support for knowledge development. President Obama appointed a council of corporate CEOs to advise on how to boost U.S. economic productivity and proposed a program of investment in R&D, technology, and education.[39] The proposal was consistent with competitiveness measures advocated by his predecessors.

Tax credits for private companies investing in R&D activities have often been used in the United States to promote knowledge development. The R&D tax credit was first introduced in 1981 as a temporary measure to encourage more private R&D.[40] That temporary credit was allowed to expire, but then was renewed annually until 2014. Several attempts over the years to make the tax credit permanent through authorizing legislation failed. Finally, in 2015, the R&D tax credit was made permanent as part of a spending bill.[41]

The impact of the direct and indirect actions of government on improving the productivity of the economy can be measured only in the long run. For example, even if businesses substantially increase their expenditures for R&D as a result of government incentives, the payoff in productivity terms will show up only years into the future. Most U.S. states offer a variety of general tax credit programs for businesses. A few additional states have more targeted tax credit programs for R&D investments in specific geographic areas of the state, or for specific industries or technologies, such as encouraging the growth of the biotechnology industry.[42]

Worldwide, the focus is somewhat more on the factors that make an economy attractive for foreign direct investment and that facilitate domestic investment than on direct stimulative activities. **Exhibit 3-2** describes research on measuring the ease of doing business in economies around the world as a way of evaluating the effects of government regulations and interventions, or lack thereof for some issues, in order to target changes that would improve the business climate.

A Government Technology Policy

It is important to differentiate between government investment in infrastructure that is of a more public nature, such as transportation, water, sanitation, and promoting knowledge development, and deliberate government investment in targeted industries or technologies, such as solar energy technologies. Investment in infrastructure has a multiplier effect—infrastructure investment boosts private sector output.[43] On the other hand, there is less consensus on the value of government investing in targeted industries and technologies. This question of whether the government should be more active in protecting and promoting critical high-technology industries first emerged in the late 1980s, when the U.S. economy began to lose ground in all areas, not just markets dominated by inexpensive labor.

The concept has persisted as a key policy issue. President Clinton made stimulation of high-technology development an economic policy priority. President George W. Bush designated corporate tax reduction, repeal of taxes on dividends, and the R&D tax credits as the most important tools with which to support economic development. President Obama made technology promotion, particularly in developing green energy and other advanced environmental improvement technologies, a focal point in his first budget proposals and as part of separate stimulus packages to combat the Great Recession.[44] President Trump focused less attention on technology promotion and more on regulatory reform to rebuild basic industries such as energy extraction and production and manufacturing. Trade negotiations with major competitors such as China absorbed much of the Trump administration's attention.[45] Congress has been reluctant to support most of these initiatives, though as noted above, R&D tax credit programs have been "temporarily" extended periodically and made permanent in 2015.

Exhibit 3-2 The Ease of Doing Business Around the World

Greater emphasis in recent decades has been placed on reducing the barriers to private economic investment and activity than on direct promotional activities of government. The World Bank produces an annual report, *Doing Business*, that ranks nearly 200 countries on the ease of doing business. Ten subjects are the basis for the measurement:

1. Starting up a business (how long it takes, how much red tape, how many actors must be involved)
2. Dealing with licenses (construction permitting, renewals, inspections)
3. Getting electricity (number of procedures, time, costs, reliability of supply)
4. Commercial property registration (time it takes, cost, clarity on property rights)
5. Access to credit (legal/regulatory practices, access to information about credit)
6. Minority investor protection (shareholder suits, disclosures on company transactions)
7. Taxes (complexity/time taken to file, total taxes as percentage of income)
8. Trading across borders (time to export and import, cost to export and import)
9. Enforceability of contracts (time, cost of enforcing, sanctity of contract)
10. Resolving insolvency (recovery rate, strength of insolvency framework)[a]

The five top-ranked economies in 2018, in order, were New Zealand, Singapore, Denmark, Hong Kong SAR (China), and Korea. The United States ranked 8th in 2019. The five lowest-ranked economies were Somalia, Eritrea, Venezuela, Yemen, and Libya.[b] The World Bank program aims at transforming economies in part by changing the rules and conditions in which economic activity takes place. Looking at the entire set of rankings, it is not just that overall level of economic development measured by size matters, but government actions and failure to take action to create a favorable climate have a great influence on the productivity of the economy.

a. World Bank (2019). *Doing business: 2019*. Retrieved August 31, 2019, from https://www.worldbank.org/content/dam/doingBusiness/media/Annual-Reports/English/DB2019-report_web-version.pdf, pp. 127-138.

b. World Bank (2011). *Doing business*, 5.

The problem with providing more support to one segment of the economy than to another is that government, rather than the marketplace, "picks winners and losers," and there is little evidence that governments are good in that role. The federal support for the Solyndra Corporation, a solar panel technology developer and manufacturer, is a case in point. As part of a larger federal push to commercialize green energy technologies, the Solyndra Corporation was a recipient of a major federal loan program. When Solyndra's solar panel technology proved commercially not viable, at least in the context of energy prices prevailing at the end of the first decade of 2000, the company declared bankruptcy.[46]

The decades of Japan's double-digit growth seemed to many observers enough evidence that government-led development was the proper path, but recent decades have altered that view considerably. Singapore is sometimes held up as an example of successful and significant government intervention, as the World Bank's *Doing Business* annual report seems to suggest. Singapore perennially ranks in the top five, often first or second as Exhibit 3-2 notes for 2018. Singapore's success, at least based on the factors measured in the *Doing Business* index, seems more likely the result of the climate created by government than by government choosing and directing industry targets for growth. Governments have difficulty determining what particular elements in a volatile industry such as electronics or alternative energy technologies will be the most important determinants of global competitiveness in high-technology markets 5 or 10 years later.[47] The more widely accepted view is that government actions, rather than overtly promoting particular industries, should be directed toward improving the human and capital base; should encourage savings and investment; and should promote the international exchange of ideas, goods, and services.

Equilibrium in International Trade and Financial Flows

Actions designed to affect the balance of trade and investments among nations are important elements of government policy in this era of the global marketplace. That balance of trade and investments includes all purchases of goods and services from individuals and institutions in other countries and all purchases made in the U.S. economy by individuals and institutions in other countries. To those goods and services must be added financial investment flows, including purchases of physical assets such as factories and financial assets such as stocks and bonds, plus other financial flows across borders such as remittances and other payments. A key component of the financial flows is the U.S. government's reliance on world capital markets to finance a major part of its budget deficit. The U.S. economy's financial position vis-à-vis the rest of the world is discussed in this section. A review of the overall deficit situation and debt management follows.

Balance of Trade and Investments

The components of the U.S. trade and investment position in the international economy are explained in **Table 3-1**.

The trade and investment position of an economy in relation to the rest of the world is a combination of three types of transactions. First, and most talked about, is the international trade in goods and services. The value of goods and services exported by the U.S. economy to the rest of the world, minus the value of goods and services imported into the U.S. economy, is the simple trade balance on goods and services. Those two sets of transactions are shown in the first two lines in Table 3-1. The U.S. economy imports more than it exports, producing a simple trade balance in 2018 of negative $628 billion, the result of $2.5 trillion in U.S. exports and $3.1 trillion in U.S. imports.[48] The United States has experienced a negative balance of trade since the mid-1970s.

The second type of transaction is income flow to the United States from investments made in other countries and income flow out to other countries from investments made in the U.S. economy by foreign parties. These are called primary income receipts and payments. In both directions, these receipts (and payments) are either direct investments in private assets such as property, factories, and so forth or portfolio investments in stocks and bonds. When U.S. investors make direct investments in capital assets (factories, buildings, land, and so forth) and portfolio investments in stocks and bonds, the income flow from those to the United States is primary receipts. When external investors make similar investments in the United States, the income from those investments flows out of the United States and is called primary income payments. The United States enjoys a favorable balance in these transactions, $254 billion in 2018. More dollars flow to the U.S. economy from U.S. financial investments abroad than flow to other economies from their investments in the United States.

The third type of transaction is income flow to the United States, mainly to individuals, such as pension and other retirement payments, social security (or other country equivalents) payments, and private remittances. The equivalent flows out of the United States are similar payments, again mainly to individuals. These respectively are called secondary income receipts and secondary income payments. The money paid to individuals currently living outside the U.S. receiving pension payments paid by U.S. sources is accounted for as secondary payments to other countries in the Current Account (see Table 3-1). Similarly, Social Security payments earned by individuals while living in the United States who then retire to live in another country and receive their Social Security there are accounted for as secondary payments to other countries. U.S. retirees who decide to live abroad after retirement would be on the receiving end of such secondary payments. The sum of these three balances—the trade balance, the primary income balance, and the secondary income balance—is the *balance on current account,* almost a $500 billion deficit in 2018. The current account balance for 2018 is not as negative as the simple trade balance because direct and portfolio

Table 3-1 U.S. International Trade and Financial Transactions: 2018

Current Account	2018 ($billions)
Exports of goods and services	2,501
Imports of goods and services	3,129
Balance on goods and services	**−628**
Primary income receipts (1)	**1,084**
Primary income payments (2)	830
Balance on primary income	254
Secondary income receipts (3)	150
Secondary income payments (4)	267
Balance on secondary income	**−117**
Balance on Current Account	**−491**
Capital Account	
Capital transfer receipts and other credits	3
Capital transfer payments and other debits	
Balance on Capital Account	3
Net Current and Capital Account	**−488**
Financial Account	
Net U.S. Acquisition of financial assets (increase in assets (+))	311
Net U.S. Acquisition of financial liabilities (increase in liabilities (+))	−736
Financial Derivatives, net transactions	−21
Statistical discrepancy	−42
Net lending (+) or borrowing (−), financial account transactions	**−488**

Data from U.S. Department of Commerce, Bureau of Economic Analysis (2019). *U.S. International Transactions, Tables 1-9.* Retrieved September 2, 2019, from https://www.bea.gov/data/intl-trade-investment/international-transactions.

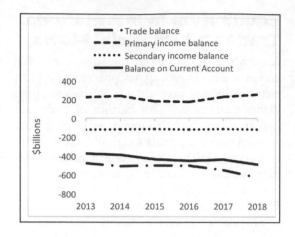

(1) Primarily flows to U.S. from direct and portfolio investments made in other countries
(2) Primarily flows to other countries from direct and portfolio investments made in the U.S.
(3) Primarily flows to U.S. from withholding taxes received, pensions, fines & penalties, and private remittances
(4) Primarily flows outside U.S. of pension payments, social security and retirement benefits to former U.S. residents

investment receipts and payments produced a positive balance of $254 billion, offset somewhat by secondary income receipts and payments.

The negative current account balance grew by about 33% from 2013 through 2018 as shown in the graph accompanying Table 3-1. That was an average annual increase in the negative trade balance of over 6%.

There also are small (relative to the transactions in the current account) capital transactions that have only a small impact on the U.S. international trade and investment position in the international economy. Capital account transactions may include copyright and trademark transactions, transfers of drilling rights, and, infrequently, insurance payments.[49] These transactions are captured in the *capital account.*

If the current and capital accounts, taken together, like one's own household accounts, have a negative balance, then the economy, or the household, dips into savings or borrows to bring the accounts back in balance. The U.S. economy has had a negative balance in the current and capital accounts, taken together, almost every year since the 1970s. To manage that negative balance, the United States has reduced savings (discussed in the next section) and borrowed. A major part of the borrowing is U.S. government borrowing from foreign governments and financial institutions abroad to finance the annual budget deficit. That borrowing is accomplished primarily by the sale of U.S. Treasury bonds. The larger the government budget deficit, the more the government borrows from the capital markets. Not all the federal borrowing is from external sources; significant purchases of federal debt are made by individuals and institutions within the United States.

Balance of Payments

The policy objective is to maintain equilibrium in the international transactions of the U.S. economy. Equilibrium is not synonymous with *balanced*, although in public discourse it often seems that way. Historically, the balance of payments policy objective was to avoid the situation in which a negative balance of trade in goods and services plus financial transactions threatened the possibility of drawing down on the U.S. gold reserve, transferring part of the gold reserve externally to pay the current and capital account deficit. Today, with the rate of exchange between the U.S. dollar and other currencies freely set by the market and unrelated to gold reserves, the balance of payments objective is primarily a matter of maintaining equitable trade relationships between the United States and other countries. Trade negotiations between the United States and China, Mexico, and Canada, for example, are contentious because of the much larger value of goods that U.S. businesses and citizens purchase from those countries than customers in those countries purchase from the United States.

To remedy the large net current and capital account deficit shown in Table 3-1, the U.S. economy would have to (1) produce and sell more goods and services abroad, which would mean an increase in GDP; (2) consume less of the goods currently produced in the United States so they could be sold abroad, assuming there is demand

for them; (3) reduce consumption of goods from abroad; or (4) achieve some combination of the first three. If the economy fails to achieve any of those possibilities, then the deficit must be addressed through borrowing.

Fortunately, investments in the U.S. economy, including purchases of U.S. private and government bonds and other debt instruments, are attractive to foreign investors, and they have been especially attractive during world financial crises such as the Asian and emerging-market collapses of the late 1990s and the more recent Great Recession. There is a demand in other countries to invest in assets and lend to the United States, independent of its trade position with the rest of the world. However, this means that the United States is relying on savings generated by other economies, rather than relying on a healthy national savings rate in this economy (discussed later).

The risk of consistently resorting to external borrowing with an ever-growing national debt is that the U.S. economy may not always be as attractive as it historically has been to foreign investors. A major shock to the U.S. economy that causes investors from abroad to pull out large amounts of funds would both decrease the funds available for investment and decrease current consumption. The post–September 11, 2001, period initially did lead to some pullback from the U.S. capital market, but that was short lived, in part due to actions by the Federal Reserve Board (discussed later in this chapter) to hold down interest rates. Even with as bad a situation as the U.S. financial markets experienced following the 2007 market collapse, by 2011 the United States was again a more attractive target of financial investors than most other countries.

Financing the U.S. Economy

Table 3-1 illustrates how, in 2018, the U.S. economy "balanced" the net current and capital accounts deficit. The financial account section captures the acquisition of financial assets and the incurrence of financial liabilities. The financial accounts display the purchases and sales of financial assets. In 2018, the United States acquired net $311 billion in financial assets (foreign assets purchased net of foreign assets sold). Also, in 2018, the United States had a net increase in financial liabilities, mainly loans undertaken, of $736 billion, reflecting the way the economy financed the current and capital account deficit. The sum of the increase in financial assets, the increase in financial liabilities plus two small adjustments,[50] makes up the Financial Account. This Financial Account must balance the net Current and Capital Account balance. Thus, in 2018, the U.S. economy incurred a net liability in financial transactions matching the amount that had to be financed to balance the net current and capital account.

The situation illustrated in Table 3-1 and the accompanying figure has not always been the case. When the U.S. current and capital account deficit was positive, or near balanced, this economy was financed largely from an even flow of goods, services, and financial investments between the United States and other countries. From the mid-nineteenth century until the mid-1980s, the U.S. economy was financed domestically. National saving was enough to provide funds for national investment, with the surplus national saving being invested abroad.

To the extent that households spend heavily on consumer goods and save little, and the government budget is in deficit, investment must be financed from sources outside the economy. An important part of the U.S. economy for most of the last four decades has been financed less by domestic savings and more by foreign lending to the U.S. government. These foreign investments represent a future claim on U.S. assets that are not matched by equal U.S. claims on foreign assets.

The upside of foreign investments and foreign lending to the United States is that they represent foreign confidence in the economy. In the market turmoil of 2011, the confidence in the U.S. economy relative to other countries might not have been as much the strength of the U.S. economy overall, but the relatively weaker investment choices offered in other countries still made the United States attractive.[51] Foreign investors have found U.S. Treasury notes an attractive investment because of the interest rates offered and because of their safety. The main threat to that confidence has been directly linked to the

politics of the U.S. budget deficit. The U.S. Treasury legally cannot borrow without limit. The Congress sets a debt ceiling periodically, and if that debt ceiling is reached, the Treasury cannot borrow more, risking default. Congress acts in crisis mode as the debt begins to reach the ceiling, and it is often only a last-minute bargain in which the two political parties and the White House agree to raise the debt ceiling. Although the U.S. Congress has stalled several times until the last possible moment raising the ceiling on the amount of debt the U.S. government can legally incur, a compromise has been reached each time. Usually a political bargain is reached, such as tying the increase in the debt ceiling to a plan to reduce the federal deficit (see discussion later in this chapter).[52] The limitation on debt is not a constitutional requirement for a debt ceiling.[53] It is strictly imposed by the Congress. First implemented by Congress in World War I, it does not limit the actual debt that may be incurred; it limits repayment of debt incurred.[54]

It is the repayment issue that can set off alarms among investors, especially foreign investors, if the debate in Congress pushes the limit. In 2018, the compromise did not really address the federal deficit in any meaningful way. The budget *deal* increased spending for military and domestic programs and agreed to a very modest $75 million in budget cuts. Congress avoided what otherwise would have been required budget sequestration—budget cuts—by the tried and true methodology of kicking the debt ceiling down the road by suspending the ceiling for 2 years. As a result, federal spending agreed to in the deal was increased by $320 million more than it otherwise would have been.[55]

The Decline in National Savings[56]

Except for the four budget surplus years from 1998 to 2001 (see the chapter on budget approval and the U.S. Congress), the U.S. economy has generated decreasing amounts of savings to finance investment in the economy, relative to the size of the economy. National savings represent the source of funds for new investment in equipment, plants, and other physical facilities that allow total production to grow. Economists generally measure savings as gross and net national savings as a percentage of GDP. *Gross national savings* is the sum of household saving, corporate saving, and government saving. Household saving may be literally in the form of savings accounts or, more likely, in investment in securities through individual investments and individual and corporate contributions to pension plans. Government saving may be in the form of investment in fixed assets such as roads and bridges or, though rare, a budget surplus. Corporate saving is investment in fixed assets such as factories, equipment, land improvement, and so forth, plus net changes in inventory. These government and corporate investments, financed by purchases of equity and debt in companies or taxes in the case of government, create the economy's capacity to produce goods and services.

Not all investments by governments and corporations produce an increase in productive assets, of course. As discussed earlier, a portion of investments is used to replace older facilities and equipment. Machinery purchased to replace obsolete equipment would not result in an increase in productive capacity. The term *net*

national savings captures the difference between investment in productive capacity, whether government or corporate, that adds to new production by subtracting the value of fixed assets replaced, as discussed in Exhibit 3-1.

The U.S. gross national savings rate has ranged from a high of 22% in 1965 to a low of just under 14% in 2009. However, considering the consumption of fixed capital (see Exhibit 3-1), the net national savings rate hit its low in 2009, a negative 2.5%. The previous high net savings rate since the early 1960s was in 1965 (12%).

Figure 3-5 shows U.S. gross and net national savings rates (savings as a percentage of GDP) from 1997 through 2018. Both savings rates have declined steadily, with occasional bumps upward. The net national savings rate, which removes the effects of inflation, in 2017 was less than half the rate in 1997 (2.9% versus 6.3%). Typically, it has not been an increase in personal savings that has caused the savings to go up temporarily, but decreases in the government budget deficit, such as the increased savings rate in the late 1990s and the economic boom following the Great Recession. The data indicate that the United States is increasingly a

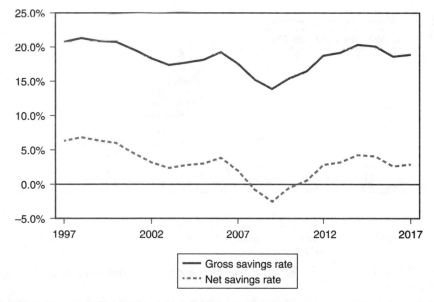

Figure 3-5 U.S. Gross and Net National Savings Rates: 1997–2017.

Note: Savings rates are gross and net savings respectively as % GDP.

Calculated from U.S. Council of Economic Advisers (2019). *Economic report of the president, Appendix B: statistical tables, Table B-19: 2019.* Retrieved September 5, 2019, from https://www.govinfo.gov/app/collection/erp/2019

consumption-based economy, with declining private sector and public sector investments that would support future growth.[57] (See the chapter on capital assets for a discussion on low levels of public investment in infrastructure.)

How does the U.S. savings rate compare with that of other industrialized countries? **Figure 3-6** compares the United States with the United Kingdom, Japan, South Korea, Germany, plus the entire Euro area (inclusive of Germany)[58] from 2000 to 2015. It is clear that except for 2000, when the United States experienced a federal budget surplus, the United States lagged behind each of the other countries and the Euro area. South Korea's net savings rate was comparable to that of other more recently advanced industrial economies, benefiting from substantial increases in labor productivity due to investments in manufacturing technology and electronics and a shift in the labor force from less to more productive occupations, such as from small-scale agriculture to manufacturing. Overall, as noted earlier, most of the capital formation that occurred in the U.S. economy was absorbed by replacing obsolete or unusable assets.

The substantial decline in U.S. net national savings has been relatively unique, based on the small sample in Figure 3-5. Even countries like the United Kingdom that run a capital account surplus typically have higher savings rates than the United States, except for 2015. While the United States experienced strong growth after the Great Recession, the United Kingdom has not. In the economic boom of the 1990s, U.S. net national savings was relatively high, in part because of substantial investment in the U.S. capital markets and in part because of low government budget deficit, including some years of budget surplus.

The compensating factor that offsets some of the problems that might otherwise be created by a sustained low savings rate is in the technology advantage that the U.S. economy has enjoyed relative to most other countries. The measures of savings discussed in this section capture those elements in the economy that are investments in fixed assets (i.e., physical or tangible objects). Classically, land, labor, and capital were the three elements that combine to produce goods and services. Increasingly, however, the main factor that still enables the United States to have the highest GDP, and one of the highest levels of GDP per capita, is technology.[59]

Typically, when a company replaces an obsolete piece of equipment, the new equipment is

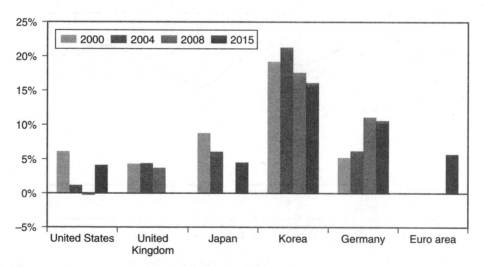

Figure 3-6 Net National Savings Rates for the United States and Selected Other Industrial Countries: 2000, 2004, 2008, and 2015.

Compiled from Organization for Economic Cooperation and Development. OECD statistics, V. 2.6, Paris: OECD. Retrieved July 15, 2006, from http://stats.oecd.org/wbos/degault.aspx?datasetcode=ANA TABLE 2. Japan data is 2000 and 2003; 2008 source: Net saving rate: percentage of GDP, Paris: OECD, Retrieved November 14, 2011, from http://www.oecd-ilibrary.org/economics/national-accounts-at-a-glance-2009/net-saving-rate_9789264075108-table7_1-en; 2015 source: OECD national accounts statistics at a glance, net national savings rate 2015. Retrieved September 5, 2019, from https://data.oecd.org/natincome/saving-rate.htm. Note: tables for 2000, 2004, and 2008 are no longer available at those URLs.

most likely to be much more productive than what it replaced. Net national savings would not capture this increased productive capacity due to the more sophisticated knowledge built into the new equipment. If one were able to measure the production of both the old and new equipment when operating at full capacity, then one would not fully subtract the cost of the replacement equipment from gross national savings. But in the total economy, the measurement problems in capturing the value of technology are currently insurmountable. To the extent that new technology built into new fixed assets is not measured in terms of contribution to productivity, net national savings understates the ability of the economy to continue to produce goods and services. The value of knowledge generated within the economy and the attractiveness of the U.S. economy are what have enabled the U.S. economy, despite lower savings rates and almost continuous government budget deficits, to enjoy higher standards of living than almost any other country in the world. However, other countries are catching up, and the advantage the United States enjoyed in information technology is no longer unique.[60]

Deficits and Debt Management

State and local debt are primarily tools for financing long-term investment in physical infrastructure and other capital assets. It is therefore prudent for state and local governments to use short-term borrowing only for meeting the demands of short-term contingencies and to ensure that long-term borrowing is linked to the expected life of the investments financed (discussed in detail in the chapter on capital finance and debt management). Federal debt policy, in contrast, is more affected by macroeconomic policy considerations, the disconnect between the public's desire for services and the willingness to pay for them, and the inability of Congress and the president to agree to either reduce the budget or increase taxes. In recent decades, except for the Great Recession period, the size of the debt

has been even less about macroeconomic policy objectives. (See the chapter on the Congress and budget approval for detailed discussion of the politics of deficits and debt.)

Deficits in the federal budget accumulate as spending exceeds revenues, regardless of whether the spending finances investments in long-term growth, meets operating expenses, pays interest on previous debt, provides transfer payments, or pays the costs of defense. While it is possible to make a numeric comparison between the investment levels in the federal budget and the size of the deficit, federal budget deficits have not been the result of conscious investment planning.

Developing countries' debt-management issues are generally not comparable to those of the United States or other longtime industrialized economies that incur substantial public debt as fiscal policy measures. For developing countries, prudent debt management is more comparable to that of U.S. state and local governments. Developing countries, as a rule, have excess or idle labor capacity. For these countries, the long-run economic strategy is to invest in education to improve the productivity of labor and in physical infrastructure to facilitate the production and flow of goods and services produced by the private sector. Typically, a shortage of physical infrastructure, such as transportation and communications facilities, retards the economic investment that would employ the excess labor capacity. Governments in developing countries borrow from donor agencies, such as the World Bank, and from banks in industrial countries to increase their physical infrastructure and other capital investments. If they are economically sound, the investments will produce long-run economic growth enough to repay the indebtedness.

Often, developing countries encounter debt troubles when borrowing is used to finance current consumption rather than investment and when physical infrastructure assets that have been built are not maintained. The economy then does not maintain an adequate level of growth, revenues do not increase as expected, and debt exceeds capacity to repay.

U.S. Government Debt and Debt Management

The annual federal budget *deficit* represents the amount the government must finance, usually by borrowing, to meet the year's spending requirements. Government *debt*, or the cumulative effect of budget deficits, represents the total amount the government is obligated to repay over time. Although the U.S. government debt gets a lot of attention in the media, not everyone realizes that there are different measures of the size of the debt. The two most common are total (or gross) federal debt and debt held by the public. Total federal debt represents all the government's indebtedness, with a few exceptions. Debt held by the public excludes the debt owed by the government to itself, or intragovernmental debt.

Most intragovernmental debt is the result of government borrowing from trust funds, the largest being Social Security. The government finances the annual deficit by borrowing from the public and borrowing from federal trust funds. Borrowing from the public consists of treasury securities purchased by individual and institutional investors such as pension funds and other governments, including U.S. state and local and foreign governments. Intragovernmental borrowing means using monies that are in a fund such as the Social Security trust fund to meet some of the current year's spending requirements. On its books, the trust fund records an asset consisting of the amount borrowed plus interest, matching the federal government's liability to repay the amount borrowed plus interest.[61]

Total federal debt represents the amount of revenue the government would have to raise to repay all its debt obligations. There is a legal distinction between the obligation to repay intragovernmental debt and the external debt owed to the public. Legally, the government cannot refuse to pay debt held by external parties without being in default. Politically, the government can repudiate debt owed to itself without being legally in default, although practically speaking, it is likely that repudiation of debt owed to trust funds such as Social Security would be an act of political suicide. Congress can address debt owed to

trust funds by reducing expenditures or increasing taxes, freeing up funds to repay debt owed to trust funds such as Social Security. Congress could decide, and the president could approve, to reduce Social Security payments to future recipients. That action would reduce the debt obligation to that fund, and total federal debt would decline. Not politically palatable, but legal. The chapter on Congress and budget approval discusses in detail the unwillingness of Congress and the president, in all recent administrations, to make the political decisions to reduce expenditures and/or increase taxes.

Size of the U.S. Federal Debt

Figure 3-7 shows federal debt as a percentage of GDP since the 1950s, using both total debt and debt held by the public.

Total federal indebtedness in 1950 equaled 92% of GDP, reflecting the financing of World War II. Through 1985, the difference between the two debt measures was usually around 10% or less, meaning most of the annual borrowing was from external parties. Both measures of debt steadily declined until total debt reached postwar lows around 33% of GDP between 1970 and 1982. Other than a dip in the balanced budget period in the Clinton administration, total federal debt has climbed regularly. Within that climb, there are two steep points—the period of and immediately following the Great Recession and, more recently, the effects of the 2017 tax cut. Though the tax cut was expected to stimulate economic growth, and therefore pay for itself with increased tax revenue, it did not do so, and both the Congressional Budget Office (CBO) and the Government Accountability Office projected continued increases in debt as a percentage of GDP for at least another decade after the tax cut took effect.[62]

The budget deficit reached at the end of FY 2019 was $984 million; 1 month later (November 2019), the deficit exceeded $1 trillion for the first time since 2012.[63] The CBO's 2019 projections were that annual budget deficits would exceed $1 trillion every year through 2029. The average deficit for the 2020 to 2029 period would be 4.7% of GDP, which is substantially higher than the

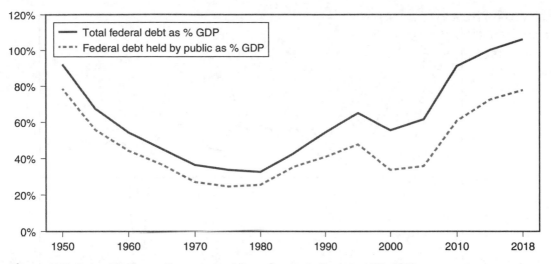

Figure 3-7 Federal Debt as a Percentage of Gross Domestic Product, 1950–2018.

U.S. Council of Economic Advisers (2019). *Economic report of the president, Appendix B: statistical tables, Table B-46: 2019.* Retrieved September 5, 2019, from https://www.govinfo.gov/app/collection/erp/2019

average of 2.9% of GDP for the previous 50 years. Over the same period, the debt held by the public would rise from $17.8 trillion (79% of GDP) in 2020 to $29.3 trillion (95% of GDP) in 2029. By 2029, the total federal debt of $34.4 trillion (which includes internal obligations, such as funds owed by the rest of the government to the Social Security trust funds) would exceed the GDP.[64] None of these debt projections take into account the large federal stimulus packages approved in early 2020, when the economy went into a steep decline as a result of measures to limit the spread of the coronavirus infection.

Figure 3-7 illustrates an important difference between total federal debt and debt held by the public. Since the early 1990s, federal borrowing from itself increased at a more rapid rate than borrowing from the public. In 1985, there was about a 7% differential—total debt was about 43% of GDP and debt held by the public was about 36%. In 1990, the difference was nearly 14% and it has risen steadily to about 30%. What this means is that since the 1990s, the federal government has relied increasingly on borrowing from itself to finance the deficit.

Borrowing from itself means the Treasury does not have to issue as much debt in the marketplace, at least in the short term, as otherwise

would be required to finance the deficit. Spending financed from internal borrowing has the effect of a fiscal stimulus to growth without affecting, in the short term, the cost of borrowing. Government debt secured from the public competes with private borrowing in the financial markets, making private investment more expensive. As discussed later in the chapter, monetary policy actions can be taken to affect interest rates, as they have been since the Great Recession, keeping interest rates low.

Effects of Economic Performance on the Size of the Federal Debt

Two circumstances explain the rapid rise in the federal government's debt at the end of the last century and into the twenty-first century. First, the federal budget, in terms of both revenues and expenditures, is affected by the overall performance of the economy. **Figure 3-8** captures this relationship comparing change in GDP with change in federal revenue from 1978 to 2018.

Oil price shocks and high inflation led to unbalanced federal budgets throughout the 1980s. Overall growth in the economy in real terms was virtually zero for that decade. This lack of growth created pressure on the budget because

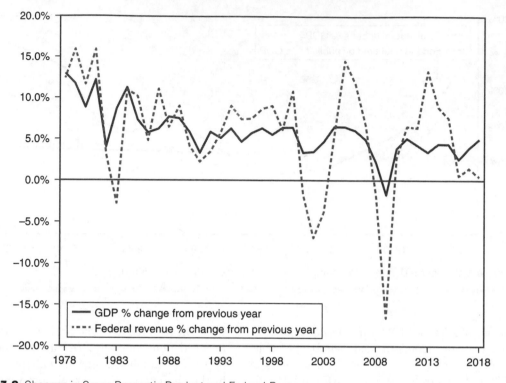

Figure 3-8 Changes in Gross Domestic Product and Federal Revenue.

U.S. Council of Economic Advisers (2019). *Economic report of the president, Appendix B: statistical tables, Table B-45: 2019*. Retrieved September 5, 2019, from https://www.govinfo.gov/app/collection/erp/2019

of automatic increases in expenditures for some social welfare programs that expand as unemployment goes up. It also caused a decline in federal revenues. The growth in entitlement spending, fueled by demographic and cost changes, threatens to overwhelm the federal budget over the next 30 years. Because of demographics and increased costs, the major entitlement programs—Social Security, Medicare, and Medicaid—have highly uncertain fiscal futures. Because Social Security and Medicare represent transfers between current workers (who pay the payroll taxes) and current retirees (who receive the benefits financed by those taxes), the retirement of the baby boomers was already having a substantial effect on the finances of these programs in 2019. At the same time, individuals are living longer, thus receiving benefits from these programs for a longer period. More importantly, Medicare and Medicaid are affected by the same cost growth as the rest of the health care system.

CBO's 2019 long term outlook extended to 2050. All told, CBO's long-term model suggested that, under plausible scenarios that would extend current law, spending would rise to 28% of GDP by 2049 (from 21% in 2019), revenues would rise to 19.5% of GDP (from 16.5% in 2019), and debt held by the public would rise from 78% of GDP in 2019 to 144% of GDP by 2049.[65] There is a great deal of uncertainty in these projections— higher or lower interest rates or higher or lower economic growth would have a substantial and compounding effect on these specific estimates. There is little question, however, that the debt will rise under current policies. and most recently the 2017 tax cuts renewed the longer-term trend toward higher deficits.

But does it matter? CBO's analysis suggests that there are several negative consequences that would result from this magnitude of debt expansion. First, the agency estimates that the need for the federal government to acquire debt to finance its operations would "crowd out" private investment. In other words, private businesses seeking to acquire capital to improve their productivity would find less capital available to do so. This would have the effect of lowering the compensation of workers, and potentially increase unemployment. Second, interest payments would become a higher percentage of federal spending, possibly forcing reductions in government services. Third, and related, a fiscal crisis could occur if investors have less confidence in U.S. Treasury securities. Higher levels of debt can constrain the options available to the government to respond to a fiscal crisis such as the Great Recession.

A contrary view is expressed by what came to be called *Modern Monetary Theory* (MMT). Although *modern* implies new or recent, MMT's emphasis on deficit financing to finance investment during recession has roots at least as old as the Great Depression and Keynesian macroeconomics.[66] In the conventional Keynesian prescription, deficit financing projects and programs to stimulate demand and increase employment during a recession period has been seen as a temporary measure. That is, once the economy recovers from a downturn, deficit spending is no longer necessary as a stimulus measure. The Great Depression–era public works programs to address unemployment and build essential, or at least useful, infrastructure were seen as temporary measures. The stimulus packages of the Great Recession, discussed in a later section of this chapter, were also temporary deficit-financed investments to boost economic growth over the long term. Running a long-term deficit is considered, in this conventional view, to have negative effects on economic growth due to potential inflationary pressures from continuing to stimulate demand. Monetary policy is a companion tool to deficit spending. Should the economy overheat, and inflation threatens, various monetary policy tools such as interest rates can dampen inflationary pressures.

Modern Monetary Theory differs in at least two respects. First, MMT proponents argue that the concern about negative effects of running a long-term deficit are misplaced, or at worst,

exaggerated. There are numerous policy options to ensure that deficits do not crowd out private investment. Second, key to MMT is the understanding that a country that controls its own currency has the *monetary* policy tools it needs to finance the deficit (monetary policy tools also are discussed later in this chapter in the section on tools available to affect the economy). Economics professor Stephanie Kelton, a strong MMT proponent, argues that "the potential risk with the national debt increasing over time is inflation. And to the extent that you don't believe the U.S. has a long-term inflation problem, you shouldn't believe that the U.S. is facing a long-term debt problem."[67]

What helped bring MMT more out of academic circles and into the national press during the Trump administration were the programs proposed by candidates for the Democratic Party nomination for the 2020 election, notably Senators Bernie Sanders and Elizabeth Warren, and the election of vocal, highly visible new Democrats to the House of Representatives in 2018, notably Representative Alexandria Ocasio-Cortez. Professor Kelton was an advisor to Senator Sanders, who was one of several candidates arguing for large federal spending increases, although tempered by tax increase proposals. Representative Ocasio-Cortez introduced advocacy for large programs with the position: "Modern Monetary Theory, which holds that the government doesn't need to balance the budget and that budget surpluses actually hurt the economy, absolutely needed to be a larger part of our conversation."[68]

Although more visible because of attention in the Democratic party nominating process and vocal political progressives elected to the 116th Congress (2019–2020), "mainstream economists"[69] have not embraced the notion of monetary sovereignty (ability to print money) to allow for large, sustained deficit spending. To control inflation, critics argue, MMT relies on the government to raise taxes and lower spending. In effect, fiscal policy carried out by Congress and the White House would substitute for the Federal Reserve in order to reduce or increase the money supply. Critics of MMT point out that simply assuming political leaders will do the right thing flies in the face of our recent experience, and these critics express much more faith in monetary policy than they do in the political system.[70]

Anticipating Change in the Economy

Both the private and public sectors need tools to measure economic change and anticipate economic trends. If businesses are to make sound investment decisions (including the decision to hire new workers or build new plant capacity), they must anticipate future economic developments. If interest rates are expected to fall, it is not the time to borrow to buy new production equipment. If a tax incentive that reduces overall tax liability when funds are invested in new productive capacity is about to expire, it is a good time to make new investments before the expiration. Some of these events can be predicted with relative certainty. Key tax cuts in the 2017 Tax Cuts and Jobs Act are set to expire after 2025, but those affecting businesses for the most part have no expiration date. Experience has shown that Congress is reluctant to give up tax credits, continually renewing them until finally making them permanent, such as the R&D investment tax credit. Based on the history of Congress renewing so-called temporary tax cuts or tax credits, businesses may be optimistic going forward that they will continue. In contrast, it may not be so easy to predict how much change will occur in interest rates, because those are affected by factors outside the direct control of political leaders in any one country.

Forecasting tools are a vital ingredient in business economic planning. If the federal government is to achieve its economic policy objectives, it needs sensitive and valid measures with which to monitor and to predict the direction of the economy. Likewise, it needs models of change that predict what will happen if specific policy changes, such as a change in the maximum corporate income tax rate or changes in major entitlement programs such as Social Security,

are enacted. Although forecasting techniques are beyond the scope of this text, some familiarity with the measures that are watched closely by business and government and with the analytical models used by forecasters is important for understanding government economic policy.

Business and government forecasters watch closely several individual economic indicators. Historically, the Bureau of Labor Statistics (BLS) regularly drew upon data about the economy from its own statistical work, the Bureau of the Census for survey-based data, and the Bureau for Economic Analysis to prepare a set of closely watched indicators that came to be known as the U.S. Composite Economic Indexes. Some data series also come from the Federal Reserve system, the stock market, and other organizations. In 1995, BLS outsourced the indicators project to the Conference Board, a nonprofit corporation founded in 1916 by CEOs of some of the United States' largest and most important companies. The indicators in these indexes are best thought of as monitoring indicators that describe the status of the American economy and give some indication about potential changes in the economy. **Table 3-2** lists the three economic indexes and each index's component data series.

The 21 indicators in the composite economic indexes are grouped into 3 categories as shown in Table 3-2: *leading, coincident,* and *lagging*. Each component and each index are statistical measures of a point in time. Some measures capture weekly averages, such as initial claims for unemployment. The composite indexes are updated monthly, and what analysts watch are changes over time in the individual components and the composite indexes. Observed over time, the composite indexes paint a picture of the volume of activities measured in each component. Rising weekly claims for unemployment insurance may reflect employers' waning confidence, causing them to start reducing the labor hours, laying off workers, and potentially cutting back on investments in production facilities.

Another way of looking at the individual indicators in a composite index is to see how many of the indicators are changing in the same direction.

Table 3-2 Composite Economic Indexes[a] Summarizing the U.S. Economy

Leading Economic Index

1. Average weekly hours, manufacturing
2. Average weekly initial claims for unemployment insurance
3. Manufacturer's new orders, consumer goods and materials
4. Institute of Supply Management (ISM) new orders index
5. Manufacturers' new orders, nondefense capital goods excluding aircraft
6. Building permits, new private housing units
7. Stock prices, 500 common stocks
8. *Leading Credit Index*™
9. Interest rate spread, 10-year Treasury bonds less federal funds
10. Average consumer expectations for business conditions

Coincident Economic Index

1. Employees on nonagricultural payrolls
2. Personal income less transfer payments
3. Industrial production
4. Manufacturing and trade sales

Lagging Economic Index

1. Inventories to sales ratio, manufacturing and trade
2. Average duration of unemployment
3. Consumer installment credit outstanding to personal income ratio
4. Commercial and industrial loans
5. Average prime (interest) rate
6. Labor cost per unit of output, manufacturing
7. Consumer price index for services

[a]Current component factors shown in the table are revised as of February 2019.

The Conference Board (2019). *The Conference Board leading economic index (LEI) for the United States and related economic indexes.* Retrieved September 8, 2019, from https://www.conference-board.org/pdf_free/press/US%20LEI%20-%20Tech%20Notes%20AUGUST%202019.pdf; The Conference Board (2019). *Description of components.* Retrieved September 8, 2019, from https://www.conference-board.org/data/bci/index.cfm?id=2160

For example, if average weekly hours in manufacturing are increasing, average weekly claims for unemployment are decreasing, new building permits issues are increasing, and so forth, then there is a strong signal from the leading indicators composite index that the economy is moving in a particular direction. Agreement among the indicators is measured in a *diffusion index*. A diffusion index calculates the proportion of individual components of the index that are moving in the same direction. The numerical value of a diffusion index is equal to the percentage of components of the index that are moving in the same direction. For example, the diffusion index of the leading composite index assigns values of 1, 0.5, or 0 to each component based on a change of 5% or more, less than 5%, or no change or drop, respectively.[71] Stock analysts and trade publications also compute and publish indexes of the major markets.

Leading Index

The leading index is intended to capture turning points in the economy that presage a directional change in the economy, such as a downturn in production of goods and services (GDP). The coincident index occurs at about the same time as measures of aggregate economic activity. The coincident index may confirm that a change in the economy suggested by changes in the leading index, or perhaps may fail to confirm indicating that the turning point in the economic cycle may not happen. Turning points in the lagging index show up after the aggregate economic activity has occurred.

Employment-Related Indicators

A key leading indicator is the *average weekly hours in manufacturing*. Its usefulness is based on the practice of most manufacturers of cutting back on the length of the workweek rather than laying off workers if the demand for production starts to decline. A somewhat later indicator is the *average weekly initial claims for unemployment insurance*. This indicator provides evidence of the extent to which layoffs are increasing or decreasing. Both measures indicate employers' estimates of the direction of change in the economy.

Housing Starts

Private, non-farm housing starts, measured by the number of building permits issued for new private housing units, provide a measure of the faith of builders and financial investors in the health of the economy. A decline in the number of starts can signal future economic decline. Housing is thought to be especially sensitive in that it reflects willingness to tie up investment dollars for several months to a year in an expensive commodity for which there may be no buyer at the time construction begins.

Stock Markets

Independent of the Leading Economic Index, stock markets are watched closely by the business community and government analysts, but their volatility makes them difficult to use as leading indicators. The New York Stock Exchange historically has been the market most carefully watched. The NASDAQ (National Association of Security Dealers Automated Quotation), where most technology stocks are traded, has become as important—and to some, more important—due to the substantial increase in the information and

communications technology sector's share of the economy. The Tokyo and London markets are watched as well. A substantial increase in investments in emerging markets and the swings in these markets have given prominence to several other markets. The Hang Seng (Hong Kong) stock market index is reported daily, for example.

Several composite indexes of stock exchange transactions are watched, the most notable being the Dow Jones Industrial Average (DJIA) and Standard & Poor's (S&P) indexes. Changes are infrequent in the stocks listed in these indexes, although they became more frequent in the late 1990s as stock values for some of the companies included in these indexes fell to near zero and some went out of business. Giants such as the Walt Disney Company and ExxonMobil Corporation have been mainstays in the DJIA. As the U.S. economy continues to rely on service industries and technology industries, more frequent additions and deletions are necessary. For example, Walmart was added to the index to capture more of the services component of the economy, and companies like Microsoft and Intel which represent information technology, have been added as well. Walgreens Boots Alliance, Inc. replaced General Electric in 2018.

Stock transactions are useful as leading indicators in that they reflect the faith of investors in the stocks traded on the open market and thus in the companies whose stocks are traded. The prices for 500 common stocks are the S&P index component. Stock transactions may be helpful as a barometer of investor confidence. In principle, the value of a stock reflects the health of the firm. Stocks may surge or decline wildly as a result of corporate takeover attempts and fights to prevent takeover or as a function of irrational investor behavior showing faith in unlimited growth potential in stock prices. To the extent that stock prices reflect factors other than the economic health of the corporations, prices will be misleading as an economic indicator. The *Leading Credit Index* is a trademarked index of six major credit measures, including, for example, LIBOR, the rate for lending among banks in the London interbank market.

Coincident Index

Coincident indicators, which report what the economy is doing now, are the indicators that most commonly reach the public's attention. Four indicators make up the coincident index. From the BLS, the number of employees on nonagricultural payrolls reflects hiring and firing in nonagricultural establishments. The industrial production index, prepared by the Federal Reserve System, is a measure of the manufacture of durable and nondurable goods. The durable portion of manufacturing is watched closely, particularly key industries such as steel. Sales of steel and other hard inputs into manufacturing reflect future intentions of manufacturing concerns. Rising sales may indicate the possibility of future investments in capital facilities, while falling sales may indicate lack of confidence in the economy and attempts by firms to keep inventories low. The value of this index has declined somewhat as the size of the manufacturing segment of the economy relative to the services segment has declined.

Lagging Index

Prices

Earlier, this chapter described the basic measures of national product and income that indicate what is happening to the levels of production and income. Prices are another measure of what is happening. Changes in the *consumer price index* (CPI) for services is one of seven components of the lagging index.

The CPI is based on the cost of goods and services bought by urban wage and clerical workers. It is produced by the BLS. The agency estimates the CPI from actual prices charged for a market basket of purchases from a sample of outlets determined by household surveys. A periodic sample survey of about 50,000 housing units and 23,000 retail establishments in 87 urban areas around the country estimates buying habits. Monthly calls and visits to retail establishments and other vendors collect price information on most commodities. The household sample includes two population groups—all urban consumers and urban wage earners and clerical workers. Change in the CPI is widely cited as an indicator of inflation. One of its most important uses is to adjust various government benefit programs, most prominently Social Security, for the effects of inflation. Social Security payments are automatically increased based on increases in the CPI, because the CPI is thought of as a cost of living index.

Changes in the CPI are not the major variables that affect budget forecasts. The CBO focuses on changes in real GDP growth, interest and inflation rates, and wage and salary share of GDP in its long-term (10-year) budget projection.[72]

Unemployment

Unemployment, a percentage measure of the people within the labor force who are not employed, is a common public policy target indicator. Unemployment measures are politically charged. A change in the unemployment rate of 0.5% up or down is enough to send the president before the news media to announce significant economic progress or to have opposition leaders charge that the economy is failing. The unemployment component in the lagging index measures the average duration (weeks) that unemployed individuals have been out of work.

Forecasting

The 21 indicators in the leading, coincident, and lagging indexes are only a subset of data that business and government forecasters use to predict change in direction and strength of change in the economy. Despite the availability of a wide range of indicators and extensive historical series, forecasting remains a risky business. It is common to find two or more major federal organizations in disagreement over expected economic trends. Rarely do the Office of Management and Budget (OMB) and the CBO agree, for example, on the forecast of the federal deficit, and often these differences have their basis in variation in assumptions about future economic growth. The CBO calculated that the mean percentage error in forecasts of more than a dozen economic indicators was rarely more than 1% for the CBO, administration forecasts, and private economic forecasters. While 1% does not seem large, when forecasting trillions of dollars, the difference is not small. The CBO has observed that its estimates of interest rates and wage and salary growth tend to be higher than actual values, and somewhat higher than OMB and the consensus forecasts of private forecasters, called the *Blue Chip Consensus*.[73]

To the extent that discrepancies arise, forecasts by the president's advisers, reflected in the annual budget, have tended to overestimate economic performance. When that happens, government receipts fall short of forecasts, and expenditures tend to be higher due to programs such as unemployment benefits that kick in automatically. When an administration has advocated and won acceptance of tax cuts or investment programs, there is a tendency to interpret forecasts favorably, or even choose which indicators and forecasts to publicize. The CBO, though an arm of Congress, has a strong degree of independence from congressional or White House pressures to reach favorable conclusions. CBO estimates are often more accurate than OMB.

Economic forecasting independent of government agencies also is a robust, if small, industry. The Blue Chip Economic Indicators program is a commercial enterprise that relies on forecasts from approximately 50 economic forecasters from major companies in the U.S. finance industry. Each expert in the survey makes forecasts of changes in 15 variables, such as real GDP, the CPI, industrial production, corporate profits, and personal consumption expenditures.[74] Like the Conference Board's economics indexes, the Blue Chip Consensus also computes diffusion indexes measuring the degree to which the 50-plus forecasters are in agreement on the strength and direction of change in the 15 indicators. Other consensus forecasting surveys include the Federal Reserve Bank of Philadelphia's (FRBP's) quarterly survey of several hundred economists and finance professionals. It originated with the American Statistical Association and the National Bureau of Economic Research before being taken up by the FRBP in 1990. Numerous international organizations, such as the International Monetary Fund, the World Bank, and the OECD also produce forecasts based on polling economists.

Another approach to economic forecasting is the use of sophisticated econometric models. Large-scale econometric models typically originate in academia and/or collaborations between universities and private firms, mainly in the finance sector. These models rely substantially on time series data, such as some of the main economic indicators already discussed throughout this chapter, but with the addition of sometimes as many as hundreds of additional indicator series. Among the more famous private models was DRI-WEFA, a 2001 merger of Data Resources, Inc., and the former Wharton Econometric Forecasting Associates.[75] The DRI-WEFA forecasting model went through several corporate transitions, most recently incorporated in Global Insight (HIS Markit).[76] Several organizations, including the Institute for Survey Research at the University of Michigan, conduct surveys of ordinary consumers and expert analysts to obtain estimates of economic trends. Judgment is regularly used to adjust the sophisticated mathematical models.

Not surprisingly, during major economic changes both business and government are sometimes criticized for not having anticipated the degree of change or sometimes even the direction of change. Models seem to fail when major structural changes are occurring, such as OPEC's gain of control over oil production in the early 1970s or the 2007 market collapse when the complex derivatives that had fueled the housing finance growth came unraveled.

Given the conflicting interpretations possible even with sound information, economic forecasters as well as political leaders interpret the data from their own perspectives. The technical problems involved are great, but inevitably, forecasting succumbs not to technical problems but to political resolutions. The president and his staff may focus on one set of indicators that show signs of progress, while members of Congress from the opposing party may focus on another set of indicators that challenge the president's interpretation. State and local political leaders are just as susceptible to coloring judgment with hope by trying to appear confident in the economic future while sometimes failing to address serious underlying economic and fiscal weaknesses. The next section returns to the issues involved in conflicting theories of economic behavior and the implications for government economic policy.

Tools Available to Affect the Economy

This section first discusses the actions government may take to affect the economy. Some are not deliberate actions, but rather occur automatically. Most of the focus in this section, however, is on deliberate actions taken by government. These fall into two categories: fiscal policy and monetary policy. Following separate discussions of fiscal and monetary policy is an illustration of the combined application of these tools to the most recent economic crisis that unfolded beginning in 2007.

Automatic Stabilizers

Government actions intended to achieve economic policy objectives can be either discretionary or automatic. In the case of discretionary actions, policy makers discuss alternatives and reach a decision as to how to intervene in specific circumstances. Automatic or built-in stabilizers, in contrast, do not require policy makers to take any special steps. Some government revenues and expenditures rise or fall automatically with changes in the economy. Revenues are especially sensitive to economic performance, with tax revenues falling due to falling incomes. State and local government revenues rise and fall without intervention as economic conditions change. In some cases, the requirement that states balance their budgets forces them to cut expenditures as revenues from sales and income taxes fall. The federal government, in contrast, historically does not immediately reduce expenditures to match a revenue decline.

Figure 3-8, discussed earlier, shows the relationship between the change in GDP and the change in federal revenues from 1978 through 2018. With few exceptions, GDP declines were matched by declines in revenues, and vice versa, though not always at the same rate. For example, the 6% increase in GDP from 1987 to 1988 was exceeded by a much larger 11% increase in federal revenue. Similarly, the drop in GDP from 2008 to 2009 was accompanied by a much larger drop in federal revenue, 2% GDP drop and 17% federal revenue drop. In most of the years illustrated in the series, the directional changes occurred in the same year. There is little lag between a declining GDP and a decline in federal revenue because much of federal revenue derives from taxes on components of GDP (corporate and personal income). Lag between these two is more noticeable in monthly and quarterly figures. Government expenditures, at least at the federal level, do not automatically fall with declining economic performance. In fact, they tend to increase because of increases in some social programs and unemployment insurance. The combined tax revenue declines and expenditure increases have an automatic stimulative effect tending to encourage economic growth.

The progressivity of the tax structure is another example of a built-in or automatic stabilizer. As the economy declines, corporate profits decline, and workers' salaries decrease. Both corporate and personal taxes go down, with the result that proportionately more funds are left available to the private sector for investment, stimulating demand. Similarly, tax revenues rise as the economy expands, providing some brake on growth so it does not lead to inflationary pressures. Unemployment insurance is another example of an automatic stabilizer, as it kicks in within 2 or 3 weeks after initial filing for benefits.

Nongovernmental stabilizers are also an inherent part of the economy and individual economic behavior. Effects of recessions are resisted when individuals and corporations use savings to maintain established levels of activities. Conversely, expansionary trends also can be tempered by consumer savings patterns. As income rises, greater proportions of income are placed in savings rather than being used for consumption.

Discretionary Policies

Discretionary interventions vary widely. They are based on economic theories of behavior, both individual and institutional, that anticipate the economy's responses to government actions involving taxing and spending and alterations in the money supply and the flow of funds through the monetary system. The former actions are called fiscal policy, while the latter are dubbed monetary policy. Fiscal policy and monetary policy are first reviewed separately, and then their integration into an overall strategy is discussed. A separate section then follows to illustrate how these tools were used to combat the effects of the recession, starting with a fiscal policy stimulus package in late 2008 endorsed by the outgoing President George W. Bush and the incoming President Barack Obama.

Fiscal Policy Instruments

The essential tools of fiscal policy are revenues, expenditures, and the implied surplus or deficit. Their use evolved during the twentieth century and has continued into the twenty-first, changing as different views of the role of government in the economy have held sway. The prevailing view had been that little government intervention was necessary. If the economy seemed to be faltering, the government's role should be limited to an incremental increase in expenditures over revenues to "prime the pump." In recent decades, both expenditure increases and tax decreases frequently are used to boost the economy. During the Great Depression of the 1930s, demand fell so rapidly and to such a depth, however, that small actions by the government had virtually no effect. It was only the extraordinary production demands of World War II, financed largely by federal budget deficits, that stimulated enough growth to pull the economy out of its freefall. The immediate postwar period rode on the demand for consumer goods that had been in short supply during the war, and there seemed to be little for the government to do for the economy one way or the other.

Keynesian Economics

Ideas about what the government should do in the event of a downturn have not stood still. John Maynard Keynes had argued in 1936 that the main cause of downturns was lack of demand.[77] According to this view, the government's aim should be to stimulate demand by spending, thereby ensuring that idle productive capacity is used. By 1946, the federal government had assumed a formal, legislatively mandated role in the economy, and that role was guided by the prescriptions of Keynesian economics.

Keynes focused on the problem of cuts in production in response to declining demand. Such cuts result in less purchasing power for consumers, which further reduces demand for goods and services. This still further decline in demand results in further reductions in production levels. The emphasis, according to Keynesians, should be on maintaining demand levels. The way to maintain demand levels, in their view, is for the federal government to spend at a level higher than revenues—in other words, to incur a deficit whenever economic fluctuations threaten to reduce demand to levels that will generate unemployment and general economic decline. President Richard Nixon famously declared during the major recession of his administration: "I am a Keynesian in economics."[78] President Obama, in his first Economic Report to Congress, stressed the need to stimulate demand—falling short, however, of declaring himself a Keynesian.

Supply-Side Economics

Keynesian economics was widely accepted until the 1970s, when a contrasting view of the basic problem in a fluctuating demand cycle was given wide circulation. Some economists argued that the basic problem lay not on the demand side, but on the supply side.[79] So-called *supply-side economics* became the dominant viewpoint of the Reagan and George H. W. Bush administrations and continued as a major precept of subsequent Republican tax-cut policies. The supply-side view holds that high tax burdens are the major contributor to reduced economic performance. The more taxes are collected, the less money is available for private investment and the less incentive there is to produce. If taxes are cut, production will be stimulated and additional workers will be hired.

Although the tax rates are lower, the actual revenue yield will be higher because of increased corporate profits and increased take-home pay for workers. Furthermore, the increased supply of goods and services available should have a dampening effect on inflation. Instead of stimulating demand with federal expenditures, the supply-side approach emphasizes stimulating the economy by increasing the income available to consumers to spend by reducing taxes.

The supply-side view had its first major impact on tax policy with the 1981 tax cuts (Economic Recovery Tax Act of 1981). However, the expected revenue windfall did not materialize. Consumer spending, and to some degree corporate spending, did increase, but the gain in federal revenue from the growth stimulated by the reduced taxes did not offset the tax losses, and the deficit increased. As noted earlier, the tax cuts of the George W. Bush administration similarly did not produce the desired effects in increased revenues from economic growth, and the early evidence from the Trump administration cited previously in the chapter also challenges the stimulative effect of tax cuts on economic production. The prevailing explanation of why tax cuts have not produced consumer and business spending enough to make up for the loss in revenue is not necessarily inconsistent with the theory that tax cuts generally stimulate growth. The response of political proponents of supply-side tax cuts is that the tax cuts were not enough to generate the expected revenue growth from stimulating investment.

This explanation is complicated by the circumstances surrounding the major tax cuts of the 1980s, the early 2000s, and 2018. In the first two periods, tax-cut packages were introduced during economic downturns so that federal revenues fell not only as a result of the tax cuts, but also because of the general decline in economic activity (discussed later in this chapter). Furthermore, the economic period of the George W. Bush administration was dominated much more by the September 11 attacks and the subsequent wars in Afghanistan and Iraq than by tax cuts and other economic programs.

The 2010–2011 period shows that a closely divided Congress does not portend well for addressing the combination of expenditure and revenue decisions. Public opinion polls seemed to indicate that most Americans would have accepted an increase in taxes. For example, the *Washington Post/ABC News* opinion survey conducted in July 2011 found that 34% of Americans said they preferred to see the budget deficit solved by spending cuts alone, 2% by revenue increases alone, and 62% by a combination of both.[80] Nevertheless, Congress was unable to agree on any budget package that included tax increases, influenced most heavily by promises made by many Republicans to never vote for a tax increase.

As noted earlier, the Tax Cut and Jobs Act of 2017 was passed during deep divides in Congress, on strictly party lines. Unlike the two previous tax cut packages discussed above, the economy in 2017 to 2018 was growing, as Figure 3-7 illustrates—a 5% increase in GDP year over year. However, the tax cuts did not yield increases in federal revenue, at least not early on. Projections were that the federal deficit would continue to grow through 2029, unless the tax cuts were allowed to expire and/or savings on the expenditure side were achieved.[81] The impact of the unexpected global coronavirus pandemic on the U.S. economy makes it almost impossible to separately assess the effects of the 2018 tax cuts.

It is impossible to evaluate the supply-side versus demand-side theories about the effects of simultaneous tax and expenditure cuts. The most recent three major tax cut packages have all been adopted without corresponding expenditure cuts, although the Reagan administration tax reform initially included cuts in expenditures, but they quickly fell by the wayside. At least at the macroeconomic level, tax cuts absent expenditure cuts have unambiguously resulted in larger federal deficits. However, the circumstances surrounding the tax cuts were not really in the context of macroeconomic conditions. Tax cuts in recent history were introduced by Republican administrations and were adopted when there were enough Republican votes to attain congressional approval. Expenditure increases generally are introduced by Democratic administrations and passed when there are enough Democratic votes to attain congressional approval.

The middle-of-the-road view is that specific and directed tax decreases or reductions in tax liabilities can be helpful, such as investment tax credits to encourage businesses to invest in capital facilities and an R&D tax credit to encourage private expenditures on research. A major multiplier effect, in which tax reductions yield tax revenue increases, is unlikely, however. Prevailing views since the Reagan administration have tended to emphasize somewhat more the supply-side view than efforts to stimulate demand until the Great Recession, in which initially bipartisan efforts produced the first in recent decades of multiple programs to stimulate demand through major expenditure increases.

Multiplier Effects

Extracting taxes from the economy or adding expenditures will have not only immediate effects but also multiplier effects, as any transaction will generate several other transactions. For each government expenditure resulting in payments to industry or an individual, part is taxed, while the remainder is divided between consumption and investment. The private citizen or firm spends and, in doing so, places dollars in the hands of others. Some of those dollars will in turn be taxed and the rest spent or invested. Therefore, an increase of $100 in government expenditures will be multiplied in its effect on the economy.

Expenditures have a stimulative effect when they exceed revenues. An initial government expenditure financed by the deficit puts money in the hands of producers and consumers, who in turn pay a portion in taxes, save a portion, and spend a portion. An excess of revenues over expenditures has a dampening effect. An extremely large federal deficit, however, confounds the fiscal policy effects, such as was experienced between 2007 and 2019.

Response Lags in Fiscal Policy

One problem with implementing a modest fiscal policy is the gap between the time a revenue or expenditure response is seen as necessary and the time it can occur. The lack of complete information about the economy produces a *perception lag*, the time that elapses between an event—such as the beginning of an inflationary or a recessionary period—and its recognition. The perception lag contributes to a *reaction lag*, the time between recognition and the decision to act. Pluralistic or decentralized political systems, as well as systems characterized by deep partisan divides, are often unable to avoid substantial reaction lags. In addition, once agreement is reached, there is typically an *implementation lag*, the time required before the action taken affects the economy. Tax measures are clearly felt within a short period of time. The Economic Stimulus Act of 2008 contained tax rebates to taxpayers, some of whom received their rebates within 3 to 4 months of the act's passage.[82] The introduction of a new tax does require time to establish the specific regulations and mechanisms for collection. Once the tax is established, however, comparatively little time is required to make the necessary adjustments to the tax rate.

In contrast, extended implementation lags are likely when expenditures are increased for fiscal policy purposes. An example is the American Recovery and Reinvestment Act of 2009, which contained an infrastructure spending component intended to go to *shovel ready* projects—projects that state or local governments were already executing, but which could be expanded or speeded up without major engineering design and procurement steps.[83] While funds were allocated rapidly in many instances, unexpended funds remained in the program even after the economy showed strong recovery signs.

In the short term, the apportionment process that allocates funds to agencies may have some marginal influence on spending patterns during the various quarters of the fiscal year (see the chapter on budget execution). Potentially more powerful tools include budget impoundments, which, within certain limits, allow the president to defer or rescind expenditures (see the chapter on budget approval and the U.S. Congress). Many expenditures, however, are basically uncontrollable in the immediate future because of previous commitments (for example, entitlement programs that aid the elderly and low-income individuals). Furthermore, an increasing component of the federal budget is now devoted to meeting interest payments on the debt or to refinancing previous debt. Interest on the national debt was 8.5% of the federal budget in 2008 and is projected to be 13% in 2029.[84]

Effects of Global Capital Flows

As noted at the outset of the chapter, in the United States, changes in world markets were of little consequence for most of the twentieth century. Changes in the U.S. economy, such as occurred during the Great Depression and other serious recessions, rippled through other economies, but economic declines in other countries had less effect on the U.S. economy. Already discussed are the current interdependencies among the United States and other economies. The Asian and emerging-market financial crisis of the late 1990s had ripple effects through financial markets around the world as portfolio investors rapidly pulled their funds from investments in the region. Severe economic distress in Greece and Italy in 2010–2012, continuing to some degree throughout the decade, created similar ripple effects in other economies.

Unlike the Asian financial collapse in the 1990s, some of the continuing problems in some countries in the European Union have come since the U.S. economy emerged from the Great Recession. U.S. government borrowing from the central banks of several nations, including Japan and China, has caused concern. Reliance on borrowed dollars from central banks of other countries that hold large dollar reserves is unprecedented in modern U.S. economic history. In 2018, foreign investors held just over $6 trillion of outstanding federal debt (held by the public), or almost 39% of all such federal debt. Over one-third of that was held by Japan and China, in equal measure.[85] Many analysts continue to argue that the underlying strength of the United States is still attractive. Those countries whose central banks hold large dollar reserves are willing to continue to lend because their economies depend substantially on purchases by the U.S. economy. Some other analysts express real concern about this unprecedented borrowing from central banks.

There is no historical base from which to understand what could make those central banks lose confidence and reduce their levels of lending to the U.S. government.[86] If other emergent economies such as the BRICS countries[87] become major economic powers, some central banks of other countries may see alternative investments sufficient to reduce their appetite for U.S. government debt. Were that to happen, federal borrowing from the U.S. markets would have to increase, causing interest rates to rise, or dramatic tax increases and/or expenditure decreases would have to occur to reduce the deficit. That concern was voiced as early as the 1990s but has not materialized as the U.S. economy continues to be the single most attractive external investment target for investors in other countries.

Monetary Policy
Control of the Money Supply

Both demand-side and supply-side economists focus on the role of taxing and spending in the economy. Although supply-side economists did not launch a major critique of demand-side theories until the late 1970s, other economists since the 1950s have argued that the government's main effect on the economy should not come through fiscal policy at all. Originally led by Milton Friedman, these economists argue that the main effects of government policy on the private sector should come through control over the money supply. In a simple economy, a government controls the money supply through its monopoly power over the printing of money. As the economy expands, the demand for money increases, and government ultimately meets this demand by printing more money. In a sense, the government can literally print currency and use that currency to meet its spending requirements.

The increase in the money supply (over and above printing replacements for worn currency) is called *seignorage*. Clearly, if the government resorts to printing money without regard to demand, the value of the currency printed declines. U.S. news media in the early 1980s showed film footage of individuals in Bolivia pushing carts full of currency to pay for a few dollars' worth of goods as the annual inflation rate reached several thousand percent. Inflation affected currencies so much in Russia and Poland shortly after the demise of the Soviet Union that the governments issued new currency, eliminating three zeros to ease the use of currency in ordinary transactions. Five countries in 2019 had 3-year cumulative inflation rates exceeding 100%: Angola, Argentina, Democratic Republic of Congo, South Sudan, and Venezuela.[88]

The main money supply is characterized by the Federal Reserve as M1 and M2. To the average citizen, money is cash—paper money and coinage—and the amount of that is strictly controlled by the government. In the United States, only the U.S. Treasury Department may print currency or mint coins. However, in any complex economy, paper money and coinage in circulation are not the major component of the money supply. In the United States, less than 50% of the readily circulating money supply takes the form of paper money and coinage. Slightly more than 50% of the readily circulating money consists mainly of checkable deposits in banking institutions. Together, currency, coinage, demand deposits such as checking accounts, and small-time deposits constitute the component of money supply called M1. In mid-2019, M1 was at about $3.9 trillion and represented about 26% of the total money supply in circulation.

To M1 would be added savings deposits and small denomination time deposits, including retail money market accounts. M1 plus these additional components is called M2. M2 is considered the measure of total money supply in circulation, which in 2019 was approximately $14.9 trillion. Familiar paper money and coins thus are about 10% of total money in circulation. Excluded from M2 are large time deposits and institutional money market accounts, individual retirement and Keogh accounts, deposits that are attributable to foreign institutions, and U.S. federal deposits. These exclusions amounted to approximately $0.8 trillion in mid-2019. Added

to M2, these additional accounts measure total money supply in the economy, which stood at $15.6 trillion in 2019.[89] Digital currencies or cryptocurrencies, such as Bitcoin, are not counted in any measure of the money supply. The Federal Reserve considers these as "investments" as opposed to money.[90]

The banking deposit component of the money supply expands through credit or borrowing. When an individual borrows to purchase a new car, the bank increases the individual's bank balance though the individual has not deposited funds in the bank for this increase. The individual then can write a check to the car dealer. When corporations borrow from financial institutions or issue debt in the stock market, they secure funds for investment. In this case, the money supply grows by the amount of the loan. If interest rates are low, both consumer and business borrowing are encouraged, and the economy expands. Similarly, depository banks can borrow from the Federal Reserve System, which also adds to the money supply. Deregulation of the banking industry and the growth of various stock and bond funds have further increased the number and types of negotiable instruments that constitute the money supply. The money supply thus grows ever more complicated.

Role of the Federal Reserve System

In the United States, control over the money supply and interest rates, and hence monetary policy, is exercised by the Treasury Department (supply of currency and coinage) and the Federal Reserve System (often called the Fed), a quasi-public institution.[91] The Fed has five functions: (1) conduct the nation's monetary policy, (2) promote stability in the financial system, (3) promote safety and soundness of individual financial institutions, (4) foster the payment and settlement system safety and efficiency, and (5) promote consumer protection and community development.[92] The system is headed by a board of governors consisting of seven members appointed by the president with the advice and consent of the Senate. The Board of Governors is an independent agency of the federal government. The chairperson and vice chair are designated from among the seven members by the president, also with the advice and consent of the Senate. Board members may serve only one term of 14 years, although a member can serve the remainder of a term of a person who leaves the Board, plus a full term of 14 years. The chair and vice chair serve only 4-year terms, though they continue on the Board unless their 14-year term expires. Although appointed by the president, the Board of Governors reports to and is directly accountable to the Congress. The Federal Reserve Bank and its 12 branches are augmented by all national banks and by state banks and trust companies that wish to join the system.

The Federal Reserve serves as a bank to the banking community. Financial transactions among banks and other financial institutions are cleared through the Federal Reserve. The system lends money to the member banks, which the banks can then relend to their customers. In setting its lending rates to banks, the Federal Reserve influences the direction and magnitude of interest rates in the entire economy, in turn dampening or stimulating the credit system. The system also buys and sells government bonds ranging from short-term Treasury notes to long-term bonds (open market operations). In addition, the Federal Reserve controls the reserve requirements for member banks—the amount of money a bank must have available as a proportion of the total demand deposits of customers.

Using these three tools—lending, open market operations, and control of reserve requirements—the Federal Reserve controls the money supply. In this way, it attempts to moderate demand that might lead to inflationary pressures by reducing the growth in the money supply, or to stimulate demand when the economy is faltering by allowing the money supply to grow. The board, in describing the purposes of the Federal Reserve System, refers explicitly to the 1978 Full Employment and Balanced Growth Act (discussed earlier in this chapter) describing the three main monetary policy objectives of "maximum employment, stable prices and moderate long-term interest rates" contributing to the legislatively mandated government roles in the economy.[93]

Discount Rate

The Federal Reserve's means to directly influence the level of borrowing is through its lending rate to member institutions (the banks). Called the discount rate, this tool has increased in prominence as a monetary tool. Banks borrow from the Federal Reserve to meet customers' demands for money. As the Federal Reserve increases the interest rate, the rate charged to final borrowers increases, which in turn decreases the demand for funds. Since the 1980s, these operations have become the focus of Federal Reserve actions to control inflation in rapid-growth periods such as the late 1990s and again in 2004–2006. Beginning in 2000, the Fed steadily reduced the federal funds rate from more than 6% in 2000 to less than 2% by the end of 2001, declining further to around 1% in 2004. Proponents of MMT rely more on the actions of Congress and the president through taxing and spending decisions to influence demand.

In 2004, the Fed began raising interest rates to slow the rate of growth in the economy out of concern that inflation would get out of control, mainly because of increased consumer spending and borrowing by the government to finance the deficit. The first increase in June 2004 was followed by regular quarterly increases until August 2006, the longest period of consecutive increases in recent history. The rate at that point in August 2006 was 5.25%, meaning that banks borrowing from the Fed to meet their obligations and maintain required reserves repaid the Fed at an annual rate of 5.25%.[94] Discussed later in this chapter, during the Great Recession the Fed steadily lowered interest rates, at one point below 0, to restore the capacity of major financial institutions to invest in the economy. The Fed maintained low interest rates between March 2018 and September 2019, never exceeding 2.5%. Actions by the Fed to adjust the interest rate are watched closely by the stock markets. How the Fed chairman announces a rate change or announces that there will be no rate change at this time can create rapid reaction in the markets.

Open Market Operations

Open market operations do not get as much citizen attention, but are highly visible to the financial community because they occur daily. In open market operations, the Federal Reserve buys or sells government bonds (or, less frequently, gold or foreign currency) on the open market. Open market operations can be particularly important when the federal funds rate drops to near zero or actual zero, as it did between 2009 and 2015. At the zero federal funds rate, lowering interest rates has reached the limit in terms of expanding the money supply. However, the Fed's purchase or sale of long-term securities, or open market operations, also can expand or contract the money supply. As the Federal Reserve purchases bonds from the banking system, it increases the reserve holdings of the member institutions selling the bonds and hence increases their ability to lend money. This increase in turn stimulates economic activity, because more investment funds are made available. As member banks buy bonds from the Federal Reserve, their cash reserves decrease, reducing their ability to loan and thereby reducing the total supply of funds available to the economy. When the Fed (or any other country's central bank) purchases bonds from member banks, it does so with electronic cash that previously did not exist. The reserves in banks in the economy increase, which enables them to lend more. The purchase of long-term securities is described as *quantitative easing*.[95]

Another tool available to the Federal Reserve is changing the reserve requirements of member institutions. This is not frequently used. For every dollar in deposits, member banks are required to retain a specific percentage. By increasing this percentage, the Federal Reserve can immediately curtail the amount banks can lend and thus the amount of money available. Historically changed only every few years, the reserve requirement in the 1980s became a more prominent feature of monetary policy, with adjustments often occurring on an annual basis.

Putting all of these monetary tools together, the government's monetary policy is described as *loose* or *tight* (or as *expansionary* or *contractionary*). Loose monetary policy usually involves lowering the prime rate, purchasing securities from member banks, and perhaps lowering reserve requirements. These actions permit banks to lend more to customers. As a result, private investment goes up and unemployment falls. The side effects are lower interest rates and higher prices.

A tight monetary policy entails the reverse: the prime rate increases, the Federal Reserve sells securities, and reserve requirements may increase. These actions reduce the ability of banks to lend. Tight monetary policy is pursued generally to dampen inflationary pressures and to slow down a speeding economy. In contrast, loose monetary policy is pursued to stimulate growth and reduce unemployment.

Role of the Chair of the Federal Reserve Board

For much of the history of the Federal Reserve, it seems unlikely that many Americans ever knew the name of an incumbent or former chair. That changed with Chairman Alan Greenspan. His was almost a household name in the 1990s, especially to the millions of Americans who became first-time investors in the stock market or started paying attention for the first time to the value of their company pension fund investments in the market. Ben Bernanke was appointed chair in 2006, just prior to the Great Recession. He stepped out as a member of the Board in 2014 and was replaced as chair by Janet Yellen. She in turn was replaced in 2018 by Jerome Powell. Each of these chairs has enjoyed sometimes long, and sometimes brief, periods in the public limelight, for varying reasons. Bernanke was highly visible as a key participant in the government's efforts to break out of the Great Recession and resume growth. Yellen to some degree, and Powell especially, enjoyed the unenviable position of becoming a target of the president's criticism. In the case of Powell, President Trump demanded that he step down and threatened regularly to fire him. During the Trump administration, the position of chair of the Federal Reserve Board became politicized as never before in the history of the Fed, singled out for not dropping interest rates back toward zero as the economy's numbers began to look unfavorable to the president.[96] Today, the news media and the investing public are now highly sensitive to actions by the Federal Reserve, and hence the chair, as the spokesperson, is watched carefully for indications of where the Federal Reserve is going. Internally, the chair presides over a seven-member group and wields his or her influence through personality, force of argument, and relative prestige. The chair and the Federal Reserve are not synonymous.

Political Criticism of the Federal Reserve Board

Although the Federal Reserve Board is protected from direct coercion from the president and the Congress because its members' terms are fixed without threat of removal, the board is periodically criticized for appearing to respond to political pressure. While there is little evidence of overt behavior in support of incumbent presidents, some evidence indicates that the Federal Reserve Board has done less than it could in some periods (for example, in the 1960s and 1970s) to offset cyclic movements in the money supply and that this lack of action coincided with the interests of incumbent administrations.[97] While Board members are relatively insulated from political criticism, the chair and vice-chair are more susceptible, and their leadership terms as chair and vice-chair are shorter than their 14-year Board position.

Combining Fiscal and Monetary Policy

Although economists differ on the emphasis given to fiscal versus monetary policy, the two sets of tools operate at the same time, whether deliberately or not. Sometimes they are complementary. At other times, the effects of fiscal policy actions are offset by monetary policy actions. Many analysts are wary of advocating frequent changes in fiscal or monetary policy in response to changing economic conditions. The inability to predict economic change sufficiently far in advance and the slow response of governments suggest to many economists that fiscal policy should be oriented toward long-term economic objectives and

that monetary policy should be used for effecting short-term adjustments.

Who Is in Charge?

When it comes to combining fiscal and monetary policy, different organizational entities are involved, sometimes raising the question, "Who is in charge of overall economic policy?" Monetary policy is somewhat clear-cut in that the Federal Reserve System is in charge. The monetary policy tools that were discussed are under the control of the board with the leadership of the chair.

Fiscal policy is more complicated. The president is responsible for recommending policy and Congress for setting it through legislation. The Council of Economic Advisers as well as other key advisers provide input into the president's decision making as to what to recommend to Congress. Historically, about the only time Congress has looked at the total picture of the budget and economic policy is during the annual budget resolution (see the chapter on budget approval and the U.S. Congress). Target revenue and spending levels are set, along with a projected deficit (or, infrequently, surplus). Tax rates are set by law periodically, with continuing debate over whether they should be adjusted upward or downward. The Treasury Department, then, has responsibility for administering the taxes. Spending is set by a series of appropriation bills handled by separate appropriation subcommittees, with each executive agency being responsible for carrying out the mandates specified in these bills. The OMB has some influence on spending patterns through the apportionment process (see the chapter on budget execution).

Recognizing the importance of the federal government's role in economic affairs, President Clinton created the National Economic Council (NEC) in 1993. The NEC is responsible for coordinating economic policy; its parallel organizations, the National Security Council (NSC) and the Domestic Policy Council, are responsible for national security concerns and for all domestic policy issues other than economic, respectively. The NEC serves as a coordinator among the numerous cabinet and Executive Office of the

President agencies advising the president, including the Council of Economic Advisers, the OMB, and the Department of the Treasury.[98] The NEC functions to ensure that actions of the executive branch affecting the economy are consistent with the president's economic policy.

In recent times, the inability to pass a complete set of appropriations bills; the apparently unmanageable, in a political sense, federal deficit; and the deep division between expenditure cuts and revenue enhancements have all focused most of the attention onto the overall budget and economic picture. The apparent power to reach compromises, or at least to negotiate in pursuit of compromise, has narrowed the focus to the president, speaker of the House, Senate majority leader, and a few other key members of Congress, along with the Federal Reserve Board chair.

Public Investment Role of Government

Government Investment in Infrastructure

Fiscal policy and monetary policy are basically tools of central governments. State and local governments typically have balanced budget requirements, making it impossible or at least inadvisable to incur debt strictly for fiscal policy reasons, and neither type of government has a major influence on the overall money supply. However, state and local governments have significant impacts on regional economies, and state and local governments are increasingly adopting explicit economic development strategies. In this regard, state and local governments pursue strategies to create an effective climate to foster economic growth.

Also, these governments inevitably change taxes and spending in response to general economic conditions, which, whether deliberate or not, has at least regional economic effects. Because state and local budgets typically need to be balanced, these governments must respond to economic trends. When an economic downturn leads to reduced revenues, expenditures need to be reduced and taxes possibly need to be increased. Consequently, citizens may find that services they

need are no longer available or are in scarcer supply. In the case of local governments, one of the biggest problems during recessions is that many people fall in arrears with their local property taxes. For state governments, economic downturns often lead to decisions to raise tax rates at a time when people can least afford tax increases. States often look first at temporary revenue measures, such as using rainy-day funds, securitizing tobacco settlement revenue (see the chapter on capital finance and debt management), and postponing expenditures. Nonetheless, the Great Recession required many states to raise taxes. For example, in fiscal year 2010, 29 states enacted net revenue increase measures in the amount of $24 billion. Annual fiscal surveys conducted by the National Association of State Budget Officers since the recession show stabilizing and then increasing revenues from economic recovery, mitigating the need for tax measures.[99]

One of the major strategic elements available is public sector investment in the physical infrastructure necessary for business expansion. Serious concern emerged in the United States during the early 1980s and remains to this day regarding the loss in economic productivity due to deterioration in the infrastructure base of roads, bridges, streets, water and sewer systems, and other public facilities. According to some, fewer technological innovations, decreases in labor productivity, and inadequate capital investment in infrastructure were major contributors to an overall worsening of the U.S. economy.[100]

State and Local Incentives for Private Sector Investment

Governments are a major source of total capital formation in many developing countries. Public sector investment in infrastructure, including state-owned enterprises, historically accounted for most of the capital formation in developing countries. With privatization of state enterprises and growth of the private sector, however, the public sector role in capital formation has diminished. Although state and local governments in the United States do not invest as high a proportion of their finances in infrastructure, their role in creating a favorable economic climate is important. Some state employee pension funds, for example, have been used as sources of venture capital and to capitalize industrial development funds to attract new business. Federal policies, such as giving municipal bonds tax-exempt and other tax-preference status, also influence state and local investment spending. (See the chapter on capital finance and debt management.)

Similarly, even in the face of reduced federal financial assistance and difficult fiscal circumstances, state and local governments have over the past several decades increased both their relative share of infrastructure financing and the absolute amounts spent on public infrastructure. This stimulative effect, of course, required state and local tax increases.

State and local governments also actively compete over the location of major industrial facilities[101] (see discussion on competition among states for private investment in the chapter on intergovernmental relations). However, to the extent that state and local governments offer special incentives, such as tax breaks and below-market-cost facilities for industrial expansion, little national economic growth is stimulated. Certainly, it may be possible to induce a business to relocate or to locate a planned expansion by offering special incentives, but such a move represents for the national economy only a relocation of economic activity rather than net new economic growth. Of course, from a national point of view, attracting firms from other countries results in net growth within the national economy, albeit at the potential expense of some other country. More generally, however, attracting an investment to a particular location may readily benefit that region, but if it is not net new investment, but rather is due to the closing of a facility in another U.S. location, then the net economic benefit to the national economy is limited.

Link Between Public Infrastructure and Economic Growth

The causal link between public infrastructure investment and real economic growth depends on two conditions: The lack of facilities or infrastructure must be a barrier to private investment, and the costs of the investment must be, in principle, recoverable through economic gains.[102] For example, if poor road conditions slow the movement of goods and services, then the costs of those goods and services increase. In addition, firms may hold back on new investments because of the expected difficulty in transportation. Investment in road improvements under these conditions reduces transportation costs, which in turn either provides additional funds for investment or is passed on in savings to consumers, who can subsequently increase either savings or investment. If the economic returns on the road improvements exceed their costs, the result is a net economic gain to the economy. Conversely, if there are insufficient centers of production and consumption linked by those roads, then the volume of transportation will not be enough to yield enough economic gain, and the investment will not have been warranted. This topic is discussed more extensively in the section on asset management in the chapter on capital assets.

Unfortunately, determining when an investment will yield enough economic return is often difficult. Many local governments in the United States have invested in downtown revitalization, business incubator facilities, industrial parks, and other facilities without appropriate analysis of the local economy and have been disappointed with the returns. Some investments that seem to have substantial benefits initially turn out later to be white elephants when the businesses some years later decide to relocate elsewhere. Charlotte, North Carolina, lost its first National Basketball Association team to New Orleans because it would not build a new stadium, though other factors—such as less-than-full arenas—were cited by the owners. Seattle similarly lost its professional basketball team, which moved to Oklahoma City. An expansion team was later awarded to Charlotte, but Charlotte first had to promise to build a new facility. One study of U.S. highway investments suggested that instead of significant new capital investment in highways, greater economic impact could occur from decreasing congestion and other planning improvements—for little more spending than current levels. Other studies have reached similar conclusions about a wide range of infrastructure investments.[103] In developing countries, inadequate consideration of whether there are genuine economic opportunities to be stimulated by an infrastructure investment at times has led to indiscriminate construction of roads where there were no real market and production centers to link.

Combining Fiscal and Monetary Policy Actions to Combat Economic Downturn

The previous sections separately discussed fiscal and monetary tools to achieve the economic objectives of full employment, price stability, and steady economic growth. During a period when the economy is growing steadily, as measured by GDP, little attention is paid to the need for overt fiscal and/or monetary policy actions. As businesses and consumers start to react to underlying economic conditions by changing their consumption and investment patterns, the change indicators discussed in the section on anticipating change in the economy begin to show signs of downturn. Particularly if the period preceding noticeable decline in key indicators has been a lengthy period of growth, the media, business economists, federal economic policy makers, and ultimately the public begin to discuss the possibility of an economic downturn into the next recession, if for no other reason than the fact that economic growth does not seem sustainable indefinitely.

Through July 2019, the U.S. GDP had grown for 126 consecutive months, marking the longest period of economic expansion in U.S. history, surpassing the previous 120-month record from 1991 to 2001. The headlines in the summer of 2019 reflected growing concern about how long it might last; a sample of headlines follows:

- PBS News Hour: Can the longest economic expansion in U.S. history last?
- CNBC: This is now the longest U.S. economic expansion in history

- *New York Post*: U.S. economy marks longest expansion in American history
- *USA Today*: Recession? Really? This 10-year economic expansion won't die just of old age[104]

And it wasn't old age that ended the longest economic expansion in history. It was the shock of an emerging, worldwide pandemic, the coronavirus. On March 12, 2020, the Dow experienced its largest percentage drop, 10%, since the largest single day drop in history on October 19, 1987.[105]

This section discusses economic downturns, when they officially turn into serious recessions, and how fiscal and monetary policy tools are deployed by the government to temper the downturn and ultimately turn it around. The illustrations are from the most serious recession in U.S. history since the Great Depression: The Great Recession of 2007–2009. This section starts with a description of the characteristics of the recession, showing the information that led the press, policy makers, and the public to describe the situation informally as a recession and then to make official pronouncements of a recession. The discussion then turns to the combination of legislative and nonlegislative actions to combat the recession. These interventions are described in the same terms as the previous section's discussion of fiscal and monetary policy actions. The section concludes with a discussion of the results achieved by those interventions. An Appendix has been added at the end of the book to discuss the early economic impacts of the coronavirus crisis and the fiscal and monetary actions taken during the first quarter of 2020 to combat the negative economic conditions.

What Is a Recession?

Figure 3-9 illustrates the key economic indicators that marked the beginning and end of the Great Recession. The indicators selected represent the specific indicator that, by consensus, defines the beginning and end points of a recession (change in GDP), and three indicators particularly reflecting the Great Recession. Two of those indicators measure change in residential and nonresidential fixed investment. The fourth indicator measures change in personal consumption.

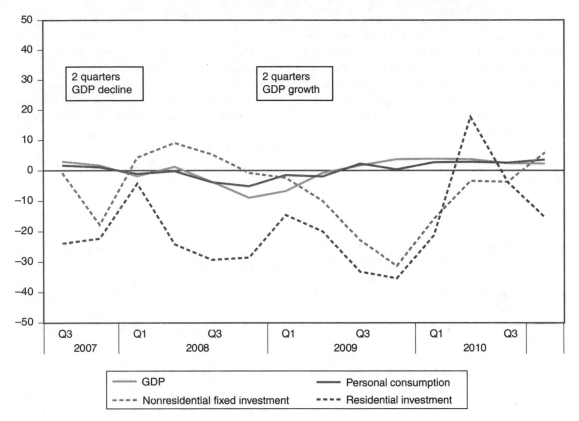

Notes: All data points are percent change from previous quarter; figures are revised for 2007 through first quarter 2010.
Source: Data from Bureau of Economic Analysis, U.S. Department of Commerce (2011).
Overview of the economy: tables. Retrieved November 16, 2011, from http://www.bea.gov

Figure 3-9 Quarterly Changes in Key Indicators Related to Recession: 2007–2011.

Notes: All data points are percentage changes from previous quarter; figures are revised for 2007 through first quarter 2010.
Data from Bureau of Economic Analysis, U.S. Department of Commerce (2011). *Overview of the economy: tables.* Retrieved November 16, 2011, from http://www.bca.gov/newsreleases/glance.htm. Note: the news release cited here is no longer available at the cited URL. The historical data from which the four change indicators depicted in the figure are still available in individual historical series from the Bureau of Economic Analysis.

The quarterly data in Figure 3-9 show that GDP growth fell every quarter—except for the second quarter of 2008—from the third quarter of 2007 to the first quarter of 2009. For most of that period, not only was each quarter's growth rate lower than the previous, but there was also an absolute drop in GDP. There is no legal definition of a recession, but a simple rule of thumb is often cited in the media: When the economy, measured by GDP change, drops two consecutive quarters, then it is a recession. By that definition, the United States entered a recession in 2007, as illustrated in Figure 3-9.

More variables than just GDP are involved in a recession, of course. The National Bureau of Economic Research (NBER) looks at a more-inclusive range of economic indicators as well as GDP growth, including indicators such as changes in consumption, income, and investment. NBER's Business Cycle Dating Committee dates the beginning of the recession as the last quarter of 2007. Though GDP growth started increasing again in the fourth quarter of 2008, the dating committee's analysis of the more comprehensive set of indicators determined that the recession ended in June 2009.[106] That definitive statement does not mean that the economic indicators described a strong economy by mid-2009—it means only that the indicators had turned in a positive direction for long enough to say formally that the recession was over. Indeed, a large portion of the general population felt no relief by then and was convinced the recession continued unabated.

Figure 3-9 also charts other variables, including residential and nonresidential investment. Of the two, residential investment shows the most volatility. By the end of the second quarter of 2008, residential investment had fallen by greater than 20%. Notably, personal consumption showed little variance. There was little growth, and little decline, in personal consumption throughout the latter part of 2007 through three quarters of 2011. Some of that pattern may be attributable to the provisions of various stimulus packages that included temporary tax reductions and extensions of unemployment benefits, and to households maintaining consumption levels by reaching into savings. As discussed earlier (Figure 3-2), unemployment rates grew rapidly to nearly 10% during the recession and remained at around 9% through 2011.

Fiscal and Monetary Policy Responses to the Recession

The first response to the financial market's collapse was measures to deal with the drop in the value of assets held by major investment banks and other financial industry giants. Major financial institutions were heavily invested in the housing mortgage market, particularly in speculative derivatives that were literally gambles on changes in the mortgage market as opposed to actual lending operations. Washington Mutual Bank became the largest bank failure in the United States. Lehman Brothers became the largest bankruptcy filing in U.S. history. Merrill Lynch was acquired by Bank of America. Bear Stearns collapsed and was acquired by JPMorgan Chase. The two government-sponsored enterprises (GSEs) that were the mainstay of the U.S. housing mortgage market, Fannie Mae and Freddie Mac, were bailed out of their losses by commitments from the Federal Reserve Bank.

Both GSEs, though sponsored by the federal government, were private firms that had been operating independently, and their shares were traded publicly on the New York Stock Exchange. The bailout involved the United States acquiring 80% of their stock, and the two entities were taken under conservatorship by the Federal Housing Finance Agency. These early steps were intended to deal with the asset values of institutions in the housing industry.

Starting in 2008, actions were taken to address the losses faced by a much broader swath of the economy: consumer spending dropped, credit dried up for both individuals and businesses, exports dropped, unemployment rose rapidly, and the economy went into full recession. Major programs to support the automobile industry, including both credit and government purchase of equity in General Motors and loans to Chrysler and Tesla, were among those actions. Among the major U.S. automakers, only Ford Motor Company survived without an infusion of government support, although Ford did borrow through one of the programs that combined economic stimulus and environmental objectives. Seven separate acts were enacted and signed into law as primary fiscal policy responses to the recession, as documented in **Exhibit 3-3**.

Exhibit 3-3 documents the major fiscal and monetary policy actions to address these two profound facets of the crisis: financial sector collapses and broader economic losses across most of society. When unemployment benefits started running out, legislation extended unemployment benefits in some cases up to 99 weeks and beyond, depending on individual state laws. To stimulate employment, programs were put in place to support infrastructure construction through grants to state and local governments. Federal agency spending that could be speeded up, such as research and development funds, was put on a faster track.

The Federal Reserve periodically reduced the federal funds rate, the rate that member banks pay to borrow from the Fed, and purchased securities in open market operations to enable banks and other financial institutions to issue more credit.

Exhibit 3-3 U.S. Fiscal and Monetary Policy Actions: 2007–2011

Beginning with the collapse of the mortgage market in 2007, the federal government undertook a number of fiscal, monetary, and regulatory actions to stimulate the economy back into growth, and to address the market failures that caused the slump. The following table lists the fiscal and monetary policy actions with a brief description of each program.[a]

Stimulus	Description
Fiscal Policy Legislated Actions to Stimulate Demand: Public Spending and Tax Incentives	
Economic Stimulus Act of 2008 (P.L. 110-185)	Provided tax rebates to low- and middle-income taxpayers and gave tax credits to employers to hire workers.
Emergency Economic Stabilization Act of 2008 (P.L. 110-343)	Troubled Assets Relief Program (TARP) provided up to $700 billion to purchase troubled assets, primarily intended for mortgages and mortgage instruments. Provided tax credits for electric hybrid vehicles and other energy efficiency initiatives. Reduced number of taxpayers subject to Alternative Minimum Tax. Extended unemployment insurance.
Toxic Asset Purchase Program 2009 (uses authorization in Emergency Economic Stabilization Act of 2008)	Allocated approximately $100 billion to entice private sector financial institutions to purchase troubled or toxic assets.
American Recovery and Reinvestment Act of 2009 (P.L. 111-5)	Provided an estimated $787 billion, mostly grants to state and local governments for infrastructure projects. Included other tax credits and tax relief measures.
Consumer Assistance to Recycle and Save Act Provisions incorporated in the Supplemental Appropriations Act of 2009 (P.L. 111-32)	So-called *Cash for Clunkers* program provided rebates to consumers purchasing more fuel-efficient new cars or light trucks.
Worker, Homeownership and Business Assistance Act of 2009 (P.L. 111-92)	Extended tax credits for first-time homebuyers, extended unemployment insurance, and extended small-business tax credits.
Tax Relief, Unemployment Insurance Reauthorization, and Job Creation Act of 2010 (P.L. 111-312)	Extended for 2 years cuts in personal and corporate income tax rates and 1-year reduction in Social Security tax.
Monetary Policy Actions to Affect Supply of Credit, Money Supply, and Support Participants in Credit Markets	
Actions to improve liquidity of member banks and other financial institutions ■ Changes in federal funds rate to member banks ■ Primary credit lending ■ Secondary credit lending ■ Seasonal credit lending ■ Term Auction Facility (TAF)	Federal funds rate reduced effectively to zero (from 5.25% at outset in 2007). Opened access to borrowing to financial institutions other than banks.

(continues)

Exhibit 3-3 U.S. Fiscal and Monetary Policy Actions: 2007–2011 *(continued)*

Operations to increase money supply, quantitative easing	Purchased Treasury bonds, Fannie Mae and Freddie Mac securities, and other securities to expand the monetary base.
Actions to restore liquidity of financial institutions	Variety of temporary programs lending to primary dealers in the credit market.
Fiscal Policy Actions to Rescue Financial Institutions	
Actions to support specific institutions ■ Bear Stearns ■ AIG ■ Citigroup ■ Bank of America	Federal Reserve Bank of New York created special credit facility to support to support JPMorgan Chase acquisition of Bear Stearns assets. $85 billion line of credit to American International Group to meet its credit requirements, enabling AIG restructure and divestiture of major assets.
Actions for mutual support of liquidity in dollar reserves and foreign currency reserves in Federal Reserve and other central banks	Extended, and received, liquidity credit to and from other central banks to stabilize fluctuations in demand for the dollar and other currencies.
Term Asset-Backed Securities Loan Facility	One-year program to stimulate highly rated (AAA) asset-backed securities such as credit card and student loan securities.

a. Congressional Budget Office (2011). *Budget and economic outlook: fiscal years 2011–2010* (pp. 33–36). Washington, DC: Government Printing Office; White House (2009). *Fact sheet: the worker, homeownership, and business assistance act of 2009.* Retrieved November 17, 2011, from http://www.whitehouse.gov /the-press-office/fact-sheet-worker-homeownership-and-business-assistance-act-2009; Federal Reserve (2011). *The Federal Reserve's response to the crisis* (follow links on overview page to each program carried out by the Fed during the crisis). Retrieved November 16, 2011, from http://federalreserve.gov /monetarypolicy/bst_crisisresponse.htm; Laeven, L., & Valencia, S. (2010). Resolution of banking crises: the good, the bad and the ugly. Washington, DC: International Monetary Fund. Retrieved November 17, 2011, from http://www.imf.org/external/ pubs/ft/wp/2010/wp10146.pdf; Binder, A. (2010). *How the great recession was brought to an end.* Retrieved November 18, 2011, from http://www.economy.com/mark-zandi/ documents/End-of-Great-Recession.pdf. Sources also consulted included online archives of news stories from *Washington Post, New York Times,* and *Wall Street Journal,* in addition to press releases from the White House. Some of these sources are cited in endnotes in the chapter. Where descriptive information is repetitive of main sources cited here, individual URLs are not listed here.

Quantitative easing, discussed earlier in the section on the Federal Reserve, was practiced when real interest rates converged on zero. The Federal Reserve also purchased asset-backed securities in a variety of financial institutions other than Fannie Mae and Freddie Mac, without the federal government taking management control.

Exhibit 3-3 shows the legislative authority under which each action was taken where appropriate. Actions taken by the Federal Reserve under its statutory authority did not require specific individual statutes as did almost all the other stimulus packages.

Nonbudgetary and Budgetary Effects of Fiscal and Monetary Policy Actions

This section discusses the effects of the actions taken to combat the Great Recession at two levels. The first view is a big picture analysis of several key economic and budgetary indicators in a time series from 2006 through 2018, preceding and following the recession. Three of these four indicators, or very similar indicators, are part of the NBER's leading, coincident, and lagging indexes discussed in the forecasting section of this chapter. Change in GDP is a key indicator, as the marker for defining the beginning and duration of the recession. Two indicators are measures related to employment: (1) changes in total civilian employment and (2) the unemployment rate. The fourth indicator is the contribution of the annual budget deficits to the total federal debt as a percentage of GDP during and continuing since. After this overall picture, a second view focuses on attempts to attribute changes in the economy to the specific actions taken by Presidents George W. Bush and Barack Obama, Congress, and specific federal agencies.

Macroeconomic Picture

Figure 3-10 plots the four selected indicators on an annual basis beginning with the year prior to the start of the recession and ending with 2018. The change in real GDP indicator reflects what had already been apparent in Figure 3-8. Change in GDP, a leading indicator, was already showing signs of an economic downturn as early as 2006.

Whereas GDP rose by 2.9% in 2006 over 2005, the rate of increase had already started falling in 2006.[107] Real GDP in 2007 was approximately $14.5 trillion, and only $14.7 trillion in 2008. Year over year, 2007 to 2008 and 2008 to 2009 were both declines in GDP. The recovery from 2009 to 2010, about $500 billion, was the steepest single year increase in the years covered by Figure 3-10. From 2010 on, GDP wobbled from year to year, with another fall from nearly 3% growth in 2015 to just over 1.5% growth in 2016.

Employment plummeted leading up to and early in the recession. Total civilian employment fell from approximately 144 million in 2006 to a low of 139 million in 2010. By 2018, civilian employment had increased to nearly 156 million. Note that the graph plots year-to-year change, demonstrating that the percentage drop was greatest in 2009. Total employment had recovered to pre-recession levels by 2014, over 146 million employed, and then climbed relatively steadily to the 2018 figure.

The change in the unemployment rate mirrors the opposite pattern to total employed as one would expect. The peak unemployment

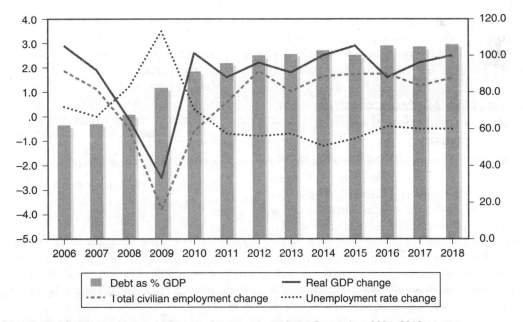

Figure 3-10 Selected Indicators of Change Pre– and Post–Great Recession: 2006–2018.

Calculated from U.S. Department of Commerce, Bureau of Economic Analysis (2019). *Economic report of the president: 2019, Appendix B, statistical tables.* Debt as % GDP, Table b-46; Real GDP change, Table b-9; Total civilian employment, Table b-24; Unemployment rate change, Table b-27. Retrieved September 14, 2019, from https://www.govinfo.gov/app/collection/erp/2019

rate occurred in 2010: 9.6%. From there, the unemployment rate fell by about one percentage point each year through 2015, and then followed a more gradual path toward lower unemployment rates. Again, note that the figure plots change in the unemployment rate, indicating that most of the improvement in lowering the recession unemployment rate had occurred by 2011–2012. Thereafter, the year-to-year changes were smaller. By analyzing the year-to-year change rates, it makes it clearer that the main recovery in employment/unemployment was within 2 to 3 years after the worst year, 2009.

Debt as a percentage of GDP is plotted as a series of bars, on the secondary vertical (or y) axis. The total federal debt was 62% of GDP in 2006, rose sharply from 2009 to 2012, and continued to increase at a slower rate of increase through 2018. Not shown in the graph, but discussed previously in this chapter, are the forecasts by both OMB and CBO that debt will continue to increase relative to GDP growth at least through 2029 unless significant policy changes are made to reverse that trend. The pattern in the graph reflects both reduced federal revenues and increased expenditures that were primarily the result of specific fiscal stimulus actions to increase demand in the economy, discussed in Exhibit 3-3.

Attributing Macroeconomic Changes to Legislative and Policy Actions

The four indicators in the figure capture only a small part of the economic picture in the 13 years graphed. Making cause and effect statements about actions taken and results as measured by a few indicators is not just risky—it is not good science. Descriptively, however, it is obvious that the federal government incurred significant deficits during the recession, a move deliberately intended to increase demand and production, and production did increase. The inference that there is a one-to-one causal relationship, however, stretches the point; the relationships among factors are complex and go beyond the scope of this text.

Exhibit 3-3 and the discussion are not nearly the full picture. As previously discussed, a major problem in the Great Recession was the collapse of key, large financial institutions and the near-collapse of others. As Exhibit 3-3 describes, numerous measures were taken to assist the financial markets and major financial and industrial institutions to recover. Almost all the temporary credit facilities shown in Exhibit 3-3 that were put in place by the Federal Reserve either ended early or were allowed to lapse at the end of the planned temporary period. Many intended beneficiaries (such as, for example, the Ford Motor company) did not need to use the credit facility made available to the auto industry. Most of the authorized credit did not reach the limit—many banks and other financial institutions, after the initial industry restructuring that took place, no longer needed the special programs.

The Federal Reserve's self-description of its programs in response to the crisis, also shown in Exhibit 3-3, were described as the deployment of three tools:[108]

1. Provision of short-term liquidity to banks and depository institutions, primarily through changes in the discount rate and temporary short-term lending facilities. These actions effectively reduced the borrowing rate to member banks to zero.
2. Provision of liquidity directly to credit market participants other than depository institutions; these programs enabled credit to major investment institutions and other large industry players.
3. Open market operations to purchase mortgage-backed securities and other assets to effectively reduce the borrowing rate below zero.

Information on the Federal Reserve website and hundreds of published briefings and reports were the result of congressional requirements that the actions of the Federal Reserve be reported to Congress in detail.[109] The website documents the repayment of most of the loans extended and the repurchase of stock acquired by the government, such as General Motors stock. The major exception to the government's recapturing loans and investments in financial institutions are the two GSEs, Fannie Mae and Freddie Mac, which remain under federal conservatorship.[110] However, the balance of federal funds pumped into the two GSEs is outweighed by their repayment to the federal treasury in profits. Fannie Mae's bail-out money totaled $119.8 billion; Freddie Mac's bail-out money was $71.6 billion. The two institutions, respectively, as of 2018 had returned to the treasury $167.3 billion and $112.4 billion.[111] The Troubled Asset Relief Program (TARP) that provided over $412 billion to banks, the automobile industry, and other companies was fully repaid, with a small profit of $12 billion.[112]

The banking industry underwent considerable consolidation. About 2% of U.S. banks failed in 2009, compared with twice that number in the 1989 Savings and Loan crisis. The banks that failed in the Great Recession held about 6% of total deposits, considerably less than the deposits held by failed financial institutions in the 1989 S&L crisis. The rapidity and breadth of the responses appear to account for both the reduced severity and the accelerated recovery of the banking sector.[113]

In summary, at the macro level, the U.S. economy recovered from the Great Recession. All the macro indicators point to that conclusion, and most of the credits initially lent by the federal government to financial, commercial, and industrial sector institutions were repaid. How much of the recovery is due directly to the fiscal and monetary policy actions taken at the time of and shortly after the crisis, and how much is attributable mainly to the general health of the economy that in more recent years is unrelated to the deliberate policy actions? The CBO was tasked in one of the major relief statutes, the American Recovery and Reinvestment Act (ARRA), to monitor and report to Congress on the relief programs.[114] In its final report in 2015, the CBO was fairly conservative in assigning cause and effect credits.[115] The CBO estimated the recovery operations of ARRA added over $800 billion to the deficit from 2007 through 2019. For that same time period, the sum of the annual federal budget deficits was $10.4 trillion (2019 estimated).[116] To put it another way, the CBO attributes responsibility for only about 8% of the federal deficit to the main financial assistance in the stimulus programs.

The CBO report estimated the impact of the ARRA programs on several macroeconomic indicators. CBO estimated that the unemployment rate was less than it otherwise would have been by 0.2% to 1.8% per year from 2009 through 2014. In other words, CBO's conclusion is that unemployment in 2010 would have been 11.4% were it not for the stimulus package, an impact of an equivalent 1.8-point reduction in the unemployment rate. The CBO estimates of impact on real GDP, employment years, and full-time equivalent employment years are similarly low.

The CBO report contains strong caveats on the source of data for its estimates of impact (reports from recipients of ARRA assistance), noting possibilities for both under- and over-reporting. But a more important caveat is that it took somewhat heroic assumptions to go from the micro-level reported data from ARRA stimulus recipients to an effect on a macro indicator of the total economy. As large as the stimulus efforts may have seemed to the public at the time, they were small relative to the size of the economy. Perhaps the best way to interpret the results is to say that the fiscal stimulus programs targeted a small proportion of the total economy and could not be expected to show up as large impacts on total economy measures. The economy's own momentum likely accounts for the magnitude of the recovery once the economy turned around.

Another way the CBO went about assessing impact was to estimate the multiplier effect of stimulus expenditures. For example, transfer payments to state and local governments for infrastructure were estimated to have a multiplier effect of 1.4 to 2.2. A million-dollar grant had roughly a $1.4 to $2.2 million effect. Similar effects were estimated for federal purchases of goods and services and transfer payments to individuals. Tax cuts were estimated to have somewhat lower multipliers.

An additional interpretation of the way monetary and fiscal policy responses to the recession contributed to the turnaround is that the programs assisted both individuals and institutions at the margins to get back on their feet. Jobs reopened; individuals were rehired; factories, notably automotive, started increasing production; retail sales climbed; and state and local revenues increased as spending increased. The substantial part of the recovery may be more due to the sheer size of the economy once it turned in the right direction to maintain its own momentum. This is somewhat analogous to changing the course of a modern aircraft carrier underway. It is a matter of applying relatively small amounts of energy to leverage small incremental changes that gradually redirect the momentum of the carrier; until the relatively small amounts on energy are applied to the carrier, momentum continues on the present course.

Equity Considerations for Government Economic Policy

The formal, legislatively mandated objectives of government economic policy for the United States include only full employment, price stability, and steady economic growth, as discussed early in this chapter. Except in the indirect results of employment policy, attention to the distribution of gain from growth in the economy is not a formal economic policy objective for the United States. However, data have been collected by the Federal Reserve and reported quarterly since 1989 on the distribution of household wealth in four groups: top 1%, next 9%, next 40%, and bottom half (below 50th percentile).[117] In many other countries, economic growth *and* equity are formal objectives of government policy. The World Bank's 2006 world development report, *Equity and Development*, noted the importance to many countries of equity as a formal policy objective. The report defined equity as "equal opportunity . . . and . . . avoidance of deprivation in outcomes."[118] Even though the United States does not have a legislatively mandated equity objective, government economic policy actions do have redistributive effects.

Unintentional Redistributive Effects

Fiscal and monetary policy actions taken to manage overall economic growth and price stability are not necessarily neutral in their effects on individuals and industries. If the government lowers corporate tax rates to stimulate business investment but increases other taxes to neutralize the effects on the budget balance, then those for whom taxes are raised are paying for the economic benefits whether they share in those benefits or not. Many developing country governments have attempted to address problems of low-income urban areas by imposing price controls on agricultural products. While the short-run effect may be to lower food prices in urban areas, the longer-run effect is to decrease agricultural production. In the short run, economic costs are imposed on one group, rural producers, for the benefit of another group, urban consumers. In the long run, overall economic performance declines.

Economic policies aimed at stabilization also can have unintentional redistributive effects. Under inflationary conditions, persons on fixed or relatively fixed incomes lose purchasing power. This is especially true for retired persons living on pensions, but it is also true for workers who cannot command increases in wages. If the government takes no action to slow the rate of inflation, its inaction "redistributes" income from those on fixed incomes to those whose wages or other income rises with inflation. Higher interest rates favor income earnings from investments, usually held by upper-income families. Large federal deficits, which ultimately impose repayment costs on future generations, may also create intergenerational inequity (see the chapter on financial management).

Addressing Inequality

Equity as a concept of "equal chances" is easy to describe, but difficult to measure. Inequality in absolute terms is somewhat easier to measure and therefore is often used in discussions of equity and inequity, such as inequality in the distribution of income. Measuring inequality involves comparison between a norm that is hypothesized to represent equality and deviations from that norm. **Exhibit 3-4** illustrates the concept of equity and discusses several different measurements. Some measures compare the United States with other countries, and some are restricted to the United States. The idea is to measure the extent to which inequity exists, and then devise deliberate government policies to reduce the inequity. Since

---

Exhibit 3-4 Measuring Income Inequality and Selected Country Results

For governments that endorse an overt policy to reduce inequality, or advocate for decreasing inequality, at the macro level, how does one best characterize the degree of inequality? One approach is to use the *Gini index*.

The Gini index concept is illustrated graphically in what is called a *Lorenz curve* as the area between a line that depicts perfect equality and a line (curve) that depicts the actual measured distribution in a specific society or economy **Figure E-1**. The line depicting perfect equality is a measurement concept, not some kind of universal norm. It is a social and political question in any given society as to what extent deviation from the line is reasonable and acceptable.

A Lorenz curve plots the cumulative percentage of income (or other valued good) held by income groups against the cumulative percentage of income groups. For example, in a perfectly equal distribution of income, the lowest population decile in income would have 10% of the income, the first and second lowest deciles would have 20% of the income, and so forth. That perfectly equal distribution would plot as a straight 45-degree line on an *x, y* graph. The difference between the actual plotted Lorenz curve and the perfectly equal distribution is measured as the area between the two curves: the *Gini coefficient of inequality*.

Figure E-2 looks at the income distribution of a selected group of OECD countries for the years 2007 and 2017. The Gini indices reported essentially measure the distance between the theoretical construct of exactly equal distribution and the actual distribution of income. The higher the index number, the greater the deviation from a perfectly equal distribution.

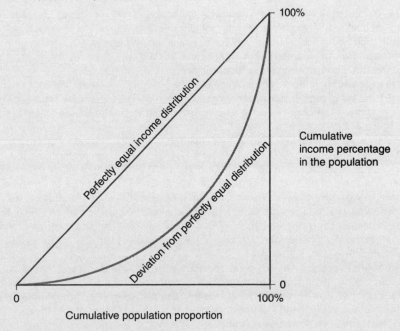

Figure E-1 Lorenz Curve for Illustrating Inequality.

(continues)

Exhibit 3-4 Measuring Income Inequality and Selected Country Results (*continued*)

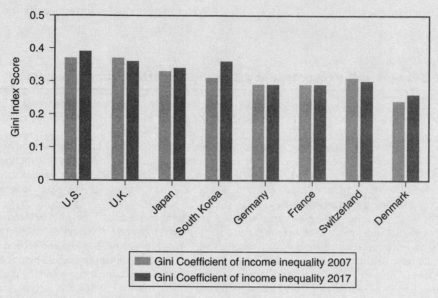

Figure E-2 Gini Index of Inequality 2007 and 2017: Selected OECD Countries.

Organization for Economic Cooperation and Development (2019). *OECD income distribution database (IDD): Gini, poverty, income, methods and concepts.* Retrieved September 14, 2019, from http://www.oecd.org/social /income-distribution-database.htm

Figure E-2 is helpful in visualizing the differences among countries. The United States has the highest index of income inequality, with the United Kingdom a close second. Japan and South Korea form a cluster closer to 0.3, although South Korea's inequality coefficient is the only one with a significant increase from 2007 to 2017. France, Switzerland, and Germany are close to each other, and Denmark is the lowest in the group, at 0.26. The OECD average across 36 countries was 0.32 in both years.

Another way of considering the concepts of equity and equality is to look at the distribution of household wealth across groups. Income is earnings in a given period; wealth is a measure of the accumulation over time. The Federal Reserve's reports show change in the United States over 30 years, illustrated in **Figure E-3**.

Figure E-3 displays the percentage of total household wealth for four income groups: top 1%, next 9%, next 40%, and bottom 50% of households. Included in household wealth are property, savings, retirement accounts, stock and bond portfolios, and so forth. During the 30 years covered by the illustration, the top 1% increased its share of household wealth by about 38%, from just over 21% to 29%. The share of the next 9% stayed almost the same, increasing only 3%. The next 40% of households decreased from 37% of total household wealth to about 30%, or a decline of almost 20%. The bottom 50% in terms of household wealth declined by about 14%, from 7% of the total to 6%. It is also clear from the figure and the underlying data that the top 10% from 1989 through 2019 concentrated the total share of U.S. household wealth from 55% to 64%.

Major international development organizations such as the World Bank and the OECD, and international cooperative forums such as the World Economic Forum have begun publishing and discussing more comprehensive measures of growth and well-being. These measures emphasize the picture of economic and social health of an economy that relate to the quality of life, distribution of income and wealth, and environmental sustainability. The World Economic Forum published in 2018 the *Inclusive Development Index 2018: Summary and Data Highlights*.[a] The Index is a "snapshot of the gap between the rich and the poor."[b] The Index groups 12 individual indicators into three groupings

Exhibit 3-4 Measuring Income Inequality and Selected Country Results (*continued*)

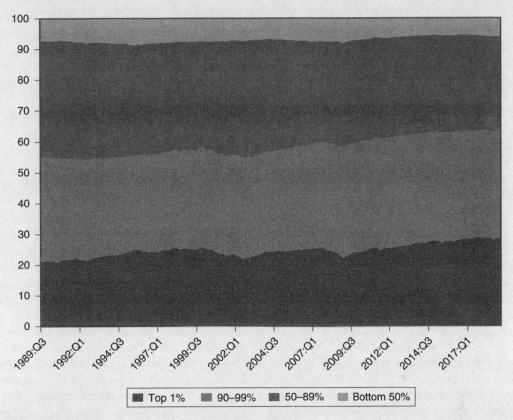

Figure E-3 U.S. Distribution of Household Wealth, 1989–2019.

Board of Governors of the Federal Reserve System (2019). *Distributional financial accounts: shares of wealth by wealth percentile groups* (downloadable CSV). Retrieved December 17, 2019, from https://www
.federalreserve.gov/releases/efa/efa-distributional-financial-accounts.htm

of national performance. Some of the indicators include Growth & Development, Inclusion, and Intergenerational Equity & Sustainability. Growth and development include common growth measures such as GDP per capita, labor productivity, and health life expectancy. Inclusion measures include net income Gini trend, poverty trend, and wealth trend. Equity and sustainability includes carbon intensity (kilogram per dollar of GDP), public debt, and dependency ratio. Of 29 advanced economies, the United States ranks 23rd, above only Japan, Israel, Spain, Italy, Portugal, and Greece.[c] The U.S. rankings on the 12 indicators are in either the top or top two quintiles on only half of the indicators, the highest ranking being GDP per capita growth. The United States is in the lowest quintile in three of the indicators: healthy life expectancy, net income Gini index trend, and median income trend.[d] Ten years prior to the 2018 index, in the United States and Western Europe, the top 1% income share was near 10%; in the 2018 index, Western European countries rose to about 12%, whereas the United States jumped to 20%.[e]

It is a near certainty that in coming decades, income and wealth distribution, environmental sustainability impact, and health and similar indicators will become focal points for political discourse and political competition. Even as early as the U.S. campaign to select a Democratic party candidate for

(*continues*)

Exhibit 3-4 Measuring Income Inequality and Selected Country Results *(continued)*

the 2020 election, variables representing issues such as inequality and environmental issues had become major issues both within the party and contrasts with the Republican party. The concern is not only the possible political and social consequences of rising inequality. An International Monetary Fund report stated "...if the income share of the top 20% (the rich) increases, then GDP growth actually declines...while an increase in the income share of the bottom 20% (the poor) is associated with higher GDP growth."[f]

a. World Economic Forum [WEF]. (2018). *The inclusive development index: 2018*. Retrieved December 21, 2019, from https://www.weforum.org/reports/the-inclusive-development-index-2018.
b. Global Finance. (2019). *Wealth distribution and income inequality by country: 2018*. Retrieved December 21, 2019, from https://www.gfmag.com/global-data/economic-data/wealth-distribution-income-inequality.
c. WEF. (2018). *Inclusive development index*, 3.
d. WEF (2018). *Inclusive development index*, 19.
e. Global Finance (2019). *Wealth distribution*.
f. As quoted in Global Finance. (2019). *Wealth distribution*.

the 1960s, the degree of inequality of income and wealth distribution in the United States has increased significantly.

Exhibit 3-4 shows the United States (and the United Kingdom) is somewhat higher than other major industrial countries measured by the Gini coefficient of income inequality. Some pundits and economists argue that one of the consequences of excessive income inequality is polarization in the population.[119] In the United States, the recession starting in 2007 and its aftermath brought inequality and equity issues to a head in the political arena. Since then, wealth has become increasingly concentrated at the top of the income distribution. In 2017, the top 20% of the income distribution held 43% of total income. The share held by the bottom 20% of the U.S. population was just over 5%.[120] One of the reasons behind the growing gap is that there is not the same access across all income classes to the sources of wealth that have grown most quickly in the last 40 years. Since 1979, the top quintile has experienced 99% growth in average income, compared to only 33% growth in the lowest and middle three quintiles.[121] The main explanation is that the lowest four quintiles earn income primarily from wages and salaries, whereas the highest quintile has a much larger share of income from stock and bond investments, in addition to salaries and bonuses. Figure E-3 in Exhibit 3-4 documents that household wealth in the United States has become increasingly concentrated at the upper income level. The top 10% of households measured on household wealth held 55% of total household wealth in 1989, compared with 64% in 2019.[122]

The political challenge with income transfers and a progressive income tax structure partially mitigating the gap between the top and the bottom is the strong differences between the two parties on transfer programs and tax rates. Republicans generally argue that the rich are the primary sources of investment to fuel economic growth and job creation. Accordingly, the more progressive the income tax rates, the less those most likely to invest will invest.[123] Furthermore, transfer programs are the most politically vulnerable with the general Republican belief that these are the very programs that should be cut to reduce deficits. Democrats generally argue that tax cuts enacted during Republican administrations disproportionately favor the wealthy. An analysis published by the Brookings Institution cited several consequences of the 2017 Tax Cut and Jobs Act (TCJA).[124] TCJA reduced federal revenues, without any expenditure reductions; took resources from lower- and middle-income families; and made wealthy households wealthier.[125] The primary campaigns to select the Democratic party candidate for president in the 2020 election notably featured these arguments, with significant retorts from the Republican party incumbents in the White House and the Congress.

Income Stabilization Policies

Income stabilization policy is one way to address the problem of economic inequality, with the most deliberate approach being a negative income tax. This would involve determining an appropriate income guarantee, a benefit reduction rate, and a break-even income. The income guarantee is the amount of the transfer when the family income is zero, the benefit reduction rate is the rate at which the amount transferred is reduced as family income increases, and the break-even income is the point where family income reaches a level beyond which the family no longer qualifies for a transfer. The United States has no negative income tax, but its principles are incorporated to varying degrees in several income-related transfer programs. The earned income tax credit acts somewhat like a negative income tax; low- to moderate-income households with income from work are eligible for the credit, including refunds in the amount of the credit even to households that owe no taxes.[126]

Transfer Programs

Several transfer programs (the Supplemental Nutrition Assistance Program and Medicaid) provide a minimum or floor level of benefits comparable to the income guarantee. Major reforms in the welfare system, however, have severely curtailed benefits by imposing lifetime limits on the amount individuals may receive and imposing strict work requirements (see the chapter on intergovernmental relations). The CBO report on the distribution of household income discussed in Exhibit 3-4 documents some mitigating effects of transfer programs on income inequality. Means-tested transfers; social insurance benefits (mainly Social Security and Medicare); and other federal, state, and local transfer programs modify the picture of income inequality, though not enough to lessen the focus of partisan political differences. After accounting for transfer programs and the income tax structure, the income growth rate from 1979 to 2016 for the lowest quintile, including income transfers, was 85%, compared to the top quintile's 101%. The gap between the highest and lowest income groups still widened, but not as much as would be suggested by the 99% versus 33% growth before considering transfers and taxes. Middle-income households (the middle three income quintiles) grew at a much slower rate over that time period—only 47%.[127]

Tax Policies

Expenditure programs are not the only form of income redistribution. Different taxes have different impacts on various groups. In addition, the overall structure of the entire tax system may operate to redistribute income among different groups. In the Tax Reform Act of 1986, lower-income groups benefited from sharply reduced taxes, middle-income groups benefited from modest reductions, and upper-income individuals and corporations experienced tax increases. In 1993, there were sharp increases in the top tax bracket. In 1997, tax decreases focused on both ends of the income spectrum. Since 1997, income tax changes have substantially benefited the highest income group more than lower- and middle-income groups.

Tax expenditures, discussed in the chapter on budgeting for revenues and taxes, are often redistributive in effect. Not taxing interest on municipal bonds redistributes income toward the purchasers of municipal bonds, who tend to be retirees, either directly or through pension fund investments. Allowing interest on mortgages, including second homes, to be deducted from taxable income has a redistributive effect toward middle- and upper-income individuals. The problem with the redistributive effects of tax expenditures is that they are much less transparent as a policy instrument. A tax expenditure does not appear plainly as an expenditure, nor does it appear directly as a tax reduction.

Combined Effects of Transfer and Tax Policies

One of the most prominent policy issues differentiating the two major political parties during and since the 2016 election is the extent to which transfer programs and income tax structure should, or should not, have a major redistributive effect. The first Obama administration was caught up in the financial and economic crisis even before the 2009 inauguration. During the second term, the economy experienced sustained economic growth. As evidence accumulated that the growth was not benefiting all income groups equally, and was disproportionately lodged in the highest income group, income inequality became a key focal point through the election of Donald Trump. **Figure 3-11** captures income distribution and demonstrates that the concentration of wealth in the highest income has not been significantly affected by transfer programs and tax structure, and these programs have not had significant impact on lower- and even middle-income groups.

With the effects of existing redistributive policies, the lowest 20% of the population in terms of income had, in 2016, a 6.9% share of the nation's income, compared to a 3.6% without those policies. There are slight improvements comparing with and without redistributive policies for the next three population quintiles. The highest 20% of the population clearly lost some share of the nation's income, from 55% to 49%. Proponents of more aggressive redistributive policies point to the almost 49% share of total income as a dangerous

gap. Opponents point to the almost 7% negative impact on the wealthiest 20%.[128]

While economic policy affects the distribution of income, it cannot be expected to address structural features of the labor market. For example, workers with minimal or obsolete skills have difficulty finding employment even during periods of rapid growth. Economic policy is also of limited assistance in coping with readjustments in the economy, such as might occur with changes in homeland security and defense operations in the United States and overseas. Other policies, of course, are designed to deal with more basic structural problems. Expenditures on education, both academic and vocational, are expected to increase the overall human resource base for the economy. Regulatory policies are expected to reduce private incentives to pollute the environment, a problem that imposes an eventual economic cost when the environmental damage is repaired. No redistributive policy is neutral in its economic impact. Indeed, no economic act, no matter what its intended effects, is automatically neutral regarding distribution of income.

Designing redistributive policies should consider the potential reduction in economic

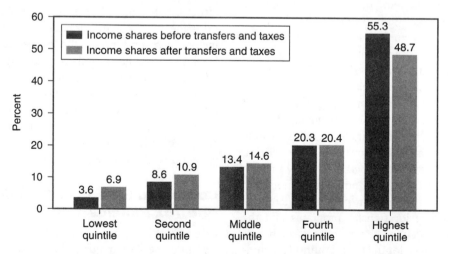

Figure 3-11 Income Shares by Population Before and After Income Transfer and Tax Benefits: 2016.

Data from Congressional Budget Office (2019). *The Distribution of Household Income, 2014*. Retrieved September 14, 2019, from https://www.cbo.gov/publication/53597.

efficiency and try to mitigate any losses. During a recessionary period, both the labor force and total plant capacity are underemployed, so that government action to stimulate the economy may do just that without causing significant unintended redistributive effects. At some point, political unrest results when public policy is seen as inequitable. The 2018 midterm election brought into Congress, especially the House of Representatives, strong vocal first-time national office holders who brought a much sharper, and highly visible, focus on income inequality and other issues such as environmental degradation that divide the major parties. It seems highly likely that these issues will pervade future national, and local, elections and may bring greater demand for expanding the formal objectives of economic policy.

Summary

Representing more than 32% of total economic activity in the United States, federal, state, and local government budgets have a tremendous combined effect on the economy. The federal government deliberately intervenes in the economy to achieve aggregate economic objectives. The major economic policy objectives of most central governments include economic growth, full employment, stable prices, and balance in the flow of funds into and out of the economy. Increasingly, as national economies become more interdependent, governments, including the U.S. federal government, are including specific competitiveness objectives as part of national economic policy. Because federal budget deficits sometimes soar to unacceptable (politically and economically) heights, management of the deficits and the overall government debt also has been added as a major economic policy objective in the United States. For some countries, achieving some degree of equity in income and social status is a formal policy objective. Although equity is not a legislatively mandated policy objective in the United States, income inequality has become a major political issue and a focal point of fairness arguments about alternative means to addressing the federal budget deficit.

Fiscal policy and monetary policy are the main tools used to influence macroeconomic performance. Fiscal policy encompasses the use of the government's taxing and spending powers to stimulate or dampen economic activity. An excess of expenditures over revenues (a deficit) stimulates demand and thus employment. A possible consequence, however, may be inflation. An excess of revenues over expenditures (a surplus) has a dampening effect on the economy. Monetary policy affects economic activity through control over the money supply. By changing interest rates and reserve requirements and by buying or selling bonds, the Federal Reserve can speed up or slow down the pace of economic activity. The federal response in two administrations to address the financial market crisis and the 2007–2009 recession was the most extensive combination of fiscal and monetary policy actions since the Great Depression.

Although state and local governments do not exercise fiscal and monetary control, their role in providing the basic infrastructure required for private sector business activity is important to regional economic performance. In this respect, state and local governments and developing country governments pursue similar ends. For developing country governments, their effective use of borrowed funds from donor agencies and commercial banks depends on putting the funds to use in increasing economic productive capacity.

Government policy interventions also have consequences for income redistribution. Changes in tax policy and increases or decreases in expenditures are almost never neutral as regards income distribution. In addition, there is general agreement that some level of redistribution of income is appropriate to address the problems of individuals with very low incomes. How extensive these programs should be, however, remains perennially controversial. Income and wealth inequality and environmental sustainability increasingly are focal points of debate on what the appropriate objectives are for government policy, and these issues are likely to be more prominent than they have in the past.

Notes

1. U.S. Bureau of Economic Analysis (2019). Calculated from U.S. Bureau of Economic Analysis, Government total expenditures [W068RCQ027SBEA], retrieved December 8, 2019, from FRED, Federal Reserve Bank of St. Louis, https://fred.stlouisfed.org/series/W068RCQ027SBEA (total government expenditures); U.S. Bureau of Economic Analysis, Federal Government: Current Expenditures [FGEXPND], retrieved December 8, 2019, from FRED, Federal Reserve Bank of St. Louis, https://fred.stlouisfed.org/series/FGEXPND (federal expenditures); U.S. Bureau of Economic Analysis, Gross Domestic Product [GDP], retrieved December 7, 2019, from FRED, Federal Reserve Bank of St. Louis, https://fred.stlouisfed.org/series/GDP (GDP).

2. World Bank (2020). *WDI Data Catalogue*. Retrieved August 26, 2019, from https://data.worldbank.org/indicator/NY.GDP.MKTP.CD and https://data.worldbank.org/indicator/BX.TRF.PWKR.CD.DT. Note: WDI Data Catalogue searchable online by country or downloading selected databases.

3. World Bank (2019). *World Development Indicators dataset.* Retrieved September 15, 2019, from http://datatopics.worldbank.org/world-development-indicators/themes/economy.html.

4. U.S. Department of Energy, Energy Information Administration (2019). *How much oil consumed in the United States comes from foreign countries?* Retrieved August 27, 2019, from https://www.eia.gov/tools/faqs/faq.php?id=32&t=6.

5. FocusEconomics (2020). *The world's top 10 largest economies.* Retrieved August 26, 2019, from https://www.focus-economics.com/blog/the-largest-economies-in-the-world.

6. European Central Bank (2016). Transmission of output shocks-the role of cross border production chains. *Economic Bulletin,* Issue 2. Retrieved August 27, 2019, from https://www.ecb.europa.eu/pub/economic-bulletin/articles/2016/html/index.en.html.

7. Olorunnipa, T., et.al. (2019). G7 summit ends with little consensus amid Trump's mixed messaging on the trade war. *Washington Post,* August 26. Retrieved August 27, 2019, from https://www.washingtonpost.com/politics/g-7-summit-set-to-end-with-little-consensus-amid-trumps-mixed-messaging-on-the-trade-war/2019/08/26/c73b49ac-c76d-11e9-a1fe-ca46e8d573c0_story.html; World Wildlife Federation (2019). *Climate change in the Amazon: a changing Amazon.* Retrieved August 27, 2019, from http://wwf.panda.org/knowledge_hub/where_we_work/amazon/amazon_threats/climate_change_amazon/.

8. United Nations Conference on Trade and Development (2019). *World Investment report: 2019* (pp. X–XI). Retrieved August 27, 2019, from https://unctad.org/en/PublicationsLibrary/wir2019_en.pdfRetrieved November 13, 2011, from http://www.unctad.org/sections/dite_dir/docs/ WIR11_web%20tab%207.pdf.

9. U.S. Council of Economic Advisers (2019). *Economic report of the president: 2020, Table B4.* Retrieved August 27, 2019, from https://www.govinfo.gov/app/collection/erp/2019.

10. Chen, V. (2011). Fed economists: 2012 recession odds top 50%. *Bloomberg News,* November 14. Retrieved November 15, 2011, from http://www.bloomberg.com/news/2011-11-14/fedeconomists-say-odds-of-2012-u-s-recession-exceed-50-on-europe-crisis.html.

11. U.S. Department of Commerce, Bureau of Economic Analysis (2019). *U.S. Net International Investment Position at the end of the period 2018,* International Investment Position tables. Retrieved August 27, 2019, from https://apps.bea.gov/histdata/fileStructDisplay.cfm?HMI=13&DY=2018&DQ=Q4&DV=Preliminary&dNRD=March-29-2019.

12. U.S. Council of Economic Advisers (2019). *Economic report of the president: 2020,* 313.

13. I wouldn't start from here. (2011). *The Economist, 401,* October 15, 80–81.

14. America is deploying a new economic arsenal to assert its power (2019). *The Economist.com,* June 6. Retrieved August 27, 2019, from https://www.economist.com/leaders/2019/06/06/america-is-deploying-a-new-economic-arsenal-to-assert-its-power; Weapons of mass disruption (2019). *The Economist, 431,* June 8, 13.

15. Macrotrends (2019). *Euro dollar exchange rate (EUR USD) – historical chart (all years).* Retrieved August 27, 2019, from https://www.macrotrends.net/2548/euro-dollar-exchange-rate-historical-chart.

16. Can China become a scientific superpower? (2019) *Economist.com.* Retrieved August 27, 2019, from https://www.economist.com/science-and-technology/2019/01/12/can-china-become-a-scientific-superpower.

17. Has BRICS lived up to expectations? (2018). *Economist.com.* Retrieved August 27, 2019, from https://www.economist.com/free-exchange/2018/07/27/has-brics-lived-up-to-expectations. Note, South Africa sometimes is included as a fifth country.

18. Malhotra, V., & Manyika, J. (2011). Five misconceptions about productivity. *McKinsey Quarterly,* March, 1. Retrieved November 3, 2011, from https://www.mckinseyquarterly.com/Five_ misconceptions_about_productivity_2760.

19. Huang, Y. (2019). U.S. dependence on pharmaceutical products from China. *Council on Foreign Relations* [blogpost]. Retrieved December 8, 2019, from https://www.cfr.org/blog/us-dependence-pharmaceutical-products-china.

20. Pereira, C., & Teles, V. (2011). *Political institutions, economic growth, and democracy: the substitute effect.* Brookings Institution. Retrieved August 29, 2019, from https://www

.brookings.edu/opinions/political-institutions-economic-growth-and-democracy-the-substitute-effect/.

21. Brookings Institution (2019): *Tracking deregulation in the Trump era.* Retrieved August 29, 2019, from https://www.brookings.edu/interactives/tracking-deregulation-in-the-trump-era/.

22. Employment Act of 1946 (P.L. 79-304); Full Employment and Balanced Growth Act of 1978 (P.L. 95-253).

23. Musgrave, R. A., & Musgrave, P. B. (1989). *Public finance in theory and practice* (5th ed.). New York, NY: McGraw-Hill; Hyman, D. N. (2013). *Public finance: a contemporary application of theory to policy* (11th ed.). Winfield, Kansas: Southwestern College.

24. U.S. Department of Labor, Bureau of Labor Statistics (2019). *How the government measures unemployment.* Retrieved August 29, 2019, from https://www.bls.gov/cps/cps_htgm.htm#where.

25. U.S. Department of Labor, Bureau of Labor Statistics (2019). *Current employment statistics – CES (National).* Retrieved August 29, 2019, from https://www.bls.gov/ces/home.htm.

26. Baldash, D. (2019). *Trump's claims about his performance on jobs just got destroyed by one of his own federal agencies.* New Civil Rights Movement, August 22. Retrieved August 29, 2019, from https://www.thenewcivilrightsmovement.com/2019/08/trumps-claims-on-jobs-just-got-eviscerated-by-one-of-his-own-federal-agencies/.

27. Bartash, J. (2019). *U.S. created 501,000 fewer jobs since 2018 than previously reported, new figures show.* MarketWatch, August 24. Retrieved August 29, 2019, from https://www.marketwatch.com/story/us-created-500000-fewer-jobs-since-2018-than-previously-reported-new-figures-show-2019-08-21.

28. ATBS (2018). *Self-driving trucks: are truck drivers out of a job?* Retrieved December 8, 2019, from https://www.atbs.com/knowledge-hub/trucking-blog/self-driving-trucks-are-truck-drivers-out-of-a-job.

29. U.S. Council of Economic Advisers (2019). *Economic report of the president: 2019, Table B-27.* Retrieved August 29, 2019, from https://www.govinfo.gov/app/search/%7B%22query%22%3A%22economic%20report%20of%20the%20president%20b-27%22%2C%22offset%22%3A0%7D.

30. McCue (2018). 57 million U.S. workers are part of the gig economy. *Forbes.com*, retrieved March 12, 2020, from https://www.forbes.com/sites/tjmccue/2018/08/31/57-million-u-s-workers-are-part-of-the-gig-economy/#643452e67118.

31. Federal Reserve Bank of San Francisco (1998). *Economic Letter 98–28: The natural rate, NAIRU, and monetary policy.* San Francisco, CA: Author. Retrieved August 2003, from http://www.frbsf.org/econrsrch/wklyltr/wklyltr98/el98–28.html. Discussion and examples of NAIRU in this paragraph rely on this source. See also Mitchell, M., & Nyusken, J. (2008). *Full employment abandoned; shifting sands and policy failures.* Cheltenham, UK: Edward Elgar.

32. Montes, J. (2017). *Labor market projections.* Congressional Budget Office. Retrieved August 29, 2019, from https://www.cbo.gov/publication/52393.

33. Federal Reserve Bank of St. Louis (2019). *Natural rate of unemployment (short term): 1975 – 2018.* Retrieved August 29, 2019, from https://fred.stlouisfed.org/series/NROUST.

34. The ravages of time. (2011). *The Economist, 401,* October 1, 33.

35. U.S. Council of Economic Advisers (2019). *Economic report of the president: 2019, Table B-27*; Lambert, L. (2020). Real unemployment rate soars past 20%-and the U.S. has now lost 26.5 million jobs. *Fortune online,* retrieved April 25, 2020, from https://fortune.com/2020/04/23/us-unemployment-rate-numbers-claims-this-week-total-job-losses-april-23-2020-benefits-claims/.

36. Malhotra, V., & Manyika, J. (2011). Five misconceptions about productivity.

37. World Bank (2019). *Databank: microdata data catalog,* Retrieved December 10, 2019, from https://data.worldbank.org/indicator/NY.GDP.MKTP.KD.ZG?. (data file download all countries).

38. MacMillan, M., et al. (2014). Globalization, structural change and productivity growth, with an update on Africa. *World Development, 63,* 11–32. Retrieved August 30, 2019, from https://drodrik.scholar.harvard.edu/files/dani-rodrik/files/globalization_structural_change_productivity_growth_with_africa_update.pdf.

39. Obama White House Archives (2019).

40. Economic Recovery Tax Act of 1981. P.L. 97-34.

41. Protecting Americans from Tax Hikes (PATH) Act of 2015, P.L. 114-113, 129 Stat 2242.

42. State Science and Technology Initiative – SSTI (2014). *How effective are state R&D tax credits?* Retrieved August 31, 2019, from https://ssti.org/blog/how-effective-are-state-rd-tax-credits.

43. Bivens, J. (2017). *The potential macroeconomic benefits from investing in infrastructure investment.* Economic Policy Institute. Retrieved August 29, 2019, from https://www.epi.org/publication/the-potential-macroeconomic-benefits-from-increasing-infrastructure-investment/.

44. White House (2011). *Blueprint for a secure energy future.* Washington, DC: U.S. Government Printing Office.

45. White House (2019). *President Donald J. Trump will work with G7 allies to build a future of opportunity and promise for all our nations.* Retrieved August 31, 2019, from https://www.whitehouse.gov/briefings-statements/president-donald-j-trump-will-work-g7-allies-build-future-opportunity-promise-nations/.

46. Solyndra and the White House: letting sunlight in. (2011). *The Economist, 401,* September 24, 36.

47. The Economist (2010). *Picking winners, saving losers.* Retrieved August 31, 2019, from https://www.economist.com/briefing/2010/08/05/picking-winners-saving-losers; The Economist (2013). *The new interventionism.* Retrieved August 31, 2019, from https://www.economist.com/britain/2013/09/21/the-new-interventionism.

48. U.S. Department of Commerce, Bureau of Economic Analysis (2019). *Table 1-U.S. international transactions: exports and imports of goods and services.* Retrieved September 1, 2019, from https://www.bea.gov/data/intl-trade-investment/international-transactions.

49. U.S. Department of Commerce, Bureau of Economic Analysis (2019). *U.S. international transactions, first quarter 2019 and annual update.* Retrieved September 5, 2019, from www.bea.gov/news/2019/us-international-transactions-first-quarter-2019-and-annual-update.

50. There are two additions to the financial account in Table 3-1. Financial derivatives are not actual purchases or sales of assets, so they do not directly add to or subtract from the value of goods and services produced by the economy. They net out of the financial accounts. The statistical discrepancy shown in the table reflects the impossibility of directly measuring all elements in the economy's current, capital and financial transactions.

51. Nowhere to hide. (2011). *The Economist, 401,* October 15, 15.

52. The debt ceiling deal: no thanks to anyone. (2011). *The Economist, 401,* August 6, 24.

53. Joyce, P., & Meyers, R. (2012). Raze the debt ceiling. *Baltimore Sun,* September 19. Retrieved December 12, 2019, from https://www.baltimoresun.com/opinion/bs-xpm-2012-12-19-bs-ed-debt-ceiling-20121219-story.html.

54. General Accounting Office (2011). *Delays create debt management challenges and increase uncertainty in the Treasury Market.* Washington, DC: U.S. Government Printing Office.

55. Sandler, R. (2019). What Congress is doing by suspending the debt ceiling. *Forbes,* July 21. Retrieved September 16, 2019, from https://www.forbes.com/sites/rachelsandler/2019/07/22/what-congress-doing-when-it-suspends-the-debt-ceiling/#36b2119e2065; Cochrane, E. et al. (2019). Federal budget would raise spending by $320 billion. *New York Times,* July 22. Retrieved September 16, 2019, from https://www.nytimes.com/2019/07/22/us/politics/budget-deal.html.

56. The tern "national" refers not to savings of the U.S. government, but to total savings in the economy. Government savings is only achieved by a surplus in the annual budget.

57. Rosenberg, J. (2019). Crumbling infrastructure is costing businesses. *Wilmington Star News (AP),* May 30, A10.

58. The Euro Area is the 16 countries in the European Union whose currency is the *euro.* Germany is one of those countries, but is used in this and other comparisons in this chapter that also include the Euro area because it is one of the United States' major trading partners and competitors. Germany is included in the Euro area data points.

59. Walsh, D. (2006). *Knowledge and the wealth of nations: a source of economic discovery.* New York, NY: Norton.

60. Mellow, C. (2019). The great productivity slowdown. *Global Finance, 33,* June 2015, 12–15.

61. A good primer on gross debt versus debt held by the public is from the Committee for a Responsible Federal Budget (2019). *Q&A: gross debt versus debt held by the public.* Retrieved September 7, 2019, from https://www.crfb.org/papers/qa-gross-debt-versus-debt-held-public#targetText=The%20gross%20federal%20debt%20is,the%20public%20and%20intragovernmental%20debt.

62. U.S. Congressional Budget Office (2019). *The budget and economic outlook: 2019 to 2029.* 1; Dodaro, G. (2019). *The nation's fiscal health: actions needed to achieve long-term fiscal sustainability.* Testimony before the Committee on Budget, U.S. Senate, June 26. Retrieved September 7, 2019, from https://www.budget.senate.gov/imo/media/doc/GAO-19-611T%20The%20Nation's%20Fiscal%20Health-%20Actions%20Needed%20to%20Achieve%20Long-Term%20Fiscal%20Sustainability.pdf.

63. U.S. Department of the Treasury (2019). *Monthly treasury statement: receipts and outlays of the United States Government for FY 2020 through November, 2019.* Retrieved December 15, 2019, from https://fiscal.treasury.gov/files/reports-statements/mts/mts1119.pdf.

64. Congressional Budget Office (2019). *An update to the budget and economic outlook 2019-2029:* August 2019. Retrieved December 15, 2019, from https://www.cbo.gov/publication/55551.

65. Congressional Budget Office (2019). *Long term budget outlook: June, 2019.* Retrieved December 15, 2019, from https://www.cbo.gov/publication/55331.

66. Is modern monetary theory nutty or essential? (2019). *The Economist.* Retrieved December 15, 2019, from https://www.economist.com/finance-and-economics/2019/03/14/is-modern-monetary-theory-nutty-or-essential?

67. As quoted in Shiller (2019). *Modern monetary theory makes sense, up to a point.* New York Times, March 29. Retrieved December 15, 2019, from https://www.nytimes.com/2019/03/29/business/modern-monetary-theory-shiller.html; Kelton, S. (2019). Modern monetary theory is not a recipe for doom. *Bloomberg Online.* Retrieved December 17, 2019, from https://www.bloomberg.com/opinion/articles/2019-02-21/modern-monetary-theory-is-not-a-recipe-for-doom.

68. Relman, E. (2019). Alexandria Ocasio-Cortez says the theory that deficit spending is good for the economy should 'absolutely' be part of the conversation. *Business Insider,* January 7. Retrieved December 15, 2019, from https://www.businessinsider.com/alexandria-ocasio-cortez-ommt-modern-monetary-theory-how-pay-for-policies-2019-1.

69. For example, Krugman, P. (2019). What's wrong with functional finance: The doctrine behind MMT was smart but not completely right. *New York Times.* Retrieved December 16, 2019, from https://www.nytimes.com/2019/02/12/opinion/how-much-does-heterodoxy-help-progressives-wonkish.html; Summers, L. (2019). The left's embrace of modern monetary theory is a recipe for disaster, *Washington Post.* Retrieved December 16, 2019, from https://www.washingtonpost.com/opinions

/the-lefts-embrace-of-modern-monetary-theory-is-a
-recipe-for-disaster/2019/03/04/6ad88eec-3ea4-11e9
-9361-301ffb5bd5e6_story.html.

70. Moller, Z. (2019). *What is MMT, and why isn't it practical?* Third Way, July 18. Retrieved December 15, 2019, from https://www.thirdway.org/memo/what-is-mmt-and-why-isnt-it-practical.

71. The Conference Board (2011). *How to compute diffusion indexes.* Retrieved September 8, 2019, from http://www.conference-board.org/data/bci/index.cfm?id=2180. (Note: the Conference Board 2011 document still is the reference document for explaining the computation of diffusion indexes.)

72. U.S. Congressional Budget Office (2019). *Budget and economic outlook: fiscal years 2019–2029.*

73. U.S. Congressional Budget Office (2017). *CBO's economic forecasting record: 2017 update* (p. 1). Washington, DC: U.S. Government Publishing Office.

74. For a full list of the indicators and a sample report of a quarterly report, see Moore R., et al. (2018). *Blue Chip Economic Indicators: top analysts' forecasts of the U.S. economic outlook for the year ahead, 43,* 1 (January 10). Baltimore, MD: Aspen Publishers. Retrieved September 10, 2019, from https://lrus.wolterskluwer.com/media/2444/bcei0118email.pdf.

75. DRI-WEFA (2011). *DRI-WEFA's macroeconomic models.* Retrieved November 13, 2011, from http://www.iccfglobal.org/pdf/DRI_WEFA_USMacroModel.pdf.

76. HIS Markit (2019). *Economics and country risk.* Retrieved September 10, 2019, from https://ihsmarkit.com/industry/economics-country-risk.html.

77. Keynes, J. M. (1936). *The general theory of employment, interest and money.* New York, NY: Harcourt Brace.

78. Variously quoted in newspapers and other media on several occasions. Most commonly cited is a speech at Harvard University, January 4, 1971.

79. Laffer, A., & Seymour, J. (Eds.). (1979). *The economics of the tax revolt: a reader.* New York, NY: Harcourt Brace Jovanovich.

80. *Washington Post–ABC News poll.* (2011). Retrieved November 15, 2011, from http://www.washingtonpost.com/wp-srv/politics/polls/postabcpoll_071711.html.

81. U.S. Congressional Budget Office (2019). *The budget and economic outlook: 2019 to 2029.*

82. Economic Stimulus Act of 2008 (P.L. 110-185).

83. American Recovery and Reinvestment Act of 2009 (P.L. 111-5).

84. White House, Office of Management and Budget (2019). *Fiscal year 2020: budget of the U.S. government* (pp. 107, 110). Washington, DC: U.S. Government Publishing Office.

85. U.S. Department of the Treasury (2019). *Major foreign holders of treasury securities.* Retrieved September 10, 2019, from https://ticdata.treasury.gov/Publish/mfh.txt.

86. McBride, J., & Chatzky, A. (2019). *The national debt dilemma.* Council on Foreign Relations Backgrounder. Retrieved September 10, 2019, from https://www.cfr.org/backgrounder/national-debt-dilemma#targetText=Foreign%20investors%2C%20mostly%20governments%2C%20hold,have%20more%20than%20%241%20trillion.

87. Brazil, Russia, China, India, and South Africa.

88. Deloitte IAS*Plus* (2019). *Hyperinflationary economies.* Retrieved September 10, 2019, from https://www.iasplus.com/en/news/2019/07/hyperinflationary-economies.

89. Federal Reserve Board (2019). *Federal Reserve money stock measures H.6.*, July 2019. Retrieved September 10, 2019, from https://www.federalreserve.gov/releases/h6/current/default.htm.

90. Wolla, S. (2018). *Bitcoin: money or financial investment?* Federal Reserve Bank of St. Louis, March. Retrieved September 17, 2019, from https://research.stlouisfed.org/publications/page1-econ/2018/03/01/bitcoin-money-or-financial-investment.

91. The Federal Reserve Board (2019). *The federal reserve system: purposes and functions:* 10th ed. Washington, DC: U.S. Government Publishing Office, and downloadable version retrieved September 10, 2019, from https://www.federalreserve.gov/aboutthefed/pf.htm.

92. The Federal Reserve Board (2019). *The federal reserve system: purposes and functions:* 10th ed. 2–3.

93. The Federal Reserve Board (2019). *The federal reserve system: purposes and functions,* 10th ed. 20.

94. The discount rate or federal funds rate at different time periods is readily accessible from various historical statistical series and current weekly and quarterly reports from the system's website, www.federalreserve.gov. Daily reports are also accessible.

95. *What is quantitative easing? And how does it work?* (2015). *The Economist.* Retrieved September 10, 2019, from https://www.economist.com/the-economist-explains/2015/03/09/what-is-quantitative-easing.

96. Smialek, J. (2019). Trump calls for Fed's 'Boneheads' to slash interest rates below zero. *New York Times.* Retrieved December 16, 2019, from https://www.nytimes.com/2019/09/11/business/economy/bonehead-trump-jay-powell.html.

97. Beck, N. (1991). The Fed and the political business cycle. *Contemporary Policy Issues 9,* 25–38.

98. Exec. Order No. 12835 of January 25, 1993, 3 C.F.R. 6189; National Economic Council (2011). *Overview.* Retrieved November 14, 2011, from http://www.whitehouse.gov/administration/eop/nec.

99. National Association of State Budget Officers (2011). *Fiscal survey of the states: 2011* (p. 40). Lexington, KY: National Association of State Budget Officers; see annual reports of this survey since 2011 to observe the gradual economic recovery at the state level.

100. Muoio, D. (2017). The U.S. will need to invest more than $4.5 trillion by 2025 to fix its failing infrastructure. *Business insider,* March 9. Retrieved July 13, 2019, from https://www.businessinsider.com/us-invest-over-4-trillion-by-2025-to-fix-infrastructure-2017-3.

101. Parilla, J., & Liu, S. (2018). *Examining the local value of economic development incentives.* Washington, DC: Brookings Institution. Retrieved July 30, 2019, from

https://www.brookings.edu/wp-content/uploads/2018/02/report_examining-the-local-value-of-economic-development-incentives_brookings-metro_march-2018.pdf.

102. Bivens, J. (2017). *The potential macroeconomic benefits from increasing infrastructure investment.* Economic Policy Institute, July 18. Retrieved December 16, 2019, from https://www.epi.org/publication/the-potential-macroeconomic-benefits-from-increasing-infrastructure-investment/

103. Small, K., et al. (1989). *Road work.* Washington, DC: Brookings Institution; Krohl, R. (2001). The role of public capital in the economic development process. *International Journal of Public Administration, 24,* 1041–1060; U.S. Congressional Budget Office (2010). *Public spending on water and transportation infrastructure* (p. 14). Washington, DC: U.S. Government Printing Office; Congressional Budget Office (2018). *Public spending on transportation and water infrastructure, 1956 to 2017.* Washington, DC: U.S. Government Publishing Office.

104. PBS News Hour (2019). *Can the longest economic expansion in U.S. history last?* July 1. Retrieved September 13, 2019, from https://www.pbs.org/newshour/economy/making-sense/can-the-longest-economic-expansion-in-u-s-history-last; Li, Y. (2019). This is now the longest U.S. economic expansion in history. *CNBC,* July 2. Retrieved September 13, 2019, from https://www.cnbc.com/2019/07/02/this-is-now-the-longest-us-economic-expansion-in-history.html; Moore, M. (2019). U.S. economy marks longest expansion in American history. *New York Post,* July 1. Retrieved September 13, 2019, from https://nypost.com/2019/07/01/us-economy-marks-longest-expansion-in-american-history/; Fisher, K. (2019). Recession? Really? This 10-year economic expansion won't die just of old age. *USA Today,* July 1. Retrieved September 13, 2019, from https://www.usatoday.com/story/money/2019/07/28/recession-economic-expansion-longest-age-kill/1817563001/.

105. Stevens, P., & Imbert, F. (2020). Historic market plunge: traders describe a day that went from 'uncertainty to panic.' *CNBC.com.* Retrieved March 15, 2020, from https://www.cnbc.com/2020/03/12/historic-market-plunge-traders-describe-a-day-that-went-from-uncertainty-to-panic.html.

106. National Bureau of Economic Research (2010). *Business cycle dating committee report,* September 20. Retrieved November 12, 2011, from http://www.nber.org/cycles/sept2010.html.

107. All data references in this and following paragraphs discussing Figure 3-10 are from the underlying data for the graph and the sources cited with the figure, unless otherwise noted.

108. Board of Governors of the Federal Reserve System (2011). *The Federal Reserve's response to the financial crisis and actions to foster maximum employment and price stability.* Also see other links in that document. Retrieved September 14, 2019, at https://www.federalreserve.gov/monetarypolicy/bst_crisisresponse.htm.

109. A provision in the American Recovery and Reinvestment Act of 2009 (P.L. 111–5).

110. Weinberg, J. (2013). *The Great Recession and its aftermath.* Retrieved September 14, 2019, from https://www.federalreservehistory.org/essays/great_recession_and_its_aftermath.

111. Merle, R. (2018). A guide to the financial crisis – 10 years later. *Washington Post,* September 10. Retrieved September 14, 2019, from https://www.washingtonpost.com/business/economy/a-guide-to-the-financial-crisis—10-years-later/2018/09/10/114b76ba-af10-11e8-a20b-5f4f84429666_story.html.

112. Merle, R. (2018). A guide to the financial crisis.

113. Laeven, L., & Valencia, F. (2010). *Resolution of banking crises: the good, the bad and the ugly.* International Monetary Fund (IMF) Working Paper no. 10/146, 19.

114. Note: Though there were dozens of other programs as documented in this chapter, the ARRA programs were the primary contributors to grant and other non-loan financial assistance to individuals and institutions, including state and local governments.

115. Congressional Budget Office (2015). *Estimated impact of the American Recovery and Reinvestment Act on employment and economic output in 2014.* Retrieved September 14, 2019, from https://www.cbo.gov/sites/default/files/114th-congress-2015-2016/reports/49958-ARRA.pdf.

116. Calculated from U.S. Department of Commerce, Bureau of Economic Analysis (2019). *Economic report of the President: 2019, Appendix B, Statistical Tables, Table b-45.*

117. Board of Governors of the Federal Reserve System (2019). *Distributional financial accounts:shares of wealth by wealth percentile groups* (downloadable CSV). Retrieved December 17, 2019, from https://www.federalreserve.gov/releases/efa/efa-distributional-financial-accounts.htm.

118. World Bank (2005). *World development report 2006* (p.vii). New York, NY: Oxford.

119. Rugaber, C. (2019). Wealth gap increasing despite long growth, *Wilmington Star News,* July 2, A6; Samuelson, R. (2019). Is the welfare state now indestructible? *Wilmington Star News,* August 5, A9.

120. Organization for Economic Cooperation and Development (2019). *OECD income distribution database (IDD): Gini, poverty, income, methods and concepts.* Retrieved September 14, 2019, from http://www.oecd.org/social/income-distribution-database.htm.

121. Congressional Budget Office (2019). *The distribution of household income, 2016.* Retrieved September 14, 2019, from https://www.cbo.gov/system/files/2019-07/55413-CBO-distribution-of-household-income-2016.pdf.

122. Board of Governors of the Federal Reserve System (2019). Distributional functional accounts.

123. Diving into the rich pool. (2011). *The Economist, 401,* September 24, 83.

124. Tax Cut and Jobs Act, P.L. 115-97.

125. Gale, W. (2019). *A fixable mistake: the tax cut and jobs act,* Brookings Institution. Retrieved December 17, 2019, from https://www.brookings.edu/blog/up-front/2019/09/25/a-fixable-mistake-the-tax-cuts-and-jobs-act/.

126. Mathur, A., & Kallen, C. (2017). *AEI tax brief: the child tax credit vs. the earned income tax credit,* AEI Tax Briefs. Retrieved December 17, 2019, from https://www.aei.org/research-products/one-pager/aei-tax-brief-ctc-vs-eitc/?gclid=CjwKCAiAluLvBRASEiwAAbX3GRatzX8tKLJfRVUOpuxSaIxk8M0tcA4thqvOdwrV8LOafymimnEKaxoCA-4QAvD_BwE.

127. Congressional Budget Office (2019). *The distribution of household income, 2016,* 4 and 13.

128. Congressional Budget Office (2019). *The distribution of household income, 2016.*

CHAPTER 4

Budget Cycles

Public budgeting systems consist of numerous participants and various processes that bring the participants into interaction. The purpose of budgeting is to allocate scarce resources among competing public demands so as to attain societal goals and objectives. Those societal ends are expressed not by philosopher kings, but by mortals who must operate within the context of some prescribed allocation process—namely, the budgetary system.

This chapter provides an overview of the participants and processes involved in budgetary decision making. First, the phases of the budget cycle are reviewed. Any system has some structure or form, and budgetary systems are no exception. The budgetary decision-making process has several phases. The chapter then discusses the intermingling of budget cycles across different budget years. The full budget cycle is longer than 12 months, which means budget planning and preparation for one cycle overlap with execution and audit for one or more other budget years. This chapter outlines the process and discusses the intermingling of the budget's cycles, both within government and among governments.

The Budget Cycle

The discrete activities that constitute budgeting are geared to a cycle. The cycle provides the timetable for the system to absorb and respond to new information and, therefore, allows government to be held accountable for its actions. Although any budget system may be less than perfect in guaranteeing adherence to this principle of accountability, periodicity contributes to achieving and maintaining limited government. The budget cycle consists of four phases: (1) preparation and submission, (2) approval, (3) execution, and (4) audit and evaluation.

Preparation and Submission

The preparation and submission phase is the most difficult to describe because it has been subjected to the most reform efforts. Experiments in reformulating the preparation process abound. Although the institutional units may exist over time, both procedures and substantive content vary from year to year.

Chief Executive Responsibilities

The responsibility for budget preparation varies greatly among jurisdictions. Budget reform efforts in the United States have pressed for executive budgeting, in which the chief executive has exclusive responsibility for preparing a proposed budget and submitting it to the legislative body. At the federal level, the president has such exclusive responsibility, although many factors curtail the extent to which the president can make major changes in the budget from one year to the next. In parliamentary systems, the prime minister (chief executive) typically has responsibility for budget preparation and submits what is usually called the "government budget" to the parliament.

Preparation authority, however, is not always assigned to state governors, mayors, and other local chief executives. While a majority of governors have responsibility for preparation and submission, some share budget-making authority with other elected administrative officers, civil service appointees, legislative leaders, or some combination of these parties. In Texas, for example, a Legislative Budget Board (LBB), created by the legislature, prepares a budget and appropriations bills. State government agencies submit budget requests both to the LBB and the Governor's Office of Budget, Planning and Policy. Instructions and forms for budget submission are issued by the LBB.[1]

In parliamentary systems, if a coalition of several parties is necessary to form a government, and the coalition is held together by each of the main parties in the coalition controlling one or more ministries, the prime minister may have very little control over budget preparation. At times, it may be difficult to form a government in a multiparty parliamentary system when no party has a majority. Belgium holds the modern record for parliamentary systems for failure to form a government and thus name a prime minister—541 days from the 2010 federal election to form a government. Iraq held the previous record of 289 days in 2010.[2]

At the municipal level, the mayor may or may not have budget preparation powers. In cities where the mayor is strong—has administrative control over the executive branch—the mayor normally does have budget-making power. This is not necessarily the case in weak-mayor systems and in cities operating under the commission plan, where each councilor or commissioner administers a given department.[3] Usually, city managers in council-manager systems have responsibility for budget preparation, although their ability to make budgetary recommendations may be tempered by their lack of independence.

City managers are appointed by councils and commonly lack tenure. Even in a city in which the mayor or chief executive does not have budget preparation responsibility, this duty is still likely to be in the hands of an executive official such as a city finance director. Thus, a majority of cities follow the principle of executive budget preparation.

Location of Budget Office

Budget preparation at the federal level is primarily a function of the budget office that was established by the Budget and Accounting Act of 1921[4]—the Bureau of the Budget (BOB), initially placed in the Treasury Department. Over time, the role of the BOB increased in importance. In 1939, the BOB was moved out of the Treasury to become part of the newly formed Executive Office of the President. Given that the BOB was thought to be the "right arm of the president"—a common phrase in early budget literature—the move out of the Treasury, a line department, into the Executive Office of the President placed the BOB under direct presidential supervision. In 1970, President Nixon reorganized the BOB, giving it a new title, the Office of Management and Budget (OMB). The OMB's policy role in budget preparation varies from president to president depending on the advisors in whom the president has the most confidence. Some presidents rely heavily on the director of OMB for advice on budget systems; some rely somewhat more on advisors within the White House staff.

The state budget office is contained within the governor's office in only 10 states in the United States. It is a freestanding agency in 12 other states. Most commonly (in 21 states), the budget office is within an office of management and/or administration. Notably, in 39 of the 50 states, the governor's office sets budget targets for executive branch agencies.[5] Information about professional personnel in state budget offices is presented in **Table 4-1**. Given the significant variation in state sizes, the number of personnel assigned to budget agencies, not surprisingly, varies widely. In 2015, there were 7,951 staff positions assigned to budget agencies in the 50 states. Of those, 1,461 were assigned to the budget function.[6] The largest

Table 4-1 Functional Roles of Budget Agency Personnel in the Fifty States, 2015

	Budget Analysts	Tech/Computer Specialists	Administrative Support Staff	Other
Average Number	20	6	5	30
Most	203 (NY)	88 (MS)	27 (MS)	303 (CA)
Fewest	4 (WVA)	1 or 0 (28 states)	1 or 0 (15 states)	1 or 0 (8 states)
Total Budget Staff	995	284	222	1,511

Adapted from National Association of State Budget Officers (2015). *Budget processes in the states*, 28. Washington, DC: National Association of State Budget Officers.

number assigned to a specific function were budget analyst positions, as shown in Table 4-1. Another 284 were in technology or computer-related positions. New York had the most personnel classified as budget analyst—203—and West Virginia the fewest, with only four. Notably, the National Association of State Budget Officers, in the report cited in Table 4-1, observed that budget analyst and administrative positions in budget offices have shrunk while information technology positions have grown since the same survey was taken in 2008.

Steps in the Preparation Stage

In the federal government, budget preparation starts in the spring, a full year and a half before the budget year starts, or even earlier for large agencies. Agencies begin by assessing their programs and considering which programs require revision and whether new programs should be recommended. At approximately the same time, the president's staff makes estimates of anticipated economic trends to determine available revenue under existing tax legislation. The next step is for the president to issue general budget and fiscal policy guidelines, which agencies use to develop their individual budgets. In late summer/early fall, these budgets are submitted to the OMB. Throughout the fall and into the later months of the year, OMB staff members review agency requests and hold hearings with agency spokespersons. Not until late in the process, usually in

November, December, and into January, does the president become deeply involved in the process, although some presidents never become deeply involved. It culminates in February with the submission of a proposed budget to Congress for the forthcoming fiscal year that starts October 1 of that same calendar year.

At the state and local levels, a similar process is used where executive budgeting systems prevail. The central budget office issues budget request instructions, reviews the submitted requests, and makes recommendations to the chief executive, who decides which items to recommend to the legislative body. In jurisdictions not using executive budgeting, the chief executive and the budget office play minor roles. In this type of system, the line agencies direct their budget requests to the legislative body.

Political Factors

The preparation phase, as well as the other three phases in the budget cycle, is replete with political considerations, both bureaucratic and partisan. Each organizational unit is concerned with its own survival and advancement. Line agencies and their subunits attempt to protect against budget cuts and may strive for increased resources. Budget offices often play negative roles, attempting to limit agency growth or imposing agency budget cuts. Budget offices are always conscious of the fact that the chief executive (the governor or mayor, for example) can overrule whatever they propose. All members of the executive branch are concerned with their relationships with the legislative branch and the general citizenry. The chief executive is especially concerned about partisan calculations: Which alternatives will be advantageous to his or her political party? Of course, there is concern for developing programs for the common good, but this concern plays out in a complicated game of political maneuvering.[7]

Fragmentation

One complaint about the preparation phase is that it tends to be highly fragmented. Organizational units within line agencies tend to be concerned primarily with their own programs and frequently fail to take a broad perspective. Even the budget office may be myopic, focusing more on budget considerations than overall budget policy. Some agencies also will privately, and some not so privately, engage in separate discussions with the legislative branch to try to restore cuts made by the budget office, thereby weakening the notion of the *executive* budget. Only the chief executive is unquestionably committed to viewing the budget in its entirety in the preparation phase.

Approval
Revenue and Appropriation Bills

The budget is approved by a legislative body, such as Congress, a state legislature, a county board of supervisors, a city council, or a school board. The important role of the legislature in the United States traces back to the American rebellion against "taxation without representation." For this reason, the "power of the purse" is considered to be a crucial responsibility of the people's representatives. The legislature reviews the executive's budget recommendations and often has access to the original agency budget requests, which enables it to make comparisons. At the federal level, revenue measures are enacted separately and are controlled by House and Senate committees other than the appropriations committees.

Congress is normally not privy to original budget requests, although ways are often found to obtain this information, such as questions being put to agency representatives in committee hearings. The fragmented approach to budgeting in the preparation phase is not characteristic of the approval phase at the local level. A city council may have a separate finance committee, but normally the council as a whole participates actively in the approval process. Local legislative bodies may take several preliminary votes on pieces of the budget but then adopt the budget as a whole by a single vote.

Most states, like the federal government, separate tax and other revenue measures from appropriations or spending bills. Some states place most or all of their spending provisions in a single appropriation bill, whereas others create hundreds of appropriation bills. Most state legislatures are free to augment or reduce the governor's budget, but some are restricted in their ability to increase the budget. Likewise, many parliamentary systems allow the parliament to modify—but not increase—the government's budget proposal.

At the federal level, the revenue and appropriation processes have been markedly fragmented and involve numerous committees and subcommittees. Not only have revenue raising and spending been treated as separate processes, but the expenditure side is handled in many different major appropriation bills instead of being treated as a whole. Reforms introduced in 1974 attempted to overlay an integrated process on top of these divergent processes and pieces of legislation, but the system had numerous flaws.[8] Numerous proposals have been advanced in recent years to reform a process that is now approaching 50 years old. The chapter on budget approval and the U.S. Congress discusses in detail both these flaws and efforts at reforming the congressional budget process.

The legislature holds a series of hearings at which the central budget office and the individual agencies testify. These hearings can be lovefests in which the committees that oversee agencies are eager to recommend increased appropriations for the agencies' programs. Conversely, tensions are common in such hearings. An executive may emphasize the need to restrain expenses, while legislators may seek expansion of various programs and corresponding increases in expenditures. Tensions are sometimes particularly keen between Congress and the president's budget director, especially during periods of divided government in which the president is of one party and Congress is controlled by the other.

In both the preparation and the approval phases, one or two issues often dominate budget deliberations. If a state government is projecting a major decline in revenues due to a weakening economy, closing the gap between low revenues and higher expenditures will be a major concern. At the federal level, wrestling with huge budget deficits has been a primary focus in budgeting since the 1980s, with the exception of the late 1990s when there was a brief period of balanced federal budgets. Neither major political party in recent years has emphasized a balanced budget, as is apparent in the annual budget deficit (see Government and the Economy).

Executive Signature or Veto Powers

The final step of the approval stage is signing the appropriation and tax bills into law. The president, governors, and, in some cases, mayors have the power to veto. A veto sends the measure back to the legislative body for further consideration. Most governors (43 of them) have item-veto power, which allows them to veto specific portions of an appropriation bill but still sign it. In no case can the executive augment parts of the budget beyond that provided by the legislature. However, 33 governors have the authority to withhold appropriations in the enacted budget from executive agencies without legislative approval.[9] The president was given a form of item veto that took effect in 1997, but it was invalidated by the Supreme Court the following year (see the chapter on budget approval and the U.S. Congress).

Execution
Apportionment Process

Execution, the third phase, commences with the beginning of the fiscal year—October 1 for the federal government and July 1 for most state governments. Some form of centralized control during this phase is common at all levels of government and is usually maintained by the budget office. Following congressional passage of an appropriation bill and its signing by the president, agencies must submit to the OMB a proposed plan for apportionment (see the chapter on budget execution). This plan indicates the funds required for operations, typically on a quarterly basis. The apportionment process is used in part to ensure that agencies do not commit all their available funds in a period shorter than the 12-month fiscal year. The intent is to avoid the need for supplemental appropriations from Congress.

The apportionment process is substantively important in that program adjustments must be made to bring planned spending into balance with available revenue. Because an agency most likely did not obtain all the funds requested, either from the president in the preparation phase or from Congress in the approval phase, plans for the coming fiscal year must be revised. To varying degrees, state and local governments also use an apportionment process.

Impoundment

The chief executive may assert control in the apportionment process through a form of item veto known as "impoundment," which is basically a refusal to release some funds to agencies. Thomas Jefferson often is considered the first president to have impounded funds. President Nixon impounded so extensively that Congress took legislative action. The 1974 legislation, in a sense, was a treaty between Congress and the White House allowing limited impoundment powers for the president. These limited impoundment powers have resulted in little reduction in spending.

Allotments

At the federal level, once funds are apportioned, agencies and departments make allotments. This process grants budgetary authority to subunits such as bureaus and divisions. Allotments are made on a monthly or quarterly basis, and, like the apportionment process, the allotment process is used to control spending over the course of the fiscal year. Control is often extensive and detailed, requiring approval by the department budget office for any shift in available funds from one item to another, such as from travel to wages. Some transfers may require clearance by the central budget office. At other levels, it is a one-stage allotment process, typically without using the term *apportionment.*

Preaudits

Before an expenditure is made, a form of preaudit is conducted. Basically, the preaudit ensures that funds are committed only for approved purposes and that an agency has sufficient resources in its budget to meet the proposed expenditure. The responsibility for this function varies widely, with the budget and/or accounting office being responsible for it in some jurisdictions and independently elected comptrollers being responsible for it in others. Later, after approval is granted and a purchase is made, the treasurer or other responsible official issues a check or makes an electronic fund transfer for the expenditure.

Execution Subsystems

During budget execution, several subsystems are in operation. Taxes and other debts to government are collected. The Internal Revenue Service (IRS) in the Treasury Department is responsible for this set of tasks at the federal level. Cash is managed in the sense that monies temporarily not needed are invested. Supplies, materials, and equipment are procured, and strategies are developed to protect the government against loss or damage of property and against liability suits. Accounting and information systems are in operation. For state and local governments, bonds are sold and the proceeds are used to finance construction of facilities and the acquisition of major equipment.

Audit and Evaluation

The final phase of the budgetary process is audit and evaluation. The objectives of this phase are undergoing considerable change, but initially the main goal was to guarantee executive compliance with the provisions of appropriation bills, particularly to ensure honesty in dispensing public monies and to prevent needless waste. In accord with this goal, accounting procedures are prescribed and auditors check the books maintained by agency personnel. In recent years, the scope of auditing has been broadened to encompass studies of the effectiveness and efficiency of government programs.

Location of the Audit Function

In the federal government, considerable controversy was generated concerning the appropriate organizational location of the audit function. In 1920, President Woodrow Wilson vetoed legislation that would have established the federal budget system on the grounds that he opposed the creation of an auditing office answerable to Congress rather than to the president. Nevertheless, the General Accounting Office (GAO) was established in 1921 by the Budget and Accounting Act and was made an arm of Congress, with the justification being that an audit unit outside of the executive branch should be created to provide objective assessments of expenditure practices.

The GAO, over the years, underwent a gradual and major set of changes that led to its name being changed in 2004 to the Government Accountability Office.[10] It obviously retained its initials of GAO.

GAO Functions

The GAO is headed by the comptroller general, who is appointed by the president, upon the advice and consent of the Senate, for only one term of 15 years. The comptroller general can be removed by Congress only by impeachment or joint resolution. There has never been such an effort and, as of 2019, only eight people have held this position since its creation in 1921.

The GAO audits the accounts of operating agencies and evaluates their accounting systems. With major reforms in accounting and auditing undertaken by the executive branch at the direction of Congress, and especially with the creation of independent inspectors general within executive departments and agencies, the GAO conducts far fewer audits than it once did.

The GAO provides a variety of other services. It gives Congress opinions on legal issues, such as advising on whether a particular agency acted within the law in some specific instance under consideration. It also resolves bid protests over the awarding of government contracts. As the highest-level audit institution in the United States, the GAO sets auditing standards and guidance standards that are looked to by state and local governments as guidance for their audit processes.

Where the GAO has gained major responsibility is in the arena of assessing the results of government programs. Eugene Dodaro, the eighth Comptroller General, whose term expires in 2025, has emphasized that much of the GAO's work has shifted to "...performance audits that look at various federal programs and investments in such areas as major weapons systems, IT systems, and satellite systems,"[11] as well as other programs. The possibilities for fraud, waste, and mismanagement are major areas of GAO concern. Every 2 years, at the beginning of a new congressional session, the GAO issues a list of *high-risk* programs and operations to bring attention to this concern.[12] This responsibility for evaluating government programs has sometimes led to criticism of the GAO; in particular, some members of Congress have claimed that the office has lost its neutrality and become a policy advocate.

The authority of the GAO to seek information from the executive branch in fulfilling its audit and performance assessments is limited. In 2002, the GAO engaged in an historic conflict with the White House. President George W. Bush had created the National Energy Policy Development Group (NEPDG) to recommend a new energy policy for the government. Vice President

Dick Cheney chaired the group. After the group completed its work, the GAO asked to see important records. Of particular concern was the list of companies and individuals from industry that had supplied advice. The energy giant Enron had collapsed, leaving many stockholders with huge losses and company employees without retirement benefits. Some suspected that Enron, which had close ties to President Bush before he left Texas for Washington, had exerted undue influence on the design of the energy policy.

The White House refused to release the requested documents, which prompted the GAO to file suit in U.S. district court against Vice President Cheney and the NEPDG.[13] This move marked the GAO's first suit in its history against a high-ranking government official. The GAO contended that taxpayers' dollars were used by the group and, consequently, the GAO had a right to know how those dollars were spent. The White House's position was that it had a right to obtain information and advice on a confidential basis and should not be required to release the documents. A U.S. district court ruled that the Comptroller General had not been harmed by the withholding of information and therefore lacked standing—namely, the right to bring suit.[14] Considerable congressional pressure to not appeal the ruling, including threats of cuts to the GAO budget, may have been influential in the GAO's decision not to appeal *Walker v. Cheney*.

The Trump Administration also refused some GAO requests for information. In 2018, the GAO general counsel Thomas Armstrong requested the House Committee on Oversight and Government Reform to conduct hearings on the refusal of the White House to respond to numerous GAO request for records. Mr. Armstrong wrote:

> Over the past year, GAO has requested information and meetings when preparing reports on topics clearly involving White House interests and expertise. These reports concern such diverse topics as the role of the NSC in the coordination of conflict prevention, mitigation, and stabilization efforts abroad;

Inspector General vacancies; and the cost of presidential travel and related security measures.[15]

The GAO's focus, of course, can change over time as the result of specific congressional direction, or more generally to resonate with the most critical issues of the time. The current Comptroller General, Eugene Dodaro, reflected in his opening statement at his confirmation hearing the criticality of the size of the budget and budget deficits:

It is critical for GAO to provide insights into the government's financial condition and outlook and to seek ways to contribute to a more efficient and fiscally sustainable government. This includes working to help agencies identify and reduce billions of dollars in improper payments; identifying areas of duplication, overlap and fragmentation, as well as other opportunities to save money and enhance revenue; and helping promote more effective financial, information technology, acquisition, and performance management practices that can lead to eliminating wasteful approaches, provide greater efficiency, and ensure better accountability of taxpayer dollars.[16]

Since Dodaro became Comptroller General, much of his testimony before Congress and other public presentations has focused on fiscal sustainability issues, concerned that the federal government "…is on an unsustainable long-term fiscal path."[17]

State and Local Auditors

At the state and local levels, the issue of organizational responsibility for auditing has been resolved in different ways. The alternatives are to have the audit function performed by a unit answerable to the legislative body, to the chief executive, to the citizenry directly, or to some combination of these. The use of an elected auditor is defended on the grounds that objectivity can be achieved

if the auditor is independent of the executive *and* legislative branches. The opposing arguments are that the electorate cannot suitably judge the qualifications of candidates for auditor and that the election process necessarily forces the auditor to become a biased rather than an objective analyst. States primarily use elected and legislative auditors.

Sample Cycle

Figure 4-1 is a sample budget cycle. It is the one used in Pennsylvania, which, like most states, has a fiscal year beginning July 1. As can be seen, preparation begins with budget instructions being issued in August. Pennsylvania also issues Program Policy Guidelines (PPGs), which provide substantive policy guidance to agencies for preparing their budget requests. Submission by the agencies occurs in October, followed by budget office analysis and the governor's review from October through January. In February, the governor submits the budget to the legislature, which deliberates through the spring. The budget is adopted by the legislature by July 1, the beginning of the new fiscal year. Agencies then submit to the budget office what Pennsylvania calls a "rebudget." This is a reworking of their budget requests to reflect what the legislature, approved as distinguished from what the agencies requested. The diagram does not show the audit phase that begins at the end of the fiscal year.

States that operate with biennial budgets—there are 22 of these states—operate with a 24-month cycle. However, only two of those states adopt a single budget for 2 years, North Dakota and Wyoming. The other "biennial budget" states either adopt separate budgets, one for each of the 2 years, or they adopt a 2-year budget and provide for revisions in the second year.[18] North Carolina, for example, adopts a 2-year budget in odd-numbered years during which the legislature meets in full session. In even-numbered years, the legislature meets in a limited purpose, so-called *short session.* By April, in the short session, the governor submits to the legislature recommendations for adjustments necessary for the second

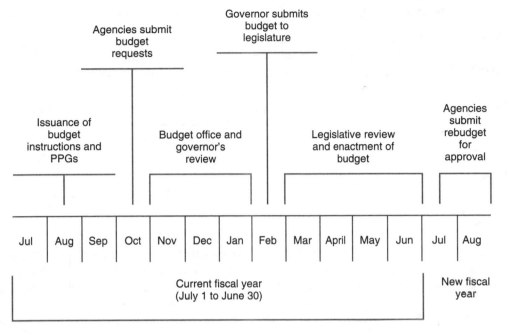

Figure 4-1 Budget Cycle in Pennsylvania.

Pennsylvania Office of the Budget (2019). *The budget process in Pennsylvania*, 7. Harrisburg, PA: Commonwealth of Pennsylvania, retrieved July 4, 2019, from https://www.budget.pa.gov/PublicationsAndReports/Documents /OtherPublications/Budget%20Process%20In%20PA%20-%20Web.pdf

year of the budget. Constitutionally the legislature can deal with only a limited number of issues, primarily making adjustments to the 2-year budget adopted in the previous year.[19]

Scrambled Budget Cycles

Although it is easy to speak of a budget cycle, no single cycle actually exists. Instead, a cycle exists for each budget period, and several cycles are in operation at any given time. The decision-making process does not simply proceed from preparation and submission to approval, execution, and finally audit. Decision making is complicated by the existence of several budget cycles for which information is imperfect and incomplete.

Overlapping Cycles

A pattern of overlapping cycles can be seen in **Figure 4-2**, which shows the sequencing of five budget cycles typical of a large state with an annual budget process. Only cycle 3 in the diagram

displays the complete period covering 39 months. The preparation and submission phase requires at least 9 months, approval 6 months, execution 12 months, and audit 12 months. The same general pattern is found at the federal level, except that the execution phase begins on October 1, giving Congress approximately 8 months to consider the budget. As indicated by the diagram, three or four budget periods are likely to be in progress at any point in time.

Budget preparation is complicated by this scrambling or intermingling of cycles. In the first place, preparation begins perhaps 15 months before the budget is to go into effect. Moreover, much of the preparation phase is completed without knowledge of the legislature's actions in the preceding budget period.

Federal Experience

At the federal level, this problem has proved especially thorny. Congress historically has been slow to pass appropriation bills, and the approval

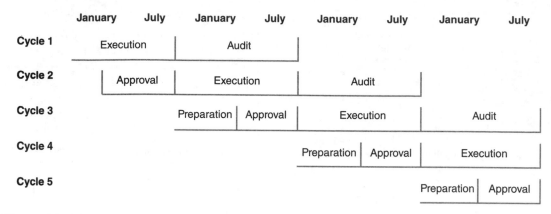

Figure 4-2 Scrambled Budget Cycles.

phase was rarely completed by the start of the fiscal year when it began July 1. The usual procedure was to pass a continuation bill permitting agencies to spend at the rate of the previous year's budget while Congress continued to deliberate on the new year's budget. The budget calendar adopted in the 1970s gave Congress an additional 3 months by moving the start of the fiscal year from July 1 to October 1. That change was expected to permit completion of the approval phase by the new October 1 deadline. However, agencies' preparation problems with the following year's budget request persisted. Congress rarely completes the full budget on time (see chapter on budget approval: the role of the U.S. Congress).

In any given year, an agency begins to prepare its budget request during the spring and summer, even as Congress deliberates on the agency's upcoming budget. Despite the additional time granted to Congress to act on the budget, work on the budget was completed on time in only 3 out of 43 years from FY 1977 through 2019 (1989, 1995, 1997).[20] This obviously compounds the problem of scrambled budget cycles.

Links Between Budget Phases

While a budget is being prepared, another one is being executed. The budget being executed may be for the immediately preceding budget year, but it can also be for the one before. As can be seen in Figure 4-2, in the early stages of preparation

for cycle 4, the execution phase is in operation for cycle 2. Under such conditions, the executive branch may not know the effects of ongoing programs, but is nevertheless required to begin a new budget, recommending changes upward or downward. Sometimes a new program may be created and an agency must then recommend changes in the program for inclusion in the next budget without any opportunity for assessing its merits.

Length of Preparation Phase

The cycle, particularly the preparation phase, may be even longer than indicated above, especially when agencies must rely upon other agencies or subunits for information. For example, in preparing the education component of a state budget, a department of education will require early budget information and requests from state universities and colleges in order to meet deadlines imposed by the governor's budget office. The reliability and validity of data undoubtedly decrease as the lead time increases. Therefore, the earlier these schools submit their budget requests to the state capital, the less likely it is that such requests will be based on accurate assessments of future requirements.

Other Considerations

Besides the factors already mentioned, other issues further complicate budget cycles—most notably, intergovernmental considerations and the timing of budget years.

Intergovernmental Factors

Another problem arises from intermingled budget cycles because the three main levels of government are interdependent. For the federal government, the main problem is assessing needs and finding resources to meet these needs. A state government must assess its needs and those of local governments and must then search for funds by raising state taxes, providing for new forms of taxation by local governments, or obtaining federal revenues. In preparing budgets, governors take into account whatever information is available on the likelihood of certain actions by the president and Congress. For instance, the president may have recommended a large increase in programs to assist states and localities dealing with the opioid crisis by including expenses for health and crime prevention programs. The program, if enacted, might significantly increase funds flowing to the states, but considerable doubt will exist as to whether Congress will accept the recommendation. Alternatively, the president may propose considerable funding increases for border security, including assistance to state agencies, but the likelihood of Congress appropriating the funds may be in real doubt. In such cases, how should a governor shape the health and public safety portions of the state budget? The problem is even worse at the local level, which is dependent on both the state and federal governments for funds.

Budget Years

Budget cycles are further complicated by a lack of uniformity in the budget period. Although most state governments have budget years beginning July 1, four states do not: New York's begins April 1; Texas's begins September 1; and Alabama's and Michigan's begin the same day as the federal fiscal year—October 1.[21] Consistency does not even exist within each state. It is common for a state to begin its fiscal year on July 1 but to have to deal with local governments operating with different start dates, such as January 1, April 1, or September 1.

Annual and Biennial Budgets

Not only is there inconsistency in the date on which budget years begin, but the length of the budget period also varies. Whereas the federal government and most local governments operate under annual budgets, as noted above, 22 states have biennial (2-year) budgets. Such a system violates the principle of annuality.[22] The argument is that annual budgets allow for careful and frequent supervision of the executive by the legislature and that this approach serves to promote greater responsibility in government. The problem with the annual budget, however, is that little breathing time is available. Both the executive and legislative branches are continuously in the throes of budgeting. The biennial approach, on the other hand, relieves participants of many routine budget matters and may allow greater time for more thorough analysis of government activities.

One of the greatest dangers of a biennial system is that it may obstruct—if not prohibit—a prompt response to new conditions. The costs of not being able to adjust to changing conditions may far outweigh any benefits accruing from time saved. This consideration may explain why most of the more populous states are on annual budget systems and why many states with biennial budgets make provision for "reopening" the 2-year budget at midpoint. Many states abandoned biennial budgeting in the latter half of the twentieth century. Only one-half of the forty-four states with biennial budgeting in 1940 still budget for 2 years.[23]

Still another consideration is whether under "normal" conditions sufficient amounts of new information become available to warrant annual systems. If program analysis were a well-established part of the budgetary process, then conceivably, new insights into the operation of programs would continually occur. In such instances, an annual process might be preferable. In other cases, in which decision makers operate one year with virtually the same information as was available the preceding year, there seems to be little need for annual budgets. Partially for this reason, proposals have been made for selectively abandoning the annual budget cycle. Under such a system, new programs or proposed changes in existing programs would be submitted in any given year for legislative review, whereas continuing programs would be reviewed only periodically.

Summary

The four phases of the budget cycle are preparation and submission, approval, execution, and audit and evaluation. In general, the first and third phases are the responsibility of the executive branch, and the second is controlled by the legislative branch. The fourth phase in the federal system is directed by the GAO, which is answerable to Congress and not the president, and a set of agency-based independent auditors known as inspectors general. Auditing at the state and local levels is normally the responsibility of either independently elected officials or officials who report directly to the legislature.

A standard criticism of budgeting, especially at the federal level, is that the budget is seldom considered in its entirety during its preparation phase. Within the executive branch, only the president and his or her immediate staff view the budget as a whole. Agencies are primarily concerned only with their own portions of the total. The same disjointed approach has been characteristic of the approval phase at the federal level. More basically, the budget is rarely adopted in its entirety by the beginning of the fiscal year, requiring a series of continuing appropriations either for some agencies or for the entire federal government.

Budget cycles are intermingled. As many as four budget cycles may be in operation at any time in a single government. This phenomenon complicates decision making. For example, budget preparation is often forced to proceed without knowledge as to what action the legislature will take on the previous year's budget. Moreover, the interdependent nature of the three levels of government contributes to a scrambling of cycles. One possibility would be conversion to biennial budgets, a practice that is common at the state level, although far less common than 50 years ago. It is introduced frequently in proposed reform legislation at the federal level, but the idea has never gained traction.

Notes

1. (Texas) Legislative Budget Board (2020). *About legislative budget board*. Retrieved March 14, 2020, from https://www.lbb.state.tx.us/.
2. Brussels Express (2018). *Fun fact: Belgium owns world record for longest period without a government*. Retrieved July 1, 2019, from https://brussels-express.eu/fun-fact-belgium-owns-world-record-longest-period-without-government/.
3. For additional information and sources on strong-mayor versus weak-mayor systems, see National League of Cities (2019). *Mayoral powers*. Retrieved July 3, 2019, from https://www.nlc.org/mayoral-powers; also, for commission form versus strong- and weak-mayor systems see National League of Cities (2019). *Forms of municipal government*. Retrieved July 3, 2019, from https://www.nlc.org/forms-of-municipal-government.
4. Budget and Accounting Act of 1921. Ch. 18, 42 Stat. 20.
5. National Association of State Budget Officers (2015). *Budget processes in the states* (p. 28). Washington, DC: National Association of State Budget Officers; White, K. V. (2017). *State budget processes: a comparative analysis*. Retrieved July 3, 2019, from https://knowledgecenter.csg.org/kc/content/state-budget-processes-comparative-analysis.
6. National Association of State Budget Officers (2015). *Budget processes in the states*, 28.
7. Wildavsky, A., & Caiden, N. (2004). *The new politics of the budgetary process* (5th ed.). New York, NY: Longman; Anessi-Pessina, et al. (2012). Budgeting and rebudgeting in local governments: Siamese twins? *Public Administration Review*, 72, November/December, 875–884.
8. Congressional Budget and Impoundment Control Act of 1974. P.L. 93-344.
9. National Association of State Budget Officers (2015). *Budget processes in the states*, 41.
10. GAO Human Capital Reform Act of 2004. P.L. 108-271.
11. Tidrick, D. E. (2017). A conversation with U.S. Comptroller General Gene L. Dodaro. *The CPA Journal*, June 2019. Retrieved July 3, 2019, from https://www.cpajournal.com/2017/04/21/conversation-u-s-comptroller-general-gene-l-dodaro/; Mihm, J. C. (2013). *Performance auditing: the experiences of the United States Government Accountability Office*. Washington, DC: U.S. Government Accountability Office.
12. U.S. General Accountability Office (2019). *High Risk List: 2019*. Retrieved January 18, 2020, from https://www.gao.gov/highrisk/overview.
13. U.S. General Accounting Office (2002). *Decision of the Comptroller General concerning NEPDG litigation*. Retrieved February 24, 2012, from http://www.gao.gov/cgdecnepdg.pdf.

14. *Walker v. Cheney* (2002). 230 F. Supp. 2d 51 (D.D.C.).

15. House Committee on Oversight and Government Reform, 115th Congress (2018). *Letter to Committee Chairman Trey Gowdy: May 29, 2018.* Retrieved January 18, 2020, from https://oversight.house.gov/sites/democrats.oversight .house.gov/files/2018-05-29.OGR%20Dems%20to%20 Gowdy%20re%20GAO%20Hearing%20Request.pdf.

16. Dodaro, E. (2010). *Testimony of Eugene L. Dodaro to be comptroller general of the United States U.S. Government Accountability Office.* Retrieved August 15, 2011, from http://www.gao.gov/new.items/testimony_confirmation _hearing2010nov18.pdf.

17. Dodaro, E. (2019). *Testimony before the Senate Committee on the Budget – the nation's fiscal health: actions needed to achieve long-term sustainability*, 2. Washington, DC: U.S. General Accountability Office.

18. Buff, B. (2015). *Annual versus biennial budgeting.* Council for Community and Economic Research. Retrieved July 3, 2019, from http://blog.c2er.org/2015/04/annual-versus -biennial-budgeting/

19. Huaman, J., & McLean, C. (2019). *North Carolina state budget.* Raleigh, NC: North Carolina State Government Publications Collection. Retrieved July 3, 2019, from http://ncgovdocs.org/guides/budget.htm.

20. Desilver, D. (2018). *Congress has long struggled to pass spending bills on time.* Pew Research Center. Retrieved from https:// www.pewresearch.org/fact-tank/2018/01/16/congress -has-long-struggled-to-pass-spending-bills-on-time/.

21. National Association of State Budget Officers (2015). *Budget processes in the states*, 9.

22. Sundelson, J. W. (1935). Budgetary principles. *Political Science Quarterly, 50*, 236–263.

23. Snell, R. K. (2011). *State Experiences with annual and biennial budgeting.* National Conference of State Legislatures. Retrieved July 4, 2019, from http://www.ncsl .org/documents/fiscal/BiennialBudgeting_May2011.pdf.

CHAPTER 5

Budgeting for Revenues: Income Taxes, Payroll Taxes, and Property Taxes

This chapter and the next one describe the principles of taxation and the institutional characteristics of the major revenue sources used by governments. This chapter covers income taxes, payroll taxes, and property taxes while the next one covers sales taxes, user fees, and gambling revenues. The availability of revenues sets the tone for deciding on the level of expenditures and the decision process for allocating expenditures among competing priorities.

Historically, taxation has been a fundamental concern of the citizenry. Citizens may be less concerned about how government spends its money than about how that money is raised to support programs. The property tax bill, federal income tax return, and the water bill are more visible than most of the services citizens receive. The tax bill also almost always seems larger than the value of any individual service, so it is a stark reminder of the cost of government. In developing a budget package, political leaders are always mindful that program initiatives leading to higher expenditures and, therefore, to higher taxes may have negative effects on the possibility of winning reelection to their offices.

This chapter includes two sections. The first section discusses principles of taxation, covering such issues as the adequacy of various revenue sources, equity considerations, economic efficiency concerns, and the ability to collect revenues at a relatively low cost. The second, and longer, section details various revenue sources that rely on income or property as a base, including the individual income tax, the corporate income tax, payroll taxes, and property taxes. The discussion of each of these taxes focuses on such characteristics as their adequacy as a revenue source, their fairness, ease of collection, and so forth and on the mechanics of how the tax base and tax rates are determined.

Principles of Taxation

A chief concern that public officials have for any tax is the extent to which that tax will generate adequate revenue to fund the services provided by the government. The major revenue sources used by governments—income taxes, property taxes, and sales taxes—are used in large part because the number and value of taxable events or the value of the base is so large and therefore has the potential to generate so much income. There are reasons aside from the adequacy of revenue, however, to choose one particular revenue source over another. These can include the equity (or fairness) of the revenue source, the extent to which the revenue source distorts economic choices, the cost of administering the tax, and the political feasibility of particular revenue sources. Few, if any, governments rely on a single source of revenue, and therefore, issues arise over how much any one source should contribute to the total budget of a government.

Adequacy of Revenue

Not all revenue sources have the same potential for growth. In general, as an individual's wealth or income goes up, he or she tends to demand more from government. For this reason, governments normally seek to avoid sources of revenue that do not have the potential to grow as fast as income or wealth. In addition, as noted previously, some sources of revenue can produce large amounts of income for the government, at relatively low rates, because of the sheer size of the tax base. To illustrate these points, consider the federal income tax and taxes on cigarettes. The federal income tax runs off a large tax base, and because of its progressive rate structure, higher levels of income are taxed at higher rates. A tax on cigarettes, on the other hand, runs off a relatively smaller base (sales of cigarettes), and demand for cigarettes does not tend to grow with income. For this reason, the progressive income tax is a much more productive revenue source than the cigarette tax. Taxes on cigarette sales, however, do not generate nearly as much controversy among a majority of voters and therefore may be more attractive to lawmakers.

In addition to the sheer size of the base, it is important for tax policy makers to take into account the potential of the tax base to respond to changes in tax rates. For many taxes, as tax rates increase, they discourage engaging in the taxed activity. Thus, a higher sales tax increases the price of goods (thus possibly decreasing the amount of goods sold), and high marginal income tax rates may encourage some individuals to choose "leisure" over work, at least at the margin.[1] Conversely, where demand for a given good is "inelastic" (that is, where demand does not respond to price), an increase in the tax rate is much less likely to discourage consumption. This tends to be true, for example, of the cigarette tax, because many people are addicted to the good in question. However, there is evidence that higher prices do discourage consumption among some smokers, including young adults age 18 to 24 years.[2] The important implication for the adequacy of revenue is that behavioral responses to taxes must be factored in when doing revenue estimates, lest these estimates overstate the amount of revenue that will be generated for a given tax rate.

Equity

As important a question of how much money is going to be raised from a tax is the question of who will pay that tax. In fact, the question of "who pays" is often the central question of taxation. Consider the debate about the Trump tax cuts enacted in 2017. One of the main debates concerned the extent to which the benefits of the tax reduction would accrue to a greater degree to higher-income individuals. Most independent analyses of the effects of these tax cuts have found that, indeed, higher-income people enjoyed more of a tax reduction than lower- or middle-income households. The Tax Policy Center estimated that the taxpayers in the top quintile would receive a tax cut of about 2.2%, while those in the bottom quintile got only a 0.4% tax cut.[3] Many Democrats who ran for the nomination for president in the 2020 election suggested that their policy proposals (some of which are very costly, such as Medicare for All or free college tuition) should be paid for by raising taxes on higher-income individuals.

There are two general principles of tax equity. The first is the ability to pay principle, which says that the taxpaying capacity of different taxpayers should be taken into account in designing the tax system. The second is the benefit principle, which says there should be some relationship between the benefits received by the taxpayer and taxes paid.

Ability to Pay

Different taxpayers have different levels of income and wealth and, therefore, may have different capacities to bear the cost of financing government.[4] One sense of equity relates to the "ability to pay" principle. A tax should be related to the taxpayer's income or wealth or, more generally, to the taxpayer's ability to pay the tax. A taxpayer who can afford to pay more should pay more. Some consider that equitable. This principle implies that a tax imposes the same loss of utility for each taxpayer or, as economists refer to it, the *equal absolute sacrifice*. Equity has both horizontal and vertical dimensions.

Horizontal Equity

Horizontal equity refers to charging the same amount to different taxpayers whose ability to pay (usually measured by income levels) is the same. If two taxpayers living in the same jurisdiction are the same on relevant dimensions, and they pay different levels of tax, that tax would violate the principle of horizontal equity. That can occur, for example, because the way a tax is administered may erroneously identify two taxpayers as being the same, when in fact they are different. This can be a particular problem for the property tax, because the level of tax paid is usually a direct function of assessed values of property. If two parcels are erroneously valued the same, when in fact one could sell for more on the market, then these two taxpayers are being treated as if they are the same, when they in fact may be quite different. It is important to note that whether two taxpayers are "the same" is frequently in the eye of the beholder. If two taxpayers have the same level of income, for example, but one is supporting a family of five on that income while the other is a single taxpayer, simply differentiating tax paid on the basis of income fails to account for real differences in ability to pay. In this case, a tax that appears to be horizontally equitable may not be at all.

Vertical Equity

While there is nearly universal agreement that horizontal equity should be adhered to, vertical equity is a somewhat harder principle on which to obtain consensus. Put simply, vertical equity has to do with "treating different taxpayers differently." Normally, this implies knowledge of how a given tax affects different people, or income groups, in the society. Vertical equity is normally measured by computing the *effective tax rate*, which is computed by dividing the tax paid by a given individual by some measure of wealth or income. The computation of the effective tax rate can yield conclusions that a given tax, or tax system, is one of the following:

- *Progressive*, if effective tax rates are higher for higher-income taxpayers than for lower-income taxpayers;
- *Proportional*, if effective tax rates are essentially the same across different income categories; or
- *Regressive*, if lower-income taxpayers experience higher effective tax rates than higher-income taxpayers.

Knowing whether a tax is progressive, proportional, or regressive involves knowing more than just the tax rate. For example, a flat rate sales tax on purchases seems to treat all taxpayers equally, but is often actually regressive in that low-income families may spend a greater proportion of their incomes on taxed items than wealthier families do.

Most people would argue for tax systems that are either proportional or progressive. However, even if there is general agreement that a tax system should be progressive (as is generally true for the federal income tax), this does not mean that there is agreement concerning *how* progressive the tax should be. Because debates about progressivity are actually debates about the portion of the tax burden to be borne by different taxpaying groups, the debates are important and can create substantial controversy. In addition to the direct tax burden borne by different taxpayers, some Republicans in Congress have wanted to make the income tax less progressive, arguing that many upper-income taxpayers are "job creators" and that lower tax rates therefore have a positive effect on employment.[5]

Overall, the entire U.S. system of revenue, at the national level, is progressive, but that masks some variation by revenue source. While the federal income tax is quite progressive, the payroll tax (for Social Security and Medicare) is actually regressive, because there is an income ceiling above which Social Security taxes are not paid. In 2019, taxpayers and employers were assessed the payroll tax only on the first $132,900 of payroll income.[6] The revenue system cannot be judged independently of certain government expenditure programs. Transfer payments, such as various forms of aid to low-income families, are somewhat like "negative" taxes in their effect and increase the progressivity of the tax and transfer system considered together.

A Congressional Budget Office (CBO) study compared the average tax rate paid for all federal taxes—individual income, social insurance, corporate income, and excise taxes—in 2016 (before the Tax Cuts and Jobs Act) and projected for 2021 (after that law took effect). It found that the top 1% of income earners paid an overall effective tax rate of 33.3% in 2016, but that this would fall to 30.4% by 2021. Similarly, the average tax rate would fall from 26.8% in 2016 for the group in the 96th through 99th percentiles to 24.8% by 2021, from 23.6% to 22.5% for those in the 91st to 95th percentiles, and from 21.2% to 20.2% for households in the 81st to 90th percentiles. Effective tax rates continue to drop as incomes decline. The average tax rate declined from 17.9% in 2016 to 16.9% in 2021 in the fourth quintile, and from 1.7% in 2016 to less than 1% in 2021 for the lowest quintile.[7] A separate study found that, for the first time in history, the 400 richest families (all billionaires) paid a lower effective tax rate than the bottom 50 percent of taxpayers (what might largely be considered to be the "working class").[8]

Benefit Received

Another concept to keep in mind is that of benefit received. Some revenue is derived from payments by recipients for services rendered or benefits received. User charges or fees are notable examples—for example, municipal parking garage fees, bus fares, and water and sewer charges. People who park in the garage pay for that service. The principle of payment for services

results in an efficient allocation of public sector resources, because people will use only the amount of a particular service for which they are willing to pay. This process is similar to the way in which the private market works—that is, the private market produces no more of those goods than people are willing to purchase.

However, if all government services were paid for by fees, some people would be unable to pay and necessarily would be excluded from the benefits provided by those services. Elementary and secondary education, for example, is the most expensive local government service. If government provided this service entirely by charging parents and students the cost of providing education, many parents would be unable to send their children to school. This situation would lead to segments of the society being uneducated and unable to secure employment that required the ability to read, write, and the like. Because of the *spillover effects* (the fact that lack of education would adversely affect others in the society), many government services cannot be appropriately supported solely through user fees.

In addition, the public supports education for equity reasons. Everyone should have access to at least some level of education regardless of their ability to pay for it. Similarly, public goods have positive *externalities*—that is, they benefit all citizens regardless of whether one actually uses the service. Education, for example, benefits the entire community by making it more attractive to businesses making location decisions, and it benefits the entire economy by increasing the productivity of the workforce. The benefit received principle simply cannot be applied uniformly to all government services.

Moreover, particular taxes may be structured to permit the overall tax system to better adhere to the benefit principle. For example, the state of Florida has a sales tax, but no income tax. This permits substantial taxation of visitors to the state to obtain revenue from individuals who are causing state services to be provided, but might otherwise not pay the cost of any of these services. Tourists would not pay income taxes were the state to have one, yet tourists impose burdens on government services. Therefore, sales taxes help to make tourists pay for the costs they impose. Of course, tourists not only generate costs, but also generate jobs and income for Florida. If the state were to impose what was perceived as an onerous sales tax rate, that might drive tourists away to other states.

The problem of nonresident service provision is also the justification for nonresident income taxes (so-called commuter taxes) in many metropolitan areas, which tax income earned in a jurisdiction, even by nonresidents, as a means of exacting payment from them for services provided. Some major metropolitan areas with a significant population of suburban commuters impose commuter taxes. An important exception is Washington, DC, which has been prohibited by Congress from levying such a tax and is prohibited by the federal courts from imposing such a tax without the approval of Congress.[9]

Economic Efficiency

According to the related concept of efficiency, an efficient tax is one that does not appreciably affect the allocation of resources in the private sector, such as between consumption and saving or among competing items for consumption. Taxes on alcohol, for example, seem to have no appreciable effect on consumption of alcoholic beverages. However, taxes can be used for regulatory purposes, as opposed to purely efficient revenue-raising purposes. Other tax provisions that exclude some items from taxation, such as selected tax deferrals on personal income saved for retirement, are designed to influence behavior and may not be neutral or simply efficient.

Tax systems that are progressive (especially highly progressive) can be inefficient and have unintentional consequences. If tax rates are particularly high for wealthy persons, for instance, then the system may encourage them to spend more time on leisure and less on working and earning more income. In many European countries, that effect—encouraging people to spend more time on leisure and less on purely income-earning activities—might be perceived as a positive outcome of the tax.[10]

Tax system design generally tries to consider both equity and efficiency objectives. Use of taxes to regulate behavior, as in increased tobacco taxes, is generally not considered in the overall design of a tax system, but rather is typically legislated separately. Extensive research has focused on how to consider both principles simultaneously while developing optimal tax structures that are designed to achieve an optimal balance between efficiency and equity objectives.[11]

Cost of Administration

Generally, taxes that are expensive to administer should be avoided. Money spent to collect taxes represents a net loss to society; therefore, the less spent on tax administration, the better. There are a number of specific costs associated with tax collection. Some costs are to the government, some to the taxpayer, and some to an intermediary, such as the shopkeeper who collects the sales tax. The individual income tax, for example, may be relatively cheap for the government to administer (given the level of revenue produced), but it can be quite costly for individuals to comply with all of the specific requirements of reporting income and calculating taxes owed. These high compliance costs occur primarily because of the complexity of the tax system. But this complexity, in part, represents the cost of attempting to promote equity. Most of the allowable deductions and credits for the federal income tax, for example, stem from attempts to adjust the tax to allow for individual taxpayer conditions.

On the other hand, there are taxes where the cost of compliance is relatively low, but the cost of initial collection by the government is high. Consider the case of the local property tax. Because the government is obliged to place a value on properties, it needs to expend substantial resources to identify the amount of taxes required to be paid and to collect those taxes in the first instance.

In addition to the cost of initial collection, there is the separate cost to the government of enforcement. Enforcement tends to be more difficult and costly in cases where the laws and rules surrounding the revenue source are complex, and where the responsibility for initial collection (for determining the amount of tax to be paid) lies with the taxpayer. Thus, the income tax is relatively costly to enforce, while the property tax is much less costly. In the latter case, there is much less room for interpretation by the taxpayer—the amount is not normally in dispute. (See the chapter on budget execution, which includes a section on tax administration that goes into greater detail on particular techniques and issues.)

Political Feasibility

Even taxes that score well on adequacy, equity, efficiency, and ease of administration still may fall short if they cannot be raised in a given political environment. States without an income tax will probably find it almost impossible to enact one, despite whatever other appeals such a tax may have. Tobacco-growing states probably will find it difficult to raise cigarette taxes, while such taxes may be relatively appealing in states that do not grow tobacco. In fact, it is not surprising that there is wide variation in the per-pack tax rates in different states. For example, Missouri taxed cigarettes at 17 cents per pack in 2018; Virginia (a major tobacco growing state that is also home to several cigarette companies) had the next lowest rate at 30 cents per pack. In contrast, New York and Connecticut each taxed them at $4.35 per pack.[12]

Income, Payroll, and Property Taxes

Many of the major revenue sources used by governments are based on income or wealth—property values being the primary wealth that is taxed in the United States to generate revenue. These bases are partially desirable because they are large; a relatively large amount of revenue can be raised at relatively low rates. They are also used because it is easy to adjust the tax to individual taxpayer conditions—that is, those taxpayers with relatively higher incomes have a relatively greater ability to pay taxes. Similarly, taxpayers with a great deal of property wealth may be viewed as having an extraordinary ability to pay, though that

is not necessarily true for the elderly, who may have a valuable residence but after retirement have much less income with which to pay the tax. The major revenue sources in this category are the personal income tax, the corporate income tax, the payroll tax (primarily used for Social Security and Medicare), and the property tax.

The Personal Income Tax

The income tax is a relatively recent, but important, addition to the revenue sources used by governments. Until the passage of the 16th Amendment to the Constitution, ratified in 1913, the taxation of income was not permitted in the United States.[13] Since that time, the income tax has become the most important revenue source for the federal government, in addition to being an important source for many state and local governments. By tradition and for convenience, state and local income taxes tend to operate in a way that is similar to the federal income tax, albeit with substantially different rate structures. This section describes the structure of the federal income tax system, and then discusses briefly the particular characteristics of state and local personal income tax systems. The Tax Cut and Jobs Act (TCJA) of 2017 made major changes in both the individual and corporate income taxes at the national level.

Income taxes, in general, have the following structure:

1. The computation of income (in the case of the federal income tax, *adjusted gross income*, or AGI), which is the initial calculation of the tax base.
2. Reductions to adjusted gross income because of individual taxpayer characteristics. These take the form of *deductions* (standard or itemized) or *exemptions* (for the taxpayer and dependents).
3. The application of *tax rates* (graduated in the case of the federal income tax) to taxable income, which is the result of AGI minus deductions and exemptions.
4. Reductions in the tax paid as a result of *tax credits*, which are dollar-for-dollar reductions in taxes paid.

Computing Adjusted Gross Income

Not all income is taxed. In the case of the federal government, decisions have been made about precisely which types of income should be subject to taxation and which should not. Economists have historically embraced a broad definition of income, called the *Haig-Simons definition*, which defines income as any increase in an individual's potential ability to consume.[14]

This includes some of the income used in the federal definition, including salaries, wages, commissions and tips, dividends, interest, rents, alimony, and unemployment compensation. Excluded from the federal definition, however, are most employee benefits (such as employer-provided health insurance and contributions to pension funds), disability retirement, workers' compensation, food stamps, and interest earned on some state and local bonds.

This arguably advantages people who have more of the excluded income. For example, two individuals whose adjusted gross income is the same may in fact be not equally well off, if one of them is being provided a subsidy by his employer for health insurance and retirement benefits (not counted in adjusted gross income, and therefore not taxed), while the other is not. For this reason, the more sources of income included in the tax base, the more equitable the income tax. When the base excludes sizable segments of income, vigorous debates immediately arise over whether some interests are receiving undue favoritism as a result of legislative lobbying.[15]

Tax codes also provide for adjustments to gross income that typically have the effect of removing portions of income from the base. For example, the federal tax code excludes expenses for moving to accept a new job, some job-related educational expenses, and some employer-paid business reimbursements. The result is that the components of income that are included (above), less these adjustments, becomes the base from which exemptions and deductions are subtracted, or AGI.

Exemptions and Deductions

Individual exemptions and deductions may further reduce the individual income tax base. Exemptions are reductions to the tax base that literally result from one's existence. Historically, the more dependents that a taxpayer claimed on his or her return, the more exemptions, and therefore the greater the dollar amount from exemptions. In 2017, the federal exemption was $4,050 for most taxpayers. This means that a married couple filing jointly could claim $8,100 in exemptions. These exemptions were subject to a phase-out, however, for individuals whose income reached a particular level. The TCJA took that to another level starting in 2018 by eliminating personal exemptions entirely, as a part of a reform that increased the standard deduction (more on this later).

Historically, deductions were even more important than exemptions for many people. This is particularly true, of course, now that exemptions have been eliminated. Each taxpayer is permitted to claim a *standard deduction* without providing any documentation. This standard deduction varies according to the filing status of the taxpayer. In 2017, the standard deduction was $6,350 for a single person and $12,700 for married people filing jointly (regardless of the number of dependents). The TCJA, however, increased the standard deduction significantly (to $12,000 for individuals and $24,000 for married couples), in large part to account for the elimination of the personal exemption.

Itemized deductions are much more complicated. These deductions literally attempt to adjust taxable income to reflect differences in individual taxpayer conditions. As such, they can vary widely from one taxpayer to another, but they also require that the taxpayer maintain supporting evidence for the deduction. Taxpayers itemize their deductions when their totals are greater than the standard deductions. The main itemized deductions include the following:

- *Home mortgage interest*—the interest paid on borrowed funds for a taxpayer's first two properties can be deducted from income. This represents an important subsidy for homeowners and establishes a significant incentive for home ownership. It decreases the progressivity of the federal income tax system, however, as more tax benefits are provided to higher-income individuals, a higher proportion of whom are homeowners.[16]

- *Unreimbursed health expenses*—health care expenses, to the extent that they are not reimbursed, may be deducted from income. An important caveat, however, is that, starting in 2019, only those unreimbursed expenses that exceed 10% of adjusted gross income can be deducted. This means that a taxpayer with an AGI of $100,000, and unreimbursed medical expenses of $11,000, could deduct only $1,000 from taxable income (prior to 2019, the rate had been 7.5% for many years).
- *State and local taxes*—many taxes paid to state and local governments have been exempt from federal taxation. This includes all state and local income and property taxes, and many vehicle licensing and registration fees. Since 2004, it has also included sales taxes paid (an earlier sales tax deduction had been repealed in 1986), but taxpayers are not permitted to deduct both income taxes and sales taxes. Historically, the real property tax and state income taxes have been the taxes most frequently claimed as deductions from federal taxes. Under the TCJA, deductions for state and local taxes were capped at $10,000. This limited substantially the ability of taxpayers from high tax states to deduct taxes. For example, taxpayers from a state with a progressive income tax that also has high property values might find that they were able to deduct either property taxes or income taxes, but not both.
- *Charitable contributions*—payments made by cash or check to recognized nonprofit organizations are deductible. In addition, items donated to such institutions may also be deducted (provided there is evidence of both the donation and its value), as well as miles driven on behalf of a charity. The TCJA did not change the deductibility of charitable contributions, but to the extent that the increases in the standard deduction reduced the number

of taxpayers who itemize deductions, this could have the effect of discouraging (or failing to encourage) charitable contributions. According to the Internal Revenue Service taxpayers claimed $54 billion less in charitable deductions in the 2018 tax year, compared to 2017.[17]

- *Business expenses*—particularly for self-employed individuals, a wide variety of business expenses can be deducted. These include the cost of providing for retirement and health benefits, and even a portion of home mortgage costs provided the taxpayer uses the deducted portion of his home solely for business. Even non-self-employed individuals can deduct a variety of expenses, especially related to unreimbursed job costs and certain entertainment expenses. The Internal Revenue Service (IRS), however, has been relatively vigilant concerning unwarranted business expense deductions.

These exclusions, inclusions, adjustments, and deductions to the income base are intended to yield income figures for individuals and families that further horizontal and vertical tax equity. These factors together are meant to recognize variations in total income and the circumstances involved in earning that income and meeting living expenses. Individuals earning the same income but having different numbers of family members and expenses will be treated differently, while others with unequal gross incomes ultimately may have the same ability to pay when adjustments and deductions are taken into account.

Rate Structure

The vertical equity of the tax system at the federal level is also affected by the use of a progressive rate structure. In 2017, before the TCJA, there were seven tax brackets, which varied from 10% (for the first $18,650 in taxable income for a married couple) to 39.6% (for taxable income in excess of $418,400 for married taxpayers). The TCJA maintained seven tax brackets, but changed the thresholds and tax rates, to 10% (for the first $19,050 for a married couple filing jointly),

12%, 22%, 24%, 32%, 35%, and 37% (for amounts over $600,000 for jointly filing married couples). It is important to note that the nature of the income tax is such that different portions of income are taxed at different rates. Therefore, even someone with taxable income of $1,000,000 will see the first $19,050 of that income taxed at only 10%. This taxpayer would experience each of the tax brackets for various portions of income. **Exhibit 5-1** shows a tax calculation for a hypothetical taxpayer, demonstrating the sequence of taxation, from the calculation of AGI, to taxable income, to tax paid.

Exhibit 5-1 **Example of Computation of the Federal Income Tax in 2018**

John and Bernadette Public are a married couple who file their taxes jointly. They have two dependent children. Their adjusted gross income, consisting of $150,000 in salaries and $20,000 in interest, was $170,000 in 2018. They claim a $1,600 tax credit for the care of their dependent children. They itemize deductions, and have three such deductions in 2018: $25,000 in home mortgage interest, $2,000 in state and local taxes, and $1,000 in charitable contributions. The calculation below shows how they compute their federal income tax liability for 2018.

In calculating the Publics' taxes, we first compute their taxable income. Next, we reduce the taxable income by their itemized deductions (they have chosen to itemize because their itemized deductions exceed the standard deduction) to arrive at taxable income. Tax liability is then computed by applying the tax rates from the tax table below to their taxable income (recall that in doing this, different portions of their income are taxed at different rates). Finally, the tax liability is reduced by the tax credit in order to arrive at the total tax paid.

Step 1: Adjusted Gross Income
Salaries—$150,000
Interest—$20,000
Total AGI—$170,000

Step 2: Taxable Income
Adjusted Gross Income—$170,000
Less: Itemized Deductions—$28,000
Total Taxable Income—$142,000

Step 3: Tax Liability
Total taxable income—$142,000
Calculating tax paid for different components of income:
$19,050 × 0.10 = $1,905
$58,350 × 0.12 = $7,002
$64,600 × 0.22 = $14,212
Total Tax Liability—$23,119

Step 4: Total Tax Paid
Tax Liability—$23,119
Less: Tax Credit—$1,600
Total Tax Paid—$21,519

2018 Tax Table: Married Filing Jointly, 2018		
If Taxable Income Is Over	**But Not Over**	**Marginal Tax Rate Is**
$0	$19,050	10%
$19,051	$77,400	12%
$77,401	$165,000	22%
$165,001	$315,000	24%
$315,001	$400,000	32%
$400,001	$600,000	35%
$600,001	No limit	37%

Some have proposed a flat rate income tax, or alternatively a national sales tax, to replace the existing federal income tax system. Either of these taxes would likely impose relatively high rates in order to replace the revenue from the existing income tax. In addition, both would be less progressive than the current federal system, although research suggests that taxpayers who support such a change do not believe the current system is as progressive as it is, and do not believe that a "reformed" system would be as regressive as it would be.[18]

Tax Credits

Unlike tax deductions, tax credits are dollar-for-dollar reductions in taxes that are applied after all the preceding steps have been completed. Perhaps the largest tax credit is the *earned income tax credit* (EITC), established in 1975. This is a tax credit for the "working poor" and can behave like a *negative income tax*, in that individuals can receive a credit in excess of the tax that they are required to pay. In this case, they receive a check from the government for the amount by which the credit exceeds their liability.[19] Research shows that the EITC is heavily used by low-income individuals because it has been around so long, and because it is effectively targeted to low-income individuals.[20] Other tax credits exist as well. One is for children (provided that the taxpayer's income is less than $400,000 for married taxpayers filing jointly, or $200,000 for single taxpayers; if incomes are greater than that amount, the credit is subject to a phaseout). Another is for child and dependent care expenses (for example, having a caregiver come into your home to care for a child or an aging relative).

The Alternative Minimum Tax

The *alternative minimum tax* (AMT) is a feature of the federal income tax system. First introduced in 1969, its intent is to collect taxes from wealthy individuals who might be able to shelter their income from the regular income tax system.[21] The AMT is literally a shadow income tax system. Taxpayers are required to calculate their taxes in two ways—under the regular tax system and the AMT—and are required, in effect, to pay the higher amount.

The AMT became controversial in recent years because it applied to more and more taxpayers. The CBO estimated that 4 million people paid the AMT in 2009. The AMT expanded its reach for two reasons. First, unlike many of the features of the regular tax system, the parameters of the AMT were not indexed for inflation. Second, because many people experienced reduction in taxes under the regular tax system due to tax cuts enacted in the first decade of the 2000s, they were pushed onto the AMT.[22] Because more people have been affected by the AMT over time, there has been substantial pressure to reform or eliminate the AMT. This is particularly true because more and more taxpayers who do not consider themselves wealthy were nonetheless paying the AMT. For example, until 2000 there was never any

year in which the AMT affected more than 1% of taxpayers. The vast majority of those taxpayers had very high levels of income. The CBO estimated that, without changes to the law, by 2010, 84% of taxpayers with incomes between $100,000 and $200,000 would have paid the AMT.

Despite some pressure to eliminate the AMT, the TCJA did not go this far. Instead, it substantially narrowed its scope by making a number of changes that reduce the odds that a given taxpayer will be required to pay the shadow tax. The new tax law increased the AMT exemptions and raised substantially (to $1 million for joint filers) the level at which those exemptions are phased out. The result of these changes is that, while an estimated 5 million taxpayers paid the AMT in 2017, that number was estimated to drop to only 200,000 in 2018. According to an article in *Forbes* explaining the changes, the reform "returned the AMT to being primarily a millionaire's tax."[23, 24]

State and Local Income Taxes

Most personal income taxes levied by the states and local governments are modeled on the federal tax. The states sometimes use the federal base or a modification of it. Some state income taxes, such as Colorado, Illinois, Indiana, and Pennsylvania, are simply a proportion of the federal tax owed. Most states have some kind of graduated rate structure, although the marginal tax rates are uniformly lower than federal marginal rates. California had the highest marginal tax rate (13.3%) in 2019, while Hawaii had the most tax brackets (12).[25]

When the federal government modifies its tax laws, changes inadvertently occur in state taxes. This happens mainly because states frequently use the federal definition of income (gross income or taxable income) in computing the tax liability of state taxpayers. Because the TCJA broadened the definition of income at the federal level, many states would have experienced a windfall in state tax revenue unless they made changes in state tax law. The Tax Foundation did an analysis of "state tax conformity" and concluded that, in 19 of 22 states for which they had data, the result of the TCJA would have been to increase revenue, absent a responding change by the state to reduce state taxes. In fact, several states—including Arkansas, Georgia, Idaho, Missouri, and Utah—have responded to the federal tax law by adjusting their taxes to offset the federal changes.[26]

Local income taxes tend to be simple to calculate and involve flat, rather than progressive, tax rates.

Indexing

The federal government and some states use indexing in various forms to adjust income taxes in accordance with changes in price levels. If tax brackets are not altered and prices subsequently rise, then inflation will produce higher tax revenues because rising incomes will place citizens in higher tax brackets without any real increase in buying power. Besides adjusting tax brackets, other indexing techniques include modifying the standard deduction. A controversial issue is the measure of inflation used to adjust tax brackets (and many other revenue and expenditure elements). The consumer price index historically has been used, but many now feel that it overstates inflation, causing taxes to be lower than they should be and, more importantly, causing federal benefit programs to extend benefits farther than they should. (See the chapter on government and the economy for further discussion.)

Enforcement

A key income tax issue is enforcement. As noted above, the individual income tax relies heavily on honest self-reporting by taxpayers. Although employers withhold an important proportion of total individual income taxes paid, thereby enforcing tax collection for the IRS, enforcement remains a problem—and an especially difficult problem when taxpayers think the tax is unfair. Much income is never identified and thus never becomes part of the tax base. A large underground economy operates in which transactions occur in trade, payments in kind, and unrecorded payments in cash that never become part of the income tax base. Measuring the size of that invisible economy is naturally difficult, but the World

Bank estimated in 2010 that the "informal sector" for Organization of Economic Cooperation and Development (OECD) countries was 16.6% of gross domestic product (GDP).[27] According to this same study, for the United States, income equal to an estimated 8.4% of GDP is unrecorded and therefore untaxed. Clearly the role of the informal sector is increasing with the rise of the "gig economy"; a later study estimated that almost one-fourth of adults in the U.S. earn their income in this informal sector.[28] In addition to this unrecorded income, the U.S. income tax relies heavily on self-reporting, which may also contribute to an exaggeration of deductions, which also has the effect of reducing the tax collected. The informal sector is likely even larger in emerging-market and developing economies; a more recent study estimated that it accounted for about one-third of the economy and 70% of employment in these countries.[29] The last estimates of the "tax gap" from the IRS estimated that 1 out of every 6 dollars owed in federal income taxes was not collected. There are particular categories of income that are more likely to escape taxation, including farm income (underreported by an estimated 71%) and rents and royalties (underreporting by more than 60%).[30] In 2016, the IRS estimated that the gap was $458 billion for the 2008–2010 period, and that the voluntary compliance rate had dropped from 83.1% in their previous (2006) study to 81.7% in the 2016 study.[31]

Tax Expenditures

Revenues that could be, but are not, collected constitute tax expenditures and can aid or hinder attempts to achieve an optimal balance. According to federal law, tax expenditures are "revenue losses … which allow a special exclusion, exemption, or deduction from gross income or which provide a special credit, a preferential rate of tax, or a deferral of tax liability."[32]

Tax expenditures are not new. Home mortgage interest payments (now up to two homes) have been deductible from income since 1910, for example. While tax expenditures may exist for any tax, the individual income tax, at the national and state levels, includes by far the largest number of tax expenditures, primarily because of the significant number of permitted deductions from gross income. Numerous exemptions from taxation or deductions from income for corporations have crept into law over the years as well.[33]

The largest income tax expenditures in the federal budget (with estimates of fiscal year 2019 revenue losses) are the exclusion of employer contributions for medical insurance ($203 billion), the exclusion of net imputed rental income ($121 billion), capital gains exclusions ($103 billion), contributions to 401(k) plans ($76 billion), and certain defined benefit employer plans ($71 billion). Together, these five income tax expenditures were estimated to cost the federal government almost $600 billion in 2019.[34]

Tax expenditures are not automatically bad. The public policy goal for the home mortgage interest deduction and the exclusion of imputed rent from income is to encourage and enable individual family home ownership. Exclusion of employer pension and medical insurance contributions is meant to increase savings for pensions and reduce the cost of health care. The housing exemption may help make housing affordable to moderate-income families, but it also benefits more affluent taxpayers and may be of no benefit to low-income families. Is the housing exemption, then, a factor that furthers or detracts from equity? Given the wave of foreclosures that followed the Great Recession, there is also some reason to believe that the mortgage interest deduction, along with other policies that reduced the cost of housing, encouraged people who could not afford homes to buy them.

Since the 1970s, tax expenditures have become an important issue in debates over tax reform. These measures reduce the revenue flowing into government treasuries and can represent "loopholes" for the wealthy. Increasingly, policy makers and analysts also recognize that these tax expenditures represent an alternative form in which to confer benefits to citizens. That is, if the goal of a program is to encourage affordable housing, there is no difference between sending a potential developer a check for $50,000 or giving the same developer a $50,000 tax break. Benefits conferred on the spending side, however, tend to be much more transparent than those provided through the tax code. One of the effects of the broadening of the tax base under the TCJA was to reduce the cost of some tax expenditures. For example, the home mortgage interest deduction, which cost almost $100 billion in fiscal year 2012, is estimated to cost only $27 billion in fiscal year 2019, presumably because the expansion of the standard deduction has resulted in many fewer taxpayers choosing to itemize deductions.

Like the federal government, some state governments routinely report estimates of tax expenditures as a part of their budgets.

Corporate Income Taxes

Taxes on corporate earnings have been defended as appropriate given the size of corporate economic power and the fact that some individuals might be able to escape taxation by "hiding" their income in corporations. On the other hand, corporate income taxes seem to result in double taxation. First a corporation is taxed, and then individuals are taxed on dividends paid on their corporate stock holdings. There have been proposals to replace the corporate income tax with a tax on net business receipts to avoid this double taxation, but these proposals have not attracted much interest. Proposals to exclude dividends from individual income taxation also have been unsuccessful.

Tax Base

Corporate taxes use net corporate earnings as a base. Whereas the individual income tax base basically considers income before expenses, except for some deductions and exclusions, corporate income taxes apply only to net profit after operating expenses. In addition, some deductions are allowed for capital losses, operating losses, depreciation of capital investments, charitable contributions, and expenditures for research and development. How these deductions are applied is often controversial, such as how rapidly a corporation can depreciate capital investments. The federal corporate tax rate, prior to the TCJA, was graduated (ranging from 15% to 35% as net earnings increase) but the new tax law changed this to one flat rate of 21%, regardless of net earnings.

As a percentage of GDP, receipts from the federal corporate income tax at 2.0% are actually substantially lower than the average of other OECD countries, which average 2.9% of GDP from corporate taxes.[35] Measured differently, however, the U.S. federal government before TJCA had one of the highest corporate tax rates when measured as total corporate taxes paid as a percentage of corporate income, third behind only Argentina and Indonesia.[36] Many states have corporate income taxes as well, although the importance of the corporate income tax has declined at the state level in recent years. In 2018, corporate income taxes accounted for approximately 5% of overall state revenues, about one-half of the level of two decades earlier.[37] In 2017, including both national and state/local government corporate taxes, the United States corporate tax rates, at 38.9%, were the fourth highest in the world; only the United Arab Emirates, Comoros, and Puerto Rico (for the purpose of the study, considered separately even though it is a U.S. territory) had higher rates.[38]

The relatively high rate of corporate taxation in the United States contributed to a desire by President Trump and Republicans in Congress to reduce the corporate income tax rate as a part of the tax reform enacted in 2017. The following changes, affecting business taxation, were included in the TCJA:[39]

- The TCJA reduced the top corporate rate from 35% and created a flat rate of 21%, bringing the United States to 17th out of 36 OECD countries in 2019. Coupled with the average of state corporate rates, the United States dropped to 24th among the 36 OECD countries with a combined federal plus subnational rate of 25.9%.[40]
- Businesses were permitted to deduct the full cost of qualified new investments in the year in which those investments are made, for the first 5 years under the new law. This so-called "bonus depreciation" is reduced in 20% increments starting in 2023, and it is fully eliminated by 2026.

- The law doubled the small business expensing limit, such as for capital investments, from $500,000 to $1,000,000.
- The TCJA limited the net interest that businesses can deduct to 30% of business income before interest, depreciation, and amortization. Previously, interest paid was fully deductible.
- The corporate AMT was repealed.
- Pass-through businesses, whose income is subject to the individual income tax, are permitted to deduct 20% of their qualified business income, lowering the effective top marginal tax rate from 37% to 29.6%.

All but five states have corporate income taxes, which are levied in addition to the federal corporate tax. For the states with such a tax, the rates range from a low of 3% (North Carolina) to 12% (Iowa). In 2018, the average state corporate income tax rate was 6%.[41]

The primary issue as regards corporate taxation is who actually carries the burden of corporate taxes, or the incidence of the tax. Corporations may be able to increase prices and, in effect, make consumers pay the tax, or they may limit wage increases to workers and, in effect, have them pay the tax. Another option is to take taxes out of profits, thereby reducing dividends for investors. Corporations probably use some combination of these shifts.

An issue involving state corporate taxes is whether they affect decisions to locate and expand operations in one state over another. Legislators and executives in a state government fear that any increase in their corporate income taxes will discourage corporations from locating in the state and encourage others to move out of the state. The expectation is that what a state loses in tax revenue, it will gain from companies already there expanding their operations in the state and from companies relocating to the state. *Corporate inversion*, in which American companies move overseas to avoid taxes, is an important political issue.[42] The Trump administration claimed that tax incentives changed so that American companies that had moved jobs overseas were bringing them back to the United States.[43]

Payroll Taxes

Insurance trust funds, which are separate accounts set up to hold certain earmarked revenues, are financed by means of charges on salaries and wages (the charges are paid by employees, employers, or both). These are typically referred to as payroll taxes, and they are differentiated from income taxes because they are taxes on wages and salaries only, as opposed to more comprehensive taxes on income. These charges are not general taxes inasmuch as they do not generate revenue to be used to pay for a range of services allocated in the budget process; instead, the taxes are earmarked to pay for the particular benefits to the people who are covered by these programs. Employers and employees pay into these systems, and people earn benefit credits through contributions made during their working careers.

As of 2019, the full rate paid for Social Security taxes was 12.4%, and for Medicare taxes it was 2.9%. Each of these was equally divided between employees and employers (self-employed individuals pay the full amount). In the case of Social Security taxes, however, there is a ceiling above which the taxes are not collected; in 2019, that ceiling meant that these taxes were only collected on the first $132,900 of payroll income. This means that while Social Security taxes appear to be proportional, they are in reality regressive taxes, in the sense that higher-income taxpayers above the threshold pay a lower effective tax rate.

Social Security and Supplemental Security Income

Social Security is a program of vast proportions. Its complexities far exceed the scope of this text. Here we sketch its overall structure.

Three major programs are administered directly by the Social Security Administration. The first, Old Age and Survivors Insurance (OASI), is a benefits program for retired workers and their survivors. The second program, Social Security Disability Insurance (SSDI), provides benefits for covered workers who are disabled and cannot work. In 2017, the Social Security Administration paid out benefits to 61.9 million individuals, including 42.4 million retired workers; 8.7 million disabled workers; and 9.8 million spouses, children, or survivors of retired, deceased, or disabled workers. In fiscal year 2010, benefits paid out for OASI benefits totaled $798.7 billion. Total benefits for SSDI in the same year totaled $142.8 billion.[44]

The third major program under Social Security provides monthly benefits to people who are aged, blind, and disabled. This program is known as Supplemental Security Income (SSI).[39] SSI funds come from general tax revenues, rather than from employer-employee contributions. Unlike SSDI, SSI does not require work credits for eligibility but does require that recipients be needy. It is possible to qualify for both programs, although qualifying for SSDI has the effect of reducing SSI benefits. In 2017, 8.2 million people received $54.5 billion in benefits under the SSI program.[45]

For some time, various analysts have projected that the point would come when Social Security benefit outlays would exceed payroll taxes in the trust fund. That time has come. In fiscal year 2018, outlays from the OASI Trust Fund exceeded income to the fund by $101 billion, meaning that the balance in the trust fund began to decline. In fact, the OASI trust fund is projected to be in deficit every year from 2019 to 2029, regardless of whether the calculation included interest to the fund (cumulative deficits of $1.8 trillion) or excludes these interest payments (cumulative deficits of $2.5 trillion). The SSDI Trust Fund is also projected to be in deficit over this same period, to the tune of $133 billion (including interest) or $149 billion (excluding interest).[46] The CBO estimates that the OASI Trust Fund will be exhausted in 2032 (the Social Security Administration puts that date at 2034); the SSDI Trust Fund will be exhausted even sooner, in 2028.[47] After the trust funds are exhausted, unless there is an additional infusion of funds into the trust funds, such as an annual appropriation that would be over and above collections, Social Security will be able to pay only a percentage (around 75%) of the full amount of current projected benefits.[48] Such a change would inevitably create a political crisis of overwhelming magnitude.

Several issues have fueled the debate over Social Security reform, and the motivations for reform among many groups are not necessarily consistent. First is the issue we might label "violation of trust." This issue is based on a misunderstanding in some circles concerning the nature of the Social Security trust funds. Many citizens assume that the funds they and their employers contribute to the system are being held in trust, invested much like pension funds to yield the benefits that will be paid out to them in the future. Politicians make a similar claim in their criticisms of Social Security. In reality, each year's payments into the Social Security Trust Fund are used to pay claims to beneficiaries in that year. Until recently, the payments into the fund exceeded payments to beneficiaries out of the fund. Those excess payments created a surplus in the fund, and that surplus, in turn, has been lent to the U.S. Treasury at the equivalent of the 30-year Treasury bond to finance part of other federal spending. The alternative to the Treasury borrowing from the Social Security fund is to force the Treasury to borrow from the U.S. and overseas capital markets (see the chapter on government and the economy). Under such a scheme, the surplus Social Security funds would need to be invested rather than sit idle—perhaps in the stock market (discussed below).

Thus, one motivation for reform is the political point of view that the fund should behave as a revolving fund, with proceeds paid into the fund being invested, as in most pension funds. That view somewhat naively assumes that private pension funds pay out benefits commensurate with the results of investment of funds paid in. That statement is true of defined contribution plans (retirement plans where individuals pay a set amount into a retirement plan, but are not guaranteed a specific return), but defined benefit plans pay out specific levels of benefits regardless of whether the fund investments are sufficient to meet those benefit payouts. Just as an employer with a defined benefits pension fund is obligated to meet the benefit payouts defined in the plan, from business net profits if necessary, so the federal government is obligated to meet whatever Congress determines will be the benefit structure, first from the Trust Fund itself and then from other federal revenues as necessary. Unless Congress fails to appropriate funds to meet legislated benefits (if and when the surplus in the fund turns into a deficit) or passes legislation so as to lower benefits, then the Trust Fund issue really is not an issue. Instead, it is a convenient political football for both parties to kick around.

A second motivation for reform is closely linked to the debates on the federal budget surplus or deficit. To the extent that the fund showed a surplus, and all revenue to the fund counted as part of the federal government's revenue total, the size of the federal deficit was lower than if Social Security figures were excluded. Critics have argued that such a practice represents a nontransparent imposition of taxes, as tax payments that were advertised as supporting Social Security are, at least in the short run, used to finance other government spending. While this was true historically (at least since a 1983 reform designed to infuse the trust funds with more revenue in anticipation of the retirement of the baby boomers), the CBO estimates that 2018 is the last year in which there are surpluses in the so-called "off budget" funds that reduce the size of the unified deficit. Starting in 2019, and continuing for the foreseeable future, there are both "on budget" deficits and "off budget" deficits.

A third issue discussed by advocates for reform is that the funds being paid into Social Security should be earning more than the implicit 30-year Treasury bond rate. The bull market of the 1990s particularly fueled this aspect of the debate, as stocks earned dramatic returns—two and three times the rate of the 30-year Treasury bond. Proposals have been advanced to invest the funds flowing into the trust fund in the stock market, so as to earn higher benefits for future pensioners. This notion lost a lot of traction since the recession of 2007 to 2009; the volatility of the U.S. stock market makes one think twice when it comes to the investment of Social Security assets in riskier equities than U.S. Treasury securities.

Medicare

Medicare, the largest federal health insurance program, is administered by the Centers for Medicare and Medicaid Services (CMS) in the Department of Health and Human Services. Medicare provides basic health insurance to the elderly, with a separately funded catastrophic coverage component, and is funded by payroll tax contributions, premiums paid by persons covered under the program, and general revenues. Medicare also covers people on SSDI once they have been receiving SSDI benefits for 24 months; these beneficiaries are younger than age 65 years.

Medicare has become one of the major contributors to rapidly rising federal expenditures for health care. Medicare outlays totaled more than $700 billion in fiscal year 2018.[49] In 2002, Congress and the George W. Bush administration passed the Medicare Modernization Act, which established, for the first time, a prescription drug benefit for Medicare that took effect in 2006. Estimates of the 10-year cost of this entitlement expansion ranged from $400 billion to $500 billion, although subsequent estimates suggested that this original cost assumption was overstated.[50]

The combination of the same demographic factors that are driving the Social Security imbalance and the pace of medical care inflation contribute to an even bleaker long-term outlook for Medicare than for Social Security. In fiscal year 2018, the two Medicare trust funds combined had a surplus of $33 billion, consisting of a surplus of $28 billion in the Supplementary Medical Insurance (Part B) fund and a surplus of $5 billion in the Hospital Insurance (Part A) fund. Part A covers hospitalization, and Part B covers medical care such as doctor visits and laboratory tests. People eligible for Part A due to having paid into the system for ten years, receive benefits without any monthly fee. Part B had a monthly premium of $144.60 for most beneficiaries in 2020. The surplus situation was expected to turn around by fiscal year 2020, when the surpluses would no longer exist, and cumulative deficits were projected to be $546 billion between 2020 and 2029, almost entirely driven by deficits in the Part A fund.[51]

Reform proposals have been especially aimed at reducing the incentives for physicians and hospitals to order expensive treatments for Medicare patients and to reduce the possibilities for fraudulent charges. Holding down reimbursement rates slowed the slide toward a Medicare deficit, and on the agenda for longer-term reform is moving more people into managed care organizations and away from individual physicians. A couple of controversial reform proposals have surfaced in recent years. On one end of the spectrum was the reform suggested by Congressman Paul Ryan (R-WI), as part of the House budget resolution in 2011. The Ryan plan would have created a cap on the amount that the federal government could spend on each beneficiary. Spending over the amount of the cap would be the responsibility of the consumer. This proposed change would have fundamentally altered Medicare and shifted much of the financial risk to beneficiaries. In addition, the House budget resolution considered in 2011 advocated increasing the Medicare eligibility age from 65 to 67 years, beginning in 2022.[52]

At the other end of the continuum is a proposal referred to as "Medicare for All," which in reality is a proposal for a government-run health care system that would guarantee coverage for all Americans. (The Patient Protection and Affordable Care Act of 2010, or Obamacare, had expanded insurance coverage, but still left 27 million Americans without insurance.[53]) The Medicare for All proposal was most closely identified with the Presidential campaigns of Senator Elizabeth Warren (D-MA) and Senator Bernie Sanders (I-VT) but was embraced by several other candidates. While there were no official estimates of the cost of this plan, there is no question that it would substantially increase federal costs for health care, even as it might be able to lower societal health care costs.

The second-largest federal health program, but one that is not funded by the payroll tax, is Medicaid. Medicaid is a federal–state matching grant program to insure the categorically needy, those who meet various eligibility criteria defined in legislation. Most of the program funding comes from federal grants to the states, as opposed to payroll taxes. (See the chapter on intergovernmental relations for discussion of the Medicaid program.)

Unemployment Insurance

The second largest insurance trust for state governments is Unemployment Insurance (UI). This program is administered by the states within a framework imposed by the federal government. A floor on benefits is set nationally, with states having the option of exceeding the floor. The program is supported by payroll taxes paid mainly by employers, although in a few states employees are required to make supplementary payments. It is expected to generate sufficient revenues during prosperous periods to cover payments to unemployed workers during recessionary periods. State programs can sometimes run into a deficit situation, such as during a sustained recession or occasionally because of temporary timing differences between payments into the funds and payments out. In such cases, the federal government lends money to the states, but expects repayment with interest. Obviously, a state with a declining tax base can face severe problems in financing its UI program. In addition, a sustained period of unemployment will deplete state resources and will typically require the federal government to step in and extend unemployment benefits beyond the regular UI benefits. In fact, during the Great Recession, state governments had to borrow $42 billion from the federal Treasury just to finance their UI costs.[54] At the end of 2011, states still owed the federal government $40 billion, but various state actions (along with a strong economy) resulted in a substantial turnaround, with net reserves of $36 billion as of June 2016.[55]

Workers' Compensation

Another important insurance trust at the state level is workers' compensation, which provides cash benefits to persons who, because of job-related injuries and illnesses, are unable to work. Accidents at work may disable people temporarily or permanently. Poor working conditions can cause physical and mental health problems. In addition to cash benefits, the program pays for medical care and rehabilitation services.

Property Taxes

Taxes on wealth are based on accumulated value in some asset rather than on current earnings from the asset. Real and personal property, financial assets, and equipment are important types of wealth that sometimes are subject to taxation. The wealth tax that is most important in the eyes of taxpayers, however, is the real property or real estate tax. The property tax is the one most reviled by taxpayers, largely because it is regarded by many as the most unfair.[56]

This tax is the almost exclusive domain of local governments. Despite forecasts of its demise, the property tax remains the largest single own-source generator of revenue for local governments (it is exceeded only by intergovernmental revenue), although it has declined in recent years relative to other state and local taxes.

According to the National Center for Education Statistics, the property tax funded 81% of locally raised school district revenues in the 2015/16 fiscal year. The highest levels were in Connecticut (98%) and Rhode Island (97%). Local school districts also receive substantial intergovernmental revenues (see the chapter on intergovernmental relations), which reduced their reliance on local property taxes. The national average in terms of total school district revenues from property taxes was 36%, from a high of 60% in Illinois to virtually zero in Vermont and Hawaii.[57] Since 1973, when the Supreme Court declined to impose a federal remedy for school financing inequities, the state courts have been the locus of legislation challenging school financing, with cases filed in 45 of the 50 states.[58] The argument is that despite state aid to local school districts, almost sole reliance on the property tax to finance education at the local level means unequal education opportunities across the state. The property tax is also the most important source of local own-source revenue for funding urban services in developing countries, although user charges have been described as a faster growing source of local revenue in the more prosperous emerging-market economies.[59] (See the chapter on budgeting for transaction-based revenues.)

There are two main justifications for using the property tax as the major revenue source for local government. The first is that the services provided by local government supposedly increase the economic value of one's property. It is widely thought that people select their place of residence based on the quality of local schools and other public services. In high-quality service jurisdictions, housing costs are typically higher, reflecting higher costs for delivering services and higher expectations of home buyers for quality services. Property taxes make possible higher-quality services at the local level. The argument goes as follows: If more general taxes, such as the sales tax, were used to finance services that benefit property owners, then property owners would be less aware of the costs of those services and therefore insist on more and higher-quality services. Evidence has been found to support this argument in developing countries, where demand for urban services is much higher in cities that do not use property and other local taxes and charges to finance those services.[60]

Second, because the property tax is less susceptible to tax avoidance than other broad-based taxes, it represents an appropriate charge for local public services. Property is clearly visible and is immobile. People can buy goods in other jurisdictions or order goods over the Internet and easily avoid paying sales tax. Property taxes, by comparison, are difficult to avoid. To the extent that they operate as a quasi-price for the public services provided in a given jurisdiction, property taxes are justified on the basis of the benefit principle, as described previously. An argument providing evidence for that view is that homeowners understand that the value of local public services substantially affects the value of their homes, and that they are vigilant in their control of local government largely for that reason.[61]

One way to tie the benefits of services affecting property values to taxes on property is through *tax increment financing* (TIF—see the chapter on capital finance and debt management for discussion of bond issues backed by expected tax incremental increases). Tax increment financing has been used in redevelopment of inner cities to capitalize on the economic and financial gains that stem from a major rehabilitation project for a contiguous area usually characterized by urban blight and abandoned properties. Prior to city government action, many property owners in such areas derive no benefits from their properties, and the city is able to collect little or no property tax. A redevelopment project changes conditions so that the property in the redeveloped area attains new value, and the property tax gains from that new value are set aside to pay for financing the redevelopment. Some use also has been made of tax increment financing in rural areas, but it is not as valuable a tool there. Property tax rates are typically much lower in rural areas, land values are more volatile, and investors in bonds to support rural infrastructure with tax increment–funded projects perceive higher risks.[62] Despite the substantial use of TIF, a 2018 study suggests that there is little evidence that the tool actually improves economic development.[63]

The main policy issue with the property tax is that it tends to be regressive. Higher-income taxpayers tend to have a larger proportion of their wealth in assets that are not subject to the property tax. As a consequence, these taxpayers generally pay a disproportionately lower property tax (as a percentage of their income) as compared with middle- and lower-income taxpayers, whose only major asset may be their homes. For middle- and lower-income taxpayers, most of their wealth is being taxed each year. For renters, the regressive effects of the property tax depend on the extent to which the landlord can pass on the property tax through the rent that is charged for the property. For all these reasons, the regressive nature of the property tax fuels controversy. In addition, the property tax is relatively complicated to implement and to maintain. Because the local jurisdiction must establish the tax base (the value of each property within the jurisdiction) rather than basing it on some external objective source, updating the tax base for the property tax is always controversial when carried out.

Tax Base

The base of the real property tax is the assessed value of the land and any improvements on it, such as homes, factories, and other structures. The goal is to establish a value that is equivalent to what the property would sell for if placed on the market.

An issue often arises with the property tax because while assessed values are intended to reflect market values, most homeowners do NOT sell their property in a given year, but still must come up with the resources to pay the tax. In situations where the assessed value of property (and therefore, the tax that is required to be paid) may increase beyond the ability of taxpayers to afford the tax bills, a given taxpayer may be "property rich, but income poor." There may be a period of rapidly rising property values, and long-time, possibly retired, residents (who might not be able to afford to buy their houses in the current market) experience ever-increasing tax bills whether or not their incomes rise sufficiently to pay the increasing taxes. An example is the neighborhood surrounding the long-abandoned Michigan Central train station in Detroit, which was purchased in 2018 by Ford Motor Company and is being renovated for a future campus for new vehicle technology. Property sales jumped from an average of $35,000 in 2008 to $250,000 in 2018.[64]

Many states and localities have instituted *homestead exemptions* to address this sort of problem. Under these exemptions, a set initial amount is excluded from assessed valuation. This would tend to benefit those individuals with homes that have lower assessed values, since a higher percentage of the assessed value would be exempt from the property tax for those properties.

Farmland is often valued using a different method than residential property or other land. Frequently this method attempts to determine the income stream generated by that farmland.[65] A specific issue, however, is how to deal with farmland in metropolitan areas. As metropolitan areas expand and encroach upon farming areas, the value of the land increases even though the use remains unchanged. Situations emerge in which taxes rise beyond what farmers can afford and create a market incentive for the land to be sold and subdivided for homes and other development. All states provide some form of protection for farmland as a means of preserving rural land and discouraging urban sprawl, with reduced tax assessments for farming and other undeveloped land being the most common method. Often these tax breaks are really postponements. If the land is later sold for subdivision and housing at a value much higher than the land's worth as farmland, the seller must then pay back property taxes reflecting the residential use tax rate. While such exemptions often have the intended effects of protecting farmers from rapidly escalating property tax bills at the same time that crop prices and demands for agricultural products are declining, they can also encourage some close-in residents to establish "fake farms" for the purpose of lowering their tax bills.[66]

Many properties are completely tax exempt in the United States. Federal and state land is normally exempt from local property taxes, for example, although these jurisdictions may make payments in lieu of taxation. Places of worship, such as churches, synagogues, and mosques, are tax exempt, as are most parsonages and other related properties. Nonprofit hospitals, YMCAs and YWCAs, nonprofit cemeteries, and the like are usually tax exempt as well.

When tax-exempt properties account for a large proportion of a jurisdiction's potential tax base, the effects of tax exemption can be severe. Some governments have aggressively challenged the tax-exempt status of some nonprofit organizations. The basis for the challenge is that some nonprofit organizations produce for-profit goods and services. Federal law, in fact, permits nonprofits to engage in commercial, fee-generating activity. In order to maintain its federal tax-exempt status, however, the fees generated must directly or indirectly be related to the charitable purpose of the organization. State and local governments, however, have their own standards as it relates to property tax exemptions. Some states and localities, for example, prohibit any commercial activity for a nonprofit to maintain its property tax exemption. In this context, so-called social entrepreneurship institutions, which blur the line between nonprofit and for-profit, have been the target of efforts to attack the property tax exemption. Generally, the rules governing property tax exemptions at the state and local level have relied on factors related to ownership (the owner must use the property for an exempt purpose) and use (that use must be for a noncommercial purpose).[67]

A different situation may exist in cases where state governments grant blanket local property tax exemptions. In this case, the state government makes decisions that cost local governments money, and these exemptions may not be directly targeted toward those individuals that most need tax relief. In many such instances, the lost local property tax revenue is replaced by the state government. A study of a homestead exemption program in New York State suggests that local governments are less efficient in the provision of local public services because those services are funded to a lesser extent by local taxes than by state assistance. The argument here is that, to the extent that state taxes are financing these services, this reduces pressure on local officials to cut back on costs to provide a given level of output.[68]

Assessment

After registering all properties in the taxing jurisdiction, the first major step to generating revenue from the tax is to assess the value of the properties. Local governments do not, in fact, have a direct way of measuring the actual market value of all properties in their jurisdiction. At any given time, the local government can know directly what recent properties have sold for, but this is only a small fraction of all the properties in the registered base. This creates a substantial challenge, in that they need to establish an assessed value for each property absent real information on the sales price of most properties.

Many governments use the *market data approach* to assessment. In this method, properties that have not sold are assessed by comparison to similar properties where a market price can be observed. The greatest challenge here is ensuring that properties that are assumed to be comparable are comparable in fact. The probability of doing

this can be improved by inspecting individual properties and cataloguing their characteristics, but this is a time-consuming process, particularly if done on an annual basis. Adjustments to property values may be done annually or only once every several years. An interesting recent development is that online real estate companies, such as Zillow, now estimate the level of property tax likely to be paid on a given property, in addition to monthly mortgage payments.[69]

While the goal in many jurisdictions is to assess each property at its full market value, in practice many jurisdictions assess parcels at a percentage or fraction of the full market value. The ratio of the assessed value to the market value is known as the *assessment ratio*. A home whose market value is $120,000 would be assessed at only $24,000 if the assessment ratio were 20%. In practice, it should make no difference whether the full value or a fraction of it is used. Fractional assessment simply requires a higher tax rate than market value assessment to produce the same revenue.

Taxpayers may find some psychological solace in fractional assessment, but problems arise in cases where properties within the same jurisdiction are assessed at different fractions of their market values. This occurs, for example, if reassessments are done on different properties at different times. If some properties are assessed at one percentage of market value and other properties at a different percentage, then the tax burden is no longer proportionate to the value of the property. This is less likely to be an issue where properties are assessed at 100% of market value, particularly because taxpayers are much more likely to know whether their property has been overassessed in this case. Even where the goal is assessing at full market value, fractional assessment may be used to differentiate types of properties. For example, rural property may be assessed at a lower fraction than highly developed property.

Inaccurate and inconsistent assessment practices can cause problems of both horizontal and vertical equity. Horizontal equity problems exist when properties that have the same market value are assessed at different rates, resulting in a situation where taxpayers who should be paying the same level of tax are paying different levels. Numerous studies have found evidence of horizontal inequity because of lack of data, assessor error, or bias.[70] Vertical equity concerns exist when properties of different market values are assessed at different percentages of those market values. A study found that, in particular, lower-valued houses were assessed at closer to their full market value than higher-valued houses. This means that less-affluent taxpayers pay a higher percentage of local property taxes than would be the case were all properties valued at the same percentage of full market value.[71]

For a local government instituting the property tax for the first time, the valuation process is almost overwhelming. Traditional valuation procedures involve comprehensive tax mapping to locate every property. An assessor must visit each property, measuring the foundation to determine square footage, noting construction details, and recording information about the condition of the structure.

For most jurisdictions in the United States, properties have been constructed under building permits that require supplying information about construction details to the local jurisdiction. Periodic inspections of the properties when under construction, conducted by local code enforcement officers or building inspectors, provide additional information. A database, then, can be devised using existing building records and information about sales of properties when deeds are transferred. As new structures are built, they can be added to the database.

Exhibit 5-2 shows a property tax valuation system in Orange County, North Carolina, that is considered a model for the country. Techniques

records and tax administration system to administer the local property tax.

It is fully computerized and includes diverse information about each property in the county. Besides information about the location of each lot, the size of the structure, and the number of baths, a drawing of the lot and the location of the structure on it are included in the computerized file and can be displayed onscreen. Of course, printed maps of properties are available as well. Property owners must fill out annually a Property Tax Listing Form, updating any changes in key characteristics of the property used in assessing the value of the property. Characteristics considered by the assessor's office include the following:

- Property address
- Plot map and reference to deed register
- Area of lot (square footage)
- Occupancy (single-family dwelling, two-family, multifamily)
- Size of dwelling (square footage of living space)
- Number of structures
- Number of stories of each structure
- Basement, slab, or crawl space
- Foundation construction method
- Exterior construction method
- Roof type and roofing materials
- Number of rooms
- Number of bathrooms
- Number of bedrooms
- Year built
- Number of fireplaces
- Interior finish
- Floor type
- Built-in appliances
- HVAC system
- Special features (spas, etc.)
- Landscaping
- Land topography
- Utility connections
- Paved or unpaved driveway
- Last sale price and date

Exhibit 5-2 **Property Tax Valuation in Orange County, NC**

Orange County, North Carolina, was an early adopter of an integrated property records and tax administration system that is illustrative of what most local jurisdictions now use. Small jurisdictions typically rely on a county property

Orange County, NC (2019). Office of Tax Administration: Property Taxes. Retrieved October 20, 2019, from https://www.orangecountync.gov/867/Property-Taxes. Also see the form for appealing an assessment for more details on variables affecting appraisal, page 2 of 4, https://www.orangecountync.gov/DocumentCenter/View/1950/Formal-Notice-of-Appeal-Form-PDF?bidId=

such as those used in Orange County help to foster a perception of fairness among taxpayers. Property owners conclude that they are paying their fair share and are not being overcharged while other taxpayers are being undercharged. If these equity considerations are met, then the likelihood of a taxpayer revolt is minimized. However, it does not make the property tax popular, as it is likely that it is the most hated tax in the country.

Tax Rates

Property tax rates are a percentage of assessed value. As applied to property taxes, the rate is expressed in mills; a one-mill rate yields $1 of revenue for every $1,000 of assessed value. A property tax rate of 68.5 mills as applied to a $120,000 property assessed at 20% of market value would yield $1,644 (120 × 0.2 × 68.5 = 1,644).

Local jurisdictions often determine the annual property tax rate by calculating backward from projected expenditures minus other revenues. The property tax increase is then expected to make up the budget gap. The community's decision makers simply determine how many additional mills will be needed to close the gap. Of course, attempts are made to avoid such tax increases by keeping expenditures as low as considered possible. The process of adjusting the tax rate to match expenditure requirements probably accounts for the great popularity of the property tax among local officials, and the great unpopularity among property owners. This tax is one over which officials have considerable control (unless there are tax and expenditure limitations that lessen that control—this is discussed later), unlike other taxes that depend on the economy (income and sales taxes) or intergovernmental aid.

Many local governments in areas of rapidly increasing property values have found that they are able to accommodate budgetary increases above the base level at declining property tax rates. In most of these cases, the rate of assessment increase exceeds the percentage of rate reduction, thus resulting in a rising tax bill. The key decision for any local government involves how often to reassess properties. With the housing boom

of the 1990s and 2000s, substantial incentives existed to reassess properties frequently in order to take advantage of increasing property values and therefore be able to produce increasing levels of revenue at declining property tax rates. This may result from increased demands on the part of citizens for additional services, or from desires by government officials to expand government.[64]

As noted above, these trends toward "easy money" from the property tax at declining rates reversed themselves dramatically after 2008. Taxpayers expected governments to downgrade the assessed value of their property because they knew that, in many cases, there had been precipitous declines in market values. Even though property values had dropped, however, this did not decrease the need that local governments had for property tax revenue. This left most local governments in the difficult position of having to raise property tax rates, reduce service levels, or both. Property values in many areas have recovered since the Great Recession, but there are still some parts of the country where values are lower than they were prior to the downturn. The fact that the 2007–2009 recession was fueled by the overvaluing of housing, of course, made property taxes particularly vulnerable.

Circuit Breakers

As taxes rise, some property owners may encounter considerable difficulty in paying their tax bills and may even be forced to sell their homes and move into rental housing. To alleviate this problem, several states use *circuit breaker* systems that set a limit on taxes, particularly for low-income elderly persons. A qualified homeowner pays an amount up to the limit, and the state pays any additional amount owed. Often a state bases the limit on some income criterion. When property taxes exceed a specified percentage of the taxpayer's income, the state pays the difference.[72] A 2018 analysis identified 31 states (including the District of Columbia) that had some form of property tax relief program based on the income of the taxpayer; of those, 18 of these programs were classified as circuit breakers. In order to qualify as a circuit breaker program, the tax relief must be targeted toward taxpayers based on the level of property tax they pay relative to their income, rather than simply based on income as a single factor.[73]

Personal Property

Besides taxing real property, some jurisdictions tax personal property. For individuals, such property includes furniture, vehicles, clothing, jewelry, and the like. Intangible personal property includes stocks, bonds, and other financial instruments such as mortgages. For corporations, personal property includes equipment, raw materials, and items in inventory. Taxes on personal property are unpopular and subject to considerable evasion.

Taxing and Spending Limitations

Although historically citizens seemingly had little opportunity to affect taxing and spending other than through the process of selecting elected representatives, 1978 changed all that. In that year, California voters approved Proposition 13, an initiative that limited the property tax rate to 1% of market value. That provision by itself would have required a rollback in taxes, but an additional provision further cut taxes. Property assessments were to be returned to their values in 1975, when property was considerably less expensive.

Although tax limitation measures were not new, Proposition 13 began a new era in which government officials were forced to consider taxpayer reaction and to limit taxing and spending.[74] Many state and local governments followed California's lead during the late 1970s and early 1980s by passing statutory limits or, in some cases, adding restrictions to state constitutions. California voters approved Proposition 4 in 1979, which limited both state and local government expenditures. In the following years, restrictive measures were adopted in about half of the states. Massachusetts, which had come to be known as "Taxachusetts," gained notoriety in 1980 as a result of its passage of Proposition 2 1/2. This measure required that local governments reduce taxes by 15% each year until they equaled 2.5% of market value.[75]

A 2015 report by the Lincoln Institute of Land Policy reviewed the history of the adoption of property tax and expenditure limitations (TELs) since the first ones were adopted in the 1850s. From the adoption of the first TEL in 1852 (in Delaware, applying to a single county) through the 1960s there were 55 such limits. As noted prior, however, TELs really took off in the 1970s, with a total of 30 adopted in that decade alone, by 25 different states. Another 52 have been adopted since 1980. According to this study, "In 2013, nearly 130 state-authorized limitations (property tax rate limits, levy limits, and assessment limits) were on the books in 46 states and the District of Columbia. Only four states—Hawaii, New Hampshire, Tennessee, and Vermont—have no major state provision limiting property taxation."[76]

The original stimulus behind what came to be known as the taxpayers' revolt was the sharp rise in property values and, consequently, tax bills, but a more generally negative attitude emerged—the attitude that government officials have an insatiable appetite for spending. This attitude has been on display once again in recent years, in particular with the movement of the Republican party to the right, which is most clearly identified with the Tea Party movement of the first decade of the 2000s. The current orthodox Republican view has, as one of its core values, the notion that virtually all taxes, at all levels of government, are too high. Besides taxing too much, governments allegedly use the revenues to interfere needlessly in the lives of citizens and the operations of corporations. Property taxes remain one of the most criticized forms of taxation. This is probably because of dissatisfaction with the results school systems are producing, which are funded almost entirely by property taxes.[77] The result has been several types of tax and expenditure limitations. One review classified them into five categories:

1. Overall property tax limitation (for example, limit maximum annual percentage increase)
2. Specific property tax limitation (for example, limit use of property tax to finance education)
3. Property tax levy limit (for example, implement ceiling on amount of tax)

4. General revenue or general expenditure increase limit (for example, limit annual expenditure increase to a specific limit)
5. Property tax assessment increase limit (limit the assessed value increase)[78]

The effects of these limitations have varied, but in most cases local governments made up for the revenue loss through other sources, usually non-general-revenue sources. In particular, there is a general consensus in the literature that TELs have reduced the reliance of local governments on the property tax. Rather than constraining overall spending, however, usually TELs have simply encouraged movement to other sources of revenue, or increases in state aid.[79] This is not to suggest that local jurisdictions are always able to make up for the loss of property tax revenue through these other sources; whether they are or not depends on many factors, including the political or legal restrictions on these other sources. There is some evidence, however, that these limitations are more constraining on local property taxes in the long run than in the short run.[80] The main effects seem to have been sevenfold.

First, state legislatures and local governments are much more reluctant to initiate new programs and especially to propose tax increases or new taxes. In the case of new programs, this is presumably because there is more uncertainty surrounding the affordability of these programs in the future. The reluctance to impose tax increases probably relates to knowledge of the underlying disposition of taxpayers toward these increases in states with TELs.

Second, combined with major cutbacks in federal aid to states and localities, as well as state aid to local governments, the limitation movement set these governments on an imaginative hunt for alternative finance measures. The significantly greater use of impact fees, discussed earlier, and other direct charges to those benefiting from services was an outgrowth of the tax revolt. However, this broadening of revenue sources may come at a cost. One study of the Colorado Taxpayer Bill of Rights (TABOR) found that this particular TEL increased the volatility of revenues.[81]

Third, states provided increased financial assistance to hard-pressed local governments. For example, when Michigan ran into problems with property tax funding for education, the state increased the sales tax and, in turn, used state funds for formerly local education funds. A more explicit example is Oregon's experience with Ballot Measure 5, which required the state to replace lost property tax revenue with state aid, thus shifting many of the fiscal effects of the initiatives to the state government.[82] A 2012 study found that the stricter the TEL, the more state aid increased.[83]

Fourth, overall expenditures have been cut somewhat and some services have been reduced, either in quality or quantity, as a means of curbing spending.[84] Essential services such as law enforcement and fire protection have been maintained, albeit at decreased levels. A study of Illinois local government experiences with TELs found that local governments reduced overall spending, but not instructional spending for schools.[85] Budget problems forced cutbacks in maintenance of buildings and purchase of new vehicles and equipment.[86] Overall, however, TELs did not materially change the relative amounts that state and local governments spend on government functions.[87] Some evidence indicates that spending cuts have produced long-term quality decline, at least in some services. For example, public school student performance has declined in several states that have imposed expenditure limitations, even after controlling for a number of other possible influences.[88] In fact, there is a movement in California to reverse some of the most restrictive aspects of Proposition 13, in part because younger taxpayers view the limitation as having led to a decline in public education. A result of Proposition 13 is viewed, therefore, by some of these taxpayers as a cost imposed by older generations on younger generations.[89] Moreover, a 2006 study argues that TELs tend to have had a positive increase on economic growth at the state level, while local-level effects on economic growth have been negative, but only in the short run.[90]

Fifth, TELs have had differential effects on service delivery and policy outcomes. Here much of the research focuses on schools and school performance, with studies finding that TELs negatively affect many school and student performance measures; TELs are found, for example, to lead to higher student–teacher ratios, lower performance on standardized tests, and alter the quality of new teachers.[91] A nationwide study found that these limitations do not offer a uniform constraint across jurisdictions, but rather represent a greater constraint for some than others. In the case of both general purpose governments (cities or counties) and school districts, there is significant variation across these jurisdictions within single metropolitan areas. In particular, the effects seem to be "greatest within counties comprising the urban core and those with relatively more disadvantaged populations."[92] An interesting finding in a study focused on the most fiscally constrained California cities was that homeowners associations were more common in the more fiscally constrained cities, presumably because these associations were able to provide some services that had been previously provided by local governments.[93]

Sixth, tax TELs enacted through citizen referenda have been found to be more constraining than those enacted through legislation. A 2010 study concluded that the legislatively enacted TELs are more likely to have loopholes that enable governments to wiggle out of them when they become too constraining.[94]

Seventh, studies of the effects of TELs on local fiscal condition have found that TELs are "positively associated with key measures of fiscal condition: higher fund balances, better-funded pensions, and lower debt," perhaps because TELs contribute to more effective fiscal management and multi-year fiscal planning.[95] One specific example of the contribution of TELs to fiscal condition focused on pension and other post-employment benefits obligations and found that funding ratios were higher in states with more stringent TELs.[96]

One clear conclusion that can be reached about TELs is that their effects are complex and go far beyond simply constraining taxing and spending. This conclusion has been sustained over 30 years of research and experience with TELs. A 2009 Lincoln Institute of Land Policy study surveyed officials in municipalities that had enacted TELs, and the results were decidedly mixed. While 36% said that their TELs had impacted budgets, 40% said they had had no clear effect. Furthermore, while 20% said that the TELs in their cities had reduced service provision, 13% said that they had sought out new revenue sources.[97] It is difficult to reach the conclusion that tax and expenditure limitations clearly limit either taxes or spending; their effects are much more complicated.

Much has changed in California since passage of Proposition 13. One notable change is that Republicans have lost power to Democrats who are more interested in local governments providing perceived needed services and consequently are more amenable to tax increases. Those who voted for Proposition 13 are aging and being replaced by younger voters, including many who moved to California, and these voters are demanding better services and may be willing to pay higher taxes.[98] A proposal appeared on the November 2020 ballot that would require commercial and industrial properties be taxed at their current market value.[99]

Summary

Governments use numerous revenue sources to support their operations, with taxes obviously being one of the most important types. In devising a tax system, governments need to consider the adequacy of the tax revenue being produced, the equity of the tax system (on both ability-to-pay grounds and on the basis of who benefits from local public services), economic efficiency, collectability, and political feasibility. Taxes on personal and corporate income are important sources of income for the federal government and state governments. They are highly complex taxes, and the personal income tax in particular is usually adjusted to individual taxpayer conditions. Payroll taxes are typically used to finance particular services and are earmarked for those purposes. By far the largest payroll taxes are for Social Security and Medicare. The property tax, which is the largest tax for local governments, is heavily influenced by assessment practices, which can substantially affect the equity and the production of the tax. The use of property taxes is constrained by the imposition of constitutional or statutory limitations.

Notes

1. Tax Policy Center (2019). *Briefing book: a citizen's guide to the fascinating (though often complex) elements of the U.S. tax system* (pp. 2, 6). Retrieved October 16, 2019, from https://www.taxpolicycenter.org/briefing-book/how-do-taxes-affect-economy-long-run.
2. Farrelly, M. (2008). The impact of tobacco control programs on adult smoking. *American Journal of Public Health, 98,* 304–309; Ho, L-M, et al. (2018). Raising cigarette excise tax to reduce consumption in low- and middle-income countries of the Asia-Pacific region: a simulation of the anticipated health and taxation revenues impacts. *BMC Public Health.* Retrieved October 16, 2019, from https://www.ncbi.nlm.nih.gov/pmc/articles/PMC6194546/.
3. Masur, M. (2018) Does the Tax Cuts and Jobs Act pass the tests of good tax policy? April 18. Retrieved November 23, 2019, from https://www.taxpolicycenter.org/taxvox/does-tax-cuts-and-jobs-act-pass-tests-good-tax-policy.
4. Lambert, P., & Naughton, H. (2009). The equal absolute sacrifice principle revisited. *Journal of Economic Surveys, 23*(2), 328–349.
5. The House Republican plan for America's job creators (2011). *GOP.gov.* Retrieved February 21, 2012, from http://www.gop.gov/indepth/jobs/taxes.
6. Thompson Reuters. (2019). Social Security wage base increases to $132,900 for 2019. Retrieved November 23, 2019, from https://tax.thomsonreuters.com/news/social-security-wage-base-increases-to-132900-for-2019/.
7. Congressional Budget Office (2019). Projected changed in the distribution of household income, 2016 to 2021. December. Retrieved March 14, 2020, from https://www.cbo.gov/system/files/2019-12/55941-CBO-Household-Income.pdf.
8. Ingraham, C. (2019). For the first time in history, U.S. billionaires paid a lower tax rate than the working class last year. *Washington Post,* October 8. Retrieved October 16, 2019, from https://www.washingtonpost.com/business/2019/10/08/first-time-history-us-billionaires-paid-lower-tax-rate-than-working-class-last-year/.
9. Weiss, E. (2005). D.C.'s bid to impose commuter tax denied. *Washington Post,* November 5.
10. See Mocan, N. (2015). Taxes and culture of leisure: Impact on labor supply in Europe. *Journal of Comparative Economics, 47*(3), 618–639.
11. Brendan, C. (2013). Efficiency, equity, and optimal income taxation. European University Institute, November.
12. Tax Foundation (2019). How high are cigarette taxes in your state? Retrieved July 10, 2019, from https://files

.taxfoundation.org/20180125120524/CigTaxes-01.png; New York City adds an extra $1.50 per pack, or a total of $5.85 per pack for state and city taxes combined.
13. Buenker, J. (1981). The ratification of the federal income tax amendment. *Cato Journal, 1*(1), 183–223.
14. Nelson, S. C., & Cronin, J. (2006). Adjusted gross income. In J. Cordes, R. Ebel, & J. Gravelle (Eds.), *Encyclopedia of taxation and tax policy.* Washington, DC: The Urban Institute Press, 3.
15. Pollack, S. (1996). *The failure of U.S. tax policy: revenue and politics.* University Park, PA: Pennsylvania State University Press.
16. Green, R. (2005). Mortgage interest deduction. In J. Cordes, R. Ebel, & J. Gravelle (Eds.), *Encyclopedia of taxation and tax policy,* 260–261.
17. Albrecht, L. (2019). Americans slashed their charitable deductions by $54 billion after Republican tax-code overhaul. MarketWatch. July 11. Retrieved March 14, 2020, from https://www.marketwatch.com/story/americans-slashed-their-charitable-deductions-by-54-billion-after-trumps-tax-overhaul-2019-07-09.
18. Slemrod, J. (2006). The role of misconceptions in support for regressive tax reform. *National Tax Journal, 59,* 57–75.
19. Dowd, T. (2005). Distinguishing between short-term and long-term recipients of the earned income tax credit. *National Tax Journal, 58,* 807–828.
20. Dickert-Conlin, S., et al. (2005). Utilization of tax credits by low-income individuals. *National Tax Journal, 58,* 743–785.
21. Weiner, D. (2006). Alternative minimum tax. In J. Cordes, R. Ebel, & J. Gravelle (Eds.), *Encyclopedia of taxation and tax policy,* 11.
22. Congressional Budget Office (2010). *The individual alternative minimum tax* (p. 1). Washington, DC: U.S. Government Printing Office.
23. Congressional Budget Office. (2010). *The individual alternative minimum tax.*
24. Carlson, B. (2018). What you need to know about the new alternative minimum tax. *Forbes,* September 29. Retrieved July 10, 2019, from https://www.forbes.com/sites/bobcarlson/2018/09/29/what-you-need-to-know-about-the-new-alternative-minimum-tax/#da4ce3f4822d.
25. Loughead, K. & Wei, E. (2019). State individual income tax rates and brackets in 2019. *Tax Foundation Fiscal Fact Number 643,* March.
26. Blankley, B. (2019). Tax day: in response to federal tax reform, several states lowered their individual income tax rates. April 15. Retrieved July 20, 2019, from https://www.thecentersquare.com/national/tax-day-in-response-to-federal-tax-reform-several-states/article_939ccaa0-5f9c-11e9-9499-0b86a77d2212.html.
27. Schneider, F., et al. (2010). Shadow economies all over the world. *World Bank,* July, 24.
28. Edison Research (2018). *Americans in the gig economy,* December 12. Retrieved March 14, 2020, from https://www.edisonresearch.com/americans-and-the-gig-economy/#:~:text=24%25%20of%20Americans%20earn%20some,the%20gig%20economy%20than%20women.

29. Yu, S., & Ohnsorge F. (2019). The challenges of informality, January 18. Retrieved July 20, 2019, from https://blogs.worldbank.org/developmenttalk/challenges-informality.

30. Gale, W., & Krupkin, A. (2019). How big is the problem of tax evasion? *Brookings Institution*, April 19. Retrieved July 20, 2019, from https://www.brookings.edu/blog/up-front/2019/04/09/how-big-is-the-problem-of-tax-evasion/.

31. Clark, C. S. (2016). Uncollected taxes now total $458 Billion, IRS estimates. *Government Executive*, April 29.

32. Congressional Budget and Impoundment Control Act of 1974 (P.L. 93–344, 88 Stat.), 297, 299.

33. Gravelle, J. G. (2006). Tax expenditures. In J. Cordes, R. Ebel, & J. Gravelle (Eds.), *Encyclopedia of taxation and tax policy,* 406–408.

34. Office of Management and Budget (2019). *Budget of the United States government: fiscal year 2020: analytical perspectives* (p. 195).

35. Organization for Economic Cooperation and Development (2018). *OECD: revenue statistics 1965–2018, Table II.1.* Retrieved October 19, 2019, from https://stats.oecd.org/index.aspx?DataSetCode=Table_II1.

36. Congressional Budget Office (2017). *International comparisons of corporate income tax rates* (p. 2). Washington, D.C.: U.S. Government Printing Office.

37. Cornia, G., et al. (2005). The disappearing state corporate income tax. *National Tax Journal, 48,* 115–138; United States Bureau of the Census (2018). *State government tax collections: summary report.* Washington, DC: Bureau of the Census.

38. Jahnsen, K., & Pomerleau, K. (2017), *Corporate income tax rates around the world, 2017,* Tax Foundation, September. Retrieved March 15, 2020, from https://taxfoundation.org/corporate-income-tax-rates-around-the-world-2017/.

39. Tax Policy Center Briefing Book (2019). *How did the Tax Cut and Jobs Act change business taxes?* Retrieved July 10, 2019, from https://www.taxpolicycenter.org/briefing-book/how-did-tax-cuts-and-jobs-act-change-business-taxes.

40. Economic Cooperation and Development (2018). *OECD: revenue statistics 1965–2018, Table II.1.*

41. Pomerleu, K. (2018). *The United States' corporate income tax rate is now more in line with those levied by other major nations.* Tax Foundation, February 12. Retrieved March 15, 2020, from https://taxfoundation.org/us-corporate-income-tax-more-competitive/.

42. Kagan, J. (2019). Corporate inversion. *Investipedia,* December 1. Retrieved January 2, 2020, from https://www.investopedia.com/terms/c/corporateinversion.asp.

43. Margolis, J. (2018), Trump hypes jobs relocating back to the US. Are they? *PRI,* December 26. Retrieved January 2, 2020, from https://www.pri.org/stories/2018-12-26/trump-hypes-jobs-relocating-back-us-are-they.

44. Social Security Administration (2019), *Annual Statistical Supplement, 2018.* Retrieved October 19, 2019, from https://www.ssa.gov/policy/docs/statcomps/supplement/.

45. Social Security Admnistration *Annual Statistical Supplement, 2018.*

46. Congressional Budget Office (2019). *The budget and economic outlook, fiscal years 2019–2029* (p. 143). Washington: U.S. Government Publishing Office.

47. Congressional Budget Office (2019). *The 2019 long-term budget outlook* (p. 23). Washington, DC: U.S. Government Publishing Office.

48. Congressional Budget Office (2019). *How changing Social Security could affect beneficiaries and the system's finances.* Retrieved July 20, 2019, from https://www.cbo.gov/publication/54868.

49. Congressional Budget Office (2019). *The budget and economic outlook, fiscal years 2019–2029,* 62.

50. See Chapter 4 of Joyce, P. (2011). *The Congressional Budget Office: honest numbers, power and policymaking.* Washington, DC: Georgetown University Press.

51. Congressional Budget Office (2019), *The budget and economic outlook, fiscal years 2019–2029,* 141.

52. U.S. House of Representatives, Committee on the Budget (2011). The path to prosperity. April 5. Retrieved February 21, 2012, from http://budget.house.gov/UploadedFiles/PathToProsperityFY2012.pdf.

53. Henry J. Kaiser Family Foundation (2018). *Key facts about the uninsured population.* December 7. Retrieved July 20, 2019, from https://www.kff.org/uninsured/fact-sheet/key-facts-about-the-uninsured-population/.

54. Burtless, G. (2011). The administration's new plan to revamp the unemployment insurance tax: a good policy that can be greatly improved [blog post]. *Brookings Up Front Blog,* March 20. Retrieved March 15, 2020, from https://www.brookings.edu/blog/up-front/2011/02/09/the-administrations-new-plan-to-revamp-the-unemployment-insurance-tax-a-good-policy-that-can-be-greatly-improved/.

55. Vroman, W. (2018). State UI financing response to the great recession. In S. A. Wandner (Ed.), *Unemployment insurance reform: fixing a broken system* (pp. 103–130), Kalamazoo, MI: W.E. Upjohn Institute for Employment Research.

56. Fisher, G. W. (1996). *The worst tax? a history of the property tax in America.* Lawrence, KS: University Press of Kansas; Taxes [Gallup poll]. (2011). *Gallup.com.* Retrieved December 20, 2011, from www.gallup.com/poll/1714/taxes.aspx?.

57. National Center for Education Statistics (2019). *Public school revenue sources.* Updated May 2019. Retrieved July 20, 2019, from https://nces.ed.gov/programs/coe/indicator_cma.asp.

58. SchoolFunding.Info, a project of the Center for Educational Equity at Teachers College. Retrieved January 3, 2020, from http://schoolfunding.info/school-funding-court-decisions/.

59. Johnson, R. W., & McCullough, J. S. (1996). *Case study on urban local government finance.* Paper presented at the Asian Development Bank seminar on Urban Infrastructure Finance in Asia, Research Triangle Park, North Carolina, Research Triangle Institute, April 17.

60. Bahl, R. W., & Linn, J. F. (1992). *Urban public finance in developing countries.* New York, NY: Oxford University Press; Bird, R. M. (1992). *Tax policy and economic development.* Baltimore, MD: Johns Hopkins University Press.

61. Fischel, W. (2001). Homeowners, municipal corporate governance, and the benefit view of the property tax. *National Tax Journal, 54,* 157–173.

62. Petersen, J. E. (2000). TIFs in the hinterlands. *Governing, 13,* August, 68.

63. Merriman, D. (2018). *Improving tax increment financing for local government.* Lincoln Institute for Land Policy. Retrieved March 15, 2020, from https://www.brookings.edu/blog/up-front/2011/02/09/the-administrations-new-plan-to-revamp-the-unemployment-insurance-tax-a-good-policy-that-can-be-greatly-improved/.

64. Marcus, J. (2019). Michigan Central and the rebirth of Detroit. *BBC,* July 11. Retrieved July 20, 2019, from https://www.bbc.co.uk/news/extra/KnxBMVGAcn/michigan_central_detroit.

65. Anderson, J. E. (2012). Agricultural use-value property tax assessment: estimation and policy issues, *Public Budgeting & Finance, 32*(4), 71–94.

66. Povitch, E. S. (2017). After long fight, some farmers get relief from high property taxes. *Stateline,* September 21. Retrieved July 20, 2019, from https://www.pewtrusts.org/en/research-and-analysis/blogs/stateline/2017/09/21/after-long-fight-some-farmers-get-relief-from-high-property-taxes.

67. Kelley, T. A., & McLaughlin, C. B. (2017). North Carolina's nonprofit property tax exemption conundrum, 96 N.C. L. Rev. 1769. Retrieved October 19, 2019, from https://scholarship.law.unc.edu/nclr/vol96/iss6/4.

68. Eom, T., & Rubenstein, R. (2006). Do state-funded property tax exemptions increase local government efficiency? An analysis of New York State's STAR program. *Public Budgeting & Finance, 26,* Spring, 66–87.

69. See https://www.zillow.com/mortgage-calculator/. Retrieved December 31, 2019.

70. Sirmans, G. S., Gatzlaff, D. H., & Macpherson, D. A. (2008). Horizontal and vertical inequity in real property taxation, *Journal of Real Estate Literature, 16*(2) 167–180.

71. Allen, M. (2003). Measuring vertical property tax inequity in multifamily property markets. *Journal of Real Estate Research, 25,* 171–184.

72. Anderson, J. (2012). *Income-based property tax relief: circuit breaker tax expenditures.* Lincoln Institute of Land Policy: working paper. Retrieved October 20, 2019, from https://www.lincolninst.edu/sites/default/files/pubfiles/2278_1617_Anderson_WP13JA3.pdf.

73. Davis, A (2018). *Property tax circuit breakers in 2018.* Institute of Tax and Economic Policy Policy Brief, September. Retrieved March 15, 2020, from https://itep.org/wp-content/uploads/091318-Property-Tax-Circuit-Breakers.pdf.

74. Rueben, K. (2000). The impact of initiatives on state and local government finance. *Municipal Finance Journal, 20,*

20–25; Hoene, C. (2004). Fiscal structure and the post-proposition 13 fiscal regime in California's cities. *Public Budgeting & Finance, 24,* Winter, 51–72.

75. Ladd, H. F., & Wilson, J. B. (1983). Who supports tax limitations: evidence from Massachusetts' proposition 2 1/2. *Journal of Policy Analysis and Management, 2,* 256–279; Moscovitch, E. (1985). Proposition 2 1/2. *Government Finance Review, 1,* October, 21–25; Wallin, B. (2004). The tax revolt in Massachusetts: revolution and reason. *Public Budgeting & Finance, 24,* Winter, 34–50.

76. Paquin, B. P (2015). Chronicle of the 161-year history of state-imposed property tax limitations. *Lincoln Institute of Land Policy Working Paper WP15BP1,* April. Retrieved March 15, 2020, from https://www.lincolninst.edu/publications/working-papers/chronicle-161-year-history-state-imposed-property-tax-limitations.

77. Bradbury, K. L., et al. (1998). School quality and Massachusetts enrollment shifts in the context of tax limitations. *New England Economic Review,* July/August, 3–20.

78. Mullins, D., & Joyce, P. (1996). Tax and expenditure limitations and state and local fiscal structure, an empirical assessment. *Public Budgeting & Finance, 16,* Spring, 77.

79. Stallman, J., et al. (2017). Surveying the effects of limitations on tax and expenditures: what do/don't we know? *Journal of Public and Nonprofit Affairs 3*(2), 197–222.

80. Dye, R., et al. (2005). Are property tax limitations more binding over time? *National Tax Journal, 58,* 215–225.

81. St. Clair, T. (2012), The effect of tax and expenditure limitations on revenue volatility: Evidence from Colorado, *Public Budgeting & Finance, 32*(3), 61–78.

82. Thompson, F., & Green, M. (2004). Vox populi? Oregon tax and expenditure limitation initiatives. *Public Budgeting & Finance, 24,* Winter, 73–87.

83. Kioko, S. N., & Martell, C. R. (2012). Impact of state-level tax and expenditure limits (TELs) on government revenues and aid to local governments. *Public Finance Review, 40,* 736–766.

84. Brown, T. (2000). Constitutional tax and expenditure limitation in Colorado: the impact on municipal governments. *Public Budgeting & Finance, 20,* Fall, 29–50.

85. Dye, R. F., & McGuire, T. J. (1997). The effect of property tax limitation measures on local government fiscal behavior. *Journal of Public Economics, 66,* 469–487.

86. King-Meadows, T., & Lowery, D. (1996). The impact of the tax revolt era state fiscal caps: a research update. *Public Budgeting & Finance, 16,* Spring, 102–112.

87. Joyce, P. G., & Mullins, D. R. (1991). The changing fiscal structure of the state and local public sector: the impact of tax and expenditure limitations. *Public Administration Review, 51,* 244–245.

88. Downes, T. A., & Figlio, D. N. (1999). Do tax and expenditure limits provide a free lunch? evidence on the link between limits and public sector service quality. *National Tax Journal, 52,* 113–128.

89. Garafoli, J. (2018). Proposition 13 is no longer off-limits in California. *San Francisco Chronicle*, December 27. Retrieved December 31, 2019, from https://www.sfchronicle.com /politics/article/Proposition-13-is-no-longer-off-limits -in-13492400.php.

90. Deller, S., & Stallman, J. (2006). Tax and expenditure limitations and economic growth. *Marquette Law Review, 90*, 497–554.

91. This research is summarized in Stallman, J., et al. (2017). Surveying the effects of limitations on tax and expenditures: what do/don't we know?

92. Mullins, D. (2004). Tax and expenditure limitations and the fiscal response of local government: asymmetric intra-local fiscal effects. *Public Budgeting & Finance, 24*, Winter, 111–147.

93. Cheung, R. (2008). The effect of property tax limitations on residential private governments: The case of proposition 13. *National Tax Journal, 61*, 35–56.

94. New, M. (2010). U.S. state tax and expenditure limitations: a comparative political analysis. *State Politics and Policy Quarterly, 10*, 25–50.

95. Stallman, J., et al. (2017). Surveying the effects of limitations on tax and expenditures: what do/don't we know?, 211.

96. Maher, C. S., Park, S., & Harrold, J. (2016). The effects of tax and expenditure limits on municipal pension and OPEB funding during the great recession. *Public Finance and Management, 16*(2), 121–146.

97. Brooks, L., & Phillips, J. (2009). Municipally imposed tax and spending limits. *Land Lines*. Lincoln Institute of Land Policy, April.

98. Garofoli, J. (2018). Proposition 13 is no longer off limits in California. *San Francisco Chronicle*, December 27. Retrieved March 16, 2020, from https://www.sfchronicle .com/politics/article/Proposition-13-is-no-longer-off -limits-in-13492400.php.

99. Ballotpedia. (2020). *California Tax on Commercial and Industrial Properties for Education and Local Government Funding Initiative*. Retrieved March 16, 2020, from https://ballotpedia.org/California_Tax_on_Commercial _and_Industrial_Properties_for_Education_and_Local _Government_Funding_Initiative_(2020).

CHAPTER 6

Budgeting for Revenues: Transaction-Based Revenue Sources

In addition to income, payroll, and wealth-based taxes, governments raise revenue from a number of sources that are based on largely voluntary transactions. The largest and most important of these is the general retail sales tax. There are also a number of sales taxes levied on specific goods, including taxes on luxury goods such as expensive automobiles, so-called sin taxes on liquor and cigarettes, and benefit-based excises on items like motor fuel. Governments have expanded their use of fees and charges, many of which are used to finance related services. Over the past 35 years, the use of lotteries and games of chance as a revenue source for state governments has mushroomed. Although having grown over the years, neither charges nor gambling revenues represent a primary source of revenue for general-purpose governments. However, many special districts such as water and sewer authorities get the majority of their revenue from charges. New transaction-based taxes are emerging as well; these include taxes on marijuana in states where it is legal and taxes on so-called "gig economy," or temporary work, transactions.

This chapter reviews each of these revenue sources, discussing their applications and the political and economic issues surrounding them.

In doing so, we discuss how these revenue sources stack up relative to other criteria.

Retail Sales and Other Consumption Taxes

Sales taxes are one of the most important sources of revenue for state governments. Forty-five of the 50 states (all but Alaska, Delaware, Montana, New Hampshire, and Oregon) plus the District of Columbia levy a general sales tax, and it is the largest state-generated source of revenue for many of them.[1] All states have at least some selective sales taxes. Overall, the general and selective sales taxes account for more than 34% of total state own-source general revenues from all sources (excluding intergovernmental revenues). Income taxes are the second largest single own-source general revenue source, at 30%, followed by user charges, which account for about 16% of own-source general revenues. If one looks at the sales tax as a proportion of tax revenues only, sales taxes account for almost one-half of state tax revenue. Local governments also often levy sales taxes, although they are less important overall to local governments, accounting for just over 11% of own-source general revenue. The largest revenue source for local governments is the property tax, which brings in about four times as much revenue for them as the sales tax.[2]

There are two types of sales taxes: general and specific. The general sales tax is a tax on all (or most) consumed goods and sometimes services, while specific sales taxes are taxes on a particular type of good or service. There are also two varieties of sales taxes. *Ad valorem* taxes are levied as a percentage of the purchase price of an item. If an item subject to a sales tax costs twice as much as another item subject to a sales tax, the tax paid is twice the amount as well. General sales taxes are *ad valorem* taxes. *Unit* taxes, on the other hand, are levied per unit of the item sold, without regard to price. This means that more expensive brands are taxed at the same level as less expensive brands. Gasoline, cigarette, and liquor taxes are usually unit taxes because taxation is based on the gallons (in the case of gasoline), milliliters (in the case of liquor), or packs (in the case of cigarettes) sold. The production from *ad valorem* taxes, for obvious reasons, tends to rise as prices increase, while unit taxes yield relatively flat revenues.

General Sales Taxes

The general sales tax is the largest revenue source for state governments and is used by many local governments as well. Many state governments raise as much as one-fourth to one-third of their tax revenue from this source. Some states raise as much as one-half. Sales tax revenues result from the size of the tax base—in this case, the value of the taxed goods that are sold—and the rates applied to that base.

Tax Base

While all three levels of government rely on some form of consumption tax, state governments are the most dependent, particularly on retail sales taxes. The base of any consumption tax is a product or class of goods (sometimes services) whose value is measured in terms of retail gross sales or receipts. The base is a function of which products and services are included and excluded.

All states except Illinois exempt prescription medicines (Illinois taxes these at a lower rate of 1%), and 40 of the 46 states (counting the District of Columbia) with sales taxes exclude food (some of these permit local taxes on food) except for that sold in restaurants, delis, or some specialty foods sold in grocery stores. All of the states that tax food have opted for reducing the sales tax rate on food compared to other taxed items, rather than eliminating it altogether. Others—including Hawaii, Idaho, Kansas, Oklahoma, and South Dakota—tax food, but allow a rebate or income tax credit to compensate low-income households.[3]

Other commonly excluded items are clothing, household fuels, soaps, and some toiletries. Some items may be exempt from the general sales tax only because they are subject to another sales tax. Cigarettes, gasoline, and alcoholic beverages are examples of specific goods exempted from the general sales tax for this reason. However, states generally are not precluded from levying two taxes on one sale. Such double taxation may occur, for example, when a general sales tax and a specific sales tax are placed on cigarettes and alcoholic beverages. States sometimes implement sales tax holidays to encourage the purchase of particular items at particular times of the year. At least 20 states have sales tax holidays. North Carolina, for example, before the beginning of the school year declares a sales tax holiday on items that are frequently purchased as part of back-to-school shopping, including school supplies, basic computers, and children's clothing. Florida even has a pre-hurricane season tax holiday on disaster preparedness supplies, including generators.[4]

The justification for these commodities' exemptions is typically that they make the sales tax less regressive, to the extent that the non-taxed items are necessities. The clearest case is food, where lower-income persons spend a larger percentage of their income on this commodity than higher-income persons. This same justification applies to the exemption for prescription and other medicines. Tax exemptions for clothing are less clear on vertical equity grounds, although some states exempt only a portion of the cost of a given article of clothing (the first $100, for example) in an effort to offset this problem.

While goods represent the main tax base for the sales tax, there is also substantial taxation of services by the states. A 2017 survey by the Federation of Tax Administrators (FTA) asked states about their service taxation by requesting information on whether specific services were taxed. The survey found that most states tax some services, although only two states—Hawaii and New Mexico—tax most of the services tracked in the FTA survey. Delaware and Washington also tax a large number of services. The services taxed by most states include utilities, business and computer services, amusements, and repairs and installations. The most notable items not included in most sales tax bases are professional services, such as the services of doctors and lawyers, dry cleaners, or accountants. The FTA survey found that only seven states taxed any professional services in 2017; the four states mentioned previously taxed all of the nine professional services tracked by the survey, while South Dakota taxed five, and West Virginia and Texas taxed only one.[5] An earlier Council of State Governments study found that consumption expenditures for tangible goods are less than those for services.[6] States that exclude services from the sales tax base may forgo considerable revenue, depending on the distribution between the "goods" and "services" economy in that state.

However, applying the sales tax to professional services is so unpopular that few states have implemented that option. In fact, when the state of Florida passed a law that applied the sales tax to services in 1986, it was forced to repeal that tax the next year when citizens and affected interests "discovered" the tax. Many states have recently considered the expansion of service taxation, but have been unsuccessful. The Pew Charitable Trusts, in a 2017 article, noted that 23 states had considered expanding service taxation in 2017, but no bill had passed to that point.[7]

The most debated current issue regarding the application of the sales tax concerns the ability of states to tax Internet sales. As more and more commerce has switched from traditional retail outlets to (first) mail-order and (currently) Internet outlets, state and local governments have lost substantial revenue because of the difficulty in enforcing the use tax (a tax paid by the purchaser on items where sales tax was not paid at purchase). **Exhibit 6-1** discusses the issues surrounding the

---

Exhibit 6-1 Taxation of Mail-Order and Internet Sales

A 2018 Supreme Court decision, in the case of *South Dakota v. Wayfair*, substantially changed the landscape for taxation of transactions conducted over the Internet.[a] The Court ruling expanded the ability of states to collect the sales tax on such transactions, paving the way for states to realize much more revenue than had been the case previously. Prior to this ruling, states had only limited authority to tax Internet (or, previously, mail-order) sales. States instead relied on a "use" tax, which required taxpayers to voluntarily remit tax revenue on transactions where they had not paid the sales tax at the point of purchase. These use taxes were unenforceable, and most taxpayers did not comply with them.

Previous U.S. Supreme Court interpretations of the due process and interstate commerce clauses had been fairly restrictive on states' ability to tax interstate sales. A 1967 case (*National Bellas Hess, Inc. v. Department of Revenue, State of Illinois*) concluded that a mail-order firm had to have a substantial nexus of business in a state in the form of a physical presence. A 1992 case (*Quill Corporation v. North Dakota*) relaxed the so-called nexus doctrine, holding that the due process clause of the Constitution does not bar enforcement of North Dakota's use tax on the Quill Corporation, but on other grounds it still refused to overrule *Bellas Hess*.[b]

The use of the Internet as a mechanism to place orders shipped interstate has become a significant mode of commerce, one that is likely to grow as more users gain access to electronic sources and more merchants turn to e-commerce as a primary sales mode. In particular, the rise of Amazon substantially expanded sales over the Internet, but even companies that have a traditional "brick-and-mortar" presence have expanded their e-commerce presence. An earlier estimate put national losses for states from the

(continues)

Exhibit 6-1 **Taxation of Mail-Order and Internet Sales**   *(continued)*

failure to tax Internet sales nationwide at $11 billion in 2012, and at least $52 billion over the 6-year period between 2007 and 2012.

Not surprisingly, estimated sales tax losses have been increasing; a recent article cited an estimate from the National Governors Association that argued that states could collect $26 billion annually from online and mail-order purchases.[c] If true, this would represent almost 10% of the total amount collected by states from the general sales tax. Further, effects may be greatest in those states with the highest tax rates. Earlier research demonstrated a small, but statistically significant, relationship between the state sales tax rate and the propensity of consumers to purchase online, with higher sales tax rates leading to more online spending.[d]

Several significant policy problems are raised by the mail-order and Internet sales issue. First, as noted above, is the sheer magnitude of the revenue loss. This puts those states that rely more heavily on the sales tax (for example, those with only a sales tax) at a significant disadvantage compared to states with both an income and a sales tax, or only an income tax. Second, there is the problem that it creates for traditional "brick-and-mortar" businesses, whose costs—rent, for example—are higher than for online businesses, and who must include the tax in the cost of the price of their goods. Third, to the extent that some taxpayers can avoid paying the sales tax through Internet or mail-order purchasing, the tax burden is shifted to those who do not engage in these kinds of transactions. To the extent that traditional sales fall more heavily on lower-income individuals without access to the Internet, this would tend to make the sales tax more regressive.

The earlier *Quill* decision concluded that the nexus, or physical presence, rule was needed in order to facilitate interstate commerce. This, as noted, constrained substantially the ability of states to access sales taxes from individuals who purchased goods from a retailer that did not have a physical presence in the same state as the customer. The state of South Dakota flouted that conclusion by passing a law requiring all e-commerce sites (except for small businesses) to collect the sales tax from South Dakota residents, regardless of whether they had a nexus. Apparently, the South Dakota law was designed as a test of the viability of the *Quill* decision in the current environment; in a separate opinion on a similar 2015 case, Justice Anthony Kennedy had virtually invited this test, stating that he hoped that "[t]he legal system should find an appropriate case for this Court to reexamine *Quill* and *Bellas Hess*."[e]

Wayfair, Inc., an affected firm, challenged the constitutionality of the South Dakota law. As expected, the South Dakota Circuit Court and South Dakota Supreme Court found for Wayfair. The South Dakota Supreme Court acknowledged that the state's arguments might be "persuasive" but that, as a matter of law, *Quill* was still the controlling precedent.

Ultimately, the 5-4 decision of the U.S. Supreme Court overturned the earlier *Quill* rule on nexus, arguing that "*Quill* has come to serve as a judicially created tax shelter for businesses that decide to limit their physical presence and still sell their goods and services to a state's consumers." In effect, the Court ruled in *South Dakota v. Wayfair, Inc. (2018)* that *both* local and interstate businesses with a physical presence had been placed at a competitive disadvantage relative to those without such a physical presence, and that the *Quill* nexus rule was out of step with e-commerce as it had developed since that 1992 decision.[f] The decision paved the way for states and localities to mandate many retailers who were not currently required to do so to collect sales taxes and remit these taxes to the governments who levied those taxes. This decision will be particularly important for those states that rely to a greater extent on the sales tax, especially those that do not have an income tax.

a. *South Dakota v. Wayfair*, 504 U.S. 298 (2018).

b. Coleman, H. A. (1992). Taxation of interstate mail-order sales. *Intergovernmental Perspective 18*, Winter, 9–14; *National Bellas Hess, Inc. v. Department of Revenue, State of Illinois* (1967). 386 U.S. 753; *Quill Corporation v. North Dakota* (1992). 504 U.S. 298.

c. Povitch, E. (2018). Big states missing out on online sales taxes for the holidays. *Stateline*, December 5. Retrieved March 30, 2020, from https://www.pewtrusts.org/en/research-and-analysis/blogs/stateline/2018/12/03/big-states-missing-out-on-online-sales-taxes-for-the-holidays. Other estimates have put the cost as high as $33 million.

d. Alm, J., & Melnik, M. (2005). Sales taxes and the decision to purchase online. *Public Finance Review, 33*, 184–212.

e. Harvard Law Review. (2018). *South Dakota v. Wayfair, Inc.* Retrieved June 3, 2019, from https://harvardlawreview.org/2018/11/south-dakota-v-wayfair-inc/

f. Bergman, A. (2018). Dissecting Supreme Court's internet sales tax decision. *Forbes*, June 26. Retrieved March 30, 2020, from https://www.forbes.com/sites/greatspeculations/2018/06/26/dissecting-supreme-courts-internet-sales-tax-decision/#7d2e6e1c3fbe taxation of mail-order and Internet sales. A 2018 Supreme Court decision has substantially affected the landscape for such taxation by expanding the ability of states to levy these taxes.

Tax Rates

State sales tax rates vary from as low as 2.9% (Colorado) to as high as 7.25% (California).[8] To avoid levies of a fraction of a cent, bracket systems are used in which a set amount is collected regardless of the specific sale. For example, a 5% tax might yield 5 cents on any purchase between 81 cents and 90 cents. With computers and electronic scanners at checkout counters in stores, determinations can be quickly made as to whether an item is taxable and how much tax, if any, should be charged.

Many states permit a separate local sales tax on top of the state sales tax. Local sales tax rates vary widely, from an average low of only 0.03% in Idaho to a high of 5.14% in Alabama.[9] Local sales taxes are typically collected by the state and remitted to the local treasury. However, states may or may not remit the full amount of sales tax collected to the local jurisdictions where the tax was collected. For example, North Carolina uses a portion of the sales tax collected in prosperous counties that have a high volume of tourism, specifically the coastal counties and the western mountain counties, to assist other counties not so blessed with tourism revenue. A legislatively determined proportion of the 2.25% maximum local option sales tax is retained by the state and redistributed by a per-capita population formula.[10] That formula is frequently a battle in the state legislature as senators and representatives from districts with less tourism push to increase the sharing and counties with higher rates of tourism fighting to preserve the tax to pay for the services they provide to tourists.[11] **Exhibit 6-2** presents a graphic from the Tax Foundation that shows the combined state and local sales tax rates, by state, as of January 1, 2019.

Sales taxes are regressive in that higher-income consumers typically have more discretionary income and may spend it on items not subject to sales taxes. As noted above, the more the base of the sales tax excludes necessities (such as food and prescription drugs) and includes luxury or nonessential goods and services, the less regressive the tax is likely to be.

This regressive nature of the sales tax may represent a somewhat counterintuitive result, because sales taxes almost always employ a single rate (as opposed to the federal income tax, for example, which has graduated rates). Because of that single rate, some people may think of them as not regressive at all, but rather proportional. Even though sales taxes are levied on a flat-rate basis, however, that does not mean that everyone pays the same portion of their income in tax. On the contrary, the vertical equity implications of the tax are substantially dependent on the portion of an individual's income that is spent on taxed items.

Consider a case of a 5% tax where one taxpayer earns $50,000 in income and spends $40,000 of that on items subject to the sales tax, while a second taxpayer earns $80,000 and spends $60,000 of that on taxed items. The first taxpayer will pay $2,000 in tax ($40,000 times 5%), which represents an effective tax rate of 4% ($2,000/$50,000). The second taxpayer pays more in tax ($3,000, or $60,000 times 5%), but for an effective tax rate of 3.75% ($3,000/$80,000). Even if the sales tax rate is 5% for each taxpayer, the lower-income taxpayer will have a higher effective tax rate than the higher-income taxpayer. Thus, a tax that appears proportional may actually be regressive. As noted previously, the exemption of necessities such as food and drugs tends to have the effect of making the tax less regressive.

The general sales tax continues to be a widespread form of taxation and more popular than the property or income taxes, but state and local governments increasingly see threats to the sales tax as a revenue source, for several reasons. First, as noted in Exhibit 6-1, the threat to the productivity of the tax resulting from sales to remote vendors is a real one. Second, the trend in the overall economy is toward more services (that tend not to be taxed) and fewer goods (that are subject to the tax), which impacts the productivity of the tax. Third, the aforementioned tax holidays, as well as other tax exemptions, may not achieve enough economic benefit to justify what may be substantial revenue losses. For these reasons, one noted sales tax expert

Exhibit 6-2 State and Local Sales Tax Rates, by State, January 2019

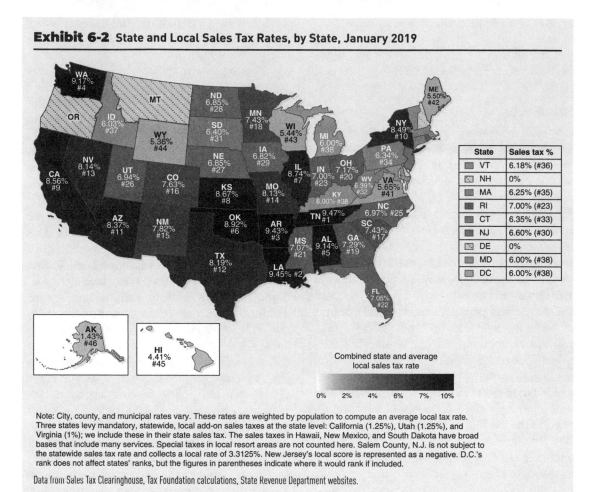

State	Sales tax %
VT	6.18% (#36)
NH	0%
MA	6.25% (#35)
RI	7.00% (#23)
CT	6.35% (#33)
NJ	6.60% (#30)
DE	0%
MD	6.00% (#38)
DC	6.00% (#38)

Combined state and average local sales tax rate

Note: City, county, and municipal rates vary. These rates are weighted by population to compute an average local tax rate. Three states levy mandatory, statewide, local add-on sales taxes at the state level: California (1.25%), Utah (1.25%), and Virginia (1%); we include these in their state sales tax. The sales taxes in Hawaii, New Mexico, and South Dakota have broad bases that include many services. Special taxes in local resort areas are not counted here. Salem County, N.J. is not subject to the statewide sales tax rate and collects a local rate of 3.3125%. New Jersey's local score is represented as a negative. D.C.'s rank does not affect states' ranks, but the figures in parentheses indicate where it would rank if included.

Data from Sales Tax Clearinghouse, Tax Foundation calculations, State Revenue Department websites.

is concerned about the viability of the sales tax as a revenue source and sees those states that rely heavily on the sales tax as having a more difficult time keeping pace with demands for services.[12]

The Value-Added Tax

Increased concerns about the robustness of the U.S. tax system, especially the intergovernmental system of taxation and revenue transfers, have led some to advocate adoption of a value-added tax (VAT).[13] The United States is one of the few industrialized countries without a VAT. A 2015 study found that 140 countries had imposed a VAT (for example, every country in western Europe and Scandinavia has one) and that the rates average about 15% (higher in Europe, at 20%).[14] As its

name implies, a VAT is a consumption tax on the value added by producers and distributors at every stage in the production, distribution, and sales process. While most VATs are collected only at the national level, the Canadian experience with the VAT indicates that it is possible to impose a VAT at multiple levels of government in a federal system.[15] Interest in the VAT in the United States seemed to peak in the early 1990s. Proposed during the 1992 election by then-candidate Bill Clinton, the VAT did not get serious attention in Congress. During the 2016 presidential campaign, a version of the VAT was proposed by Senator Ted Cruz (R-TX). Tax professionals argue that it is superior to many other forms of consumption taxation, but it just has not generated much enthusiasm in the United States.[16]

Efforts to reduce the federal budget deficit have revived calls for some kind of national sales tax in the United States. The highest profile of these was proposed by the Bipartisan Policy Center's (BPC) debt reduction proposal. This BPC initiative of 2010–2012 was headed by former Senator Pete Domenici (R-NM) and CBO founding director Alice Rivlin. The Domenici-Rivlin proposal was for a 6.5% "debt reduction sales tax," phased in over 2 years.[17]

Selective Sales Taxes

Selective sales taxes are normally referred to as *excise taxes*. There are three general categories of excise taxes: luxury excises, sumptuary excises, and benefit-based excises. They differ according both to the specific types of sales that are taxed and to the fiscal or social goals of the tax.

Luxury Excises

These excise taxes are levied on items that are "uniquely or predominantly consumed by the rich," meaning that the act of purchasing the good itself is considered to be evidence of an extraordinary ability to pay taxes.[18] At one time, federal excise taxes were levied on a wide range of luxury goods, such as jewelry, yachts, and expensive automobiles. The logic of these taxes rests on the assumption that the purchase of such goods is prima facie evidence that the consumer can afford the tax. The overall effect of these taxes, then, is to make the tax system more progressive. There are some problems created by luxury excises. One problem is that the definition of what is a "luxury" is in no way fixed. A watch or car in and of itself is not a luxury, but an "expensive watch" or "expensive car" may be. The problem, of course, is that there is no standard definition for "expensive," so any definition used is by necessity somewhat arbitrary. Some families may have a need to purchase a more expensive car in order to accommodate their family. Some sale personnel, such as real estate agents, may argue that a more expensive car is necessary in order for them to be successful in their businesses. On the other hand, for a single person, the purchase of such a vehicle

for personal use may be a luxury. Thus, the definition of a luxury item is clearly open to debate and interpretation.

Another issue with luxury excises is that they can create distortions between taxed and untaxed goods. The luxury tax itself changes the relative price of the luxury item compared to items that are not subject to the tax. This means that tax policy is discriminatory against these luxury items relative to other goods that may be purchased. This has the effect of discouraging, at the margin, purchases of these items, which has the related effect of disadvantaging retailers and producers of luxury goods, perhaps to the point of driving them out of business. In 1990, a new federal luxury tax on yachts was criticized as bankrupting yacht producers and sellers, although it was difficult to evaluate the specific cause of the problems experienced by producers and sellers because the imposition of the tax occurred virtually simultaneously with the economic recession of the early 1990s.

Luxury excise taxes tend not to exist at the state level, and the federal luxury tax has ebbed and flowed according primarily to political factors. The last experience with expanding federal luxury taxation was under the Omnibus Budget Reconciliation Act of 1990, when luxury taxes on boats (over $100,000), automobiles (over $30,000), airplanes (over $250,000), and furs and jewelry (over $10,000) were imposed. These taxes proved unpopular, however, and all have since been repealed.[19]

Sumptuary Excises

These sales taxes are regulatory in nature. Taxes on alcohol and tobacco have been justified as deterring people from consuming these commodities. In reality, the evidence suggests that the demand for these products is relatively *inelastic*, casting doubt on whether taxes discourage usage. The demand for these items tends to be relatively inelastic in large part because they are addictive in nature. Therefore, heavily addicted smokers are unlikely to stop smoking, or even cut back, because of higher taxes on a pack of cigarettes. However, among new smokers, especially youth, price does seem to be a deterrent.

In the 1990s, a substantial tax increase on tobacco was proposed as an important source of financing for federal health care reform. The rationale was that smokers are one of the major sources of health care insurance utilization and that those who create those costs should be the ones to pay taxes to fund them—a sort of reverse benefit principle. The proposal, however, did not get serious review in Congress. Nevertheless, some states have substantially increased tobacco taxes both as a revenue measure and as a health regulatory measure. Large increases in tobacco taxes have reportedly discouraged youth from smoking.

Sumptuary excises, regardless of their regulatory nature, tend to be somewhat regressive, for two reasons. First, there is a tendency toward greater alcohol and cigarette consumption among lower-income groups than higher-income groups. Second, and perhaps even more important, because these taxes are unit taxes instead of ad valorem taxes, effective tax rates are higher for lower-priced brands. While this is likely less of an issue for cigarettes (because the price difference between brands is not great), it is a much larger issue for alcoholic beverages, where there is a huge price range for bottles of wine or spirits (or even six-packs of beer). As an example, if the tax on wine amounted to $1 per bottle, this would represent a 10% tax on a $10 bottle, but only a 2% tax on a $50 bottle.

The federal tobacco tax is a tax collected when products (cigars, cigarettes, snuff, chewing tobacco, pipe tobacco, and roll-your-own tobacco) leave the manufacturer for domestic distribution. The resulting tax adds about $1 to a pack of 20 cigarettes. There is a federal alcohol beverage tax, and many states levy liquor taxes as well. Both federal and state alcohol taxes are levied on a unit basis. In fiscal year 2017, the federal tax was $13.50 per "proof gallon" (about $2.14 for an 80-proof bottle) of distilled spirits, $18 per 31-gallon barrel of beer (or $0.58 per gallon, and roughly 5 cents per can), and $1.07 per gallon (about 21 cents per bottle) of table wine (provided that the alcohol content was 14% or less).[20]

Table 6-1 shows the state tax rates for both the cigarette tax (per pack of cigarettes) and the tax on distilled spirits (per gallon) in 2019 (as well as

Table 6-1 State Gasoline, Cigarette, and Alcohol Taxes, 2019

	Gas Tax (Per Gallon)[a,b]	Cigarette Tax (Per 20-Pack)	Spirits Tax (Per Gallon)
Alabama	$0.21	$0.68	$19.15[c]
Alaska	0.15	2.00	12.80
Arizona	0.19	2.00	3.00
Arkansas	0.22	1.15	7.73
California	0.61	2.87	3.30
Colorado	0.22	0.84	2.28
Connecticut	0.42	4.35	5.40
Delaware	0.23	2.10	4.50
Florida	0.42	1.34	6.50
Georgia	0.35	0.37	3.79
Hawaii	0.48	3.20	5.98
Idaho	0.33	0.57	10.95[c]

Table 6-1 State Gasoline, Cigarette, and Alcohol Taxes, 2019 *(continued)*

	Gas Tax (Per Gallon)[a,b]	Cigarette Tax (Per 20-Pack)	Spirits Tax (Per Gallon)
Illinois	0.55	1.98	8.55
Indiana	0.46	1.00	2.68
Iowa	0.31	1.36	13.07[c]
Kansas	0.24	1.29	2.50
Kentucky	0.26	1.10	8.04[d]
Louisiana	0.20	1.08	3.03
Maine	0.30	2.00	12.00[c]
Maryland	0.37	2.00	5.02
Massachusetts	0.27	3.51	4.05
Michigan	0.42	2.00	11.99[c]
Minnesota	0.29	3.04	8.96
Mississippi	0.18	0.68	8.15[c]
Missouri	0.17	0.17	2.00
Montana	0.33	1.70	9.78[c]
Nebraska	0.31	0.64	3.75
Nevada	0.34	1.80	3.60
New Hampshire	0.24	1.78	0.00[c]
New Jersey	0.41	2.70	5.50
New Mexico	0.19	1.66	6.06
New York	0.46	4.35	6.44
N. Carolina	0.36	0.45	14.63[c]
N. Dakota	0.23	0.44	4.92
Ohio	0.39	1.60	9.87[c]
Oklahoma	0.20	2.03	5.56
Oregon	0.37	1.33	21.98[c]
Penn.	0.59	2.60	7.24[c]
Rhode Island	0.35	4.25	5.40
S. Carolina	0.21	0.57	5.42
S. Dakota	0.30	1.53	4.67

(continues)

Table 6-1 State Gasoline, Cigarette, and Alcohol Taxes, 2019 **(continued)**

	Gas Tax (Per Gallon)[a,b]	Cigarette Tax (Per 20-Pack)	Spirits Tax (Per Gallon)
Tennessee	0.27	0.62	4.46
Texas	0.20	1.41	2.40
Utah	0.30	1.70	15.96[c]
Vermont	0.31	3.08	7.72[c]
Virginia	0.22	0.30	19.93[c]
Washington	0.49	3.03	32.52
West Virginia	0.36	1.20	7.67[c]
Wisconsin	0.33	2.52	3.25
Wyoming	0.24	0.60	0.00[c]
District of Columbia	0.24	4.50	6.19

[a]In addition to the 18.4 cents per gallon federal gasoline tax.

[b]The American Petroleum Institute (API) has developed a methodology for determining the average tax rate on a gallon of fuel. Rates may include any of the following: excise taxes, environmental fees, storage tank fees, other fees or taxes, general sales tax, and local taxes. In states where gasoline is subject to the general sales tax, or where the fuel tax is based on the average sale price, the average rate determined by API is sensitive to changes in the price of gasoline. States that fully or partially apply general sales taxes to gasoline: CA, CT, GA, IL, IN, MI, NY. Rates shown are as of July 2018.

[c]States where the state government controls all sales. The implied excise tax rate is calculated using methodology designed by the Distilled Spirits Council of the United States (DISCUS). In the case of New Hampshire and Wyoming, the implied excise tax rate as calculated by DISCUS is less than zero.

[d]There is an additional 11% wholesale sales tax on all alcoholic beverages.

Cammenga, J. (2019). How high are spirit taxes in your state? *Tax Foundation*, June 19. Retrieved March 30, 2020, from https://taxfoundation.org/state-distilled-spirits-taxes-2019/; Cammenga, J. (2019). How high are cigarette taxes in your state? *Tax Foundation*, April 10. Retrieved March 30, 2020, from https://taxfoundation.org/2019-state-cigarette-tax-rankings/; Loughead, K. (2019). State gasoline tax rates as of July 2018. *Tax Foundation*, August 8.

gasoline tax, which will be discussed later). Several things are notable from this table. First, while every state taxes cigarettes, the cigarette tax varied widely from state to state. Missouri had the lowest tax in the nation, at only 17 cents per pack, while New York and Connecticut's cigarette tax was 25 times that level, at $4.35 per pack (the District of Columbia's rate is even higher, at $4.50). Overall, there were 38 states (including the District of Columbia) with a tax of more than $1.00 per pack, and 5 states with taxes of less than 50 cents per pack. On average, state cigarette taxes added $1.73 to the cost of a pack of cigarettes.[21] Distilled spirits showed substantial variation but not as much as cigarettes, with a range from no taxes at all (New Hampshire and Wyoming) to $32.52 per gallon (Washington).

In addition to the taxes on distilled spirits listed in Table 6-1, most states also tax beer and wine. The Beer Institute argues that taxes are the single most expensive ingredient in beer. Research seems to bear this out; approximately 40% of the cost of a six-pack is accounted for by the cost of taxes (federal and state). As with the other taxes discussed in this chapter, these taxes can differ substantially from state to state. Beer taxes range from a low of 2 cents per gallon in Wyoming to a high of $1.29 per gallon in Tennessee. Other states with relatively high beer tax rates (more than 50 cents per gallon) include Alabama, Alaska, the District of Columbia, Hawaii, Kentucky, Maryland, North Carolina, and South Carolina.[22] Wine taxes are also highly variable, with a high of

$3.26 per gallon in Kentucky, followed by Alaska ($2.50), Florida ($2.25), Iowa ($1.75), and Alabama and New Mexico (tied at $1.70). The lowest taxes per gallon are found in California and Texas (20 cents), Wisconsin (25 cents), and Kansas and New York (both 30 cents).[23]

One of the arguments in favor of liquor taxes is that they reduce alcohol consumption. Studies have shown that heavy and moderate drinkers tend to reduce their consumption in response to higher taxes because these taxes affect the price of a fifth of liquor, a bottle of wine, or a six-pack of beer. Young and underage drinkers are thought to be particularly responsive to price.[24] The tax, then, is thought to assist in helping these individuals to recognize the external costs that their drinking has on society.[25]

Benefit-Based Excises

These taxes are justified on the basis of the "benefit received" concept discussed in the prior chapter on budgeting for revenues. The assumption here is that the tax should be levied on individuals who cause particular services to be provided and that the proceeds from the tax should go to finance that particular service.

Motor vehicle fuel taxes are the classic case. In most states and for the federal government, revenues from taxes on gasoline and diesel fuels are used for transportation purposes. This includes road and bridge construction and maintenance, as well as mass transportation in many cases. The argument here is a simple one: Those individuals who purchase more motor fuel tend to use the highways more than those who purchase a lesser amount of motor fuels; to the extent, then, that the motor fuel tax is used to finance these transportation services, the result is that a greater portion of the cost of financing these services is borne by users. Furthermore, the greater the service consumption, the more the tax paid. Even in cases where gasoline taxes are used to finance mass transportation, the argument holds because encouraging use of mass transportation creates benefits for drivers who are driving on roads that are less congested.

Taxes are typically levied on different types of motor fuels, such as gasoline, diesel, and gasohol. The federal gasoline tax is 18.4 cents per gallon and has been at that level since 1993.[26] On top of that tax, there are state motor fuel taxes in every state. Table 6-1 includes a column showing the state tax rates for gasoline only. As with the excise taxes discussed earlier, gasoline tax rates per gallon differ from state to state, although the range here is much narrower, from a low of 15 cents (Alaska) to a high of 59 cents (Pennsylvania). The tax rates in about three-fourths of the states (38 out of 51, including the District of Columbia) fall somewhere between 20 and 40 cents per gallon.

The rise of hybrid and other fuel-efficient vehicles has led to a stagnation of gasoline tax revenues. Because these are unit taxes levied on a per-gallon basis, greater fuel efficiency leads to less revenue collected, absent increases in rates. The need for increasing revenue, however, is obvious, given the sorry state of the nation's infrastructure. Many governors, especially in the Midwest, have called for big increases in the gas tax (for example, an increase of 45 cents per gallon on top of the existing 26 cents in Michigan, and an increase of 18 cents on top of the existing 28 cents in Ohio).[27] Forcing polluters to pay carbon taxes, an approach favored by environmentalists, has faced opposition where it has been attempted. In November 2018, Washington state voters rejected, for the second time in 2 years, what would have been the nation's first carbon tax.[28] These increases are, however, difficult for politicians and taxpayers to swallow. For this reason, some states are considering moving to a system that bases taxes on the miles that are driven, rather than the gallons of gas consumed.[29] Certainly this would be consistent with the benefit principle, as it is the miles driven that represent the benefit received, rather than the number of gallons of gas consumed. Such a system can be difficult to implement, however, because it requires the state to know how many miles a given driver has driven.

Other such excises include taxes on airline tickets. The revenues from these taxes are used to maintain airports and airport security. There are numerous such taxes at the national level in the United States, including the U.S. Domestic Transportation Tax (7.5%), the U.S. International Arrival and Departure Tax ($18.60), and a $4.20 Federal Flight Segment Tax (all figures 2019).[30]

New Excise Taxes

Changes in the economy, and in legal and regulatory structures in some states, have led to the imposition of new excise taxes on transactions that either did not exist in the past or activities that were not legal. Among the services now subject to taxation in some states are ride-sharing services (such as Uber and Lyft) and rental hosting (such as Airbnb). A longer-standing practice, in many more states, is the taxation of wireless (cell phone) service. As widespread use of wireless services has become commonplace, states and localities have begun applying these taxes. Including the federal Universal Service Fund surcharge (6.64% in July 2018), these wireless taxes were estimated to raise $16 billion in revenues in 2018. They represented, on average, about 19% of a customer's bill in that same year. State and local rates average 12.5% and vary from a low of 2.1% in Oregon to a high of 20.9% in Illinois.[31]

The "new" tax that has raised the most interest and the most interesting policy issues, by far, is the tax on the use of recreational marijuana. Despite the fact that marijuana sale, possession, and use are still against federal law, 11 states (Alaska, California, Colorado, Illinois, Maine, Michigan, Massachusetts, Nevada, Oregon, Vermont, and Washington) plus the District of Columbia have legalized the use and possession of the drug. Two of these jurisdictions (Maine and Vermont) had not yet (as of June 2020) created a legal market and therefore do not yet tax these transactions. Of the remaining nine states, Alaska is the only state without a sales tax collected from the consumer; that state collects a $50 per ounce tax from growers when they sell their product to retailers (presumably that cost is passed on to the consumer). The other eight states have excise or sales taxes that range from 17% (Oregon) to

37% (Washington).[32] In 2018, the states with legal markets and taxes raised approximately $1.1 billion in revenues, with 85% of that coming from three states—California ($345 million), Washington ($319 million), and Colorado ($267 million).[33] Many states that have not yet legalized marijuana are considering doing so in part because of the revenue-raising potential that would accompany legalization. The fact that marijuana is legal at the state level, but still against federal law, has led to at least one interesting budgeting problem, as banks are reluctant to work with states because of a concern that deposits of revenue from marijuana sales will cause these banks to run afoul of federal regulators.[34]

User Charges

All governments have user charges, and almost all public sector functions are partially supported by user charges. As noted earlier, user charges and fees for services are the fastest growing state and local revenue sources. For example, admission fees are charged to national and some state parks and to local tennis courts, other recreational facilities, and exercise and athletic programs. Some elementary and secondary schools charge for textbooks, and higher-education institutions charge tuition. Hospitals, transit systems, water and sewer operations, and refuse collection revenues come mainly from fees and charges. Some jurisdictions own electric and telephone facilities, which they finance through user fees. Police departments charge fees for fingerprinting and special assignments, such as patrolling at sports events.

Rationale for Charges and Fees

The employment of user charges to raise revenues is based on the principle that citizens ought to pay for the cost of public services as a control on the demand for services, which in turn affects the level of services that need to be produced. The more technical argument for their employment holds that the amount of a service provided is closer to the *optimal level of service*, as determined by consumer preferences, when the cost of service is borne directly by the consumer.[35] If the cost of a service is part of general taxes, then citizens tend to demand more of that service than they are actually willing to pay. Furthermore, user charges adhere very closely to the benefit principle, in that it is the beneficiaries of the service in question that pay for that service.

At the federal level, the growth in user charges and fees began with the Reagan administration's opposition to tax increases. With massive annual federal deficits and a president opposed to raising taxes, federal agencies in need of additional revenues selectively considered fees as an alternative. The philosophy of federal user charges, that "each service, sale, or use of Government's goods or resources provided by an agency to specific recipients be self-sustaining," is expressed in Office of Management and Budget Circular A-25.[36] Presidents and members of Congress have found it financially useful and politically acceptable to increase user fees while holding taxes steady or even cutting taxes. President Trump's fiscal year 2020 budget proposed new or expanded user fees that would have resulted in more than $125 billion in additional revenue between fiscal year 2020 and fiscal year 2029.[37]

Types of Charges

Fees vary in the extent to which they are voluntary. Charges for entrance into a museum or a municipal swimming pool are clearly voluntary; other leisure options are available if citizens prefer not to pay for these public services. On the other hand, charges for sewers and trash collection are usually mandatory. If a municipal sewer system exists, citizens normally have no choice but to use it and pay the requisite fee. The largest federal user fees are levied by the U.S. Postal Service. (These charges may be considered partially voluntary in that alternatives for at least some postal services exist.) Other services lie between these extremes. Paying a bus or subway fare may be voluntary, but for many people without other transit options, the fees are required. Differentiating between a mandatory fee and a tax is difficult.

The federal government classifies user charges as *offsetting collections* and *offsetting receipts*. Generally speaking, the former represent collections from the public that the Congress authorizes agencies to spend when collected, while the latter are authorized to be spent by a law enacted subsequent to their collection. Between these two types of charges, the U.S. government collected $564 billion in user charges in fiscal year 2018. **Table 6-2** lists the most common of these fees. The largest two sources of fees were

Table 6-2 Major Federal User Charges, Fiscal Year 2019

Department/Agency	Description	$Billions
Health and Human Services	Medicare premiums	100.1
Postal Service	Stamps and other fees	70.0
Tennessee Valley Authority	Sale of energy	47.7
Various	Employee contributions for health	16.46
Federal Deposit Insurance Corporation	Deposit Insurance	16.3
Pension Benefit Guarantee Corporation	Pension fees from corporations	10.5
Total Offsetting Collections and Offsetting Receipts		564.0

Data from U.S. Office of Management and Budget (2019). *Budget of the United States government, fiscal year 2020, analytical perspectives* (p. 158). Washington, DC: U.S. Government Publishing Office.

the Department of Health and Human Services, whose Medicare insurance premiums accounted for $100 billion, and the Postal Service, which collected fees worth $70 billion. Other significant charges were for Tennessee Valley Authority sales of energy ($48 billion), federal employee insurance premiums ($17 billion), and Federal Deposit Insurance Corporation payments ($16 billion). Taken together, these five sources represent more than $251 billion of the total $564 billion in user charges, or 45% of the total.[38]

State and local governments also generate substantial user charges. In fiscal year 2016, state governments in aggregate collected $208 billion in these levies. Of this amount, almost $104 billion (50%) was for higher education, primarily for tuition and room and board. The other large user charge area was hospitals, at $63 billion (30%). States also collected $10.5 billion (5% of the total collected by states) in charges for highway travel (through tolls). Other charges were for use of natural resources, recreation, air transportation fees, and numerous other activities, but none of these other individual categories accounted for more than 2% of total state charges. Local governments collected $289 billion in charges in the same year, with hospitals as the largest single source ($87.5 billion, or 30%). Other significant local charges were for sewerage ($55 billion, or 19%), education ($24 billion, or 8%), and air transportation ($21 billion, or 7%). The aforementioned four categories accounted for almost two-thirds of all local charges.[39]

Some fees are continuous, whereas others are applied only for special occasions. Transit fares and sewer and water charges are examples of continuous fees. Special-occasion charges include a building permit fee that a contractor has to pay prior to erecting a house, an office building, or some other structure. Although many jurisdictions use general tax revenues to repave and improve streets, other communities levy special assessments on the property owners whose streets will be improved. Similarly, when a community installs a sewer system for the first time, property owners are assessed connection or hookup fees. These charges are calculated on a front footage basis—namely, the number of linear feet that a lot faces or fronts a street. User charges are increasingly being seen as effective revenue sources for social and human services as well.

Special assessments are used in more general ways to support municipal services. Firms that construct new office buildings in a city may have an option to provide on-site parking or pay a fee that is used to construct municipal parking facilities. The state of Virginia, for example, permits high-growth areas to impose "Road Impact Fees." These fees are used to "offset the cost of transportation improvements that are necessary due to new development."[40]

User charges have had a limited role to play in financing local education services, despite the fact that education is the largest area of expenditure at the local level. Fees for school lunches represent the single case where substantial use has been made of charges to recover costs for local public services, although there is increasing pressure to provide school lunches for all students in response to enforcement problems that involve denying students lunch when families cannot pay the fees.[41] Other fees that could be charged, but often are not, are for services such as transportation, textbooks, or activities. Some have argued that education fees could be expanded substantially, particularly for auxiliary services (services over and above the basic educational market basket), including such services as transportation, after-school care, and other services beyond the scope of a typical K–12 curriculum. Some schools also charge, or fundraise, for items such as athletic or band uniforms. The argument for charging for these services is usually made on the basis of efficiency The argument is that parents are more likely to demand careful accounting for the costs of these services if they are required to pay these costs. This would have the effect of reducing overall costs for those services.[42]

Charges and Tax Subsidies

Although user charges can be substantial, they often fail to cover the costs of the services they support. Entrance fees for a municipal swimming pool usually do not provide adequate funds to operate the pool. Therefore, tax revenues are used to supplement funds collected from those fees. An important example of such a subsidy is in the operation of municipal transit systems. If transit fares were set high enough to generate the required operating revenues, the rates would be so high that low-income commuters could not afford to use the system and higher-income commuters would shift to alternative modes of travel—private vehicles and taxicabs. Pricing policies for some services can be quite complicated, making it difficult to determine whether the actual costs are fully recovered by the fee structure.[43] Furthermore, recovery of the capital cost of constructing facilities such as swimming pools and transit systems would increase the cost still more than just fees to recover operating costs. However, the failure to include capital cost recovery in user charges also likely leads to underinvestment in capital facilities, or significant subsidy from the general fund, at the expense of all taxpayers.

Subsidies aid all who use a service, without regard to ability to pay. If transit fares remain artificially low because of a tax subsidy, then both wealthy and low-income individuals who use the system benefit, though the wealthier could certainly afford to pay for the service. Alternative mechanisms include providing free service based on income, such as free bus tokens, or setting fees on a sliding scale. For example, a government-operated mental health clinic might charge low- and moderate-income families little or nothing for services while charging higher-income families at a rate that covers costs.

Some local governments that own profitable utilities, such as public electricity companies and sometimes water enterprises with substantial industrial customers, use utility fee revenue to decrease the taxes otherwise needed to finance other, unrelated services. For those local governments owning such profitable enterprises, the overall cost of other government services to citizens is often lower per capita than for other comparable local governments. Caution is in order, however, before one automatically assumes that local governments should seek to become utility owners. The sometimes hidden costs of diverting

public management talent to the operation of an essentially private business could adversely affect the municipality's overall management efficiency, although that may be difficult to quantify.

Besides the various revenue sources discussed so far, there are still others that can be mentioned only briefly here. Governments operate revolving loan programs that produce revenue as borrowers make principal and interest payments. Licenses are issued that usually require fees. The purpose of these fees may be to cover costs (for example, building permit fees are used to pay the salaries of building inspectors) or to raise revenues beyond costs. Charitable contributions, such as gifts to municipal hospitals, county nursing homes, state universities, and the like, constitute another revenue source.

Lotteries, Casinos, and Other Forms of Gambling

For the past 40 years in the United States, state governments have increasingly operated lotteries and other games of chance in an effort to raise revenues. In addition, more and more states have permitted casino gambling and slot machines and have taxed and regulated these activities. Governments had taxed gambling activities, such as horse and dog racing, for many years earlier, but with the advent of lotteries in the 1960s the states became more directly involved in the operation of games of chance. A recent development, after a 2018 Supreme Court decision, is the expansion of states into the sports betting arena; such betting will be regulated and taxed by states in which it occurs.[44]

Lotteries and Other Gambling Revenues

Since 1963, when New Hampshire began the first modern state lottery, all but eight states have launched lottery programs. In 2016, states generated $23 billion in net revenue from all lottery games.[45] This represented just under 2% of overall state revenues from their own sources (that is, excluding grants and other intergovernmental revenues).

There is wide variation from state to state in the importance of the lottery as a revenue source. The state of New York raised $3.2 billion from the lottery in 2016, or 3.19% of its own-source general revenue of $108 billion. Income from lotteries in other large states varied substantially, with California collecting about 1% and Florida just over 3% of their own-source general revenue from lotteries. Some states with smaller budgets raise substantial sums from their lotteries. Rhode Island raised 7.5% of its own-source general revenue from the lottery in 2016, while the figure was 6% in West Virginia.[46]

Revenues generated from the programs can vary considerably from year to year, depending on lottery activity in adjacent states, the size of jackpots, and the extent to which a lottery has "matured" and lost the public's interest. State lottery revenues rose rapidly in the late 1980s and early 1990s, then leveled off by the mid-1990s. Recent years have seen a resurgence in interest by the public, attracted in part by very large, multi-state payouts (from games such as MegaMillions and Powerball). With the advent of new lottery games—especially LOTTO and other "pick your own" games—and the expansion of the number of states with lotteries, sales more than tripled between 1985 and 1995. They have continued to rise at a relatively stable rate, exceeding the rate of inflation, after 1995. Lottery sales, which were just under $30 billion in 1995, rose to $46 billion by 2005, and to almost $83 billion by 2016. Over that same period, new revenues from the lottery rose from $10.7 billion (1995), to $15.6 billion (2005), and to almost $23 billion in 2016.[47]

As noted above, even with all of this activity, the lottery is not a significant revenue source for most states. There is research suggesting not only that lotteries do not raise much revenue, but they also provide evidence that the revenue that is raised from the lottery often comes at the expense of revenues from other sources, especially sales and excise taxes. Put simply, either taxpayers may substitute spending on the lottery for other spending subject to the sales

tax, or politicians may feel less pressure to raise taxes from other sources because of the revenue generated by the lottery.[48]

Lotteries can be regressive in that lower-income individuals are more likely to participate than middle- and upper-income individuals.[49] A review of the research on lotteries consistently found the lottery to be among the most regressive "taxes" at the state level. This same article went a step further and argued that, in states with lotteries, the regressive nature of the tax contributed to the concentration of wealth toward higher-income taxpayers.[50] A partial exception to this trend was found in the high-stakes "Powerball" game, where, for higher jackpots, the lottery tends to become significantly less regressive, suggesting that higher-income people are willing to play the lottery if the potential returns are high enough.[51] The regressive nature of the lottery is considered particularly problematic given the substantial effort—in the form of advertising—that is made by states to convince citizens to play the lottery. The regressiveness of the lottery is particularly problematic in lieu of the fact that the odds against winning substantial sums from playing the lottery are astronomically high.

In addition to their regressive nature, one factor that distinguishes lotteries from other forms of taxation is their relatively high administrative costs. According to data from the U.S. Census Bureau, in 2016, out of the total money spent on lottery tickets, 64% of those funds went back to lottery players in the form of prizes, 31.5% went to the state in net revenue, and the remaining 4.5% went for administrative costs.[52] This means that, given conventional ways of calculating administrative costs of taxes (administrative costs as a percentage of revenue), the lottery, at 14%, is a very expensive tax to administer. This tax costs so much to administer primarily because of the high cost of advertising. Again, as noted above, there is no other tax where the government expends so much time and money trying to convince people to pay it.

In the past decade, several states have privatized their lotteries or contracted out significant administrative functions. These privatization schemes typically take two forms. In the first, a state may turn over all operations of the lottery to a private firm, in exchange for a share of the profits. This form of privatization has occurred in states such as Illinois, Indiana, and New Jersey. Normally, in these cases the private firm estimates the net revenue that will flow to the state over the term of the contract when the contract is initially entered into. The other form, which is probably more appropriately referred to as outsourcing, is more limited. It involves contracting out particular lottery activities (marketing, for example) to a private firm, with the state still maintaining overall operational control. It is fair to say that lotteries, like most government activities, have increasingly turned to outsourcing; here the variation from state to state is more one of degrees. Outsourcing and privatization of services, such as solid waste collection and toll roads, are discussed separately in the chapter on capital finance and debt management.

In September 2010, Illinois became the first state to hand over management of its lottery to a private firm, although the state (as required by the Justice Department) retained "ownership and regulatory oversight" (this was required by a 2008 Justice Department decision, which held that states could not enter into long-term leases with non-state actors to operate lotteries.[53] Northstar Lottery Group took over day-to-day lottery operations as of July 1, 2011. Northstar ran lottery operations until January 1, 2018, when another private firm (Camelot Illinois) took over the lottery. In fiscal year 2018, the Illinois Lottery sold $2.9 billion in tickets and paid out $1.9 billion in prizes, with $722 million in net revenue to the state. The balance of $300 million represented administrative expenses; relative to sales, that represents a little more than 10% of total sales.[54] A before-and-after-privatization comparison indicates a substantial increase in administrative costs since 2009; in 2009, administrative costs represented only a little more than 3% of total sales. Curiously, however, this tripling of administrative costs occurred between 2009 and 2010, thus predating the privatization of the operations of the lottery. It certainly does appear, however, based on Census Bureau data, that the privatization of the Illinois lottery has been of questionable

benefit, at least in terms of overall revenue. In 2010, the year before the lottery was privatized, the state realized net revenue of $647 million out of about $2.2 billion in sales (29.4%). By 2016, the state realized $717 million out of $2.9 billion in sales, or 25%.[55] The 2018 figures from the lottery's annual report cited earlier suggest almost identical percentages as these 2016 numbers. Thus, while revenue has increased, it is unclear whether the privatization of the lottery has been a good investment for the state overall.

Casino Gambling

In addition to lotteries, a number of states have legalized casino gambling and similar forms of amusement, such as slot machines. While in 1988, legalized casino gambling existed only in Nevada and New Jersey, in 2011, 29 states had Native American casinos and 25 states had non–Native American casinos as standalone properties or casinos at racetracks (in four of those states, casinos were only at racetracks; in two others they were only on riverboats).[56] Native American casinos operate substantially differently than non–Native American casinos. In the case of the former, states negotiate with tribes for the state "take" of casino revenues. In the latter case, taxes are levied on gross receipts or adjusted gross receipts (gross receipts less winnings). Some states use a flat scale, while others use an adjusted scale. States also raise money from licensing fees and fees for gaming devices, such as slot machines. The chapter on intergovernmental relations discusses the relationships between states and Native American tribes concerning casino gambling.

While states do not raise substantial revenue from taxing gaming, such revenue has become more important as more states have legalized casino gambling. In 2017, according to the American Gaming Association, a total of $9.2 billion was raised from direct taxes on gaming (this does not include income or sales taxes paid that are attributable to the industry). While traditional leader Nevada still raises significant revenue ($867 million in 2017), it has now been eclipsed by two more populous states, as Pennsylvania raised more than

$1.4 billion from gaming taxes and New York raised more than $1 billion. These three states—plus Illinois, Indiana, Louisiana, Maryland, and Ohio—accounted for approximately two-thirds of all of the gaming revenues produced in 2017.[57] Nationwide research suggests that, while there is significant "cannibalization" of lottery revenues from casinos, states as a whole seem to benefit, from a revenue perspective, from having both lotteries and casino gambling.[58]

One of the selling points often used to market the lottery and other forms of gambling revenues is that their proceeds will be used to support spending for some specific (usually popular) policy area. For example, many states earmark lottery revenues, or other gaming revenues, for education or senior citizen programs. It is frequently difficult, however, to make the case that this earmarking actually leads to a net increase in funding for these areas. In cases where funds are dedicated to education, for example, lottery earmarking may simply have the effect of freeing up other revenues that would have been spent on education to be used for other purposes.[59] This is because of the *fungibility* of revenues, given that some sources can be substituted for others without increasing spending for particular programs. In some states where lottery earnings are earmarked to support education, state legislatures have cut other state education spending by commensurate amounts.[60] (See the chapter on intergovernmental relations.)

An exception was found to this general rule in Georgia, where lottery revenues, at least initially, stimulated additional spending in the areas advertised by lottery proponents. According to one study, this occurred because of the specific structure of the earmark, the transparency of the budget process, and the commitment of the governor to increase funds rather than substitute them.[61]

Pari-Mutuel Wagering Taxes

In addition to lottery and amusement taxes, some states allow betting on sporting competitions, primarily horse racing (although some states also have legalized dog racing and jai alai). These are more similar to amusement taxes than lotteries in the sense that the activity is not operated by the state but is regulated and taxed by the state. Nationwide, pari-mutuel taxes generated only $232 million in 2007. This represented only 0.02% of total own-source revenue for states in that year. Only California ($37.5 million), New York ($28.1 million), Florida ($28.1 million), and Pennsylvania ($24.7 million) raised more than $20 million in that year, but in each of these cases, the revenue from this source made an inconsequential contribution to state revenues.

Sports Betting—The Gaming Tax of the Future?

One source of revenue that has generally not been available to states is that associated with betting on sporting events. With the exception of Nevada and New Jersey (which were grandfathered in as a result of activity already permitted in Las Vegas and Atlantic City), states have not been permitted to legalize, and thus tax, sports betting. The U.S Supreme Court, in *Murphy v. National Collegiate Athletic Association*, ruled in 2018 that the 1992 Professional and Amateur Sports Protection Act was a violation of the 10th Amendment to the Constitution, as it illegally interfered with the ability of states to allow and regulate gambling on sporting events. This freed states to pass legislation that would permit sports betting in those states. Ultimately, this sports betting could be subject to taxation, just like casino gambling or horse racing.[62]

As of June 2019, sports betting was legal in eight states—Delaware, Mississippi, Nevada, New Jersey, New Mexico, Pennsylvania, Rhode Island, and West Virginia. Bills had been passed by at least one house of the legislature in six other states (Arkansas, Indiana, Iowa, Montana, New York, and Tennessee), plus the District of Columbia. There were bills introduced, but not passed, in 29 other states, leaving only seven states where there has been no legislative activity.[63]

Summary

Some revenue sources, instead of being taxes on income or wealth, are taxes on individual transactions. Among these are general and specific sales taxes; user charges; and revenue raised from games of chance, such as lotteries. These revenue sources have in common that they are levied on a more or less voluntary basis. That is, individuals have relatively more "choice" in whether they engage in the transaction or pay the tax.

The general sales tax is the largest single revenue source for state governments and is also used by many local governments. The tax is levied on sales made at the retail level. Many states exclude particular transactions from the tax base; among the most frequent exclusions are food and prescription drugs. By and large, these exclusions make the tax less regressive, as they are necessities and thus tend to represent a larger percentage of total spending for lower-income taxpayers than for higher-income taxpayers. In recent years, the viability of the sales tax has been threatened by the increased spending by consumers from remote vendors, including both mail-order and Internet sales. States and local governments lack a reliable way to collect taxes on these transactions.

Sales taxes are also levied on particular types of transactions. There are three general categories of these selective sales, or excise, taxes. First, luxury excises are levied on items (such as boats or luxury automobiles) the purchase of which is viewed as evidence of an extraordinary tax-paying ability. Second, sumptuary excises (so-called sin taxes) are levied on items such as cigarettes and liquor, ostensibly to discourage consumption of these goods that are thought to cause harm to both the individual who consumes them and society as a whole. Third, benefit-based excises operate as a quasi-price by taxing individuals and then using the proceeds of those taxes to finance benefits used by the specific taxpayers on whom the tax is levied. A classic example of this is gasoline taxes used to finance transportation projects, especially highways. Changes in the economy or in some state laws have created the opportunity for the taxation of other activities or products, such as marijuana.

Increasingly, governments charge citizens directly for their purchase of individual services or have dedicated revenue from charges for particular spending programs or functions. In this way, government services can be made to resemble market transactions. User charges have been growing at all levels of government and include such varied items as federal postal service fees, state university tuition, and local water and sewer fees.

Many state governments rely on revenue from gambling to finance a portion of state government services. While most states do not raise much money from gambling, games of chance have been a growth industry for states. There are substantial differences between lotteries and other forms of gaming revenue. In the case of lotteries, the games are operated directly by the government, with games marketed, tickets sold, and proceeds paid directly to state coffers. In the case of other games of chance, such as casino gambling, the games are not operated by the state but are taxed by the government. Casino gambling has been on the increase in recent years, including both Native American and non–Native American components. As the result of a 2018 Supreme Court decision, several states have already begun to tax gambling on sporting events, and even more are sure to follow.

Notes

1. Cammenga, J. (2019). *State and local sales tax rates, January 2019*. Washington, DC; Tax Foundation.
2. U.S. Census Bureau (2019); *2016 Annual surveys of state and local government finances summary tables*. Retrieved January 3, 2020, from https://factfinder.census.gov/faces/tableservices/jsf/pages/productview.xhtml?src=bkmk#.
3. Federation of Tax Administrators (2020). *State sales tax rates and food and drug exemptions*, January. Retrieved March 30, 2020, from https://taxadmin.memberclicks.net/assets/docs/Research/Rates/sales.pdf.
4. Federation of Tax Administrators (2019). *2019 state sales tax holidays*. Retrieved October 24, 2019, from https://www.taxadmin.org/2019-sales-tax-holiday.
5. Federation of Tax Administrators (2017). *FTA survey of services taxation—update*. Retrieved July 23, 2019, from https://www.taxadmin.org/btn-0817_services.
6. CanagaRetna, S. (2010). *State fiscal issues*. Presentation at the Southern Legislative Conference of the Council of State Governments, at the 2010 Division of Insurance and Research Economist and Analyst Meeting Federal Deposit Insurance Corporation (FDIC), Dallas, Texas, October 7. Retrieved December 7, 2011, from http://knowledgecenter.csg.org/drupal/content/state-fiscal-issues.

7. Povitch, E. (2017). *Why states are struggling to tax services.* Pew Charitable Trusts, July.

8. Cammenga, J. (2019). *State and local sales tax rates*, p. 3.

9. Cammenga, J. (2019). *State and local sales tax rates*, p. 4.

10. Afonso, W., et al. (2016). LOSTS in detail: a comparison of North Carolina's local option sales tax policy with those of other states. *UNC School of Government.* Retrieved October 24, 2019, from https://www.sog.unc.edu/sites /www.sog.unc.edu/files/reports/2016-08-23%202014 1101%20LOSTs%20in%20Detail.pdf.

11. Khrais, R. (2015). NC Senate approves bill that would redistribute sales tax revenue. *WUNC Public Radio.* Retrieved October 24, 2019, from https://www.wunc.org /post/nc-senate-approves-bill-would-redistribute-sales -tax-revenue.

12. Mikesell, J. (2004). The prospects for general sales taxation in American state and local government finance: challenges for a fiscal workhorse unready for the new millennium. *Journal of Public Budgeting, Accounting and Financial Management, 16*, 63–79.

13. Rivlin, A. M. (1992). *Reviving the American dream: the economy, the states and the federal government.* Washington, DC: Brookings Institution.

14. Pomerleau, K. (2015). How many countries in the world have a value-added tax. *Tax Foundation*, November 19. Retrieved March 30, 2020, from https://taxfoundation.org /how-many-countries-world-have-value-added-tax/.

15. Bird, R., & Smart, M. (2014). VAT in a federal System: lessons from Canada. *Public Budgeting & Finance, 34*, Winter, 38–60.

16. Zodrow, G. R. (1999). The sales tax, the VAT, and taxes in between—or, is the only good NRST a "VAT in drag"? *National Tax Journal, 52*, 429–442.

17. Debt Reduction Task Force (2010). *Restoring America's future* (pp. 20–43). Washington, DC: Bipartisan Policy Center.

18. Davie, B., updated by D. Zimmerman (2005). Luxury taxes. In J. Cordes, R. Ebel, & J. Gravelle (Eds.), *Encyclopedia of taxation and tax policy*, 245–247.

19. Davie, B., updated by D. Zimmerman (2005). Luxury taxes.

20. Tax Policy Center (n.d.). *What are the major federal excise taxes, and how much money do they raise? Key Elements of the U.S. Tax System.* Retrieved June 1, 2020, from https:// www.taxpolicycenter.org/briefing-book/what-are-major -federal-excise-taxes-and-how-much-money-do-they -raise.

21. Cammenga, J. (2019). *How high are cigarette taxes in your state?* Tax Foundation, April 10. Retrieved March 30, 2020, from https://taxfoundation.org/2019-state-cigarette-tax -rankings.

22. Cammenga, J. (2019). *How high are beer taxes in your state?* Tax Foundation, June 5. Retrieved March 30, 2020, from https://taxfoundation.org/state-beer-taxes-2019/.

23. Cammenga, J. (2019). *How high are wine taxes in your state?* Tax Foundation, June 12. Retrieved March 30, 2020, from https://taxfoundation.org/state-wine-taxes-2019/.

24. Chaloupka, F., Grossman, M., & Saffer, H. (2002). The effects of price on alcohol consumption and alcohol-related problems. *National Institute on Alcohol Abuse and Alcoholism of the National Institutes of Health.* Retrieved December 7, 2011, from http://pubs.niaaa.nih .gov/publications/arh26-1/22-34.htm.

25. Pogue, T. (2005). Alcohol beverage taxes, federal. *Encyclopedia of taxation and tax policy*, 5.

26. Thorndike, T. J. (2013). Tax history: how Congress broke the gas tax. *Tax History Project, Tax Analysts, Inc.*, October 13. Retrieved July 23, 2019, from http:// www.taxhistory.org/thp/readings.nsf/ArtWeb/1B663 ACC1F6D710F85257D1B00412409?OpenDocument.

27. Vock, D., & Greenblatt, A. (2019). 45 cents a gallon? 20? 18? Midwest governors float major gas tax hikes. *Governing*, February 26. Retrieved June 25, 2019 from https://www.governing.com/topics/transportation -infrastructure/gov-gas-tax-minnesota-ohio-governor -funding-roads.html.

28. Vock, D. (2018). Voters reject, again, what would have been the nation's first carbon tax, *Governing*, November 7. Retrieved June 25, 2019 from https://www.governing.com /topics/transportation-infrastructure/gov-washington -nations-first-carbon-tax.html.

29. Vock, D. (2018). With gas taxes in peril, more states study alternatives. *Governing*, January 16. Retrieved June 25, 2019, from https://www.governing.com/topics /transportation-infrastructure/gov-gas-tax-oregon -california-mileage.html.

30. Federal Aviation Administration (2019). *Current aviation excise tax structure.* Retrieved June 27, 2019, from https:// www.faa.gov/about/budget/aatf/media/Excise_Tax_Rate _Structure_2019.pdf.

31. Mackey, S., & Bishop-Henchman, J. (2018). *Wireless taxes and fees climb again in 2018.* Tax Foundation Fiscal Fact Number 626, December. Retrieved March 30, 2020, from https://www.dontmesswithtaxes.com/2018/12/wireless -taxes-and-fees-jump-again-2018.html.

32. Cammenga, J. (2019). *How high are taxes on recreational marijuana in your state?* Tax Foundation, April 24. Retrieved March 30, 2020, from https://taxfoundation .org/2019-recreational-marijuana-taxes/.

33. Lotus, J. (2019). States reap tax rewards from legalized marijuana sales. *UPI*, June 14. Retrieved January 3, 2020, from https://www.upi.com/Top_News/US/2019/06/14 /States-reap-tax-rewards-from-legalized-marijuana-sales /7721560462729/.

34. Quinton, S (2019). Despite state support, marijuana banking bill may sink again in Congress. *Stateline*, May 30. Retrieved January 2, 2020, from https://www.governing .com/topics/finance/sl-safe-banking-act-cannabis -bill.html.

35. Johnson, R. W., & McCullough, J. S. (1996). *Case study on urban local government finance.* Paper presented at the Asian Development Bank Seminar on Urban Infrastructure Finance in Asia. Research Triangle Park, NC: Research Triangle Institute.

36. U.S. Office of Management and Budget (1993). *Circular A-25*. Retrieved January 21, 2007, from http://www.whitehouse.gov/omb/circulars/a025/a025.html.

37. U.S. Office of Management and Budget (2019). *Budget of the United States government: fiscal year 2020: analytical perspectives*, March, 168–169.

38. U.S. Office of Management and Budget (2019). *Budget of the United States government: fiscal year 2020, analytical perspectives*, 158.

39. U.S. Census Bureau (2019). *2016 annual surveys of state and local government finances summary tables*. Retrieved January 3, 2020, from https://factfinder.census.gov/faces/tableservices/jsf/pages/productview.xhtml?src=bkmk#.

40. *House Bill 3202: Road impact fees*. (2007). Retrieved February 24, 2012, from http://www.hb3202.virginia.gov/roadimpactfees.shtml.

41. FitzSimons, C. (2019). School lunch debt and lunch shaming is a problem that needs a national solution. *NBC News Essay*. retrieved October 26, 2019, from https://www.nbcnews.com/think/opinion/school-lunch-debt-lunch-shaming-problem-needs-national-solution-ncna1066461.

42. Wassmer, R., & Fisher. R. (2002). Interstate variation in the use of fees to fund K–12 public education. *Economics of Education Review, 21*, 87–100.

43. Foster, B. D., & Fujita, G. (2000). Rate setting for municipal utilities: Detroit's combined sewer overflow facilities. *Government Finance Review, 16*, June, 33–40.

44. *Murphy v. National Collegiate Athletic Association*, 138 S.Ct.1461 (2018).

45. U.S. Census Bureau (2019). *Income and apportionment of state-administered lottery funds: 2016*. Retrieved July 13, 2019, from https://www.census.gov/data/tables/2016/econ/state/historical-tables.html.

46. Calculations by the author from U.S. Census Bureau (2019). *Income and apportionment of state-administered lottery funds: 2016*. Retrieved July 13, 2019, from https://www.census.gov/data/tables/2016/econ/state/historical-tables.html.

47. Calculation by author from U.S. Census Bureau (2019). *Income and apportionment of state-administered lottery funds: 1995, 2005, 2016*. Retrieved July 13, 2019, from https://www.census.gov/data/tables/2016/econ/state/historical-tables.html.

48. Fink, S., Marco, A., & Rork, J. (2004). Lotto nothing? The budgetary impact of state lotteries. *Applied Economics, 36*, 2357–2367.

49. Clotfelter, C. T., & Cook, P. J. (1990). On the economics of state lotteries. *Journal of Economic Perspective, 4*, Fall, 105–119.

50. Freund, E., & Morris, I. (2005). The lottery and income inequality in the states. *Social Science Quarterly, 86*, 996–1012.

51. Oster, E. (2004). Are all lotteries regressive? Evidence from the Powerball. *National Tax Journal, 57*, 179–187.

52. U.S. Bureau of the Census, U.S. Department of Commerce (2019). *Income and apportionment of state-administered lottery funds: 2016*. Retrieved June 27, 2019, from https://www.census.gov/data/tables/2016/econ/state/historical-tables.html.

53. Illinois lottery goes private. (2010). *NBCChicago.com*, September 15. Retrieved February 24, 2012, from http://www.nbcchicago.com/news/business/illinois-lottery-privatization-103016309.html.

54. KPMG (2019). *Illinois State Lottery Financial Audit, Fiscal Year 2018* December 21. Retrieved March 30, 2020, from http://www.ilga.gov/reports/ReportsSubmitted/246RSGAEmail551RSGAAttachFY18-Lottery-Fin-Full.pdf.

55. Calculation by author from U.S. Census Bureau, *Income and apportionment of state-administered lottery funds: 2010, 2016*.

56. American Gaming Association (2019). *State of the states 2018: The AGA Survey of the Commercial Casino Industry*, pp. 12–14. Retrieved January 3, 2020, from https://www.americangaming.org/wp-content/uploads/2018/08/AGA-2018-State-of-the-States Report_FINAL.pdf.

57. American Gaming Association (2019). *State of the states 2018: The AGA survey of the commercial casino industry, 2018*, 15.

58. Elliott, D. E., & Navin, J. (2002). Has riverboat gambling reduced state lottery revenue? *Public Finance Review, 30*, 235–247.

59. Gribbin, D., & Bean, J. (2006). Adoption of state lotteries in the United States, with a closer look at Illinois. *The Independent Review, 10*, 360.

60. Broadwater, L., & Green, E. (2017). Maryland casinos are pumping out billions for education. So why are there school budget deficits? *Baltimore Sun*, January 22, Retrieved January 2, 2020, from https://www.baltimoresun.com/maryland/bs-md-casino-education-20170121-story.html; Tyko, K., & Beegan, G. (2017). Lottery not the education jackpot you may think. *TCPalm*, March 8. Retrieved January 2, 2020, from https://www.tcpalm.com/story/news/2017/03/08/florida-lottery-not-education-jackpot/98265030/.

61. Lauth, T., & Robbins, M. (2002). The Georgia lottery and state appropriations for education: substitution or additional funding? *Public Budgeting & Finance, 22*, Fall, 89–100.

62. Edelman, M. (2018). Explaining the Supreme Court's recent sports betting decision. *Forbes*, May 16. Retrieved March 30, 2020, from https://www.forbes.com/sites/marcedelman/2018/05/16/explaining-the-supreme-courts-recent-sports-betting-decision/#d6700fa537cb.

63. Rodenberg, R. (2019). United States of sports betting: an updated map of where every state stands. *ESPN.com*, June 26. Retrieved July 13, 2019, from https://www.espn.com/chalk/story/_/id/19740480/the-united-states-sports-betting-where-all-50-states-stand-legalization.

CHAPTER 7

Budget Preparation: The Expenditure Side

Since the late 1990s, the federal government's Office of Management and Budget (OMB) has been engaged in various efforts focused on strategic planning, performance measurement, and program evaluation, all of which are designed to assist in allocating resources in the budgetary process. State and local governments similarly have been using program information in their budget processes. These were the outgrowth of changes that began in the early 1900s. While challenges remain in using these measures for decision making, budgeting has come a long way from the times when all that mattered to decision makers was the dollars being spent, rather than how they were being used.

In the budget preparation phase, important decisions about expenditures are made simultaneously with decisions concerning revenues. The two general types of information relevant for budgeting are program and resource information. Program information consists of data on what government does and what those activities accomplish, while resource information consists of the inputs necessary to perform those activities. The inputs include dollars, facilities, equipment, supplies, and personnel and have been a long-established feature of budgetary systems. The use of program information, on the other hand, has slowly emerged as an integral part of budgeting.

The critical argument relating to these two types of information is that they must be considered in combination if budgeting is to be a sensible process of allocating resources. Because resources are finite, the budget is expected to relate the accomplishments of government to the resources available. The history of budgetary reform can be viewed as a struggle to create such budget systems.

This chapter examines the various approaches used in assembling the expenditure side of budgets. The first section of this chapter discusses early reform efforts. The second section describes the types of program information used to varying degrees in budget systems. The last section explores the numerous budget systems that have been used, including performance, program, zero-base, and hybrid budgeting systems.

Early Developments

Budgeting can focus on expenditure control, management of resources, and planning for future allocation decisions.[1] By "planning," we are specifically referring to efforts to associate means with ends in order to attain goals and objectives in the future. While the development of these three emphases has been sequential over time to some extent, they are not rigidly fixed to specific time periods, and both the management and planning phases have involved greater utilization of program information. Not only is there a blurring of distinctions between these stages in terms of the dates of their popularity, but use of planning coupled with program information also was advocated at least as far back as the early part of the twentieth century.

Program Information

1910–1939

Before the establishment of the federal budgetary system in the early part of the twentieth century (see the chapter on budgeting in the Congress), budgeting was often advocated as a means of allocating resources to obtain program results.[2] Two of the most notable proponents were President Taft and the 1912 Taft Commission on Economy and Efficiency.[3] At one point in its report, the Commission stated, "In order that he [the administrator] may think intelligently about the subject of his responsibility he must have before him regularly statements which will reflect *results in terms of quality and quantity*; he must be able to measure quality and quantity of results by units of cost and units of efficiency" (emphasis added).[4]

Other important spokespersons for program results in budgeting in the 1910s included Frederick A. Cleveland[5] and William F. Willoughby.[6] The 1920s and 1930s brought more proponents for program results being included in budgets, including Lent D. Upson,[7] A. E. Buck,[8] Wylie Kilpatrick,[9] and the 1937 President's Committee on Administrative Management.[10] A. E. Buck's classic *Public Budgeting* (1929) admittedly lacked a strong program information orientation, but Buck did express interest in reforms that would concentrate on measuring the products of government activities.

1940–1960

Although the use of program information and planning was advocated throughout the first four decades of the twentieth century, this issue received far greater attention beginning in the 1940s. V. O. Key, Jr., challenged previous budgetary literature as largely mechanical and criticized it for failing to focus on the "basic budgeting problem" of comparing the merits of alternative programs: "On what basis shall it be decided to allocate X dollars to activity A instead of activity B?"[11] The 1949 Commission on Organization of the Executive Branch of the Government, commonly known as the First Hoover Commission, recommended that the federal budget be "based upon functions, activities, and projects: this we designate as a performance budget." Budgeting should be in terms of "the work or the service to be accomplished."[12]

More proponents of the same viewpoint emerged in the 1950s. Noted scholars included Verne B. Lewis,[13] Frederick C. Mosher,[14] Catheryn Seckler-Hudson,[15] and Arthur Smithies.[16] The Second Hoover Commission supported the recommendations of its predecessor.[17] Smithies suggested the use of program information in budgeting as a primary means of improving both executive and legislative decision making. Jesse Burkhead's *Government Budgeting* (1956), while basically descriptive rather than normative, devoted considerable discussion to performance and program budgeting.[18]

An alternative school of thought led by David Novick, Charles J. Hitch, Roland McKean, and others was rooted in a set of theoretical and technological fields that developed after World War II. These fields and technologies, which included operations research, economic analysis, and general systems theory, were highly compatible with the budget reform movement and served as the theoretical foundation for planning-programming-budgeting (PPB) systems attempted in the 1960s.[19]

By the 1950s and 1960s, the use of program information in budgeting had become a mainstream reform issue. At the same time, another school of thought led by Charles E. Lindblom, Aaron Wildavsky, and others challenged the budget reform movement on the grounds that political decision systems like budgeting were not readily adaptable to program planning. Lindblom advanced the "muddling through" model of decision making that ran counter to budgetary reform efforts.[20] Wildavsky was to become the most outspoken skeptic of the feasibility of using program information in budgeting. In the same vein as Lindblom, he pioneered a description of budgeting referred to as "incrementalism," arguing that budgets, like the political process, tended to change little from one year to the next. In 1969 he concluded, "No one knows how to do program budgeting."[21]

The reform efforts from the early 1900s to 1960 that emphasized the use of program information, coupled with this series of other non-budgetary developments, constitute the foundation for more recent budget system innovations and for contemporary budget systems. State and local governments continue to emphasize the importance of considering what programs accomplish in making budget decisions. 41 states require outcome data in the budget process. Among those 41 states, results measures are used more in human services programs than in complete application of results measures across the entire budget.[22]

Structuring the Request Process

Except in the smallest organizations, a central budget office alone cannot prepare a budget. As noted in the chapter on budget cycles, budget preparation begins with the almost simultaneous amassing of supporting information in the operating agencies and the issuance of budget instructions from a central budget office.

The information developed at this stage depends partially on how each agency chooses to make its case and partially on the way decisions are expected to be made within an organization. If only dollar requests are prepared, obviously no information will be available with which to make judgments on program effectiveness. On the other hand, a central budget office may not necessarily use program information in its deliberations, even if it requires its submission. Still another factor determining what information will be prepared is the known information demands from other budget participants, most notably, the legislative

body. Much data may be amassed, not because the agency or the chief executive has any intention of using them for decision purposes, but simply because each year the legislative body demands that information. Program efficiency or effectiveness information may be used in executive branch decisions about appropriations requests sent to the legislature, but that information may be largely ignored by the legislative body in the actual appropriations process.

Preparation Instructions

Budget preparation practices vary considerably within agencies. Different degrees of participation by field office staff and other line personnel occur, but while such variation exists, the overall process is guided by a set of instructions issued by a central budget office of a government.

At the federal level, such instructions are contained in OMB Circular A-11, *Preparation, Submission, and Execution of the Budget*. This document, issued annually, contains considerable detail about most aspects of federal budgeting and, counting text and supporting illustrations, runs approximately 1,000 pages in length. The circular is available on the Internet, and agencies can submit much of their budget request information online.[23] **Table 7-1** indicates the vast array of materials that agencies must submit. Much of this information is mandated by various statutes, such as performance information being required by the Government Performance and Results Modernization Act of 2010 and its predecessor, the Government Performance and Results Act of 1993.[24]

Table 7-2 provides a comparable summary of budget preparation instructions for New York State. One striking characteristic is the attention devoted to capital expenditures, such as monies for the purchase of land, buildings, and large pieces of equipment—10 of 18 required budget request schedules pertain to capital assets. This is not a surprising contrast to federal budget instructions, as New York State, like almost all state governments and unlike the federal government, has a separate capital budget. (See the chapter on capital assets.)

Table 7-1 **Selected Materials That Federal Agencies Must Submit as Part of Their Budget Requests: 2018**

Section Title of OMB Circular A-11	Description
I. General Policies and Requirements	
25 – Summary of Requirements	Overview of materials they must submit
31 – Compliance with Administrative Policies and Other General Requirements	Confirm that budgets comply with president's spending levels, president's management agenda, management improvement agenda, and other requirements
32 – Personnel, Compensation, Benefits, and Related Costs	Estimate expenditures for employee pay and benefits
32 – Estimates Related to Specific Types of Programs and Expenditures	Estimate expenditures for construction, leases of capital assets, hospitals, advisory committees, taxes, and tax expenditures
II. The Budget Submission	
51 – Basic Justification Materials	Summarize justification of programs, analysis of resources, agency restructuring, performance goals, measures and indicators, loan and loan guarantee programs, and acquisition of capital assets
52 – Information on Financial Management	General reporting requirements, policies addressed by reports, description of required Report on Resources for Financial Management Activities
53 – Information Technology and E-Government	Report information technology spending and efforts to expand public access to information through technology (e-government)
54 – Rental Payments for Space and Land	Show expenditures for rental of buildings, other structures, and land; justification of budget for space requirements
III. MAX Data and Other Materials Required after Passback	
79 – Budget Data System	Overview of MAX budget system, which provides computer support for the budget process and account identification codes
80 – Development of Baseline Estimates	Overview of preparing baseline estimates on discretionary and mandatory spending, supplemental requests, and governmental receipts
81 – Policy and Baseline Estimates of Budget Authority, Outlays, and Receipts	Project budget authority, outlays, and receipts for future years based on existing laws (current services projections)
82 – Combined Schedule X	Budget obligations by program activity, budgetary resources available for obligation, and other detailed resource accounting
83 – Object Classification	Submit information about personnel, contractual services, acquisition of assets, and grants and fixed charges
84 – Character Classification (Schedule C)	Report expenditures as to whether they are investments or non-investments and whether they provide funding to state and local governments

Table 7-1 Selected Materials That Federal Agencies Must Submit as Part of Their Budget Requests: 2018 *(continued)*

Section Title of OMB Circular A-11	Description
III. MAX Data and Other Materials Required after Passback	
85 – Estimating Employment Levels and the Personnel Summary	Estimate the full-time equivalent (FTE) of personnel by program activity
86 – Special Schedules	Provide balance sheets that summarize financial transactions
95 – Budget Appendix and Print Material	Instructions on detailed appropriations language, narratives, and more detailed budget request supporting information

Data from U.S. Office of Management and Budget (2019). *Preparation, submission, and execution of the budget,* Circular No. A-11. Retrieved July 5, 2019, from https://www.whitehouse.gov/wp-content/uploads/2018/06/a11.pdf

Table 7-2 Selected Materials That New York State Agencies Must Submit as Part of Their Budget Requests for FY 2021 Budget

Subject	Description
Commissioner's Statement	Indicate agency's mission, funding requirements, and changes requested
Agency Summary Recapitulation	Show appropriations by fund type, aid to localities, capital projects, and debt service
Program Recapitulation	Summarize current appropriations by program/fund and show requested changes
Miscellaneous Receipts	Report miscellaneous receipts
State Operations and Aid to Localities	Provide expenditures for each state program and report aid to localities (each by fund)
State Operations Nonpersonal Services	Submit information on all equipment and real property that requires installment payments out of state bond proceeds
Federal Funds Requested Appropriations	Report existing and requested federal funds
Request to Reappropriate Existing State Operations and Aid to Localities Appropriations	Request reappropriation when an existing appropriation will not be expended by its expiration date
Commissioner's Capital Plan Overview	Report major changes in 5-year capital plan
Capital Projects Summaries	Provide detailed data on capital projects
Non Highway and Highway Appropriation Request	Request approval of new capital projects
Capital Commitments	Report expected dollar value of contracts expected to be awarded

(continues)

Table 7-2 **Selected Materials That New York State Agencies Must Submit as Part of Their Budget Requests for FY 2021 Budget**   *(continued)*

Subject	Description
Capital Projects Codes	Supply departmental and budget codes for each capital project
Capital Maintenance Plan Report	Provide overview of plans for maintenance of capital
Description of Maintenance Projects	Show detailed information about planned maintenance projects
Requested Maintenance Appropriations, Reappropriations, and Disbursements	Request approval of maintenance appropriations
Summary of Capital Assets	Indicate age, useful life, and value of agency assets
Summary of Maintenance Plan Evaluations	Supply narrative discussing the evaluation of plans to maintain agency assets

Adapted from New York State Division of the Budget (2019). *Budget request manual: FY 2021 budget request manual updates.* Retrieved July 5, 2019, from https://www.budget.ny.gov/guide/brm/index.html. Individual schedules available separately.

Instructions such as those contained in federal Circular A-11 and New York State's budget instructions include forms to be completed, reducing uncertainty among agencies as to what the budget office expects of them. Typically, a calendar will be provided explaining when requests are due for submission to the budget office and indicating a period when agencies may be called for hearings with the budget office (see the chapter on budget cycles). The instructions, then, determine the type and amount of information that will be required of the agencies, although the budget office may request additional information from particular agencies.

In the case of the federal government, Circular A-11 describes a two-step process. The circular is released in the summer, and agencies have varying deadlines to submit their requests. Then the agencies receive feedback, or "passback," on their proposals. This often leads to a negotiation between OMB and the agency prior to determining the ultimate level of funding that will be included in the President's budget. Agencies then must submit revised and more detailed requests using the MAX computer support system. This second stage occurs sometime in the November–December time period, leading up to the president's submission of the budget to Congress, which is required by law to occur in February.

No matter what the jurisdiction, standard items can be found in virtually all budget instruction manuals. Where appropriate, agencies are asked to submit revenue data (e.g., an agency operating a loan program with a revolving fund, or an agency that collects fees, such as a state park agency). Most of the instructions, however, concentrate on expenditures. The expenditures are normally keyed with an accounting system, using objects of expenditures such as personnel and supplies (see the chapter on financial management). There may also be detailed breakouts on the number of persons in each unit, their job titles, and their current salaries. The instructions usually allow for the agencies to provide narrative statements to justify their requests.

Separate sets of instructions may be provided for the operating and capital fund budgets as well as other funds, as Table 7-2 illustrates for New York State. Instructions for the latter, which are used extensively at the state and local levels, are required to distinguish requests for appropriations that must be accounted for in different funds, other than the state general fund. Examples include funds meant primarily for major fixed assets such as buildings and equipment, special funds that segregate certain federal revenues, revenues from state enterprises, and others. Federal agencies are required to separate out their investments in fixed assets, although no distinctions are made between investments in assets, or capital, and operating or current expenses when Congress appropriates funding for the agencies. (See the chapters on capital assets and capital financing.)

Program Information

Budget systems are making increased use of program information, starting with the emphasis on planning reforms that began in the latter half of the previous century. Preparation instructions specify which types of program data are to be supplied. The measures typically will have been negotiated between the budget office and the agencies before budget preparation time. In other words, when the agencies receive the request instructions, they already know what program information they need to submit. Determining what information to collect and present in budget requests is a concern at all levels of government in the United States and abroad. The umbrella term most often used to describe the overall field of program information is *performance measurement*.[25] Such measurement is seen as a means for holding agencies accountable for the results of the expenditure of tax dollars and other public resources.

Social Indicators

Of the variety of program information that might be required, social indicators are the broadest or most general type. These measures of the physical, social, and economic environments are intended to reflect what sometimes is called *quality of life*.[26] The percentage of the workforce unemployed broken out by age, sex, race, and income constitutes a set of important social indicators. Other commonly used social indicators gauge educational level attained, air or water quality, income for individuals and families, and health-related topics such as infant mortality. Measures of this type

are useful in assessing past and current trends and provide decision makers with some insights into the need for programs.

Social indicators are rarely used as measures of program performance because they are so broad as to defy demonstrating causal linkage between a specific program expenditure and a change in one of these indicators. However, they are important in identifying the problems on which government may need to focus and in identifying long-term trends, whether the trends are positive or negative. Part of the *Analytical Perspectives* document in the president's annual federal budget includes a section on social indicators. The section acknowledges that social indicators do not link directly to specific federal program performance: "They do not measure the impacts of Government policies. Instead, they provide a quantitative picture of the baseline on which future policies are set and useful context for prioritizing budgetary resources."[27]

Broad social indicators are used at state and local levels as well. One nonprofit volunteer organization in the Seattle area developed, in 1993, for the Central Puget Sound area a set of 40 such indicators to determine whether the region is maintaining "sustainability"—namely, preserving its "cultural, economic, environmental and social" conditions. In the 1990s, the group found that the region was declining in sustainability in such areas as wetlands, energy use, and children living in poverty. In the 2000s, the City of Seattle strove for sustainability while at the same time fostering development. The current iteration of Sustainable Seattle identifies a mission to "build a thriving future through initiatives that deliver environmental, economic and community benefits, promote equity, and build resilience."[28] One limitation of Seattle measures, as well as other social indicators, is their lack of direct linkage with any given government service, meaning that the indicators may be of little use for making yearly budget decisions. Children live in poverty as a result of many factors, and no government program alone could be expected to solve the problem.[29] At the same time, social indicators about communities in a state may give rise to decisions about how to help each of the communities in need.[30]

Sustainable Seattle has sought to develop indicators at a lower level of aggregation, including down to the neighborhood level, to make it more possible to link indicators with actions to improve conditions.[31]

Outcomes

Measures of more direct relevance to budgeting are outcomes, which are also referred to by some as *impacts*, Measures of this type concentrate on *effectiveness*—whether desired effects or consequences are being achieved. When a government action has affected "individuals, institutions [or] the environment," an outcome has occurred.[32] In the case of employment, an outcome measure might be the average earnings of nonwhite men who completed a job training program or, even more narrowly focused, the average increase in hourly earnings after completion of the program compared with prior earnings. Such a measure needs to be assessed carefully because earnings may have increased in a given time period for reasons having nothing to do with job training, such as inflation or an upturn in the economy. Outcomes can be seen as a method of gauging the value of government services or determining whether expenditures are accomplishing what decision makers wished to achieve. A Pew Foundation project found that seventeen states use outcome or benefit measures to compare the costs of programs versus the results achieved; sixteen of those states formally use cost-benefit analysis techniques in these comparisons.[33]

One approach may be to think of some outcomes as "raw" and others as "adjusted." Raw outcomes might be various measures of performance by school children on a standardized achievement test. Adjusted measures might consider the children's characteristics, their families' socio-economic backgrounds, and the neighborhoods in which they live.[34]

Myths or doctrines sometimes lead to problems in the selection of outcome measures. For example, in providing funds to police departments, the assumption is often made that crime will be controlled. This assumption leads to selection of crime rates as outcome measures even though police have only limited control over crime, or that reported or discovered crime might increase as a result of an increased number of police officers. In this latter case, public safety may have improved, even though crime statistics might suggest the opposite.

Outputs

In contrast with outcome measures, output measures reflect the immediate products or services being provided. Returning to the employment example, the number of graduates of the training program would be the output. The number of graduates may be able to tell you something about the achievement of the program, but this measure is limited in its ability to convey information about the quality of the program. Similarly, a health clinic may keep track of how many individuals receive a flu vaccine in a given year, but that does not tell us anything about the health effects of that vaccine. Output measures have the advantage of being far easier to calculate than many outcome measures because the data sources are within the organization—one needs simply to keep accurate records (in the above examples enrollments or immunizations). If we want to move beyond outputs to outcomes, we would need (at a minimum) to follow up with clients in order to see what happened to them after they left the program.

Similarly, a program to spray for malaria is easy to measure in terms of the number of households sprayed, because the agency responsible for spraying keeps track of the output. However, it may be a different part of the same agency, or sometimes a different agency altogether, or even a private party, that measures health status, the presumed intended outcome. Furthermore, there may be many additional factors involved in reducing the incidence of malaria, and it can be difficult to measure the extent to which the outcome is attributable to the spraying program or some other program or change in environmental conditions, such as a drought reducing the opportunity for the next season of mosquitoes to breed.

When it is known that a relationship exists between outputs and outcomes, then allocating resources may be straightforward. For example, if research has demonstrated that measles inoculations are known to prevent the disease, then allocating funds for the inoculations is warranted, presuming a disease threat exists. Measles has made something of a comeback, the largest in the United States since measles was declared eradicated in 2000. The outbreak is not because any evidence has been found suggesting that inoculations no longer are effective, but because of religious or political objections to government mandating vaccination for measles.[35] Similarly, in the case of smallpox, vaccination programs ceased when the disease was basically eradicated, though recent recurrences in isolated regions of the world have stimulated new smallpox vaccination programs.

One drawback of using output measures alone is that an erroneous assumption can be made about causal relationships. Focusing on the number of graduates of a job training program makes sense only if it is known that training improves employability. Unless data are collected to verify anticipated results (i.e., a higher rate of employment at the end of the job training), the program is being maintained without outside corroboration of its goal.

Outputs, then, may encourage *suboptimization*, or the improvement of operations for attaining subobjectives, while risking the substitution of those more controllable, easier to measure outputs for the broader societal outcomes that are the ultimate goals of the program. If the job training program was ineffective but the emphasis was placed on outputs, then decision makers would focus attention on increasing the quantity of outputs at reduced unit costs without realizing that the expenditures were altogether ineffective—not producing the desired employment results.

Activities and Workload

Activities represent the work that is done to produce outputs. The total hours of instruction could be a measure for a job training program, or the measure might be more tightly focused, such as hours of instruction in 3-D printer operations. Activities are sometimes measured as workload. The number of applications processed and the number of enrollees in a program are both workload measures. If the number of applicants increases even though enrollments are kept constant because of space limitations, the workload will still increase, because more applications must be screened. Both activities and outputs are far easier to measure than outcomes, a factor that contributes to the extensive use of the former and more limited use of the latter in budgeting as well as other public decision processes.

Productivity

Productivity is a term that has many different meanings. It is sometimes used to cover virtually all forms of program measurement. A different approach is to limit the concept of productivity to comparisons of resource inputs and work. Ratios are typically used for productivity measurement, such as the total cost of a job training program divided by the number of graduates, yielding an average cost per graduate. If average cost remains constant from one year to another despite increases in salary rates and various supplies, then the assumption is that the unit is more productive. OMB Circular A-11 provides that agencies should report gains in *efficiency*, which is sometimes a synonym for productivity.

Productivity measures often require extensive recordkeeping. If a group of employees together performs several different activities, then a reporting system is needed to account for the hours committed to each activity by each employee. This accounting is sometimes accomplished by means of daily report forms. State and local police often must submit daily reports on hours spent patrolling, investigating, testifying in court, and report writing itself. Less complicated systems may use weekly, monthly, or quarterly report forms. On the cost side, accounting systems need to capture nonpersonnel expenditures related to activities.

Need

A final type of measure gauges the need for a program. This measure indicates the gap between the level of service and the need for it. In the case of the job training program, one need measure would be the number of persons who are without adequate job skills and, therefore, require training.

In discussing need, we have come full circle back to social indicators, prompting a few words of caution. We have relied here on several examples to show differences among types of measures, but the differences might not always be so obvious. For example, the dollar value of fire damage in a city might be considered a social indicator, an outcome for the fire department, and an indicator of fire service need.

Using Program Measures

A major challenge facing any budget system is deciding how to use these diverse types of information. Which types of information will be used, in what combination, and to what extent? An initial temptation is to use every imaginable measure of government operations. Such an approach is doomed to failure. If carefully and thoroughly executed, it would produce massive amounts of data that could not be comprehended by decision makers. Indeed, such data produce what is called "noise" rather than information.

Although scholars and practitioners in the field of budgeting have yet to reach any consensus on what constitutes a goal as distinguished from an objective, one approach is to think of goals as broadly stated ideal conditions, such as the absence of crime, or zero deaths due to automobile collisions with bicyclists in an urban area. *Goals*, under this definition, may be unlikely to be achieved but function as desired states that governments can continuously work toward attaining. Distinctions are sometimes made, however, between goals and "stretch" goals, with the stated goal being one that is believed to be realistically achievable, but the stretch goal representing a goal that is hard to achieve, but ultimately desirable. *Objectives*, on the other hand, are more focused and immediate, and outcome data are used to gauge whether a program is moving toward achieving its objectives. A jurisdiction might focus on reducing burglaries and could specify a quantitative target for the future, such

as a 10% reduction in burglaries. In setting goals and objectives, decision makers must understand that some desired results can be achieved in a comparatively short period, such as a year, whereas other results will require many years of effort to achieve.[36]

Selecting measures for any given program depends on perceptions about the program's mission. Individuals may differ widely on what they consider to be a specific program's mission. In a broad sense, the vision one has of a program is related to one's perception of what the public interest is. In a narrow sense, individuals may have specific expectations of what government programs should accomplish. Renters may want a city housing program to focus on affordable rental housing, while homeowners may be largely concerned with city policies that will protect property values and keep taxes low. Owners of rental properties, in contrast, may be chiefly interested in achieving substantial returns on their financial investments. Ultimately, the success of many, if not most, government programs will be evaluated in terms of several measures rather than only one or two. The need to use multiple measures makes analysis of a program's achievements more challenging than if a single measure is used.

Interpreting measures, especially social indicators and outcomes, poses an additional problem. Because conditions in society result from a wide assortment of variables, isolating government's contribution to any given situation is difficult. One of the most difficult tasks in developing program measures is to select those that reflect what a particular government, government agency, or government program accomplishes. The federal government faces considerable challenges in this arena, because national programs are carried out through a variety of means. Means and actors vary, such as direct action of multiple federal agencies or indirect actions of other parties who are assisted through grants—for example, state and local governments and nonprofit organizations—and providing or guaranteeing credit. If a given program is successful, to what extent is the success due to funding by a federal agency, actions by state or local governments, or actions that are outside of government control entirely?

Choosing Among Program Results

Inevitably some tradeoffs occur when trying to decide among programs. Consequently, *equity* becomes a concern: Are different segments of the citizenry benefiting according to some standard of fairness? The perceived severity of a problem to be addressed by government enters such deliberations, such as the perception that a community has a major illegal drug problem or that the nation must address the problem of conquering the opioid crisis. Variations across the country, and the world, in the speed and severity of coronavirus infections in the 2020 pandemic challenged federal and international decision makers allocating scarce resources such as testing materials and protective clothing and masks for health care workers and first responders.[37] In these examples, a tempering factor is whether government programs can use infusions of resources effectively. Large budget allocations for combating drug abuse, or opioid addiction, will not necessarily resolve such problems.

Governments are at a disadvantage in making these difficult choices in comparison with private corporations, which have the profit motive as their primary concern. Put simply, a private corporation will invest in those product lines that are expected to yield the highest rate of return on investments. Governments utilize some combination of the types of program information discussed here but cannot readily convert them into a single measure of profit. Instead, they must choose among disparate commodities such as fire protection, air pollution reduction, and public transit. Making comparisons may help in this situation. Where government actions such as physical capital investments can be measured more easily on the cost and result side with a common metric, such as monetary, then a single measure of return on investment comparable to private sector metrics can be and is used. (See the chapter on capital assets.)

Systems of Budgeting

If the central budget office simply instructed agencies to request budgets for the coming year, the result most likely would be several different types of responses based on different assumptions about the coming budget year. One agency might respond by requesting what it felt was needed. Another might respond considering what resources it thought were available, resulting in a much lower request. Others might use combinations of these and other approaches. The consequences would be budget requests based on varied assumptions, and these requests would require different reactions from the budget office. To avoid such disparities in the assumptions made by requesting agencies, budget instructions often provide guidance to agencies.

Preparation Assumptions
Current Services Budgeting

One type of guidance is to assume essentially no change in programs. A department's current budget is considered its base, and any increases are to be requested only to cover additional operating costs, such as increased costs for salary increases for personnel, inflation of supply costs, increasing fuel prices, and so on. An assumption is made that the government is committed or obligated to continue existing programs. Often, this base approach has been used only implicitly, but since the 1960s and 1970s, many governments have had their budgets explicitly indicate levels of commitment for agencies and programs.

The federal budget has included current services estimates since the 1970s. For the federal government, current services estimates are frequently referred to as "baseline" budget estimates. A baseline budget, like a current services budget, estimates the effects of continuing current tax and spending policies into the future. North Carolina segregates *continuation budgets* from *expansion budgets*, requiring agencies to submit on separate forms and worksheets their budgets for *continuation* of current programs at current levels and their proposed budgets for new or *expanded* programs.[38] The chapter on the budget decision process presents a variety of samples from budget documents, including baseline estimates for the federal government.

Nonprofit organizations sometimes consider the base, or current services, budget to be last year's budget less specific projects that were intended to have a starting and stopping point. Other special projects may be included in the new budget request, but the baseline total budget does not include the costs of projects that have been completed in the previous year. For example, a youth nonprofit organization might have received a 3-year grant for after-school programming for teens. The grant money, because it is temporary, would not be considered part of the base and would be budgeted accordingly.

Explicitly determining the current commitments is difficult because programs often are created without any forthright statement of commitment. In the easiest cases, there is an obligation to serve all claimants on the system. School districts, for example, are obligated to serve all eligible children. Therefore, budget requests from units within the school district would be based on the expected number of enrolled children, or perhaps on maintaining the same average class size from the prior year. Budget changes, then, can be seen as adding increments to or subtracting them from the base level of service provision, or the current services level.

Fixed-Ceiling Budgeting

One alternative to the current commitment approach is fixed-ceiling budgeting. Under this system, a dollar limit is set government-wide, then factored into limits for departments, bureaus, and other subunits. The advantage is that budget requests are created that do not, when totaled, exceed the desired ceiling. The disadvantage is that some organizational units may receive inadequate funding and others may be overfunded in terms of overall program priorities for the government or organization. This imbalance can result from the unavailability of adequate information about program requirements when limits are set. This disadvantage can be offset somewhat by setting different ceilings for different agencies or programs, but doing so would require such knowledge about different needs and priorities up front.

Fixed-ceiling budgeting is most useful during periods of stability, although fixed-ceiling approaches are used quite frequently by governments to encourage line agencies to make fewer expenditure demands during periods of fiscal stress. A weakness of both the current services and fixed-ceiling approaches is that by themselves they offer no suggestions for program changes. If the budget office and chief executive have only these types of budget requests, they lack information about alternative resource allocations. In response to this lack of information, several "what-if" approaches to budget requests have been devised. These approaches ask agencies to develop alternatives by asking, for example, "What if more dollars were available?" or "What if program improvements were to be made in specific areas?"

Open-Ended Budgeting

One of the most common what-if approaches is open-ended budgeting. The question is asked, "What if resources were available to meet all anticipated needs?" This approach is sometimes called "blue sky" budgeting, in which the sky is the limit in requesting new funds. Agencies are expected to ask for what they think they need to deal with problems assigned to them. Open-ended budgeting should not be confused with the absence of guidance, in which some agencies might request "needed" funds and others might ask for lesser amounts. The advantage of the open-ended approach is that it brings perceived needs for services to the surface. The open-ended budget, in contrast with the current services budget, can serve as the basis for discussions of preferred funding levels. The disadvantage is that open-ended requests almost always exceed the economic and political capabilities of the jurisdiction, making the requests sometimes seem like fanciful wish lists. The harsh realities at federal, state, and local levels during any time of economic downturn, such as during the Great Recession, can render notions of open-ended budgets, for all practical matters, useless.

Hybrid Techniques

Many of the techniques discussed here can be used in combination to form hybrid systems. A government may use fixed-ceiling budgeting to allocate monies among major departments but then allow each department to use entrepreneurial budgeting—namely, allocating funds within the department with only a minimum of control from the central budget office.[39] Target-base budgeting is also sometimes used, such as in California. In this type of budgeting, agencies prepare budget requests based on fixed ceilings but then may propose budget increases above the ceilings.[40] Governments can use a current services budget in conjunction with priority listing of decision packages in an approach akin to the Carter administration's version of zero-base budgeting, a form of budgeting that requires each agency to start from zero and rejustify the program for which funding is requested (discussed in more detail later in the chapter). The base approach can be combined with open-ended budgeting, in which agencies request funds for what they perceive to be their needs. Program guidance can be linked with priority listings.

Performance Budgeting

A flurry of budget reform activity aimed at bringing greater program data into the budget decision-making process occurred in response to the First Hoover Commission (1949), which proposed the use of performance budgeting. In response to the Commission's recommendation, Congress specifically provided in the National Security Act Amendments of 1949 that performance budgeting be used in the military.[41] The following year saw passage of the Budget and Accounting Procedures Act, which in essence required performance budgeting for the entire federal government.[42] State and local governments followed suit.

Among federal, state, and local agencies, performance budgeting was geared mainly toward developing workload and unit cost measures of activities. For the postal service, the number of letters that could be processed by one employee was identified. Armed with this knowledge and an estimate of the number of letters to be processed, postal officials could calculate the personnel required for the coming budget year.[43] This, of course, was in the period before automation when mail was sorted by hand.

While the 1950s-era performance budgeting never became the basis upon which decisions were made in federal, state, or local budget processes, it did introduce the use of program information in budget documents as well as the use of performance information for various purposes. The term *performance*, however, rather narrowly referred to outputs, and this iteration of performance budgeting did not focus on results. It did pave the way, however, for such a focus, which followed in the 1960s.

Planning-Programming-Budgeting and Program Budgeting

The origin of the term *planning-programming-budgeting* is uncertain, although Mosher used it in his 1954 book on Army program budgeting.[44] By 1965, when President Lyndon Johnson extended the system to civilian agencies, PPB had come to mean planning-programming-budgeting. Today, PPB is generally used to refer to a series of budgetary reform efforts in the 1960s. The terms *program budgeting* and *performance budgeting* are more generic and apply to systems intended to link program costs with results.

Defense

There are several reasons why PPB started in the Department of Defense (DOD). Probably the most important one was that, despite having the authority to manage the military, the secretary of defense did not have the necessary management support. Defense Secretary Robert S. McNamara, in 1961, brought with him several people from the RAND Corporation who earlier had done extensive work related to program budgeting. McNamara and his

DOD colleagues made use of the development of operations research, computers, and systems analysis, all of which were complementary to the mainstream of budgetary reform.

The central component of the DOD system is the Future Years Defense Program (FYDP), which projects costs and personnel according to missions or programs over a 5-year period. The programs form the *program structure*, a classification system that begins with broad missions and factors them into subunits and activities. The structure groups like activities together regardless of which branches of the service conduct them, thereby allowing for analyses across organizational lines. The main program elements are generally consistent over time. **Exhibit 7-1** explains the relationship between program elements and budget appropriations accounts and lists the most recent DOD program elements.

Changes in the FYDP are accomplished by the Office of the Secretary of Defense issuing guidance, to which the services respond by preparing *program objective memoranda*, which contain budget proposals for modifying the FYDP.[45] The program objective memoranda suggest programmatic and resource incremental changes to the base established in the FYDP. In addition to this elaborate process, the DOD undergoes a Quadrennial Defense Review (QDR) every 4 years. The results feed into DOD strategic planning, which in turn feed into the budget process.

PPB in Civilian Agencies

Turning to the civilian side of government, use of PPB by federal agencies was announced in 1965 by President Johnson, who had been impressed with the DOD budget system. This action sparked massive reform efforts throughout all levels of government in the United States.

The federal civilian system was intended to be like the DOD model. Multiyear plans, known as program and financial plans, were to be devised for each department. Changes were to be made through the submission of program memoranda. However, by 1969, when Richard M. Nixon became president, PPB had not been fully implemented by the civilian agencies. In 1971, OMB relieved agencies of the duty to prepare program and financial plans and program memoranda. As a major budget system, PPB was allowed to die quietly.[46]

Exhibit 7-1 **Department of Defense Future Years Defense Program**

The Future Years Defense Program (FYDP) relates the appropriated funds and other resources to the Department of Defense's major programs. Resource requirements are specified in three broad categories: dollars, manpower, and forces (either equipment or combat units). The FYDP considers the following 12 program elements the *outputs* purchased by the resource requirements (inputs):

MFP 01* - Strategic Forces
MFP 02* - General Purpose Forces
MFP 03* - Command, Control, Communications, Intelligence, and Space
MFP 04* - Mobility Forces
MFP 05* - Guard and Reserve Forces
MFP 06 - Research and Development
MFP 07 - Central Supply and Maintenance
MFP 08 - Training, Medical, & Other Personnel Activities
MFP 09 - Administration and Associated Activities
MFP 10 - Support of Other Nations
MFP 11* - Special Operations Forces
MFP 12 - National Security Space

*Combat force programs

Data from Congressional Research Service, *Defense Primer: Future Years Defense Program (FYDP)*. Updated December 13, 2018.

A study conducted by the Bureau of the Budget (now OMB) found 6 factors that characterized the more successful efforts to introduce PPB:[47]

1. The number of analysts was enough.
2. Analysts were well qualified.
3. Analysts had formal access to agency heads and managers.
4. Analysts had informal access.
5. Agency heads and managers gave strong support for use of analysis.
6. Analysis was viewed as a valuable tool by agency heads and managers.

This study and others found that lack of understanding of and commitment to program budgeting on the part of leadership tended to deter success, as did an agency's general "underdevelopment" in the use of analytic techniques. Agencies administering "soft" social programs had difficulty devising useful program measures. Bureaucratic infighting also reduced the chances of successful implementation. These findings are instructive for any government that undertakes to restructure the operations of its budget system.[48]

State and Local Reforms

The use of PPB or program budgeting did not revolutionize state and local decision making in the 1960s any more than it revolutionized federal decision making. Most of the states that experimented with PPB emphasized the development of program structure, multiyear plans, and program memoranda, while only a few concentrated on analysis as their main thrust. In the 1960s, many states and municipalities took only cautious first steps and established no timetable for completion of the installation process. Others began the effort on a pilot basis, attempting PPB in one department before expanding its use.

By the close of the 1960s, it was difficult to identify many ongoing PPB systems at the state and local levels. The reasons for failure or lack of major success were like those already mentioned for federal agencies. State and local governments usually did not have sufficiently sophisticated management practices to be able to undertake the expected transformation. Additionally, people

simply expected too much to result from conversion to PPB and did not realize the financial and administrative costs associated with the conversion. Legislative bodies often showed little support for the new budget system, and this fact was interpreted by some as legislative hostility toward change.[49]

Change, however, did occur as a result of efforts to introduce PPB systems. Perhaps the biggest single achievement was that governments began to make greater use of program information in budgetary decision making, albeit information largely of the output variety.[50]

Zero-Base Budgeting

Zero-base budgeting (ZBB) is another form of "what-if" budgeting. "Traditional" ZBB asks, "What if a program were to be eliminated?" Rather than if a base exists, the approach asks what would happen if a program were to be discontinued. Each program is challenged to justify its very existence in every budget cycle.

The disadvantage of ZBB is analogous to that of open-ended budgeting: Both approaches make basically unrealistic assumptions. Whereas open-ended budgeting assumes unlimited resources, the zero-base approach assumes that decision makers have the capacity to eliminate enough programs to justify the time spent in evaluating them. In reality, the political forces in any jurisdiction are such that few programs in any given year can be abandoned. For this reason, ZBB may be better applied to selective programs in any one year rather than government wide. A cycle of reviews can be established such that some programs are thoroughly reviewed each year using ZBB, and all programs are reviewed in any 5-year period. The ascendancy of ZBB at the federal level coincided with the election of Jimmy Carter as president. Carter had been governor of Georgia, which used a version of ZBB, and brought the reform to the federal government upon becoming president in 1977.[51] The Carter administration's version had three major characteristics:[52]

1. *Decision units* were identified for which budget requests, called decision packages, were

to be prepared. Approximately 10,000 of these were prepared each year.

2. Alternative funding levels were used for each package:

  • The *minimum level*, which entailed providing services below present levels;

  • The *current level*, which maintained existing services and reflected increased costs for personnel, supplies, and the like; and

  • An *enhancement level*, which provided for upgraded services.

3. Alternative funding levels of decision packages were to be ranked by importance.

The ZBB experiment at the federal level was criticized on several counts. The most frequently heard complaint related to the amount of time required to prepare requests and the corresponding deluge of paperwork. The ZBB system, contrary to what President Carter had promised, did not require agencies to justify every tax dollar they received. Administrators puzzled over how a minimum level below current operations could exist when the statute under which an agency operated specified benefits, as in the case of Social Security.

Rarely did ZBB eliminate unnecessary programs, curtail their growth, or result in reassigning priorities among programs.[53] The system was seen as involving excessive paperwork that ultimately had little or no impact on policy making. Shortly after President Reagan took office in January 1981, the new administration announced that ZBB would no longer be practiced.

The experience at the state and local levels was comparable to that of the federal government. Although ZBB initially seemed to hold great promise, ultimately it was abandoned, even if some governments continued to describe their budget systems as founded on the concept.

One observation was that ZBB efforts in the 1970s were doomed because of the immense amount of data that needed to be processed with technology that would seem ancient compared with today's standards. An extension of such reasoning is that today's technology may make possible ZBB and other reforms that failed in earlier times.[54] That observation seems reasonable with

respect to the steady increase in the use of program information in budgetary decision making, but does not gainsay the pessimism based on many attempts for total systemic reform in budgetary processes.[55] However, the main reason ZBB, at least in its original form, is unlikely to be considered seriously again is that literally starting with base zero on an essential function, such as police services, is nonsensical.

Interestingly, ZBB resurfaced in Georgia, starting with legislative passage in 2010 and eventually becoming law when Governor Nathan Deal signed legislation in 2012 reestablishing ZBB in the state budget process. There were significant differences, however, between "the new ZBB" in Georgia and the Carter-era reform. The current version does not attempt to build a budget from the ground up, but rather requires agencies to justify their activities and programs using measures of effectiveness, workload, and efficiency. An analysis concluded that "(a)although these procedures were identified as zero-base budget analysis, in reality they are fairly standard performance-budgeting reviews."[56] The same analysis suggests that the new ZBB is much more ideologically driven—specifically designed to cut the budget—than the Carter reform, which was about management and efficiency.

Strategic Planning and Guidance

Planning

Many governments, in part following the lead of private sector organizations, have engaged in strategic planning efforts, which focus attention on missions, goals, and objectives. In strategic planning, options are identified and chosen considering fundamental values and purposes. Annual budgeting is then used to allocate resources according to the established priorities. Some have called budget systems that use strategic planning and performance measurement *performance-based budgeting*,[57] but that is an overly broad way to conceive of performance-based budgeting. A strategic plan and performance measures do not necessarily have anything to do with the budget process.

Strategic planning can be an extremely time-consuming process in which various plans, often presented in detail, are drafted, reviewed, and then modified. This process usually involves developing an overall plan and then revising the plan annually to reflect new information and revised priorities. Comparisons can be drawn here with the DOD's FYDP, mentioned earlier. The process of devising and revising plans is sometimes considered as valuable as the actual written plans themselves, in that the process fosters extensive thinking within a government about its core values in serving the citizenry.

Policy and Program Guidance

A less ambitious but nevertheless useful approach is to provide broad policy guidance or more narrowly focused program guidance to departments and agencies before they begin to prepare their budget requests. At the federal level, the OMB often instructs specific agencies regarding which program funding proposals are likely to receive favorable review and instructs them to prepare issue papers on specific programs for which concern exists about the efficacy of resource utilization. OMB also conducts a spring review prior to the issuance of Circular A-11 to start a dialogue concerning what issues or policies are likely to be highlighted in the coming budget submission. Some state and local budget offices provide program guidelines that indicate to agencies the concerns of their governors or mayors—namely, the issues that have high priority for the coming budget year.

In response to such guidance, agencies prepare detailed program requests. A discussion of the range of available alternatives is likely to take place, possibly with detailed costing and the expected results of each. Where guidance is not directed at any one agency, two or more may submit competing requests, each attempting to show how its proposed alternative would deal with a problem. For example, both the city police and the recreation departments might submit budget proposals for dealing with juvenile gangs.

The advantage of preparation guidance is that agencies prepare requests that are likely to be favorably received by the chief executive and are spared many hours of needless work in preparing requests that are fated for rejection. Policy or program guidance, however, does not ensure executive approval of agency requests. The requests may be rejected simply because of inadequate funds or because the arguments for the proposed changes fail to persuade decision makers.

Multiyear Requests

All budget requests are multiyear in that they cover at least the current year plus the coming budget year and normally include data on experience in the past year. States with biennial budgets obviously have multiyear requests. One issue is whether budget requests should extend beyond the budget year and, if so, how such a multiyear perspective is to be included in the budget. The argument for multiyear requests is simple: Without looking beyond the budget year, commitments of resources may be made that were never intended. This argument applies particularly to proposed expansions and new programs. A key distinction is between multiyear budget forecasting, or estimating, and multiyear appropriations requests. The DOD's QDR, for example, is a 5-year planning perspective estimating future year budget requirements, but the DOD appropriations request, like all other federal agencies, is for a single year.

Time Horizons

In theory, the time horizon of a budget request should be geared to the life cycle of each program. This life cycle is clearest in specific projects or programs that have an obvious beginning and conclusion. A weapons system is one of the best examples. The cycle begins with research and concludes when the system is judged to be obsolete.

On the other hand, many government programs have no foreseeable conclusion. The need for education, roads, law enforcement, recreation, and the like will always exist. Each may have unique properties that suggest possible time horizons. Given the length of time required to design and construct schools, projections of several years are needed. Multiyear requests can reveal when roads will require major repairs, redesigns, and expansions. Indeed, the necessity for multiyear planning is often part of the justification for the separate capital budgeting processes pursued by many governments.

Because an appropriate life cycle for multiyear requests is often not obvious, an arbitrary set of years may be imposed. The most common is the budget year plus the 4 succeeding years, known as a 5-year projection. In the case of the federal government, budget baselines have typically covered 10 years, at least since the late 1990s. The further into the future that projections are attempted, the more difficult it is to have faith in the (even approximate) accuracy of those projections. Using the road example, it may be largely unknown what the typical commuting pattern will be 10 or more years from now. Furthermore, political leaders have limited incentives to focus on costs or benefits that occur many years in the future, because these future costs and benefits will likely arise outside of their electoral window.

Cost and Program Projections

Assuming they can be made, projections can be limited to finances or can include program data projections. The state of the art tends to limit projections to finances, showing anticipated future financial requirements. When program outputs and outcomes are projected, the requests show what resources will be needed in future years as well as the benefits that will be accrued.

Multiyear projections using cost and program data can prove helpful in coping with severe economic conditions. Where program reductions are necessary, agency requests can illustrate the consequences over a longer time period. Cuts in an agency's budget made this year may seem essential, but produce undesirable future consequences. To live within available revenues, a city may reduce its road maintenance program, with no noticeable reduction in road quality in the first year. However, by the second or third year following these cuts, the city may have a road network of substantially lower quality than before, and

that in turn can lead to more costly capital investments to rehabilitate the road network.

Federal Performance Budget Reforms

Numerous congressional and presidential initiatives over the past two decades have continued the pattern of planning reforms by emphasizing the use of program measures, either or both output and outcome measures, to improve program performance. The desire to make more explicit connections between performance information, on the one hand, and the allocation of resources, on the other, has a long history in the United States. In fact, the story of budget reform in the United States has, as backdrop, the desire to both promote the production of information on program and agency effectiveness and the use of that information for decision making. As budgeting is one of the key loci of decision making, it has been at the center of these efforts.

Each recent administration has put its own emphasis on budget reform, generally rejecting the primary label attached to the previous administration's reform initiative and introducing at least a new description of how the new administration intends to improve governmental performance. During that same time period, Congress has weighed in with two major government performance improvement statutes. Each presidential and congressional initiative is discussed in brief in the following subsections.

GPRA and the GPRA Modernization Act

The current wave of performance budgeting efforts at the federal level began in the 1990s, with the passage of the Government Performance and Results Act (GPRA) of 1993.[58] GPRA required strategic planning, annual performance planning, and performance reporting. This law resulted from a congressional and presidential concern about "waste and inefficiency" in government and "insufficient articulation of program goals and inadequate information on program performance." It was based on the premise that agencies

(1) need to define their missions and desired outcomes, (2) measure performance, and (3) use the performance information to revise programs.[59] While GPRA's ultimate stated goal was the use of performance data in the budget process, its main legacy, starting during the Clinton administration and continuing to the Trump administration, has been an increase in the supply of performance information.

In late 2010, GPRA was amended by the GPRA Modernization Act (GPRMA).[60] This modernization was the accumulation of several years of congressional effort, stimulated by a major Government Accountability Office (GAO) analysis of GPRA's accomplishments and shortcomings. The GAO reported that GPRA:

- "established a solid foundation of results-oriented performance planning, measurement, and reporting in the federal government"; and
- had "begun to facilitate the linking of resources to results"; but
- had issues such as "federal managers continue to have difficulty setting outcome-oriented goals, collecting useful data on results, and linking institutional, program, unit, and individual performance measurement and reward systems."[61]

In the Clinton administration, the White House established a formal structure for implementing GPRA. The president designated deputy secretaries in the various departments to serve as chief operating officers and assigned to them responsibility to direct implementation of GPRA. Subsequent administrations continued that practice, and by executive order, the Bush administration created the role of performance improvement officer (PIO).[62] These structures were not formalized in the legislation, however. This was corrected by GPRMA, which conveys a statutory requirement for the PIOs, and for the Performance Improvement Council, also previously established under presidential authority prior to GPRMA. Circular A-11, which instructs agencies on how to prepare their budgets, provides guidance on the implementation of GPRMA.

GPRA required federal agencies to have strategic planning processes and plans in place, starting by the end of fiscal year 1997. GPRMA requires that agency strategic plans be published annually on their agency websites, reflecting an increasing emphasis in both the executive and legislative branches to give more public visibility to planning and budgeting, with a focus on results accomplished, or not, by federal programs. According to Circular A-11, plans must cover at least 6 years—the budget year plus the next 5 years. Plans must show agency mission, strategic goals, and means and strategies planned for achieving goals. Updates and revised plans must be submitted to the president (i.e., OMB) and Congress at least every three years.

Given the diversity of agencies within the federal government and the immensity of the task of implementing GPRA, unevenness in the quality of the annual plans was inevitable. GAO reviewed weaknesses in the implementation of GPRA that were intended to be resolved by GPRMA's enhancements of the original act. GAO identified five major areas for improvement:

- Greater coordination across overlapping and crosscutting programs;
- Improved management capabilities in the areas of financial, human capital, information technology, procurement, and acquisition;
- Improved quality and usefulness of performance information;
- Sustained leadership commitment to accountability for results; and
- Partnering with Congress to shape agency goals, identify appropriate performance measures, and increase consultation.[63]

National Performance Review

The Clinton administration also pursued a separate reform agenda embodied by the National Performance Review (NPR), which was spearheaded by Vice President Al Gore.[64] The NPR's initial report, issued in 1993, contained a host of recommendations intended to streamline all aspects of the government.[65] Later in the Clinton administration, NPR became known as the

National Partnership for Reinventing Government and had as its focus *reengineering* or *reinventing* government. The intent was to redesign processes carried out by agencies to improve their efficiency and effectiveness. *Benchmarking* was an important component in which best practices elsewhere, whether in government or the private sector, were identified and used as a guide for revising how government operates.[66]

Performance Budgeting in the George W. Bush Administration

The George W. Bush administration put its own stamp on federal budget reform upon coming into office, arguing that GPRA had failed to have the desired impact on budgeting. In response, President Bush unveiled two separate initiatives. The first, called the President's Management Agenda (PMA), was published in September 2001.[67] It included five government-wide management reforms; the one most directly related to budgeting was "budget and performance integration" (BPI), designed to continue to improve performance information while also allocating and managing resources to achieve results. For each of these management areas, the Bush administration created a "traffic light" scorecard, judging each of 26 federal agencies as red, yellow, or green, depending on the level of progress toward prescribed management objectives. The apparent progress in these areas can be demonstrated by the fact that the initial 2001 scorecard on BPI included 3 yellow scores and 23 reds, while by 2008 there were 19 greens and 7 yellows.[68]

The second significant reform initiative of the Bush administration was the creation of the Program Assessment Rating Tool (PART), first unveiled for use in the FY2004 budget process. The PART took the "program" as the unit of analysis, and evaluated these programs (because there was no standard definition of "program," part of the challenge was one of identification; eventually there were approximately 1,000 identified) through the use of a questionnaire that requested information from agencies on characteristics of their programs.[69] Agencies filled out the questionnaire, with their answers reviewed

(approved) by OMB. The program was eventually "scored" as falling within one of five categories: effective (85–100), moderately effective (70–84), adequate (50–69), ineffective (0–49), and results not demonstrated (if a program lacks adequate measures, it falls into this category regardless of its score).[70]

The specific goal of the PART was to evaluate every program; thus, the Bush administration sacrificed evaluation depth to gain a comprehensive view. While the percentage of ineffective programs stayed roughly the same (at 3% to 5%) over the 7 years of the PART, in 2002, 30% of programs were rated effective or moderately effective; in 2008, that figure was 51%. Perhaps as significantly, the results not demonstrated category decreased by two-thirds from 50% in 2002 to 17% in 2008).[71]

The PART program ultimately got mixed reviews. It was generally perceived as more useful in the executive budgeting process, but of more limited utility in congressional appropriations decision making, in part because committee staff did not feel the process of developing performance measures included congressional consultation.[72] The PART did force agencies to be mindful about justifying their programs through specific measures. At the same time, OMB did not generally use PART results to slash underachieving programs.

An assessment after the first 3 years of implementation concluded that PART had an impact on agency resource allocation decisions, but had not caused significant changes in program and agency management. Still, the PART may well have influenced budget decisions by OMB. One study found that PART scores were related to OMB budget recommendations, particularly for small- and medium-sized programs.[73] Another study found that the PART enhanced OMB's control over the budget, which is important in that the agency is responsible for overseeing the budget on behalf of the president. A third study suggested, perhaps not surprisingly, that the PART was not applied in a neutral manner by the Bush administration, but rather that "liberal" programs and agencies got more scrutiny than those that were traditionally considered to be more "conservative."[74] Congress, on the other hand, "generally ignored the OMB-initiated PART performance evaluations."[75]

The Obama Administration

President Obama took office in January 2009 at one of the most challenging times in U.S. history. The initial Obama performance agenda was dominated by a focus on those activities undertaken by the government in response to the Great Recession, chiefly the American Recovery and Reinvestment Act (ARRA, or "stimulus bill") that was passed in early 2009. In addition, as part of a demonstration of the Obama administration's desire to cut back on spending, it identified programs in its first budgets that it believed should have funding reduced or eliminated because of inadequate performance. In the context of the overall budget, these proposals were relatively modest, adding up to less than 1% of total federal spending.

As has often been the case in the United States, the new administration jettisoned the reforms of its predecessor; neither the PART nor the Bush PMA approach survived in the Obama administration. The Obama administration shifted the focus away from comprehensive analysis to more targeted attention to priority goals. It also focused a bit less on top-down, one-size-fits-all efforts in favor of providing general guidelines and permitting a bit more flexibility to agencies. As a part of this effort, the administration asked each agency to identify the goals that it viewed as the highest priorities over the next several years. Some of these goals cut across agencies, while others were specific to particular departments. By requiring agencies to participate in identifying their highest priority goals, OMB was more successful in engaging the leaders of these agencies in the process of performance improvement than was true in the Bush administration, where agency heads frequently delegated the work of PART and the PMA to lower-level officials.

One important change from the PART approach used in the Bush administration was the Obama administration's focus on the strategic objective, rather than the program, as the unit of analysis. Strategic objectives tend to be more cross cutting, and more focused on outcomes, than are programs. Further, multiple programs often support a single strategic objective. While the PART process was often focused on the potential for the elimination of programs, the U.S. experience has in fact shown that the elimination of a program is perhaps the least likely result of a strategic review. The focus on strategic objectives, conversely, does not question the appropriateness of the objective itself, but focuses attention on the tools that are employed to attempt to meet the objective. It is thus more likely for a strategic review to result in changes in program design, tools used to achieve objectives, or program management.

Finally, the Obama team devoted a significant amount of time and resources to program evaluation, in part to assist with the identification of what works and what does not. The Obama administration argued that as important as performance goals and performance measures can be, performance information "can answer only so many questions. More sophisticated evaluation methods are required to answer fundamental questions about the social, economic, or environmental impact of programs and practices, isolating the effect of Government action from other possible influencing factors."[76]

The Commission on Evidence-Based Policymaking

One of the key recent developments, not only for the federal government but more broadly, is descriptive. Instead of "performance management" or "performance budgeting," the term du jour is "evidence-based policy making." Consistent with this, a 2016 law created a federal Commission on Evidence-Based Policymaking. It was established by the bipartisan Evidence-Based Policymaking Commission Act of 2016, jointly sponsored by Speaker Paul Ryan (R-WI) and Senator Patty Murray (D-WA), and signed by President Barack Obama.[77] The act "recognizes that better use of existing data may improve how government programs operate. The mission of the Commission was to develop a strategy for increasing the availability and use of data in order to build evidence about government programs, while protecting privacy and confidentiality."[78]

Relative to budget reform, what is most notable about the final report of the Commission is how little discussion there was of budgeting—or even management—reforms, or of the use of evidence for decision making. Most of the attention in the final report of the Commission focused on the production of data for evidence-based policy, rather than on the use of that data. The report included no mention of GPRA or GPRAMA, or any other government-wide performance regime. It did embrace some organizational reforms, such as the creation of chief evaluation officers in each agency. It recommended that OMB coordinate the development of a more robust information architecture for the government, but did not mention OMB's role in fostering the use of this information. Thus, as the Commission noted, its brief is about "evidence building," not about how to create systems and incentives for its use.[79]

Trump Administration Initiatives

While the Trump administration might not generally be thought of as one that might embrace efforts to make government work better, the real story is more nuanced than that. First, it is important to note that the fact that the GPRAMA is a statute that, to a degree, acts as a stabilizing influence on federal management efforts. GPRAMA established the architecture for performance management, including cross-agency priority (CAP) goals, agency priority goals (APGs), and strategic goals and objectives; an alignment of planning processes with election cycles; and specific defined roles for OMB, agency chief operating officers, and PIOs.

The fiscal year 2019 President's budget, issued in February 2018, included a chapter entitled "Building and Using Evidence to Improve Government Effectiveness." This was explicitly not an attempt to articulate a general performance strategy for the administration, but rather it laid out the necessary elements of what it called an "infrastructure for evidence-based policymaking."[80] The chapter, in particular, stressed the need to have consistent and rigorous program evaluation in federal agencies, and noted the inconsistent practice and capacity of federal agencies toward that end. It argued that "(m)any agencies do not understand or undertake evaluation or conduct poor-quality evaluation that is of limited utility or may provide misleading or incorrect information." It stressed the establishment of evaluation offices, interagency coordination, and funding set-asides as essential elements on an improved capacity. It also stressed the need for improved data and data management to support evidence-based policy making. In addition, every major agency published an updated strategic plan with the budget.

This action was followed in March of 2018 by the President's Management Agenda (PMA), which presented the comprehensive performance approach that had not been presented in the budget a month earlier. The PMA stressed a vision that included three elements: mission, or achieving results; service, focusing on delivering "a customer experience that compares to—or exceeds—that of leading private sector organizations"; and stewardship, arguing for the necessity of providing "(t)taxpayer dollars…to successful programs that produce results efficiently." Like the budget a month earlier, and the evidence-based policy commission recommendations, the PMA argued for information technology modernization and an improved data infrastructure. It also built on proposals in the budget that would reform human capital management to make hiring and dismissal easier and create reforms in the management of the workforce to focus on performance.

The PMA also listed each of the cross-agency priority goals permitting attention to the challenges of dealing with problems that require action from more than one agency in order to achieve success.[81] The Obama administration had focused on its own set of CAP goals, but the new administration established 14 new goals since taking office. **Exhibit 7-2** presents the Trump administration CAP goals.[82]

Each of these goals has a designated goal leader, who has responsibility for coordinating the activities of the multiple agencies whose collaboration is necessary for the accomplishment

Exhibit 7-2 Cross-Agency Priority Goals in the Trump Administration, 2018

Building on the creation of CAP goals that were required by GPRAMA, and first established by the Obama administration, the Trump administration identified the following CAP goals as part of the President's Management Agenda, which was unveiled in March 2018. These goals include the following:

1. Modernize IT to Increase Productivity and Security
2. Leveraging Data as a Strategic Asset
3. Developing a Workforce for 21st Century
4. Improving the Customer Experience with Federal Services
5. Sharing Quality Services
6. Shifting from Low-Value to High-Value Work
7. Category Management: Leveraging Common Contracts and Best Practices to Drive Savings and Efficiencies
8. Results-Oriented Accountability for Grants
9. Getting Payments Right
10. Improving Outcomes Through Federal IT Spending Transparency
11. Improve Management of Major Acquisitions
12. Modernize Infrastructure Permitting
13. Security Clearance, Suitability & Credentialing Reform
14. Improve Transfer of Federally Funded Technologies from Lab-to-Market

At an agency level, the two most important initiatives focused on the APGs and the strategic reviews. In the former case, each agency was asked to identify three to eight APGs that were "ambitious, meaningful, and measurable" and could be accomplished within the confines of current legislation and current resources. For each of the APGs, action plans and quarterly targets were required, and OMB conducted quarterly data-driven performance reviews. A couple of examples of APGs will illustrate:

- Department of Veterans Affairs: "By September 30, 2019, Veterans' positive responses will increase from 67 percent (FY17, Q4) to 90 percent to the statement, 'I trust VA to fulfill our country's commitment to Veterans.'"
- Social Security Administration: "By September, 30, 2019, SSA will complete 97 percent of the cases that begin the fiscal year 350 days old or older (complete ~385,000 cases)."[a]

The annual strategic reviews probably mapped most closely to the timetable of the budget process. Shortly after the submission of the budget for the prior fiscal year, agencies developed a method for assessing progress toward their strategic goals. Reviews were then conducted in the spring, with the goal of each agency determining proposed changes, including budget changes. This led to feedback provided by OMB that is used by the agency as an input into policy and budget development and informed the budget proposal that submitted to OMB in September. The President's budget, transmitted in February, then reflected the key proposals necessary to improve results. This process (strategic reviews in the spring, feeding into budget preparation) was also used in the FY20 budget preparation process.[b]

An additional resource that should be mentioned is the website, managed by OMB, where information on federal performance initiatives and performance data can be found. Performance.gov (www.performance.gov) was launched in the Obama administration, and at that time was mainly a portal through which various department documents (such as GPRA strategic plans and performance plans) could be found. Some users found it is not very user friendly, particularly if a goal was to enable citizens to locate information on the performance of particular programs. As the result of feedback from users, the site was revised substantially, with emphasis on overarching goals and links to videos and other more accessible content. The site still includes the agency-specific information that was included previously, but overall appears to be improved, in look and content, over the previous iteration.

a. Brown, D. (2018). *The Federal Performance Framework*. [Unpublished presentation.] Washington, DC: Office of Management and Budget.
b. Brown, D. (2018). *The Federal Performance Framework*.

of the goal. The Trump administration also continued to support a $15 million annual fund (the fund had been established in the Obama administration) to support cross-agency collaboration. While not related to the budget directly, clearly many of these CAP goals track to a more efficient and effective use of resources, particularly those related to issues such as grants management, improper payments, and contracting.

GPRAMA Assessment

The GAO has done several studies on the strategic review process, post GPRAMA. A 2015 study done in response to a specific requirement included in GPRAMA examined several agencies to determine the most effective practices for conducting strategic reviews.[83] The office concluded that establishing a process, with a clear timetable and connection to stakeholders, contributed to successful reviews. In addition, the office stressed the development of clearly measurable outcomes, and the strategies that affect those outcomes.

A later study looked at the strategic review process in given agencies—the General Services Administration, the Small Business Administration, the Department of State, the U.S. Agency for International Development, and the Department of the Treasury—and concluded that the reviews were being conducted as part of existing performance and management processes, rather than separately. Perhaps most relevant to our discussion, a separate GAO study emphasized that there had been little change in the use of data in decision making over a 20-year period despite all the efforts made since the passage of the original GPRA. GAO recommended that OMB redouble its efforts, through the Performance Improvement Council, to encourage managers to use performance data to make decisions.[84]

There has been scant attention paid to the use of evidence for decision making by the Congress, except for a two-volume report published in March and April 2018 by the Bipartisan Policy Center. The study suggested that evidence could be used to inform several key congressional decisions and activities, including those related to program authorization, appropriations, and

oversight. The study went on to lay out several impediments to congressional uses of evidence. Some of these are related to perceptions about the usefulness of information, including inconsistent goals of programs, limited credibility of some of the providers of information, and differences of opinion concerning how useful and relevant the information is considered to be. Institutionally, the Congress can be hamstrung by partisan concerns, lack of coordination between the branches, and insufficient expertise to produce and interpret evidence. Finally, evidence may not be produced in timely enough manner, and in a large enough supply, to allow it to enter the policy process at the appropriate time.[85]

The second volume suggested several reforms that could be attempted in order to increase both the supply of, and use of, evidence by the Congress. It specifically addressed the authorizing and appropriations processes, suggesting 19 separate reforms that would increase the capacity of the Congress to use evidence, change institutional structures to promote evidence-based decision making, and establish incentives to make it more likely that the Congress would find it in its interest to use information on program and policy success when making funding and other decisions.[86]

Performance Budgeting in State and Local Governments, and in Other Countries

State Experiences

As noted previously, many states adopted performance budget reforms in the 1960s and 1970s at roughly the same time that the federal government was experimenting with budget reform. There have been several comprehensive evaluations of performance budgeting over the past 20 years. The first was the Government Performance Project (GPP), which reviewed "Managing for Results" and then later "Information" as one of several categories of management reviewed in the process of assessing the management capacity of state governments. There were full reviews of the

50 states published four times—in 1999, 2002, 2005, and 2008.[87]

In the most recent of these, published in 2008, states were "graded" in part on their production and use of performance information for both budgeting and management. In the category of "Budgeting for Performance," 10 states were identified as particularly strong—Delaware, Iowa, Louisiana, Missouri, New Mexico, Oregon, Texas, Utah, Virginia, and Washington. In an overview article on the use of information by the states, Barrett and Greene pointed out that

> (o)ne of the biggest obstacles to progress in managing for performance is the disconnect between the production of performance information and its use in the budgeting process, particularly by legislators. Michigan and Georgia, for example, produce a great deal of excellent performance information, but officials report that the data seem more a burden than a tool to many legislators.[88]

In fact, the key difference between these top 10 states and those in the next tier had to do with the extent to which performance information was actually used in the budget process.

An additional study, by Yilin Hou and colleagues, looked at the extent to which states considered performance information when making budgetary decisions (especially budget reductions) during the Great Recession. The prevailing theory had been that it was particularly important for governments to have performance information during times of budget reductions, as it would assist them in deciding which programs or agencies to cut. This study found, to the contrary, that the states reviewed tended to resort to across-the-board cuts and other similar strategies, rather than targeting those programs for reduction that had failed to demonstrate results.[89]

Several studies and resources about state performance budgeting have surfaced since 2014. A 2014 study by the National Association of State Budget Officers (NASBO) focused on case studies of five of the same states that had been identified as leaders by the GPP (Iowa, Oregon, Utah,

Virginia, and Washington), adding Connecticut, Minnesota, and Nevada to the mix. The study did not attempt to evaluate the states in terms of the extent of performance budgeting, but rather used state case studies and convened sets of state officials to reach some general conclusions concerning factors that contribute to successful performance budgeting, including the following:[90]

- The importance of "high level leadership" that champions the effort, both in the central government and at the top of state agencies.
- The need to establish, for agencies, the real benefits that will accrue as a result of the practice, and the necessity that it is not viewed as only a budget-cutting exercise.
- The desirability of having a statutory framework in order to promote the sustainability of the practice in changing political climates.
- The need to focus on a few useful measures so as not to overwhelm decision makers with data that have questionable value for the decisions they need to make.
- The need for patience, and flexibility, if the system is to be sustained.

Following up on this study, the NASBO 2015 version of its annual *Budget Processes in the States* volume asked all 50 states plus the District of Columbia to identify whether performance budgeting was either a primary or secondary budget approach in constructing the state budget. For this purpose, performance budgeting was defined as follows:

> Similar to program budgeting, this budgeting approach also uses programs or activities as budget units and presents information on program goals and performance. This budget system places emphasis on incorporating program performance information into the budget development and appropriations process, and allocating resources to achieve measurable results.[91]

Given this definition, three states (Texas, Louisiana, and New Jersey) plus the District of Columbia identified performance budgeting as their primary approach, while 25 others said it was a secondary approach. The remaining 22 apparently did not believe that they used it enough to justify either response. Most states identified incremental budgeting as their dominant approach, although almost all states said that they collected outcome data.

In 2018 NASBO developed an inventory of "Statewide Initiatives to Advance the Use of Data & Evidence for Decision-Making," which categorizes these state efforts into five types: data analytics, evidence-based policy making, performance budgeting, performance management, and process improvement. NASBO acknowledged that it is difficult to draw a bright line between these actions and classify them according to the one that appears to be the dominant. Further, in some states there are separate initiatives that are catalogued, so that some states have one initiative identified, and others may have three or four.

In total, this inventory included, as of this writing (it is a "living" inventory and is thus updated as additional practices are discovered), 108 separate state initiatives. Of these, the raw counts of practices are as follows:

- Performance management—31 initiatives in 26 states
- Process improvement—23 initiatives in 21 states
- Performance budgeting—19 initiatives in 17 states
- Data analytics—18 initiatives in 12 states
- Evidence-based policy-making—17 initiatives in 13 states

The Pew Charitable Trusts, in a 2017 study, described most states as engaged in evidence-based policy-making. While this finding would seem to be at odds with the results from the NASBO inventory, the Pew study, however, had a much narrower focus, as it only addressed the use of evidence-based policymaking across several specific human services areas. Many fewer states are engaged in statewide efforts.[92]

Focusing on the 19 performance budgeting initiatives, the inventory identifies 17 of the 19 as being in the budget office, while 2 are in the legislature. All but one is a statewide initiative. In terms of the age of the initiative, Pennsylvania reports that its performance budgeting effort (which involves the reporting of performance in the Governor's budget) started in 1971, while the next most recent efforts (in Delaware, Louisiana, and Maryland) started in 1996 or 1997. New Mexico's system got its start in 2000, while all the others have started since 2010 (including four identified as starting between 2017 and 2019). Twelve of the initiatives have their basis in either legislation or executive order.[93]

This inventory provides a useful catalogue of what states report they are doing. It does not, nor does it intend to, present any information on how data are used in the budget process. It would be necessary to dig into decision processes at the state level in order to determine the extent to which there are real budgetary actions (at any stage of the budget process) that are being taken to use performance data to allocate or manage resources. That is, it seems obvious that there is a lot going on out there. There is much less information on what difference it is making.

Local Experience

While some of the earliest examples of the development of performance measures (going back to the early part of the twentieth century, and associated with the New York Bureau of Municipal Research) occurred at the local level, the use of program information at the local level is more limited than at the state level, but there has been progress since the 1990s.[94] Some organizations, such as the International City/County Management Association, were strong advocates for greater integration of budgetary and performance information.[95] A mid-1990s study of members of the Government Finance Officers Association found that 51% of local governments still used line-item budgeting.[96] Performance budgeting and zero-base/target-base budgeting were used by 2% to 3%, while program budgeting was used by 10% of the local governments. Thirty-five percent reported using a hybrid system. In contrast, a survey of city and county administrators and budgeters done in the early 2000s found performance measurement to be "pervasive."[97] A case study analysis of Indianapolis documented the importance of the role of performance measures in departmental budgeting.[98]

In addition to grading the states, the Government Performance Project graded the nation's largest cities and counties in 2000 on several factors, including managing for results.[99] Though the 2000 study has not been repeated, at that time it found cities lagging behind state governments, not surprisingly, but increasing in the use of performance measures, especially in reporting to the public. Milwaukee, which earned a high grade in the GPP 2000 study, has attracted attention as a city that successfully achieved comprehensive management and budget reform.[100] A National League of Cities database of city practices shows about 24% of almost 150 entries include performance reports to citizens or other performance measurement dissemination practices.[101] Atlanta has gained recognition for its "Atlanta Dashboard" system. Its CitiStats program is designed to create a "performance management culture in the City of Atlanta"[102] through its performance management system designed to identify the effectiveness of city programs.[103] Baltimore also has a well-regarded CitiStat program.

While performance measurement has clearly gained ground at the local level, the use of program information in decision making may be more limited. A study of counties found that of those reporting usage of performance measurement in budgeting, 78% said measures were used in preparing departmental budget requests, 68% said measures helped county commissioners review the executive budget, and 80% said measures were used for monitoring the efficiency and effectiveness of services.[104] A study of cities and counties found that administrators had doubts about the extent that program measurement was being used in decision making.[105]

The city of Baltimore practices what it calls outcome budgeting, arguing that "(i)nstead of starting from last year's spending allocations up or down, in Outcome Budgeting we start with what results matter most to citizens."[106] A case study of the Baltimore system noted that the impetus for the new system was an environment of significant budget constraints that existed after the Great Recession. The city organizes its budget around a set of priority outcomes that are informed by input from the public, including from a citizen survey. The priority outcomes in the fiscal year 2018 budget, for example, included Thriving Youth and Families; Safe Neighborhoods, Healthy Communities; Vibrant Economy; Sustainable Infrastructure; and High Performing Government. The mayor and city leadership determine spending allocations not by department but by priority areas. By focusing on gaps between desired spending to achieve target outcomes and actual spending, the city has been able to reprioritize spending. Proposals from agencies focus on how their requested funds would achieve results in the priority areas, and the city then tracks outcomes to see whether the reallocation is achieving the desired results.[107]

Experience of Other Nations

Efforts to include performance measurement in budgeting are common in other countries.[108] In the mid-1990s, New Zealand was said to be furthest along in developing a resource allocation system that relied heavily on quantified performance.[109] The financial and fiscal crisis in the United States and most industrialized countries brought on by the recession starting in 2007, as noted earlier in this chapter, has focused more attention on the efficiency side of governmental performance. Local governments in the United Kingdom underwent a performance management initiative in the 1990s that produced a data set known as the Best Value Performance Indicators. These were replaced in 2008 by a single set—the National Indicators Set. This was revised again in 2011 to produce the Single Data List for Local Government.[110] A survey of local governments in the Australian state of Victoria found that 50% of the respondents thought budget reforms changed attitudes in favor of planning, and 47% thought the reforms influenced resource allocations.[111] Singapore has made extensive use of performance information and is increasing its emphasis on outcome measures. However, Singapore, while using program information in budgetary decision making, does not attempt to directly link performance and budget data.[112] A study of five governments in Canada, England, and the United States found that performance reporting was being used in strategic planning and agency decision making.[113]

Management reforms, including those in the budgeting arena, in Australia, New Zealand, the United Kingdom, and to a lesser extent, Canada, have been called the *New Public Management* (NPM).[114] This concept is generally associated with the concern that public sector management theories gave almost exclusive attention to technological reforms, neglecting the role of values and the political process through which values affect decisions. Over time, the movement spread throughout Europe, especially into Austria, Germany, and Switzerland. NPM has reached the United States from the standpoint of scholars trying to understand what constitutes NPM, whether it has accomplished anything in other countries, and whether it is on the upswing or downswing. For example, some scholars have declared NPM dead, though that is disputed.[115] It should be noted, at a minimum, that NPM is more than a budgeting reform. It typically covers myriad other changes, including privatization and increased flexibility for managers.

A recent book examined performance budgeting from an international perspective, studying its use both in developed and less developed settings. This book, *Performance Budgeting Reform*, represents the most comprehensive and current treatment of performance budgeting throughout the world.[116] One chapter in the book examined the reform in two countries—Australia and the Netherlands—that have been viewed as leaders. In Australia, for example, the reform movement started with program budgeting in 1976. Program budgets in Australia coupled program objectives with firm caps on program spending and forward estimates. The estimates represented not only fiscal limits, but also established program objectives going out multiple years. Both spending and performance measures are reported on annually relative to the plan. In the Netherlands, the adoption of performance-oriented reforms followed 1980s fiscal reforms intended to address the chronic Dutch problem of cost overruns and revenue shortfalls. It was not until the late 1990s that the Netherlands embraced performance budgeting. After that point, budget documents had to specify general goals, operational objectives, and performance indicators.[117]

Low- and middle-income countries have embraced performance budgeting as well, albeit more sporadically and with greater challenges than higher-income states. *Performance Budgeting Reform* included case studies of eight of these countries—Afghanistan, Chile, China (limited to analysis of national or provincial governments), Indonesia, Kenya, Mexico, the Philippines, and Tunisia. In the interest of space, it is useful to highlight just a few of these experiences:

- The Philippines, which was the first country outside of the United States to adopt program budgeting, undoubtedly because of the U.S. influence after World War II, in the period between 2008 and 2014 implemented a new budgeting system focused first on outputs, and then later outcomes.[118]

- Mexico, after its national economic crisis of 1994, embraced "serious fiscal and administrative reforms, including performance budgeting." A 2006 law codified the move from an input-focused model to one that is focused on results and was followed by a specific effort at "results-based budgeting" in 2006. Implementation has faced some challenges, including establishing a culture of performance and achieving success at the state and local levels.[119]

- Chile has perhaps gone further than other middle- and low-income countries in integrating formal program evaluation into its performance budgeting system. In addition to program evaluation, the Chilean reforms were characterized by the awarding of bonuses to individual civil servants in institutions that achieved performance targets. The analysis of the Chilean system suggests that there is limited use of performance measures for allocating budgets, except for the analysis of requests for budget expansions.[120]

- Tunisia ousted its president, Ben Ali, in 2011, ending a quarter-century of his autocratic rule. Even prior to his removal from office, however, Tunisia embraced a version of performance budgeting, as part of a public financial management modernization program supported by the International Monetary Fund. The Tunisian reform is designed to improve the effectiveness of spending and strengthen parliamentary oversight of public finance. While Tunisia has a strong civil service with substantial capacity to implement a performance budgeting reform, it has lacked a champion at a high enough place in the government.[121]

Reasons for Adopting Reforms

Why do some governments adopt budget reforms while others do not—or adopt them at a slower pace?[122] Researchers have identified several factors:

- Fiscal stress caused by the inability of governments to finance all programs at what seems to be a minimal standard stimulates searches for alternative budget techniques. Improved budgeting is seen as a means for improving the "health" of the government and the economic health of the economy.[123] On the other hand, when fiscal stress becomes severe, governments may simply attempt to cope during a crisis rather than improve their ability to manage themselves.[124]
- Governments search for techniques that facilitate dealing with the knottiest of problems and provide them with the sense of being in control of current and future operations. Emphasis is on increasing the efficiency and effectiveness of operations. The concern is to link programmatic goals with results.[125] When an agency is under pressure from higher-level decision makers about its effectiveness and even existence, the agency may initiate budget changes using performance measures on its own as a means of strengthening its position in the political-administrative arena.[126]

- Government structure is sometimes important. Local governments with professional managers are more likely to adopt program and performance budgeting than are those with strong mayor systems.[127] This seems to be true internationally with national governments.[128]
- Having an elected and appointed political leadership that is committed to budget reform is another important ingredient, because reforms that are generated exclusively from lower levels in the bureaucracy are unlikely to be effective. Leadership not only must be committed but must also have the leadership skills necessary to forge ahead.[129]
- Governments need trained professional staffs and technical capabilities to undertake many budget reforms.[130] Involvement by employees and incentives for their involvement may increase the chances for success.[131] Agencies led by "prospectors" as distinguished from "defenders" and "reactors" may be more likely to introduce performance management and be successful in the endeavor.[132] Any such changes that are undertaken should be expected to take time. Expectations of quick results are likely to lead to disappointments.
- A desire on the part of legislators for enhanced information as an aid in exercising oversight of the executive branch is another important factor.[133] On the other hand, when the budget structure and appropriations are not aligned with performance information, the legislature may send a signal to the executive branch that performance is not all that important.[134]
- Legal requirements, such as the 1993 and 2010 federal legislation (GPRA and GPRMA) instructing agencies to prepare strategic and annual performance plans, and other mandates and incentives are important.
- Budget reforms sometimes are seen as aids to controlling or reducing corruption. The international development community initiatives on public financial management (PFM) reforms are in part intended to reduce public sector corruption in developing countries.[135]

- Another potential influence of major proportions relates to professions. The professional accounting field has shown interest in mandating that accounting systems be linked to program measurement. The Governmental Accounting Standards Board strongly encourages voluntary reporting of *service efforts and accomplishments* and in 1994 moved toward adopting a requirement that governments link *service efforts and accomplishments* to their accounting systems.[136]

This listing is in no way exhaustive, but simply illustrates some of the factors that can be important in whether a government successfully implements some form of budget reform that is results oriented.

Impediments to Reform

Perhaps one of the most difficult barriers to reform is overcoming the past. So-called new management practices arise with great frequency. Governments may feel pressure to jump on the most current bandwagon, but then later they jump from that bandwagon to another. Any person involved in policy making and administration can easily become cynical about the prospects for any new management practice being implemented. Experienced administrators inevitably question whether the latest technique will have any real effect on how decisions are made and what outcomes they produce. Administrators may also feel that the only reason for adopting the latest technique is the desire for a new administration to put its own identity stamp on the budget process.

Other factors that complicate or deter reform include the following:

- Major difficulties can be expected in setting goals and measures and gaining acceptance of those goals.[137] For example, environmental and conservation interests hold differing views on which goals the U.S. Forest Service should pursue.[138] This lack of clarity would be much less of a problem for an agency such as the U.S. Weather Service, which operates with the luxury of an agreed-upon mandate—to forecast the weather in an accurate and timely manner. Even when there is agreement on the goal, operationalizing it so that it is clear when it has been achieved can be a thorny problem. For instance, there is no easy method for determining how much defense is enough, as defense is as much about deterrence and preparedness as it is about success in waging war.

- When multiple federal agencies are required to accomplish a set of objectives, it can be too complicated to arrive at a clear set of common objectives. When state, local, and private agencies are part of the equation, identifying a clear set of performance objectives and the appropriate measures of success defy imagination. Natural and environmental disasters require federal, state, and local government agencies and nongovernmental organizations to work together to respond.

- Another concern is whether strategies lead to accomplishment of goals. Substantial additional resources have been put into the Department of Homeland Security since the beginning of the Trump administration to reduce the influx of undocumented persons entering the United States. GAO or other internal and external evaluations have yet to be completed assessing the success of those efforts.

- More generally, producing believable data presents a major problem. Simple errors can occur in collecting and tabulating data. Organizations and individuals may be tempted to falsify or misrepresent their accomplishments or may feel under such great pressure to perform that they cheat on performance measures. For example, teachers and administrators in numerous districts from New York City to Atlanta from New Jersey to Washington, DC, have exaggerated student performance on standardized achievement scores or even reported exaggerated results obtained by assisting students with the test.[139] Data need to be valid (measures are appropriate) and verified (for completeness, accuracy, consistency, and the like).[140]

- Agencies have overlapping missions, and consequently any outcomes or impacts may result from several agencies' work. Managing for results suggests prospects for collaboration across agencies but can work in the other direction, leading to battles over administrative "turf."[141]

- Measuring the accomplishments of regulatory agencies is particularly challenging, and much of what the federal government does is of a regulatory nature.[142] The regulatory units are located both in departments, such as the Food and Drug Administration in the Department of Health and Human Services, and in stand-alone bodies, such as the Environmental Protection Agency, the Securities and Exchange Commission, and the Federal Communications Commission. The banking crisis that began in 2008 raised the question of whether it could have been avoided had the regulators not, in effect, been asleep on the job.

- Obtaining accurate data in a uniform format and on a timely basis can be a nightmare for federal agencies that depend on information from state and local governments and private enterprises. The same problem arises for state agencies in obtaining data from local governments.

- Some governments have used adjusted performance measures that attempt to consider the extent to which external factors (i.e., those outside an organization's control) influence outcomes. These techniques are themselves subject to criticism, but with attention to methodology they can yield more accurate results.[143]

- Linking program data with cost data is complicated by the limited abilities of accounting systems and inconsistencies across accounting systems. Accounting systems may track financial transactions in formats that do not match up well with the needs of a program manager. Comparisons between units may be thwarted because the units use different accounting system rules.

- The lack of incentives can doom efforts to use performance measurement in budgeting. If high-level executives and legislators show little or no interest in using performance data for decision making, lower-level administrators will consider data collection and program planning to be merely a paper exercise.[144] Equally as troublesome is holding executives and managers accountable for results but not giving them the means to accomplish the desired outcomes. Due to revenue declines, budgets may be cut, but departments may be expected to accomplish what was originally planned.

- Managers often find it unpleasant, if not downright repulsive, to have their operations compared with operations in other departments or in other governments. Yet benchmarking is frequently regarded as a desirable technique. As discussed earlier, benchmarking involves comparing one's operations with those of others. Serious problems of comparison arise in that governments operate in different environments, may measure their activities differently, and may account differently for their use of resources. The federal government's No Child Left Behind Act of 2001, for example, required testing of individual students to hold teachers and administrators accountable for educational outcomes. As noted previously, the pressure to meet the act's requirements generated considerable controversy and numerous instances of false reporting and cheating by threatened school administrators, teachers, and entire districts. The law was basically replaced by the Every Student Succeeds Act of 2015, which continued the testing requirement but left specifics up to the states.[145] The Trump administration, in 2017, substantially weakened testing programs.[146] Citizen satisfaction can be measured across governmental boundaries, such as determining whether one community is more satisfied with its recreation services than other communities.[147]

Finally, the question must be asked whether budget reforms aimed at fostering performance management have any bearing on global rethinking about the purposes of government and how those purposes or goals are pursued.[148] Yes, budget systems may be tied to strategic planning, but do these systems address, in any real sense, fundamental questions about government and draw attention to key issues, such as immigration, terrorism, international trade imbalance, and the like?

Summary

One of the main themes running through the budgetary literature has been the need to use the budgetary process as a vehicle for planning. This need has facilitated an attempt to incorporate program data into the system along with resource data, such as dollar and personnel costs.

During and after World War II, a set of theoretical fields and technologies emerged that had a great influence on budgetary reform. These include operations research, economic analysis, general systems theory, cybernetics, computer technology, and systems analysis.

Budget requests are prepared by agencies in accordance with instructions provided by the central budget office. In addition to data on finances and personnel, request instructions increasingly require program data, including social indicators, impacts, outputs, workloads, and activities, as well as data on the need or demand for services. Productivity measures are used to relate resource consumption, as measured in dollars and personnel, to the work accomplished and the product of that work.

Budget request manuals take varied approaches to providing guidance on how agencies should request resources. These approaches include current commitment, fixed-ceiling, and open-ended budgeting. Reform efforts since the 1960s have focused on PPB systems, or more generally program budgeting. Strategic planning and policy and program guidance have also proved popular. Current emphasis is on performance budgeting, which attempts to make connections between the use of resources, on the one hand, and the achievement of results, on the other.

Notes

1. Schick, A. (1966). The road to PPB: the stages of budget reform. *Public Administration Review, 26,* 243–258; Caiden, N. (2010). Challenges confronting contemporary public budgeting: retrospectives/prospectives from Allen Schick. *Public Administration Review, 70,* 203–210.
2. Williams, D. W. (2004). Evolution of performance measurement until 1930. *Administration & Society, 36,* 131–165; Meyers, R., & Rubin, I. (2011). The executive budget in the federal government: the first century and beyond. *Public Administration Review, 71,* 334–344.
3. Taft, W. H. (1912). *Economy and efficiency in the government service.* House Doc. No. 458, 16.
4. Commission on Economy and Efficiency (1912). *The need for a national budget.* House Doc. No. 854, 4–5.
5. Cleveland, F. A. (1915). Evolution of the budget idea in the United States. *Annals, 62,* 15–35.
6. Willoughby, W. F. (1918). *The problems of a national budget.* New York, NY: Appleton.
7. Upson, L. D. (1924). Half-time budget methods. *Annals, 113,* 69–74.
8. Buck, A. E. (1929). *Public budgeting.* New York, NY: Harper and Brothers.
9. Kilpatrick, W. (1936). Classification and measurement of public expenditures. *Annals, 183,* 19–26.
10. President's Committee on Administrative Management (1937). *Report.* Washington, DC: U.S. Government Printing Office.
11. Key, V. O., Jr. (1940). The lack of a budgetary theory. *American Political Science Review, 34,* 1138–1144. See Light, P. C. (2006). The tides of reform revisited: patterns in making government work, 1945–2002. *Public Administration Review, 66,* 6–19; and Posner, P. (2009). Introduction to the mini symposium on the federal budget process: the persistence of reform. *Public Administration Review, 69,* 207–210.
12. Commission on Organization of the Executive Branch of the Government (1949). *Budgeting and accounting* (p. 8). Washington, DC: U.S. Government Printing Office; U.S. Office of Management and Budget (2010). *Budget of the U.S. government: analytical perspectives,* 10. Social indicators (pp. 95–102). Washington, DC: U.S. Government Printing Office.
13. Lewis, V. B. (1952). Toward a theory of budgeting. *Public Administration Review, 12,* 42–54.
14. Mosher, F. C. (1954). *Program budgeting: theory and practice with particular reference to the U.S. Department of Army.* Chicago, IL: Public Administrative Service.
15. Seckler-Hudson, C. (1952). Performance budgeting in the government of the United States. *Public Finance, 7,* 327–345.
16. Smithies, A. (1955). *The budgetary process in the United States.* New York, NY: McGraw-Hill.
17. Commission on Organization of the Executive Branch of the Government (1955). *Final report to Congress.*

Washington, DC: U.S. Government Printing Office; Commission on Organization of the Executive Branch of the Government (1955). *Budgeting and accounting.* Washington, DC: U.S. Government Printing Office.

18. Burkhead, J. (1956). *Government budgeting* (pp. 133–182) New York, NY: Wiley.

19. For an early survey of the economic analysis field, see Prest, A. R., & Turvey, R. (1965). Cost-benefit analysis: a survey. *Economic Journal, 75,* 683–735.

20. Lindblom, C. (1959). The science of muddling through. *Public Administration Review, 19,* Spring, 79–88.

21. Wildavsky, A. (1969). Rescuing policy analysis from PPBS. *Public Administration Review, 29,* 193.

22. Pew-MacArthur Results First. (2017). *How states engage in evidence-based policymaking: a national assessment.* Pew Research Center. Retrieved February 9, 2020, from https://www.pewtrusts.org/en/research-and-analysis /reports/2017/01/how-states-engage-in-evidence-based -policymaking

23. Office of Management and Budget. (2019). *Circular A-11, Preparation, Submission, and Execution of the Budget.* Retrieved from https://www.whitehouse.gov/wp-content /uploads/2018/06/a11.pdf.

24. Government Performance and Results Act of 1993 (P.L. 103-62); Government Performance and Results Modernization Act of 2010 (P.L. 111-352).

25. Joyce, P. (2011). The Obama administration and PBB: building on the legacy of federal performance-informed budgeting? *Public Administration Review, 71,* 356–367. For historical reviews, see Hatry, H. P. (1999). *Performance measurement: getting results.* Washington, DC: Urban Institute; Walters, J. (1998). *Measuring up: governing's guide to performance measures for geniuses (and other public managers).* Washington, DC: Congressional Quarterly; Klitgaard, R., & Light, P. C. (Eds.) (2005). *High-performance government: structure, leadership, incentives.* Santa Monica, CA: RAND Corporation; U.S. Government Accountability Office (2005). *Performance measurement and evaluation: definitions and relationships.* Washington, DC: GAO.

26. See the *Social Indicators Research* journal, which has been publishing research and information on social indicators since 1974.

27. Office of Management and Budget. (2019). *Budget of the United States Government: Fiscal Year 2020, Analytical Perspectives,* March, 45. Retrieved September 21, 2019, from https://www.whitehouse.gov/wp-content/uploads/2019 /03/spec-fy2020.pdf.

28. Website for Sustainable Seattle, at http://sustainableseattle .org/about-us/. Retrieved July 5, 2019.

29. Aristigueta, M. P., et al. (2001). The role of social indicators in developing a managing for results system. *Public Performance & Management Review, 24,* 254–269.

30. Murphey, D. A. (1999). Presenting community-level data in an "outcomes and indicators" framework: lessons from Vermont's experience. *Public Administration Review, 59,* 76–82.

31. For a list of all indicators, see SustainableSeattle.org (2006). *Sustainable Seattle: ecology, economy, community, celebrating 15 years.* Retrieved September 21, 2019, from https:// communityindicators.net/wp-content/uploads/2018/01 /SustainableSeattleSustainabilityReport2006.pdf.

32. Mowitz, R. J. (1970). *The design and implementation of Pennsylvania's planning, programming, budgeting system.* Harrisburg, PA: Commonwealth of Pennsylvania.

33. Pew-MacArthur Results First (2017). *How states engage in evidence-based policymaking: a national assessment.*

34. Rubenstein, R., et al. (2003). Better than raw: a guide to measuring organizational performance with adjusted performance measures. *Public Administration Review, 63,* 607–615.

35. McNeil, D. G. (2019). Religious objections to the measles vaccine? Get the shots, faith leaders say. *New York Times,* April 26. Retrieved September 21, 2019, from https://www .nytimes.com/2019/04/26/health/measles-vaccination -jews-muslims-catholics.html.

36. Spicer, M. (2004). Public administration, the history of ideas, and the reinventing government movement. *Public Administration Review, 64,* 353–362; Kim, P. S., et al. (2005). Toward participatory and transparent governance: report on the sixth global forum on reinventing government. *Public Administration Review, 65,* 646–654.

37. Ezekiel, J., et al. (2020). Fair allocation of scarce medical resources in the time of Covid-19. *New England Journal of Medicine,* March 23. Retrieved March 26, 2020, from https://www.nejm.org/doi/full/10.1056/NEJMsb2005114.

38. North Carolina Office of Management and Budget (2019). Budget 101, retrieved July 18, 2019, from https://www .osbm.nc.gov/budget/budget-process.

39. Kobrak, P. (1996). The social responsibilities of a public entrepreneur. *Administration and Society, 28,* 205–237.

40. Alderete, J. (2007). *Budget practices and state expenditures: lessons for California.* Public Policy Institute of California, 10. Retrieved December 3, 2019, from https://www.ppic .org/publication/budget-practices-and-state-expenditures -lessons-for-california/.

41. National Security Act Amendments of 1949. Ch. 412, 63 Stat. 578.

42. Budget and Accounting Procedures Act of 1950. Ch. 946, 64 Stat. 832.

43. Schick, A. (1966). *The road to PPB,* 252–253.

44. Mosher, F. C. (1954). *Program budgeting,* 34–47.

45. Jones, L. R. (1991). Policy development, planning, and resource allocation in the Department of Defense. *Public Budgeting & Finance,* 11, Fall, 15–27; U.S. General Accounting Office (2004). *Future Years Defense Program: actions needed to improve transparency of DOD's projected resource needs.* Washington, DC: GAO.

46. Schick, A. (1973). A death in the bureaucracy: the demise of the federal PPB. *Public Administration Review, 33,* 146–156.

47. Harper, E. L., et al. (1969). Implementation and use of PPB in sixteen federal agencies. *Public Administration Review, 29,* 634.

48. Kelley, J. (2005). A century of public budgeting reform: the "key" question. *Administration and Society, 37,* 89–109; see also Fabrizio, S., & Mody, A. (2006). Can budget institutions counteract political indiscipline? *Economic Policy, 21,* 689–739, for similar conclusions in other countries.

49. Casselman, R. C. (1973). Massachusetts revisited: chronology of a failure. *Public Administration Review, 33,* 129–135.

50. Sallack, D., & Allen, D. N. (1987). From impact to output: Pennsylvania's Planning-Programming-Budgeting System in transition. *Public Budgeting & Finance, 7,* Spring, 38–50; Tat-Kei Ho, A. (2011). PBB in American local governments: it's more than a management tool. *Public Administration Review, 71,* 391–401.

51. Lauth, T. P., & Rieck, S. C. (1979). Modifications in Georgia zero-base budgeting procedures: 1973–1981. *Midwest Review of Public Administration, 13,* 225–238.

52. U.S. General Accounting Office (1979). *Streamlining zero-base budgeting will benefit decision making.* Washington, DC: U.S. Government Printing Office.

53. Schick, A. (1978). The road from ZBB. *Public Administration Review, 38,* 177–180.

54. Metzgar, J., & Miranda, R. (2001). Bringing out the dead: can information technology resurrect budget reform? *Government Finance Review, 17,* April, 9–14.

55. Posner, P. (2007). The continuity of change: public budgeting and finance reforms over 70 years. *Public Administration Review, 67,* 1018–1029.

56. Lauth, T. P. (2014). Zero-base budgeting redux in Georgia: efficiency or ideology? *Public Budgeting & Finance, 34,* Spring, 6.

57. Willoughby, K. G., & Melkers, J. E. (2000). Implementing PBB: conflicting views of success. *Public Budgeting & Finance, 20,* Spring, 105–120; Lu, Y., et al. (2011); Performance budgeting in the American states: what's law got to do with it? *State and Local Government Review, 43,* 79–94.

58. Government Performance and Results Act of 1993 (P.L. 103-62).

59. U.S. General Accounting Office (1996). *Effectively implementing the Government Performance and Results Act.* Washington, DC: U.S. Government Printing Office; Long, E., & Franklin, A. L. (2004). The paradox of implementing the Government Performance and Results Act: top-down direction for bottom-up implementation. *Public Administration Review, 64,* 309–319.

60. Government Performance and Results Modernization Act of 2010 (P.L. 111-352).

61. U.S. Government Accountability Office (2004). *GPRA has established a solid foundation for achieving greater results.* Washington, DC: U.S. Government Printing Office.

62. Exec. Order No. 13450, 72 Fed. Reg. 64519 (signed November 13, 2007).

63. U.S. Government Accountability Office (2011). *GPRA Modernization Act provides opportunities to help address fiscal, performance, and management challenges.* Washington, DC: U.S. Government Printing Office.

64. Joyce, P. G. (2003). *Linking performance and budgeting: opportunities in the federal budget process.* Washington, DC: IBM Center for the Business of Government.

65. National Performance Review (1993). *From red tape to results: creating a government that works better and costs less.* Washington, DC: U.S. Government Printing Office.

66. Howard, M., & Kilmartin, B. (2006). *Assessment of benchmarking within government organization.* Note: this report is no longer accessible on the website where originally located.

67. U.S. Office of Management and Budget. (2001). *The President's Management Agenda.* Washington, DC: OMB.

68. Joyce, P. G. (2011). Transparency and accountability in the federal budget: How is the Obama Administration building on the legacy of federal performance-informed budgeting? *Public Administration Review, 71,* May/June, 356–367.

69. Mark, K.,& Pfeiffer, J. R. (2011). *Monitoring and Evaluation in the United States Government: An Overview.* Evaluation Capacity Development Working Paper Number 26, Independent Evaluation Group. Washington, DC: World Bank.

70. Gilmour, J. (2006). *Implementing OMB's Program Assessment Rating Tool: Meeting the challenges of integrating budget and performance.* Washington, DC: IBM Center for the Business of Government. Retrieved March 26, 2020, from http://www.businessofgovernment.org/sites/default/files/GilmourReport.pdf.

71. Joyce, P. G. (2011). "The Obama Administration."

72. U.S. Government Accountability Office (2011). *GPRA Modernization Act provides opportunities to help address fiscal, performance, and management challenges,* 10.

73. Gilmour, J. B., & Lewis, D. E. (2006). Assessing performance budgeting at OMB: the influence of politics, performance, and program size. *Journal of Public Administration Research and Theory, 16,* 169–186.

74. Lavertu, S., Lewis, D. E., & Moynihan, D. P. (2013). Government reform, political ideology, and administrative burden: the case of performance management in the Bush Administration. *Public Administration Review, 73,* 845–857.

75. Rubin, I. (2009). Budgeting during the Bush administration. *Public Budgeting and Finance, 29,* Fall, 1–14.

76. Office of Management and Budget (2011). *Budget of the United States Government, Fiscal Year 2011: Analytical Perspectives,* 90–92. Washington, DC: U.S. Government Printing Office, 90–92.

77. Evidence-Based Policymaking Commission Act of 2016. P.L. 114-140.

78. Commission on Evidence-Based Policymaking (2017). *Final report: the promise of evidence-based policymaking.* Report of the Commission on Evidence-Based Policymaking, September 2017. Retrieved March 26, 2020, from https://www.govexec.com/media/gbc/docs/pdfs_edit/090617cc1.pdf.

79. Commission on Evidence-Based Policymaking, 2017.

80. Office of Management and Budget. (2018). *Building and Using Evidence to Improve Government Effectiveness, Budget*

of the United States Government, Fiscal Year 2019: Analytical Perspectives (p. 60). Washington, DC: OMB.

81. U.S. Office of Management and Budget. (2018). *The President's Management Agenda.* Washington, DC: OMB.

82. Brown, D. (2018). *The Federal Performance Framework* [unpublished presentation]. Washington, DC: Office of Management and Budget.

83. Government Accountability Office (2015). *Managing for Results: Practices for Effective Agency Strategic Reviews.* GAO-15-602. Washington, DC: GAO.

84. Government Accountability Office (2018). *Managing for Results: Government-wide Actions Needed to Improve Agencies' Use of Performance Information in Decision Making.* Washington, DC: GAO.

85. Bipartisan Policy Center. (2018). *Evidence Use in Congress: Challenges for Evidence-Based Policymaking.* Washington, DC: Bipartisan Policy Center.

86. Bipartisan Policy Center (2018). *Evidence Use in Congress: Options for Charting a New Direction.* Washington, DC: Bipartisan Policy Center.

87. Ingraham, P., Joyce, P., & Donahue, A. (2003). *Government Performance: Why Management Matters.* Baltimore, MD: Johns Hopkins University Press; Governing Magazine, *Grading the States: 2005*; Governing Magazine. *Measuring Performance: The State Management Report Card for 2008.*

88. Barrett, K., & Greene, R. (2008). The mandate to measure. *Governing,* March, 24–34.

89. Hou, Y., et.al. (2011). State performance-based-budgeting in boom and bust years: an analytical framework and survey of the states. *Public Administration Review, 71,* 370–388,

90. National Association of State Budget Officers (2014). *Investing in Results: Using Performance Data to Inform State Budgeting* (p. 17). Washington, DC: NASBO.

91. National Association of State Budget Officers. (2015). *Budget Processes Spotlight: How States Use Performance Data* (p. 2). Washington, DC: NASBO.

92. Pew-MacArthur Results First (2017). *How states engage in evidence-based policymaking: a national assessment.*

93. National Association of State Budget Officers. (2018). *Using Data and Evidence in the States.* Retrieved December 3, 2019, from https://www.nasbo.org/reports-data/using-data-and-evidence.

94. Kelly, J. M., & Rivenbark, W. C. (2003). *Performance budgeting for state and local governments.* Armonk, NY: M. E. Sharpe.

95. Ho, A., & Ni, A. (2005). Have cities shifted to outcome-oriented performance reporting? A content analysis of city budgets. *Public Budgeting & Finance, 25*(2), 64.

96. O'Toole, D. E., et al. (1996). Current local government budgeting practices. *Government Finance Review, 12,* December, 25–29.

97. Melkers, J., & Willoughby, K. (2005). Models of performance-measurement use in local governments: understanding budgeting, communication, and lasting effects. *Public Administration Review, 65,* 180–190.

98. Ho, A. (2011). PBB in American local governments: it's more than a management tool. *Public Administration Review, 71,* 391–401.

99. Barrett, K., & Greene, R. (2000). Grading the cities: a management report card. *Governing, 13,* February, 22–88.

100. Hendrick, R. (2000). Comprehensive management and budgeting reform in local government: the case of Milwaukee. *Public Productivity & Management Review, 23,* 312–337.

101. National League of Cities (2011). *City knowledge network: database.* Retrieved October 25, 2011, from http://www2.nlc.org/examples/cknsearchtest.htm.

102. ATLStat website, http://web.atlantaga.gov/atlstat/index.shtml. Retrieved October 28, 2011.

103. Mackie, B. (2008). *Organisational performance management in a government context: a literature review.* Retrieved October 28, 2011, from www.scotland.gov.uk/Resource/Doc/236340/0064768.pdf.

104. Wang, X. (2000). Performance measurement in budgeting: a study of county governments. *Public Budgeting & Finance, 20,* Fall, 102–118.

105. Melkers, J., & Willoughby, K. (2005). Models of performance-measurement use in local governments: understanding budgeting, communication, and lasting effects. *Public Administration Review, 65,* 180; see, more generally, the budget reform survey article Pagano, M., & Mullins, D. (2005). Local budgeting and finance: twenty-five years of developments. *Public Budgeting and Finance, 2,* Fall, 3–45.

106. City of Baltimore, Bureau of the Budget and Management Research (2019). *Outcome Budgeting* retrieved December 3, 2019, from https://bbmr.baltimorecity.gov/outcome-budgeting.

107. Results for America (2018). *Baltimore's Advanced Outcome Budgeting System Allows City Leaders to Invest Taxpayer Dollars in Programs and Services that Matter Most.* Retrieved December 3, 2019, from https://bbmr.baltimorecity.gov/sites/default/files/bbmr_baltimorecity_gov/attachments/Final-Baltimore-Case-Study-Results-for-America.pdf; see also Kleine, A. (2018), *City on the Line.* Lanham, MD: Rowman and Littlefield.

108. Organization for Economic Cooperation and Development (2009). *Evolutions in budgetary practice: Allen Schick and the OECD senior budget officials.* Paris, France: OECD.

109. Organization for Economic Cooperation and Development (1995). *Budgeting for results: perspectives on public expenditure management* (p. 55). Paris, France: OECD; OECD (2007). *Performance Budgeting in OECD Countries.* Paris, France: OECD.

110. Audit Commission (2011). *National Indicator Set: single list for local governments.* Retrieved October 28, 2011, from www.audit-commission.gov.uk/localgov/audit/nis/pages/default.aspx.

111. Kluvers, R. (2001). An analysis of introducing program budgeting in local government. *Public Budgeting & Finance, 21,* Summer, 29–45.

112. Blondal, J. (2006). Budgeting in Singapore. *OECD Journal on Budgeting, 6*, 45–86.

113. Cunningham, G. M., & Harris, J. E. (2005). Toward a theory of performance reporting to achieve public sector accountability: a field study. *Public Budgeting & Finance, 25*, Summer, 15–42.

114. Barzelay, M. (2001). *The new public management.* Berkeley, CA: University of California Press; Page, S. (2005). What's new about the new public management? Administrative change in the human services. *Public Administration Review, 65*, 713–727; Pollitt, C., et al. (Eds.). (2007). *The new public management in Europe: adaptations and alternatives.* New York, NY: Palgrave.

115. De Vries, J. (2010). Is new public management really dead? *OECD Journal on Budgeting, 10*, 1–6.

116. Ho, A. T-K, de Jong, M., & Zhao, A. (2019). *Performance Budgeting Reform: Theories and International Practices.* Abingdon, UK: Routledge.

117. Podger, A., & de Jong, M. (2019). The evolution of performance budgeting amidst other public financial management reforms: The Experience of Australia and the Netherland. In Ho, A., et al. (Eds.), *Performance Budgeting Reform: Theories and International Practices.* Abingdon, UK: Routledge, 71–92.

118. Venner, M. (2019). The long history of performance budgeting in the Philippines. In Ho, A., et al. (Eds.), *Performance Budgeting Reform: Theories and International Practices.* Abingdon, UK: Routledge, 133–143.

119. Ramirez de la Cruz, E. Y., & Gabriel, P. (2019). Performance-based budgeting system and performance evaluation in Mexico. In Ho, A., et al. (Eds.), *Performance Budgeting Reform: Theories and International Practices.* Abingdon, UK: Routledge, 144–164.

120. Martinez Guzman, J. P. (2019). The evolution of performance budgeting in Chile. In Ho, A., et al. (Eds.), *Performance Budgeting Reform: Theories and International Practices.* Abingdon, UK: Routledge, 165–176.

121. De Jong, M. (2019). Performance budgeting reform in Tunisia. In Ho, A., et al. (Eds.), *Performance Budgeting Reform: Theories and International Practices.* Abingdon, UK: Routledge, 242–252.

122. Forrester, J. P., & Adams, G. B. (1997). Budgetary reform through organizational learning. *Administration and Society, 28,* 466–488; Fernandez, S., & Rainey, H. G. (2006). Managing successful organizational change in the public sector. *Public Administration Review, 66,* 168–176; Kasdin, S. (2010). Reinventing reforms: how to improve program management using performance measures. Really. *Public Budgeting and Finance, 30,* Fall, 51–78.

123. Walters, J. (2000). Raising Alabama. *Governing, 14,* October, 28–32.

124. Hou, Y. (2011). State performance-based budgeting in boom and bust years: an analytical framework and survey of the states. *Public Administration Review, 71,* 370–388.

125. U.S. Government Accountability Office (2005). *Managing for results: enhancing agency use of performance information for management decision-making.* Washington, DC: U.S. Government Printing Office.

126. Barzelay, M., & Thompson, F. (2006). Responsibility budgeting at the Air Force Materiel Command. *Public Administration Review, 66,* 127–138

127. Lu, H., & Facer, R. L., II. (2004). Budget change in Georgia counties: examining patterns and practices. *American Review of Public Administration, 34,* 67–93.

128. Andrews, M. (2005). Beyond "best practice" and "basics first" in adopting performance budgeting reform. *Public Administration and Development, 26,* 147–161.

129. U.S. General Accounting Office (2000). *Managing for results: federal managers' views show need for ensuring top leadership skills.* Washington, DC: U.S. Government Printing Office; Klitgaard, R., & Light, P. C. (Eds.) (2005). *High-performance government: structure, leadership, incentives.* Santa Monica, CA: RAND Corporation; Ho, A. (2011).

130. Ingraham, P. W., et al. (2003). *Government performance: why management matters.* Baltimore, MD: Johns Hopkins University Press.

131. Boyne, G. A., et al. (2004). Toward the self-evaluating organization? An empirical test of the Wildavsky model. *Public Administration Review, 64,* 463–473; Swiss, J. E. (2005). A framework for assessing incentives in results-based management. *Public Administration Review, 65,* 592–602.

132. Andrews, R., Boyne, G. A., & Walker, R. M. (2006). Strategy content and organizational performance: an empirical analysis. *Public Administration Review, 66,* 52–63.

133. Mihm, J. C., U.S. General Accounting Office (2001). *Using GPRA to assist oversight and decision making; Testimony before the House Subcommittee on Government Efficiency, Financial Management and Intergovernmental Relations.* Washington, DC: U.S. Government Printing Office. Retrieved February 24, 2012, from http://comptrollerlegal2001.tpub.com/d01872t/d01872t0001.htm. (no longer accessible at this source).

134. U.S. Government Accountability Office (2005). *Performance budgeting: efforts to restructure budgets to better align resources with performance.* Washington, DC: GAO.

135. French, B. (2013). *The impact of PFM interventions on corruption.* GSDRC Applied Knowledge Services. Retrieved March 26, 2020, from https://gsdrc.org/document-library/impact-pfm-interventions-corruption/.

136. Governmental Accounting Standards Board (1994). *Concepts statement no. 2: service efforts and accomplishments reporting.* Norwalk, CT: Governmental Accounting Standards Board; Epstein, P. et al. (2005). *Government service efforts and accomplishments performance reports: a guide to understanding.* Norwalk, CT: Governmental Accounting Standards Board.

137. Nicholson-Crotty, S., et al. (2006). Disparate measures: public managers and performance-measurement strategies. *Public Administration Review, 66,* 101–113.

138. Peckenpaugh, J. (2001). Linking performance goals to budgets won't be easy, experts say. *Govexec.com*. Retrieved August 3, 2006, from http://www.govexec .com/dailyfed/0301/032201p1.htm. (reference no longer available at this source)

139. Otterman, S. (2011). In cheating cases, teachers who took risks or flouted rules. *New York Times*, October 18. Retrieved October 29, 2011, from http://www.nytimes .com/2011/10/18/nyregion/how-cheating-cases-at -new-york-schools-played-out.html?_r=2&adxnnl =1&ref=education&pagewanted=1&adxnnlx =131896806254qgwtseUQe5lTB9njoxCg. (reference no longer available at this source)

140. Holtzer, M., et al. (2009). *Literature review and analysis related to measurement of local government efficiency: a report to the local unit alignment, reorganization and consolidation commission (New Jersey)*. Newark, NJ: Rutgers University School of Public Affairs and Administration; Berman, B. (2008). Involving the public in measuring and reporting local government performance. Retrieved December 3, 2019, from http://venus.fcny.org/cmgp/press/National _Civic_Review_Article.pdf.

141. Simeone, R., et al. (2005). A systems approach to performance-based management: the national drug control strategy. *Public Administration Review, 65*, 191–202.

142. U.S. General Accounting Office (1999). *Managing for results: strengthening regulatory agencies' performance management practices*. Washington, DC: U.S. Government Printing Office. For specific examples, see U.S. Government Accountability Office (2011). *Environmental Protection Agency: management challenges and budget observations*. Washington, DC: GAO.

143. Rubenstein, R., et al. (2003). Better than raw: a guide to measuring organizational performance with adjusted performance measures. *Public Administration Review, 63*, 607–615.

144. Kasdin, S. (2010). "Reinventing reforms: how to improve program management using performance measures. Really."

145. Every Student Succeeds Act of 2015, P.L.114-95, 20 U.S.C. §6301.

146. Goldstein, D. (2017). Obama education rules are swept aside by Congress. *The New York Times*, March 9. Retrieved September 21, 2019, from https://www.nytimes .com/2017/03/09/us/every-student-succeeds-act-essa -congress.html; Camera, L. (2017). Trump nixes Obama-era rules for new federal K-12 law. *U.S. News and World Report*, March 2). Retrieved September 21, 2019, from https://www.usnews.com/news/education-news /articles/2017-03-27/trump-nixes-obama-era-rules-for -new-federal-k-12-law

147. Van Ryzin, G. G., et al. (2004). Drivers and consequences of citizen satisfaction: an application of the American Customer Satisfaction Index Model to New York City. *Public Administration Review, 64*, 331–341; Swindell, D., & Kelly, J. (2005). Performance measurement versus city service satisfaction: intra-city variations in quality? *Social Science Quarterly, 86*, 704–723.

148. U.S. Government Accountability Office (2005). *Strategic budgeting: risk management principles can help DHS allocate resources to highest priorities*. Washington, DC: GAO; U.S. Government Accountability Office (2011). *GAO's perspectives on fiscal and performance challenges facing government*. Washington, DC: GAO.

CHAPTER 8

Budget Preparation: The Decision Process

Budget preparation is like a giant juggling act. Many balls are tossed up into the air—some by agencies, some by the budget office, some by the chief executive, and some by others—and surprisingly, in some years they do not all come crashing down. Instead, often a proposed budget comes out of this dizzying assortment of taxing and spending initiatives, on time.

Preparing a budget in an executive budget system involves having agencies prepare requests and then assembling those requests; however, the process involves much more. Indeed, the request process is simple compared with the difficult task that remains—making decisions on the recommended levels for revenues and expenditures. Is a tax increase needed? What programs should be expanded, and what programs should be reduced? In systems that do not centralize budget preparation in the executive, the same concerns prevail. A legislative committee or a joint group of executives and legislators may be responsible for weighing the citizens' joint demands for increased services and possibly lower taxes and for proposing a budget package that balances these competing demands.

This chapter includes two sections. The first section considers how a proposed executive budget is assembled. Deliberations on the revenue and expenditure sides of the budget are examined.

The second section reviews the products of budget preparation—namely, the various types of budget documents and their formats.

Decisions on Budget Requests

Budget preparation involves participation by a variety of individuals and organizations, all of whom have myriad values regarding taxing and spending. In an *executive budget system*, the chief executive has the overall responsibility for the preparation process. Numerous other actors play roles as well, including the central budget office and other units such as the treasury office. Not all governments have executive systems. For example, many county governments do not have a county executive or manager. As a consequence, their budgets are prepared jointly by several different executive and legislative officials. Legislators or their staffs may be involved in budget preparation. On occasion, state legislative staff members may be allowed to attend executive budget hearings that review the proposed budgets of line agencies. This practice helps the legislative branch become aware of the budget proposals being developed and the rationales behind these proposals prior to the budget actually reaching the legislature. In small local governments, budget preparation may be a relatively fluid process that is characterized by close links between executive and legislative officials. Even when legislative officers are not involved, their views on taxing and spending are taken into account. For example, a mayor will think twice about recommending a budget increase for a program when it is known that perhaps two-thirds of the city council has serious doubts about the program's worth.

Concerns of the Chief Executive

The chief executive—president, governor, mayor, city manager, county executive, or the like—may have official responsibility for budget preparation, but usually will have only limited direct involvement until the later stages of preparation. This system allows the chief executive time to take care of other duties. Having the budget office and other units, such as treasury, involved early in the process provides for the application of professional administrative talent in analyzing problems and options that will later come before the chief executive for review. A professional budget staff endeavors to take preliminary actions on budget requests that are in keeping with the policy objectives of the chief executive, thereby allowing the chief executive to avoid dealing with minor problems and reserving time to deal with major ones.

Strategic Concerns

The chief executive needs to convey to the departments, bureaus, and offices involved, and especially to the central budget office, a sense of priorities so that effort is not needlessly wasted on proposals that will later be rejected. Several concerns arise, with a major one at the national level being the overall philosophy of the role of government in contemporary society. What is the overall public interest, and how large should the public sector be in the total economy? Parallel questions at the regional (state or province) and local (city, county, or school district) levels

are usually related to a few key issues such as the quality of the education system; the condition of roads or other infrastructure; and taxes, especially the property tax.

Another concern for many chief executives is the effect that the budget may have on the economy. Cities, counties, states, and the national government are concerned about budgetary influences on the economy and about the economy's influences on the budget. For local and state chief executives, their concern tends to focus on whether current or proposed taxes will deter businesses from locating or expanding operations in their jurisdictions. Perhaps equally important is the quality of government services. While school districts and special districts may have little or no official role in economic development, the quality of education, water systems, sewers, and so on is critical in the location decisions of corporations. The national government has these same concerns and others as well, including international implications and price stability.

The chief executive sets ground rules on policies and program priorities. The president conveys an overall sense of priorities to the Office of Management and Budget (OMB) regarding national security and domestic spending and a sense of priorities within each of these categories. Election campaign promises are important in that chief executives usually attempt to pursue the objectives outlined in their bids for voter approval. For many chief executives, the budget serves as a vehicle for strategic planning for the government. For example, President Trump's budgets focused on such policy areas as national defense, border security and immigration, and international trade.[1] Program priorities also can be viewed from the perspective of achieving some degree of social justice or equity.[2]

While space constraints prohibit any extensive discussion of what constitutes social justice, it can be said that budget deliberations include an overall assessment of how different segments of the society will benefit or be burdened by governmental actions. One way of viewing this situation is to think of government as redistributing income among the various segments of society.

Funding one set of programs at a high level will obviously benefit those programs' clients. If, for example, the elderly benefit from a program, then the young may not. Providing income maintenance checks to the needy redistributes money from the middle and upper classes to low-income persons. Redistribution also occurs through tax measures, including tax expenditures, such as the policy of not taxing home mortgage interest payments. Proposed tax cuts are always debated in part based on whether the direct beneficiaries will be upper-, middle-, or lower-income individuals and households. Concerns about distributing the burden of taxes on the rich versus middle- and lower-income groups also hinge on the argument that it is the wealthier individuals who create jobs and economic growth.[3]

A major concern of most states and particularly southern and western border states is social justice as it pertains to persons who are illegally in the country. When taxes are high and available revenues cannot keep pace with funding needs, one view holds that immigrants who are illegally in the country should be denied access to government services like health care and various social services. For example, complaints from citizens began to arise when they realized that most mothers giving birth at the Los Angeles County Hospital were not in the country legally.[4] Providing free services to such persons is seen by many people as imposing an unfair burden on taxpayers. While the consensus of studies reviewed by the Congressional Budget Office (CBO) in 2007 was that illegal immigration does impose a net cost on state and local governments, there is no consensus on the size of that effect.[5] On the other hand, there are estimates that show that undocumented workers pay an estimated $9 billion in Social Security taxes annually, even though they are ineligible to receive benefits.[6] Many employers are eager to hire undocumented workers who can be paid "under the table" below minimum wage, thereby reducing employers' production costs.

Another suggestion whose popularity is growing is that budgeting should be concerned with its generational effects—the extent to which current actions will improve or harm the conditions

that older, younger, and future generations must confront.[7] For example, the federal government has reported generational effects in terms of taxes and transfers.

Today, science plays a major role in strategic decision making—namely, what scientific information can be brought to bear on problems? For example, what is the threat of an *E. coli* outbreak on the vegetable or meat industry and the health of the public, and what roles should federal, state, and local governments play in fighting it? How likely is a disease pandemic, and what actions should government be taking to prevent one? Is the evidence persuasive, as most scientists would say, that the world is facing massive problems due to global warming, or is the evidence still inconclusive (as President Trump suggested) that climate change is a result of man-made factors?[8] The COVID-19 pandemic of 2020 underscored the need for scientific input into planning and budgeting for potential catastrophes.

Budget preparation also uses, to some extent, available program analyses, such as cost-effectiveness analysis and cost-benefit analysis.[9] Issues exist over how best to use analysis in decision making. Questions need to be asked, such as: Who conducted the analysis? Can the results be trusted? If an agency evaluated its own program, are the results believable, or was the analysis designed in such a way as to produce favorable results? For example, what items were included as costs and what ones as benefits? If efforts are made to minimize reported costs and maximize benefits, the resulting cost-benefit ratio is likely to be well above the 1.0 level. Even when the analyses are considered valid, questions remain. If results from a program analysis are discouraging, should that be used to cut an agency's budget or to increase the budget so as to get better performance?

Surplus or Deficit?

The dynamics of decision making are greatly affected by whether a current services budget would be expected to yield a surplus or a deficit. In other words, if current revenue sources and spending patterns continue, will a surplus or a deficit result? In budget preparation, the projection of a budget deficit becomes an overriding issue that cannot be ignored. For state and local governments, chief executives are often required to submit balanced budgets, so any projections of a deficit must be resolved.[10]

As a result of recessions, such as the Great Recession that started in 2007, many state and local governments need to adjust what may have been previously balanced budgets in order to deal with projected budget deficits. During recessions, deficits (whether at the national or state and local levels) tend to result from a combination of substantially reduced tax revenue and increases in spending for recession-driven programs such as unemployment insurance and Medicaid. In the case of the Great Recession, there were substantial reductions in the value of housing, leading to depressed property tax revenues at the local level.

For years, the state of California was the poster child for the fiscal problems faced by state governments. Its budgets were chronically late, and when former Governor Jerry Brown took office in 2007, the state budget was in deficit to the tune of $27 billion. By the time Brown left office in early 2019, however, the budget was back in surplus, and budgets were being enacted on time.[11] California was replaced, as a symbol of budget dysfunction, by Illinois, where a budget impasse between Governor Bruce Rauner and the General Assembly left the state without a budget for fiscal years 2016, 2017, and a portion of 2018. The budget crisis was brewing for more than 20 years, spurred on by a number of factors, including chronic underfunding of pensions and two consecutive governors (Republican George Ryan and Democrat Rod Blagojevich) who ended up in prison for various forms of public corruption. This ultimately paved the way for the election of Rauner, a business executive who promised to right the ship, but ultimately was unable to reach agreement with Democrats in the General Assembly. By the time the state was able to enact a fiscal year 2018 budget (over Governor Rauner's veto) in the summer of 2017, the state had a backlog of almost $17 billion in unpaid bills and

had unfunded pension liabilities of $129 billion. Moreover, the state had the worst credit rating in the nation, nearing "junk bond" status.[12]

At the local level, the City of Detroit perhaps best exemplifies the plight of northern Rust Belt cities, whose manufacturing base was eroded for decades. Detroit saw the problems of a reduced tax base deepen after the Great Recession. The city was forced to declare bankruptcy in July 2013, which ultimately led to a takeover by a state-appointed financial review commission.[13] This situation was similar to what New York City faced in the 1970s and Washington, DC, in the 1990s. Detroit emerged from this crisis in a stronger position, however, and three consecutive years of balanced budgets (for fiscal years 2015, 2016, and 2017) led to a return of financial control to the city; the city was expected to maintain this control unless deficits returned.[14]

Tactical Concerns

In addition to a "philosophical" approach to taxation and expenditures, the chief executive conveys a tactical view. An assessment must be made of political reactions to any possible proposed tax increase or cut. Of course, increases are more likely to produce negative reactions than are tax cuts.

For governors and the president, intergovernmental relations constitute an important component of budget preparation deliberations. Presidents may prefer, where possible, to carry out policies through state and local governments rather than directly through federal agencies. Likewise, governors may prefer to work through local governments. Mandating that state and local governments deliver services, adopt standards, or otherwise implement federal programs is seen by some as a way of achieving a federal policy goal without paying for it. These *unfunded mandates* are extremely unpopular with governors, state legislatures, mayors, and city councils.[15] (See the chapter on intergovernmental relations.)

Another set of considerations involves relationships with the legislative body. Stated simply, the chief executive assesses the chances of various recommendations receiving the approval of Congress, the state legislature, or the city council. Executives must decide whether to push for proposals that will meet with certain opposition from some legislators in alliance with interest groups. In making such calculations, chief executives do not recommend only policies likely to be approved. A doomed recommendation may be put forth as a means of preparing the legislature to approve the proposal in some future year, or the chief executive may be strongly committed to a proposal despite legislative opposition. An executive may want to score political points by advocating a proposal that has no chance with a legislature controlled by another political party, then using the disapproval of the legislature to score political points in subsequent elections. President Trump, before the midterm elections of 2018, found his path to getting policies approved substantially easier than after that election, when the opposition party had taken over one house of Congress. Many proposals put forward by Democratic House and Senate members in 2019 and 2020 had no chance of actually becoming law because of the Senate and White House being controlled by Republicans, but were rather put forward to stake out a position in preparation for the November 2020 presidential election.

Perceived citizen preferences regarding service and tax levels constitute another consideration. Chief executives have a keen sense of what the general citizenry and interest groups desire. What services do citizens demand, and what are they willing to pay for those services through either taxes or fees? Results from national and state polls are watched in an effort to identify important trends. Some cities conduct surveys of citizens and hold public hearings at which citizens may testify as a means of identifying prevailing attitudes about existing and desired services.

In preparing a budget for the upcoming fiscal year, the executive must also consider the current budget. Supplemental appropriations are standard at the federal level. Supplemental appropriations, simply called supplementals, are when an agency's budgets are selectively augmented during the fiscal year to meet unanticipated needs. During the George W. Bush administration, supplementals were the standard means for providing spending authority for the wars in Afghanistan and Iraq. None of the Bush administration budgets ever included the costs of those wars and the civilian reconstruction efforts in the regular departmental budget proposals. An even more routine cause of supplemental appropriations is spending for recovery from natural disasters, such as hurricanes or floods. For example, federal supplemental appropriation for fiscal year 2019 was identified as providing "$17.2 billion in FY2019 supplemental appropriations to several federal departments and agencies for expenses related to the consequences of recent wildfires, hurricanes, volcanos, earthquakes, typhoons, and other natural disasters."[16] Supplemental appropriations like these may throw the existing budget out of balance (or further out of balance) as the president and the budget office begin preparing a deficit budget for the next fiscal year. This kind of situation can play into the hands of the president's political opponents.

Revenue Deliberations
Revenue Estimates

Central to deliberations on the revenue side of budget preparation are revenue estimates.[17] Revenue estimating is sometimes assigned to the organization responsible for collecting revenues, most often a treasury or revenue department. Such an arrangement may place that unit in competition with the budget office because the two may offer different revenue projections. The budget office may essentially be forced into developing a budget package that is perceived to be unnecessarily constrained because of an estimate that anticipates little or no growth in revenue or even a downturn in revenue collections. This problem is especially troublesome in some developing countries where the local treasurer is a central government appointee. At the federal level, the revenue-estimating function is handled jointly by OMB, the Council of Economic Advisers, and the Treasury Department. The CBO makes independent revenue estimates for congressional consideration.

Revenue estimates tend to cover three time periods—the current year (for projecting cash flows), the budget year (for immediate budget planning), and the "outyears" (for determining the longer-term fiscal condition of the government).[18] For any of these purposes forecasting is, as much as anything, a technical process. If a government is required to have a balanced budget, as state and local governments are, then accurate revenue forecasts become critical. Estimates that are too high can create major crises during the execution phase, at which time expenditures must be cut so as not to exceed revenues. Low estimates also cause problems, in that programs may be needlessly reduced at the beginning of the fiscal year.

Perhaps the easiest method of revenue forecasting involves deterministic models that manipulate the revenue base and tax rate to produce a desired level of revenue. Property tax forecasts are deterministic in that a government can adjust assessments and tax rates to meet desired revenue levels. The main problems to address in such forecasting are the extent that (1) overall property values will rise or possibly decline, (2) new properties will be added to or removed from the tax rolls, and (3) properties will fall into default. Old and deteriorating properties are usually the ones most likely to fall into default, but during the Great Recession, defaults were common across all types of properties. Deterministic models are useful for revenue sources over which a jurisdiction has substantial control. They are not useful for taxes on such items as personal income and retail sales, which depend on economic conditions.

In cases where jurisdictions do not have control over the revenue source, but have substantial data on past performance of the source, a more appropriate form of revenue estimate involves simple trend extrapolation. Both formal and informal trend extrapolations are used in revenue estimating. In an informal situation, an assumption may be made that a particular revenue source will increase by 5% because that is what has occurred for the past several years. In most cases, of course, revenues do not increase or decrease by a set percentage or remain constant. Revenue growth may increase on average by 5%, but in some years the growth may be 10% and in others only 1% or 2%. Given this information, what percentage estimate should be used for the upcoming budget year?

One method of dealing with this problem is to use *simple linear regression*, a statistical technique that fits a straight line to a series of historical data. The formula used is $y = mx + b$. In the equation, y, the forecast revenue, is a function of a coefficient m multiplied by a known value x plus a constant b. In the formula, m is the slope of the straight line, x is the actual revenue generated the previous year, and b is a scale factor that adjusts for orders of magnitude differences between values. Computer software is readily available for making the appropriate calculations, but such projections can also be made using a simple calculator.

Besides linear regression, other techniques exist for smoothing out fluctuations in a historical series into a straight line. The method called *moving averages* calculates an average value for each point in the historical series. Starting with a series of, say, 8 years, the revenues for years 1, 2, and 3 are averaged. This average becomes the new smoothed value for year 2. Then, actual values for years 2, 3, and 4 are averaged to create a new "smoothed" year 3. Similar averages are calculated for the remaining years. A variant of this technique weighs the most recent years more heavily than the early years in calculating the moving average, on the grounds that recent years are better predictors.

Underlying these techniques is the premise that the future will be like the past. The purpose of any projection technique is to reduce historical information to a discernible pattern and then extend that pattern into the future. One way of testing how well the technique works is to "predict" several recent time periods and compare those predictions with what actually occurred. Most local governments, except large cities, still rely on one form or another of *trend extrapolation*. Evidence suggests that when used in combination with other tools, trend extrapolations produce reliable estimates for local governments.[19] Extrapolation methods are not helpful when there are significant and abrupt changes in economic conditions such as occur during economic declines, such as the one precipitated by the COVID-19 crisis. These can cause rapid reversal from state and local budget surpluses to severe fiscal pressures.

A more complex method than simple regression or trend extrapolation involves using econometric modeling to project revenues. Several types of econometric techniques for forecasting revenues exist.[20] One of the most popular is *multiple regression*. In multiple regression models, independent variables are sought that can serve as predictors of revenue yield. The assumption is that a linear relationship exists between each predictor and the dependent variable of forecast revenue. Another assumption is that each independent variable is unrelated to the others. A model for sales tax receipts might include the independent variables of population, personal income, and the consumer price index. As the values of each of these variables increases, estimated revenues increase.

Multiple predictor variables are also used in *simultaneous equation models* (multiple regression models rely on a single equation). In simultaneous equation models, individual equations relate each independent or predictor variable to the revenue to be forecast. These individual equations are solved simultaneously. The advantage of simultaneous equation models is that, unlike multiple regression models, they do not assume that each predictor variable is independent of each other predictor variable. Because many of the variables one would use to make a revenue forecast would be expected to be related to one another, the simultaneous equation approach is both more realistic and computationally more valid.

Revenue forecasts can be made using *microsimulation models* that are dependent on large databases. Individual taxpayers and corporations are included in the models and exhibit behavior changes in response to projected changes in the economy, tax laws, price levels, personal income, and the like. The models use data based on the historical performance of actual taxpayers in the jurisdiction.[21]

All of these models necessarily use variables that are sensitive to changes in economic conditions. Sales and income tax receipts rise and fall according to economic trends. Many user charges are affected, too. When people are unemployed, they curtail their use of public transportation, parking facilities, museums, and zoos. Therefore, these models are most vulnerable with regard to the assumptions made about future economic trends. Also critical are basic demographic shifts. Changing population patterns due to shifting birth rates and migration can undermine the effectiveness of forecasting models that previously had shown themselves to be extremely accurate.[22] Projecting national trends is quite difficult, and state and local trends are no easier to predict, especially given that each subnational jurisdiction has its own economic characteristics and is influenced by national trends.

Even though revenue estimating is a highly technical process, it is not immune from politics. Presidents, governors, and mayors are loath to forecast economic hard times and low revenue levels. Political executives tend to campaign for election in part on the promise that they will achieve economic growth. Presidents have the additional problem that the forecast of a recession may be a self-fulfilling prophecy. State and local executives must limit expenditures to available revenue. Pessimistic estimates force executives to make difficult choices as to where to cut programs so as to reduce overall expenditures. In general, there seems to be a tendency to underestimate revenues more often than to overestimate them. Apparently, politicians feel the political risks of underestimating and producing a surplus at the end of the year are less dire than the consequences of overestimating and having to make program cuts or raise taxes unexpectedly during the year. Further, where the "official" revenue estimates are done in the executive branch, chief executives may use underestimating as a strategy to discourage legislatures from spending money.[23] However, overestimating revenues is the more likely problem during economic downturns.[24] Because revenue estimates can rarely, if ever, be guaranteed to come true, establishing *contingency reserves* or *rainy day funds* may be a useful method of protecting against possible shortfalls and the political problems that ensue from them; these reserves proved very useful, yet inadequate, during the Great Recession. (See the chapter on budget execution.)

Taxing Limitations

Since the 1970s, taxing limitations have constituted a major consideration at the state and local levels.[25] In addition to any statutory or constitutional limitations, government officials who assemble budget proposals may be politically constrained by having to present a balanced budget that allows for no increases in tax revenues. Limited in their ability to increase revenues, decision makers are sometimes forced to fund programs at less than optimal levels and even may have to cut programs.[26]

Balanced Budgets

For state and local governments, revenue estimating is particularly critical because of the standard requirement that they have balanced operating budgets. Indebtedness is possible, but is typically used only for capital investments and other selected expenses. If a budget is built on revenue estimates that are too high, crises will ensue during execution as the government attempts to bring expenditures down so as to balance them against actual revenues. One of the reasons for the popularity of the property tax among revenue departments, but not taxpayers, is that in the short run, revenue from the property tax is easily forecast and budget shortfalls can be made up by resetting the property tax rate—although of course, that may be constrained by previous voter-approved limitations and may be the end of incumbents' political careers.

In addition to legal restraints, the bond markets impose some budgetary discipline on state and local governments. Some states or localities may lack structural balance between revenues and spending or may resort often to extraordinary means to bring budgets into balance. Such jurisdictions may experience lower bond ratings and higher borrowing costs, creating strong incentives for sound fiscal management. (See the chapter on capital finance and debt management.)

Although most states have requirements for a balanced budget, the requirements are not uniform across all states. In the first place, "balance" means that expenditures may not exceed revenues,

but not all available revenues must be appropriated and spent. Coverage is not all-inclusive, and trust funds and capital expenditures are often excluded.[27] Consequently, as little as one-half of all state funds may be covered by the balanced budget requirement. Balancing requirements also vary as to when they apply in the budget process, such as when the budget is presented to the legislature or when it is adopted. Similar variations are found at the local level.

Achieving balance in a state or local budget is a political process. The obvious alternatives are to seek revenue increases or impose spending decreases, but balance can also be attained through other means. Budget reserves, rainy day funds, or savings from previous years may be drawn upon to cover expenditures.[28] It is possible that some governments may continue spending at high levels, when helped by rainy day funds, at a time that budget cuts are really needed. Payments from one fiscal year may sometimes be shifted to the next, even though resources are actually used in the earlier year. Political leaders use this technique and others to make budgets appear to be balanced when the opposite is true.

Elimination or reduction of tax expenditures can yield additional revenues without officially raising tax rates by expanding the base of activities subject to taxation. For instance, adding products or services to the list of items subject to a state sales tax can increase revenues. Decision makers are concerned with whether each tax expenditure serves any major public purpose, and all tax expenditures are particularly subject to challenge when revenues are needed to balance a budget.[29] At the federal level, the Tax Cut and Jobs Act of 2017 broadened the tax base by substantially reducing tax expenditures and marginal tax rates, but not in a deficit neutral manner. (See the chapter on budgeting for income, property, and payroll taxes.)

One commonly used alternative to raising taxes is raising user fees or adding new fees. A school district might consider imposing new or higher fees for student parking, school trips, lost textbooks, and physical education. Of course, there are limits on how much can be realistically collected from such fees. Could the new fee revenue cover a projected revenue shortfall and alleviate a need for a tax increase?

Budget gimmickry is also used during economic boom times. By estimating revenues to be lower than are most likely to occur, decision makers later in the year can "discover" that a budget surplus exists and then use the money for some combination of tax relief and new spending.

Tax earmarking often constrains efforts to balance budgets without necessarily helping the programs officially decreed to be beneficiaries. Receipts from state lotteries, for instance, are often earmarked for such good causes as public education or aid to senior citizens. While there are no comprehensive data on the effects of earmarking, a 2002 study found that education spending did appear to be greater in states where lottery proceeds were earmarked for education, and that this substantially exceeded the effect that earmarking had in other cases.[30] Indeed, earmarking is sometimes used as an excuse for not providing more funds to a program because it is expected to operate within available revenue from the earmarked source. The supposed program that benefits from a lottery, then, may receive no greater funding than it would have without the lottery. Earmarking in effect "Balkanizes" governments' finances and can greatly hamper efforts to resolve budget problems when revenues decline, because monies are compartmentalized and cannot be treated as part of the total resources available for creating an overall balanced budget.[31]

In addition, revenue gaps are sometimes closed with public employee pension monies. A government may simply not make its full contribution to the employee pension funds or may even have the freedom to withdraw monies in an effort to balance the budget. Typically, financial penalties must be paid for such actions, including negative reactions by the financial markets for municipal bonds issued by jurisdictions engaging in such practices. More subtle methods involve adjusting actuarial assumptions. By making an assumption that retired employees will die comparatively early in life, fewer dollars will be needed to cover expected retirees when benefit levels

are predetermined. Also, by assuming that investments on retirement monies will result in comparatively high returns, more dollars will become available to cover expected retirement benefits and the government will need to contribute less to the retirement fund.[32] The Pew Charitable Trusts estimated in 2018 that the total unfunded liability across the states for retiree pension benefits was almost $1.3 trillion nationally.[33]

Whereas the decision makers responsible for state and local budgeting spend substantial time and energy balancing their budgets, the situation is quite different at the federal level. Whether to require a balanced federal budget has long been a controversial issue, but a constitutional amendment requiring an annually balanced budget has yet to be adopted. (See the chapter on the public sector in perspective and the chapter on budget approval and the U.S. Congress.)

One general rule of thumb is that one-time revenues should not be the basis upon which long-term commitments are made.[34] This concern arose after the enactment of the American Recovery and Reinvestment Act (ARRA) of 2009 when some governors expressed hesitation in accepting ARRA funds because they offered only temporary relief, and therefore put off hard decisions for the future.[35] It also was the stated reason that some states declined to participate in the expansion of Medicaid under the Affordable Care Act, but this may have been an excuse provided by Republican legislators and governors who simply did not want to comply with the signature accomplishment of the Obama administration.[36]

Spending Deliberations
Entitlements and Other Commitments

Much of the spending side of any budget is determined in advance of budget preparation deliberations. Interest on the debt must be paid, and prior commitments to employees, such as set levels of contributions to retirement plans, must be met. Entitlement programs that guarantee benefits to various groups, such as the needy, the elderly, and the ill, determine much of the spending side

---

of a budget, where the amount spent is a function of the numbers of people qualifying for various programs, and the amount each would be paid under existing law. At the state and local levels, Medicaid and unemployment insurance spending are heavily caseload driven, and these caseloads expand greatly during times of recession. Local education spending, while not an entitlement in a classic sense, is still heavily driven by the size of the school-age population that a given school district needs to educate at a given point in time. The same could be said for other caseload-driven spending, such as that associated with state prisons, which is heavily driven by the size of the prison population and the sentencing behavior of judges; states have recognized, for example, that the only way to make a significant dent in prison spending was to control the population, often through early release programs.[37] The Nebraska legislature mandated that the state corrections department reduce its inmate population to 140% of what its facilities were designed to hold, with a deadline of July 1, 2020. If the department failed to meet that deadline, they would be forced to grant early release to eligible inmates until the target was reached.[38]

Organizational Competition

Just as central administrative organizations compete in trying to influence revenue decisions, so organizations vie with one another on the spending side of the budget. At the top level of a government, personalities become important. The roles of various participants at the federal level depend upon a president's administrative style, his or her confidence in the abilities of key figures, and the roles that these figures seek for themselves. A president, governor, or mayor is not obligated to rely on the advice of any individual and may seek guidance from anyone inside or outside government.

Cabinet officers seek to gain acceptance and financial support for their agencies' programs. At the federal level, central advisers to the president are other contenders for attention. In addition to advice provided by the White House Office staff, advice is available from the Domestic Policy Council, the National Economic Council, the Council of Economic Advisers, and the National Security Council. At these high levels of government as well as elsewhere throughout the government, heated debates occur over such topics as Social Security and health care funding.[39]

Some have suggested that at the federal level of government, but also at lower levels, misrepresentation and other ethically questionable behaviors prevail.[40] The competitive nature of budgeting may emphasize self-interest, both personal and collective, to the detriment of the public interest. As C. W. Lewis noted, "The process depends on and rewards deceit."[41]

Agencies may misrepresent their situations to budget offices—for example, by claiming dire consequences unless budgets are increased for programs that are highly visible and favored by the public. At a higher level, political leaders may deceive the public—for example, by downplaying the importance of budget deficits and rationalizing the need for greater spending on pet projects even though the budget is out of balance. Financial managers, in serving their political bosses, are often ethically stressed during times of budget crises.[42]

Budget Office Roles

The central budget office has numerous roles. Not only does it recommend policies on spending, but it participates in the review of legislative proposals, economic policy, administrative regulations, evaluation of programs, collection of data by agencies, and agency management studies and management improvement efforts. When OMB examines an agency's budget requests, all of these forces come into play. Agency budget proposals will be seen in the context of what legislative changes will be necessary, what regulatory actions will be required by the agency, and whether the agency is perceived as well managed.

Agency Expectations and Deliberations

In approaching the budget process, including the preparation phase, agencies have expectations about what constitutes success. Until the latter half of the 1970s, success was often measured in terms of budget increases approved by the executive and ultimately by the legislative body. This approach of adding increments to a base has since been discarded in many locales. Where taxing and spending limits have been imposed at the state and local levels, agencies have been forced instead to concentrate on defending their bases and minimizing the extent of cuts imposed on their budgets. The period from the late 1970s to the early 1990s was dubbed the decremental age.[43] Budgets tended to grow after that point, but recessions in general (such as the Great Recession) can usher in decremental periods at all levels of government.

By the time a budget request reaches the central budget office, an extensive series of discussions has been completed within the line agency. In large agencies having several layers of organizational units, those at the bottom will have attempted to persuade their superiors to approve requests for additional funding. The force being exerted from the top downward tends to be negative—in the sense that pressure is applied to limit the growth of programs and the corresponding rise in expenditures. This does not mean that there is simply a set of petitioners and a set of rejecters who do battle within each agency or department. Middle managers up through department heads are required to take positive and negative positions, rejecting many of the proposals brought to them by subordinates and, in negotiating with their superiors, advocating those proposals that they accept.

Part of the influence within an agency is a function of superior levels attempting to determine what is likely to be salable to the budget office and the chief executive. Agencies are aware that they are likely to get less than they request. Therefore, they will avoid requesting too little, but will not ask for exorbitant sums unless an open-ended budget system is in use.

The amount eventually requested by a department is necessarily a function of the type of budget system in place. Some systems provide for a base budget and then permit requests for additions to that base. Others use a current services budget and require that an agency include information about possibly funding activities below and above the current services level. Some budget systems may require reductions. President Trump (as had President Obama before him) called for agencies to offer up reductions in spending in their budget requests. In the case of the Trump budget, the President asked domestic agencies to propose budgets demonstrating how they would cut 5% from previous levels.[44] However, though the Republican party controlled both the Senate and the House, Congress actually approved higher spending levels than the last Obama administration budget.[45] State and local governments have also needed to reach into the base for budget reductions. For example, the effects of the Great Recession resulted in Texas asking its agencies to cut their budgets by more than $3 billion during fiscal year 2010.[46]

Across-the-board cuts are sometimes imposed during budget preparation, although, as was noted previously, those can be far more harmful to some agencies than others and result in harm to the clients of the agencies that suffer reduced funding. Prioritization, therefore, is sometimes used. Washington State has used a process called "priorities of government" to drive budget decisions.[47]

Budget Office and Agency Relations

Just as the interplay within an agency is extensive and vociferous during budget preparation, so is the interplay between the central budget office and the agencies. The central office, serving as the agent of the chief executive, must assert a unifying influence over the diverse interests of administrative units. These, in contrast, can be expected to favor greater autonomy. Operating departments and agencies will, of course, favor the advancement of their particular programs (seeking greater funds or defending programs against cuts), while the budget office usually will be forced to say no to program growth and to enforce needed cutbacks during times of fiscal scarcity.

When the budget office receives agency budget submissions, analysts or examiners are assigned to review these documents. The examiners serve as the main link between the budget office and these agency line units. These professionals must balance a variety of factors, such as being expected to be thorough but having limited time available for their work and being sensitive to political matters but serving professional values.[48] With the passage of time, examiners gain considerable knowledge about their agencies, providing substantive expertise within the budget office. They often become advocates for the agencies they review and frequently even shift their employment to an operating agency. Still, the accusation is commonly made by the agency officials that budget analysts are not program oriented and are insensitive to the needs of operating units. Legislative analysts may also be part of the budget development process, particularly in state governments.[49] Sometimes budget office analysts may consult informally with legislative analysts during the preparation phase.[50]

The structure of budget offices varies from government to government and from time to time. One key concern is whether the central function of examining agency budget requests should be integrated with other functions, notably management functions, program analysis, and planning. The argument for their integration is that it gives budget analysts much broader exposure to the operations of government and enhances the analysts' opportunities to make valuable inputs into budget deliberations. The argument against integration is that budget examination activities all too often take top priority, leaving all other activities on the sidelines.

The desire to better integrate the management and budget functions of OMB led to a reorganization, called "OMB 2000," under Director Alice Rivlin.[51] The purpose of this reorganization was to try to better integrate management improvements into the budget process. Since this reform, the budget review function at OMB has been organized into five resource management offices:

1. Natural resources (including agriculture, energy, science, and space)
2. National security (including international affairs)
3. Education, income maintenance, and labor programs
4. General government (including housing, justice, transportation, and treasury)
5. Health

Each resource management office is responsible for budgeting, management, and planning/policy issues within its particular arena.

Budget office discussions with agencies involve how services are to be delivered to the citizenry, as well as the funding for those services. The deliberations include whether services should be provided directly by agencies, by private corporations or other governments operating under contract with government, or through some combination of these and other modes.

The nature of the dialogue between the budget office and agencies hinges in large measure on the extent to which the latter consider the former to be an important ally or an opponent. Only minimal information can be expected from an agency that is suspicious of the central budget office. A common concern is that an agency will not release data that could be used to its detriment. In contrast, if an agency can win the confidence and support of the examiner, then it in effect gains a spokesperson for its program on the chief executive's staff.

The budget office typically holds hearings with agency representatives. Whereas earlier in the process the examiners may have contacted agencies by phone, e-mail, or in person to clarify detailed items included in requests, hearings tend to focus on broader concerns. The budget office must decide whether agencies can accomplish what they propose and whether the anticipated accomplishments are worth seeking. The burden of proof rests with the agencies. The operating agency that has a reputation for requesting excessive sums and for overpromising on results will be suspect.

At the same time, winning budget office approval does not guarantee success for the agency. The resistant or recalcitrant agency may, indeed, be able to increase the caution with which the examiner makes recommendations to reduce the agency's budget. At the federal level, the significance of OMB action is mitigated by the fact that Congress is a strong legislature that jealously guards its power to pass appropriations. Opposition by the budget office to some agencies' requests for funds may sometimes be helpful in winning legislative support.

The agencies, not OMB, have had major responsibility for defending their budget requests before Congress, and therefore the OMB's utility to the agencies has been greater in the preparation phase than in the approval phase of the budget cycle. Some organizational units, such as the Federal Bureau of Investigation in the 1950s and 1960s and the National Institutes of Health more recently, have been able to secure extensive support in Congress, thereby providing them with some autonomy vis-à-vis their departments and OMB. Of course, agencies can fall out of favor when their heads lose public and congressional confidence, making the agencies more vulnerable to OMB control. Beginning in the 1980s, OMB gained greater responsibility for explaining and defending the president's budget before Congress. This role, however, often was negative in the sense that the main task was to explain how and why reductions should be made in agencies' budgets.[52] In the Trump administration, OMB has been in the position of defending large budget cuts for many domestic programs, while at the same time advocating increases for national defense and homeland security (especially border protection).

Legal requirements and court decisions may force increases in expenditures and preclude some decision making by agencies and the central budget office. For instance, state government mandates may require local governments to establish recycling programs for solid waste. Federal officials may require a city to upgrade its sewage treatment facilities. Federal and state court decisions may force a state government to expand prison facilities to accommodate increased numbers of prisoners, or may declare certain programs to be illegal or unconstitutional. Court cases may be filed against governments, forcing them to spend considerable sums on legal representation. Such suits may be filed by private citizens or corporations or by one government against another.

Budget Office Recommendations

The response of the budget office to agency requests is, in part, a function of the office's assessment of its own powers and responsibilities in relation to the operating agencies and other central units. Few would deny to a budget office the ministerial or bookkeeping functions of assembling requests and carrying out the mechanical duties of designing, tabulating, and overseeing the printing of the budget. At the same time, how many additional responsibilities the budget office has depends largely on the competition from other units and the management style of the chief executive.

In an executive budgeting system, the chief executive has the final say on what to recommend to the legislative body. Thus, the budget office attempts to formulate recommendations thought to be in keeping with the executive's priorities. As part of the calculation of what to recommend, it assesses the chances of agencies making direct appeals to the chief executive or, in the extreme case, to the legislature, and thereby overturning the budget office's recommendations. If this strategy—making an end run around the budget office—is successful, it can severely weaken the budget office's role. If an agency knows it can get what it wants by appealing directly to the chief executive or the legislature, the agency is likely to consider the budget office as merely a bookkeeper that can be largely ignored. Normally the budget director will communicate to the chief executive the importance of keeping the budget office in the loop and resisting unilateral appeals from agencies.

As a staff unit of the chief executive, the budget office is expected to develop recommendations that are consistent with executive priorities. A central budget office is typically headed by a political appointee who is closely aligned with the chief executive, both in terms of priorities and politics. At the federal level, there have been cases (most notably Leon Panetta in the Clinton administration and Mick Mulvaney in the Trump administration) where the OMB director eventually became the President's chief of staff. Other staff in the budget office, however, are often career staff and as professionals have a responsibility to report to the chief executive their views on the worthiness of programs. To report that a given program is operating well simply because the chief executive wants to hear that message does a disservice, as does recommending severe budget cuts to the chief executive when the budget office knows that these cuts could have devastating results on the affected programs or on programs that have proven to be effective. *Neutral competence* has been proposed as the appropriate role for the budget office: The office should retain its professional approach in developing its budget recommendations but simultaneously should develop recommendations in tune with executive priorities.[53]

As the budget is being developed by the budget office and when it is released, the budget office may engage in a public relations campaign that is intended to reach not only the public but also administrative agencies. At the federal level, the OMB director may issue press releases, hold press conferences, appear on television talk shows, and speak before such groups as the National Press Club. In this way, the budget director communicates on a broad scale the priorities of the administration and in effect warns agencies to beware of pushing for other priorities.

Downsizing, Rightsizing, and Spending Cutbacks

The Great Recession marked the return to a budgetary theme that first surfaced in the 1980s, referred to as "cutback budgeting." The impetus for cutbacks comes in particular from the imperative that comes from reduced revenues and increased spending on countercyclical programs that accompany periodic recessions. State and local governments, which are forced to balance their budgets, typically see it as imperative, both legally and practically, to make cuts during a recession. Some of these governments' problems derive from extended declines in their economies. Other problems stem from a temporary lack of robustness in the national economy. When the economy slumps, state and local sales and income tax revenues fall. So-called Rust Belt states, especially Michigan, Ohio, and Pennsylvania, face a different set of economic woes—namely, a long-term erosion in their tax bases. Pressure often exists, in such a downsizing regime, as agencies try to provide the same or even more services with fewer personnel and other resources.

The tax revolt movement has imposed additional constraints on spending. In some instances, a jurisdiction's economy may have been vibrant, but the government was precluded from taxing that economic base to the extent it perceived was needed to fund government programs. (See the chapter on budgeting for income, payroll, and property taxes.)

The tactics used to deal with a budget shortage depend in part upon its perceived duration. If the shortage is considered to be short term, perhaps lasting only for the current year, then modest adjustments can be made, such as imposing temporary cuts on programs and drawing on budget reserves or rainy day funds. During the Great Recession, rainy day fund balances proved inadequate to shield states and local governments from substantial budget reductions. In a sense this is no surprise, as rainy day funds were never intended to permit states to weather a recession of the length and depth of the Great Recession without being required to take any policy actions. These funds are rather intended to buffer states against the need to take precipitous and draconian actions for short-term economic problems.

When long-term budget retrenchment is seen as necessary, then decision makers must manage the immediate problems of the current and upcoming budget years and anticipate problems in future years. When budget cuts must be imposed several years in a row, decision makers must be prepared to make extraordinarily difficult choices. Sometimes across-the-board cuts are ordered. These uniform cuts can have the effect of inappropriately freezing current priorities in place rather than taking a hard look at which lower-priority programs deserve larger reductions or even terminations.

Which budget cuts will be made ultimately hinges on the extent to which various groups in the society will suffer from program reductions or eliminations. Budget cuts are less likely to be imposed on groups that are politically organized and vocal than on other, less visible groups. Applying the budget knife to programs for the elderly is often politically dangerous, for instance, whereas cutting programs for low-income individuals, who tend to be politically less active, may seem "safer" for decision makers. This is, in part, what has led to the adage that Social Security and Medicare are the "third rail" of American politics—"touch them and you die."[54] In relatively homogeneous communities, budget cutback procedures do not pit one segment of the community against another.

Budget Office Roles During Cutbacks

When jurisdictions confront fiscal stress, the decision process initially tends to be centralized. After all, without central instruction to begin a process of cutting, agencies might well submit budget requests based on unrealistic assumptions. The central budget office, working with the chief executive, attempts to instruct departments as to priorities for funding. Often some version of an across-the-board cut strategy is implemented because it is easy and perceived as fair. In many European countries, such an approach is referred to as "cheese slicer" budgeting, as it involves taking a uniform piece off the top.[55] Such a strategy, however, is anathema to priority setting, as it makes the implicit assumptions that all programs are of equal priority, at least at the margin. If programs are set aside as immune from budget cuts, they may have few incentives to be efficient in their spending. Moreover, achieving the level of budget reductions needed to balance a budget may be impossible if many key programs are protected from cuts. For example, since the George W. Bush administration, defense and homeland security spending have been largely viewed by many as exempt from serious budget review in light of the wars in Iraq and Afghanistan and post–September 11, 2001, domestic security concerns. At the state level, funding for elementary and secondary education is often viewed as

sacrosanct, meaning that cuts by definition need to come from the rest of the state budget.

In a retrenchment environment, agencies normally feel fortunate if the budget office approves even their projected current services budget. In other situations, the central budget office may provide specific budget ceilings to each department. These figures, which most likely are below the current services levels, are used in preparing budget requests. This process has all the strengths and the weaknesses of fixed-ceiling budgeting. Where such approaches are taken, the process of cutting often starts earlier in the calendar than in a budget situation when growth predominates.[56] More time may be needed to determine which programs will be cut than to introduce new programs or expand existing ones, although some governments may find themselves in crisis situations in which cuts must be imposed immediately to avert a collapse of their financial situations. (See the chapter on the expenditure side of public budgeting.)

Legislative Roles

If legislative preferences can be identified at the beginning of budget preparation, then cuts can be planned that are ultimately likely to meet with legislative approval. Some communities have used confidential questionnaires and other techniques for soliciting legislative input when budget cutting must be part of the preparation phase. Members of local legislative bodies, however, may prefer not to reveal their preferences until later, when more is known about the options for cutting and about citizens' attitudes. Of course, legislatures are frequently not on the "cutting" side of the budget process, in that legislatures are sometimes in the position of restoring cuts proposed by the executive, or providing their own add-ons to the budget.

Items to Cut

When reductions in expenditures become necessary, certain standard areas are considered. One of them is personnel costs. Because much of any government's operating budget covers personnel costs, it is difficult to make any appreciable reduction in expenditures without reducing personnel budgets. Several specific techniques are used for reducing personnel costs:

- Holding down general pay increases for workers
- Delaying filling of vacant positions and leaving other positions empty as they become vacant
- Laying off workers
- Providing financial incentives for workers to induce them to retire and (presumably) be replaced by lower-salaried workers
- Reducing government contributions for benefits, particularly costly retirement packages

The National Association of State Budget Officers, in its 2011 Fiscal Survey of the States, catalogued the budget reductions that had been made in the fiscal year 2011 state budget process. The most frequently used strategy was targeting cuts to individual programs (34 states), followed by across-the-board cuts (20 states) and layoffs (20 states). Interestingly, 19 of the states reporting that they had employed across-the-board cuts also employed targeted reductions. Other frequently used strategies included reducing local aid (16 states), imposing user fees (14 states), and furloughs (19 states).[57] Fiscal year 2011 was a year in which state governments were still reeling from the effects of the Great Recession.

A look at similar data for the fiscal year 2020 state budget processes suggests that many of these same strategies were used, but often to a much lesser extent. For example, across-the-board cuts were only used by four states in the FY20 budget process, and local aid was also cut by only four states. Only one state (Kentucky) imposed furloughs in fiscal year 2020.[58] Governments also tend to make cutbacks in equipment and facilities during times of fiscal stress. Decisions may be made to delay the purchase of major equipment and to defer maintenance, such as postponing the repair of city-owned sidewalks, roofs on government buildings, and potholes in city and state roads. The savings here can be short-lived: The failure to repair a roof, for example, might result in water damage costing

many thousands of dollars. There may be a tendency to use the deferred maintenance approach on less visible facilities, especially water and sewer lines, although highways and bridges have suffered notably due to state and local fiscal problems. States may also cut back on resources promised to local governments. Michigan, for example, has balanced its budget by not providing as much revenue to local governments as is required by law.[59]

In so-called tight budget periods, major emphasis is given to making operations as efficient as possible. The expectation is that organizational units should be able to operate with fewer resources while maintaining existing service levels. On the other hand, no single agency is eager to relinquish resources through increased efficiency if other agencies are not compelled to take the same route. Each agency is fearful of being the first to show how savings can be accomplished in its operations. This same attitude prevails in the approval phase among legislators, who are not eager to agree to budget cuts in their favored programs even though it is well understood that major cuts will be necessary.

Governments sometimes allow agencies to carry forward unspent money into the next fiscal year. This technique is seen as giving agencies incentives to use their resources efficiently. In a cutback period, however, the budget office and the legislature may be tempted to cancel out any carryover monies. Agencies mindful of such possible action, then, may avoid carrying forward any monies during economic recessions.

Budget cutting creates havoc, low morale, and some inefficiency in agencies. Personnel rightfully become concerned that their positions will be eliminated in the agency's budget request. Political appointees in an agency may be at odds with career personnel over which activities are essential and which are expendable. Some budget cuts necessitate agency reorganization, which disrupts operations. Uncertainty in funding can require stretching out the completion of projects. Defense is a major example of this problem, where changes in project schedules can result in billions of dollars of increased costs.

Budget Systems and Cutbacks

A final consideration regarding cutback budgeting is how the various budget systems (fixed-ceiling budgeting, open-ended budgeting, and current services budgeting) assist in retrenchment efforts. As already noted, central budget offices use variations on fixed-ceiling budgeting to indicate to agencies what funding levels are acceptable in the budget preparation process. Perhaps most other budget systems have been developed on the stated or unstated premise that budgets will increase from year to year, and therefore these budget systems are less central to decision making when budget cuts must be imposed. At the same time, program budgeting and various forms of zero-base budgeting in theory should be highly useful in budget-cutting situations. During prosperous times, budgeting may be largely a process of considering possible incremental additions to the budget bases of programs. During declining times, the process may become one of subtracting increments from the base.

Final Preparation Deliberations

Chief executives and their staffs become most active in the budget preparation phase during its final weeks, a frustrating period for the budget office. Decisions are seemingly reached but then may be reversed. The chief executive may instruct the budget office to include an agency's proposed change in the budget but later reject the proposal after considering revenue estimates. Alternatively, some spending initiative may be added at the last minute, forcing the budget office to scramble to fit that new spending in the budget. The chief executive may tentatively decide to recommend tax increases and then reverse that decision. Materials prepared during evenings and weekends by the budget office may find their way to the paper shredder as decisions are changed. The process may seem haphazard—and it probably is in many respects—but it is necessarily complicated because of the numerous factors being evaluated simultaneously.

A common complaint about the preparation phase is that only the chief executive, perhaps a top staff person (such as the governor's chief of staff), and the director of the central budget office consider the budget as a whole. An organizational unit in a department or agency is concerned primarily with its own piece of the budget, and the same is true of a department vis-à-vis other departments and the rest of the budget. Even in the central budget office, budget examiners focus mainly on one or a few segments of the budget and not on the total package. The chief executive, assisted by the budget director, must pull together pieces of information and intelligence provided by various sources into a set of decisions that can be defended as a whole. The budget that is to be submitted to the legislative body is the chief executive's creation.

The decision process necessarily involves tradeoffs. Assuming that there is a fixed budget constraint (like a balanced budget requirement), a $1 million increase in a city police department's budget means there is that much less available for other departments in the government. An increase in property taxes makes more money available to provide services that citizens want, but at the same time may anger those same citizens who face an increase in their tax bills. Planning personnel layoffs may seem a reasonable choice for avoiding tax increases, but will layoffs be imposed on all agencies, including highly visible units like the police and fire departments? Chief executives take seriously the justifications that agencies make for increasing budget amounts or for avoiding budget cuts, and perceptions about the effectiveness of agencies' programs and activities influence executive decisions in the preparation phase of budgeting.

In this final stage of preparation, the chief executive must decide to what extent to include initiatives that may be opposed by the legislature. For example, with the end of the Cold War and the advent of global terrorism, the Department of Defense has insisted on the need to transform itself. The argument is made that the military needs to invest in new technologies and scrap old ones. Closing unneeded military bases is part of this argument, but it runs counter to the interests of key members of Congress, who want to preserve bases in their jurisdictions. The president, then, must decide what to include in the budget on this sensitive matter, balancing the needs of national security with the reality of politics. Sustained combat operations also rapidly speed up the need for equipment replacement and spare parts, and in every war, new threats are identified that lead to research and development expenditures for new technologies and tools to defeat the threats, such as the need to reduce damage from improvised explosive devices. In addition, cybersecurity concerns, almost unheard of two decades ago, are now front and center as officials think about threats to national and homeland security.[60]

Chief executives often include items in their budgets that they do not wholeheartedly support, because they know that the legislature is likely to fund the initiatives in any event. In this type of situation, an executive may include the item to get a more realistic picture of ultimate expenditures and budget tradeoffs.

Budget Documents

The final product of the preparation phase of budgeting is a budget document (or documents) that contains the decisions reached during the months of agency requests and executive reviews. The budget at this point is only a proposal, a set of recommended policies and programs set forth by the chief executive. It remains a proposal until the legislative body acts on it.

Number and Types of Documents

The budget for any government may consist of one or several documents. Small jurisdictions often have one-volume budgets, whereas larger governments usually package their budgets in several volumes. The size of a jurisdiction's budget, as measured in receipts or expenditures, does not always determine the size of its documents, however. Some volumes contain mainly text and tables, while others include charts, graphs, photographs,

and narrative discussions of special topics and initiatives.

The preparers of budget documents are paying increasing attention to making the documents more "user friendly," reflecting the fact that these documents are expected to communicate the proposals contained within not only to technical budget analysts but also to executive and legislative political leaders, the news media, and the general citizenry. Budget documents often include glossaries that define technical terms in everyday language. Explanations are provided as to how tables should be read. Sections are sometimes color-coded and tabbed or have markings on page edges to help readers find the topics of interest to them. Since 1984, the Government Finance Officers Association has given its Award for Distinguished Budget Presentation to thousands of state and local governments.[61]

A government may produce one main document as well as one or more additional documents. A *budget-in-brief* may be prepared for general consumption that places emphasis on graphics and readability. The government can enhance its documents' interest to general readers by using attractive formats made possible by the widespread availability of affordable desktop publishing computer software. Of course, many governments have their budgets online, which increases their accessibility. Nashville has an online *Citizen's Guide to the Metro Budget*.[62]

Federal Documents

In some years, the federal government publishes numerous budget documents. In other years, it provides far fewer documents. The main budget document is the *Budget of the United States Government*,[63] which is backed up by a second and much larger document—the *Budget Appendix*.[64] In addition to preparing these documents, OMB prepares *Analytical Perspectives*, which provides more detailed information about specific aspects of the budget.[65] The content of this document varies over time but often includes discussions of crosscutting programs, such as homeland security, economic assumptions that are the foundation for the budget, budget reform proposals, and the current services budget. *Historical Tables* provides multiyear financial data on a variety of subjects.[66]

OMB produces other important documents, such as budget circulars (for example, Circular A-11) and annual publications covering procurement and the midyear status of the budget. Some documents may be prepared for a few years but then are replaced or superseded by other documents. For instance, separate annual volumes have sometimes been prepared that describe the policy initiatives being advocated by the president and the information being collected by federal agencies. OMB's website (*www.whitehouse.gov/omb*) provides links to other documents it issues as well as a discussion of other sources of budget-related information.

The *Economic Report of the President* is prepared by the Council of Economic Advisers and is released at about the same time as the other main budget documents.[67] The report discusses expected economic trends for the coming fiscal year and is the basis upon which the president's economic policy is formulated. The economic assumptions reflected in this report are used for estimating revenues and expenditures for the budget year.

The Treasury Department has an extensive publishing program and produces several documents specifically related to budgeting. The *Financial Report of the United States Government* reports on the financial condition of the government.[68] The *Treasury Bulletin*, issued quarterly, reports information about the economy, government receipts and outlays, and federal debt.[69] This document provides details on the various forms of federal securities. In addition to these documents, the Treasury Department publishes monthly and daily reports on the government's financial transactions and separate reports on trust funds, such as the unemployment, highway, and disability insurance trust funds.

Other Specialized Documents

Governments sometimes publish specialized budget-related documents in addition to those already mentioned. Some states and many local governments publish capital budgets, showing planned construction projects and major pieces of equipment to be purchased, and some publish separate volumes on personnel. (See the chapter on capital assets for more on nonpersonnel expenditures.)

The federal government and some states publish discussions of tax expenditures, which are losses in government revenue due to tax provisions that exempt some items from taxation or provide favorable tax rates. In its annual publication *Analytical Perspectives*, OMB provides an extensive discussion of the effects of various tax provisions on receipts—namely, how these provisions create tax expenditures. Massachusetts publishes a separate volume on tax expenditures annually.[70] (See the chapters on budgeting for revenues for more on tax expenditures.)

Budget Messages

Another feature of budget documents is the budget message, in which the chief executive highlights the major recommendations in the budget. This message is sometimes presented orally to the legislature. The president's budget message is included in the *Budget of the United States Government* itself. State governments vary widely in this regard, with some having no message and others having lengthy ones, sometimes as long as 100 pages. **Exhibit 8-1** shows the budget message of Massachusetts Governor Charlie Baker included with his fiscal year 2020 budget proposal. State and local jurisdictions occasionally publish their budget messages as separate documents.

Approved Budgets

Some jurisdictions publish their approved budgets (i.e., budgets that reflect action taken by the legislative bodies). New Mexico, for example, publishes a *Post-Session Review*.[71] The federal government does not provide such a volume, making it difficult for citizens and other interested parties to track the trajectory of the budget from the president's budget proposal, to congressional action, to actual results.

Exhibit 8-1 2020 Budget Message, State of Massachusetts

January 23, 2019

To the Honorable Senate and House of Representatives,

We are pleased to present our Fiscal Year 2020 (FY20) House 1 budget recommendation, the fifth budget of our Administration. This fiscally-responsible proposal builds on our collaborative and productive relationship with the Legislature over the past four years to keep state spending in line with revenue growth and to reduce our reliance on non-recurring sources of revenue. A growing economy and continuing commitment to fiscal discipline have enabled investments in key priorities including education, substance misuse services and treatment, housing, climate change adaptation and resiliency, transportation, economic development, and our local communities.

Our FY20 House 1 proposal anticipates a $297 million deposit into the Stabilization Fund which, in addition to the anticipated year-end deposit in Fiscal Year 2019, would bring the Commonwealth's reserves to nearly $2.8 billion, an increase of 150% since the Baker-Polito Administration took office. We are proud to partner with the Legislature on this shared commitment to building our reserves and protecting the Commonwealth against recession or other disruption in the economy.

House 1 proposes $42.7 billion in gross spending, an increase of 1.5% over Fiscal Year 2019 projected spending, excluding transfers to the Medical Assistance Trust Fund.

Through separate legislation being filed alongside the budget today the Administration is proposing a major, multi-year school finance reform initiative, which includes an overhaul of the school funding formula. This proposal is accompanied by an increase of $200 million in Chapter 70 education aid in the FY20 budget. The reforms will assist districts in managing the rising cost of health care and of educating English language learners and students with special education needs, and will provide an influx of new funding support for school districts with higher concentrations of poverty. The initiative is funded with existing revenues, and is implemented gradually to ensure it can be sustained over time.

Along with increased investments in Chapter 70 aid for education House 1 proposes additional funding for schools, including a proposed new formula for reimbursing school districts for charter school tuition and an increase of $16 million for those reimbursements in FY20. House 1 also includes a sales tax modernization proposal that will generate significant one-time revenues. This money will be used to seed education investments, including $100 million for college scholarships, $50 million for a new trust fund to help drive quality improvements in low-performing schools, $30 million to help local school districts address their school safety needs, and $20 million to help districts eliminate lead from their school drinking water.

Continuing our strong partnership with the Commonwealth's cities and towns and consistent with immediate past budget years, House 1 increases unrestricted local aid by 2.7%, equal to 100% of the consensus revenue tax growth estimate percentage. This investment will provide cities and towns with $1.129 billion in unrestricted general government aid in FY20. The budget also includes $6.8 million to support Community Compact-related programs, which have provided all 351 cities and towns with access to important grant funding and have led to the adoption of more than 800 best practices to help enhance the delivery of local services.

As part of the continuing effort to manage MassHealth costs House 1 proposes significant MassHealth pharmacy reforms to reduce the high cost of prescription drugs, a major driver of program costs. We project $80 million in gross savings from these reforms.

The budget supports $266 million in funding across several state agencies for substance misuse treatment and services. To address the significant and growing state costs associated with opioid misuse, House 1 proposes a tax on gross receipts of manufacturers of opioids from the sale of their opioid products. The budget also ensures consistency with state tax policy as it applies to tobacco and marijuana, by proposing a retail tax on electronic cigarettes and an excise tax on vapor products.

The FY20 budget proposal also supports a total of $23.9 million in funding to increase opportunities in education, job training, and business development consistent with recommendations of the Administration's Black Advisory Commission (BAC) and Latino Advisory Commission (LAC).

Exhibit 8-1 2020 Budget Message, State of Massachusetts *(continued)*

The broader budget package includes a separate legislative proposal to amend the state gaming law to allow legal sports wagering at Category 1 and Category 2 gaming facilities in Massachusetts. The proposal would also allow those facilities and other duly-licensed online vendors to offer on-line sports wagering. This proposed legislative change is projected to generate $35 million in FY20.

To save taxpayers from having to cover the cost of excessive sick time payouts to workers who retire from state service House 1 once again includes a proposal to cap accrued sick time for Executive Branch and Higher Education employees, bringing the Commonwealth in line with other states and private sector employers.

Finally, House 1 anticipates a reduction in the state income tax rate from 5.05% to 5% on January 1, 2020, in accordance with state law, returning $88 million to taxpayers in FY20 — and representing the final milestone on a two-decade journey to achieve a 5% income tax rate.

We are proud of the partnership we have built with the House and Senate to develop responsible budgets that reflect the needs of Massachusetts residents. We look forward to working with you on this proposal in the coming months.

Sincerely,
Charles D. Baker, Governor
Karyn E. Polito, Lieutenant Governor

Governor Charles D. Baker's Budget Recommendation, Fiscal Year 2020 Commonwealth of Massachusetts. Retrieved January 5, 2020, from https://budget.digital .mass.gov/bb/h1/fy20h1/msg_20/hdefault.htm

Coverage

Budget documents vary with regard to the extent of their coverage. All report information about government receipts and expenditures. Likewise, intergovernmental transactions are reported. A state budget highlights the funds it receives from the federal government and the funds it provides local governments within the state. Issues arise over how much detail to provide on these items.

State and Local Budgets

Confusion is common in the handling of funds in budget documents. State and local governments are major users of special funds, which basically are financial accounts for special revenue sources, such as the Casino Revenue Fund in New Jersey, and which can be used only for specific purposes. A jurisdiction's general fund consists of revenue that can be used for all functions of the government. Many jurisdictions have a general fund budget document plus one or more documents for special funds. One result of having separate budgets can be confusion over the size of the total budget and the amount spent by any given

agency, because the agency may be receiving support from several funds. These different types of funds are discussed in the chapter on financial management.

The Federal Budget

The coverage issue at the federal level is similar. Until the late 1960s, there were really three types of federal budgets: the administrative budget, the consolidated cash statement, and the federal sector of the national income accounts. Using three types of budgets resulted in much confusion. Since 1969, there has been a single consolidated (unified) budget, that includes all federal agencies and programs, with some important exceptions noted later.[72] Receipts, budget authority (funds made available for obligation), outlays (expenditures), and the resulting deficit or surplus are shown. Information is supplied for the means of financing the deficit and about the size of the federal debt.

Since adoption of the unified budget, important changes have occurred. One trend is toward greater use of moving some items out of the reported budget totals, what is known as *off-budget* totals. Congress determined what was off-budget, which could vary somewhat from year to year. The U.S. Postal Service, for example, was moved off-budget because it was expected to operate like a business, largely independent of the government. The Social Security trust funds were moved off-budget because the surpluses in those trust funds were perceived as being "saved" for future generations. Being "off-budget" has more of a political than a budgetary effect. The transactions of the off-budget entities are still part of the budget. There are other transactions, however, that have been considered to be outside of the budget. These transactions are referred to as non-budgetary because they do not involve federal taxes and spending. These have included entities that were removed from the budget because they operated largely with revolving funds rather than annual appropriations and made direct loans to the public. Government-sponsored enterprises (GSEs), such as the Federal National Mortgage Association (Fannie Mae) and the Federal Home Mortgage Corporation (Freddie Mac), were historically neither on-budget nor off-budget. With the bailout by the government of Fannie and Freddie in 2009, they are now wholly part of the government. The Board of Governors of the Federal Reserve System is also not included in the budget.

Coverage—The Special Case of Credit and Insurance Liabilities

In assembling a proposed budget, both obvious and not-so-obvious expenditures must be anticipated. Much of any budget will be committed to funding the operations of government, either for direct services provided by the government's departments or through grant programs, as in the case of state aid to local school districts. Monies also must be set aside for making payments on the principal and interest for any outstanding debt. Sustained federal budget deficits have yielded an increasingly large total federal debt that requires massive interest payments every year—so massive that they now constitute one of the most important components of federal expenditures.

In addition to debt accumulated through borrowing by the Treasury Department, federal debt has grown through borrowing by federal agencies such as the U.S. Postal Service and the Tennessee Valley Authority.

Beginning in the late 1980s, political leaders, public administrators, leaders in private financial institutions, and the citizenry became painfully aware that the federal government had other liabilities that until then had seemed innocuous or almost nonexistent. Hundreds of savings and loan institutions failed, forcing the federal government to meet its financial commitments to depositors. The Resolution Trust Corporation was established, as a temporary agency, to manage the resources of thrifts going into receivership at a staggering cost to taxpayers. Further liabilities were encountered when the government had surviving banks acquire many of the failed thrifts.[73] Similarly, the federal government during the Great Recession lent money to a wide variety of private financial institutions, issued credit guarantees to others, and took stock and other securities in exchange for loans to such private corporations as General Motors. Many of those credit programs ended by 2011 with the federal government having been repaid, or with corporations like General Motors repurchasing their stocks from the government. Loans still outstanding, however, represent contingent liabilities on future budgets. While these contingent liabilities are reported publicly, as in the Federal Reserve's reports on each of the numerous different credit programs it operates, they do not enter into the budget except in the event of default.

Types of Liabilities

Appreciating the nature of government liabilities is difficult due to the complex nature of the institutions involved. The most common method, for the federal government, of differentiating between types of liabilities is to look at them in terms of the type of instrument involved.

As outlined in **Table 8-1**, the instruments used and the consequent categories of liabilities are direct loans, guaranteed loans, insurance, and government-sponsored enterprises.

Table 8-1 Long-Term Federal Government Obligations and Risks, 2017

1. Direct Loans
   - Federal Student Loans
   - Farm Service Agency (excluding Commodity Credit Corporation), Rural Development, Rural Housing
   - Rural Utilities Service and Rural Telephone Bank
   - Housing and Urban Development
   - Export-Import Bank
   - Advanced Technology Vehicle Manufacturing, Title 17 Loans
   - Transportation Infrastructure Finance and Innovation Act Loans
   - International Assistance
   - Disaster Assistance
   - Education Temporary Student Loan Purchase Authority
2. Guaranteed Loans
   - Federal Housing Administration–Mutual Mortgage Insurance Fund
   - Department of Veterans Affairs Mortgages
   - Federal Student Loan Guarantees
   - Federal Housing Administration—General and Special Risk Insurance Fund
   - Small Business Administration
   - Export Import Bank
   - International Assistance
   - Farm Service Agency (excluding Commodity Credit Corporation), Rural Development, Rural Housing
   - Commodity Credit Corporation
3. Insurance
   - Deposit Insurance—Federal Deposit Insurance Corporation
   - Pension Guarantees—Pension Benefit Guaranty Corporation
   - Disaster Insurance—Flood, Crop
   - Insurance Against Security-Related Risks—Terrorism, Aviation War
4. Government-Sponsored Enterprises
   - Federal National Mortgage Association (Fannie Mae)
   - Federal Home Loan Mortgage Corporation (Freddie Mac)
   - Farm Credit System
   - Federal Home Loan Banks

Data from U.S. Office of Management and Budget (2019). *Analytical perspectives, budget of the United States government, fiscal year 2020* (pp. 276–293). Washington, DC: U.S. Government Publishing Office.

Before discussing these instruments, we should note that other major liabilities are omitted from the table, such as the costs of environmental cleanup of nuclear weapon production plants, defense installations that are being closed both in the United States and overseas, the future unfunded liabilities of Social Security and Medicare, cost associated with climate change, and other federal agency facilities.

Direct loans involve operations at home and abroad. Monies are available to help farmers acquire homes, electrify their farms, and engage in overseas commerce. Loans are provided directly to students to help them finance the cost of college.

International operations include loans to support the defense and economic development of other nations and to stimulate the growth of the private sectors in these countries. Immense political risks exist with such instruments because a change in a government may lead to the renunciation of previous commitments to repay loans. In other situations, developing countries may not possess the wealth to repay loans, so these become de facto grants. *Guaranteed loans* entail agreement by the government to pay loans when customers default. A major segment of the housing mortgage market in the United States is backed by federal government loan guarantees. The category has also included student loans, which have had a history of high rates of default.[74] In the international arena, the federal government has guaranteed billions of dollars of loans made by U.S. financial institutions to developing countries under the former Housing Guaranty Loan Program and loans by host country financial institutions in other programs such as the Development Credit Authority.

Federal insurance programs cover deposits in financial institutions and private pension deposits. While the huge bank failures of the 1980s were mopped up long ago, bank failures continue to occur.[75] Pension guarantees present other problems. Corporate failures leave pensioners and employees with credits into pension plans that lack adequate financial backing. The Pension Benefit Guarantee Corporation deals with these problems, with the support of the federal government. Other programs include crop insurance for farmers.

GSEs are another source of liability. These institutions have historically involved largely secondary credit markets, in which these institutions purchase debt instruments, such as mortgages, and in turn release funds to lending institutions for further loan activity.[76] GSEs have always had somewhat of a "neither fish nor fowl" quality. They have been owned privately, but their loans have been backed implicitly by the federal government.

This implicit guarantee became an *explicit* one in 2009 when Fannie Mae and Freddie Mac were taken over by the federal government. The total budgetary effect of this takeover by the federal government is somewhat uncertain and controversial. The CBO estimated in June 2011 that the total cost to the federal government from the loans guaranteed by Fannie and Freddie prior to 2009 would total $291 billion and that there were additional losses associated with later loans.[77] A 2018 estimate by an independent researcher put the cost of the bailout at $311 billion; in fact, according to that analysis, the cost of bailing out the GSEs represented more than 60% of the total bailout costs, for all industries, in the Great Recession.[78] Conversely, the OMB has estimated that the federal government may have made a slight profit by the time one offsets the repayments from the GSEs against the funds provided in the initial bailout. The Federal Reserve seemed to reach the same conclusion in a 2013 report.[79] The difference between the CBO and the OMB/Federal Reserve estimates has to do with the accounting assumptions used. The latter are simply counting the cash flows in and out of the budget, while the former estimates use a "fair value" approach that accounts for the time value of money as well as an estimate of market risk.

Federal Liability Reforms

Efforts are under way to bring some clarity to what liabilities the government has, and proposals exist for reforming this immense area of finance. The concerns about such liabilities are not new but rather date back to 1945, when Congress passed the Government Corporation Control Act.[80] At the time, there was concern that government corporations were operating without sufficient guidance and control by the government. The argument can be made that despite the numerous revisions Congress has made in the law over the years, the law remains inadequate in controlling these major institutions.

The Financial Institutions Reform, Recovery, and Enforcement Act of 1989 dealt with failed thrift institutions and required the General Accounting Office (now the Government Accountability Office [GAO]) to investigate the financing of government-sponsored enterprises.[81] The GAO has designated some programs, such as the Department of the Interior's management of oil and gas resources, as "high risk." The GAO's intent is to train attention on those programs that have the potential for creating large economic losses for the government. The list in 2020 included such big-ticket and sensitive items as the Government-wide Personnel Security Clearance Process, the Medicare Program and Improper Payments, the National Flood Insurance Program, and Postal Service Liability.[82]

The Federal Credit Reform Act of 1990 required the government to upgrade its accounting for credit programs.[83] OMB issued Circular A-129

(1993, rev. 2013), which provides a uniform set of procedures for agencies engaged in loan programs, both direct and guaranteed. The procedures indicate how agencies should estimate the costs of loans and loan guarantees, a function that is difficult to accomplish. The purpose of Circular A-129 is to reduce risks and place the federal government's credit operations on a better financial foundation.[84] Agencies that guarantee loans must estimate potential defaults and include those estimates in their current appropriations requests. This requires the annual costs of credit programs to represent the present value of the long-term costs to the federal government. This reform places potential defaults in direct competition with current spending requests, a practice expected to make decision makers more cautious in extending loans and loan guarantees.

It has proved difficult, however, to obtain reliable estimates of these long-term costs because of the uncertainty associated with forecasting the long-term liabilities associated with a given program.[85] On the other hand, the Treasury Department makes estimates of country risk for some agencies, such as the Development Credit Authority, and then the U.S. Agency for International Development has little problem in calculating the appropriation it needs to cover any potential default.

Efforts are now under way to improve the collection of debts rather than simply writing off bad debts. The Debt Collection Improvement Act of 1996 strengthened the government's ability to retrieve monies owed.[86] Agencies may refer bad debts to private collection companies and may share information with one another in locating those borrowers who are in arrears.

These significant changes, however, have not addressed the main issue—namely, what should be the federal government's responsibilities in this area, and how can liabilities and risks be curtailed? One line of criticism states that the federal government has been too generous. Fostering a credit market is important to national economic growth, but should the federal government have such a major role?

Credit programs subsidize risk-taking on the part of individuals and corporations. When the federal government provides full backing for a venture, then it assumes 100% of the risk. Crop insurance, for example, is available at comparatively low cost to farmers. Only about one in four farms uses the insurance, however, because when droughts, floods, and other conditions destroy crops, the government usually passes legislation that fully covers all damage. Similarly, were government to cover all of the damage from hurricanes and their related floods, then there would be little incentive to purchase insurance. As severe weather events become more frequent and costly as a result of climate change, it will become more and more difficult for the government to cover all associated costs from storms, thus compelling property owners to purchase insurance.

Prescriptions for reform, therefore, tend to favor increasing the risk of the private sector and decreasing that of the public sector. Such action was taken in 1996 with the passage of the Student Loan Marketing Association Reorganization Act, which provided for the privatization of Sallie Mae (student loans) and Connie Lee (college construction loans).[87] Connie Lee was converted to a private entity in 1997, and Sallie Mae was converted in 2004.[88] In 2005, Congress passed the Terrorism Risk Insurance Extension Act, which extended coverage available through the Treasury Department.[89] The Dodd-Frank Wall Street Reform and Consumer Protection Act of 2010 included provisions that require financial institutions supervised by the Federal Reserve to increase their reporting to the Fed on their exposure to other companies and to maintain a reserve of at least 25% of such exposure, and that such institutions reveal off-balance-sheet liabilities such as participation in purchases of securities, repurchase agreements, and a long list of other types of participation in the securities market. The last provision is intended to reduce the risk of the Fed having to bail out financial institutions that engage in complex securities instruments, such as those involved in the collapse of the mortgage market during the Great Recession.[90] The Trump administration pursued a deregulatory agenda, including attempting to reduce federal regulation of financial institutions.[91] The U.S. Senate voted in 2018 to exempt many banks from the provisions of Dodd-Frank, but the bill did not pass the House.

Although one line of concern insists that government credit and insurance institutions have become burdensome on government, perhaps suggesting that they should be totally privatized, the reality is that they serve important functions. Proposals exist for creating still more of these bodies. Government corporations have been proposed for air traffic services, management of petroleum reserves, and development of national infrastructure.

State and Local Governments

Similar liability and risk problems exist at the state and local levels. The Governmental Accounting Standards Board has prescribed how these governments should report risks and insurance. Potential losses can be due to "torts; theft of, damage to, or destruction of assets; business interruptions; errors or omissions; job-related illnesses or injuries to employees; acts of God; and any other risks of loss assumed under a policy or participation contract issued by a public entity risk pool."[92]

Torts are civil wrongs that occur independent of contract, as when a city refuse truck accidentally backs into a person's vehicle and causes personal harm and property damage. Among the greatest liabilities of state and local governments are their pension systems, which are sometimes actuarially unsound.

Information Displays
Revenues

Budget documents present both revenue and expenditure data. The coverage of receipts or revenues is usually substantially less extensive than the coverage of expenditures. Budgets show receipts from taxes, such as individual and corporate income taxes; from user charges, such as water service fees; and from other governments, such as state grants to local government. Budget documents also typically discuss proposed changes in tax laws, especially proposed tax rate changes. For the federal government, some revenues are treated as expenditures. OMB treats receipts generated by an agency in the form of user fees as an *offsetting collection* and deducts them from outlays rather than treating the amount as revenue. **Table 8-2** shows the various sources used to finance the state of Oregon's budget.

Table 8-2 All Funds Revenue by Major Source, State of Oregon ($ millions), 2015–2021

	2015–17 Actuals	2017–19 Approved	2019–21 Budget
Taxes	21,551.0	27,566.3	28,634.2
Federal Funds	21,538.5	22,314.5	23,614.3
Federal Funds as Other Funds	1,022.8	1,139.8	1,367.3
Donations and Contributions	3,421.9	4,820.7	4,619.4
Other	3,385.9	3,324.6	4,218.3
Bond Sales	3,013.9	2,218.2	2,795.0
Interest Earnings	9,759.9	14,911.7	10,742.1
Liquor and Other Sales Income	923.2	951.8	1,094.0
Loan Repayments	709.7	491.1	659.1

Table 8-2 All Funds Revenue by Major Source, State of Oregon ($ millions), 2015–2021 *(continued)*

	2015–17 Actuals	2017–19 Approved	2019–21 Budget
Lottery Distributions	1,235.4	1,387.2	1,432.0
Charges for Services	3,775.2	5,722.7	5,336.4
Licenses, Fines and Fees	1,522.7	1,647.9	1,863.4
Total	**71,860.0**	**86,496.5**	**86,375.5**

Governor's Budget, State of Oregon, 2019–2021, p. 340. Retrieved August 1, 2019, from https://www.oregon.gov/das/Financial/Documents/2019-21_gb.pdf

Expenditures

The bulk of the budget document is devoted to the expenditure side of government finance, with the main classification usually based on organizational unit. Each department presents a budget within which subunits are given separate treatment. A generally uniform format is used for each subunit, including a brief narrative description of the subunit's responsibilities and functions. Narratives contained in the federal *Appendix* also contain proposed appropriations language that may be quite specific—for the Department of Agriculture's Risk Management Agency's recommended budget of more than $63 million, a provision stated that not more than $1,000 was to be used for "official reception and representation expenses."[93]

In addition to the narrative are various tabular displays. Expenditures are reported by object classes, such as personnel, equipment, and travel. These financial tables may be primarily for informational purposes, or they may later be incorporated into the appropriation bill. When this practice is used, the legislative body is said to have adopted a *line-item budget*, which reduces the president's, governor's, or mayor's flexibility in executing the budget.

Personnel

The main component of an operating budget often consists of salaries, wages, and employee benefits. For that reason, budget documents sometimes include specific information about personnel.

Sometimes the budget may even go so far as to list the number of people employed for each position title in an agency. **Table 8-3** shows budget changes in less detail by presenting the costs of personnel and other expenses for fire rescue in the city of San Diego. Carefully studying the table will give the reader a sense of the effort in calculating such budget tables and how they might be used by decision makers, both executive and legislative.

Budget presentations sometimes show for the past fiscal year the budgeted amounts and actual amounts, for both receipts and expenditures. This information is important in understanding the accuracy with which the government is able to estimate its revenues and keep its expenditures within budgeted amounts. Budgets typically show the most recently completed fiscal year, the estimate of revenues and expenditures for the current fiscal year, and the proposed budget for the next fiscal year.

Current Services

Governments sometimes provide current services budget data, which are intended to show decision makers what receipts and expenditures will be without any changes being made in tax laws, other revenue sources, and spending levels. **Table 8-4** shows current services projections for the federal government from 2018 through 2023. In addition to receipts, the table reports outlays subdivided into discretionary spending and mandatory or entitlement spending. It also shows the differences between on-budget and off-budget receipts and

Table 8-3 Expenditure Detail, Fire and Rescue Department, City of San Diego, California, Fiscal Year 2019 ($ thousands)

	FY2017 Actual Budget	FY2018 Budget	FY2019 Adopted	FY2018–2019 Change
PERSONNEL				
Personnel Cost	$124,443	$128,376	$137,011	$8,635
Fringe Benefits	82,653	93,553	97,352	**3,799**
PERSONNEL SUBTOTAL	**$208,096**	**$221,929**	**$234,363**	**$12,434**
NONPERSONNEL				
Supplies	$4,869	$4,291	$4,118	($173)
Contracts	17,039	17,357	16,383	(974)
Information Technology	3,606	5,471	4,573	(898)
Energy and Utilities	5,491	5,938	6,518	580
Other and Transfers Out	189	696	176	(520)
Capital Expenditures	801	155	481	326
Debt	1,140	1,775	3,122	1,347
NONPERSONNEL	**$33,134**	**$35,682**	**$35,370**	**($312)**
Total	**$241,230**	**$257,611**	**$269,733**	**($12,122)**

Modified from City of San Diego (2019). *Fire and rescue budget: fiscal year 2019* (p. 278).

Table 8-4 Current Services Estimates, Budget of the United States Government, Fiscal Year 2020 ($ billions)

	Actual	Estimated				
	2018	2019	2020	2021	2022	2023
Receipts	$3,330	$3,438	$3,643	$3,874	$4,126	$4,415
Outlays:						
Discretionary:						
Defense	623	674	671	674	674	686
Non-Defense	639	685	669	654	658	662
Subtotal, Discretionary	1,262	1,359	1,340	1,328	1,332	1,348
Mandatory:						
Social Security	982	1,041	1,102	1,166	1,235	1,309
Medicare	582	645	702	762	861	892
Medicaid and CHIP	406	437	443	461	486	516

Table 8-4 Current Services Estimates, Budget of the United States Government, Fiscal Year 2020 ($ billions) *(continued)*

	Actual	Estimated				
	2018	2019	2020	2021	2022	2023
Other Mandatory	552	660	640	658	702	703
Subtotal, Mandatory	2,522	2,783	2,887	3,047	3,284	3,419
Net Interest	325	394	482	548	611	666
Total, Outlays	4,109	4,536	4,709	4,923	5,228	5,434
Unified Deficit(+)/Surplus(−)	779	1,098	1,067	1,049	1,102	1,019
On-Budget	(785)	(1,100)	(1,047)	(1,021)	(1,062)	(965)
Off-Budget	(−6)	(−2)	(20)	(28)	(40)	(54)

Reprinted from U.S. Office of Management and Budget (2019). *Analytical perspectives, budget of the United States Government, fiscal year 2020* (p. 315). Washington, DC: U.S. Government Publishing Office.

outlays for each year. The off-budget surplus is due to the Social Security system bringing in more revenue than it pays out. This phenomenon will be reversed when the baby boomer generation starts to draw Social Security, unless rates are substantially increased or benefits are cut.

Program Information

Increasingly over the past several decades, budget documents have included information on the workload and performance of programs. These program data may represent information that was used in the process of making budget decisions, or they may simply reflect information on the past performance of programs or agencies. More than 40 state governments reported in 2008 that their documents contained performance measures for their respective agencies.[94] A January 2017 survey by The Pew Charitable Trusts reported that 42 states included outcome data related to several defined human service policy areas in their budget documents.[95]

Future Years

Budget reformers have tended to advocate multiyear projections as a method for helping decision makers understand the long-term implications of policy and program issues. However, given the uncertainty of the future, one might expect few governments to attempt to make projections beyond the budget year or biennium. However, the use of multiyear projections has increased over time. This, in part, results from the fear that elected officials will make policies for the budget year where future costs explode, whether intentionally or through ignorance. Internationally, multiyear budgeting, often manifested through the use of medium-term expenditure frameworks, has become a best practice, and one that is advocated by organizations such as the World Bank and International Monetary Fund.[96] The obvious downside of multiyear projections is that the further into the future that forecasts are attempted, the more likely they are to be prone to errors, which can result in making policies based on faulty information.

Summary

In beginning the preparation phase, the chief executive conveys to agencies some sense of priorities, either formally in writing or by more subtle means. The executive's view of the role of government in society is indicated to agencies, along with more specific priorities.

The revenue side of the budget is examined carefully, especially because state and local governments are generally prohibited from having operating budgets that exceed available revenues. One of the key components of budget preparation on the revenue side is revenue forecasting, which is a technical exercise that may have intense political ramifications. Budget preparation begins in agencies and involves extensive debate. Similar debate develops between agencies and the central budget office, which in turn must compete with other central staff units. Because little formal authority is granted to a central budget office, it must always be concerned with being overruled by the chief executive.

The 1980s ushered in a new era in budgeting, where the focus was on budget cutbacks rather than program expansion. Fiscal stress, taxing and spending limitations, and an increase in anti–big government attitudes among political leaders have resulted in retrenchment efforts. A respite in cutbacks occurred in the second half of the 1990s, when the booming economy produced budget surpluses. With two recessions in the first decade of the 2000s, cutback management became necessary once again. Decision makers have come to realize that they can be forced to deal with immense problems associated with credit and insurance liabilities. The collapse of hundreds of federally backed thrift institutions amply demonstrated the risks that are involved. At the federal level, decision makers can be forced to decide whether to commit government resources to deal with the woes of private corporations, as occurred in 2007–2008 with the banking and auto industry crises and in 2020 with the COVID-19 crisis.

The product of the preparation phase is a budget or a set of budget documents that reflect executive decisions on policies and programs. The federal government has what is called a unified budget. Revenue and expenditure data are treated in all budgets, but the latter receive much more extensive treatment. One common budget format has a structure based on organizational units and includes supporting narratives and tabular displays that present revenue, costs, personnel, and program data.

Notes

1. Office of Management and Budget, *Budget of the United States Government: Fiscal Year 2019*. Washington: U.S. Government Publishing Office, 2018.
2. Hampton, G. (1999). Environmental equity and public participation. *Policy Sciences, 32*, 163–174; Rubin, M. M., & Bartle, J. R. (2005). Integrating gender into government budgets: a new perspective. *Public Administration Review, 65*, 259–272; Midgley, J. (2005). *Women and the U.S. budget: where the money goes and what you can do about it*. Gabriola Island, BC, Canada: New Society. See also Clinton, W. (2011). *Back to work: why we need smart government for a strong economy*. New York, NY: Knopf.
3. Diving into the rich pool. (2011). *The Economist, 401*, September 24, 83; Hunting the rich. (2011). *The Economist, 401*, September 24, 13.
4. Mathesian, C. (1994). Immigration: the symbolic crackdown. *Governing, 7*, May, 52–57.
5. Congressional Budget Office (2007). *The impact of unauthorized immigrants on the budgets of state and local governments*, December 6. Retrieved March 1, 2012, from http://www.cbo.gov/publication/41645.
6. Ferris, S. (2019). Trump justifies shutdown, wall by bashing immigrants, role in economy. What's true? *The Center for Public Integrity*, January 8. Retrieved January 2, 2020, from https://publicintegrity.org/immigration/ask -immigration-decoded/trump-shutdown-wall-immigrants -economy.
7. Williamson, J., et al. (2003). Generational equity, generational interdependence, and the framing of the debate over Social Security reform. *Journal of Sociology and Social Welfare, 30*, 3–14; Gokhale, J., & Smetters, K. (2003). *Fiscal and generational imbalances: new budget measures for new budget priorities*. Washington, DC: AEI Press.
8. Friedman, L. (2018). "I don't know that it's man made," Trump says of climate change. It is. *New York Times*, October 14. Retrieved January 3, 2019, from https://www .nytimes.com/2018/10/15/climate/trump-climate-change -fact-check.html.
9. Weimer, D. L., & Vining, A. R. (2004). *Policy analysis: concepts and practice* (4th ed.). Upper Saddle River, NJ: Pearson Prentice Hall; Royse, D., et al. (2006). *Program evaluation: an introduction*. Belmont, CA: Thomson Brooks/ Cole.
10. Balanoff, H. R., & Pinto, C. W. (1999). What do you do when your city is looking at a million-dollar deficit in the current fiscal year? *Public Productivity & Management Review, 23*, 83–88.
11. Lazo, A., & Malas, N. (2018). Jerry Brown's legacy: A $6.1 billion budget surplus in California. *Fox Business*, January 10. Retrieved August 3, 2019, from https://www .foxbusiness.com/features/jerry-browns-legacy-a-6-1 -billion-budget-surplus-in-california.
12. Vock, D. C. (2018). Who ruined Illinois? *Governing*, May. Retrieved August 3, 2019, from https://www.governing.com /topics/politics/gov-illinois-rauner-budget-rating.html.

13. Laitner, B. (2018). Detroit has third year of balanced budgets; state oversight could end soon. *Detroit Free Press,* February 1. Retrieved August 3, 2019, from https://www.freep.com/story/news/local/michigan/detroit/2018/02/01/detroit-balanced-budget-state-oversight/1088486001/.

14. Cwiek, S. (2019). Duggan: Detroit budget balanced, but "tight." *WUOMFM Weekend Edition,* March 7. Retrieved August 3, 2019, from https://www.michiganradio.org/post/duggan-detroit-budget-balanced-tight.

15. Congressional Research Service (2020). *Unfunded Mandates Reform Act: history, impact, and issues,* January 2. Retrieved March 30, 2020, from https://fas.org/sgp/crs/misc/R40957.pdf.

16. H.R. 2157 (2019). Supplemental Appropriations Act, 2019. Retrieved January 10, 2020, from https://www.congress.gov/bill/116th-congress/house-bill/2157.

17. Cornia, G. C., et al. (2004). Fiscal planning, budgeting, and rebudgeting using revenue semaphores. *Public Administration Review, 64,* 164–179.

18. Williams, D. W., & Calabrese, T. (2016). The status of budget forecasting. *Journal of Public and Nonprofit Affairs,* 2(2), 127–160.

19. Williams, D. W., & Kavanagh, S. (2016). Local government revenue forecasting methods: competition and comparison. *Journal of Public Budgeting, Accounting & Financial Management,* 28(4), 488–526.

20. Cirincione, C., et al. (1999). Municipal government revenue forecasting: issues of method and data. *Public Budgeting & Finance, 19,* Spring, 26–46.

21. Williams & Calabrese (2016) present a more detailed summary of techniques for revenue forecasting.

22. Mullins, D. R., & Wallace, S. (1996). Changing demographics and state fiscal outlook: the case of sales taxes. *Public Finance Quarterly, 24,* 237–262.

23. Rodgers, R., & Joyce, P. (1996). The effect of underforecasting on the accuracy of revenue forecasts by state governments. *Public Administration Review, 56,* 48–56.

24. Pew Charitable Trusts and Nelson Rockefeller Institute of Government (2011). *States' revenue estimating: cracks in the crystal ball,* March. Retrieved March 30, 2020, from https://www.pewtrusts.org/~/media/assets/2011/03/01/003_11_ri-states-revenue-estimates-report_v1040711.pdf.

25. Mullins, D. R., & Wallin, B. A. (2004). Tax and expenditure limitations: introduction and overview. *Public Budgeting & Finance, 24,* Winter, 2–15; Mullins, D. R. (2004). Tax and expenditure limitations and the fiscal response of local government: asymmetric intra-local fiscal effects. *Public Budgeting & Finance, 24,* Winter, 111–147.

26. James, F. J., & Wallis, A. (2004). Tax and spending limits in Colorado. *Public Budgeting & Finance, 24,* Winter, 16–33.

27. Hou, Y., & Smith, D. L. (2006). A framework for understanding state balanced budget requirement systems: reexamining distinctive features and an operational definition. *Public Budgeting & Finance, 26,* Fall, 22–45.

28. Joyce, P. G. (2001). What's so magical about five percent? A nationwide look at factors that influence the optimal size of state rainy day funds. *Public Budgeting & Finance, 21,* Summer, 62–87.

29. Jen, K. I. (2002). Tax expenditures in Michigan: a comparison to federal findings. *Public Budgeting & Finance, 22,* Spring, 31–45; Brixi, H. P., et al. (2004). *Tax expenditure: shedding light on government spending through the tax system.* Washington, DC: World Bank.

30. Novarro, N. (2002). Does earmarking matter? The case of lottery profits and educational spending. *Stanford Institute for Economic Policy Research Discussion Paper 2-19,* December 9. Retrieved March 30, 2020, from https://siepr.stanford.edu/sites/default/files/publications/02-19_0.pdf.

31. Anderson, S. H., & Smirnova, N. V. (2006). A study of executive budget-balancing decisions. *American Review of Public Administration, 36,* 323–336.

32. Schneider, M., & Damanpour, F. (2001). Determinants of public pension plan investment return. *Public Management Review, 3,* 551–573; Peng, J. (2004). Public pension funds and operating budgets: a tale of three states. *Public Budgeting & Finance, 24,* Summer, 59–73.

33. Moran, D. (2018). Pension fund outlook brightens in 41 states. *Bloomberg,* October 12. Retrieved January 10, 2020, from https://www.bloomberg.com/graphics/2018-state-pension-funding-ratios/; Pew Charitable Trusts (2019). *The state pension funding gap: 2017,* June. Retrieved January 10, 2020, from https://www.pewtrusts.org/-/media/assets/2019/06/statepensionfundinggap.pdf.

34. Ingraham, P. W., et al. (2003). *Government performance: why management matters* (p. 34). Baltimore, MD: Johns Hopkins University Press.

35. GOP's anti-bailout South Carolina Governor Mark Sanford ordered to take federal stimulus funds. (2009). *New York Daily News,* June 5. Retrieved September 24, 2011, from https://www.nydailynews.com/news/world/gop-anti-bailout-south-carolina-governor-mark-sanford-ordered-federal-stimulus-funds-article-1.376618; Condon, S. (2009). Texas gov. who refused stimulus funds asks for loan. *CBS.com,* July 16. Retrieved September 24, 2011, from http://www.cbsnews.com/8301-503544_162-5166310-503544.html.

36. For the status of state action on Medicaid expansion, see Kaiser Family Foundation State Health Facts (2020). *Status of state action on the Medicaid expansion decision,* January 2. Retrieved January 10, 2020, from https://www.kff.org/health-reform/state-indicator/state-activity-around-expanding-medicaid-under-the-affordable-care-act.

37. Archbold, R. (2010). California, in financial crisis, opens prison doors. *New York Times,* March 23. Retrieved September 24, 2011, from http://www.cbsnews.com/8301-503544_162-5166310-503544.html.

38. Schulte, G. (2019). Nebraska prisons head says overcrowding emergency is likely. *AP News,* January 18. Retrieved August 3, 2019, from https://www.apnews.com/bed6772a5abc4261a0c297c5be8afa8b.

39. Rivlin, A., & Sawhill, I. (Eds.) (2005). *Restoring fiscal sanity, 2005: meeting the long-run challenge.* Washington, DC: Brookings Institution.

40. Jones, L. R., & Euske, K. J. (1991). Strategic misrepresentation in budgeting. *Journal of Public Administration Research and Theory, 1*, 437–460; Peterson, P. G. (2004). Running on empty: how the Democratic and Republican Parties are bankrupting our future and what Americans can do about it. New York, NY: Farrar, Straus and Giroux.

41. Lewis, C. W. (1992). Public budgeting: unethical in purpose, product, and promise. *Public Budgeting and Financial Management, 4*, 667–680.

42. Miller, G. J., et al. (2005). How financial managers deal with ethical stress. *Public Administration Review, 65*, 301–312.

43. Schick, A. (1983). Incremental budgeting in a decremental age. *Policy Sciences, 16*, 1–25.

44. O'Brien, M. (2010). White House wants federal agencies to cut spending by 5 percent. *The Hill's Blog Briefing Room*, June 6. Retrieved April 29, 2011, from http://thehill.com /blogs/blog-briefing-room/news/101897-white-house -wants-agencies-to-cut-spending-by-five-percent; Hughes, S., & Rubin, R. (2018). Trump seeks 5% budget cuts from cabinet agencies. *Wall Street Journal*, October 17. Retrieved March 30, 2020, from https://www.wsj.com /articles/trump-seeks-5-budget-cuts-from-cabinet -agencies-1539800152.

45. Berman, R. (2018). A domestic budget to make Barack Obama proud. *The Atlantic*, March 25. Retrieved October 5, 2019, from https://www.theatlantic.com/politics/archive /2018/03/trump-obama-omnibus-spending-budget /556436/.

46. Fikac, P. (2010). State agencies asked to find more cuts. *San Antonio Express News*, November 16. Retrieved April 29, 2011, from http://www.mysanantonio.com/default/article /State-agencies-askedto-find-more-cuts-817261.php.

47. Governing (2005). Grading the states 2005: a management report card. *Governing*, Volume 18, Number 5 (February), p. 92.

48. Goodman, D., & Clynch, E. J. (2004). Budgetary decision making by executive and legislative budget analysts: the impact of political cues and analytical information. *Public Budgeting & Finance, 24*, Fall, 20–37; Lidman, R., & Sommers, P. (2005). The "compleat" policy analysts: a top 10 list. *Public Administration Review, 65*, 628–634.

49. Hoffman, K. U. (2006). Legislative fiscal analysts: influence in state budget development. *State and Local Government Review, 38*, 41–51.

50. For a comprehensive discussion of the role of budget analysts in state budgeting, see Thurmaier, K., & Willoughby, K. (2015). *Policy and politics in state budgeting*. New York: Routledge.

51. U.S. General Accounting Office (1995). *Changes resulting from the OMB 2000 reorganization*. Washington, DC: U.S. Government Printing Office.

52. Stockman, D. A. (1986). *The triumph of politics: how the Reagan revolution failed*. New York, NY: Harper & Row; Wildavsky, A., & Caiden, N. (2004). *The new politics of the budgetary process* (5th ed.). New York, NY: Pearson/ Longman.

53. Heclo, H. (1975). OMB and the presidency: the problem of "neutral competence." *Public Interest, 38*, 80–98; Posner, P. (2008). Can't ideology and policy expertise just get along? *Governing*, March 26. Retrieved January 6, 2020, from https://www.governing.com/columns/mgmt -insights/Cant-Ideology-and-Policy.html.

54. Hiltzik, M. (2015). Column: Still the third rail? Social Security, Medicare mostly unharmed in budget deal. *Los Angeles Times*, October 27. Retrieved August 13, 2019, from https://www.latimes.com/business/hiltzik/la-fi-mh -social-security-medicare-20151027-column.html.

55. See Sorensen, E. M., Hansen, H. F., & Kristiansen, M. B. (2018). *Public management in times of austerity*. New York: Taylor and Francis.

56. Schick, A. (1986). Macro-budgetary adaptations to fiscal stress in industrialized democracies. *Public Administration Review, 46*, 124–134.

57. National Association of State Budget Officers (2011). *Fiscal survey of the states*, April, 16–17.

58. National Association of State Budget Officers (2019). *Fiscal survey of the states*, Spring, 16–17.

59. Oosting, J. (2019). How Michigan's revenue sharing 'raid' cost communities billions for local services. *mslive.com*, January 20. Retrieved January 6, 2020, from https://www .mlive.com/lansing-news/2014/03/michigan_revenue _sharing_strug.html.

60. Office of the Secretary of Defense (2015). *Department of Defense cybersecurity culture and compliance initiative*, September 30. Retrieved January 6, 2020, from https:// dod.defense.gov/Portals/1/Documents/pubs/OSD011517 -15-RES-Final.pdf.

61. Government Finance Officers Association (2019). *Distinguished budget presentation award*. Retrieved August 3, 2019, from https://www.gfoa.org/award-programs /distinguished-budget-presentation-award-program -budget-awards-program.

62. City of Nashville (2020). *Citizens' guide to the metro budget*. Retrieved January 7, 2020, from https://www.nashville .gov/Finance/Management-and-Budget/Citizens-Guide-to -the-Budget.aspx.

63. U.S. Office of Management and Budget (2019). *Budget of the United States government, fiscal year 2020*. Retrieved August 2, 2019, from https://www.whitehouse.gov/omb /budget/.

64. U.S. Office of Management and Budget (2019). *Appendix, budget of the United States government, fiscal year 2020*. Retrieved August 3, 2019, from https://www.whitehouse .gov/omb/appendix/.

65. U.S. Office of Management and Budget (2019). *Analytical perspectives, budget of the United States government, fiscal year 2020*. Retrieved August 3, 2019, from https://www .whitehouse.gov/omb/analytical-perspectives.

66. U.S. Office of Management and Budget (2019). *Historical tables, budget of the United States government, fiscal year 2020*. Retrieved August 3, 2019, from https://www .whitehouse.gov/omb/historical-tables/.

67. Council of Economic Advisers (2019). *Economic report of the President: fiscal year 2020*. March. Retrieved January 7,

2020, from https://www.whitehouse.gov/wp-content/uploads/2019/03/ERP-2019.pdf.

68. U.S. Treasury Department (2019). *Financial report of the United States government*. Retrieved August 3, 2019, from https://www.fiscal.treasury.gov/reports-statements/financial-report/index.html.

69. U.S. Treasury Department (2019). *Bulletin*. Retrieved August 3, 2019, from https://fiscal.treasury.gov/reports-statements/treasury-bulletin/.

70. Executive Office of Administration and Finance (2019). *Commonwealth of Massachusetts, Tax Expenditure Budget: Fiscal Year 2020*, January. Retrieved August 3, 2019, from https://www.mass.gov/files/documents/2019/03/07/dor-fy-2020-tax-expenditure-budget.pdf.

71. State of New Mexico (2019). *Report of the Legislative Finance Committee to the Fifty-Fourth Legislature. Post-Session Review*, May. Retrieved August 1, 2019, from https://www.nmlegis.gov/Entity/LFC/Documents/Session_Publications/Post_Session_Fiscal_Reviews/May%202019.pdf.

72. President's Commission on Budget Concepts (1967). *Report* (p. 1085). Washington, DC: U.S. Government Printing Office.

73. Feldman, R. (1996). How weak recognition and measurement in the federal budget encouraged costly policy: the case of "supervisory goodwill." *Public Budgeting & Finance, 16*, Winter, 31–44.

74. U.S. General Accounting Office (2001). Student loans: direct loan default rates. Washington, DC: U.S. Government Printing Office.

75. Ennis, H. M., & Malek, H. S. (2005). Bank risk of failure and the too-big-to-fail policy. *Economic Quarterly, 91*(2), 21–44.

76. U.S. General Accounting Office (2004). *Government-sponsored enterprises: a framework for strengthening GSE governance and oversight*. Washington, DC: U.S. Government Printing Office.

77. Congressional Budget Office (2011). *The budgetary cost of Fannie Mae and Freddie Mac and options for the future federal role in the secondary mortgage market. Statement of Deborah Lucas before the House Committee on the Budget*, June 2. Retrieved March 30, 2020, from http://www.cbo.gov/sites/default/files/112th-congress-2011-2012/reports/06-02-gses_testimony.pdf.

78. Lucas, D. Measuring the cost of bailouts. Prepared for the Annual Review of Financial Economics, November 2018. Retrieved March 30, 2020, from https://www.cfainstitute.org/en/research/multimedia/2018/2008-financial-crisis-measuring-cost-bailouts.

79. Weinberg, J. (2013). *The Great Recession and its aftermath*. Retrieved September 14, 2019, from https://www.federalreservehistory.org/essays/great_recession_and_its_aftermath.

80. Government Corporation Control Act of 1945, Ch. 557.

81. Financial Institutions Reform, Recovery, and Enforcement Act of 1989 (P.L. 101-73).

82. U.S. Government Accountability Office (2019). *GAO's 2019 high-risk list*. Retrieved August 13, 2019, from https://www.gao.gov/highrisk/overview.

83. Federal Credit Reform Act (1990). P.L. 101-508, as part of the Omnibus Budget Reconciliation Act.

84. Office of Management and Budget. (2013). *Circular A-129, Policies for Federal Credit Programs and Non-tax receivables*. Retrieved June 1, 2020, https://www.whitehouse.gov/sites/whitehouse.gov/files/omb/circulars/A129/a-129.pdf.

85. Phaup, M. (1996). Credit reform, negative subsidies, and FHA. *Public Budgeting & Finance, 16*, Spring, 23–36.

86. Debt Collection Improvement Act of 1996 (P.L. 104-34); see also Federal Debt Collection Procedures Act of 1990 (P.L. 101-647).

87. Student Loan Marketing Association Reorganization Act of 1996 (P.L. 104-208, 2009-275), as part of the Omnibus Consolidation Appropriations Act of 1997.

88. U.S. Department of Treasury (2004). Treasury announces successful privatization of Sallie Mae. Retrieved August 8, 2006, from http://www.treasury.gov/press/releases/js2173.htm (link no longer active); Corder, J. K., & Hoffman, S. M. (2004). Privatizing federal credit programs: why Sallie Mae? *Public Administration Review, 64*, 180–191.

89. Terrorism Risk Insurance Extension Act of 2005 (P.L. 109-144).

90. Wall Street Reform and Consumer Protection Act of 2010 (P.L. 111-203).

91. Lebovitch, M., & Spaid, J. (2019). In corporations we trust: ongoing deregulation and government protections. *Harvard Law School Forum on Corporate Governance*, February 6. Retrieved January 10, 2020, from https://corpgov.law.harvard.edu/2019/02/06/in-corporations-we-trust-ongoing-deregulation-and-government-protections/.

92. Governmental Accounting Standards Board (1989). *Accounting and financial reporting for risk financing and related insurance issues*, Statement No. 10. Norwalk, CT: Financial Accounting Foundation.

93. U.S. Office of Management and Budget (2019). *Budget of the United States Department of Agriculture: fiscal year 2020*. Appendix, 283. Washington, DC: U.S. Government Publishing Office.

94. National Association of State Budget Officers (2008). *Budget processes in the states*, Summer, 57. Washington, DC: National Association of State Budget Officers.

95. Pew Charitable Trusts. (2017). *How states engage in evidence-based policymaking: A national assessment,* January. Washington, DC: The Pew Charitable Trusts.

96. Brumby, J., & Hemming, R. (2013). Medium-term expenditure frameworks. In Allen, R., Hemming, R., & Potter, B. H., eds, *The international handbook of public financial management*. London, UK: Palgrave-MacMillan, 219–236.

CHAPTER 9

Budget Approval: The Role of the Legislature

The tradition of legislative "power of the purse" is perhaps as strong in the United States as in any other country. This means that the struggle over the budget has only begun when the budget document goes to the legislative body. Executive budget preparation at the state and federal levels will have consumed months, but the product of the process is simply a proposal. The distinction between preparation and approval is alluded to by the phrase "the executive proposes and the legislature disposes." The process of legislative disposition is often not pretty. Like the federal government, some states have had difficulty enacting their budgets on time. The state of California, for example, was 100 days late in enacting its budget for fiscal year 2010; this was the 23rd time in 24 years that the state missed the deadline.[1] Later that same year, however, California voters approved Proposition 25, which removed the requirement that the state House and Senate approve the budget by a two-thirds majority. Since then, budgets have routinely become law before the beginning of the fiscal year.[2]

Illinois replaced California as the poster child for state budget dysfunction by going more than two years (from July 1, 2015, to August 31, 2017) without a state budget. A dispute between then-Governor Bruce Rauner and House Speaker Michael Madigan led to a budget impasse that resulted in the courts intervening to avoid basic state services halting, state employees and contractors either receiving late paychecks or going without entirely, and credit rating agencies threatening to lower the states' credit rating to "junk bond" status. In the end, the state only was able to enact a budget (for fiscal year 2018) because the legislature overrode the governor's veto, by the slimmest of margins.[3]

The process in the United States differs from that used in parliamentary governments such as the British one, in which the executive and legislative functions are controlled by the same political party or coalition of parties. In such systems, the approval phase is largely pro forma. Parliaments generally can alter the government's budget but are often prohibited from increasing it, and party discipline helps to ensure that the changes made by a parliament are typically minor. In the United States, in contrast, the legislative body may approve a budget that diverges in important respects from the budget proposed by the executive. Two studies of Organization for Economic Cooperation and Development countries by the International Monetary Fund characterized countries in terms of the roles of the legislature in the budgetary process and the legislature's power vis-à-vis the executive.

The United States ranked as the one with the most legislative budgetary power, far ahead of the Westminster countries (notably Great Britain and Australia), but also more powerful than others, such as Germany, Mexico, and Spain.[4] While these studies focused on national governments, the tradition of legislative independence in the United States tends to apply to states and localities as well. In this chapter, major emphasis is given to the similarities in the approval phase across levels of government—local, state, and federal. The next chapter focuses exclusively on Congress, because that body is unique in the American political system and has unique budgetary roles, procedures, and problems.

This chapter has three main sections. The first discusses the parameters that constrain how legislative bodies operate and the processes used in approving government budgets. The second section examines the legislative budget process itself, including relationships between the legislative and executive branches, and the procedures used by the legislature. The third discusses the changing role of the legislature as an overseer of the executive branch.

Constraints on Legislatures

General Characteristics of Legislatures

Legislative bodies—city councils, school boards, state legislatures, and Congress—sometimes have had a reputation for being relatively weak bodies (in terms of the powers granted to them or asserted by them), but that perception has changed in recent times. Legislative bodies at all levels of government are reasserting their authority to set policy and are taking measures to increase their ability to wield the powers granted to them. This has gone as far in recent years as legislatures attempting to take away powers from an incoming governor of a different political party, as happened in Wisconsin in 2018.[5] There are certain underlying trends and characteristics that affect

the environment for legislative deliberation on the budget. These include the following:

- the role of the legislature as, first and foremost, a representative body;
- trends in how legislators are selected for their jobs;
- the movement toward limiting legislative terms; and
- the deep partisan divides that have developed throughout the country.

Representation of Interests

Both socioeconomic and political diversity influence legislative behavior. At the national level, Congress must deal with a broad range of issues and associated interest groups. States tend to be less diverse and have fewer interest groups that press their preferences upon legislatures. This situation can allow for a relatively small number of interests to influence legislation.[6] The concentration of influence can be even greater at the local level, as in the case of a town that is dominated by a single employer.

Citizen initiatives, allowable in many states, constitute another set of parameters that can have major impacts on the legislative bodies responsible for approving budgets.[7] Under the initiative process, citizens have the power to initiate changes, often by making amendments to state constitutions. If citizens become dissatisfied with tax rates, as was frequently the case in the 1970s, voters may approve new limits on taxes that force jurisdictions to cut tax rates and spending.

Voters in some states have recall powers. When legislators take action disapproved of by their constituents, they can be voted out of office before their terms expire. Michigan allows this for both local and state elective officers, including the governor as well as the legislature.[8] Legislative recalls do not happen frequently and are not even attempted very often. The website *ballotpedia* lists only 13 attempts of state legislative recalls in calendar year 2019. None was successful, although one legislator did resign her seat.[9]

The news media are also important influences on legislatures. The media bring issues to the public's attention, help frame those issues and their solutions, and focus attention on legislatures in their efforts to resolve issues. However, newspapers, local radio and television stations, and news networks vary in their abilities to understand complex budget matters and to convey information to the public.[10] As a consequence, the media can be important sources of misinformation as well as information regarding public budgeting and finance.

Though young adults, by a clear margin, use the Internet as a basic source of information more than any other age group, the Internet is a rapidly increasing source of both information and misinformation for everyone. Individuals can create their own blogs, and there is considerable volunteerism creating opinions and information on the web. Sources like *Wikipedia* publish unvetted information on a large array of topics, and it is often difficult on these websites to distinguish fact from opinion or error. The fact that foreign powers were able to use misinformation in an attempt to influence the 2016 Presidential election is just one example of where the Internet became a platform for influencing public opinion. In addition, the use of Twitter as a primary information vehicle by President Trump demonstrates the power of the medium. Many people take his statements at face value, in spite of the fact that many have been demonstrated to be false. In fact, the *Washington Post* asserted in June 2019 that the President had made more than 10,000 false or misleading statements in his first 869 days in office, or approximately 12 per day.[11] The misinformation alleging that President Obama was not born in the United States is another recent example of this phenomenon, where something that is not true—and that had been repeatedly disproved—was repeated often enough to cause some people to accept it as fact, including Donald Trump before becoming president.

A responsibility—if not the chief responsibility—of legislators is to represent their constituents. Decisions on the budget can have major positive and negative effects on a legislator's constituents and on the legislator's prospects for reelection. Although a legislator may generally favor reduced government spending, one common exception arises with any budget reduction proposed for the legislator's district. Positive budget decisions—increases in government spending or fending off possible decreases in spending—are seen by every officeholder as essential for gaining reelection, which itself is seen as of paramount importance. Some research suggests that not all public preferences are for decreased spending and that decisions about capital spending are more important to voters in local elections than current operating expenditures.[12]

Legislative Apportionment

How the duty of representation is met is influenced by how legislators are elected to their jobs. In the 1960s, the U.S. Supreme Court ruled that state legislatures must draw district lines that are proportional to population. The effect of this ruling has been to apportion legislative election districts on a population basis and to reduce substantially what was once overrepresentation of rural interests and to increase representation of urban and suburban areas in states.[13]

Local governments are undergoing similar changes. City councils are changing from using at-large seats because this procedure tends to result in underrepresentation of minority interests. Instead, the movement is toward single-member districts based on neighborhood populations, or a combination of these and at-large seats.[14] Legislative bodies are increasingly diverse in terms of gender and minority representation, although the distinct influence that women and minority legislators have on the legislative process is uncertain. A 2015 study by the National Conference of State Legislatures found that the representation of women and African Americans in state legislatures had increased between 1971 and 2009. Women made up 25% of state legislators in 2009 (up from 4% in 1971), and African Americans made up 9% of state legislators in 2009 (up from 2% in 1971). The same study argued that the progress of both groups had stalled after 2009.[15] Other historically underrepresented groups, such as Arab Americans, Hispanics, and LGBTQ individuals, have also seen their ranks increase. Like women and African Americans, however, they still make up a much smaller portion of state legislatures than they represent in the larger society.

In an earlier time, when efforts were deliberately made to underrepresent the interests of minorities, boundaries were drawn such that minority neighborhoods were carved into small segments and then apportioned to several districts. This approach ensured that a minority candidate would never be elected to represent any of the districts. In contemporary times, efforts have been made to help ensure minority representation by drawing boundaries to encircle minority neighborhoods. The Supreme Court has held through a series of rulings that when race becomes the dominant factor in deciding on district boundaries, that action is a violation of the Equal Protection Clause of the 14th Amendment.[16] The result has been considerable confusion when state legislatures have redrawn district boundaries for their own election districts or for congressional districts.

Beyond any racial justification for redistricting, however, there is the pure political motivation for drawing or redrawing district lines. In an infamous case in advance of the 2004 election, then–House Majority Leader Tom Delay aggressively pursued the redrawing of Texas congressional boundaries in a way that would make it easier for the Republican Party to keep its majority in Congress. Democratic legislators attempted to thwart this effort by fleeing the state in an effort to prevent a vote occurring on this plan. Ultimately the U.S. Supreme Court upheld the redrawn Texas districts as constitutional, but questionable ethical behavior by Delay in his pursuit of the new congressional boundaries led to his resignation from the Congress and ultimately his conviction of laundering corporate money in an effort to influence state-level elections.[17] A landmark 5-4 decision by the Supreme Court in 2019, however, dealt a severe blow to opponents of gerrymandering by ruling that the federal courts have no authority to rule on cases where gerrymandering is practiced for purely partisan purposes.[18] The effect of that ruling was to throw challenges to electoral district boundaries

based on political partisan criteria back to state courts for resolution. North Carolina in 2019 went back to state Supreme Court rulings to overturn congressional districts drawn to favor one party over another.[19]

Term Limits

A related concern regarding legislators is that they not become so entrenched in their positions that they lose a sense of responsibility to the citizens who elected them. One response to this concern has been moves to limit the number of years a person may serve.[20] The limits typically involve consecutive years of service, such as no more than two terms of 4 years in a state senate and no more than six terms of 2 years in a state house. Limits also can be on a lifetime basis, such as limiting the total number of years a person may serve in the house or senate for one's entire life. As of 2018, 15 states had term limits for membership in their state legislative bodies.[21] Term limits have been proposed at all levels of government, and many governments now have such limits. Of the 10 largest cities in the United States, 9 of them (all but Chicago) have term limits.[22] As for the federal government, the Supreme Court has ruled that term limits to be imposed on Congress must be carried out through a constitutional amendment.[23] Proposals are advanced regularly for constitutional amendments to impose congressional term limits.[24]

Term limits are, as one might imagine, controversial. Advocates of term limits argue that term-limited representatives are more likely to embrace the ethic of the "citizen-legislator" as opposed to a careerist politician who may lose touch with their constituency. In addition, some argue that the reform has led to more women and Latinos being elected. Between 1996 and 2007, for example, there was a 37% increase in Hispanic elected officials.[25] The academic studies on the effects of term limits on female and minority participation, however, reached rather mixed conclusions.[26] A 2006 study focused on the state of Florida provided some evidence that, at least in that state, term limits had not led to an increase in diversity among elected officials.[27]

Term limits have their downside. Political bodies are automatically denied the experience that can be gained only from long years of service in a legislature. People do not automatically change their family doctors and dentists every 6 years, so why should they do so with their elected representatives? Effective representatives presumably should be retained in office, while ineffective ones should not be reelected. Reducing the length of time that someone may stay in office may deter some more qualified people from running for office in the first place. Term limits, in addition to denying a legislative body experienced legislators, may also increase the influence of staff who know vastly more about particular issues than inexperienced members. In fact, given the complexity of government, many legislators find that their learning curves have just reached a peak at about the time that their legislative careers are drawing to an end.[28]

A study sponsored by the National Conference of State Legislatures concluded, after a detailed comparison of states with term limits to those without, that term limits led to inexperienced lawmakers, polarized legislatures, and a shift in the balance of power toward the executive branch. The same study concluded that these costs have not come with the associated benefits of greater representative diversity.[29]

To counter this problem, some states have established "training" and "mentoring" programs for new legislators to try to increase their effectiveness.[30] Citizens may support term limits less because of any dissatisfaction with their representatives and more because of a general cynicism about government itself.[31] A study about the effects of term limits internationally found that term limits have no significant effects on either overall spending or budget deficits, while in the United States previous studies had found that term limits tended to make government revenue and spending increase.[32] A further study studied the effects on spending by U.S. states with more restrictive and less restrictive term limits. The authors found that "more restrictive term limits that greatly change the distribution of seniority within the legislature increase the amount of spending, while less restrictive term limits that slightly change the distribution of seniority have little effect on the amount of spending."[33]

Increased Partisanship

It has become much more difficult in recent years for legislators to reach agreement with each other on policies, as a result of the increasing polarization of politics at all levels of government. The parties have developed intractable, orthodox views on policy issues. Republicans, for example, are expected to oppose all tax increases, as a result of a pledge taken by many of them. This promise has been exacted as a result of the efforts of Grover Norquist, whose organization (Americans for Tax Reform) has argued for many years that the only way to curb the size of government is to reduce its revenue. Moderate Republicans, who might be supportive of tax increases in some circumstances, have increasingly been threatened by attacks from their right, and many moderate Republicans have been defeated in primary elections. The so-called "Freedom Caucus" in the House of Representatives is the current manifestation of this anti-tax movement at the national level. Similarly, Republicans expect of one another opposition to the Affordable Care Act (which they refer to as Obamacare), even though the party, when it controlled the House, Senate, and White House in 2017, was unable to adopt a replacement for the health care program. Democrats, in contrast, have been reluctant to cut spending and have been very protective of social safety net programs and public employee unions, both of which tend to be supported by core Democratic constituencies.

In a sense, the Republican antipathy toward taxes and the Democratic protection of social programs are not new phenomena. What makes the environment different now, however, than in the past is the near vanishing of the political moderates in legislative bodies at all levels of government. Moderates, while never a majority, at one time wielded great power in legislative bodies because they represented "swing" voters whose support could mean either victory or defeat for a given initiative. In a 2017 analysis, 51 of the 53 most conservative U.S. Senators (and the 46 most conservative) were Republicans, and 46 of the 47 most liberal Senators were Democrats. In the House, 235 of the 236 most conservative members were Republicans, and the 188 most liberal members were Democrats.[34] Both the redistricting phenomenon and the need to adhere to party orthodoxy have made compromise almost impossible, especially at the national level.[35]

Factors Affecting Legislative Decisions

Beyond these general characteristics of legislative bodies that affect their selection and tenure in office, there are other factors that influence the manner in which they deliberate on the budget. Legislatures tend to differ from one another in terms of many of these characteristics, such as the extent of fragmentation, the role of party leadership, the amount of time available to legislate, and the availability of staff. The capacity to legislate—and consequently to budget—is heavily influenced by these factors.

Fragmentation

An overriding characteristic of state legislatures and Congress is fragmentation in budgeting. Constitutionally imposed bicameralism divides the legislature into two chambers, a house and a senate, that seek to establish their own identities and powers but that must be coordinated if a budget is to be approved. Local governing bodies, in contrast, are usually unicameral and do not face this fragmentation problem. Fragmentation is also apparent within each chamber of a legislative body and between the executive and legislative branches.

Political parties can serve as a unifying force between branches, between legislative chambers, and within chambers. According to conventional practice, whichever party wins a majority of seats in a chamber controls the leadership positions, has a majority of its members on each committee, and

has each committee chaired by a member of the party. In theory, if the Republicans hold a majority of the seats in a state senate, then the Republican Party has control of that chamber in handling all legislative matters. Sometimes a ruling party may have the narrowest possible majority or no majority at all. In the 2019 legislative session, Virginia Republicans held two-seat majorities in both the Senate and the House (both houses later switched party control in the November 2019 election), and Arizona Republicans also held only a two-seat majority in the House. Republicans held even a slimmer edge of one seat in the Minnesota Senate.[36]

Political Party Leadership

In the United States, political parties are relatively weak (compared with parliamentary systems), meaning that party leadership cannot control their own party members by telling them how to vote (with notable exceptions in practice, as indicated by the previous discussion on Republican positions on taxes). On any given issue there may be no guarantee that all or even most of the party's members will vote as a bloc. Many members of the legislative body, especially those who have gained seniority through numerous reelections, are not always amenable to supporting the policies pursued by their party's leadership, whether in the legislature or in the executive branch. Furthermore, in term-limited legislatures, the assistance that leaders can offer rank-and-file members with reelection is much less important. For this reason, leaders do not have as much to offer these members in exchange for toeing the party line. In addition, regional differences sometimes trump partisan differences. In the Illinois Senate, for instance, a Republican from the Chicago area may be as likely to vote with a Chicago Democrat on some issue that affects the Chicagoland region as to vote with a Republican from "downstate" Illinois. Studies have also found evidence that interpersonal ties influence legislators' votes independent of partisanship.[37] In a situation where party control is weak, leaders must try to persuade members to win their votes, unlike in earlier times when legislative leaders may have ruled with iron fists.[38]

Parties attempt to exert influence on their legislators by providing or withholding privileges or by taking party positions in caucuses. Legislative leaders have different levels of institutional control over rank-and-file members. They may, for example, differ substantially in terms of their ability to appoint members to key committees or to provide resources.[39] Republicans in a state house of representatives, for example, will meet periodically to develop party positions on issues and then attempt to exert their influence on party members to vote accordingly. The positions approved in caucus meetings do not always coincide with the views of the party's leadership.

The situation is further complicated by the fact that the two chambers can be controlled by different parties. Even if both are controlled by one party, the chief executive might be of another party. In 2019, for example, 13 states had divided governments in which the governor, the lower legislative chamber, and the upper legislative chamber were not all controlled by the same political party.[40]

This condition is sometimes seen as leading to gridlock, which is one oft-cited cause for the inability of government to deal with pressing problems. While gridlock has a negative connotation, however, it should be noted that "checks and balances" (which leads to gridlock) is a principle firmly ingrained in the political philosophy of the United States and its citizens. Divided government, as will be seen in this chapter, should not be considered the sole explanation of why governments sometimes fail to address major problems.[41]

Legislative Committees

The extensive use of legislative committees is essential in that acting as a committee of the whole is impractical, but committee structures add to fragmentation. Committees become little legislatures in their own right.[42] Given that the U.S. House of Representatives has 435 members and the Senate has 100 members, a committee structure is inevitable. Among the states, New Hampshire has the largest legislature, with 424 members, and Nebraska the smallest, with 49 members in its single chamber. In 42 of the 50 states, there are at least 100 legislators.[43]

In a bicameral legislative body, legislation is handled by parallel committees in each chamber. These committees report out bills that are acted upon by the full membership of the house and senate. When differences exist in the two bills, a conference committee is usually appointed, which reports a revised bill that again is acted upon by both houses. The conference committee consists of members from the two committees that prepared the legislation. Once the chambers have passed identical bills, the legislation is ready for signing or vetoing by the governor or president.

At the local level, where unicameralism prevails, a budget committee often assumes the main responsibility for reviewing and amending the executive's proposed budget and for submitting a set of recommendations to the full legislative body, such as a city council or school board.

Committees that continue on a permanent basis are known as standing committees, whereas ad hoc committees are usually created to deal with specific problems and are then disbanded. Most standing committees consist of selected members of one house of a legislature, but standing committees can be joint in nature, consisting of selected members from both chambers. In 2019, state legislatures usually had 15 to 20 standing committees in each chamber. The range was 5 (the Maine Senate) to 47 (Wisconsin Assembly).[44]

Legislators seek to serve their district's or state's interests by gaining appointment to appropriate legislative committees. Someone from a farming community may seek appointment to a state senate's agriculture committee. A member of the U.S. House of Representatives from a district that includes major military installations may seek appointment to the Armed Services Committee to help ensure that military funds continue to flow into the district. Similarly, members of the House and Senate will seek appointment to key subcommittees (organized in line with key constituencies—i.e., defense, agriculture, transportation, and so forth) of their chamber's appropriations committee.[45]

Availability of Time

How a legislative body operates is greatly influenced by whether it continues in session throughout the year. City councils usually hold meetings once, twice, or even more times per month throughout the year. Congress is in session much of each year except for holidays and recesses during election periods.

State legislatures vary widely. While about a dozen states have no limits on the length of legislative sessions, the rest control whether the legislature can meet each year, for how many days, and whether the legislature may call itself back into session after adjournment. The legislatures in California, Idaho, Illinois, Iowa, Michigan, New Jersey, New York, North Carolina, Ohio, Pennsylvania, Rhode Island, Vermont, and Wisconsin hold sessions that are not limited as to their length, and thus may run during much of the year.[46] However, some states such as North Carolina have what are known colloquially as a *long session* in one year and a *short session* in the next year. The difference in duration is a biennial budget. The state adopts a 2-year budget, and during the short session the only budget actions are modification, usually leading to a much shorter legislative session.[47]

When legislatures have time limitations, procedural limits are used to "budget" the available time. For example, a common practice is to set a cutoff date for the introduction of bills, as late submission would carry deliberations beyond the required adjournment.

Similarly, time limits are set on the budget process. Some states allow their spending and taxation committees only a few weeks to consider their relevant portions of the budget, while other states allow 20 or more weeks. In some states, the entire budget approval process must be completed by the legislature within 6 weeks or less. Other states allow 20 weeks, 30 weeks, or even more.

A major problem facing Congress is not that it has limits on the time that it may be in session, but rather that it has difficulty approving the budget within the available time. This problem has existed periodically for some states and localities (such as California in the past or Illinois more recently, as indicated in the beginning of this chapter). One study cited the timeliness of budget adoption in New York State as a chronic phenomenon.[48] Late budgeting by states and localities, however, is much more the exception than the rule. The reason for this relative timeliness for states and localities may be more that they face a separate external force that does not exist at the national level. They may discover that the failure to enact bills on time can have an adverse effect on bond ratings and, therefore, increase borrowing costs. Indeed, as of 2019, Illinois had the lowest general obligation bond rating of any state in the nation (certainly late budgets contribute only partially to this result). Lower bond ratings translate into higher borrowing costs, amounting to millions of extra dollars over the years. (See the chapter on capital finance and debt management for discussion of the effects of bond ratings on the cost of borrowing.)

Compensation and Staff

Closely associated with time limits on legislatures is the issue of compensation for their members. Annual compensation is low in many states. For example, in 2019, Maine, Nebraska, New Hampshire, North Carolina, South Carolina, South Dakota, and Texas paid their legislators $15,000 or less.[49]

In these states and others, however, members might be eligible for per diem payments, travel expenses, and other payments. Nevertheless, pay for state legislators overall is low, so most legislators need other income sources, such as from law practices or other alternative employment, in order to make ends meet. In contrast, members of Congress earn incomes and receive other benefits, such as travel expenses, that allow the legislative job to be a full-time occupation. One of the most important forms of compensation afforded members of Congress is generous pension benefits that can be an incentive for continuing to stand for reelection. Fees for speeches and other appearances are lucrative for some legislators, although these are generally prohibited to be paid to members of Congress.

Staffing is another factor that influences legislative behavior. Staff dedicated to assist legislators presumably can help them perform more effectively and reduce their reliance on the executive branch and lobbyists for information. Although local legislators, such as county commissioners or city council members, rarely have sizable staffs at their disposal, Congress does. So do many state legislatures, although some states have small staffs. A predominantly rural state, such as Wyoming, will have a legislative staff of less than 100, while a large state, such as New York, will have staff in the thousands. These personnel serve individual members, committees, and persons holding leadership positions, as in the case of the speaker of a state house of representatives. In addition, some legislative staff units serve a variety of individuals and committees in both chambers. The Congressional Budget Office (CBO) is a notable example of such a unit, but many states have similar legislative budget offices. California's Office of the Legislative Analyst, in fact, is one of the most highly regarded of such offices, and it served as a model for the development of the CBO at the national level.[50] Since the 1960s, staffs in state legislatures and Congress have greatly increased their professional training. Many staff members now have graduate degrees, including doctorates.

Legislative fiscal committee staffs provide a host of services. For example, most state legislatures' fiscal committee staffs conduct fiscal research studies, prepare reports on revenues and taxes, and prepare reports on expenditures and the budget. Other important staff functions include making revenue projections, analyzing budget trends during the fiscal year, and preparing reports on economic conditions. States also differ as to whether they maintain separate fiscal staffs for each house or one joint legislative fiscal office that serves both houses.[51]

The National Conference of State Legislatures (NCSL), in 2017, sorted the 50 state legislatures into three categories:[52]

- Green (10 states), representing those legislatures that are full time, well paid, with a large staff. Most legislatures from populous states fit into this category, including four that were identified as the most professional—California, Michigan, New York, and Pennsylvania. Six other states were identified as "green lite" because they had full-time legislatures, but typically with lower salaries and fewer staff.
- Gray (26 states), representing a middle majority category where legislators may or may not be full time, but do say that they spend more than two-thirds of their time being legislators. These tend to be from mid-level states according to population and also have medium-sized staffs.
- Gold (14 states), which are part time legislatures where legislators spend an average of one-half of their time being legislators and need to earn substantial additional compensation from other work. This is the "citizen legislator" model. These tend to have small staffs and are in rural, less populated states. Within this category, NCSL identified four states—Montana, North Dakota, South Dakota, and Wyoming—as being the most extreme examples of relatively weak, part-time legislatures.

Professionalism, however, is no guarantee of a smoothly operating legislature, as has been evident in such states as California and New York. One view is that professionalism attracts better-informed individuals who inevitably clash with one another, yielding conflict that is not necessarily productive.[53]

The Legislative Budget Process

This section examines what happens to the executive budget when it reaches the legislature. Legislatures are not integrated wholes but rather consist of numerous subunits, and this section considers how the executive branch relates to those subunits, especially to the two legislative chambers and their committees.

General Relations Between the Branches

The executive and legislative branches of government in the United States are typically said to be coequal.[54] The separation of powers—in this case, between the executive and legislative branches—is a fundamental feature of U.S. governments. Because political power tends to be a somewhat "zero-sum" game, the two branches tend to be wary of possible diminution of their powers and may seek strategies for demonstrating their independence. Confrontations between the two are sometimes akin to tests of strength with each branch showing it is not subservient to the other.

Authority

In earlier days, the legislature was considered to be responsible for setting policy. Today, both the legislative and executive branches are inextricably engaged in policymaking. Conflicts arise, not over whether the executive should be involved in policy making, but rather to what extent and in what ways. The movement toward executive budget systems has placed the executive four-square in the policymaking process, because the preparation of budget proposals by the executive is, in effect, the drafting of proposed policies. Congress, state legislatures, and city councils have often found themselves in the position of having to react to executive recommendations instead of formulating policy. To demonstrate their independence, then, legislators may feel a compulsion to alter a proposed budget no matter how compatible its recommendations are with their own preferences.

Not all governments have executive budgeting systems. In some governments, budgeting powers overlap between the branches. In others, legislatures dominate the budgeting process. Those states where legislatures are weaker are likely those where there are shorter legislative sessions, or where the legislature has fewer staff. In fact, in a study of the budget practices of 13 states, only 3 were characterized as states where the executive is dominant, while 4 were judged as states where the legislature is dominant. In the rest, budgetary power was viewed as

relatively equal between the branches.[55] Regardless of the distribution of powers, tensions will exist between the branches of government.

Constitutional and legal constraints greatly affect the extent of executive and legislative powers in budgeting. The Budget and Accounting Act of 1921 and comparable legislation at the state level have granted substantial budgetary powers to the president and governors. Yet, in some states, the governor must share budget-making authority with other relatively independent executive officers or legislative bodies. In most states, the legislature is free to adjust the governor's budget either upward or downward, but in three states—Maryland, Nebraska, and West Virginia—the legislature has limited or no authority to appropriate amounts above those recommended by the governor.[56] Even in states where the legislature is not constrained, however, legislative authority is offset by the fact that governors often (in 44 states) have item-veto power, as is discussed more fully later in this chapter.[57]

Relationships between the branches change over time. Changes in political leadership have both short- and long-term effects. When a new executive takes office, inevitable discontinuities occur during the transition period that can last from a few weeks to months. In addition, personalities and the political clout of leaders influence executive–legislative relations. The election of a highly popular political leader to the legislature can lead to diminished executive powers. A newly elected governor who is more assertive than his or her predecessor may succeed in demanding that the legislature yield some of its budgetary powers. Either the executive or the legislative branch may change its partisan makeup (as occurred, for example, in the 2018 election, when the Democrats took the Senates of Colorado and Connecticut, as well as the the Minnesota House, and the 2019 by-elections that culminated in Democrat control of Virginia's Office of the Governor and both chambers of the legislature for the first time since 1994.[58] In periods of fiscal crisis and other challenging times, the executive may tend to garner greater budgetary powers at the expense of the legislature.[59]

Constituency Differences

The legislative and executive branches have different constituencies and, as a result, have different perspectives on the budget. One common interpretation has been that the chief executive, being elected by the jurisdiction's entire constituency, has a broader perspective on the budget. A governor will attempt to satisfy the diverse needs of citizens throughout the state. Legislative bodies, on the other hand, have been seen as consisting of parochial individuals who may be less impressed with government-wide problems and, therefore, more likely to cut budgets. The legislature, then, is seen as a protector of the treasury and as a budget cutter.

A competing view of legislative bodies is that, in their desire to represent constituents, they tend to be eager to spend resources far beyond what is financially sound and that, while the requirement for a balanced budget keeps that desire to spend in check at the state and local levels, few constraints are evident at the national level. *Pork barrel*, a basic term of U.S. politics, refers to legislatively approved government projects that are aimed at helping home districts and states.[60] In fact, some prominent political scientists have suggested that pork barrel spending and constituent casework (intervening on behalf of constituents with administrative agencies) have become more valued than legislating because they offer a more certain path to reelection.[61] A standard complaint of many pork barrel projects is that they have limited utility beyond winning votes for legislators seeking reelection. The line-item veto, discussed below, may help to reduce the wastefulness of pork barrel spending.

Factors Constraining Legislative Deliberations on the Budget

Members of the legislature or their staffs often participate in budget preparation deliberations by the executive branch. When the budget reaches the legislature, it may contain relatively few surprises in terms of proposals being advanced because many of the key legislators will already be familiar with the budget's main proposals. Legislative involvement during preparation can help build support for executive budget recommendations. In addition to the political and institutional characteristics discussed previously, the deliberation of any legislature is constrained by some factors outside of its control, such as the state's economic environment and the effect of previous budget decisions. Operating within those constraints, the legislature then makes the decisions necessary for the chief executive's budget proposal to become law.

Economic and Political Environment

As with all human enterprise, legislative bodies must operate within a set of parameters that greatly constrain how they approve the budgets. One of the most important constraints is the economic environment in both the short and the long term. How a legislative body approaches the task of passing a budget is influenced greatly by whether a surplus of revenues is projected or whether sizable cuts must be made to bring expenditures down to meet anticipated reductions in revenues. At the height of the Great Recession during fiscal years 2009 and 2010, an average of 40 states per year needed to cut the budget in midyear.[62] During fiscal year 2018, however, such midyear reductions only occurred in seven states.[63] COVID-19 is sure to usher in several years in which the state funding environment will return to one in which there is substantial economic and budgetary uncertainty, perhaps restoring the kind of instability that leads to midyear reductions.

Furthermore, the legislature is constrained by whether the political environment would permit additional revenues to be raised, whether the level of revenues under current law represents a revenue ceiling, or even whether tax cuts have already been promised. In the current political environment, where conservative activists have forced candidates for political office to pledge not to raise taxes, this can make for some very challenging budgeting.

Previous Decisions

Before a local legislative body commences considering the budget, many decisions will already have been made. The state will have imposed a variety of mandates. A school district will be told how many days it must operate in a school year, possibly what the minimum salaries should be for teachers at different levels, and what courses must be taught. More than one-half of a school district's budget typically comes from state aid, which greatly reduces what the school district can decide on its own. The state will also have imposed limits on the taxation and borrowing authority for each type of local government and may deny taxing power to some jurisdictions, as is sometimes the case with special districts.

Whether the legislative body is Congress, the state legislature, or a local legislature, many decisions will already have been made before legislative deliberations begin. Entitlement laws that provide open-ended benefits to individuals, such as guaranteed payments to all persons qualifying for disability benefits under Social Security, greatly curtail what Congress can do in a given year. Programs such as Medicaid, where many rules that affect state and local costs have been made by the federal government, may seem uncontrollable at the state or local level. The Trump administration, for example, proposed large cuts in Medicaid in its fiscal year 2020 budget; one of the potential effects from this proposal is the fiscal benefit that reduced Medicaid costs could have for the states.[64] These cuts were not adopted by Congress.[65] Additionally, courts force legislative bodies to take actions, such as legislatures having to revise state funding formulas for school districts to comply with court orders. If tax increases must be approved by voters, as is sometimes the case with sewer taxes on property, and voters reject proposed increases, then the sewer board may be faced with finding revenues in some other forms, such as raising monthly or quarterly sewer fees.

The Legislature Adopts the Budget

The legislative budget process typically involves several sequential types of actions:

- Committee action, where committees, or sometimes subcommittees, hold hearings and collect other information on proposed agency budgets, and then use their expertise to draft bills that reflect their judgment concerning funding levels for programs and agencies under their jurisdiction;
- Action by the legislature as a whole, which must vote on proposals coming out of committees, frequently modify those proposals, and resolve differences that usually exist between the chambers; and
- Action by the chief executive, whose assent is often necessary (and always necessary at the state and federal levels) in order for any budget legislation to have the force of law.

While the process is sequential, actions are simultaneous. Several committees work simultaneously on bills but report out on them at various times. Committees work on bills at the same time the full chambers act on others and the executive considers signing or vetoing others.

Committee Action

Legislatures—especially in a large government with many responsibilities—are not typically in a position to deal with the budget in a unified way. Frequently when a budget reaches a state legislature or Congress, the document is divided into numerous pieces and sent to committees. Proposals that require new substantive legislation to implement them will be sent to substantive standing committees. These committees exist for areas such as environmental protection; health; education; recreation; welfare; and, at the federal level, defense and international relations. For programs to be implemented, these committees must report bills that will be approved eventually by the two chambers of the legislature. Legislation of this type authorizes the existence of programs, while appropriations provide the necessary funding.

While deliberations proceed on these substantive matters, other committees deal with the financial aspects of the budget. A regular practice is to assign taxing and other revenue matters to one group of committees and spending or appropriations to another. Appropriations may be handled at the full committee level, or in subcommittees, each of which provides appropriations for a portion of the government.

Coordination problems and terrain battles among committees are common. A person typically achieves the position of chair of a committee by serving on the committee for a long time and, once made chair, is unlikely to look favorably on threats to the committee's powers. Nevertheless, some coordinating mechanisms are essential to ensure that realistic budgets are adopted. For example, if separate revenue and expenditure committees are free to act independently, then there may be little relation between how much revenue comes into the government and how much is spent.

It was precisely this situation that led the federal government to enact the Congressional Budget and Impoundment Control Act of 1974, creating the Budget Committees and budget resolution to better coordinate action on the budget. The budget resolution, which is under the jurisdiction of the Budget Committees, sought to address the fragmentation of the budget process at the federal level by requiring Congress to vote on the whole budget, rather than considering it only in pieces. This type of fragmentation may be less likely to occur at the state and local levels, particularly in smaller and less complex governmental units. Local governments—especially those in jurisdictions with smaller populations—are particularly unlikely to have specific committees focused on the budget.

Hearings

In local governments with elected boards or councils, hearings and budget reviews are typically conducted with the entire legislative body present. Directors of city or county departments are asked to defend budget proposals in the same way that similar officials defend their budget requests at the state and national levels. The public, however, may be more involved in local budget issues at a much greater level of detail than is the case for national or state budgets, because citizens are likely to be more knowledgeable about local issues and more directly affected by the budget.[66] In fact, specific provision for direct citizen input into the budget process is a common feature of local government budgeting.[67]

While an executive budget system provides the chief executive with control over budget preparation, there is no guarantee that all units within the executive branch will subscribe fully to the budget's recommendations. The chief executive will not be uniformly in support of all portions of the budget. Some recommendations will have been approved because of political considerations. Typically, the chief executive will single out a few major recommendations for which approval is sought, with other recommendations being considered low priority. The budget office will be expected to make general presentations on the overall recommendations contained in the budget even though it may be lukewarm toward many of those recommendations. Hearings may be held by budget or appropriations committees, or for the legislative body as a whole, in an effort to discern the overall fiscal and policy direction implied in the budget.

More detailed hearings with executive branch agencies, however, typically dominate the budget process. In advance of these hearings, executive branch agencies may be requested to provide budget justification documents to legislative committees with jurisdiction over the budget. These documents may simply be the sections of the chief executive's budget that deal with the agency, or agencies may be required to present budget data in an entirely different format than was included in the executive budget document. Agencies usually know in advance what data the committees want and in what formats and prepare accordingly during the budget preparation phase.

Hearings may generate more heat than light. It is normally the responsibility of executive branch officials to defend the chief executive's agency-by-agency budget recommendations to the legislature. The heads of the agencies in a strong executive system are the appointees of the chief executive and have an obligation to defend the budget recommendations, even though higher funding levels may be preferred.[68] Agency representatives, however, may have little enthusiasm for defending budget proposals that call for deep cuts in programs. As a result, agencies attempt to calculate the extent to which they can reveal their preferences for greater resources to the spending committees in the legislature and still remain "faithful" to the chief executive. They do not always calculate correctly. In 2002, President George W. Bush's appointed civilian head of the Army Corps of Engineers, former Representative Mike Parker, was fired for being a bit too honest in his responses to questions from Congress about the adequacy of the Corps' budget.[69] Agencies also seek to head off any budget cuts being contemplated by the appropriations committee and are willing to engage in conflict if necessary to protect their budgets.[70]

During the approval phase, central budget offices may have responsibility for exercising some control over agencies that might seek to garner financial support beyond what the executive is recommending to the legislature and may serve as a major negotiator for the executive in sensitive discussions with legislative leaders. Since the early 1980s, the Office of Management and Budget (OMB) has played a much more prominent role in legislative relations. This role includes activities not just of the OMB director, but also of individual budget examiners.[71]

Strategies

Regardless of what level of government is considered, executive–legislative relationships inevitably can be characterized as cat-and-mouse games, although it is not always clear who is the cat and who is the mouse. Strategies are devised in each branch to deal with the other. On the executive side, an almost ubiquitous strategy is to cultivate

clientele who will support requests for increased funding. Agencies are sensitive to where they locate buildings and other facilities. A new facility in a key legislator's district may gain the support of that legislator. Agencies pursue such strategies continuously as a matter of course.[72]

Contingent strategies, on the other hand, are limited to particular situations. No comprehensive cataloguing of them is possible because they vary from agency to agency and from circumstance to circumstance. They arise out of perceptions of what is possible in a given budget period. In growth periods, when revenue surplus or slack is evident, agencies may seek to expand existing programs or gain approval for the creation of new ones. Even when revenues are scarce, agencies whose areas are favored by the chief executive may seek expansion, as occurred with the expansion of defense spending and the creation of the Department of Homeland Security in the aftermath of the September 11, 2001, terrorist attacks. Sometimes obtaining approval for a new program may be easier than obtaining approval for expansion of an existing one. Executives and legislators alike prefer being able to take credit for creation of a new program over simply improving an existing one.

A ploy used by supporters of programs may be to start a new project with a small appropriation, get the legislature accustomed to the program, and then seek much greater appropriations in subsequent years. This tactic has been referred to as the "camel's nose" strategy. Under this imagery, the majority of the "camel" (the new program) is outside the tent, and thus obscured from view. The camel's nose is visible, but the nose represents a small percentage of the total camel (the eventual cost of the program). The assumption is that once the first part (the nose) of the program is funded, funding for the rest (the remainder of the camel) will follow.[73]

When funds are less plentiful, one strategy is to defend programs against cuts and to maintain what is called the base. An agency's existing budget is often regarded as the base, with the budget process adding or subtracting increments to the base. Agencies have been known to warn that the slightest of budget cuts would necessarily diminish popular programs and thereby erode electoral support of legislators.

When cuts are perceived as inevitable, often because of declining tax revenues, one strategy is to minimize cuts in the base and to obtain fair share funding. An agency will argue, on the one hand, that its programs are essential and should not be cut at all. On the other hand, it will insist that, if cuts must be made, they be no greater than cuts imposed on programs in other agencies.

Strategies used by proponents of government programs can be highly situational. A thorough study of the strategies used by federal agencies in dealing with OMB and Congress catalogued 35 different strategies used at various times. These included some that have been well documented in the budgeting literature, such as establishing earmarked funding sources, portraying the disastrous consequences of failing to spend money, and stressing the needs of a particular group that will be served. They also include many more arcane strategies that have been less well documented: establishment of a government sponsored enterprise, creation of a loan guarantee program, establishment of a tax expenditure, and leasing instead of purchasing a capital asset.[74] There are, in short, many different "tools" available to governments to satisfy the desire for social action. Increasingly, these tactics involve less direct means than government expenditures, for strategic as well as substantive reasons.[75] Some changes in the budget process, such as federal credit reform, have occurred specifically to lessen the incentives to provide resources through less direct and apparently less costly means. (See the chapter on financial management.)

While various strategies may be influential, there are limits to their effectiveness. Legislatures are influenced by personal values and committee role expectations as well as by agency budget strategies and presentations. Agency strategies may also backfire and create negative feelings on the part of members of the appropriations committees, perhaps because they suspect they are being exploited.

In response to agency pressure, legislators devise a number of strategies for dealing with their budgetary responsibilities. A major problem is the capacity of agencies to produce vast amounts of information in support of their requests—more information than the legislature can process.

Legislative hearings are often used as opportunities for members of key committees to collect what is often anecdotal information from agencies in an attempt to determine how much confidence they have in the ability of the agency to use resources effectively. They may place much of the burden for calculation on the executive branch and demand that an agency justify its need for certain funds in response to probing questions. Detailed questions that may seem petty and trivial to outsiders are designed to determine how much confidence the subcommittee can place in the executive's stewardship of public funds. Legislators have "discernible patterns" in their line of questioning, suggesting that they have their own strategies for dealing with different agencies and that these strategies depend in part on changes in fiscal conditions.[76] How the various strategies affect the outcomes of appropriations is uncertain and no doubt varies among jurisdictions and over time.

Fiscal Notes

One important mechanism that has been adopted is the requirement that fiscal notes be developed for most draft legislation reported out of legislative committees. A fiscal note is a report that addresses the current and future costs of implementing a proposed bill. It may include analysis of the purpose of the legislation, the proposed sources of funding, and the impact on other governments, as in the case of a state law affecting local government budgets.

Fiscal notes are typically prepared by legislative staff. At the state level, appropriations committees often have this responsibility. At the federal level, the CBO prepares fiscal notes (referred to as cost estimates) to any bill that is reported out of a House or Senate Committee. CBO is required to estimate the marginal cost of the proposed legislation to the federal government, relative to the baseline, which is the estimate of costs under current law. It also estimates the costs of legislation to state and local governments. The Unfunded Mandates Reform Act of 1995 requires that Congress consider the possible financial effects of draft legislation on state and local governments and creates hurdles to considering legislation that does not include an estimate of potential unfunded mandates.[77] (See the chapter on intergovernmental relations.)

The fiscal note is intended to help decision makers be better informed about the implications of draft legislation. For example, if a proposal provides for revising a state program for teenagers to include 13-year-olds, whereas only those 14 years old and older are currently included, the revision could greatly increase the number of clients served and heighten the demand on resources. Fiscal notes are also prepared for revenue proposals, as in the case of forecasting the extra income that would be generated by increasing a state sales tax by one percentage point.

Fiscal notes are particularly important at the state and local levels, where balanced budgets are required. Indeed, the revenue estimates prepared by the chief executive, coupled with any fiscal note on proposed revenue increases, will greatly influence what spending programs the legislature will be able to approve. Some states require that fiscal notes be prepared for tax expenditure proposals, while others do not. (See the chapter on income, property, and payroll taxes.)

A 2015 study of state fiscal note practices suggested the following as desirable elements of a state fiscal note process as of that year:

- Preparing fiscal notes for all legislative proposals; this happens in 38 states plus the District of Columbia;
- Assigning the fiscal note process to a nonpartisan entity, as happens in 33 states plus DC;
- Revising estimates as needed, as occurs in 27 states plus DC; and
- Posting fiscal notes online; only four of the states that prepare fiscal notes do NOT do this.

This same study, by reviewing state practices, categorized states into three categories (best, needs improvement, and worst). Six jurisdictions were identified as "best" based on their use of all of the above best practices—the District of Columbia, Iowa, Louisiana, Maryland, Oregon, and Texas. On the other hand, California, Hawaii, Illinois, Massachusetts, Mississippi, New York, and Pennsylvania were identified as having the worst fiscal note processes.[78]

In addition to fiscal notes, other mechanisms are devised to link together the work of committees and ensure that "reasonable" budgets are developed. Some states have used a system by which lump-sum amounts are assigned to program areas, and these funds then are distributed among programs within each area by standing committees and reported back to the appropriations committee for inclusion in their budget bills. Congress uses a variation of this approach. Local governments generally have less of a coordination problem because most of the budget work is handled by a single committee.

The Committee Adopts the Budget

Once committees have gathered and processed all of the information collected as a part of the hearing process, they turn to drafting and approving the budget legislation itself. This is best seen as the starting point for later legislative deliberations on the budget. The initial committee proposal can be quite influential, depending on how much interest or power the rest of the legislature has to amend bills after they emerge from committee. From the perspective of executive branch agencies and interest groups, it is highly desirable to receive favorable budget treatment in draft committee legislation.

Obtaining Overall Legislative Approval

All of the previous activity implies that legislative action is taking place in one committee of the legislature. In a bicameral legislative system, all of the previous activity takes place not in one set of legislative committees, but in committees in both chambers. Because differences almost always exist between the two legislative chambers, a bicameral system complicates the ultimate approval of the budget. Another complicating factor is that there may be multiple committees with jurisdiction over legislation that affects the budget. Thus, many different bills may be required in order to finally pass the entire budget.

One set of considerations from both the executive and the legislative branch perspectives involves the relative roles of the two chambers. At the federal level, the Constitution (Article I, Section 7) requires that revenue or tax bills begin in the House of Representatives. This means, given the current organization of the House, that revenue bills start in the Ways and Means Committee. Until the 1974 reform legislation, the normal procedure was for the Senate Finance Committee to wait until the House completed action before taking up the tax bill. Appropriations were handled in a similar manner, although the practice was based on custom and not the Constitution. Appropriation bills began in the House and were later referred to the Senate. Under that system, strategists were able to concentrate their attentions on first one committee and then another, and on one chamber and then the other, as the legislation worked its way through Congress. Since 1974, the House and Senate have simultaneously commenced work on the budget—or not, given the rather dismal record of the Congress on budget time lines. (See the chapter on budget approval in the Congress.)

In either legislative house, once the budget or a component of the budget has been approved by the appropriate committee, it is considered by the relevant house where that committee is housed. The overall house may or may not substantially revise or amend the budget as approved by the relevant committee depending on the rules of that particular legislature. In some legislatures, the practice is for quite substantial amendment of committee proposals, whereas in others there is a great deal of deference to the approved committee budgets.

One factor that influences legislative deliberations on the budget is the relative roles played by the two legislative chambers. Where appropriations are handled sequentially (that is, beginning in the lower chamber and then moving to the upper chamber), the two chambers tend to take on different roles. Because a house of representatives tends to have more members than a senate, a house appropriations committee tends to have more members than its counterpart in the senate. As a result, house committee members can specialize in segments of the budget, whereas senators must attempt to become informed on a larger number of areas and consequently may be viewed as amateurs. Members of the senate committee, however, might consider themselves to have a broader awareness of total budget needs than house members.

A vital and complicating factor in bicameral systems is the necessity to resolve the inevitable differences that result from the deliberations of the two legislative bodies. Almost invariably, because of the difference in constituencies between the chambers or because the chambers may be controlled by different political parties, a conference committee or some other institution will be required to work out these disputes. The conference committee process is often a delicate balancing act where the members attempt to draft legislation that can gain enough votes in each chamber without costing votes of members who may find that their preferred project or funding level did not survive in conference.

Chief Executive Action on the Budget

Once a revenue or expenditure bill has passed the legislature, it typically (at least in states and in the federal government) will go to the chief executive for approval. Deadlock between the branches is a common phenomenon. When the two cannot agree on a budget, commuters can be greatly inconvenienced due to shutdowns in public transit, assistance recipients can be forced to eke out an existence without their checks, and public employees may have to endure payless paydays. At the national level, the best recent example of the effects of an interbranch budget stalemate was the 35-day partial government shutdown that commenced in late 2018 and continued through much of January of 2019. The shutdown was the longest in U.S. Government history, had many negative effects on service delivery, and caused great hardship for employees and contractors who had to go without paychecks.[79] The shutdown was said to have cost the economy at least $11 billion.[80] At the state level, the best (worst?) recent example was the 2-year budget impasse in Illinois that led to substantial disruptions in the service provided by and operations of state government.[81]

Budget offices commonly perform a clearinghouse function by reviewing all proposed legislation and bills that have been passed by the legislature and forwarded to the chief executive for signing. OMB Circular A-19, *Legislative Coordination and Clearance*, prescribes for federal agencies that they submit to OMB an annual set of proposals for legislation.[82] If these proposals are not submitted in time for consideration during budget preparation, then they are excluded from the president's budget and therefore not endorsed by the president and his administration. Circular A-19 provides that when Congress passes a bill, OMB distributes copies of the enrolled bill to affected agencies for their comments. The agencies must respond promptly, either endorsing or opposing the enrolled bill, to be considered within the president's limit of 10 days. If the president does not act within the 10 days (including holidays but excluding Sundays), the bill automatically becomes law.

Line-Item Veto

Once appropriation and revenue bills are adopted by the legislature, the approval phase is not completed. In 44 states, governors have item-veto power, which permits reductions in amounts that have been appropriated.[83] In 10 of these states, the Governor also has reduction veto power, which permits approval of a reduced amount for a line item without the necessity of vetoing the entire item.[84] In some cases, governors may eliminate selected language in appropriation bills that can have substantial effects on policy. State legislatures may seek to override these vetoes. Usually a supermajority vote of both houses—three-fifths or two-thirds—is required for an override. As with the general veto power, the threat of the line-item veto may be as important as its eventual use, in that legislators may avoid including some measures in an appropriation bill on the assumption that they would be excised eventually by the governor.

The line-item veto has three uses:[85]

1. It allows chief executives to keep total expenditures within the limits of anticipated available revenue.
2. The executive can reduce or even eliminate funds for projects or programs considered to be unworthy. The line-item veto can help curtail the excesses of pork barrel projects mentioned earlier.
3. The veto can be used for partisan purposes. This kind of use often occurs in situations where the governor is of one political party and one or both chambers of the legislature are of another party.

Studies have found that the item-veto power sometimes, but not always, has a negative effect on spending. This is especially true for pork barrel highway projects and can be particularly important when at least one chamber is under the control of a political party that differs from the governor's party.[86] From a practical standpoint, the line-item veto allows action by the governor without forcing the legislature to react unless it chooses to do so. Indeed, legislators may be privately pleased to have the governor veto some projects that were included in an appropriation bill to satisfy strong lobbying pressure. In spite of the constitutional foundations underlying state line-item vetoes, state courts have been at times very active in interpreting their application and these court decisions have had substantial effects on the "reach" of a governor's item-veto power.[87]

At the federal level, the president has always been able to exercise the standard veto power, meaning that he can veto an entire appropriation bill. When this power is exercised, the House and Senate may override the veto by a two-thirds vote. Should the veto be sustained, the legislation is referred back to the committee for further review. The disadvantage of the veto power for both

Congress and the president is that much time and energy may be consumed in redrafting the legislation and negotiating an agreement between the two branches.

Every president since Ulysses S. Grant, including Barack Obama and Donald Trump, has requested the item-veto power or a variant of it.[88] In 1996, Congress granted that wish by passing the Line Item Veto Act.[89] The law was ultimately declared unconstitutional by the Supreme Court in 1998.[90] (See the chapter on U.S. Congress.)

Legislative Oversight

Not only are the executive and legislative branches typically separated in U.S. governments, but each branch is also provided with powers that can be used to limit the powers of the other. The basic structure of this checks-and-balances system is set forth in the U.S. Constitution, state constitutions, and city charters. However, constitutional and statutory provisions must be implemented on a daily basis, and the extent to which one branch limits the other may fluctuate over time. In this section, we consider the increasing interest being given to the legislative body's oversight of executive operations.[91]

Influences on Oversight

When revenues are limited and the demands for expenditures are seemingly limitless, legislators perceive a need for greater efficiency and effectiveness in government operations. Such perceptions increase the interest in oversight operations, which in turn increases the pressure on administrative agencies to improve their operations while curtailing or even reducing expenditures. Agencies are required to provide masses of information to legislative committees to support their quest for ferreting out mismanagement and saving tax dollars.[92]

There are, of course, other reasons for the current legislative oversight movement. Financial crises in major cities have contributed to the interest in oversight. When perceived or real scandals or problems occur at the federal level, such as the failure of the technology undergirding the Affordable Care Act, the alleged Internal Revenue Service's harassment of conservative organizations, or travel irregularities by Trump cabinet officials, this can stimulate interest in greater legislative oversight. This can be particularly true if there is turnover in the party controlling the legislature, such as occurred when the Democrats took the House of Representatives in the 2018 midterm elections and began an aggressive oversight campaign in early 2019. This ultimately led to an affirmative vote by the House to impeach President Trump, leading to only the third-ever trial by the Senate. Legislators have not been immune from their own scandals, raising the question of whether they have the appropriate credentials to oversee executive branch operations. A study of all congressional resignations since 1901 concludes that scandals involving members of Congress have become a more important factor in explaining resignations over time. The most high profile of these was the campaign donation-fueled Abscam scandal in 1980 and 1981 and the sexual harassment scandals after 2016.[93]

Legislators may be sincerely interested in using government to alleviate societal problems. Frustrated by what is perceived as inept administration, they are attracted to the idea of expanding their oversight roles in the hope of improving government operations. Of course, oversight of the executive branch can also provide an opportunity for legislators to score political points. In fact, legislatures have often been criticized for engaging in oversight designed to take an agency to task for some particular perceived offense, rather than using this opportunity to attempt to understand programs in detail so that they can be reformed constructively.

This legislative interest in oversight occurs at a time when executives feel increasingly frustrated with their own efforts to control public bureaucracies. Elected executives often complain that they lack the authority needed to control and redirect agencies. Merit systems that protect civil service employees are often cited as weakening executives and protecting lazy and incompetent employees from disciplinary actions.

In states that allow strong collective bargaining for public workers, both state and local executives often complain that they cannot make needed changes in administration because of collective bargaining agreements and that unions refuse to yield to essential changes such as cutbacks in wages and benefits when revenues are down. The tensions that this creates were brought into sharp relief in 2010 and 2011 when the governors of both Wisconsin and Ohio took high-profile stands against public employee unions in their states. In Ohio, this approach led to a backlash from voters, who approved a referendum in 2011 that repudiated a union-curbing law passed only 1 year earlier.[94]

Methods

Legislative oversight can be performed using numerous methods. Legislation that provides authorizations, revenues, and appropriations constitutes one set of methods. Other familiar devices are laws that prescribe the structure of executive agencies and personnel policies regarding hiring, promotion, and dismissal. An informal type of oversight occurs when a legislator or a legislative staff member contacts an agency about specific day-to-day operations. Although legislators may have no official power to command any action by an agency, their wishes will be treated carefully and with some urgency by agency personnel. Oversight is important in advise-and-consent proceedings in which a senate committee screens a nominee for an executive position. Commitments made by a nominee in response to questions asked during such nomination hearings can influence that person's actions once in office.

Legislative investigations and just the simple threat of investigation are other instruments of oversight. A legislative committee chair may greatly influence an agency by suggesting that investigative hearings will be scheduled unless certain practices are changed within the agency.

Greater specificity of legislative intent is being used to reduce executive discretion. In the past, ambiguous language was used as a deliberate tool for delegating responsibilities to the executive and increasing executive flexibility in carrying out policies. The opposite is common today. State legislatures attempt to establish legislative intent through the use of wording contained in line items, footnotes, and concluding sections to appropriation bills; the use of committee reports; and the use of letters of intent delivered to the governor.

Legislatures often find it difficult to enforce legislative intent. What if an agency stays within the legal prescriptions of legislative intent but violates its spirit? The punitive action of cutting the agency's budget often is not possible—citizens benefiting from agency programs would be harmed as well as the agency itself. Therefore, the main punitive alternative may be to impose more restrictions on the agency, such as making legislative intent more explicit, specifically prohibiting various practices, and increasing the number of line items in the agency's budget to hamstring its flexibility.

The legislature may also attempt to enforce legislative intent by requiring agencies to collect and provide specific information to the legislature. This practice denies agencies the tactic of confessing ignorance about their own programs. If legislation indicates that an agency is to collect specific data, the agency will be expected to deliver it at designated times every year.

Congress often adopts appropriation bills that have detailed language. Sometimes the disagreements that delay action on the budget, or threaten government shutdowns, are as much about these policy riders as about the level of appropriations. For example, House Republicans have sometimes successfully included restrictions on using family planning funds for abortions in the District of Columbia and to remove certain animals from the endangered species list.[95]

Use of Program and Performance Information

Legislatures can also, in performing their oversight function, use information on the results that are obtained from government programs. Some reforms, such as zero-base budgeting, have this as a goal. Sometimes legislatures also establish specific deadlines for the existence of programs.

These are typically referred to as sunset provisions, where programs are authorized to exist for a given period, after which they expire (the sun sets on them). Beyond these specific reforms, however, legislatures are increasingly demanding output and outcome data from agencies. Such demands have reinforcing effects on chief executives' efforts to install program budgeting. There is limited evidence, however, that performance data are important in allocating resources. (See the chapter on budget preparation.)

Legislatures have sometimes given little attention to oversight, and the function has fallen to audit agencies that at the state level are often headed by independently elected auditors. When legislative bodies later develop their own analytic capabilities, turf issues arise.[96] Virginia's Joint Legislative Audit and Review Commission and Florida's Office of Program Policy Analysis and Government Accountability are examples of state legislative analysis units.[97]

At the federal level, the Government Accountability Office (GAO) has an extensive ongoing research agenda that examines the full gamut of government programs.[98] The fact that the GAO works for Congress often brings it into conflict with the executive branch. One case involved the GAO's desire to obtain records of Vice President Dick Cheney's contacts with outsiders in the process of developing the administration's energy policy. This issue became particularly salient politically after the collapse of Enron, which had ties to some high-ranking officials in the Bush administration.[99] The White House, however, maintained executive privilege, and the requested documents and names were not provided to the GAO.

Information technology also makes possible greater legislative oversight. Congress and state legislatures have developed their own information systems that allow them to tap into a variety of databases, including those maintained by agencies. The application of this technology is limited by the quality of data being maintained. Computer hardware and software cannot compensate for agency neglect in collecting important information.

Legislative Veto

Legislatures are making increased use of their power to veto proposed executive actions. For instance, an agency may be granted authority to issue regulations, but a stipulation in the legislation can require the agency to obtain legislative approval prior to implementing the regulations.[100] Depending on the governing legislation, a proposed action can be vetoed by a vote in either or both chambers of a legislature, or it can be implemented only with a vote of approval from both chambers. Sometimes legislative committees have veto powers. According to the NCSL:

> (f)orty-one states have some type of authority to review administrative rules, although not all of them have the power to veto rules. In the states that have veto authority, the action may be required through enactment of a statute (13 states) or passage of a resolution (15 states). State courts have heard challenges to legislative veto of administrative rules in at least 11 states, with all but two ruling that the power—or the process being used—was unconstitutional.[101]

The legislative veto is used as a means of furthering policy. Legislative intent is served presumably by allowing the full legislature or designated committees to oversee executive implementation. The veto process can steer executive agencies away from actions that are contrary to what the legislature wishes to see implemented.

Not surprisingly, executives have a less positive view of legislative vetoes. The process often delays implementation of actions because the legislature is ensured a given number of weeks to consider whether to support or veto a proposal. These vetoes are seen as giving authority to legislatures to meddle needlessly in the details of administration and, more significantly, to infringe upon the constitutional administrative powers of the executive.

A crisis seemed to develop in 1983 when the Supreme Court handed down one of its most controversial decisions, in *Immigration and*

Naturalization Service v. Chadha.[102] The case dealt with congressional veto power involving the deportation of aliens. What was significant was not that the Court struck down that legislative veto, but rather that it struck down most, if not all, such vetoes at the federal level. The Court's reasoning was simple: The Constitution provides for the House and Senate to set policy subject to veto by the president and does not allow for the opposite procedure.

Following the *Chadha* decision, Congress did not rush to adopt statutory measures or seek constitutional revisions that would reinstate the legislative veto. Instead, it dealt with matters as they arose and, in some instances, largely ignored the Court's ruling. For example, subsequent appropriation bills have included legislative vetoes. In 1996, Congress passed the Congressional Review Act, which provides a form of legislative veto of agency draft regulations.[103] Decades later, Republicans in Congress and the Trump administration sought to eliminate regulations that were imposed by past presidents, particularly Democratic ones. In attempting to do so, they invoked a little-used provision of the Congressional Review Act that permits any regulation that had not previously been submitted for review to be now submitted by the Trump administration and be subject to veto. This potentially permitted the nullification of rules that have been in place for decades.[104]

Oversight Limitations

While numerous methods of oversight are available, the organizational locus of oversight remains a problem because of the fragmentation discussed earlier. A coherent approach to oversight is not possible when committee powers overlap. Every federal agency must deal with at least one (and often more) substantive committee plus the Appropriations Committee and the Budget Committee in each chamber of Congress. That is six committees at a minimum, not counting subcommittees. These committees may disagree with each other and may not have the backing of the full legislative body. Turf battles among committees are routine. Authorizing and appropriations committees frequently compete for control of spending, including earmarks. The committees responsible for transportation policy have been particularly prone to conflict over which one gets to control local transportation projects. For example, the authorizing legislation may include specific earmarks that are substantially different from those included in the appropriations bill for the same year.[105]

One approach to overcoming fragmentation might be to concentrate oversight in a staff unit of the legislature. For example, GAO at the federal level could be given greater oversight responsibilities. GAO already attempts to assist in establishing the oversight agenda for Congress, partially through establishment of its "high risk" list of federal activities.[106] Another option would be to give oversight duties to committee staffs. The problem with these suggestions is that they tend to conflict with legislators' desire to have staff units act in subordinate and inferior capacities. For a staff unit to evaluate a program enacted by the legislative body, to find the program inadequate, and to suggest means of improving it is likely to be viewed by many legislators as an affront to their authority in setting policy. For this reason, legislative analytic units tend to be cautious in program analysis and tentative in reaching conclusions and recommendations.

A final limitation on oversight is the priorities that legislators set for themselves. Reelection is always paramount, and legislators often regard oversight activities as not contributing appreciably to their prospects for winning voter approval. In that sense, the limited oversight role performed by legislatures is seen as a completely rational response to the incentives facing them. If voters are more supportive of legislators who initiate new programs than of those who serve as watchdogs over the executive branch, legislators will respond accordingly.

Summary

A variety of factors constrain the budgetary role of legislatures. First and foremost, legislatures are representative bodies. As such, they are constrained by the methods through which individual members are selected, often by limits on their terms, and increasingly by the intense partisan nature of politics. In addition to these constraints, there are others that affect how they make budget decisions. The factors that may affect how legislatures budget include the extent of fragmentation, the role of party leadership, the amount of time available to legislate, and the availability of staff.

When the budget reaches the legislature, the availability of revenue greatly influences how the legislature approaches budget approval. Previously reached decisions, such as established entitlement programs, limit action, as do numerous socioeconomic and political factors, such as the influence of interest groups. The budget is approved through the work of substantive standing committees, appropriations committees, and revenue or finance committees. These committees hold hearings and produce draft legislation that is then considered by each legislative house. In interacting with these committees, agencies use numerous strategies in seeking approval of their budgets. An administrator's initial objective may be to obtain increased funding for a program. If that is not possible, then the administrator will concentrate on protecting the base and preventing budget cuts beyond those that constitute a fair share. Fiscal notes have become important tools for tracking the financial implications of proposed legislation. Once the legislature adopts the budget, it is sent to the chief executive for approval. In many states, chief executives make use of the line-item veto to strike individual projects or activities from the legislative budget.

Legislative oversight has become increasingly popular. Prior legislative approval of some administrative decisions may be required. Legislative investigative hearings serve the oversight function, along with detailed specification of legislative intent. Legislatures are increasingly using performance data in performing oversight, and information technology can be useful to elected officials and their staffs when seeking data on the operations of executive agencies.

Notes

1. Goldmacher, S. (2010). State again misses budget deadline. *Los Angeles Times*, June 16. Retrieved March 25, 2020, from https://www.latimes.com/archives/la-xpm-2010-jun-16-la-me-state-budget-20100616-story.html.
2. Myers, J. (2016). Remember when California's budget was always late? Here's why fiscal gridlock is a thing of the past. *Los Angeles Times*, June 18. Retrieved August 10, 2019, from https://www.latimes.com/politics/la-pol-sac-california-budget-gridlock-over-20160618-snap-story.html.
3. National Public Radio (2017). *Illinois approves spending plan, ending nation's longest budget stalemate*, July 6. Retrieved August 10, 2019, from at https://www.pbs.org/newshour/nation/illinois-vote-end-nations-longest-budget-stalemate.
4. Lienert, I. (2005). *Who controls the budget: the legislature or the executive?* IMF Working Paper. Washington, DC: International Monetary Fund; Liener, I. (2010). *Role of the legislature in budget processes*. Washington, DC: International Monetary Fund. Retrieved November 3, 2019, from https://www.imf.org/external/pubs/ft/tnm/2010/tnm1004.pdf.
5. White, L. (2019). Wisconsin Supreme Court sides with GOP lawmakers to limit Democratic governor's power. *WAMU 88.5*, June 21. Retrieved January 15, 2020, from https://www.npr.org/2019/06/21/734722167/wisconsin-supreme-court-sides-with-gop-lawmakers-to-limit-democratic-governors-p.
6. Keefe, W. J., & Ogul, M. S. (2000). *The American legislative process: Congress and the states* (10th ed.). Upper Saddle River, NJ: Prentice-Hall.
7. Kurfirst, R. (1996). Direct democracy in the sunshine state: recent challenges to Florida's citizen initiative. *Comparative State Politics, 17*, August, 1–15.
8. National Conference of State Legislatures. (2011). *Recall of state officials*. Retrieved December 12, 2011, from http://www.ncsl.org/default.aspx?tabid=16581.
9. Ballotpedia. (2019). *State legislative recalls*. Retrieved April 5, 2020, from https://ballotpedia.org/State_legislative_recalls#2019.
10. Swoboda, D. P. (1995). Accuracy and accountability in reporting local government budget activities: evidence from the newsroom and from newsmakers. *Public Budgeting & Finance, 15*, Fall, 74–90.
11. Kessler, G., Rizzo, S., & Kelly, M. (2019). President Trump has made 10,796 false or misleading claims over 869 days. *Washington Post*, June 10. Retrieved August 10, 2019, from https://www.washingtonpost.com/politics/2019/06/10/president-trump-has-made-false-or-misleading-claims-over-days/?noredirect=on&utm_term=.932ff1cfc170.
12. MacManus, S. (2004). "Bricks and mortar" politics: how infrastructure decisions defeat incumbents. *Public Budgeting & Finance, 24*, Spring, 96–112.
13. *Baker v. Carr* (1962). 369 U.S. 186; *Reynolds v. Sims* (1964). 377 U.S. 533.

14. *Reno v. Bossier Parish School Board* (1997). 520 U.S. 471.

15. Kurtz, K. (2015). Who we elect: the demographics of state legislatures. *State Legislatures Magazine*, December 2015. Retrieved August 13, 2019, from http://www.ncsl.org/research/about-state-legislatures/who-we-elect.aspx.

16. *Shaw v. Reno* (1993). 509 U.S. 630; *Miller v. Johnson* (1995). 515 U.S. 900; *Shaw v. Hunt* (1996). 517 U.S. 899; *Bush v. Vera* (1996). 517 U.S. 952.

17. Greenhouse, L. (2006). Justices uphold most remapping in Texas by G.O.P. *NY Times*, June 29, 2006. Retrieved March 25, 2020, from https://www.nytimes.com/2006/06/29/washington/29district.html; Smith, R. J. (2011). Tom Delay, former U.S. House leader, sentenced to 3 years in prison. NYtimes.com, January 10, 2011. Retrieved March 25, 2020, from https://www.nytimes.com/2011/01/11/us/politics/11delay.html.

18. Liptak, A. (2019). Supreme Court Bars Challenges to Partisan Gerrymandering. *New York Times*, June 27. Retrieved March 25, 2020, from https://www.nytimes.com/2019/06/27/us/politics/supreme-court-gerrymandering.html.

19. Ross, K. (2019). State court blocks current House districts in North Carolina for 2020 elections. *Washington Post*, October 29. Retrieved November 3, 2019, from https://www.washingtonpost.com/politics/state-court-blocks-current-house-districts-in-north-carolina-for-2020-elections/2019/10/28/cd9e8b5a-f9dc-11e9-8190-6be4deb56e01_story.html.

20. Sundquist, J. L. (1992). Constitutional reform and effective government. Washington, DC: Brookings Institution, 144–198; Axelrod, T. (2019). GOP Senators propose congressional term limits. *The Hill*, May 14. Retrieved November 3, 2019, from https://thehill.com/homenews/senate/443746-gop-senators-propose-congressional-term-limits.

21. U.S. Term Limits (2018). How many states have term limits on their legislatures? June 8. Retrieved August 13, 2019, from https://www.termlimits.com/state-legislative-term-limits/.

22. U.S. Term Limits (2017). City term limits, October 25. Retrieved August 13, 2019, from https://www.termlimits.com/city-term-limits/.

23. *U.S. Term Limits, Inc. v. Thornton* (1995). 514 U.S. 779.

24. Axelrod, T. (2019). GOP senators propose congressional term limits. *The Hill*.

25. National Association of Latino Elected Officials. (2011). *2011 Directory of Latino elected officials*. Retrieved June 6, 2011, from http://www.naleo.org/directory.html.

26. Carroll, S., & Jenkins, K. (2001). Increasing diversity or more of the same? Term limits and the representation of women, minorities, and minority women in state legislatures. Paper presented at the 2001 annual meeting of the American Political Science Association, San Francisco, CA, August 30.

27. Schraufnagel, S., & Halperin, K. (2006). Term limits, electoral competition, and representational diversity: the case of Florida. *State Politics & Policy Quarterly, 6*(4), 448–462.

28. Burgat, C. (2018). *Five reasons to oppose congressional term limits.* Washington, DC: Brookings. Retrieved November 3, 2019, from https://www.brookings.edu/blog/fixgov/2018/01/18/five-reasons-to-oppose-congressional-term-limits/.

29. National Conference of State Legislatures. (2006). Term limits erode effectiveness of legislative branch, new study finds. *NCSL.org*, August 15. Retrieved August 22, 2006, fromhttps://www.ppic.org/press-release/term-limits-eroding-effectiveness-of-state-legislature/.

30. Greenblatt, A. (2001). Term limits: crash course. *Governing*, November. Retrieved January 20, 2007, from http://www.governing.com/archive/2001/nov/term.txt (source no longer accessible).

31. Karp, J. A. (1995). Explaining public support for legislative term limits. *Public Opinion Quarterly, 59*, 373–391.

32. Nogare, C., & Ricciuti, R. (2008). *Term limits: do they really affect fiscal policy choices?* CESIFO working paper number 2199, January.

33. Asako, Y., Matsubayashi, Y., & Ueda, M. (2013). Seniority, term limits, and government spending: theory and evidence from the United States. *SSRN Electronic Journal*. DOI: 10.2139/ssrn.2105006.

34. Govtrack. (2017). Senate ideology. Retrieved March 25, 2020, from https://www.govtrack.us/congress/members/report-cards/2017/senate/ideology; Govtrack. (2017). House ideology. Retrieved March 25, 2020, from https://www.govtrack.us/congress/members/report-cards/2017/house/ideology.

35. Boulard, G. (2011). The great divide. *NCSL.org*, February. Retrieved December 12, 2011, from http://www.ncsl.org/?tabid=22082; Pfiffner, J. (2006). Partisan polarization, politics, and the presidency: structural sources of conflict. In James A. Thurber (Ed.), *Rivals for power* (3rd ed., pp. 33–58). Lanham, MD: Rowman and Littlefield.

36. National Conference of State Legislatures (2019). *2019 State and Legislative Party Composition*, February 1. Retrieved August 13, 2019, from http://www.ncsl.org/Portals/1/Documents/Elections/Legis_Control_2019_February%201st.pdf.

37. Arnold, L. W., Deen, R. E., & Patterson, S. C. (2000). Friendship and votes: the impact of interpersonal ties on legislative decision making. *State and Local Government Review, 32*, 142–147.

38. Jewell, M. E., & Whicker, M. L. (1994). *Legislative leadership in the American states*. Ann Arbor, MI: University of Michigan Press.

39. Clucas, R. A. (2001). Principal-agent theory and the power of state house speakers. *Legislative Studies Quarterly, 26*, May, 319–338.

40. National Conference of State Legislatures (2019). *2019 State and Legislative Party Composition*, February 1. Retrieved August 13, 2019, from http://www.ncsl.org/Portals/1/Documents/Elections/Legis_Control_2019_February%201st.pdf.

41. Cox, C. W., & Kernell, S. (Eds.). (1991). *The politics of divided government*. Boulder, CO: Westview Press.

42. Goodwin, G., Jr. (1970). *The little legislatures: committees of Congress.* Amherst, MA: University of Massachusetts Press; Deering, C., & Smith, S. (1997). *Committees in Congress.* Washington, DC: CQ Press.

43. National Conference of State Legislatures (2019). *2019 state and legislative partisan composition.*

44. Council of State Governments (2019). *The book of the states*, Table 3.23, Standing Committees Appointment and Number. Retrieved January 15, 2020, from http://knowledgecenter.csg.org/kc/system/files/3.23.2019.pdf.

45. Gryski, G. S. (1991). The influence of committee position on federal program spending. *Polity, 23,* 443–459.

46. Council of State Governments (2019). *The book of the states*, Table 3.2, Legislative Sessions: legal provisions. Retrieved January 15, 2020, from http://knowledgecenter.csg.org/kc/system/files/3.2.2019.pdf.

47. North Carolina General Assembly (2019). *Legislative Calendar.* Retrieved November 5, 2019, from https://www.ncleg.gov/LegislativeCalendar/.

48. The website of the California State Treasurer includes a comparison of California's bond rating with the ratings of other states. See State of California Treasurer, Public Finance Division, Comparison of Other States' General Obligation Bond Ratings. Retrieved July 24, 2019, from https://www.treasurer.ca.gov/ratings/current.asp.

49. National Conference of State Legislatures, (2018). *2018 Legislator Compensation Information*, April 16. Retrieved August 14, 2019, from http://www.ncsl.org/research/about-state-legislatures/legislator-compensation-2018.aspx.

50. Joyce, P. (2011). *The Congressional Budget Office: honest numbers, power, and policymaking* (p. 26). Washington, DC: Georgetown University Press.

51. Chadha, A., et al. (2001). The consequences of independence: functions and resources of state legislative fiscal offices. *State and Local Government Review, 33,* Fall, 202–207.

52. National Conference of State Legislatures (2017). *Full- and part-time legislatures*, June 14. Retrieved August 14, 2019, from http://www.ncsl.org/research/about-state-legislatures/full-and-part-time-legislatures.aspx.

53. Mahtesian, C. (1997). The sick legislature syndrome. *Governing, 10,* February, 16–20.

54. Loftus, E. (1994). The art of legislative politics. *Congressional Quarterly Press*, 61–75; Gill, J. (1995). Formal models of legislative/administrative interaction: a survey of the subfield. *Public Administration Review, 55,* 99–106.

55. Ballotpedia (2020). Dates of 2020 State Legislative Sessions. Retrieved April 3, 2020, from https://ballotpedia.org/Dates_of_2020_state_legislative_.

56. National Conferences of State Legislatures (2006). *Legislative budget procedure: a guide to appropriations and budget processes in the states, commonwealths and territories.* Retrieved August 21, 2006, from http://www.ncsl.org/programs/fiscal/ibptabls/index.htm.

57. Council of State Governments (2019). *The book of the states 2019*, Table 4.4, the Governors: Powers. Retrieved January 15, 2020, from http://knowledgecenter.csg.org/kc/system/files/4.4.2019.pdf.

58. Stewart, E. (2018). State legislatures Democrats have flipped so far in the 2018 elections. *Vox.* Retrieved March 20, 2020, from https://www.vox.com/policy-and-politics/2018/11/7/18071410/democrat-state-legislature-colorado-minnesota-election-results; 2019 Virginia General Election Results. *New York Times.* Retrieved November 6, 2019, from https://www.nytimes.com/interactive/2019/11/05/us/elections/results-virginia-general-elections.html.

59. Clynch, E. J., & Lauth, T. P. (Eds.). (1991). *Governors, legislatures, and budgets.*

60. Payne, J. L. (1991). *The culture of spending: why Congress lives beyond our means.* San Francisco, CA: ICS Press; Klingensmith, J. Z. (2019). Using tax dollars for re-election: the impact of pork-barrel spending on electoral success. *Constitutional Political Economy, (30)*1, 31–49.

61. Fiorina, M. (1989). *Congress: keystone of the Washington establishment* (2nd ed.). New Haven, CT: Yale University Press.

62. National Association of State Budget Officers (2011). *Fiscal survey of the states.* Retrieved March 3, 2012, from https://higherlogicdownload.s3.amazonaws.com/NASBO/9d2d2db1-c943-4f1b-b750-0fca152d64c2/UploadedImages/Fiscal%20Survey/Spring%202011%20Fiscal%20Survey.pdf.

63. National Association of State Budget Officers (2019). *Fiscal survey of the states*, Spring. Retrieved August 14, 2019, from https://higherlogicdownload.s3.amazonaws.com/NASBO/9d2d2db1-c943-4f1b-b750-0fca152d64c2/UploadedImages/Fiscal%20Survey/NASBO_Spring_2019_Fiscal_Survey_of_States_-_S.pdf, pp. 10–11.

64. Golshen, T. (2019). Trump said he wouldn't cut Medicaid, Social Security, and Medicare. His 2020 budget cuts all 3. *Vox*, March 12. Retrieved March 25, 2020, from https://www.vox.com/policy-and-politics/2019/3/12/18260271/trump-medicaid-social-security-medicare-budget-cuts/.

65. Clark, D. (2019). Trump signs massive two-year budget deal into law. *NBC News*, August 2. Retrieved November 6, 2019, from https://www.nbcnews.com/politics/politics-news/trump-signs-massive-two-year-budget-deal-law-n1038786.

66. Bland, R. L. (2013). *A budgeting guide for local governments* (3rd ed.). Washington, DC: International City/County Management Association.

67. Ebdon, C., & Franklin, A. (2006). Citizen participation in budgeting theory. *Public Administration Review, 66,* 437–447.

68. Dobel, J. P. (1995). Managerial leadership in divided times. *Administration and Society, 26,* 488–514.

69. Rosenbaum, D. (2002). Official forced to step down after testifying on budget cut. *New York Times*, March 7, A22.

70. Johnson, C. M. (1992). *The dynamics of conflict between bureaucrats and legislators.* Armonk, NY: M. E. Sharpe.

71. Johnson, B. (1989). The OMB budget examiner and the congressional budget process. *Public Budgeting & Finance, 9*, Spring, 5–14.

72. Wildavsky, A., & Caiden N. (2000). *The new politics of the budgetary process* (4th ed., pp. 47–55, 59–64). New York, NY: Longman.

73. Wildavsky, A. (1988). *The new politics of the budgetary process* (p. 115). Glenview, IL: Scott Foresman and Company.

74. Meyers, R. T. (1994). *Strategic budgeting.* Ann Arbor, MI: University of Michigan Press.

75. Salamon, L. T. (2002). *The tools of government: a guide for the new governance.* Baltimore, MD: Johns Hopkins Press.

76. Stanford, K. A. (1992). State budget deliberations: do legislators have a strategy? *Public Administration Review, 52,* 16–26.

77. *Unfunded Mandates Reform Act of 1995* (P.L. 104-4). For a discussion of CBO's role in implementing the act, see Joyce, P. (2011). *The Congressional Budget Office,* 114–117.

78. McNichol, E., Lav, I., & Masterson, K. (2015). *Better cost estimates, better budgets: improved fiscal notes would help states make more informed decisions.* Center on Budget and Policy Priorities. Retrieved March 25, 2020, from https://www.cbpp.org/research/state-budget-and-tax/better-cost-estimates-better-budgets.

79. Zaccarina, J., & Zhou, L. (2019). The astonishing effects of the shutdown, in 8 charts. *Vox,* January 14. Retrieved August 15, 2019, from https://www.vox.com/policy-and-politics/2019/1/11/18177101/government-shutdown-longest-workers-agencies-charts.

80. Rappepoprt, A., & Appelbaum, B. (2019). Government shutdown cost U.S. economy $11 Billion, C.B.O. says. *New York Times,* January 28. Retrieved January 15, 2020, from https://www.nytimes.com/2019/01/28/us/politics/shutdown-cost-us-economy-11-billion-cbo-says.html.

81. O'Connor, J., & Tareen, S. (2017). Illinois approves spending plan, ending nation's longest budget stalemate. *PBS Newshour,* July 6. Retrieved March 25, 2020, from www.pbs.org/newshour/nation/illinois-vote-end-nations-longest-budget-stalemate.

82. U.S. Office of Management and Budget (2019). *Legislative coordination and clearance, Circular A-19.* Retrieved July 24, 2019, from https://www.whitehouse.gov/wp-content/uploads/2017/11/Circular-019.pdf.

83. National Association of State Budget Officers (2015). *Budget processes in the states,* Spring, 49.

84. American Legislative Exchange Council. (2016). *Item-reduction veto constitutional amendment.* Retrieved March 25, 2020, from https://www.alec.org/model-policy/item-reduction-veto-constitutional-amendment-2/.

85. Abney, G., & Lauth, T. P. (1985). The line-item veto in the states. *Public Administration Review, 45,* 372–377; Lauth, T. P. (1996). The line-item veto in government budgeting. *Public Budgeting & Finance, 16,* 97–111.

86. Alm, J., & Evers, M. (1991). The item veto and state government expenditures. *Public Choice, 68,* 1–15; Berch, N. (1992). The item veto in the states: an analysis of the effects over time. *Social Science Quarterly, 29,* 335–346; Thompson, P., & Boyd, S. R. (1994). Use of the item veto in Texas, 1940–1990. *State and Local Government Review, 26,* 38–45.

87. Lee, R. D., Jr. (2000). State item veto legal issues in the 1990s. *Public Budgeting & Finance, 20,* Summer, 49–73.

88. Bellamy, C. (1989). Item veto: dangerous constitutional tinkering. *Public Administration Review, 49,* 46–51; Sundquist, J. (1992). Constitutional reform and effective government, 281–294. For the Obama proposal, see Office of Management and Budget (2011). *Budget of the United States government: fiscal year 2012, analytical perspectives,* 156–157. Retrieved December 15, 2011, from http://www.whitehouse.gov/omb/budget/overview. For the Trump proposal, see Nelson, L. (2018). Trump, unhappy with omnibus bill, calls on Congress to reinstate line-item veto, *Politico,* May 23. Retrieved August 18, 2019, from https://www.politico.com/story/2018/03/23/trump-line-item-veto-482192.

89. Line Item Veto Act of 1996 (P.L. 104-130).

90. Joyce, P. G. (1998). The line item veto act: after the Supreme Court decision, what's next? *Public Budgeting & Finance, 18,* Winter, 3–21.

91. Aberbach, J. B. (1990). *Keeping a watchful eye: the politics of congressional oversight.* Washington, DC: Brookings Institution; Evans, D. (1994). Congressional oversight and the diversity of members' goals. *Political Science Quarterly, 109,* 669–687.

92. Lewis, B. J., & Ellefson, P. V. (1996). Evaluating information flows to policy committees in state legislatures. *Evaluation Review, 20,* 29–48.

93. Rakich, N. (2018). We've never seen congressional resignations like this before. *Fivethirtyeight.com,* January 18. Retrieved January 29, 2020, from https://fivethirtyeight.com/features/more-people-are-resigning-from-congress-than-at-any-time-in-recent-history/.

94. Bauer, S. (2011). Scott Walker's collective bargaining law keeping Wisconsin unions from seeking recertification. *Huffington Post,* September 22. Retrieved December 12, 2011, from http://www.huffingtonpost.com/2011/09/22/scott-walker-collective-bargaining_n_976376.html; Kornblut, A., & Wallsten, P. (2011). In Ohio collective-bargaining vote, Democrats see some hope for 2012. *Washington Post,* November 9. Retrieved December 12, 2011, from http://www.washingtonpost.com/politics/in-ohio-collective-bargaining-vote-democrats-see-some-hope-for-2012/2011/11/09/gIQAJzll6M_story.html.

95. Should Congress take the gray wolf off the endangered species list? (2011). *Washington Post,* April 12. Retrieved March 3, 2012, from http://www.washingtonpost.com/opinions/should-congress-takethe-gray-wolf-off-the-endangered-species-list/2011/04/12/AFp9SlSD_story.html.

96. Walton, K. S., & Brown, R. E. (1990). State legislators and state auditors: is there an inherent role conflict? *Public Budgeting & Finance, 10,* Spring, 3–12.

97. See the websites of the Joint Legislative Audit and Review Commission, Commonwealth of Virginia, at http://jlarc .state.va.us, and of the Office of Program Policy Analysis and Government Accountability, State of Florida, at www.oppaga.state.fl.us.

98. Havens, H. S. (1990). *The evolution of the General Accounting Office: from voucher audits to program evaluations*. Washington, DC: U.S. Government Printing Office; National Academy of Public Administration (1994). *The roles, mission and operation of the U.S. General Accounting Office*. Washington, DC: U.S. Government Printing Office.

99. Denniston, L. (2002). GAO sues for access to Cheney records. *Boston Globe*, February 23, A1.

100. Gibson, M. L. (1992). *Weapons of influence: the legislative veto, American foreign policy, and the irony of reform*. Boulder, CO: Westview Press.

101. National Conference of State Legislatures (2020). *Separation of powers—legislative oversight*. Retrieved January 15, 2020, from http://www.ncsl.org/research /about-state-legislatures/separation-of-powers-legislative -oversight.aspx#Veto.

102. *Immigration and Naturalization Service v. Chadha* (1983). 462 U.S. 919.

103. Congressional Review Act of 1996 (P.L. 104-121).

104. Larking, P. J. (2018). The Trump Administration and the Congressional Review Act. *Georgetown Journal of Law & Public Policy* 16, Summer, 505–520; Scott, D. (2018). The new Republican plan to deregulate America, explained. *Vox*, April 25. Retrieved March 25, 2020, from https://www.vox.com/policy-and-politics /2018/4/25/17275566/congressional-review-act-what -regulations-has-trump-cut.

105. Schick, A. (2007). *The federal budget: politics, policy, process* (3rd ed.). Washington, DC: Brookings Institution.

106. U.S. Government Accountability Office (2019). *High risk list*. Retrieved August 20, 2019, from https://www.gao .gov/highrisk/overview.

CHAPTER 10

Budget Approval: The U.S. Congress

The United States Congress is perhaps the most powerful legislature in the world. Relative to the budget process, the Congress has unique powers and capacities, in particular because the U.S. Constitution provides that money cannot be raised or spent without first being approved by the Congress. The special case of the U.S. Congress necessitates that we devote an entire chapter on its role in the budget process, which in turn requires a discussion of the peculiarities of the federal budget process in general.

Even casual observers of federal policy in recent years will have noticed the general dysfunction of decision making, and the budget process has been at center stage in that dysfunction. Since 2013, there have been four government shutdowns, including one in late 2017 and early 2018 that was the longest in history, lasting 35 days. Besides the problems that these shutdowns cause for those who rely on government for support, they hardly inspire confidence in the ability of the Congress to address the nation's problems. In addition, these shutdowns are costly to the taxpayer. An analysis by the Senate of the FY2014, 2018, and 2019 shutdowns estimated the cost to taxpayers as at least $4 billion in back pay to furloughed workers and additional administrative costs. Those estimates were only partial, as several large government agencies could not give the Senate committee any estimates.[1] A later estimate from the Congressional Budget Office put the estimate for the 2018/19 shutdown alone at $11 billion.[2] Government shutdowns, however, are only the tip of the iceberg. The last time that the federal government had all of its appropriations on time was more than two decades ago, for fiscal year 1997. It is no wonder, given this performance, that many view the federal budget process to be fundamentally broken.

The chapter has four sections. The first section reviews the legal underpinnings of the modern budget process by reviewing the main laws that affect the current operations of the budget process, including the Budget and Accounting Act of 1921, the Congressional Budget and Impoundment Control Act of 1974, and the various deficit-based budget process reforms beginning in 1985 with the Gramm-Rudman-Hollings reform and continuing through the Budget Control Act of 2011. The second section reviews the timetable for the resulting budget process, from presidential budget submission to budget resolution to committee action, including reconciliation, authorizations, and appropriations. The third section discusses the biggest current problems and challenges facing the budget process. The chapter concludes by discussing a variety of possible reforms that have been suggested that might improve both the budget process and budget outcomes.

Evolution of the Federal Budget Process

The federal budget process has evolved since the early part of the twentieth century as it has been used to achieve particular objectives and to solve particular problems. For that reason, understanding this history is crucial to demystifying the budget process. Most of the current procedures result from two laws: the Budget and Accounting Act of 1921 and the Congressional Budget and Impoundment Control Act of 1974. In addition, there were a number of deficit-based budget reforms (such as the Gramm-Rudman-Hollings law in 1985, the Budget Enforcement Act in 1990, and the Budget Control Act in 2011) over roughly a quarter decade after the mid-1980s. The first of these laws, the Budget and Accounting Act of 1921, had three main purposes. First, it created a requirement that the president submit a budget to Congress each year. Prior to the Budget and Accounting Act, federal agencies submitted their budget estimates directly to Congress. Second, it created the Bureau of the Budget (now the Office of Management and Budget) to assist the president in preparing the budget.[3] Third, it created the General Accounting Office (now the Government Accountability Office), initially to help control agency spending but later to do programmatic and performance audits of federal agencies and programs.[4]

Congress, like the legislatures discussed in the chapter on budget approval, conducts its work in committees. Subcommittees are especially important in the appropriations process. One group of committees, as explained in the chapter on budget approval and the legislature, has responsibility for substantive legislation. These committees develop authorizing legislation, which establishes departments and agencies and the programs they operate. An authorization provides a dollar amount as a ceiling for spending. Approval to commit the government to spend, however, is given through the appropriations process.[5]

Another set of committees provides the wherewithal for the government to operate.[6] The Ways and Means Committee in the House and the Finance Committee in the Senate fashion legislation that generates revenue for the government. In addition to being responsible for tax legislation, these committees are responsible for some substantive measures with dedicated revenue sources, such as Social Security and Medicare. They handle legislation permitting increases in the federal debt. Such legislation is necessary because the government typically accumulates debt by spending more than it collects in revenues (see discussion on annual deficits and national debt in the chapter on government and the economy). Raising the debt limit is a sensitive matter, partially because members of Congress assume that voting for debt increases is itself evidence of fiscal irresponsibility.

The Ways and Means Committee, as of 2020, included 42 of the 435 members of the House, and the Finance Committee included 28 of the 100 members of the Senate. The number of seats held by each party on the committees is generally proportional to total party membership in the chambers.

Discretionary, or nonentitlement, spending is under the aegis of the Appropriations Committee in each house.[7] In 2020, there were 53 members on the House committee and 31 on the Senate committee. The spending side of the budget is currently divided among 12 subcommittees in the House and the same number in the Senate that report out appropriation bills. Appropriations permit agencies to commit the government to expenditures, with some spending occurring in subsequent budget years as a result of contracts signed in the current year.

Starting in the 1940s, two major problems with this process became abundantly clear. First, because Congress dealt with the budget through a variety of bills, the budget was handled piecemeal, making it difficult to set comprehensive policy. This problem became particularly acute after the 1960s because the passage of new mandatory spending programs such as Medicare and Medicaid (along with the already existing entitlement for Social Security) meant that a larger and larger portion of the budget was made outside of the annual appropriations process. Second, the piecemeal approach meant that various subcommittees, committees, and the two chambers had to exercise discipline over themselves to complete their work in time for the beginning of the fiscal year. The delays in the budget process created unpredictability and disruptions in funding for federal agencies and recipients of federal funds. These twin problems—the lack of a comprehensive approach to the budget and the lack of timely action—led many to call for fundamental changes in the budget process.

The other factor that brought budget reforms to the forefront in the early 1970s was a political disagreement over spending priorities between the president and the Congress. As a means of controlling spending, President Richard Nixon vetoed appropriation bills on the grounds that they included too much spending, but that action pleased neither Congress nor the agencies that were covered by the bills. Later in his administration, Nixon went ahead and signed the bills but refused to spend all of the money, a process known as impoundment. The lack of a coordinating mechanism for the budget, combined with a desire to limit impoundments, led to passage of the Congressional Budget and Impoundment Control Act of 1974.[8]

The 1974 Budget Reform

The 1974 reform legislation had many objectives. One objective was to provide Congress with a means for controlling the budget as a whole—namely, taking a comprehensive view of spending, including not only all appropriation bills but legislation affecting mandatory spending as well, and linking spending with revenue measures. Controlling the budget as a whole was seen as essential if Congress was to influence economic policy. Resolving conflict between Congress and the president was another important objective that required dealing with the impoundment problem. Members of Congress wished to assert their policy-making role vis-à-vis the presidency. A process was needed by which Congress could complete its work on the budget by the beginning of the fiscal year.

Taken as a whole, the Budget Act of 1974 had four main effects. First, it created a new mechanism, the budget resolution, to express the overall will of Congress on budget issues. Second, it created Budget Committees to marshal the budget resolution through Congress. Third, it created the Congressional Budget Office, a new agency intended to provide Congress with information on the budget and the economy. Fourth, it changed the start of the fiscal year from July 1 to October 1. Finally, it established a new procedure for dealing with presidential impoundments.[9]

The Budget Resolution

Under the procedures established by the Budget Act of 1974, Congress would adopt a concurrent budget resolution that established the overall outline of the budget (a concurrent resolution is an action that is taken by both houses of Congress that does not require the president's signature). The resolution would represent a "blueprint" for the budget, showing aggregate budget numbers—revenues, budget authority (the authority to commit the government to spend money), outlays (the actual spending of funds out of the Treasury), the overall target (budget deficit or surplus, if any), and government debt.

Following passage of the concurrent resolution in the spring, Congress then reverted to its old procedures. Committees in Congress needed to adopt individual pieces of legislation affecting revenues and spending within the constraints imposed by the budget resolution. Subcommittees of the Appropriations Committees considered specific appropriation bills, and the revenue committees considered their portion of the budget. The budget resolution also was permitted to include reconciliation instructions. Reconciliation is a process in which committees are instructed to adjust spending and revenue measures upward or downward to conform to the overall budget plan. The beginning of the fiscal year was shifted from July 1 to October 1, thereby giving Congress three additional months for its annual budgetary work.

The Budget Committees

To provide for coordination among the various components of Congress, the 1974 law established House and Senate Budget Committees. Initially the members of these committees tended to come from the other committees that controlled taxes and spending, but increasingly committee membership has tended toward more junior members, especially in the House. As of 2020, there were 36 members on the House Budget Committee and 21 on the Senate Budget Committee. The budget committees were to serve two functions. First, they had jurisdiction over the development of the budget resolution itself, putting them in the center of macro-level budget policy. Second, they were to serve as watchdogs, making sure that legislation was not substantially at variance with the resolution, although they lacked authority to overrule other committees. The resolution could be enforced through points of order, which would make legislation not consistent with the resolution more difficult to enact.

The Congressional Budget Office

The law also provided Congress with additional staff support by creating the Congressional Budget Office (CBO) to serve as overall staff to the Budget Committees, the other four money committees, and any other committees or individuals in Congress that need assistance in the area of budgeting. CBO's charge was to serve Congress in a nonpartisan manner.[10] Given that charge, CBO decided that it would refrain from providing policy recommendations. It was to play three main roles:

1. Developing the budget baseline (a current services estimate) that would prove to be the starting point for the resolution;
2. Estimating the costs of proposed legislation; and
3. Conducting policy research on issues before Congress.[11]

The CBO currently has a staff of about 250. It has had 10 directors from its creation through 2019: Alice Rivlin, Rudolph Penner, Robert Reischauer, June O'Neill, Dan Crippen, Douglas Holtz-Eakin, Peter Orszag, Douglas Elmendorf, Keith Hall, and Phillip Swagel, who was named director in May 2019.

Impoundment Control

Prior to the passage of the 1974 legislation, the Nixon administration claimed it was simply following in the footsteps of virtually every president since Thomas Jefferson in deciding not to spend all of the funds that were appropriated.[12] The Anti-Deficiency Act of 1950, allowing the executive to establish agency reserves in the apportionment process (see the chapter on budget execution), was used as further justification for impounding monies.[13]

The Congressional Budget and Impoundment Control Act represented a compromise between the legislative and executive branches, albeit one that the Nixon administration was forced to accept. Two forms of impoundments were permitted: rescissions and deferrals. When, in the judgment of the president, part of or all the funds of a given appropriation were not needed, a rescission proposal (a proposal to cancel budget authority already provided) was to be made to Congress. The rescission would not take effect unless approved by Congress within 45 working days. The other type of impoundment, deferral, was a proposal to delay obligations or expenditures. Like rescissions, deferral proposals had to be submitted to Congress, but they became effective unless either the House or the Senate passed a resolution disapproving them. In 2020, impoundment control took center stage in the attempt to impeach President Donald Trump, as the Government Accountability Office argued that his withholding of military funds to Ukraine represented an unlawful impoundment as defined by the act.[14]

Deficit-Focused Budget Reforms

While the 1921 Budget and Accounting Act and the 1974 Congressional Budget Act established a framework for presidential submission and congressional consideration of the budget, there was nothing about these laws that attempted to force the President and Congress to address overall fiscal imbalances. Therefore, when large deficits began to emerge in the early 1980s as a result of both an early-1980s recession and tax cuts and increases in defense spending pushed by the administration of President Ronald Reagan, there was a move in the Congress to adjust the budget process to address these deficits.

Gramm-Rudman-Hollings

In 1985, both because of yearly deficits and because of the resulting need to raise the nation's borrowing limit, or debt ceiling, the Congress adopted the Balanced Budget and Emergency Deficit Control Act of 1985.[15] The chief authors were Senators W. Philip Gramm (R-TX), Warren B. Rudman (R-NH), and Ernest F. Hollings (D-SC). The main objective of Gramm-Rudman-Hollings was simple: to reduce the size of the budget deficit annually until expenditures were in balance with revenues. Target figures were set, and if the president and Congress could not reach agreement on a budget package that met the target figure for a given fiscal year, then automatic across-the-board reductions in expenditures were to occur—a process known as sequestration. Senator Rudman described the law as "a bad idea whose time has come."[16] The law later was revised as a result of a legal challenge. The main effect of the amended law was to delay the goal for balancing the budget from fiscal year 1991 to fiscal year 1993.[17]

Gramm-Rudman-Hollings created a new procedure—called sequestration—that was to impose budget reductions if budget deficit targets were not reached. Some cuts were to be taken from appropriated spending and some from mandatory spending. Of the appropriated cuts, half were apportioned to defense and the other half to domestic programs. On the mandatory side, special rules, limiting the reach of sequestration, applied to some domestic programs, such as Medicare and guaranteed student loans. Other parts of the budget were totally protected from sequestration. These included the basic retirement program under Social Security, Aid to Families with Dependent Children, civil service retirement funds, and the like.

The 1980s closed without Gramm-Rudman-Hollings having appreciably affected the government's overall budget outlook.[18] In fact, the Gramm-Rudman-Hollings targets were routinely met by basing presidential budgets and congressional budget resolutions on unrealistically optimistic economic assumptions. Nothing in the act required the president and the Congress to do anything when (invariably) these projections did not come true. This led to a second attempt in the 1990s to address the deficit through deciding on spending cuts and tax increases and using the budget process to enforce these changes.

Changes in the 1990s: The Budget Enforcement Act

President George H. W. Bush was elected in 1988 and almost immediately faced a rapidly deteriorating budget outlook. While the process limped along under the Gramm-Rudman-Hollings Act during 1989, by late summer 1990, the budget situation had reached another crisis stage. If Congress were to live within the constraints imposed by Gramm-Rudman-Hollings, it would have required a massive reduction in the deficit in a single year. Because this result was not credible or possible, political leaders of both parties became convinced that another approach to deficit reduction was necessary. A budget "summit" was held between Bush administration officials and key members of Congress in late 1990, which ultimately resulted in the passage of the Omnibus Budget Reconciliation Act of 1990 (OBRA 1990). OBRA 1990 included a combination of revenue increases, reductions in mandatory spending, and budget enforcement procedures estimated to reduce cumulative deficits by almost $500 billion between FY1991 and FY1995.[19]

The Budget Enforcement Act (BEA), which was established by Title XIII of OBRA 1990, provided for a new budget process that shifted emphasis away from fixed annual targets for the budget deficit. In effect, it was based on the premise that Congress had little control over the total annual deficit and that the emphasis should therefore be on those areas over which control was possible. Entitlement program expenditures were allowed to fluctuate according to shifts in the eligibility pools. The law also exempted the budget from emergencies.[20] Spending limits, or caps, were set for the discretionary portion of the budget. These caps were considered to be reductions in the deficit because they did not allow discretionary spending to grow as fast as inflation.

The BEA also created a pay-as-you-go (PAYGO) process affecting laws governing revenues and entitlement programs. The PAYGO system required that, in a given Congress, the overall effect of policies that would expand entitlement spending or decrease revenues relative to the baseline should be deficit-neutral. In practice, it was intended to focus attention not only on the cost of the policy change but also on tradeoffs with existing tax or spending programs. PAYGO gave an advantage to those programs already budgeted and made difficult the inclusion of new or expanded initiatives. The BEA, along with OBRA 1990, successfully kept the budget process under control through the 1992 presidential election, a primary objective of many political leaders. Members of Congress came to the realization that whatever proposals they wished to advance, a price was to be placed on them. Neither tax cuts nor spending increases could be advocated without taking into account their effects on the overall deficit.

OBRA 1990, while it did not promise a balanced budget, was projected to put the budget on a path to that budgetary promised land. But while a CBO analysis done immediately after the passage of OBRA 1990 projected a deficit of only $29 billion by fiscal year 1995, an analysis done only 13 months later projected a deficit in excess of $200 billion by mid-decade.[21] This deterioration resulted from the effects of economic recession, not because of any policy actions. Because the deficit had not been eradicated as promised, there were two more efforts in the 1990s to build on and extend the procedures agreed to in the BEA in order to continue to address the deficits.

The first of these was the Omnibus Budget Reconciliation Act of 1993, adopted in August 1993. This bill was notable because, unlike OBRA 1990 that was passed with bipartisan support, this legislation was passed without any Republican votes (neither on the reconciliation bill nor on the budget resolution that preceded it) and with considerable pressure applied by Republican members to have their Democratic colleagues join them in opposition. The law included a combination of additional tax increases (especially in individual income taxes for the wealthiest Americans), spending cuts (with some increases), and an extension of the discretionary caps and PAYGO process through fiscal year 1998.[22]

The second revision of the BEA occurred after the Congress was taken over by the Republicans in the November 1994 elections (in the case of the House, the Republicans had not been in control for 40 years). There was a period of intense conflict between President Clinton and the Congress in 1995 and 1996 that led to two government shutdowns ostensibly over how much and how fast to cut spending. After President Clinton was re-elected in 1996, however, there was a third deficit-focused reconciliation bill, building on the 1990 and 1993 efforts. In May 1997, President Clinton and the Republican leadership in Congress agreed on the outline for a package of decisions that was supposed to balance the budget by 2002.[23] The agreement was followed by passage of two key laws—the Balanced Budget Act (a set of spending cuts in mandatory spending and an extension of the discretionary caps and PAYGO through fiscal year 2002) and the Taxpayer Relief Act (a tax cut)—both of which were signed by President Clinton at a special ceremony on August 5, 1997.

The sustained growth of the economy that continued into the late 1990s accelerated the timetable for the achievement of surpluses. Fueled in large part by increases in federal revenues (which grew by an average of 8.4% per year between fiscal years 1995 and 2000 with no changes in rates), the budget surplus arrived a full 4 years earlier than had been projected. The federal government ran a unified budget surplus of $69 billion in fiscal year 1998. The surplus, which was the first since FY1969, grew to $129 billion in 1999 and to $236 billion in 2000.[24] The arrival of surpluses—and a projection that these surpluses would continue through the first decade of the 2000s—paved the way for a pair of tax cuts enacted by Congress and implemented by the George W. Bush administration in 2001 and 2003.

The Return of Deficits and the Budget Control Act of 2011

The recession that started in 2001, coupled with increases in defense spending that occurred after the attacks of September 11, 2001, led to a return of deficits in fiscal year 2002. While deficits continued through the first decade of the 2000s, the Great Recession had a substantial effect on the deficit outlook. The lowered economic output reduced tax revenues, especially for the individual and corporate income taxes. On the spending side, a combination of increases in spending for automatic stabilizers—such as unemployment compensation, Medicaid, and food assistance under the Supplemental Nutrition Assistance Program (formerly food stamps)—increased budget deficits. In addition, however, Congress and the president took a series of legislative actions to combat the recession, with the stated goal of warding off another depression (see discussion in the chapter on government and the economy). These included a bailout of financial institutions and other sectors as a result of the Troubled Asset Relief Program; the passage of an economic stimulus package called the American Recovery and

Reinvestment Act; and the bailout by the federal government of the mortgage giants Fannie Mae and Freddie Mac, which had guaranteed a large number of subprime mortgages and compounded that exposure by making risky investments of their own, and ultimately had to be taken over by the government.[25]

The deficits that resulted from the combination of the Great Recession and these policy changes, and the need to enact legislation to extend the Bush tax cuts (which had been scheduled to expire) and to again raise the debt ceiling, led to the passage of the Budget Control Act of 2011, which was the first deficit-focused budget reform law passed since 1997. The Budget Control Act created new discretionary spending caps, covering fiscal years 2013 to 2021. It also created a new committee, the Joint Select Committee on Deficit Reduction. This "supercommittee," as it came to be called, was a committee of 12 members (six from each house, and six from each party) tasked to identify an additional $1.5 trillion in deficit savings by November 23, 2011. The supercommittee's recommendations were to be voted on, without amendment, by the rest of Congress. Absent an agreement on at least $1.2 trillion in savings, further reductions in the spending caps would kick in. This occurred when the supercommittee announced that it had failed to reach agreement.[26]

Table 10-1 shows the trend in deficits and surpluses for the federal government from fiscal

Table 10-1 Federal Deficits and Surpluses, Fiscal Year 1985 Through Fiscal Year 2019 ($ billions)

Fiscal Year	Surplus or Deficit
1985	−212
1986	−221
1987	−150
1988	−155
1989	−153
1990	−221

(continues)

Table 10-1 Federal Deficits and Surpluses, Fiscal Year 1985 Through
Fiscal Year 2019 ($ billions) *(continued)*

Fiscal Year	Surplus or Deficit
1991	−269
1992	−290
1993	−255
1994	−203
1995	−164
1996	−107
1997	−22
1998	69
1999	126
2000	236
2001	128
2002	−158
2003	−378
2004	−413
2005	−318
2006	−248
2007	−161
2008	−459
2009	−1,413
2010	−1,294
2011	−1,296
2012	−1,077
2013	−680
2014	−485
2015	−442
2016	−585
2017	−665
2018	−779
2019	−985

Congressional Budget Office (2019). *The budget and economic outlook: fiscal years 2020–2030* (p. 150).

Table 10-2 Comparing Discretionary Spending Caps under the Budget Control Act to Actual Budget Authority (billions)

Fiscal Year	Original Budget Control Act Caps	Actual Budget Authority	Difference
2013	$1,090.0	$1,140.2	+$50.2
2014	$1115.0	$1,133.7	+$18.7
2015	$1,138.0	$1,116.7	−$21.3
2016	$1,161.0	$1,166.7	+$5.7
2017	$1,188.0	$1,220.0	+$32.0
2018	$1,216.0	$1,422.8	+$206.8
2019	$1,246.0	$1.321.0	+$75.0
2020	$1,276.0	$1,370.0	+$94.0
2021	$1,306.0	$1,372.0	+66.0
Total 2013–2021	**$10,736.0**	**$11,263.1**	**+$527.1**

year 1985 through fiscal year 2019. The table clearly demonstrates the rise in the deficit, the four years of budget surplus from 1998 through 2001, the return of the deficit after 2002, and the explosion of deficits after the Great Recession. The table does not include estimates of deficits from 2020 and beyond that will be affected by the federal response to COVID-19, although estimates are that the 2020 deficit alone may approach $4 trillion.[27]

The Budget Control Act caps were very tight and would have required large cuts in defense and nondefense spending relative to the baseline. In reality, however, the Congress has just routinely increased these caps, including finally reaching an agreement in the summer of 2019 that raised the caps for the remaining two years—2020 and 2021.[28] In point of fact, then, the Budget Control Act has been a massive failure with respect to its stated intentions, as is obvious from **Table 10-2**, which shows the original (post-supercommittee failure) caps compared to actual spending (through 2018) and projected spending through 2021 with the caps raised for those years (positive numbers indicate higher actual budget authority than in

the original caps). The revision of the caps has added more than half a trillion dollars to deficits over these 9 fiscal years.

The Resulting Congressional Timetable

When put together, laws prescribe the rules and the timetable for enacting the federal budget each year. This section of the chapter summarizes the steps in the budget process as a chronology of events. Each year, the budget process begins (not quite in earnest, but it begins) with the president's budget submission in early February. It continues (with luck) only until October 1, with all appropriations enacted prior to the start of the fiscal year. Almost always (specifically, in 40 of the 43 years between 1977 and 2019), the process continues beyond October 1, as one or more bills fail to become law by the statutory deadline. **Table 10-3** shows the timetable for budgetary action as applied to the fiscal year 2020 budget process.

Table 10-3 Federal Budget Process Timetable, Fiscal Year 2020

Date	Action to Be Completed
Between the first Monday in January and the first Monday in February	President transmits the budget
Six weeks later	Congressional committees report budget estimates to Budget Committees
April 15	Action to be completed on congressional budget resolution
May 15	House consideration of annual appropriation bills may begin
June 10	House Appropriations Committee to report the last of its annual appropriations bills
June 15	Action to be completed on reconciliation
June 30	Action on appropriations to be completed by House
July 15	President transmits mid-session review of the budget
October 1	Fiscal year begins

Reprinted from U.S. Office of Management and Budget (2017). *The budget system and concepts, budget of the United States government, fiscal year 2018: analytical perspectives* (p. 71). Washington, DC: U.S. Office of Management and Budget.

Submission of the President's Budget Request

As noted earlier, chief executives submit their budget proposals hoping that the legislature will "rubber stamp" the plans, but expecting (except in cases where the legislature is very weak) that significant changes will be made. Congress is an extremely strong and professional legislative body, so the president's budget is viewed as only the "first shot" in what is almost invariably an annual budgetary war.

The law provides that a president submit his budget to Congress no later than the first Monday in February. In practice, this schedule has been met except for cases where new presidents have just taken office on January 20. In this case, OMB normally submits current services estimates by the February deadline, and the new president submits policy proposals, in the form of amendments to the budget, within 2 months. The FY2020 budget submitted by the Trump administration was not submitted until March 11, 2019. The stated reason for the delay was the 2018/19 government shutdown, where many of the people who needed to work on the budget were furloughed and unable to work during a crucial period in budget development.[29]

The Budget Resolution and Reconciliation

Congress responds to the president's budget request by producing its overall plan for the budget, in the form of its budget resolution. As noted earlier, the budget resolution, created as a coordinating mechanism by the 1974 Budget Act, serves as the overall blueprint for the budget. It also may result in reconciliation, an optional process used to make changes in revenues and mandatory spending.

The Budget Resolution

Under the current timetable, Congress is to complete work on the budget resolution by April 15 of each year. The groundwork for the development of the budget resolution is typically done by the CBO, whose annual report, *The Budget and Economic Outlook*, presents baseline budget estimates 10 years into the future.[30] This is designed to give Congress a reasonable idea of the starting point for its deliberations. The budget resolution ultimately includes aggregate budget targets (total revenue, total budget authority, and the like), functional budget targets, and allocations of budget authority and revenue authority to congressional committees. Committees are not permitted to exceed these targets—called Section 302(a) allocations—and face procedural points of order on the House and (particularly) Senate floor if they attempt to do so.[31]

The budget resolution, in practice, is a tricky annual spring ritual in which the House and Senate Budget Committees must each work with other committees and members to forge an agreement that will withstand later challenges as the details of the budget are prepared. In many years, the budget resolution has not been adopted by the statutory deadline because of difficulties in reaching agreement within one house or (in particular) between both houses. An extreme version of this problem would be the failure to adopt a budget resolution. For example, in more than half of the fiscal years between FY2000 and FY2020, no budget resolution was enacted at all. The current budget timetable provides that, if Congress has not enacted a budget resolution prior to May 15, the appropriations committees can begin to act on appropriation bills without any limits that would have been imposed by the budget resolution. It is common, however, for one or both houses of Congress to pass what is called a "deeming" resolution that establishes that the 302(a) allocations to the appropriations committees in the House-passed or Senate-passed budget resolution are deemed to be those that were included in the budget resolution passed by that house.[32]

Reconciliation

Reconciliation, an optional procedure, has been used since 1980, primarily during years when some major change is anticipated to affect either mandatory spending or revenues. When the procedure is used, reconciliation instructions are included in the budget resolution that will tell committees to produce legislation that has the effect of reducing spending and increasing revenues.[33] At least seven major observations can be made about the use of reconciliation:

1. The size and complexity of these bills defy individual comprehension. When these bills are assembled, even the members of the originating committees may not be familiar with all the details spread across hundreds of pages.

2. Large bills are open invitations to pork barrel politics (see the chapter on budget approval). Some members will succeed in adding pet projects or programs that, if required to stand by themselves for approval, might not be accepted by Congress.

3. Large bills place presidents at a distinct disadvantage in that they must either accept or reject the bills in their entirety. On the other hand, reconciliation bills differ from appropriations in that there is no immediate negative consequence for failing to pass them, and Congress has sometimes been hard-pressed to get the president to go along with them on reconciliation.

4. Large bills are compatible with congressional desires to avoid blame. Members of the House or Senate cannot be held accountable for their votes supporting any one aspect of a bill, because they can say they felt compelled to vote for the bill even though it admittedly was flawed in numerous respects.

5. Because of a provision known as the Byrd Rule (named after former West Virginia Democratic Senator Robert C. Byrd), the House sometimes feels disadvantaged relative to the Senate by the reconciliation process. The rule (specifically Section 313 of the Congressional Budget Act) limits "extraneous" matters in reconciliation legislation. A provision is considered extraneous, for example, if it does not produce a change in outlays or revenues, increases the deficit in a year beyond that covered by reconciliation, or is outside the jurisdiction of the committee proposing the change.[34]

6. The use of large bills and Congress's pre-occupation with budgeting since the 1980s has contributed to centralization of decision making at a time when Congress had been democratized. Power was redirected to those members of Congress most closely associated with the budget process. Furthermore, because reconciliation bills cannot be filibustered, some have argued that they changed the operations of the Senate in a way that no longer gives sufficient protection to legislative minorities.[35] In fact, the protections offered by reconciliation caused the Trump administration to use reconciliation bills as a means to ease passage of its legislative agenda (including attempting to repeal the Affordable Care Act and the passage of its signature tax cuts enacted in the Tax Cuts and Jobs Act of 2017 (see the chapter on income and property taxes) without the normal hurdles that such changes would face, particularly in the Senate.[36]

7. Members of the Appropriations Committees have sometimes expressed concern that their powers are diminished through the reconciliation process, which is under the direction of the Budget Committees. In reality, reconciliation involves other members of Congress besides those who serve on the House and Senate Budget Committees. In working out a conference bill between the two chambers, the numerous subconference committees created include conferees who are not members of either the House or Senate Budget Committees. Nevertheless, the Appropriations Committees see the situation as centralizing power in the hands of the Budget Committees.

The Authorization Process

Theoretically, federal programs must be authorized and appropriated. Authorizations play an important role in federal budgeting. They establish or change federal programs, and they create the terms and conditions under which those programs operate. Authorizations can be provided for 1 year (as is common for defense programs), for multiple years, or permanently (many mandatory spending programs). In the case of mandatory spending programs, authorizations provide spending directly. Major entitlement programs are authorized and appropriations are provided simultaneously. An entitlement such as Social Security, for example, is created by an authorization, and the authorization itself creates the obligation for the federal government to spend money that goes to program beneficiaries.

For discretionary spending, the authorization does not provide the appropriation directly, but rather creates a program that may or may not later be funded in the appropriation process. These authorizations typically include what are called "authorizations of appropriations," which are intended to provide guidance to the appropriations committees but are not binding on them. In fact, the appropriations committees routinely enact appropriations for programs that have no authorization at all. In fiscal year 2019, Congress appropriated $307 billion for programs whose authorizations had expired.[37] Even where there are authorizations for discretionary programs, they typically represent something like a "bid" for future resources, and the appropriations are often less than the amount that is authorized to be appropriated.

The Appropriations Process

While the reconciliation process is optional and the authorization process does not happen for all programs in all years, there is nothing optional about the process of enacting annual appropriations. In fact, enacting the regular appropriation bills is the only budget action that Congress has to take each year. Without appropriations, federal agencies cannot pay staff or contractors and cannot deliver basic benefits. For this reason, in most years the main focus of the budget process is on the fate of appropriations. The appropriations process itself involves several kinds of activities, including action in subcommittee, action in committee, action by the full House and Senate, conference committee action, and negotiation with the White House.

Both the House and the Senate have Appropriations Committees. Historically, the Appropriations Committee in each house was divided into

Table 10-4 Appropriations Subcommittees in Houses of Congress, 2019

Agriculture, Rural Development, and Related Agencies
Commerce, Justice, and Science and Related Agencies
Defense
Energy and Water Development and Related Agencies
Financial Services and General Government
Homeland Security
Interior, Environment, and Related Agencies
Labor, Health and Human Services, Education, and Related Agencies
Legislative Branch
Military Construction, Veterans Affairs, and Related Agencies
State, Foreign Operations, and Related Programs
Transportation, Housing and Urban Development, and Related Agencies

U.S. Senate, Committee on Appropriations (2019). *Subcommittees*. Retrieved August 19, 2019, from https://www.appropriations.senate.gov/subcommittees.

13 subcommittees, which do the substantive work of crafting the detailed bills that fund each individual budget account. Each subcommittee produces a bill that funds various cabinet departments and (sometimes) related agencies. Except for a brief period starting in 2005, the jurisdiction of the appropriations subcommittees has virtually always matched between the House and the Senate.

Table 10-4 lists the jurisdiction of the current 12 subcommittees (that is, which federal agencies are financed by which subcommittees, as of 2019) in the House and the Senate.

As noted earlier, the Appropriations Committees receive a 302(a) allocation as a part of the budget resolution. The allocation effectively tells the committees how much money they have to divide up in aggregate. At an early stage of the process, the committees divide these allocations by subcommittee by establishing the so-called 302(b) allocations. These allocations tell Congress how much money will be available to divide among the various agencies funded as a part of each subcommittee's bill. In other words, the 302(a) allocations establish the size of the appropriated pie, while the 302(b) suballocations tell each subcommittee how large a slice it will have.

After the suballocations have been set, the subcommittees work to produce appropriation bills. Appropriation bills become law in the same way that other bills become law: They must ultimately be passed by both houses in identical form and approved by the president. For appropriation bills, getting to this point involves a lengthy process:

- *Subcommittee action*—where hearings are held (see the chapter on budget approval) and initial allocations are made to each account in each appropriation bill. Each subcommittee is headed by a chairperson who exercises substantial influence over the operations of agencies under the subcommittee's jurisdiction. In fact, the subcommittee "chairman's mark" represents the starting point for deliberations on the appropriation bill, and the bill is considered by the full committee under a process known as the "mark-up," where amendments to the bill are considered in the subcommittee.
- *Full committee action*—where typically the actions of the subcommittee are ratified with very little change.
- *Floor action*—where procedural limitations may (especially in the House) restrict what amendments may be proposed, and where amendments that add money normally need to be offset by reductions.
- *Conference action*—where selected members of appropriations subcommittees in each house convene to work out differences between bills.
- *Presidential action*—where the president exercises constitutional authority to approve or veto appropriation bills.

The process of getting through these steps is time consuming, and this (coupled with the high political stakes that can accompany appropriations) means that often one or more appropriation bills do not become law prior to the beginning of the fiscal year. There were only three years between 1977 and 2019 when all appropriations cleared Congress prior to the start of the fiscal year.[38] The government shutdown that stretched from late 2018 into 2019 over the failure to enact fiscal year 2019 appropriations is only the most recent evidence of this failure. During that shutdown, some appropriation bills (most notably the defense and homeland security bills) had become law, but much of the rest of government was shut down. Moreover, even when there are not government shutdowns, it is now routine for appropriations to be enacted after the start of the fiscal year. Government by continuing resolution is now an annual event that creates costly disruption for federal agencies and recipients of government funds.

Another source of conflict in the appropriation process has to do with items that are added to the budget by Congress but were not in the president's budget. The incentives facing Congress and the president lead them to pursue different types of priorities. While not confined to the appropriations process, pork barrel politics is perhaps most visible in the appropriation process. The pursuit of these special-interest priorities has led to the effort to provide the president with the line-item veto, as discussed in the last section of this chapter.[39]

After an appropriation bill passes both houses of Congress and differences are resolved between the two bodies in conference, then and only then is a bill sent to the president for action. The president has only two options—to approve the bill in its entirety or to veto it. If a bill is vetoed, it is sent back to the Congress and the veto can only be overridden by a vote of two-thirds of both houses. Because the veto is such a blunt instrument and because appropriation bills are often being passed at the last minute (and beyond), presidential vetoes of appropriation bills are relatively rare. The White House, however, does inform the Congress during the appropriations process of changes it would like to see made in appropriation bills, sometimes threatening to veto the bills if those changes are not made.

Issues and Challenges

Despite whatever logic may exist in the described budget process, all is not well with either the federal budget or the process of enacting it. The growth in deficits described earlier has led to a doubling of the debt as a percentage of gross domestic product (GDP) in a relatively short period of time (see the chapter on government and the economy). Moreover, without changes, both the medium-term (10 years) and long-term projections show a debt trajectory that most view as unsustainable. This was true even before the federal response to COVID-19, but that response by itself is projected to add trillions of dollars to the federal debt over the next 10 years. The process identified previously is not followed in practice, with the clearest procedural indictment in the appropriations process, where brinksmanship and government by continuing resolution have become the norm, and government shutdowns have occurred as often as four times in 5 years (2013 to 2018).

Partisan Disagreement and Lack of Consensus

Most federal budget experts agree that it will not be possible to put the country on a fiscally sustainable path without simultaneously raising taxes and reducing entitlement spending. The increasing political partisanship in the Congress (and in the country) works against reaching any kind of agreement that would include those two elements. One party (the Republicans) opposes tax increases as an article of faith, while the other (the Democrats) protects spending on the largest three entitlements—Social Security, Medicare, and Medicaid. Moreover, compromise is considered a dirty word, and the divide between the two parties in Congress is so wide that anyone in the middle of the political spectrum is likely to find him- or herself to be an endangered species.

Moderates from both parties, as has been seen in recent elections, are vulnerable to challenges from either the far left (Democrats) or the far right (Republicans).

Moreover, there is no consensus on a fiscal goal for the country. For many years, a balanced budget was considered a fiscal norm. This is an imperfect norm, in that there are times when deficits are necessary, especially at the national level, but there was at least general agreement that the budget should be balanced over the business cycle. That norm has completely broken down. For example, the period after the Great Recession was the longest period of sustained economic growth between downturns in U.S. history, but it still did not see a return to fiscal discipline. Instead, the 2017 tax cut provided economic stimulus in a period of low inflation and robust economic growth, when arguably no stimulus was necessary. Other goals or fiscal rules have been suggested, such as a target debt-to-GDP ratio. The fact remains, however, that policy makers can neither agree on where we are going nor on how to get there. This challenge has been made even more difficult by COVID-19, since the economic downturn caused by the virus has no certain endpoint, and the necessary fiscal policy response to the coronavirus has made the hole even deeper.

Procedural Failures

In addition to the substantive and political problems faced by the federal government, the budget process itself does not work anywhere close to as intended. The government shutdown of 2017 and 2018 is only one recent high-profile example of a dysfunctional budget process. The Congress routinely fails to pass budget resolutions. Even when they do pass, they are normally just opportunities for one house or the other to take partisan positions that have little chance of becoming law rather than as vehicles to set overall congressional fiscal policy.

More important, and damaging, is the failure to enact appropriation bills anywhere close to on time. When appropriation bills are late, agencies financed through the appropriations process no longer have the funds to operate and are forced

to shut down. To avoid this situation, Congress passes one or more continuing appropriation bills (often called continuing resolutions). These bills permit the affected agencies to operate for a specified time period, usually spending at the same level as they did in the just-completed fiscal year. Typically, no new programs can begin spending while the agency is operating under a continuing resolution, even if budget savings have been achieved by having proposed elimination of other programs or reduction in size of other programs. When the federal government's fiscal year began on July 1, it was common for many or most appropriation bills not to have cleared Congress by the deadline, and agencies often operated for an entire fiscal year with continuing rather than regular appropriations. Changing the fiscal year to begin October 1 was thought to be a solution, giving more time for budget preparation, congressional review, and approval. As history has demonstrated, however, appropriation bills have been approved on time even less often since the fiscal year change.

Government by continuing resolution has a number of negative impacts, and these have been getting worse over time. First, the uncertainly created by late appropriations disrupts service delivery; hiring freezes rob high-priority programs of staff because employee turnover is not even across all programs. Further, furloughs lower morale, which encourages employees with other options—the ones we would least likely want to lose—to leave government. Second, continuing resolutions freeze priorities in place. Agencies have difficulty responding to new threats and problems, and they are required to keep funding outdated or ineffective programs. Third, continuing resolutions may require governments to engage in short-term contracting, as agencies have to squeeze 12 months of contracting work into perhaps less than half a year. Moreover, it is widely believed that many contractors dealing with the federal government include a "risk premium" in the rate that they charge for contractual services, because they cannot negotiate reliable multiyear commitments without fear of funding interruption. Fourth, agencies waste a great deal of time preparing for potential government shutdowns and continuing resolutions, and then complying with them after the fact. Finally, agencies defer investments—in people or in physical assets—which compromises their effectiveness and leads to higher future costs. For example, there were measurable reductions in training in federal agencies, perhaps especially the Department of Defense, in some recent years because of continuing resolutions.[40]

Proposed Reforms and Their Prospects

Because the current results of the federal budget process are so dysfunctional, there are numerous cries for reforms of the process. Some of these reforms focus on attempting to come to grips with the fiscal imbalance exemplified by the large and growing federal debt. Others focus on helping the nation better set priorities. Still others attempt to address the problems created by the lack of timeliness of the process. In 2018, a joint select committee was appointed to make recommendations on reforms of the budget process. After several months of hearings, the committee adjourned unable to come to agreement on any significant reforms and was itself simply another failed attempt to do anything with respect to the budget.[41] Subsequent to this, in 2019, Chairman Mike Enzi of the Senate Budget Committee unveiled his own comprehensive set of budget reforms.[42] While none of these changes has yet become law, it is nonetheless reasonable in a chapter on federal budgeting to ask what changes might be made to the budget process, and even whether the whole idea of establishing a congressional budget process was doomed from the start.[43]

Budget process reform proposals are hardy perennials in Congress. Many members, convinced that the current process is fundamentally broken, propose changes in budget procedures or institutions as solutions to fiscal problems. In fact, both the House and Senate Budget Committees did thorough reviews of the budget process in 2016 and made a number of recommendations

concerning changes that could be made.[44] There are many more of these proposals than can be catalogued on these pages, but among the most common are reforms that would give the president a line-item veto, would amend the Constitution to require a balanced budget, would reorganize Congress as it deals with the budget, would convert Congress to a biennial budget process, and would change the kinds of information provided to policy makers on the reported cost of programs in the budget.

The Line-Item Veto

Most governors (44 out of 50) have line-item veto power, allowing them to reduce or eliminate line items in appropriation bills.[45] The president of the United States has historically lacked such power. The power could be provided in a statute or, as many would advocate, in an amendment to the Constitution. Thomas Jefferson may have been the first president to refuse to spend money appropriated by Congress, and Ulysses S. Grant was apparently the first president to ask for the item-veto power: He called for the line-item veto in his fifth State of the Union address in 1873.[46]

One of the main justifications cited for the line-item veto is that the president needs the authority to reduce or eliminate funding of pork barrel projects that have little merit other than pleasing specific constituent groups of individual members of Congress. However, what constitutes excesses in spending is necessarily a function of one's values and priorities, and the executive branch is not immune from advocating spending for programs and projects of questionable utility to appease a particular advocacy or constituent group. One aspect that is clearly not a purpose of the line-item veto is to reduce the budget deficit. The spending cuts that might be made by a president would be unlikely to have any appreciable effect on total spending.[47]

Critics of the line-item veto contend that it gives the president an unwarranted increase in power, allowing for presidential policy preferences to supplant congressional preferences. If a president needed to muster senatorial votes for an initiative, he could privately threaten to item-veto favored projects of individual senators. When the White House is controlled by one political party and Congress by the other, White House priorities might prevail. One can speculate that if Presidents Reagan and Trump had been able to wield item-veto power, then several agencies and programs would have been eliminated or severely cut, such as the Economic Development Administration, the Appalachian Regional Commission, and urban mass-transportation formula grants (in the Reagan administration) or the Environmental Protection Agency or the Department of Housing and Urban Development (in the Trump administration).

Members of Congress have continued to push for a constitutional amendment to permit the president to exercise a line-item veto. Given the difficulty of amending the Constitution, however, efforts turned in the mid-1990s to a statutory substitute for the item veto, using the rescission process created by the impoundment control provisions of the 1974 Congressional Budget Act.

After decades of debate, the Republican-controlled Congress enacted the Line Item Veto Act (LIVA) of 1996, which took effect in January 1997, giving President Clinton a tool to use against Congress during the 1997 legislative session. The 1996 law explicitly recognized that many earmarks (another name for pork barrel items) are listed not in the legislation itself (an appropriation bill or a tax bill, for example) but in committee reports accompanying those bills. Significantly, then, the LIVA gave the president power to cancel three types of provisions: (1) new items of discretionary spending (found either in appropriation bills or in committee reports accompanying these bills), (2) new entitlements or increased entitlements, and (3) tax provisions that would benefit 100 or fewer individuals or corporations. The president was required to veto an entire item and not just reduce an amount, and he could not veto existing entitlement programs and other forms of mandatory spending. The law had a sunset provision, withdrawing this power from the president on January 1, 2005.[48]

The line-item veto was first used by President Clinton to cut three items from the Balanced Budget

Act of 1997 and the Taxpayer Relief Act of 1997, just 5 days after signing these laws. The vetoes covered (1) tax shelters for financial service companies; (2) a Medicaid provision that specifically would benefit New York State and New York City; and (3) a tax benefit that would go to a small number of agribusinesses, including large corporations that in his view did not need such a tax advantage. President Clinton also used the line-item veto power in the appropriation process. By far the most aggressive use of this power was on the military construction appropriation bill, where he cancelled 38 projects totaling $287 million. Congress used the procedures contained in the act to pass a disapproval bill, which was ultimately vetoed by President Clinton. His veto was overridden by Congress, thereby restoring funding for these projects. Clinton was much more restrained in his use of the veto on other appropriation bills, canceling only $190 million in total budget authority from those other 12 bills.[49]

The LIVA included a section for judicial review, allowing for members of Congress and others to file suit in the U.S. District Court for the District of Columbia, with its decision being appealable directly to the Supreme Court. While the District Court agreed with Senator Robert C. Byrd (the law's main critic) that the law had unconstitutionally delegated congressional powers to the president, the Supreme Court reversed that decision, noting that Byrd lacked standing because no injury had yet been imposed. After President Clinton exercised the power, however, two legal challenges were brought by the City of New York and the Snake River (Idaho) Potato Growers over Clinton's cancellation of items in the Balanced Budget Act and the Taxpayer Relief Act, respectively. The law was found unconstitutional in U.S. District Court, and in 1998, the Supreme Court, in a 6 to 3 decision, sided with the District Court in the case of *Clinton v. City of New York*.[50] The Court ruled that the act ran afoul of the Presentment Clause of the Constitution because it permitted the president to unilaterally unmake law that had been made by both houses of Congress in concert with the president. The majority argued that providing the president with the kind of power envisioned in the act would require an amendment to the Constitution. Thus, the LIVA was relegated to a 1-year experiment—a blip on the federal budgeting radar screen.[51]

Subsequently, presidents have proposed a reduced form of line-item veto authority through what is referred to as "expedited rescission." Under this proposal, a president would be guaranteed a vote on rescission proposals that he proposed, and individual items would be subjected to an "up-or-down" vote on the Senate or House floor. The presumption is that these items would be subject to greater scrutiny, making it harder for the more egregious pork barrel projects to survive.[52] None of these expedited rescission proposals as of 2019 ever passed either house of Congress.

Proposed Balanced Budget Requirement

A persistent proposal has been for the federal government to adopt a balanced budget requirement.[53] Proponents typically refer to the successful use of this requirement at the state level—46 states currently require some form of balanced budget.[54] Note that balanced budget requirements in most states do not preclude borrowing for capital investments, and few state budgets are annually balanced when both current and capital expenditures are taken into account.

Having some set of enforcement mechanisms is essential for successful implementation, although such mechanisms do not exist at the state level, where the balanced budget process is regarded as generally successful. The states, however, have an externally imposed imperative for bringing revenues and expenditures into structural balance: Failing to do so would have adverse effects on their bond ratings and borrowing costs.

Skeptics of congressional abilities to reach agreement on a balanced budget fear that Congress would resort to "smoke and mirror" techniques that merely give the illusion of a balanced budget. Such devices might include overestimating revenues to be collected and moving some expenditures off-budget so that they would be excluded from official total spending. These are precisely the kinds of tricks that resulted under Gramm-Rudman-Hollings, the federal government's prior failed experiment with fixed deficit targets. Attempting to prohibit such practices by outlawing them in the constitutional amendment would be cumbersome, and creative minds might always be able to find loopholes in the amendment's language. In addition, detailed provisions in the amendment could create an inflexibility that later might prove detrimental to the nation's best interests.

A major concern regarding implementation of a balanced budget requirement at the federal level is that the measure might impose unwarranted restrictions in times of economic hardship or national security emergencies. Some form of override mechanism must be included for situations when the federal government needs to spend more to counteract economic recessions and to wage war. In fact, the necessary response of the federal government to the economic disruptions caused by COVID-19 provide a stark reminder of exactly why it would be dangerous to require the budget to be balanced in every year. The Congress and the President needed to pump funds into the economy to provide relief to individuals and small businesses; to require that taxes be raised on those same people and businesses would have been counterproductive.

Critics of the balanced budget amendment contend that it would unduly enhance the powers of the president. A typical requirement of balanced budget proposals is that the president would have to submit a balanced budget, similar to most states' requirements, thereby setting the agenda from which Congress might have little latitude to veer. Often at the state level, the legislative waiver of such a requirement (for economic or national security reasons) would require a vote of 60 percent, two-thirds, or a majority of all members (rather than a simple majority of those voting).[55] This would put the President in a stronger position, since a balanced budget would only require a simple majority.

Furthermore, to the extent that the balanced budget amendment is sought as a means to avoid deficit spending, it seems useful to point out that it is not self-enforcing. The spending cuts and tax increases, and enforcement mechanisms, would still need to be enacted. It is these actions, not the Constitution, that are central to getting control of the nation's debt.[56]

The Congress has, at times, come close to passing a constitutional amendment. An amendment originating in Congress requires a two-thirds vote in each chamber. In 1995, for example, the House passed a version of the amendment, only to see it fall one vote short of the two-thirds necessary in the Senate. A majority of House members voted in favor of the amendment again in 2018, but the legislation fell 50 votes short of the two-thirds necessary for passage.[57] Even were Congress to approve a balanced budget amendment, the measure would still require three-quarters of the states to approve it, a great hurdle to overcome.

Proposed Congressional Reorganization

One way that the Congress could change its approach to the budget would be to reorganize its committee structure in a way that might lead to better decision making. A typical reorganization proposal is to reduce the number of congressional committees and subcommittees. These various bodies create problems in coordination because their domains often overlap and subject areas are needlessly segmented among committees and subcommittees. Power becomes diffuse, and setting overall policy is complicated by the split jurisdictions. The greater the number of committees, the greater the number of committee assignments members have, meaning that they can easily be scheduled to attend two or more committee meetings at the same time. This problem is even more acute in the Senate, where 100 members must handle the same work that is done by the 435 members in the House.

Although considerable agreement may exist that Congress needs to reduce the number of committees and subcommittees, the task is difficult. Chairing one of these committees provides power, prestige, and perquisites, so any chairperson or other senior member on the committee is likely to defend continuance of the committee and repel efforts to diminish the committee's powers. Members in both houses have historically sought seats on committees dealing with the various aspects of the budget as a means of gaining power over congressional actions.

One controversial suggestion has been that the budget process could be streamlined by eliminating the two Appropriations Committees and assigning their duties to the committees that handle authorizations. Rather than appropriation bills emanating from one committee, they would arise from the standing substantive committees in each chamber. Critics of this proposal contend that such a reform would worsen the budget situation, because the Appropriations Committees are far more likely to restrict government spending than the substantive committees, which are often seen as having been captured by the executive branch agencies that they oversee. Furthermore, the Appropriations Committees currently wield great power, and they vigorously oppose any efforts to reduce that power. They would not be abolished without a fight.

Some have proposed a reform known as portfolio budgeting explicitly to address the fragmentation of the budget. The logic behind the portfolio approach is that the current budget process does not encourage consideration of tradeoffs between the various tools that are available to the Congress for meeting particular policy objectives. Because these tools are under the jurisdiction of different committees (tax expenditures by the tax committees, mandatory spending by the authorizing committees, and discretionary programs by the appropriations committees) it discourages consideration of these different kinds of tools as alternatives for achieving desired outcomes. Advocates of portfolio budgeting contend that the budget process should be organized in a way that encourages this more comprehensive approach.[58] The 2019 Enzi proposed reform embraced the idea of portfolio budgeting.

Other committee-related proposals involve reconfiguring the House and Senate Budget Committees (possibly even merging them into a joint committee) or making them into leadership committees by including chairs and other ranking members on the budget committees. The assumption behind this proposal is that including the leadership would provide greater incentives for the budget resolution to be enacted and for other committees to make a more good-faith effort to comply with its strictures.[59] Some argue that these committees should be eliminated on the grounds that they have merely added to the complexity of congressional budgeting and have recently failed to accomplish their major objective in any event.[60]

A more far-reaching proposal would eliminate the concurrent nature of budget resolutions, which do not require presidential signature, and substitute a joint resolution or law to be signed by the president.[61] In effect, budget summitry would be employed at the outset of the budget process. The hope is that the president and key congressional leaders would develop an annual budget resolution that all would support, thereby helping to ensure more timely action as the details of the budget are worked out at a later time. Budget summits bind all participants so that a president who endorsed a summit agreement could not later renege when Congress passed appropriation bills in conformance with the agreement. The downside of a joint budget resolution is that conflict would be "front loaded." Obtaining the agreement of both houses without having the president involved has often proved difficult. After control of the House was won by the Democratic party in the 2018 congressional election, Senate majority leader Mitch McConnell often refused to hold a floor vote on any legislation originating in the House, appropriations related or otherwise, until he got clear indication from the White House that the president would sign the bill. That clear guidance rarely came. Allowing the president to have a veto over the budget resolution might be the practical equivalent of ensuring that no budget resolution will occur in many years.[62]

Biennial Budgeting

One frequently mentioned proposal is to change over to a biennial budget.[63] Because Congress has such difficulty acting on a budget, why not simplify the problem by requiring action only

every other year? The idea of moving the federal government from an annual to a biennial process is not a new one. Representative Leon Panetta (D-CA) introduced the first bill proposing such a change in 1977, and the proposal has been more or less an annual entry in the budget reform sweepstakes since then. Most biennial budgeting proposals would have the president submit the budget biennially and would also feature biennial budget resolutions and appropriations.

Proponents of biennial budgeting argue that the current annual process features repetitive votes on many fiscal issues that eat up valuable committee and floor time. For example, there may be three votes on the budget for defense: one associated with the budget resolution, one associated with the annual defense authorization bill, and one on the annual defense appropriation bill. Second, in a related issue, supporters note that time spent on budgeting cannot be spent on other activities, particularly detailed oversight of federal programs. In particular, these advocates of a biennial process indicate that the need for Congress to review agency performance under the Government Performance and Results Act necessitates spending more time on such detailed oversight. Third, supporters point to the dismal record of Congress and the president in enacting annual appropriation bills prior to the start of each fiscal year. Finally, executive branch officials decry the time-consuming nature of the annual process from their perspective. The sequence of developing an agency budget request, having that budget undergo review by the Office of Management and Budget and the president, and justifying the budget to Congress is continuous in an annual process.[64]

There are also numerous arguments offered by skeptics of biennial budgeting. First, the federal government has a rather checkered history of budget forecasting. Producing a budget every 2 years would increase the probability that budgets would be based on erroneous information. A 2-year budget resolution adopted in April, for example, would be adopted a full 30 months before the end of the second fiscal year of the biennium. The agencies would have begun developing their budgets for that fiscal year at least 10 months prior to the passage of the budget resolution, or more than 3 years from the end of the second fiscal year of the biennium. Second, opponents argue that the benefits of biennial budgeting (decreased time on budgeting, more time for oversight) are overstated. The biennial process may degenerate into an annual process, given the uncertainties associated with budgeting for a $4 trillion enterprise (Congress already engages in an annual process of adopting supplemental appropriations) and the likelihood that Appropriations Committee members will want to act on the budget every year. Third, an increase in oversight under biennial budgeting would occur only if the current lack of oversight results from a lack of time. Opponents argue that even if members of Congress had more time to do oversight, they would not be likely to do more of it simply because they do not have any incentives to do so. Understanding more about how federal programs work in great detail is not politically sexy, nor does it offer any specific benefits in terms of helping members get reelected.[65]

Perhaps the high-water mark for biennial budgeting came in 1993, when both the Joint Committee on the Organization of Congress and Vice President Gore's National Performance Review recommended that the federal government adopt a biennial timetable for the process. Most recently, biennial budgeting was the key proposed reform that the Joint Select Committee on Appropriations and Budget Reform endorsed in 2018, even though that recommendation was never considered by the full House or Senate.[66] The Enzi proposal in 2019 also embraced biennial budgeting. When the supercommittee died, so did this proposal. Despite this long history of support, in fact, no bill to create a biennial process has ever passed either the House or the Senate.

Especially because one of the purported benefits of biennial budgeting is greater predictability and timeliness of the budget process, and especially on the heels of the 2018/19 government shutdown, some have also proposed that continuing resolutions become automatic. Under this proposed reform, if Congress failed to pass an appropriation bill, the agencies affected would operate with a continuing appropriation without Congress having to act. Because congressional failure to act on the budget in a timely fashion has become the norm, the obvious advantage of an automatic continuing resolution is that it would eliminate the crisis handling of appropriation bills.[67] The disadvantage of the proposal is that incentives for Congress to adopt regular appropriation bills would be reduced. Critics of the proposal argue that the damage caused by routine continuing resolutions may be greater than that caused by an occasional shutdown, meaning that making them automatic may be a step in the wrong direction.[68] Automatic continuing resolutions were also included in the Enzi package of reforms in 2019.

Improving the Information Provided about Programs and the Reported Costs of Programs

While the previously mentioned changes have been the most frequently debated, they are by no means the only reform proposals put forth. A number of reforms put forward by budget experts—but not usually by members of Congress—would change the information provided to members of Congress about federal programs. Some of these would go as far as to change the reported cost of programs in the budget. Reforms to provide more performance information in the budget process fall into this category (see the discussion in the chapter on the expenditure side of the budget). In fact, because there are so many changes that have occurred since the 1967 President's Commission on Budget Concepts issued its report, some have suggested that it might be time for a new commission.[69] At least three such reforms are worthy of discussion—capital budgeting, increasing the number of programs that are budgeted for on an accrual basis, and requiring more information on the long-term effects of federal tax and spending decisions.

Adoption of a capital budgeting system is advocated as a way of helping to put the deficit into perspective, because it would show that much of federal spending is of an investment nature and not simply annual consumption. However, the federal budget has very little investment in it, if one excludes major defense systems and intergovernmental transfers to state and local governments for infrastructure (see the chapter on capital assets and capital budgeting for a discussion of the pros and cons of capital budgeting). Capital budgeting presumably would encourage better planning of expenditures. On the negative side, capital budgets could be used to downplay the true magnitude of federal budget deficits and total debt. The President's budget every year includes in the *Analytical Perspectives* portion of the budget a section on Federal Investment. Many of the investment categories included in that section, such as research and development and education and training, are not at all candidates for inclusion in a capital budget, but the temptation would be to include some of the items in a capital budget to reduce the apparent size of a deficit. More and more of the budget could be "capitalized" as a method of making desired spending appear to be less costly. Furthermore, if a balanced budget constitutional amendment were adopted, Congress most likely would move capital expenditures off-budget, just as states permit indebtedness for investments but not for operating expenses.[70]

Accrual budgeting, of course, has already been brought into the budget process as a result of the *Federal Credit Reform Act of 1990* (for more details, see the chapter on accounting and financial management). Federal loan programs, however, are far from the only federal programs where cash budgeting potentially sends misleading signals to policy makers concerning the real cost of programs. Federal insurance programs (such as deposit insurance, pension insurance, and flood insurance) could also be candidates for accrual treatment in the budget. In addition, the costs of federal retirement programs might send more accurate signals if reported on an accrual basis. The CBO, in a 2018 report, argued that transactions might be good candidates for accrual treatment if three conditions were present—current 10-year cash-based cost estimates provide misleading information about the cost of the programs, the future commitments are firm enough to be confident of the future costs, and the future costs can be measured and discounted accurately enough to enable them to be "reliably used in the budget process."[71] Even among those who recognize that an accrual basis of budgeting might send more accurate signals, however, a difference of opinion has emerged concerning how future costs or savings should be discounted. Credit reform discounting uses the Treasury borrowing rate; an alternative, called fair value accounting, would use a higher discount rate based on market risk.[72]

Given the long-term fiscal imbalance facing the country, some reformers also advocate incorporating longer-term costs more explicitly into budget deliberations.[73] These individuals argue that even the 10-year costs that are currently used in the process for cost estimating and for budget enforcement hide what are potentially large costs that occur outside of the 10 year estimating window. Even though the CBO, for example, periodically provides a long-term forecast (which extends for 30 years), these numbers are not formally incorporated into the budget process when individual bills are being considered. This means that, for some programs, the costs that policy makers are confronted with when decisions are made can be misleading and understated. Opponents of incorporating more long-term estimates into the budget process point at the difficulty present in even projecting medium-term costs and wonder whether providing policy makers with inaccurate information about the 20- or 30-year costs will really bring about an improvement in federal budgeting.

Summary

Congress has an elaborate system for approving the budget. An authorization process exists independently of appropriations. Meanwhile, the House Ways and Means Committee and the Senate Finance Committee have power to deal not only with tax measures but also with much entitlement spending. The Appropriations Committees in the two houses operate by developing a series of bills through subcommittees.

The current budget process resulted from two main laws. The Budget and Accounting Act of 1921 prescribes the executive budget process. The Congressional Budget and Impoundment Control Act of 1974 attempted to deal with several problems, including congressional tardiness in adopting the budget, impoundments, and piecemeal handling of the budget. A budget resolution process, Budget Committees, and the Congressional Budget Office were established. Other laws have been passed since the mid-1980s in an attempt to control the deficit, including the Gramm-Rudman-Hollings law in 1985, the Budget Enforcement Act in 1990, and the Budget Control Act in 2011.

The resulting budget process has several stages. First, the president submits a budget on or before the first Monday in February. Congress then adopts a budget resolution that establishes a blueprint for the budget. Committee action follows the constraints established by the budget resolution. In some years, reconciliation bills, which make changes to government revenue and entitlement legislation, are enacted. In each year, much of the budget process focuses on the fate of the regular appropriation bills.

There are a number of future challenges, both substantive and procedural, facing the federal budget. Substantively, the imbalance between revenues and spending (made worse by recent tax cuts and the growth of entitlement spending) is projected to grow both over the next 10 years and reach even more alarming levels over a 30-year period. Procedurally, the budget resolution is only adopted about half the time and appropriation bills are chronically late, sometimes resulting in partial shutdowns of government operations. Numerous proposals exist for further revising how the federal government adopts the budget. Major proposals include giving line-item veto power to the president, passing a constitutional amendment requiring that the budget be balanced, restructuring congressional committees, moving the government to a biennial budget cycle, or changing the kinds of information provided to policy makers when the budget is being considered.

Notes

1. U.S. Senate Permanent Subcommittee on Investigations. (2019). *The true cost of government shutdowns: staff report.* Retrieved September 24, 2019, from https://www.hsgac.senate.gov/imo/media/doc/2019-09-17%20PSI%20Staff%20Report%20-%20Government%20Shutdowns.pdf.

2. Rappeport, A., & Appelbaum, B. (2019). Government shutdown cost U.S. economy $11 billion, C.B.O. says. *New York Times*, January 28. Retrieved January 15, 2020, from https://www.nytimes.com/2019/01/28/us/politics/shutdown-cost-us-economy-11-billion-cbo-says.html.

3. Tompkin, S. (1998). *Inside OMB: politics and process in the President's budget office.* Armonk, NY: M. E. Sharpe.

4. Hughes, J. (1998). General Accounting Office. In J. M. Shafritz (Ed.), *International encyclopedia of public policy and administration* (pp. 969–972). Boulder, CO: Westview Press.

5. Fisher, L. (1987). *The politics of shared power: Congress and the executive* (2nd ed., pp. 91–217). Washington, DC: Congressional Quarterly Press; Schick, A. (2007). *The federal budget: politics, policy, process,* 3rd ed. Washington, DC: Brookings Institution.

6. Manley, J. (1970). *The politics of finance: the House Committee on Ways and Means.* Boston, MA: Little, Brown.

7. Fenno, R., Jr. (1966). *The power of the purse: appropriations politics in Congress.* Boston, MA: Little, Brown; Shuman, H. (1992). *Politics and the budget: the struggle between the president and the Congress* (3rd ed.). Englewood Cliffs, NJ: Prentice-Hall; Wildavsky, A., & Caiden, N. (2004). *The new politics of the budgetary process* (5th ed.). New York, NY: Longman.

8. Schick, A. (1980). *Congress and money.* Washington, DC: The Urban Institute Press; Congressional Budget and Impoundment Control Act of 1974 (P.L. 93–344).

9. Schick, A. (2007). *The federal budget: politics, policy and process,* 3rd ed. Washington, D.C.: Brookings Institution Press; Joyce, P., & Reischauer, R. (1992). Deficit budgeting: the federal budget process and budget reform. *Harvard Journal on Legislation, 29,* 429–453.

10. Joyce, P. (2011). *The Congressional Budget Office: honest numbers, power and policymaking.* Washington, DC: Georgetown University Press.

11. Crippen, D. (2002). *Informing legislators about the budget: the history and role of the U.S. Congressional Budget Office.* Speech to parliamentary officials of the OECD, Washington, DC, June 7.

12. Fisher, L. (1970). The politics of impounded funds. *Administrative Science Quarterly, 15,* 361–377.

13. Anti-Deficiency Act of 1950. Ch. 510, §3, 34 Stat. 49.

14. Rascoe, A. (2020). Trump broke the law in freezing Ukraine funds, watchdog report concludes. *NPR.org,* January 16. Retrieved January 17, 2020, from https://www.npr.org/2020/01/16/796806517/trump-broke-the-law-in-freezing-ukraine-funds-watchdog-report-concludes.

15. Balanced Budget and Emergency Deficit Control Act of 1985 (P.L. 99-177), Title II; Havens, H. (1986).

Gramm-Rudman-Hollings: origins and implementation. *Public Budgeting & Finance, 6*, Fall, 4–24; LeLoup, L., et al. (1987). Deficit politics and constitutional government: the impact of Gramm-Rudman-Hollings. *Public Budgeting & Finance, 7*, Spring, 83–103.

16. Rudman, W., as quoted in Wehr, E. (1985). Congress enacts far-reaching budget measure. *Congressional Quarterly Weekly Report, 43*, 2604.

17. Balanced Budget and Emergency Deficit Control Reaffirmation Act of 1987 (P.L. 100-119), Title I.

18. Schier, S. (1992). *A decade of deficits: congressional thought and fiscal action.* Albany: State University of New York Press; Thelwell, R. (1990). Gramm-Rudman-Hollings four years later. *Public Administration Review, 50*, 190–198.

19. U.S. Congressional Budget Office (1993). *The economic and budget outlook: fiscal years 1994–1998* (p. 85). Washington, DC: U.S. Government Printing Office.

20. The Budget Enforcement Act was a component of the Omnibus Budget Reconciliation Act of 1990 (P.L. 101-508); Joyce, P., & Reischauer, R. (1992). Deficit budgeting.

21. U.S. Congressional Budget Office (1990). *The 1990 budget agreement: an interim assessment.* Washington, DC: U.S. Government Printing Office; U.S. Congressional Budget Office (1992). *The economic and budget outlook: fiscal years 1993–1997.* Washington, DC: U.S. Government Printing Office.

22. Oak, D. (1995). An overview of adjustments to the Budget Enforcement Act discretionary spending caps. *Public Budgeting & Finance, 15*, Fall, 35–53.

23 Hager, G. (1997). Clinton, GOP Congress strike historic budget agreement. *Congressional Quarterly Weekly Report, 56*, 993, 996–997.

24. U.S. Congressional Budget Office (2001). *The budget and economic outlook: fiscal years 2003–2012* (p. 158). Washington, DC: U.S. Government Printing Office.

25. U.S. Congressional Budget Office (2011). *Report on the Troubled Asset Relief Program*, March, 4; Stolberg, S. G. (2009). Signing stimulus, Obama doesn't rule out more. *New York Times*, February 18. Retrieved April 22, 2020, from https://www.nytimes.com/2009/02/18/us/politics/18web-stim.html; Lucas, D. (2011). *The budgetary cost of Fannie Mae and Freddie Mac and options for the future federal role in the secondary mortgage market.* Statement before the Committee on the Budget, U.S. House of Representatives, June 2, 7.

26. Meyers, R. (2014). The implosion of the federal budget process: triggers, commissions, cliffs, sequesters, debt ceilings, and shutdown. *Public Budgeting & Finance 34*, Winter, 1–23.

27. Taylor A. (2020). Coronavirus relief pushing US deficits to staggering heights. *AP News*, April 24. Retrieved April 27, 2020, from https://apnews.com/b483d9691de2b83a8b35951508c3b4d1.

28. House of Representatives, Committee on the Budget, Democratic Staff. (2019). The budget agreement to raise the caps supports critical investments for the American people, July 23. Retrieved April 22, 2020, from https://budget.house.gov/publications/report/budget-agreement-raise-caps-supports-critical-investments-american-people.

29. Elis, N. (2019). Trump's 2020 budget delayed by shutdown. *The Hill*, January 29. Retrieved April 22, 2020, from https://thehill.com/policy/finance/427523-trumps-2020-budget-delayed-by-shutdown.

30. U.S. Congressional Budget Office. (2019). *The budget and economic outlook: fiscal years 2019–2029.* Washington, DC: U.S. Government Publishing Office.

31. Schick, A. (2007). *The federal budget.*

32. Congressional Research Service (2019). *Deeming resolutions: budget enforcement in the absence of a budget resolution.* Updated April 29. Retrieved April 22, 2020, from https://fas.org/sgp/crs/misc/R44296.pdf.

33. Doyle, R. (1996). Congress, the deficit, and budget reconciliation. *Public Budgeting & Finance, 16*, Winter, 59–81.

34. U.S. Senate, Committee on the Budget, Republican Staff (2005). *Informed budgeteer*, September. Retrieved March 17, 2012, from http://budget.senate.gov/republican/public/index.cfm/2005/9/issue-5-hurricane-katrina-the-byrd-rule; Heniff, B. (2016). The budget reconciliation process: The Senate's "Byrd rule. *Congressional Research Service*, November 22. Retrieved April 22, 2020, from https://www.senate.gov/CRSpubs/95a2a72a-83f0-4a19-b0a8-5911712d3ce2.pdf.

35. Dauster, W. (1998). The monster that ate the United States Senate. *Public Budgeting & Finance, 18*, Summer, 87–93.

36. Collender, S. (2001). Repeated reconciliation. *Government Executive.* Retrieved January 10, 2001, from http://www.govexec.com/dailyfed/0101/011001bb.htm.

37. U.S. Congressional Budget Office (2019). *Expired and expiring authorizations of appropriations: fiscal year 2019* (p. 3).

38. Congressional Research Service (2019). *Continuing resolutions: overview of components and practices*, April 19. Retrieved April 22, 2020, from https://fas.org/sgp/crs/misc/R42647.pdf.

39. Dennis, S., & Higa, L. (2006). Conservatives frustrated in earmarks crusade. *CQ Today*, June 14. Retrieved August 30, 2006, from http://oncongress.cq.com.

40. Statement of P. G. Joyce (2016). U.S. Senate, Committee on the Budget, Hearing on Fixing the Budget Process & Restoring Stability to Govt. Operations, April 20.

41. Joyce, P., & Meyers, R. (2019). *The problem and the process are both problems: why the Joint Select Committee on Budget and Appropriations Process failed.* [Unpublished manuscript.]

42. Committee for a Responsible Federal Budget (2019). Enzi-Whitehouse budget process bill includes important reforms. November 19. Retrieved January 17, 2020, from https://www.crfb.org/blogs/enzi-whitehouse-budget-process-bill-includes-important-reforms.

43. Meyers, R., & Joyce, P. (2005). Congressional budgeting at age 30: Is it worth saving? *Public Budgeting & Finance, 26*, Special Issue, 68–82.

44. Price, T. (2016). Proposed rewrite of the congressional budget process: summary of selected provisions, November 30. Retrieved April 22, 2020, from https://republicans-budget .house.gov/uploadedfiles/bpr-longsummary-30nov2016 .pdf; Enzi, M. (2016). Fixing America's Broken Budget Process. *U.S. Senate, Committee on the Budget*, December 7. Retrieved April 22, 2020, from https://www.budget.senate .gov/imo/media/doc/FINAL.SBC.BPR.Leg.SUMMARY.pdf.

45. National Association of State Budget Officers (2015). *Budget processes in the states*, Spring, p. 49.

46. Gryski, G. S. (1991). The influence of committee position on federal program spending. *Polity, 23*, 443–459.

47. U.S. General Accounting Office (1992). *Line item veto: estimating potential savings.* Washington, DC: U.S. Government Printing Office.

48. Line Item Veto Act of 1996 (P.L. 104-130); Joyce, P., & Reischauer, R. (1997). The federal line-item veto: what is it and what will it do? *Public Administration Review, 57*, 95–104.

49. Joyce, P. (1998). The line-item veto experiment: after the Supreme Court ruling, what's next? *Public Budgeting & Finance, 18*, Winter, 3–22.

50. *Clinton v. City of New York* (1998). 524 U.S. 417. *Byrd v. Raines* (1997). 6 LW 2660 (DDC); *Raines v. Byrd* (1997). 521 U.S. 811 (1997).

51. Joyce, P. (1998). The line-item veto experiment.

52. Statement of Donald B. Marron before the United States Senate Committee on the Budget, May 2, 2006.

53. Hager, G. (1997). Country comes full circle on balancing the budget. *Congressional Quarterly Weekly Report, 55*, 278–285.

54. National Association of State Budget Officers (2015). *Budget processes in the states*, Spring, 52.

55. U.S. Congressional Budget Office (1993). *The economic and budget outlook: fiscal years 1994–1998.*

56. Joyce, P. (2011). Testimony before the Judiciary Committee, U.S. House of Representatives, October 5.

57. Kaplan, T. (2018). As deficits mount, amendment to require balanced budgets fails in house. *New York Times*, April 12. Retrieved August 19, 2020, from https://www .nytimes.com/2018/04/12/us/politics/house-balanced -budget-amendment-vote.html.

58. Redburn, F. S., & Posner, P. (2015). *Budgeting for national goals.* Paper prepared for the National Budgeting Roundtable, August. Washington, D.C.: George Mason University Centers on the Public Service.

59. Joyce, P. (2011). *Strengthening the budget committees, January.* Washington, DC: Pew Charitable Trusts.

60. Fisher, L. (1990). Federal budget doldrums: the vacuum in presidential leadership. *Public Administration Review, 50*, November/December.

61. Meyers, R. (1990). The budget resolution should be a law. *Public Budgeting & Finance, 10*, Fall, 103–112; Meyers, R. (1994). *Strategic budgeting.* Ann Arbor, MI: University of Michigan Press.

62. Committee for a Responsible Budget (2016). *The better budget process initiative: strengthening the budget resolution.* April 14, pp. 3–4. Retrieved May 4, 2020, from http:// www.crfb.org/sites/default/files/bbpi_strengtheningbudget resolution_0.pdf.

63. Meyers, R. (1988). Biennial budgeting in the U.S. Congress. *Public Budgeting & Finance, 8*, Summer, 21–32.

64. Rivlin, A. (2015). Biennial budgeting: A first step toward budget process reform. Testimony before Committee on the Budget, U.S. House of Representatives, November 18.

65. Joyce, P. (2015). Biennial budgeting. Testimony before Committee on the Budget, U.S. House of Representatives, November 18.

66. Congressional Research Service (2019). *The Joint Select Committee on Budget and Appropriations Process Reform*, Updated March 26.

67. S. 589: Prevent Government Shutdowns Act of 2019.

68. Joyce, P. (2012). *The costs of budget uncertainty: analyzing the impact of late appropriations.* Washington: IBM Center on the Business of Government.

69. Anderson, B., & Penner, R. (2016). *Time for a new budget concepts commission*, January. Retrieved August 20, 2019, from https://www.brookings.edu/wp-content/uploads /2016/07/Penner-Anderson-Draft-Layout-010516v1-2 .pdf.

70. U.S. General Accounting Office (1998). *Budget issues: budgeting for capital.* Washington, DC: U.S. Government Printing Office.

71. Congressional Budget Office. (2018). *Cash and accrual measures in federal budg*eting, January, 2. Retrieved April 22, 2020, from https://www.cbo.gov/system/files/115th -congress-2017-2018/reports/53461-cashaccrual measures.pdf.

72. Congressional Budget Office (2012). *Fair-value accounting for federal credit programs*, March. Retrieved April 22, 2020, from https://www.cbo.gov/publication/43027.

73. Peterson-Pew Commission on Budget Reform (2011). *Eyes on the horizon: multi-year budgeting and its role in the federal budget process.* December 13. Retrieved April 22, 2020, from http://budgetreform.org/document/eyes-horizon -multi-year-budgeting-and-its-role-federal-budget -process; Bipartisan Policy Center (2016). *Fixing fiscal myopia: why and how we should emphasize the long term in federal budgeting*, December. Retrieved April 22, 2020, from https://bipartisanpolicy.org/report/fixing-fiscal -myopia/.

CHAPTER 11

Budget Execution

When President Donald Trump was impeached by the House of Representatives, the popular focus was on the political story—the alleged "quid pro quo" between the release of funds to Ukraine and political favors that he had requested from his Ukrainian counterpart. At its base, however, the story is one of budget execution—that is, the responsibility of a chief executive to carry out the budget in line with the enacted law. In fact, the Government Accountability Office (GAO) found that the president had violated a law—called the Impoundment Control Act—that governs how the budget needs to be carried out once appropriation bills have become law.[1]

Budget execution is, in one sense, management by another name. It involves hiring and managing people, procuring capital and other resources that can be used to produce the outcomes of the organization, collecting revenues, and carrying out other activities. As there is a voluminous management literature, the focus of this chapter is on those parts of management that are most closely related to budgeting. The first section of the chapter deals with interactions between the central budget office and the line agencies. Then, four subsystems of the execution phase are discussed—tax administration, cash management, procurement, and risk management.

Budget Office and Agency Relations

As would be expected, relationships—both direct and indirect—are extensive between the central budget office and the line agencies during the execution phase of the budget. These relationships involve interactions that relate directly to carrying out revenue and spending plans, but also coordinating activities that are less directly related to the overall budget, such as the organization of the government, its day-to-day management, information technology resources, and regulatory control.

Interactions on Budgeting

Every budget, either explicitly or implicitly, contains plans for the work to be done and the achievements to be made. Execution involves converting those plans into operations. During this phase, budget office personnel gain important insights into the operations of agencies, and this knowledge later becomes important for the next round of budget preparation.

Legislative Intent

The legislature provides some indication of legislative intent through a variety of mechanisms, some legally binding and some advisory. Legislative intent is what the legislators had in mind when creating and funding programs. It begins with the creation of a governmental unit and programs for it to administer: For example, a state legislature will have created an organization to deliver special education and one or more programs for that unit to administer. Besides these provisions are a host of other legal requirements pertaining to legislative intent. At the federal level, the GAO has a manual known as the *Red Book* that discusses these requirements.[22]

Agencies prefer as much flexibility as they can get in budget execution, such as would occur with *lump-sum* appropriations, meaning monies that are in one overall pot and not broken into smaller ones. The more the budget is focused on detailed line items, the less flexibility the agency will have to spend money as it sees fit.

The legislative intent contained in legislation is by definition legally binding during budget execution, but beyond this is a further gray area of legislative intent. Bills reported out of legislative committees are accompanied by committee reports that explain what provisions were considered and why the committees are recommending specific provisions. These reports can run to hundreds of pages in length. In addition, the legislative history of a bill will include statements by legislators specifying how money is intended to be spent. There may be a separate explanatory report prepared after passage of the bill.

Except for two critical factors, statements contained in committee reports, statements made on the floor of the legislature, and statements made in reports subsequent to passage of bills are not legally binding on agencies—but woe to the agency that ignores these sources of information on legislative intent.

First, these statements have the effect of putting the budget office and the affected agencies on notice of what is expected in the implementation of the laws. To ignore these informal provisions, an agency runs the risk of raising the ire of legislators, people who may have the power to cut their budgets next year or to hamstring them with specific provisions in law.

The second factor involves legal challenges. Some laws and how they are administered are challenged in court by private citizens, state and local governments, interest groups, and even legislators themselves. Courts, in deciding legislative intent, first turn to the statutes involved and use a "plain language" interpretation. In other words, how does the law read using standard usage of the English language? If ambiguities remain, then courts turn to the unofficial forms of legislative intent—namely, committee reports before passage, floor debates, and committee reports after passage.

Legislative intent was at the center of the recent controversy over the Trump administration's border wall. After Congress explicitly rejected the appropriation of additional funds for the wall, President Trump directed that $3.6 billion in funds that had been appropriated to the Department of Defense be diverted to supplement funds to be used for border wall construction. This diversion was challenged in court, but the 5th District of the U.S. Court of Appeals sided with the administration and allowed the repurposing of the funds to go forward.[3]

Both legislators and executives realize that legislative language needs to be worded somewhat generally so as to provide flexibility over time. Bills often cover multiple years. As time passes, executive agencies need flexibility to adapt to changes in their environments and therefore need flexibility in the laws under which they operate. This flexibility, then, creates an opening for further decision making at the onset of the new fiscal year. Once an agency's appropriation is passed by the legislature, the agency is not simply in the position of routinely commencing administration with its new funding.

Apportionments and Allotments

At the state and federal levels, an apportionment process is used in which line agencies submit plans to the central budget office for how appropriated funds will be used. The plans often indicate proposed expenditures for each month or quarter of the fiscal year. Office of Management and Budget (OMB) Circular A-11 governs this process at the federal level. According to OMB,

> Apportionment is a plan, approved by OMB, to spend resources provided by

one of the annual appropriations acts, a supplemental appropriations act, a continuing resolution, or a permanent law (mandatory appropriations). Resources are apportioned by Treasury Appropriation Fund Symbol (TAFS). The apportionment identifies amounts available for obligation and expenditure. It specifies and limits the obligations that may be incurred and expenditures made (or makes other limitations, as appropriate) for specified time periods, programs, activities, projects, objects, or any combination.[4]

A primary purpose of apportionment is to ensure that agencies spend at a rate that will keep them within limits imposed by their annual appropriations. A further purpose, especially at the state and local levels, may be to attempt to match spending with inflows of revenues—in other words, to promote positive cash flow. Another purpose is to guide agencies so that the desired program accomplishments are achieved. As A-11 indicates, "An apportioned amount may be further subdivided by an agency into allotments, suballotments, and allocations."[5]

The apportionment plan, therefore, should seemingly be linked closely with performance plans, although that is not always the case. Agencies are required to defend their proposed apportionment plans in terms of the work that they expect to accomplish over the course of the fiscal year. A third purpose may be to guide agencies in using resources efficiently. At the federal level, agencies use Standard Form 132 to submit their apportionment plans; OMB then approves, modifies, or disapproves. Spending cannot begin until approval is granted.[5]

In the apportionment process, chief executives and their budget offices have greater power to deny authority than to grant authority to agencies. The executive cannot approve apportionments for projects prohibited in the appropriation, but may be able to reduce or eliminate some appropriated items. As noted in the chapter on budgeting in the U.S. Congress, presidents have impounded appropriated funds. Another executive means of denying spending authority

is to exercise the line-item veto. That is common among the states and is also used in some local governments; the president does not have the power of the line-item veto.

Initial Planning

At the outset of the fiscal year, agencies must accommodate differences between the actual appropriations and the original requests for funding. In addition, some substantive changes may be specified in the appropriations, or an informal understanding may have developed between an agency and legislators over how a program will be redirected.

For agencies that were fortunate enough to obtain increased funds for improving or expanding existing programs or for new programs, the budget office plays a key role. Mindful that the legislature will expect a detailed reporting of how these new funds were used, the budget office exercises oversight in implementing the program revisions or new programs.

Control of Agencies

From the perspective of the central administration, agencies must live within their budgets. Otherwise, the budget process becomes an empty exercise. Therefore, various central controls are imposed upon agencies, including the *preaudit*. After approval of an apportionment plan and granting an allotment, an agency still is not free to spend at will, but rather must submit a request to obligate the government to spend resources. The request is matched against the unit's budget to determine whether the proposed expenditure is authorized and whether sufficient funds are available in the agency's budget.

Several different units may carry out the preaudit function. Not only the budget office, but also an accounting department, may be involved. At the state and local levels, independent comptrollers, controllers, treasurers, or auditors general often have preaudit responsibilities. These officials have the duty of providing another, presumably independent, check on financial transactions.

In the case of an agency proposing to hire new staff, not only will the usual preaudit procedure be used, but a central personnel office also may review the request. Such a review, known as *personnel complement control*, is used in part to avoid increasing personnel commitments and corresponding increases in budget requirements over what has been appropriated.

Midyear Changes

As the year progresses, the budget office conducts reviews of agency operations. One all-too-common problem is that the need or demand for services far exceeds the funds appropriated. Such conditions may be known at the outset of the fiscal year, with allotment plans being used in effect to ration services across the year. In some situations, the need or demand may rise unexpectedly and sharply during the year; in other cases, service demands may be as expected, but the cost of meeting those demands may change, as would occur for a state police department if gasoline prices increased suddenly. Any of these situations may prompt a request for a supplemental appropriation from the legislative branch. In other circumstances, the budget office will work with agencies to stay within funding limits.

Many governments track and report on revenues and spending throughout the year. At the federal level, each summer the OMB issues the *Mid-Session Review of the Budget*, which discusses economic trends and the ways in which these trends are affecting receipts, spending patterns, the activities of credit programs, and whatever other procedures are in place to attempt to limit the budget deficit. The Congressional Budget Office (CBO), in mid-summer, updates its *Budget and Economic Outlook*. These reports cover some of the same ground as the OMB midsession document. The Treasury Department issues a *Monthly Treasury Statement of Receipts and Outlays of the U.S. Government*, which is another tool for tracking government finances during budget execution (CBO also publishes an analysis of the *Monthly Treasury Statement*).

Midyear crises may arise because of an unfavorable revenue situation. Government budgets that depend heavily on a single commodity export—like Indonesia's budget, which relies on oil—may experience significant fluctuation during the year as the world price of the commodity fluctuates. This can also be true of a state that is dependent on a particular industry, such as Texas on oil or Nevada on tourism. In the United States, a downturn in a state's economy can have devastating effects on sales tax and income tax receipts, forcing (because of balanced budget requirements) across-the-board cutbacks in spending, as happened in the Great Recession. Because personnel costs are usually the largest single item in operating budgets, these costs must be curtailed when revenues fall below projected levels. Personnel hiring freezes are common in government. Another, more extreme, technique is to furlough employees, resulting in less pay but also less work. Depending on the chief executive's authority, they may be able to cut back on agency spending to bring outgo in line with income, or they may need approval from the legislature to take such action.

The Great Recession resulted in many states cutting their budgets in midyear, employing a number of specific strategies, such as across the board cuts, furloughs, hiring freezes, and cutbacks on funds to state and local governments. In all, 43 states reduced their budgets in midyear during fiscal year 2009, 39 states did so during fiscal year 2010, and 23 did so during fiscal year 2011.[6] These sorts of cutbacks have been less common since the Great Recession ended. A 2019 report of the National Association of State Budget Officers (NASBO) indicated that only 7 states made budget reductions to the fiscal year 2018 budget after the budget initially passed.[7]

When more resources are needed in midyear, this frequently results in the enactment of supplemental appropriations. At the state and local levels, balanced budget norms usually require supplemental funding to be offset by some reduction in another part of the budget. At the federal level, response to some natural disaster or national security emergency is less likely to be offset by other reductions. For example, the Bush administration funded the wars in Iraq and Afghanistan almost entirely through supplementals. The administration took the position that even though it was known that vast sums would be needed in these endeavors, the specific needs could not be forecast at regular budget time. Between 2001 and 2011, a total of almost $1.3 trillion was spent on the wars, and most of this was provided through supplemental appropriations. A more recent example was represented by the Additional Supplemental Appropriations for Disaster Relief Act of 2019, which provided $19 billion in assistance for victims of disasters that occurred over a 3-year period. The act included funds for agriculture-related losses, losses from flood damage, timber restoration, and wildfire suppression, among many other purposes.[8]

When an agency wishes to shift existing resources to meet new needs during the fiscal year, or when an agency receives a supplemental appropriation, it must prepare a revised apportionment or reapportionment plan. The budget office then has an opportunity to exercise some guidance over how the agency will spend its monies. This process is sometimes known as *budget revision* or *rebudgeting*.

Just because a government is experiencing a downturn in revenues and needs to cut expenditures does not mean there will be no need for supplemental appropriations. In other words, budget increases and decreases occur simultaneously during budget execution. Some agencies' budgets of necessity may be augmented, while others are cut to try to make up the difference. For example, many state government departments may have their budgets trimmed, while the state's labor department budget is being augmented to cope with an increased caseload of unemployed workers. Any recession is likely to simultaneously affect revenues and spending. Revenues will decline because the tax base for a major tax (income, sales, or property) may be eroded because of reduced economic activity. Spending may increase because some anti-poverty programs (such as Medicaid or unemployment insurance) are designed to expand in times of economic dislocation.

During the execution phase, agencies are required to supply periodic reports on their budgets. At the federal level, quarterly reports are required by law (Standard Form 133). Also, cabinet departments and some independent agencies must supply outlay reports that are used to monitor trends in budget deficits or surpluses.

End-of-Year Spending

As the fiscal year approaches its end, agencies will attempt to zero out their budgets. An agency having unexpended funds at the end of the fiscal year may be considered a prime candidate for cuts in the upcoming budget. Also, unexpended or unencumbered funds often lapse at the end of the budget year. From the agency's perspective, it is a now-or-never situation for spending the available money. Another factor is that an agency may have delayed some expenditures, saving a portion of its budget for contingencies. This delay results in a spurt in expenditures at the end of the year, with some spending being highly appropriate and other spending being utterly wasteful. An alternative is to allow surplus funds to be transferred to the agency's new budget without requiring a reappropriation. Some jurisdictions allow this kind of transfer within limits, such as a small percentage of each unit's total budget. While end-of-year spending is decried by many as inherently wasteful, it is only truly wasteful if it results in spending that is only to use any unspent funds and is for items that do not advance the mission of the agency. It is particularly difficult to fault federal agencies for a desire to spend all the money they have available in any fiscal year, given the uncertainty of the federal appropriations process.[9]

Reorganizing, Downsizing, Privatizing, and Outsourcing

Budget offices have historically played central roles in examining the structures of departments and agencies, with an eye toward possible reorganization as a means for increasing the efficiency of operations. In addition to structural arrangements, budget offices often seek improvements in management processes as a means of garnering savings. When the Department of Homeland Security was created in 2002, for example, OMB played a key role in orchestrating the massive reorganization of units from various federal departments into the new department.[10] More recently, President Trump tasked his son-in-law, Jared Kushner, to head an effort to reorganize the federal government. Kushner was tasked with heading up a new White House Office of American Innovation designed to create a more efficient federal government. Much of the early focus on this new office was on information technology modernization.[11]

Downsizing, rightsizing, and similar efforts may be aimed simply at reducing the size of government on the assumption that the bureaucracy is bloated and that cutbacks are possible without really altering the level of service. Other efforts to reduce the size and role of government may be based on the premise that certain functions are necessary but that most likely are not well run and could be performed better by the private sector. One option to achieve this reduced role of government in favor of the private sector is *privatization*. While definitions vary, the core of any definition of privatization or privatizing is the reassignment of government activities to the private sector. There are two forms of privatizing public services. One is the outright sale of government assets to the private sector and turning over the responsibility of providing services to the private purchasers. Sale of a previously municipally owned power company to a private party is one example of sale of assets and making service provision a private responsibility. Utility customers become customers of the private company and the municipality no longer is involved, other than possibly in a regulatory capacity (see the chapter on capital financing). The other form of privatization is contracting out to private parties to provide services that are still *public* services. A dramatic example is the National Aeronautics and Space Administration's (NASA's) effort to replace its own programs in development of manned space rockets and some launch programs with contracting to private corporations.[12]

In *contracting* or *outsourcing*, a private firm provides a product or service to the government at an agreed quantity, quality, and price. Other means of encouraging private sector involvement in the provision of public services include grants, loan guarantees, tax expenditures, social

regulation, and government corporations. Outsourcing of government services is intended to increase government efficiency and reduce government spending. It should be kept in mind that outsourcing may officially result in a reduction in the number of government employees, but that many private sector employees will have jobs only because of government contracting. Outsourcing can be used for so-called business services such as janitorial housekeeping, but also for more fundamental basic services such as water, roads, prisons, and the like.[13]

Although the procedures used in contracting are reviewed later in this chapter, we note here that OMB Circular A-76, *Performance of Commercial Activities*, provides for a review process to determine when activities of the government should be contracted out. Two main criteria apply: that the activity be a "commercial" one and not "governmental," and that the cost be lower in the private sector than in government. Examples of commercial activities include guarding public buildings and providing cafeterias for employees. Policymaking activities may not be contracted out.[14]

Contracting out has at least two types of supporters. One group wants to increase the efficiency of government operations through utilization of the private sector.[15] Circular A-76 uses an efficiency standard—namely, contracting out should be used when the unit cost for a service is lower outside government than inside it. The second group adheres to the view that the population is better served if service delivery is left, where possible, to the private sector. Advocates of outsourcing contend that government should be proactive in seeking opportunities for turning functions over to the private sector.

Although critics reason that sometimes too much faith is placed in private enterprise and that outsourcing supports nonunionized firms that pay low wages, private sector contracting has become a familiar form of service delivery in the United States and abroad.[16]

Contracting out is routinely used for such services as refuse pickup and towing of illegally parked vehicles. Private sector firms under government contract now handle services once thought to be exclusively the responsibility of the public sector, such as welfare services and the operation of prisons. During the wars in Iraq and Afghanistan, many security and intelligence activities, previously conducted exclusively by federal employees, were carried out by contractors.

Several lessons have been learned as governments have ventured into outsourcing, with one of the most important being the need to conduct a thorough analysis before taking the plunge.[17] There is a need to consider whether cost efficiencies will be attained, whether the private firm will be held accountable for its performance, whether any cost efficiency is attained at the expense of quality, and whether equity or fairness in treating citizens and employees will be achieved.[18] Another important question is whether companies in the market can provide the agreed-upon services in a timely fashion and can respond to unforeseen problems that may arise. Do any legal barriers prohibit privatizing a given service? And what liability risks may be created by having a private firm deliver a government service?

The analysis needs to include projected costs for monitoring a firm in its delivery of a service. A government must be able to assure itself that a firm is abiding by its commitments and be able to respond when citizens complain about a service. Part of the monitoring process includes determining whether the cost savings that were predicted in the original analysis did, indeed, materialize. Some local governments that contract out for solid waste collection also retain some capacity inside government. In a given city, waste is collected in some areas by private contractors and in some areas by city employees. That way, the city retains some capability if the private service provider does not live up to its obligations, and it ensures that there will be at least one competitor if only one private firm ventures a bid.

Management Controls

Budget offices have been assigned a variety of management-related duties beyond the core activities of assembling proposed budgets and overseeing their execution. For instance, budget offices may be partially responsible for establishing standards to be used in accounting systems

(OMB Circular A-127). Of course, other units, such as the GAO at the federal level, also play major roles in this area. Information systems and procurement are other important areas in which budget offices have key roles. Procurement is discussed later in this chapter.

Some budget offices have responsibility for studying agency procedures and for recommending or prescribing new procedures. These organization-and-management studies can recommend changes in the department's management processes.

Budget offices set ground rules for many of the routine activities of line organizations. For example, limitations are set for paying employee travel costs. Centrally imposed standards also circumscribe the use of consulting services.

Some budget offices are charged with performing a legislative clearinghouse function. Before an agency may endorse a proposal for new or revised legislation, the proposal must be vetted through the budget office. This practice helps ensure that what is proposed is consistent with the views of the chief executive, both substantively and financially (see OMB Circular A-19).

The OMB also oversees agency compliance with the Federal Managers' Financial Integrity Act of 1982, which requires safeguarding financial systems, particularly accounting and payroll, from fraud.[19] OMB Circular A-123 is used to implement the law; it was revised in 2004 and portions have been revised since then. The circular emphasizes that managers should be held accountable for producing government services that yield desired results as well as providing these services free of fraud and abuse of resources.[20] Similar controls are established at the state and local levels.

Besides these areas mentioned, budget offices may have some responsibility for other management controls over agencies. For example, budget offices may be involved in some or all of the following activities:

- implementing government-wide diversity and inclusion plans;
- ensuring compliance with right-to-know laws that require employers, both public and

private, to inform their employees if they are working with hazardous materials;

- assisting with the implementation of hiring freezes and other personnel reduction plans;
- calculating the effect of federal or state laws on the budgets of lower levels of governments or the private sector; and
- implementing freedom-of-information laws.

Control of Information Collection, Quality, Security, and Dissemination

Budget offices are heavily involved in government collection and dissemination of information. A chief concern is that government agencies heap huge burdens on individuals and corporations and, in the case of the federal government, on state and local governments in requiring them to submit information. The Paperwork Reduction Act (PRA), originally passed in 1980 and thoroughly rewritten in 1995, provides an elaborate process by which the federal government handles information.[21] The process is under the supervision of OMB's Office of Information and Regulatory Affairs (OIRA). The law is implemented by OMB Circular A-130. Each department is required to have a chief information officer (CIO) appointed by the department head and directly accountable to the head. These officers meet periodically as the CIO Council.[22]

The PRA, as its title suggests, requires agencies to reduce the information collection burdens that they impose. Agencies are required to calculate the thousands of "burden hours" that the collection process demands of those required to submit information to them. The law requires the OIRA to review requests for information or data from federal agencies that will impose burdens on those who are required to produce it. The PRA applies in all circumstances except where the request affects fewer than 10 people, involves open-ended requests for feedback, requests information from federal employees, or involves requests made at a public hearing.[23]

Any new collection of information must be approved by OIRA, but before that can occur,

an agency must go through an elaborate analytic process. Factors to consider include the importance to the agency in collecting the information (the practical utility of the information), a realistic assessment of the burden imposed on those who would be required to submit the information, and a determination that the information does not exist already in some other form or in another agency. Once all of this activity is completed, the agency must post a notice about the proposed collection process in the *Federal Register* and then go through a period in which it accepts comments from the public. The CIO of an agency must review and certify the proposal. Only after these steps are completed may the proposal be submitted to the OIRA. That office can reject the agency's proposal on grounds such as that the information is nonessential, that the information already exists, that the process would impose an undue burden, or simply that the proposed forms are unacceptable. After OMB approves a proposal, a notice must be posted once again in the *Federal Register*.

The process of disseminating information also is of concern. OMB provides guidance so that the dissemination process does not invade the privacy of citizens or reveal trade secrets of corporations. Circular A-130 provides guidance on when and how much agencies may charge for their information. The PRA requires that information be made available in a timely fashion.

Information security has been particularly troublesome. For example, electronic filing of tax returns poses important challenges in safeguarding the security of data.[24] In 2015, the Office of Personnel Management acknowledged that two breaches of its records on individuals resulted in the loss of highly confidential data including social security numbers, addresses, and phone numbers on as many as 25 million individuals. The breach was considered so serious that the Office of Personnel Management contracted for a security firm to monitor and notify individuals for at least a decade, at no cost to the individuals affected, any suspicious appearance of data stolen in the breach on the Internet and other sources. Free identity and credit restoration services also are provided.[25] Concerns over the hacking of U.S. databases by foreign governments has led to an increase in the investment in cybersecurity. The most highly publicized example was the foreign interference in the 2016 presidential election, followed by additional efforts to influence the 2018 congressional midterms. The Trump administration's fiscal year 2020 budget included more than $17 billion in requested funds for cybersecurity efforts, with almost $10 billion of that going to the Department of Defense.[26] However, two bills on election security passed in 2019 by the Democratic-controlled house were blocked by the Republican Senate majority leader.[27]

Enterprise Architecture and E-Government

The term *enterprise architecture* (EA) has become widely used throughout the public and private sectors and refers in general to a framework for how business processes within an organization should relate to one another. Major emphasis is given to information technology for linking these processes. The term is defined in OMB Circular A-130, *Managing Information as a Strategic Resource*, as follows:[28]

> Agencies shall develop an enterprise architecture (EA) that describes the baseline architecture, target architecture, and a transition plan to get to the target architecture. The agency's EA shall align to their IRM [Information Resource Management] Strategic Plan. The EA should incorporate agency plans for significant upgrades, replacements, and disposition of information systems when the systems can no longer effectively support missions or business functions. The EA should align business and technology resources to achieve strategic outcomes. The process of describing the current and future state of the agency, and laying out a plan for transitioning from the current state to the desired future state, helps agencies to eliminate waste and duplication, increase shared services, close

performance gaps, and promote engagement among Government, industry, and citizens.

Protecting the privacy of individuals and organizations is central to information management. OMB is responsible for overseeing this aspect of information management and works with the CIO Council, mentioned above.[29] The office has provided guidance on such matters as information sharing among agencies. On the one hand, there is a desire to share information so as to avoid two or more agencies collecting the same information and thereby increasing the paperwork burden on individuals. On the other hand, privacy can be violated when information sharing is not handled with suitable safeguards.

Electronic government, or *E-government*, is a central concern. Information technology can be and is used in data sharing with the public, procurement, the regulatory process, and the issuance of grants and their administration. The United Nations, in a 2018 study comparing the online presence of governments, found that the top 5 countries (out of 193 studied) included Denmark, Australia, Korea, the United Kingdom, and Sweden. Five African countries—Somalia, Niger, South Sudan, Chad, and Eritrea, were at the bottom of the UN index. The United States was 11th.[30] The Federal Funding Accountability and Transparency Act of 2006 required the government to create an extensive search engine and database accessible to the public.[31] The system, under the direction of the OMB, provides information about most government grants, loans, and contracts in excess of $25,000. The main means by which OMB implemented this directive was a website, *www.USAspending.gov*, where all contracts and grants awarded to organizations by federal agencies and departments are reported. For each, reports include the name of the organization, the amount of the award, and how the award will be spent. In a report released in December 2018, the GAO evaluated *USAspending.gov* relative to five desirable key practices: providing free and unrestricted data, engaging with users, providing data in useful formats, fully describing the data, and facilitating data discovery for all users.

GAO found that the system complied with most of these practices, but recommended improvements around security and description of data, as well as access for users.[32]

Control of Regulations

In addition to providing relief from paperwork, budget offices may be responsible for providing regulatory relief to businesses and governments. Critics of regulations view them as imposing needless expenses on corporations, which in turn pass these costs on to consumers, or to taxpayers in the case of state and local governments. However, one should keep in mind that regulations are issued pursuant to statutes and that both the regulations and the statutes presumably have important public purposes, such as ensuring the safety of a measles vaccine or the nation's food supply.

The regulatory process occurs at all levels of government and has its champions and critics at all levels. Few would argue that all government regulations are worthless, but regulations can be questioned over their utility considering the costs that they impose on individuals, corporations, and other governments, as in the case of federal regulations affecting state and local governments.

Beginning in the Reagan administration, OMB was given increased powers over the regulatory process, and those powers have been greatly expanded in subsequent years. Part of this movement has probably been driven by political motivations in which presidents have sought to show their concern for keeping a potentially runaway bureaucracy in check. A central line of reasoning is that thorough analysis is needed to determine whether regulations should be issued and then whether they should be retained. In 1993, President Clinton issued Executive Order 12866, which provides for a regulatory planning and review process under OIRA. Each year, agencies must submit to OIRA their proposed plans for revising, issuing, and rescinding regulations. Any proposals for new or revised regulations must be evaluated in terms of their costs and benefits. When OMB rejects a regulation, it is sent back to the agency in the form of a "return letter." OMB also may send a "prompt letter" that need not be in a response to a submission by an agency, but rather suggests that an agency has a problem with its regulations and offers suggestions for improvement.

A major thrust for reformists has been the idea that regulations should exist only if their benefits outweigh the costs they impose on society. Circular A-4, *Regulatory Analysis*, provides ground rules for the conduct of evaluations so that some degree of standardized procedures exists from one agency to another.[33] There are major technical and political issues over what gets counted as a cost and what is counted as a benefit. The budget office was charged by the Regulatory Right-to-Know Act of 1999 with reporting to Congress on the "annual costs and benefits (including quantifiable and nonquantifiable effects) of federal rules and paperwork."[34] OMB estimated that between 2000 and 2010, it reviewed regulations that together had annual costs ranging between $44 billion and $62 billion and benefits ranging between $132 billion and $655 billion.[35]

Republican and Democratic administrations have tended to have differing attitudes toward regulatory policy. Democratic administrations tend to view regulations as necessary to protect the health and safety of the public, while Republican administrations often view regulations as an overreach of government, particularly as it relates to placing constraints on businesses that cost these businesses money and potentially lead to job losses. Accordingly, the George W. Bush administration, by executive order, made it easier for political appointees in federal agencies to eliminate regulatory requirements. The Obama administration revoked those orders, as well as creating additional opportunities for public participation in the regulatory review process.

The Trump administration, consistent with its anti-regulatory agenda, issued Executive Order 13777 in February 2017, barely 1 month after taking office. The order states that "it is the policy of the United States to alleviate unnecessary regulatory burdens on the American people."[36] It seeks to reduce such burdens by directing that each agency head designate a regulatory reform officer to ensure that relevant regulatory reform orders are carried out, including Executive Order 13771 that had been issued by President Trump on January 30, 2017. This previous order had established a process for review and possible repeal of federal regulations, particularly if those regulations had adverse employment impacts, were outdated or ineffective, or imposed costs that exceeded benefits.[37] The order called for eliminating at least two regulations for each new one being proposed.

The Brookings Institution has established an online tool to track Trump administration deregulation progress. According to this inventory, the administration has been successful in repealing the following:

- emissions standards under the Clean Air Act;
- energy conservation standards related to general service lamps;
- the Environmental Protection Agency's rule concerning the Clean Power Plan;
- the nondiscrimination provisions that were included under the Affordable Care Act;
- rules associated with greenhouse gas emissions; and
- rules related to state funding for abortion providers.

This is only a partial list and does not include a large number of regulations that have had their implementation delayed or where the rule is in the process of being considered for repeal.[38] A September 2019 *New York Times* analysis of Trump administration environmental regulations found that there were 85 such regulations that either had been repealed (53) or were in the process of being repealed (32).[39] One specific example is the Trump administration's attempts to revoke the ability of California to regulate automobile pollution.[40]

Adopting a regulation or revising an existing one is an extremely complicated process in the federal government. OMB has identified nine basic steps that include drafting the regulation, publishing it in draft form, obtaining public comments, preparing it in final form, obtaining OMB approval, and publishing it in final form.[41] In addition, several other laws and executive orders may apply. If a regulation affects state and local governments, then analysis must be conducted to determine the financial implications of the regulation. This is in accord with the Unfunded Mandates Reform Act of 1995 (see the chapter on intergovernmental relations).[42] A draft regulation may be required to undergo special analysis of its impact on federalism as required by Executive Order 13132.

OMB has teamed with the General Services Administration in creating the website *www.Reginfo.gov*. The site contains the government's current and past regulatory plans and agendas. It has links to the *Federal Register*, which contains draft and final rules, and to the *Code of Federal Regulations*, which houses current regulations organized by subject. The other important website in this regard is *www.Regulations.gov*. This site, which includes information on proposed rules from more than 300 federal agencies, provides easy access to all documents that are open for public comment and allows searching of regulations by subject.

In 1996, the Congress passed a law that, among other provisions, provided for a legislative review of regulatory actions. This provision, codified in the Congressional Review Act (CRA), provides a form of legislative veto of administrative regulations.[43] Before a proposed rule can take effect, it must be submitted to Congress. Congress then has 60 days, excluding days when it is in recess for 4 days or more, to review the regulations and can pass a joint resolution disapproving or vetoing the regulations. The president may veto the resolution, and Congress may consider overriding the president's veto. A GAO study found that outgoing presidential administrations tended to issue a large number of regulatory changes prior to leaving office, and that this workload tended to interfere with the intent of the CRA. Specifically, the percentage of rules that were noncompliant with the CRA (meaning, normally, not providing the Congress with sufficient time to review significant regulations prior to their taking effect) was found to be much higher in the transition between the Obama and Trump administrations and in the prior two presidential transition years.[44]

Given all of the items discussed here—reorganization, management controls, control of information, enterprise architecture and E-government, and control of regulations—some observers have suggested that such management tasks are too great to be left to budget offices. One suggestion is to create a separate office of management that would have nonbudgetary duties ranging well beyond what OMB currently has. The argument against creating an office of management hinges mainly on the fact that the issues addressed have budgetary implications, and to assign them to a different agency would automatically create coordination problems.

In addition to relations between the central budget office and the line agencies, several other subsystems are in operation during budget execution. Taxes and other debts must be collected, the cash needs of the government must be met, items must be purchased, and the vulnerability of the government to loss of property and other problems must be managed. These topics are discussed next.

Tax Administration and Debt Collection

Tax administration, which is discussed here, and cash management, which is discussed in the next section, are two functions that are usually under the same administrative officer, typically a secretary of treasury or revenue. Having the two functions linked together administratively facilitates sharing information. The cash manager uses information generated by the tax administrator. At the federal level, the Treasury Department handles these tasks. While the two earlier chapters on budgeting for revenues discussed the nature of various taxes, here we consider how those taxes are administered over the course of the fiscal year.

Besides taxes, numerous other revenue sources must be administered. User charges are common at all levels of government. State lotteries have become important sources of revenue. Administrators responsible for lotteries focus on marketing to increase sales. As the dollar value of sales increases, the unit cost of administration declines. Governments lend billions of dollars, and loan payments frequently are delinquent. Therefore, debt collection is of great import.

Main Steps

Tax administration has four main steps:

1. Determining the objects or services to be taxed. Using the local property tax as an example, parcels of land and structures, along with their owners, must be identified.
2. Applying the tax. In the case of the property tax, this is an annual process. Governments make property tax calculations, and bills are sent to property owners. In contrast, sales tax calculations are made each time a sale occurs. Individuals have the responsibility to calculate their own income taxes.
3. Collecting the revenues. Funds are paid either directly to the government, as in the case of a corporation's paying income tax, or through a third party, as in the case of employers' remitting individual income tax withholdings to the government.
4. Enforcing the law. Audits are conducted selectively of taxpayers to verify compliance, and some taxpayers are prosecuted for tax evasion.

The chapters on budgeting for revenues have already highlighted many of the important administrative issues that are raised by initial application and collection, in the context of issues such as the determination of property tax liability and taxable income under the individual income tax. The remainder of this section highlights four issues that present challenges particular to tax administration—enforcement, the role of technology, debt collection, and taxpayer rights. Tradeoffs exist, as between collections and taxpayer rights.

Enforcement

Numerous tax enforcement measures are used, and well-trained and ethical personnel are essential for effective enforcement practices.

- The IRS verifies mathematical accuracy through the use of optical scanning. Proper design of forms and clearly written instructions contribute to improved taxpayer accuracy in filing returns. Verification has been made easier because of the extensive use of e-filing.

- Tax return information supplied by individuals is compared with information supplied by banks, employers, and other federal agencies, such as the Social Security Administration.
- Governments share computer-based data to compare information on income being reported (or not reported).[45]
- Taxpayer services are provided to help in preparing tax returns. Services may be available at designated government offices, at other facilities, by telephone, and online.[46]
- Governments draw samples of taxpayer returns to audit. Regression models are designed to identify cases that are most likely to involve noncompliance with the tax laws. In addition, some taxpayers are audited in response to tips received from the public, and others are audited at random in an attempt to encourage voluntary compliance.
- Delinquent accounts are investigated, as are accounts in which taxpayers have stopped complying altogether.
- Some taxpayers are prosecuted in court, depending on the "seriousness" of the cases and the availability of resources to pursue the cases in court.
- Special enforcement is reserved for sources of illegal income, such as gambling, prostitution, narcotics, and, more generally, organized crime.

Any government must decide how many resources to commit to these various activities and how resources should be distributed among them. The IRS has been criticized for not having a firm idea of the relative yield in tax revenue generated from these activities. Performance measures are needed to determine the relative merits of these activities.[47] Decisions must be made not only about the type of activity to conduct, but also about the distribution of tax enforcement resources across different forms of taxes. For example, a state needs to decide how many

resources to commit to tax cheating on personal income, corporate income, and motor fuels taxes.

Complaints often arise that some taxpayers are being audited more intensively than others. Increased auditing may be warranted where it is known that certain types of taxpayers are more likely to cheat on their returns than others. Politics also come into play, and particular types of tax cheating may be highlighted for this reason. The objective of having taxpayers comply with the law is having them report all taxable income. Failure to report income results in less money being paid in taxes. The difference between what taxpayers pay and what they should pay is known as the *tax gap*. The Internal Revenue Service (IRS) estimated the tax gap for tax year 2011 through 2013 to be an average of $441 billion, which dropped to $381 billion after accounting for IRS tax collections in response to the gap. This translates to a compliance rate of approximately 84%. This percentage of voluntary compliance has been relatively stable in recent years.[48] A 2019 article cited compliance figures (62% to 68%) in European countries much lower than those for the United States. This same article cited a 2017 IRS survey suggesting that 88% of Americans do not think it is "at all acceptable" to cheat on taxes.[49]

Determining compliance/noncompliance with the tax laws is, of course, a difficult task. If the IRS or any other tax agency knew that taxpayers were not complying, the agency would seek to collect the delinquent taxes owed. Noncompliance data by nature, therefore, are imprecise estimates. The IRS, for a time, used a system of super-audits that required a sample of taxpayers to substantiate every item on their tax returns, but these were determined to be ineffective in detecting unreported income and identifying unauthorized or fraudulent claims for tax deductions and tax credits. At the federal level, funds have been cut for tax enforcement, leading to questions about whether the IRS is able to effectively monitor compliance with tax laws.[50]

Another consideration is that tax administration would be far less complicated if tax laws were less complicated. Of course, the reason for their complexity is simple: Tax laws are replete with specific conditions to take into account the specific conditions of taxpayers. Some countries have tax-withholding systems that free most taxpayers from the onerous task of preparing and filing tax returns. If tax laws were simplified, people would be better able to calculate their tax bills and would have less opportunity to cheat, and tax agencies would need to spend far less than current levels on tax administration.[51]

Technology in Tax Administration

It should come as no surprise that technology is playing increasingly important roles in tax administration:

- Besides routine recordkeeping, computers are used for drawing samples for tax auditing and for cross-checking information among different sources.
- Many businesses are required to make federal tax payments through the Electronic Federal Tax Payment System.[52]
- State and local governments electronically submit federal income tax and Social Security withholdings.
- Answers to frequently asked questions pertaining to tax laws are commonly available on government websites.
- Many local governments have automated tax systems that can make withdrawals for property taxes from taxpayers' bank accounts, providing that taxpayers preapprove such withdrawals.
- In many jurisdictions, taxpayers use telephone or online services to pay their taxes.
- Many governments accept credit and debit cards for payment of taxes, fees, parking tickets, and the like.
- Many states accept electronic funds transfers for corporations making tax payments.
- Electronic auctions are used by governments to sell delinquent tax properties.
- Auditors on field assignments use portable computers with wireless Internet connections. Computers can be used to manage tax cases,

providing in any one case a variety of information and prompting the case manager with reminders about the status of the case.
- Tax office employees can work at home on confidential tax files using secure, high-speed access to networks.

One of the most important developments in this area relates to online tax filing and payments. The Internal Revenue Service Restructuring and Reform Act of 1998 mandated the rapid development of electronic filing, using the aforementioned Electronic Federal Tax Payment System that was unveiled in 2001. The IRS estimated that 92% of all taxpayers filed electronically for tax years 2016 through 2018. This was up from 86% for 2014, and 70% for 2010.[53] As of 2019, 37 states permitted state returns to be accepted through federal/state e-file.[54]

Debt Collection

One of the biggest debts owed to government is taxes, but individuals and corporations also may owe several other types of debt to government. Loans, both direct and guaranteed, result in some defaults. Federal credit programs exist for college students, low-income housing, ship construction, development in other nations, and small businesses recovering from disasters, to name only a few. Various other business transactions with government result in debts, including farmers owing on crop insurance payments and foreign countries owing on purchases of agricultural commodities. Fines are another form of debt owed to the government, as in the case of a corporation being fined for not meeting environmental standards for its mining operations.

The federal government, as discussed in the chapter on budget preparation and the decision process, is attempting to deal with the "hidden liabilities" of federal credit programs. General information on credit is contained in the *Analytical Perspectives* budget document, and more detailed information is available through other documents produced by OMB and the Treasury Department.

OMB Circular A-129, *Policies for Federal Credit Programs and Non-Tax Receivables*, lays out

15 specific requirements that agencies must follow in managing their credit programs. These cover following statutory and regulatory requirements, ensuring that changes in law and regulations are proposed that will assist the programs in meeting their objectives, establishing oversight and internal controls over program funds, providing for appropriate debt collection, and collecting and using performance data to ensure that programs meet their objectives.[55]

Federal agencies must calculate expected credit losses on both direct and guaranteed loans. These losses can reduce the amount of funding available for future loans.

The Debt Collection Act of 1982, the Debt Collection Improvement Act of 1996, and OMB Circular A-129 further require that agencies take steps to improve their credit programs. Loan applications must be examined with an eye toward uncovering the risks that government would take in approving the loans. Delinquent cases can be turned over to collection agencies and can be reported to consumer credit agencies. Salary offsets can be used in the case of federal employees who owe the government, and individuals may have income tax refunds withheld up to the amount owed. State governments have also used this latter technique.

In the mid-2000s, the IRS announced plans to turn over some tax collection to private firms.[56] As of 2019, the IRS was required to use private debt collection agencies to collect certain delinquent taxes, and the IRS website listed the four debt collection agencies. In order to protect taxpayers from unscrupulous unauthorized debt collection activity, the same site lays out the process that must be followed by these private firms. The process includes prior written notification from the IRS indicating that your case has been turned over to one of these private agencies.[57]

Taxpayer Rights

In their zeal to extract as many tax dollars as legally possible from the public, tax administrators must keep in mind that the citizens are ultimately responsible for setting tax laws and for paying the salaries of tax administrators. In other words, administrators are employees of the citizenry. To this end, governments have adopted laws that declare a set of rights for taxpayers.

The Internal Revenue Service Restructuring and Reform Act of 1998 contains more than 70 provisions that protect taxpayers and gives them rights in dealing with the IRS. The law includes such important provisions as altering the burden of proof in taxpayer cases. If the IRS challenges a taxpayer on reported income tax deductions, for example, the taxpayer need only provide some credible evidence, which then shifts the burden to the IRS to disprove the evidence. An important provision is that innocent spouses can be relieved of tax fines and other penalties. Restrictions are imposed on liens and on the seizing of taxpayer property for back taxes. The IRS, as prescribed by the legislation, maintains a taxpayer advocate office, which assists taxpayers in dealing with the agency. States also have taxpayer bills of rights.[58]

The standard view in the field is that taxpayers' privacy needs to be protected and taxpayers need to be treated equally. Some government workers have been found browsing the tax returns of celebrities and other prominent figures. The response is to restrict access to files to ensure security and avoid record tampering. One problem has been that taxpayer records are sometimes left in open areas of a tax administration office. In such situations, the records can be seen by unauthorized personnel, stolen, or lost.[59] Another concern is that the audit process not be politically motivated. The IRS, state tax agencies, and private tax professionals have been challenged by identity thefts in the filing of tax returns.[60]

Cash Management

Cash management is the process of administering monies to ensure that they are available over time to meet expenditure needs and that, when temporarily not needed, they are invested at a minimum risk and a maximum yield. Cash management involves both short- and long-term investments. The latter are used mainly in the case of pension funds that try to build up reserves for future years when employees retire. The state of the art of cash management is necessarily dependent on the state of the larger financial system.

Cash Flow

An essential aspect of cash management is forecasting when revenues will be received and in what amounts, and when expenditures will occur and in what amounts, over the course of the fiscal year and beyond.[61] A cash management plan will strive to accelerate the receipt of revenues and delay or minimize expenditures.

The chapter on financial management discusses the cash flows statement as one form of financial reporting.

Inflow of Revenues

Enforcement of tax laws is viewed as one means of maximizing inflow. Other techniques involve depositing government receipts as soon as possible into interest-bearing accounts. For example, when tax payments accompany tax returns, these checks can be immediately deposited in banks, and processing the returns can occur later. Governments attempt to minimize the *float time* between when checks and currency are received and when they are deposited. Accounts receivable, involving payments due from citizens, corporations, and other governments, are kept to a minimum. Inflow can be accelerated by prompt invoicing. For example, airlines may be invoiced on a monthly basis for their gate space at an airport terminal.

Method of Receiving Revenues

At one time, governments received all of their revenues by check. When this was true, lockboxes were an important innovation for revenue receipt. Under this system, used selectively by the federal government and some state governments, post office boxes are used that are under the control of banks. Taxpayers send their payments to designated post office boxes that are opened by banking officials, and the receipts are deposited promptly. The process reduces the amount of float time between when a check is written and when government deposits it and begins

earning interest. Increasingly, of course, a higher and higher percentage of payments are made electronically, through electronic funds transfer (EFT) or similar methods.

Expenditure Planning and Prompt Payment

Some techniques deal not with inflow, but with outflow. Here the concern is keeping money in interest-bearing accounts until it is needed to cover expenses and avoiding the need to borrow funds to cover expenses when revenues, such as tax receipts, are unavailable in the projected amounts. Cash flow planning is one reason that agencies are required to submit apportionment plans to the central budget office. Agencies may be instructed to shift expenditures in apportionment plans from one month or quarter to another. One rule is to pay promptly—that is, when bills are due and not before or after. This procedure is mandated at the federal level by the Prompt Payment Act of 1982, as amended.[62] Paying bills promptly saves money for the government, such as avoiding payment of late fees, and reduces a common problem encountered by government's suppliers—namely, not knowing when they will be paid. Small businesses are the most severely hurt when government agencies fail to pay their bills on time.[63] Prompt payment can also be thrown off by antiquated technology systems. The federal government's payments to individuals and businesses in the immediate aftermath of the COVID-19 crisis were slowed by a reliance on outdated technology, some of which dated from the 1960s.[64]

Although the vast majority of the federal government's payments to vendors are on time, that may still leave many millions of other payments that are late.[65] The Bureau of the Fiscal Service within the Treasury Department has a prompt payment web page that provides for simple interest calculations for short-term tardiness and compound interest when a government agency is in arrears by months. For example, in the last half of 2019, the government paid 2.625% interest on late payments. If a payment of $6,000,000 was overdue by 31 days, then the government would owe $13,563 in addition to the principal. The web page also provides a calculator to help an agency decide when to accept a vendor's offer of a discount for early payment.[66]

Of course, another concern is to make sure that bills are not only paid on time, but paid to the right party and in the right amount. Lax disbursement systems increase the chances that errors are made in paying vendors and that fraud occurs. Fraud can happen without a government officer being aware of the situation—or with the officer's assistance.

Borrowing

If forecasted expenditures cannot be adjusted downward to be no greater than expected revenues, then short-term borrowing becomes an important option. State and local governments borrow from banks for up to 1 year in cases where expenditures are considered essential and funds are unavailable to cover the expenses. The backing of these bank notes consists of future receipt of revenues, and the instruments are known as BANs, RANs, and TANs—*bond, revenue,* and *tax anticipation notes* (see the chapter on debt management).

Governments also may spend from their own reserves and borrow from themselves. *Unrestricted fund balances,* which are in effect contingency funds, may be drawn upon to meet unanticipated expenditure needs. Short-term borrowing from one fund to meet the cash needs of another also occurs, as in the case of a local government's borrowing from its pension funds. State laws, however, may greatly restrict such borrowing as a protection against depleting the funds.

Some governments have established *rainy day funds* or *budget stabilization funds* that can be used during years when revenues decline. Statutes or state constitutional provisions require that monies be placed in these funds when the economy improves and revenues rise and that monies may be withdrawn only when revenues decline by some set percentage. It is common for governments to have in these funds something in excess of 5% of their general funds, although the appropriate amount needed depends on many factors that vary across different units of government.[67] These funds can reduce fiscal stress during recessions, such as occurred in the early 1990s, the early 2000s, and later in the first decade of the 2000s.[68] A state that dipped heavily into its rainy day fund in one year to balance its budget might then face major problems in the following year if the economy had not recovered, perhaps forcing decision makers to increase taxes. The use of budget stabilization monies also implies the replenishment of these funds when the budgetary environment becomes more favorable.

Given the severity of the Great Recession, many states found that the balances in their rainy day funds were insufficient to prevent them from needing to take other actions. Indeed, it is not necessarily the intent that these funds enable states to weather all storms; rather, they are designed to either enable them to adequately confront relatively small disruptions or to buy them time in dealing with larger ones. In this recent recession, most states with rainy day funds used them at least to some extent. The balances in state rainy day funds dropped from a high of $35 billion in 2006, before the recession, to less than $5 billion by 2010. They were restored to pre-recession levels by 2016.[69]

Historically, the rule of thumb for rainy day funds has been 5% of the budget, although there is no reason to believe that a fund of the same size would be appropriate for each state. In reality, there are many factors that would dictate the appropriate fund size, including the volatility of state revenues.[70] In aggregate, states as of 2018 had more money set aside to weather the next recession than they had set aside prior to the Great Recession. Still, there were concerns that some states were relatively unprepared for a future fiscal disruption.[71]

Investment Planning

When forecasts show periods during the year when revenues will exceed expenditures, plans are made for investment. Virtually all governments encounter this situation. Often there are spurts in revenue receipts, such as when local property taxes are due or state sales tax receipts are paid following the Christmas shopping period.

At least seven factors must be taken into account when devising an investment strategy:

1. *Security*. Financial institutions insure some deposits only up to $100,000.
2. *Maturity date*. Some instruments mature in a few months, while others mature in 30 years.
3. *Marketability or liquidity*. If cash is needed before the maturity date, may an instrument be sold to a third party, or will the issuer convert the instrument to cash?
4. *Call provisions*. May the issuer repay the investor before the date of maturity?
5. *Denominations*. Minimum amounts for investing range from $1,000 to $100,000 or more.
6. *Yield or return on investment*. Yield is measured in terms of a percentage of the investment and often expressed as an interest rate.
7. *Legal authority*. State laws may prohibit the state government and local governments from making some types of investments.

Investment Instruments

The instruments available for state and local investments consist of three general types: federal government securities, corporate securities, and money market instruments. Any government must decide to what extent it wishes to invest in each type.

Federal Securities

Fully guaranteed federal securities include Treasury bills (T-bills), notes, and bonds. T-bills mature in 4, 13, 26, and 52 weeks. They are sold at a discount by auction and consequently have no set percentage return. Treasury notes and bonds, which range in maturity from 1 to 30 years, and mature every 6 months. In the 1990s, the Treasury Department launched two instruments that are sensitive to inflation. When inflation occurs, the yield rate increases. Treasury inflation-protected securities, known as TIPS, have their interest rate set at the time of auction. Their principal rises or falls based on the consumer price index. If the consumer price index rises in a time period, the value of the note rises and then the interest is calculated based on the new principal. If deflation occurs, investors at the time of maturity are guaranteed the original purchase price.

The other inflation-sensitive instrument is the Series I savings bond. I bonds are purchased at face value, which ranges between $50 and $10,000, and have a fixed rate of return. Inflation rates, then, are added to the calculations. TIPS and I bonds have yield rates that are somewhat lower than instruments that lack the inflation protection.

Series EE/E savings bonds are guaranteed by the government, can be cashed after 6 months, and earn interest up to 30 years. Those bonds issued before May 1, 2005, pay interest at current market rates. Bonds issued May 1, 2005, and after pay interest at a fixed rate. EE bonds exist in paper and electronic form, but the U.S. Treasury no longer issues the paper form.[72]

Other Federal-Related Securities

Other securities are issued by credit institutions created by the federal government and may have full, limited, or no backing or ambiguous backing of the government. Instruments backed by the federal government include insured notes of the Housing and Community Facilities Programs within the Agriculture Department and the Government Home Loan Mortgage Corporation, which is part of the Department of Housing and Urban Development. Instruments that do not have the expressed guarantee of the federal government but could be backed in emergency situations include Federal Home Loan Bank bonds, Federal Land Bank bonds, and Federal Intermediate Credit Bank bonds. Many of these federal-related securities involve mortgages, including mortgages on homes, farms, cooperatives, and overseas investments (Asian Development Bank notes and bonds and Export Import Bank debentures).

Corporate Securities

Corporations are another possibility for the investment of state and local monies. Corporate bonds are essentially loans made to the issuers. Stocks, in comparison, represent ownership of the corporation. In the event that a corporation goes into bankruptcy, creditors such as bondholders are paid first. If any assets remain, they are then distributed among stockholders.

Money Market Instruments

Financial institutions provide numerous investment opportunities. Interest is paid on *negotiable order of withdrawal* checking accounts and on savings accounts. Not only can government earn interest on these deposits, but other benefits may also be negotiated through *linked deposit agreements*. In these situations, banks, as a condition of receiving government deposits, may agree to make available more loans for housing in a community or for industrial development in a targeted area.

Monies can also be invested in money market instruments, with *certificates of deposit* (CDs) being one of the most popular. Issuers include banks, offshore subsidiaries of U.S. banks, and U.S. branches of foreign banks. The latter two issue what are known as *Eurodollars* and *Yankee CDs*, respectively, which are not guaranteed by the federal government.

Some, but not all, CDs are negotiable. Issuers may charge interest penalties for early withdrawal of monies. Various other instruments, used less frequently, include *bankers' acceptances* and *commercial paper*. Bankers' acceptances are agreements to purchase a bank's agreement to loan money on a short-term basis to a corporation (one usually involved in international trade). Commercial paper, also available through banks, is a corporate promissory note. A repurchase agreement (repo) is a pool of U.S. government securities held by a financial institution and sold temporarily to state and local governments and other purchasers. The institution agrees to repurchase the securities at a later date.

State and local governments may purchase combinations of various money market instruments. One technique is to invest in a money market fund that is a pool of securities. The Securities and Exchange Commission regulates these funds in an attempt to reduce the risks undertaken by investors. Despite these regulations, however, laws preclude many governments from investing in money market funds because they often include higher-risk investments such as Eurodollars.

Derivatives

One of the most controversial financial instruments is known as a derivative.[73] Derivatives are highly complex devices that are often poorly understood by both those who sell them and the state and local governments that buy them. A derivative's value depends upon some underlying security or a market index. In other words, the derivative is a bet on what future interest rates will be. Governments purchase swaps that trade in variable rates for fixed rates, with the underlying gamble by the government being that the return on investment will be better with the fixed rate. Some derivatives take the form of collateralized mortgage obligations, which entail investing in a pool of mortgages with the return being based on changes in interest rates and changes in mortgage prepayment rates (see discussion of the extensive use of derivatives in the subprime mortgage market in the chapter on government and the economy). Investments by state and local governments in derivatives created substantial problems during the recession that started in 2007. For example, a class action lawsuit in Texas alleged that the Teachers Retirement System in Texas lost $415 million because of investments in derivatives.[74]

Investment Pools

Another money management technique that has become popular is for jurisdictions to combine their investments into a state-authorized investment pool.[75] By pooling resources, smaller jurisdictions can take advantage of higher-yield investments that require larger investments than passbook savings or CDs. Liquidity is improved in that jurisdictions can often withdraw some of their monies from these pools without the financial loss that would be involved if they held securities themselves and had to liquidate them. The Governmental Accounting Standards Board has worked to establish guidelines on the operation of local government investment pools.[76]

Yield Rates

Table 11-1 provides a snapshot of yield rates for some of the instruments discussed here. As can be seen from the table, the rates varied considerably

Table 11-1 Yield Rates of Selected Investment Instruments

Instrument	2005	2011	2019
Federal Securities			
4-week bills	2.94	0.04	2.08
3-month bills	3.15	0.05	2.06
6-month bills	3.39	0.10	2.05
1-year bills	NA	0.17	1.99
Inflation Indexed			
5-year	1.50	−0.41	0.35
10-year	1.81	0.55	0.40
20-year	1.97	1.19	0.60
30-year	NA	1.47	0.78
Constant Maturities			
5-year	4.05	1.52	1.95
10-year	4.29	2.78	2.14
20-year	4.64	3.62	2.40
30-year	NA	3.91	2.58

Compiled by author from U.S. Federal Reserve Board (2020). Website. Retrieved April 23, 2020, from https://www.federalreserve.gov/datadownload/Build.aspx?rel=H15. Specific data from following URLs: Treasury Bills: https://www.federalreserve.gov/datadownload/Review.aspx?rel=H15&series=27df0e9d98c18e6bc8e5875bc74884d4&lastobs=&from=01/01/2005&to=12/31/2019&filetype=csv&label=include&layout=seriesrow; Treasury Securities inflation-indexed: https://www.federalreserve.gov/datadownload/Review.aspx?rel=H15&series=5e9b356ff76926b45c4560a4b3329726&lastobs=&from=01/01/2005&to=12/31/2019&filetype=spreadsheetml&label=include&layout=seriesrow; Treasury Securities constant maturity: https://www.federalreserve.gov/datadownload/Review.aspx?rel=H15&series=6ee28668562ab2ca26387f18d557ec5e&lastobs=&from=01/01/2005&to=12/31/2019&filetype=spreadsheetml&label=include&layout=seriescolumn. Federal Reserve. Department of the Treasury (2020), Daily Treasury Yield Curve Rates. Retrieved January 31, 2020 from https://www.treasury.gov/resource-center/data-chart-center/interest-rates/Pages/TextView.aspx?data=yieldYear&year=2018.

among the 3 years reported. Rates increase with risk, with higher-risk instruments paying higher rates. The federal inflated-indexed securities paid decidedly less than other securities, indicating a price that purchasers pay for being protected from possible inflation. Bonds usually pay a higher rate than notes, and notes pay a higher rate than bills, because of the time factor involved, but this pattern does not happen to show up in the years sampled. Note the very low rates, in particular, paid on U.S. Treasury securities in 2011; these are largely a reflection of a very loose Fed monetary policy.

Use of Investment Instruments

Most of the money (more than 90%) in state and local government trust funds, such as employee retirement systems and workers' compensation, is invested, and little is kept on hand. In contrast, the money for the rest of state and local governments is kept much more fluid (one-third in cash and deposits and two-thirds invested). Retirement systems invest mainly in corporate stocks and bonds (49.68%), government securities (12.23%), and foreign and international securities (25.3%).[77] In 2018, the California investment pool had 12.9%

of its funds in federal agency discount notes, 11.8% in certificates of deposit, 10.0% in commercial paper, 7.0% in bank time deposits, and 27.5% in federal securities. California had no funds invested in corporate bonds.[78]

As noted earlier, legal constraints affect investment programs. Illinois law, for example, had barred the state from depositing funds with financial institutions that had specific ties with Sudan, but this law was declared unconstitutional by a federal judge in 2007.[79] Such laws exist in other states as well, and a New Hampshire State Supreme Court upheld that state's divestiture act in 2010.[80] The state of Maryland, as of 2019, was considering a strategy that would take into account the carbon footprint of firms included in the state's investment portfolio.[81]

Investment Risks

Investments are not risk free to the investor. To the extent that governments are investors, they must account for this risk. One type of risk involves the creditworthiness of the issuer of a security. Bonds issued by the federal government are nearly risk free in this sense, and bonds issued by major corporations, such as Apple or Microsoft, are low risk. Another aspect of risk, however, is whether a particular instrument is volatile in terms of the yield it may produce. In this context, fixed-rate, long-term government bonds are risky investments. If a government's portfolio contains high-yield securities at a time when yield rates are declining, then the situation is generally positive. If trends reverse and yield rates climb above those in the portfolio, however, the government may have difficulty selling low-bearing securities. In that situation, a government's investments might fail to keep pace with inflation. Derivatives are often singled out as one of the most high-risk investments due to their volatility, even though the issuers of the derivatives may be creditworthy. In the 1990s, Orange County, California, was embroiled in a massive problem involving derivatives. The county had been hailed as a shrewd investor, earning close to double the rate of return on investments compared with other governments and investment pools. The county had

been so successful that 180 other local governments had deposited money with Orange County with the expectation of reaping the benefits of an investment policy that was more aggressive than the typical one. In 1994, reality hit hard. This approach resulted in a loss of nearly $2 billion. What went wrong in Orange County? The short answer is that heavy investments were placed in derivatives. Derivatives are gambles on what will happen to interest rates. When rates went in the opposite direction than expected, the county was in trouble.

The Governmental Accounting Standards Board (GASB) has issued important directives regarding investments of government monies.[82] Statement No. 3, *Deposits with Financial Institutions, Investments (including Repurchase Agreements), and Reverse Repurchase Agreements*, mandates that governments report high-risk investments in their comprehensive annual financial reports. Statement No. 9, *Reporting Cash Flows of Proprietary and Nonexpendable Trust Funds and Governmental Entities that Use Proprietary Fund Accounting*, as its title suggests, sets rules for reporting cash flows for those activities within a government that are run like businesses, such as a municipal transit system or parking garage.

While an annual report showing such investments is helpful, more short-term reporting is needed. One option is to mark or report the value of each item in a portfolio on a daily basis. GASB Statement No. 31, *Accounting and Financial Reporting for Certain Investments and for External Investment Pools*, specifies that governments account for and report "fair value" for their investments in (1) participating interest-earning investment contracts; (2) external investment pools; (3) open-end mutual funds; (4) debt securities; and (5) equity securities, option contracts, stock warrants, and stock rights that have readily determinable fair values.

Federal Cash Management

The federal government's cash management system is considerably different from those of state and local governments. Federal monies are kept with the Federal Reserve System (see the chapter on government and the economy), which pays a form of interest for deposits, and banks, which also pay interest. The Bureau of the Fiscal Service (BFS) of the Treasury Department handles transactions. BFS provides extensive information on its website about the overall aspects of cash management and about specific operations. For example, the BFS *Green Book* provides detailed instructions to financial institutions as to how they are to process federal monies using automatic clearing houses.[83] The agency's *Gold Book* gives specifics on how federal checks are to be reclaimed when they have been forged or have been issued to persons no longer eligible for payment.[84] Other departments and agencies handle many cash management transactions in accordance with instructions issued by the Treasury Department.

The inflow of federal receipts comes from taxes and other payments and from the sale of T-bills and other instruments discussed earlier. These sales are handled through the Federal Reserve and are limited according to the total debt ceiling set by Congress (see the chapter on budget approval and the U.S. Congress). T-bills are auctioned off weekly, and other instruments are sold less frequently. There is, of course, a secondary market for these securities.

Like state and local governments, the federal government is concerned about having needed cash on hand and minimizing the costs of money, such as avoiding late payment fees on government purchases and avoiding paying out funds any earlier than required. An additional consideration at the federal level is that the government's cash operations affect markets.[85]

The federal government operates under the Cash Management Improvement Act of 1990 in making payments to state and local governments, particularly grant payments.[86] BFS lists three objectives of the law:

1. Efficiency—to minimize the time between the transfer of funds to the states and the payout for program purposes
2. Effectiveness—to ensure that federal funds are available when requested

3. Equity—to assess an interest liability to the federal government and/or the states to compensate for the lost value of funds[87]

Another important consideration is that the federal government must meet its cash needs on a global basis. Sufficient amounts of money must be available at specific times in specific countries. For example, the Department of Defense (DOD) must handle large sums of foreign currency and, in doing so, exposes itself to potential problems in the value of such currency, particularly in the currency's devaluation.[88]

Currency

Since the 1990s, the federal government has been introducing redesigned currency. The bills use color-shifting ink, security threads, watermarks, large off-center portraits, low-vision features, and microprinting that greatly deter counterfeiting. Nevertheless, counterfeiting remains a concern, given the sophistication of contemporary photocopying equipment. Also, politics entered into the redesign of the $20 bill in 2019 when an image of Harriet Tubman, a former slave and major abolitionist, would have replaced that of former President Andrew Jackson, a slave owner.[89] The redesign project was put on hold.

Electronic Funds Transfers

Advances in computer technology have made possible extensive use of electronic funds transfers (EFTs). Through EFTs, monies are moved via computer communication from bank to bank and from account to account. Monies received at one bank through a lockbox system, for instance, can be moved to other accounts in distant banks. Another advantage of EFTs is that they can be used for recurring payments, such as making direct deposits of Social Security payments into retirees' bank accounts. A form of EFT is the electronic benefit transfer, which can be used to transfer funds through automatic teller machines. Some governments use electronic benefit transfers to make payments to welfare recipients. EFTs are also used by governments to transfer funds for alimony and child support in cases of divorce.

The transfers, which are processed nationally by a few large banking systems, cost much less per transaction than do conventional checks.

Congress decided, in the Debt Collection Improvement Act of 1996, to phase out most check writing by January 1, 1999. This trend toward phasing out paper checks has continued, with the U.S. Treasury announcing in April 2011 that new recipients of Social Security benefits would be required to accept electronic payments—they would no longer have the option of receiving paper checks. Current check recipients were required to switch to electronic payment by March 2013.[90] People without bank accounts may receive their payments through U.S. Treasury issued Direct Express debit cards.[91]

Letters of Credit

An important cash management technique, especially for the federal government, is the use of letters of credit. As mandated by the Cash Management Improvement Act of 1990, these letters are provided to governments and nonprofit corporations that are awarded grants and contracts. The letters allow recipient organizations to establish credit at banks without the federal government having to provide money until it is needed. Funds then are transferred electronically into these accounts by the federal government.[92]

Procurement

Procurement entails the acquisition of resources required in providing government services.[93] While this function is not at the core of budgeting, it has major budgetary implications. In fiscal year 2017, the federal government spent $510 billion (or roughly 13% of its budget) on contracted goods or services. This represents the average level of procurement spending over the past 10 fiscal years.[94] Procurement is a massive business. According to Bloomberg Government's annual listing of the top 200 federal contractors, the top five companies in federal contracting in fiscal 2019 were Lockheed Martin, Boeing, General Dynamics, Raytheon, and Northrop Grumman. All of these companies play major roles in the defense and aerospace industries.[95]

Some government agencies, such as the DOD and NASA, spend a major share of their resources on contracted products and services rather than delivering services directly on their own. In addition, most other federal agencies accomplish their missions through the actions of other parties, usually through grants and other transfers of funds (see the discussion in the chapter on intergovernmental relations). Contracting, while fundamental to the operations of government, is not always handled well in budgets. Some local governments exclude contracts from their budgets and others report them only in lump sum. With the growing emphasis on results-oriented budgeting, governments have been forced to report contracts in their budgets.

Organizational Configurations

Most jurisdictions have procurement systems that blend centralized and decentralized services. A central purchasing agency may be responsible for acquiring commonly used materials, such as office furniture and supplies, while line agencies have authority to purchase items used primarily by themselves. Centralization, at least in theory, has the advantage of providing overall controls to ensure that appropriate procedures are followed, resulting in fair competition among government suppliers and the purchase of quality goods and services at the lowest possible prices (due to savings arising from economies of scale). Decentralization, in contrast, presumably reduces red tape, allowing individual agencies to make purchases as needed and to tailor purchases to their specific needs. At the federal level, several major organizational units are responsible for procurement. The General Services Administration (GSA) provides overall support to departments by procuring buildings, equipment, motor vehicles, computer systems, telephone systems, supplies, day care centers for employees' dependents, and the like. Its operations are immense. Although GSA has numerous components, the main ones are the

Public Buildings Service (PBS) and the Federal Acquisition Service (FAS). PBS manages more than 8,700 federally owned or leased buildings; the inventory of rental space alone adds up to nearly 370 million square feet. FAS "provides Federal agencies with over 28 million different products and services, and annually delivers over $55B[illion] in IT products, services and solutions, telecommunications services, assisted acquisition services, travel and transportation management solutions, motor vehicles and fleet services, and charge card services." FAS also managed over 215,000 leased vehicles and 35 million charge cards.[96]

The PBS unit operates with appropriated funds, while FAS operates with revolving funds by buying goods and services and then selling them to federal agencies.[97] All federal line departments and agencies carry out procurement, with the DOD having one of the largest procurement operations. The Defense Logistics Agency purchases many common items centrally for the department, while the individual services and other DOD agencies also have purchasing authority.[98]

The existence of many procurement offices can result in a hodgepodge of operations, each with its own peculiar set of regulations. In 1974, Congress attempted to deal with this problem by creating the Office of Federal Procurement Policy (OFPP) within the OMB.[99] The OFPP, while not conducting purchasing activities, is responsible for overall procurement policy and coordinating the activities of purchasing offices. The GSA issues the Federal Acquisition Regulation (FAR), which sets standards for basically all federal acquisitions. The DOD and other agencies have regulations that supplement FAR.[100] Besides a central procurement office and individual agency offices, there are other possible arrangements. In some instances, one agency may piggyback on a contract issued through another agency. Another approach is for agencies to work together jointly on acquisitions. This has the advantage of increasing buying power over what any one agency would have, but has the drawback of requiring that the procurement regulations of both agencies be met.

Procurement Objectives

A procurement program has several objectives. One chief concern is having the materials and supplies available when needed and avoiding stock outages. Every agency must focus on its mission and use procurement as a means of completing that mission in a timely fashion. Because public agencies are spending public funds, they must also strive to conduct their business with integrity, fairness, and openness, and in the case of the federal government, fulfill other public policy and socioeconomic objectives.

Keeping unit costs as low as possible is another objective. The lowest costs for acquiring items are often obtained by ordering large quantities, whether large amounts of office stationery or entire fleets of automobiles. Ordering large quantities, however, conflicts with another concern: keeping stocked items to a minimum. Procurement specialists strive to determine *economic ordering quantities* or when to purchase particular types of items and in what quantities. Some purchasing offices have shifted to *just-in-time ordering*, in which items are received from vendors when needed, thereby eliminating the cost of warehousing these items. The widespread use of computer systems has greatly increased the ability of organizations—both public and private—to implement just-in-time ordering. A different concern is that lowest cost purchasing may not obtain a quality product or service. Thus, the procurement official's job is getting "best value" (considering cost, quality, and delivery).

Another objective is creating some flexibility in decision making. For example, if all personnel in a city government are on continuing appointments, then difficult choices will need to be made about possibly laying off workers during economic recessions. On the other hand, if some employees are on fixed-term contracts and expenditures need to be reduced, then these contracts simply need not be renewed when they expire. The same can be done with auxiliary services. When budget cuts are required, auxiliary contracts may not be renewed or may operate at reduced levels.

Procurement objectives often conflict with one another. Procurement policies may include numerous specific requirements that are viewed as red tape and unnecessarily hinder executives in managing their operations. At the same time, such red tape may be important in preventing fraud and waste.

Choices also must be made among purchasing, leasing, and privatizing. In some instances, there may be financial and other advantages to leasing a building rather than purchasing it. The federal government, however, may rely too heavily on leasing office space, as ownership may be less expensive in the long run. A wide range of equipment can be leased, including photocopying machines, computers, and dump trucks. The DOD has even considered leasing rather than buying its most expensive weapons systems.[101] *True* or *operating leases* are those in which the government pays for the specified period and gains no ownership of whatever is being leased, whereas *lease-purchase agreements* provide for ownership after a specified period. Leasing and other forms of contracting out are not necessarily an avenue for reducing costs.[102] One survey of state governments found that only one-third reported reduced service costs.[103] Moreover, federal scorekeeping rules require that capital leases be scored at their full cost when the lease is initiated, thus discouraging their use at the federal level.

Outsourcing, as discussed earlier, is another option and may involve contracting with a private firm to use its facilities, personnel, and other resources to deliver a service. In many cases, private contractor employees and government employees work side by side to produce services in government or contracted facilities. While many services can be contracted out, policy making is regarded as an inherently governmental function that cannot be privatized. This possibility becomes a concern in situations where government relies heavily on consulting firms to the extent that they seem to be responsible for setting policy or conducting other inherently governmental functions. A blurring of organizational boundaries occurs when a government agency works not with just one but two or more contractors on a particular program or project. In making a choice among these options, a paramount concern must be to use tax dollars effectively and efficiently, without any conflicts of interest.

When outsourcing a function currently performed by federal employees, federal agencies must follow the guidance in Circular A-76 that has procedures for competing the work between the federal employees and contractor proposals. The DOD, both because of its size and the scope of its activities, was the user with the most A-76 activity from the time of its initial release through the George W. Bush administration. The A-76 program had impressive results, producing savings that averaged above 30%, but met constant resistance from government employee unions. With the discovery of poor performance at the Walter Reed Army Medical Center, attributed in large part to the excessive time (over 6 years) the A-76 process took in this case, competitions were prohibited in DOD by the 2008 National Defense Authorization Act. This prohibition was quickly extended to the rest of the government. Practically speaking, therefore, it has been more than a decade since the A-76 process was operative.[104] There have been attempts in the Trump administration to renew A-76 competitions, but largely because of pressure from federal employee unions, these efforts have not been successful.[105]

In addition to Circular A-76, the Federal Activities and Inventory Reform (FAIR) Act of 1998 gives priority to competitive sourcing (rather than keeping them solely in-house). Each year federal agencies, under OMB's guidance, must report what activities are "not inherently governmental in nature."[106] Upward of half of all jobs analyzed have been identified as potentially being outsourced. The law does not require that some or all of these jobs actually be contracted out, but certainly there is an implication that maybe they should at least be competed (public versus private, via A-76). The lists can be challenged, however. Contractors usually contend that jobs that should have been included were not. Government employees and government unions typically contend the opposite.

By the mid-2000s, there was growing concern that competitive sourcing had become too narrowly focused and that a broader approach was needed at all levels of government and in the private sector, wherever sole-source methods were present. *Spend analysis* became popular as a method for *strategic sourcing*. The underlying idea here is that careful study of existing spending patterns can provide insights into improving the efficient and effective acquisition of services and products. GAO called on federal agencies to make use of spend analysis, but the moratorium on competitions makes this something of a moot issue, at least at the federal level.[107]

Contracting Process

Steps

Standard procedures are normally followed when contracting for products or services. Specifications for what is to be purchased are determined (this is referred to as the *requirements process*). For example, a truck might be required to have a specified ground clearance, load capacity, passenger capacity, and the like. Usually, a part of this process is *market analysis*—that is, determining what industry has available expertise. Often a formal *request for information* (RFI) is issued as a part of this process.

Then, bidding procedures begin through the issuance of *invitations for bid* (IFBs), *requests for proposal* (RFPs), and *requests for quotation* (RFQs). An IFB is used when a government has a reasonably detailed conception of what is to be purchased, such as the painting of the exterior of a building. In such cases, competitors produce largely similar products or services, so price can be the dominant discriminator. An RFP or RFQ is used in a situation where some latitude exists on the part of the bidder in terms of what is to be offered, or how it is to be provided.

Once bids are received, they are analyzed and, in the case of IFBs, awards are made to the lowest responsible qualified bidder. In a competition involving an RFP, an award might be made to a higher bidder, one that was thought to have the best approach to dealing with a problem. In this case, contracting officers are required to perform a *best value* analysis to ensure that selecting

a higher price bid yields best overall value to the government. The life cycle cost of a truck, including expected maintenance costs over the life of the truck, fuel efficiency, and so forth, would generally be included in the best value analysis. For technical services, the best value analysis might take into account which bid offers the most inputs for a given price, and the award could go to a higher bidder in order to obtain better value. Also, the best value judgment would include an estimate of the risk associated with each of the bidders achieving its claimed performance, cost, and schedule.

When the government selects a firm using an RFQ, bilateral negotiations are required before a final selection may be made. In contrast, with an RFP, the government may select a firm without further negotiations. The receipt of a product or service follows the signing of a contract or the award of a grant. Additional steps include inspecting the product or service received and paying the contractor.

Congress has encouraged government agencies to buy commercial products from firms not used to doing government business. To that end, *other transactions authority* (OTA) was created. Here, the government buyer is authorized to waive all government-unique regulations and comply only with relevant general laws. Initially, this authority was provided only to the Defense Advanced Research Projects Agency to encourage nontraditional contractors to work with the agency to develop prototypes in early research and development work. It was subsequently expanded to include other agencies and for production. Clearly, a major value of using OTA is the ability to expand the base of firms that can bid on a government procurement by including commercially oriented firms.[108]

Not all spending is handled through the bidding process. As discussed later, many small purchases can be handled through government credit cards and no bids are required. Although restricted to small purchases, the credit card transactions amount to many billions of dollars each year and pose major challenges for auditors.

In some situations, contracts are awarded not to one company but to several firms. The federal government, because it serves the entire nation, finds it advantageous to contract with several suppliers in the same industry. This *multiple-award schedule system* makes goods and services available on a standby basis, allowing agencies to order them when needed.[109]

In addition, state and local procurement agencies are permitted to take advantage of the lower prices offered in these GSA multiple-award schedules.[110] These schedules cover a wide variety of goods and services. For example, all forms of construction, ranging from simple repair and maintenance to the construction of an entire building, can be handled through a job order contracting mechanism in which suppliers agree to provide services at specified costs when needed. As another example, a painting firm might sign a contract agreeing to charge a set amount per square foot. Any agency could then hire the firm for painting services.

The federal government has experimented with *reverse auctioning* on common (interchangeable) goods and services. This technique allowed bidders during the open bidding period to see the bids made by competing firms but not the identities of the firms themselves. If a company found its bid had been undercut by another bidder, then the first bidder could consider lowering its bid to meet the competition. The GSA decommissioned its reverse auction platform at the end of fiscal year 2018.[111]

Another feature of some procurement programs is specification of performance in terms of timeliness and quality. For example, a contract for a state highway construction project may stipulate that the project must be completed by a specified date, with financial penalties being imposed for each day beyond the deadline. In a cost-conscious period, the RFP may specify the desired price the government is willing to pay, and the bidders will respond with the best offer for that price.

The 1994 Federal Acquisition Streamlining Act instructs federal agencies to develop *results-oriented* or *performance contracts* for acquisitions other than standardized commercial items.[112] In other words, when an agency buys a service, such as using a firm to process grant applications

from local governments, standards should be set for evaluating the firm's performance. Measurable performance is increasingly a part of federal contracts for research and development. These contracts may contain financial incentives (award and/or incentive fees) in which contractors achieve higher or lower fees (or profits) based on their performance. To award these contracts, agencies must be able to specify what work is to be accomplished, at what time, and with what degree of quality. That has been the rub of the matter. When agencies cannot precisely define their expectations of contractors, then accountability for performance can be elusive. The Services Acquisition Reform Act Advisory Panel found that to be the case at the federal level.[113]

One form of performance contracting is known as *share-in-savings*. Share-in-savings (SiS) allows for government to contract with a private firm that takes on much of the risk of the endeavor with the promise of financial rewards later through cost savings. For example, contracting out some aspects of debt collection, as noted earlier, can enhance revenue to a government, and a contractor can be paid with some of that newly generated revenue. The E-Government Act of 2002 authorized selective use of SiS contracting for information technology.[114] Despite this effort to promote SiS, not one SiS contract was awarded under the E-Government Act and "SiS fell by the wayside—never to be revisited again."[115]

Competition

Competition in procurement is considered one of the best means of ensuring quality products or services at minimum cost. Lack of competition may result from blatant favoritism in awarding contracts or from somewhat more subtle ploys, such as specifying a named product brand and model in the IFB. At the state and local levels, corporations have become more aggressive in challenging contract awards when they seem to violate legal requirements for competition.

It is important to emphasize the difference between "competition for an award" and "continuous competition during execution" (often called "competitive dual sourcing"). In the former case, there is a fierce rivalry for the initial award—the winning vendor knows that it will be a sole-source supplier from that point on through the remainder of the contract period, and it can bid all the changes that will come later on a monopoly pricing basis. In fact, this usually results in the winner bidding extremely low (known as a "buy-in" or sometimes more pejoratively "low-ball") and assuming that it will "get well on the changes."

With continuous competition during execution, on the other hand, the best value winner (based on cost and performance) gets a larger share of each year's award, and both contractors are motivated to deliver higher and higher performance at lower and lower costs.

Not all awards are made on a competitive basis. **Exhibit 11-1** discusses *noncompetitive* or *no-bid contracting*.

Exhibit 11-1 No-Bid Contracting

No-bid or noncompetitive contracting has generally been considered anathema to contemporary procurement, but with important exceptions. The bidding process is defended as saving taxpayers' dollars by seeking out the vendors or contractors that offer the best products and services at the best prices. Without bidding, so the argument goes, government pays top dollar and often for inferior goods and services.

No-bid contracting creates opportunities for favoritism. For example, the fact that former Vice President Cheney had been the head of Halliburton was the grounds for speculation that any no-bid awards going to Halliburton and its subsidiaries were based on favoritism.[1] The fact that defense contractors donate *millions* of dollars to political campaigns and then reap *billions* of dollars in no-bid defense contracts raises questions about whether these contracts were "bought" (at least indirectly) by the companies.[2]

There have been a number of subsequent questions about no-bid contracts, at all levels of government, since that time.

- Former Baltimore Mayor Catherine Pugh was forced to resign from office when it was revealed that the University of Maryland Medical System had a $500,000 no-bid contract with Pugh for the purchase of a children's book that she had authored. Pugh was a member of the medical system's Board of Directors at the time.[3]
- The Washington, D.C., City council approved a $215 million, no-bid contract with a Greek gaming company to manage its online sports betting and lottery operations. The approval of the contract, on close 7-5 vote, came despite the fact that one of the council members (Jack Evans, who has subsequently been forced to resign as a result of an ethics probe) had close ties to the company.[4]
- Puerto Rico's bankrupt public utility signed a no-bid contract with a firm to restore power after Hurricane Maria devastated the island in 2017. The firm failed to deliver the promised results and charged far in excess of the going rate for such services. It was ultimately canceled and the entire episode triggered a congressional investigation.[5]

If noncompetitive contracting is considered faulty, then why use it? There are at least two main factors. One is that sometimes there is only one possible bidder, such as when government needs the services that only one company can provide. Then, going with a "sole-source" contract is the only option. The other reason is that of speed. In times of emergency, there may be no time to allow for a lengthy bidding process. A particular project needs to get under way, as in recovering from a flood or tornado.

What governments enter into no-bid contracts? Basically all of them, and basically all are challenged from time to time on their decisions to use such contracts. For example, in 2006, California entered into $51 million of no-bid contracts for sending prison inmates out of state to other facilities.[6]

Federal no-bid contracting received widespread attention with spending on the wars in Afghanistan and Iraq and for recovery from Hurricane Katrina.[7] The Department of Homeland Security awarded most of its Katrina funds with contracts valued at less than $500,000, and 55% of those awards were no-bid. Only 19% were full-and-open competitions, with the remainder falling in other categories.[8] The Government Accountability Office studied Iraq reconstruction spending between 2003 and 2006 and found that only 10%

Exhibit 11-1 No-Bid Contracting   *(continued)*

of State Department contracting was awarded competitively compared with 99% for the U.S. Agency for International Development and 82% for the Defense Department.[9] Of course, State Department spending in total was small compared with Defense Department spending. According to GAO, federal agencies obligated approximately $170 billion on noncompetitive contracts in fiscal year 2009 alone.[10]

No-bid contracting is based on negotiations. A government worker or team of workers is responsible for hammering out the details of a contract with a sole-source vendor. This process can be done in a matter of minutes or, if time allows, can extend to months. During the negotiations, there can be bargaining over prices and services. No-bid contracts often involve situations in which the quantity of services is yet unknown, as is the timeline for such services.

The immensity of no-bid contracting in the mid-2000s has resulted in some key recommendations. Both the Government Accountability Office (GAO) when looking at the experience with Hurricane Katrina and the Special Inspector General for Iraq Reconstruction (SIGIR) when looking at the war situation have recommended better prior planning for emergencies.[9] SIGIR recommended the creation of an enhanced Contingency Federal Acquisition Regulation (CFAR) that would be developed on an interagency basis and eventually enacted into law. When planning for emergencies, contracting staff needed to be included. The contracting staff should not be brought into a situation after the fact. Another recommendation was that responsibilities needed to be specified within agencies and across agency lines.

Adequate numbers of qualified government contracting staff are needed in all aspects of procurement but particularly in no-bid situations, where it is important to have staff alert to possible contractor failures and mismanagement. One observer said that the lack of adequate staff led to extensive waste in Iraq: "People were blowing cash around Iraq like they had leaf-blowers."[11] SIGIR recommended creation of a reserve contracting corps that could be deployed to wherever it was needed in the world.

1. Morris, D. (2003). Criticism grows of no-bid work for Iraq reconstruction. Government Executive. Retrieved May 21, 2012, from http://www.govexec.com/defense/2003/04/criticism-grows-of-no-bid-work-for-iraq-reconstruction/13872/; Avery, A. H. (2006). Weapons of mass construction: the potential liability of Halliburton under the False Claims Act and the implications to defense contracting. Alabama Law Review, 57, 827–852.
2. Strohm, C. (2004). Major defense contractors reap billions in no-bid contracts, report finds. Government Executive. Retrieved October 22, 2006, from http://www.govexec.com/dailyfed/0904/092904c1.htm.
3. Broadwater, L. (2019). Review of Maryland hospital network finds more no-bid contracting, faults former CEO for 'Healthy Holly' deal. The Baltimore Sun, June 12. Retrieved February 7, 2020, from https://www.baltimoresun.com/politics/bs-md-umms-nygren-report-20190612-story.html.
4. Nirrapil, F. (2019). D.C. Council approves no-bid sports gambling contract. Washington Post, July 9. Retrieved February 7, 2020, from https://www.washingtonpost.com/local/dc-politics/dc-council-approves-no-bid-sports-gambling-contract/2019/07/09/fdd994fe-a1d5-11e9-bd56-eac6bb02d01d_story.html.
5. Campbell, A. C., and U. Irfan (2017). Puerto Rico's deal with Whitefish was shady as hell, new records show. Vox.com, November 15. Retrieved February 7, 2020, from https://www.vox.com/policy-and-politics/2017/11/15/16648924/puerto-rico-whitefish-contract-congress-investigation.
6. California to transfer inmates out of state (2006). Associated Press, October 21, 2006. Retrieved October 22, 2006, from http://www.nytimes.com/aponline/us/AP-California-Prisons.html?_r=1&oref=slogin (link no longer active).
7. Miller, T. C. (2006). Blood money: wasted billions, lost lives, and corporate greed in Iraq. New York, NY: Little, Brown and Company.
8. Office of the Inspector General, U.S. Department of Homeland Security (2006). 9th PCIE Hurricane Katrina Report. Retrieved October 22, 2006, from http://www.dhs.gov/xoig/assets/katovrsght/OIG_PCIE_033106.pdf.
9. Special Inspector General for Iraq (2009). Hard lessons: the Iraq reconstruction experience. Washington, DC: U.S. Government Accountability Office.
10. Government Accountability Office (2010, July). Federal contracting: Opportunities exist to increase competition and assess reasons when only one offer is received (p.11). Retrieved March 21, 2012, from http://www.gao.gov/products/GAO-10-833.
11. Miller, T. C., as quoted in Mandel, J. (2006). Iraq reconstruction failures tied to contracting breakdowns. Government Executive. Retrieved October 22, 2006, from http://www.govexec.com/dailyfed/1006/101306m1.htm.

There are two general types of contracts: cost reimbursable and fixed price. A major distinction is that with a cost-reimbursable contract, the contractor commits to best effort and is reimbursed for costs incurred, whereas with a fixed-price contract, the contractor delivers the contracted product or service for the price negotiated in the contract. Both fixed-price and cost-reimbursable contracts can be coupled with additional inducements to incentivize contractors in areas that include cost performance, schedule or delivery performance, and quality performance. Subjective incentives include award fees, and objective incentives include incentive fees. There are substantial subcategories within each of the categories of fixed-price and cost-reimbursable contracts.[116]

Fixed-price contracts in general refer to the category of contracts in which a price is negotiated for the delivery of the good or service, and the contractor is obligated to deliver the service for that price. In a classic fixed-price contract, the risk is entirely on the contractor, as cost overruns negatively affect the contractor's bottom line, but not the government's. There are, however, many variations of fixed price contracts, including firm fixed-price (FFP), fixed-price economic price adjustment (FPEPA), fixed-price award fee (FPAF), fixed-price incentive firm (FPIF), fixed-price incentive with successive targets (FPIS), fixed-price contract with prospective price redetermination (FPRP), fixed-ceiling price contract with retroactive price redetermination (FPRR), and firm fixed-price level of effort term contract (FFPLOE). A discussion of each of these contracting variations is beyond the scope of this chapter, but often whether one type or another is chosen depends on expected market conditions. For example, the FFEPA contract is often used when there is an unstable market for labor or materials. It allows the price to fluctuate up or down depending on those conditions. The FPAF contract includes fees for failing to meet performance targets that provide a meaningful incentive for the contractor to deliver the promised performance, as scheduled.

Cost reimbursement contracts generally carry a greater risk for the government, as the contractor is reimbursed for allowable costs under the contract, rather than agreeing to perform the service or deliver the product at a fixed price. The contracts will include estimates of costs and a ceiling price that cannot be exceeded without prior approval. Within this category are the following types of contracts: cost-reimbursement, cost-sharing, cost-plus-fixed-fee (CPFF), cost-plus-award-fee (CPAF), and cost-plus-incentive-fee. In a CPFF contract, for example, the award simply provides that the vendor's costs will be covered, plus the vendor will receive a fixed fee or profit on top of the costs; if cost increases are authorized by the agency, the contractor will be reimbursed, but not receive

additional fee or profit. In a CPAF contract, the contractor's costs are reimbursable just as in CPFF, but the amount of the award fee is not completely fixed at contract negotiation. A contractor may receive a higher or lower award fee depending on performance, and performance metrics can include cost management.

In addition to fixed-price and cost-reimbursement contracts, there are two other types of contracts that do not fit completely in either of these categories. Labor-hour and time-and-materials contracts fix the labor rates but provide only estimates of the number of hours required to complete the contract. Because they do not require the work to be completed for an agreed-upon price, they are more like cost-reimbursement than fixed-price contracts.

The Competition in Contracting Act of 1984 was passed to encourage greater competition in federal contracting and specifically enhanced the powers of losing bidders to mount legal challenges to the awards.[117] In addition to filing a protest with the contracting agency itself or with the GAO, a losing bidder may be able to appeal to the General Services Board of Contract Appeals, the Court of Federal Claims, or a federal district court.[118] Cooperative agreements and grants awarded as the result of a competitive process are not subject to protest, nor are task orders in a master task order contract. The original master award for the task order contract, or subsequent task awards, may each be protested. In addition, the 1994 Federal Acquisition Streamlining Act contains important provisions that limit bid protests that are often perceived as needlessly delaying the awarding of contracts.

Several factors discourage competition among would-be contractors. Lack of knowledge about how contracts are awarded and how to prepare a bid excludes some companies from bidding, although that problem is somewhat mitigated today given the vast amounts of information on contracting available on government websites. The DOD has established Procurement Technical Assistance Centers in many states. These centers assist business firms in understanding the process by which they can sell their goods and services to the government.[119] Many procurements are so large and complex that companies would have to make major investments in personnel and technology just to become competitive in the bidding process. *Design-and-build contracts*, in which several contract awards may be made for the design phase, with the best design being selected for the build or implementation phase, enable more firms to compete for much larger, more complex contracts. But, as noted above, they become sole-source after the best design selection is made.

Competition is restricted in other ways as well. A close and long-term relationship between a government agency and a contractor can develop over time. When a contract is to be rebid for a new time period, the company already holding the contract usually has a decided advantage.

Contract bundling tends to prohibit smaller companies from competing for contracts, whether this be at the local, state, or federal level. In contract bundling, several would-be small contracts are put up for bid as a single, large contract. The advantages to government are at least twofold. First, the administrative costs of handling the bidding and contracting processes are reduced. Second, the item or service being purchased is often less expensive when it is ordered in bulk as in a bundled contract than when it is purchased through several smaller contracts. Combining efforts into larger and larger contracts is often an agency response to budget cuts or cuts in personnel complement. Fewer procurement officers and fewer government staff to oversee contracts increase the pressure on the agency to make fewer but larger awards. However, such bundled contracts can involve a diverse set of products and services, many of which are beyond the scope of a single small company, thereby excluding smaller companies from the bidding process.[120] Nonetheless, the empirical data for past competitions for bundled contracts show clear increases in savings as the size of the effort increases.[121]

Companies become reluctant to participate in competitions when, if they win, they might have to wait for weeks or months to receive the money owed them. Delays in payments can bankrupt a small firm. Even when payments occur promptly, small firms may face other problems. If payments are made but then later an audit agency determines that the costs incurred are unallowable due to lack of adequate documentation, the small firm may be unable to comply due to weak recordkeeping. Whatever the situation, it will be costly from the standpoint of the time consumed in trying to comply with the government's requests.

Government contracting also opens up contractors to liability over their compliance with various employment laws, such as equal employment opportunity based on race, gender, and the like. The Rehabilitation Act of 1973 requires affirmative action in government hiring of people with disabilities, and this law is extended to private companies when they become government contractors.[122] Similarly, affirmative action is required in the hiring and promoting of veterans under the Vietnam Era Veterans' Readjustment Assistance Act of 1974.[123] Requirements such as these may discourage companies from bidding on federal contracts, not because the companies oppose equal opportunity or hiring veterans but because they fear lawsuits or the threat of lawsuits.

The widespread use of the Internet beginning in the 1990s has posed major challenges in the procurement arena. Expectations have developed that procurement should be an essential component of E-government. Governments at all levels have worked diligently to convert their paper-based processes for procurement to ones that include electronic processing. These efforts are complicated by the massiveness of procurement programs in large governments, by statutory restrictions that specify processes to be used, and by rapidly changing technology. At the federal level, much acquisition information has been consolidated under the contracting portion of *USA.gov*. There are, however, several other websites with relevant information for contractors and potential contractors:

- *Acquisition.gov* is focused specifically on procurement and provides links to a variety of government websites. This site is hosted by the E-government initiative.
- *FPDS.gov* is the Federal Procurement Data System. It provides access to a wealth of information about government awards. The

system is managed by a team of agencies led by the GSA.

- *USASpending.gov* is an accessible, user-friendly website that allows a wide variety of queries about recipients of government awards, patterns over time, agency procurement trends, geographic distribution of awards, and other information of interest to organizations that compete for awards and organizations and individuals who keep watch over government awards.

- *GSA e-Buy* (www.ebuy.gsa.gov) allows federal buyers to post RFQs and RFPs (see above) and vendors to respond electronically.

Increasingly, federal agencies that issue research grants have implemented online grant application systems. The National Science Foundation and the National Institutes of Health were early leaders, and information about programs in these and other agencies can be found at *www.grants.gov*. Once grant applications are received, agencies forward through electronic means the relevant portions of the applications to extramural panels that review the proposals. The review process in which the extramural panels evaluate proposals is also conducted online.

State and local governments and the private sector have become deeply involved in information technology as a vehicle for communicating between the business community and government procurement. For example, California maintains a website for state, federal, and local contracting.[124] One example of a commercial site is *GovCB.com*, Government Contract and Bid, which helps businesses win government contracts and find potential teaming partners online.

Computer technology is as important to government agencies that consume products and services as it is to firms that sell to government. The GSA operates GSA Advantage! (*gsaadvantage.gov*), an online shopping center. Agencies can not only compare prices on products and place orders, but also configure products and add accessories. GSA offers to agencies similar services in the information technology realm.

Contract management is another critical component of the procurement process.[125] What good

is a contract if government procurement officers fail to follow up to be sure that a business met its obligations under the contract? One occasional problem has been for contractors to meet their obligations but for government to overpay the contractors. Congress has required agencies to use recovery auditing to identify overpayments and recoup money that was misspent.[126]

Reforms

Procurement procedures become increasingly complex as additional, well-intended requirements are imposed. One prescription might be to simplify the government procurement process. Off-the-shelf purchasing of commercial items may be less expensive than specifying items that then might require special designs and types of construction. As an example of the rigidity in government purchasing, the GSA once had elaborate specifications for the design and durability of "ash receiver[s], tobacco (desk type)" when commercially available ashtrays probably would have been suitable, especially given that smoking is banned in most government buildings. The Federal Acquisition Reform Act (FARA), or Clinger-Cohen Act of 1996, broadened the definition of commercial services, bringing more purchasing activities under the simplified procedures.[127] Ten years' experience with the law found that the expected cost savings were not realized.[128] In addition, numerous barriers to buying commercial goods and services were found to continue to exist.

Workforce Quality

Another reform frequently mentioned is a move to upgrade the quality and sometimes quantity of the procurement workforce. The argument is that upgrades are necessary to reflect the increasing size of contracting and its complexity, particularly in procurements for high-tech goods and in professional services. This shortage has been found across the federal government. The DOD, which engages in massive contracting, has perhaps the most acute shortages. The Procurement and Supply Chain Benchmarking Association awards governments "best in class" status for excellence in procurement (*www.pasba.com*).

At the federal level, efforts are under way in dealing with perceived acquisition workforce problems. One concern is workforce turnover and retirements. A 2018 GAO report discussed the establishment of the Defense Acquisition Workforce Development Fund in 2008. This led to an increase of about 24% in the size of the DOD acquisition workforce from 2008 to 2016. Even though DOD has seen an overall growth in the contractor workforce, GAO found that it has not reached its growth targets in several career fields, such as contracting, business, and engineering.[129] In fact, GAO has identified DOD contract management as one of its "high risk" areas, and listed "the acquisition workforce" as one of three key challenges faced by the Department.[130]

Shortages in staff may result in procurement officers devoting their time almost exclusively to the awarding of contracts at the expense of overseeing the implementation of the awards.[131] The Federal Acquisition Institute, a branch of the GSA, was established in the 1970s to further the development of the procurement workforce. It delivers online and classroom training and serves as a link to other training providers.

Fraud, Waste, Abuse, and Scandals

Despite sustained efforts to improve procurement practices, the field has been plagued with scandals involving fraud, waste (as in the case of toilet seats that cost the military hundreds of dollars), and abuse (as in the case of the Federal Emergency Management Agency being sued for fraud in the recovery effort after Hurricane Maria devastated Puerto Rico).[132] While illegal actions represent only a very small percentage of procurement dollars, these come at a high price in terms of public faith in government. Because the acquisition function at DOD, NASA, and the Department of Veterans Affairs appears on the GAO's high-risk list, the government is exposed to the possible loss of large sums of resources, more as a result of waste than fraud.[133]

Fraud comes in many forms. Frauds involving state highway contracting can occur in the following ways:

- Specifications that are written by government workers to favor particular contractors and suppliers;
- Conflicts of interest, such as acquisition officials having financial interests in road construction companies;
- Collusive bidding and price fixing (while extremely rare, these actions involve some contractors not bidding on a contract so as to swing the award to a favored company);
- Questionable documentation from contractors, such as altering or modifying critical information like the contractor's bond and pre-qualifications;
- Production substitution, such as mismarking and mislabeling products and materials; or
- Cost mischarging for materials and labor, such as cost overruns due to intentional underestimating or underbidding.[134]

Safeguards against such practices exist. Federal agencies have inspectors general offices to ferret out corruption, and similar units exist at the state and local levels. Governments sometimes cooperate with one another, as in the case of the Federal Emergency Management Agency working with New York State to combat fraud related to regional flooding in 2006.[135] The Procurement Integrity Act of 1996 prohibits federal employees from releasing "contractor bid or proposal information" that in some way would unfairly benefit competitors.[136] Many acquisition employees are prohibited from receiving compensation from contractors that they had direct contact with for 1 year or more after they leave government service. While working for government, they are to report any employment offers by contractors. Federal agency personnel in positions other than procurement are often precluded from representing their new private employer with their old agency for 1 year after leaving government service, although this does not prohibit their being employed by a company that does business with their old agency. Under restrictions established by the Obama administration, and continuing into the Trump administration, no former federal employee can work for a contractor for at least 1 year after federal employment if the position would put the former employee in direct contact with his or her agency.

One of the most notorious fraud situations involved David Safavian, who was chief of the Office of Federal Procurement Policy within OMB. Prior to joining OMB, he had been chief of staff at the GSA. He was indicted and convicted for obstructing a GSA investigation into possible illegal business relations with lobbyist Jack Abramoff. He was convicted in 2006, had his conviction overturned on appeal, but then was retried and convicted in 2008. He was sentenced to 18 months in prison in late 2009.[137]

Contractors can be sanctioned. They can be suspended from government contracting for a fixed period or barred permanently. The GAO has stepped up pressure on federal agencies to revise and use their procedures for suspending or even debarring contractors.[138]

Short of these measures, contractors can have restrictions imposed on them on bidding on contracts and executing them. Nevertheless, abuses still occur too frequently. The GAO reported that one of the most widespread abuses of contractors was failure to pay federal taxes owed.[139] In the mid-2000s, the Boeing Company engaged in bribing an Air Force contractor over tanker procurement and paid $615 million to settle the case. This largest defense contracting scandal in decades resulted in people from the Air Force and Boeing going to prison.[140] In the aftermath of the scandal, the Justice Department created a special task force against fraud in defense and homeland security.[141]

Problem Areas and Innovations

Procurement is undergoing extensive changes too numerous to discuss here, but a few can be noted. One major change is the growing importance of contracting for services as distinguished from acquisition of products. The field began to show significant growth, and in 1972 a group of industry leaders in government contracting formed a professional association known as the Professional Services Council (PSC).[142] The PSC promotes private contracting by government, creates opportunities for networking between companies and government agencies, and provides training for contractors in how to work with governments at all levels. Service contracting presents special challenges of determining what services, of what quality, and what quantity are to be delivered. After delivery, the challenge is in monitoring the process to ensure that the contract requirements are met and that only appropriate expenses are charged for those services.

Measuring the costs of services is particularly troublesome due to variations in accounting rules used by companies doing business in the private and public sectors. This situation complicates efforts to compare the costs of producing a service by a corporation with those done for a government agency. Furthermore, when such service contracts are awarded to nonprofit entities, important problems may arise over how government expects operations to be managed and how the nonprofits normally manage themselves.

Credit Cards and ID Cards

Government-issued credit cards have become standard components of acquisition systems. Some governments now provide employees with credit cards so that they may charge their travel expenses and be reimbursed later, rather than use travel advances or their personal funds to cover costs until being reimbursed. The federal government has what it calls "micro-purchase thresholds" that limit the size of a credit card transaction. This limit had been set at $3,500, but a rule proposed by DOD, GSA, and NASA would raise the threshold to $10,000.[143]

The cards in the federal government are helpful in remote areas that lack ready access to GSA supply centers. Today's technology allows credit cards to work or not work for specified sales. For example, the cards can be programmed not to work for liquor sales where bar code systems are used. The GSA reported $32.5 billion of card purchases for fiscal year 2019 and claimed it saved nearly $70 on every transaction due to reduced processing costs—thus saving $1.7 billion yearly for the government.[144]

With millions of cards in circulation in the federal government, abuse can be expected. The GAO and the Inspector General of the Department of Homeland Security (DHS) found that DHS employees had purchased "a beer brewing kit, a 63" plasma television costing $8,000 which was found unused in its original box 6 months after being purchased, and tens of thousands of dollars for training at golf and tennis resorts."[145] More recently, a general was found to have used his card at multiple overseas strip clubs and was subsequently disciplined for these and other actions.[146]

Procurement Actions Affecting Historically Disadvantaged Groups

As highlighted earlier, one of the objectives of federal acquisition is to fulfill public policy objectives, which includes supporting socioeconomic programs. These include supporting businesses owned by minorities, women, disabled veterans, and other historically disadvantaged groups. The Small Business Administration negotiates goals for these various categories with the other federal agencies. In 1995, the Federal Acquisition Streamlining Act set nonbinding goals of contracting with minority-owned businesses, and Executive Order 12928 called upon agencies to develop methods for encouraging minority businesses and historically black colleges and universities to bid on contracts with the government.[147] Executive Order 13360, issued by President George W. Bush, expects agencies to create opportunities for service-disabled veterans to contract and subcontract with the government.[148] To avoid charges of reverse discrimination, agencies do not use quotas, but rather pursue outreach and other programs to help make minority businesses aware of contracting opportunities and provide advice on how to prepare procurement proposals.

Acquisition programs are often expected to provide special opportunities to small businesses that otherwise might be locked out of selling to the government by large corporations. Executive Orders 13169 and 13170 require federal agencies to increase opportunities for small businesses, especially disadvantaged ones.[149]

Labor–Management Relations

In the contracting process, labor–management issues may arise, such as whether a contractor will enter into agreements with labor unions. Executive Order 12871 established the National Partnership Council and required federal agencies to work cooperatively with unions. In 2001, President George W. Bush revoked this order by issuing Executive Order 13202. The new order called for "neutrality towards government contractors' labor relations on federal and federally funded construction projects." The Davis–Bacon Act of 1931 is a United States federal law that requires paying the local prevailing wages on public works projects for laborers and mechanics. It applies to "contractors and subcontractors performing on federally funded or assisted contracts in excess of $2,000 for the construction, alteration, or repair (including painting and decorating) of public buildings or public works."[150]

"Buy American" Concerns

International interests have always been of concern, and with economic threats to the U.S. economy has come renewed interest in requirements to "buy American." Congress, from time to time, has required federal agencies to report on their purchases of products made abroad but has stopped short of blocking such purchases. The purchase of defense components from overseas suppliers has been particularly sensitive. In 2006, there was a brouhaha when the federal government announced plans to award a contract to manage six seaports to Dubai Ports World of the United Arab Emirates.[151] Considerable alarm was expressed over whether port security was being turned over to a Middle Eastern company, given terrorism and unrest in that part of the world. Dubai Ports World, faced with the furor, withdrew from the proposed contract. More generally, foreign-owned, U.S.-located firms doing national security work get special reviews and oversight. In order to do any classified work, these firms must have a government-approved board of directors with a majority of members from the United States. The Trump administration, which has made "America first" one of its central concerns, has issued at least three executive orders related to either "buy American" or "hire American" concerns—EO 13788 (April 18, 2017—Buy American and Hire American), EO 13858 (January 31, 2019—Strengthening Buy-American Preferences for Infrastructure Projects), and EO 13881 (July 15, 2019—Maximizing Use of American-Made Goods, Products, and Materials). A specific example of concerns over the acquisition of services supplied by foreign firms involved Huawei, a Chinese firm pioneering 5G technology. This raised concerns that the company's equipment could threaten national security.[152]

Procurement During Crises

The war in Iraq after 2003 and natural disasters, such as Hurricanes Katrina and Rita in 2005, or Florence, Harvey, Irma, and Maria more recently, test the limits of how procurement programs operate under extreme circumstances. Contracts for Iraq's reconstruction worth billions of dollars were awarded to be carried out in extraordinarily difficult situations. In simple terms, how can contractors be held accountable for results when shells are literally falling around them? Additionally, during these crises there were charges of favoritism in awarding contracts and just simple mismanagement. Congress created the Office of Special Inspector General for Iraq (and later Afghanistan) Reconstruction to audit the government's activities.[153] One of the audits found "millions of reconstruction dollars stuffed casually into footlockers and filing cabinets, an American soldier in the Philippines who gambled away cash belonging to Iraq, and three Iraqis who plunged to their deaths in a rebuilt hospital elevator that had been improperly certified as safe."[154] In the case of natural disasters, the need to move quickly sometimes results in ignorance or misunderstanding of contracting rules. For example, the GAO found that, in the particularly difficult 2017 disaster season, federal agencies failed to follow laws that, in particular,

required them to give preference to local business when contracting for cleanup and rebuilding.[155]

Risk Management

To provide services, governments must have property and personnel. Arising from this simple fact are a series of exposures or risks, such as the risk of property being damaged or lost owing to natural disasters, employee error, and fraud by employees and others. Property damage can lead to major repair or replacement costs and to loss of income (e.g., structural problems in a municipal stadium may force its closing). The Chicago flood of 1992, in which water from the Chicago River entered buildings throughout the downtown area, is an example of how inattention to a problem—in this case, leakage into a tunnel system caused by faulty construction under government contract—can have disastrous consequences.

Risk management considers what threats exist, the probability of each happening, and the likely consequence if the threat or disaster materializes. Until September 11, 2001, the probability of commercial aircraft being used as devices to destroy major landmark buildings would have been considered quite low. Since then, risk managers have had to reexamine the vulnerability of food supplies, water systems, nuclear power plants, ports, and the like to deliberate acts of terrorism. Anthrax in powder form was shipped in the mail in 2001, causing a shutdown of delivery to many offices, especially government offices. As of the mid-2000s, many federal agencies had systems in place to help safeguard against future anthrax attacks. E-government, by which much of government's work is done today, has the advantage of avoiding the anthrax threat but faces the disadvantage of malicious computer hacking. The National Security Council's directorate for global health and security and bio-defense in the White House was responsible for preparing for pandemics but was disbanded in 2017, three years prior to the COVID-19 crisis.[156]

Other risks pertain to financial guarantees. The federal government strives to identify the extent of its exposure in loan programs and other activities, such as mortgage guarantees. Perhaps the highest-profile cases associated with the financial crisis after 2007 were the costly takeovers of Fannie Mae and Freddie Mac and the bankruptcy of the solar energy company Solyndra.

Liability

Governments are vulnerable to suits brought by employees or by corporations and private citizens. Negligence is often the basis of suits in which government is alleged not to have acted the way a "reasonable" person would and inflicted harm as a result. Court-awarded financial settlements can be extraordinarily large. In some suits against local governments, the awards have been greater than the governments' total annual budgets.

Laws govern liability cases. The federal government may be sued only in federal court. One of the most important federal laws is the Federal Tort Claims Act of 1946, which selectively permits suits against the government in cases not arising out of contract.[157] State and local governments may sometimes be sued in federal courts as well as in state courts. Antitrust cases against local governments, for example, are the domain of federal courts. Discrimination cases can be filed in federal and state courts.

Managing Risks

Governments need a management strategy for dealing with exposures. Risk management planning begins by identifying risks and, where possible, eliminating them. A faulty woodworking machine in a school shop should be repaired; the repair will improve the safety of the machine, thereby eliminating some risk when students use it. A road intersection widely known to be dangerous can be redesigned. A community that is subject to hurricanes obviously cannot avoid these fierce storms, but it can take steps to be prepared for such emergencies.

Having eliminated or reduced risks, governments must be prepared to deal with the remaining areas of exposure. Commercial insurance is used by governments and awarded through a bidding process similar to that for any other purchasing arrangement. Another option is self-insurance, where a government sets aside funds on a regular basis to cover awards or simply expends funds from the current budget to cover abnormal expenses (for example, the costs of repairing police cars damaged in the line of duty). In some instances, governments help cover each other's risks through self-insurance pooling.

Insurance premiums for liability coverage have become extremely expensive, sometimes so expensive that insurance is beyond the reach of governments—if it is available at all. Costs are a function of the nature of a policy. Salient factors include the number of employees and officials of a government, the services covered, the deductibles included, and the loss experienced. The latter is not just the experience of a particular government. A given city might have had no major suits filed against it, but because some cities have encountered major legal problems, as in cases involving landfills, all cities pay heavily for coverage.

The costs of risk management are typically handled centrally. That is, the costs of insurance premiums, court-mandated awards to injured parties, out-of-court settlements, and the like are handled by the central government budget and not charged to department budgets. Were line agencies charged for these costs, managers would be more aware of the costs of their operations and would have greater incentives to reduce risk. Faced with staggering insurance premiums, a government may choose to discontinue a service, such as operating a community swimming pool.

The GASB has several pertinent statements:

- Statement No. 10, as amended by Statement No. 30, covers risks associated with torts, thefts, business interruptions, errors or omissions, job-related illnesses or injuries of employees, and acts of God.
- Statement No. 27 requires governments to report pension plan risks.
- Statement No. 31 covers the reporting of investment risks.

- Statement No. 40 requires reporting of deposit and investment risks.
- Statement No. 42 expects governments to report impairment of capital assets and insurance recoveries for situations such as when a building becomes unexpectedly unusable.
- Statement No. 53 covers accounting and financial reporting for derivative investments in order to ensure that the reporting of them is done at fair market value.
- Statement No. 58 sets financial and accounting guidance for governments that have filed for Chapter 9 bankruptcy protection.

The federal government has taken steps toward integrating risk management into its overall system of management. The OMB, in Circular A-123, outlines desired risk management strategies for federal agencies.[158] The GAO has recommended that risk assessment be used to prioritize threats and that it be used in conjunction with performance budgeting for the allocation of scarce resources. Specifically, in 2017, the GAO issued a report on enterprise risk management (ERM) that encouraged federal agencies to adopt the following approach:[159]

- Align the ERM process to goals and objectives—The agency should make sure that its leaders communicate the importance of ERM for its key mission areas;
- Identify risks—In each of these areas, agencies should develop a culture that encourages employees to discuss risks openly;
- Assess risks—Strategic planning and performance management processes should include attention to ERM;
- Select risk response—Actions in response to risk should be adjusted to the structure and culture of the agency;
- Monitor risks—Performance indicators should be used that allow the tracking of identified risks, and whether additional actions are necessary; and
- Communicate and report—Stakeholders, both internal and external to the agency, should be made aware of the risks, the actions taken to combat them, and the progress made.

Summary

Execution is the conversion of plans embodied in the budget into day-to-day operations. At stake are factors such as interpreting and complying with legislative intent as prescribed in appropriations and providing the services that have been authorized. Control over line agencies is exercised through apportionment planning and preauditing of expenditures.

Since the 1980s, there has been a resurgence of interest in achieving economy and efficiency. Outsourcing of services has been used as one means of increasing the efficiency of operations.

Budget offices are involved in a host of activities other than preparing budgets. On the federal level, OMB exercises major powers related to information collection and dissemination and to agencies issuing regulations.

Tax administration and cash management, which are usually under the direction of a secretary of treasury, are processes aimed at maximizing revenues and minimizing costs. Numerous mechanisms are used to enforce tax laws, ranging from offering assistance in preparing tax returns to prosecuting delinquent taxpayers.

Cash management is the process of administering monies to ensure that they are available to meet expenditure needs and that monies, when temporarily not needed, are invested at a minimum risk and a maximum yield. Many instruments exist for investing state and local funds. The U.S. Treasury Department handles federal cash management through the Federal Reserve System.

Procurement entails the acquisition of resources required to provide government services, while risk management is concerned with protecting those resources. Governments often have a central purchasing office but allow individual departments some independence in purchasing products and services. A procurement program attempts to purchase only what is needed, avoid stock outages, and keep unit costs low.

Risk management attempts to eliminate or reduce risk exposure and to prepare for such events as damage to government property and liability suits arising out of government operations.

Notes

1. Beavers, O., & Karr, R. (2020). GAO finds Trump administration broke law by withholding Ukraine aid. *The Hill*, January 16. Retrieved February 28, 2020, from https://thehill.com/homenews/administration/478557-gao-finds-trump-administration-broke-law-by-withholding-aid-from.

2. Government Accountability Office (2016), *Principles of federal appropriations law*, 4th ed. GAO-16-464SP, March. Retrieved April 23, 2016, from https://www.gao.gov/legal/appropriations-law-decisions/red-book/.

3. Allyn, B. (2020). Appeals court allows Trump to divert $3.6 billion in military funds for border wall. *NPR.org*, January 9. Retrieved February 28, 2020, from https://www.npr.org/2020/01/09/794969121/appeals-court-allows-trump-to-divert-3-6-billion-in-military-funds-for-border-wa.

4. Office of Management and Budget (2019). *Circular A-11, Section 20, page 2*. Retrieved February 6, 2020, from https://www.whitehouse.gov/wp-content/uploads/2018/06/a11_web_toc.pdf.

5. Office of Management and Budget (2019). *Circular A-11, Section 20, page 2*. Retrieved February 6, 2020, from https://www.whitehouse.gov/wp-content/uploads/2018/06/a11_web_toc.pdf.

6. The National Governors Association and the National Association of State Budget Officers (2011). *Fiscal Survey of the States*. Spring, p. 8. Retrieved March 20, 2012, from http://www.nga.org/files/live/sites/NGA/files/PDF/FSS1111.PDF.

7. National Association of State Budget Officers (2019). *Fiscal Survey of the States*. Spring, p. 11. Retrieved April 23, 2020, from https://higherlogicdownload.s3.amazonaws.com/NASBO/9d2d2db1-c943-4f1b-b750-0fca152d64c2/UploadedImages/Fiscal%20Survey/NASBO_Spring_2019_Fiscal_Survey_of_States_-_S.pdf.

8. The White House. (2019). *Statement from the Press Secretary Regarding the Signing of H.R. 2157 – Additional Supplemental Appropriations for Disaster Relief Act, 2019*, June 6. Retrieved January 31, 2020, from https://www.whitehouse.gov/briefings-statements/statement-press-secretary-regarding-signing-h-r-2157-additional-supplemental-appropriations-disaster-relief-act-2019/.

9. Subcommittee on Federal Spending Oversight and Emergency Management, Committee on Homeland Security and Governmental Affairs, United States Senate (2015). *Prudent planning or wasteful binge?: A look at the end of the year spending*, September 30. Retrieved April 23, 2020, from https://www.hsgac.senate.gov/hearings/prudent-planning-or-wasteful-binge-a-look-at-end-of-the-year-spending.

10. Peckenpaugh, J. (2002). OMB to manage Homeland Security reorganization. *Government Executive*. Retrieved August 13, 2006, from http://www.govexec.com/dailyfed/071702p1.htm (source no longer available).

11. Bur, J. (2018). Innovation at Scale: What has the White House Office of American Innovation accomplished? *Federal Times*, March 14. Retrieved April 23, 2020, from https://www.federaltimes.com/it-networks/2018/03/14/innovation-at-scale-what-has-the-white-house-office-of-american-innovation-accomplished/.

12. Beames, C. (2019). Commercial competition: the rocket science of the space force. *Forbes*, September 30. Retrieved February 28, 2020, from https://www.forbes.com/sites/charlesbeames/2019/09/30/commercial-competition-the-rocket-science-of-the-space-force/#f78d2e077014.

13. Prison Policy Initiative (2020). *Privatization*. Retrieved February 28, 2020, from https://www.prisonpolicy.org/research/privatization/.

14. Office of Management and Budget. (2003). *Circular A-11*. Retrieved from https://www.whitehouse.gov/sites/whitehouse.gov/files/omb/circulars/A76/a76_incl_tech_correction.pdf

15. Savas, E. S. (1982). *Privatizing the public sector*. Chatham, NJ: Chatham House; Savas, E. S. (2005). *Privatization in the city: successes, failures, lessons*. Washington, DC: CQ Press.

16. Sinn, W., & Whalley, J. (Eds.) (2006). *Privatization experiences in the European Union*. Cambridge, MA: MIT Press; The World Bank (2019). *2018 private participation in infrastructure (PPI) annual report*. Washington, DC: Author.

17. Renn, A. (2016). The lessons of long-term privatizations: why Chicago got it wrong and Indiana got it right. *The Manhattan Institute*. Retrieved July 23, 2019, from https://www.infrastructureusa.org/the-lessons-of-long-term-privatization-why-chicago-got-it-wrong-and-indiana-got-it-right/.

18. Schiffler, M. (2015). *Water, politics and money: a reality check on privatization*. Springer International Publishing: Switzerland. Retrieved February 28, 2020, from https://www.governing.com/topics/mgmt/pros-cons-privatizing-government-functions.html.

19. Federal Managers' Financial Integrity Act of 1982 (P.L. 97-255); Robert, N., & Candreva, P. J. (2006). Controlling internal controls. *Public Administration Review*, 66, 463–465.

20. Office of Management and Budget (2004). *Circular A-123*. Retrieved January 31, 2020, from https://www.whitehouse.gov/omb/information-for-agencies/circulars/; Office of Management and Budget (2018). *Memorandum from Mick Mulvaney to the heads of federal departments and agencies, Appendix A to OMB Circular No. A-123, Management of Reporting and Data Integrity Risk*, June 6. Retrieved January 31, 2020, from https://www.whitehouse.gov/wp-content/uploads/2018/06/M-18-16.pdf.

21. Paperwork Reduction Act of 1980 (P.L. 96-511); Paperwork Reduction Act of 1995 (P.L. 104-13).

22. Chief Information Officers Council website, www.cio.gov.

23. Digital.gov (2020). *A guide to the Paperwork Reduction Act*. Retrieved February 9, 2020, from pra.digital.gov/?dg.

24. U.S. Government Accountability Office (2006). *Information security: continued progress needed to strengthen controls at the Internal Revenue Service.* Washington, DC: Author; Pulliam, D. (2006). OMB steps up data security reporting requirements. *Government Executive.* Retrieved March 20, 2012, from http://www.govexec.com/technology/2006/07/omb-steps-up-data-security-reportingrequirements/22261.

25. Office of Personnel Management (2020). *Cybersecuity incidents.* Retrieved February 13, 2020, from https://www.opm.gov/cybersecurity/cybersecurity-incidents/.

26. Corrigan, J. (2019). Under the president's 2020 budget proposal, the Pentagon's cyber coffers would grow while funds for some civilian agencies dry up. *Nextgov*, March 18. Retrieved January 31, 2020, from https://www.nextgov.com/cybersecurity/2019/03/white-house-requests-more-174-billion-federal-cyber-efforts/155638/.

27. West, D., & Gambhir, K. (2019). Why won't the Senate protect American elections? *Brookings Institution.* Retrieved February 16, 2020, from https://www.brookings.edu/blog/fixgov/2019/08/02/why-wont-the-senate-protect-american-elections/.

28. Office of Management and Budget (2016). *Circular A-130, Managing Federal Information as a Strategic Resource.* Retrieved January 31, 2020, from https://www.whitehouse.gov/sites/whitehouse.gov/files/omb/circulars/A130/a130revised.pdf.

29. U.S. Chief Information Officer Council (2006). *Federal enterprise architecture: security and privacy profile.* Retrieved August 16, 2006, from http://www.cio.gov/documents/Security_and_Privacy_ Profile_v2.pdf.

30. United Nations (2018). *U.N. E-Government Knowledge Base.* Retrieved November 1, 2019, from https://public administration.un.org/egovkb/en-us/Data/Compare-Countries,

31. Federal Funding Accountability and Transparency Act of 2006 (P.L. 109-282).

32. Government Accountability Office (2018). Open Data: Treasury Could Better Align USAspending.gov with Key Practices and Search Requirements. GAO 19-72, December. Retrieved April 23, 2020, from https://www.gao.gov/products/GAO-19-72.

33. U.S. Office of Management and Budget (2003). *Regulatory analysis,* Circular A-4. Retrieved August 16, 2006, from http://www.whitehouse.gov/omb/circulars/a004/a-4.pdf.

34. Regulatory Right-to-Know Act of 1999, as contained in Treasury and General Government Appropriations Act for Fiscal Year 1999 (P.L. 106-58).

35. U.S. Office of Management and Budget (2011). *2011 report to Congress on the benefits and costs of federal regulation and unfunded mandates on state, local, and tribal entities.* Retrieved March 20, 2012, from http://www.whitehouse.gov/sites/default/files/omb/inforeg/2011_cb/2011_cba_report.pdf.

36. Executive Office of the President (2017). Executive Order 13777, *Enforcing the Regulatory Reform Agenda,* February 24. Retrieved February 29, 2020, from https://www.federalregister.gov/documents/2017/03/01/2017-04107/enforcing-the-regulatory-reform-agenda.

37. Executive Office of the President (2017). Executive Order 13771, *Reducing Regulation and Reducing Regulatory Costs.* Retrieved November 1, 2019, from https://www.federalregister.gov/documents/2017/02/03/2017-02451/reducing-regulation-and-controlling-regulatory-costs.

38. Brookings Institution (2020). *Tracking deregulation in the Trump Era.* Retrieved January 31, 2020, from https://www.brookings.edu/interactives/tracking-deregulation-in-the-trump-era/.

39. Popovich, N., Albeck-Ripka, L., & Pierre-Louis, K. (2019). 95 Environmental rules being rolled back under Trump. *New York Times*, December 21. Retrieved January 31, 2020, from https://www.nytimes.com/interactive/2019/climate/trump-environment-rollbacks.html.

40. Davenport, C. (2019). Trump to revoke California's authority to set stricter auto emissions rules. *New York Times*, September 17. Retrieved February 28, 2020, from https://www.nytimes.com/2019/09/17/climate/trump-california-emissions-waiver.html.

41. Steps available at the U.S. General Services Administration & U.S. Office of Management and Budget websites, RegInfo.gov; West, W. F. (2004). Formal procedures, informal processes, accountability, and responsiveness in bureaucratic policy making: an institutional policy analysis. *Public Administration Review, 64,* 66–80.

42. Unfunded Mandates Reform Act of 1995 (P.L. 104-4).

43. Congressional Review Act of 1996 (P.L. 104-121).

44. Government Accountability Office (2018). *OMB Should Work with Agencies to Improve Congressional Review Act Compliance during and at the End of Presidents' Terms.* GAO 18-183, March. Retrieved January 31, 2020, from https://www.gao.gov/assets/700/690624.pdf.

45. U.S. Government Accountability Office (2005). *Tax administration: systematic information sharing would help IRS determine the deductibility of civil settlement payments.* Washington, DC: Author.

46. Gruber, A. (2006). IRS plan to close service centers based on faulty data. *Government Executive.* Retrieved December 19, 2011, from http://www.govexec.com/story_page.cfm?filepath=/ dailyfed/0306/032406a1.htm.

47. U.S. Government Accountability Office (2005). *Tax administration: IRS can improve its productivity measures by using alternative methods.* Washington, DC: Author; Klun, M. (2004). Performance measurement for tax administrations: the case of Slovenia. *International Review of Administrative Sciences, 70,* 567–574; Sera, P. (2005). Performance measures in tax administration: Chile as a case study. *Public Administration and Development, 25,* 115–124.

48. Department of the Treasury, Internal Revenue Service (2019). *IRS releases new Tax Gap estimates; compliance rates remain substantially unchanged from prior study,* September 26. Retrieved November 1, 2019, from https://www.irs.gov/newsroom/irs-releases-new-tax-gap-estimates-compliance-rates-remain-substantially-unchanged-from-prior-study.

49. Chun, R. (2019). Why Americans don't cheat on their taxes. *The Atlantic,* April. Retrieved November 1, 2019,

from https://www.theatlantic.com/magazine/archive/2019/04/why-americans-dont-cheat-on-their-taxes/583222/.

50. Jacoby, S. (2019). High cost of IRS cuts: weakened tax enforcement. *Center on Budget and Policy Priorities.* Retrieved February 28, 2020, from https://www.cbpp.org/blog/high-cost-of-irs-cuts-weakened-tax-enforcement.

51. U.S. Government Accountability Office (2006). *Tax compliance: opportunities exist to reduce the tax gap using a variety of approaches.* Washington, DC: Author; U.S. Government Accountability Office (2006). *Individual income tax policy: streamlining, simplification, and additional reforms are desirable.* Washington, DC: Author.

52. Department of the Treasury, Internal Revenue Service (2019). *EFTPS: The Electronic Federal Tax Payment System.* Retrieved November 1, 2019, from https://www.irs.gov/payments/eftps-the-electronic-federal-tax-payment-system.

53. Department of the Treasury, Internal Revenue Service (2019). *Income tax return statistics.* Retrieved November 1, 2019, from https://www.efile.com/efile-tax-return-direct-deposit-statistics.

54. Moreno, T. (2018). Save Time: E-File your federal and state tax return together. *The Balance,* December 31. Retrieved November 1, 2019, from https://www.thebalance.com/e-file-federal-state-tax-return-together-3192895.

55. Office of Management and Budget (2013). Circular A-129: Policies for federal credit programs and non-tax receivables. January. Retrieved June 4, 2020, from https://www.whitehouse.gov/sites/whitehouse.gov/files/omb/circulars/A129/a-129.pdf.

56. Mandel, J. (2006). IRS announces first contracts for debt collection work. *Government Executive.* Retrieved December 19, 2011, from http://www.govexec.com/story_page.cfm?filepath=/dailyfed/0306/030906m1.htm.

57. Department of the Treasury, Internal Revenue Service (2019). *Private collection agencies.* Retrieved November 1, 2019, from https://www.irs.gov/businesses/small-businesses-self-employed/private-debt-collection.

58. Department of the Treasury, Internal Revenue Service (2019). *Taxpayer rights.* Retrieved November 1, 2019, from https://www.irs.gov/advocate/taxpayer-rights.

59. U.S. Government Accountability Office (2007). *Management report: improvements needed in IRS's internal controls.* Washington, DC: Author. Retrieved March 20, 2012, from http://www.gao.gov/products/GAO-07-689R.

60. Internal Revenue Service (2020). *Taxes. Security. Together. We all have a role to play in protecting your data.* Retrieved February 28, 2020, from https://www.irs.gov/individuals/taxes-security-together.

61. Dropkin, M., & Hayden, A. (2001). *The cash flow management book for nonprofits: a step-by-step guide for managers, consultants, and boards.* San Francisco, CA: Jossey-Bass; Fight, A. (2005). *Cash flow forecasting.* Boston, MA: Elsevier.

62. Prompt Payment Act of 1982 (P.L. 97-177).

63. U.S. Government Accountability Office (2006). *DOD payments to small business: implementation and effective utilization of electronic invoicing could further reduce late payments.* Washington, DC: Author.

64. Long, H., Stein, J., Rein, L., & Romm, T. (2020). Stimulus checks and other coronavirus relief hindered by dated technology and rocky government rollout. *Washington Post,* April 18. Retrieved April 17, 2020, from https://www.washingtonpost.com/business/2020/04/17/stimulus-unemployment-checks-delays-government-delays/.

65. Pulliam, D. (2006). Pentagon late payments hurt small contractors. *Government Executive.* Retrieved October 21, 2006, from http://www.govexec.com/dailyfed/0506/052206p1.htm.

66. Department of the Treasury, Bureau of the Fiscal Service (2019). *Prompt payment.* Retrieved November 1, 2019, from https://fiscal.treasury.gov/prompt-payment/.

67. Joyce, P. G. (2001). What's so magical about five percent? A nationwide look at factors that influence the optimal size of state rainy day funds. *Public Budgeting & Finance, 21,* Summer, 62–87.

68. Hou, Y. (2004). Budget stabilization fund: structural features of the enabling legislation and balance levels. *Public Budgeting & Finance, 24,* Fall, 38–64; Marlowe, J. (2005). Fiscal slack and counter-cyclical expenditure stabilization: a first look at the local level. *Public Budgeting & Finance, 25,* Fall, 48–72; Schunk, D., & Woodward, D. (2005). Spending stabilization rules: a solution to recurring state budget crises? *Public Budgeting & Finance, 25,* Winter, 105–124.

69. Tax Policy Center (2019). What are state rainy day funds and how do they work? Retrieved November 1, 2019, from https://www.taxpolicycenter.org/briefing-book/what-are-state-rainy-day-funds-and-how-do-they-work.

70. Gramlich, J. (2011). Rainy day funds explained: how much money should states have in the bank? *Stateline.org,* May 4. Retrieved March 20, 2012, from www.stateline.org/live/details/story/?contentId=572171; Joyce, P. (2001). What's so magical about five percent?

71. Pew Charitable Trusts (2019) *Budget surpluses are helping many states boost their savings.* Retrieved November 1, 2019, from https://www.pewtrusts.org/en/research-and-analysis/data-visualizations/2014/fiscal-50#ind5.

72. TreasuryDirect (2020). *Series EE savings bonds.* Retrieved February 28, 2020, from https://www.treasurydirect.gov/indiv/products/prod_eebonds_glance.htm.

73. Strong, R. A. (2005). *Derivatives: an introduction* (2nd ed). Mason, OH: Thomson/South-Western; Hinkelmann, C., & Swidler, S. (2005). State government hedging using financial derivatives. *State and Local Government Review, 37,* 127–141; McDonald, R. L. (2006). *Derivatives markets* (2nd ed). Boston, MA: Addison-Wesley.

74. Barton, P. (2010). Derivative disaster spreads to local governments. *CNC News,* May 10.

75. Office of the State Treasurer, State of Wisconsin (2006). *Local government investment pool.* Retrieved August 18, 2006, from http://www.ost.state.wi.us/home/lgip.htm; Treasury Department, Tennessee (2006). *Local government investment pool.* Retrieved August 18, 2006, from http://www.treasury.state.tn.us/lgip/index.htm; Sims, R. (2006). *King County*

investment pool receives highest rating from Standard & Poor's [press release]. Retrieved March 23, 2012, from http://your .kingcounty.gov/exec/news/2006/0109investmentpool.aspx.

76. Governmental Accounting Standards Board (2020). *What you need to know: local government investment pools.* Retrieved February 28, 2020, from https://gasb.org/jsp /GASB/Page/GASBSectionPage&cid=1176165972807.

77. Department of Commerce, Bureau of the Census (2019). *2018 Annual survey of public pensions: state & local tables.* Retrieved November 3, 2019, from https://www.census.gov /data/tables/2018/econ/aspp/aspp-historical-tables.html.

78. Treasurer, State of California (2019). *Pooled money investment board, 62nd annual report,* Fiscal Year 2017–18, p. 3. Retrieved April 23, 2020, from https://www.treasurer .ca.gov/pmia-laif/reports/annual/2018.pdf.

79. Stern, A. (2007). Judge voids Illinois law barring Sudan investment. *Reuters,* February 24. Retrieved March 23, 2012, from http://www.reuters.com/article/2007/02/24 /investment-sudan-rulingidUSN2335511320070224.

80. Wolfe, A. (2010). Court upholds Sudan Divestment Act. *Nashua Telegraph,* October 28. Retrieved March 20, 2012, from http://www.nashuatelegraph.com/news/891914-196 /story.html.

81. Kurtz, J. (2019). Kopp: State may look into divesting from fossil fuels. *Maryland Matters,* July 8. Retrieved April 23, 2020, from https://www.marylandmatters.org/2019/07/08 /kopp-state-may-look-into-divesting-from-fossil-fuels/.

82. Governmental Accounting Standards Board (2020). *Summary of statement no. 3: deposits with financial institutions, investments (including repurchase agreements), and reverse repurchase agreements* (issued 4/86). Retrieved February 2, 2020, from https://www.gasb.org/st/summary /gstsm3.html

83. Bureau of the Fiscal Service (2020). *Green book.* Retrieved January 31, 2020, from https://fiscal.treasury.gov/reference -guidance/green-book/.

84. Bureau of the Fiscal Service (2020). *Gold book.* Retrieved January 31, 2020, from https://fiscal.treasury.gov/reference -guidance/gold-book/.

85. U.S. General Accounting Office (2001). *Federal debt: debt management actions and future challenges.* Washington, DC: U.S. Government Printing Office; U.S. General Accounting Office (2004). *Debt ceiling: analysis of actions taken during the 2003 debt issuance suspension period.* Washington, DC: U.S. Government Printing Office.

86. Cash Management Improvement Act of 1990 (P.L. 101-453).

87. Financial Management Service, U.S. Department of Treasury (2011). *Cash Management Improvement Act (CMIA).* Retrieved December 7, 2011, from http://fms.treas.gov /cmia/index.html.

88. Groshek, G. M. (2000). Foreign currency exposure in the Department of Defense. *Public Budgeting & Finance,* 20, Winter, 15–35.

89. Rappeport, A. (2019). See a design of the Harriet Tubman $20 bill that Mnuchin delayed. *New York Times,* June 14. Retrieved February 28, 2020, from https://www.nytimes .com/2019/06/14/us/politics/harriet-tubman-bill.html.

90. Financial Management Service (2011). *U.S. Treasury to "retire" Social Security paper check option* [press release], April 26. Retrieved March 20, 2012, from http://www .godirect.org/media/release/ustreasury-retires-paper -check-option/.

91. U.S. Treasury (2020). U.S. *Treasury Introduces Direct Express® Debit Card.* Retrieved February 28, 2020, from https://fiscal.treasury.gov/godirect/media/release/us -treasury-introduces-direct-express-debit-card/index. html.

92. U.S. Treasury, Bureau of the Fiscal Service (2020). *Chapter 5000: Letter of credit-Federal Reserve Bank system operational requirements.* Retrieved February 28, 2020, from https://tfm.fiscal.treasury.gov/v2/p4/c500.html.

93. Cooper, P. J. (2003). *Governing by contract: challenges and opportunities for public managers.* Washington, DC: CQ Press; Seddon, N. (2004). *Government contracts: federal, state, and local* (3rd ed.). Annandale, NSW, Australia: Federation Press; Emanuelli, P. (2005). *Government procurement.* Markham, Ontario: LexisNexis Butterworths; Brown, T. L., et al. (2006). Managing public service contracts: aligning values, institutions, and markets. *Public Administration Review,* 66, 323–331.

94. Datalab (2020). *Contract spending analysis; How has federal contract spending changed over time.* Retrieved January 31, 2020, from https://datalab.usaspending.gov/contracts -over-time.html.

95. Bloomberg Government (2019). *Top 10 federal contractors.* Retrieved January 31, 2020, from https://about.bgov .com/top-10-federal-contractors/.

96. General Services Administration (2019). *FY 2020 performance plan and FY 2018 annual performance report.* Retrieved February 2, 2020, from https://www.gsa.gov /cdnstatic/GSA%20FY%202020%20Annual%20 Performance%20Plan%20and%20FY%202018%20 Report_FINAL.pdf.

97. Harris, S. (2002). GSA lacks hard data on inter-agency competition. *Government Executive.* Retrieved December 19, 2011, from http://www.govexec.com/story_page.cfm ?filepath=/dailyfed/1006/041102h1.htm.

98. Defense Logistics Agency, U.S. Department of Defense website, www.dla.mil.

99. Office of Federal Procurement Policy Act of 1974 (P.L. 93-400).

100. U.S. General Services Administration (2020). *Federal acquisition regulation.* Retrieved February 2, 2020, from https://www.gsa.gov/policy-regulations/regulations /federal-acquisition-regulation-far; Department of Defense (2020). *Defense pricing and contracting,* January 15. Retrieved February 2, 2020, from https://www.acq.osd .mil/dpap/dars/dfarspgi/current/.

101. Wilson, G. C. (2002). Rent-a-weapons. *Government Executive.* Retrieved December 19, 2011, from http:// www.govexec.com/story_page.cfm?filepath=/dailyfed /0202/020502db.htm.

102. U.S. Department of Energy (2020). *Leasing arrangements.* Retrieved February 28, 2020, from https://www.energy .gov/eere/slsc/leasing-arrangements.

103. Brudney, J. L., et al. (2005). Exploring and explaining contracting out: patterns among the American states. *Journal of Public Administration Research and Theory*, 15, 393–419; Nemec, J., et al. (2005). Contracting-out at local government level: theory and selected evidence from the Czech and Slovak Republics. *Public Management Review*, 7, 637–648.

104. Bartels, F. (2018). *Renewing OMB Circular A-76 Competitions: Savings and Greater Effectiveness*. The Heritage Foundation, August 2. Retrieved February 3, 2020, from https://www.heritage.org/defense/report/renewing-omb-circular-76-competitions-savings-and-greater-effectiveness.

105. Clark, C. (2017). House Rejects Outsourcing of Federal Jobs in Vote to Block Revival of Circular A-76. *Government Executive*, July 28. Retrieved February 3, 2020, from https://www.govexec.com/management/2017/07/house-rejects-outsourcing-federal-jobs-vote-block-revival-circular-76/139829/; Fedweek (2019). *Spending bill would block OPM breakup, address other issues*, June 5. Retrieved February 3, 2020, from https://www.fedweek.com/fedweek/spending-bill-would-block-opm-breakup-other-issues/.

106. Federal Activities and Inventory Reform Act of 1998 (P.L. 105-270).

107. U.S. General Accounting Office (2004). *Best practices: using spend analysis to help agencies take a more strategic approach to procurement*. Washington, DC: U.S. Government Printing Office.

108. Dunn, R. L. (2009). *Injecting new ideas and new approaches in defense systems: are "other transactions" an answer?* Center for Public Policy and Private Enterprise Report, July. Retrieved March 20, 2012, from http://www.acquisitionresearch.net/files/FY2009/NPS-AM-09-088.pdf.

109. U.S. General Services Administration (2020). *GSA Award Schedules*. Retrieved February 28, 2020, from https://www.gsa.gov/buying-selling/purchasing-programs/gsa-schedules; U.S. Government Accountability Office (2005). *Contract management: opportunities to improve pricing of GSA multiple award schedules contracts*. Washington, DC: Author.

110. General Services Administration (2011). *GSA order 4800.2G: Eligibility to use GSA sources and supplies of services*, February 16. Retrieved March 20, 2012, from http://www.gsa.gov/graphics/fas/GSAOrder4800.2G_FSSUA_FINAL_2-2-11.pdf.

111. General Services Administration (2018). *GSA Reverse Auctions*. Retrieved February 28, 2020, from https://reverseauctions.gsa.gov/reverseauctions/reverseauctions/.

112. Federal Acquisition Streamlining Act of 1994 (P.L. 103-355).

113. Mandel, J. (2006). Panel finds performance-based contracts poorly implemented. *Government Executive*. Retrieved December 19, 2011, from http://www.govexec.com/story_page.cfm?filepath=/dailyfed/0606/062906m1.htm.

114. U.S. Government Accountability Office (2005). *Federal contracting: share-in-savings initiative not yet tested*. Washington, DC: Author.

115. Cairns, C., & Read, R. (2016). A brief history of IT Share-in-savings contracting in the federal government. *Medium.com*, December 22. Retrieved February 3, 2020, from https://medium.com/@ccairns/a-brief-history-of-it-share-in-savings-contracting-in-the-federal-government-d6f13f00e874.

116. The discussion below relies on a description included in Defense Acquisition University (2020). *Tools catalog, Chapter 1*. Retrieved February 9, 2020, from https://www.dau.edu/tools/Pages/Guidebook-Viewer.aspx?source=https%3a//www.dau.edu/guidebooks/Shared%20Documents%20HTML/CPRG_Vol4.aspx. For a full description of these subcategories, Federal Acquisition Regulations (2020). *Part 16—Types of contracts*, January 15. Retrieved February 9, 2020, from https://www.acquisition.gov/content/part-16-types-contracts.

117. Competition in Contracting Act of 1984 (P.L. 98-369), Title VII.

118. U.S. Government Accountability Office (2020). *Bid protests*. Retrieved February 3, 2020, from https://www.gao.gov/legal/bid-protests.

119. See the Association of Procurement Technical Assistance Centers website at https://www.aptac-us.org/.

120. For a report on the practice, see Small Business Administration (2019). *Contract bundling report to Congress: fiscal year 2017*, April 2. Retrieved February 3, 2020, from https://www.sba.gov/sites/default/files/resources_articles/Final_Contract_Bundling_Report_to_Congress_FY_17.pdf.

121. Gansler, J. S. (2003). Moving toward market-based government: the changing role of government as the provider. *IBM Center for the Business of Government*, June. Retrieved March 20, 2012, from http://www.businessofgovernment.org/report/moving-toward-market-based-government-changing-rolegovernment-provider.

122. Rehabilitation Act of 1973 (P.L. 93-112).

123. Vietnam Era Veterans' Readjustment Assistance Act of 1974 (P.L. 93-508); Committee on Veterans Affairs, U.S. House of Representatives (2006). *NASA extends contract proposal deadline for service-disabled veteran-owned small businesses*. Retrieved August 21, 2006, from http://veterans.house.gov/ news/109/8-3-06.html.

124. Department of General Services, State of California (2020). *Federal and local government contracts, bids, and RFPs in the State of California (CA)*. Retrieved February 28, 2020, from https://www.bidcontract.com/State-County-City-Bids/government-contracts-bids-California-State-CA.aspx.

125. Romzek, B. S., & Johnston, J. M. (2005). State social services contracting: exploring the determinants of effective contract accountability. *Public Administration Review*, 65, 436–449.

126. National Defense Authorization Act for Fiscal Year 2002 (P.L. 107-107).

127. Federal Acquisition Reform Act/Clinger-Cohen Act of 1996 (P.L. 104-106), section 4001.

128. Andrues, W. (2006). The Clinger-Cohen Act, 10 years later: measuring efficiency. *Government Executive*. Retrieved August 22, 2006, from http://www.govexec.com/story_page.cfm?filepath=/dailyfed/0706/071806cc.htm.

129. Government Accountability Office (2018). *Federal acquisitions: Congress and the executive branch have taken steps to address key issues, but challenges endure*, September, p. 35. Retrieved February 3, 2020, from https://www.gao.gov/assets/700/694457.pdf.

130. Government Accountability Office (2020). *DOD contract management – high risk issue*. Retrieved February 3, 2020, from https://www.gao.gov/key_issues/dod_contract_management/issue_summary.

131. Mandel, J. (2006). Panel agrees OMB needs official dedicated to acquisition workforce. *Government Executive*. Retrieved March 20, 2012, from http://www.govexec.com/defense/2006/07/panelagrees-omb-needs-official-dedicated-to-acquisition-workforce/22265/.

132. Kim, S. (2019). FEMA official arrested for fraud over Hurricane Maria recovery effort in Puerto Rico. *CNBC*, September 10. Retrieved February 28, 2020, from https://www.cnbc.com/2019/09/10/fema-official-arrested-for-fraud-over-hurricane-maria-recovery-effort-in-puerto-rico.html.

133. Government Accountability Office (2020). *High risk list*. Retrieved February 3, 2020, from https://www.gao.gov/highrisk/overview.

134. Compiled from Federal Highway Administration, U.S. Department of Transportation (2006). *The reporting and detecting of fraud*. Retrieved August 22, 2006, from http://www.fhwa.dot.gov/programadmin/contracts/fraud.htm.

135. Federal Emergency Management Agency, U.S. Department of Homeland Security (2006). *FEMA and state alert to fraud* [press release]. Retrieved August 22, 2006, from http://www.fema.gov/news/ newsrelease.fema?id=28298.

136. Procurement Integrity Act of 1996 (P.L. 104-106).

137. Palmer, K. (2005). Former OMB official indicted. *Government Executive*. Retrieved December 19, 2011, from http://www.govexec.com/story_page.cfm?filepath=/dailyfed/1005/100505k1.htm; Palmer, K. (2006). Ex-procurement chief argues for new trial. *Government Executive*. Retrieved December 19, 2011, from http://www.govexec.com/story_page.cfm?filepath=/dailyfed/0806/081706k1.htm.

138. Government Accountability Office (2014). *Federal contracts and grants: agencies have taken steps to improve suspension and debarment programs*. May 21. Retrieved February 3, 2020, from https://www.gao.gov/products/GAO-14-513.

139. U.S. Government Accountability Office (2005). *Financial management: thousands of civilian agency contractors abuse the federal tax system with little consequence*. Washington, DC: Author.

140. Smith, R. J. (2006). Tanker inquiry finds Rumsfeld's attention was elsewhere. *Washington Post*, June 20. Retrieved August 22, 2006, from http://www.washingtonpost.com/wp-dyn/content/article/2006/06/19/AR2006061901090.html.

141. Cahlink, G. (2005). Justice forms procurement fraud task force. *Government Executive*. Retrieved December 19, 2011, from http://www.govexec.com/story_page.cfm?filepath=/dailyfed/0205/022305g1.htm.

142. See the PSC website at https://www.pscouncil.org/.

143. Weber, G. (2019). FAR update: simplified acquisition threshold and micro-purchase threshold are going up. *SmallGovCon*, October 7. Retrieved February 3, 2020, from http://smallgovcon.com/statutes-and-regulations/the-simplified-acquisition-threshold-and-micro-purchase-threshold-are-going-up/.

144. General Services Administration (2020). *About GSA SmartPay*. Retrieved February 3, 2020, from https://smartpay.gsa.gov/content/about-gsa-smartpay.

145. U.S. Government Accountability Office (2006). *Purchase cards: control weaknesses leave DHS highly vulnerable to fraudulent, improper, and abusive activity*. Washington, DC: Author.

146. Cooper, H. (2016). Army general used government credit card at strip clubs, Pentagon says. *New York Times*, October 6. Retrieved February 3, 2020, from https://www.nytimes.com/2016/10/07/us/general-ron-lewis-credit-card-gentlemens-club.html.

147. Executive Office of the President (1994). Executive Order 12928, *Promoting Procurement With Small Businesses Owned and Controlled by Socially and Economically Disadvantaged Individuals, Historically Black Colleges and Universities, and Minority Institutions*.

148. Executive Office of the President (2004). Executive Order 13360, *Service-Disabled Veterans*.

149. Gangemi, J. (2006). Winning the federal contracting game. *Businessweek Online*, July 26. Retrieved August 21, 2006, from http://www.businessweek.com/smallbiz/content/jul2006/sb20060726_724414.htm?chan=search (source no longer available).

150. U.S. Department of Labor (2020). Davis-Bacon and Related Acts. Retrieved February 28, 2020, from https://www.dol.gov/agencies/whd/government-contracts/construction.

151. Bumiller, E., & Hulse, C. (2006). Panel saw no security issue in port contract, officials say. *New York Times*, February 23. Retrieved August 22, 2006, from https://www.nytimes.com/2006/02/23/politics/panel-saw-no-security-issue-in-port-contract-officials-say.html; Cloud, D. S., & Sanger, D. E. (2006). Dubai company delays new role at six ports. *New York Times*, February 24. Retrieved August 14, 2006, from http://select.nytimes.com/gst/abstract.html?res=F10912FC345AOC778EDDAB0894DE404482.

152. Gold, H. (2020). UK will allow Huawei to help build its 5G network despite US pressure. *CNN Business*, January 28. Retrieved February 28, 2020, from https://www.cnn.com/2020/01/28/tech/huawei-5g-uk/index.html.

153. U.S. Office of the Special Inspector General for Iraq Reconstruction (2006). *SIGIR: independent and objective oversight*. Retrieved August 22, 2006, from www.sigir .mil/; U.S. General Accounting Office (2004). *Contract management: contracting for Iraq reconstruction and for global logistics support*. Washington, DC: U.S. Government Printing Office.

154. Glanz, J. (2006). New U.S. audit describes misuse of funds in Iraq projects. *New York Times*, January 25. Retrieved August 22, 2006, from http://select.nytimes .com/gst/abstract.html?res=F00F16FC3B5B0C768 EDDA80894DE404482.

155. Government Accountability Office (2019). *2017 disaster contracting: actions needed to improve the use of post-disaster contracts to support response and recovery*. April 24. Retrieved February 3, 2020, from https://www.gao.gov /products/GAO-19-281.

156. Reichmann, D. (2020). Trump disbanded NSC pandemic unit that experts had praised. AP, March 14. Retrieved April 23, 2020, from https://apnews.com/ce014d94 b64e98b7203b873e56f80e9a.

157. Federal Tort Claims Act of 1946, Ch. 753, 60 Stat. 842.

158. Office of Management and Budget (2016). *OMB Circular no. A-123, management's responsibility for enterprise risk management and internal control*, July 15. Retrieved February 9, 2020, from https://www.whitehouse.gov /sites/whitehouse.gov/files/omb/memoranda/2016/m-16 -17.pdf.

159. Government Accountability Office (2016). *Enterprise risk management: selected agencies' experiences illustrate good practices in managing risk*, December. Retrieved February 6, 2020, from https://www.gao.gov/assets/690 /681342.pdf.

CHAPTER 12

Financial Management: Accounting, Reporting, and Auditing

The term *creative accounting* and the older term *cooking the books* refer to deliberate manipulation of accounting systems and accounting reports in order to hide the actual financial condition of an entity. A particular form of creative accounting in popular culture is what is referred to as Hollywood Accounting, which represents the practice of manipulating the costs and revenues of a film in order to avoid reporting a profit and sharing that profit with actors and other filmmakers. A notorious example of this is the 1983 film *Return of the Jedi*. The film is estimated to have grossed $475 million on a $32 million budget, which in some worlds (but apparently not the Star Wars universe) would mean that the movie turned a profit of more than $440 million. However, because of Hollywood Accounting, the film reported no profits and therefore the actors (at least as of 2011) had received no residuals.[1]

While some may not feel any sympathy for well-compensated Hollywood types, it is serious business when taxpayers must pay up through higher taxes due to bad accounting practices and fraud in their governments.

There were accounting scandals uncovered at the mortgage giants Fannie Mae and Freddie Mac in 2003. These scandals led to the resignations of the heads of both of these organizations after they were discovered, but they seemed even more significant in light of the costly federal bailout of both of these institutions in 2008.[2] Even if no fraud exists, an estimating error that simply fails to recognize in advance that not all taxes owed will be collected can throw a budget badly out of balance, forcing stringent measures on spending and possibly giving decision makers no choice but to adopt a tax increase in order to correct the mistake. Budget execution requires accounting systems that track projected and actual revenues and expenditures during the budget year.

Accounting is the process of recording all financial transactions—revenues and expenditures—according to clear and usually precise rules, in such a manner that all transactions can be audited independently. As will be seen in the following sections, accounting serves a variety of purposes, but one of the most important has always been maintaining honesty and integrity. Accounting is also important to the functions discussed in the preceding chapter—namely, tax administration, cash management, procurement, and risk management. Accounting systems provide the financial information components of more comprehensive management information systems.

This chapter has three sections. The first is devoted to accounting systems, and the second to reporting—that is, the types of documents that flow from accounting data. The third section discusses government auditing.

Governmental Accounting

"A standard definition of accounting is the art of analyzing, recording, summarizing, evaluating and interpreting an organization's financial activities and status, and communicating the results."[3] Accounting is one type of information system, one that contains mostly financial information on transactions involving the receipt of funds and their expenditure.

In this section, we explore several aspects of accounting systems, beginning with the purposes and standards of accounting and the organizations that shape accounting systems. Fund accounting, the structure of accounting systems, the classification of expenditures, and the bases for accounting are considered.

Organizational Responsibilities and Standards
Purposes

Accounting systems have been devised for a variety of purposes. **Exhibit 12-1** lists the main ones, including the ever-present one of ensuring honesty in the handling of public monies—keeping the rascals honest. As will be seen, accounting systems are based on details, but those who operate accounting systems should never lose sight of the main purposes. Accounting systems, in meeting the purposes noted here, are valuable tools in running the government rather than simply being additional costs of government operations.[4]

Exhibit 12-1 Purposes of Accounting

Here are some of the main purposes of accounting:

- Perhaps the primary purpose is the maintenance of honesty. Through accounting, people who have wrongly intercepted monies being paid to government or who have channeled expenditures to their own advantage can be detected. Accounting serves as a deterrent to fraud and corruption and prevents inadvertent loss.
- A related purpose is to prevent expenditures from straying beyond legal parameters. Illegal expenditures can occur that do not involve corruption, as in the case of agency expenditures that exceed an appropriation or are used for purposes other than those permitted in authorizing legislation. Accounting serves to control agencies so that they act in accordance with policy and administrative directives and appropriation legislation.
- Accounting systems are intended to provide complete, timely, and accurate information concerning receipts and expenditures. The information is used in billing taxpayers and receiving tax payments, paying employees, ordering goods, receiving goods, and paying vendors or contractors. Accounting systems help control inventory by providing accurate records of what items have been purchased.
- Another important purpose is to report on the management of funds that are held in custody or trust. For example, accounting systems are used to handle contributions to employee retirement funds and outlays to beneficiaries.
- Decision making is facilitated by accounting systems, which report historical data on revenues and expenditures that are essential for forecasting financial transactions. Without accurate information from an accounting system, decision makers are unable to determine whether a gap exists between proposed spending for the budget year and available revenue. Accounting information is important in determining whether a budget deficit exists and in what amount. Data are used in determining the size of the government's total debt, including those debts that are part of credit programs. Accounting data can help identify historical trends and current costs, and this information is essential in identifying funds required for proposed changes in service levels and service quality.

Exhibit 12-1 Purposes of Accounting *(continued)*

- Accounting is used internally to help managers increase efficiency and effectiveness in delivering services. The utilization of resources is monitored to avoid waste and to help ensure that desired programmatic outcomes are achieved. Managerial accounting focuses on calculating the costs associated with providing services to citizens. These derived costs can also be used for setting schedules for service charges. Office of Management and Budget (OMB) Circular A-123, *Management's Responsibility for Internal Control*, emphasizes that management should be held accountable for achieving results and not just for using resources efficiently and honestly.
- Information from accounting systems is used in communication between a government and its citizens, investors, and other governments. Financial reports derived from detailed accounting information can help citizens gain confidence that the government's resources are well supervised. The federal government, in making grants to state and local governments, wants to be assured that the recipient governments have accounting systems that will protect the assets being invested.
- Accounting in the public sector is being increasingly used to identify financial condition or the relative fiscal health of a government and the environment in which it operates. Investors in such commodities as state and local bonds and federal Treasury bills use accounting-based information to understand the financial condition of the governments whose bonds they are buying.

Federal Government Accounting Organizations

For accounting systems to serve these purposes, certain conventions or standards must be established, or else chaos would reign as each government or department within a government established its own standards and practices. Numerous organizations establish the ground rules for accounting.

Both the Government Accountability Office (GAO), which is an agency of Congress, and the OMB, which is an arm of the Executive Office of the President, set guidelines for federal agencies and to some extent compete with one another over control of accounting.[5] The Federal Managers' Financial Integrity Act of 1982, which amended the Accounting and Auditing Act of 1950, requires that each executive agency establish internal accounting and administrative controls in accordance with standards prescribed by GAO and that the agency conduct annual reviews to determine the extent of compliance with those standards.[6] However, because the Supreme Court has ruled that GAO cannot be in a position of instructing agencies in what they must do (see the chapter on budget approval and the U.S. Congress), OMB has the upper hand in establishing financial management practices.

OMB's deputy director for management oversees the Office of Federal Financial Management, which is headed by the controller. The Chief Financial Officers Act of 1990 created similar offices and chief financial officer (CFO) positions within the major agencies of the government.[7] Agency CFOs have responsibility for all financial operations, including budgeting, and the CFOs, along with OMB's deputy director for management, the controller, and the fiscal assistant secretary of Treasury, meet periodically as the Chief Financial Officers Council for the purpose of coordinating their activities.[8] OMB Circular A-136, revised as of June 2019, lays out specific financial reporting requirements that federal agencies must follow.[9]

In addition to the Chief Financial Officers Act, 1990 also brought the formation of the Federal Accounting Standards Advisory Board (FASAB).[10] As its title suggests, this entity is strictly advisory, but its recommendations have indeed had major impacts on federal accounting. The board consists of representatives of GAO, OMB, and the Treasury Department plus a representative from the Congressional Budget Office (CBO), representatives from civilian agencies and the Department of Defense (DOD), and nonfederal members. The board's mission is to develop consensus on accounting standards that can then be adopted by GAO, OMB, and the Treasury Department. FASAB has issued numerous standards, such as ones pertaining to the accounting of assets and liabilities (the first standard that it adopted), to others dealing with inventory, managerial cost accounting, and social insurance accounting. OMB reviews each standard issued and in effect incorporates all standards into government policy through Circular A-134, *Financial Accounting Principles and Standards*.[11]

Chief financial officers are to some extent in competition with another set of key officers— namely, chief information officers. The latter were established by the Clinger-Cohen Act (Information Technology Management Reform Act) of 1996 and have overall responsibility for information technology in their respective organizations.[12] The catch arises in that accounting systems are necessarily part of information technology operations, which creates issues over who is in charge whenever any accounting matter is at hand.[13]

The General Services Administration (GSA) is another player in the accounting game at the federal level. GSA, as described in the chapter on budget execution, is the federal government's central purchaser for buildings, materials and supplies, vehicles, and computers. In 2006, GSA had responsibility for preparing, under OMB's supervision, the Common Government-wide Accounting Code, which was expected to be the foundation for future accounting systems.[14] This effort is part of the Financial Management Line of Business initiative currently being driven by the Treasury department's Bureau of the Fiscal Service.[15]

State, Local, and Related Organizations

State and local accounting systems are influenced by several sources. State auditors and comptrollers set standards for their state and local systems, as do individual state legislatures. These systems also are influenced by GAO and OMB, which determine how federal grant monies are handled.

Professional organizations have periodically attempted to establish standards of accounting in the public sector. The blue book, or GAAFR (Governmental Accounting, Auditing, and Financial Reporting), which is published by the Government Finance Officers Association, is designed to assist governments at all levels achieve what are considered the standards in the field.[16] The Government Finance Officers Association issues a variety of policy statements not only on accounting, auditing, and financial reporting, but also on budgeting, cash management, debt management, and retirement and benefits administration.

In 1984, the Governmental Accounting Standards Board (GASB) was established. GASB, usually pronounced "gas-bee," speaks for accounting practices by government entities.[17] GASB is under the umbrella of the Financial Accounting Foundation and issues accounting standards, known as statements, first as exposure drafts available for public comment and then in final form. The organization also issues technical bulletins that provide guidance on the implementation of the standards. The Governmental Accounting Standards Advisory Council provides advice to GASB.[18]

Private Sector Accounting Organizations

The private sector has long had a well-established standards-setting organization. The Financial Accounting Standards Board, established in 1973, issues authoritative pronouncements on accounting for private profit and nonprofit organizations.[19] Also, private accounting firms have major input into determining what constitutes good accounting. The Big 4 accounting firms are Deloitte Touche Tohmatsu, Ernst & Young, Klynveld Peat Marwick Goerdeler, and Pricewaterhouse Coopers.[20]

Another large accounting firm, Arthur Andersen, was brought down by scandal. Energy giant Enron went bankrupt in 2001 when it came to light that the company had been cooking the books, making the firm's financial situation look far better than it actually was. Enron officials were eventually convicted. Andersen was involved, because it had been Enron's auditor. The company was found guilty of shredding key documents about Enron, and because a felon cannot be an auditor, the company was forced to relinquish its certified public accountant licensure. That was effectively the end of Andersen as an accounting firm, although the consulting arm of Andersen continues as a company known as Accenture.[21]

The Enron situation and other major scandals involving accounting practices and major corporations' auditors led to widespread criticism of companies that performed both an auditing function and served as financial consultants to the corporations. At the time of the Enron collapse, Andersen was receiving more payments from Enron for consulting and financial advice than for auditing. Such situations may create conflicts of interest in which the consulting arm of a company is eager to see that the auditing arm finds no serious problems in the manner that accounting is conducted by the client. The Securities and Exchange Commission has authority in this area. The Sarbanes-Oxley Act of 2002, discussed later, limits greatly this cozy relationship between consulting and auditing. None of the major management accounting firms now has management and financial consulting practices.

Standards and Principles of Accounting

While GAAFR is useful to state and local governments in evaluating their accounting systems, it is not regarded as an authoritative document. In contrast, GASB annually issues a document that is authoritative regarding the standards to be used in public accounting: Codification of Governmental Accounting and Financial Reporting Standards.[22] The Government Finance Officers Association's blue book includes discussions of how it is related to GASB's pronouncements.

GASB and its predecessors have recognized what are considered generally accepted accounting principles (GAAP). At the federal level, the GAAP are established by the Federal Accounting Standards Advisory Board (FASAB), having been granted this authority by the American Institute of Certified Public Accountants (AICPA).[23] FASAB issues an annual document summarizing its pronouncements with respect to federal financial reporting.[24] From that statement, FASAB has promulgated numerous statements

and interpretations that constitute the first tier in the hierarchy, technical bulletins that are second, and the other documents that make up third and fourth tiers. Together, these constitute GAAP for the federal government.

Organizational Arrangements and Fraud

Creating organizational arrangements that deter fraud is of paramount interest in accounting. Fraud can be committed by workers handling receipts. An employee might hold taxpayer A's money for personal use and use taxpayer B's money to cover A's taxes and subsequently C's money to cover B's taxes. Employees may steal from petty cash or from inventory. Employees may pay vendors or provide travel reimbursement checks to employees who are due nothing. In Michigan, a county official was caught having filed false travel expense claims for years. What was significant was that he was the finance chairman for the county government commission, the very person who should have been alert to possible financial wrongdoings.[25] Financial control systems rely upon the principle of segregation of authority, such that a person who can authorize a financial transaction cannot also approve of paying out the actual cash when it is time. A county official should not be able to approve incurring a travel expense for himself and then approving its payment, but segregation of duties is not always complete.

Fraud can involve one or two individuals or can be systemic. The Accountant General of the Federation of Nigeria complained about public servants systematically looting the treasury, particularly through the payroll systems. He said this was done in part with the cooperation of the international community in that stolen funds were transferred overseas to international financial institutions that readily accepted new deposits regardless of their source.[26] A more recent, and higher profile, example involved a lack of sufficient controls to ensure that aid provided by the United States to Afghanistan did not end up being siphoned off for personal use by Afghani officials.[27]

One prescription is that accounting systems need to be *transparent*. How they operate and the products of their operations, specifically their various reports, need to be available to interested parties and the public in general. This is of widespread concern in both highly developed countries and less developed ones. The International Monetary Fund uses its *Code of Good Practices on Fiscal Transparency* in working with developing nations.[28] United Way International has adopted global standards that include financial accountability and transparency as a key requirement when working with participating nongovernmental organizations.[29] Simply getting officials to make public their accounting reports can be controversial, as has been the situation in Uganda, for instance. Officials there, when called to testify about their reports, sometimes switched off their phones so as not to be reached or claimed they had gone to burials.[30]

To prevent fraud and to reduce other losses due to errors, internal controls that specify organizational arrangements and procedures are established. OMB Circular A-123, for example, "provides guidance to federal managers on improving the accountability and effectiveness of federal programs and operations by establishing, assessing, correcting, and reporting on internal control."[31]

Responsibility needs to be assigned to individuals, and any delegations of responsibility need to be detailed in writing. One standard practice is to segregate duties, so that one individual may have only limited authority over monies and two or more people may be required to approve some financial transactions. The presumption is that if two or more individuals are part of a particular process, they will monitor each other's behavior and limit various abuses. For example, two or more signatures may be required in approving the issuance of checks or in transferring money through electronic funds transfers.

Employees are trained in how to enter transactions properly in accounting systems and what their ethical and legal responsibilities are in handling public resources. Individuals who handle funds may be subject to more extensive background checks before hiring and may be bonded.

Downsizing can force the elimination of personnel and increase the risk that funds are vulnerable to theft or accidental loss due to the reduced oversight of financial operations.

Auditing bodies are important in preventing and detecting fraud. GAO selectively conducts financial as well as program audits and on occasion finds losses in the billions of dollars. GAO audits the financial statements for the government as a whole, for departments (for example, the Treasury Department), for independent commissions (for example, the Securities and Exchange Commission), and for federally chartered corporations (for example, the Boy Scouts of America, which incidentally filed for bankruptcy in 2020). The heavy-duty workload of auditing at the federal level is handled by the inspectors general in their respective departments and agencies. When discrepancies are identified through audits, follow-up is necessary to determine their causes, and corrective measures need to be initiated.

Fund Accounting

One of the main differences between public and private sector accounting is the definition of the accounting entity. For the typical private sector organization, the entity is the organization itself because accounts are designed to reflect its entire resources. Governments, in contrast, separate financial resources into distinct accounting entities called *funds*. Each fund is set up to record and account for the uses of a specific group of assets or sources of revenue or collection of a specific type of costs. As provided for by GASB, there are 3 general classes of public sector funds and 11 different particular types of funds.[32]

The following are the funds that state and local governments use:

1. *Governmental Funds*.
   - The *general fund* is the most important governmental fund. Several revenue sources may flow into a government's general fund, such as property tax and income tax receipts at the local level. The resources in the fund are available for expenditure for virtually any purpose

that the jurisdiction is legally empow-
ered to pursue. Most municipalities, for
instance, may use general fund receipts
for police and road services but not
schools, because the latter are the domain
of independent school districts. The other
fund types within the governmental class
are available for what are thought of as
normal government operations, but these
types have receipt and/or expenditure
restrictions.

- *Special revenue funds* receive monies
from special sources and are earmarked
for special purposes. Gasoline taxes are
typically accounted for in a special revenue fund, with expenditures limited
to transportation, especially roads and
highways.
- *Capital projects funds* account for receipts
and expenditures related to capital
projects, such as construction of a new
park or city hall, or for major pieces of
equipment, such as vehicles for a city
fire department. Monies may come into
these funds from bond sales that will be
paid for with general fund tax receipts.
- *Debt service funds* are used to account
for interest and principal on general-
purpose long-term debt. The revenue
received by this type of fund is usually
from the general fund.
- *Permanent funds* are used in cases where
only the earnings may be expended and
the principal may not.
2. *Proprietary Funds.* The second class of funds
consists of those that are proprietary or
business-like in nature.
- *Enterprise funds* operate as businesses
whose customers are external to government. Such funds are established for toll
roads, bridges, and local water systems.
Numerous proposals have circulated
recommending that various federal operations be converted to government corporations that would be run as enterprises.[33]
- *Internal service funds* operate as businesses whose customers are internal to

government. A central purchasing office
or a vehicle maintenance garage may
operate as an internal service fund, with
revenues coming from other departments as services are rendered.
- When bonds are sold to support the
activities of a proprietary fund (for
example, bond proceeds might be used
to renovate a city sewage system), capital
expenditures and payment of debt are
handled through the proprietary fund,
not through a capital project or debt service fund.
3. *Fiduciary Funds.* The third class, known
as fiduciary funds, consists of four types.
The first, called *custodial funds* (sometimes
also referred to as agency funds), consists
of accounts that are held by one entity for
another (such as a city government collecting
taxes for the local school district). The last
three are separate categories of trust funds,
including pension trust funds, investment
trust funds, and private purpose trust funds.
- *Pension trusts* for government employees are often the largest set of fiduciary
funds.
- *Investment trust funds* are used for tracking and reporting the external portion of
local government investment pools.
- *Private purpose trust funds* cover all other
trust-type arrangements of the government in which principal and earnings may
be expended. An increasingly large set of
fiduciary funds at the state level are savings held in trust for when children grow
up and enroll in college or university.[34]

Account Groups

Governmental funds include only financial
assets—namely, assets that will be converted to
cash—and therefore the general fixed asset account
group (GFAAG) is used to report assets that will
not be converted to cash, such as buildings, swimming pools, aircraft hangars, and airport terminals. The GFAAG is simply a reporting of assets
and does not involve transactions. Fixed-asset
account groups are increasingly important to the

description and analysis of the financial health of government agencies and entire government jurisdictions (see the chapter on capital assets).

The second account group is the general long-term debt account group. This group reports government debt that is not part of proprietary or fiduciary funds. In other words, the account group reports liabilities of the entity as a whole, as distinguished from specific funds. This account group and the fixed-assets group, in effect, are memoranda that report assets and liabilities that otherwise would not be reported.

Structure and Rules of Accounting Systems

Ledgers

Accounting systems use ledgers as a means of organization or structure. Each fund has a general ledger and subsidiary ledgers. The general ledger records the overall status of revenues and expenditures, while subsidiary ledgers are established for each revenue source and type of expenditure. In a general fund having several tax sources of revenue, a subsidiary revenue ledger is used for each source. The OMB and the Treasury Department have established a U.S. Government Standard General Ledger that indicates how agencies are to organize their ledgers.[35] OMB Circular A-123, Appendix D, requires agencies to comply with the standards of the general ledger.[36]

Expenditure subsidiary ledgers control expenditures by appropriation, organizational unit, object of expenditure, and sometimes purpose or activity. Accounting systems are used to track expenditures according to provisions in appropriations. Often these appropriations are specific to organizations, as in the case of $2 million appropriated to a city housing department. The appropriation may also contain limitations on how funds will be spent, such as expenditures for personnel or equipment. This aspect of accounting is explained later. Some jurisdictions track expenditures by program or activity (this is done if a government's program budget structure does not match its organizational structure).

Accounting Formula

Accounting systems use equations that allow systematic recording of transactions and double-checking that the transactions have been properly recorded. The basic equation that is used is:

$$assets = liabilities + fund\ balance$$

In the formula, *assets* can be the money or other resources that reside, or come into, a fund. *Liabilities* are the monies owed others, such as suppliers of office equipment and tires for police cars. The *fund balance* comprises the residual, uncommitted monies. Specific accounts are established for each of the three components of the formula. Asset accounts, for example, can include those showing cash on hand as well as monies owed by taxpayers (taxes receivable). FASAB has recommended standards for assets and liabilities.

In the mid-2000s, the GASB began work not to revise this fundamental formula, but to revise its components. GASB Concept Statement No. 4, *Elements of Financial Statements*, defines key terms that state and local governments are to use in developing their financial statements. Among the concepts defined by the statement are the following:

- *Assets*, which are resources with present service capacity that the government presently controls.
- *Liabilities*, which are present obligations to sacrifice current resources or future resources that the entity has little or no discretion to avoid.
- An *outflow of resources*, representing a consumption of net resources by the entity that is applicable to the reporting period.
- An *inflow of resources*, representing an acquisition of net resources by the entity that is applicable to the reporting period.
- A *deferred outflow of resources*, which is a consumption of net resources by the entity that is applicable to a future reporting period.
- A *deferred inflow of resources*, which is an acquisition of net resources by the entity that is applicable to a future reporting period.
- *Net position* (fund balance) is then the residual of all other elements presented in a statement of financial position.[37]

Why go through all of this work simply defining the elements to be used in accounting? The answer is simple: Unless terms are defined, there is no consistency from jurisdiction to jurisdiction and even from department to department within a jurisdiction. As a result, financial statements, to be discussed later, become largely worthless in that they are unclear as to how transactions have been recorded. Furthermore, the lack of consistency makes pointless any efforts to draw comparisons across departments, across jurisdictions, and over time. For example, it is important to handle separately resources flowing immediately into a jurisdiction as distinguished from resources that are deferred and presumably will flow into the jurisdiction at some later reporting period. Also, the inflow concept means that the resources are coming into the government and are not merely being transferred from one fund to another within the government. The latter activities are known as transfers and are discussed later.

In addition to its work on the *Elements of Financial Statements*, GASB in 2009 issued a new statement (Number 54), *Fund Balance Reporting and Governmental Fund Type Definitions*.[38] This document was the result of concerns over inconsistencies across jurisdictions as to how they were treating fund balance. Statement 54 separates fund balance between amounts that are nonspendable as restricted, committed, assigned, or unassigned. It is only this last category, which can be spent for any purpose, that can add to the fund balance in the general fund.[39]

Double-entry accounting, in which any single transaction is recorded twice (at a minimum), is used as a cross-check. For instance, if taxes are received and no additional obligations are incurred, then both assets and the fund balance increase, and the accounting system will record these two events. The double-entry approach can also be used within one portion of the overall formula. If taxes are received but were already noted in an asset account called taxes receivable, then that account would be reduced while an asset account for cash would be increased. That particular set of transactions would not affect liabilities or the fund balance.

Transactions are recorded in a T, in which the left side of the T constitutes debits and the right side constitutes credits. The terms *debits* and *credits* refer only to the left and right sides of the T. Contrary to their use in everyday conversation, the term "debits" is not negative in the sense of expenses or debts owed, and the term "credits" is not positive in the sense of receipts or money to be paid to government. Rules exist as to when an account should be debited and when credited. In any transaction, the amount debited to one or more accounts must equal the amount credited to other accounts.

Specified Procedures

Flowing out of accounting standards and principles are procedures that determine how transactions will be recorded and in what accounts. These procedures are typically specified in manuals or handbooks so that employees involved in whatever aspects of accounting know how to meet their responsibilities. Manuals explain the handling of receipts and purchases, including, for example, overall purchasing policy, purchase orders, contract payments, and emergency purchases. Payroll procedures will be specified in some detail in a manual and are likely to require the approval of specific individuals, possibly including written signatures confirming which employees are to be paid what amounts.

The typical accounting cycle is as follows.[40] An event occurs and a source document is prepared. The event might be a decision to tax property, and the document might be a tax bill sent to a citizen. When the citizen pays the bill, another transaction occurs, and the accounting system needs to reflect the receipt of payment. On the expenditure side of the budget, one event might be placing an order for office supplies, and a later event might be receipt of the supplies and the invoice. These types of transactions will first be posted in a *journal*, which is a chronological listing of events or transactions. The journal entry indicates both the credits and the debits involved in the transaction. For example, tax monies received would increase a cash account and decrease a taxes receivable account. Entries once recorded in the journal are posted to ledgers, and from time to time the debits and credits of these accounts are totaled to obtain trial and final balances. The balances are used in preparing financial reports (which are discussed later).

Classification of Receipts and Expenditures

Receipts and expenditures are classified in a variety of ways, and elaborate coding systems are used to monitor and control financial transactions. Such coding devices help hold government officials responsible for honestly managing the government's business.

Receipts

The monies that government receives need to be recorded according to the source. The money derived from each tax source, such as property and income taxes, needs to be recorded separately and in distinction from user fees, such as charges for using a municipal golf course. The federal government treats user fees as offsetting collections. Money derived from fees, as in the case of the Tennessee Valley Authority, is used to offset expenditures for Tennessee Valley Authority operations. The net differences in such transactions are reported in the budget. The practice of netting receipts against expenditures in the budget for enterprise operations, while perfectly appropriate, hinders the transparency of financial reporting because it means that one cannot use the government budget alone to gauge the size of government.

GASB has had to deal with a relatively recent phenomenon in the realm of revenues. Some governments strapped for cash have borrowed against outstanding receivables, such as taxes owed, and have actually sold such receivables, an act known as *securitizing* a stream of receivables (see the chapter on capital finance and debt management). In 2006, GASB released Statement No. 48, which requires these governments to report such transactions as liabilities in that they have pledged collateral against borrowed resources.[41]

Fund and Appropriation

Expenditures are accounted for in a variety of ways. One set of characteristics is the fund and appropriation. An appropriation is a legislative approval to spend from a specific fund. Because several bills may be passed that appropriate out of the general fund, the dollar stipulations in each of these bills must be observed vis-à-vis the total assets available in the general fund. Even if a jurisdiction uses only one appropriation bill, each of the expenditure limits in the bill must be observed and consequently must be monitored by the accounting system. When an expenditure is made, it is charged against the appropriated amount and the remaining available balance is shown. In this way, an accounting system can be used to keep agency expenditures within budgeted figures.

If the legislative body earmarks expenditures in detail, then the accounting system becomes increasingly complex. For example, Congress, in its annual foreign assistance appropriation bill, typically appropriates funds for programs within the Agency for International Development in great detail, specifying amounts to be available in each country receiving aid. The accounting system, therefore, must monitor expenditures by program (e.g., child survival) and by country to adhere to the stipulations in the appropriation bill.[42]

Organizational Unit

Expenditures are made by organizational units, and accounting systems must track expenditures accordingly. Appropriation bills are usually specific to agencies so that, instead of the government simply being authorized to spend an amount on forest preservation, a specific unit within a department is appropriated the money. Large governments, then, account for expenditures not only at the department level but also at the bureau, office, division, or regional unit level.

Objects of Expenditure

Accounting systems invariably account in terms of the objects acquired or the objects of expenditure. Broad groupings of objects are called major objects, and their subdivisions are called minor objects. **Exhibit 12-2** illustrates the object classes

Exhibit 12-2 Federal Objects of Expenditure Classification

Code	Classification Title
10	**Personnel Compensation and Benefits**
11	**Personnel Compensation**
11.1	Full-Time Permanent
11.3	Other Than Full-Time Permanent
11.5	Other Personnel Compensation
11.6	Military Personnel Basic Allowance for Housing
11.7	Military Personnel
11.8	Special Personal Services Payments
11.9	Total Personnel Compensation
12	**Personnel Benefits**
12.1	Civilian Personnel Benefits
12.2	Military Personnel Benefits
13	**Benefits for Former Personnel**
20	**Contractual Services and Supplies**
21	**Travel and Transportation of Persons**
22	**Transportation of Things**
23	**Rent, Communications, and Utilities**
23.1	Rental Payments to General Services Administration
23.2	Rental Payments to Others
23.3	Communications, Utilities, and Miscellaneous Charges
24	**Printing and Reproduction**
25	**Other Contractual Services**
25.1	Advisory and Assistance Services
25.2	Other Services
25.3	Other Goods and Services from Federal Sources
25.4	Operation and Maintenance of Facilities
25.5	Research and Development Contracts
25.6	Medical Care
25.7	Operation and Maintenance of Equipment
25.8	Subsistence and Support of Persons
26	**Supplies and Materials**
30	**Acquisition of Assets**
31	**Equipment**
32	**Land and Structures**
33	**Investments and Loans**
40	**Grants and Fixed Charges**
41	**Grants, Subsidies, and Contributions**
42	**Insurance Claims and Indemnities**
43	**Interest and Dividends**
44	**Refunds**
90	**Other**
91	**Unvouchered**
92	**Undistributed**
94	**Financial Transfers**
99	**Subtotal Obligations**
99.5	Below Reporting Threshold
99.9	Total New Obligations

Data from U.S. Office of Management and Budget (2019). *Preparation, submission, and execution of the budget*, Circular No. A-11 (sec. 83, pp. 4–22). Washington, DC: Author. Retrieved February 14, 2020, from https://www.whitehouse.gov/wp-content/uploads/2018/06/a11.pdf.

used by the federal government. The object series begins with the major object class number 10, for example, which contains object classes 11, 12, and 13 covering all personnel compensation and benefits. The other major object classes are contractual services and supplies, acquisition of assets, grants and fixed charges, and other as illustrated in the exhibit.

Accounting systems can become unwieldy in their use of minor objects. For instance, travel as a major object can be subdivided in numerous ways:

- Mode (personal automobile, government automobile, commercial airline)
- Type of person traveling (elected official, political executive, career executive, employee, client)
- Purpose (meeting, conference, training, inspection)
- Location (in state, out of state, out of country)
- Type of expense (lodging, meals, transportation)

The number of possible permutations is great. When an accounting system uses such detail, the entry of many transactions may be delayed due to classification ambiguities.

Despite the administrative problems of detailed minor objects, legislative bodies often incorporate such details in appropriation bills. These line items in an appropriation allow control when there is concern that funds may be abused. Restrictions may be inserted regarding the purchase of newspaper subscriptions, the number of automobiles, and government employee travel. When minor object restrictions are embedded in appropriations, the limits are legal mandates, and the accounting system must ensure compliance.

Purpose and Activity

Program-oriented budgets that focus decision-making attention on specific program goals and objectives also require accounting-based information on how much each program costs. The federal government uses broad functional categories, such as national defense, energy, and income security, which are divided into subfunctions. For example, energy is subdivided into supply, conservation, emergency preparedness and energy information, policy, and regulation.[43] If a budget based on program classifications cuts across agency lines, then the accounting system needs to cut across agency lines to accumulate the costs according to program. Similarly, preparing a budget that allocates funds according to detailed work activities requires an accounting system that tracks expenditures by those activities. The problem of accounting for finances by program or activity is discussed more fully in the next section in regard to cost accounting.

Performance Measurement

While practitioners and academics in the field of budgeting have long been concerned about how to measure the results of government programs, accountants only became particularly concerned starting in the 1980s.[44] They came to recognize a need for measuring outputs, outcomes, efficiency, effectiveness, and the like (see the chapter on the expenditure side of budget preparation). What is significant here is that accountants now back the notion that financial accounting should be tied to performance measurement. If one wishes to determine the efficiency of an organization in delivering a service over time, then there needs to be a measurement of the service provided (outputs) and the costs (the latter obtained through accounting).

GASB, since 1987, has had a project that encourages state and local governments to engage in *service efforts and accomplishments* (SEA) reporting as part of *general-purpose external financial reporting*. There have been numerous debates concerning whether such SEA reporting should be required or voluntary. GASB issued guidelines for voluntary SEA reporting in July 2010.[45]

Accounting for performance and then auditing for it require going beyond the boundaries of the organization to where results are produced. In contrast, traditional accounting systems have been structured to capture financial transactions within organizations. Once the accounting system has to take measurements outside the organization, as it must with performance accounting, major problems arise over how to collect information and how to audit it. Measurement errors inevitably occur in such systems, raising issues about their accuracy and utility.

The federal government has taken major steps in the direction of greater utilization of performance measurement. The Chief Financial Officers Act of 1990 instructs agency CFOs to develop reporting systems that provide for "the integration of accounting and budgeting information and the systematic measurement of performance." The Government Performance and Results Act (GPRA) of 1993 requires federal agencies to develop annual performance plans that are integral to the budget.[46] The GPRA Modernization Act of 2010 revised those requirements in an effort to make the reports more useful.[17] Of course, including performance information in accounting systems and having that information actually influence decision making are two different things. For the federal government, more strides have been made in performance reporting than in using performance information in decision making (see the chapter on the expenditure side of budget preparation).

Perhaps equally difficult is the direct challenge that connecting performance and the budget creates for accounting systems themselves. Connecting performance information and cost information implies the ability to appropriately measure both. Proper cost measurement requires a level of accounting sophistication that has proved difficult for governments to achieve. They have attempted to remedy this problem through greater attention to cost accounting, as discussed later.

Basis of Accounting

The *basis of accounting* refers to the timing of transactions, or when a revenue item is recorded as received by the government and when an expenditure is recorded as having occurred. There are several methods for determining when a revenue or expenditure item is recorded, and each has a different purpose.

Cash Accounting

The oldest system is cash accounting, which is still used today, particularly in small governments. In general, all governments have a cash aspect to their accounting systems. In a cash accounting system, tax receipts are recorded when they are actually received by the government, and expenditures are recorded when payments are made. Minor variations exist. Some systems record expenditures when checks are written, but others record expenditures when checks clear the banking system. The major advantages of the cash system are that it is simple in comparison with alternatives and that it presents an accurate picture of cash on hand at any point in time.

The major disadvantage of the cash system is that it does not provide information about the future—namely, anticipated receipts and expenditures.[48] The cash on hand may seem to suggest that one's financial situation is reasonably secure, but a different picture may emerge when considering obligations that must be met, such as payrolls. Another major disadvantage of cash accounting is that it can be manipulated—for example, by making payments more quickly or more slowly—in a way that makes a government's financial condition appear better or worse at a point in time than it really is.

Encumbrance Accounting

A step in the direction of anticipating future transactions is encumbrance accounting. Expenditures are recorded when purchase orders are written or contracts are signed. Some of the cash on hand, then, is said to be encumbered and not available for covering other expenditures. In the case of a multiyear contract, all of the expenditures for a year may be encumbered at the outset of the fiscal year, or amounts may be encumbered each month as work is completed by the contractor. An encumbrance system helps ensure that a government unit will not overspend its appropriation.

Accrual Accounting

In accrual systems, financial transactions are recognized when the activities that generate them occur.[49] Revenues are recorded when the government earns the income, as when a local government sends tax bills to property owners. Expenditures are recognized when the liabilities are incurred, regardless of when payment for those goods or services might actually be made during the year.

The accrual basis has been required of federal agencies for more than 40 years, but few federal accounting systems actually use accrual accounting. The obstacle has been the diversity of accounting systems. Large departments, such as the DOD, for example, have many different accounting systems. Where accrual accounting is used in state and local governments (particularly for the general fund and other governmental funds), it is normally on a *modified accrual* basis: Not all transactions are accrued, and some remain on a cash basis. Under modified accrual accounting, revenues are recognized when they are "measurable and available" for obligation (this typically means that the revenues will be available to meet expenditures in the same fiscal year), and expenditures are recognized when an obligation to spend has occurred. A standard interpretation of this is that the cash would need to be received within 60 days of the end of the fiscal year in order to be "counted" under modified accrual. Expenditure treatment under modified accrual focuses on "obligations" rather than focusing on the consumption of resources, as occurs under full accrual. Thus, modified accrual records an expenditure when the government is obligated to pay for the resource. Under full accrual, an expense would be recorded when the resource was actually consumed, regardless of when the obligation to pay for it occurred.[50] Full accrual, however, is recommended for proprietary funds (enterprise and internal service funds) and pension trusts.

Despite the obstacles to implementation, the accounting profession continues to endorse strongly the accrual basis of accounting. GASB's Statement No. 11, *Measurement Focus and Basis of Accounting: Governmental Fund Operating Statements*, provides for extending the accrual process to cover items previously not covered.[51] For instance, the costs of employees' vacations are to be recognized when employees earn their vacation time. When employees are allowed to accumulate vacation leave, the accounting system needs to recognize that government's liabilities have increased. Particularly controversial is the provision that employee pension funds should recognize future payments owed to future retirees by recording them in the governmental funds rather than as normally reported in the general long-term debt account group. These provisions are controversial in that they negatively affect fund balances, pushing some governments into negative balances.

Not recording future obligations in the accounting system gives a false picture of the financial condition of the governmental entity. In the private sector, future pension payouts must be accounted for now to control for the possibility that the company will not have the funds to pay out the pension obligations when members of its workforce retire. Government presumably is in a somewhat different situation in that at least in principle, government can use its taxing power in the future to obtain the funds necessary to meet pension fund payout obligations. However, the fact that the government in principle can use its taxing power to meet pension obligations does not relieve government of the obligation to report what its pension fund liabilities are. Taxpayers are in for a rude shock when their jurisdiction's pension obligations have not been funded as employees earn future pension payouts and the accounting system does not record the future payouts that will be due.

Cost Accounting

While the cash, encumbrance, and accrual bases of accounting focus attention on resources coming into government and being expended, cost accounting is concerned with when resources are used, and by whom, in the production of goods and services.[52] For example, gasoline purchased for a state highway department could be accounted for when the order is made (encumbrance), when the goods are received (modified accrual method), or when the vendor is paid (cash method). The cost approach, in contrast, records the transaction when the gasoline is consumed.

Managerial cost accounting can be viewed as providing key information needed by managers in conducting their operations and, in addition to this internal function, providing information to external parties such as the legislative body, taxpayers, and investors in governmental securities.[53] In a cost accounting system, costs of providing services are matched with measures of those services. For example, a school district might want to know the average cost of graduating someone from the general population compared with the average cost of graduating a student with special needs—for instance, a student with physical disabilities.

Activity-based costing and *activity-based management* concentrate on collecting costs of delivering services to citizens.[54] The costs of delivering services can be monitored over time, thereby giving an impetus for increased efficiency of operations. Such accounting can determine the costs of producing activities, outputs, and outcomes.

The incentives for using cost accounting are different in the private and public sectors. To determine their profitability, corporations need to know the cost of providing each product or service. The costs of production can be subtracted from sales receipts to determine a corporation's profit or loss, something that every investor wants to know about a company. Governmental programs, such as police and fire departments, obviously do not seek a profit and consequently may see less need for cost accounting. Contemporary public safety managers want to know whether desired outcomes are being achieved and want to know from their accounting systems what the costs are for outputs and work (see the chapter on the expenditure side of budget preparation).

Other programs, particularly enterprise and internal service funds, while not seeking a profit, do endeavor to break even and consequently have an incentive to know the costs of their services. For example, a centralized office supplies agency has an incentive to calculate its costs so as to set appropriate fee schedules for charging departments for products. A central maintenance garage for city vehicles needs an accurate understanding of its costs for maintaining

garbage trucks, police cars, and buses. Keeping costs down in each of these areas is important in linking the production of services with costs. Cost accounting systems should be able to provide insight into marginal costs, such as the extra expense of repairing each additional police car damaged in the line of duty.

Besides the reduced incentives to use cost accounting in government, several other impediments to its implementation exist. One such obstacle is that purposes and objectives are not neatly compartmentalized into organizational units, resulting in situations in which one organization may be serving multiple purposes and another organization may be serving some of those same purposes. To resolve this problem, *cost centers* must be used in which the accounting system records financial information for each activity performed within an organizational unit. In a bureau that engages in three activities and that has its personnel working at various times on the three activities, records must be maintained regarding the amount of time each worker spends on each activity. Other bureau costs, such as those for supplies, telephones, and furniture, must be distributed among the cost centers.

Other impediments to cost accounting being used in government pertain to how various financial transactions are currently conducted. Government agencies sometimes provide services to one another at no charge, resulting in a form of subsidy to the recipient agencies and a consequent understatement of the costs of the services that those agencies provide. Salaries, wages, and other personnel expenses, such as pension contributions and health benefits for employees and retirees, often appear in central budgets and not in the budgets of units that deliver services. Likewise, other support services involving budgeting, legal assistance, janitorial services, and computer support may not be charged to line agencies. The result is that organizational budgets typically fall short of fully reflecting the costs of activities.

Cost accounting requires that special attention be given to the acquisition and utilization of *fixed assets*—land, structures, and major pieces of equipment. Fixed assets are sometimes financed centrally and, consequently, do not appear in the budgets of the organizational units that actually use these assets. Additionally, purchases of fixed assets or capital goods should not be considered costs in the year of purchase, but rather should be depreciated over the life span of the goods. From a cost standpoint, the cost of police patrol cars might be spread over 3 years. From a cash standpoint, the purchase will be recorded in the first year when the purchase is made. Buildings and vehicles then are depreciated over time, showing a truer picture of the cost of services than the cash method does.

The life cycle of an asset needs to be considered—that is, how long an asset has utility before it needs major renovation or complete replacement. Federal law and OMB Circular A-131 instruct agencies to use value engineering as a management technique in determining how long assets will be of use. The circular defines *value engineering* as

> a systematic process of reviewing and analyzing the requirements, functions and elements of systems, project, equipment, facilities, services, and supplies for the purpose of achieving the essential functions at the lowest life-cycle cost consistent with required levels of performance, reliability, quality, or safety.[55]

Depreciation is essential in cost accounting, and depreciation rules need to be applied differently according to the fixed assets involved. FASAB has identified four types of *property, plant, and equipment* (PP&E):[56]

- The *general PP&E* category includes buildings for which a market value can be derived, such as an office building.
- The category of *federal mission PP&E* is for the uniquely federal functions of defense and space exploration. Depreciating these assets is extremely difficult because it requires estimating the assets' useful lives. How long will a weapons system be of use, or how long will a space satellite continue to operate?
- The *heritage PP&E* category includes education, culture, and artistic endeavors.[57] The Washington Monument and the White House are in this grouping, as they have special significance and are not just ordinary government buildings.
- The last category, *stewardship PP&E*, covers government holdings that are entrusted to the government for safekeeping. It includes federal land held by the National Park Service and the U.S. Forest Service.

In addition to fixed assets, other investments pose major challenges for the use of cost accounting in government. When a government bureau pays for several of its workers to attend a training program, is it an investment, and, if so, what is the life of that investment? When a state government provides a grant to a local government for construction of a sewage treatment plant, how should the state record the investment given that the new plant will belong to the local government and not to the state?

Project-Based Accounting

Another option that is not as elaborate as cost accounting is project-based accounting. Accounts can be established on a temporary basis to track costs for selected activities. Private firms, both for-profit and nonprofit, keep detailed accounting records for contracts, including costs at task or subtask levels. If a consulting firm has been awarded a government contract, a separate set of accounts is established showing which personnel worked on which tasks for what length of time in a given reporting period (weekly, biweekly, or monthly). Accounts of this type are important for reimbursement purposes. Federal cost accounting standards require strict adherence to project cost accounting. Charging time or other costs to a project when that time or other resources were not actually contributing to the project, if determined to be deliberate and significant, can result in severe penalties, including debarment from future government contracting.

Project-based accounting is also used for monitoring internal operations. If a corporation is developing a new product or group of products, separate accounts can be established to gauge the developmental costs of the project.

Cost Finding

In some instances, governments may be satisfied with something less than a complete cost
accounting system or even project-based accounting. Rather than having an ongoing cost information system, governments sometimes selectively
study costs of specific activities that may be
contained within a single organization or spread
across several units. The cost of delivering family
planning services to teenagers might be derived
through analysis of expenditure records and a
sampling of employee time commitments. A far
more elaborate cost-finding endeavor would be to
try to derive the costs of the opioid addiction to a
state government. The analysis would attempt to
determine the costs of prevention and treatment
activities that most likely are not encoded in the
accounting system. For example, opioids may
well increase health care costs for prisoners, but
such costs would not routinely be segregated in
the accounting system.

The analysis of cost data can be useful in
identifying *fixed costs* and *variable costs*. There
may be a minimum or fixed cost for providing a
given service up to some level, above which costs
increase as units of service increase. For example,
a preschool program for disadvantaged children
begins with a fixed set of costs for essentials such
as a schoolroom, a teacher, and some supportive
services—costs that are incurred whether 1 or 10
children are taught. As the number of children in
the class increases, variable costs increase, such
as those for teaching materials and supplies, and
perhaps teacher aides. Fixed costs, however, do
not rise unless the number of children grows to a
level that another classroom, another teacher, and
so forth are required.

Allowable Costs

In the awarding of grants and contracts, governments need to determine what costs are allowable. The federal government's Cost Accounting
Standards Board, located within OMB's Office of
Federal Procurement Policy, has attempted to set
parameters for costs in defense and related contracts.[58] OMB Circular A-87 specifies in great
detail what costs are allowable in grants to state
and local governments.[59] Unallowable costs include
entertainment; alcoholic beverages; interest on
debt (such as working capital borrowings); and
donations, as in the case of volunteer services.

Risk and Credit Accounting

Public sector officials have come to recognize that
risks arise in carrying out public duties. Not only
are revenues raised and expenditures made, but
other factors create conditions that can result in
major financial loss and/or expenditures. Risk
management involves assessing the risk exposure
of a government (see the chapter on budget execution). On the one hand, in making and guaranteeing loans, the federal government assumes
risks that can have major financial consequences,
as evidenced by the forced bailout of failed savings and loan associations. On the other hand,
credit programs can yield savings or negative subsidies, particularly at some point in the future.
Estimating such savings poses considerable technical problems, and agencies that administer such
programs may be biased in favor of forecasting
such savings.

The OMB, as prescribed by the Federal Credit
Reform Act of 1990, oversaw a thorough revamping of how the government accounts for credit
programs and how decisions are made about
these programs. The law was intended to "place
the cost of credit programs on a budgetary basis"
so that they compete with all other programs for
scarce resources.[60] Prior to the enactment of the
Credit Reform Act, the budget "charged" costs
based on the cash that would flow out of or into
the budget in a given year. This meant that direct
loans appeared to be the budgetary equivalent
of grants, even though many of the funds would
be repaid in later years. Loan guarantees, on the
other hand, appeared to be cost free because third
parties were disbursing the funds in the budget
year (the government sometimes made money,
in the budget year, because of up-front payments
that came from borrowers). However, the federal
government was liable for costs—sometimes substantial costs—in future years when loan recipients defaulted on their obligations. By focusing
on the long-term costs to the federal government

from both kinds of programs, the Credit Reform Act put them on an equivalent budgetary basis.

OMB requires agencies to supply data on direct loans, loan subsidies, guaranteed loans, and guaranteed loan subsidies as part of the agencies' budget submissions (Circular A-129). Prior to passage of the Federal Credit Reform Act, many federal agencies could borrow from the Federal Financing Bank, but they now must borrow from the Treasury Department to finance their direct and guaranteed loan programs. When the law was implemented in the 1990s, federal agencies encountered considerable difficulty in complying because their existing accounting systems and supporting staff were often inadequate.[61]

A more recent controversy concerns not the implementation of credit reform, but how the costs of federal credit are estimated. Under credit reform, the cost of credit programs is calculated as the net present value of the budgetary effect of loans or loan guarantees over the life of the loan in question. Another method, called fair value scoring, has been argued to be a more accurate measure. Fair value scoring attempts to account for the cost of the risk that taxpayers are taking when they commit to providing benefits under a credit program. Under the fair value argument, credit reform scoring understates the true cost because it assumes that future cash flows are discounted only at a risk-free Treasury rate, as opposed to a market rate, which is viewed to be more realistic in terms of the actual risks.

In fact, the CBO has taken to presenting both costs when it estimates the effect of a given change in credit policy. The difference between estimates produced by the two methods can be large. For example, in 2014, the CBO reported that federal student loan programs would save $135 billion over 10 years under credit reform scoring, while fair value scoring would result in a loss of $88 billion over the same period.[62] There has been no resolution to this debate, and budget technicians continue to disagree over how to appropriately score credit programs. Congressional support agencies have taken different views on the debate, with CBO continuing to argue for fair value accounting, while GAO siding with those who advocate more traditional credit reform scoring.[63]

Generational Accounting

Of growing interest are the potential effects of government finances on different generations.[64] Expenditures for elementary and secondary education obviously help children, whereas alcohol programs help adults and programs such as Medicare mostly help the elderly. In addition, at the federal level, generational accounting considers the effects that current budget deficits have on future generations because those deficits represent a deferral of the costs of current benefits across generations. Although accounting systems have not been devised for identifying the costs or the benefits of government activities for different age groups, some reporting of such effects occurs. Generational accounting has not taken hold in the United States, but several other countries have explored how generational accounting might change the way that budgetary effects of various policies are calculated.[65]

Need for Different Bases

These different approaches to the basis of accounting are not substitutes for one another. Rather, each satisfies a different type of need.

- From the standpoint of a treasury department, a cash basis for recording receipts and expenditures is necessary because the department has the legal responsibility to receive revenue and issue checks to cover expenses. This responsibility extends to determining that there are sufficient funds to cover checks to be issued.

- The encumbrance basis is important in showing the current status of assets and liabilities, including liabilities that will place a demand on cash in the future.

- Cost accounting is valuable in identifying resources consumed, as distinguished from resources acquired and placed in inventory.

- Risk accounting provides a more comprehensive overview of obligations than is available through accounting systems that cover only revenues and expenditures.

- Generational accounting provides insights into the implications of government finances for different generations, from the elderly to the young and to those not yet born.

Private Sector Reforms in Accounting and Implications for Government Accounting

The discussion has shown that government accounting has undergone considerable reform, but it is worth giving special attention to efforts to extend the Sarbanes-Oxley Act to privately held companies, nonprofit organizations, and governments.

The Sarbanes-Oxley Act, formally the Public Company Accounting Reform and Investor Protection Act and commonly referred to as *SOX*, was passed in 2002 in the wake of the financial scandals involving Enron and WorldCom.[66] As its official title indicates, it was aimed at upgrading accounting practices in publicly traded companies in order to protect investors.

SOX's complex provisions include the following:

- Creation of the independent Public Company Accounting Oversight Board, which sets standards and oversees the accounting profession
- Requirement for chief executive officers and chief financial officers of companies to take personal responsibility for the content of financial statements
- Prohibition of ongoing use of lead auditors (that is, auditors primarily responsible for audits of particular firms) and instead requires that they be rotated at least every 5 years
- Internal controls and requirement that structure of such controls be audited by the company and assessed by auditors and reported to the Securities and Exchange Commission
- Increased penalties for fraud in terms of fines and imprisonment
- Protection to company employees who report wrongdoing (whistleblowers)
- Illegalization of the destruction of documents that are routinely needed in investigations and legal actions

In response to Sarbanes-Oxley, the OMB launched a review of federal financial management. This process was already ongoing as required by the Federal Financial Management Improvement Act of 1996.[67] Circular A-123, dealing with internal controls, was revised in 2008, and subsequent guidance has been provided since. Among the specific changes over the past few years are the following:

- Appendix B (last amended in 2019) establishes procedures to improve internal controls and eliminate fraud and waste in the use of government charge cards. The Appendix provides guidance intended to assist in avoiding improper payments and appropriately disciplining employees. It also requires that the government be reimbursed by employees or supervisors in the case of inappropriate or erroneous payments.[68]
- Appendix C, I-II (last amended in 2018), outlines steps to implement the Improper Payments Information Act of 2002, the Improper Payments Elimination and Recovery Act (IPERA) of 2010, and the Improper Payments Elimination and Recovery Improvement Act of 2012. These laws require agencies that are deemed to be susceptible for significant improper payments to report annually to OMB; requires all agencies to implement appropriate internal controls; and requires any agency expending at least $1 million per year to implement recapture audits, if such audits are cost effective to the agency.[69]

Reforms in Private Sector Pension Plans and Implications for Government Plans

The other major topic for possible reform is that of state and local pension plans. There are almost 300 state-administered plans, some of which include local government employees as well as state employees, and more than 5,000 locally administered plans.[70] In addition, there are thousands of other small plans involving annuity policies with private insurance carriers.

Retirement systems—both public sector and private sector—must comply with federal laws. The Employee Retirement Income Security Act (ERISA) of 1974 governs private sector plans.[71] Sections 415 and 457 of the Internal Revenue Code exert major controls over public retirement systems. In 1996, Congress amended these provisions to allow greater flexibility on the part of state and local systems in complying with federal law.[72]

Retirement systems are generally based on an assumption that a person will use a variety of measures to cover living expenses during retirement besides pension checks. First, living expenses may decline as the individual becomes less active and has fewer demands on income, such as support for dependents. Second, savings are used to cover expenses. Third, many government workers are covered by Social Security (including Old-Age and Survivors Insurance and disability insurance), as well as Medicare.

Defined Benefit and Defined Contribution Plans

Pension systems in the public sector historically used *defined benefit plans*, in which benefits normally are determined according to some combination of years of services, wages or salaries (for example, average salary of the last 3 years of service), and age at time of retirement. The longer one has worked for a government and the higher one's salary, the higher pension benefits will be. State and local government retirement systems have historically used the defined benefit plan.

In addition to initial retirement benefits, cost-of-living allowances (COLAs) are sometimes assigned to pensioners, in some cases on an automatic basis according to an economic barometer, such as the consumer price index, and in other cases on an ad hoc basis. In the latter instance, a government might decide one year to increase retirement benefits by the same percentage as salary increases being awarded current employees. When governments face difficult financial situations, retirees may go for years without COLA increases. Other benefits are provided for disability retirement (for people who retire early because of poor health) and for survivors' benefits (covering family members who continue to live after the death of retirees). The vast majority of benefits paid each year go to elderly retirees, with the

remainder divided between disability retirees and survivors.

Defined benefit plans coupled with COLAs provide income security to employees and retirees and place investment risks on employers. Because benefits are determined in advance of retirement, employers must take steps necessary to ensure that sufficient funds will be available when employees retire. Cost accounting standards require that private sector companies "fund" the future liabilities created by these defined benefit programs. If projected earnings from investments of a company's pension fund are less than projected payouts, then the company must take an accounting adjustment, generally a write-down of profits, to cover the projected difference.

An alternative to defined benefits is the *defined contribution plan*. Under this plan, benefits are not defined in advance of retirement, but rather the employer commits to contributing regularly to an employee's retirement account (usually a percentage of compensation). The benefits received at the time of retirement are a function of the employer's and employee's contributions plus investment earnings on these contributions. 401(k) plans (named after the section of the Internal Revenue Code that defines their tax treatment) are the most common examples of defined contribution plans; 403(b) plans are the nonprofit company equivalent. Both typically involve employer and individual contributions. Private companies may also have plans that are based solely on employer contributions. Most private employers use defined contribution plans, and while public employers are shifting to defined contribution plans, many still use defined benefit plans.

A key advantage of a defined contribution plan for an employer is its predictability. All that needs be done each year is to set aside a percentage of salaries and wages for depositing into retirement accounts. A key disadvantage for the employee is that the benefits to be paid are not predictable and not guaranteed. Indeed, many employees in defined contribution plans saw the value of their assets decline precipitously as a result of the global financial crisis that began in 2007 and again in the coronavirus-related drop in the stock market in 2020. In many cases, this meant that these employees had to delay retirement because the value of their assets was insufficient to permit them to retire on the planned timetable. They continued to work, providing their jobs had not been eliminated.

Funding

Pension plans are funded by a combination of contributions from government and employees and investment earnings on those contributions. In some cases, the retirement program is financed exclusively by government, but that practice is an exception to the rule.

For the defined benefit pension plan, there are basically two methods of financing: *pay as you go* and *advance funding*. With the pay-as-you-go method, all that is required in any one budget year is to raise sufficient revenue to cover retirement benefit checks. This method is generally discouraged because it allows for the accumulation of debt. Persons in the future will be owed benefits, and taxpayers at that time will be forced to meet those costs. This is particularly problematic in cases where many employees may be eligible to retire at the same time, as is happening as baby boomers begin to retire.

The preferred method is advance funding, in which monies are accumulated for workers while they are working and those monies generate income through investments while workers are on the payroll and during retirement as well. When using this method, a retirement system must invest prudently but effectively to avoid any unfunded actuarial accrued liability so that the system is "actuarially sound." Advance funding uses the concept of present value—that is, future receipts, particularly contributions and investment earnings, are compared with anticipated costs (benefits) in terms of current dollars.

Liabilities

Until the 1970s, many public retirement systems were woefully underfunded. Over the years, governments had made pension plan commitments to employees but had failed to follow through by contributing sufficient funds to the plans. For those governments that do have underfunded pension plans, serious problems loom. Meeting current operating needs and covering the costs of retiree benefits can easily put a budget out of balance and force a tax increase. Where jurisdictions are at their legal or political limits on tax rates, severe program cuts may be the only alternative. Pension fund liabilities can increase the cost of doing business, as interest rates may be higher for jurisdictions that have large outstanding pension debts.

After the 1970s, the outlook improved for government pension plans. These were spurred by accounting requirements, such as those issued by GASB that improved the transparency of financial reporting for pension systems. By the early 2000s, however, a new pension threat had emerged, particularly for state and local governments. This was precipitated by the chronic underfunding of pension systems by these governments, in addition to the discovery of the financial implications of the promises made to retirees for what GASB referred to as Other Post-Employment Benefits (OPEB). These OPEB benefits were mostly related to retiree health costs, which were rising rapidly because of the number of retirees and the impact of medical care inflation.

The Pew Charitable Trusts has done substantial work on the pension financing problem at the state level. Many local pension systems, such as those for teachers and police officers, are administered at the state level. In a 2019 report, Pew estimated the total 2017 unfunded liabilities of state pension systems to be $1.28 trillion, a decline from the previous year's gap of $1.35 trillion. In total, states had funded 69% of their future pension liabilities. This aggregate shortfall number masked a substantial amount of variation across states, with 8 states at more than 90% funded, while 24 states were below 70% funded. The three states with the highest funding ratios—averaging 97%—were South Dakota, Tennessee, and Wisconsin. On the other hand, the bottom three—Illinois, Kentucky, and New Jersey—had funding ratios of just over 50%.[73]

State pension systems, however, are much better funded than OPEB. At the end of 2016, state OPEB assets nationwide covered only about 7% of OPEB liabilities ($46 billion, compared with $696 billion). Only six states (Arizona at 95%; Oregon at 80%; and Alaska, North Dakota, Ohio, and Utah at between 50% and 60%) had funded liabilities greater than 50%. In stark contrast, there were 20 states that had effectively set no money aside for OPEB liabilities at all—in other words, they had unfunded liabilities of somewhere between 99% and 100%.[74]

Similar estimates are not available, in aggregate, for local pension and OPEB liabilities. There is no question, however, that many localities that fund their own pension and retiree health benefits (there are many cases, as noted above, where the local employees are covered under state systems) have systems that are similarly underfunded. New York City, as an example, had a net OPEB liability of $90 billion in 2018, which was greater than the OPEB liability for New York State in the same year.[75]

The reporting, and therefore the understanding, of OPEB liabilities has been accelerated by the issuance of GASB Statement No. 45, which requires state and local governments to disclose their OPEB liabilities.[76] GASB No. 45 does not require these governments to fund these liabilities or even to explain how they are planning to. Once financial statements are required to disclose them, however, it is inevitable that bond rating agencies will focus attention on plans to fund them. GASB issued two other statements—Statement No. 74 and Statement No. 75—that further clarified how OPEB liabilities were to be disclosed in financial statements.[77] Ignoring them, therefore, will have real costs to state and local governments.

Several options are available for improving the funding situation of retirement systems and OPEB benefits:

- An obvious option is to increase government and employee contributions.
- A jurisdiction can take advantage of economies of scale by combining systems. This technique may reduce administrative costs and make possible more lucrative investments.
- Retirement systems can pool their funds for investment purposes.
- A jurisdiction can make investments that are riskier but also have higher rates of return. The Orange County, California, bankruptcy of 1994 (see the chapters on budget execution and capital finance) and the stock market crash during the Great Recession, however, are sobering reminders of the loss that can result from nonguaranteed investments. Models are available that suggest how to balance high returns with acceptable levels of risk.
- Some jurisdictions have sold bonds to obtain the funds needed to cover retirement liabilities.
- A pension system can have its creditworthiness rated in terms of the system's ability to meet its financial obligations. This rating then can be used to back other entities for fees, consequently increasing the revenue for the pension system.
- An increasingly common response, particularly for OPEB liabilities, is to reduce the generosity of retiree health care benefits, to both current employees and current retirees. Many jurisdictions will have little choice but to take this approach as the need to finance the gap between resources available and promises made becomes more acute.[78]

Private pension plans have their own funding problems. Starting in 2006, it became woefully obvious that despite ERISA protecting private sector workers, private pension plans were underfunded. For example, giant Delphi Corporation, which was General Motors' primary parts supplier and had once been part of it, went into bankruptcy and left in doubt the pension plans of current workers and those already retired. This caused substantial losses for the federal Pension Benefit Guaranty Corporation (PBGC), which insures private pension plans.

Congress passed the Pension Protection Act of 2006 in response to this situation. In general, the law gave private companies 7 years to get their pensions up to a standard of being fully funded.

The financially troubled airlines were given longer to comply. Plans that are deemed "at risk" have tougher funding standards to meet. Workers were given new incentives to save on their own through individual retirement accounts and 401(k) plans. The law can be seen as a balancing act of being tough with companies about their pension funding but not being so tough as to have them eliminate traditional pension systems.[79] Indeed, many companies have phased out pensions for new hires and/or shifted to greater use of part-time employment with few, if any, benefits such as pensions or health care. In fact, while more than 80% of state and local governments still have defined benefit plans, fewer than 4% of private companies provide this sort of retirement benefit.[80] Future funding of guaranteed health insurance benefits has also been an issue for private companies. Accounting reforms require private companies to fund through accrual the estimated costs of these health insurance payouts.

Despite this law, however, the deterioration of the economy has had substantial negative effect on private pension plans, and therefore on PBGC. In 2019 alone, PBGC assumed responsibility for 75,000 additional workers, bringing the total number of participants receiving benefits from PBGC to more than 1.5 million. By the end of fiscal year 2019, PBGC had a deficit of more than $56 billion, up from $51 billion in 2018.[81] Furthermore, this represents a continued deterioration of the PBGC situation since 2001, when PBGC had a surplus of almost $8 billion.[82] The deterioration in PBGC's financial position caused the GAO to put the PBGC on its "high risk" list.[83] Given the fragile condition of many private pension plans, the financial condition of PBGC, and therefore its potential drain on the federal budget, remains a legitimate area of concern.

Pension Accounting and Reporting

Government requirements have influenced the reporting of both state and local governments and private firms, regarding their pension plans. The following 10 statements and a technical bulletin have been issued by the GASB as the governing documents for accounting and reporting of state and local pension systems:

- Statement No. 25, *Financial Reporting for Defined Benefit Pension Plans and Note Disclosures for Defined Contribution Plans* (later amended by Statement No. 67).
- Statement No. 26, *Financial Reporting for Postemployment Healthcare Plans Administered by Defined Benefit Pension Plans* (later amended by Statement No. 68).
- Statement No. 27, *Accounting for Pensions by State and Local Governmental Employers*
- Statement No. 45, *Reporting on Post-Employment Benefits Other Than Pensions*
- Statement No. 50, *Pension Disclosures—an amendment to GASB Statements No. 25 and No. 27*
- Technical Bulletin 96-1, *Pension Disclosure Requirements for Employers*
- Statement No. 73, *Accounting and Financial Reporting for Pensions and Related Assets That Are Not within the Scope of GASB Statement 68, and Amendments to Certain Provisions of GASB Statements 67 and 68*
- Statement No. 74, *Financial Reporting for Postemployment Benefit Plans Other Than Pension Plans*
- Statement No. 75, *Accounting and Financial Reporting for Postemployment Benefits Other Than Pensions*
- Statement No. 78, *Pensions Provided through Certain Multiple-Employer Defined Benefit Pension Plans*
- Statement No. 82, *Pension Issues—an amendment of GASB Statements No. 67, No. 68, and No. 73*

Overall, these documents require an annual reporting of assets, changes in assets from year to year, and actuarial information on the long-term prospects of pension funds and retiree benefits.

Financial Reporting

Accounting systems generate reports that are used by managers, policy makers, and people outside of government. In state and local governments,

GAAP 12 calls on jurisdictions to prepare both interim and annual reports (see above). Interim reports, such as daily and weekly reports, serve internal purposes, as in the case of checking on appropriated funds that are neither spent nor encumbered. These reports are useful in monitoring budget execution and anticipating situations in which agencies might lack sufficient funds to operate their programs throughout the fiscal year. A fundamental expectation of all financial reports is that they can be audited, meaning that accounting records back up the data in the reports.

Annual reports are particularly useful to people and organizations outside of government. Reports can show taxpayers how revenues have been used to support services, for example. Annual reports of local governments are helpful for businesses that are considering locating, relocating, or expanding existing facilities. Such reports are used to help discover the financial condition of governments and decide whether to purchase their bonds. The Government Finance Officers Association issues certificates of achievement for excellence in financial reporting. The association also issues awards for outstanding popular annual financial reporting. These reports are prepared for use by the general public and not accountants and budgeteers.[84]

GASB prescribes a *comprehensive annual financial report* that has three sections: introduction, finances, and statistics.[85] The first section includes a letter of transmittal and general information about the government. It lists the principal officials and provides an organization chart indicating lines of authority and responsibility.

The second section contains a variety of financial statements. As governments make extensive use of funds, several different types of statements may be provided on each fund. These statements by themselves can be confusing in that they do not provide an overall perspective on the finances of the government. For this reason, GASB and other professional accounting organizations prescribe the use of condensed statements that offer a comprehensive picture of a jurisdiction and omit some of the confusing detail.

One particularly troubling aspect of these statements is the use of *transfers* among funds. Monies can be moved from one fund to another without affecting the overall assets of a jurisdiction, but if transfers are not carefully noted, they may appear as expenditures in one fund and as new assets or receipts in another fund. These transfers need to be clearly identified not only to avoid confusion, but also to provide important information about a government's operations. Transfers may indicate that enterprises are subsidizing general government operations, as when proceeds from a city airport are used in part to support a city's general fund. This type of transfer may be welcome relief to local taxpayers, but may raise concern among holders of airport bonds. Good financial reports clearly label transfers—showing the source of receipts and the recipient of transfers—so that false impressions of asset creation or usage are avoided.

The third section of a financial report contains statistical data. Some tables present trend data assembled from earlier financial reports, such as general revenues by source over the most recent 10-year period. Other tables provide demographic data and indicate the principal taxpayers in the jurisdiction.

Balance Sheets

Of the numerous types of financial statements, balance sheets are one of the most common. A balance sheet can be thought of as a snapshot of a government's finances at a point in time, such as at the end of a quarter or fiscal year.

A balance sheet is organized according to the accounting formula discussed earlier. Assets are first listed, showing cash on hand (bank deposits) and taxes receivable. For proprietary funds and fiduciary funds, fixed assets (buildings, land, and so forth) are also reported as assets. The balance sheet then indicates liabilities—namely, accounts that are payable and bonds outstanding—followed by the fund balance, showing items such as monies that are encumbered. **Exhibit 12-3** is an example of a balance sheet from the State of Maryland.

GASB's Statement No. 11 on measurement focus and the basis of accounting requires governments to recognize items as liabilities that were previously excluded. As a result of complying with this requirement, balance sheet bottom lines went from positive to negative for many governments. When numerous governments complained about the potential political and economic

harm of such balance sheets, GASB allowed governments to use the term *fund equity* for the difference between revised assets and liabilities. The term *fund balance* can be used for calculating

Exhibit 12-3 Balance Sheet, State of Maryland

	Governmental Funds June 30, 2019 (Expressed in Thousands)			
	General	Special Revenue Maryland Department of Transportation	Other Governmental Funds	Total Governmental Funds
Assets:				
Cash	$ 448,450	$ 3,854	—	$ 452,304
Equity in pooled invested cash	$ 2,281,961	$ 36,845	$ 266,807	$ 2,585,613
Investments	—	—	$ 253,332	$ 253,332
Prepaid items	$ 558,368	$ 162,276	—	$ 720,644
Taxes receivable, net	$ 1,410,199	$ 189,149	—	$ 1,599,348
Intergovernmental receivables	$ 1,120,263	$ 542,688	—	$ 1,662,951
Other accounts receivable	$ 626,555	$ 94,474	$ 130	$ 721,159
Due from other funds	$ 299,059	$ 94,695	—	$ 393,754
Due from component units	$ 5,950	—	—	$ 5,950
Inventories	$ 24,951	$ 94,763	—	$ 119,714
Loans and notes receivable, net	$ 27,873	—	—	$ 27,873
Restricted assets:				
Cash with fiscal agent	—	—	$ 46,835	$ 46,835
Equity in pooled invested cash	—	—	$ 114,224	$ 114,224
Investments	$ 1,530	—	$ 26,264	$ 27,794
Taxes receivable, net	—	—	$ 26,744	$ 26,744
Other accounts receivable	—	—	$ 477	$ 477
Loans and notes receivable, net	—	—	$ 1,252	$ 1,252
Total assets	$ 6,805,158	$ 1,218,744	$ 736,065	$ 8,759,967

(continues)

Exhibit 12-3 Balance Sheet, State of Maryland   (*continued*)

| | | Governmental Funds June 30, 2010 (*Expressed in Thousands*) | | |
	General	Special Revenue Maryland Department of Transportation	Other Governmental Funds	Total Governmental Funds
Liabilities:				
Salaries payable	$ 149,315	$ 25,319	—	$ 174,633.93
Vouchers payable	$ 847,352	—	$ 53,824	$ 901,177
Accounts payable and accrued liabilities	$ 1,068,579	$ 466,310	$ 42,605	$ 1,577,494
Due to other funds	$ 1,006,047	$ 166,140	$ 25,493	$ 1,197,680
Due to component units	$ 410	—	—	$ 410
Accounts payable to political subdivisions	$ 93,756	$ 45,657	$ 6,768	$ 146,180
Unearned revenue	$ 142,306	$ 32,725	—	$ 175,031
Accrued self-insurance costs	$ 122,610	—	—	$ 122,610
Total liabilities	$ 3,430,375	$ 736,151	$ 128,690	$ 4,295,216
Deferred inflows of resources	$ 681,415	$ 233,881	—	$ 915,296
Fund balances:				
Nonspendable	$ 610,281	$ 257,039	—	$ 867,320
Restricted	$ 8,186	—	$ 215,796	$ 223,982
Committed	$ 2,094,213	$ 8,908	$ 618,245	$ 2,721,366
Unassigned	$ (19,312)	$ (17,235)	$ (226,666)	$ (263,213)
Total fund balances	$ 2,693,368	$ 248,712	$ 607,375	$ 3,549,455
Total liabilities and fund balances	$ 6,805,158	$ 1,218,744	$ 736,065	$ 8,759,967

The accompanying notes to the financial statement are an integral part of this financial statement.

Office of the Comptroller, State of Maryland (2019). Comprehensive Annual Financial Report, p. 28.

balance sheets in the format that preceded Statement No. 11.

Although the federal government does not produce a balance sheet using the same rules as state and local governments, the Treasury Department produces a financial statement for the U.S. government that includes a balance sheet that reports assets and liabilities. In **Exhibit 12-4**, net

Exhibit 12-4 United States Government Balance Sheets as of September 30, 2018, and 2017

(In billions of dollars)	2018	Restated 2017
Assets:		
Cash and other monetary assets (Note 2)	$ 507.5	$ 271.2
Accounts and taxes receivable, net (Note 3)	$ 144.9	$ 143.3
Loans receivable, net (Note 4)	$ 1,419.1	$ 1,350.2
Inventories and related property, net (Note 5)	$ 337.5	$ 326.7
Property, plant and equipment, net (Note 6)	$ 1,090.5	$ 1,087.0
Debt and equity securities (Note 7)	$ 110.3	$ 116.2
Investments in government-sponsored enterprises (Note 8)	$ 113.2	$ 92.6
Other assets (Note 9)	$ 113.7	$ 147.7
Total assets	$ 3,836.7	$ 3,534.9
Stewardship land and heritage assets (Note 24)		
Liabilities:		
Accounts payable (Note 10)	$ 86.7	$ 70.8
Federal debt securities held by the public and accrued interest (Note 11)	$ 15,812.7	$ 14,724.1
Federal employee and veteran benefits payable (Note 12)	$ 7,982.3	$ 7,700.1
Environmental and disposal liabilities (Note 13)	$ 577.3	$ 464.5
Benefits due and payable (Note 14)	$ 211.1	$ 218.8
Insurance and guarantee program liabilities (Note 15)	$ 170.2	$ 202.5
Loan guarantee liabilities (Note 4)	$ 38.2	$ 42.9
Other liabilities (Note 16)	$ 479.0	$ 473.1
Total liabilities	$ 25,357.5	$ 23,896.8
Contingencies (Note 18) and Commitments (Note 19)		
Net Position:		
Funds from Dedicated Collections (Note 20)	$ 3,462.0	$ 3,419.5
Funds other than those from Dedicated Collections	$ (24,982.8)	$ (23,781.4)
Total net position	$ (21,520.8)	$ (20,361.9)
Total liabilities and net position	$ 3,836.7	$ 3,534.9

The accompanying notes are an integral part of these financial statements.

United States Treasury, Bureau of the Fiscal Service (2019). Financial Report of the U.S. Government, FY18, p. 59.

liabilities for 2018 are reported at $21.5 trillion. This consists of total assets of $3.8 trillion, offset by liabilities of $25.4 trillion.

Operating Statements

A second major type of financial statement is the operating statement, which shows the monies received and expended during a specified period of time. State and local governments refer to these as "statements of revenues, expenditures, and changes in fund balance." Revenues can be reported by source—sales tax and income tax. Expenditures can be reported by major objects, organizational units, or other means. **Exhibit 12-5** is an operating statement for the State of Utah. This table shows these transactions for all governmental funds. Tables such as this one and others shown in the chapter typically have notes that explain what is included and excluded in specific entries in the statements. These notes are essential components of the statements.

Cash Flow Statements

A third form of financial statement details cash flows. The purpose is to show how cash entering and leaving a fund affects an entity's operations. These statements cover cash and cash equivalents, such as short-term investments (U.S. Treasury bills; see the chapter on budget execution). Controversy exists over how these statements should be organized and whether they should be extended from just covering enterprise funds to include basically all funds. **Exhibit 12-6** is a cash flow statement for the State of Wyoming, covering the enterprise and internal service funds.

Other Reports and Reporting Requirements

In addition to balance sheets, operating statements, and cash flow statements, governments issue other important financial reports (e.g., disclosures on securities). Governments provide statements when issuing bonds and other securities that are intended to help would-be purchasers

understand what is being offered for sale in terms of the backing of the securities and what risks are involved. GASB Statement No. 34, issued in 1999, has imposed dramatic changes on state and local government financial reporting, including the following:

- Statements must have *management's discussion and analysis* (MDA) indicating, in an objective way, the current financial situation in understandable English.
- Government-wide financial statements must be provided and must show the current and prior year.
- Full accrual accounting for all government activities is mandated.
- All capital assets must be shown and depreciated, including infrastructure assets.
- Analysis must be shown of significant changes in fund balance for the various governmental, proprietary, and fiduciary funds.
- Note disclosures are required to show important accounting policies. Disclosures must show changes in long-term liabilities and in capital assets.
- GASB No. 34 reconfigured the types of funds to be used. The new configuration was presented earlier when we discussed governmental, proprietary, and fiduciary funds.[86]

Given that we have more than 20 years' experience with GASB Statement No. 34, more research has begun to surface concerning its impacts. A 2016 study asked municipal finance analysts if they thought that financial reporting had improved as a result of GASB No. 34, and how it might have changed the way that they analyze municipal debt issuances. They concluded that it had improved reporting, but that they still tended to use the individual fund statements to a greater extent than the government-wide financial statements. They did generally think that the MDA was beneficial, particularly when it went beyond boilerplate discussion to highlight the peculiarities of a given jurisdiction.[87] A separate study from 2017 found that the requirement that states and localities report more information regarding infrastructure had

Exhibit 12-5 State of Utah Statement of Revenues, Expenditures, and Changes in Fund Balances

Statement of Revenues, Expenditures and Changes in Fund Balances Governmental Funds
(Expressed in Thousands)

For the Year Ended June 30, 2019	Special Revenue Funds			Capital Projects Fund	Permanent Fund	Nonmajor Governmental Funds	Total Governmental Funds
	General Fund	Education	Transportation	Transportation Investment	Trust Lands		
REVENUES							
Taxes:							
Sales and Use Tax	$ 2,147,235	$ —	$ 65	$ 634,888	$ —	$ 23,430	$ 2,805,618
Individual Income Tax	—	$ 4,336,437	—	—	—	—	$ 4,336,437
Corporate Tax	—	$ 534,977	—	—	—	—	$ 534,977
Motor and Special Fuels Tax	—	—	$ 521,199	—	—	—	$ 521,199
Other Taxes	$ 342,048	$ 27,000	$ 13,546	—	—	$ 16,090	$ 398,684
Total Taxes	$ 2,489,283	$ 4,898,414	$ 534,810	$ 634,888	$ 0	$ 39,520	$ 8,596,915
Other Revenues:							
Federal Contracts and Grants	$ 3,103,195	$ 428,881	$ 386,374		—	$ 54,576	$ 3,973,026
Changes for Services/Royalties	$ 501,910	$ 1,152	$ 55,193		$ 50,757	$ 171,778	$ 780,790
Licenses, Permits, and Fees	$ 25,664	$ 6,449	$ 98,682	$ 89,177	—	—	$ 219,972
Federal Mineral Lease	$ 77,607	—	—	—	—	—	$ 77,607
Intergovernmental	—	—	—	—	—	$ 16,029	$ 16,029
Investment Income	$ 43,630	$ 17,556	$ 9,591	$ 20,833	$ 97,690	$ 28,777	$ 218,077

(continues)

Exhibit 12-5 State of Utah Statement of Revenues, Expenditures, and Changes in Fund Balances *(continued)*

Statement of Revenues, Expenditures and Changes in Fund Balances
Governmental Funds
(Expressed in Thousands)

For the Year Ended June 30, 2019	Special Revenue Funds			Capital Projects Fund	Permanent Fund	Nonmajor Governmental Funds	Total Governmental Funds
	General Fund	Education	Transportation	Transportation Investment	Trust Lands		
Miscellaneous Other:							
Liquor Sales Allocated for School Lunch	—	$ 48,024	—	—	—	—	$ 48,024
Miscellaneous and Other	$ 268,298	$ 38,127	$ 49,345	—	—	$ 29,939	$ 385,709
Total Revenues	$ 6,509,587	$ 5,438,603	$ 1,133,995	$ 744,898	$ 148,447	$ 340,619	$ 14,316,149
EXPENDITURES							
Current:							
General Government	$ 420,062	—	—	—	$ 14,362	$ 58,376	$ 492,800
Human Services and Juvenile Justice Services	$ 908,593	—	—	—	—	$ 10,634	$ 919,227
Corrections	$ 322,230	—	—	—	—	$ 6,356	$ 328,586
Public Safety	$ 300,839	—	—	—	—	$ 39,371	$ 340,210
Courts	$ 159,098	—	—	—	—	$ 6,271	$ 165,369
Health and Environmental Quality	$ 2,995,463	—	—	—	—	$ 1,576	$ 2,997,039
Higher Education—State Administration	$ 96,323	—	—	—	—	—	$ 96,323

Exhibit 12-5 State of Utah Statement of Revenues, Expenditures, and Changes in Fund Balances *(continued)*

Statement of Revenues, Expenditures and Changes in Fund Balances
Governmental Funds
(Expressed in Thousands)

For the Year Ended June 30, 2019	General Fund	Special Revenue Funds		Capital Projects Fund	Permanent Fund	Nonmajor Governmental Funds	Total Governmental Funds
		Education	Transportation	Transportation Investment	Trust Lands		
Higher Education — Colleges and Universities	$ 1,063,258	—	—	—	$ 4,073	$ 34,979	$ 1,102,310
Employment and Family Services	$ 744,336	—	—	—	—	$ 11,277	$ 755,613
Natural Resources	$ 247,042	—	—	—	—	$ 4,503	$ 251,545
Heritage and Arts	$ 31,145	—	—	—	—	$ 836	$ 31,981
Business, Labor, and Agriculture	$ 97,919	—	—	—	—	$ 21,572	$ 119,491
Public Education	—	$ 4,138,708	—	—	—	$ 1,555	$ 4,140,263
Transportation	—	—	$ 994,803	—	—	$ 1,925	$ 996,728
Capital Outlay	—	—	—	$ 612,407	—	$ 253,134	$ 847,541
Debt Service:							
Principal Retirement	—	—	—	—	—	$ 260,949	$ 260,949
Interest and Other Charges	—	—	—	—	—	$ 103,417	$ 103,417
Total Expenditures	$ 7,386,308	$ 4,138,708	$ 994,803	$ 612,407	$ 18,435	$ 798,731	$ 13,949,392
Excess Revenues Over (Under) Expenditures	$ (876,721)	$ 1,299,895	$ 139,192	$ 132,491	$ 130,012	$ (458,112)	$ 366,757

(continues)

Exhibit 12-5 State of Utah Statement of Revenues, Expenditures, and Changes in Fund Balances   *(continued)*

Statement of Revenues, Expenditures and Changes in Fund Balances
Governmental Funds
(Expressed in Thousands)

For the Year Ended June 30, 2019	Special Revenue Funds			Capital Projects Fund	Permanent Fund	Nonmajor Governmental Funds	Total Governmental Funds
	General Fund	Education	Transportation	Transportation Investment	Trust Lands		
OTHER FINANCING SOURCES (USES)							
General Obligation Bonds Issued	—	—	—	$ 127,715	—	—	$ 127,715
Premium on Bonds Issued	—	—	—	$ 22,688	—	$ 620	$ 23,308
Payment to Refunded Bond Escrow Agent	—	—	—	—	—	$ (27,770)	$ (27,770)
Sale of Capital Assets	$ 3	—	$ 31,134	—	$ 34,192	$ 2	$ 65,331
Transfers In	$ 1,501,574	S 94,074	$ 44,027	$ 38,147	$ 19	$ 903,740	$ 2,581,581
Transfers Out	$ (441,552)	$ (1,335,011)	$ (110,400)	$ (305,565)	$ (82,663)	$ (165,530)	$ (2,440,721)
Total Other Financing Sources (Uses)	$ 1,060,025	$ (1,240,937)	$ (35,239)	$ (117,015)	$ (48,452)	$ 711,062	$ 329,444
Net Change in Fund Balances	$ 183,304	$ 58,958	$ 103,953	$ 15,476	$ 81,560	$ 252,950	$ 696,201
Fund Balances - Beginning	$ 1,055,216	$ 1,144,738	$ 407,653	$ 654,819	$ 2,596,245	$ 777,440	$ 6,636,111
Adjustment to Beginning Fund Balances	—	—	—	—	$ (15,469)	—	$ (15,469)
Fund Balances - Beginning As Adjusted	$ 1,055,216	$ 1,144,738	$ 407,653	$ 654,819	$ 2,580,776	$ 777,440	$ 6,620,642
Fund Balances - Ending	$ 1,238,520	$ 1,203,696	$ 511,606	$ 670,295	$ 2,662,336	$ 1,030,390	$ 7,316,843

The notes to the financial statements are an integral part of this statement.

State of Utah (2019). Comprehensive Annual Financial Report: 2019, p. 40.

Exhibit 12-6 Statement of Cash Flows, State of Wyoming

Statement of Cash Flows
Proprietary Funds
For the Year Ended June 30, 2019

	Enterprise Funds			
	Workers' Compensation Insurance Fund	Nonmajor Enterprise Funds	Total	Internal Service Funds
CASH FLOWS FROM OPERATING ACTIVITIES				
Cash Receipts from Customers	$ 220,190,558	$ 206,012,331	$ 426,202,889	$ 150,001,260
Cash Receipts from Interfund Charges	—	—	—	$ 175,357,598
Cash Payments to Suppliers for Goods and Services	$ (180,835,367)	$ (154,378,966)	$ (335,214,333)	$ (330,471,577)
Cash Payment to Employees for Services	$ (13,623,729)	S (3,063,800)	$ (16,687,529)	$ (7,684,331)
NET CASH PROVIDED BY (USED IN) OPERATING ACTIVITIES	$ 25,731,462	$ 48,569,565	$ 74,301,027	$ (12,797,050)
CASH FLOWS FROM NONCAPITAL FINANCING ACTIVITIES				
Grants Received	—	$ 2,391,918	$ 2,391,918	—
Transfers In	—	—	—	$ 5,421,388
Transfers Out	$ (8,900)	$ (16,650,000)	$ (16,658,900)	—
NET CASH PROVIDED BY (USED IN) NONCAPITAL FINANCING ACTIVITIES	$ (8,900)	$ (14,258,082)	$ (14,266,982)	$ 5,421,388
CASH FLOWS FROM CAPITAL AND RELATED FINANCING ACTIVITIES				
Purchase of Capital Assets	$ (77,324)	v(35,009)	$ (112,333)	$ (1,335,613)
NET CASH PROVIDED BY (USED IN) CAPITAL AND RELATED FINANCING ACTIVITIES	$ (77,324)	(35,009)	$ (112,333)	$ (1,335,613)

(continues)

Exhibit 12-6 Statement of Cash Flows, State of Wyoming

Statement of Cash Flows
Proprietary Funds
For the Year Ended June 30, 2019

(continued)

	Workers' Compensation Insurance Fund	Enterprise Funds		Internal Service Funds
		Nonmajor Enterprise Funds	Total	
CASH FLOWS FROM INVESTING ACTIVITIES				
Investment Income	$ 179,154,761	$ 8,895,356	$ 188,050,117	$ 2,739,419
Securities Lending Collateral	$ 13,803,800	$ 768,737	$ 14,572,537	$ 114,822
Change in Pooled Investments Trade Receivable	$ (29,879,882)	$ 1,400,062	$ (28,479,820)	$ 1,897,875
Change in Pooled Investments Trade Payable	$ 8,233,969	$ (1,837,671)	$ 6,396,298	$ (2,491,098)
NET CASH PROVIDED BY (USED IN) INVESTING ACTIVITIES	$ 171,312,648	$ 9,226,484	$ 180,539,132	$ 2,261,018
NET INCREASE (DECREASE) IN CASH AND CASH EQUIVALENTS	$ 196,957,886	$ 43,502,958	$ 240,460,844	$ (6,450,257)
CASH AND CASH EQUIVALENTS, JULY 1, 2018	$ 2,233,820,116	$ 391,376,879	$ 2,625,196,995	$ 95,967,683
CASH AND CASH EQUIVALENTS, JUNE 30, 2019	$ 2,430,778,002	$ 434,879,837	$ 2,865,657,839	$ 89,517,426
OPERATING INCOME (LOSS)	$ 7,119,696	$ 48,335,145	$ 55,454,841	$ (19,306,725)
Adjustments to Reconcile Operating Income (Loss) to Net Cash				
Depreciation	$ 1,397,827	$ 96,643	$ 1,494,470	$ 2,561,084
Change in Deferred Outflows of Resources	$ (3,462,353)	$ (784,074)	$ (4,246,427)	—
Change in Net Pension Liability	$ 3,155,435	$ 719,260	$ 3,874,695	—
Change in Deferred Inflows of Resources	$ (249,610)	$ (80,946)	$ (330,556)	—
Change in Net OPEB Obligation	$ 1,802,031	$ 430,011	$ 2,232,042	—

(continued)

Exhibit 12-6 Statement of Cash Flows, State of Wyoming

Statement of Cash Flows
Proprietary Funds
For the Year Ended June 30, 2019

	Enterprise Funds			Internal Service Funds
	Workers' Compensation Insurance Fund	Nonmajor Enterprise Funds	Total	
Changes in Assets and Liabilities				
(Increase) Decrease in Accounts Receivable and Taxes Receivable	$ 1,594,155	$ (805,550)	$ 788,605	$ 8,333
(Increase) Decrease in Due from Other Funds	$ 46,434	$ 1,173,958	$ 1,220,392	$ 10,264
(Increase) Decrease in Due from Other Governments	$ 4,552,781	$ 126,845	$ 4,679,626	—
(Increase) Decrease in Due from Component Unit	$ 644,647	—	$ 644,647	$ 40,118
(Increase) Decrease in Inventories	—	$ (1,419,011)	$ (1,419,011)	$ 9,746
(Increase) Decrease in Prepaid Expense	—	$ (16,794)	$ (16,794)	—
Increase (Decrease) in Unearned Revenue	—	$ (27,444)	$ (27,444)	$ (228,744)
Increase (Decrease) in Due to Other Funds	$ 561,230	$ 197,485	$ 758,715	$ 1,630
Increase (Decrease) in Due to Other Governments	—	$ 75,359	$ 75,359	$ 2,530
Increase (Decrease) in Accounts Payable	$ (1,110,344)	$ 890,833	$ (219,511)	$ (88,646)
Increase (Decrease) in Claims and Benefits Payable	$ 9,772,357	$ (352,095)	$ 9,420,262	$ 4,236,793
Increase (Decrease) in Compensated Absences	$ (92,824)	$ 9,940	$ (82,884)	$ (43,433)
Total Adjustments	$ 18,611,766	$ 234,420	$ 18,846,186	$ 6,509,675
NET CASH PROVIDED BY (USED IN) OPERATING ACTIVITIES	$ 25,731,462	$ 48,569,565	$ 74,301,027	$ (12,797,050)

(continues)

Exhibit 12-6 Statement of Cash Flows, State of Wyoming *(continued)*

Statement of Cash Flows
Proprietary Funds
For the Year Ended June 30, 2019

	Enterprise Funds			Internal Service Funds
	Workers' Compensation Insurance Fund	Nonmajor Enterprise Funds	Total	
Reconciliation of Cash and Cash Equivalents to Amounts Shown on Statement of Net Position				
Cash and Pooled Investments	$ 2,279,547,115	$ 71,285,563	$ 2,350,832,678	$ 82,544,042
Cash and Investments with Trustee	$ 151,230,887	$ 5,864,599	$ 157,095,486	$ 6,973,384
Amounts on Deposit with U.S. Treasury	—	$ 357,729,675	$ 357,729,675	—
Total Cash and Cash Equivalents shown on Statement of Net Position	$ 2,430,778,002	$ 434,879,837	$ 2,865,657,839	$ 89,517,426

The notes to the financial statements are an integral part of this statement.

State of Wyoming (2020). Comprehensive Annual Financial Report: Financial year 2019, p. 42.

led to an increase in capital spending, but not spending on maintenance of assets.[88] Finally, and perhaps most significantly, a separate 2017 paper concluded that, after governments implemented GASB No. 34, this led to less debt issuance, and that these governments had less debt outstanding than those that had not yet implemented the reform.[89]

In addition to GASB No. 34 and the various statements related to pensions and OPEB obligations listed above, GASB issued several other statements between 2008 and 2019 that have affected financial reporting:

- Statement No. 53, issued in 2008, and GASB No. 64 (2011) are concerned with derivatives, and specifically provide that they should be reported at fair value, with changes in fair value reported either as investment revenue or in the statement of net assets as a deferral.
- Statement No. 56, issued in 2009, incorporates into GASB requirements specific accounting and financial reporting guidance presented by the AICPA.
- Statement No. 58, issued in 2009, sets financial and accounting guidance for governments that have filed for Chapter 9 bankruptcy protection.
- Statement No. 60, issued in 2010, provides for the accounting and financial reporting of *service concession agreements* (SCAs). SCAs are public–private or public–public agreements where a government allows an operator to use public assets or infrastructure, with the operator receiving a fee.
- Statement No. 63, issued in 2011, provides financial reporting guidance for deferred outflows of resources (consumption of net assets applicable to future reporting periods) or deferred inflows of resources (acquisition of net asset to the government applicable to future reporting periods).
- Statement No. 65, issued in 2012, reclassifies certain items that were previously reported as assets and liabilities as instead deferred outflows or deferred inflows of resources.
- Statement No. 69, issued in 2013, establishes accounting and financial standards that clarify how government mergers and government acquisitions should be treated, and how to identify the distinction between the two.
- Statement No. 70, issued in 2013, relates to when a liability should be recognized in cases where qualitative factors and historical data indicate that it is more likely than not that the nonfinancial guarantee will result in a financial obligation.
- Statement No. 77, issued in 2015, clarifies reporting requirements related to tax abatements, which are limitations on a government's ability to raise revenues, normally as result of a specific policy decision aimed at forgiving what would otherwise be a tax obligation that would exist for a citizen or corporate entity.
- Statement No. 79, issued in 2015, establishes criteria that address how certain external investment pools should account for, and report on, their financial transactions.
- Statement No. 80, issued in 2016, amends Statement No. 14 to clarify the financial status of certain component units of a reporting entity.
- Statement No. 81, issued in 2016, relates to donor agreements where the donor is providing funds to multiple beneficiaries (including governments). In these cases, assets, liabilities, and deferred inflows must be recognized at the inception of the agreement.
- Statement No. 83, issued in 2016, addresses accounting and financial reporting for asset retirement obligations, identifying the timing for recognition of such activities.
- Statement No. 84, issued in 2017, improves guidance with respect to the reporting of fiduciary activities by specifying more clearly the circumstances under which a fiduciary activity exists.
- Statement No. 86, issued in 2017, addresses accounting and financial reporting requirements in cases where cash and other monetary assets provided with existing resources are placed in an irrevocable trust for the sole purpose of extinguishing debt.
- Statement No. 87, issued in 2017, addresses the accounting and financial reporting requirements associated with the use of leases by governments.

- Statement No. 88, issued in 2018, provides guidance intended to improve the information that is disclosed in financial statements related to debt.
- Statement No. 89, issued in 2018, relates to the reporting of interest cost incurred before the end of a construction period, with the intent of both enhancing the relevance and comparability of information about capital assets and simplifying accounting for interest costs.
- Statement No. 90, issued in 2018, is intended to improve the consistency and comparability of financial reporting in cases where a government has majority equity interest in a legally separate organization.

Federal Financial Reporting

As noted above, the OMB issues an annual series of tables that together report on the financial condition of the government. In addition, OMB works with federal agencies in their preparation of agency-specific reports. The Chief Financial Officers Act of 1990 and the Government Management Reform Act of 1994 required agencies to prepare a series of auditable financial statements by March 1, 1997, and every year thereafter.[90]

Circular A-136, which OMB updates annually, is the governing document in this process.[91] Federal entities are required to prepare both annual financial reports and annual performance reports that are mandated by law. For many years, OMB required these reports to be consolidated into a single performance and accountability report (PAR). More recently, however, agencies have been given more discretion in terms of whether this information is presented in a single PAR, or whether financial and performance information is presented in separate reports.

Government financial reporting has clearly become much more extensive in recent decades, but this expansion has come at a cost. Questions arise regarding whether accounting systems have become overloaded and whether some of the resources spent on financial reporting might be better spent on the delivery of services to citizens. Demands for the streamlining of financial reports are increasing. To date, Congress has authorized OMB to waive some reporting requirements imposed on federal agencies. The accounting profession itself has shown some awareness that reporting requirements can create overwhelming burdens.

Governmental Auditing

Auditing serves a variety of functions and consequently exists in many different forms, all over the world.[92] One distinction made is between *preaudits* and *postaudits*—that is, between reviewing transactions before and after they occur. The preaudit occurs before the government commits itself to a purchase and is used to verify, for example, that the police department has sufficient funds to purchase a piece of equipment and that the department is authorized to have that equipment. Not only the budget office but also an accounting department may be involved in preaudits. If personnel are to be hired, a personnel office may have some preaudit responsibility. Often at the state and local levels, independent comptrollers, controllers, or auditors general have preaudit responsibilities.

Postaudits generally involve more extensive procedures and often more participants. The following discussion concerns the function of postaudits in government budgeting and finance. This form of auditing has been defined as "a systematic collection of the sufficient, competent evidential matter needed to attest to the fairness of management's assertions in the financial statements, or to evaluate whether management has efficiently and effectively carried out its responsibilities."[93]

Audit Objectives and Organizational Responsibilities
Purposes

Auditing in the private sector is used largely to ensure that the financial statements issued by a firm fairly reflect its financial status, and this same concern exists in the public sector. Auditing provides some assurance to investors (or taxpayers) in both the private and public sectors that their investments are secure and are being well managed.

Another purpose of auditing is ensuring that funds are not subject to fraud, waste, and abuse, or subject to error in reporting. When financial reports cannot be verified by checking accounting records, the opportunities for dishonesty, waste, or just poor management of funds may exist. Auditing in government is used for compliance purposes as well. As has been noted, accounting systems track receipts and expenditures to ensure that they are handled in conformance with restrictions contained in revenue and appropriation bills. Auditing helps ensure that an agency does not spend funds on an activity that, while beneficial to society, simply has not been authorized. Compliance auditing can include ensuring that an agency has accomplished programmatically what it was instructed to do. Another form of compliance auditing involves grants and contracts. The federal government, for example, needs to check that only appropriate charges have been made by a state government in the case of a federally funded project or program, such as Medicaid, or by a university in the case of funded research. Similarly, government contracts are audited regularly for compliance with financial provisions of the contracts to ensure that billed costs are within the scope of the contracts and that adequate records exist to support the legitimacy of these billed costs.

Auditing Organizations

Nationally, several organizations influence the practice of governmental auditing. The AICPA issues generally accepted auditing standards (GAAS).[94] AICPA's Auditing Standard Board now promulgates auditing, attestation, and quality control standards for auditors.[95] GASB, in the process of identifying standards for accounting, inevitably becomes involved in auditing. GASB Statement No. 34, discussed earlier, created several issues about auditing in state and local governments.

The GAO issues *Government Auditing Standards* (GAS, known as the Yellow Book). The standards are applied to federal agencies and may be applied to state and local governments that receive federal financial assistance. GAO uses an Advisory Council on Government Auditing to assist in reviewing and revising the Yellow Book. The council's members come from all levels of government, the private sector, and academia.[96] GAO and the Council of the Inspectors General on Integrity and Efficiency issue the *Financial Audit Manual,* which provides a methodology for federal auditing.[97] The OMB is deeply involved in auditing, a relatively new role for the organization. The key documents are Circular A-123 on internal controls; Circular A-136 on reporting requirements; and Bulletin No. 19-03, *Audit Requirements for Federal Financial Statements.*[98]

Auditing within a government is often performed by several organizations. Audits are conducted periodically by officers within an agency to provide information to management. These internal audits help maintain managerial control over operations. Other audits are conducted by external officers, who can be from a unit answerable to the legislative body (such as GAO being answerable to Congress), a unit headed by an independently elected officer, or an independent private corporation that has a contract to conduct an audit.

The federal government ratcheted up the auditing function during the 1970s and 1980s by creating *inspectors general* in major federal agencies. Appointed by the president with the advice and consent of the Senate, inspectors general are located within agencies but can be removed only by the president. According to the Inspector General Act of 1978 and the Chief Financial Officers Act of 1990, inspectors general are responsible for conducting audits and for investigating possible cases of fraud, waste, and abuse of government resources.[99] Most of the burden of federal auditing rests with these inspectors general rather than the GAO. The Chief Financial Officers Act, by creating CFOs in major agencies, greatly increased the attention that agencies devote to sound accounting practices and to the auditing of accounts. Agencies have redesigned their central staff units, consolidating considerable powers under the CFOs. Other federal agencies not covered by the 1978 legislation also have inspectors general.

All levels of government use the Big 4 and other accounting firms to conduct or assist in auditing. Depending on the state, a local government may have a choice of paying either the state auditor or a private firm for audit services. State services may be less expensive, but private services may perform audits in a timelier fashion. When a private firm is to be used, a government will employ a bidding process to give competing firms an opportunity to indicate what services they can provide, in what time frame, and at what cost.

A practice often recommended for the public sector is the use of independent *audit committees*. These bodies typically consist of administrators, legislators, and financial experts from outside the government. The committees can serve as useful interfaces between finance offices and auditors. The Sarbanes-Oxley Act required such committees of publicly traded corporations, but the committees are used only on a limited basis in the public sector.

Sometimes the number of organizations involved in auditing in a given situation can seem overwhelming. An agency may have two or more auditors. In the DOD, for instance, audit functions are performed by the Defense Contract Audit Agency (which audits contractors), the inspector general, the comptroller, and the CFO. Five outside contractors assisted the inspector general in auditing the DOD's 2018 financial statements.[100] Large state and local agencies may have similar internal auditors, and all levels of government have their central auditors, such as the Auditor General of Illinois. As noted, private accounting firms may have responsibilities as well. Additional auditing occurs because of intergovernmental financial transactions. State government agencies, for example, may be audited by federal funding agencies and the GAO, although this level of auditing has changed since passage of the Single Audit Act of 1984 (see below).

Types of Audits and Standards

Audit Types

As already noted, there are preaudits and postaudits, and internal and external audits. Another means of categorizing audits is by considering the purposes to be served. The definition of auditing provided earlier suggests that audits can be directed toward finance and performance.

Financial audits focus on whether financial statements prepared by a government accurately reflect financial transactions and the government's or agency's status. The standards of auditing provide a framework for conducting an audit.

Financial audits also review how financial matters are handled or whether suitable internal controls exist to protect resources. Auditors are concerned with the vulnerability of a financial management system to potential fraud. Are organizational lines of responsibility clearly established to ensure that whoever is in charge has the authority to protect the government's or agency's finances? Are policies and procedures established for maintaining records, and are those policies and procedures adhered to in practice? Are computer systems that handle financial transactions protected against potential fraud?

Identification of risks is the first step in eliminating problems. Auditors make risk assessments to determine which accounting activities or operations to audit, as only a sample of financial activities can be audited, given the auditors' limited resources. The risk assessment determines which activities are most vulnerable to fraud, waste, and abuse and therefore should be audited.

As of 2019, the GAO's high-risk list included 35 items, with some items, such as defense weapons systems acquisition, having been on the list for many years. Many of the items on the list involve substantial current or future costs to the government, such as Medicare, Medicaid, the Social Security Administration's Disability Insurance programs, DOD and NASA acquisitions activities, and the PBGC, whose problems were discussed above. There are several items that have been added in recent iterations of the list: the U.S. government's environmental liability and the decennial census (added in 2017), the government's personnel clearance process (2018), and veterans affairs acquisition management (2019).[101]

The other major auditing function served is performance or program auditing, which deals with whether resources are being used efficiently and whether results or objectives are being achieved (see the chapter on the expenditure side of budget preparation). In GAO's case, it has moved largely away from financial audits and conducts mostly performance audits. Several states have been cited as actively engaged in program audits. These include Florida's Office of Program Policy Analysis and Government Accountability, Missouri's Auditor's Office and the Oversight Division of the Committee on Legislative Research, Pennsylvania's Department of the Auditor General and the Legislative Budget and Finance Committee, and Virginia's Joint Legislative Audit and Review Commission.[102]

Any audit agency faces the difficult choice of deciding how much effort and resources should be devoted to the competing functions of financial and performance auditing. If major emphasis is given to performance auditing, fraud and other abuses may become more prevalent. Conversely, placing greater emphasis on financial auditing may keep government honest but does little to encourage agencies to fulfill their missions.

Auditing Standards

The federal Government Auditing Standards provide overall guidelines as well as standards for conducting fieldwork and preparing audit reports. Overall standards call for auditors to be independent of the agencies under review and to be fully trained in the auditing function. The Securities and Exchange Commission oversees accounting firms to ensure that private auditors are independent of the entities that they audit. Fieldwork is to be planned adequately in advance and sufficiently staffed to meet the requirements of the work plan. Auditors must keep accurate records of their fieldwork to answer questions that may arise at a later time.

Field auditing involves verifying sample transactions to ensure that transactions did occur as recorded. For example, an expense report of a trip taken by a city employee to a national conference, among numerous expense reports, might be selected for review. The auditor may (1) call the travel agent or airline to verify the ticket price, (2) check that the trip was an authorized budget expenditure, (3) interview the employee to verify unreceipted miscellaneous expenses, and (4) review other receipts and documents to determine the accuracy of the report. The purpose of this fieldwork is not particularly to find cases of fraud, waste, and abuse, but rather to verify that the jurisdiction has procedures in place to protect against them.

The Single Audit Act

A concern of the federal government for many years has been the large volume of federal financial transfers to state and local governments and to nongovernmental organizations, and verification of whether these transfers are being suitably audited. The OMB has six circulars that detail how these organizations are to arrange their accounts:

- A-21, *Cost Principles for Educational Institutions* (2004)
- A-87, *Cost Principles for State, Local, and Indian Tribal Governments* (2004)
- A-102, *Grants and Cooperative Agreements with State and Local Governments* (1994, as amended in 1997)
- A-110, *Uniform Administrative Requirements for Grants and Agreements with Institutions of Higher Education, Hospitals, and Other Non-Profit Organizations* (1993, as amended in 1999)
- A-122, *Cost Principles for Non-Profit Organizations* (2004)
- A-133, *Audits of States, Non-Profits, and Local Organizations* (1997, with revisions and supplements in 2003 through 2007)

The Single Audit Act of 1984, as amended, requires recipients of federal assistance amounting to $750,000 or more in a fiscal year to undergo a single audit of their accounting systems and the way federal funds are handled.[103] Audits must be submitted within 9 months of the audit period's close. The law applies to state and local governments as well as to nonprofit organizations. It has had the effect of requiring tens of thousands of audits annually. These audits, normally conducted by private firms, are intended to help ensure that recipients use federal resources in accordance with federal laws and regulations. The act is implemented through OMB Circular A-133. The Single Audit Act has undoubtedly improved the handling of federal financial assistance, but it may have had only a limited impact on overall financial management in these governments.

GAAS, GAS, and the Single Audit Act set standards for audit reporting. Of course, one of the chief concerns with regard to any report is that financial statements be in accordance with GAAP. Audit reports are expected to indicate deficiencies, such as inconsistent use of accounting procedures. Reports indicate whether internal controls exist to protect against fraud, waste, and abuse.

Four types of conclusions can be drawn by the auditing body:

1. The audit might be *unqualified*, providing an unqualified or "clean" opinion—that is, the accounting system meets all standards.
2. The report may be *qualified*, indicating there are problems but that the system generally meets standards. A qualified audit of a local or state government might be interpreted unfavorably by would-be investors in the government's bonds.
3. A *disclaimer of opinion* indicates that the accounting system is inadequate and that conducting an audit is impossible.
4. An audit can be *adverse* or *negative*, indicating that the financial statements fail to provide an accurate report of the entity's finances.

For fiscal year 2018, the federal government as a whole received a disclaimer of opinion from the GAO's audit of consolidated financial statements. This was the 22nd year of such disclaimers, covering every year since GAO first started carrying out these audits for the fiscal year 1997 financial statements. GAO, in its report accompanying the financial statements, highlighted the federal government's material weaknesses in internal control, including improper payments, information security problems, and problems with loan programs. The largest single obstacle to the federal government's ability to receive a clean audit opinion is the continued financial management challenges of the DOD. The audit news out of federal departments has been encouraging. For fiscal year 2018, unqualified opinions were issued for all federal departments, with the important exceptions of the Departments of Defense and Housing and Urban Development.[104]

Improper Payments

Erroneous or improper payments have been one of the biggest problems detected through auditing. The governing legislation at the federal level was the Improper Payments Information Act of 2002.[105] The law required federal agencies to (1) conduct risk assessments, gauging the possibility and likelihood of making improper payments; (2) estimate the annual amount of such payments; and (3) report recouped funds. This information was to be included in the agencies' performance and accountability reports or financial reports.

In 2010, Congress passed the IPERA. The IPERA adds to the 2002 act by (1) lowering the permitted threshold of susceptibility to improper payments over time; (2) expanding the types of programs required to be audited for payment recovery; (3) enabling agency heads to use funds they recover for additional uses such as improvement of financial management, support of their Office of Inspector General, and the original funding purpose; and (4) establishing repercussions for agencies that are noncompliant.[106] In 2019, GAO estimated that federal agencies made about $151 billion in improper payments during fiscal year 2018. This represented about 4% of all federal spending during that year and was an increase of $10 billion over the fiscal year 2017 number.[107] Of course, the federal government is not the only government subject to wrongful spending. State auditors check on both state spending and state grants to local governments. The federal government cannot get a handle on the extent of overpayment of federal money if such overpayments go undetected in state programs administering federal money. When state auditors find improper payment errors in the administration of state money by local governments, the grant payments can be halted. This indeed happened to a Florida opportunity council that provided services to the poor and had poorly organized accounting records, preventing the auditor from issuing an opinion.[108] In extreme cases, when local governments' finances are in disarray, states have the authority to take over the jurisdictions on a temporary basis.

Follow-up after an audit is essential to ensure that weaknesses are corrected. Without such follow-up, auditing is an empty exercise. OMB Circular A-50, *Audit Followup*, sets guidelines for checks to be made after audits have been completed at the federal level.

Summary

Governmental accounting is characterized by procedures intended to prevent fraud and to guarantee agency conformance with legal requirements. Information from accounting systems is used in decision making and can help improve the efficiency and effectiveness of services. The Governmental Accounting Standards Board was established to help improve state and local government accounting systems, and the Federal Accounting Standards Advisory Board has similar responsibilities at the federal level. Generally accepted accounting principles allow the use of several different types of funds, with the general fund usually the most important for any government.

Accounting systems are structured by having a general ledger and subsidiary ledgers. They follow a relatively simple formula: assets equal the total of liabilities and fund balance. Within the ledgers, expenditures are accounted for in a variety of ways, including major and minor objects of expenditures.

Bases of accounting include cash, encumbrance, accrual, and cost. Some jurisdictions use project-based accounting and cost finding instead of the more comprehensive cost accounting methods. Regardless of the basis for accounting, reports summarizing transactions are prepared at specified intervals. Three of the most common types of reports are balance sheets, operating statements, and cash flow statements.

Auditing attempts to determine whether financial statements accurately reflect the status of accounts and/or whether an organization is operating efficiently and effectively. It is used for compliance purposes—namely, to ensure that financial transactions are in accordance with revenue and appropriation legislation. Generally accepted auditing standards constitute the guidelines for auditing in the public sector.

Notes

1. Thompson, D. (2011). How Hollywood accounting can make a $450 million movie 'unprofitable'. *The Atlantic*, September 14. Retrieved February 12, 2020, from https://www.theatlantic.com/business/archive/2011/09/how-hollywood-accounting-can-make-a-450-million-movie-unprofitable/245134/.
2. Joyce, P. (2011). *The Congressional Budget Office: honest numbers, power and policymaking* (p. 142). Washington, DC: Georgetown University Press.
3. Norvelle, J. W. (1997). *Introduction to fund accounting* (5th ed.). Eaton Rapids, MI: RIA Professional Publishing; see Harris, J. (2005). The discourse of governmental accounting and auditing. *Public Budgeting & Finance*, 25, Supplement 1, Winter, 154–179.
4. U.S. General Accounting Office (2000). *Executive guide: creating value through world-class financial management.* Washington, DC: U.S. Government Printing Office.
5. Mosher, F. C. (1984). *A tale of two agencies.* Baton Rouge, LA: Louisiana State University Press.
6. Federal Managers' Financial Integrity Act of 1982 (P.L. 97-255); Accounting and Auditing Act of 1950, Ch. 946, Title I.
7. Chief Financial Officers Act of 1990 (P.L. 101-576).
8. U.S. Chief Financial Officers Council website, www.cfo.gov.
9. Office of Management and Budget (2019). *Circular A-136, Financial reporting requirements*. June 28. Retrieved February 12, 2020, from https://www.whitehouse.gov/wp-content/uploads/2019/08/OMB-Circular-A-136-new.pdf.
10. Federal Accounting Standards Advisory Board website, www.fasab.gov.
11. Office of Management and Budget (2020). *Circular A-134, Financial Accounting Principles and Standards*. Retrieved February 12, 2020, from https://www.whitehouse.gov/wp-content/uploads/2017/11/Circular-A-134-2.pdf.

12. Clinger-Cohen Act (Information Technology Management Reform Act) of 1996 (P.L. 104-106).

13. Palmer, K. (2005). Chief financial officers highlight their job challenges. *Government Executive*. Retrieved December 20, 2011, from http://www.govexec.com/story_page.cfm?filepath=/dailyfed/0205/020805k1.htm&oref=search.

14. Mitchell, M., Deputy Associate Administrator, U.S. General Services Administration (2006). *GSA's role in implementing FMLoB government-wide*. Retrieved December 20, 2011, from http://www.gsa.gov/portal/content/102185.

15. U.S. Department of the Treasury, Bureau of the Fiscal Service (2020). *Managing the financial management line of business (FMLoB)*. Retrieved February 12, 2020, from https://fiscal.treasury.gov/fit/managing-the-fmlob.html.

16. Gauthier, S. J. (2012). *Governmental accounting, auditing, and financial reporting*. Chicago, IL: Government Finance Officers Association (a supplement was published in 2014).

17. Governmental Accounting Standards Board website, www.gasb.org.

18. Governmental Accounting Standards Board website, www.gasb.org.

19. Financial Accounting Standards Board website, www.fasb.org.

20. AccountingVerse (2020). *Big 4 Accounting Firms*. Retrieved February 12, 2020, from https://www.accountingverse.com/articles/big-4-accounting-firms.html.

21. Andersen guilty in Enron case. (2002). *BBC News*, June 15. Retrieved August 26, 2006, from http://news.bbc.co.uk/2/hi/business/2047122.stm; Brown, R. E. (2005). Enron/Andersen: crisis in U.S. accounting and lessons for government. *Public Budgeting & Finance, 25*, Fall, 20–32; Accenture website, www.accenture.com.

22. Governmental Accounting Standards Board (2019). *GASB Codification as of June 30, 2019*. Norwalk, CT: Author.

23. American Institute of Certified Public Accountants website, www.aicpa.org.

24. Federal Accounting Standards Advisory Board (2019). *FASAB handbook of federal accounting standards and other pronouncements, as amended*. Retrieved February 12, 2020, from https://fasab.gov/accounting-standards/.

25. Smith, J. L. (2005). Lapeer official says "sorry." *Flint Journal*, December 2, A1, A2.

26. Abuja, F. M. (2006). How public servants loot treasury—accountant general. *AllAfrica.com*, August 25. Retrieved August 27, 2006, from http://allafrica.com/stories/printable/200608250483.html.

27. Glenger, B., & Capaccio, T. (2011). Afghan aid tracking suffers on Karzai, U.S. failures, audit says. *Bloomberg*, July 20. Retrieved March 22, 2012, from http://www.bloomberg.com/news/2011-07-20/afghan-aid-tracking-suffers-on-karzai-u-s-failures-audit-says.html.

28. International Monetary Fund (2019). *Fiscal transparency code*. Retrieved February 12, 2020, from https://www.imf.org/external/np/fad/trans/Code2019.pdf.

29. United Way International (2020). *Global standards for United Way organizations*. Retrieved February 12, 2020, from https://www.unitedway.org/about/public-reporting/global-standards#.

30. Odyek, J. (2006). Uganda: accounting chiefs warned. *New Vision*, August 21. *AllAfrica.com*. Retrieved March 22, 2012, from http://allafrica.com/stories/200608220488.html.

31. Office of Management and Budget (2016). *OMB Circular No. A-123, Management's responsibility for enterprise risk, management and internal control*. Retrieved February 12, 2020, from https://www.whitehouse.gov/sites/whitehouse.gov/files/omb/memoranda/2016/m-16-17.pdf.

32. American Institute of Certified Public Accountants (2018). *A basic background & overview of state and local government accounting*. Presentation, February 6. Retrieved February 12, 2020, from https://www.aicpa.org/content/dam/aicpa/interestareas/governmentalauditquality/resources/downloadabledocuments/slgbasicspart1.pdf.

33. U.S. General Accounting Office (1995). *Government corporations: profiles of recent proposals*. Washington, DC: U.S. Government Printing Office; Bunch, B. S. (2000). Changes in usage of enterprise finds by large cities. *Public Budgeting & Finance, 20*, Summer, 15–29.

34. McCoskey, M. G., et al. (2003). Trust, trusts, and accountability: the role of states in college saving plans. *Public Budgeting & Finance, 23*, Fall, 49–63; College Savings Plan Network website, www.collegesavings.org.

35. Bureau of the Fiscal Service, U.S. Department of Treasury (2019). *USSGL implementation guidance*. Retrieved February 14, 2020, from https://fiscal.treasury.gov/ussgl/resources-implementation.html.

36. Office of Management and Budget (2013). *Appendix D to Circular No. A-123, Compliance with the Federal Financial Management Improvement Act of l996*. Retrieved February 22, 2020, from https://www.whitehouse.gov/sites/whitehouse.gov/files/omb/memoranda/2013/m-13-23.pdf.

37. Governmental Accounting Standards Board (2007). *Defining the fundamental elements of financial reporting*, June, 1. Retrieved March 22, 2012, from http://www.gasb.org/cs/BlobServer?blobcol=urldata&blobtable=MungoBlobs&blobkey=id&blobwhere=1175820452682&blobheader=application %2Fpdf.

38. Governmental Accounting Standards Board (2009). Statement No. 54, *Fund balance reporting and governmental fund type definitions*. February. Retrieved March 22, 2012, from http://www.gasb.org/st/summary/gstsm54.html.

39. Governmental Accounting Standards Board (2009). *GASB improves the usefulness of reported fund balance information*. March 11. Retrieved March 22, 2012, from http://www.gasb.org/cs/ContentServer?c=GASBContent_C&pagename=GASB/GASBContent_C/GASBNewsPage&cid=1176156695762.

40. Norvelle, J. W. (1997). *Introduction to fund accounting*, RIA Professional Publishing, 43.

41. Governmental Accounting Standards Board (2006). Statement No. 48, *Sales and pledges of receivables and*

future revenues and intra-entity transfers of assets and future revenues, September 29. Retrieved March 22, 2012, from http://www.gasb.org/cs/ContentServer?c=GASBContent_C&pagename=GASB%2FGASBContent_C%2FProjectPage&cid=1176156655051.

42. U.S. Congress. (2019). *S. Rept. 115-282, Department of State, foreign operations, and related programs appropriations bill, 2019.* Retrieved February 14, 2020, from https://www.congress.gov/congressional-report/115th-congress/senate-report/282/1.

43. U.S. Office of Management and Budget (2020). *Historical tables, table 3.2-outlays by function and subfunction* (downloadable xls file). Retrieved April 20, 2020, from https://www.whitehouse.gov/omb/historical-tables/.

44. Roberts, A. (1999). Accounting for results, 1997: government-wide performance plan, fiscal year 1999. *Journal of Policy Analysis and Management, 18,* 187–191; Cunningham, G. M., & Harris, J. (2005). Toward a theory of performance reporting to achieve public sector accountability: a field study. *Public Budgeting & Finance, 25,* Summer, 15–42; Berman, B. J. (2006). *Listening to the public: adding the voices of the people to government performance measurement and reporting.* New York, NY: Fund for the City of New York.

45. Governmental Accounting Standards Board (2020). *Basic facts about service efforts and accomplishments reporting.* Retrieved April 20, 2020, from https://www.gasb.org/cs/ContentServer?c=Document_C&cid=1176156714761&d=&pagename=GASB%2FDocument_C%2FDocumentPage.

46. Government Performance and Results Act of 1993 (P.L. 101-576).

47. Government Performance and Results Modernization Act of 2010 (P.L. 111-352).

48. Musso, D. (2006). Social Security: reliance on cash flow accounting and projections disguises an inherent upside cash flow bias. *Public Budgeting & Finance, 26,* Spring, 143–156.

49. Van der Hoek, M. P. (2005). From cash to accrual budgeting and accounting in the public sector: the Dutch experience. *Public Budgeting & Finance, 25,* Spring, 32–45; Organization for Economic Cooperation and Development (2017). *Accrual practices and reform experiences in OECD countries.* Retrieved February 14, 2020, from https://www.oecd.org/publications/accrual-practices-and-reform-experiences-in-oecd-countries-9789264270572-en.htm.

50. Finkler, S., et al. (2017). *Financial management for public, health and nonprofit organizations* (5th ed; pp. 445–450). Thousand Oaks: CQ Press.

51. Governmental Accounting Standards Board (2020). *Summary of statement no. 11: measurement focus and basis of accounting-governmental fund operating statements.* Retrieved April 20, 2020, from https://www.gasb.org/st/summary/gstsm11.html.

52. Kinney, M. R., & Raiborn, C. A. (2013). *Cost accounting; foundations and evolutions,* 9th ed. Mason, OH: Southwestern Cengage Learning; Brock, H. R., et al. (2007). *Cost*

accounting: principles and applications (7th ed.). Boston, MA: McGraw-Hill.

53. Rivenbark, W. C. (2005). A historical overview of cost accounting in local government. *State and Local Government Review, 37,* 217–227.

54. Activity-based costing and activity-based management symposium. (1999). *Public Budgeting & Finance, 19,* Summer, 3–58; Kaplan, R. S., & Andersen, S. R. (2004). Time-driven activity-based costing. *Harvard Business Review, 82,* 131–140; Rozlocki, N. (2006).

55. Office of Management and Budget (2013). *Value engineering,* December 26. Retrieved February 14, 2020, from https://www.whitehouse.gov/sites/whitehouse.gov/files/omb/circulars/A131/a131-122013.pdf.

56. Federal Accounting Standards Advisory Board (1995). *Accounting for property, plant, and equipment,* Statement of Federal Financial Accounting Standards 6. Retrieved February 14, 2020, from http://files.fasab.gov/pdffiles/handbook_sffas_6.pdf.

57. Federal Accounting Standards Advisory Board (2005). *Heritage assets and stewardship land.* Statement of Federal Financial Accounting Standards 29. Retrieved April 20, 2020, from http://files.fasab.gov/pdffiles/financacctstandards29.pdf.

58. U.S. Office of Management and Budget, Office of Federal Procurement Policy (2020). *Cost Accounting Standards Board.* Retrieved February 14, 2020, from https://www.whitehouse.gov/omb/management/office-federal-procurement-policy/#_Office_of_Federal_5.

59. U.S. Office of Management and Budget (2004). *Cost principles for state, local and Indian tribal governments, Circular No. 87.* Retrieved February 14, 2020, from http://www.whitehouse.gov/sites/default/files/omb/circulars/a087/a87_2004.pdf.

60. Federal Credit Reform Act of 1990 (P.L. 101-508), Title XIII.

61. U.S. General Accounting Office (1993). *Federal credit programs: agencies had serious problems meeting credit reform accounting requirements.* Washington, DC: U.S. Government Printing Office.

62. Sastry, P., & Sheiner, L. (2015). Credit scoring and the scoring of risk. *Hutchins Center on Fiscal and Monetary Policy, Brookings Institution,* May 27. Retrieved February 16, 2020, from https://www.brookings.edu/wp-content/uploads/2016/06/cbo-credit-score-background-paper.pdf.

63. Congressional Budget Office (2019). *Fair-value estimates of the cost of federal credit programs in 2020,* May 30. Retrieved February 16, 2020, from https://www.cbo.gov/publication/55278; Kogan, R. (2016). GAO agrees: current accounting method beats fair value approach. *Center for Budget and Policy Priorities,* February 29. Retrieved February 16, 2020, from https://www.cbpp.org/blog/gao-agrees-current-accounting-method-beats-fair-value-approach.

64. Collard, D. (2004). Generational accounting and generational transfers. *Ageing Horizons,* 1. Retrieved

December 20, 2011, from http://www.ageing.ox.ac.uk/system/files/AH1%20Collard.pdf; Eschker, E. (2005). Generational accounting and the saving rate decline, 1960–2000. *Public Budgeting & Finance, 25,* Spring, 46–65.

65. Spies-Butcher, B., & Stebbing, A. (2019). Mobilising alternative futures: generational accounting and the fiscal politics of ageing in Australia. *Ageing and Society,* 9, July, 1409–1435; Thomson, I., et al. (2018). Review: Time machines, ethics and sustainable development: accounting for inter-generational equity in public sector organization. *Public Money and Management,* 38, 5, 379–388.

66. Sarbanes-Oxley Act (Public Company Accounting Reform and Investor Protection Act) of 2002 (P.L. 107-204).

67. Federal Credit Reform Act of 1990 (P.L. 101-508), Title XIII.

68. Office of Management and Budget (2019). *Appendix B to Circular no. A-123, A risk management framework for government charge card programs,* August 27. Retrieved February 20, 2019, from https://www.whitehouse.gov/wp-content/uploads/2019/08/Issuance-of-Revised-Appendix-B-to-OMB-Circular-A-123.pdf.

69. Office of Management and Budget (2018). *Transmittal of Appendix C to OMB Circular A-123, Requirements for Payment Integrity Improvement.* June 26. Retrieved February 16, 2020 from https://www.whitehouse.gov/wp-content/uploads/2018/06/M-18-20.pdf.

70. Urban Institute (2020). *State and local government pensions.* Retrieved February 16, 2020, from https://www.urban.org/policy-centers/cross-center-initiatives/state-and-local-finance-initiative/projects/state-and-local-backgrounders/state-and-local-government-pensions.

71. Employee Retirement Income Security Act of 1974 (P.L. 93-406).

72. Small Business Job Protection Act of 1996 (P.L. 104-188).

73. Pew Charitable Trust (2019). *The state pension funding gap: 2017,* June 27. Retrieved February 16, 2020, from https://www.pewtrusts.org/en/research-and-analysis/issue-briefs/2019/06/the-state-pension-funding-gap-2017.

74. Pew Charitable Trusts (2018). *Update: 50-state survey of retiree health care liabilities,* December 21. Retrieved February 16, 2020, from https://www.pewtrusts.org/en/research-and-analysis/fact-sheets/2018/12/update-50-state-survey-of-retiree-health-care-liabilities.

75. Powers, T. (2019). Post-employment benefits in New York, New Jersey, and Connecticut: the case for reform. *Manhattan Institute,* October 3. Retrieved February 16, 2020, from https://www.manhattan-institute.org/post-employment-benefits-opeb-ny-ct-nj.

76. Governmental Accounting Standards Board, *GASB 45.*

77. Governmental Accounting Standards Board (2020). *Implementation Guide for Statements 74 and 75 on Other Postemployment Benefits.* Retrieved February 16, 2020, from https://www.gasb.org/jsp/GASB/GASBContent_C/ProjectPage&cid=1176166904842.

78. National League of Cities (2017). *How cities can prepare for the new OPEB accounting requirements,* January 18. Retrieved February 16, 2020, from https://www.nlc.org/article/how-cities-can-prepare-for-the-new-opeb-accounting-requirements.

79. Pension Protection Act of 2006 (P.L. 109-280); BNA Tax Management (2006). *Pension Protection Act of 2006.* Retrieved December 20, 2011, from http://subscript.bna.com/pic2/ppa.nsf/id/RSAR-6SSJ5X?OpenDocument; CCH (2006).

80. CNN Money (2020). *Ultimate guide to retirement.* Retrieved February 29, 2020, from https://money.cnn.com/retirement/guide/pensions_basics.moneymag/index7.htm.

81. Pension Benefit Guaranty Corporation (2019). *Annual report.* Retrieved February 16, 2020, from https://www.pbgc.gov/sites/default/files/pbgc-fy-2019-annual-report.pdf, p. 24.

82. Pension Benefit Guarantee Corporation (2010). PBGC annual report. Retrieved April 20, 2020, from https://www.pbgc.gov/about/annual-reports/pbgc-annual-report-2010.

83. Government Accountability Office (2019). *High-risk list,* January. Retrieved February 16, 2020, from https://www.gao.gov/high-risk-list.

84. Government Finance Officers Association (2006). *Preparing popular reports.* Retrieved December 20, 2011, from http://www.gfoa.org/index.php?option=com_content&task=view&id=1467.

85. Governmental Accounting Standards Board (2006). *Codification of governmental accounting and financial reporting standards.*

86. Governmental Accounting Standards Board (1999). *Basic financial statements—and management's discussion and analysis—for state and local governments, Statement No. 34.* Retrieved December 20, 2011, from http://www.gasb.org/cs/ContentServer?c=Pronouncement_C&pagename=GASB%2FPronouncement_C%2FGASBSummaryPage&cid=1176156699453; Kravchuk, R. S., & Voorhees, W. R. (Eds.) (2001). Governmental Accounting Standards Board (GASB) Statement No. 34 symposium. *Public Budgeting & Finance, 21,* Fall, 1–87.

87. Bloch, R. (2016). Assessing the impact of GASB statement No. 34: the perceptions of municipal bond analysts. *Municipal Finance Journal, 37,* 2, 51–71.

88. Kim, J., & Ebdon, C. (2017). Have the GASB no. 34 infrastructure reporting requirements affected state highway spending? *Journal of Public Budgeting, Accounting & Financial Management, 29,* 3, 347–374.

89. St. Clair, T. (2017). *The impact of the GASB 34 reporting model on municipal debt issuance: a regression discontinuity approach.* Unpublished working paper.

90. Government Management Reform Act of 1994 (P.L. 103-356).

91. Office of Management and Budget (2019). *Circular A-136, Financial reporting requirements,* June 28. Retrieved February 21, 2020, from https://www.whitehouse.gov/wp-content/uploads/2019/06/OMB-Circular-A-136.pdf.

92. Carlos, S. (2006). Banking on accountability? Strengthening budget oversight and public sector auditing in emerging economies. *Public Budgeting & Finance, 26,* Summer, 66–100.

93. Government Finance Officers Association (1994). *Governmental accounting, auditing, and financial reporting* (p. 314). Chicago, IL: Government Finance Officers Association.

94. American Institute of Certified Public Accountants (2020). *Statements on auditing standards*. Retrieved February 21, 2020, from https://www.aicpa.org/research /standards/auditattest/sas.html.

95. Auditing Standards Board (2020). *Clarified statements on auditing standards*. Retrieved February 21, 2020, from https://www.aicpa.org/research/standards/auditattest /asb.html.

96. Government Accountability Office (2020). *Yellow book*. Retrieved February 21, 2020, from https://www.gao.gov /yellowbook.

97. Government Accountability Office (2020). *Financial audit manual*. Retrieved February 21, 2020, from https:// www.gao.gov/financial_audit_manual.

98. U.S. Office of Management and Budget (2019). *Audit requirements for federal financial statements, bulletin no. 19-03*, August 27. Retrieved February 21, 2020, from https://www.whitehouse.gov/wp-content/uploads /2019/08/OMB-Bulletin-No.-19-03-Audit-Requirements -for-Federal-Financial-Statements.pdf.

99. Inspector General Act of 1978 (P.L. 95-452).

100. Department of Defense, Office of the Inspector General (2019). *Understanding the results of the audit of the DoD FY 2018 financial statements*. Retrieved February 29, 2020, from https://fas.org/man/eprint/dodig-audit.pdf.

101. Government Accountability Office (2019). *High risk list*. Retrieved February 21, 2020, from https://www.gao.gov /high-risk-list.

102. Government Performance Project (2008). *Grading the states 2008*. Retrieved December 20, 2011 from http:// www.pewcenteronthestates.org/gpp_report_card.aspx.

103. Single Audit Act of 1984 (P.L. 98-502); Single Audit Act Amendments of 1996 (P.L. 104-156); National Council on Nonprofits (2020). *Federal law audit requirements*. Retrieved February 21, 2020, from https://www.council ofnonprofits.org/nonprofit-audit-guide/federal-law -audit-requirements.

104. Government Accountability Office (2019). *Did you know the government gets audited too?* March 28. Retrieved February 21, 2020, from https://blog.gao.gov/2019/03/28 /did-you-know-the-government-gets-audited-too/.

105. Improper Payments Information Act of 2002 (P.L.107-300).

106. Improper Payments Elimination and Recovery Act of 2010 (P.L. 111-204).

107. Government Accountability Office (2020). *Action tracker: government-wide improper payments*. Retrieved February 21, 2020, from https://www.gao.gov/action -tracker/general-government-government-wide -improper-payments-2011-46.

108. Rousos, R. (2006). Agency under fire: a Q and A. *The Ledger*, August 25. Retrieved December 20, 2011, from http://www.theledger.com/article/20060825/NEWS /608250370.

CHAPTER 13

Capital Assets: Planning and Budgeting, Analysis, and Management

This chapter examines systems developed to plan and budget for capital projects, to analyze capital project selection, and to manage the government's portfolio of assets. Every year, governments spend resources on the construction of facilities or the purchase of equipment and other assets that will continue in use for many years beyond the year of purchase. The construction of a new water treatment plant will serve a community for decades, although the actual construction itself may take less than 2 or 3 years. By constructing the water treatment plant, the community has acquired a capital facility: It has purchased a long-term asset that will provide services many years into the future. This chapter focuses on the decision to build such a facility or purchase such an asset and related systems for managing long-lived facilities or equipment once they are in place.

In this chapter, we examine both the rationale for public sector capital budgeting and the general form of capital plans and budgets. We see that it differs for the U.S. federal government, and most national governments, when compared with state and local governments. Furthermore, because the cost of capital projects is large, especially relative to a state or local government's annual operating budget, capital projects are subject to more detailed analysis, often with formal criteria for determining whether the benefits of the project are worth the cost. The chapter concludes with a section on asset management. This final section focuses on how governments ensure that the capital assets they own (that they have built or purchased) are managed effectively and are maintained so that they achieve the long-life cycle for which they were designed.

Capital Planning and Budgeting

In this section, we define capital and capital investments, discuss the reasons for considering capital spending separately from annual spending in operating budgets, describe the general form for a capital investment planning and budgeting process, and discuss the issues involved in separating capital from operating budgets. We focus mainly on state and local governments. While there is much discussion in annual federal budgets of investments and capital expenditures, and the federal government has considered several times having a formal capital budget, it has never adopted one.

Capital Investments Versus Current Expenditures

Capital Investments

The purchase or construction of a long-lasting physical asset or facility is a capital investment. Businesses invest to have new capacity, to replace assets such as production machinery that have reached or exceeded their usefulness, and to replace existing capacity with more efficient methods of production. These investments are intended to increase the efficiency of the businesses' output and possibly increase total output in the future. Many public sector physical facilities also represent investment in the ability to provide more or higher-quality services in the future. While the term *assets* is commonly used in the public sector also, most public sector assets are infrastructure facilities such as sewer and water systems.

Public sector assets differ in important respects from private sector assets. In conventional private sector accounting, "assets are defined as economic resources" and they are the accounting counterpart to liabilities that are "amounts owed to outside entities and employees."[1] Current assets may consist of cash; investments; and a variety of items that can be readily converted into cash, such as inventory. Capital assets in the private sector have the capacity to generate future revenues for the enterprise. In the public sector, assets typically do not have as a primary purpose the generation of future revenues. Nonprofit organizations in the private sector, such as homeowners' associations formed to manage the assets of a planned community, in most states are required to develop and manage multiyear reserve, or capital, accounts to provide for the repairs and eventual replacement of community physical assets, such as stormwater drainage systems.[2]

Although a government facility that provides a service to citizens, such as a wastewater treatment plant, may not have as an objective generating future revenues, the facility, once built, does provide a continuing service through many future years. In that sense, an expenditure on a facility that will provide benefits for many years after its construction is an investment, and the investment creates a long-lasting asset. According to Statement No. 34 of the Governmental Accounting Standards Board (GASB; see the chapter on financial management), "infrastructure assets have long lives and are usually stationary. Examples are roads, bridges, tunnels, sewer systems, and lighting systems."[3] Buildings also are long-term assets but are not classified as infrastructure. This long-lived investment aspect helps explain why many governments distinguish capital expenditures from current expenditures and have capital budgeting processes, in addition to budgeting processes for current (operating) expenditures.

For governments, it is useful to distinguish among three types of investments. First, a government may purchase physical assets for its own use over many years in the future—assets such as office buildings, heavy equipment, and machinery. Second, governments may make investments in physical facilities that enhance public health and safety, private economic development, and deliver needed public services—for example, roads and water systems. Third, governments may invest in intangibles, such as education and research. The federal government, in the chapter on *federal investment* in the *Analytical Perspectives* volume of the President's annual budget, considers expenditures on physical assets, research and development, and education as investment, but excludes what may be called *social investments*, such as childhood immunization programs, although they also have long-term benefits.[4] Capital budgeting processes deal only with the purchase of physical assets. Capital budgets assist in deciding how much of each type of investment is necessary and assist in evaluating available revenues (including loans and other sources) to finance those investments.

With or without a formal capital budget, focusing some attention on the investment component of a government budget is politically useful because it draws attention to the fact that many public spending programs build for the future. Taxpayers should be informed about government spending that occurs in one year, but then has benefits over many future years. There is some evidence indicating that voters are much more sensitive to infrastructure decisions reflected in capital budgets than to operating budget decisions. The type of capital project—for maintenance and rehabilitation versus building or acquiring new capacity—makes a difference in voter approval in economically distressed periods. Voters tend to prefer maintenance or rehabilitation capital investments in tight budget circumstances.[5] The clearer the impact of a bond issue on taxes, typically property taxes, the more likely voters are to vote against bond issues that result in tax increases.[6] Brick-and-mortar decisions also can be decisive in whether incumbents are reelected.[7] Attention to capital assets reminds citizens that public assets, like highways, may deteriorate to the point of uselessness if not regularly rehabilitated. Governments with formal capital budgets often draw attention in the operating budget to expenditures that are necessary to preserve the value of a previously constructed or acquired asset.

State and local governments also stress the importance of public capital investment in stimulating economic growth. Not only are obvious facilities such as convention centers or improved water services for water-intensive industries the focal point of economic development investments, but state and local governments also increasingly invest in quality-of-life facilities, such as parks and other recreational facilities, and even open space to attract companies to the area.[8] States and local governments compete with each other in offering facilities, tax concessions, and other inducements to attract economic growth (see the chapter on government and the economy), requiring in many cases significant capital investments. Competition among localities in building youth sports complexes that host local, regional, and sometimes even national tournaments can be fierce because of the expected benefits to both government and private parties such as restaurants, hotels, retail stores, concession operators, and others whose sales volumes increase during such tournaments. One such study estimated residents' income increased by over $30 for every $1.00 of local investment in a facility to host girls' amateur softball tournaments, including a national softball championship.[9]

Sometimes it is difficult to draw the line between investment and consumption expenditures. The federal budget's definition of investment is very broad, including such human capital investments as education, research, and development expenditures, but still it does not include many other elements that it logically could. For example, mental health programs, programs for juveniles, and family counseling programs may be considered investments that help prevent future social and economic problems. A major rationale for the Children's Health Insurance Program, which provides federal assistance to states for uninsured children, is that the investment in health helps prevent some future federal expenditures for Medicaid. These types of investments have not historically been considered investments, with the exception that some administrations describe social investment programs such as these. The President's FY2020 budget explicitly excluded "social investment items like health care or social services where it is difficult to separate out the degree to which the spending provides current versus future benefits."[10]

Although it is useful to think of government expenditures as investment or consumption in economic terms, for budgeting purposes the more meaningful distinction is that between capital and current (operating) expenditures. Investments in social capital such as health and education do not fall into the capital category in any budgeting system. Because capital expenditures differ from current expenditures, many state and local governments therefore distinguish between capital and current budgets.

Physical Nature and Time Duration

Businesses think of capital expenditures as the purchase of physical assets or the construction of facilities that will be used over a period of several years. Public sector capital expenditures likewise involve the purchase of physical assets whose use extends over several years, often 30 to 50 years with proper maintenance and replacement programs, as in the case of sewage treatment plants.

Examples of capital expenditures are easy to find. A school building is physically present and will last for many years. In contrast, paper, pens, pencils, and staples, although physical, are used up and must be purchased anew each year. The purchase of a laboratory is easy to classify as a capital expenditure, and the purchase of the supplies that will be used in it is clearly a current expenditure. Similarly, water mains extending from a treatment plant to neighborhood lines have a physical presence and will serve for many years. Their construction is a capital expenditure. In contrast, chemicals used in the water treatment process will be used up and need to be purchased again and again. Purchase of these chemicals is an operating or current expenditure.

Conventionally, debt service payments for both principal and interest for long-term bonds or loans used to finance a capital facility also are included in the capital budget, as opposed to the operating budget. Debt service accounts may be used to segregate these payments (see the chapter on financial management), but they are regarded as capital budget items.

Classification Problems

These examples illustrate that capital expenditures normally are for purchases of physical assets that have a long life. Other examples, however, show that the distinction between capital and current expenditure is sometimes ambiguous. A big-city police department may purchase more than 50 vehicles per year, and many of those vehicles may replace vehicles purchased the previous year. That city may classify the purchase of the police cars as a current expenditure, both because many vehicles are purchased annually and because they are not likely to have a multiyear life span. A small town may purchase two police cars of the same type as the big city, but expect those two cars to last for 3 to 5 years. The small town probably would consider purchase of the police cars to be a capital expenditure.

Even within the same city, some classification problems occur. Books and periodicals bought for a library are expected to be used for many years, and their purchase can be treated as a capital investment. In contrast, purchase of a periodical by a department of public works, if the periodical has a short useful life, would be an operating expense.

Every government and every business establish arbitrary cutoff points that distinguish current from capital expenditures. In most cases, the cutoff is a combination of the size of the expenditure and the useful life of the asset. Purchase of anything expected to be consumed (or destroyed) in the course of 1 year normally will be a current expenditure, no matter how large it is. In addition, small expenditures, even for goods that will last several years, also are classified as current. The size of the government's budget usually determines how small is small. A small town may classify expenditures of less than $1,000 as current regardless of the useful life, while a larger city may use $25,000 as a cutoff. Below $25,000 is a current expenditure regardless of its useful life in the larger city. Although some purchases may be classified arbitrarily one way or the other, the issue of what constitutes a capital purchase and what constitutes a current one usually is not controversial.

Another classification issue involves expenditures for major repairs on an existing asset. When is an expenditure to repair hurricane-damaged storm drains, dams, and other storm water management systems a capital expenditure, and when is it an operating (or current) expenditure? The damages may be so severe that the useful life of the asset may have become effectively zero; it is no longer functional. That situation is most likely to be considered the creation of a new capital asset to replace a previous asset. However, when repairs involve replacement of important system components, such as drain culverts under roadways, the decision to classify as capital or operating may depend upon whether the repair is enough to keep the drains functional through the planned life span or the repair extends the expected life span. A planned maintenance expenditure to preserve the expected life span of the component may be classified as an operating expenditure. There is no rule that fits all situations; what is a capital versus an operating expense is to some degree a matter of judgment.

Capital Decisions Versus Current Decisions

Separate Capital Budgets

The size of the expenditure and the longevity of the asset or facility purchased distinguish a capital expenditure from a current one. A third distinction of importance to decision making, the method of financing the expenditure, causes most state and local governments to pay at least some separate attention to capital expenditures in the annual budget decision-making process. Most states distinguish capital from current expenses in the form of either capital improvement plans or budgets or both, and most larger counties and cities as well as some smaller ones make similar distinctions.

Table 13-1 shows state and local capital expenditures for 2017 as a proportion of total expenditures. Considering only direct capital outlays, about 8% of state and local expenditures are for capital purposes. That is lower than the 10% to 13% level sustained by state and local governments for almost two decades. The actual expenditures do not tell the whole story, however, because most of the capital outlays at the state and local levels are financed by borrowing and hence have interest costs. With interest included,

the figure is 11%. Local government capital outlays (combined capital and interest) are a higher proportion of total outlays than state government outlays—13% and 9%, respectively. These gross percentages can obscure the real nature of the decisions to undertake capital projects. Capital expenditures cluster in only a few government functions. For local governments, school construction; utilities such as electricity, roads, sewerage, and water; and housing construction account for most direct capital outlays.

State government capital outlays also cluster in only a few functional categories, and decisions made in one year affect future budgets. More than $168 billion, or 41% of state and local public works expenditures, went to highway construction in 2015. Of that, 55% was for capital expenditures. An amount almost equal to new capital investments (45%) in highways was spent on operations and maintenance of highways built in prior years.[11]

These examples demonstrate that decisions about capital spending at the state and local levels are consequential in the year they are made and can have major consequences for future budgets. As discussed in previous chapters, it is difficult to incorporate a long-run perspective into budget decisions, especially when the decisions tend to

Table 13-1 Direct Capital Outlays as a Proportion of Total State and Local Expenditures, 2017 (Billions of Dollars)

Government	Total Direct Outlays (a)	Capital Outlays	Capital as Percentage of Total	Interest on Debt (b)	Combined Capital Outlays	Combined Capital as Percentage of Total
State and Local	3,660.1	310.4	8%	106.4	416.9	11%
State	1,764.9	122.7	7%	43.9	166.6	9%
Local	1,895.2	187.8	10%	62.5	250.3	13%

(a) Outlays here exclude duplicative intergovernmental transfers so that the figures shown are for the level of government making the expenditure even if the source of finance is a transfer from another level of government.

(b) Interest on general debt plus interest on utility borrowing is attributed in this table to borrowing for capital investment.

Compiled from Bureau of the Census original data, U.S. Department of Commerce (2017). Table 1. State and Local Government Finances by Level of Government and by State: 2017, *2017 Census of Governments*. Retrieved November 7, 2019, from https://www.census.gov/data/datasets/2017/econ/local/public-use-datasets.html. (downloadable xls file: US Summary & Alabama-Mississippi) focus in large part on personnel expenditures and only on the current-year implications of starting new programs. The fact that current-year capital budget decisions have significant implications for future operations and maintenance suggests that the effects of capital decisions on future operating budgets must be considered in any budgeting process. For state and local governments, the logic of having processes for examining capital spending decisions in more detail seems compelling. That does not necessarily entail separate capital budgets, however. In the next section, we describe capital investment planning as a set of tools that focus on capital expenditures and help consider cost implications of capital expenditures for future-year operating budgets.

Capital Investment Planning

Few governmental jurisdictions ignore the distinction between capital costs and current costs. The form in which capital and current costs are planned and budgeted varies greatly across jurisdictions. For most governments, some form of long-term capital investment plan is the starting point. Even for those without formal capital budgets, capital investment planning is still the norm. Private nonprofit associations, such as homeowners' associations, with both capital and current expenses also typically have a capital asset investment plan and differentiate between capital and current costs in their annual budgets. Illustrating with examples from different types of institutions, the following discussion focuses on a general framework for capital investment planning that highlights the data that inform capital decisions.

Multiyear Capital Investment Plans

Most governments and other organizations that distinguish between capital and current budget decisions have an established process for developing a multiyear capital investment plan (CIP) and incorporating elements of that plan into either separate capital budget and operating budgets or single budgets with capital and operating sections. Likewise, governments that do not have a capital budget still have a multiyear investment plan. Five years is a common period for projecting capital expenditures, although a longer period is often included in the statements of long-range programs. The Orange Water and Sewer Authority in Carrboro–Chapel Hill, North Carolina, has a rolling 5-year Capital Improvements Program that is updated annually, detailing a 5-year investment program. Annually, a Capital Project Resolution is adopted for the forthcoming year's capital expenditures.[12]

Michigan's Planning Enabling Act (2008 as amended 2010) requires counties, townships, cities, and villages to develop 6-year CIPSs and to update those plans annually. The CIP includes budget estimates for the full 6 years, with adoption annually only of the portion required for the next fiscal year. Michigan's CIP is integrated into an overall asset management system. For a project to be included in Michigan's capital budget, it must already have gone through the investment planning process and have been included in the CIP.[13]

Not everything included in a CIP will necessarily make its way into the capital budget, as the financial resources simply may not be available for every investment that the planning process has identified, or something in the capital investment plan may be deferred beyond the immediate 5-year plan when financing, hopefully, becomes available. **Exhibit 13-1** from the City of Durham, North Carolina, illustrates the way a capital improvement program typically contains items for which the financing is already secured as well as items for which the financing sources are not yet known and, in some cases, may never become available.

Preparation of a CIP varies considerably depending largely on the size of the town, city, public utility, or other organization. A nonprofit property owners association may hire an engineering firm to conduct a reserve or capital facilities study to evaluate the current condition of all capital assets, including roads, sidewalks, paths, swimming pools, tennis courts, amenity centers (clubhouses), beach houses, storm drains,

Exhibit 13-1 City of Durham, North Carolina, Capital Improvement Program, 2020–2025

The City of Durham, North Carolina, produces a multiyear capital improvement plan (CIP) that reports on the most recent prior year's capital investments, identifies financing that already has been approved—which could be voter approved bond issues, federal grants, or other sources—and illustrates the difference between a plan and a budget. The first table is the plan for FY2019 through FY2024 including any costs that will be incurred beyond 2024. The second table summarizes the revenue sources for those investments. To be included in the Durham CIP, the asset must have a useful life of 10 years or more and must have an investment value of over $100,000.

City of Durham
Capital Improvement Program

FY 2020 – 2025 Capital Improvement Program Summary
Summary By Project Category

Category	Prior Year	FY 2019–20	FY 2020–21	FY 2021–22	FY 2022–23	FY 2023–24	FY 2024–25	Future Years	Total Request
Culture & Recreation	26,489,448	4,454,000	75,000	2,475,000	75,000	2,475,000	75,000	2,475,000	38,593,448
General Services	56,172,597	8,801,611	0	0	0	0	0	0	64,974,208
Other Enterprise Funds	2,108,570	4,250,000	0	0	0	0	0	0	6,358,570
Public Protection	1,258,582	8,300,770	0	0	0	0	0	0	9,559,352
Solid Waste	14,923,543	4,024,020	0	0	0	0	0	0	18,947,563
Stormwater	43,969,769	6,234,000	21,300,000	8,150,000	6,025,000	1,875,000	0	0	87,553,769
Technology	7,410,209	3,200,000	0	0	0	0	0	0	10,610,209
Transportation	98,123,378	27,390,318	10,348,859	2,807,298	3,461,455	1,500,000	0	0	143,631,308
Wastewater	459,799,974	66,300,000	125,400,000	80,700,000	71,500,000	43,700,000	0	0	847,399,974
Water	278,337,240	53,855,000	54,480,000	144,249,999	25,300,000	13,400,000	5,500,000	0	575,122,239
	$988,593,310	**$186,809,719**	**$211,603,859**	**$238,382,297**	**$106,361,455**	**$62,950,000**	**$5,575,000**	**$2,475,000**	**$1,802,750,640**

[continues]

Exhibit 13-1 City of Durham, North Carolina, Capital Improvement Program, 2020–2025

(continued)

Summary By Revenue Source									
Source	Prior Year	FY 2019–20	FY 2020–21	FY 2021–22	FY 2022–23	FY 2023–24	FY 2024–25	Future Years	Total Request
GOB Authorized	11,482,325	0	0	0	0	0	0	0	11,482,325
GOB Unauthorized	239,342	0	0	0	0	0	0	0	239,342
Impact Fees	23,963,761	0	0	0	0	0		0	23,963,761
Installment Sales	69,244,459	40,848,806	0	0	0	0	0	0	110,093,265
Intergovernmental	27,547,618	2,750,000	0	0	0	0	0	0	30,297,618
Other	86,277,843	14,169,541	7,000,000	0	0	0	0	0	107,447,384
Pay-As-You-Go	221,688,638	74,114,000	112,900,000	57,250,000	52,525,000	40,075,000	0	0	558,552,638
Rev Authorized	9,533,654	0	0	0	0	0	0	0	9,533,654
Rev Unauthorized	537,765,670	54,927,372	88,280,000	175,849,999	50,300,000	18,900,000	5,500,000	0	931,523,041
Unidentified	850,000	0	3,423,859	5,282,298	3,536,455	3,975,000	75,000	2,475,000	19,617,612
	$988,593,310	**$186,809,719**	**$211,603,859**	**$238,382,297**	**$106,361,455**	**$62,950,000**	**$5,575,000**	**$2,475,000**	**$1,802,750,640**

Source: *City of Durham: Fiscal Year 2020-2025 Adopted Capital Improvement Program Plan* (tables reproduced). Retrieved November 8, 2019, from https://durhamnc.gov/DocumentCenter/View/27413/FY20-Final-CIP.

Exhibit 13-2 Capital Facilities Planning and Budgeting

---

1. Identify present service characteristics (inventory facilities and service levels)
   a. Coverage (quantity)
   b. Quality
   c. Cost per unit of service (efficiency)
2. Identify environmental trends
   a. Population growth projections
   b. Changing regulatory environment
   c. Employment and economic development trends
3. Develop service objectives
   a. Extension of service to new population or area (coverage)
   b. Improvement in quality of service
   c. Opportunities to stimulate economic growth
4. Develop preliminary list of capital projects and cost estimates
   a. Rehabilitation of existing facilities
   b. Replacement of existing facilities
   c. Addition of new facilities
5. Identify financial resources
   a. External assistance
   b. Projected growth in present revenue base
   c. Potential for direct cost recovery for individual projects
   d. Use of credit
6. Select subset of projects for inclusion in 5-year capital investment plan (CIP)
7. Identify future recurrent cost impact of CIP on operating budget
8. Include first year of CIP in annual budget estimate

---

and retention ponds. That analysis estimates the remaining useful life of these facilities, including the separable components of buildings such as roofs, HVAC systems, and pool water treatment systems. Using current cost information for replacement of the assets with estimated price inflation for the remaining life of those assets, the reserve study produces a capital needs planned replacement program with cost estimates. Such a plan flows into the association's capital reserve schedule so that annual budgets will include adequate funds to build up the association's reserve funds to meet future capital costs. It is not unusual for lenders to evaluate financing a mortgage for a family buying or building a home in a planned community whose assets are owned and managed by the homeowners, association if the association's budget includes reserves for future costs such as repaving roads or replacing the roof of the amenity center.

A CIP for a homeowner's association, compared to even small local governments, is a much simpler task. However, the elements are essentially the same. **Exhibit 13-2** illustrates a general model of the steps in a local government's capital investment planning process. In larger governments, including state governments, the overall capital investment plan is a high-level summary of more detailed capital investment plans for each department. Practices vary considerably from city to city and state to state. Exhibit 13-2 outlines a general model for a capital investment planning process consisting of eight steps. A brief description of each step follows.

Step 1: Identify Current Service Characteristics

The first step is to make an inventory of existing physical or infrastructure facilities and to assess the services provided. That assessment includes coverage and measures of quality and efficiency of service provided. For a state or local government that has not previously conducted an inventory, this first step is complex and expensive, although maintaining the inventory once established is not as burdensome. Such an inventory involves listing all physical facilities and elements of the physical infrastructure and such related information as date of construction; date of last major rehabilitation; type of construction material (such as type of road surface); and, where relevant, characteristics such as size and capacity. For a building, information may be collected on electrical wiring, fiber optics for computer hookups, plumbing, and elevators. All capital asset inventory systems offered by a variety of information technology solutions providers to the public sector contain an asset inventory module.

Quantity of service includes such characteristics as the number of people served; the proportion of total population served; the geographic area covered (area, density, and spatial distribution); and various socioeconomic groupings related to coverage, such as number of clients served by a facility. Different quantity measures are appropriate for different services.

Quality of service in part is a function of the level or the type of service provided. For example, water treatment systems that remove only bacteriological contaminants are qualitatively less effective than those that remove toxins and heavy metals as well as bacteria. Quality may also be indicated by such things as the age of the facility and its condition. The latter may be measured by the frequency-of-repair record. Qualitative measures of service, including records of citizens' complaints and structured citizen satisfaction surveys, are as appropriate as other measures.

Step 2: Identify Environmental Trends

The second step looks toward the future. Most city and state governments develop long-range planning forecasts to estimate future service requirements. These forecasts, which project population growth, commercial and industrial growth, demographic and economic changes, and so forth, are linked to the capital facilities planning process in order to develop plans for required service expansion or contraction. In addition, more detailed analyses of trends in business locations may predict possible shortages or other problems in critical areas, such as the water supply. The capital

facilities planning process can provide a means for the jurisdiction to plan expansion of services in an orderly way and can help convince potential investors that the jurisdiction is anticipating future business and residential requirements.

School buildings serve as a good example. When the school-age population of a community is increasing, the school district must plan for having, in the future, the appropriate number of buildings of the appropriate sizes and in the appropriate locations. When the population is declining, the district must plan for decommissioning school buildings. When buildings are in surplus, should they be sold off to bring in revenue for the district, or should they be converted to other purposes? Keeping a building in inventory, even though it is not used as a school, may be advantageous if the district thinks the population will increase in coming years and necessitate reopening the building, or the building may be repurposed for a completely different use.

Step 3: Develop Service Objectives

The third step is to develop level of service objectives. The process of defining the need for capital investments can take numerous forms. Not only is the technical judgment of government staff important, but so are citizens' preferences and willingness to pay. Typical ways to include citizen input include representation on long-range planning groups, open forums to discuss the need for community facilities, and referendums to approve a specific bond issue to finance a capital investment (see the chapter on capital finance and debt management). Even in jurisdictions with established channels for citizen input, a special group often convenes every 2 to 3 years just to review the current CIP and establish new priorities. Thus, a key step is to determine the service objectives that capital investments will need to satisfy.

Step 4: Develop Preliminary List of Capital Projects and Cost Estimates

Based on the first three steps, a preliminary list of capital projects can be developed, along with a timetable for completing the projects. Typically, the preliminary list includes the rehabilitation of existing facilities to improve the quality and/or efficiency of service; the replacement of existing facilities, also for the purpose of improving quality and efficiency; and the addition of new facilities or expansion of existing facilities to meet expansion objectives. The preliminary list typically will not be screened for financial feasibility at this stage.

Step 5: Identify Financial Resources

With a preliminary list of projects and cost estimates in hand, identifying the financial resources potentially available to carry out the preliminary list of capital projects is a critical next step. This step involves analyzing the jurisdiction's overall financial condition and some of the individual capital projects for possible sources of financing specific to them. Since the 1980s, an important aspect of overall financial management has been the evaluation of the financial condition of local governments.[14] In the wake of public pressure to hold steady or to cut back state and local taxes, major new revenue initiatives in the form of tax increases often are not possible, even when the need to build up infrastructure and rehabilitate existing facilities is obvious. When economic conditions improve, tax bases expand, yielding more revenue. However, sustained economic problems such as general economic recessions or locally specific economic decline due to factory closings make general tax base financing for infrastructure tenuous to plan. More commonly, state and local governments (and particularly the latter) rely increasingly on revenue sources specific to individual capital projects. User fees and property assessments have traditionally been used to finance the major portion of water and other utility capital investments as well as operating expenses. More recently, cities have exacted special impact fees and other charges from residential and commercial developers to pay for roads, water, and sewer lines and drainage intended to serve new developments (see the chapter on transaction-based revenues). Other sources of revenues tied to particular projects include grants from other levels of government and borrowing (typically involving the issuance of bonds).

Federal and state grants to local governments may help fund local government capital projects, although the federal role has declined since the 1980s with the exception of assistance during the Great Recession (see the chapter on intergovernmental relations).

Step 6: Select Projects for Inclusion in 5-Year Capital Investment Plan

Step 6 involves matching available financial resources with the set of projects included in the preliminary investment plan. Steps 3 through 6 may be iterated to eventually narrow down the list of projects and select a feasible set. Reevaluation of desired service objectives sometimes is necessary during this iterative process, because financial realities can make it clear that some objectives are impossible without major new financial initiatives. For most state and local governments, the application of complex analytical tools such as cost–benefit analysis or rate-of-return analysis plays only a small role in the selection of projects. Instead, the ranking of priorities is often based on the principle that replacing deteriorated facilities should be the first concern, meeting population growth requirements should be the second, and improving quality of services should be last.

Contemporary management tools such as the *balanced scorecard* have been adapted to help in the project selection process. This approach emphasizes balancing selection criteria among four factors—financial information, customer requirements, internal management processes, and innovation and learning—with the notion being that a structured process to balance several criteria in different categories can lead to better choices and more successful implementation than overreliance on any one set of factors.[15]

Step 7: Identify Implications for Future Recurrent Costs

Decision makers frequently neglect the recurrent cost implications of capital investments.[16] It is sometimes difficult to anticipate the costs of keeping a facility operating, and the usually valuable public relations aspects of a new project tend to overshadow the longer-run impact on the general fund budget. The problem is exaggerated by the fact that the operating and maintenance costs of any new project or facility are lower in the early years of operation, and the heavier costs fall outside the range of normal 5-year capital planning cycles. Without an analysis that takes this fact into account, a state or local jurisdiction may find itself facing the dilemma 10 or 20 years down the road of either forgoing new capital investments because of the need to budget greater funds for maintenance or neglecting maintenance in favor of more politically popular capital projects.

The analysis of future operation and maintenance costs is not all negative. If the analysis of the current capital facilities base in step 1 has been carried out well, the jurisdiction will have an idea of the current operation and maintenance costs of existing facilities. Replacing some facilities that require expensive maintenance expenditures may produce significant reductions in operation and maintenance costs in the operating budget.

Step 8: Include the First Year of the Capital Investment Plan in the Capital Budget

Once a feasible set of investments has been selected and the short- and long-term costs have been determined, the final step is to incorporate the first year of the CIP into the budget. To this point, the process, which has been one of planning and programming, may have involved input from the legislative body, but no legal appropriation of funds will have taken place. Some jurisdictions submit the CIP to the legislative body (e.g., state legislature, city council) for formal approval, but the CIP rarely includes actual appropriation of funds. Some states appropriate the full costs of capital projects, at least for smaller projects, whereas other states appropriate only the annual costs of each project. In the latter case, only a single year's cost shows up in the appropriation act. Exhibit 13-1 earlier in the chapter illustrates the link from the capital investment plan to appropriating annually a single year's capital costs.

The eight steps outlined in this section represent a generic process description. Governments may use different names for the various steps,

and likely will combine one or more steps. Most governments will, to varying degrees of intensity, carry out some aspects of each of these steps. Some may have very involved processes for garnering input from citizens. Others may only hold a public hearing at the end of a process carried out by city staff or merely publish the capital investment plan. Office of Management and Budget (OMB) Circular A-11 instructions to federal agencies on the preparation of capital requests contain requirements quite similar to these steps, starting with analysis of existing assets that are being used, or potentially could be used, to fulfill the function for which additional or new capital spending is being requested and concluding with required analysis of future operating costs.[17] The main difference between the federal budget preparation of capital investment requests and governments with capital budgets is that there is no overall federal capital investment plan and capital budget. Each federal agency prepares requests for capital as well as current expenditures, and a summary compilation and analysis are completed in the OMB, for information purposes only.

Capital Budgeting

Even though most governments of any size have some formal capital investment planning process, and the results of that process feed into budget decisions, not all governments have a formal capital budget and capital budgeting process. This section discusses capital budgeting as a decision process or budget system.

Much of the argument over the value of capital budgeting at any level of government hinges on whether there should be a separate capital budget. There is little argument over the need to examine fully the long-term implications of capital spending and not focus just on a single budget year. It is possible to have a comprehensive capital planning process that concludes with a capital investment and financing plan or a capital investment statement without a separate capital budgeting process, such as that contained in the federal *Analytical Perspectives* budget document. The amount a city council, state legislature, or U.S. Congress is then asked to appropriate may be for only 1 year, but the budget request is made in the context of future-year requirements.

Pros and Cons of Separate Capital Budgeting

Capital budgets and statements indicate the extent to which investments are being made with current expenditures. From a political perspective, this gives capital budgets a certain public relations value because government officials can show citizens that government funds are being used for the acquisition of useful assets and not solely for the payment of civil servant salaries.

On the negative side, capital budgeting can encourage political logrolling, in which various political interests agree to help each other. A capital budget can be a political grab bag, a fund where every interest can find a project. A state capital budget may provide highway projects in every county, even though the greatest need is concentrated in a small number of counties. In providing everyone with something, some important needs will not be met, while less pressing needs will be satisfied. Furthermore, if capital costs are presented in a separate budget, particularly when financed by borrowing, it may appear as if capital decisions are "costless" in the current year.

On balance, however, the arguments in favor of paying special attention to capital spending, at least at the state and local levels, seem overwhelming. Although capital budget decisions are no less political than other budget decisions, the logic of focusing attention on long-run financial and economic consequences of spending or failing to spend for capital facilities is compelling. More than current operating budget decisions, decisions to invest in infrastructure help shape the future direction, location, and extent of private economic investments in the community. A bad capital investment decision as a consequence of poor investment planning will be around to haunt a government's budget for years to come.

Local governments' capital investments may in some cases play a leading role in encouraging future local economic development, as discussed in the chapter on government and the economy. The combination of strategic planning

and capital budgeting at the state and municipal levels has been found in some studies to be positively related to overall financial performance of the municipality.[18] State and local governments compete for location of major facilities, and they sometimes offer large incentive packages comprising infrastructure projects and financial assistance to induce private companies or federal agencies to locate facilities in their jurisdictions.

Once built, major facilities will largely be limited to the uses for which they were designed. Inadequate planning of facilities can result in inadequate services, major financial burdens, or the need for expensive alterations. Excess capacity built into a community sewer system cannot be converted into other uses. Too little acquisition of land for parks in a rapidly growing suburban area may later result in a shortage of recreational opportunities or may force the local government to pay far more for space than it might have earlier.

These arguments do not mandate that capital budgets be separate from operating budgets. Although capital spending requires attention to some issues that are not germane to operating budgets, capital and operating expenditures are intertwined. As noted earlier, the mistake governments often make even with separate capital budgets or a distinctive capital planning/budgeting process is not considering long-term operation and maintenance costs. And as governments, cash strapped as a result of Covid-19, experience revenue problems, maintenance expenditures begin to be neglected. Capital budgeting, even if formalized and well done, must clearly link back to the operations and maintenance implications in the future for current capital spending.[19]

The main reason state and local governments formally segregate capital and current into two distinct, formal budgets is related to the primary means of financing large-scale infrastructure. State and local governments rarely have enough revenue to finance large capital items from regular revenues, described as a *pay-as-you-go* basis of financing, but a few do operate this way. But to appropriate the entire portion of capital facilities to be built in a given year from current revenue would typically leave insufficient funds for all the recurring expenses of state and local governments. Typically, state and local governments borrow to finance capital infrastructure, and this debt (as opposed to the annual cost of financing the debt) does not "count" in determining budget balance. Furthermore, financing capital projects through borrowing permits the annual cost of capital to be borne by the specific residents who benefit in the future from facilities as they are used to provide services each year.

Federal Capital Budgeting

Forty-nine states (excluding Alabama) and most local governments other than small towns and townships have a separate capital budget.[20] Unlike state and local governments, federal capital and current expenditures are budgeted expenses in a single year. One implication of this for the federal government is that capital expenditures, like current expenditures, are subject to discretionary spending caps placed on budget authority and outlays.[21] Despite that concern, the logic of capital budgeting is less compelling for the federal government. First, more than half of the "capital" side of the federal budget goes toward defense acquisitions—56% in 2018 and an estimated similar 57% in the 2020 budget proposal. The remainder is divided between direct federal physical capital expenditures and grants to state and local governments for capital spending. Around 13% to 14% for 2018 and 2020,

respectively, was for nondefense direct federal capital investments. Approximately one-third of the federal physical capital outlays are grants to state and local governments. **Table 13-2** shows the distribution of federal physical capital outlays in the 2020 budget. These percentages have been stable (+/−3%) for almost two decades.

If one examines only direct physical capital, excluding federal grants to state and local governments, defense physical acquisitions are about 80% of the federal total.[22] These are not investments in the same sense as state and local expenditures for water systems or highways. This statement does not mean that the purchase of nuclear-powered aircraft carriers, for example, has no implications for future operations and maintenance; rather, the need to replace a weapons system often is generated not so much by it wearing out, but by its inability to cope with new offensive or defensive systems of a potential enemy or its being destroyed or damaged beyond recovery in a combat or training situation.

Furthermore, the federal government may undertake many nondefense capital expenditures more for macroeconomic policy reasons than for investment purposes. Because of the federal government's role in stimulating the economy, capital spending sometimes has the primary objective of assisting a state or local economy rather than providing a needed facility. This was clearly

Table 13-2 Federal Physical Capital Outlays, 2018 and 2020 (est.) (in Billions of Current Dollars)

| | Total Federal Physical Capital Outlays | Direct Federal | | Federal Grants to States/Local | Federal Exclusive of Intergovernmental Grants |
		National Defense	Nondefense		
FY2018 actual	260.5	146.0	34.6	79.9	180.6
FY2020 est.	323.3	183.4	46.3	93.6	229.7
FY2018 actual	Percentage of Total	56.0%	13.3%	30.7%	69.3%
FY2020 est.	Percentage of Total	56.7%	14.3%	29.0%	71.0%

Compiled from U.S. Office of Management and Budget (2019). *Budget of the United States Government for 2020: analytical perspectives.* Washington, DC: U.S. Government Printing Office, 262.

demonstrated in the fiscal stimulus programs to address the Great Recession (see the chapter on government and the economy). So-called *shovel-ready* projects funded by federal grants to state and local governments were a major feature of the stimulus program.[23] Unfortunately, this use of capital spending often leads to earmarking or pork barrel decisions that place expensive projects in many congressional districts where the need does not really justify the expenditure.

There have been periodic calls for federal capital budgeting. At the time the unified budget was adopted at the recommendation of the 1967 President's Commission on Budget Concepts, a capital budget for the federal government was rejected.[24] There was a resurgence of calls for capital budgeting at the federal level in the 1980s and again in the 1990s, and the recession at the end of the first decade of the 2000s was a principal stimulus to renewed recommendations for a federal capital budget.

The federal budget for fiscal year 1996, for the first time, included a capital budget presentation in the *Analytical Perspectives* chapter on investment spending. The Government Accountability Office (GAO) and others argued that the federal government must adopt more contemporary financial management practices to improve the efficiency of government operations. According to these critics, federal management practices are inadequate for the task of achieving efficiency or effectiveness in government operations. This does not mean that GAO was or is in favor of a separate federal capital budget, but rather that much more systematic attention should be given to physical capital investments, to the value of those assets, and to their management.[25]

The second cause for renewed interest in federal capital budgeting is the concern that the nation as a whole—at the federal, state, and local levels—is not investing sufficiently in basic infrastructure, to the long-run detriment of the economy. More than three decades ago, Congress established the National Council on Public Works Improvement and gave it the mandate to assess the state of the nation's capital infrastructure and make recommendations for improvement. In 1988, the Council published the influential

Fragile Foundations: A Report on America's Public Works.[26] In the same year, the National Academy of Sciences published the results of a major study of American cities' infrastructure facilities.[27] Both studies expressed grave concerns about the inadequate level of infrastructure investment at all levels of government in the United States. The section on Asset Management later in this chapter discusses this continuing concern for inadequate infrastructure investment in more detail.

Many of those concerned that the level of investment in infrastructure is too low have argued that the federal budget is biased against such capital investments because it must show the full cost of the capital outlays in the construction years instead of showing only the annual depreciation of the investments over their long lives.[28] A capital budgeting statement might show only 1 year's depreciation value in the current year budget, spreading the budget implications of such an investment over the expected years of benefits. This approach would more clearly isolate how much of the federal deficit is due to investments that will pay for themselves through future economic growth and might reduce some concern for the size of the deficit.

In 1997, President William Clinton appointed the President's Commission to Study Capital Budgeting. That commission examined primarily federal capital spending, but also considered the larger question of the nation's total investment in productive capital. The commission concluded that the federal budget process does not give enough attention to the long-term implications of capital spending, given that capital investments are expensed in the federal budget in the years in which the costs are incurred. However, the commission also did not recommend the creation of a separate federal capital budget, or a capital budgeting process. The recommendation focused on providing information in the annual federal budget to focus congressional decisions and public awareness on the physical infrastructure stock; the investments proposed in a given year for capital investments, especially nondefense; and the longer-term maintenance requirements implied in proposed investments, as well as the maintenance costs in the budget for previous investments.[29]

In 2008–2009, the Brookings Institution undertook an examination of a federal capital budget and the implementation of the stimulus programs during the early stages of the recession. The study evaluated both the question of the adequacy of the nation's spending on capital investments and the question of whether a federal capital budget would improve upon the way federal investments are evaluated and funded. Specifically included in the study was the possibility of creating a National Infrastructure Bank, discussed in the chapter on capital finance and debt. The study's findings were consistent with the general view of many other analyses that infrastructure investment combined across federal, state, and local governments is not keeping up with the combined effects of population and economic growth and the deterioration of aging infrastructure. However, the report concluded that a federal capital budget would not do much to solve the problems.[30]

The various discussions of improved presentations of capital investments and the serious concerns about underinvestment in infrastructure have not led to the adoption of capital budgeting at the federal level. Outlays for acquisition of assets or construction of facilities are still recorded fully in the year acquired or constructed. In contrast, in state and local capital budgets, full investment cost is shown, albeit in connection with the method of financing. So, when a state government borrows (typically issues bonds) to finance highways, the bond issuance and construction costs are fully disclosed, but the only impact of the project in the operating or general budget is the cost of debt service—principal and interest payments (see the chapter on capital finance and debt management).

Federal capital budget presentations, by contrast, are not linked to any specific method of financing, and they do record in the budget the full construction or acquisition cost incurred in that year. That is unlikely to change soon.

In the *Analytical Perspectives* volume of the annual federal budget, a chapter on federal investments continues to discuss the nature of federal expenditures on physical capital, and other types of investments such as research and development funding and education. But there has been no resurgence of interest in a federal capital budget or capital budgeting process. **Table 13-3** is the

Table 13-3 Federal Investment Outlays, All Investment Purposes, 2018–2020 (Billions of Dollars)

	2018	2020
Major public physical capital investment:		
Direct federal:		
National defense	146.0	183.4
Nondefense	34.6	46.3
Subtotal, direct major public physical capital investment	180.6	229.7
Grants to state and local governments	79.9	93.6
Subtotal, major public physical capital investment	260.5	323.3
Conduct of research and development		
National defense	49.1	64.3
Nondefense	65.2	70.3
Subtotal, conduct of research and development	114.3	134.6
Conduct of education and training		
Grants to state and local governments	56.1	59.7
Direct federal:	54.5	69.0
Subtotal, conduct of education and training	110.6	128.7
Total, major federal investment outlays	**485.4**	**586.7**

Compiled from U.S. Office of Management and Budget (2020). *Budget of the United States Government: fiscal year 2020, analytical perspectives.* Washington, DC: U.S. Government Publishing Office, 262.

federal investment outlays table, including all types of investments—physical capital, research and development, and education and training—from the fiscal year 2020 budget.

Capital Project Analysis

In this section, we discuss methods for analyzing prospective capital investments. Some of the tools discussed can be used for nonphysical capital investments as well. Many social programs, for example, are discussed in terms of the costs of the programs and measures of effectiveness that may be output oriented (the number of participants in a workforce training program, for example) or outcome oriented (the reduction in morbidity and mortality from introducing an immunization program against a specific disease). In this chapter, we are concerned with analytical approaches to the investment and return on investment from physical capital expenditures, such as water treatment plants, highways, elementary schools, and so forth. Conceptually, the overall approach most often used is a form of cost–benefit analysis.

Cost–Benefit and Cost-Effectiveness Analysis

We can distinguish between cost–benefit and cost-effectiveness analysis. Both types attempt to relate costs of projects or programs to performance, and both quantify costs in monetary terms. They differ, however, in the way they measure the outcomes of programs.

Cost-effectiveness analysis measures outcomes in quantitative but nonmonetary form. For example, an investment in redesign and construction of a dangerous highway intersection might focus on such outcomes as accidents prevented, deaths averted, and reduction in time lost to lengthy traffic delays from accidents at that intersection. Cost–benefit analysis, by contrast, measures program outcomes in monetary form, thereby allowing for measuring the extent to which economic returns exceed economic costs, or vice versa. In the case of constructing a multilane, divided highway, for example, cost–benefit analysis would estimate the

dollar value of reduced wear and tear on vehicles and time saved to travelers and would use that figure to calculate the economic value of the gains. It would then compare those benefits to the dollar value of the cost of building and maintaining the highway.

A national nonprofit transportation research group, TRIP, conducted a study of the costs of aging and congested roads that concluded California drivers spend an additional $22.1 billion annually in vehicle operating costs. The study also calculated the financial cost of accidents and of time lost due to congestion; those costs were $9.8 billion related to safety and $29.1 billion related to congestion.[31] If these costs could be saved by capital investment projects to alleviate road segments, a bridge, or bottlenecks, such as those reported in the TRIP report, then those savings would be counted as benefits in performing a cost–benefit analysis.

Large numbers often cited in studies such as the TRIP report on California may seem almost fantastical. It may be hard for decision makers to relate to such aggregate numbers without seeing it as it affects individuals or small companies. A concrete example is the story of The Advance Group trucking company that runs 40 trucks daily into Manhattan. That company estimated pothole damages to the fleet at $65,000 each winter. Staff of AdvantaClean, a company that services air systems in large buildings, spend about half of their time traveling to their jobsites in the New York City area. The president of Advanta-Clean estimated that infrastructure investments could save as much as 35% of the time cost of employee travel to jobsites and increase company revenue by 25%.[32] Of course, estimates such as those may or may not be the result of careful measurement, but they do illustrate real examples of what is behind the large numbers produced in statewide or even national studies.

Attaching monetary value to some things, however, can be controversial. Some investments in physical infrastructure may have as the primary impact a reduction in morbidity (disease) or mortality (death), or both. For example, controlling or eliminating environmental conditions that breed mosquitoes, such as an investment in draining a low-lying area, may have the aim of reducing illness and death from malaria and other mosquito-borne diseases. A cost-effectiveness analysis of that program might compare the environmental intervention with an indoor residual spraying program or the issuance of insecticide-treated bed nets that intend to kill or ward off mosquitoes from being able to infect household residents. The analysis would focus on monetary costs of the various interventions and nonmonetary results such as reduction in the number of malaria cases, deaths averted, reduction in days lost to debilitating disease, and so forth.

A cost–benefit analysis of the same investment comparisons would place monetary value on deaths averted, workdays not lost to debilitating illness, and so forth. The potential technical merit of cost–benefit analysis over cost-effectiveness analysis is that the former allows for analysis across subject areas. When the expressed ratio of benefits to costs of a program is 1.0, costs are equal to benefits. As the ratio increases, the benefits outweigh the costs. In theory, if government investment in a new high-efficiency airplane yielded a ratio of 1.7 and a highway traffic control program yielded a ratio of 2.5, then, based on the standard of economic efficiency (and assuming the magnitude of the programs is similar), government would be advised to favor the traffic control program over the air transportation program. Cost-effectiveness analysis, in contrast, would not allow such direct comparisons because the effects would be expressed in time saved for one program and lives saved for the other.

For a private sector company, capital projects can be evaluated and choices made in terms of the financial results to the company's owners, such as the stockholders. General Electric (GE) can make choices between investing in the aviation jet engine business and the electric turbine business and can let the monetary returns relative to the monetary costs guide the decision. A local government cannot as easily make the same kinds of tradeoff decisions as a private company. A local government responsible for both water and sewer service cannot just decide that because the economic returns on a water project are greater than they are for the sewer project, it will just not

provide sewer service. What the local government typically must do in this kind of comparison is decide what possibilities exist for redesigning both projects, for changing the timing of when water and sewer projects will be implemented, and what possibilities exist for more favorable financing terms. But even though compromises will be made, the local government cannot simply decide that citizens do not get sewer service the way GE can decide to go into or to exit a line of business. Regulatory matters may be more important that economic decisions. A local government may be forced to install a sewer system or upgrade an existing system because of state and federal regulations. An economic analysis in that situation could not focus on performing the sewer system upgrade or not, but economic analysis could be used to evaluate the most efficient alternative design among several to meet the regulatory requirement.

The following paragraphs discuss the various issues that arise in public sector decision making on capital projects within an overall economic and financial framework. We make the distinction between *economic analysis* and *financial analysis* to emphasize that there are some differences between a project being valuable (generating returns) for economic reasons and being valuable because it generates direct financial returns to the organization making the investment.

Financial benefits and economic benefits are almost never entirely the same thing. A *financial analysis* is limited to the direct, actual revenue the company would be expected to earn or decreased costs as a result of an investment. For a local government, the financial return may be the increased tax revenues that are estimated to accrue to a jurisdiction as a result, for example, of a major urban renewal investment, which increases property values. An *economic analysis* includes the financial benefits, but also estimates other benefits, such as the dollar value of savings from reduced workdays lost to alcohol abuse. Those dollars saved would not typically be realized in terms of additional revenue flow, and hence would not typically count as financial returns.

Every public sector capital project has both kinds of returns. Financial returns are the actual cash flow returns to the government that are direct results of the investment. Economic returns may also be measured in dollar terms, but some economic returns do not come in the form of direct cash flow to the jurisdiction making the investment. Extending the distribution of the water system has direct financial returns in the form of user payments for the water, but it also may make water using commercial activities more efficient than the means they relied upon before they got service from the utility. Economic analysis would attempt to measure the value of those efficiency gains in dollars, but these would not be cash flow to the water utility. The World Bank, in appraising a loan for a capital investment program in a developing country, would require that both economic and financial returns be measured.

Identifying Costs and Benefits

The first basic issue in an economic or financial analysis of a capital project is deciding what counts as a cost and what counts as a benefit. It is usually different for an economic analysis versus a financial analysis. Determining the financial costs of existing programs is often difficult because accounting systems are designed to produce information by organizational unit and not necessarily by program. Only if all the costs of a program are captured in one organizational unit in the accounting system will the financial costs be easy to measure. For capital projects, the acquisition or purchase price and the construction costs are relatively easier. The engineering specifications lead to cost estimates that are based on the labor, materials, technology, and other inputs, and the actual construction or acquisition costs are easily captured in the accounting system.

Even when the costs are identified in this manner, all that is produced are the direct financial expenditures of government in executing the project. There are other possible costs that must be incorporated in the analysis. Purchasing the right of way for a road project may stretch over several years, and original cost estimates in the analysis may not be accurate with the market value and willingness of owners to sell. Indeed, critics often charge that analyses overlook the costs imposed on others. Failure to consider all costs tends to weight the analysis in favor of the proposed project under review. If personal residences have to be acquired and demolished to secure the right of way for a road project, the cost of purchasing those properties can be measured, but subsequent lawsuits may award larger amounts to the property owners, and those additional costs may or may not ever be attributed back to the construction project. Furthermore, even if they are, they may be too late to influence the decision itself, as the suits likely will not be resolved before the project is finished. Similarly, the money paid to property holders for their condemned property may not fully reimburse them for their purchase of a comparable property and moving, and those additional costs imposed on the property owners never will be measured in the cost analysis. Similarly, the psychological costs of uprooting families from long-established neighborhoods will not be measured formally in economic terms.

Externalities

A capital project may have indirect effects that are not directly measured. There may be indirect costs as well as benefits, called *externalities,* that affect individuals, businesses, the public in general, and the local or regional economy. These *spillover, secondary*, and even *tertiary* costs and benefits affect parties other than the ones directly involved. In the private sector, air and water pollution from industrial plants are externalities. The main concern of a private enterprise is making a profit, but part of the cost of production may be imposed on persons living in the area. Residents of areas downstream and downwind of the plant may pay the costs of discomfort, poor health, and loss of water recreation opportunities. They may also experience an actual decrease in the value of their assets, such as their homes, if the pollution is bad enough to make it difficult to sell property. If a municipality downstream has to treat water that has been polluted by the plant, there are financial costs to the treatment authority that are easy to identify, but the costs imposed on consumers, particularly health effects, even after increased treatment may be unknown for years or decades, as illustrated by

---

Exhibit 13-3 The Direct and Indirect Costs of Chemical Releases in the Cape Fear River

GenX is a chemical developed to replace a former key ingredient discovered to be toxic in the manufacture of Teflon, the coating used in many brands of nonstick cookware and industrial products such as sealants. In 2018, GenX was discovered in the water supply of towns and cities drawing their water from the Cape Fear River, including more than 250,000 customers in the Wilmington, North Carolina, area. Investigations led to discovery that Chemours, the manufacturer of Teflon, had been dumping GenX in the Cape Fear River from its plant near Fayetteville for decades.

GenX is a regulated chemical with determined levels above which its presence is a health threat. Frequent monitoring starting in 2018 of the levels of the chemical in the river, in the air near the plant, and in private wells supplying individual homes with drinking water found the levels to be substantially in excess of that considered safe, and in excess of the levels specified in operating permits issued Chemours by North Carolina.

The externalities from this chemical discharge illustrate the broad range of spillover effects:

- Costs to state and local agencies in increased monitoring and analysis costs;
- Costs to water utilities to install new treatment methods; and
- Costs to individuals who, in some cases, had to acquire safe water from new sources.

The costs of those externalities are relatively easy to measure in dollars. Other, not easily measured, externalities potentially[a] include the following:

- Costs of short-term illnesses such as respiratory infections from exposure to GenX in the air and well water;
- Costs of potential long-term illnesses, such as various cancers, that may not show up in more than a decade; and
- Costs of developmental disabilities that may show up in children consuming GenX in their water supply since birth.

a. These potential costs are possible consequences of ingesting or coming into contact with GenX. The science of measuring and determining safe exposure levels and the degree of culpability of Chemours as the source are all matters of pending and future lawsuits, unlikely to be resolved for many years.

Various articles in the news media, particularly the *Wilmington Star News* and *Raleigh News and Observer*; television reporting and coverage of public officials' press conferences over the period January 2018 to the publication of this book; public hearings and testimony of expert witnesses; and national media coverage, an example of which is Otterbourg, K. (2018). Teflon's river of fear. *Fortune*, May 24. Retrieved July 10, 2018, from https://fortune.com/longform/teflon-pollution-north-carolina/.

---

the dumping of chemicals used in the manufacture of nonstick coatings (see **Exhibit 13-3**).

Most government capital expenditure decisions involve similar spillover effects. The costs of an urban redevelopment program are not just the financial outlays required for purchasing and clearing land, but also the costs imposed on the families and businesses that must relocate. One government's decision can affect thousands of individuals; businesses; nonprofit organizations such as churches, synagogues, and mosques; and other governments.

Some argue that there are no such things as secondary or spillover effects, that all effects of a program should be part of the explicit benefits and costs of that program. This idea is sometimes expressed as the belief that every affected individual or organization should have *standing* and should thus be taken into account in any analysis of the program.[33] Affected parties are said to be *stakeholders* in that they have interests regarding the outcomes of the program and any decisions that may change it.

Redistributive Effects

Related to spillover costs and benefits are redistributive effects, which analysts once tended to ignore. Today, consideration of major infrastructure projects encompasses their potential redistributive effects. For infrastructure projects, the question is whether some groups in society will benefit more than other groups. In the example of the high-efficiency airframe investment mentioned earlier, the program presumably would benefit middle- and upper-income groups, who would be the ones more likely to take advantage of this means of transportation. However, benefits from reduced fuel consumption, while directly benefiting airlines and passengers, indirectly benefit all of society from the reduced air pollution and reduced contributions to global warming. Other criteria for judging redistribution include race, educational level, and occupational class.[34] The effects of programs on different generations in the population have increasingly become a focus of attention.

Common tools exist for analyzing redistributive effects, including *Lorenz curves* and *Gini coefficients* of inequality (see chapter on government and the economy for explanation of Lorenz curves and Gini coefficients and their calculation). For capital infrastructure projects, an analysis of the current situation in a jurisdiction before the project is built and after the project is completed could see if the existing Gini coefficient measure of income inequality improves, worsens, or is unaffected. However, note that a project must be large relative to the population of the jurisdiction undertaking the project to even imagine that income distribution would be affected enough to warrant the analysis. See the chapter on government and the economy for descriptions of Gini coefficients of inequality.

Subjective Information

Analyses often must rely on subjective, attitudinal data as distinguished from data that gauge behavior. One objective measure in the city road example discussed above might be the miles of roads resurfaced, while an attitudinal measure of the same program might be citizen satisfaction with road conditions. It is indeed possible for citizens (stakeholders) to exhibit no increase in satisfaction even though road conditions may have improved markedly. The same type of situation can develop regarding police protection. Citizens' fear of being burglarized may not decrease despite a decline in the burglary rate brought on by the acquisition of city surveillance technology. In addition to not feeling safer, citizens may also feel that the surveillance system is an invasion of privacy.

Analytical models such as cost–benefit and cost-effectiveness analyses are based on rational behavior models in which individuals are presumed to respond to choices based on the desire to maximize their personal utility. Behavioral research calls into question these underlying assumptions, with the consequence that a supposedly rational result of analysis still may not be the actual preferred result of those affected by the project. Methodologies to consider these more subjective perspectives involve surveying preferences of stakeholders or those with presumed interests in a potential project and assessing their subjective values. *Contingent valuation* surveys, discussed later, are one contemporary approach to measuring how much value survey respondents place on alternative possibilities.

The generic capital investment planning process discussed in the first section of this chapter, typical of many local governments, incorporates several opportunities for citizen involvement. For some, the CIP itself is the product of a joint government and citizen advisory committee, whereas the government's capital budget is the operationalization of that CIP.

Internal Validity

When costs, benefits, and expected relationships among them are defined, analysis must consider whether other possible variables may influence outcomes. Such influence is a threat to internal validity.[35] The example in Exhibit 13-3 of the chemical GenX in the drinking water supply of customers downriver from the chemical plant includes possible future health effects on infants consuming water with higher than permitted levels of GenX. Developmental disabilities that may develop years in the future in some children exposed to GenX conceivably could have other causes, including access to regular medical care both pre- and postpartum, dietary factors unrelated to drinking water, and so forth. If the incidence of developmental disabilities that do arise are in a small proportion of the population exposed to the chemical, the number of instances may not be enough to demonstrate GenX exposure causality. If the number is large, then analyses of differences among those exposed with and without developmental disabilities may be able to eliminate some of the other possible explanations.

Similarly, a school construction program to build facilities for vocational education to increase employment among disadvantaged teenagers may seem to be effective when, in fact, it may have little influence on employment. Any increase in employment might be attributable not to school district investments but to some other program, such as one operated by a nonprofit agency or church. Whether the analysis of a capital project is rigorously quantitative in economic terms or not, every effort must be made to state clearly the causal relationships between the project(s) and the expected outcomes and then to determine the possibility of variables not related to the capital project affecting the result.

Problems of Quantification

Even if an ideal model is designed displaying all the relevant types of costs and benefits or effects of a program, the problem of quantifying them remains. What are the monetary costs imposed on families relocated by urban redevelopment activities? Part of the costs will consist of moving expenses, perhaps higher rents, and greater costs for commuting to work. These measurements go well beyond the physical investment cost of the redevelopment program. Although these items can be measured, it is much more difficult to set a dollar value on the mental anguish of having to move and leave friends behind. For the financial analysis of the urban redevelopment project, only the direct payments to families for purchasing their homes, moving expenses, and so forth will count. For the economic analysis, the higher rents they will have to pay after the move, their greater commuting costs, and so forth will also count.

Shadow Pricing

Much of the problem of setting dollar values in the analysis stems from the fact that the results of many government investments do not have market prices. Despite various limitations, the private market does provide some standard for

measuring the value of goods and services by the prices set for those. Much of analysis in the public sector, however, must impute the prices or values of programs. One such method is known as shadow pricing.[36]

Suppose an analyst is given the task of predicting the benefits of a proposed outdoor recreation project such as a community swimming facility. The average hourly value (the shadow price) to a person attending the proposed new public facility can be assumed to be what individuals on average spend per hour for similar forms of outdoor recreation. This figure multiplied by the number attending will yield an approximate value of the recreational opportunities to be provided by the facility under study.

The geographic area presumably affected by the analysis of shadow prices can complicate the analysis. For example, if there are no nearby swimming facilities, citizens are presumed to benefit from a new facility and the shadow price analysis yields a reasonable estimate of the economic benefit. However, if there are facilities nearby that charge for use, and a new public facility is built, then the value to users of current facilities that switch to the new, public facility represents value lost to the operators of the old facilities. The economic gain to society will thus be less, and perhaps even nonexistent. In contrast, if there are consumers who could not afford to pay for the current, fee-for-service swimming facilities who use the new facilities, their use does not represent lost business to the operators of current facilities, and thus there is economic value gained from the investment. Spatial considerations have become an important feature of economic analysis of investment projects.[37]

More detailed approaches can examine each form of outdoor recreation: hiking, swimming, tennis, golfing, picnicking, and so forth. In the case of swimming, the average spent per person for 1 hour of swimming at a private beach can be imputed to be the value of swimming at a public beach. One danger of such an assumption, however, is that it ignores the possibility that the quality of swimming may be different at the two beaches. If such a difference exists, the shadow price should be adjusted accordingly. Another danger is that building the new public swimming facility will change the overall market value of swimming in the area. With the additional supply—the public swimming facility—people may now be less willing to pay the price charged by the private facility. In that instance, the shadow price must reflect the changes in demand.

Shadow pricing becomes increasingly difficult and the analysis more tenuous when the subject matter for study involves functions that are primarily governmental. There is no apparent method by which a dollar value can be set for the defense capability of killing via intercontinental missiles X million people of an aggressor nation within 1 hour. Similarly, it is difficult to calculate the dollar value of avoiding one traffic fatality. The standard calculations employed require assessing what kinds of people are killed in automobile accidents, how old they are, and what income they would have earned in their remaining lifetimes.

Given the possibly questionable assumptions that must be made in estimating the dollar value of saving a life, cost-effectiveness analysis may be preferable to cost–benefit analysis. The former does not attempt to place a dollar value on life but leaves the estimation of that value to decision makers. The disadvantage is that cost-effectiveness analysis, unlike cost–benefit analysis, seldom will yield a single measure of effectiveness. A traffic safety program might be measured by the number of lives saved and by the dollar value of property damage caused by crashes. Like apples and oranges, these benefits cannot be compared.

Contingent Valuation

The amount the public is willing to pay for a particular benefit or to avoid a cost also can be measured by means of formal surveys. The methodology, known as contingent valuation, describes to survey respondents a particular service or government action and asks through various contingency statements what the respondent would be willing to pay.[38] For example, "Would you be willing to pay a fee of $0.75 per day per family to avoid the smoke and other pollution emitted by a

nearby power plant?" Depending on the response, subsequent questions would increase or decrease the $0.75 per day until the maximum price the individual would be willing to pay is identified, or how low the price has to go before the respondent says yes (including $0.00, meaning the respondent is not willing to pay anything to avoid the smoke). Guidelines for federal government cost–benefit analysis, contained in OMB Circular A-94, recommend willingness to pay as an appropriate concept for measuring costs and benefits.[39]

It is important to note that a response to a question about willingness to pay is not the same thing as observing actual behavior. Nonetheless, contingent valuation is used by both government and private industry in the valuation of resource losses due to damages, gaining prominence in its application to the *Exxon Valdez* oil spill in Alaska, and by government to assess the benefits of projected recreational and natural resource preservation programs.[40] The British Petroleum oil spill in the Gulf of Mexico in 2010 (blowout of the Deepwater Horizon rig) gave impetus to the value of the methodology in estimating the value of damage to real estate.[41] Contingent valuation studies are now almost universally required in designing multilateral donor agency–funded infrastructure construction projects that are predicated on user fees to ensure project financial viability.

Discount Rates

Another problem for analysis involves the diversion of resources from the private to the public sector and from current consumption to investment in future returns. From an economic point of view, investment in a public project is warranted only if the returns are greater than they would be if the same funds were left to the private sector and if the future returns are worth the current sacrifice. Thus, the relevant concept of the cost of a public expenditure is the value of the benefits forgone by not leaving the money in the private sector to be consumed or invested.

A dollar diverted from the private sector to the public sector is not just an equivalent dollar cost or dollar benefit forgone. Presumably, had the dollar not been collected as taxes, it would have been available for the private citizen's use in some enjoyable, immediate consumption, or it would have been available for the private citizen to invest in an interest-bearing security. If the tax is used to finance a public project that produces a benefit to that citizen, or to citizens in general, then the benefit may offset the sacrifice the taxpayer had to make in private consumption or investment. This is the concept of *opportunity cost*—the public project comes at the expense of other opportunities. How do we analyze that tradeoff? If the tax is used to finance a public project that produces a benefit to citizens, then the benefit may offset the sacrifice taxpayers had to make in private consumption or investment.

The second problem is that the public benefit typically occurs at some future time, whereas the private consumption would have been in the more immediate time period. The future public benefit, even if it could be said to be exactly equal to the benefit of private consumption, will not be as valuable because of the simple fact of its being postponed. People typically are not willing to put their money in a savings account, deferring its immediate use for some future situation, without the financial institution paying interest for the privilege of holding, and using, those savings. In the project analysis situation, as an analogue to interest paid to the saver, some charge must be made against the dollars removed from consumption for an investment in order to arrive at the current value of future consumption forgone. This charge is known as the discount rate.

The discount rate addresses both problems: the opportunity cost and the time value of money, two sides of the same coin. First, it is like an interest charge that reflects the cost of removing a dollar from private sector use and diverting it to the public sector. If a dollar could earn 4% in the private sector, investment in the public sector would be warranted (in a strictly economic sense) only if the rate of return from the public investment would be at least 4%. Second, the discount rate takes into consideration the time pattern of expenditures and returns. In general, people prefer present consumption to future consumption. A dollar that might be spent for current

consumption is worth more than a dollar that might be consumed 10 years from now.

Clearly, the choice of a discount rate has an important influence on investment decisions. Too low a rate understates the value of current consumption or of leaving the money to the private sector. Too high a rate uneconomically favors current consumption over future benefits and results in less investment than is worthwhile. The choice of a discount rate may thus determine the outcome of the analysis.

Selecting appropriate discount rates is difficult. Returning to the GE example, when choosing between investing in the jet engine business or in the power turbine business, the discount rate typically would be the cost of capital to the corporation. Because GE's capital includes both equity (stock values) and debt (loans, bonds), weighted cost of capital would be ascertained, and that weighted cost of capital typically would be used as the discount rate. GE then would, if evaluating strictly on financial returns, require that the returns (financial only) must exceed the cost of capital. That would be referred to as the *hurdle rate*. But a private corporation would typically have a higher hurdle rate because it would not just be comparing the investment with the cost of capital: It would be comparing the two different investments in many cases and would more likely select the one with the higher rate of return. Of course, many other factors would go into the investment decision.

For the public sector, private market rates are inappropriate because they include calculations of the risks of loss that lenders must consider in making a loan to a private company. In contrast, interest rates charged to governments are often lower because of the presumed lower risk of default (see discussion of public sector borrowing costs and risk in the capital finance and debt management chapter). Also, interest cost to government often is artificially low because of various guarantees against defaults and sometimes the loan's tax-exempt status. The appropriate discount rate lies between these extremes. OMB annually provides guidance to federal agencies on the discount rates that should be used for federal projects (Circular A-94, Appendix C).

In 2019, the discount rate for costs and benefits ranged from 4.1% for a 3-year period to 4.9% for a 30-year period, the equivalent nominal interest rates for federal Treasury bonds with 3- and 30-year maturities, respectively.[42]

Several discount rates may be applied to program alternatives to determine the sensitivity of the analysis to discounting. If the cost–benefit ratios of a project are well above 1.0, regardless of the discount rate used, there is little problem. A different situation arises if some plausible discount rates yield results well below 1.0. In other situations, one discount rate might result in a favorable cost–benefit ratio for alternative A and another ratio for alternative B. The point is that an arbitrary choice of a discount rate without consideration of other ranges can produce misleading results.

The relationships among costs, returns, and time are depicted graphically in **Figure 13-1**. Most investment projects involve heavy capital costs early on, followed by a tapering off to operating costs. Returns are nonexistent or minimal for the first few years and then increase rapidly. The shape of the return curve after the initial upturn depends on the nature of the particular investment and is drawn arbitrarily for illustrative purposes in the figure. The comparison of costs to benefits over time makes the necessity for discounting obvious. Higher costs occur earlier in most projects. The higher benefits that occur later are valued less because they occur later in time.

Costs and benefits must therefore be compared for each time period (usually each year), and the differences summed over the life span of the project. That is what a discount rate accomplishes. The longer it takes for returns to occur, the more their value is discounted. In effect, the situation involves compound interest in reverse. Costs occurring earlier are subject to less discounting. Thus, for a project to be economically feasible, total discounted benefits must exceed total discounted costs. This excess of discounted benefits over discounted costs is known as the *net present value* (NPV). Government expenditures are efficient allocations of a society's resources when the NPV is positive. Any spreadsheet software contains built-in functions for calculating the NPV, the internal rate of return, and similar concepts useful in assessing the value of benefits occurring over time in comparison with the costs of the investment.

Measuring the Return on Investment

Two forms of calculating the rate of return on investment are typically used in capital project analysis. If the project is similar to what a private

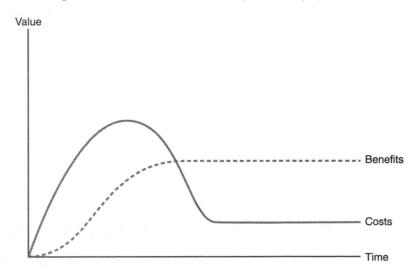

Figure 13-1 Relationship of Costs and Benefits to Time.

company might do, such as build a parking garage for which customers will pay fees to cover the costs of the facility, then the first analysis will be a financial rate of return (sometimes called a *financial internal rate of return* or FIRR). The full costs of the project are measured on the cost side, and the financial returns in the form of charges to customers over the life span of the garage are the measures on the benefit side. The expectation is that the garage would earn revenues, considering the long time period over which those revenues would be earned as exhibited in Figure 13-1, that would yield a positive FIRR.

Similarly, the extension of water lines into a new neighborhood would yield revenue in the form of hook-up charges and regular charges for water use. A FIRR analysis would inform the decision makers if the planned costs for hook-up fees and regular usage fees would yield a positive financial rate of return. Because private providers build and run parking garages and private companies may provide water services, the financial analysis of a project is important in order to evaluate whether the public investment in either facility pays for itself through future revenue generation. If it does not, then decision makers would in effect need to approve a government subsidy for the project to go forward.

The results of the financial analysis, if the financial return is less than an equivalent privately provided option, do not automatically mean the project should not be done. There may be good reasons to go forward anyway, including, as discussed earlier, positive externalities of a nonfinancial nature or redistributive benefits such as a subsidy element for low-income families. But the strict analysis of financial costs and financial returns makes the value of these other considerations apparent even if they were not directly measured.

Of course, not all projects yield direct revenue. Construction of a recreation facility from which the public could not be excluded or regulated through charging fees for use would yield benefits to the community, but if it is open to the public without charge, it would yield no revenue. As noted in the discussion of shadow pricing

previously, imputed prices, the prices people might pay for other recreational opportunities, may be used nonetheless to calculate a rate of return. That rate of return would be called an *economic internal rate of return* (EIRR).[43]

These examples might seem as if economic and financial rates of return are just two names for the same thing—that an analyst may use either one or the other indifferently. For some projects, both an FIRR and an EIRR are likely to be calculated, and the results are likely to be different. For example, if the water line extension example includes health benefits to the previously unserved neighborhood whose well water contained some levels of toxic substances, such as illustrated in Exhibit 13-3, then there would be value to society from the project that would be additional to the financial cash flows from the hook-up and usage fees.

If a reduction in illnesses means fewer days lost to productive work and fewer costs for health care, then the monetary value of those additional workdays and the reduction in health care costs would be added to the financial returns, even though there would be no attempt actually to *charge* the individuals in their water rates for those health benefits. Similarly, if the project imposed costs on other individuals, or the government as a whole, such as the additional costs to people who had to relocate from their homes, then those costs would be added to the project costs. The economic rate of return analysis typically includes all the financial costs and benefits, but also adds in economic costs and benefits that are not reflected in the financial structure of the project. Some financial benefits, such as any tax gains a government may gain from a capital project, are excluded from an economic rate of return calculation. The calculation methods are identical; the difference is what is put into the cost stream and the benefit stream.

Asset Management

Asset management historically was not tied directly to budgeting, not even in the context of capital budgeting. However, the increasingly sophisticated financial management systems that larger governmental jurisdictions employ may blur the lines as comprehensive systems link modules for capital budgeting, asset management, and operating (current) budgeting. Examples cited earlier in this chapter of the City of Durham, the Orange Water and Sewer Authority, and Michigan's requirements for local governments all demonstrate the practice, and in some cases the mandate, that capital budget preparation is a component of a larger program of capital asset planning and management. Two factors have contributed to the much greater emphasis now given to the role of asset management in public sector organizations—the concern beginning in the 1980s that many state and local governments had allowed critical infrastructure to deteriorate without any adequate planning for its replacement, and the 1999 release of GASB Statement No. 34, amended and updated several times since then.

Asset Decline
Asset Decline in the United States

Concern for the condition of America's deteriorating infrastructure base emerged in the early 1980s. In that decade, spectacular incidents, such as the collapse of the Mianus River Bridge in Connecticut, drew national public attention for perhaps the first time to dangerous conditions with the nation's infrastructure. Since then, the 2007 collapse of an interstate highway bridge in Minnesota that killed 13 people further dramatized infrastructure problems. The discovery of lead throughout the Flint, Michigan, water system that required far more investment than the city could afford is still another example. Infrastructure disasters and investment needs were a large issue in the 2016 presidential campaign, with both candidates promising major increases in federal infrastructure spending.

Advocacy groups regularly publicize estimates of investment needs. For example, the American Society of Civil Engineers (ASCE) in 2017 estimated that the combined public infrastructure deficit in facilities such as water systems, schools,

airports, and highways required a $4.5 trillion investment through 2025.[44] That figure was one-third larger than the total amount of municipal debt outstanding that year ($3.7 trillion).[45]

There are legitimate concerns about estimates of such large numbers. Advocacy groups representing industries in transportation, water and wastewater systems, and so forth may promote their interests by only presenting worst case scenarios. One report compared the ASCE estimates with estimates from the agencies responsible for federal efforts. The report cited ASCE's estimate of $2 trillion needed in roads and bridges, in contrast to the Federal Highway Administration's estimate of $836 billion. Similarly, the ASCE estimate of $1 trillion for drinking water systems contrasted with an Environmental Protective Agency (EPA) estimate of $400 billion.[46] Comparisons among these large-scale estimates are difficult. ASCE's 2017 report projects need through 2025. CNNMoney's contrasting figure was for an unspecified time target. EPA's own estimate in a 2018 report estimated drinking water systems investments needed over a 20-year investment period (through 2035) as $500 billion.[47] A GAO report in 2017 cited an EPA estimate of a slightly different 20-year needed investment (2012–2032) in both water and wastewater systems as $700 billion.[48]

A different slant that benchmarks U.S. infrastructure investments with China is a 2018 Congressional Budget Office report that total public spending on infrastructure was 2.5% of gross domestic product (GDP) in the United States, contrasted with China spending an estimated 9% of GDP.[49] Despite the differences in the magnitude of investments, and the potential biases that may be built into some estimates, there are no serious research-based estimates that do not show a significant gap between investment spending to remedy infrastructure problems and actual and planned spending.

All the studies define an infrastructure deficit as facilities that have outlived their usefulness and need replacement as well as facilities needed to address unmet needs of unserved and underserved populations. For example, some sewer systems still in use are more than 100 years old.

An earlier Congressional Budget Office study noted that sewer pipes, for example, have an average asset life of 50 years, and that many systems in major U.S. cities had reached or were approaching that age.[50] In addition, when governments do not spend adequately for maintenance and rehabilitation, facilities may not last anywhere near their useful life span. But budgeting enough amounts in the operating budget for repairs and maintenance in order to avoid or reduce capital costs 20 years hence is not easy for elected executive and legislative officials.

Asset Decline in Other Countries

Concerns over infrastructure deficits are not limited to the United States, causing similar concern for improved systems for planning and budgeting and then managing the assets once built. European Union countries and especially developing and emerging market countries experience shortages of capital to construct physical facilities and often also fail to support existing capital facilities with adequate operation and maintenance. The collapse of Asian financial markets in the 1990s and the later scandal-related collapse of Enron staggered what had been a growth market in global private investment in infrastructure in booming Asian economies, leaving many countries increasingly concerned that public infrastructure could not keep up with demand for services. The 2007–2008 financial markets collapse exacerbated the problem for the world's industrial economies, but China, India, Brazil, and some other emerging economic powers were able to sustain needed infrastructure investments. Public infrastructure investments in emerging market economies has again become a more attractive focus, especially for U.S. investors, particularly those with long-term investment targets such as major pension funds.[51]

Spending on Infrastructure

The U.S. physical infrastructure asset base exists primarily because of state and local government investments. As far back as the mid-1950s, state and local capital spending greatly exceeded federal capital spending. In 1956, state and local capital spending on infrastructure amounted to almost $28 billion, whereas federal capital spending was less than $10 billion. A gradual climb in federal spending led to its overtaking state and local capital spending in 1976, and it remained higher until significant federal budget cutbacks affected capital spending in 1986.[52] **Figure 13-2** documents for selected years since 1980 federal (nondefense), state, and local government

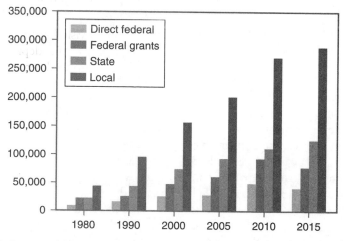

Figure 13-2 Federal, State, and Local Roles in Public Works Funding, 1980–2015, Selected Years (Millions of Dollars).

Compiled from Federal from Office of Management and Budget (2019). *Budget of the United States, FY 2020: historical tables* (pp. 173 and 237). Washington, DC: U.S. Government Printing Office; State from ProQuest LLC (2019). *Statistical abstract of the United States: 2019* (p. 299). Lanham, MD: ProQuestLLC.

expenditures for public works facilities specifically. This includes highways, airports, water transport and terminals, sewage, solid waste, water supply, and mass transit.

Figure 13-2 gives some indication of the relative roles played by federal, state, and local governments in public works funding. The amounts for the three sources are all for direct spending on capital assets. By far, local governments exceed both federal and state governments, and even exceed federal and state combined. As can be seen in Figure 13-2, more than 50% of the total is local government spending in each of the six selected years starting in 1980. States are next, at around 24%, and federal direct (spent directly by federal agencies on capital projects) is, in all the years in the figure, less than 10%. The federal grants figure shows the contribution the federal government makes, for nondefense capital investments only, through intergovernmental grant transfers. Federal grants for physical capital investment historically were a relatively small contribution. Programs introduced in the 1970s caused federal grants to state and local governments for physical capital investments to double between 1975 and 1980 and then drop after 1980. In Figure 13-2, federal grants in 1980 for capital projects carried out at the state or local level were just over 23% of total physical capital expenditures. In the other three years depicted, federal grants have been around 15% of the total. When federal direct spending and federal grants are combined, federal finance support for capital investment in 1980 was just over 31%. For the remaining years in the figure, combined federal capital spending was 23% to 27% of total capital investment. There was a jump in federal grants and direct spending for public works in the Great Recession, but as the figure shows with the 2015 data, the federal increases were temporary.

The concern for deterioration of existing physical assets and corresponding inadequate investment levels prompted larger city governments and the more populous states as early as the early 1980s to begin developing, or purchasing from financial information services firms, more sophisticated approaches to planning and

managing the infrastructure base. But the introduction of GASB Statement No. 34 in 1999 raised the bar on financial reporting standards for state and local governments, forcing more rigorous attention to the condition of the asset base in reporting on the overall health of the institution. Here we discuss its impact on capital asset reporting.

Capital Assets in GASB Statement No. 34

Statement No. 34 requires that governments report their capital assets in a *statement of net assets* and requires that the report show the depreciation in the value of those assets. Specific asset reporting requirements include the following:

- Depreciation of assets must begin when the asset, equipment, or facility is acquired or put in service;
- Accumulated depreciation for all assets must be reported; and
- Assets acquired or built prior to 1980 are not required to be reported, but once a major renovation of an older asset has been carried out, then the rehabilitated asset must be included in the statement of net assets.[53]

The difference that this makes to capital and operating budget practices is substantial.[54] GASB No. 34 gives visibility to the expected life span of facilities and the depreciation of the assets through the financial reporting process. In turn, citizens may observe the adequacy of the operating budget's provisions for operation and maintenance and provision for future replacement costs. Realistically, citizens are unlikely to pay attention to those details unless it becomes an electoral issue. However, bond rating agencies do consider the adequacy of operation and maintenance programs and provision for timely rehabilitation expenditures to avoid larger capital costs in the future (see the chapter on capital finance and debt management). The financial reporting requirements for physical assets more readily expose to financial institutions and bond underwriters the overall health of a jurisdiction's infrastructure and the adequacy of budget planning to preserve those assets. That, in turn, can affect the bond rating and therefore the interest the jurisdiction will have to pay on a bond issue. As a result, an increasing number of state and local governments have adopted comprehensive systems for assessing physical asset conditions and linking those conditions to the budgeting process, both capital budgeting and recurrent budgeting. San Diego uses a computerized inventory and mapping system to keep track of maintenance schedules on 3,000 miles of water and sewer pipes. For example, one of the features is mapping of facilities by date installed and by current condition.[55]

Requirements like GASB No. 34 in other countries also have produced similar changes. The United Kingdom Accounting Standards Board recognizes as a Standard of Recommended Practice local government asset accounting that includes asset inventories, depreciation of those assets, and changes in valuation of the assets.[56] Standard accounting practices in New Zealand, noted for its progressive public sector budgeting and financial management practices, "records state highways at depreciated replacement cost based on the estimated present cost of constructing the existing asset by the most appropriate method of construction."[57]

Asset management practices are not limited to state and local governments. At the federal level, OMB Circular A-11 was modified in 2006 in Part 300 (focusing on planning, budgeting, acquisition, and management of capital assets) to give greater emphasis to the management of federal assets. When proposing in their budget to acquire a new capital asset or significantly improve an existing asset, agencies must include with their budgets a capital asset plan and business case summary.[58] The *business case summary* explains the rationale for the investment in terms of mission and alternatives considered, and provides detailed management information on the acquisition process and subsequent management of the asset. At least three viable alternatives to the asset acquisition must be presented as part of the business case. Operations and maintenance milestones are identified in the business case

in order to ensure that there has been adequate planning to preserve the value of the asset once acquired and put into service. A plan for measuring the performance of the asset to be acquired provides the basis for subsequent monitoring to ensure that operations and maintenance activities are taking place to maximize the asset's useful life.

Summary

Governments plan and budget for the recurring expenditures for the myriad of services they provide, and governments plan and budget for major investments in infrastructure systems and equipment and other capital assets. The latter investments are the focus of capital planning and budgeting. Most state and local governments have formal systems for making capital budget decisions and segregate capital investments into separate capital budgets or statements. The reasons are twofold: state and local capital investments are a major share of their total budget decisions in any given year, and state and local governments generally rely upon various forms of borrowing (discussed in the chapter on capital finance and debt) to finance capital investments. Both reasons make capital budgeting a best practice for state and local governments.

The rationale for federal capital budgeting, despite being evaluated several times in the past four decades, has never been persuasive. Capital investments are a much smaller share of the federal budget, and much of the capital costs incurred by the federal government are for defense expenditures that are not normally considered investments or grants to state and local governments to support their capital investments. Despite not adopting capital budgeting, however, the federal government has continued to adopt financial management and reporting practices to improve upon how capital costs are communicated to Congress and the public, and how they are managed.

Whether it is a formal capital budgeting process or not, federal, state, and local governments use formal analysis tools to assist in evaluating capital investments. These tools use both economic and financial measures to assess the value of the investment to the government and consider that these are long-term investments with long-term payoff. The analytical tools do not substitute quantitative analysis for judgment in decision making, but they do expose for decision makers and the public the underlying assumptions, costs, and benefits so that good judgments can be made.

Also independent of whether capital budgets are employed or not, other pressures since the 1980s have generated demand for better decision making and better reporting on investments. Deterioration of major infrastructure systems that might have lasted much longer before having to be replaced started creating demand in the United States for better management of infrastructure systems and more informed attention to maintenance costs and the depreciating value of infrastructure. Government cost accounting standards, particularly GASB No. 34, require financial reporting of physical assets that basically demand more sophisticated and integrated planning, budgeting, and financial management systems that include a focus on asset management. This has relegated arguments about whether to have capital budgets to the back seat as, regardless of formal capital budgeting, governments must do a better job of managing the entire capital investment process.

Notes

1. Wang, X. (2014). *Financial management in the public sector: tools, applications, and cases* (3rd ed., pp. 116–119). Abingdon, Oxfordshire, UK: Routledge.
2. For example, North Carolina (2019). North Carolina General Statutes, Chapter 47 Planned Community Act (1998 as amended through 2018).
3. Governmental Accounting Standards Board (2020). *Statement of Governmental Accounting Standards No. 34, Basic financial statements—and management's discussion and analysis—for state and local government*. Norwalk, CT: Author. Retrieved April 21, 2020, from https://www.gasb.org/st/summary/gstsm34.html; Sage (2019). *Government accounting for fixed assets: GASB guidelines for your organization* (p. 4). Irvine, CA: Sage Publications.
4. U.S. Office of Management and Budget (2019). *Budget of the United States government for 2020: analytical perspectives, 20. federal investment* (p. 261). Washington, DC: U.S. Government Publishing Office.
5. Zimmer, R., et al. (2011). What types of school capital projects are voters willing to support? *Public Budgeting and Finance, 31*, Spring, 37–55.
6. Brunner, E. J., et al. (2018). Information, tax salience, and support for school bond referenda. *Public Budgeting and Finance, 38*, Winter, 52–73.
7. MacManus, S. (2004). "Bricks and mortar" politics: how infrastructure decisions defeat incumbents. *Public Budgeting & Finance, 24*, Spring, 96–112.
8. McDonald, R., & Bailly, A. (2017). *What investors want. Centre for Cities*, July 19. Retrieved July 7, 2019, from https://www.centreforcities.org/reader/investors-want-guide-cities/makes-city-attractive-investors/.
9. Crompton, J. L. (2010). *Measuring the economic impact of park and recreation services* (p. 7). Ashburn, VA: National Recreation and Park Association. Retrieved July 7, 2019, from https://www.nrpa.org/globalassets/research/crompton-research-paper.pdf.
10. U.S. Office of Management and Budget (2019). *Budget of the United States government for 2020. analytical perspectives, federal investment*. Washington, DC: U.S. Government Publishing Office, 261.
11. Calculated from ProQuest (2019). *ProQuest statistical abstract of the United States: 2019* (p. 299). Bethesda, MD: ProQuest LLC. Based on Bureau of the Census Annual Surveys of State and Local Government Finances.
12. Orange Water and Sewer Authority (2020). *Capital improvements program: fiscal years 2020–2024*. Carrboro, NC: Author. Retrieved April 21, 2020, from https://www.owasa.org/wp-content/uploads/2019/12/cipfy20-24.pdf.
13. Michigan Planning Enabling Act (2008 as amended 2010). P.A. 33 of 2008, as amended, M.C.L. 125.3801 et. seq. See for an example City of Marquette (2017). *Capital improvement plan: 2017–2022*. Retrieved July 19, 2019, from https://www.marquettemi.gov/how-do-i/view/capital-improvement-plan/.
14. Berne, R., & Schramm, R. (1986). *The financial analysis of governments*. Englewood Cliffs, NJ: Prentice Hall; McDonald III, B. (2017). Measuring the fiscal health of municipalities. *Lincoln Institute of Land Policy*. Retrieved April 21, 2020, from https://www.lincolninst.edu/sites/default/files/pubfiles/mcdonald_wp17bm1.pdf.
15. QuickScore (2019). *What is the balanced scorecard: a short and simple guide for 2019*. Retrieved July 12, 2019, from https://balancedscorecards.com/balanced-scorecard/#learn-perspectives.
16. Sorrels, J., & Walton, T. (2017). *Cost estimation: concepts and methodology*. Research Triangle Park, NC: Air Economics Group, U.S. Environmental Protection Agency. Retrieved July 12, 2019, from https://www.epa.gov/sites/production/files/2017-12/documents/epaccmcostestimationmethodchapter_7thedition_2017.pdf; Irving, S. (2011). *Budget process: enforcing fiscal choices*. Washington, DC: U.S. Government Accountability Office; Office of Management and Budget (2017). Circular A-11: Planning, budgeting and acquisition of capital assets – appendix 6: principles of budgeting for capital

investments. Retrieved April 21, 2020, from https://www
.whitehouse.gov/sites/whitehouse.gov/files/omb/assets
/a11_current_year/a11_2017/capital_programming
_guide.pdf.

17. Office of Management and Budget (2017). Circular
A-11, *Capital programming guide, appendix 6: principles of
budgeting for capital investments.*

18. Ermasova, N. (2013). The improvement of capital
budgeting at the state level in the USA. *Public Administration
Research,* 2, 2, 92–104.

19. City of Durham, North Carolina (2019). *Capital improvement
program process (2019).* Retrieved July 12, 2019, from
https://durhamnc.gov/223/Capital-Improvement-Plan-CIP.

20. National Association of State Budget Officers (2014).
Capital budgeting in the states. Retrieved July 12, 2019,
from https://higherlogicdownload.s3.amazonaws.com
/NASBO/9d2d2db1-c943-4f1b-b750-0fca152d64c2
/UploadedImages/Reports/Capital%20Budgeting%20
in%20the%20States.pdf.

21. Vesey, K. (2012). Capital budgeting by the Federal
Government. *Journal of the Washington Institute of China
Studies,* 7, 2, 36–44. Retrieved July 10, 2019, from https://
www.bpastudies.org/bpastudies/article/view/176/331.

22. U.S. Office of Management and Budget (2020). *Budget of
the United States government for 2020: analytical perspectives,
federal investment,* 262.

23. Copeland, C., et al. (2011). *The role of public works
infrastructure in economic recovery.* Washington, DC:
Congressional Research Service.

24. U.S. Office of Management and Budget (1967). *Report
of the President's Commission on Budget Concepts* (p. 34).
Washington, DC: U.S. Government Printing Office.

25. U.S. Government Accountability Office (2014). *Capital
financing: alternative approaches to budgeting for federal real
property.* Washington, DC: U.S. Government Publishing
Office.

26. National Council on Public Works Improvement (1988).
Fragile foundations: a report on America's public works.
Washington, DC: U.S. Government Printing Office.

27. Ausubel, J., & Herman, R. (Eds.) (1988). *Cities and
their vital systems: infrastructure past, present, and future.*
Washington, DC: National Academy of Sciences.

28. U.S. General Accounting Office (1995). *Budget structure:
providing an investment focus in the federal budget.*
Washington, DC: U.S. Government Printing Office.

29. President's Commission to Study Capital Budgeting (1999).
Report. Washington, DC: U.S. Government Printing Office.

30. Israte, E., & Puentes, R. (2009). *Investing for success:
examining a federal capital budget and a National Infrastructure
Bank.* Washington, DC: Brookings Institution.

31. Powell, J. (2018). Bad roads cost Calif. drivers $61B a
year, TRIP research shows. *Equipment world's better roads,*
August 20. Retrieved July 11, 2019, from https://www
.equipmentworld.com/bad-roads-cost-calif-drivers-61b
-a-year-trip-research-shows/.

32. Rosenberg, J. M. (2019). Crumbling infrastructure is
costing businesses. *Wilmington Star News,* May 30, A10.

33. Dobes, L. (2017). A cross-border perspective on 'standing'
in cost-benefit analysis. *Crawford School Working Paper
1711.* Australian National University Crawford School
of Public Policy. Retrieved July 13, 2019, from https://
crawford.anu.edu.au/sites/default/files/publication
/crawford01_cap_anu_edu_au/2017-12/a_cross-border
_perspective_on_standing_in_cost_benefit_analysis.pdf;
Whittington, D., & MacRae, Jr., D. (1986). The issue
of standing in cost-benefit analysis. *Journal of Policy
Analysis and Management* 5, 665–682; Whittington, D., &
Hanemann, W. (2006). *The economic costs and benefits of
investments in municipal water and sanitation infrastructure:
a global perspective,* CUDARE Working Paper Series
1027, University of California at Berkeley, Department of
Agricultural and Resource Economics and Policy.

34. Johnson, R., & Pierce, J. (1975). The economic evaluation
of policy impacts: cost-benefit and cost effectiveness
analysis. In F. Scioli & T. Cook (Eds.), *Methodologies for
analyzing public policies* (pp. 131–154). Lexington, MA:
Lexington Books.

35. Campbell, D., & Stanley, J. (1963). *Experimental and quasi-
experimental designs for research.* Boston, MA: Houghton
Mifflin; Shadish, W., et al. (2002). *Experimental and quasi-
experimental designs for generalized causal inference.* New
York, NY: Houghton Mifflin Harcourt.

36. Accounting Tools (2018). *Shadow pricing.* Retrieved
July 13, 2019, from https://www.accountingtools.com
/articles/2017/5/16/shadow-pricing; McKean, R. N. (1968).
The use of shadow prices. In S. B. Chase, Jr. (Ed.), *Problems
in public expenditure analysis* (pp. 33–65). Washington,
DC: Brookings Institution.

37. World Bank (2013). *Investment project financing: economic
analysis and guidance note.* Washington, DC: World Bank.
Retrieved July 13, 2019, from http://siteresources.worldbank
.org/PROJECTS/Resources/40940-1365611011935
/Guidance_Note_Economic_Analysis.pdf.

38. Winden, M., et al. (2017). A contingent valuation study
comparing citizen's willingness-to-pay for climate change
mitigation in China and the United States. *Environmental
Economics, 20,* 2451–2475.

39. U.S. Office of Management and Budget (2019). *Circular
A-94 revised, Guidelines and discount rates for cost benefit
analysis of federal programs.* Washington, DC: Author.

40. Carson, R. (2012). Contingent evaluation: practical
alternative when prices aren't available. *Journal of Economic
Perspectives, 26,* 4, 27–42.

41. Lipscomb, C. (2011). Contingent valuation and real estate
damage estimation. *Journal of Real Estate Literature,* 19,
2. Retrieved July 13, 2019, from https://www.jstor.org
/stable/24884127.

42. U.S. Office of Management and Budget (2019). *Circular
A-94 revised, Appendix C.* Retrieved November 10, 2019,
from https://georgewbush-whitehouse.archives.gov/omb
/circulars/a094/text/a94_appx-c.html.

43. Brigham, E., & Ehrhardt, M. (2016). *Financial management: theory and practice* (15th ed.). Mason, OH: South-Western Cengage Publications. This is a business-oriented text, as are most texts that provide detailed analysis of rates of return and related concepts, but the analytical framework is the same whether private sector or public sector oriented.

44. Muoio, D. (2017). The U.S. will need to invest more than $4.5 trillion by 2025 to fix its failing infrastructure. *Business Insider Online*, March 9. Retrieved July 13, 2019, from https://www.businessinsider.com/us-invest -over-4-trillion-by-2025-to-fix-infrastructure-2017-3; American Society of Civil Engineers (2017). *2017 Infrastructure report card: America's infrastructure scores a D+*. Retrieved November 10, 2019, from https://www .infrastructurereportcard.org/.

45. Securities Industry and Financial Market Association (2017). *Municipal bond credit report*. Retrieved July 13, 2019, from https://www.sifma.org/wp-content/uploads /2018/02/US-Municipal-Report-2018-02-23-SIFMA.pdf.

46. Frank, T. (2017). Civil engineers say fixing infrastructure will take $4.6 trillion. *CNNMoney*, March 9. Retrieved July 13, 2019, from https://money.cnn.com/2017/03/09 /news/infrastructure-report-card/index.html.

47. U.S. Environmental Protection Agency, Office of Water (2018). *Drinking water infrastructure needs survey and assessment: sixth report to Congress*. Washington, DC: U.S. Government Publishing Office.

48. U.S. Government Accountability Office (2017). *Drinking water and wastewater infrastructure: information on identified needs, planning for future conditions, and coordination of project funding* (p. 15). Washington, DC: U.S. Government Publishing Office.

49. Congressional Budget Office (2018). *Public spending on transportation and water infrastructure, 1956 to 2017*. Washington, DC: U.S. Government Publishing Office.

50. U.S. Congressional Budget Office (2002). *Future investment in drinking water and wastewater infrastructure* (p. 8). Washington, DC: U.S. Government Printing Office.

51. Reynard, C. (2018). Building infrastructure in emerging markets. *Forbes*, July 5. Retrieved July 13, 2019, from https://www.forbes.com/sites/cherryreynard/2018 /07/05/building-infrastructure-in-emerging-markets /#293915051fa2.

52. U.S. Congressional Budget Office (1992). *Trends in public infrastructure outlays and the president's proposals for infrastructure spending in 1993* (p. 15). Washington, DC: U.S. Government Printing Office; Congressional Budget Office (2010). *Public spending on transportation and water infrastructure* (p. 3).

53. Governmental Accounting Standards Board (2006). *Statement of Governmental Accounting Standards No. 34, Basic statements—and management's discussion and analysis—for state and local government*.

54. Pridgen, A., & Wilder, M. (2013). Relevance of GASB No. 34 to Financial Reporting by Municipal Governments. *Accounting Horizons, 27, 2*, 175–204.

55. County of San Diego (2015). *County of San Diego Sewer System Management Plan*. Retrieved July 13, 2019, from https://www.sandiegocounty.gov/content/dam/sdc/dpw /SAN_DIEGO_COUNTY_SANITATION_DISTRICT /SDCSD_SSMP_2015.pdf.

56. Ellwood, C. (2002). The financial reporting (r)evolution in the UK public sector. *Public Budgeting, Accounting and Financial Management, 14*, 572.

57. Santiso, C. (2006). Banking on accountability? Strengthening budget oversight and public sector auditing in emerging economies. *Public Budgeting & Finance, 26*, Summer, 57.

58. U.S. Office of Management and Budget (2011). *OMB Circular A-11, Capital assets* (Section 300, pp. 9–11). Washington, DC: U.S. Government Printing Office.

CHAPTER 14

Capital Finance and Debt Management

In this chapter, we discuss the means for financing capital projects. As noted in the chapter on capital planning and budgeting, capital investments are *lumpy*. That is, financing a large infrastructure project requires a large amount of capital up front, whereas the benefits and the revenue from that up-front investment are spread over many years—20 to 50 years in the case of significant infrastructure such as a sewer system. Not only will current taxpayers, or service charge payers, benefit from the investment, but future generations will too, and they should help pay for the investment.

For such large projects, few governments other than national governments have the capital or taxing power to finance the acquisition and construction of large infrastructure assets at one time. Even national governments that have massive infrastructure needs are typically unable to finance all their requirements without resorting to some form of long-term financing. The same is true of large private corporations wishing to undertake a major expansion of their production facilities, as well as most households when it comes to purchasing something as large as a home. Consequently, most governments, corporations, and households look to other sources of funds—investors or lenders—to finance up front the capital investment, and in exchange agree to

pay a financial return to those lenders/investors at a future time or times.

The primary source for governments financing large capital projects is borrowing from investors: individuals and financial institutions. In the United States, state and local governments borrow from individuals and institutions such as banks, capital market funds, and other institutional investors by issuing bonds. The generic term that is used to describe such financing instruments is *municipal bonds*. Accordingly, throughout this chapter, for securities issued by state governments, local governments, and special districts such as school and water districts, we use the term *municipal* without implying that the word municipal always refers to local governments.

At the end of the second quarter of 2019, the outstanding value of municipal securities held by various investors was more than $3.8 trillion.[1] That is almost 9% of total U.S. domestic bond market debt outstanding, a figure that has held steady since the early 2000s. From 1980 to the mid-1990s, municipal debt was 15% to 20% of total U.S. domestic debt. The decline of municipal debt as a proportion of total bond market debt is not the result of less municipal borrowing, it is the result of a substantial increase in mortgage-related bonds as a proportion of total bond market debt. (See the chapter on government and the economy for discussion of the mortgage-backed securities market collapse in the Great Recession.)

Bonds and bond issuance by governments are a major focus of discussion in this chapter. In other industrialized countries, specialized lending institutions that serve as bankers for municipalities often substitute for bond issues by individual states and municipalities. Since the 1970s, state infrastructure banks in the United States have been an important source of debt financing at the U.S. state and local levels, but they still do not approach the importance of the municipal bond market.

This chapter stresses that capital financing is not about how infrastructure is paid for. Taxpayers of a jurisdiction in general, including the entire United States at the federal level; the specific users of a service; or both, for the most part, pay for services, and that includes the costs of financing the up-front investment. This chapter on financing is about how the capital is raised for the initial investment in new facilities or rehabilitated existing facilities.

After a brief introduction to types of finance, we focus on state and local debt financing for infrastructure. Federal government borrowing is mainly for other purposes than infrastructure investment and therefore is not discussed in this chapter. The second focus of this chapter is governments' debt management practices and what happens when the borrower does not or cannot repay. Even with robust capital markets and governments in sound financial condition, borrowing is not always enough, nor is it always the best way to finance infrastructure.

The final section of the chapter focuses on private sector equity investment in public infrastructure. Over the past 40 years, there has been a substantial increase in private equity investments in public infrastructure projects worldwide, including in the United States. Private equity investments have quite different implications for financing and managing public facilities than government borrowing to finance investments. The various forms in which the private sector makes an equity investment in public services involve the government turning over part or all of the responsibility for constructing and operating some public services. As with the rest of the chapter, the emphasis on private equity investment is only for services that require large capital investments.

Types of Finance

In the private sector, there are three sources of financing capital assets: *debt*, *equity*, and *retained earnings*. Debt is available to both public and private institutions, and to households. Equity comes in the form of stock issuance in the case of publicly traded companies. Companies whose stock is traded on one of the stock exchanges—the New York Stock Exchange, for example—sell stock in order to raise capital for investment or operating purposes. Purchasers of stock then literally *own* a fraction of the corporation. They are not entitled to any *repayment* of the money invested in purchasing the stock. Rather, they are entitled to a share of the value of the corporation. They may benefit from that value if the corporation pays dividends, or they may sell the stock later for whatever it is worth at the time. If the company has performed well in the market, the value of the shares sold will have appreciated. Equity investors, of course, also may experience a decline in value and sell their stock for less than they originally invested.

The other two forms of equity capital are owners' equity investments, in the case of privately held companies, and retained earnings. In a family-owned company in which 100% of the ownership is private, not available for public sale through publicly traded shares of stock, the investments these private owners have made both initially in founding the company and potentially later as additional capital is needed are *owners' equity*. Partnerships such as law firms are privately held, and the owners' investments (partners in the firm) are the source of equity capital. Cargill, an agribusiness company, is the largest U.S. privately held company, with revenues in 2018 of more than $109 billion.[2] When a privately held company, including a state-owned enterprise that does not offer stock shares for sale, seeks equity investment, it comes either from the current owners inviting additional private owners to put capital into the company, in exchange for partial ownership, or from the existing owners contributing additional capital from their own sources.[3]

Retained earnings, essentially profits not distributed to owners, are the third source of equity capital. (Retained earnings are what households think of as *savings*.) For private companies, revenues in excess of cost may be distributed to the owners as their share of the profits, or they may be reinvested in the company for a variety of purposes, including capital facilities expansion. These *retained* earnings, earnings kept in the company for investment, are an important source of finance for capital investment.[4] Retained earnings also are achieved in the operations of public utilities such as water authorities, typically in the form of depreciation costs included in the calculation of water rates. Because a public water authority is not set up to make a profit, and certainly would not be expected to pay dividends to the owners (citizens), *excess* revenues (retained earnings) are expected to be reinvested in replacement and construction of new infrastructure assets.

In some countries, including the United States, a utility may be *owned* by the municipality it serves. In the Philippines, in the 1990s, municipalities owning water utilities expected dividends to be paid back into the municipal treasury. That practice almost decapitalized some water utilities because the *parent* municipality took capital out of the enterprise as dividends, capital that should have been retained to replace deteriorating facilities.[5] This practice of treating utilities as a revenue source for other municipal services is not unusual for municipally owned utilities in developing countries. Many U.S. cities also own some of the utilities that provide services to residents, including, for example, electricity and water. Municipally owned utilities in the United States are more tightly regulated and do not subsidize general government operating costs with excess or retained earnings intended for future capital investment in the utility.

Creditors who have lent money to a public or private enterprise legally have first recourse

to being repaid; they have the first claim on the assets of the borrower. Equity investors come in only after all debts are satisfied. In some countries, the state owns companies that are listed on that country's stock exchange(s). For example, oil and gas companies in some countries may be owned solely by the state, or in part by the state and in part by private investors. Public transportation companies, such as airlines, telecommunications, and some utilities such as electric power generation and water supply, may be organized as state-owned enterprises (SOE) with partial, usually minority, ownership in the hands of private investors. The SOE may also be fully owned by the state, with no shares traded in the market.

All three sources of finance—credit, equity, and retained earnings—are used by public sector institutions to secure the capital needed to finance investments that may be used for rehabilitating aging infrastructure or other facilities or building new capacity in order to meet the needs of a growing population, as discussed in the capital assets chapter.

State and Local Debt Financing

State and local governments rely upon debt capital to finance many types of public facilities and infrastructure. In the United States, the main source of debt financing is issuing bonds in the securities market to finance major infrastructure investments. Commonly referred to as municipal bonds, bonds are issued by state and local general-purpose jurisdictions as well as many nonprofit public institutions, such as hospitals, and single-service authorities, such as school and water districts. Municipal bonds are debt instruments in that the issuer incurs an obligation to repay and the buyer becomes a lender with a claim on future repayments. The buyer, however, has no direct claim on the assets of the issuer. The exemption from federal taxes of the interest earned from many of these bonds, discussed below, is a critical feature of their success and a controversial one.[6]

Types of Bonds

Guaranteed and Non-Guaranteed Bonds

The two main categories of long-term bonds are *full faith and credit bonds* (or *general obligation bonds*) and *non-guaranteed* (or *revenue*) *bonds*. General obligation (GO) bonds are generally described as *guaranteed* because they are backed by the full faith and credit of the issuing government. That means that the issuer pledges to repay the debt using its resources (all the assets available to the issuer to satisfy the debt), including the jurisdiction's legal authority to raise taxes if necessary. Non-guaranteed bonds are those that are backed by specifically identified revenue sources and do not have the legal backing of a larger governmental entity with taxing power. If a municipality offers the full faith and credit guarantee, it is obligated to raise taxes or reduce services to pay back the credit. What happens when a municipality refuses to raise taxes or cut services is covered later in the discussion of defaults and bankruptcies.

GO (full faith and credit) bonds typically are considered safer investments than non-guaranteed bonds because they have the full backing of the jurisdiction's resources. These bonds typically, therefore, carry lower interest rates than non-guaranteed bonds. The interest rate the issuer must pay bond purchasers is critical in large bond issues, for which a difference of 0.1% can affect total interest payments by millions of dollars. However, GO bonds do not always carry a lower interest cost. Revenue bonds from a well-managed special-purpose authority, such as a water district, with an excellent record of previous borrowing are likely to have a lower interest rate than a GO bond from a municipality with a declining property tax base and low personal income. With states and localities facing much more severe fiscal constraints in the recession of the latter part of the first decade of the 2000s, the difference in rate or yield on GO versus revenue bonds has converged somewhat.[7]

Bonds not backed by the general revenue resources of a state or local government have become much more common as special districts

such as water and sewer authorities, economic development zones, and so forth have grown in number and size. In addition, state limitations on general tax revenues, such as Proposition 13 in California (see the chapter on income and property taxes), have forced state and local governments to favor revenue bonds over GO bonds. Such non-guaranteed bonds do not have the full backing of the issuing jurisdiction's resources.

Whatever security is offered, such as a pledge of the revenues from the services delivered by the new facility, no resources other than specifically pledged revenues are available to the creditor/investor. In that case, if the revenues fail to materialize, then the investor has no recourse to other sources of repayment. For both guaranteed and non-guaranteed bonds, the investor is typically paid, except in the case of default, at a fixed rate of interest, although variable rate bonds also are increasing in frequency.

Revenue bonds are politically easier to issue, for two reasons. First, voter approval is required in almost every jurisdiction to issue a full faith and credit bond, but typically is not required for revenue bond issues. Second, revenue bonds are repaid by the charges made to only those who consume or benefit from the services provided by the debt-financed facility or infrastructure, so taxpayers not using the service are not required to help pay off the debt. As voter approval has become more difficult to achieve, the proportion of revenue bonds versus GO bonds has increased. In 2018, about $197 billion in revenue bonds were issued by state and local governments (and utilities) and $123 billion in GO bonds—62% and 38%, respectively.[8]

Non-guaranteed debt is generally repaid from funds restricted to the revenue earnings of the specific facility created by the investment. Many sources are used to repay these so-called non-guaranteed bonds. In the case of revenue bonds, the most common revenue, charges to users, generates the funds necessary to repay the loans. Other sources include special assessments, in which the properties affected by an investment are assessed charges. For example, property owners might be assessed hook-up charges for sewer installations.

Revenue bonds pledging the revenue from a specific tax or fee have the advantage of placing the burden for financing a facility on those who will use it. For example, using the parking fees from a parking garage to finance its construction places the burden on those who park in the garage. From an intergovernmental perspective, the revenue bond device also forces nonresidents who use the parking garage or the highways to pay their fair share regardless of where they reside.

Traditionally, municipalities and local utilities issued bonds in a local market with the main purchasers being local or regional banks. A general-purpose municipal government or school district almost always issued a GO bond, backed by the jurisdiction, mainly by property tax proceeds. Water and other utilities issued non-guaranteed revenue bonds backed by the future revenue streams from user charges. In recent times, these conditions have changed radically. The number of different instruments for debt, while still falling within the two general categories, has increased dramatically, and banks are no longer the largest holders of municipal debt. In addition, in the electronic age, information about municipal debt issues is widely available across the country, and for that matter across the world. Large bond issues may be purchased by institutional investors who are remote from the issuing jurisdiction.

Table 14-1 shows the composition of holders of outstanding municipal debt from 1996 through 2018. Individuals held between 32% and 54% of total municipal debt during that time period. Since 2008, the proportion held by individuals has varied only from 47% to 49%. On the other hand, banking institutions held less than 10% of the value of bonds issued until the last 3 years shown in the table, when the share rose to 12% to 15%. This is in striking contrast to the history of municipal debt purchasers: In 1985, commercial banks held 27% of the total outstanding municipal securities. Property and casualty insurance companies also began to purchase more municipal bonds in the 1990s to diversify their investment portfolios. Mutual funds and money market funds were more heavily invested in municipal debt prior to the early 2000s, before their shares as a proportion of the total fell off. Table 14-1 combines mutual and money market funds into one category. Many of the investors in these funds

Table 14-1 Holders of Municipal Debt: 1996–2018 ($ billions)

	Individuals	Mutual Funds[1]	Banking Institutions[2]	Insurance Companies[3]	Other[4]	Discrepancy	Total
1996	449	455	107	189	56	7	1,262
2000	475	583	129	209	77	8	1,481
2004	1,596	746	180	320	118	−84	2,876
2008	1,533	922	263	444	125	378	3,666
2012	2,016	1,050	408	504	134	−188	3,924
2016	1,870	899	573	536	142	−148	3,872
2018	1,853	960	526	482	145	−138	3,828

[1] Includes mutual funds, money market funds, close-end funds and exchange traded funds.
[2] Includes commercial banks, savings institutions and brokers and dealers.
[3] Includes property-casualty and life insurance companies.
[4] Includes nonfinancial corporate business, nonfarm noncorporate business, state and local governments and retirement funds, government-sponsored enterprises and foreign holders.

Securities Industry and Financial Markets Association (2019). *Holders of U.S. municipal securities*. Retrieved November 14, 2019, from https://www.sifma.org/resources/research/us-municipal-securities-holders/.

are also individuals, through their pension programs or their own individual investments. If we could separate out the individual from the institutional investors in these mutual funds, the role of the individual investor in Table 14-1 would be still more prominent.

Importance of Bond Financing for Infrastructure
Debt Financing Versus Pay-as-You-Go

State and local governments finance a major portion of their capital investment spending through long-term debt instruments. In 2017, state and local governments, including special districts, issued $425 billion in new long-term bonds. Of that amount, $152 billion was in the form

of GO bonds and $273 billion took the form of revenue bonds.[9] **Table 14-2** illustrates the trend in issuer and type of issue from 1995 through 2017. States through those years issued from 8% to 12% of all new municipal debt. General-purpose local governments (municipalities, counties, townships) were in the 19% to 26% range, with special districts such as water and sewer authorities and school districts issuing the most bonds, from 64% to 73%. GO bonds, from 1995 through 2017, accounted for a little over or under one-third of all debt issues, whereas revenue bonds, at two-thirds of all issues, reflect the trends of the past 30 years for revenue bonds to dominate the issuance market. Overall municipal bond issuance went down in 2018, attributable mainly to a fourth-quarter surge in issuance in 2017 of bonds originally scheduled for 2018. Issuers were

Table 14-2 New Bond Issues by Issuer and Type of Issue: 1995–2017 ($ billions)

Issuer	1995	2000	2005	2010	2016	2017
State	15	20	32	55	na	na
Special District incl. School Districts	94	121	299	295	na	na
Municipality, county or township	38	39	79	87	na	na
	147	180	410	437	431	425
Type of Issue						
General Obligation	57	65	146	138	161	152
Revenue	88	116	264	323	270	273
	145	181	410	461	431	425
Issuer	% of total					
State	10.2%	11.1%	7.8%	11.9%	na	na
Special District incl. School Districts	63.9%	67.2%	72.9%	64.0%	na	na
Municipality, county or township	25.9%	21.7%	19.3%	18.9%	na	na
General Obligation	39.3%	35.9%	35.6%	29.9%	37.4%	35.8%
Revenue	60.7%	64.1%	64.4%	70.1%	62.6%	64.2%

na: not available separately by state, special district and municipality; special district includes school district 2010 discrepancy between total by type of issue and issuer is from source.

ProQuest (2019). *ProQuest Statistical Abstract of the United States: 2019* (7th ed), p. 300. Lanham, MD: ProQuest LLC.

uncertain about the impact of the Tax Cuts and Jobs Act introduced in November 2017, fearing that tax exemptions for municipal bonds might be eliminated.[10] Data observed in 2019 seemed to support the interpretation that it was a temporary uncertainty, as municipal issues rebounded in the first two quarters.

Most state constitutions or statutes limit the issuance of long-term debt for both state and local governments to capital investment–type expenditures. Some local governments try to avoid indebtedness as much as possible and work on a *pay-as-you-go* system. That means saving funds in advance until there is enough cash to build the infrastructure facility. These governments are like car buyers who save money until they have enough funds in the bank to purchase their cars for cash. The motivations are similar: both the government and the consumer avoid the interest costs for borrowing. If the jurisdiction can afford to wait for the facility or can plan far enough in advance to have the funds available when needed, then the prospect of financing without interest costs is attractive. Indeed, as the government is saving funds, it can invest them in interest-earning opportunities, which are becoming increasingly sophisticated for government investors.

Pay-as-you-go local governments typically are smaller jurisdictions with relatively stable annual capital investment requirements. For example, if a small local government generally needs to spend about $500,000 per year on capital facilities and goods and that figure is not expected to change much from year to year, over time it will need to spend that same amount, plus interest, each year in debt repayment if it borrows for the capital facilities. So, if the jurisdiction can plan far enough ahead or can afford to wait for the facility, by establishing a capital investment sinking fund it can accumulate the funds necessary to meet the annual $500,000 per year capital spending requirement.[11] Future citizens of the jurisdiction will then benefit from the services and will not have to pay for the capital costs of previous investments. That, of course, means that current residents/taxpayers of the jurisdiction are paying for the benefits enjoyed by others in the future.

Utilities that operate on a commercial basis— capital and operating costs are financed by fees charged to the users of the service—typically include enough depreciation cost in the user charges to accumulate amounts to pay for rehabilitation expenses as the infrastructure wears out. But these utilities, unless small, still require large capital infusions when a major expansion or a major technology change is needed, such as shifting to a more efficient and environmentally friendly energy source. These capital infusions will most likely be through bond issues.

The pay-as-you-go approach does not work as well for larger jurisdictions, which tend to have less predictable requirements, and it does not work well for lumpy investment patterns where large amounts are needed in some years for big construction projects and smaller amounts in other years. Pay-as-you-go is also a problem during sustained periods of fiscal distress. In those times, saving for investment or even investment itself often is sacrificed to make up for declining tax revenues.[12] State or local "rainy day" funds provide a cushion in downturns. They are almost always the highest priority to replenish after a downturn, which may make it difficult for pay-as-you-go governments to keep up the pace of building up a fund for future investments. Some form of credit financing for most state and local jurisdictions is a necessity, especially in rapidly growing areas where, regardless of size, pay-as-you-go financing cannot keep up with population growth and service demands.[13]

Role of the Tax System and State and Local Bond Financing

A key reason for the attractiveness of bond financing for state and local government capital borrowing is that federal tax law allows deduction from the taxpayer's gross income of interest earned on many government bonds. The federal tax exemption is not unlimited. For individuals (or married filing jointly) in the highest tax bracket (as of 2020) of 37%, earning 3% interest on a municipal bond is equal to earning more than 4.7% taxable interest.

In addition to the federal exemption, most states with income taxes exempt interest earnings from state or local bonds for government entities within that state, but do not exempt from state income taxes the interest earned on bonds issued by other states and their municipalities. Only Illinois, Iowa, Oklahoma, Utah, and Wisconsin do not exempt all interest earned on bonds issued by qualifying government jurisdictions in their states.[14]

Because the tax exemption for interest earnings attracts investors to the state and local bond market, a ready source of capital for infrastructure financing exists for state and local government. The tax-exempt status of the earnings also enables jurisdictions to offer bonds at lower interest rates than they could get by borrowing from commercial lenders or issuing taxable debt securities. Tax exemption for the interest earnings on bonds, then, is a cornerstone of the U.S. system for financing public infrastructure for state and local governments. **Exhibit 14-1** illustrates the value to the investor of federal tax exemption.

Municipal bonds' tax-exempt status is somewhat controversial. A wave of expansion in the

---

Exhibit 14-1 Federal Tax Exemption for Municipal Bond Yields

Municipal bonds are attractive to investors in part because the earnings to the investor on the bond are exempt from federal income taxes. The wealthier the taxpayer, the more valuable the exemption is because wealthier taxpayers generally pay a higher marginal tax rate on their income. In that sense, the tax exemption on municipal bonds is a regressive feature in the federal income tax.

Arguments against this tax exemption are its regressive nature, which favors wealthier taxpayers, and the lost federal revenue that must be made up for in the form of either other taxes or higher marginal rates on the individual income tax. The 2020 federal budget estimates that exemption of interest from municipal bonds will mean more than $30 billion in lost federal revenue.[a]

Arguments in favor of this exemption are that it enables badly needed public sector infrastructure to be constructed at a lower cost, and that lower cost is of greater benefit to lower-income individuals. That is because the amount lower-income people would otherwise spend on public utilities such as water and sewer would be a higher proportion of their income than it would be for wealthier households.

The table below illustrates the tax advantage, using as an example a married couple filing a joint return. For each marginal rate for the federal 2019 tax year, the cells in the table show the return (yield) the couple would have to achieve in a taxable bond to be equivalent to the value of the tax-exempt bond. The table does not consider state taxes.

Value to Taxpayer of Federal Income Tax Exemption on Municipal Bond Yields

Marginal Tax Rate, Married Joint Return	Tax-exempt Yield	3.00%	3.50%	4.00%	4.50%	5.00%	5.50%	6.00%
10%		3.33%	3.89%	4.44%	5.00%	5.56%	6.11%	6.67%
12%		3.41%	3.98%	4.55%	5.11%	5.68%	6.25%	6.82%
22%		3.85%	4.49%	5.13%	5.77%	6.41%	7.05%	7.69%
24%		3.95%	4.61%	5.26%	5.92%	6.58%	7.24%	7.89%
35%		4.62%	5.38%	6.15%	6.92%	7.69%	8.46%	9.23%
37%		4.76%	5.56%	6.35%	7.14%	7.94%	8.73%	9.52%

a. U.S. Office of Management and Budget (2019). *Analytical perspectives: tax expenditures,* Washington, DC: U.S. Government Publishing Office, 180.

use of tax-exempt bonds to finance private purposes, such as industrial development parks, incubator facilities to woo private developers to invest in local areas, and a wide variety of other essentially private endeavors, led to significant curbs on state and local governments' authority to issue tax-exempt bonds in the Tax Reform Act of 1986 (TRA86). Private purpose bonds are discussed in more detail in a following section. Other features of that tax reform also made municipal bonds a much less attractive investment for commercial banks, accounting in part for the trend noted in Table 14-1.

The securities industry clearly recognizes that there is a strong individual/household appetite for municipal bonds, as evidenced by the increasing availability of bonds as part of money market and mutual funds as well as the creation of tax-exempt bond funds. Concern for equity in taxation leads some to question whether interest on government and certain nonprofit bonds should be exempt. It is generally thought that mostly higher-income taxpayers benefit from this exemption, as they are the most likely purchasers of tax-exempt bonds and, therefore, that this exemption unfairly benefits those who can most afford to pay higher taxes. The illustration in Exhibit 14-1 seems to bear this out, at least in terms of the increasing value of the tax exemption as the marginal tax rate increases. However, the growth of mutual funds in which middle-class individuals are making more investments is mitigating this equity argument.

If and when efforts to reduce federal debt, or slow its growth, are successful, this will lead to renewed challenges to the tax exemption for interest on municipal bonds. The National Commission on Fiscal Responsibility in 2010 recommended the elimination of interest exemption for municipal debt.[15] The Obama administration in 2011 made elimination of part of the tax exemption for higher-income taxpayers one of the revenue components of a proposed jobs program.[16] There was discussion during hearings in 2017 on the Tax Cut and Jobs Act about tax exemption of municipal bond interest, but no serious support for eliminating the exemption emerged.[17]

It is likely that challenges to this tax exemption will continue during difficult budget deficit conditions, but unless it is replaced by other mechanisms that are equal to the challenge of financing trillions of dollars in infrastructure, it is unlikely that this fundamental feature of state and local finance in the United States will go away. At the same time, it is likely that the federal government will continue to increase regulations regarding the issuance of tax-exempt bonds in order to restrict the tax favorability to the essential purposes of financing public infrastructure. The state of South Carolina challenged the constitutionality of any federal regulation of state governments' tax-exempt debt issuance in the 1988 *South Carolina v. Baker* case, questioning a law that denied tax-exempt status to bearer bonds (as opposed to registered bonds; see the discussion of bond features later in this chapter).[18] The Supreme Court ruled that the Tenth Amendment did not prohibit federal regulation of state and local governments and that there is no constitutional right to state and local immunity from federal tax provisions.[19]

Nontraditional Bond Financing

The municipal bond finance system has developed several variations in how to use bond financing for public infrastructure. Securitization, special facility user charges, and tax increment bond financing have been used extensively and are discussed below.

Securitizing Future Revenue Streams

Securitizing the future revenue stream from some activity or of a set of receivables is an innovation introduced in the private sector in the late 1970s. For example, credit card companies often issue a bond or borrow against the stream of receivables that will be flowing in from credit card users. The card company gets immediate revenue instead of waiting for the stream of repayments. This technique is called securitization because the credit card company issues a security (a bond) against the future payments that are already known because the credit card holders have already incurred the debt. Or, the securitization may involve a known value for the revenue stream such as outstanding credit card debt, plus estimated additional payments for credit card debt not yet incurred. On a larger scale, banks and housing finance companies may package a group of mortgages and issue a security (a bond) that is repaid by the known stream of revenues from those future mortgage payments.

Securitization involves a stream of payments that already are legal commitments. Any assured, meaning legally obligated, revenue stream that will accrue to the issuer over future years is susceptible to securitization. Securitization may involve different risks than straight revenue bonds and, therefore, may be priced higher if considered by the market as riskier investments. However, if the revenue stream is clearly known, that security may be considered less risky than a partly speculative future revenue stream. Among the riskier forms of securitizing future revenue streams is selling pieces of the future stream to different investors. The collapse in the mortgage finance market during the Great Recession of some of the major players, such as Washington Mutual, is an example of both packaging mortgage revenue streams and selling and buying such packages. The original mortgages may have been highly risky in the first place, as happened in the lead up to the recession. Selling packages of mortgages, which in turn may have been traded again several times, compounded the problem by distancing the original assets, mortgages, from the purchaser, who was buying only a portion of a group of mortgages packaged for securitization (for a more detailed discussion of that market collapse, see the chapter on government and the economy).

Because of the turmoil in the financial markets that erupted in 2007, the Securities and Exchange Commission (SEC) issued new regulations in 2011 to strengthen the disclosure requirements for issuers of asset-backed securities. Municipal asset-backed securities—for example, bonds for single-family housing—fall under SEC Rule 15Ga-1 that imposed on issuers more rigorous disclosure rules, designed to provide more detailed and more accurate information on the underlying assets being pledged.[20]

Bonds issued against pools of tax liens are another form of securitization states and municipalities use to sell a stream of future revenue from liens placed on property for failure to pay taxes, user charges, or other obligations. New York City, in 2018, sponsored a sale of tax lien asset bonds turning a long-term revenue stream into a pool of finance available for other investments. Moody's Investor Services rated the bond provisionally as Aaa.[21] New Jersey, Florida, and Connecticut have used this as an alternative to directly foreclosing on properties against which tax liens have been issued. Governments holding the liens capitalize on the value of those liens immediately, with the market issuer acquiring the value of the liens.

A somewhat unusual revenue stream available to many states and some large cities was the proceeds from successful suits against tobacco companies. New York City issued a $709 million bond in 1999 that entitled the purchasers of the bond to the proceeds the city received under the tobacco litigation settlement funds.[22] The tobacco settlement funds are payments to states from large tobacco companies as settlement for a class action suit filed by more than 40 states to recover the costs the states were incurring for health care for illnesses and chronic conditions attributable to tobacco usage. The near future may see a similar phenomenon with successful state lawsuits against drug manufacturers and distributors of opioids.

Airport Passenger Facility Charges (PFCs)

Airport PFCs involve the pledge of specific charges for use of the airport facility collected from the airlines through increments to ticket prices. These charges apply to every eligible passenger transiting through an airport, generating a stream of revenue that may be pledged as security for a bond issue.[23] Cleveland, as the owner of the Cleveland Hopkins International Airport, issued in 2011 a $75 million bond based on passenger facility charges.[24] Broward County, Florida, used a different wrinkle to the passenger facility charge instrument. In 1998 and 2001, the airport issued bonds totaling more than $150 million secured by passenger facility charges. These were charges added to the price of tickets of passengers emplaning or deplaning at the airport, estimated at a cost of just over $5 per passenger. In 2012, the pledged security for the bonds shifted from the passenger facility charge to a lien on total airport system revenues until maturity in 2023. This so-called convertible lien bond device gives added security to the investors. Broward regularly incorporates planned revenues from PFCs and PFC collateralized loans in its capital investment plans and budgets.[25]

Tax Increment Financing Bonds

Tax increment bonds combine features of revenue bonds and GO bonds. They are used to finance local economic development and urban renewal by pledging future increases in property taxes of areas targeted for development or redevelopment. A city may decide to build libraries or renovate parks or redevelop an area of the inner city through construction of housing or commercial facilities and may issue a bond to finance that redevelopment. Because the redevelopment will not directly generate revenues, it is not suitable for revenue bond financing. At the same time, the city may not wish to obligate its full resources to repay the bonds, may be at state debt-limit ceilings for full faith and credit bonds, or may wish to confine the repayment obligations to the direct beneficiaries of the redevelopment. A tax increment financing bond backs up the debt issue with the pledge of the incremental increase in property tax revenue from the area being developed (the property taxes will rise because the property in the redevelopment area will become more valuable and thus have a higher taxable value).

Private Purpose Bonds

Private purpose bonds are state and local issues to finance construction and ownership of facilities that may serve both public and private purposes.[26] Bonds for single- and multifamily housing, industrial development, and municipal purchases of private utilities, such as electric utilities, are generally classified as private activity bonds that may or may not be eligible for tax-exempt status. For these types of activities, tax-exempt status is limited by a federal cap on the total private activity bonds that may be issued annually by all governmental units within a state. The formula for calculating the cap for 2019, applied to each state, was $105 multiplied by the population of the state or $3,166,875, whichever is greater.[27] An example is a bond issued for the construction of a municipal parking garage by a private operator, which is then leased back to the municipality. Similar use has been made of private activity bonds for lease and subsequent purchase of privately constructed facilities. In some cases, government bonds have been issued to finance a facility that then is leased to or purchased by the private sector.[28]

A state must approve each private activity bond issued by local jurisdictions, utilities, or, in some cases, nonprofit companies that are serving a public as well as private purpose. When the cap is reached during the year, no more tax-exempt private activity bonds may be issued that year regardless of their merit. Private activity bonds may still be issued when a state's total private activity bonds issued for the year is over the cap, but newer issues do not enjoy tax-exempt status. Some private activity bonds are treated differently with respect to the cap. Regardless of the cap, private activity bonds for construction of facilities such as airports, docks and wharves, hazardous waste treatment plants, and water supply facilities retain their tax-exempt status, although interest is included in the alternative minimum tax base. In 2016, almost 30% of all municipal tax-exempt debt issues involved these private purpose activities.[29]

Private purpose bonds also have been used in special circumstances, such as reconstruction following a natural disaster. The Gulf Opportunity Zone Act of 2005 was passed after major hurricanes devastated Louisiana, Mississippi, and Alabama.[30] The act relaxed some of the restrictions on the volume of tax-exempt private activity bonds that could be issued by those states hard hit by the hurricane. The act's relaxation of restrictions for these purposes was limited to only a few years.

Tax Credit Bonds

Tax-exempt bonds reduce the purchaser's tax liability by allowing exemption of interest earned on the bonds. A tax credit bond reduces the purchaser's tax liability by allowing a credit against taxes owed. Tax credit bonds were created for a narrow range of investments designed to assist primarily school construction and energy production and conservation. From time to time, Congress also enacted legislation for a limited, time bound purpose, such as the Gulf Tax Credit Bonds, established by the Gulf Opportunity Zone Act of 2005, to assist in Hurricane Katrina recovery, discussed in **Exhibit 14-2**. The Tax Cuts and Jobs Act of 2017 eliminated the tax credit exemption, although attempts continue in Congress to reinstate the tax credit deduction for some purposes.[31] It would not be surprising to see temporary reinstatement in the case of some future circumstance involving unexpected and catastrophic damage to public infrastructure, but reinstatement of tax credit bonds on a longer-term basis is not likely, as such a change lacks any significant support from either party in Congress.

Municipal Minibonds

Most purchasers of municipal bonds are large purchase investors, including financial institutions that develop tax-exempt investment funds that may then be purchased by both large and small investors. Generally, it has been more difficult for all but higher-income individuals to get directly involved in purchasing bonds from their own jurisdictions because purchases often involve

---

Exhibit 14-2 Private Purpose Bonds Address Hurricane Losses to State and Municipal Infrastructure and the Tax Base

---

Hurricanes Katrina and Rita in 2005 devastated the Gulf Coast of the United States, causing damages estimated in excess of $140 billion. Losses to government infrastructure alone amounted to between $13 billion on the low end and $25 billion on the high end.[a] At least $16.7 billion in face value of insured bonds were directly affected by the hurricanes, but as of a year after the hurricanes, only a little over $17 million in claims on insured bonds had been paid out, and most of that was thought likely to be recovered as it was mostly late payments as municipalities and special districts struggled to get their records back in order in the immediate aftermath.[b]

The City of New Orleans and other bond issuers faced long-term problems, however, in rebuilding the lost infrastructure by issuing new debt and at the same time meeting payments on previous bonds that financed now destroyed or damaged capital assets. The Gulf Opportunity Zone Act of 2005 (P.L. 109-135) relaxed some of the restrictions on private activity bonds in order to permit tax-exempt issues for housing and other facilities that are not necessarily for public use and waived other requirements that otherwise would potentially have impeded issuance of new bonds to refund existing bonds or to refinance infrastructure on which existing bonds already were outstanding. One provision of the act also extended authority to the affected states to issue *tax credit* bonds to pay interest on or to repay debt previously issued, subject to a maximum per state—$200 million for Louisiana—and requiring that the state match the tax credit issue with an equal amount of state resources, financed by debt or otherwise.

The state of Louisiana, for example, in 2006 issued $200 million in tax credit bonds to be used to pay debt service and to repay bonds issued prior to Hurricanes Katrina and Rita in affected areas. The fact sheet from this bond issue, following, shows the debt rated AAA by Fitch and similarly by other rating agencies. While there have been major municipal bond defaults in U.S. history, they are rare and, when significant, often result in solutions to work out the losses through a variety of financing options and with extended oversight by regulatory agencies or appointed oversight commissions.

a. Holtz-Eakin, D. (2005). *Macroeconomic and budgetary effects of Hurricanes Katrina and Rita*. Washington, DC: Congressional Budget Office, 3.
b. Dorsey and Company. (2006). *Hurricane Katrina: One year later the municipal bond market remains resilient*. Retrieved December 5, 2006, from http://www.dorseyco.com/documents/GKSTResearch-HurricaneKatrinaOneYearLater_000.pdf. Note: the article referenced is no longer archived on the Dorsey and Company website and is not retrievable.

minimum amounts of $5,000 to $10,000 or more. However, mutual funds consisting entirely of municipal bonds have brought them in reach of more investors as smaller investments may be made in these mutual funds. However, tax exemption of the earnings on these mutual funds is tricky. If the fund mixes tax-exempt bonds with taxable bonds, such as private activity bonds that exceed the cap or do not fit the requirements for tax exemption, figuring out the value of the tax exemption for the fund as well as the investor is difficult.

Another option for smaller investors is municipal minibonds. Some cities have issued bonds in smaller denominations. Denver, Colorado, was one of the first issuers of *minibonds*, a $5.9 million issue in $1,000 denomination bonds in 1990.[32] The minibonds were issued directly by the city without an underwriter (see the discussion later on bond issuance), and purchase was possible only by Colorado residents. Almost 2,000 citizens purchased more than twice the amount initially expected. A 2014 Denver $12 million minibond issue sold out in less than 20 minutes.[33]

While not appropriate for large-scale bond issues because it becomes uneconomical to sell and track bonds in small denominations, minibonds have proved popular for financing smaller projects that especially interest local residents. Bond issues that combine both large denomination and small denomination (mini) bonds attract different kinds of investors. Minibonds do not make an impact in the overall size of the municipal bond market, but they do open the door to more widespread participation. Cities such as Denver and Cambridge, Massachusetts, have deliberately used minibonds as a means of encouraging local residents to invest in their community. Madison, Wisconsin, issued minibonds in 2018, considering the value of direct participation by their residents as worth some additional cost to issue the bonds.[34]

Certificates of Participation

Another form of small-scale municipal issuance is the use of certificates of participation (COPs). A municipality may issue a bond for the construction of a revenue-generating facility, such as a parking garage or a utility within that municipality. The issuing jurisdiction leases the facility for a specified period and sells COPs to investors in the lease revenues. The investor buys a share in the revenue stream generated by the project, but not a specific number of bonds.[35] The investors may defer receiving their share of the lease revenues or may receive them periodically during the lease. The investors in the COPs have a legal interest in the lease facility in the event of a default. At the end of the lease period, the bond has been retired through the lease payments, investors have been paid off, and the facility belongs to the issuing jurisdiction. COPs became especially popular in California after Proposition 13 placed severe restrictions on the ability of local governments to borrow. COPs have the same legal status as revenue bonds as far as legal limitations on borrowing. COPs can be risky investments if the facility financed is not as successful financially as anticipated, and lease payments or other mechanisms to generate a revenue stream to pay off investors are insufficient.

E-Trading Municipal Bonds

Just as online trading in the private sector has become a common practice, so securities dealers offer information about municipal bonds and offer the bonds for sale online. Issuance costs have come down somewhat compared with trading through securities dealers. Purchasing municipal bonds online is as commonplace as any other online investing. Of equal or perhaps greater importance to purchasing is access to online information for individual investors about possible bond investments that are then purchased either online or through regular securities dealer channels, or sometimes directly from the underwriter. Information readily available online includes trading prices and detailed information on the issuers, for both original issues and previously issued bonds offered on the secondary market. Municipal bonds of one variety or another are now as accessible an investment choice to investors as any other security.[36] This is a far cry from the days when most municipal bonds were issued locally or regionally and known only to local or regional investors.

Bond Banks, State Revolving Funds, and Other Intermediaries

Large city and state governments, unless there are underlying problems with the jurisdictions' financial status, generally have ready access to the U.S. capital markets to issue their own bonds. However, smaller cities and municipalities, and many municipalities in developing countries where there is only a limited market in fixed-income securities and generally no track record for municipal debt, have greater difficulty issuing debt at competitive prices. In most industrialized European economies, the banking sector is the primary source of finance to subnational governments. In some countries, municipally owned banks, such as the De Nederlandsche Bank (BNG) in the Netherlands, in addition to managing the accounts and financial transactions of owner municipalities, lend long term to municipalities. Half of BNG's share capital is owned by the national government and half by provincial, municipal, and water utilities.[37] In other countries, commercial and investment banks are the primary lenders. In still other European countries, specialized financing institutions somewhat like U.S. state revolving loan funds, and infrastructure banks have been established to provide credit to municipalities. In many emerging market countries, such as Brazil and Poland, municipalities have emerged as good credit risks, and a variety of credit systems have developed, including bond markets, specialized financing institutions, and direct lending from commercial and investment banks.[38] Several institutional structures are prevalent, and have been for decades, in the United States and other Organisation for Economic Co-operation and Development countries to assist smaller governments. Some of these structures have become popular in developing country public finance. The most common forms of borrowing from intermediaries in both the United States and Europe, and in some developing countries, are revolving loan funds and bond banks or infrastructure banks. In many European countries, borrowing from banks or financing institutions especially created to lend to local governments is the most common means by which local governments secure debt capital.

In the United States, several actions contributed to the invention of and growth in state revolving loan funds and bond banks. The original stimulus for many of these funds was federal environmental funding programs for water and sewerage systems. All 50 states plus Puerto Rico operate Clean Water State Revolving Loan Fund programs. Similarly, all 50 states and Puerto Rico operate Drinking Water State Revolving loan funds. They were partially capitalized with grants from federal and state budgets. Federal assistance to these programs was authorized under the Clean Water Act of 1972 (previously known as the Federal Water Pollution Act of 1948).[39]

The Clean Water Act has not been reauthorized since 1987. The Safe Drinking Water Act of 1974, last reauthorized in 2003, contained provisions for the Environmental Protection Agency to provide financial assistance to states to set up drinking water revolving funds.[40] In 1996, amendments to the Safe Drinking Water Act created the Drinking Water State Revolving Fund. Additional amendments expanded the scope of the act, including drinking water security provisions in the Public Health Security and Bioterrorism Act of 2002.[41]

A revolving fund is created with some initial capitalization, such as grants from the federal government plus state government bond issues, to lend to municipal borrowers. The premise is that the state government can get better credit ratings both because it is in better financial condition and because it can issue debt in larger amounts than individual small local governments. Repayments from the local governments that borrow from the fund keep the capitalization intact, allowing lending and borrowing to continue on a revolving basis.

One of the model state revolving loan funds created initially with federal environmental grants is the New York State Environmental Facilities Corporation (EFC). The New York State EFC is a public-benefit state corporation financially independent from the state government. Its transactions are not backed by state budget authority.

It operates several state revolving loan funds, the largest of which are the Clean Water State Revolving Fund (CWSRF) and the Drinking Water State Revolving Fund (DWSRF). As of 2018, the CWSRF had lent approximately $28 billion since its inception in 1990. Projects financed focus on point and non-point source water development projects, stormwater management projects, and sewer and wastewater treatment facilities. The DWSRF, created in 1996, through 2018 had provided over $6 billion to public water systems.[42] Even without continuing financial assistance from the federal government, state clean water and drinking water revolving funds continue to function.

Other state bond banks or infrastructure banks are like the New York State EFC. A state bond bank may pool the borrowing needs of numerous, smaller municipal borrowers into a single state bond issue and then finance the individual borrower's requirements from the proceeds of the single state issue. Some state bond banks issue bonds to capitalize a fund for lending, which then is a form of revolving fund. Others accumulate individual municipalities' borrowing needs until a sufficiently large amount is reached and then issue a single bond to meet those specific needs. Generally, for the smaller municipal borrowers, bond banks reduce the cost of issuance.

Most state infrastructure banks were stimulated and continue to be assisted by federal programs, particularly federal transportation funding acts beginning in 1995.[13] The original 1995 federal transportation legislation—the National Highway System Designation Act—created a pilot program to provide federal grant funding to capitalize *state infrastructure banks* (SIBs) to finance transportation projects. Initially, 10 pilot states were authorized, but the program was later extended to all states. Subsequent reauthorizations of the Transportation Equity Act of 1998 and the Safe, Accountable, Flexible, Efficient Transportation Equity Act: A Legacy for Users of 2005 extended a variety of financing tools, including continued support to the SIBs.[44] Thirty-two states and Puerto Rico have some form of operational SIB. Two—Kansas and Georgia—are capitalized exclusively by state funds, and three—Florida, Ohio, and Pennsylvania—have separate facilities within the SIB for state and federal sources of capital.[45]

Overall, the use of bonds to finance state and local investments, both in the United States and in other countries, continues to increase as state and local financial conditions improve and federal transfers to assist state and local governments decrease. The Great Recession only temporarily interrupted what had been a more general pattern of improvement in state and local financial conditions. The distinction between GO bonds and limited revenue bonds is less important in practice than the financial condition of the borrowing entity. In fact, many water utilities and other users of more limited revenue bonds are in better financial shape than states and general-purpose local governments.

Bond Issuance Process

The process of issuing municipal bonds involves numerous steps, and the number of participants in these steps is quite large.[46] **Exhibit 14-3** lists the major participants, ignoring some of the minor players (for example, bond printers).

Bond Issuance Costs

With so many steps and participants in the process, the costs to the issuing jurisdiction can be high. Numerous legal steps must be followed, numerous documents must be prepared, and numerous transactions with various financial and legal institutions must occur. These transactions require considerable personnel time or the purchase of consulting services. Some of the costs are absorbed by the municipality directly, and some are built into the bond price. Among the former costs are financial advisory fees, bond counsel fees, rating agency costs, bond insurance, trustee fees, and a few minor fees. The underwriter's fees are built into the price of the bond. They are the difference between the price at which the underwriter sells the bond to investors and the price paid by the underwriter to the issuer. The difference between these two prices is known as the *gross spread*.[47]

Exhibit 14-3 Participants in the Municipal Bond Market

Issuers: General-purpose municipalities, counties, and states; special-purpose governmental entities such as school districts and water authorities; and unique public service entities such as airports and transportation terminals.

Financial Advisors: Finance specialists used by bond issuers to structure features of the issue to increase attractiveness to borrowers and/or to address a special need of the issuer—features such as issuer options to call the bond before maturity and structuring debt retirement to match cash flow circumstances of the issuer.

Bond Counsel: Legal advisors to offer legal opinion on the legal authority of the issuer to borrow, on the tax-exempt status of the issue, and the legal obligation of the issuer to repay.

Underwriters: Investment firms, banks, and other financial institutions licensed to trade in municipal securities who sell the issuers' bonds.

Trustee: Institution that serves mainly bondholders by securing from the issuers bond repayment cash flows and paying out to bondholders when due.

Investors: Individuals, investment banks, commercial banks, and other financial institutions.

The inclusive cost to the issuer includes those paid out by the issuer plus the gross spread. One study of issuance costs found that some financial services, such as Bloomberg, consider the issuance cost to be only the underwriters fees. Considering only that cost, Bloomberg estimated the national average issuance cost in 2014 at about 0.5%.[48] This average varied widely by state, from 0.2% in Wyoming to 1.0% in Alaska. On the other hand, Internal Revenue Service data on municipal issues and reported issuance costs for the same year are just over 0.8%, a figure closer to the California Debt and Investment Advisory Commission estimate of 0.7% for large issues.[49]

Costs vary by issue based on characteristics of the issue itself—size, complexity, the issuer (financial condition, experience with previous debt issues), market conditions, and general familiarity of investors with the issuer. These can cause large differences in issuance costs, from averages as low as 0.9% for large issues to as high as 2.4% for smaller issues.[50] Variations by state are affected by state policies; the general economic climate; experience with defaults or other financial troubles; and, of course, market conditions. Intense political factionalism and high turnover of elected public officials have been

found to increase the borrowing costs of affected jurisdictions as investors apparently worry about the stability over time of policy decisions that may affect the issuer's financial viability.[51]

Voter Approval

In most states, a GO (full faith and credit) bond requires a referendum to secure voter approval. Revenue bonds and other forms of limited obligation financing generally do not require voter approval. In some cases, to avoid state limitations on general municipal borrowing, cities have established nonprofit building authorities to issue bonds and construct facilities. Such facilities are then rented to the municipality, and the rental payments secure the bond principal and interest. These special authorities, because they do not legally obligate in a direct way the general revenues of the municipality, can issue bonds without voter approval and without the debt counting as part of the municipality's overall debt. Of course, the source of funds used by the municipality to pay for renting the facility is, in fact, the general revenue fund. Voters approve far more bond issues than they reject. In the 2016 general elections across all states, voters approved over 80% of all bond issues.[52]

Underwriting

Typically, the authority issuing a bond will secure the services of an underwriter, whose role is to arrange the actual sale of bonds to financial institutions. The underwriter for a small issue may well be a local bank or a major regional bank. Such firms as Goldman Sachs, Bank of America Merrill Lynch, Morgan Stanley, Wells Fargo, and other investment bankers and securities dealers typically handle major issues that are marketed nationally (and internationally). Individuals, banks, insurance companies, and mutual and money market funds invest in state and local bonds, as shown previously in this chapter in Table 14-1.

Most issuers, except those with strong market recognition themselves, such as states and major cities, rely upon an underwriter. Underwriters have client lists and access to a wide range of investors and typically can sell a borrower's bond issue more quickly than the borrower. The underwriter collects the fee from the issuer by discounting back to the issuer the value of the bonds. For example, an underwriter on a $100 million bond issue, charging 50 basis points as the underwriting fee, will pay to the issuer $99.5 million. The underwriter literally *owns* the issue at that point. If the market responds favorably to the bond issue, the underwriter may earn more than the 50 basis points or, in this example, $500,000. But if the underwriter has misjudged the market's appetite for the issue, or the market changes while the underwriter is still selling some of the issue, the underwriter may not realize enough profit to fully offset the underwriting fee.

Public Sale Versus Negotiated Sale

Issuers may approach the market to sell their bonds in one of two ways: public competitive bidding and negotiated sale. Historically, bonds were offered for public sale, with purchasers such as larger financial institutions, which might be purchasing for their own portfolio or for resale, effectively determining the interest rate by their offers. A *public sale* is initiated by a widely published official notice of sale. The notice of sale typically includes information such as the denomination of the bonds, bid conditions and requirements, and provisions for payment. The issuer will have worked with a financial adviser to establish the amount of the issue, the maturity date(s), obtaining (typically) a rating (discussed below), and all other characteristics of the sale. Investors then, in effect, determine the interest rate through their bids, with the issuer free to choose the investor or potentially several investors who offer the lowest rates. More detailed information is provided in the bond prospectus.

Sealed bids are submitted by interested institutional investors, brokerage firms, and even individuals, although individuals typically purchase through intermediaries. The issuing jurisdiction then is free to accept the lowest bid interest rate or to reject the bid according to the terms and conditions of sale. Jurisdictions with good ratings prefer this method, as they are likely to attract numerous bidders and thus be able to choose lower interest rates.

The *negotiated sale* overtook competitive sales in the 1990s. In 2017, negotiated sales were three times the value of competitive sales and almost the same in 2018. Negotiated sales are conducted between underwriters such as the large investment banks and the issuing government. The issuer typically issues a request for proposals (RFP) specifying the objectives of the issue (amount, time period, and so forth). Responders to the RFP present to the issuer their best case for why they should be selected based on track record, fees, and so forth. Once the underwriter, or often several underwriters, is selected, the issuer then works with the underwriter to develop the bond issue. The underwriter acts as a broker between the issuing jurisdiction and the investment community. If the issuer thinks the rates quoted by potential buyers are too high, the issuer is free to reject the bids, as in a public sale.

A key advantage of a negotiated sale is that the bond issue can be spread over a longer period. If the interest rates in bids are high but the issuer cannot postpone the project, the issuer may sell only a portion of the total issue to start the project while the underwriter continues to seek additional bids. One disadvantage of negotiated sales is that some investors, including some pension funds, cannot purchase state or municipal securities except through public sale.

Although it has been argued that negotiated sales seem to cost about 30 basis points more than competitive bids, other research has presented evidence that it is more the characteristics of the issuers that determine whether competitive versus negotiated sale is selected by the issuer, and that in turn explains any interest differences. Poor credit risk, unusually large issues, unusual financial structure or offered security, market volatility, and unusual financing terms are some of the factors that may argue for negotiated sale.[53]

Bond Features

Bonds differ from one another in a variety of ways. *Term bonds* may be due and payable to the investors on a single date. Investors holding term bonds obviously must be concerned with whether a jurisdiction is annually setting aside enough funds to be able to repay its debt. Underwriters typically require that the issuer establish a *sinking fund* and pay into that fund semiannually or annually amounts that will be enough at maturity to repay the principal on the bonds. *Serial bonds* are due according to a specific schedule of payments over several years. Serial bonds have largely replaced term bonds, in part because of statutory prohibitions against term bonds, but mainly because they allow the issuer to schedule sales over time to match the issuer's financial situation. For example, an issuer may have other previously issued bonds being paid off over time. Payment schedules for serial bonds could be timed to increase as older bonds are retired.

Historically, bonds could be *coupon bonds* or *registered bonds*. Coupon bonds have coupons attached indicating the bond's maturity date and the amount of payment. Coupon bond payments are paid out to whomever presents the coupon, and not to a named purchaser. Registered bonds require that the owner register with the government issuing the bonds. States and municipalities historically preferred coupon bonds because the issuing jurisdiction was not responsible for keeping records of the purchasers. Electronic registration and a federal tax law changes have rendered coupon bonds almost obsolete. The use of coupon bonds has all but disappeared, although state and local governments continue to lobby for federal legislation that would permit issuing nonregistered bonds that are tax exempt.

Another feature of bond sales is *discounting*. A bond is discounted when it is sold at some fraction of its face value. For example, a $10,000 bond may be sold for $9,800. It is thus discounted below par (meaning below face value). When it matures and the principal is paid out, the investor will receive $10,000 in return for the $9,800 investment in addition to the interest payments the investor would have been receiving over the years.

At times, a bond may be sold at a premium over its par value. This can happen when a bond whose fixed interest rate was set in a period of high interest rates becomes available for sale after interest rates have fallen. A potential investor will be attracted to the higher interest rate bond, but the seller has less incentive to sell the bond because of the low return offered by other choices now available on the market. So, the seller charges the new investor, say, $10,200 for a bond that will repay principal of only $10,000 at maturity. The bond investor must consider both the selling value—discounted, at par, or at a premium—as well as the interest rate in determining the return on investment. The secondary market, in which bonds already sold once are resold to other investors, rarely has bonds that are sold at their face value. Conditions at the time of sales in the secondary market are almost always different from the time of issue, causing the bonds to be valued at either more or less than their face value.

Bonds are becoming increasingly complex in the structure of their terms. Traditionally, debt issuers were concerned primarily with the *interest* or *coupon rate* of the bond and the various costs of debt issuance. Today, however, issuers are incorporating detailed features, usually with the help of financial advisory services, to vary the conditions of sale, the conditions under which the issuer may pay off the bond early, and variations in cash flows at different points in the life of the bond. For example, one feature is a collateral structure in which an asset-backed security is issued, and collateralized by a bundle of underlying securities, such as several municipal bonds. The risk and therefore pricing of those different bonds varies, and thus the new asset-backed security may smooth out the different risks. A different form or structure is when an issue is divided and sold in different *tranches* or portions, each sold at different times, each tranche having different repayment schedules.

Zero-Coupon Bonds

The typical municipal bond pays interest at specified points until the maturity date, when the principal is paid. Zero-coupon bonds are an option that is attractive to investors who are looking to maximize the long-term return and are not particularly seeking annual or semi-annual interest payments until maturity. The coupon rate, in finance terminology, is the interest rate that the bond will pay. A zero-coupon bond pays out no interest until maturity, when both the principal and the interest are paid at once. Attractive to the issuer because they have no annual cash flow requirements, zero-coupon bonds naturally require some incentive to attract investors away from the more typical municipal bond, which pays in regular installments through the years until maturity. The usual means of attracting investors to zero-coupon bonds is to sell the bonds for much less than their stated value—to discount the bond from face value. Zero-coupon bonds typically call for the issuer to set aside funds with a trustee, on a regular basis, enough to pay off the debt at time of maturity.

Interest Rates

Interest rates, of course, are one of the most critical elements of bonds for both the issuer and potential buyers. As a hedge against changing interest rates or financial condition, the state or municipal authority may sometimes use a *call feature*. This means the authority may call or repay the bond in part or in full before the maturity date. The issuer

can thus take advantage of falling interest rates by paying off all or part of the bond issue. Exercising this feature usually involves the payment of some premium. Callable bonds typically carry a higher rate of interest because investors would otherwise be less attracted to an investment that may be repaid sooner and therefore at a lower profit. A similar feature that favors the bond buyer is the *put option*. It allows the buyer, at specified intervals, to require paying off the bond. For this feature, the buyer agrees to specified discount rates at the different put options.

The actual interest that the jurisdiction will have to pay on a bond issue depends on many factors related to the financial condition of the jurisdiction and the general market for other investments at the time of the issue. The tax-exempt status of the interest earned by state and local bonds means that the interest rate paid will be lower than comparably safe investments that do not enjoy tax-exempt status. If the jurisdiction has a good record of previous debt management, it will be perceived as a lower risk than one that has experienced trouble meeting its financial obligations. Likewise, if the jurisdiction is in a good regional economy with low unemployment rates and a high tax base, it will be able to sell its bonds at lower interest rates. If the issuer embodies recognized good management practices, that will have a positive impact on bond pricing. The issuing jurisdiction also will provide potential investors with information about other long-term obligations, including other debt and unfunded pension liabilities. A reputation for good financial management is cited as evidence of creditworthiness.[54]

Bond Ratings

Investors rely heavily on standard ratings provided by independent services, such as Fitch Investors Service L.P. (Fitch), Moody's Investor Service (Moody's), and Standard & Poor's (S&P). Although the rating agencies use somewhat different labels for their ratings, they are quite similar.

The importance of ratings is illustrated by an S&P downgrade of the Chicago Sales Tax Securitization Corporation after adding to its credit rating practice accounting for the risk that governments in distress may raid pledged revenue streams. This downrating was prompted by actions of the Puerto Rico highway agency, approved by a circuit court ruling, to divert tolls and fees pledged to bondholders. The downgrade for Chicago caused investors to demand an additional 0.8 percentage points in yield from investments of the Tax Securitization Corporation.[55]

Exhibit 14-4 discusses how rating agencies evaluate potential borrowers and potential debt issues.

The terminology used by different rating organizations differs with respect to speculative

---

Exhibit 14-4 How Do Rating Agencies Evaluate Municipal Bond Issues?

There are several U.S. financial services firms that rate municipal bond issues in the United States, and increasingly the subnational debt issues in developing countries. Moody's, Standard & Poor's, and Fitch are the largest. They all use quite similar rating categories and similar criteria. The lower the grade, the riskier the bond issue, and therefore, in general, the higher the interest rate the issuer will have to pay to attract investors.

Note that the rating is for an individual bond issue, not the issuer. The same issuer may have a variety of bonds in the market, and they may be rated differently, though because overall financial condition and management of the issuer are important factors in determining a rating, issues with similar characteristics from the same issuer are likely to be rated close to each other.

The table below lists the rating categories for those three major organizations with short adjectival phrases used by the organizations to describe the rating.

Rating Categories from the Three Major U.S. Rating Organizations

Moody's	Standard & Poor's	Fitch
Aaa Strongest creditworthiness	AAA Extremely strong capacity	AAA Highest credit quality
Aa Strong creditworthiness	AA Very strong capacity	AA Very high credit
A Above average	A Strong capacity	A High credit
Baa Average	BBB Adequate capacity	BBB Good credit quality
Ba Below average	BBB− Lowest investment grade	
B Weak creditworthiness	BB+ Highest speculative grade	BB Speculative
	BB Near-term less vulnerable, but long-term vulnerable	B Highly speculative
	B More vulnerable, but current capacity ok	
Caa Very weak	CCC Currently vulnerable	CCC Substantial credit risk

Exhibit 14-4 How Do Rating Agencies Evaluate Municipal Bond Issues? *(continued)*

Ca Extremely weak	CC Highly vulnerable	CC Very high-risk levels
C Weakest	C Highly vulnerable	C Exceptionally high risk
		RD Restricted default
	D Payment default	D Default/bankruptcy proceedings

Municipal Securities Rulemaking Board (2019). *Credit rating basics for municipal bond investors.* Retrieved July 20, 2019, from http://www.msrb.org/~/media /Files/Education/Credit-Rating-Basics-for-Municipal-Bond-Investors.ashx??

and below investment grade quality. Such a rating does not mean the issuer cannot sell the bonds. It means that investors, in the view of the rating agency, should be cautious and aware of the considerable risk associated with the issue before purchasing. The interest premium will be higher, or the issuer may have to sell the issue below par (below face value). Issues are almost never offered at below investment grade. However, outstanding issues may be re-rated to below investment grade quality if changes in conditions warrant.

Selling below par means the issuer will perhaps have to sell the issue at a percentage, illustratively 92%, of the face value of the bond. Discounting below par to 92% on a $100 million issue will net $92 million, but that is not what the issuer receives. Instead, the underwriter possibly might charge $500,000 in fees, netting only $91.5 million for the issuer. But at maturity, the issuer will be expected to repay the full $100 million.

In developing a rating for a specific issue, all rating agencies consider similar quantitative and qualitative information. A long list of basic information requirements from the issuer is common, such as the following:

1. Several recent years of annual audited financial statements
2. Several years of budget history and forecasts for the next several years
3. Capital improvement program
4. Sources of major revenues if general-purpose jurisdiction, and revenue source for the issue if a revenue bond
5. Complete statement of all outstanding debt and terms of debt
6. Basic economic conditions in the region of the issuing jurisdiction, including employment rates, employment by major employers, literacy and other education characteristics, property valuation, and sources of regular intergovernmental revenue (determined by formula)
7. Debt management policies
8. Basic institutional characteristics such as background and experience of key administrative and elected (if relevant) officials; mechanisms (electoral, appointment) and frequency for replacing key officials; and relevant national or state regulations that affect the operations of the issuer.

These are only examples drawn from the current public websites and published materials of the major rating agencies. The processes by which the rating agencies combine the various types of information are proprietary, but generally are relatively transparent to the issuer in that lengthy interviews and time onsite by professionals from the rating agencies explain the information requirements and the way the information is used in constructing a rating. For a rating agency that has previously rated debt from an issuer, a new issue may require only a modest update of the previously submitted information, especially if recent.

Rating agencies periodically review bond issues because conditions may change for the issuer, and/or changes may occur in the markets that affect the outstanding bonds. Because bonds are marketable for secondary resale—original purchasers may elect to sell the bonds before maturity—a regular reconfirmation or change in the rating is necessary to secure continued investor interest.

Credit Enhancement

One device that state and local governments may use to control the costs of debt and debt issuance is *insurance*. The issuer purchases bond insurance guaranteeing the principal of a bond issue to the purchaser. Before the financial market collapse of 2007–2008, there were nine companies insuring municipal bonds. Only two large companies survived as of 2018: Assured Guaranty and Build America Mutual.[56] The rating companies in the market before the market collapse suffered serious losses in the complex derivatives and structured finance fiascoes of that period and were either bought out by other firms or simply went out of business. In 2018, Assured Guaranty insured just under $11 billion in municipal issues; Build America Mutual insured just over $8 billion in new issues. Only about 6% of the value of new bond issues in 2018 were insured, up slightly from 2017.[57]

The near collapse of the municipal bond insurance industry was a function of the risky investments and business practices in the period leading up to the Great Recession combined with increasing evidence that insurance is not worth that much to most municipal bond issuers. A key conclusion from a study of over 700,000 municipal issues over 30 years was that prior to the recession, the high credit ratings of municipal insurance companies wrapped around the issues they insured saved about 0.1 percentage point

in borrowing costs After the recession, borrowers have found little to no effect from purchasing insurance on the price of the bond, and may cost more than any savings achieved.[58] Bond insurance is a shadow of its former importance and is used now for more specialized and often highly risky situations where the issuer may be unable to garner purchasers without the bond insurance.

Another type of credit enhancement is a *bank-issued line of credit*. The line of credit assures the bond buyer that the issuer will not be delayed in meeting payments even if short-term fluctuations in cash flow cause a temporary problem. The line of credit can be accessed if needed to meet the short-term cash flow problem. Bank lines of credit have been used successfully by new issuers in bond markets in strong emerging market economies.

There are also federal programs to enhance the credit of states and municipalities, assisting them in securing financing from the capital markets. The Fixing America's Surface Transportation of 2015 continued earlier federal programs, including some temporary programs enacted specifically to support infrastructure investment to stimulate growth during and shortly after the recession of 2007–2009.[59] The mechanisms are direct loans to state or local agencies, loan guarantees, and standby lines of credit. Except for a few projects, the limit of federal assistance is 33% of total project cost. These mechanisms enhance the creditworthiness of projects that might otherwise have difficulty securing 100% financing from bond issues and other credit mechanisms. Many of the projects assisted are public-private partnerships that involve both government and private actors in not only financing, but also operating and even owning the assets produced, such as toll roads. Public-private partnerships are the subject of the last section of this chapter.

Disclosure and Regulation

Municipal bond issuance is subject to the general regulatory functions of the SEC, as are all other public debt and equity issues in the U.S. financial markets. For decades, municipal debt instruments were specifically exempt from SEC regulation.

Beginning in the 1970s, however, Congress began to increase the role of the SEC in regulating municipal bond issues. Amendments to the Securities Exchange Act created the Municipal Securities Rulemaking Board (MSRB) in 1975 in the wake of New York City's financial crisis and the revelation that some dealers in state and municipal securities were involved in unethical and "dangerous" conduct.[60] The MSRB, the Financial Industry Regulatory Authority, and federal bank regulators all oversee aspects of the municipal bond market.

SEC regulations, for all underwriting and disclosure, focus on the underwriter's role and set disclosure requirements that affect the type and quality of information that underwriters must provide to potential investors. Significant new disclosure rules were adopted in 1990 (SEC Rule 15c–12) that pertain to the consistency and timeliness of an underwriter's release of information provided by the bond issuer. The quality of the information itself and all releases by the bond-issuing jurisdiction are still considered to be the jurisdiction's responsibility. The underwriter does not assume any liability properly borne by the issuer. Evidence suggests that disclosure improves the investor's ability to judge credit and hence improves credit ratings for creditworthy municipalities.

The MSRB was created to provide focus to the SEC's functions in regulating financial institutions in the municipal bond market. MSRB is the standard-setting body for all municipal securities dealers. Its authority extends only to dealers and others involved in municipal bond transactions, not to the actual issuing governments themselves. MSRB functions under the general authority of the SEC to ensure that the disclosure information is as accurate and timely as possible. It requires bond dealers to file repository copies of all official documentation on a municipal bond issue to make the information more widely available to all potential investors (Rule G-32). That rule requires any dealer selling municipal securities to deliver the issuer's official disclosure statement to the customer no later than the settlement date of that transaction.

MSRB also makes bond pricing information more widely accessible. Rule G-14 requires securities dealers to report daily to the Transactions Reporting Database all transactions in municipal securities, including both interdealer transactions and retail transactions in municipal bonds. MSRB provides a publicly accessible daily report on pricing and volume of municipal securities, enabling investors to get up-to-date information to guide investment decisions.[61]

A large step in imposing public disclosure requirements on the issuing jurisdictions themselves was the implementation of Nationally Recognized Municipal Securities Information Repositories. These repositories were sites for mandatory registration of municipal issues, accessible to the public. Four national repositories existed, including such financial services organizations as Bloomberg Financial Markets and Standard & Poor's as well as DPC Data and FP Interactive.[62] They played an important role in the era when disclosure documents were mainly paper documents. Since 2009, municipal security disclosure information must be sent also through the Electronic Municipal Market Access website, which replaced the role of the Repositories.[63] Municipal debt issuers must at least annually—and more often if conditions change—report on their financial condition. This reporting requirement extends for as long as the issuer has outstanding debt in the market, providing potentially valuable information to subsequent secondary market purchasers of municipal securities. Also, municipal debt issuers are required to maintain and report regularly on their overall financial condition, not just on the status of specific debt issues.

The additional disclosure requirements initially caused considerable consternation among many of the participants in the municipal bond market.[64] One particular requirement that securities dealers thought was too vague is the requirement that brokers and dealers must judge whether a client is capable of understanding the risk involved in an investment before they issue a recommendation to the client. The requirement (Rule G-17) persists. After the landmark Orange

County, California, financial fiasco (discussed later), there were far fewer attempts to reduce disclosure requirements of both issuers and dealers in the municipal securities market.

Debt Capacity and Management

Because the federal government borrows mainly for purposes other than capital investment, we focus in this chapter only on state and local governments. The chapter on government and the economy discusses federal debt. Media discussions of the federal debt and the size of the federal deficit raise citizens' consciousness of government debt, but locally, people are more interested in bond issues that finance local assets ranging from schools to new fire stations to water system expansion. The questions to be addressed in this section involve measuring debt (size and distribution), debt capacity (how much debt can be managed safely), and debt management practices to help ensure sound future financial condition.

Size of Debt

The size of debt can be assessed in several ways. The total amount of debt is probably the least meaningful measure. The fact that state and local governments' total outstanding debt in early 2019 was nearly $3.8 trillion, although this figure may sound staggering, is not really instructive.[65] Interest on state and local general debt in 2017 amounted to $44 billion, or only 2% of state and local general expenditures, and interest payments have declined over recent years.[66] This figure does not seem excessive when considering that many households commonly devote far more than 2% of their total expenditures to interest payments for home mortgages, car loans, and credit card debt.

Per Capita Debt

Per capita debt figures also help put the total government debt in perspective. How much per capita do state and local governments owe? In 2005, they owed $7,055 per capita, up 66% from 1995. In the first quarter of 2019, state and local governments owed $9,271 per capita.[67] Is that too much, too little, or just right? Is it growing, declining, or remaining stable? Per capita debt is one way of assessing size of the debt.

Figure 14-1 charts outstanding state and local per capita debt from 1975 through the first quarter of 2019. Per capita debt has risen at both the state and the local government levels, with local debt rising somewhat more rapidly than state debt. Since 2010, both have almost leveled off. Is the rapid rise through 2010 a cause for alarm, or does the 9-year trend since 2010 of little to no growth per capita alleviate the concern?

Ratio of Debt to Personal Income

Relating debt to personal income instead of population clears the picture somewhat. Calculating total debt outstanding per $1,000 of personal income is one way of assessing whether debt is in danger of becoming an unreasonable economic burden. Over time, debt in relation to personal income is a measure of affordability. For 50 years, combined state and local debt per $1,000 in personal income has remained relatively stable, ranging from $160 per $1,000 personal income to just over $200 per $1,000 in personal income. **Figure 14-2** charts that 50-year period. In 2017, state and local government debt per $1,000 in personal income was $187, almost identical to what it was in 1962. This pattern is considerably less alarming than the per capita data in Figure 14-1. Figure 14-2 shows that the debt has remained stable when measured in terms of per $1,000 in personal income, meaning that increases in personal income have kept up with debt levels for state and local governments.

One should use caution in interpreting the two figures. The data are aggregated across all 50 states, so it is an average. State and local debt per capita varies by state, as does debt per $1,000 in personal income. In addition, any analysis of total state and local debt is somewhat misleading in that the debt consists of both general obligations of state and local governments and revenue-backed obligations that do not encumber the taxing power of governments.

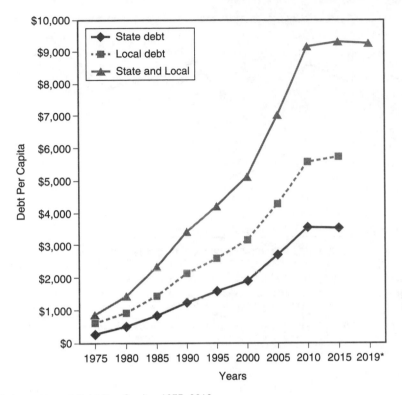

Figure 14-1 State and Local Debt Per Capita, 1975–2019.

*2019 data from FRBSL (2019) does not break out state and local.

Compiled from: Data for 1970–1990 from U.S. Bureau of the Census. (1985). *Statistical Abstract of the United States: 1985.* Washington, DC: U.S. Government Printing Office, 274; Data for 1990–2015 from ProQuest LLC. (2019). *ProQuest Statistical abstract of the United States: 2019.* Lanham, MD: ProQuest LLC, 298; 2019 data from Federal Reserve Bank of St. Louis (2019). *State and local government debt outstanding.* Retrieved July 20, 2019, from https://fred.stlouisfed.org/series/SLGSDODNS.

Revenue-backed obligations for services such as water and sewer do not create a tax burden on individuals; rather, those obligations are paid by the users of the services. GO bonds are only approximately one-third of total state and local debt outstanding. Thus, taxpayers were obligated for about $62 per $1,000 in personal income through taxes in 2017.

Ultimately, whether the size of state and local debt is reasonable is a subjective judgment. The main factors used in making such an appraisal are the financial burden on individual taxpayers and the economy and the perceived value of the facilities and services purchased by the debt. Generally, debt varies somewhat with income and with the amount of state and local services. California had the highest debt outstanding in 2015 at $421 billion. This was an average of $10,794 per

capita. Massachusetts, a considerably less populous state and with outstanding debt only about one-third that of California had much higher per capita debt $13,722. Personal income per capita in Massachusetts was $58,159, compared with California's $51,201.[68] Both states are in approximately the same position comparing personal income per person and outstanding debt per person. Of course, the debt figures are total debt outstanding, not the amount of debt the state must repay in a single year.

States with higher incomes in general have higher debt, by almost any measure, and states with lower incomes have lower debt. In the end, it is a judgment call as to what state and local governments can afford, a judgment that is ultimately made by voters in general elections and referendums. A good way to understand how state and

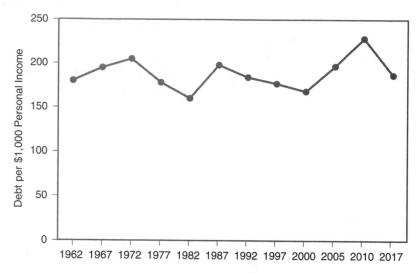

Figure 14-2 State and Local Debt per $1,000 Personal Income, 1962–2017.

Data for 1962–1982 compiled from U.S. Bureau of the Census (1984). *Historical Statistics on Governmental Finances and Employment.* Washington, DC: U.S. Government Printing Office, 113; Data for 1987 from U.S. Advisory Commission on Intergovernmental Relations (1992). *Significant Features of Fiscal Federalism, Vol.1: Revenues and Expenditures.* Washington, DC: U.S. Government Printing Office, 245; Data for 1992–1997 from U.S. Bureau of the Census. (2012). *Statistical Abstract of the United States: 2012.* Washington, DC: U.S. Government Printing Office, 443; personal income data for 2000–2017 are from ProQuest LLC. (2019). *ProQuest statistical abstract of the United States: 2019.* Lanham, MD: ProQuest LLC, 459; indebtedness data for 2000–2015 from ProQuest LLC. (2019). *ProQuest statistical abstract of the United States: 2019.* Lanham, MD: ProQuest LLC, 300; 2017 indebtedness data from U.S. Bureau of the Census. (2017). *State and local government finances by level of government and state: 2017.* Retrieved November 16, 2019, from https://www.census.gov/data/datasets/2017/econ/local/public-use-datasets.html.

local governments, including special districts, have fared with managing their debt historically is to look at defaults and bankruptcies.

Debt Default, Bankruptcies, and Financial Oversight

It is important to remember that the figures on debt do not reflect the full scope of future financial obligations of governments. Pension programs for public workers constitute a form of debt and are often inadequately funded. Debt defaults are correlated with economic cycles, but it should be noted that there have been few defaults on state or local indebtedness since the Great Depression of the 1930s. In that decade, about 4,800 state and local units defaulted on their obligations.[69] While that number may seem large, the total number of governments then was 150,000. Most of the defaults involved small jurisdictions. Fewer than 50 of these defaulting governments had populations of more than 25,000.[70]

Since that time, the number of defaults has been quite low. From 1970 to 2011, the average, cumulative default rate was less than 0.1%.

There were only 71 defaults during that period on debt rated by Moody's. Three of these were GO bonds[71]—Baldwin County, Alabama, in 1988; Jefferson County, Alabama, in 2008; and Sierra Kings Health Care District, California, in 2009. In the period 2010 through the first quarter of 2019, only nine general purpose local governments filed for bankruptcy. Sixty other entities filing for bankruptcy between 2010 and 2019 were mainly special purpose districts. Many of these entities were small, such as the Natchez Regional Medical Center (county owned) and numerous other hospital authorities.[72]

Averages can mask wide variation. Riskier issues, such as multifamily housing and nonprofit health care organizations—including some hospitals—experience much higher default rates, whereas municipal GO bonds and water and sewer and similar revenue-backed bonds experience default rates in the range of less than 0.05%. Even more interesting is the fact that, since the Great Depression, no state has defaulted on a debt (even then, only Arkansas postponed payments). Even municipalities that go into bankruptcy proceedings typically emerge with creditors paid off, at least on GO bonds. More often, the cases are ones in which the issuing jurisdiction or authority is delinquent (late) in debt payments, rather than default. That is the case in the Sierra Kings Health Care District example above.

School district issues almost never default, in part because they are typically full faith and credit bonds backed by the independent school district's taxing authority, or in the case of city or county school Districts, the taxing authority of the full

jurisdiction. Overall, Moody's Investor Services research shows that the default rate for bonds rated Baa or better is virtually nil. For all rated securities, a 10-year average through 2016, which includes the effects of the Great Recession, was 0.15% for rated securities.[73]

Exhibit 14-5 describes in more detail some of the major historic and recent examples of municipal bankruptcies, defaults, or jurisdictions temporarily placed under the control of a state agency to deal with debt and financial crises.

Exhibit 14-5 Famous (or Infamous) Defaults and Bankruptcies

Few public bond issuers have faced financial insolvency, although the exceptions have been noteworthy. In 1963, debt service payments on $100 million in revenue bonds for the Calumet Skyway in Chicago were interrupted. In the mid-1970s, New York City came close to bankruptcy as a result of extensive borrowing to meet operating budget requirements and defaulting on some of its short-term debt. As a result, New York City was partially placed under the supervision of a financial control board (see the chapter on intergovernmental relations). Only this intervention by the state government and the banking community prevented outright default on several bond issues. Also, in the 1970s, Cleveland defaulted on just over $15 million in tax anticipation notes, largely because of poor financial management practices and inadequate accounting procedures.[a]

The largest failure until the recession that started in 2007 was that of the Washington Public Power Supply System (WPPSS). In 1983, after a more than decade-long program of construction of five nuclear power generating plants, WPPSS defaulted on more than $2 billion in revenue bonds. The revenue bonds were issued in anticipation of the sale of electricity. WPPSS got caught in the situation faced by the power industry in many parts of the country in the 1970s—a combination of slower rates of growth in electricity demand, rapid escalation in the costs of nuclear power plant construction, and rising interest rates.[b] In 1993, WPPSS successfully issued $800 million in bonds to refund the debt and was later reorganized into a new entity.[c]

The largest city to file for bankruptcy is Detroit, in 2013, putting at risk about $18.5 billion. The city was placed under state financial oversight for a 5-year period ending in 2018. During the oversight period, the city was able to shed some $7 billion of its liabilities and return to balanced annual budgets.[d]

Cuyahoga County, Ohio, and Orange County, California, became mired in financial difficulties as a result of their investment activities with their own pension funds and other sources of cash, plus those of numerous other local governments for which the counties acted as investment managers. Cuyahoga County lost $114 million on a $1.8 billion investment pool, but subsequently repaid most of the local government co-investors. Orange County invested its own pension funds and acted as the investor for almost 200 other local government units, with investments totaling more than $7 billion at the peak.[e] Orange County had a several-year history of achieving significant returns on its pension funds invested and acted as the investor for numerous other local government pension funds. The string of successful investment years perhaps blinded the investment managers, and Orange County borrowed in order to invest still more. A series of bad market years left the county with insufficient resources to repay the borrowed funds. Taxpayers refused to increase taxes to pay off the debt, and the county entered bankruptcy proceedings (see the financial management chapter for additional discussion). Neither the Cuyahoga County nor the Orange County cases had anything to do with municipal bond issuance.

(continues)

Exhibit 14-5 **Famous (or Infamous) Defaults and Bankruptcies** *(continued)*

Harrisburg, Pennsylvania, filed for bankruptcy in November 2011, owing more than $360 million, on which it had missed $65 million in payments due as of the bankruptcy filing. The debt was from financing a major renovation of a solid waste incinerator. Pennsylvania's Department of Economic and Community Development put in place an emergency plan to ensure that city services did not lapse.[f] In 2011, Jefferson County, Alabama, filed for bankruptcy protection with more than $3 billion in defaulted sewer debt. Most of the debt was the result of debt refinancing packages in 2002 and 2003, swapping variable rate debt for the previous fixed debt to avoid a large increase in sewer rates.[g]

These examples are exceptional, as the low municipal bankruptcy figures cited in this chapter document. The examples also illustrate that many major municipal or special district bankruptcies or financial takeovers are not caused by problems with a bond issue or even a portfolio of bond issues. Many are caused by disastrous local or regional financial conditions that overwhelm a municipality, including the ability to raise revenue to continue providing city services, or by poor financial management and sometimes corrupt practices

a. Cohen, N. (1989). Municipal default patterns: an historical study. *Public Budgeting & Finance, 9*, Winter, 62.

b. Leigland, J., & Lamb, R. (1986). *WPP$$: who is to blame for the WPPSS disaster?* Cambridge, MA: Ballinger.

c. Sitzer, H. (1994). The Washington Public Power Supply System: then and now. *Municipal Finance Journal, 14*, Winter, 59–78.

d. Farmer, L. (2018). Detroit may be out from under state oversight, but its problems are far from over. *Governing (online)*. Retrieved July 20, 2019, from https://www.governing.com/week-in-finance/gov-finance-roundup-detroit-exits-state-oversight.html.

e. Halstead, J., et al. (2004). Orange County bankruptcy: financial contagion in the municipal bond and bank equity markets. *Financial Review, 39*, 293–315.

f. Burton, P. (2011). Attorney for Harrisburg, Pa., puts bondholders first. *The Bond Buyer*, November 9. Retrieved November 10, 2011, from http://www.bondbuyer.com/issues/120_216/harrisburgpa-bankruptcy-1032952-1.html; Burton, P. (2011). Pa. emergency action plan ensures services for Harrisburg. *The Bond Buyer*, November 4. Retrieved November 10, 2011, from http://www.bondbuyer.com/news/harrisburg-emergency-action-bankruptcy-1032821-1.html.

g. Sigo, S. (2011). Jefferson county finally files for bankruptcy. *The Bond Buyer*, November 9. Retrieved November 10, 2011, from http://www.bondbuyer.com/news/jeffco-1032991-1.html.

Although for residents of these various communities and investors the headlines are often dramatic, the lesson from the history of municipal bond defaults and municipal bankruptcies is that services almost always continue uninterrupted and investors typically get at least the principal back from their investments. Typically, refinancing is worked out, and investors suffer a loss on the return they had expected but do not suffer the same fate as often faced by investors in corporate bonds.

In the section below on debt capacity, we discuss measures that are often used as norms for what state and local governments should be able to afford based on government revenues and expenditures for various purposes.

Debt Capacity
Measuring Debt Capacity

Measuring debt capacity is an art rather than a science. Since the 1980s, the public finance and budgeting profession has paid considerably more

attention to improving that art. Three main factors influence debt capacity: expenditure pressures, resource availability, and the commitment of government officials to use resources to meet debt requirements.[74] To these might be added voters' willingness to accept the actions of their elected officials. Expenditure analysts look at the present and potential future commitments of jurisdictions. Population growth, changing economic conditions, the state of the current capital facilities and infrastructure base, and the socioeconomic characteristics of the population are important influences on potential future expenditures.

Assessing resource availability involves analyzing all potential sources of revenue, including own-source revenues; transfers from other levels of government; and types of self-financing, including user charges, special assessments, impact fees, and a variety of other measures to collect fees or revenues sufficient to support the specific project or facility (see the chapter on budgeting for revenues). The willingness of lenders to purchase debt is reflected ultimately in the interest rate they will require to lend. Revenue and expenditure analyses are used by state and local governments to support capital budgeting and debt management. Fiscal capacity analysis, focusing on the ability to generate revenues and on expenditure needs, is used to determine present fiscal conditions and estimate future conditions. Against that backdrop, the financial requirements and budgetary impact of possible capital investments and debt financing alternatives can be assessed.

Debt Burden

There are two common ratios used to measure overall debt burden:

1. the ratio of debt service (payments for principal and interest) to total expenditures of the debt issuer, and
2. the ratio of debt service to current revenues.

It is most common to look only at a municipality's own-source revenues as the denominator in the debt service to current revenues ratio. Own-source revenues are those the jurisdiction controls itself, mainly revenue from property taxes. In most cases, municipalities determine the property tax rate, except in situations such as California's where there are constitutional limits on the amount that may be increased (see chapter on income, payroll, and property taxes). State legislatures typically determine local jurisdictions' shares of the sales tax generated within those jurisdictions' boundaries. Own-source revenue does include sales tax revenues (from state sales taxes), but if the legislature is considering changing the redistribution formula, an analysis with share of state sales tax under current law and under proposed alternatives is appropriate. Respectively, these ratio measures indicate how much of the issuer's revenue, once the new debt is incurred, will be required to pay debt service.

Another, less common, ratio measure is debt service to expenditure.[75] Although there are no hard-and-fast rules, the County of Riverside, California, in 2015–2016 was upgraded in its credit rating as stable by Fitch, and a Standard & Poor's stable rating was reaffirmed for improving the level of debt service to total expenditures.[76] The City of Alexandria, Virginia, used S&P's rating criteria in a financial management self-assessment, noting debt service as a percentage of general government expenditures target at 8% with a 10% limit and debt as a percentage of total personal income at a 3.2% target with a 4.5% limit.[77]

One caution is that analysis of state debt that focuses only on borrowing for infrastructure and other capital investments may neglect an important component of possible future debt: unfunded pension and retiree health costs. States, and many large cities and counties, have varying types of pension funds that fall mainly into two categories: defined benefit and defined contribution. Although accounting standards for government entities have become much more rigorous in the last half century, there are still many states and some large cities that have defined benefit programs for which sufficient funds have not been set aside or for which investments are lagging behind payment obligations (see chapter on financial management, accounting, and reporting). If future payouts will exceed likely revenue, these plans are said to have unfunded liabilities. Some states have large unfunded retiree obligations that exceed liabilities from debt. **Table 14-3** illustrates the importance of unfunded pension and retiree health benefits in relation to state GO debt. The table considers only GO debt, excluding debt secured by user charges to customers, pledged revenue streams, and other sources that are not a legal obligation of the state's general funds.

Alaska is the state with the highest ratio of unfunded pension and retiree health benefits to GO debt.[78] Their unfunded liabilities as a percentage of state personal income is 16 times the liability for GO debt as a percentage of state personal income. At the other end is Wisconsin; their unfunded obligations are just over 10% of their GO debt. The average across all 50 states is 3. For some states and cities, unfunded retiree-related benefits are a serious impediment to funding capital infrastructure. All the rating agencies consider unfunded future obligations a reason for rating a GO debt issue lower than it might be otherwise,

Table 14-3 **State GO Debt, Unfunded Pension, and Unfunded Retiree Health Benefits as a Share of State Personal Income**

	GO Debt	Unfunded Pension	Unfunded Retiree Health Benefits	Total GO Plus Unfunded
50 State Average	3.7%	6.9%	4.2%	14.8%
Highest Risk—Alaska	3.1%	23.7%	26.2%	53.0%
Lowest Risk—Wisconsin	4.3%	0.1%	4.0%	8.4%

Pew Charitable Trust (2018). *Fiscal 50: state trends and analysis, debt and unfunded retirement costs as a share of state personal income, 2013.* Retrieved July 22, 2019, from https://www.pewtrusts.org/en/research-and-analysis/data-visualizations/2014/fiscal-50#ind4.

adding to the cost of the bond issue to the issuer. This is one reason the trend has been steadily down in GO debt issues in favor of revenue-backed bonds and other debt that does not pledge the jurisdiction to use all its resources, if necessary, to pay off the debt.

Internationally, the World Bank often looks at the ratio of debt service to current revenues, the ratio of capital expenditures to total expenditures, and the excess of current revenues over ordinary operating expenditures as indicators of the ability of a city to incur additional debt. More refined measures focus not on actual revenues, but on the revenue base itself. U.S. local governments commonly use the ratio of debt to the assessed value of taxable property, because that assessed value reflects a local government's basic ability to generate revenues. These quick indicators are all useful, but ultimately, they are interpretable only in the context of a jurisdiction's overall debt management strategy.

For enterprise-like operations, such as water authorities, conventional ratio measures of debt burden are in common use. The *debt-to-equity ratio* is a measure of the extent to which a utility is financing itself through debt relative to equity. The higher the ratio, the more risk there is in additional debt issues, as lenders want to see borrowers also making significant commitments of their own resources (equity). Another common ratio, *interest share of operating income*, measures the amount of debt as a percentage that operating income must cover.

Debt Management

In general, sound debt management at the state and local levels involves restricting debt primarily to financing long-term investments. A general rule is that borrowing should not be used to meet current operating expenses. The much-publicized 1970s financial crisis experienced by New York City involved short-term borrowing to finance current expenses. State regulations and in some cases statutory limitations generally prohibit short-term borrowing for operating expenses, except for good cash-flow management practices. Occasionally, short-term borrowing is used to deal with emergencies, but is often refinanced as part of a long-term debt issue. Moreover, as a rule of thumb, the payout period of the debt should correspond to the useful life of the facility or infrastructure financed.

The rule to restrict debt to long-term capital financing does not apply to financial emergencies resulting from major flooding or unusually heavy snows during the winter or states' emergency responses to the Gulf of Mexico Deepwater Horizon oil spill and Puerto Rico's situation after Hurricane Maria. But this rule, along with the rule to match the payout period for the debt with the expected life of the facility, should generally be followed. Adherence to these two rules ensures that the jurisdiction will match the benefit flows from capital facilities with the opportunity costs. One of the major positive results of the financial difficulties of cities such as New York has been an increase in the sophistication of the tools used in analyzing the financial condition of governments. These developments have been of great value in preventing significant financial crises and almost no collapses at the state and local levels after the 2007 financial markets collapse (see Exhibit 14-5). Furthermore, state governments have become quite involved in regulating local government debt, not only by means of the more traditional statutory and constitutional provisions that govern the powers and authority of local governments but also by means of extensive state programs of technical assistance. Effective debt management requires the balancing of competing claims against the current annual budget and future annual budgets. Therefore, state and local governments increasingly rely on methods to assess overall financial health and place potential bond issues in that context.

Debt Refinancing

From time to time, substantial swings in market conditions bring interest rates down and spur a round of refinancing bonds. Municipalities may issue a new bond during a period of lower interest rates and use the proceeds to pay off an older bond that has higher interest costs. This is known as advance refunding. Prior to the 2017 Tax Cuts and Jobs Act (TCJA), the interest earned on these advance refunding bonds was tax exempt even when the proceeds were held for a considerable period of time.[79] After TCJA, the interest earned by the purchaser is tax exempt only if the advance refunding bond is used to retire debt within ninety days of the advance refunding issue date.[80] Issues for new capital versus for refunding existing municipal securities has varied considerably over time. In 1990, the value of new capital issues was 80% of total issues, but only 46% in 2017. When interest rates are falling, and municipal issuers have outstanding debt at higher interest rates, refunding issues are attractive.[81]

An alternative that does not require any actual transaction with outstanding bonds is an *interest rate swap*. In this type of transaction, the borrowing authority agrees to pay a third-party financial investor a variable rate of interest over a fixed period in exchange for payment of a fixed rate of interest by the third party. This is a synthetic variable rate financing deal in that the bonds themselves remain as they were with the terms and conditions unchanged.

The interest rate swap works by introducing a third party into the transactions between issuers and investors. During a period of high interest rates, for example, bond issuers try several strategies to control the effects of high interest. One strategy is to issue serial bonds, breaking the total issue into several annual tranches. If interest rates do fall from the high at the time the choice is made to issue a bond over a series of years, then the later tranches carry lower rates. Another strategy is to issue variable interest rate bonds tied to some short-term rate index. The issuer then may enter into a contract with a third party in which, for a fee, the third party agrees to swap fixed rate payments for the variable rate payments. The issuer decides from time to time whether to take the swap. The issuer "bets" that the fee paid for the swap option over time will be less than what the issuer saves by exercising the swap option.

Interest rate swaps can help or hurt. When variable rate securities are swapped for fixed rate, and interest rates then fall, issuers find themselves with higher interest costs. Harvard University, for example, paid investors almost $500 million to get out of $1.1 billion in interest rate swaps.[82] In contrast, the Cleveland Airport bond issue described earlier in this chapter included a successful refinancing that lowered overall future interest costs for the city-owned airport.[83]

Typically, a debt swap is neutral with respect to bondholders. The state or local authority is simply trading in the financial market based on judgments about future interest rates. The original bond issue is not affected, in that investors will be paid according to the original terms. The borrowing authority, through a separate transaction, hedges against future interest rate changes and achieves, through a third party, a gain or a loss based on the marginal interest rate differences. The risk analysis focuses on whether the overall portfolio of the borrowing authority has been exposed to higher or lower future interest payments.

Public-Private Partnerships (PPPs) for Public Capital Assets

The preceding sections of this chapter have focused on the traditional approach to state and local government infrastructure finance: long-term borrowing. The last section of this chapter focuses on direct private participation as a source of finance for public infrastructure. Private equity investments in public infrastructure involve some form of partnership between the private and public sector. A substantial amount of public infrastructure finance around the world now involves such public-private partnerships (PPPs). The World Bank's database of projects financed by a combination of private debt, private equity, and public funds lists nearly 7,000 projects with a total investment value of almost $2 trillion in the period 1990–2018.[84]

The aim of PPPs is to bring private capital and private sector operating expertise to build and operate public infrastructure. Each project in the World Bank database has a minimum of 15% private equity investment in the project, from either one or more private companies or foreign state-owned enterprises. This section discusses the various forms in which private equity and operational expertise become involved in infrastructure projects, and the benefits and risks to the public sector in PPPs.

Not all forms of PPPs are considered in this section. For example, contracting with private companies to perform a public service, such as contracting out solid waste collection, may not involve private equity capital investment in public infrastructure. If such a contracting arrangement does involve service contracting plus equity investment, such as contracting for solid waste collection *and* licensing a company to use its own capital to build and operate a solid waste disposal facility, then it is considered in this section. Likewise, if an arrangement involves a contract turning over the assets of an existing infrastructure system or other capital asset to a private party, either for a fixed period or permanently, it is also considered in this section.

The terminology of PPPs can seem mysterious, emphasizing what are sometimes subtle distinctions. There is not a universal vocabulary in which everyone agrees on exactly what to call any given PPP structure. To describe PPPs, this chapter uses the terms *concession contracts*, including build-operate-transfer (BOT) contracts and build-own-operate-transfer (BOOT), and *divestiture*.

Concession Contracts

Concession contracting involves a substantial change from conventional public sector financing and operation of public service facilities. Concession contracting involves the government awarding a contract with one or more companies for construction and operation of a service, such as a water utility, for a fixed concession period.[85] For a public utility, 15 to 30 years is a common time frame. Large transportation projects such as toll roads may be much longer, as much as 99-year concessions. After the concession period, operation of the facility reverts to the public authority (for example, a city or a public utility).

Concessions have several variations. The simplest is one in which the private contractor constructs or reconstructs *and* operates the facility for the contract period. In this structure, the contractor is not involved in the capital financing, and there is no private ownership. A public bond issue, for example, may provide the financing. A second variant does require private contractor involvement in financing, but not ownership. This variant is often called a *Build-Operate-Transfer (BOT)* contract. The private party constructs the facility, often including participating in the financing; operates during the concession period; and then transfers operations back to the public authority.

In a more complex concession, the contractor is responsible for all debt and equity capital financing to rehabilitate an existing facility and/or to expand the service to new users. This type of concession is often called a *Build-Own-Operate-Transfer (BOOT)* project. For the equity financing, the private party secures ownership, for the duration of the concession contract. A common BOOT project is a so-called *greenfield* project. A greenfield project is physically and contractually separate from an existing facility or system. It involves private financing, both debt and equity, and the construction and operation of an entirely new and separately managed facility. For example, a public water utility may operate the existing water supply system and award a concession contract for a complete, independent water system to provide water to a previously unserved area. The private party owns that new facility for the duration of the concession. A BOOT project also may be awarded for substantial rehabilitation of an existing service, extension of service to new areas including ownership and operation of the entire public utility for the period of the concession.

Build-Operate-Transfer (BOT) Concessions

An example of a BOT is the New Jersey Hudson-Bergen Light Rail (HBLR). A Phase I contract valued at $1.1 billion was awarded in 1996 to a private consortium consisting of an infrastructure construction company and two railway car and other railway products manufacturers and operators to build and operate for a 15-year period the first (9.5 miles) segment of an eventual 25-mile light rail system along the Hudson River in two counties. The private contractor was responsible for designing, building, and operating for the 15-year contract period the entire system, including construction of the railway and the stations and provision of the rolling stock. Financing was public, and ownership remained public.

Two additional phases were added: Phase II in 2002–2006 with a contract value of $1.2 billion and Phase III in 2011–2016 with a contract value of $100 million. Phase III was completed and operational in 2011 with the operating concession continuing through 2019. In July 2019, the New Jersey Transit Corporation approved extending the concession through 2021.[86]

The private consortia consisted of a U.S.-owned construction and engineering firm (AECOM) and two Japanese companies specializing in railway car construction operations (Itochu Rail Car and Kinkisharyo USA). The consortia assumed an operating responsibility for HBLR but assumed no responsibility for capital finance. The state of New Jersey issued bonds to finance the project, secured by a pledge of future federal transit grants—*grant anticipation note*—authorized under federal transportation support programs. If these discretionary grants were not awarded, or were insufficient, a secondary pledge of funds in the New Jersey State transportation trust fund secured the bonds, though the secondary pledge was not needed.

BOT contracts have been common in the electric power generation and bulk water supply industries for decades, especially in developing countries where the existing power supply often is either inadequate or nonexistent. A BOT concession is awarded to a private contractor to build, operate, and, at the end of the contract period, transfer to the public sector the new facility. In the bulk water supply industry, the BOT contract is used to build and operate for a designated period a new impoundment, a new deep well system, or a new extraction/treatment plant to obtain bulk water from an existing source such as a river. Malaysia has used the BOT mechanism extensively for new bulk water and treatment facilities.

BOT concessions often are characterized by what is called a *take-or-pay mechanism* for determining payments to the contractor. That is, the contractor agrees to deliver a minimum volume, for instance, kilowatts of electricity or cubic meters of water, and the public utility agrees to buy at least that minimum amount. Price per unit is based on that minimum. The public utility will *take* that minimum for which the private contractor likely will be paid by tariffs paid by the consumers. But if the minimum is not actually required by the utility's customers, the utility will nonetheless *pay* the contractor for that minimum. The contractor has the assurance of the minimum, but if demand is there, the contractor may sell more than the minimum.

BOT contracts commonly require some minimum proportion of the capital investment to be the private operator's equity investment, meaning the contractor cannot limit investment only to borrowed funds. This equity investment is intended to protect the public sector against the contractor terminating the agreement early. With no equity investment, the contractor has nothing invested to lose, and should anything go wrong; the debt suppliers are the ultimate losers, along with the public utility executing the deal in the first place and its customers.

BOT structures often involve public funding as well as private funding, or they may require that the contractor finance the entire project. The contractor needs assurances of operating the facility for a period enough to achieve a return on its equity and to repay debt financing. The public agency needs to ensure that the prices charged are reasonable in the market and that the facility is still in operating condition at the time of the transfer. Contract negotiations revolve around these two sets of provisions.

Build-Own-Operate-Transfer (BOOT) Concessions

The distinguishing feature of a BOOT concession is that the private investor/operator, for the concession period, owns the capital assets. BOOT contracts have provisions for transfer to the public entity without cost to the public or the public entity's buying the facility at a negotiated price at the end of the contract period. Note that this is not a salvage price, the residual value of an asset whose useful life has for the most part been exhausted. The utility at transfer is expected to be fully operational, to have been well maintained, and to be able to provide service continuously into the future.

BOOT concession contracts with publicly owned and operated water and wastewater systems are common. **Exhibit 14-6** is a case study of the Buenos Aires water concession awarded in 1993. It is an important case because long-term concession contracts are decades in planning and implementation, illustrating the complexities of large concessions. The case study illustrates the main characteristics of concession contracting involving private equity investment and ownership. The concession also has sufficient history to consider outcomes separate from the publicity and euphoria surrounding the award of major concessions.

Exhibit 14-6 Buenos Aires Water Concession

Under the Buenos Aires contract, all bidders were required to invest $240 million per year for the first 5 years in infrastructure. This compares with only about $10 million per year in capital investments in the preceding several years by the public sector utility. The competition was decided based on which bidder offered the largest rate reduction. The winner contracted to reduce water rates by 26.9%, slightly above the 26.1% proposed by the second closest bidder.[a]

The Buenos Aires concession illustrates many of the features typically designed to ensure that the public sector's responsibility for the public service is treated by the concessionaire as a *public* responsibility and that consumers' interests are protected by provisions in the contract:

1. Water quality and quantity requirements such as volume and water pressure
2. Operating improvements such as installing a metering system
3. New capital facilities such as building sewage treatment plants
4. Increased population coverage for water and sewerage services
5. Tariffs fixed for 5 years at a time, and otherwise renegotiable only as a result of situations beyond the concessionaire's control
6. Preservation of employment and negotiation of union contracts
7. Significant capital investment; in the Buenos Aires case, this was at least $4 billion over the life of the concession, more than $1 billion of which was to be invested in the first five years. The project was subsequently augmented with the investment target just over $2 billion in the first 10 years.[b]

In this concession-type arrangement, the concessionaire is responsible for all financing, both capital and operating. The public sector is not required to provide capital grants or to raise debt capital for the program. One of the main features, aside from specific contract provisions of the type listed above, is that

---

Exhibit 14-6 Buenos Aires Water Concession   *(continued)*

---

the concession contract stipulates the minimum amount of the capital investment that must come from concessionaire's equity participation. This has the effect of ensuring the concessionaire's performance over the concession period. The public sector is interested in seeing the concessionaire finance as large a proportion of the cost as can be negotiated as equity investment, whereas the private party is usually interested in minimizing the equity investment. Typical outcomes are 15% to 30% equity investment.

The economics of the concession was built around extension of services to almost one-third more water supply customers and nearly 40% more sewerage customers. However, not enough consideration was given to the fact that most of the new customers were low-income households who would at best pay the basic life rate only. There were immediate gains in water rate cuts of almost 27%, but gradually rate increases were necessary to balance the large increase in customers paying only the basic life rate. Initially favorable public opinion turned negative within a decade of project inception. Some of the negative public perception was due to layoffs of almost 60% of the grossly overstaffed water and sewer utility.[c] Overall, the concession proved successful in expanding water and sewerage service as well as reducing unit costs of production and delivery of services. The International Finance Corporation in 2017 provided additional financing for further expansion and system upgrades.[d]

a. The World Bank (2001). *The Buenos Aires concession: the private sector serving the poor* (pp. 1–2). Washington, DC: World Bank.

b. The World Bank (2001). *The Buenos Aires concession*, 3; Delfino, J., et al. (2007). *How far does it go? The Buenos Aires water concession a decade after the reform* (pp. 5–6). New York, NY: United Nations Social Policy and Development Programme.

c. Alcazar, L. et.al. (2000). *The Buenos Aires Water Concession*. Retrieved November 19, 2019, from https://www.researchgate.net/publication/23722302_The_Buenos _Aires_Water_Concession.

d. International Finance Corporation (2017). *IFC approves three infrastructure projects in Argentina: new investments in water, power and port sectors*. Retrieved November 19, 2019, from https://ifcextapps.ifc.org/ifcext/pressroom/ifcpressroom.nsf/0/03E3C97C6D6A50708525696C0051FD25?OpenDocument.

What the public sector gains from the equity investment is that the concessionaire has contributed its own capital and will not be able to make a profit unless it manages the utility efficiently and effectively to generate the return on equity. The more debt financing, the more other people's money other than that of the concessionaire is in the enterprise, the less incentive there is to maintain the physical infrastructure. And in the worst case, the concessionaire going bankrupt in an all debt-financed enterprise would leave the concessionaire without a significant capital loss, having no equity in the enterprise, and the public holding the bag with a dysfunctional public service.

The difficulties inherent in negotiating contracts involving private ownership of a public utility or service, including addressing public concerns for turning over an asset to the private sector even temporarily, are apparent in the case of Edison Township, New Jersey's negotiations in 2019 for an $811 million, 40-year water and wastewater BOOT concession contract with Suez North America. The concessionaire would have made substantial investments in infrastructure improvements. In exchange, Suez would operate the facility and retain water rate payments for the 40-year period. The degree of ownership and control that would have been conceded to Suez ultimately proved to be too much for township residents. A public referendum in late 2019 failed to approve the concession by a large margin.[87]

Edison Township's negotiations were for a very modest concession contract. Major concession contracts typically take 3 to 5 years to design, bid, and negotiate. To protect the public interest, the negotiating public entity spends considerable capital on legal and financial advisory fees. The concessionaires, of course, are sophisticated in the business of private investment in the specific service and in operating the business. Developing countries especially, but also smaller jurisdictions in industrialized countries, can be at a significant disadvantage in negotiating the concession contracts.

Divestiture/Privatization

Divestiture or privatization differs from concession contracts by complete sale or turnover of control of public assets to a private party. A public sector entity may decide upon divestiture of a set of assets because the facility is deteriorating, needs significant investment, or is perhaps at the periphery of what the public now thinks of as a "public sector responsibility." Not all *privatizations* involve an irrevocable sale of assets. Municipally owned parking garages are an example of a public asset that sometimes is irrevocably sold to a private party, with the municipality retaining no interest in the garage. Other so-called privatizations are actually leasing for a period, such as 99 years, that for all practical purposes are seen by the public as permanent.

For example, in 2006, Chicago executed a 99-year lease on the Skyway, an expressway connecting Chicago and Indiana, to an international consortium for $1.83 billion. The other bids were considerably smaller, suggesting that Chicago made a good deal with the lease. That observation seems born out in that Chicago was able to pay off bonds issued to construct the Skyway, pay off other city debt, and put money into a long-term reserve fund.[88] Though there were suggestions that the original consortium's bid much higher than other competitors' bids was not such a good deal for the winner, a decade later, the original consortium sold its lease to a consortium of three Canadian pension plans, for $2.8 billion, a tidy profit. As of 2016, half of the funds received from the privatization remained unspent in a city reserve fund.[89] The contract for the privatization contained limits on the amount by which tolls could be increased over time by the concession contractor.

Also in 2006, the state of Indiana leased for 75 years the Indiana East-West Toll Road, which feeds into the Chicago Skyway, at a cost of $3.8 billion, to the same two international companies that originally won the Skyway project.[90] In contrast, efforts by New Jersey to privatize the New Jersey Turnpike did not materialize.[91]

At the heart of the divestiture decision on the part a of governmental institution is whether the assets being divested are a fundamental public sector responsibility that can or should be turned over to the private sector. If a service is regarded as a fundamental public sector responsibility, why bring in the private sector, which lacks traditional public service values? But there is no clear answer in many cases, as only a few public sector goods meet the test of a pure public good (see the introductory chapter). Many public services may have varying degrees of private sector involvement without real consequence to the public one way or the other. Many cities own and operate parking garages, for example. Many other cities have no public parking garages but leave parking entirely in the hands of the private sector. There is no obvious criterion that says parking garages should clearly be public, or clearly be private—or at least there is no criterion upon which everyone agrees.

Historically, many county governments owned their local hospitals. As the health care sector became increasingly complicated, smaller publicly owned hospitals, just like smaller private hospitals, became uneconomical. Local governments, not able to afford subsidizing the hospital to keep them open, have resorted to divestiture—outright sale of the hospital to private for-profit and nonprofit health management companies. New Hanover County, North Carolina, in 2019 started exploring the possible sale of county-owned New Hanover Regional Medical Center (NHRMC). NHRMC at that time was the third largest county-owned hospital in the country, with estimated asset value to the county of $1 to $1.5 billion.[92] Unlike many local government–owned hospitals, NHRMC was self-supporting, receiving no funding from the county government. The county motivations for considering sale were perhaps a $1 billion revenue windfall. For the hospital, merging with a larger health care industry player could bring needed investment capital to keep up with changes in health care technology. Hospitals, electric power–generating companies, and airports all have been active targets for municipal divestiture or privatization of businesses that serve a public purpose but operate like self-sustaining businesses that may benefit from better access to capital and technology.

Appraisal of Private Equity Investment and Divestiture Experience

The controversy over privatization or divestiture usually arises when citizens or interest groups feel the city, or other governmental entity, is turning over a fundamental public interest to the private sector and leaving citizens (especially poorer citizens) unprotected in the aftermath. The failure of the Edison Township, New Jersey, water concession is a good illustration of a decision made by public officials who were then forced by public opinion to hold a referendum, a referendum that failed to support the concession.[93] Similarly, the success of the Indiana East-West toll road contract is attributed in large part to a high level of public involvement and legislative/executive checks and balances in full play.[94]

In every developing country, water sector public-private partnerships of any of the forms above lead to higher prices to some consumers. But, this is often in the context of systems that have been previously heavily subsidized with the utility rarely recovering capital costs, and often not even fully recovering operating costs. The utility usually faces a major need for renovation and expansion as a result of urbanization, and the capital is just not available to the public sector.

Typically, in these developing countries, the wealthy and middle-income segments have been the only ones receiving direct piped service to their residences, and they enjoy low, subsidized rates. The extremely poor segment of the population pays for bottled water or buys from vendors who travel through impoverished neighborhoods, and the price they pay per liter is generally 5 to 10 times more than the per-liter cost to a middle-income household connected to the public system. The concession contract or divestiture can be quite controversial because current customers almost always experience rate increases, although the average rate may go down because of the addition of lower-income, low-volume users. One of the remedies for protecting the lowest income segment is what is sometimes called the *life support* tariff. The first several cubic liters of water

service, an amount estimated to be the amount needed to live, is free or billed at a very low cost. Rates then go up as consumption goes up, and the middle- and upper-income groups thus pay more.

In some of the examples cited in this chapter, such as the Buenos Aires case in Exhibit 14-6, the concession is for services in which the existing management of the utility has become inefficient, including possibly employing a much larger workforce because the utility was serving not only to provide water, but to provide the social good of employment whether the employees were required or not. In those cases, the concession contract may lower the marginal cost of the service.

Certainly, there are examples of high expectations not being met.[95] A famous, sometimes considered infamous, case of failed expectations were two water concession contracts executed in 1997. The metropolitan District of Jakarta was split into two parts, with separate concession contracts competed for east and west Jakarta. The projects were financed with debt and equity capital from the private investors and World Bank and International Finance Corporation assistance. The initial lead international partners in the two concession contracts were Thames Water and Suez Lyonnaise des Eaux, respectively. Thames was one of the U.K. private water companies resulting from the divestiture of public water authority assets in the United Kingdom in the 1980s. Suez Lyonnaise was a French private water operator. Both lead international companies started as public utilities. Each had developed, over decades, formidable technical and financial expertise in constructing and operating water systems by the time of concession awards. As is common in concession contracts with private financing and a lengthy operating contract, the concession awards for Jakarta included targets to increase service coverage and reduce water losses.

The Jakarta concessions were awarded only months before the overthrow of the Suharto regime and less than a year before the 1997–1998 Asian financial collapse that caused the Indonesian rupiah to devalue against the U.S. dollar from about 3,700 to 1 to about 20,000 to 1.

Water consumers in Jakarta paid their water tariffs in rupiah, whereas much of the debt and equity financing the concessionaires brought to the contracts were denominated in various international currencies, mainly the dollar, pound, and franc. The immediate problem as the concessions started to go sour was to renegotiate the tariffs on the grounds of a *force majeure* clause (unforeseeable external events outside the control of the contractors) that made the original contracts untenable. The Jakarta concessions were especially controversial because at the time the contracts were awarded, both international lead firms had joint ventures with companies owned and directed by members of the then-ruling Suharto family. Ultimately, the Supreme Court of Indonesia in 2017 upheld a lower court ruling that the Jakarta water contracts were illegal because they were awarded by the central government without involvement of Jakarta authorities.[96]

The 2007 financial market collapse similarly put a damper on long-term concession arrangements and full privatizations because of the lack of debt capital available to private investors seeking concession opportunities. Considerable experience has amassed in both the public and private sectors in the past three decades, and sophisticated expertise is more readily available to both sectors to protect the public interest and to ensure a fair return on investment to the private party. The 2007–2009 recession that affected capital markets worldwide, and serious problems that arose in some of the earliest PPPs for major infrastructure, dampened the number and value of PPPs for almost a decade. The World Bank, in its tracking of PPPs, has noted that the 335 projects valued at $90 billion in 2018 investments show a recovery from the 10-year low.[97]

Public interest groups and other watchdogs are actively engaged in informing the public, sometimes dispassionately and sometimes with a strong bias. We can confidently say, however, that various forms of private equity financing for major capital facilities providing public services will continue. The first driver is capital market expansion. As capital markets expand, investors such as pension funds look for attractive long-term investments. The second driver is the inability of governments to find enough capital themselves to meet the demand for infrastructure. As governments face pressures to focus on vital public services, they will likely consider divesting themselves of enterprise-like operations that are easily converted to private operations.

On the other hand, privatized or long-term concessions for public services that have significant nonmonetary value attached to public ownership and operation, such as water supply, in 2017–2019 may have started a trend toward *remunicipalization* (a municipality takes back over a utility it had previously privatized), at least in some developing countries where major projects have experienced problems, such as the Buenos Aires and Jakarta examples.[98] It seems certain that three decades of experience has produced much greater public scrutiny of concession contracts. This accumulated experience will equalize the knowledge and experience of both public and private parties and make the negotiation of major concessions more of a contest of equals. It also is fair to say that major PPPs are not for the faint of heart unless the public entity is prepared with enough independent advisors and willing to spend sometimes years and significant sums to reach a satisfactory contract.

Summary

Because of the long life of capital facilities and infrastructure, extensive use is made of long-term financing in various forms. Both the public and private sectors combine debt and equity financing to satisfy capital investment needs, with equity financing for public sector infrastructure a phenomenon that has emerged in the past 30 years. Some local governments still consider it financially prudent to borrow little or not at all, but state governments and virtually all large cities are unable to provide the services demanded by citizens without resorting to some debt financing for capital investments. Although it is generally accepted that future generations should not be saddled with unreasonable debt burdens about which they have no say, most citizens recognize that capital facilities will be enjoyed by future generations. Debt financing provides a means for those future generations to share the costs as well as the benefits.

Governments typically lack the resources to fully finance the infrastructure requirements alone, although some smaller local governments do use *pay-as-you-go* financing. Governments have historically relied on long-term capital for financing, either securing debt capital through issuing bonds or borrowing from specialized public sector lending institutions, or in recent years private equity capital. The municipal debt market has undergone remarkable changes in the past decade. Sophisticated structured financing tools developed for private debt and equity transactions are being applied to municipal debt issues. In addition, municipalities are using increasingly sophisticated money management techniques to minimize their cost of debt and to maximize the returns on their own investments. Occasionally these techniques result in major financial disasters. As a result, the SEC, which once had a hands-off attitude toward the municipal debt market, has adopted increasingly stringent disclosure requirements, and Congress has increased the SEC's regulatory role regarding municipal debt.

Effective debt management requires that the amount of debt incurred not impose hardships on future taxpayers and that it not force future cutbacks in operation and maintenance expenditures necessary to maintain capital facilities. State governments, through constitutional provisions and statutory requirements, regulate their own borrowing as well as that of local governments. These regulations focus mainly on the commitment of the "full faith and credit" of the jurisdiction. Partly because of the restrictions imposed on general obligation bonds and partly because of the efficiency of tying repayment of debt to specific revenues generated by the investment, there has been tremendous growth in the use of a wide variety of debt instruments. Overall, however, state and local debt has grown little over the past 30 years in relation to personal income. State and local governments also have become more sophisticated in their financial analysis of capital investments and debt financing.

Even with innovations in municipal bonds and other means for governments to access the capital markets for credit, debt financing has not been enough. Beginning largely with the privatization of the United Kingdom's water utilities, the involvement of public-private partnerships in financing and operating public infrastructure has become commonplace in both industrialized and developing countries. Various forms of concession contracting, including structures that feature private operating concessions only to structures that feature significant private debt and equity financing, are increasing. This industry has had significant problems with many of the earliest large concession-type contracts, but with experience, sophistication on the sides of both private investors and the public sector has made various forms of private financing more attractive to both investors and public agencies.

Notes

1. Securities Industry and Financial Markets Association (2019). *U.S. Fixed Income Issuance and Outstanding: 2020 (downloaded report)*. Retrieved May 12, 2020, from https://www.sifma.org/search/?aq=Fixed%20Income%20Outstanding&hPP=10&idx=prod_wp_searchable_posts&ap=0&is_v=1.
2. Forbes. (2019). *The 20 largest private companies in America*. Retrieved July 17, 2019, from https://www.forbes.com/pictures/eimh45hlig/the-20-largest-private-companies-in-america-2/#7f51791056c7.
3. For simplicity's sake, we do not discuss forms of ownership here. A private limited liability company (LLC) also has shares, and additional investors may be allowed to contribute equity capital by purchasing shares. But the shares are not listed publicly and are not available for sale to the public.
4. Capital investments are not the only use of retained earnings, of course. A privately held company may use retained earnings to acquire the assets of another company, including that company's capital facilities, accounts receivable and payable, and so forth. Similarly, publicly traded companies may use retained earnings for acquisitions other than capital investments.
5. Johnson, R. (1996). *Capital financing for municipal infrastructure: choices as viewed by the enterprise and the investor*. Research Triangle Park, NC: RTI International; Brinkerhoff, D., Johnson, R., & Hill, R. (2009). *Guide to rebuilding public sector services in stability operations: a role for the military*. Carlisle, PA: Strategic Studies Institute, U.S. Army War College.

6. Congressional Research Service (2018). *Tax-exempt bonds: a description of state and local government debt.* Washington, DC: U.S. Government Publishing Office.

7. Hayes, P. (2016). The case for favoring revenue bonds over general obligation bonds. *Investment News.* Retrieved July 17, 2019, from https://www.investmentnews.com /article/20160613/FREE/160619980/the-case-for-favoring -revenue-bonds-over-general-obligation-bonds.

8. Securities Industry and Financial Markets Association (2019). *U.S. municipal issuance.* Washington, DC: SIFMA. Retrieved July 19, 2019, from https://www.sifma.org /resources/research/us-municipal-issuance/.

9. ProQuest (2019). *ProQuest statistical abstract of the U.S. 2019* (7th ed). Lanham, MD: ProQuest, p. 300.

10. Larosiliere, S. (2018). Limited supply has supported municipal bonds in 2018. *Invesco.* Retrieved May 9, 2020, from https://www.advisorperspectives.com/commentaries /2018/08/27/limited-supply-has-supported-municipal -bonds-in-2018.

11. Marlowe, Justin (2013). How to make 'pay as you go' work for large capital projects. *Governing*, December. Retrieved July 18, 2018, from https://www.governing.com/columns /public-money/gov-how-to-make-paygo-work.html.

12. Martell, C., & Kravchuk, R. (2012). The liquidity crisis: the 2007-2009 market impacts on municipal securities. *Public Administration Review, 72*, 5, 668–677.

13. Wang, W., et al. (2007). Determinants of pay-as-you-go financing of capital projects: evidence from the states. *Public Budgeting and Finance, 27*, Winter, 18–42.

14. Pylpczak-Wasylzszyn, D. (2015). Are municipal bonds exempt from state taxes? *MuncipalBonds.com.* Retrieved July 18, 2019, from https://www.municipalbonds.com /tax-education/tax-exemption-from-state-income-taxes/.

15. The White House (2010). *The moment of truth: report of the national commission on fiscal responsibility and reform.* Washington, DC: U.S. Government Printing Office.

16. Hume, L., & Temple-West, P. (2011). Obama proposal stuns market: market participants weigh impact of tax-exempt interest cap. *The Bond Buyer*, September 14. Retrieved November 6, 2011, from http://www.bondbuyer .com/issues/120_177/muni-reaction-obama-jobs-bill -1031028-1.html.

17. Public Law: 115-97.

18. *South Carolina v. Baker* (1988). 485 U.S. 505.

19. For a discussion of the history of legal actions concerning state and local tax immunity, see Wrightson, M. (1989). The road to *South Carolina*: intergovernmental tax immunity and the constitutional status of federalism. *Publius, 19*, Winter, 39–55.

20. Municipal Securities Rulemaking Board (2016). *About municipal asset-backed securities.* Retrieved July 19, 2019, from http://www.msrb.org/msrb1/pdfs/Municipal-Asset -Backed-Securities.pdf.

21. Moody's Investor Service (2018). *Moody's assigns provisional rating to NYC-sponsored tax lien collateralized bonds.* Retrieved July 19, 2019, from https://www.moodys .com/research/Moodys-assigns-provisional-rating-to -NYC-sponsored-tax-lien-collateralized--PR_386954.

22. Lemov, P. (2000). Tobacco bonds draw a market. *Governing, 14*, January, 54.

23. U.S. Department of Transportation, Federal Aviation Administration (2019). *Passenger facility charge (PFC) program: airports.* Retrieved July 19, 2019, from https:// www.faa.gov/airports/pfc/.

24. Deavitt, C. (2011). Cleveland airport offering $75 million in a rare deal. *The Bond Buyer*, October 31. Retrieved November 8, 2011, from http://www.bondbuyer.com /issues/120_209/clevelandhopkins-revenue-bond-deal -1032601-1.html. Note: *Bond Buyer* older issues no longer accessible online.

25. Broward County Aviation Department (2019). *Recommended budget: fiscal year 2019.* Retrieved July 19, 2019, from https://www.broward.org/Budget/Archives/Documents /FY19-AviationBudgetPresentation.pdf.

26. Maquire, S., & Hughes, J. (2018). Private activity bonds: an introduction. *Congressional Research Service.* Washington, DC: U.S. Government Publishing Office.

27. U.S. Department of the Treasury, Internal Revenue Service (2018). *Revenue procedure 2018-57.* Retrieved May 9, 2020, from https://www.irs.gov/pub/irs-drop/rp-18-57.pdf.

28. Maquire, S., and Hughes, J. (2018). Private activity bonds: an introduction. *Congressional Research Service.* Washington, DC: U.S. Government Publishing Office.

29. U.S. Department of Treasury, Internal Revenue Service (2019). *Tax-exempt private activity bonds, by type and term of issue, 2016.* Retrieved July 19, 2019, from https://www .irs.gov/statistics/soi-tax-stats-tax-exempt-bond-statistics.

30. Gulf Opportunity Zone Act (2005). P.L. 109-135.

31. Tax Cut and Jobs Opportunity Act (2017). P.L. 115-97.

32. Ely, T., & Martell, C. (2016). Costs of raising (social) capital through minibonds. *Municipal Finance Journal, 37*, 3, 23–43.

33. Fu, E. (2016). Minibonds: public engagement and public investment. *Government Finance Review, 13*, 5.

34. Axelrod, J. (2018). The mini-bond issue. *American City & County*, November 7. Retrieved July 19, 2019, from https:// www.americancityandcounty.com/2018/11/07/the-mini -bond-issue/.

35. Municipal Securities Rulemaking Board (2019). *Glossary of municipal securities terms: certificate of participation (COP).* Retrieved July 19, 2019, from http://www.msrb.org /glossary/definition/certificate-of-participation-_cop _.aspx.

36. Wirz, M. (2019). Robo-trading electrifies sleepy municipal bond market. *Wall Street Journal*, May 6. Retrieved July 19, 2019, from https://www.wsj.com/articles/robo -trading-electrifies-sleepy-municipal-bond-market -11557144000.

37. BNG Bank (2019). *Ownership and structure.* Retrieved July 17, 2019, from https://www.bngbank.com/Pages /Ownership%20and%20Structure.aspx.

38. Pozhidaev, D., & Farid, M. (2017). Improving capital markets for municipal finance in least developed countries. In *Finance for city leaders' handbook: improving municipal finance to deliver better services* (Chapter 14). New York: UNHabitat. Retrieved May 9, 2020, from

https://www.academia.edu/29121959/Improving_Capital
_Markets_for_Municipal_Finance_in_Least_Developed
_Countries.

39. Clean Water Act of 1972 (P.L. 92-500).

40. Safe Drinking Water Act of 1974 (P.L. 95-523).

41. Public Health Security and Bioterrorism Act of 2002. (P.L. 107-188).

42. New York State Environmental Facilities Corporation (2019). *Disbursement guidance.* Retrieved July 19, 2019, from https://www.efc.ny.gov/Disbursements.

43. Council of State Governments (2011). *State infrastructure banks* (p. 1). Lexington, KY: Council of State Governments.

44. National Highway System Designation Act of 1995 (P.L. 104-59); Transportation Safety Act of 1998 (P.L. 105-178); Safe, Accountable, Flexible, Efficient Transportation Equity Act: A Legacy for Users (2005; P.L. 109-59).

45. Federal Transit Administration (2019). *State infrastructure banks (SIBs).* Retrieved July 19, 2019, from https://www.transit.dot.gov/funding/funding-finance-resources/state-infrastructure-banks/state-infrastructure-banks-sibs.

46. Municipal Securities Rulemaking Board (MSRB) Education Center, 2019. *The underwriting process.* Retrieved July 17, 2019, from https://www.msrb.org/EducationCenter/Municipal-Market/Lifecycle/Primary/Underwriting-Process.aspx; Feldstein, S., & Fabozzi, F. (Eds.) (2008). *The handbook of municipal bonds.* New York, NY: Wiley.

47. Municipal Securities Rulemaking Board (2019). *Costs associated with issuing municipal securities.* Retrieved July 17, 2019, from http://msrb.org/msrb1/pdfs/Understanding-Gross-Spread.pdf.

48. Joffe, M. (2015). *Doubly bound: the costs of issuing municipal bonds* (p. 7). Haas Institute for Fair and Inclusive Society, University of California Berkeley. Retrieved July 17, 2019, from https://haasinstitute.berkeley.edu/sites/default/files/haasinstituterefundamerica_doublybound_cost_of_issuingbonds_publish.pdf.

49. Joffe (2015). *Doubly bound,* 9.

50. Joffe (2015). *Doubly bound,* 13.

51. Krueger, S., & Walker, R. (2008). Divided government, political turnover, and state bond ratings. *Public Finance Review, 36,* 259–286; Devitt, C. (2011). Panelists: politics play big part in analyzing governments' credit. *The Bond Buyer,* April 28. Retrieved November 10, 2011, from http://www.bondbuyer.com/issues/120_81/-1026021-1.html.

52. National Conference of State Legislatures (2018). *Statewide ballot measures database.* Retrieved July 18, 2019, from http://www.ncsl.org/research/elections-and-campaigns/ballot-measures-database.aspx.

53 Cestau, D., et.al. (2017). *The cost burden of negotiated sales restrictions: a natural experiment using heterogeneous state laws.* Washington, DC: Brookings Institution. Retrieved July 19, 2019, from https://www.brookings.edu/research/the-cost-burden-of-negotiated-sales-restrictions-a-natural-experiment-using-heterogeneous-state-laws/; Munibondadvisor.com (2018). *Bond sale methods (competitive vs. negotiated bond sales).* Retrieved July 19, 2019, from http://www.munibondadvisor.com/SaleChoice.htm.

54. Municipal Securities Rulemaking Board (2019). *About municipal securities: investment risk.* Retrieved July 13, 2019, from https://www.msrb.org/EducationCenter/Municipal-Market/About/Financial/Investment-Risk.aspx.

55. Albright, A. (2019). Puerto Rico ruling sends shock through $3.8 trillion muni market. *Bloomberg.* Retrieved July 20, 2019, from https://www.bloomberg.com/news/articles/2019-04-12/america-s-3-8-trillion-safe-haven-market-imperiled-by-ruling.

56. Hudson, J. (2018). How to evaluate the strength and performance of Bond Insurers. *MunicipalBonds.com.* Retrieved July 19, 2019, from https://www.municipalbonds.com/bond-insurance/how-to-evaluate-the-strength-and-performance-of-bond-insurers/.

57. Weitzman, A. (2019). Top muni bond insurers of 2018. *The Bond Buyer (online).* Retrieved July 19, 2019, from https://www.bondbuyer.com/list/top-municipal-bond-insurers.

58. Cornaggia, K. et al. (2019). *The price of safety: the evolution of insurance value in municipal markets.* Paper prepared for the 2019 Brookings Municipal Finance Conference. Retrieved July 20, 2019, from https://www.brookings.edu/blog/up-front/2019/07/15/for-all-but-the-lowest-rated-state-and-local-governments-buying-bond-insurance-is-a-bad-deal/.

59. FAST, Public Law 114-94.

60. Doty, R. (1990). The role of the Municipal Securities Rulemaking Board and the central repository for public securities: dealer regulation or market regulation? *Municipal Finance Journal, 11,* 7–51.

61. Municipal Securities Rulemaking Board (2019). *Rule G-14: Reports of Sales or Purchases.* Retrieved July 20, 2019, from http://www.msrb.org/Rules-and-Interpretations/MSRB-Rules/General/Rule-G-14.aspx.

62. U.S. Securities and Exchange Commission (2008). *SEC, MSRB: new measures to provide more transparency than ever before for municipal bond investor.* Retrieved July 20, 2019, from http://www.sec.gov/news/press/2008/2008-286.htm.

63. Electronic Municipal Market Access (EMMA). https://emma.msrb.org/.

64. Lemov, P. (1996). A new investment rule requires "suitable" advice. *Governing, 10,* October, 57.

65. Federal Reserve Bank of St. Louis (2019). *State and local government debt outstanding.* Retrieved July 20, 2019, from https://fred.stlouisfed.org/series/SLGSDODNS. Note, excludes employee retirement funds, debt securities, and loans.

66. U.S. Bureau of the Census (2017). *State and local government finances by level of government and state: 2017.* Retrieved November 16, 2019, from https://www.census.gov/data/datasets/2017/econ/local/public-use-datasets.html.

67. Federal Reserve Bank of St. Louis (2019). *State and local government debt outstanding.*

68. All figures in this paragraph are from *ProQuest statistical abstract: 2019,* 17, 304–305, and 459.

69. Dickson, S. (1993). Civil war, railroads, and road bonds: bond repudiations in the days of yore. In J. Lamb et al.

(Eds.), *The handbook of municipal bonds and public finance* (pp. 166–173). New York, NY: New York Institute of Finance.

70. Mitchell, G. (1975). Statement before the Committee on Banking, Housing and Urban Affairs. *Federal Reserve Bulletin, 61*, 729–730.

71. Pylpczak, D. (2011). *Default rates of municipal bonds.* MunicipalBonds.com. Retrieved May 12, 2020, from https://www.municipalbonds.com/education/read/77/default-rates-of-municipal-bonds/.

72. Governing Data (2019) *Bankrupt cities, municipalities list and map.* Retrieved May 12, 2020, from https://www.governing.com/gov-data/other/municipal-cities-counties-bankruptcies-and-defaults.html.

73. Bourgi, SS. (2018). How municipal bonds can help you during volatile markets. *MunicipalBonds.com.* Retrieved July 10, 2019, from https://www.municipalbonds.com/investing-strategies/municipal-bonds-help-during-volatile-markets/.

74. Berne, R. (1993). Governmental accounting and financial reporting and the measurement of financial condition. In J. Lamb et al. (Eds.), *The handbook of municipal bonds and public finance* (pp. 257–315).

75. Standard & Poor's Ratings Services (2015). *U.S. public finance criteria: tax-secured and utilities.* McGraw-Hill Financials, online. Retrieved July 20, 2019, from https://www.spratings.com/documents/20184/1282625/USPF+Criteria+-+Tax-Secured+and+Utilities/87b1f173-efdc-4dae-9126-be662efc4a9a, 4.; S&P Global Ratings (2019). *S&P global ratings U.S. public finance criteria.* Retrieved July 21, 2019, from https://www.standardandpoors.com/en_US/web/guest/ratings/ratings-criteria/-/articles/criteria/governments/filter/table-of-contents.

76. County of Riverside (2015). *Adopted budget: 2015/16.* Retrieved July 21, 2019, from https://countyofriverside.us/Portals/0/Government/Budget%20Information/2015-2016%20Adopted%20Budget/9FY15-16_Adopted_BudgetBook.pdf, p. 2.

77. City of Alexandria (2009). *Financial management assessment using S&Ps rating criteria.* Retrieved July 21, 2019, from https://www.alexandriava.gov/uploadedFiles/budget/Self%20Assessment%20-%20Financial%20Management.pdf.

78. States with less than $1 billion in general obligation debt are excluded from the analysis because the small sizes lead to odd figures. Eight states therefore are excluded. For example, Nebraska had $22.7 million in GO debt, no unfunded pension liabilities, and 2.4 billion in unfunded retiree health benefits. Nebraska's ratio is 105.7. Wyoming's ratio is 70.7. This is a big deal to residents of those two states, but they do not look like most of the other states.

79. Tax Cuts and Jobs Act of 2017 (Public Law 115-97).

80. Government Finance Officers Association (2019). *Refunding municipal bonds*, Retrieved July 22, 2019, from https://www.gfoa.org/refunding-municipal-bonds.

81. Federal Reserve (2019). New security issues, state and local governments. Retrieved July 22, 2019, from https://www.federalreserve.gov/data/govsecure/current.htm; ProQuest LLC (2019). *ProQuest statistical abstract, 2019*, p. 300.

82. Business-Standard.com (2013). Harvard's bet on rate rise cost $500 million to exit. Reference to *Bloomberg.com*, January 20, 2013. Retrieved May 12, 2020, from https://www.business-standard.com/article/economy-policy/harvard-s-bet-on-rate-rise-cost-500-mn-to-exit-109101900034_1.html.

83. Deavitt, C. (2011). Cleveland airport offering $75 million in a rare deal. *The Bond Buyer*, October 31. Retrieved May 9, 2020, from https://www.bondbuyer.com/news/cleveland-airport-offering-75-million-in-a-rare-deal.

84. Author compilation from The World Bank (2019). *Private participation in infrastructure database.* Washington, DC: World Bank. Retrieved July 23, 2019, from https://ppi.worldbank.org/data.

85. World Bank (2019). *Concessions, build-operate-transfer (BOT), and design-build-operate (DBO) projects.* Retrieved July 23, 2019, from https://ppp.worldbank.org/public-private-partnership/agreements/concessions-bots-dbos.

86. Federal Highway Administration, U.S. Department of Transportation (2019). *Project profile: Hudson-Bergen Light Rail.* Retrieved July 23, 2019, from https://www.fhwa.dot.gov/ipd/project_profiles/nj_hudson_bergen.aspx.

87. Chang, K. (2019). Public may have a say on proposed water and wastewater concession agreement with Suez North America. *CentralJersey.com*, June 11. Retrieved July 23, 2019, from https://centraljersey.com/2019/06/11/public-may-have-a-say-on-proposed-water-and-wastewater-concession-agreement-with-suez-north-america/; Warren, M. (2019). Edison's voters force public control of water after yearlong political drama. *nj.com.* Retrieved November 16, 2019, from https://www.nj.com/news/2019/09/edisons-voters-force-public-control-of-water-after-yearlong-political-drama.html.

88. Engel, E., et al. (2004). *The economics of public-private-partnerships: a basic guide* (pp. 48–49). Cambridge, UK: Cambridge University Press.

89. Chicago Sun-Times (2016). Canadian consortium buys Chicago Skyway lease rights for $2.8 billion. June 24, 2016. Retrieved May 12, 2020, from https://chicago.suntimes.com/2016/6/24/18448534/canadian-consortium-buys-chicago-skyway-lease-rights-for-2-8-billion.

90. Renn, A. (2016). The lessons of long-term privatizations: why Chicago got it wrong and Indiana got it right. *The Manhattan Institute.* Retrieved July 23, 2019, from https://www.infrastructureusa.org/the-lessons-of-long-term-privatization-why-chicago-got-it-wrong-and-indiana-got-it-right/. The reference to Chicago getting it wrong concerns not the Skyway privatization, but a long-term lease of the city's parking meters.

91. Bary, A. (2009). The long and binding road. *Barron's*, May 11. Retrieved November 3, 2011, from http://online.barrons.com/article/SB124183159872002803.html.

92. McGrath, G. (2019). New Hanover County to explore sale of hospital. *Wilmington Star News,* July 23. Retrieved July 25, 2019, from https://www.starnewsonline.com/news/20190723/new-hanover-county-to-explore-sale-of-hospital.

93. Chang, K. (2019). Public may have a say on proposed water and wastewater concession agreement with Suez North America; Warren, M. (2019). Edison's voters force public control of water after yearlong political drama.

94. Renn, A. (2016). *The lessons of long-term privatizations.*

95. Schiffler, M. (2015). *Water, politics and money: a reality check on privatization.* Cham: Switzerland: Springer International Publishing.

96. Charmila, W. A. (2017). Coalition opposing Jakarta water privatization wins appeal. *Jakarta Post*, October 10. Retrieved July 23, 2019, from http://www.thejakartapost.com/news/2017/10/10/coalition-opposing-jakarta-water-privatization-wins-appeal.html.

97. The World Bank (2019). *2018 private participation in infrastructure (PPI) annual report.* Washington, DC: The World Bank.

98. McDonald, D. (2019). Finding common(s) ground in the fight for water remunicipalization. *Community Development Journal, 54*, 1, 55–79.

CHAPTER 15

Intergovernmental Relations

Each level of government has discrete financial decision-making processes that determine matters of revenue and expenditure. Decisions about revenues and expenditures, however, are interdependent among different levels of government. Budgetary decisions made at one level are partially dependent on budgetary decisions made at other levels. Nonbudgetary decisions made at one level also may have dramatic impacts on budgets at another level of government.

This chapter examines the financial interdependencies among federal, state, and local governments.[1] The first section examines some of the basic economic and political problems that stem from having three major levels of government that provide various services and possess differing financial capabilities. The second section considers the patterns of interaction among the different levels, and the third section considers the main types of intergovernmental financial assistance programs. Key topics include devolution of responsibility from the federal government to state and local governments, especially welfare reform and health care for lower-income groups. The chapter concludes with a discussion of current issues and alternatives for restructuring these patterns of financial interaction, including the controversial issue of unfunded versus funded mandates, such as for state and local education

programs. The 2020 coronavirus crisis underscored confusion in federal versus state roles in such critical problems as the lack of coordinated procurement for scarce medical equipment and supplies and the authority of states versus the federal government over measures, such as stay-at-home orders, to ensure public health and safety.

Structural and Fiscal Features of the Intergovernmental System

In this section, we look beyond the simplified three-level model of government to consider the issues associated with having multiple levels and types of governments.

Areal and Functional Relations
Multiple Governments

Governments around the world and the organizations that they create constitute an intricate web of interjurisdictional relations. The United Nations, the European Union, NATO, and the like affect their member states and other states throughout the world. The European Union (EU), for example, consists of 28 European countries. Joining the EU subjects member countries to certain rules and policies affecting such sovereign practices as travel of citizens of member countries to and from other EU countries, unit of currency (with some exceptions), and some taxation matters.[2] Only recently have some countries begun to question the costs versus benefits of EU membership and consider leaving the union. The United Kingdom, in 2018, voted in a national referendum to exit the EU, a complicated and lengthy process. The World Trade Organization (WTO), another example, with about 160 member states, sets ground rules for international commerce and resolves trade disputes among member nations.[3] The WTO's actions impact governments, businesses, and individuals everywhere. These interactions are about diplomacy, trade, and global concerns that extend beyond the scope of this text, but it needs to be recognized that what occurs in intergovernmental relations in the United States is within a much broader context of governments relating with one another around the world.

In the United States, governments operate within a federal system in which power is constitutionally shared between a central or national government and 50 states, which have sovereign status, meaning they are (at least technically) independent of the national government within the division of powers in the Constitution.[4] Other countries with federal systems include Australia, Belgium, Brazil, Canada, Germany, India, and Switzerland. In contrast is a centralized or unitary system in which all power resides in a national government, with some powers then being delegated to regional units. France and the United Kingdom are examples of this form of government.

In a federal system, the national government and states almost inevitably clash from time to time over their respective powers, and legal remedies are often available. In the United States, the states may sue in federal court when they allege federal action has abrogated their constitutionally protected powers. In a unitary system, the national government has the power to create and dissolve subunits, which may or may not have any legal recourse against adverse actions taken

against them by higher authority. In other words, American states can and often do defend their rights by filing suit, claiming the federal government has usurped their powers, whereas in unitary systems, such rights are severely circumscribed at best.

Complicating the federal system in the United States is the fact that Native American tribes have independent status. Some federal actions have imposed both costs and benefits on the states with policies and rulings that circumscribe the authority of states regarding Native American tribes. In modern times, this fact has been the source of confusion, politicking, and legal wrangling since 1987, when the Supreme Court ruled that Native American tribes could operate gaming facilities. Congress passed the Indian Gaming Regulatory Act of 1988, which allowed for gaming and created the National Indian Gaming Commission to regulate the newly emerging industry.[5] The Supreme Court decision and the 1988 law set the stage for an elaborate set of intergovernmental actions.

Native American casinos are allowed only in states that otherwise allow other specific forms of gaming. In return, states benefit from tax receipts. The law has led to states having to negotiate with tribes over the construction, operation, and expansion of casinos, regardless of whether they wanted such casinos to exist at all. Native American gaming has grown dramatically. Nearly five hundred tribal casinos operate in 31 states. Revenues were $32 billion in 2017. California and Oklahoma top the list of states, with 38% of all gambling revenues from Native American casinos. Native American gaming paid $9 billion in taxes and other payments to federal state and local governments.[6]

In addition to the federal government, the 50 state governments, and more than 570 Native American tribal entities,[7] the United States includes more than 90,000 local governments and the District of Columbia.[8] The local "level" is not a single level, in that most states have county governments, and within their boundaries exist general-purpose governments such as cities, municipalities, and townships (almost 39,000). Superimposed over these are numerous independent school districts (13,000) and special-purpose districts such as irrigation and sewer districts. Special districts other than school districts, of which there are more than 38,000, are the most numerous. There are more than 13,000 school districts.

These various local governments have a decidedly different legal status from that of the states. Although the states created the national government and preserved their sovereignty through the Constitution, local governments are creatures of their respective states. They were created by the states and can be destroyed by the states. According to Dillon's Rule, as decided by the Supreme Court in 1907, local governments only have powers that are granted to them by their respective states.[9]

Whether federal or unitary, many countries in the past 30 years have granted greater autonomous authority to regional, provincial, or local governments. This autonomy does not necessarily mean shifts from unitary to federal systems. India, for example, enacted in 1991 constitutional reforms to establish certain powers and responsibilities for local governments as a matter of national constitutional authority, effectively removing some aspects of state government control over local government. In most of the Central and Eastern European states formerly part of the Soviet Union, central authority over all governmental functions gave way to increased responsibility at the regional and city levels, and that authority is defined and delimited by the central government. Having myriad governments at different levels within a nation can be defended in several ways. By having multiple governments, an omnipotent, despotic type of government is less likely. Another advantage is that the diversity of governments allows for differing responses according to the divergent needs of citizens in different locales. For instance, some communities may place greater emphasis than others on amenities, such as flower beds and other decorations along city streets, whereas other communities may prefer more utilitarian, and presumably less expensive, streets. The Federalist framers and advocates for the U.S. Constitution defended a federal structure using three arguments:

- It would promote a sense of community and affinity between citizens and the government.

- It would promote efficiency by assigning functions that had mainly local importance to local governments and functions of national importance to the federal government.
- It would promote liberty by avoiding concentration of power in the hands of a few.[10]

Anti-Federalists, concerned that the Constitution would give too much power to the central government, withheld their approval until there was agreement to include key provisions within the first 10 amendments, adopted simultaneously with the Constitution. Perhaps the most important amendment related to intergovernmental relations, the 10th Amendment, articulated the *reserved* powers doctrine: "The powers not delegated to the United States by the Constitution, nor prohibited by it to the States, are reserved to the States respectively, or to the people."

The existence of numerous units of government increases the probability that individuals will be able to find communities to live in that suit them. For example, people may locate in communities that offer desirable mixes of taxes and services. Of course, we do not suggest that such economic calculations are the sole criteria on which people base their location decisions, but the existence of multiple governments enhances that important aspect of quality of life.[11] People may choose to locate in communities with higher or lower levels of services and to live with more like-minded neighbors, reflecting the diversity in the United States.[12]

Another advantage is that having multiple governments allows the achievement of *economies of scale*. Functions may be performed by the size of government that is most efficient in carrying out the functions. Just as it may be advantageous from the standpoint of efficient resource use for private, profit-oriented organizations to grow to a large scale, so it also may be advantageous for one unit of government to conduct some government activities on a large scale.

On the other hand, to perform all government functions at the central level might result in inefficient conduct of some activities.[13] Not only did the economic woes of the former Soviet Union demonstrate that overly centralized planning of the productive sector of the economy produced many inefficiencies, but the overly centralized administrative and fiscal systems also left a legacy of weak decision making not well adapted to provision of basic local public services. Lessened flexibility of operations and other diseconomies suggest the need for some functions to be performed by units of government smaller than the central government. Geographically and economically smaller-scale activities are more efficient when carried out by smaller governments. Many services probably can be provided most efficiently at the local level.

No government, no matter what the level, is free to do whatever it pleases. In some countries, the reverse is true, with the states, regions, or provinces having enumerated powers and the national government having the remainder. In the United States, each state constitution provides for the powers of that government. Local governments have fewer constitutional protections because these governments have been created by their states. Within these constitutional and legal parameters, a higher-level government may impose standards upon lower levels.

Coordination Problems

The existence of thousands of governments results in coordination problems both geographically and functionally. Municipalities in a metropolitan area need some coordinative mechanisms. Road networks, for example, need to be planned in accordance with commuting patterns within a metropolitan area, and such plans should not be restricted to the geographic boundaries of each municipality. Before the federal government became involved in highway programs, many highways did not connect sensibly across state lines. Examples like the Chicago Skyway and the Indiana East-West Toll Road, as discussed in the chapter on capital finance and debt management, illustrate not only state-to-state coordination issues, but also the involvement of private contractors. Recreation and parks programs may be provided on a metropolitan or area basis and thereby achieve economies of scale. Numerous regional planning agencies, regional or metropolitan transportation

planning groups, and regional economic development programs exist to consolidate an otherwise fragmented approach to interjurisdictional overlaps.

The need to avoid excessive fragmentation at the local level in a decentralized system and increase efficiency by reducing overlap and duplication of services led to consideration of consolidating the local governments in a metropolitan area, such as in Miami–Dade County, Florida, and Nashville–Davidson County, Tennessee. Over a 40-year period, however, only about 100 initiatives actually led to voter referenda, and less than one-quarter of them were successful.[14] Where coordination is needed among the local governments of a metropolitan area, it seems achievable through cooperation and shared decision making rather than consolidation, although there does seem to be evidence that consolidation has benefits in the case of very small local units of government.

Federal-state, interstate, and interlocal arrangements have been developed for the provision of services (as distinguished from forums for discussion), including metropolitan councils of governments that involve officials from various communities in a region. One of the most successful interstate organizations is the Port Authority of New York and New Jersey, established in 1921 by the two participating states.[15] The authority operates terminals, bridges, and tunnels. It operated the World Trade Center until its destruction in 2001. Subsequently, the Port Authority and the Lower Manhattan Development Corporation were instrumental in approving plans for the rebuilt site.

At the local level, numerous types of cooperative arrangements exist. Some counties provide services such as water and sewage treatment on a contract basis for municipalities within their jurisdictions. The choice of such an arrangement may be at the discretion of municipalities, as in the case of the Lakewood Plan, whereby communities can contract with Los Angeles County for virtually all city services (see chapter on budget execution). In some instances, state governments may require city-county cooperation for services, such as police and fire departments having standby aid agreements during large civil disturbances or fires.

Functional coordination among different levels is also necessary because the three main levels of government share responsibilities for some of the same functions. Criminal justice, for instance, is a shared function. Some type of police, court, and prison system exists at each government level. Environmental protection similarly is a function in which federal, state, and local jurisdictions all have a stake, and all but the smallest local governments have some formal unit involved in addressing environmental problems. The independent pursuit of similar objectives by different governments can result in wasted resources and ineffective services.

Multilevel overlapping and shared responsibility can make it difficult to design federal programs to achieve national objectives. Any given federal assistance program may be a good fit for local governments in one state and not in another given the differences in how states allocate responsibilities between themselves and their respective local governments. Therefore, emphasis has been given to developing mechanisms for functional integration. Although program specialists stress functional integration, policy generalists may stress areal integration. This conflict was popularized by Deil S. Wright as "picket fence federalism"—each picket represents a function, such as mental health or education, and all three levels of government make up part of each picket.[16] Another analogy used is that of silos, that program areas are compartmentalized within each of many silos. As with pickets of a fence, silos discourage the crossover of information and integration of services that so often is needed in government operations.

Exhibit 15-1 illustrates how complicated the mosaic of intergovernmental relations can be.

Exhibit 15-1 Coordinating Air Emissions as a Case Study in Interstate Compacts

Like watersheds, airsheds respect no political boundaries. Emissions from private vehicles, public facilities, and factories within the boundaries of one political jurisdiction effectively go where the winds blow. Unlike water, which has a stable pattern of flows, emissions into the air over time span the full 360 degrees of the map.

In purely self-interested terms, it may not be rational for a local government with a strong "smokestack" industry that is employing a large percentage of the workforce to regulate emissions from that industry, especially if the prevailing winds for the most part blow the polluted air away from the jurisdiction. For this reason, the federal government has for several decades played a significant role in setting limits on emissions. However, federally imposed limits rely on states and localities to develop policies and practices to meet the standards. States and the local jurisdictions within metropolitan areas realize that they cannot act unilaterally to solve the problems if their neighbors are not also taking care of the problems. They then act to create coordinated policies and programs to impose and enforce stronger controls.

One such example is an interstate compact among New England and mid-Atlantic states to control ground-level ozone concentrations. Members of the Ozone Transport Commission (OTC) set targets for the total amount of nitrous oxide emissions allowed from sources within the states in the compact. States then allocate the allowable emissions among the major producers/sources, rewarding those that come in "below budget." Individual emitters and even states may trade in these permitted levels. Those falling below the levels may trade for various compensations with those who cannot meet the allocated amount.[a]

The EPA reports significant reductions in toxic emissions through 2015, though it is impossible to separate the effects of actions of the OTC from other causes.[b] A big issue was that the Midwestern states did not join the Commission, and prevailing winds bring large problems eastward. The attorneys general of some member states sued coal-burning power plants in several other Midwestern states. The result of that suit was a consent decree requiring the EPA to add nine "upwind" states to the Ozone Transport Region. However, failure of the EPA to add those nine states led the OTC states to file another suit in

(continues)

2017, this time against the EPA to force action.[c] The legal steps may continue several more years, and the anti-regulatory atmosphere in the Trump Administration did not favor increased regulatory actions. Nonetheless, the Ozone Transport Commission has achieved some significant progress on a common problem in intergovernmental relations.

While interstate compacts can be effective in addressing cross-jurisdictional issues, they are not easy to set up. Article I, Section 10 of the Constitution requires congressional approval of any interstate compact. Despite this step, this approach has proved a useful mechanism for creating interjurisdictional authority to address mutual interests.[d]

a. Ozone Transport Commission (2019). *What is the Ozone Transport Commission?* Retrieved July 28, 2019, from https://otcair.org/index.asp; see also *OTC model rules/regulatory & technical guidelines.* Retrieved July 28, 2019, from https://otcair.org/document.asp?fview=modelrules.

b. U.S. Environmental Protection Agency (2018). *Interstate air pollution has been reduced.* Retrieved July 28, 2019, from https://www.epa.gov/clean-air-act-overview/progress-cleaning-air-andimproving-peoples-health#interstate.

c. Szekely, P. (2017). Northeast states sue EPA over air pollution from Midwest. *Reuters online,* December 26. Retrieved July 28, 2019, from https://www.reuters.com/article/us-usa-environment-new-york/northeaststates-sue-epa-over-air-pollution-from-midwest-idUSKBN1EK1BK.

d. Law Library of Congress, Global Legal Research Center (2018). *Interstate compacts in the United States.* Retrieved July 28, 2019, from https://www.loc.gov/law/help/interstate-compacts/us-interstate-compacts.pdf.

The exhibit uses as its focus the efforts made to control air emissions in an intergovernmental context. The device illustrated in the exhibit, an interstate compact among 12 states and the District of Columbia, is one mechanism that can be used to coordinate efforts by multiple jurisdictions to combat problems that span jurisdictional boundaries. More generally, all problems dealing with the environment, whether they involve air, land, or water, need to be handled on a multijurisdictional basis, including internationally.[17] Similarly, health issues such as the opioid crisis simultaneously affect all levels of government and require coordination to address effectively.

Responses to Terrorist Attacks: Physical and Cyberwarfare

The terrorist attacks of September 11, 2001, and the cyberwarfare attacks in the 2016 presidential election dramatically underscore the need for intergovernmental cooperation and coordination. One painfully obvious fact in these events is the lack of sharing of information and coordination within federal agencies and among them. Equally important were the weak linkages existing among federal intelligence gathering and law enforcement agencies on the one hand and similar units internationally and at the state and local levels within the United States.

The federal organizational response to the 9/11 attacks was the creation of the Department of Homeland Security to pull together a variety of agencies that had been located throughout the federal bureaucracy. Among other things, Homeland Security provides grants for upgrading law enforcement and fire protection at the state and local levels. Noticeably absent, however, from Homeland Security's ranks is the Federal Bureau of Investigation (FBI), which remains within the Department of Justice. The FBI continues to be the federal government's primary criminal investigation and law enforcement unit, having responsibility for international investigations such as tracking international conduits for funding terrorist activities. The U.S. Treasury Department and the U.S. Postal Service also have key roles in investigating international financial crimes.[18]

It is impossible to assess how effective intergovernmental cooperation has been in preventing acts of terrorism and other major incidents, because many threats averted are never made public. There have been several small-scale events involving loss of life attributable to foreign-originated terrorism. These attacks have been the work mainly of isolated individuals, mostly legal immigrants with valid green cards or U.S. citizens. Domestic terror attacks, such as school shootings, have risen dramatically and for the most part have involved only U.S.-born citizens. The 2016 presidential election exposed weaknesses in U.S. electoral process and systems with large-scale cyberwarfare penetrating state voting systems and inserting attack ads with fabricated stories throughout the vast social media network. A bipartisan Senate Select Committee on Intelligence reported in 2019 that Russian hackers tried to access election systems in all 50 states, and succeeded in numerous instances.[19] Two reports commissioned by the same Senate committee detail widespread use of ads, stories, and releases of hacked e-mails and documents from presidential campaign committees to sow discord and create confusion in the electorate, using such prominent social media as Facebook, Twitter, and Alphabet.[20]

The political climate and extreme partisan disagreement in the Congress and with the White House make difficult reaching any consensus on the magnitude and the impact of the use of cyberwarfare tools and techniques to disrupt a major feature of our political system. Federal agencies have been slow in sharing information about international electoral threats with state and local officials.[21] No doubt, however, the events of the 2016 election exposed the vulnerability of our electoral systems, and the vulnerability of the public to questionable material inserted into major social media sites. More importantly, they reinforce the extent to which greater efforts to coordinate the roles and responsibilities of federal agencies, state and local organizations, the news media, and private providers of social media sites to address U.S. vulnerabilities to physical and electronic attacks.

Terrorist Threats, Disasters, and Public Health Emergencies

September 11 dramatized the need for all levels of government to cooperate in the event of catastrophic disasters. Such major events include natural disasters like the devastation inflicted in 2005 by the Gulf Coast Hurricanes Katrina, Rita, and Wilma.

Superstorm Sandy in 2012; Hurricanes Harvey, Irma, and Maria in 2017; and Hurricanes Florence and Michael in 2018 have each exposed weakness in U.S. disaster recovery systems, but also have shown that these systems have improved interagency coordination. The California wildfires of 2018 wiped out entire communities and caused approximately the same number of fatalities as the small-scale terror attacks from 2001 through 2017 noted above: approximately 100 fatalities in the wildfires and 100 fatalities in nine physical attacks.[22] In almost every instance of the larger natural catastrophes, the response systems and major agencies responsible for immediate assistance and long-term recovery have been overwhelmed. Improvement has been most notable in the immediate response period with improved relationships among federal, state, and local agencies, including the National Guard. Access to shelter, food and water, and public safety has improved since Katrina. On the other hand, coordination among those entities and others involved in longer-term recovery and rebuilding has not fared well.

The Federal Emergency Management Agency (FEMA) is the major agency responsible for federal preparation, relief, and recovery efforts from natural disasters. FEMA was an independent agency until it was brought into the newly formed Homeland Security Department in response to the September 11 disasters. Arguments have been made for retaining FEMA within Homeland Security or spinning it off once again as an independent agency, reporting directly to the president. The arguments are not especially persuasive on either side. What is persuasive is the need for a clear role for FEMA. That would seem to be one of a coordinator for all federal, state, and local units when major national disasters occur.[23] A 2018 Government Accountability Office (GAO) assessment of FEMA capabilities and performance concluded that the agency has made progress since Katrina, but has serious weaknesses in responding to catastrophes in U.S. territories, most notably Puerto Rico and the U.S. Virgin Islands. The report also emphasized that FEMA still has not fully assessed the nation's capabilities and gaps in preparedness. The GAO concluded that FEMA had, by 2019, addressed only about one-half of the concerns and recommendations GAO had made in previous GAO reports to Congress.

In addition to issues in the U.S. capacity to prepare for and address natural disasters, recent decades have exposed other significant intergovernmental policy issues. State and local governments are the parties responsible for planning that dictates where homes and business may or may not be built and building codes that dictate standards for buildings' capacity to withstand major hazards. The insurance industry is the primary provider of insured recovery funds, supplemented significantly by state flood insurance and reinsurance programs. But the proportion of properties vulnerable to flooding in south Texas, North Carolina, and South Carolina shows that individual property owners and federal, state, and local regulations are not at all prepared for what in the 2000s has been shown to be common flooding disasters. The notion of "100-year and 500-year" floods used to lull people into thinking they were likely to occur very infrequently and far into the future. The recent record shows that this magnitude of flooding occurs somewhere in the United States every 1 or 2 years. Wildfires in the West reflect similar gaps in private individual and commercial preparation and the same kinds of policy and regulatory weaknesses among federal, state, and local agencies. The time seems ripe for major examination of the intergovernmental system's ability to cope with natural disasters.

Planning for a major pandemic threat generally has been of less concern than terrorist threats and natural disasters in the United States, in part because these two threats, especially natural disasters, have been frequent and costly. The planning and preparation role for pandemic threats generally falls in the homeland security arena, with major roles for the Centers for Disease Control and Prevention (CDC), although in the early stages of the coronavirus crisis, the CDC appeared to have been pushed into a role secondary to the National Institute for Allergy and Infectious Diseases, at least with respect to policy advice to the White House. The Homeland Security Council,

established in 2001 shortly after the 9/11 attacks, is a separate but equal counterpart to the National Security Council (NSC). Both are in the Executive Office of the President, responsible to advising the president. In 2005, President George W. Bush announced the National Strategy for Pandemic Influenza, followed in a few months by the publication of the Implementation Plan for the National Strategy for Pandemic Influenza under the responsibility of the Homeland Security Council (HSC).[24] President Barack Obama in 2016 created within the NSC the Directorate for Global Health Security and Biodefense (Directorate) after the 2014 Ebola epidemic exposed weaknesses in U.S. planning and preparedness efforts for global pandemic crises. In 2017, under President Trump, the Directorate was reduced one level as part of a larger reorganization of the entire NSC, no longer reporting directly to the National Security Director.[25] None of these Councils and Directorates was tested with a full-blown global pandemic until the 2020 coronavirus pandemic. The United States was one of the most seriously affected countries, considering both health and economic impacts.

The coronavirus pandemic spread rapidly at the beginning of 2020 and exposed weaknesses in the U.S. intergovernmental system. These weaknesses were exacerbated by the intensity of political partisanship within the U.S. Congress and between Congress and the White House.[26] Recognition of the severity of the threat to the United States was slow. Initial responses at the national level, particularly the White House, downplayed the threat, likening the disease to the flu that would disappear naturally as spring and summer arrived.[27] By late March, the pervasiveness of the threat had become evident. A majority of states had issued stay-at-home orders and other restrictions of varying severity. Key issues emerged in the planning and preparedness, jeopardizing response capacity at both the federal and state level:

- The national capacity to treat critical cases, including intensive care facilities such as isolation rooms and medical personnel, seemed to be either inadequate or not distributed to match up with need.[28]

- The national supply of personal protective equipment for medical and other emergency personnel, equipment necessary for critical care patients such as respirators and ventilators, and basic medical supplies seemed to be inadequate or badly distributed.[29]
- There was little to no coordination at the national level in managing procurement of critical materials and equipment, leaving states to compete with each other and with other countries on the world market to purchase needed supplies.[30]

Other key issues emerged in the respective roles and responsibilities of federal government, including within the federal government, and of the states.

- At least four formal and informal federal task forces were created with some apparent authority to speak for the government: an official task force headed by the vice president to oversee the federal response, an economic council to focus on reopening the economy, a trouble-shooting task force headed by senior advisor and son-in-law to the president, and an unofficial "doctors group" that appeared to be set up to push back against some of the more extreme strategies floated by various advisors.[31]
- Existing federal authority, such as the Defense Production Act (1950), to influence and require private industry to produce materials critical to meet a wide range of national emergencies was invoked, but used only sparingly to increase the supply of equipment and materials.[32]
- Confusion over responsibility for a national testing strategy, testing both for the presence of the infection and for antibodies indicating a person has previously been infected and recovered.[33] Even into the early summer, with deaths over 100,000 there was still no national testing strategy, other than to leave both procurement of tests and materials and conducting testing to each state.
- Disagreement and inconsistency in authority over when states start to relax their restrictions—a battle between when is it safe

to reopen and when it is necessary for the economy to reopen, with President Trump asserting total authority and then reversing course and acknowledging states' authority, albeit noting that the federal government may come in and correct the states if they are wrong.[34]

None of these issues is easily understood or resolved in the middle of the crisis. Like a recession, much of what we learn about what worked and what did not and what should be done in advance of and during the next time is available to us several years afterward.

Fiscal Considerations
Vertical Fiscal Imbalance

The conflict between the organizing principles of geographic area and program function plays out within the context of need for services and the corresponding need for revenues, with differences in capabilities existing both within and among levels of government.[35] *Vertical fiscal imbalance*, or *fiscal noncorrespondence*, refers to the relative abilities of different levels of government to generate needed revenue and to produce specific public services. The intergovernmental fiscal problem is deciding on assignment of expenditure responsibilities and then designing an intergovernmental fiscal system of revenue authority, shared revenue sources, and transfers to match the expenditure assignments. Although one level of government may have a comparative advantage in efficiently providing a service, it may not have the same advantage in obtaining revenue. Conversely, another level of government may possess enough revenue capability but is not the most efficient unit to provide certain services.

In the United States, it is typically the federal government that possesses the greatest revenue capacity, but not the comparative advantage in providing many government services efficiently. State and local governments, on the other hand, have comparative advantages in providing local services, but have functional expenditure obligations that may exceed their ability to raise revenue.

This disparity is due largely to the different revenue sources used by governments. The federal government, relying on personal and corporate income taxes, has a more elastic tax structure in which revenues increase with any increase in economic activity. State and local revenue sources are relatively more inelastic. For example, the property tax does not change when the economy swings up and down, as discussed in the chapter on budgeting for income taxes, payroll taxes, and property taxes.

Superior fiscal capacity can be used by one level of government to entice or persuade another to provide a given service. For example, the federal government used its tremendous fiscal capacity to persuade the states to build an interstate network of freeways. Had the federal government not initially paid 90% of the cost of the system, there would be far fewer freeways today. Federal programs created by the Clean Water and the Safe Drinking Water Acts, discussed in the chapter on capital finance and debt management, initially provided grant funding for water and sewer systems, and then after some years of grant funding, provided capitalization funding for state revolving loan funds to lower the borrowing costs for water and sewer systems. Similar federal assistance to capitalize state education loan programs to induce more school construction have been proposed but not implemented. States also induce local activities through grants and loans.

Horizontal Fiscal Differences

Problems caused by differences in fiscal capacity also exist for governments at the same level. From state to state, there clearly are differences in income and wealth, which are the basic sources of government revenue. For example, U.S. per capita personal income in 2018 was $54,420, but Connecticut's was $76,456, or 140% of the national figure, and Mississippi's was $37,834, or only 70% of the national average.[36] Differences in income and wealth lead to differences in revenue-generating abilities, tax burdens, and levels of public services, although no simple correlation exists between income on the one hand and taxing and spending on the other hand.

There is disagreement over whether per capita income differences are a good measure of the differing fiscal capacities of the states. Per capita income has been widely used since the 1930s to differentiate among the states' relative needs for federal assistance. However, this measure does not fully capture ability to pay for services within states. Other measures include retail sales and gross state product. Analysts often use full market property value to assess local government and some special districts debt repayment capacity, but this measure reflects accumulated wealth and not necessarily the direct ability to generate revenues.

The ability of a state to raise revenue to meet its spending requirements is called the *fiscal capacity* of the state. *Total taxable resources (TTR)* is a more comprehensive estimate of the potential income flows produced in the state. It is more comprehensive than other measures such as *gross state product,* which is like the concept of gross domestic product calculated for a national economy (see the chapter on government and the economy). The TTR index is a calculation based on TTR per capita. The index is set with the national score of 100, and states with scores above that level have higher potential to generate revenues; states with scores below have lower abilities. For 2016, Connecticut and New York scored high on the index (137 and 132, respectively), whereas Mississippi was at the bottom (66). Other low states were West Virginia and Alabama (72 and 74, respectively). Near the middle point of 100 were Colorado, Rhode Island, Pennsylvania, and South Dakota (in the 100 to 102 range).[37] The TTR index is used by the Department of Health and Human Services in distributing Community Mental Health Service and Substance Abuse Prevention and Treatment block grant programs' funds to the states. Were the index to become widely accepted as an effective measure of states' capacity, it might well be used for a host of grant formulas.

Just because a state has a high taxable capacity does not necessarily mean the state collects taxes commensurate with their capacity. The extent to which a state taps into its available resources is called the *tax burden*. Before it was eliminated in 1996 by federal budget cuts, the U.S. Advisory Commission on Intergovernmental

Relations (ACIR) calculated a measure that estimated the revenues a state would raise if it were to use the average tax system employed throughout the country. This *representative tax system* measured tax capacity and, when divided by population, provided a gauge of a state's fiscal effort.[38] The ACIR subsequently added the concept of representative expenditures, including information about costs for public services, to help measure different states' financial abilities.[39]

There has been some reconstruction of the ACIR's work since its demise,[40] though governments in other countries have shown more interest than have those in the United States in the concepts of the representative tax system and fiscal capacity. For example, Canada has an official Expert Panel on Equalization and Territorial Formula Financing that calculates *representative tax burdens*.[41]

Several other measures are used to gauge the tax burden in the states. These include total state and local taxes as a share of personal income, as a share of total taxable resources, or as a share of gross state product. Similar measures are derived using state own-source revenue. Such measures reveal which states make more of an effort to raise revenue within their capacity. Using the own-source revenue figure as a share of total state taxable resources, Vermont in 2016 was ranked first, at 12%, compared with middle-ranked California, Ohio, Pennsylvania, and several others (each 8%) and lowest-ranked Florida (5%).[42]

Although there are plenty of arguments about the adequacy of any one measure or group of measures, the empirical research corresponds to commonsense expectations. Some poorer states in the country have greater needs for spending on services than they have the fiscal capacity to respond, and some richer states have greater fiscal capacity than their expenditure requirements. In addition, some states make more of an effort to use their own taxable resources to meet expenditure needs than others. Federal formulas such as the TTR index are used by some federal programs to calculate distribution of grant funds to states to guard against the federal government rewarding states that do not make the effort with their own

tax resources while penalizing other states that do make the effort. However, politics sometimes interferes with this principle, and as a result few federal programs use a measure of tax effort of any kind in calculating grant distributions.

Any comparisons among states or localities, whether based on income, wealth, or tax effort, cannot capture an essential feature determining levels of services and levels of taxation. Residents of each state do not make uniform demands for services. Even if the ability to tax or charge for services were distributed evenly across the country, expenditures would differ because citizens desire different levels of services. From a strict demand point of view, a state would provide only those services for which citizens are willing to pay. But willingness to pay for services, as measured by tax effort, still may not solve the problem. The need for many government services is greatest in those states where the fiscal capacity to meet those needs is lowest. Mississippi is a good example of a state that has high needs and falls short despite making a better-than-average effort to meet those needs. In the taxable effort measure discussed above (own-source revenue as a percent of total taxable resources), Mississippi ranked 5th in its actual use of its own-source revenues as a percentage of its total taxable resources, but ranked 34th in total taxable resources available to it. The problem is even more acute with respect to different local jurisdictions in the same state. Central city governments in large metropolitan areas face demands for services that increase at a faster rate than does the value of their revenue sources.

Fiscal Responsibilities

Another issue is the extent to which one government with greater revenue-generating capacity should be responsible for aiding other lower-level governments. Should governments redistribute resources among different segments of the population and geographic areas, and, if so, to what extent? Since the 1980s, there seemingly has been less support for redistributive activities, especially at the federal level, than in the decades beginning with the Johnson administration's War on Poverty. The two decades from 1960 through

1980 witnessed the largest effort ever by the federal government to redress disparities among the states and among regions within states. Since then, the willingness, especially at the federal level, to assist other levels of government has declined. On the other hand, by some measures, the need for some redistribution has increased. On one index measure, income inequality in the United States has been rising (income inequality is discussed in the chapter on government and the economy).

One governing principle is that a government should address only those problems that correspond to its level of responsibility—that is, the federal government should deal with national problems and the states with state problems. Oates made this argument in a classic work in the 1970s.[43] That principle was articulated quite clearly by President Ronald Reagan's Executive Order 12612: "It is important to recognize the distinction between problems of national scope (which may justify Federal action) and problems that are merely common to the States (which will not justify Federal action because individual States, acting individually or together, can effectively deal with them)."[44] Though there have been differences in preference for various programs since then, both Democratic and Republican administrations have tended toward devolution of responsibility with respect to federal assistance to state and local governments. Federal payments to individuals, on the other hand, have increased steadily regardless of the party controlling the White House or the Congress.

Disparities in fiscal capacity among governments at the same level lead directly to another problem, that of *external costs* and *external benefits* of government functions. People of low income moving from states with low services to states with high services create new burdens on the high-service states. This occurred, for example, with the population migration of the 1930s from impoverished areas to the West Coast and in later migrations from the rural South to cities in the North and West. Proportionately more people who move from lower-income to higher-income states receive assistance and generate

greater demands on other public services than do those moving between states with similarly high levels of income and services. The flow of undocumented immigrants into some states may exacerbate those states' difficulties in financing social services and education. However, the questions raised are complex and do not unambiguously point to one conclusion.[45]

Some of the costs of the failure to provide comparable levels of service across state lines are borne by those outside the low-service states. But the situation has positive aspects as well. Providing services at the most economic level may result in the benefits' spilling over into other areas. The most obvious example is education: Higher levels of education generally yield higher levels of income. Given the mobility of the population, the benefits produced by one local education system may spread far beyond its geographic boundaries.

Economic Competition

Governments compete in trying to attract businesses and industries.[46] Firms locate for a variety of reasons, such as access to markets, a good labor supply, a quality education system, and availability of other resources. Furthermore, they locate where there are clusters of related industries and suppliers. Because businesses seek to minimize production costs, the advantage lies with jurisdictions that have a high service level and low taxes on industry. Whether these are the main reasons businesses move or not is irrelevant. If governments compete based on taxes and services, the fiscal effects are the same.

Competition for businesses among political jurisdictions can have important consequences, including distortions in revenue and expenditure patterns. When special concessions are granted to firms, either revenues needed for other purposes must be obtained elsewhere or the level of these other services must be reduced. Devoting resources to special facilities, such as industrial parks, which are frequently financed by long-term debt instruments, may affect a community's ability to finance other capital projects, such as a civic center or a new sewage treatment plant.

The package of tax forgiveness, direct subsidies, and free services that Alabama gave Daimler-Benz in return for locating its first U.S. manufacturing facility in the state was a gamble. The state provided a direct subsidy, forgave corporate taxes to the extent the forgone taxes were used by Daimler-Benz for debt service on its physical plant investments, and allowed the company to keep up to 5% of the state income tax withheld from employee salaries, again if the withheld taxes were used instead to pay debt service. The total value of these incentives was $250 million.[47] In return, Daimler-Benz has built additional factories in Alabama since the 1993 plant, including plans announced in 2011 and 2015 to invest $2 billion and $1.3 billion, respectively, to upgrade and expand the Tuscaloosa plant.[48] In addition, other automotive companies such as Honda, subsequent to the Daimler investment, located facilities there. Each of those decisions was accompanied by additional tax concessions.

Although intense competition among some states for industrial relocation does cause problems, there are important benefits from this competition. First, it serves as a market-like regulator, preventing state and local governments from overtaxation. Second, it increases the efficiency of the allocation of public sector resources. States and localities that offer uneconomical incentives to businesses ultimately cannot sustain those incentives. There is a tendency toward equilibrium in the balance of incentives and the taxes and other charges necessary to make services available to support industrial development. Some states have backed away from the use of high-cost incentives. For example, North Carolina started competing for location of the film (television and movies) industry with tax incentives in 2005. Literally hundreds of productions were filmed in North Carolina, centering around the Wilmington area. In 2014, the state ended the tax incentive program. In 2013, before the tax incentives were abolished, there were 34 productions in North Carolina; in 2017, there was only one, a television series.[49]

Tax incentives were replaced with a much lower value grant program, which gradually brought producers back to the state, but at much reduced levels than prior to 2014.

Overlapping Taxes

The taxes of jurisdictions overlap with each other, and ultimately the same people and firms must pay the various governments. Tax overlapping also occurs when all levels of government tax the same specific source, such as when federal, state, and local governments all tax income. Overlapping or multiple taxation is unavoidable and not necessarily undesirable. It causes serious problems only when a government at one level, in effect, preempts another government's ability to raise enough revenue. This can occur if the state sales tax rate is so high that it discourages local jurisdictions from levying such a tax. Indeed, states may preclude their local governments from having sales taxes but may provide them with alternative sources of revenue. On the other hand, increasing numbers of states allow local governments to levy local sales taxes to support transportation. A study of 2001–2011 documented significant growth, although there were some variations from year to year, in voter-approved local sales taxes for transportation.[50]

The same kind of crowding-out problem occurs as a result of heavy federal personal and corporate income taxes, though corporate taxes were lowered in 2018. State and local governments, although often criticized for failing to raise enough revenue to meet needs, may be largely preempted by the federal government from major reliance on income taxes.

One proposal often advanced is a value-added tax (see the chapter on transaction-based revenue sources) and sharing corporate income and gasoline taxes. If ever implemented, this would have broad impact on the allocation of governmental responsibilities among federal, state, and local governments, potentially minimizing the issue of overlapping taxes. However, the value-added tax has never really garnered substantial political support in the United States.

Patterns of Interaction among Levels of Government

The structural and fiscal features of the U.S. intergovernmental system ensure that there will be numerous interactions among the different levels of governments. Multiple governments within the same nation interact in numerous ways that directly involve budgetary and other financial decisions as well as each government's fiscal condition. Intergovernmental revenue transfers, such as grants, are a common form of interaction, but they are by no means the only important form. Federal direct expenditures and taxes that occur within a state or local jurisdiction are also important, as is the financial assistance that one level of government gives to another. Finally, regulations, statutes, and other actions that do not directly involve taxing and spending, but nevertheless affect taxing and spending, shape budgetary decisions.

Direct Expenditures and Taxes

Discussions of intergovernmental finance too often concentrate exclusively on financial assistance and neglect the importance of direct expenditures. How much the federal government spends in a state and, in turn, how much a state spends in specific local areas have large impacts. Direct federal expenditures have varying geographic impacts, and the same is true for state expenditures.

Nongrant Spending

Locating government-owned or government-built facilities in a jurisdiction can substantially affect the jurisdiction's economy. Political considerations are crucial at the state level regarding the location of highways, state hospitals, prisons, and parks. Local and state governments work actively to obtain federal projects in their jurisdictions as one means of guaranteeing future prosperity. At the federal level, military installations, the awarding of defense contracts to corporations (which are

geographically based), and other civilian installations inspire intensive lobbying. Military base closings were especially contentious from the late 1980s to 2005 when there were five major rounds of base closures.[51]

Beyond the physical items are various programs that disburse loans and grants or make payments directly to individuals and corporations. At the federal level, these programs include Social Security, health insurance programs like Medicare, support to farmers, and small business loans. Social Security plus four health programs (Medicare, Medicaid, the Children's Health Insurance Program [CHIP], and the Affordable Care Act [ACA]) accounted for nearly 50% of all federal expenditures in 2018.[52] States also distribute large welfare and other human services payments among local jurisdictions.

Federal spending other than grants to individuals, organizations, and governments includes significant salaries and wages paid to federal employees and members of the military, a boost to state income. States having more than 100,000 federal civilian workers in 2017 included California, Maryland, Texas, and Virginia plus the District of Columbia.[53] Maryland and Virginia, of course, are contiguous with the District of Columbia. Virginia ranked highest in Department of Defense personnel spending with $16 billion in payrolls, followed by California and Texas with $14 billion and $11 billion, respectively. Iowa, Montana, New Hampshire, West Virginia, and Wyoming were at the other end, all less than $300 million.[54] Local effects can be dramatic. For example, San Diego County in 2017 had a total of 110,000 active duty military and civilian employees.[55] The county also had many military retirees receiving federal pensions. Depending upon the state, military pension may be taxed, but such taxes may be disincentives for military retirees to locate in states that tax their pensions.

Contracts with private firms and individuals for defense work totaled $272 billion, with California getting 13% of that very large pie.[56] These contracts, federal salaries, and miscellaneous other small programs are of far greater economic significance than are actual federal grants given to state and local governments.

Tax Collections

In addition to spending, tax collections have varying effects on locales, and the resulting balance between federal tax collections and expenditures has significant effects on jurisdictions. Generally, federal revenues raised in the Northeast and the Midwest have tended to be greater than the federal expenditures in these regions. The opposite pattern has existed in the South and the West, with the exception of states like Texas, California, Colorado, Nevada, and Oregon, where the federal tax burden has been greater than total federal expenditures.[57] The typical historical pattern changed with the federal programs put in place to combat the effects of the Great Recession.

Table 15-1 indicates the states with the highest and lowest ratios of federal spending per dollar of taxes for 2017. The table does not imply that there necessarily should be an equal return to each state of federal expenditures for every dollar of federal taxes collected.

Kentucky topped the list. The federal government spent $2.35 in Kentucky for every $1.00 extracted in taxes. Connecticut was at the other extreme. For every $1.00 in taxes from that state, only 74 cents flowed back into the state. In 10 states, the flow of federal funds to the state was less than the flow of taxes to the federal government. California was at the "break even" point: $1 in funds flowed to the state for every federal tax dollar collected.[58] In the remaining 39 states, flows from the federal government to the states were greater than the flow of taxes to the federal government. Clearly, whether a federal budget deficit is incurred for economic stimulus reasons, war expenditures, or just the fact that the federal budget has almost always been in deficit over the last 50 years, states generally have more federal funds spent in their states than they pay in taxes in recession years.

Figure 15-1 illustrates the relationship between net revenue flow of federal expenditures and federal taxes, for all 50 states, and state per capita personal income. If this net federal flow is generally redistributive, then we would expect the pattern to be generally downward sloping to the

Table 15-1 States with Highest and Lowest Ratios of Federal Spending per Dollar of Federal Taxes, 2017

Highest Ratios of Spending per Dollar of Taxes			Lowest Ratios of Spending per Dollar of Taxes		
Rank	State	Ratio	Rank	State	Ratio
1.	Kentucky	2.35	41.	Colorado	0.99
2.	New Mexico	2.34	42.	New Hampshire	0.98
3.	Mississippi	2.19	43.	Washington	0.98
4.	West Virginia	2.17	44.	Nebraska	0.98
5.	Alabama	1.99	45.	Illinois	0.97
6.	Virginia	1.97	46.	North Dakota	0.94
7.	Arkansas	1.77	47.	New York	0.86
8.	Maine	1.74	48.	Massachusetts	0.83
9.	South Carolina	1.73	49.	New Jersey	0.82
10.	Alaska	1.67	50.	Connecticut	0.74

Schultz, L., and Cummings, M. (2019). *Giving or getting? New York's balance of payments with the federal government.* Albany, NY: Rockefeller Institute of Government, 13

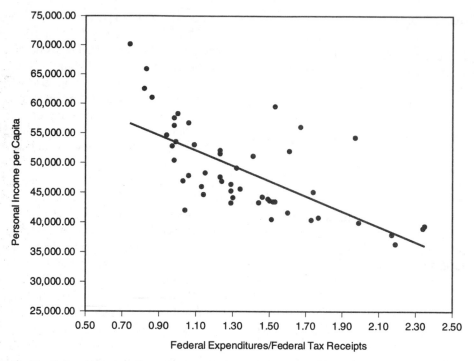

Figure 15-1 Net Federal Funds to/from States as a Function of State Personal Income Per Capita, 2017.

Ratio of federal taxes collected to federal expenditures by state from: Schultz, L., and Cummings, M. (2019). *Giving or getting? New York's balance of payments with the federal government.* Albany, NY: Rockefeller Institute of Government, 13. State personal income per capita (current dollars, 2017) from: ProQuest LLC (2019). *Statistical abstract of the United States, 2019.* Lanham, MD: ProQuest LLC, 460.

right, which indeed is what Figure 15-1 demonstrates. The lower the per capita income, the greater the net flow of federal funds to the state.

We inserted the overall, linear trend line in the figure. The correlation between net flow and per capita income is strong: –0.67, the negative sign consistent with the expectation. Although the trendline is consistent with the hypothesis that net federal revenue and expenditure actions are redistributive across the states, there is considerable variation, visible in the scatterplot with its numerous large outliers. The trend in earlier years was the same, consistent with the hypothesis. In 2004, for example, the correlation coefficient was –0.61. Of course, numerous other factors are involved. Figure 15-1 merely illustrates the general tendency of total federal activities in the states to be redistributive. Figure 15-1 is important, however, because it is not just federal grants. It includes all federal spending—for example, federal civilian payroll and payments to individuals. Total federal spending is more redistributive than federal grants alone.

Intergovernmental Assistance
State Aid

The literature on intergovernmental relations tends to overemphasize federal aid to state and local governments and underemphasize state aid to local government. In 2016, federal aid to states was $622 billion and to local governments was $69 billion. State aid to local governments was $521 billion.[59] State support of local governments, for most states, is the largest element in the state budget. Of course, state aid probably would be much smaller were states not receiving substantial federal support. As noted in the chapter on public sector in perspective, states receive nearly 30% of their revenue from the federal government. Local governments, excluding school districts, receive about 40% of their revenue from other governments, almost all of it from state governments, with only 6% from the federal government. Except for school districts, each type of local government

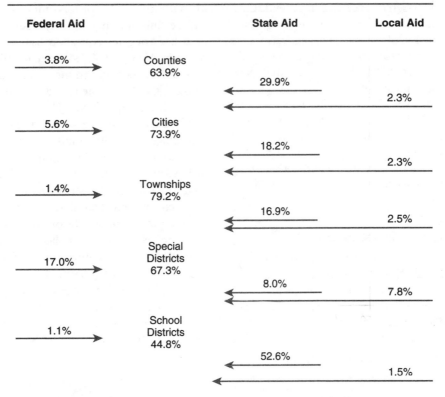

Federal Aid		State Aid	Local Aid
3.8%	Counties 63.9%	29.9%	2.3%
5.6%	Cities 73.9%	18.2%	2.3%
1.4%	Townships 79.2%	16.9%	2.5%
17.0%	Special Districts 67.3%	8.0%	7.8%
1.1%	School Districts 44.8%	52.6%	1.5%

Figure 15-2 Intergovernmental Sources of General Revenue for Types of Local Governments, 2012. Data may not equal 100% due to rounding.

Compiled from The Urban Institute-Brookings Institution Tax Policy Center (2019). State & local government finance data query system. Data from U.S. Census Bureau, Annual Survey of State and Local Government Finances, Government Finances, Volume 4, and Census of Governments (2012). Retrieved August 4, 2019, from http://www.taxpolicycenter.org/slf-dqs/pages.cfm. Note: data for different types of local governments, as in Figure 15-2, are not available for more recent years than figures for state and local combined.

obtains half or more of its revenue from its own sources. Differences in federal and state support exist among the types of local governments.

Figure 15-2 illustrates intergovernmental revenues provided to the different types of local government entities, as a proportion of those entities' total general revenues. For example, in the middle column, county revenues for 2012 were 64% from their own sources. The remaining 36% came from intergovernmental transfers: 4% from federal government, 30% from states, and 2% from other local entities. Similarly, one can see that school districts are the only local entities that receive more than half of their revenue from other governments—state governments provided most of the funds that school districts spent (53%).

Another way to look at intergovernmental aid is to consider where most of the federal intergovernmental transfers go, and similarly for state and local transfers. As of 2012, about 33% of all federal aid to local governments went to municipalities, but these monies constituted only about 6% of municipal revenues. Special districts such as sewer and water districts were the most dependent on federal aid, which constituted 17% of their budgets. Slightly more than half (55%) of state aid went to school districts, with these monies accounting for just over half of school district revenues. Most of the other state aid went to counties and municipalities, 24% and 17%, respectively.[60]

These summary figures, of course, do not convey the great variety in patterns of state aid. States vary substantially in terms of how much assistance they provide to their local governments. Some states may provide a given service and thereby make direct expenditures, whereas other states may fund local governments to provide the service. Local governments in most states receive about 20% to 35% from other governments. This is much less than New Mexico's local governments, which get almost 50% of their revenues from other governments, again almost all from the state government.[61] Hawaii's intergovernmental transfers to local governments are low because the state directly operates schools, unlike the other states, which funnel elementary and secondary school money to local districts.

State Aid to Education

Aid to elementary and secondary education, as noted, constitutes the largest portion of state aid to local governments. Local school districts have not always depended as heavily on state and federal aid. **Figure 15-3** shows that local sources in the early part of the 20th century accounted

for more than 80% of total funding, whereas it had declined to only 43% by 1980. Since then, local financing for education has varied slightly, between 43% and 48% through 2017. Just as state aid to local governments in general varies considerably from state to state, so too does state aid to education, with New Hampshire, Nebraska, South Dakota, and Texas providing the lowest percentage of funding (mid-30% range).[62]

Because of the importance of external—mainly state—funding, the way funds are distributed to local school districts is often a matter of some controversy. States use a formula for distributing these funds. Historically known as the *foundation plan*, such formulas are geared toward guaranteeing a minimum amount of educational expenditures either per pupil or per classroom. The word *foundation* suggests equality of educational opportunity, meaning that every student should have a minimum level of education—a foundation program. Formulas typically have

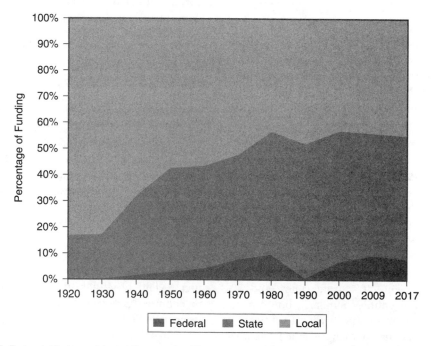

Figure 15-3 Federal, State, and Local Support for Elementary and Secondary Education, 1920–2017 (in Percent).

Compiled from Monk, D.H. (1991). *Educational finance: an economic approach.* New York, NY: McGraw-Hill, 101; Bureau of the Census, U.S. Department of Commerce. Government finances: 1989-90. Washington, DC: U.S. Government Printing Office, 7; Bureau of the Census, U.S. Department of Commerce (2002). Public education finances, 2000. Washington, DC: U.S. Government Printing Office, 1; Bureau of the Census, U.S. Department of Commerce (2006). Public education finances, 2004. Washington, DC: U.S. Government Printing Office, ix; U.S. Bureau of the Census, Public elementary-secondary school system finance data, retrieved August 4, 2019, from https://www.census.gov/data/tables/2017/econ/school-finances/secondaryeducation-finance.html, 2009 and 2017 data, respectively.

been tied to real estate property assessments, with districts having low assessments per pupil receiving more aid than districts having high assessments. Separate formulas may be used for programs serving preschool, disadvantaged, and handicapped children as well as elementary-level children and secondary-level children.

Foundation formulas were attacked in the courts starting in the 1970s as discriminatory. Foundation plans were accused of failing to equalize educational opportunity among jurisdictions. While recognizing the great importance of education, the Supreme Court, in 1973, decided in a Texas case, *San Antonio School District v. Rodriquez*, that the allocation of funds for education was a state responsibility and was not controlled by the Constitution.[63] The Court, in that case, was concerned that basing the formula on a macro measure such as the property tax base may not represent circumstances at the micro or individual level (e.g., extremely poor families might live in a wealthy district and not be receiving equal educational opportunity). Thus, the Court ruled that the reliance on the property tax did not create any inequality challengeable on constitutional grounds.

After *Rodriquez,* challenges turned to state courts. By 2016, more than 40 states experienced legal challenges, and in 30, existing systems were overturned.[64] Many states have been required to alter their education financing schemes to minimize disparities in per-pupil expenditures among districts. The California Supreme Court ruled in *Serrano v. Priest (Serrano II)* in 1976 that the state's finance system for education violated California's equal protection clause in the state constitution because it created disparities in per-pupil spending. Several subsequent suits against individual California school districts have relied on the state's equal protection clause articulated in *Serrano II.*[65]

Most states have abandoned the simplistic concept of equal funding per pupil as the basis for foundation support. Approximately 25% of state education assistance is categorical funding directed to a variety of needs, including special needs, transportation, gifted and talented, and bilingual programs. Typically, these flow to districts with relatively fewer resources and/or with greater need.[66] Equalizing spending does not ensure that spending will be enough for each child to achieve desired outcomes. Adequacy is a more profound concept that links equity to educational achievement. The equal opportunity to achieve is not necessarily ensured by equal funding.[67] *Rose v. Council for Better Education*, a 1989 Kentucky Supreme Court case, is often considered the landmark case in litigation using the adequacy concept. The court decided that the Kentucky legislature had failed to live up to the state's constitutional requirement to "provide an efficient system of common schools throughout the state."[68] That forced the state to change its school funding scheme.

Though education is primarily a state responsibility, the federal government also is involved in assistance to achieve educational performance and decrease fiscal and other inequities across the states. The No Child Left Behind Act of 2001 reauthorizing the Elementary and Secondary Education Act expressed the philosophy that individuals should have equal chances for educational achievement and mandated individual testing to measure success.[69] Strong opposition to No Child Left Behind resulted ultimately in its replacement in 2015 by the Every Student Succeeds Act (ESSA).[70] ESSA focuses on support for innovation in schools and school systems to improve educational achievement, funding demonstration projects, evidence-based assessments of educational progress, and neighborhood programs in distressed communities.[71]

Other State Aid

Other state aid programs are comparatively small. Education is followed in size by expenditures for welfare and highways. Aid for these programs is usually handed out based on some type of formula (welfare programs are often per-client reimbursement programs). Virtually all states have some form of motor fuels tax–sharing formula that benefits local government road programs as well as state roads.[72] General local government support, as opposed to specific functional aid, is higher than support for any functions other than education and welfare.

Overall, state assistance has been more predictable than federal aid because local governments are creatures of the states. Most states make extensive use of formulas that facilitate budget planning at the local level because jurisdictions from year to year need to have some knowledge of what state funds will be. The only major controversies have centered on the factors used in the formulas. Aid to local governments in many states rises and falls depending on the states' economic health. Following the Great Recession, local governments were slow to recover their finances. The National Association of Counties estimated that only 7% of U.S. counties had recovered their pre-recession economies by 2015.[73] Since that recession, almost all states have developed new monitoring frameworks or enhanced existing programs to monitor local government fiscal health.[74] Fundamentally, local governments are creatures of their respective states, and ultimate responsibility falls upon state government when local governments are unable to perform.[75] Most of the focus in state monitoring programs is aimed at ensuring sufficient financial health in local governments to avoid defaulting on general obligation bonds and avoiding bankruptcy and state takeover of a local government's finances. Local governments have shown resiliency in making up for state and federal decreases by drawing on their own resources and by placing greater reliance on user charges and other charges aimed at direct beneficiaries of programs (see the chapter on budgeting for transaction-based revenues).

Federal Aid

Federal grants have been aimed at inducing state and local governments to increase the level of services in specified functions and are not intended to replace state or local spending with federal revenues. This *inducement effect* is based on the theory that the more separation that exists between taxing and spending, the more taxpayers will not perceive the full costs of local services. Therefore, citizens at the lower level will demand or lobby for more funding from a higher level because it appears to be without cost to these citizens. This

is known as the *fiscal illusion hypothesis*. However, state and local governments may take advantage of grant funds to reduce their own resources. Grant programs contain provisions to prevent or at least minimize the substitution effect.

Matching Requirements, Fungibility, and the Flypaper Effect

Matching provisions are usually required as a means of ensuring that grants will not merely result in a lessened tax effort by the recipients of the grants. For example, a grant might require that a state government match federal aid dollar for dollar. Without a matching provision, a $1 million federal grant could be offset by an equal reduction in state or local revenues supporting a program, thereby producing no increase in the level of services.

The ability to replace local or state money for a program with grant money is known as *fungibility*. The government providing the grant usually does not want this to occur because its intent usually is to increase funding in a targeted area. For example, if grant money is targeted at crime, then the intent is to boost law enforcement expenditures and not to have federal dollars simply supplant some of the state and local money that otherwise would have been spent on law enforcement. However, sometimes substituting spending by a recipient government with a grant or transfer from another government may be the goal. States may want local governments to accept state aid and decrease reliance on the property tax. A related matter is the extent of earmarking of grant money for specific purposes, a topic addressed later in this chapter. When grants are earmarked in detail, flexibility is decreased. In the case of helping small businesses recover from the September 11, 2001, disaster in New York City, the New York City Investment Fund found it important to avoid earmarking and to provide small businesses with the flexibility that they needed in the use of the assistance.[76] In the case of donations—for example, people who donate to the American Red Cross in the wake of hurricanes and wildfires—often earmark their donations specifically for particular disasters and reduce the flexibility of the agency in meeting other needs.

Fungibility poses a major threat to analyses of the effectiveness of programs and the use of such analyses in budgetary decision making. If state or local dollars are replaced one-for-one with grant money, then no increase in funding has occurred, and any identified change in program results clearly is not associated with funding. The extent to which governments take advantage of possible fungibility relates to another concept known as the *flypaper effect*. When private citizens receive increased funding, say bonuses of $1,000 each, the typical pattern will be to spend some and save some. A family with a tight budget might spend all or almost all the $1,000, but other families might spend only $700 and put the remaining $300 in savings. The question for state and local governments is whether they tend to do the same or if there is a flypaper effect in which the money received gets spent for the intended purpose (that is, whether the money "sticks" to the grant area as planned by the donor government).

Research tends to support the flypaper effect. Recipient governments tend to spend the money received for the intended purpose, and in some cases the governments even spend more of their own funds than they otherwise would have spent.[77] Financially strapped jurisdictions, however, may view fungibility as an opportunity to free up money for other pressing services, and to do so may even use what amounts to subterfuge to hide such transactions from the granting agency.

The fiscal effect, inducing more local spending, is less when the grants are provided without any minimum requirements for tax effort or expenditure requirements. When there is no matching requirement, the greater effect may be on local tax relief—mainly property taxes in the case of education—rather than on increasing spending. The opposite situation arises also. Research shows that some increases in state aid for education forced by having to meet legal challenges result in reduced state aid to local governments in other functional areas.[78]

Where the objective is more clearly weighted toward redistributive effects, such as welfare assistance, there is the risk that states with less fiscal capacity may choose to spend less than what is considered nationally desirable. The various low-income assistance programs with which the federal government helps states and localities exhibit a range of federal involvement. The Supplemental Nutrition Assistance Program, or SNAP (known more colloquially as food stamps), is fully federally funded. The Supplemental Security Income (SSI) program for the low-income elderly and disabled is mainly federally funded. The Temporary Assistance to Needy Families (TANF) program is a block grant program with major contributions from both the federal government and the states.[79] State fiscal responses to this package of programs have been somewhat mixed, with apparent reduced efforts for cash assistance programs and overall increased state and local spending for various welfare programs, especially Medicaid.

For grant programs aimed at inducing behavior changes and not necessarily fiscal responses, the task is more difficult. To accomplish changes in program emphasis at the state and local levels with grants, one must believe that state and local preferences for service modes, such as transportation, are primarily driven by the cost and revenue availability. The Intermodal Surface Transportation Efficiency Act of 1991 and the Transportation Enhancement Act of 1998 were intended, in part, to encourage development and use of transportation modes other than cars on highways. In reality, states and localities are more likely to choose to repair and rehabilitate deteriorating highways and bridges than to fund mass transit.[80] The federal CHIP was designed to induce states to implement programs to insure low-income children.[81] CHIP focuses on children whose family incomes make them ineligible for Medicaid assistance, but cannot afford traditional insurance. The program allows for significant state flexibility in program design and implementation.[82] Designed before the ACA, CHIP and ACA assistance for children of families eligible for help in affording health insurance have been modified to help ensure complementarity and to avoid overlap.[83]

Table 15-2 Functional Distribution (%) of Federal Grants-in-Aid, 1960–2019

	1960	1970	1980	1990	2000	2010	2019 est.
Administration of Justice	*	*	1	*	2	1	1
Agriculture	3	3	1	1	*	*	*
Community and Regional Development	1	8	7	4	3	3	4
Education, Employment, Training, and Social Services	7	27	24	16	13	16	9
General Government	3	2	9	2	1	1	1
Health	3	16	17	33	44	48	61
Income Security	38	24	20	27	24	19	15
Natural Resources and Environment	1	2	6	3	2	2	1
Transportation	43	19	14	14	11	10	9
Other	*	*	1	1	1	1	1
Total	100	100	100	100	100	100	100

Totals may not equal 100 percent due to rounding.
* 0.5 percent or less.

Calculated from U.S. Office of Management and Budget (2020). Historical Tables: Table 12.2-Historical Outlays for Grants to State and Local Governments by Function and Fund Group: 1940-2025. Retrieved May 27, 2020 from https://www.whitehouse.gov/omb/historical-tables/

Federal Aid and Functional Areas

During the 1960s, about 80% of all federal aid went for transportation and income security. As can be seen in **Table 15-2**, there have been substantial shifts since that time. Transportation, which accounted for more than 40% of the aid in the 1960s, declined to just under 20% in 1970, and then continued to fall to 9% in 2019. Aid for health programs rose to 61%. Income security accounted for about 15% of the aid. It has fluctuated widely, up in the 1960s (38%), down to 20% in 1980, back up again around 27% in the 1990s, and down substantially in 2019. The decreases since 2000 are, in part, due to welfare reforms limiting the number of years during which an individual can receive assistance (TANF program). Generally, the effects of rapidly rising health care costs and the reduction in income security support explain most of the shifts that occurred between 1980 and 2019.

The amount of federal aid given to state and local governments varies among federal agencies. The Department of Health and Human Services disburses the most aid by far, accounting for 67% of all federal grants. A different perspective, however, is gained by looking at the portion of an agency's budget committed to grants in **Table 15-3**. Although the Department of Health and Human Services accounts for the largest share of federal grants to state and local governments, it spends only about 41% of its funds on grants. The Department of Transportation spends 81% of its budget on grants, and the Department of Education spends 47%.

Regional Differences

Just as total federal outlays are not uniform from state to state, so too do grants vary. In 2018, the national average was $2,039 per capita in federal

Table 15-3 Federal Agency Outlays and Grants to State and Local Governments, 2010 (in Billions of Dollars)

Agency	Total Outlays	Grant Outlays	Grants as Percentage of Total
Agriculture	129.5	32.5	25.1
Commerce	13.2	0.5	3.8
Education	92.9	75.1	80.8
Energy	30.8	2.2	7.1
Environmental Protection Agency	11.0	6.9	62.6
Health and Human Services	854.1	347.1	40.6
Homeland Security	44.5	8.9	20.1
Housing and Urban Development	60.1	44.4	73.9
Interior	13.2	4.5	34.1
Justice	29.6	4.6	15.5
Labor	173.1	11.6	6.7
Social Security Administration	754.2	0.0	0.0
Transportation	77.8	61.0	78.4
Treasury	444.3	3.9	0.9
Veterans Affairs	108.3	0.8	0.8
Other Agencies	620.0	4.4	0.7
Total*	3,456.2	608.4	17.6

*Total does not include allowances and undistributed offsetting receipts (on-budget and off-budget).

Compiled from U.S. Office of Management and Budget (2020). Historical tables: budget of the United States Government, 2020. Table 4.1—Outlays by Agency: 1962–2024 and Table 12.3—Total Outlays for Grants to State and Local Governments, by Function, Agency, and Program: 1940–2020. Retrieved August 17, 2019, from https://www.whitehouse.gov/omb/historical-tables/.

grants to state and local governments, up from $1,765 in 2009. The states receiving the highest per capita grants, other than Alaska, were New York ($3,163), Delaware ($3,036), New Mexico ($2,929), California ($2,926), and Vermont ($2,810). Three of the top five per capita recipients were sparsely populated states. The group with the lowest per capita grants consisted of Utah ($1,116), Virginia ($1,187), Kansas ($1,293), Nebraska ($1,313), and Florida ($1,352). The lowest-ranking recipients were a mix of less and more populous states. Alaska was the highest state, with $4,108, but it commonly is an outlier and is typically excluded from comparisons.[84]

These per-capita grant figures must not be interpreted simply as revealing which areas are winners and losers in the federal aid game. As noted in the previous section, a state and its local governments might receive comparatively small amounts of grants, but extensive economic support as a result of direct federal expenditures. Virginia receives relatively little in grants but benefits from having a great many federal offices and facilities located in the state.

If the federal progressive income tax has the effect of drawing proportionately greater resources from wealthy states than from less wealthy states, federal aid could amplify or dampen this effect. For example, per-capita federal aid to state and local governments might increase as state per-capita personal income declines, which would amplify the effect. This pattern, however, is not evident. Nonetheless, as already discussed, there is a general redistributive effect when the total flows to states from all federal actions and flows of taxes from the states are compared to per-capita income. Other factors explaining the distribution of federal grants include the number of Medicaid recipients and the amount of federal land in the state, which brings money from minerals, timber, and grazing rights. Again, caution is necessary when interpreting only one measure of federal economic impact on states. The lack of a clear pattern is explained by the numerous federal grant programs that tend to offset each other in benefiting types of states.

Studies that have compared federal aid and state aid to urban areas have concluded that, although both are responsive to need, state aid is more responsive. Cities with greater fiscal problems receive greater per-capita state assistance. An important factor in this area is local initiative itself. Some cities are much more aggressive and adept at securing federal and state aid, and this ability is not necessarily correlated with the extent of need. In recent years, state governments have tried to offset some of the decline in federal aid to local governments, particularly by targeting their assistance to cities with the severest problems measured in terms of need, such as prevalence of poverty and low fiscal capacity. However, state budget crises during the recent two recessions, as noted above, resulted in serious cutbacks in state assistance to all local governments, both rural and urban.

In metropolitan areas, fiscal imbalances can cause problems in the pattern of services and the ability to pay for those services. Capital flight out of central cities in the form of wealthier households and businesses moving to the suburbs exacerbates differences, especially in the older cities of the Northeast and the Midwest. One way that some metropolitan areas have combated this problem is to develop metropolitan area tax base sharing and other fiscal equalization strategies, although few governments across the country willingly share their tax bases. Some multiple municipal jurisdictions within the same metropolitan area have begun to see advantages in increased coordination as some city regions look to their potential fate in a global economy. Greater metropolitan area coordination and cooperation is likely to be an important outgrowth of the recent Great Recession, the likelihood of a weak federal assistance budget for years to come, and state governments' cutback responses.[85]

Federal aid to local communities can be provided directly to these communities or indirectly through the states. In the latter case, state officials are allowed some discretion in distributing federal funds, although federal regulations may require that a given amount pass through to localities and that some of this money be distributed according to set criteria, such as population. State *enabling legislation* often is required before a local government can receive funds directly from the federal government.

Devolution and Future Trends

The dollar volume of federal grants-in-aid continues to climb each year; but federal aid as a percentage of state and local expenditures has had a more variable pattern. **Figure 15-4** shows that since 1960, there has been a general long-term trend upward in federal grants as a percentage of state and local expenditures, except for a decade-long slump from 1980 to 1990. Two recessions, early and late in the decade of the 2000s, were major factors in seeing that percentage increase again, almost to the 1980 peak. Barring any significant economic downturn, the upward trend is unlikely to continue in the foreseeable future considering mounting federal budget deficits (see discussion in the chapter on government and the economy). The trend to low levels of federal assistance to state and local governments, except in a major crisis as in the Great Recession, and the size of the federal deficit are changing the

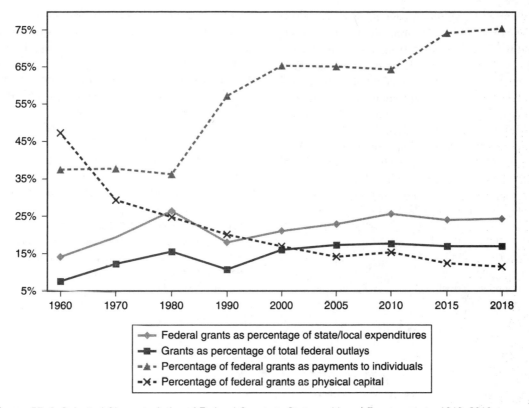

Figure 15-4 Selected Characteristics of Federal Grants to State and Local Governments, 1960–2018.

Calculated from U.S. Office of Management and Budget (2020). Historical Tables: Table 12.1- Summary Comparison of Total Outlays for Grants to State and Local Governments: 1940-2025. Retrieved May 27, 2020 **download PDF** from https://www.whitehouse.gov/omb/historical-tables/

character of intergovernmental relations in the United States.

Figure 15-4 illustrates three other comparative measures of federal grants. Grants as a percentage of federal outlays grew from 8% in 1960 to 16% in 1980. Since 2000, grants as a share of total federal outlays have stayed in the 16% to 17% range. Federal aid hovered between 2% and 4% of gross domestic product throughout the period covered by Figure 15-4.[86]

Figure 15-4, in addition to tracking changes in federal grants vis-à-vis state and local expenditures and total federal outlays, also indicates the substantial change in the character of federal aid. The most prominent change has been the growth in the percentage of federal assistance that are payments to individuals. As Figure 15-4 shows, beginning between 1980 and 1990, payments to individuals grew from the mid-30% range to

about 75%. The other noticeable trend is the decline in federal grants for physical capital. In the 1960s, nearly 50% of federal grants were for physical capital. That percentage dropped below 25% in the mid-1970s and has continued to decline to below 12% in 2018.

Figure 15-4 reveals other trends that are significant for the shape of the intergovernmental system. The shift from grants to states and local governments for physical capital investments toward payments to individuals has meant a change for state and local governments. Rather than serving as active agents in implementing federally funded programs, they now play more of a role as conduits for channeling federal funds to individuals. During the 1960s, which saw extensive federal assistance to capital infrastructure programs, state governments mainly (but also local governments) were heavily involved in selection, design, and contracting for public works financed by federal dollars. The shift toward payments to individuals channeled by the states is politically more divisive, with the fault lines lying between arguments for smaller versus larger federal roles and for less or more federal influence on state prerogatives.

Figure 15-4 examines the intergovernmental assistance patterns in federal versus state expenditures. **Figure 15-5** completes the picture with analysis of state and local revenues and federal assistance. In the figure, state and local total revenues are shown in billions of dollars on the left *y*-axis, and the percentage of state and local general revenues constituted by federal aid is shown on the right *y*-axis. From 1950 through the first decade of the 2000s, state and local governments generally maintained their overall revenue growth despite relative declines in federal grants, with the exceptions of the recessions in 2001–2002 and 2007–2009. In those two periods, state and local revenues dropped significantly, partially compensated by increases in federal grants, as the figure illustrates. In the 2001–2002 recession, federal grants increased, reaching 20% in 2002 of total state and local revenues, higher than the previous peak (1980). In the post-recession period, they fell back to 17% almost immediately.

In 2008–2009, the stimulus programs implemented to combat the Great Recession had substantial effects. The drop in the Great Recession in state and local revenues was precipitous—from $2.7 trillion in 2008 to $2.1 trillion in 2009, or 24%. Federal assistance partly filled the gap, primarily through grant programs included in the various fiscal stimulus packages and increased assistance to individuals affected by the recession. Federal aid to states increased 20% in 2009 over 2008, and the federal share of state and local revenues jumped from 17% to 27%, by far the highest share in the 1950 through 2009 period. In the

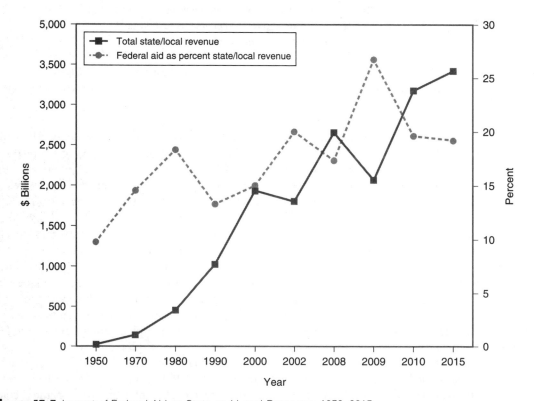

Figure 15-5 Impact of Federal Aid on State and Local Revenues, 1950–2015.

Compiled from Bureau of the Census, U.S. Department of Commerce (1952). Statistical abstract, 1952. Washington, DC: U.S. Government Printing Office, 353; Statistical abstract, 1962, 416; Statistical abstract, 1982, 275; Statistical abstract, 2006, 280; ProQuest LLC (2019). ProQuest statistical abstract of the United States, 2019. Lanham, MD: Rowman & Littlefield, 297.

post-recession period, state and local revenues resumed the trend upward, and federal assistance as a percentage of state and local revenues fell, although the dollar value of federal assistance remained about the same from 2010 to 2015.

Though federal assistance levels have increased to partially offset drops in state and local revenues, it has not alleviated state and local budget stress. The recessionary period of 1990–1992 caused enormous hardships for state and local governments. That was repeated in the two recessions since 2000. Prior to the 1960s, state and local governments had primary financing responsibility for domestic programs. Beginning with the 1960s and the antipoverty programs of the Johnson administration, the financial role of the federal government came to equal and, by the mid-1970s, even exceed the financial role of state and local governments. Not only have federal grants for capital declined, but state and local spending for capital investment as a percentage of gross domestic product has declined as well. Thus, states have been forced to scramble to keep services operating and, in many situations, have had little or no choice but to cut and sometimes eliminate programs.

The shift from federal assistance for capital projects to assistance to individuals, with the matching requirements, has increased the pressure on state budgets. When federal funding is increasing along with state and local revenues, state decision makers are hard pressed to turn down the federal dollars. Medicaid assistance is the primary pressure point. Medicaid, as well as other federal programs, come with significant state matches. When state and local revenues decrease during economic downturns, whether national in scope or only in some states, the states are faced with the hard decision to cut programs that assist individuals who need it the most during the downturn or cut other programs to meet the matching requirements. In the early 1990s, the National Association of State Budget Officers posed the dilemma: "Both the modest budget growth and the midyear budget adjustments reflect the tepid economy as well as pressures from double-digit growth in Medicaid spending and increased welfare caseloads."[87]

In addition to the matching requirements, federal aid programs, particularly those for individual assistance, have had significant regulatory requirements that restrict state and local flexibility in program design and implementation. Pressure built to reform federal assistance by devolving more responsibility and more authority from the federal to the state and local levels. Even prior to the early 1990s, there were significant federal budget cuts in assistance to states and major changes in many federal grant programs during the Reagan Administration. Since then, federal assistance programs have been reshaped along the twin fault lines of the size of the federal role and the degree of federal influence on state level decisions. During some administrations, notably the Clinton and Obama presidencies, the pendulum swung toward greater federal roles. During the two Bush administrations (George H.W. and George W.) and continuing through the Trump administration, the pendulum swung toward greater *devolution* of responsibility to state and local governments.

Devolution has meant a fundamental shift in responsibility for policy, programs, and financing. Devolution involves outright reductions in federal aid to state and local governments; changes in some programs from matching to nonmatching grants; and, of course, greater flexibility. In response to the challenges, state and local governments have taken on much more activist roles in policy formulation, program design, and program implementation in assuming responsibilities that previously had been determined by federal policy and program design since their origins.

Two program clusters involving federal and state assistance to individuals illustrate these fault lines. One cluster is federal programs to provide financial assistance to individuals that meet various program criteria, primarily focusing on income level. The most prominent program is the Aid for Dependent Children (AFDC), succeeded by TANF. AFDC had its origins in the New Deal. The second cluster includes assistance aimed at support for health care costs, the most prominent being Medicaid and the ACA, also more colloquially called Obamacare by supporters and critics alike. Each program involves federal funds used to induce states to achieve objectives determined by Congress to be in the national interest. Each program also involves mandates that states must accept in order to participate in the program. All have changed over time. **Exhibit 15-2** briefly describes these programs and the changes over time to illustrate the shifts in federal and state/local responsibilities in the federal system.

Exhibit 15-2   **Welfare and Health Care Reform: Federal Versus State/Local Roles in Individual Assistance Programs**

Welfare Reform. The most prominent shift in devolving federal assistance policy and program design in the past three decades has been reconfiguring the nation's welfare system. Welfare assistance to individuals began as a New Deal program in 1935 to provide direct payments to individual households meeting program requirements, initially white-only households headed by single mothers who did not and were not expected to work. States had wide latitude in determining income and other resources limits on eligibility, but within those boundaries had to assist all eligible households. AFDC federal funding was a matching grant program, with unlimited federal funds based on state matches. Gradual changes made in the program extended assistance to households with an unemployed father and removed the "white only" stipulation.

By the 1990s, criticisms of the program focused on growing welfare rolls swelling the impact on state budgets and on the argument that the program created a culture of welfare dependency. The number of families receiving assistance grew from less than 1 million in 1959 to a peak of more than 5 million in 1994.[a] The 1994 Republican sweep of the House and the Senate focused criticisms on the AFDC program and negotiated with the Democratic President Clinton for major reforms, leading to passage of the Personal Responsibility and Work Opportunity Reconciliation Act (PRWORA) of 1996, that created the Technical Assistance to Needy Families program. The big change in the intergovernmental system introduced by PRWORA was the shift of federal responsibility for setting welfare standards and the long-standing approach of federal matching grants to a fixed block grant program.[b] States have wide latitude in designing programs. From the point of view of welfare recipients, the major change was a maximum lifetime eligibility of five years for public financial assistance.

PRWORA provided for considerable relaxation in federal requirements through granting states waivers, thereby exempting them from many federal requirements, to develop their own policies and system designs. Some states secured waivers to contract out to private organizations such previously state functions as eligibility determination, job counseling and training, and administration of the program. Others consolidated numerous programs. States could determine eligibility, set benefit levels, and design their own program administration. State programs are funded through a combination of federal funds (through the TANF block grant) and state funds. The block grant sets a ceiling and puts states more in control of their level of commitment to the program since they are no longer required to assist every eligible household. States still are required to match at a level consistent with their historic expenditures under the PRWORA *maintenance of effort* requirement. Once funding levels are reached, eligible non-participants, based on state limits, go on a waiting list. The PRWORA reforms succeeded in relieving some state budget pressures since states determine their extent of participation. Federal funding also decreased as a result of federal budget pressures and decreased congressional policy support. Federal block grant funding was $16.5 billion in 2019, down from $21.7 billion in 2010.[c]

The law provided for limitations as to how long people could be eligible for cash assistance. Recipients of AFDC (TANF's predecessor) in 1990 totaled 11.5 million. That number had increased to 13.4 million in 1995. In 2018, total TANF cash assistance recipients numbered just over 2.2 million.[d]

Innovative policy and program reforms in welfare-to-work transition, teen pregnancy reduction, health screening, and single-parent family issues have been developed as a result of states discretion to experiment with program design. Welfare recipients themselves have had varying experiences. Clearly, some have found productive employment and are unlikely to return to public assistance. However, much of the decline in welfare rolls has been attributed to individuals and households being declared ineligible because they could not, or did not, meet the work requirements. One analysis of the number of families receiving benefits showed that for every 100 families with children meeting federal poverty levels,

Exhibit 15-2 **Welfare and Health Care Reform: Federal Versus State/Local Roles in Individual Assistance Programs**   *(continued)*

82 families received assistance in 1979 under AFDC whereas only 23 families received assistance under TANF in 2017.[e]

TANF was reauthorized in 2019, extending authorization and funding only through the end of the fiscal year. Its future is uncertain with respect to its longer-term continuation with or without changes to eligibility requirements, state discretionary authority, and federal funding in a deeply divided Congress and White House.

Health Care Reform. One of the fastest-growing budgetary components for all levels of government is the Medicaid program, which offers health assistance to the poor. Major health care reform legislation in 2010 significantly expanded eligibility for Medicaid and altered federal-state relationships in health care for low-income individuals and families.[f] The Patient Protection and Affordable Care Act of 2010, typically abbreviated to Affordable Care Act (ACA) was accomplished with significant Republican opposition and opposition by many Republican-controlled state governments.[g]

Medicaid is a federal-state matching grant program administered at the federal level by the Centers for Medicare and Medicaid Services in the Department of Health and Human Services. The program provides medical insurance to the categorically needy, including people who qualify for cash assistance under the Temporary Assistance for Needy Families (TANF) program, pregnant women and children below the poverty level, children at the poverty level, caregivers of children, disabled people receiving benefits under the Supplemental Security Income (SSI) program, and others. Beyond the categorically needy are the medically needy who cannot qualify for assistance because their incomes are too high, but they still cannot afford medical insurance. The Patient Protection and Affordable Care Act of 2010 greatly expanded eligibility, increasing the income threshold and including most uninsured adults under 65 who meet the poverty threshold.

All states participate in the Medicaid program. States are allowed considerable flexibility in designing their programs. Some states, prior to the 2010 health care reform, covered few adults; others have more extended adult coverage, some including both parents and childless adults. States also may participate in the State Children's Health Insurance Program (CHIP or SCHIP), which provides additional support and is intended to expand coverage of children beyond the standard Medicaid program, particularly to children whose families otherwise do not qualify for Medicaid.

Eligibility for Medicaid was expanded significantly by the 2010 health care reform. Not all states opted to expand Medicaid despite the attraction of federal funding. As of 2019, 17 states had not elected to expand their programs, all but 3 in the south.[h] Previously, eligibility requirements included income at or below 64% of the poverty level. The Patient Protection and Affordable Care Act increased the threshold to 133%. It also extended (effective 2014) coverage to childless adults. More than 50 million people were covered by Medicaid prior to health care reform in 2010. In 2019, nearly 66 million individuals were enrolled in Medicaid; an additional 6 million people were in combined Medicaid/CHIP programs.[i] Federal funds financed almost all of the costs, about 14% of total Medicaid spending, of the additional enrollment.[j] Numerically, the largest number of enrollees, about 75%, are children and their parents. The major beneficiaries of medical care, as measured in dollars, however, are the elderly and disabled clients—accounting for about two-thirds of expenditures. At the time of patients' discharge from nursing homes, about two-thirds of those patients are on Medicaid. The federal government spent about $345 billion on Medicaid in 2017–2018; the states' share was $212 billion.[k]

Although the ACA generated major criticism at the time of passage and has been the focus of Republican legislative and legal efforts to overturn or to invalidate the whole act, or at least major features, the impact on the access to health care is substantial. Not all states that opposed the act have found its impact as substantial or as onerous as they may have thought. States have considerable flexibility in design including determining population coverage, services covered, payment mechanisms to hospitals and physicians, and modes of health delivery. Federal matches to states have no caps, and the minimum match is 50%, higher for poorer states, 75% for the poorest state.[l]

(continues)

Exhibit 15-2 **Welfare and Health Care Reform: Federal Versus State/Local Roles in Individual Assistance Programs** *(continued)*

The most controversial aspect of the ACA reforms has been the requirement that most individuals must have health insurance or pay a penalty. That provision was challenged in the court system. The provision was upheld in the Supreme Court on the basis that the requirement falls within the congressional power to levy taxes.[m] With that Supreme Court decision, opponents of the ACA changed the focus to attempting to overturn the law through legislative action. Although control over both chambers of Congress and the White House was attained by the Republican party in the 2016 election, an attempt to overturn the ACA through legislation failed. The 2018 election resulted in Democratic control of the Senate with Republican control of the House retained. Additional legal actions have followed and likely will continue in the highly partisan climate.

a. Congressional Research Service (2019). *The Temporary Assistance for Needy Families (TANF), block grant: Responses to frequently asked questions*. Washington, DC: Author, 5.

b. Personal Responsibility and Work Opportunity Reconciliation Act of 1996 (P.L. 104-193).

c. Congressional Research Service (2019). *The Temporary Assistance for Needy Families Block Grant: Responses to frequently asked questions*, 7.

d. Administration for Children and Families, U.S. Department of Health and Human Services (2018). *Temporary Assistance for Needy Families and Children: Caseload data*. Retrieved August 17, 2019, from https://www.acf.hhs.gov/ofa/resource/tanf-caseload-data-2018.

e. Floyd, I. (2018). *TANF reaching few poor families*. Center on Budget and Policy Priorities, Retrieved August 18, 2019, from https://www.cbpp.org/research/family-income-support/tanf-reaching-few-poor-families.

f. Holahan, J., & Headen, I. (2011). *Medicaid coverage and spending in health reform: national and state-by-state results for adults at or below 133% FTL*. Washington, DC: Kaiser Commission on Medicaid and the Uninsured. Retrieved November 24, 2011, from http://www.kff.org/healthreform/upload/8149.pdf.

g. P.L. 111-148.

h. Norris, L. (2020). *A state-by-state guide to Medicaid expansion, eligibility, enrollment and benefits*. Retrieved November 30, 2019, from https://www.healthinsurance.org/medicaid/.

i. Medicaid.gov (2019). *May 2019 Medicaid and CHIP enrollment data highlights*. Retrieved August 18, 2019, from https://www.medicaid.gov/medicaid/program-information/medicaid-and-chip-enrollment-data/reporthighlights/index.html.

j. Rudowitz, R., et al. (2019). Medicaid financing: the basics. *Kaiser Family Foundation*. Retrieved August 18, 2019, from https://www.kff.org/medicaid/issue-brief/medicaid-financing-the-basics/. References to enrollment and other data in this and the next paragraph are from this source.

k. Rudowitz, R., et al. (2018). Medicaid enrollment & spending growth: FY 2018 & 2019. *Kaiser Family Foundation*. Retrieved August 18, 2019, from https://www.kff.org/medicaid/issue-brief/medicaid-enrollment-spending-growth-fy-2018-2019/.

l. Rudowitz, R., et al. (2019). 10 things to know about Medicaid: setting the facts straight. *Kaiser Family Foundation*. Retrieved August 18, 2019, https://www.kff.org/medicaid/issue-brief/10-things-to-know-about-medicaid-setting-the-facts-straight/.

m. *National Federation of Independent Business v. Sebelius*. 567 U.S. 519 (2012).

Features Not Directly Associated with Financial Assistance Affecting Intergovernmental Patterns

Direct expenditures and financial assistance provided by one level of government to another level are not the only factors in the U.S. system of intergovernmental relations that affect budgeting. In addition to restrictions and requirements built into most financial assistance, the programs financed by the assistance contain various requirements that influence how state and local governments plan and budget. Another element derives from the fact that state governments are the constitutional authorities for establishing local governments within their jurisdictions and thus have significant roles in determining which revenue sources local governments may use, which services local governments are responsible for providing, and under which circumstances local governments may enter into debt.

The federal government's authority under the Constitution has been used to *preempt* or supersede state authority, and state governments frequently preclude local action in various arenas. Since the late 1960s, coinciding with the development of many of the federal assistance programs, federal preemptions of state and local authority have increased at a rapid pace. From 1960 through 1995, more than 800 statutory actions were implemented preempting state policy or action in favor of federal policy or action.[88] Examples include the Clean Water Act amendments in 1987 and the Safe Drinking Water Act amendments of 1996. The former retained the regulatory requirements but reduced federal financial assistance to state and local governments and shifted it to assisting states to set up revolving loan funds to finance systems. The 1996 amendments to the Safe Drinking Water Act strengthened the regulatory requirements to mandate stronger scientific studies of health risks. The result of those additional requirements was increased costs to states. The 2017 Tax Cuts and Jobs Act,[89] without affecting financial assistance to state and local governments, affects state taxes for those states that substantially conform their definitions of incomes and deductions to the federal system.[90] Forty-one states have broad-based income tax systems, most of which conform their individual income tax base to the federal definition. Changes in the federal tax code that affect personal and corporate income automatically alter state income taxes for those conforming states. Changes to federal personal and corporate income in the 2017 law had a positive impact on state taxes, broadening the taxable income base. For example, eliminating the deduction of state and local taxes paid, for states that conform to the federal definition, increased the base for conforming states' personal income tax base income.[91] While welcome news to state legislatures that experienced higher tax revenues, these same legislatures had to grapple with pressure from some taxpayers to reform the state tax system. The issue was not necessarily the financial impact on states, but with the feeling in many states that changes in federal (tax) law forces reconsideration of state laws, though there was little consultation with states and little discussion in Congress about how state and local governments might be affected.[92]

In the federal system, Article VI of the Constitution declares federal law as the supreme law of the land. However, this supremacy is not unlimited. Federal powers to regulate commerce, declare war and levy taxes, and establish immigration laws are expressly federal powers. Other powers

are held to be implied. The federal court system plays a critical role in determining whether a federal law—or in many cases, regulatory standard—preempts state authority. Judicial strengthening of the federal government's preemptive right to regulate is often traced to the 1985 case of *Garcia v. San Antonio Metropolitan Transit Authority*.[93] The case focused on whether the federal Fair Labor Standards Act applied to a local government entity. The Supreme Court ruled that because the transit authority had received considerable funding from federal programs (Urban Mass Transportation Act of 1965), it must adhere to fair labor standards requirements. In this case, the Court narrowly interpreted the extent to which the Constitution protects the powers and authority of the states. In *United States v. Lopez*, the court, though not overturning *Garcia*, confirmed that the Commerce clause is not unlimited, requiring a clear and significant connection with interstate commerce.[94]

The Court has not always ruled in favor of preemption, which is welcome on the part of state and local governments but is unsettling to all parties involved because the Court has not delineated any clear doctrine as to when preemption should be upheld and when denied. In *Printz v. United States* (1997), the U.S. Supreme Court ruled that the provision of the Brady Handgun Violence Prevention Act requiring chief law enforcement officers of local jurisdictions to conduct background checks until a national system was in place was an unconstitutional requirement of state officials to enforce federal law.[95] In contrast, the Court in *Geier v. American Honda Motor Company* (2000) upheld preemption, which had the effect of protecting the automobile manufacturer from tort suits claiming that vehicles should have been equipped with airbags.[96] In 2000 and 2001, the Court ruled that the Age Discrimination in Employment Act and the Americans with Disabilities Act did not apply to the states.[97] In 2011, the Supreme Court was asked to review whether the federal government had preemptive powers over the states regarding immigration. Arizona and other states had taken actions against undocumented immigrants.[98] In 33 states, the medicinal use of marijuana is legal, including 11 states that have legalized recreational use. Under the federal Controlled Substances Act,[99] marijuana is a schedule 1 substance and thus the growing, distribution, or possession of marijuana is illegal under federal law. In addition, federally chartered banks are prohibited from dealing with money from marijuana commerce. The Obama administration issued guidance to U.S. Attorneys that generally advised noninterference in states that have legalized marijuana. In 2018, that guidance was rescinded by the Trump Administration, but no immediate actions were taken to enforce the new ruling.

The No Child Left Behind Act, a major federal education initiative to support performance measures involving extensive student testing in exchange for federal financial assistance, dominated federal secondary and elementary education support from 2001 to 2015. The law required states to implement corrective actions for schools that failed in repeated years to meet student performance expectations. After more than a decade of state and local criticism of the testing requirements and the intrusiveness of federal requirements on a fundamentally state responsibility, No Child Left Behind was repealed by ESSA that provides modest federal assistance and imposes minimal federal requirements.[100]

The National Conference of State Legislatures (NCSL) regards preemption as such a threat to state sovereignty that it had a project devoted to analyzing proposed federal legislation and working against would-be preemptions. In 2005, Congress passed a law that preempted state courts from hearing lawsuits stemming from alleged injuries caused by defective vaccines. In 2006, Congress preempted the states regarding the registry of sex offenders.[101] Despite stating in the overview page of the NCSL *Preemption Monitor* website that federal preemptive legislation is increasing, the 2010 and 2011 issues of the *Monitor* identified only two pieces of federal legislation judged to contain provisions preempting state authority in almost 2 years, both relatively minor statutes, in terms of states' rights, dealing with tobacco products transportation and distribution and public smoking, and NCSL closed the *Preemption Monitor* website in 2012.[102] The Supreme

Court's 2018 ruling in *Murphy v. National Collegiate Athletic Association* struck down a prohibition against state-supported sports betting and may have implications limiting federal authority over marijuana sales.[103]

State Control of Local Governments

These issues are not limited to federal effects on state and local governments. Because state governments have full constitutional authority over local governments, significant limitations on local authority may stem from state actions. Statutory debt limitations, usually expressed as a maximum debt to the property tax base ratio, are common (see the chapter on capital finance and debt management), as are requirements that state legislatures approve through formal legislative enactment some local taxes, such as sales taxes.[104]

A state also may assume direct control of a local government if it cannot exercise the capacity to govern itself. Instances of state takeover of municipal functions have been associated with some aspect or another of financial failure, but not usually bond debt failures. State governments watch local situations to see whether intervention is needed, although they do not consistently use specific indices of financial condition in making their decisions. A full discussion of state assumption of direct control related to debt management and financial distress is included in full in the chapter on capital finance and debt management.

State takeover of a general-purpose jurisdiction such as a city or town in financial distress is not the only kind of state control over sub-state entities. School systems are a target of state action. Texas passed a law in 1995 that would allow the state to take over schools that failed to meet specified state standards. The law was challenged in the courts, but the U.S. Supreme Court determined in 1998 that there was no need for a ruling at the time because no school takeover was imminent.[105] New Jersey was the first state to take over a school district, the Jersey City school district, in 1989. More recently, 33 states had takeover laws, and more than 20 states have taken over school districts.[106] By the mid-2000s, school takeovers were more common. In 2006, St. Louis schools were among the schools under pressure to perform or face possible takeovers.[107] While still a relatively rare event, states do use the threat by putting districts on probation when student performance fails to meet state standards over a long period of time.[108] Local governments also have used this tool. The city of Indianapolis took over management control of seven schools in the Indianapolis Public School District in 2012. By 2019, four of the seven were no longer administered by the city, but three remained under supervision.[109] While a state's assuming complete control over a city or a school district is still a rare event, it serves as a reminder that local governments are statutorily governed by state governments. Local governments have nothing comparable to the states' protection from the federal government as guaranteed by the Constitution's 10th Amendment reserving a broad array of powers to states.

Types of Fiscal Assistance

Grant Characteristics

Of the numerous aspects of grants-in-aid, at least four are particularly important: (1) the purpose of the award, (2) the recipient, (3) the amount, and (4) the method of distribution. The purposes of awards will be discussed in some detail in the next subsection, but for the moment it should be noted that purposes range from narrowly defined functions to general support.

Recipients can be individuals or families who receive financial aid, as in the case of welfare payments made directly to clients, or institutions, as in Medicaid payments made to medical providers to cover the health needs of the poor and medically needy. When programs provide guarantees of aid to individuals and families, they are referred to as entitlements. Sometimes the term *entitlement* is used for programs providing funds to state and local governments, as in the instance of the Community Development Block Grant (CDBG) program, in which 1,209 state and local units of government receive funds on a formula

basis—funds that are predictable by the cities in advance of their receipt.[110] The CDBG program was proposed for elimination in the Trump administration's 2017 and 2018 budgets, but Congress continued the programs; the program was reinstated in the President's proposed budget for 2019 and 2020.

The third aspect is the amount of aid that is made available. Some programs are open ended in the sense that aid is provided to all persons who qualify. All persons meeting a needs test based on income, for instance, might qualify for aid. If the number of qualified applicants increases, then the amount of aid available must also increase. This type of grant, of course, complicates budgeting, because administrators do not know in advance the amount of funds that will be needed. An alternative is for the legislature to predetermine an amount that will be available regardless of the number of potential recipients; the money then is on a first-come, first-served basis.

The Women, Infants, and Children (WIC) supplemental food program is an example of a program in which the amount that eligible families may receive is determined by a needs test, but funding may or may not be made available for everyone who is eligible. Once the funding limit in a state is reached, other eligible candidates are placed on a waiting list. For this program, the Food and Nutrition Service in the U.S. Department of Agriculture must annually estimate the number of eligible individuals so that federal appropriations can cover the number of people who are eligible. Actual participation rates in the 2010s have been significantly lower than eligibility rates. In 2015, 77% of eligible infants participated in the program; 46% of eligible pregnant women participated.[111]

Fourth, various methods are used in deciding whether applicants will receive funding and in what amounts. In one method, would-be recipients compete for awards by submitting proposals to indicate how funds will be used. This method is common for demonstration grants available to private and nonprofit institutions and several categories of grants available to state and local governments. Another method is to use a formula that allocates funds among eligible recipients. Formulas can be used to help target money where it is needed most. Gaining agreement on specific provisions in a formula among legislators can be difficult. For example, members of Congress evaluate proposed provisions of a formula in terms of how their home districts or states will be affected. Sometimes the distribution is set by the legislative body, particularly in instances in which funds are provided for specified public works projects.

At the federal level, the process of awarding and administering grants was spelled out in Office of Management and Budget (OMB) Circular A-102, *Grants and Cooperative Agreements with State and Local Governments*. Beginning with all grant and cooperative agreement awards issued in 2016, guidance provided by separate OMB circulars was replaced by *Title 2 Code of Federal Regulations Part 200: uniform administrative requirements, cost principles, and audit requirements for federal awards*.[112] *Cooperative agreements* are used when "substantial involvement" by federal agencies is planned, unlike *grants*, in which activities are carried out primarily by state and local governments.

Categorical Aid

At the federal level, hundreds of grant programs exist. **Table 15-4**, based on data from the 2019 online *Catalog of Federal Domestic Assistance*, provides a count of various grant programs, by type of grant, and an illustration of each type. Of the more than 2,000 federal domestic assistance programs in the catalog, more than 1,000 are colloquially called categorical aid programs. Only the grant programs (as opposed to loans and other programs) are listed in Table 15-4. It needs to be noted that the listings in the table are not mutually exclusive; a program is sometimes listed in two or even more categories. Also, not all items listed flow directly through state and local governments; some grants, such as research grants, go directly to individuals, businesses, and nonprofit organizations.

Categorical grants are a historically common designation, although no longer used as a single term in the *Catalog*. The meaning of "categorical" was that funds were targeted for expenditure in specified areas. This broad type is now separated into three in the *Catalog*: (1) *project grants*, of which there were 984 in 2018, covers such items as scholarships, research grants, and construction

Table 15-4 Federal Grant Programs by Type, with Examples, 2019

Type of Program	Number of Programs	Example
Formula Grants	245	Social Services Block Grant
Project Grants	984	21st Century Continuing Cures Act-Precision Medicine Initiative
Direct Payments for Specified Use	171	Conservation Security Program
Direct Payments with Unrestricted Use	48	Public Safety Officers' Educational Assistance
Sale, Exchange, or Donation of Property and Goods	25	Donation of Federal Surplus Property
Provision of Specialized Services	13	Disaster Legal Services
Advisory Services and Counseling	14	River, Trails, and Conservation Assistance

Compiled from U.S. General Services Administration (2019). *Catalog of federal domestic assistance*. Retrieved August 22, 2019, from https://beta.sam.gov/search ?index=cfda&assistance_type=&page=1&sort=title&keywords=&date_filter_index=0&date_rad_selection=date&inactive_filter_values=false.

grants; (2) *direct payments for specified use*, of which there were 171, is for comparatively narrowly defined projects—the category does not include contracts, such as when the federal government contracts with a local government to carry out an activity on its behalf; and (3) *direct payments with unrestricted use*, of which there were 48, is broader than the second grouping. As the example in the table indicates, payments are for a broad range of services for specific groups, such as law enforcement personnel, veterans, and veterans' families.

Sale, exchange, or donation of property and goods covers such activities as the government donating surplus food to a food bank. *Use of property, facilities, and equipment* includes lending or donating surplus military equipment (tanks, artillery, and clothing) to state-run military museums, but it is not included in the table because there is only one grant program in the category. *Provision of specialized services* covers the direct support by federal agencies in support of state and local activities, such as the example of disaster legal services. Advisory services and counseling are a small component of grant assistance.

The number of these various types of aid, of course, does not signify the amount of assistance available, but it does indicate the diversity of programs. Indeed, one frequent complaint over the years has been that there are too many specific grant programs and that they should be reduced in number. As a result, various consolidations have occurred from time to time, but later new programs are added, resulting in an ever-fluctuating number of grants.

Categorical programs have a narrow focus and target aid to deal with perceived problems. If rat infestations are a major problem in poor neighborhoods, an aid program can be established to support efforts to eliminate or control rat populations. Categorical programs presumably allow the federal government to target aid to deal with problems that are perceived to be national in scope and allow the state governments to do the same regarding state problems. Many categorical programs were created during the War on Poverty initiated by President Johnson in the late 1960s. Part of the motivation for creating categorical programs was that state legislatures,

then dominated in many states by politicians from rural areas, were unresponsive to urban needs, especially the problems of large center cities. Many categorical grant programs were intended to channel funds directly to cities, bypassing the state legislatures.[113]

Another reason for creating categorical programs was to target and restrict assistance in various ways to control the recipients' behavior.[114] For example, assistance for community development projects required extensive community participation to ensure that low-income groups had an influence over program design.

Categorical grants typically require would-be recipients to apply for aid by preparing proposals. These proposals indicate what problems exist, how the problems will be addressed, and what the expected benefits will be. During the application process, applicants must engage in considerable preplanning that is expected to help increase the chances that the money will be spent effectively. Funding agencies, by means of an application review process, presumably can weed out unsound projects.

Criticisms of categorical aid programs abound. Grants may skew local priorities. A jurisdiction might apply for funds for one type of project even though some other project, for which no grant funding was available, would provide greater benefits to the jurisdiction. Another criticism is that much time and energy are consumed in drafting grant proposals. Still another is that some jurisdictions do not obtain their "fair share" of federal dollars simply because they lack adequate staff for proposal writing. Small jurisdictions, in particular, may have little "grantsmanship" capability, although many small jurisdictions contract for grant writing assistance, providing the town with needed expertise at a small cost relative to the size of the grant being requested. Categorical grants make budget planning difficult because proposals may be held pending for months. Another problem is that grants are not coordinated. Furthermore, state legislatures dislike being bypassed, and many grant recipients—whether governmental or private organizations—resent some of the restrictions that are attached to the use of funds.

Critics frequently propose that the application process be simplified. Simplification includes reducing the amount of paperwork involved and standardizing some forms and procedures to make the process more comprehensible to applicants who may wish to seek funds from two or more agencies. In 2016, several federal guidance documents, including seven OMB guidance circulars, were consolidated.[115] Subsequent legislation reduced some duplicative audit requirements and standardized some forms and procedures. Still, preparing individual grant applications is time consuming. Most federal agencies have automated some or all their application processes, making it possible for applications to be submitted online. Of course, that step has not eliminated the actual proposal writing, but processing time has been reduced.

Revenue Sharing

Revenue sharing is often advocated as a better solution to eliminate large numbers of overlapping and highly specialized programs. These aid programs have none of the application process and restricted purpose features of categorical grants. The United States experimented with General Revenue Sharing (GRS) for a little over a decade under the State and Local Fiscal Assistance Act of 1972.[116] Under the original legislation, the federal government shared some of its revenue with states, counties, cities, and townships. In subsequent years, the states were dropped from the list of beneficiaries, in part because many had surpluses in their budgets and could hardly claim to need general federal support.

Although federal revenue sharing expired in 1986, it is worthy to note that it represents the opposite end of the spectrum from categorical grants. General revenue sharing continues to be proposed from time to time, along with shared tax systems, as a more radical overhaul to the intergovernmental fiscal system. The advantages of revenue sharing include the following:

- Pre-established amounts of aid
- Use of formulas for distributing the aid
- Considerable latitude to spend funds in terms of local priorities

GRS expired because a compelling case could not be made for its continuation. At the time, the federal government faced annual budget deficits in excess of $200 billion, so federal officials could convincingly argue that there simply was no revenue to share with local governments. Additionally, proponents faced the difficult task of identifying a national purpose being served by GRS. In the short run, eliminating the program caused serious budgetary problems for municipalities with shrinking tax bases. In addition, many local governments shifted to user charges, which in some cases were regressive (see the chapter on transaction-based revenue sources). User charges are typically based on the cost of the service rather than the ability to pay.

Although revenue sharing is no longer in operation at the national level, it persists at the state level. Many states provide funds to local governments using formulas based on population and income. Fiscal pressures on state governments in the early 1990s caused many to reduce the amounts allocated to revenue sharing. Then, after almost a decade of surpluses, a return in 2001 to severe state budget pressures again caused states to drastically reduce funding in their own programs.[117]

Block Grants

Block grants, or special revenue sharing, represent a form of compromise between GRS and categorical grants. Under this system, a higher-level government shares part of its revenue with lower-level governments, but the use of funds is restricted to specified functions, such as law enforcement or social services. A distinction is sometimes made between block grants and special revenue sharing, with the former requiring submission of an application and the latter not. More often, however, the terms are used interchangeably or the term "block grant" is used to cover both types of revenue sharing. State aid to education, using various formulas, is an example of a block grant, with the funds coming largely from state general revenue. State aid for local roads is another form of block grant, with monies coming from earmarked taxes on motor fuels.

The TANF program discussed earlier is a federal example.

Block grants at the federal level have been used as a method for consolidating categorical grant programs. These "categoricals" are grouped together so that jurisdictions have greater flexibility in specified program areas. The application process is greatly reduced, because a jurisdiction applies for only one grant instead of several. Two of the federal block grant programs with longevity are the CDBG, administered by the Department of Housing and Urban Development, and the Social Services Block Grant (SSBG) program, administered by the Department of Health and Human Services.

The CDBG program, the longest running program of the Department of Housing and Urban Development,[118] provides entitlement funding to medium and large cities using a formula and gives funds to states to award small cities on a discretionary basis. Changes in the program from time to time reflect current priorities. For example, the law phased out programs for open space, public facility loans, water and sewer grants, urban renewal, model cities, and rehabilitation loans. Under the original legislation, entitlement cities were required to apply for funding. The process was considerably less detailed than had been required for the previous categorical programs. Later, the application process was dropped for the entitlement cities. The SSBG is a noncompetitive, formula grant program that assists states to tailor their social service programming needs to their own situation.[119]

Some federal block grants awards are based on metropolitan areas, which are defined by the OMB. An area that is not classified as metropolitan may be excluded from funding, and the amount of funding to a given area may be dependent on its population size or other key characteristics. Therefore, the definition of an area becomes critical for funding purposes. In 1999, OMB redefined the concept of metropolitan area.[120] In 2010, the government again revised the standards for defining metropolitan areas, effective in 2013. The CDBG grants are affected by the metropolitan definition.[121]

Because many block grant programs, and other federal assistance, rely at least in part on population count in the criteria for determining the amount of assistance a state may receive, the decennial census count is an important variable that may cause states losing population to also lose out on grant assistance relative to states with growing population. It can become a political issue. In 2018, the Trump administration mandated that the 2020 census include a citizenship status question. The inclusion of that question might have undercounted the number of people living, working, and relying on services by frightening some people from responding. That outcome would have affected some states' counts more than others, ultimately affecting not only their potential number of representatives in Congress, but also their share of federal assistance. A three-judge panel blocked the move, and the Census Bureau removed the question from the 2020 census.[122]

Various consolidations of categorical grants into block grants have taken place over recent decades. The first wave started with the Omnibus Budget Reconciliation Act of 1981, which, among other things, consolidated many existing categorical grant programs and created nine new block grants, four in health-related services, to be administered by the states.[123] The most recent round of consolidation and relaxation of federal control created the TANF program (1996), the initial major reform of welfare assistance, in an attempt to devolve responsibilities from the federal government to states, as discussed earlier. President Donald Trump proposed in 2018 a major consolidation and collapsing of programs across such functions as food, education, social services, and others, including substantial consolidation and elimination of many grant programs. The president recommended merging the Departments of Labor and Education. Although hearings and committee work began in the U.S. Senate, no legislation was proposed during the first 3 years of the Trump Administration, and the House of Representatives never took up committee work on the proposals.[124]

The programmatic feature of federal block grants is that monies are granted in lump sums to states, which determine how the money is to be used and, when it involves local government assistance, how funds are to be divided among governments within each state. This approach has been championed as restoring power to the states. The fiscal feature of federal block grants, each time they are introduced, has been a substantial reduction in funds. These cuts are defended in part in the name of efficiency. Allowing states and localities to select the desired mix of activities and levels of quality and quantity, block grants reduce the costs of "one-size-fits-all" categorical grants, which substitute federal judgments for those at the state and local levels. Furthermore, because the block grants provide more flexibility to state and local governments, fewer federal officials are needed to administer the programs and fewer state officials are needed to oversee local government operations. Given that block grants almost always result in some degree of reduced federal financing because they are consolidating previous categorical programs, state and local governments must achieve the supposed efficiencies, make up for the losses, or reduce quality or quantity of services. This may account for the fact that there have been no further major consolidations since the 1990s.

Department of Homeland Security Illustration

Grant assistance not only changes as financial conditions at the federal, state, and local levels change. Major external events such as the terrorist attacks in 2001 resulted in the major reorganization of several federal departments and agencies to form the Department of Homeland Security (DHS). An important component of DHS programs is financial assistance to state and local governments to strengthen their ability to prevent and respond to terrorist threats.

The department carries out its functions through a mix of approaches. Unlike some departments, which are mainly in the business of achieving objectives through awarding money, such as the Department of Housing and Urban Development, DHS spends a good portion of its own funds. As noted earlier in the chapter (Table 15-3), about

22% of homeland security money is in grants and cooperative agreements, compared with Housing and Urban Development, 80% of whose budget consists of grants and contracts. The 22% figure for DHS grants is less than in the 2000s, although as noted above, disaster relief is up significantly. Additionally, DHS is a primary user of contracting for services (see the chapter on budget execution). For example, FEMA and other units contract extensively for both services and products. FEMA has special needs to be able to enter into contracts on a speedy basis.[125]

DHS administers a wide variety of grant programs. One cluster, the Homeland Security Grant Program (HSGP), provides grants to state governments, local governments (mainly large metropolitan and urban areas), and some private and nonprofit entities. All states have counterparts to DHS and receive federal funding, some of which is dispersed further to state and local units. Similarly, all states share in the Citizen Corps grants, which support activities like the old Civil Defense.

DHS, since 2010, has consolidated its grants program as it has continued to absorb and manage the disparate agencies that were brought into DHS. As of 2019, DHS categorizes its grant programs into three groups.[126] The funding amounts for the three under HSGP broke out as follows: (1) state homeland, $415 million; (2) urban security, $590 million; and (3) Operation Stonegarden (formerly law enforcement), $90 million. All those amounts are lower than 10 years earlier, with law enforcement grants reduced the most, from $396 million in 2006.[127]

Awards are made for the HSGP through a combination of formula and categorical processes. Monies do not flow automatically to state and local governments, so therefore they must apply for funding. That is done exclusively online through the cross-agency portal *Grants.gov*. In order to apply, a government needs some savvy in understanding the language and forms of grantsmanship, though the increasingly standardized grant application processes across many federal departments and agencies has simplified matters.

Some of the HSGP, as prescribed by Congress, must be distributed among all 50 states and the

District of Columbia at a minimum of 0.35% of total funds in 2019, down from 0.75% in 2011.[128] This is akin to the floor that was set under GRS, ensuring a minimum amount of funding across governmental boundaries. The remaining money is awarded on a risk-based program. DHS is required to employ a threat or risk-based methodology to determine the distribution of funding for most of its preparedness and planning programs (more than 90% of DHS grants, excluding post-disaster recovery grant programs).

The risk-based methodology naturally is controversial because no one likes to think their area is at lower risk and therefore lower priority for protection than other areas of the country. Changes in the model result in some areas no longer meeting the risk threshold, while other areas are added. For example, the department cut back on the number of metropolitan areas eligible for Urban Areas Security Initiative grants from 50 in 2005 to 31 in 2011. Recipients in urban areas eliminated from funding were eligible for continuation awards to complete the projects they had begun but were ineligible for new awards. This was called "sustained" funding. California lost two areas—Sacramento and San Diego. Others eliminated included Phoenix, Arizona; Las Vegas, Nevada; and Toledo, Ohio. Two Florida areas were added—Orlando and Fort Lauderdale.[129] The changes of dropping some areas were highly controversial with influential members of Congress whose districts or states were affected. As a result, Congress requires the GAO to review the methodology and the results of its application by DHS. The GAO concluded the following in both its 2008 and its most recent (2018) review: "FEMA has improved its risk-based grant assessment model, but additional steps could further strengthen its model."[130]

Congress, as is its rightful role, has set funding constraints on DHS grants, but those priorities are sometimes questioned. One is the 0.35% requirement for each state to receive some funding. Examples of wasteful spending are often used by critics to indict the whole program. For example, some of the law enforcement grants have been spent on physical fitness training for law enforcement and the purchase of treadmills and other training machines, seemingly aimed at making law enforcement officers buff. DHS officials have winced over such spending, but have noted that it is specifically authorized by Congress.[131]

However, the biggest concern is that Congress sets priorities on spending by allocating money to the various grant programs independent of what the "experts" in DHS think makes sense. For example, Congress determines how much money will be spent on ports versus other forms of infrastructure. Congress, as the representative of the people, has the right and responsibility to set priorities and allocate funds, but in an era in which the United States seemingly faces multiple internal and cross-border threats, should greater flexibility be afforded the DHS? Should the department have flexibility in allocating funds among ports, law enforcement, and the like? If yes, how much flexibility? This is the age-old problem of trying to reach an appropriate balance in decision making between the legislative and executive branches.

Restructuring Patterns of Intergovernmental Relations

Tax Laws

Tax Deductions and Exemptions

As we have seen to this point in the chapter, the intergovernmental system is complicated in part by a constellation of various kinds of assistance programs and controls, created over at least 75 years (since the New Deal). Reforms have come and gone, some aimed at reducing the impact on the federal budget that complements the policy views that as much as possible should be devolved to the lowest level of government that can handle the responsibility. Adding to the complexity are individual new programs responding to new needs, such as federal assistance to state and local governments to deal with the risks of foreign and domestic terrorism and increasingly devastating natural disasters.

One substantive change that could be made to simplify the system is to adjust taxes in ways that would reduce the need for financial assistance. By increasing the taxing powers of lower-level governments, the need for grants-in-aid may be reduced. For example, taxpayers historically have been able to deduct many state and local taxes from gross income before computing federal tax liabilities. Included were state and local income taxes, property taxes, and some other lesser taxes. The Tax Reform Act of 1986 (TRA86) removed the deductibility of some state and local taxes, such as sales taxes. The Tax Cuts and Jobs Act (TCJA17) further reduced deductions for state and local taxes paid and mortgage interest. (Such tax policies affect disposable income, increase state and local tax collections for those states that follow federal definitions of personal income, and alter the distribution of taxing power among levels of government.)

Some of these reforms, such as eliminating the deductibility of interest on two home mortgages and property taxes paid, are considered not so much as an intergovernmental fiscal reform but as a measure to address the federal budget deficit. While TRA86 was deficit neutral, TCJA17 is one of the causes of substantial growth in the deficit. In general, federal tax law changes generally impact on state and local revenues as a secondary result of changes made for the federal tax system. At least in principle, more comprehensive tax reform, both federal and state, could be considered in conjunction with impact on lower governmental levels to reduce assistance from one level to the next. Public finance theory considers this a more efficient revenue system because it more closely links decisions about revenue generation (taxes and charges mainly) with decisions about expenditure levels.

Tax Credits

In the same vein as tax reform to decrease reliance on assistance instruments in favor of direct revenue and expenditure decisions, tax credits would be likely to cause a more substantial shift in revenue sources than would result from changes in tax deductibility. Tax credits would allow individual taxpayers to use taxes paid to one jurisdiction to reduce the tax liability owed to another jurisdiction. A tax credit reduces tax liability dollar for dollar, whereas a deduction of taxes paid to another jurisdiction from one's taxable income is worth only the marginal tax bracket percentage, the highest being 37%. One proposal sometimes made is to allow such credits for the federal income tax. The effect would be to redistribute revenue from the federal government to state and local governments. A tax credit on income taxes could encourage those states without income taxes to adopt them because the taxpayers would be less affected. However, if the tax credit is uniform regardless of income, it would benefit the wealthier states even more than the poorer ones.

Unemployment Insurance

The federal government has enticed or forced states to impose unemployment insurance taxes on employers by providing that most monies from such taxes may stay within each state. If a state did not have an approved system, a tax presumably would be imposed by the federal government. All states adopted unemployment insurance programs because failure to do so would have made those states without such programs less attractive as places to live and conduct business. In that case, the federal government used its taxation power effectively to force a policy action at the state level. Similarly, inheritance taxes are practically forced on states by a federal tax provision deducting 80% of any state inheritance tax paid. Any state that did not adopt an inheritance tax would lose considerable appeal to retirees and other older citizens. TCJA17 raised the exemption to $11.8 million.

Tax Exemptions on Bonds

Another important benefit afforded state and local governments through federal tax law is the tax exemption on interest earned on bonds issued by these governments, discussed in more detail in the chapter on capital finance and debt management. Tax exemption has had the effect of allowing governments to pay lower interest rates to bondholders than if the bonds were taxable. In the context of the intergovernmental system, this tax exemption is effectively a transfer from the federal government to state and local governments.

Shared Taxes

Federal, state, and local governments in the United States have either exclusive or overlapping jurisdiction over various tax sources. Only the federal government may tax imports and exports. The federal government does not have a property tax or general sales tax. Federal, state, and local governments overlap in the use of personal and corporate income taxes. Many states benefit from linking their own personal income tax systems to the federal system. This simplifies administration of the system and reduces state tax administration costs. When changes in federal tax provisions occur, such as TCJA17 expansion of the federal tax base, it automatically expanded the base for most states because their systems are tied in one form or another to the federal system. However, there is no shared link between the two—the federal Internal Revenue Service collects only federal income taxes, and state and local governments collect their own income taxes. State and local governments typically share a sales tax. It is collected by the state, but revenues are allocated to local governments that also levy such taxes.

The United States, unlike most other industrialized countries, does not have a value-added tax. Alice M. Rivlin, the first director of the Congressional Budget Office (CBO) and later the director of the OMB, proposed in an influential book a value-added tax that would be shared among levels of government as one solution to improving the intergovernmental fiscal system.[132] Sharing the tax means that it would be a common tax, eliminating competition between states over the level of taxation. It would also mean shared administration, reducing the collection costs, and it would minimize the ability of one level of government to preempt other levels' use of a particular tax. State and local finance in the German federal system, for example, relies heavily on shared taxation. A national shared sales tax also would resolve the issues around states' inability to develop an effective way to tax e-commerce (see the chapter on budgeting for revenues: income, payroll, and property taxes). These ideas resurface from time to time, but such a major overhaul of the federal tax system has no traction in Congress. Any major realignment of responsibilities among levels of government must include changes in revenue systems as well.

Grant Requirements
Strings

State and local officials are all too familiar with the strings that come attached to grants. The solicitation announcements in which governments are encouraged to apply for grants are replete with notifications as to how the money may and may not be used and other requirements. For example, grants must be audited, and the audit reports supplied to the funding agency. Other progress and final reports are required. These reporting requirements for the federal government have grown as part of the yin and yang of support for programs to assist state and local governments coupled with conviction that grant funds are often wasted, or worse, misappropriated.

Grants administration sometimes involves gray areas in which funding agencies say something *should* be done but lack authority to say it *must* be done. Officials of recipient governments are wary of not following such guidance even though they think the funding agency may be stepping out of bounds. No one wants to jeopardize possible future funding by failing to follow unofficial guidance. The situation has been referred to as "soft governance."[133]

Mandates

Other proposals to improve intergovernmental fiscal relations pertain to mandates. For instance, when a state legislature passes a law requiring school districts to adopt certain procedures in dealing with gifted children or children with learning disabilities, a mandate has been established that has budgetary implications. Typically, federal mandates on state and local governments are tied to grants or other forms of federal assistance and contracts, making the stipulation that a government (or private party) must meet specified conditions to qualify for funds.

Notable federal crosscutting mandates—requirements that apply to the work of most federal agencies and grant programs—require recipients to pay locally prevailing wages; meet Americans with Disabilities Act standards for removing architectural barriers for persons with disabilities; and prevent discrimination based on race, gender, and the like. These mandates are at a basic level unrelated to the purpose of a specific grant or contract or other funding. That is, a local government carrying out an activity funded under the CDBG program related to building a community facility is required to pay minimum wages and is required to adhere to provisions of the Fair Labor Standards Act and the Davis-Bacon Act. The various requirements imposed have to do with federal policy as stated in the legislation and regulations toward work and employment conditions, including fair wages. These regulations apply to the entire local government receiving the grant, not just the department involved with the grant funded facility.

Other mandates are directly related to the grant program objectives. As noted earlier, continued TANF funding to states is contingent on their reducing the number of people on their welfare rolls. How the states accomplish that goal is open to wide latitude in this block grant program, but the states are required to achieve specific, quantitative reductions.

Medicaid is always on the firing line because of the high and increasing costs of health care and because state funds must be committed along with the federal funds. Federal mandates limit state control of Medicaid by specifying, in detail, who is eligible and what costs are reimbursable. As a result of these mandates, states have felt they are less able to make their own budgetary decisions.

Unfunded Mandates

Another category for reform has been eliminating what many term "unfunded mandates." These are federal or state requirements that are not necessarily tied to financial assistance programs. For example, federal laws and court rulings have set standards for state prison systems that in many cases require additional prisons to be built without federal assistance. These obligations are not associated with any program of financial assistance, and they are mandatory for all states (in the case of federal requirements) regardless of whether the state is a recipient of federal programs related to the justice system. They are a matter of a federal determination that it is in the national interest to require states to meet certain standards, but no help to do so is available from the federal government.

The Disabilities Education Act of 1975, later known as the Individuals with Disabilities Education Act, is implemented by regulations that include detailed requirements for states to accommodate students with disabilities to enable successful educational outcomes.[134] The act promises federal funding assistance up to 40% of the amount states spend. In principle, one might call that a "funded mandate." However, appropriations have never come close to meeting that 40% promise. Hence, the mandate is substantially unfunded. Federal clean air and water standards that are not tied to any federal financial assistance have forced local governments to build new solid waste treatment facilities, substantially change wastewater treatment systems, and adopt numerous other practices.

State and local officials argue that these mandates should be accompanied by federal funding because they appear to be attempts to achieve goals previously set by the federal government through financial assistance programs. The contrary view argues that there are genuine national goals that relate to such public purposes as health and safety, environmental regulation, minimum living standards for every family, and so forth and that these require federal action. Just because a national purpose exists, it does not necessarily mean there should be a matching federal payment to assist in achieving that purpose. The same line of reasoning is employed by states in their use of mandates for local governments.

The Unfunded Mandates Reform Act of 1995 (UMRA) requires draft legislation to be analyzed as to what unfunded mandates might be imposed on other governments or the private sector.[135] Bills below certain thresholds that are adjusted annually do not fall under the law. For a bill in 2019 to be covered by UMRA, it had to have an impact on state and local governments of $82 million or more or an impact on the private sector of $164 million or more.[136] The CBO, a staff arm of Congress, prepares the estimates, which are attached to committee reports on the bills. If the threshold is reached, a member of the House of Representatives may raise a point of order, which then requires the full House to vote on whether to consider the bill. If a point of order is raised in the Senate, the chamber is barred from considering the bill unless a vote is taken to waive the order, or the presiding officer overrules the point of order. Note that this provision goes into effect only when a point of order is raised. Otherwise, the bill's consideration proceeds with the unfunded mandate included.

Four features restrict the law's applicability. The first three are provisions of the act itself. First is that of the threshold cost figure. Second, any new conditions imposed on grant programs are excluded. Third, a wide variety of subjects of legislation are excluded from the law's coverage including national security, constitutional rights, and parts of the Social Security program. Also excluded from the law's coverage are statutory rights protecting against discrimination, such as voting and employment rights. Fourth, the CBO determined that programs like Medicaid have enough flexibility for state implementation that the provisions of UMRA do not apply.[137] Some critics have argued that the law is too restrictive in its application.[138] Federal agencies are required to estimate mandates contained in legislation they wish to see passed and estimate the mandates contained in regulations that they draft. The GAO has responsibility for reviewing the regulation estimates.

Mandates Since Passage of the Unfunded Mandates Reform Act

As might be expected, most proposed federal legislation does not include mandates. In its 2019 report on reviews conducted from 2007 through 2018, CBO noted that of 313 bills and legislative proposals reviewed, only 25 contained intergovernmental mandates at all. Of these, none had mandates exceeding the 2018 threshold. In the period since the law became effective through 2018, CBO identified mandates in excess of applicable thresholds in less than 1% of federal laws and less than 5% of private sector mandates.[139] The mandates have included the following:

- an increase in the minimum wage,
- a reduction in federal funding to administer the Food Stamp program,
- a preemption of state taxes on premiums for certain prescription drug plans,
- a temporary preemption of state authority to tax certain Internet services and transactions, and
- a requirement that state and local governments meet certain standards for issuing driver's licenses.

One of the most hotly criticized laws for excessive, unfunded mandates was the No Child Left Behind Act of 2001. As discussed earlier in this chapter, the act eventually was replaced with Every Student Succeeds Act of 2015. Among other features, ESSA removed many of the mandates that had met with significant opposition, particularly those related to student testing requirements, and allowed state and local governments substantial flexibility in meeting the act's requirements.

The fifth "official" mandate from the above list was the Real ID Act of 2005.[140] Following the September 11 disasters, there was general consensus that government needed to have better identification of people, but whereas many countries require adults to have passports regardless of any plans to travel overseas, that notion was anathema in the United States. Instead, the view was that the country would stay with state identification systems, but Congress wanted more careful attention devoted to confirming that people were who they said they were when applying for driver's licenses and identification cards. Congress also wanted more secure state cards in order to thwart counterfeiters.

The 2005 legislation, therefore, required extensive revamping of state driver's license and identification card systems. Congress did not have authority to require states to comply, and indeed some states even voiced interest in rebelling. However, there was considerable clout behind the legislation. If a state did not comply, its licenses and identification cards would be unacceptable by the federal government. In just one simple example, people with such licenses would be prohibited from passing security at airports and boarding aircraft.

The CBO estimated that Real ID would cost $100 million to implement, and Congress appropriated $40 million in fiscal 2006.[141] The states found both the CBO number and the appropriation to be wildly underestimated. Implementation was estimated to cost $11 billion according to a study done by the National Governors Association, NCSL, and American Association of Motor Vehicle Administrators.[142] Implementation of the act was delayed for almost 15 years. Implementing regulations were not issued until 2008, setting 2011 as the date by which states were to have complied with the act. Numerous extensions were issued. As of 2016, less than half of the states were fully compliant.[143] The most recent deadline, enforcing the penalty that individuals without a compliant "real ID" would be unable to board a passenger plane in the United States, was implemented in 2020.

Legislative proposals to improve the UMRA have surfaced from time to time. The Unfunded Mandates and Information Transparency Act was first introduced in 2014; a second version passed the House in 2015, but no action was taken in the Senate. The Trump administration's proposed federal government overhaul discussed earlier in the chapter would have implications for federal mandates, but that initiative stalled after the 2018 election produced a split in party control of the two chambers of Congress.

Additional Federal Mandate Issues

Federal mandates, whether funded or unfunded, have been contested in federal gun control laws, political campaign financing, civil rights, and other issues. Federal courts are often involved.

In 1995, in *U.S. v. Lopez*, the Supreme Court struck down a federal statute that regulated possessing a gun in a school zone. The decision was unique in that it was the first such decision involving the Commerce clause in over 50 years.[144] In *Citizens United v. Federal Election Commission*, the Supreme Court struck down provisions of the McCain-Feingold Act that prohibited corporations from producing and broadcasting overt messages in support of political positions or candidates.[145] This opened the door to virtually unlimited corporate funding of political campaigns.

In a 1984 civil rights–related case, the Supreme Court ruled in *Grove City College v. Bell* that only that portion of an organization affected by federal dollars had to comply with standards protecting against discrimination based on race, gender, age, and handicapping condition.[146] In that instance, the college's only federal support was for student-aid activities, so only those activities had to comply. In 1988, Congress reversed that decision by passing the Civil Rights Restoration Act, which provides that all operations of a recipient government must meet federal standards.[147] The law was passed despite a veto by President Reagan.

Title IX of the Education Amendments of 1972 addressed a different discrimination issue: the applicability of the prohibitions against discrimination in educational institutions on the basis of gender to all activities of an institution, whether or not those activities received any federal funding.[148] Title IX is applicable across the entire institution, without regard to specific links to federal funding. If a university, for example, participates in a federal student financial aid program or receives funding directly from the federal government or indirectly from state government agencies for construction of a library, then the university may not discriminate based on gender in any program. Thus, women's sports programs must be supported if men's sports programs are funded by the university. Sometimes schools have had to eliminate some sports due to funding constraints; for example, in 2006, James Madison University had to eliminate 10 sports teams. In 2011, the University of Maryland announced the elimination of eight teams due to lack of enough funds.[149]

Streamlining and Paperwork Reduction

Related to mandates are various reporting requirements that create paperwork and thereby create costs. Reporting requirements may be associated with a single federally funded program, or identical information is often required for many programs funded by the same federal agency. States require local governments to submit numerous reports each year, and the federal government requires the same of state and local governments.

The Paperwork Reduction Act, a 1995 revision of the 1980 statute, regulates agency requests for information from state and local governments, and from private corporations and individuals. The Regulatory Flexibility Act of 1980 and Executive Order 12866 of 1993 require agencies to conduct regulatory impact analyses to determine the effects of proposed rules or regulations, including the effects on state and local governments. Agencies are required to develop annual regulatory plans that must be submitted to OMB, which in effect has a veto power over regulations. The Single Audit Act of 1984, amended in 1996, is an additional paperwork reduction device (see the chapter on financial management).[150] The act allows a state or local government receiving funds through numerous different federal programs to comply with those programs' audit provisions by using a single financial compliance audit.

An outgrowth of these efforts is the creation of the website *Grants.gov*.[151] The purpose of the site is to provide one-stop shopping for grants. The site is searchable for possible grants, and application can be made online. For a state or local government agency to apply, it must obtain a DUNS number, which stands for Data Universal Number System, and must file with the Central Contractor Registry. The Department of Health and Human Services is the contact point for Grants.gov, and all federal agencies are required to post their grant announcements and other solicitations on the site. OMB, in accordance with the Federal Funding Accountability and Transparency Act of 2006, developed a search engine and database on government grants, contracts, and loans, accessible at *www.usaspending.gov*.[152]

Another useful tool is the *Catalog of Federal Domestic Assistance*, mentioned earlier. The *Catalog*, which gives capsule descriptions of grant programs, can help a local government determine whether it might be able to secure federal funding for a contemplated project, even though applications may not be received at that time.

Awarding Grants and Grants Administration

All too often, applicants for grants worry about possible bias on the part of those responsible for making awards. The fear is that regardless of the merits of grant proposals, awards will be made based on favoritism. All governments experience problems in administering grants. Communication problems are routine—for example, between what a local government thinks it needs to report to its funding agencies at the state and federal levels and what the funding sources think is required. As time passes during a grant, recipient governments frequently need to adjust changes in their environment, but these adjustments may not meet with approval of funding agencies.

A New Form of Interstate "Agreements" in the Coronavirus Pandemic

In the midst of confusion both at the federal level and between the federal government and the states in managing the coronavirus crisis, as early as 3 months into the crisis states in several regions of the country banded together in informal agreements to coordinate both policy and actions. Connecticut, Delaware, Massachusetts, New York, New Jersey, Pennsylvania, Rhode Island, and Vermont in the Northeast joined to coordinate state plans to gradually reopen their states to more economic and other public activity. On the west coast, California, Washington, and Oregon joined in a similar effort. Seven midwestern states—Illinois, Indiana, Kentucky, Ohio, Michigan, Minnesota, and Wisconsin—joined in collaboration. Other states and the District of Columbia were among those announcing various forms of collaboration early after the White House first announced that the president would order the states to reopen on a federal plan, and then a day later said that it would be left up to the states. These actions by states seemed to be taken at an intergovernmental crisis point when President Trump claimed that he had "total authority" over states and would tell them when and how to reopen.[153] The President indirectly walked that statement back the next day acknowledging state authority in some respects.

The coordination problems with the federal government, and problems states experienced competing with each other on the open market-place for scarce medical commodities and equipment, were keenly felt by many governors and public health officials. Lacking an overall coordinated and consistent approach from the federal government, informal state agreements during the crisis could be an early step in future intergovernmental reform discussions. The intergovernmental system for dealing with pandemics that strike the entire country, unlike natural disasters and terrorist attacks that are local or regional in initial impact, did not manage the early months of the coronavirus crisis.

Summary

Fundamental issues arise regarding the question of how to structure intergovernmental relations. Functional integration results in picket fence arrangements that may deter geographic integration. Fiscal capacities differ among and within levels of government, so that the government that perhaps should provide services often lacks the necessary funding capability. Failure to provide services results in externality problems.

Both direct spending and grants-in-aid are important for intergovernmental relations. Decisions by federal and state agencies on the location and expansion of capital facilities affect the economic viability of local jurisdictions. Despite more extensive attention often being devoted to federal aid programs, state aid to local government is larger. Some states provide much of their local governments' revenue while others provide little,

a point that should be stressed to avoid unwarranted generalizations. Aid to education constitutes the largest portion of state aid, with monies typically allocated on a formula basis. Federal aid is concentrated in the areas of education, income security, health, and transportation.

Major changes are occurring in the intergovernmental fiscal landscape, with substantial responsibilities for welfare reform already having been devolved to state governments. Health care reform significantly altered the joint federal-state Medicaid program. Furthermore, substantial concern has prompted legislative and executive action to mitigate the impacts of unfunded federal mandates. Though the massive stimulus programs to address the effects of the Great Recession caused a bump up in the number of mandates that required CBO review, the actual number of unfunded mandates with significant financial implications remains at very low levels, less than 1% of all legislation passed between 2010 and 2018.

Intergovernmental grants have at least four aspects: their purpose (narrow, broad, or general), the type of recipient, the amount, and the method of distribution. Categorical grants are criticized as deterring coordination, skewing local priorities, and needlessly wasting time in their proposal preparation. On the positive side, these grants are said to force planning in the preparation of their proposals and to allow for screening out poorly conceived projects. Though the federal experiment with general revenue sharing only lasted a decade, some states continue to engage in revenue sharing with their local governments. Block grants, a cross between categorical grants and GRS, have advantages and disadvantages of both.

In addition to grant programs, numerous other intergovernmental devices are employed. They include provisions in federal tax law that benefit state and local governments and review and comment processes for grant proposals. Proposals have been made for major reconfiguring of program responsibilities among the federal, state, and local governments. Since the 1980s, many state and local governments have shown a resurgence in this area, resulting in what many see as a healthy redress of balance between the federal level and the state and local levels.

Notes

1. Galston, W., & Davis, K. (2014). *21st Century federalism: proposals for reform*. Washington, DC: Brookings.
2. European Union (2019). *The EU in brief*. Retrieved July 28, 2019, from https://europa.eu/european-union/about-eu/eu-in-brief_en.
3. World Trade Organization (2019). *What is WTO?* Retrieved July 28, 2019, from https://www.wto.org/english/thewto_e/whatis_e/whatis_e.htm.
4. Pound, W. (2017). The state of federalism today. *State Legislatures Magazine*, July–August. Retrieved July 28, 2019, from http://www.ncsl.org/bookstore/state-legislatures-magazine/the-state-of-federalism-today636359051.aspx.
5. Indian Gaming Regulatory Act of 1988 (P.L. 100-497); National Indian Gaming Commission website, www.nigc.gov.
6. 500nations (2019). *Indian casinos*. Retrieved July 28, 2019, from https://www.500nations.com/Indian_Casinos.asp.
7. Bureau of Indian Affairs, U.S. Department of Interior (2019). *The tribal leaders' directory: tribal directory dataset*. Retrieved July 28, 2019, from https://www.bia.gov/tribal-leaders-directory.
8. Governing the States and Localities (2019). Number of local governments by state. Governing. Retrieved July 28, 2019, from https://www.governing.com/gov-data/number-of-governments-by-state.html.
9. *Hunter v. Pittsburgh*, 207 U.S. 161 (1907).
10. Walker, D. B. (1995). *The rebirth of federalism: slouching toward Washington*. Chatham, NJ: Chatham House.
11. Tiebout, C. M. (1956). A pure theory of public expenditures. *Journal of Political Economy*, 44, 416–424; Nallathiga, N. (2017). *Tiebout's theory/model on local public goods*. Retrieved July 28, 2019, from https://www.researchgate.net/publication/321332089_Tiebout's_TheoryModel_on_Local_Public_Goods.
12. Daniels, J. (2019). More Californians are considering fleeing the state as they blame sky-high costs, survey says. *CNBC.com*, February 13. Retrieved November 19, 2019, from https://www.cnbc.com/2019/02/12/growing-number-of-californians-considering-moving-from-state-survey.html.
13. Dilger, R. (2018). *Federal grants to state and local governments: a historical perspective on contemporary issues*. Washington, DC: Brookings; Congressional Budget Office (2013). Federal grants to state and local governments. Washington, DC: Author.
14. Pineda, C. (2005). *City-county consolidation and diseconomies of scale: summary of selected literature*. Harvard University Ash Institute for Democratic Governance. Retrieved November 25, 2011, from https://www.innovations.harvard.edu/sites/default/files/9331.pdf; Wood, C. (2006). Scope and patterns of metropolitan governance in urban America: probing the complexities in the Kansas City region. *American Review of Public Administration, 36*, 337–353.
15. Port Authority of New York and New Jersey website. Retrieved July 28, 2019, from http://www.panynj.gov/.
16. Wright, D. S. (1988). *Understanding intergovernmental relations* (3rd ed., pp. 83–86). Pacific Grove, CA: Brooks/Cole.
17. Sapat, A. (2004). Devolution and innovation: the adoption of state environmental policy innovations by administrative agencies. *Public Administration Review, 64*, 141–151; U.S. General Accounting Office (2004). *Columbia River Basin: a multilayered collection of directives and plans guide federal fish and wildlife activities*. Washington, DC: U.S. Government Printing Office; Intergovernmental Panel on Climate Change website, http://www.ipcc.ch/.
18. United States Postal Inspection Service (2019). *What we do*. Retrieved November 30, 2019, from https://www.uspis.gov/about/what-we-do/.
19. U.S. Senate (2019). *Report of the Select Committee on Intelligence: Russian active measures campaigns and interference in the 2016 U.S. Election, Volume I*. Retrieved July 28, 2019, from https://www.intelligence.senate.gov/publications/reports.
20. Howard, P., et al. (2019). *The IRA, social media and political polarization in the United States, 2012-2018*. Oxford Internet Institute, University of Oxford. Retrieved July 28, 2019, from https://comprop.oii.ox.ac.uk/research/ira-political-polarization/; DiResta, R., et al. (2018). *The tactics & tropes of the Internet Research Agency*. Retrieved July 28, 2019, from https://disinformationreport.blob.core.windows.net/disinformation-report/NewKnowledge-Disinformation-Report-Whitepaper.pdf.
21. Wines, M. (2018). State officials say they are told too little about election threats. *New York Times*, February 19. Retrieved November 30, 2019, from https://www.nytimes.com/2018/02/19/us/elections-states-hacking.html; Karmack, E. (2019). The federal-state disconnect in securing the 2016 election and how not to repeat it. *Brookings Institution*. Retrieved November 30, 2019, from https://www.brookings.edu/blog/fixgov/2019/08/23/the-federal-state-disconnect-in-securing-the-2016-election-and-how-not-to-repeat-it/.
22. Jacobs, B. (2017). America since 9/11: timeline of attacks linked to the 'war on terror.' *The Guardian: U.S. Edition*. Retrieved July 28, 2019, from https://www.theguardian.com/us-news/2017/nov/01/america-since-911-terrorist-attacks-linked-to-the-war-on-terror.
23. U.S. Government Accountability Office (2006). *Catastrophic disasters: enhanced leadership, capabilities, and accountability controls will improve the effectiveness of the nation's preparedness, response, and recovery system*. Washington, DC: Author.
24. Homeland Security Council (2006). *National strategy for pandemic influenza: implementation plan*. Retrieved April 18, 2020, from https://www.cdc.gov/flu/pandemic-resources/pdf/pandemic-influenza-implementation.pdf.
25. Kessler, G., & Kelley, M. (2020). Was the White House office for global pandemics eliminated? *Washington Post*, March 20. Retrieved April 18, 2020, from https://www.washingtonpost.com/politics/2020/03/20/was-white-house-office-global-pandemics-eliminated/.

26. Van Bavel, J. (2020). In a pandemic, political polarization could kill people. *Washington Post*, March 22. Retrieved April 18, 2020, from https://www.washingtonpost.com /outlook/2020/03/23/coronavirus-polarization-political -exaggeration/.

27. Beals, R. K. (2020). Trump believes coronavirus will vanish with April temps—experts are skeptical warm weather alone is enough. *MarketWatch*, March 16. Retrieved April 18, 2020, from https://www.marketwatch .com/story/trump-believes-coronavirus-will-vanish-with -april-temps-experts-are-skeptical-warm-weather-alone -is-enough-2020-03-12.

28. Sanger-Katz, M., et al. (2020). These places could run out of hospital beds as coronavirus spreads. *New York Times*. Retrieved April 18, 2020, from https://www.nytimes.com /interactive/2020/03/17/upshot/hospital-bed-shortages -coronavirus.html.

29. U.S. Food and Drug Administration (2020). *FAQs on shortages of surgical masks and gowns.* Retrieved April 18, 2020, from https://www.fda.gov/medical-devices/personal -protective-equipment-infection-control/faqs-shortages -surgical-masks-and-gowns.

30. Miller, H. (2020). Governors across the nation slam federal coronavirus response: 'We didn't take this seriously.' *CNBC*. Retrieved April 18, 2020, from https://www.cnbc .com/2020/03/22/governors-say-they-are-not-getting -supplies-they-need-for-coronavirus.html.

31. Parker, A., et al. (2020). Trump Administration has many task forces – but still no plan for beating covid-19. *The Washington Post*, April 11. Retrieved April 18, 2020, from https://www.washingtonpost.com/politics/trump-task -forces-coronavirus-pandemic/2020/04/11/5cc5a30c -7a77-11ea-a130-df573469f094_story.html.

32. Defense Production Act (DPA) of 1950. P.L. 81-774; Congressional Research Service (2020). *The defense production act of 1950: history, authorities, and considerations for Congress.* Washington, DC: U.S. Government Publishing Office.

33. Selin, J. (2020). Trump versus the states: what federalism means for the coronavirus response. *The Conversation*. Retrieved April 18, 2020, from https://theconversation .com/trump-versus-the-states-what-federalism-means-for -the-coronavirus-response-136361.

34. Selin, J. (2020). Trump versus the states.

35. Ter-Minassian, T. (2016). *Fiscal and financial issues for 21st century cities.* Washington, DC: Brookings Institution.

36. Federal Reserve of St. Louis (2019). *Personal income per capita: U.S.* Retrieved November 30, 2019, from https:// fred.stlouisfed.org/series/A792RC0A052NBEA; Federal Reserve of St. Louis (2019). *Release tables: per capita personal income by state.* Retrieved November 30, 2019, from https:// fred.stlouisfed.org/release/tables?rid=151&eid=257197.

37. Office of Economic Policy, U.S. Department of Treasury (2018). *Total taxable resources estimates, 2018.* Retrieved July 30, 2019, from https://home.treasury.gov/policy-issues /economic-policy/total-taxable-resources (available for download in .pdf and .xlsx formats).

38. U.S. Advisory Commission on Intergovernmental Relations (1992). *Significant features of fiscal federalism, vol. 2, revenues and expenditures: 1992.* Washington, DC: U.S. Government Printing Office.

39. U.S. Advisory Commission on Intergovernmental Relations (1990). *Representative expenditures: addressing the neglected dimension of fiscal capacity.* Washington, DC: U.S. Government Printing Office.

40. Gordon, T., et al. (2016). *Assessing fiscal capacities of states: a representative revenue system-representative expenditure system approach, fiscal year 2012.* Washington, DC: Urban Institute.

41. Library of Parliament (2013). *Canada's equalization formula.* Retrieved July 30, 2019, from https://lop.parl .ca/staticfiles/PublicWebsite/Home/ResearchPublications /InBriefs/PDF/2008-20-e.pdf.

42. Authors' calculation Tax Policy Center (2019). *State and local government finance data query system (SLF-DQS for own source).* Washington, DC: Urban Institute– Brookings Institution. Retrieved July 30, 2019, from https://slfdqs.taxpolicycenter.org/pages.cfm; Total taxable resources from U.S. Department of Treasury (2018). *Total taxable resources estimates, 2018*, http://www.treasury .gov/resource-center/economic-policy/taxable-resources /Documents/tables%202011.pdf.

43. Oates, W. E. (1972). Fiscal federalism. New York, NY: Harcourt Brace Jovanovich.

44. Executive Order 12612—Federalism. 52 FR 41685, 3 CFR, 1987 Comp., p. 252.

45. Bandyopadyay, S., & Geurrero, R. (2017). Comparing income, education and job data for immigrants vs. those born in the U.S. *The Regional Economist.* Retrieved July 30, 2019, from https://www.stlouisfed.org/~/media /publications/regional-economist/2017/second_quarter _2017/immigration.pdf.

46. Parilla, J., & Liu, S. (2018). *Examining the local value of economic development incentives.* Washington, DC: Brookings. Retrieved July 30, 2019, from https://www .brookings.edu/wp-content/uploads/2018/02/report _examining-the-local-value-of-economic-development -incentives_brookings-metro_march-2018.pdf.

47. Taylor, D. (2018). Mercedes decided 25 years ago to build in Alabama, fueling economy. *Tuscaloosa News.* Retrieved July 30, 2019, from https://www.tuscaloosanews.com/news /20180930/mercedes-decided-25-years-ago-to-build-in -alabama-fueling-economy.

48. Cremer, A. (2011). Daimler spends $2 billion on Mercedes-Benz site in Alabama as demand rises. *Bloomberg.com*, July 21. Retrieved November 28, 2011, from http://www .bloomberg.com/news/2011-07-21/daimler-spends -2-billion-on-mercedes-benz-site-in-alabama-as-demand -rises.html; Alabama Department of Commerce (2019). How Mercedes is preparing for the future in Alabama. *MadeinAlabama.com*. Retrieved July 30, 2019, from http:// www.madeinalabama.com/why-alabama/success-stories /project-gateway-how-mercedes-is-preparing-for-the -future-in-alabama/.

49. Mayer, M. (2018). North Carolina film industry regains footing with revived incentives. *The Daily Tar Heel*, October 18. Retrieved July 30, 2019, from https://www.dailytarheel.com/article/2018/10/film-incentives-1007.

50. Rainville, L. (2012). *Taxing for transit: an exploratory analysis of local option transportation taxes*. Tufts University, Urban and Environmental Policy and Planning. Retrieved July 30, 2019, from http://sites.tufts.edu/MaryDavis/files/2013/06/LRainville-Thesis.pdf.

51. Congressional Research Service (2019). *Base closure and realignment (BRAC): background and issues for Congress*. Washington, DC: U.S. Government Publishing Office.

52. U.S. Office of Management and Budget (2019). *Budget of the United States government, 2020*. Washington, DC: U.S. Government Publishing Office; Center for Budget and Policy Priorities (2018). *Where do our federal tax dollars go?* Washington, DC: Center for Budget and Policy Priorities, 2.

53. Office of Personnel Management (2017). *Federal civilian employment*. OPM.Gov. Retrieved August 3, 2019, from https://www.opm.gov/policy-data-oversight/data-analysis-documentation/federal-employment-reports/reports-publications/federal-civilian-employment/.

54. U.S. Department of Defense (2019). *Defense spending by state: fiscal year 2017*. Washington, DC: U.S. Government Publishing Office, 6. Retrieved August 3, 2019, from https://www.defense.gov/explore/story/Article/1789129/which-state-ranks-highest-in-military-spending/.

55. U.S. Department of Defense (2019). *Defense spending by state: fiscal year 2017*, 12.

56. U.S. Department of Defense (2019). *Defense spending by state: fiscal year 2017*, 6.

57. Dubay, C. S. (2006). *Federal tax burdens and expenditures by state*. Washington, DC. Tax Foundation.

58. Schultz, L., & Cummings, M. (2019). *Giving or getting? New York's balance of payments with the federal government*. Albany, NY: Rockefeller Institute of Government, 13.

59. The Urban Institute-Brookings Institution Tax Policy Center (2019). *State & local government finance data query system*. Data from U.S. Census Bureau, Annual Survey of State and Local Government Finances, Government Finances, Volume 4, and Census of Governments (2016). Retrieved August 4, 2019, from http://www.taxpolicycenter.org/slf-dqs/pages.cfm.

60. Urban Institute-Brookings Institution Tax Policy Center (2019). *State & local government finance data query system (for year 2012)*.

61. ProQuest (2019). *ProQuest statistical abstract of the United States: 2019*, 315 (data from 2015).

62. U.S. Bureau of the Census. (2017). *Public elementary-secondary school system finance data*. Retrieved August 4, 2019, from https://www.census.gov/data/tables/2017/econ/school-finances/secondary-education-finance.html.

63. *San Antonio School District v. Rodriquez* (1973). 411 U.S. 1.

64. Chingos, M., & Blagg, K. (2017). *Making sense of state school funding policy*. Washington, DC: Urban Institute, 3. Retrieved August 4, 2019, from https://www.urban.org/sites/default/files/publication/94961/making-sense-of-state-school-funding-policy_0.pdf.

65. *Serrano v. Priest (Serrano II)* (1976). 18 Cal.3d 728 (Calif.); Butt v. State of California (1992). 4 Cal.4th 668; Reed v. United Teachers L.A. (2012). 208 Cal.App.4th 322.

66. Chingos, M., & Blagg, K. (2017). *Making sense of state school funding policy*. 12.

67. Baker, B., & Green, P. (2015). Conceptions of equity and adequacy in school finance. In Ladd, H., & Goertz, M. (Eds.), *Handbook of research in education finance and policy* (pp. 213–244). New York: Routledge.

68. *Rose v. Council for Better Education* (1989). 7090 S.W.2d 186 (Ky.).

69. No Child Left Behind Act of 2001 (P.L. 107-110).

70. Every Student Succeeds Act of 2015 (P.L. 114-95).

71. U.S. Department of Education (2019). *Every Student Succeeds Act (ESSA)*. Retrieved August 4, 2019, from https://www.ed.gov/essa.

72. See Federal Highway Administration, U.S. Department of Transportation (2018). *Highway statistics, 2017*. Retrieved August 4, 2019, from https://www.fhwa.dot.gov/policyinformation/statistics/2017/.

73. Reported in PEW Charitable Trusts (2013). *The state role in local government financial distress*. Retrieved August 16, 2019, from https://www.pewtrusts.org/~/media/assets/2016/04/pew_state_role_in_local_government_financial_distress.pdf.

74. PEW Charitable Trusts (2013). *The state role in local government financial distress*. 37.

75. The PEW Charitable Trusts (2016). *State strategies to detect local fiscal distress: how states assess and monitor the financial health of local governments*. Retrieved August 16, 2019, from https://www.pewtrusts.org/en/research-and-analysis/reports/2016/09/state-strategies-to-detect-local-fiscal-distress.

76. New York City Investment Fund (2003). *Lessons learned: an analysis of the New York City Investment Fund's financial recovery fund for small businesses affected by 9/11*. Retrieved October 1, 2006, from http://www.nycif.org/RECOVERYFUND/LessonsLearned_FRF.pdf (document no longer accessible online).

77. Basfamille, M., et al. (2015). *The flypaper effect is not a puzzle*, Documentos de Trabajo 464, Instituto de Economia, Pontificia Univerisdad Catolica de Chile. Retrieved August 16, 2019, from https://ideas.repec.org/p/ioe/doctra/464.html; Deller, S. C., & Maher, C. (2005). Categorical municipal expenditures with a focus on the flypaper effect. *Public Budgeting & Finance, 25*, Fall, 73–90; Deller, S. C., & Maher, C. S. (2006). A model of asymmetries in the flypaper effect. *Publius, 36*, 213–230.

78. Baicher, K., & Gordon, N. (2006). The effect of state education finance reform on total local resources. *Journal of Public Economics, 90*, 1519–1535.

79. Benefits.gov (2019). *Temporary assistance for needy families*. Retrieved from https://www.benefits.gov/benefit/613.

80. U.S. Government Accountability Office (2008). *Surface transportation: restructured federal approach needed for*

more focused, performance-based, and sustainable programs. Washington, DC: Government Printing Office.

81. Kousser, T. (2014). How America's "devolution revolution" reshaped its federalism. *Revue Francaise de Science Politique, 64*, 265–287.

82. Peter G. Peterson Foundation (2018). *Three key things to know about CHIP*. Retrieved August 16, 2019, from https://www.pgpf.org/blog/2017/12/three-key-things-to-know-about-chip.

83. Vestal, C. (2014). ACA and the children's health insurance program. *Stateline*, May 21. Retrieved August 16, 2019, from https://khn.org/news/aca-and-the-childrens-health-insurance-program/.

84. Calculated from Office of Management and Budget (2020). *Summary of programs by state, state-by-state-fy 2020.xlsx*. Retrieved August 17, 2019, from https://www.whitehouse.gov/wp-content/uploads/2019/03/state-by-state-fy2020.xlsx; and U.S. Bureau of the Census (2020). *Annual estimates of the resident population for the United States, regions, states, and Puerto Rico: April 1, 2010 to July 1, 2018*. Retrieved August 17, 2019, from https://www2.census.gov/programs-surveys/popest/tables/2010-2018/national/totals/nst-est2018-01.xlsx?#.

85. World Bank (2015). *Competitive cities for jobs and growth: working paper 101546*. Retrieved August 17, 2019, from https://openknowledge.worldbank.org/bitstream/handle/10986/23227/Competitive0ci000what00who00and0how.pdf?sequence=5&isAllowed=y; Katz, B., & Bradley, J. (2011). Metro connection: cities, competitiveness, growth through innovation, job creation, U.S. economic growth. *Democracy: A Journal of Ideas*, March (Brookings Institution online journal). Retrieved November 25, 2011, from http://www.brookings.edu/articles/2011/03_metros_katz_bradley.aspx.

86. Office of Management and Budget (2019). *Budget of the United States government, fiscal 2020, analytical perspectives* (p. 232). Washington, DC. U.S. Government Publishing Office.

87. As quoted in Kousser (2014). *How America's "devolution revolution" reshaped its federalism*, 265.

88. Walker, D. B. (1996). The advent of an ambiguous federalism and the emergence of New Federalism II. *Public Administration Review, 56*, 271–280.

89. Public Law 115-97 (Amendment of the Revenue Code of 1986).

90. National Conference of State Legislatures (2018). *Federal tax reform and the states*. Retrieved August 20, 2019, from http://www.ncsl.org/research/fiscal-policy/federal-tax-reform-and-the-states.aspx.

91. Pomerleau, K. (2017). *Federal tax reform: the impact on states*. Retrieved August 20, 2019, from https://taxfoundation.org/federal-tax-reform-the-impact-on-states/.

92. National Conference of State Legislatures (2018). *Federal tax reform and the states*.

93. *Garcia v. San Antonio Metropolitan Transit Authority* (1985). 469 U.S. 528.

94. *United States v. Lopez* (1985). 514 U.S. 549.

95. *Printz v. United States* (1997). 521 U.S. 98.

96. *Geier v. American Honda Motor Company* (2000). 529 U.S. 861; Andrews, J. L. (2006). Saving preemption: a conflict preemption quandary resolved in *Geier v. American Honda Motor Co., Inc. Transportation Law Journal, 32*, 221–284.

97. *Kimel v. Florida Board of Regents* (2000). 528 U.S. 62; *Board of Trustees of Alabama v. Garrett* (2001). 531 U.S. 356.

98. Rivoll, D. (2011). Tough Arizona-style immigration laws pose new issues for high court. *International Business Times*, December 6. Retrieved December 6, 2011, from https://www.ibtimes.com/tough-arizona-style-immigration-laws-pose-new-issues-high-court-379250.

99. P.L. 91-513 (1970).

100. P.L. 114-95, 20015; U.S. Department of Education (2019). *Every Student Succeeds Act*. Retrieved August 22, 2019, from https://www.ed.gov/essa?src=rn.

101. National Conference of State Legislatures (2006). *Preemption monitor*. Retrieved October 3, 2006, from http://www.ncsl.organ/sclaw/PreemptionMonitor_Index.htm (no longer archived); see Galligan, T. C. (2006). U.S. Supreme Court tort reform: limiting state power to articulate and develop tort law—defamation, preemption, and punitive damages. *University of Cincinnati Law Review, 74*, 1189–1264; Kaulukukui, K. L. (2006). The brief and unexpected preemption of Hawaii's humpback whale laws: the authority of the states to protect endangered marine mammals under ESA and MMPA. *Environmental Law Reporter News and Analysis, 36*, 10712–10725.

102. Authors' review of all issues of *Preemption Monitor* for mid-2009 through mid-2011, and subsequent review in 2019 of NCSL publications on pre-emption.

103. *Murphy v. National Collegiate Athletic Association*, 584 U.S. ___ (2018).

104. Ruben, K., & Randall, M. (2017). *Debt limits: how states restrict borrowing*. Washington, DC: Urban Institute. Retrieved August 20, 2019, from https://www.taxpolicycenter.org/sites/default/files/publication/149161/debt-limits_1.pdf.

105. *Texas v. United States* (1998). 523 U.S. 296.

106. Barnum, M. (2018). When states take over school districts, they say it's about academics. *Chalkbeat*. Retrieved August 20, 2019, from https://www.chalkbeat.org/posts/us/2018/06/12/state-takeovers-book/.

107. Gay, M. (2007). State takes control of troubled public schools in St. Louis. *NYTimes online*. Retrieved May 16, 2020, from https://www.nytimes.com/2007/03/23/us/23missouri.html; Pew Charitable Trusts (2016). *The state role in local government fiscal distress*. Retrieved May 16, 2020, from https://www.pewtrusts.org/~/media/assets/2016/04/pew_state_role_in_local_government_financial_distress.pdf.

108. Chen, G. (2019). Local school districts at risk of state government takeovers. *Public School Review*, August 6. Retrieved August 22, 2019, from https://www.publics

choolreview.com/blog/local-school-districts-at-risk-of-state-government-takeovers.

109. McCoy, D. (2019). The fate of these Indianapolis schools is once again uncertain, years after state takeover. *Chalkbeat*, February 8. Retrieved August 22, 2019, from https://www.chalkbeat.org/posts/in/2019/02/08/the-fate-of-these-indianapolis-schools-is-once-again-uncertain-years-after-state-takeover/.

110. U.S. Department of Housing and Urban Development (2020). *Community Development* Retrieved May 12, 2020, from https://www.hud.gov/program_offices/comm_planning/communitydevelopment.

111. U.S. Department of Agriculture, Food and Nutrition Service (2019). *WIC eligibility and coverage rates*. Retrieved August 22, 2019, from https://www.fns.usda.gov/wic/wic-2015-eligibility-and-coverage-rates#Chart1.

112. Federal Register (2019). *Federal acquisition regulation; OMB circular citation update*. Retrieved August 22, 2019, from https://www.federalregister.gov/documents/2016/07/14/2016-16246/federal-acquisition-regulation-omb-circular-citation-update.

113. McDowell, B. D. (1991). Grant reform reconsidered. *Intergovernmental Perspective, 17*, Summer, 8–11.

114. Givel, M. (1991). *The War on Poverty revisited: the Community Services Block Grant Program in the Reagan years*. Lanham, MD: University Press of America; U.S. Government Accountability Office (2006). *Community Services Block Grant Program: HHS should improve oversight by focusing monitoring and assistance efforts on areas of high risk*. Washington, DC: Author.

115. Federal Register (2019). *Federal acquisition regulation; OMB circular citation update.*

116. State and Local Fiscal Assistance Act of 1972 (P.L. 92-512).

117. Greenblatt, A. (2002). Enemies of the State. *Governing, 16*, June, 26–31.

118. Housing and Community Development Act of 1974 (P.L. 93-383).

119. Office of the Administration for Children & Families, U.S. Department of Health and Human Services (2019). *Social Services Block Grant Program*. Retrieved August 22, 2019, from https://www.acf.hhs.gov/ocs/programs/ssbg.

120. U.S. Office of Management and Budget (1999). *Revised statistical definitions of metropolitan areas (MA) and guidance on use of MA definitions*, Bulletin 99–04. Retrieved May 12, 2020, from https://clintonwhitehouse2.archives.gov/OMB/inforeg/msa-bull99-04.html.

121. U.S. General Accounting Office (2004). *Metropolitan statistical areas: new standards and their impact on selected federal programs*. Washington, DC: U.S. Government Printing Office.

122. Wang, H. L. (2019). Why is the Census Bureau still asking a citizenship question on forms? *NPR.org*, August 9. Retrieved December 1, 2019, from https://www.npr.org/2019/08/09/743296249/why-is-the-census-bureau-still-asking-a-citizenship-question-on-forms.

123. Omnibus Budget Reconciliation Act of 1981 (P.L. 97-35).

124. Rein, L. (2018). White House proposes federal government overhaul, including a consolidation of safety-net programs. *Washington Post*, June 21. Retrieved August 22, 2019, from https://www.washingtonpost.com/politics/white-house-announces-proposed-revamp-of-federal-government-including-a-consolidation-of-social-safety-net-programs/2018/06/21/64fdb8ca-756a-11e8-9780-b1dd6a09b549_story.html?noredirect=on.

125. U.S. Government Accountability Office (2006). *Department of Homeland Security's use of special streamlined acquisition authorities in Section 833 of the Homeland Security Act of 2002*. Washington, DC: Author.

126. Department of Homeland Security (2018). *Fiscal Year 2018 homeland security grant program*. Retrieved August 22, 2019, from https://www.fema.gov/media-library-data/1526578922142-6e8ecdd336887cfb43062fcf7b374f4a/FY_2018_HSGP_Fact_Sheet_FINAL_508.pdf.

127. Federal Emergency Management Agency (2011). *FY 2018 Homeland Security Grant Program (HSGP)*. Retrieved August 22, 2019, from https://www.fema.gov/homeland-security-grant-program

128. U.S. Department of Homeland Security (2011). *FY 2011 Homeland Security Grant program*. Retrieved November 30, 2011, from http://www.fema.gov/government/grant/hsgp/.

129. U.S. Government Accountability Office (2008). *Homeland Security: DHS risk-based grant methodology is reasonable, but its current version's measure of vulnerability is limited* (p. 1). Washington, DC: Author.

130. U.S. Government Accountability Office (2018). *Homeland Security Grant Program: additional actions could further enhance FEMA's risk-based grant assessment model* (p. 14). Washington, DC: Author.

131. Hudson, A. (2006). Homeland Security grants spent on clowns and gyms. *Washington Times*, April 21.

132. Rivlin, A. M. (1992). *Reviving the American dream: the economy, the states, and the federal government* (pp. 126–152). Washington, DC: Brookings Institution.

133. Bradson, T., et al. (2006). Soft governance, hard consequences: the ambiguous status of unofficial guidelines. *Public Administration Review, 66*, 546–553.

134. P.L. 108-446; further amended by Every Student Succeeds Act, P.L. 114-95.

135. Unfunded Mandates Reform Act of 1995 (P.L. 104-4); see Dilger, R., & Beth, R. (2015). Unfunded Mandates Reform Act: history, impact, and issues. *Congressional Research Service*. Retrieved August 23, 2019, from https://nationalaglawcenter.org/wp-content/uploads/assets/crs/R40957.pdf.

136. Congressional Budget Office (2019). *CBO's activities under the Unfunded Mandates Reform Act*. Washington, DC: Author. Retrieved August 23, 2019, from https://www.cbo.gov/publication/51335.

137. U.S. Congressional Budget Office (2009). *Cost estimate for the Patient Protection and Affordable Care Act as proposed on November 18*. Retrieved May 12, 2020, from https://www.cbo.gov/publication/24998.

138. Congressional Research Service (2015). *Unfunded Mandates Reform Act: history, impact and issues.*

139. U.S. Congressional Budget Office (2011). CBO's activities under the *Unfunded Mandates Reform Act.* Washington, DC: Author. Retrieved August 23, 2019, from https://www.cbo.gov/publication/51335.

140. Real ID Act of 2005 (P.L. 109-13).

141. U.S. Congressional Budget Office (2006). *A review of CBO's activities under the Unfunded Mandates Reform Act, 1996 to 2005* (p. 5).

142. National Governors Association, National Conference of State Legislatures, and American Association of Motor Vehicle Administrators (2006). *The Real ID Act: national impact analysis.* Washington, DC: Author.

143. National Conference of State Legislatures (2016). *Countdown to REAL ID.* Retrieved August 23, 2019, from http://www.ncsl.org/research/transportation/count-down-to-real-id.aspx.

144. *U.S. v. Lopez* (1995). 514 U.S. 549; *Printz v. U.S.* (1997). 521 U.S. 898.

145. *Citizens United v. Federal Election Commission* (2010). 558 U.S. 08-205; Bipartisan Campaign Reform Act of 2002 (P.L. 107-55).

146. *Grove City College v. Bell* (1984). 465 U.S. 555.

147. Civil Rights Restoration Act of 1988 (P.L. 100-259).

148. Education Amendments of 1972 (P.L. 92-318).

149. Sander, L. (2011). James Madison U.'s elimination of 10 sports teams was legal, appeals court affirms. *Chronicle of Higher Education*, March 8. Retrieved December 1, 2019, from https://www.chronicle.com/article/James-Madison-Us-Elimination/126655; Grasgreen, A. (2011). Sports slashed at Maryland. *Inside Higher Ed*, November 22. Retrieved December 1, 2019, from https://www.insidehighered.com/news/2011/11/22/maryland-will-cut-eight-teams-mitigate-athletic-budget-deficit.

150. Single Audit Act of 1984 (P.L. 98-502).

151. U.S. Department of Health and Human Services (2011). *Grants.gov.* Retrieved December 2, 2011, from http://grants.gov/.

152. Federal Funding Accountability and Transparency Act of 2006 (P.L. 109-282).

153. Orr, G., et al. (2020). Trump tosses coronavirus shutdowns back to the states. *Politico*, April 16. Retrieved April 18, 2020, from https://www.politico.com/news/2020/04/16/trump-plan-for-reopening-economy-191073.

Appendix

COVID-19 Crisis and the Economy

This appendix on the coronavirus crisis was written at the end of the second quarter of 2020 as the initial economic effects of the crisis became obvious. On June 8, 2020, the National Bureau of Economic Research (NBER) officially determined that the U.S. economy was in recession, marking the end of a 128-month expansion in economic activity that began in June 2009.[1] Recognizing the unusual nature of this recession, NBER's Business Cycle Dating Committee noted:

> "The usual definition of a recession involves a decline in economic activity that lasts more than a few months. However, in deciding whether to identify a recession, the committee weighs the depth of the contraction, its duration, and whether economic activity declined broadly across the economy (the diffusion of the downturn). The committee recognizes that the pandemic and the public health response have resulted in a downturn with different characteristics and dynamics than prior recessions. Nonetheless, it concluded that the unprecedented magnitude of the decline in employment and production, and its broad reach across the entire economy, warrants the designation of this episode as a recession, even if it turns out to be briefer than earlier contractions."

The appendix focuses on the early economic data available in the first two quarters of the COVID-19 recession, including the initial sharp gross domestic project (GDP) drop in the first quarter, the almost immediate employment effects, and the fiscal and monetary policy actions undertaken to sustain the economy. The major focus of the appendix is comparing what the early features of this pandemic-induced recession looked like compared with the Great Recession (2007–2009). This appendix should be viewed as a companion piece to the chapter on government and the economy. Terminology introduced in that chapter is not redefined or explained here.

Economic Impacts of the Health Crisis

The growth period following the Great Recession was long and sustained—almost 11 years of sustained economic growth, measured by GDP and its major components. GDP growth ended in the first quarter of 2020 when the economy went into dramatic decline. The Conference Board's Leading Economic Index "…registered the largest decline in its 60-year history"—down 6.7% in March.[2] The speed with which the economy came to an almost sudden halt was more precipitous and deeper than the first months of the Great Recession. Over 43 million new unemployment benefit claims were filed in just over 2 months

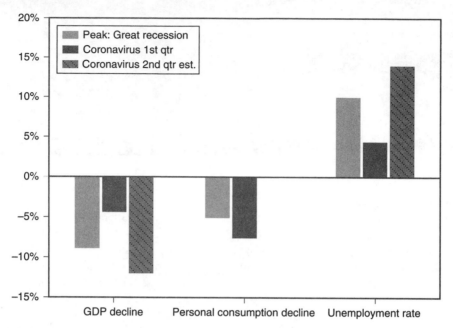

Figure A-1 Selected Economic Indicators for the Great Recession and Early 2020 Coronavirus Crisis.

Note: Economic and unemployment indicators for early 2020 in this figure are first release, subject to revision. First, second, and third official revisions generally take place within the subsequent two quarters from the first release date.

Federal Reserve Bank of St. Louis (2020). *U.S. Bureau of Labor Statistics: Unemployment Rate [UNRATE]*. Retrieved May 8, 2020, from https://fred.stlouisfed.org/series/UNRATE; U.S. Department of Commerce, Bureau of Economic Analysis (2020). *BEA News Gross Domestic Product: 1st quarter 2020, historical tables*. Retrieved April 30, 2020, from https://www.bea.gov/system/files/2020-04/hist1q20_Adv.pdf; Swagel, P. (2020). Updating CBO's economic forecast to account for the pandemic. *Congressional Budget Office*. Retrieved April 30, 2020, from https://www.cbo.gov/publication/56314.

from the first week of the 2020 economic shutdown, to the end of the second quarter of 2020, a historic labor market decline. By contrast, it was 23 months from the start of the Great Recession before 43 million new unemployment benefit claims had been filed.[3]

Figure A-1 compares several major economic indicators for the first four months (first quarter and 1 month into the second quarter) of 2020 with the worst quarter of the Great Recession (fourth quarter, 2008). The figure focuses on declines in GDP, personal consumption expenditures, and the unemployment rate.

The official first quarter decline in GDP of the COVID-19 recession, as illustrated in Figure A-1, was −4.8%, compared with −8.9%, the largest single-quarter GDP decline in the Great Recession. The Congressional Budget Office (CBO), based largely on April and early May 2020 new claims for unemployment, estimated that the second quarter 2020 GDP could drop another 12%, or down 16% total through half the year.[4]

Unemployment figures mirror the GDP comparison. The Great Recession's peak unemployment rate of 10% (several months in 2009–2010) was less than April 2020's unemployment rate of 14.7%.[5] The initial announcement of May's unemployment rate from the Bureau of Economic Analysis showed improvement to 13.3%[6] although the rate may have been higher. Some analysts noted that in analyzing the results of the survey on which the Bureau of Labor Statistics (BLS) estimates the unemployment rate, BLS counted individuals who were furloughed from their jobs as employed on the assumption that they would return to the jobs they held previously.[7] Similarly, in the first quarter of the COVID-19 recession, personal consumption had already reached a point lower than the peak rate in the Great Recession.

Figure A-2 compares quarterly changes in GDP and three of its major components: personal consumption expenditures, residential fixed investments, and nonresidential fixed investments. The quarters selected capture a full

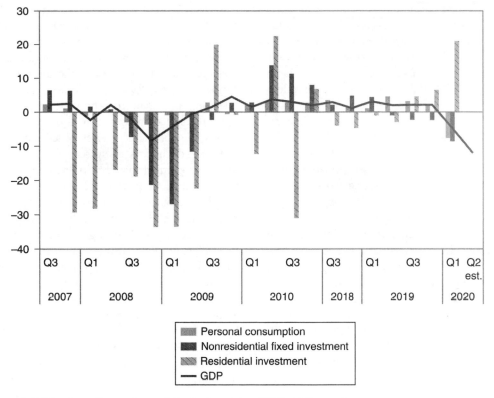

Figure A-2 The Great Recession and Beginning of the COVID-19 Recession.

For 2019–2020: U.S. Department of Commerce, Bureau of Economic Analysis (2020). *National Income and Product Accounts: Table 1.1.1, 2020.* Retrieved April 30, 2020, from https://apps.bea.gov/iTable/iTable.
cfm?reqid=19&step=2#reqid=19&step=2&isuri=1&1921=survey, for 2007–2010: U.S. Department of Commerce, Bureau of Economic Analysis (2020). *National Income and Product Accounts, Table 1.1.1: Percent Change from
Preceding Period in Real Gross Domestic Product.* Table created using interactive data search for selected years. Retrieved April 30, 2020, from https://apps.bea.gov/iTable/iTable.cfm?reqid=19&step=2#reqid=19&step=2&isuri
=1&1921=survey; Swagel, P. (2020). CBO's current projections of output, employment, and interest rates and a preliminary look at federal deficits for 2020 and 2021. *Congressional Budget Office.* Retrieved May 2, 2020, from
https://www.cbo.gov/publication/56335.

year before onset of the Great Recession through 2010 and compare that period with 2018 through the first quarter of 2020. The data graphed are percent changes from quarter to quarter.

The Great Recession was a financial market collapse caused primarily by a collapse in the housing and mortgage markets (see chapter on government and the economy). Residential investment declined between 20% and 36% for nine of the eleven quarters of the Great Recession, as illustrated in Figure A-2, and did not begin substantial recovery until 2012. Personal consumption started recovering much earlier, in 2010. The coronavirus crisis caused an abrupt shut down of major segments of the economy with both voluntary and mandated stay-at-home orders to prevent the spread of coronavirus.

By the end of the first quarter, forecasts, such as the CBO's,[8] predicted a recession much deeper than the Great Recession. The COVID-19 recession did not build up over several quarters. Shutdown of much of the economy in most states had large and immediate effects on economic activity.

The numbers are dramatic, but caution in making comparisons between the two economic declines is necessary. The COVID-19 recession was in the early stages in the United States at the time this appendix was written. The first month of 2020 had been a period of economic growth. Health effects were just beginning to be visible, and the economy was stable or growing as measured by most indicators. Most of the first quarter economic downturn in 2020 was not visible until March, the last month of the quarter. In April, the bottom dropped out, unlike the Great Recession's effects that stretched over several years. Weekly claims for unemployment insurance did not exceed 700,000 in any month of that recession. In only 6 weeks of the COVID-19 recession, from March 21 through May 2, 2020, weekly initial unemployment claims ranged from a low of 3.2 million to a high of 6.6 million; cumulative unemployment claims reached 36 million in 6 weeks.[9]

The two economic crises also differ markedly in the components of GDP that contributed the most to total GDP decline. **Table A-1** shows the relative contributions of the four major components of GDP to the change in GDP in the quarter with the largest decline in the Great Recession with the first quarter of 2020. The major components are personal consumption expenditures, gross private domestic investment, net exports of goods and services, and government consumption expenditures and gross investment. GDP fell 8.4% in the fourth quarter of 2008 and 5% in the first quarter of 2020, respectively. Growth in a component of GDP, such as 1.3% increase in net exports of goods and services in 2020, offset declines in other components.

Gross private domestic investment (residential and nonresidential fixed investment) accounted for most of the −8% drop in GDP in the fourth quarter of 2008. That was a consequence of the large decline in new home construction and, as that worsened, decline in nonresidential domestic investment. Personal consumption expenditures accounted for the rest of the drop in 2008. During the first few weeks of the COVID-19 recession, personal consumption expenditures declined more than the entire drop in GDP; net exports of goods and services offset some of the total GDP decline. A decrease in gross domestic private investment also contributed to the GDP decline in the first quarter of 2020.

The Great Recession started with massive asset losses in the housing and finance industries. Those losses rippled through to manufacturing, especially automobile production. In contrast, the coronavirus crisis started with immediate massive unemployment that then rippled through the consumption of goods and services. The Chair of the Federal Reserve characterized the sharp drop in the economy as "heartbreaking," with the expectation that it would take more than a year to recover the job losses already experienced in the first quarter.[10] The full story of the coronavirus crisis, of course, was yet to be written at the time this appendix was put together. Most predictions based on the damage to the economy already incurred in the first two quarters, even under

Table A-1 Contributions of the Four Major GDP Components to Decline in GDP: 2020 COVID-19 Recession and the Great Recession

	2008	2020
Change in GDP (quarter over quarter)	−8.4	−5.0
Contribution to change of major components of GDP		
▪ Personal consumption expenditures	−2.4	−4.7
▪ Gross private domestic investment	−6.4	−1.8
▪ Net exports of goods and services	−0.2	1.3
▪ Government consumption expenditures and gross investment	0.6	0.2

Note: The sum of the four components may not add to GDP change due to rounding.

U.S. Department of Commerce, Bureau of Economic Analysis (2020). *National Income and Product Accounts, Table 1.1.2: Contributions to Percent Change in Real GDP.* Table created using interactive data search for selected years. Retrieved April 30, 2020, from https://apps.bea.gov/iTable/iTable.cfm?reqid=19&step=2#reqid=19&step=2&isuri=1&1921=survey.

optimistic health assumptions, forecast that the economy would not be likely to show recovery in GDP until the fourth quarter of 2020, or even well into 2021.

GDP recovery does not tell the full story of economic recovery. The Great Recession officially ended in 2009 with two consecutive quarters of GDP growth, but it was several years after that before employment returned to pre-recession levels. Incomes for lower quintiles had only neared, but not reached, pre-2007 levels when the coronavirus crisis hit (see discussion of income and wealth inequality in the chapter on government and the economy). The same long recovery period in all aspects of the economy in the COVID-19 recession is highly likely. CBO's projections include a peak unemployment rate of 16% in the third quarter of 2020, gradually falling to around 9% through the end of 2021, with gradual recovery after that.[11] As personal consumption drops, the manufacturing sector declines. The Institute for Supply Management noted that new orders (for manufactured goods) dropped 15% in April, and production dropped over 27%.[12] That will not ramp up rapidly even if stock markets and GDP start to recover.[13]

Stimulus Programs to Stabilize and Restart the Economy

The federal response during the Great Recession started by helping financial institutions and then manufacturing recover from their asset losses. The initial response in the COVID-19 recession was to shore up the losses in personal income and the commercial losses in large and small businesses as people stopped traveling and reduced consumption. **Exhibit A-1** summarizes the major fiscal and monetary policy actions taken through April 2020.

COVID-19 recession fiscal measures committed through legislation, summarized in Exhibit A-1, through early May 2020 exceeded $3.5 trillion.

Exhibit A-1 Fiscal and Monetary Policy Actions to Combat the Coronavirus Crisis

Stimulus	Description
Fiscal Policy Legislated Actions to Support the Economy	
Coronavirus Preparedness and Response Supplemental Appropriations Act of 2020: Public Law 116-123.	This $8.3 billion was not primarily a stimulus act. Funds mainly were for emergency expenditures related to therapeutics and diagnostics, as well as vaccine research; public health funding to assist agencies dealing with the crisis; and medical supplies.
Coronavirus Aid, Relief, and Economic Security Act (CARES) of 2020: Public Law 116-136[a]	Up to $2.3 trillion in primarily fiscal policy actions; monetary policy actions in the act's Title IV discussed below.
■ Economic Impact Payments	Tax rebates or payments directly to households of up to $1,200 per adult and $500 per child, up to $3,400 per household; eligibility based on income and related criteria.
■ Small Business Paycheck Protection	Up to $349 billion in loans to small business, some nonprofits, and other organizations to assist them in paying employees. 75% of a loan goes to employee retention and 25% to other business expenses. Loan may be forgiven if funds are spent as required.

(continues)

Exhibit A-1 Fiscal and Monetary Policy Actions to Combat the Coronavirus Crisis   (*continued*)

Stimulus	Description
■ Employee Retention Tax Credit (firms facing foreclosure or other economic hardship)	50% tax credit on up to $10,000 on wages paid during the crisis.
■ Payroll Tax Deferral (air carriers and related businesses emphasized)	Employers and the self-employed can defer employer share of Social Security taxes owed until 2021 and 2022.
■ Grants up to $2.3 billion	Numerous targeted grants for a hodgepodge of beneficiaries, largely included because of horse trading among legislators in the House and the Senate.
■ Pandemic Emergency Unemployment Compensation	Workers able to work can received an additional 13 weeks of unemployment assistance if original benefits are exhausted. Includes self-employed, freelancers, and independent contractors.
Paycheck Protection and Healthcare Enhancement Act (aka the CARES Act 3.5) of 2020: Public Law 116-139[b]	Mainly provides additional funding for several programs within the CARES Act. The largest item was an additional $320 billion in funding for the Paycheck Protection Program (discussed above). Also included were funds for testing, relief for health providers' unreimbursed expenses or revenue losses, and additional small business disaster loans.
Monetary Policy Actions to Affect the Supply of Credit and Support Participants in Credit Markets (initial pledge of up to $1.5 trillion injection into financial system, later expanded to an undefined amount)[c]	
Fed lowered federal funds rates to near zero to improve liquidity of member banks and non-member banks	Reduces the cost of credit to banks and other financial institutions to stimulate their lending to businesses by lowering their borrowing costs.
Federal Open Market Committee (FOMC) purchases of agency (e.g., Fannie Mae and Freddie Mac)-mortgage backed securities	Called *quantitative easing*, purchases of up to $500 billion in U.S. Treasury securities and at least $200 billion in mortgage-backed securities to improve liquidity of member banks; subsequently, Fed announced removal of the $700 billion limit and included corporate bond purchases.
Title IV of the CARES Act included $500 billion to the Economic Exchange Stabilization Fund (ESF) for loans to businesses, states, and municipalities. ■ Primary Market Corporate Credit Facility (PMCCF) ■ Secondary Market Corporate Credit Facility (SMCCF)	PMCCF: Direct loans administered by the Treasury Secretary to distressed essential companies in specific industries such as air carriers and defense ($46 billion). SMCCF: Direct loans and securities purchases administered by the Fed Board of Governors for states, municipalities, and businesses and to purchase debt in the secondary market. Treasury holds direct equity position in the two credit facilities.

Stimulus	Description
Term Asset-Backed Securities Loan Facility (TALF), under authority of the Federal Reserve Act to support flow of credit to consumers and businesses	Enables issuance of asset-backed securities (ABS) backed by such lending streams as student loans, credit card loans, loans guaranteed by Small Business Administration, and others. The Fed can issue non-recourse loans to AAA-rated ASBs.
Money Market Mutual Fund Liquidity Facility (MMLF) to support flow of credit to households and businesses	MMLF mechanism is loans from Federal Reserve Bank of Boston to financial institutions to secure their purchases of assets backed by money market mutual funds.
Commercial Paper Funding Facility (CPFF) to support flow of credit to households and businesses	Like MMLF mechanism to backstop issuers of commercial paper by purchasing unsecured and asset-backed commercial paper directly from companies.

Excluded from this table are actions taken to address other coronavirus issues (e.g., health) that were not focused primarily on economic maintenance and stimulus actions. Included in these other non-stimulus actions are the Coronavirus Preparedness and Response Supplemental Appropriations Act of 2020: Public Law 116-123 ($8.3 billion) and the Families First Coronavirus Response Act: Public Law 116-127.

[a] U.S. Department of the Treasury (2020). *The CARES Act preserves jobs for American industry.* Retrieved April 28, 2020, from https://home.treasury.gov/policy-issues/cares/preserving-jobs-for-american-industry. Also includes additional detail from numerous secondary links included in the summary.
[b] Paycheck Protection and Healthcare Enhancement Act (aka the CARES Act 3.5) of 2020: Public Law 116-139.
[c] Board of Governors of the Federal Reserve System (2020). *Federal Reserve announces extensive new measures to support the economy.* Retrieved April 28, 2020, from https://www.federalreserve.gov/newsevents/pressreleases/monetary20200323b.htm. Also includes additional detail from numerous secondary links included in the Fed press release.

The anticipated impact on the federal deficit was over $2 trillion.[14] These measures were aimed at several affected groups:

- Tax rebates, deferrals, and direct payment to individuals to provide rapid relief from sudden loss of jobs
- Small and large business lending to support employee retention; extension of unemployment assistance
- Deferral, for as much as 2 years if needed, of employer share and self-employed Social Security taxes, focused initially on airlines among large employers
- Tax credits to businesses to assist in maintaining payroll during shutdown

In the Great Recession, fiscal measures, mainly the American Recovery and Reinvestment Act (ARRA), totaled less than $1 trillion. The CBO's final report assessing the impact of fiscal measures in the Great Recession summarized them into four categories:

- Funds to states and localities: transportation projects, Medicaid cost support, and education support
- Individual and family assistance: unemployment insurance, food aid
- Construction and other investment expenditures to stimulate growth and provide employment
- Tax relief for individuals and businesses[15]

Both sets of fiscal responses included emphases on assistance to individuals and families. Great Recession programs were more focused on traditional fiscal stimulus, emphasizing investments and projects that would provide employment over a longer time. coronavirus programs, at least initially, aimed at short-term relief, banking on the assumption that once health conditions permitted, the economy would pick up again rapidly without the need for longer term assistance.

Notable in the coronavirus fiscal responses, through the first quarter, was the lack of programs assisting state and local governments, hospitals, and other health facilities, in contrast to significant assistance (to state and local government) in the Great Recession. 24% of state and local revenues come from sales taxes, and 16% from individual income taxes,[16] both of which will be hard hit in 2020 (see the chapter on public sector in perspective). Though gas taxes represent a small source of total revenue to state governments, they are an important source of highway construction and repairs funding. Even with significant relief from stimulus programs in the Great Recession, state and local spending declined nearly 10%. Without federal assistance, the effects of the coronavirus pandemic on state and local governments are likely to be greater.[17]

As of the writing of this appendix, coronavirus responses were still in flux. State and local assistance almost immediately became a partisan dividing point. The National Governors Association, in mid-April 2020, requested $500 billion in assistance to the states to offset revenue shortfalls and stabilize budgets.[18] The Democratic-controlled House backed the need to assist state and local governments, passing in mid-May a $3 trillion package.[19] The Republican-controlled Senate and White House's early responses were refusal to consider the package. President Trump declared via a Tweet: "why should the people and taxpayers of America be bailing out poorly run states (like Illinois, as example) and cities, in all cases Democrat run and managed, when most of the other states are not looking for bailout help?"[20]

Only when the COVID-19 recession has run its course will it be possible to compare the two economic collapses and the remediation programs. The grim news as the unemployment problems approached Depression-era magnitude was likely to stimulate additional negotiation between the parties over more relief efforts.

The monetary policy responses to the two economic crises were similar. Federal Reserve commitments early in the crisis were over $5.5 trillion,

disbursing $2 trillion by mid-May.[21] It is important to note that the Fed's major actions in reducing the cost of borrowing and buying up debt from and lending to both member and non-member financial institutions do not have immediate implications for the federal budget and deficit except for interest on federal debt issued. The other operations are mostly within the Federal Reserve System's balance sheet.

As Exhibit A-1 describes, decreasing lending rates, quantitative easing, and opening new lending programs to both member banks (members of the Federal Reserve system) and other financial and nonfinancial institutions were the key monetary policy actions early in the COVID-19 recession. These same tools were deployed in the Great Recession (see discussion in the chapter on government and the economy). One key difference, however, is that the Fed, in 2020, did not have as much flexibility as in 2007. In mid-2007, the federal funds rate was approximately 4.5%; in mid-January, 2020, the rate was already as low as 1.5%.[22] This forced the Fed in 2020 to resort much more quickly to other methods to increase the flow of capital to financial and nonfinancial institutions. These methods are outlined in Exhibit A-1.

Conclusion

The purpose of this appendix is to provide a comparative perspective on the two most recent U.S. economic crises: the Great Recession and the COVID-19 recession. The comparisons are necessarily truncated as both the magnitude of the most recent crisis is unknown and the fiscal and monetary responses are incomplete. The perspective presented should help in understanding some of the similarities and differences. The precipitating causes are quite different in both cases: The Great Recession built over a lengthy period with a housing bubble and a mortgage market collapse, while the COVID-19 recession went from an optimistic economic picture with a GDP growth rate near 3% to an economic shutdown throwing tens of millions out of work in a matter of weeks.

The fiscal and monetary policy tools generally available to combat these two crises are generally the same. Their application differed for three reasons:

- Lending rates were already low in 2020, constraining the Fed's use of that instrument.
- The Great Recession began as the presidency transitioned from one party to the other. In 2008, President George W. Bush and President-elect Barack H. Obama collaborated to produce stimulus legislation prior to the inauguration. In 2020, the two political parties had been at loggerheads in the latter part of the Obama Administration through the Trump Administration right up to and during the crisis.
- The causes of the two crises were completely different.

This appendix focuses exclusively on the economic impact of the coronavirus crisis on the U.S. economy. The crisis was worldwide, and different countries approached the stabilization and recovery differently. Some countries implemented immediate, strict quarantine and other control measures, seeming to avoid some of the worst health and economic effects. South Korea, New Zealand, Singapore, Sweden, and Denmark were often mentioned in this respect. As of early summer, however, how successful efforts would be to develop treatments and vaccines was unpredictable. Accurate estimates of how many people were infected without showing symptoms, and even the rapid evolution of new symptoms themselves, render guesses as to what strategies will prove to be the most successful at stopping disease spread and moving economies significantly toward recovery.

Notes

1. National Bureau of Economic Research (2020). Determination of the February 2020 peak in US economic activity. Retrieved June 8, 2020, from https://www.nber.org/cycles/june2020.html. PDF also available to download from same site.
2. Ozyildirim, A. (2020). The Conference Board leading economic index for the U.S. plummets in March: largest decline in Index's 60-year history. *The Conference Board: Press Release*, April 17. Retrieved April 27, 2020, from https://www.conference-board.org/pdf_free/press/US%20LEI%20PRESS%20RELEASE%20-%20APRIL%202020.pdf.
3. Federal Reserve Bank of St. Louis (2020). *U.S. Employment and Training Administration, Initial Claims (ICSA)*. Retrieved May 7, 2020, from https://fred.stlouisfed.org/series/ICSA.
4. Swagel, P. (2020). CBO's current projections of output, employment, and interest rates and a preliminary look at federal deficits for 2020 and 2021. *Congressional Budget Office*. Retrieved May 2, 2020, from https://www.cbo.gov/publication/56335.
5. Federal Reserve Bank of St. Louis (2020). *U.S. Bureau of Labor Statistics: Unemployment Rate [UNRATE]*. Retrieved May 26, 2020, from https://fred.stlouisfed.org/series/UNRATE/.
6. U.S. Department of Labor, Bureau of Labor Statistics (2020). *News release: the employment situation- May 2020*. Retrieved June 8, 2020, from https://www.bls.gov/news.release/pdf/empsit.pdf.
7. Kelly, J. (2020). There's a glaring, misleading error in the May jobs report: U.S. may be at 20% unemployment. *Forbes online, June 8, 2020*. Retrieved June 8, 2020, from https://www.forbes.com/sites/jackkelly/2020/06/08/theres-a-glaring-misleading-error-in-the-may-jobs-report-us-may-be-at-20-unemployment/#4b9a5e4e60d3; Shapiro, R. (2020). No, the unemployment rate didn't really drop in May. *Washington Monthly online, June 5, 2020*. Retrieved June 8, 2020, from https://washingtonmonthly.com/2020/06/05/no-the-unemployment-rate-didnt-really-drop-in-may/.
8. Swagel (2020). *CBO's current projections*.
9. Federal Reserve Bank of St. Louis (2020). *U.S. Employment and Training Administration, Initial Claims (ICSA)*.
10. Long, H. (2020). Fed chair warns of 'heartbreaking' scenario as U.S. economy suffers worst first quarter since Great Recession. *Washington Post,* April 29. Retrieved April 30, 2020, from https://www.washingtonpost.com/business/2020/04/29/gdp-coronavirus/.
11. Swagel, P. (2020).CBO Interim economic projections for 2020 and 2021. *Congressional Budget Office*. Retrieved May 30, 2020, from https://www.cbo.gov/system/files/2020-05/56351-CBO-interim-projections.pdf.
12. Cahill, K. (2020). April 2020 manufacturing ISM: report on business. *Institute for Supply Management*. Retrieved May 8, 2020, from https://www.instituteforsupplymanagement.org/ISMReport/MfgROB.cfm?SSO=1.
13. Sheiner, L., & Yilla, K. (2020). *The ABCs of the post-COVID economic recovery*. Hutchins Center on Fiscal and Monetary Policy at Brookings. Retrieved May 16, 2020, from https://www.brookings.edu/blog/up-front/2020/05/04/the-abcs-of-the-post-covid-economic-recovery/; Bartash, J. (2020). Why the U.S. economy's recovery from the coronavirus is likely to be long and painful. *MarketWatch*, April 22. Retrieved May 16, 2020, from https://www.marketwatch.com/story/why-the-us-economys-recovery-from-the-coronavirus-is-likely-to-be-long-and-painful-2020-04-22.

14. Committee for a Responsible Federal Budget (2020). *COVID response: how much money has been made available so far?* Retrieved May 16, 2020, from www.crfb.org/blogs/covid-response-how-much-money-has-been-made-available-so-far.

15. Congressional Budget Office (2015). *Estimated impact of the American Recovery and Reinvestment Act on employment and economic output in 2014.* Retrieved September 14, 2019, from https://www.cbo.gov/sites/default/files/114th-congress-2015-2016/reports/49958-ARRA.pdf.

16 Data downloaded from Bureau of the Census, U.S. Department of Commerce (2018). Table 1: State and local government finances by level of government and by state: 2016. Retrieved May 19, 2019, from https://www.census.gov/data/datasets/2016/econ/local/public-use-datasets.html.

17. Beltz, S., and Sheiner, L. (2020). How will the coronavirus affect state and local government budgets? *Brookings: Hutchins Center Explains (blog).* Retrieved May 30, 2020, from https://www.brookings.edu/blog/up-front/2020/03/23/how-will-the-coronavirus-affect-state-and-local-government-budgets/.

18. National Governors Association (2020). *NGA outlines need for 'additional and immediate' fiscal assistance to states.* Press release, April 11. Retrieved May 9, 2020, from https://www.nga.org/news/press-releases/national-governors-association-outlines-need-for-additional-and-immediate-fiscal-assistance-to-states/.

19. Roll Call (2020). *House narrowly passes $3 trillion coronavirus aid bill.* Retrieved May 16, 2020, from https://rollcall.com/2020/05/15/house-narrowly-passes-3-trillion-coronavirus-aid-bill/.

20. As quoted in Edelman, A. (2020). Trump: government shouldn't rescue states and cities struggling under pandemic. *NBC News online,* April 27. Retrieved May 9, 2020, from https://www.nbcnews.com/politics/donald-trump/trump-federal-govt-shouldn-t-rescue-states-cities-struggling-under-n1193351.

21. Committee for a Responsible Federal Budget (2020). *COVID response: how much money has been made available so far?* Retrieved May 26, 2020, from www.crfb.org/blogs/covid-response-how-much-money-has-been-made-available-so-far; Karabell, Z. (2020). The Fed's unprecedented bailout of everyone and everything could prevent total collapse. *Time.com, April 1, 2020.* Retrieved May 26, 2020, from https://time.com/5813366/pandemic-financial-crisis-economic-crisis-looms/.

22. Macrotrends (2020). *Federal funds rate – 62-year historical chart.* Retrieved May 9, 2020, from https://www.macrotrends.net/2015/fed-funds-rate-historical-chart.

Concluding Remarks

Public budgeting, because it involves allocating scarce public resources, will always be at the center of debates about government. This is likely to be particularly true over the next decades as governments of all kinds, domestically and internationally, come to grips with the need to develop a sustainable fiscal policy. In many cases, political leaders will find that the promises they have made outstrip their capacity to pay for these promises. In the United States, this will necessarily mean coming to grips with mounting federal debt, exacerbated by two recessions almost in the same decade. It may entail scaling back on expenditures, augmenting revenues, or both, although even that statement is contested by some with arguments that much higher federal debt is sustainable (see the chapter on government and the economy). In the United States, to the extent that the federal government is forced to finally deal with its mounting debt, there will be ripple effects, not only on the state and local sectors, but on the private sector as well.

Although any predictions about the future should always be attempted with some humility, in this general environment of resource scarcity, recent experience leads us to conclude that the field of public budgeting and finance in the coming years will be characterized by sustained or increased attention given to several areas:

- Disagreements about the appropriate roles of government in the economy and society, including disagreements about the extent to which income and wealth inequality between higher- and lower-income families is sustainable in a democratic society
- Disagreements about the level and type of taxes, who pays them, and the viability of various revenue sources

- The role of information versus partisan preferences in budgetary decision making
- Financial management and financial reporting, including accounting rules for governments and nonprofit agencies
- Legislative–executive conflict over budgetary roles
- Setting priorities for the nation within the intergovernmental system, including the continuing need to consider the tradeoffs among the costs of security and disaster relief, emergency responses to pandemic health crises, and other pressing needs
- Promotion of economic growth in an international context
- Coming to grips with the fiscal implications of an aging society and with the consequences of promises that have been made to the elderly
- Dealing with the demands placed on public budgets from an aging infrastructure
- Responding to global climate change with the "right" resources and with enough of them to make a difference
- Budgeting for emergencies

In concluding, we would like to give brief attention to each of these areas in order to encourage readers to follow these debates for themselves.

Proper Role of Government

The first two decades of the new century were characterized by considerable debate about the proper role of government—the extent to which government should be involved in addressing income and social disparities and the extent to which government should bail out large corporations that find themselves in financial jeopardy as a result of their own decisions. Rising income and wealth inequality became a major focal point in national politics in the United States as well as many European nations. Social and constitutional issues have arisen over inequalities that differentially affect racial, ethnic, or other groups in society.

The United States ended the second decade of the 2000s with the greatest disparities in wealth and income levels between top- and bottom-income earners in more than a century, and with middle-income households realizing little income growth in more than a decade. To what extent are these disparities the proper province of government intervention, or should these matters be resolved by private markets? That question was complicated by the rapidity with which government intervened in the Great Recession (2007–2009) to save large corporations in the financial industry from the consequences of risks they had taken themselves. The issue was exacerbated by tax cuts in 2017 that reduced the average tax rate of higher-income taxpayers more than the average tax rate of middle- and lower-income taxpayers.[1] In the COVID-19 recession that began in 2020, lower income and racial and ethnic minorities experienced more difficulties in accessing health care and had more severe health outcomes. From a budgetary politics point of view, is government intervention in the economy either deliberately or inadvertently worsening disparities among different economic groups? If the government is contributing to these differences through taxing and spending decisions that may favor some segments of society and disadvantage others, does it become part of the government's responsibility to address the resulting disparities?

Resources for Financing Public Services

Financing public services is another controversial aspect of government. The resources that finance government do not just appear. In a democratic society, decisions must be made by the populace and their elected leaders to provide these resources. In a country founded in response to concerns about "taxation without representation," however, even taxation *with* representation has proved to be controversial.

There are many sources of this controversy. First, there is the question of the level of taxation. This question, although difficult, is often driven by a lack of consensus over how much money it would be necessary to raise in order to finance the desired level of services. This decision itself is quite difficult and controversial. Even after a decision about "how much" has been resolved, it does not tell us which taxes will be employed by a given government. The individual income tax and the property tax have provoked the most hostility, sometimes taking the form of specific limitations on the level of taxation and how taxes are administered. It is likely that these kinds of movements will continue.

Second, the question of who will pay what level of tax will remain the subject of great debate. Disagreements about whether a given tax should be progressive or proportional, or even how progressive it should be, are really debates about how the tax burden will be distributed across the population. If tax increases are part of the federal government's solution to its fiscal imbalance, this will lead to questions about whether the deficit should be reduced by taxing mainly higher-income people or whether there should be relatively equal sacrifice among income groups. Should corporations that achieve record earnings be able to escape paying any corporate income tax at all? The 2017 tax cuts that substantially reduced the role of the corporate income tax and the tax burden on income derived from investments is the most recent example. Republican presidents and members of Congress generally have taken the position that tax cuts to reduce the relative burden on corporations and high-income individuals repay themselves with increased economic growth. Democratic officials generally have held to the position that the benefits to the economy from tax cuts have not historically materialized, or have not trickled down to middle- and lower-income households.[2]

Third, there is the question of the viability of certain revenue sources, particularly the state and local sales tax. The popularity of Internet sales had threatened the sales tax, as states and localities found it difficult to collect the tax on items sold over the Internet and through mail-order catalogues. The recent Supreme Court decision (see the chapter on transaction-based revenue sources) permitting states to tax online sales has decreased this particular threat. A remaining threat to the sales tax is the reluctance to tax services in what is increasingly a service economy. This may eventually put pressure on these governments to turn to alternative revenue sources. Other taxes, such as those on certain forms of gambling, legalization of substances such as marijuana, and on corporations, have proven risky because the tax base for these sources is less stable than for some other sources of revenue, because the increased control of state legislatures and the governor's office by more conservative politicians has made corporate taxation politically less viable, and because (in the case of marijuana taxation) the disconnect between state and federal laws has created implementation problems.

Integrating Planning, Budgeting, Accounting, and Measurement

Although budget reform has contributed significantly to greater availability of information to executive branch personnel, elected officials, and citizens to evaluate the success of public services, the budget process itself, when it reaches legislative approval, does not seem to be influenced by information on the effectiveness, or lack thereof, of public services. This observation may be influenced more by the extreme political partisanship displayed in the U.S. Congress than is the case in some states. Budgetary decision systems in some states not only have increased capabilities to use program information when resources are allocated, but also display willingness to use program information in the decision-making process. Evidence-based policymaking in human services is a serious endeavor in a majority of states. Washington, Utah, Minnesota, Connecticut, and Oregon are among the leaders. Forty-one states require outcome data in the budget process.[3] The use of program information in the bureaucracy has been a moot question for years. The issue today is whether legislative bodies regard such information in their approval processes or are bound so tightly to partisan viewpoints that the impact on re-election to office is the more important consideration.

The integration of planning and budgeting, with the goal of informing the budget process with data on expected performance, is recognized as the crucial last step in making budgeting more performance-focused. While it is fair to say that many—perhaps the majority of—governments have made substantial progress in planning and in the supply of relevant measurements, many still fall short when it comes to the use of those measures for budgeting and management. The trend toward using performance measures does not mean that political realities will be removed from budgetary decision making. Rather, a greater array of information will be more readily available than in the past, and decision makers will have the option of considering that information in determining what positions to take on difficult problems. The desire—quite attainable—is not to have resource allocation driven by performance information in some kind of automatic sense, but to have more resource allocation decisions *informed* by considerations of performance.

Regardless of exactly how these connections are made, the movement toward performance-informed budgeting is unlikely to abate, largely because it focuses on the major budgeting question: Does the value that society receives from the public expenditure match or exceed the cost of the program or service? Growth in government programs will be accepted grudgingly, if at all, by taxpayers, who remain skeptical of the ability of governments to do many things well. Increasingly, this will mean that justifying government spending requires demonstration that "value for money" is being delivered. The overwhelming evidence from studies of performance-informed budgeting, at all levels of government domestically and internationally, is that performance information is much more likely to influence management of resources—that is budget execution—than the allocation of resources by elected officials.

Financial Management and Financial Reporting

Financial management—defined as the steward-ship of public resources after they are received—can hardly avoid being an important focus for the budget process. Particularly because these are pub-lic resources, the accountability for their use is even more important. Economic problems at the local, state, and federal levels have continued to make for "tight" budget situations that call for frugal measures. Governments frequently need to engage in midyear "rebudgeting" in response to unantici-pated spending pressures or inadequate revenues. Budget execution, therefore, will receive greater attention in the future. Can savings be achieved through closer monitoring of program spending? Can improvements in accounting systems lead to savings? What alternative financial arrangements hold promise for reducing costs? To what extent should governments pursue contracting out of ser-vices, privatization, and leasing arrangements?

The past 40 years have seen major additional requirements for accounting and financial report-ing for state and local governments. In large part, these have been spurred by the need for those external to government to have a better under-standing of government's financial position. For example, potential investors in municipal bonds desire to understand the underlying fiscal health of a given state, locality, or government enterprise. Prior to the institution of common accounting standards by the Governmental Accounting Stan-dards Board (GASB), it was difficult to draw any valid conclusions about the fiscal health of these jurisdictions based on information contained in their financial statements. Citizens and bond pur-chasers view as vital the overall performance of the entire jurisdiction, such as the local government, in maintaining and preserving the assets that have been the result of previous capital investment, much of it debt financed. At the federal level, successive presidential administrations for at least 30 years have made improving federal financial management and reporting a priority, even without the same kinds of accounting standards. Comply-ing with these rules and guidelines, however, can be complicated and costly for governments at all levels. For example, the requirement under GASB No. 45 that states and localities report the full accrued cost of employee benefits may ultimately cost these governments significant resources not just in reporting costs, but also in funding these benefits more fully in the interest of improving their stated financial position.

Legislative and Executive Roles in Budgeting

Executive and legislative bodies will continue their struggles with one another over their relative roles in budgetary decision making. Both execu-tives and legislatures may be less than assertive in dealing with the most intractable problems. Gridlock existed largely from 1981 to 1993 when Republican Presidents Reagan and Bush con-trolled the White House and Democrats largely controlled Congress. Gridlock has been a fea-ture since then with occasional exceptions—for example, in the first 2 years of the first Obama administration when Democrats controlled both houses of Congress and the White House, and the first 2 years of the Trump administration when Republicans controlled both branches. In fact, according to some analyses, the vanishing moder-ates in American politics at the federal level means that the extremes of the political spectrum have become increasingly dominant (see the discussion in the chapter on budget approval: the role of the legislature).

State and local governments have their own share of legislative–executive conflict. These con-flicts are made more or less important in a given jurisdiction by the relative budgetary power of the branches. Although some state governments have strong legislatures similar to the Congress, in other cases the legislatures are weaker because of short legislative sessions, term limits, limited staff, or a combination of all of these. It is probably the trend toward term limits that has weakened state legislatures the most, but that seemed to wane in the early 2000s.

Priority Setting in an Intergovernmental System

Governments will continue to be confronted with competing programmatic needs that must be met in a context of limited resources and intergovernmental relationships. Homeland security and natural disasters are likely to be high priorities for limited resources for the foreseeable future. Small wars, special military operations, and rebuilding at least conventional weapons systems that have been heavily depleted by the Iraq and Afghanistan wars also seem likely to continue putting pressure on the federal budget. For the defense budget, a key question will be whether forward basing of heavily armored divisions and air power in Europe and elsewhere is affordable.

Natural disasters claim an increasing amount of state and local governments' attention. The Federal Emergency Management Agency made over 6,000 emergency declarations between 2014 and 2019.[4] Federal agencies such as the Department of Housing and Urban Development have a budget to assist coastal states in preparing for disasters.

Programs for the elderly (especially Social Security) and health care will continue to demand the attention of the federal government (see more on this below), while all levels of government will be called upon to deal with emerging diseases, such as the 2020 coronavirus; drug trafficking and opioid addiction; and poverty and related conditions, such as homelessness. The coronavirus pandemic in 2020 demonstrated how quickly a thriving economy can fall into a deep recession, driving the federal budget deeper into debt and challenging the essence of the division of responsibility between federal and state governments, and the willingness of political leadership at both levels to accept responsibility. If Congress and the president ever make real spending reductions in order to lower the federal deficit, this may squeeze the funding available for all levels of government.

State and local governments, in contrast, will continue to find that financing elementary and secondary education will require new approaches as traditional sources of finance decline or are limited by taxpayer resistance. The pressures to improve the quality of education are likely to continue, both because of federal initiatives like the Every Student Succeeds Act and because of similar state-level accountability efforts. Although there is not necessarily a direct relationship between spending more money and education quality, it is nonetheless true that these efforts will put more pressure on the budgets of state and local governments. Difficult choices must be made over how other programs will operate and how they will be financed. Presidents, governors, and mayors may all lament the painful realities of dealing with a health crisis that overwhelmed some states' and cities' ability to cope, but where are funds to be obtained for dealing with these problems, and what types of preventative and treatment steps are most effective? Local governments may be willing to provide programs for the poor, but only if state and federal funds are available to support these efforts. The intergovernmental finance system will come under increasing scrutiny as the different levels of government vie for the same tax dollars.

Continued conflict among national, state, and local levels of government may be expected as new problems emerge that challenge existing intergovernmental divisions of authority and responsibility. Nowhere are the intergovernmental roles more complex than in attempting to ensure homeland security. How are security agencies at the federal level best able to relate to state and local agencies, especially given the long-standing tension that has existed among the levels of government? The confounding of immigration policy change and the financial burden on state and local governments imposed by the federal crackdown on illegal immigration in the Trump administration underscored these issues. The budget systems of all governments allocate large sums of money to security efforts, but how are agencies to be held accountable for results when buck-passing for any failures can easily be done in such a decentralized environment? The COVID-19 recession strained the understanding of what responsibilities are truly federal and what are fundamentally states' roles. Other continuing intergovernmental concerns include preemptions of authority by the federal government over areas claimed by state and local governments and mandates by the federal government to state and local governments and by states to local governments.

Promoting Economic Growth in an International Context

Promoting economic growth for the nation will continue to be a priority. In addition, states with high concentrations of industries that are technologically behind or not financially competitive, particularly with foreign firms, will continue their struggle to reorient their economies in search of new industrial niches. Other regions, such as those dependent on the price of petroleum, will continue through periods of boom and bust as petroleum supplies and prices and worldwide demand fluctuate. The extent to which state and local governments can affect their economic futures will remain uncertain because all governments are subject to the ups and downs of the business cycle. State and local governments that focus on improving the business environment in their states and communities, including education systems, living conditions, and attention to environmental issues such as climate change, are more likely to succeed in improving their competitiveness.

One of the most important sources of the uncertainty in promoting economic growth by all levels of government is the interdependence of the U.S. economy with the international economy. If there was ever any question that this interdependence existed, the two recent recessions should have resolved it once and for all. The Great Recession and the subsequent European debt crisis threatened financial markets around the world. The disease pandemic that precipitated the COVID-19 recession certainly demonstrated that political borders are easily crossed by some threats. The latter recession also exposed the potential risks of globally dispersed supply chains in which critical health supplies, such as protective equipment and medical technology, almost immediately were in short supply and depended upon manufacturers and suppliers around the world in countries also facing the same health crisis and same shortages.

What the U.S. economy makes and sells is intimately influenced by the economies of other nations. Perhaps none of these events will have a greater impact on the United States and the world than the rapid changes in the Brazilian, Russian, Chinese, Indian, and South African economies. The industrial mix of the U.S. economy and its labor force will inevitably change. These changes will arise at a time when the U.S. labor force is growing older as a whole due to the aging of the baby boomers. In addition, to the extent that more manufactured goods are produced abroad, the number of higher-wage U.S. manufacturing jobs will continue to decline. How budget systems will be able to respond to these challenges is unknown.

Dealing with the Budgetary Implications of an Aging Society

The U.S. population is getting older. As this happens, it will place pressure on the entire society—public, private, and nonprofit sectors—to deal with the budgetary implications of an older population. The most obvious implication for public budgets is at the federal level, where both Social Security and Medicare face mounting financial pressures. These pressures largely result from the nature of these programs, which transfer resources from current workers (through payroll taxes) to current retirees (through benefits). As the baby boomers retire and begin receiving benefits, the ratio of workers paying into these systems to individuals receiving benefits will decline. For Social Security, dealing with this imbalance is conceptually easy, because the federal government controls both sides of the Social Security equation—the taxes paid and the benefits received. A wide variety of fixes are possible, including tax increases and benefit cuts, but each of these is politically difficult because of the dislike for higher taxes and the popularity of the program. This comes at a time when public sentiment leans toward restricting immigration as a source of labor force growth in younger age groupings—a less restrictive immigration policy could improve the Social Security outlook.

Medicare is a different story. The financing problems of Medicare are driven in part by the aging of the population, but a more important factor affecting the future fiscal imbalance for the program is the generally high level of medical care inflation across the entire economy. This, in turn, is driven by factors such as increased life expectancy and the availability of often expensive drugs and procedures to prolong life. Medicaid—the shared federal/state/local program providing health benefits for the poor—is also substantially affected by the cost of health care. The solutions for financing both Medicare and Medicaid are also politically difficult, but perhaps the larger problem is that they are analytically insoluble. Simply put, it is hard to know how to bring down the cost of medical care without sacrificing other things that Americans hold dear, such as the choice of doctors and unfettered access to procedures.

In addition to these federal programs, state and local governments will find themselves needing to deal with rapidly increasing costs associated with employee retirement. In addition to the traditionally underfunded pension systems, the requirement that state and local governments report their "Other Post-Employment Benefit" liabilities (mainly for retiree health) has highlighted the huge gap between needs and current funding streams. As health costs continue to increase, this problem will only increase, and it will be compounded by the need for governments to provide health benefits to current employees, in addition to retirees.

Problems of an Aging Infrastructure

Particularly for state and local governments, the implications of an aging infrastructure will have important fiscal implications. The scope of this challenge is a wide one and includes roads, bridges, schools, university buildings, prisons, utilities, and numerous other capital projects. This problem has been almost continuously discussed by economists and civil engineers over the past 30 years, but little has been done to address it, with the exception of the temporary programs put in place to address the effects of the Great Recession. The infrastructure aging problem has only become worse. To the extent that a tight future fiscal situation hampers the ability of these governments to keep up with the rising infrastructure needs, this mismatch will be an ever-expanding problem. This, in turn, will create pressures for assistance from higher levels of government (federal and state governments) to assist with financing this infrastructure. In addition to the problem of having to build more infrastructure, there is the related, and costly, problem of maintaining what has already been constructed. Maintenance is an expense that is frequently underfunded, thus compromising the condition of infrastructure and accelerating the need for its replacement.

At the same time that there will be more pressure to increase infrastructure spending, the traditional sources of revenue to finance this spending may be particularly constrained. Even with the low energy prices, federal and state governments find it difficult to increase the gasoline tax at all; it will be even more difficult to raise it to a level that would be sufficient to meet the expected need. This will mean that governments will face tough choices as to whether to build new and maintain existing infrastructure at the expense of funds for other important functions.

As a result, governments will increasingly turn to creative financing arrangements—especially public–private partnerships. Although in some quarters controversial, public–private partnerships continue to grow in number simply because many elected officials will otherwise have to cut budgets or raise taxes to maintain and build infrastructure. In addition to these public–private partnerships, state and local governments will likely seek additional privatization or leasing strategies to provide needed infrastructure. This will increase substantially the need for governments to have qualified legal and contract management staff.

Responding to Global Climate Change

Although some politicians and citizens are skeptical of whether climate change is an issue requiring government intervention, or even exists, weather patterns contributing to more severe storms with changing patterns of rainfall (droughts in some regions, serious flooding in others) have created severe problems for state, local, and federal governments in the United States and around the world. Whatever one's theories or beliefs about the causes, governments at all levels in the United States have had to react to major hurricanes, larger and more extensive rain events, and larger and more extensive wildfires. These events have required greater coordination among levels of government and greater expenditures at all three levels (see the chapter on intergovernmental relations).[5] The political debate as to whether the problems are just natural cyclical weather changes that do not require governmental action or permanent changes that require immediate governmental actions has made it difficult for a coordinated response among levels of government and across political boundaries. At a minimum, budgeting sufficient resources to prevent and/or deal with the aftermath of major national disasters will likely be one of the key issues in coming decades.[6]

Budgeting for Emergencies

Increasing emphasis is likely to be given to planning *and* budgeting for emergencies in the future. Some emergencies can be more or less predicted and planned for, such as hurricanes. Others, such as wildfires, also are known to recur regularly. Although the number and location may not be predictable, areas more susceptible to the outbreak of a wildfire can take long-term preventive actions that may reduce their consequences. Governments at all levels currently have plans for handling expected emergencies such as planning to close schools during heavy snowstorms and budgeting for plowing snow and salting roads that are local and state maintained. All governments that are in wildfire and hurricane zones plan accordingly and may set aside some monies for coping with such emergencies. Similarly, other nations prepare for monsoon and typhoon seasons. The coronavirus pandemic proved to most countries that stockpiling equipment and materials and planning for a pandemic is woefully inadequate.

Mitigation may be attempted such as mandating "earthquake-proofing" of new buildings to reduce the loss of life and property damage. Humankind's crystal ball is never perfect such as Haiti not having been perceived as being earthquake-prone and then being decimated in 2010.

Stockpiling for emergencies can be helpful, but the issue always is how much is enough and how much will it cost. For example, governments have stockpiled food and water for human consumption and petroleum/gasoline for transportation.

Rainy day funds have been established in many jurisdictions to help finance essential services during crises. State governments grew their rainy-day funds after the Great Recession, but the early evidence from the COVID-19 recession suggests the rainy day funds will not be enough without federal assistance or actions by these governments to cut spending or raise taxes.[7]

The greatest problems are giant emergencies that for many decision makers seem to have a low probability, until they happen, and therefore may rationalize only limited planning and budgeting. Although some experts predicted terrorist attacks similar to what occurred on September 11, 2001, only limited planning and even scarcer budgeting were done. Recessions are part of the normal business cycle, but again decision makers were caught short being unprepared for the Great Recession that left local and state coffers drained and forced the federal government into vast spending for government services and for assisting private corporations to survive.

The most recent example is the COVID-19 recession and health emergency that began in the United States in early 2020. There had been warnings of a pandemic,[8] and since 1990 and the George H.W. Bush administration, there was a President's Council of Advisors on Science and Technology and a White House Office of Science and Technology Policy. Even so, decision makers were caught off guard for both planning and budgeting for something like the COVID-19 pandemic. State and local governments found their revenue sources drying up with people in lockdown, businesses closed, and taxes not being generated. Worse than the budget planning, there was no preparation for working within the intergovernmental system in the United States and no clear advance planning for which responsibilities would be federal and which state and local in a crisis that moved with the speed of the pandemic to shut down the economy, stress health systems, and leave people unsure about whose guidance to follow.

All emergencies challenge the abilities of decision makers to plan and budget. State and local governments with the expectation of having balanced budgets have limited abilities to cope with emergencies. The federal government's abilities to spend rapidly and with little constraint, demonstrated in 2020, comes at the price of a growing debt that over time may be unsustainable. Budget professionals are challenged by showing how they may contribute to managing major crises.

These themes do not capture all that is likely to transpire over the coming years. Based on history, the thing that is the surest is that the budgetary conflicts and decisions will mirror the conflicts and debates about priorities within the society. Much has happened since the first edition of *Public Budgeting Systems* was published in 1973. The Vietnam war ended; other wars began and ended. Three presidents were impeached: President Nixon resigned before trial in the Senate, while Presidents Clinton and Trump prevailed in their trials in the Senate and remained in office. The U.S. economy experienced periods of sustained growth and serious downturns, including the largest two recessions since the Great Depression of the 1930s. Budget systems at the federal, state,

and local levels have been challenged throughout to accommodate political processes that either explicitly or implicitly make decisions about the appropriate role of government and technical decisions about how to better inform budgetary decisions.

So what does all of this have to do with *Public Budgeting Systems*? We hope that the many exhibits, tables, and figures, as well as our analyses, almost all of which provide information over extended time periods, provide readers with both an understanding of budget systems and processes at all levels of government and the tools and data sources needed in managing budget systems from a legislative or executive perspective.

NOTES

1. United States Congress, Joint Committee on Taxation (2019). Distributional effect of Public Law 115-97, March 25. Retrieved February 24, 2020, from https://www.jct .gov/publications.html?func=startdown&id=5173.
2. Tanden, N. (2013). Burying supply-side once and for all. *Democracy, 29*, Summer. Retrieved February 24, 2020, from https://democracyjournal.org/magazine/29/burying -supply-side-once-and-for-all/.
3. Pew-MacArthur Results First (2017). How states engage in evidence-based policymaking: a national assessment. *Pew Research Center*. Retrieved February 9, 2020, from https://www.pewtrusts.org/en/research-and-analysis /reports/2017/01/how-states-engage-in-evidence-based -policymaking.
4. Brown, A. (2020). As states prepare for disasters, they acknowledge things will get worse. *Stateline*, January 29. Retrieved February 9, 2020, from https://www.pewtrusts .org/en/research-and-analysis/blogs/stateline/2020/01/29 /as-states-prepare-for-disasters-they-acknowledge-things -will-get-worse.
5. U.S. Government Accountability Office (2016). *Climate change: Selected governments have approached adaptation through laws and long-term plans*. Retrieved February 25, 2020, from https://www.gao.gov/key_issues/climate _change_funding_management/issue_summary#t=1.
6. Congressional Budget Office (2019). Expected costs of damage from hurricane winds and storm-related flooding. Retrieved February 25, 2020, from https://www.cbo.gov /system/files/2019-04/55019-ExpectedCostsFromWind Storm.pdf; Paul, K. (2018). Climate change has cost the government $350 billion: here's what it will cost you. MarketWatch, November 26. Retrieved February 25, 2020, from https://www.marketwatch.com/story/6-ways -to-prepare-your-finances-for-climate-change-2016-12-20.

7. Rosewicz, B. et. al. (2020). States' financial reserves hit record highs. Pew Charitable Trusts: State Fiscal Health Project. Retrieved July 12, 2020, from https://www.pewtrusts.org/en/research-and-analysis/articles/2020/03/18/states-financial-reserves-hit-record-highs#:~:text=Forty%2Done%20states%20grew%20their,State%20Budget%20Officers%20(NASBO).

8. Hoffower, H. (2020). Bill Gates has been warning of a global health threat for years; here are 12 people who seemingly predicted the coronavirus pandemic. Business Insider online. Retrieved July 12, 2020, from https://www.businessinsider.com/people-who-seemingly-predicted-the-coronavirus-pandemic-2020-3.

Bibliographic Note

This bibliographic note is intended to assist the reader in finding materials for further reading on public budgeting systems. Because the preceding chapters have extensive notes, we make no attempt here to recapitulate everything cited. The sources of data cited within the text and in tables, figures, and exhibits are extensively documented. Readers also will find the index to be a handy guide to references. This note is meant as an aid in identifying general references as well as sources that have produced and can be expected to continue to produce literature and data on public budgeting.

Numerous periodicals provide information about the theory and practice of administration in general, and budgeting and finance in particular. Most relevant journal articles are available online as well as in print. However, journal articles online are seldom free and many libraries no longer retain past volumes in print. Researchers, in most cases, will need access to a university library to read journal articles older than 1 year. Publishers commonly provide an abstract online, helping researchers identify articles they wish to read through public or university library subscriptions.

Online databases such as EBSCOhost, ProQuest Central, and Wiley Online Library offer full-text access to collections of journals for subscribers. JSTOR is an online full-text source for articles from over 2,000 academic and research journals, including most of the journals of interest to students of public budgeting and public sector economics. In addition to title and subject research, searching for text within the periodicals is one of the available JSTOR tools. Most university libraries as well as some large public libraries subscribe to JSTOR. Researchers need to check with their local libraries for access to these or other full-text databases, or for print copies of the journals described below.

Periodical indexes, once available in print and on CD-ROM, are now generally available to any user online without requiring the researcher to go through a library, although some require a subscription, which are typically held by large university libraries. Researchers may still need to rely on print indexes when searching for topics in older issues. Researchers should check with local libraries for access, or they may be able to pay a per-search fee individually for some databases. More specific periodical indices include *Current Contents Connect* (Web of Science platform online); *Journal of Economic Literature* (Pittsburgh, PA: American Economic Association); *Ingenta Connect; Public Affairs Information Service (PAIS) Index* (New York, NY: ProQuest [part of Cambridge Information Group]); and *EBSCO Discovery Service*, an index of journals and magazines that is published by EBSCO Information Services (Ipswich, MA: EBSCO). *EconLit* is the American Economic Association's electronic bibliography of economics literature, containing abstracts, indexing, and links to full-text articles in economics journals. *PAIS*, as its title suggests, indexes journal articles in the field of public administration and public affairs. *Ingenta* is a subscription service that provides for searches and full texts of articles.

Some of the most important journals that produce articles on budgeting and finance are as follows. *Public Administration Review* (Wiley-Blackwell Publishing for the American Society for Public Administration) often publishes scholarly articles on budgeting. *Policy Studies Journal* (Policy Studies Organization) includes occasional articles related to budgeting in its regular issues and in special symposia issues. *State and Local Government Review*

(Sage Publications) frequently includes budget-related articles that are particularly helpful to practitioners as well as scholars.

Public Budgeting & Finance (Wiley-Blackwell Publishing for the Association for Budgeting and Financial Management and the American Association for Budget and Program Analysis); *Journal of Public Budgeting, Accounting, and Financial Management* (PrAcademics Press); *OECD Journal on Budgeting* (Organisation for Economic Co-operation and Development); and *Public Finance and Management* (Southern Public Administration Education Foundation) focus especially on financial management and budgeting. *Government Finance Review* (Government Finance Officers Association) provides brief analytical pieces and news items on budgeting and finance. *Governing,* a monthly publication of e.Republic, covers U.S. state and local government and is a good source of short articles on general issues related to state and local government as well as examples from individual cities, counties, and states on contemporary issues such as a public transit privatization. The National Association of State Budget Officers (https://www.nasbo.org/home), the National Governors Association (https://www.nga.org/), and the Government Finance Officers Association (https://www.gfoa.org/) publish and allow free access online to annual reports and some publications. The Pew Charitable Trusts has several ongoing projects that publish reports and statistical series of interest to students and practitioners of state and local budgeting and finance. Of particular interest are their projects on State Fiscal Health (https://www.pewtrusts.org/en/projects/states-fiscal-health) and the Fiscal Federalism Initiative (https://www.pewtrusts.org/en/projects/fiscal-federalism-initiative).

Numerous journals cover the fields of public finance, policy analysis, and policy evaluation. Although occasional articles related specifically to budgeting systems appear in these journals, their usual focus is on specific budgetary subtopics. *National Tax Journal* (National Tax Association) and *Public Finance Review* (Sage) publish empirical and theoretical analyses of economic policy concerns, including government growth and size, tax policy, and fiscal and monetary policy, as well as economic analysis. Numerous journals are devoted to policy analysis and policy evaluation. In addition to *Policy Studies Journal*, the journals *Evaluation Review* (Sage), *Evaluation and Program Planning* (Elsevier), *Journal of Policy Analysis and Management* (Wiley for the Association for Public Policy Analysis and Management), and *Public Performance and Management Review* (Taylor & Francis Online) all share that focus.

Besides the periodicals concentrating on budgeting or related topics, other professional journals publish occasional articles of relevance. These include *Administration and Society*, *Administrative Sciences, Administrative Science Quarterly*, *American Economic Review*, *American Political Science Review*, *Journal of Public Administration Research and Theory*, *Management Science*, and *Public Management Review*. The Washington-based *National Journal* (https://www.nationaljournal.com/) and *Government Executive* (http://www.govexec.com) provide news and analysis of the federal government, including budgetary events. *Roll Call* (https://www.rollcall.com/), formerly *CQ Today,* is a daily publication covering congressional actions and politics; *CQ Magazine* (https://library.cqpress.com/cqweekly/) is a weekly publication publishing both news and analysis of congressional actions. Most of the journals listed have annual or occasional indices to facilitate general searches.

Another major source of up-to-date analysis and data is government publications. Federal documents can be located through the Government Printing Office through the federal government's main web portal, *govinfo* (https://www.govinfo.gov/). For statistical information, refer to the *American Statistics Index*, which indexes federal documents, and the *Statistical Reference Index*, which indexes state government publications. Both indices are published by the Congressional Information Service owned by LEXIS/NEXIS (Washington, DC). USA.gov contains an index of the various federal government agencies that collect and publish statistics with links to each agency (https://www.usa.gov/statistics).

Congressional documents can be identified and obtained through a variety of sources. A useful index is the *CIS Index to Publications of the United States Congress* (Washington, DC: Congressional Information Service, LEXIS/NEXIS). Many congressional documents are available through the *Thomas* database of the U.S. Library of Congress's website (http://www.thomas.loc.gov). The Government Accountability Office, which is an arm of Congress, has its reports available online as well (http://www.gao.gov).

In 2006, Congress passed the Federal Funding Accountability and Transparency Act, which provided for the creation of a federal spending database. The database, called *USAspending.gov*, is a central entry point for obtaining information about all aspects of federal government spending, including contracts and grants, by geographic area and recipient.

There are numerous online subscription databases related to government. LexisNexis Academic publishes business, news, and legal publications online in full text. LexisNexis State Capital covers all 50 states, publishing comprehensive information about state constitutions, laws and regulations, and details about state legislatures. ProQuest, in addition to taking over *Statistical Abstract* from the Bureau of the Census, publishes ProQuest *Statistical Insight,* indexing statistical data from numerous universities and private groups as well as the federal and state governments. ProQuest Congressional allows access to congressional reports, bills, and other congressional publications.

Students of budgeting and finance will find themselves returning regularly to several key government sources. The Office of Management and Budget (http://www.whitehouse.gov/omb), Council of Economic Advisers (http://www.whitehouse.gov/cea), U.S. Treasury Department (http://www.treasury.gov), Congressional Budget Office (http://www.cbo.gov), Government Accountability Office (http://www.gao.gov), the Bureau for Economic Analysis in the U.S. Department of Commerce (www.bea.gov), and the Federal Reserve (http://www.federalreserve.gov) produce publications and data of major import to the field. Each of the 12 federal reserve banks is a source of statistical series; tables and analyses from these reserve banks are referenced widely in several

chapters in this book. Reports from these agencies are available in print and on the web. Data related to international budgeting and economic issues are found in a variety of sources, including the World Bank (http://www.worldbank.org), the Organisation for Economic Co-operation and Development (http://www.oecd.org), the International Monetary Fund (http://www.imf.org), and the International Finance Corporation (http://www.ifc.org).

Several annual volumes from various agencies contain basic data on revenues and expenditures for local, state, and federal levels and intergovernmental transfers among levels. Data for state and local government revenues and expenditures from the Bureau of the Census's *Annual Survey of State and Local Government Finances* are available with a 2-year lag—data from the 2018 data were released in 2020, for example. Considerable care must be exercised when working from more than one source, as the figures do not always agree. For instance, some sources dealing with government and the economy use national income as a measure, whereas others use gross domestic product (see discussion in the chapter on government and the economy on national income accounting). In other words, users must be cautious when data are combined from two or more sources. The Census Bureau in the U.S. Department of Commerce published the widely used annual *Statistical Abstract* through 2012. The *Statistical Abstract* was outsourced to ProQuest, which has compiled and published since 2013 the *ProQuest Statistical Abstract,* containing most of the tables previously published in the Census publication. Most of the federal agencies collecting and compiling data still publish the same statistical series on which the *Statistical Abstract* relies. Researchers, including the three authors of this book, after getting used to seeking out the data series from the individual agencies and bureaus, have found most data series, including historical data on government finance, economics, the economy, employment, and so forth, readily available and convenient in downloadable data files. Students will find specific references in many of the tables and charts in this book.

The annual federal budget is available online in two formats from whitehouse.gov/omb/budget/:

1. PDF files of the entire budget including Analytical Perspectives, Appendix, Historical Tables, Supplemental Materials, Amendments and Releases, Mid-Session Review, and Fact Sheets. There are multiple PDF files covering the entire budget.
2. Excel files for many of the tables, including all Historical Tables (in a single ZIP file), and most of the supplemental materials that are in table form.

In addition, a CD-ROM of the full budget document and many supporting documents remained available through the 2019 Federal budget. The CD-ROM contains software to search, display, and print PDF files. Budget tables and the Historical Tables are included on the CD-ROM in spreadsheet format. The 2020 Budget was not made available in the CD-ROM format.

Another important source, the *Census of Governments*, is conducted every 5 years by the Bureau of the Census, U.S. Department of Commerce, and is required by law. It contains not only financial data, but also a wealth of organizational information. State and local government budget information, when released by the Bureau, is almost always 3 to 4 years out of date, except right after the Census of Governments. The Census Bureau is located on the web at http://www.census.gov. Publications in print and online of the Federal Reserve contain more up-to-date information on state and local government, but these publications do not disaggregate local from state.

Besides the Census Bureau, other providers of statistical information are located on the web. Analyses of federal budgeting and finance are published by private organizations such as the American Enterprise Institute (Washington, DC; http://www.aei.org), the Committee for Economic Development (Washington, DC; http://www.ced.org), the Heritage Foundation (Washington, DC; http://www.heritage.org), the National Bureau of Economic Research (Cambridge, MA; www.nber.org), the Conference Board (New York, NY; http://www.conference-board.org), and the Tax Foundation (Washington, DC; http://www.taxfoundation.org). The Brookings Institution (Washington, DC; http://www.brookings.edu) publishes numerous books on budgeting and taxation, as does the Urban Institute (www.urban.org). Brookings and the Urban Institute continue to collaborate on the Urban-Brookings Tax Policy Center (www.taxpolicycenter.org) and publish high-quality research related to taxation and expenditures of state and local governments. Two useful private sources of information on state and local government borrowing and the municipal bond market are the *Bond Buyer*, available in print and online by subscription only, and the public access website of the *Securities Industry and Financial Markets Association (SIFMA)* at http://www.sifma.org/. Some data are limited access to members only, but all of the data from this source in Chapters 13 and 14 were available for nonmember public access.

Books, of course, are an important source of information. Six of the classics in public budgeting, no longer subject to revision and updating, are the following:

- Willoughby, W. F. (1918). *The problems of a national budget*. New York, NY: Appleton.
- Buck, A. E. (1919). *Public budgeting*. New York, NY: Harper and Brothers.
- Smithies, A. (1955). *The budgetary process in the United States*. New York, NY: McGraw-Hill.
- Burkhead, J. (1956). *Government budgeting*. New York, NY: Wiley.
- Wildavsky, A. (1964). *The politics of the budgetary process*. Reading, MA: Addison-Wesley.
- Schick, A. (1980). *Congress and money*. Washington, DC: Urban Institute Press.

Histories of budgeting include the following:

- Browne, V. J. (1949). *The control of the public budget*. Washington, DC: Public Affairs Press.
- Lewis, C. W. (1989). History of federal budgeting and financial management from the Constitution to the beginning of the modern era. *Public Budgeting and Financial Management, 1*, 193–213.
- Meyer, A. E. (2002). *Evolution of the United States budget*, rev. ed. Westport, CT: Praeger.

- Rubin, I. S. (1993). Who invented budgeting in the United States? *Public Administration Review, 53,* 438–444.
- Webber, C., & Wildavsky, A. (1986). *A history of taxation and expenditure in the Western World.* New York, NY: Simon & Schuster.

Works on budgeting with a special focus, such as on the federal government, state governments, budget theory, and budget politics, include the following:

- Allen, R., & Tommasi, D. (2001). *Managing public expenditure: A reference book for transition countries.* Paris, France: Organisation for Economic Co-operation and Development.
- Bland, R. L. (2007). *A budgeting guide for local government.* Washington, DC: International City/County Management Association.
- Forsythe, D. W., & Boyd, D. (2012). *Memos to the governor: An introduction to state budgeting,* 3rd ed. Washington, DC: Georgetown University Press.
- Gosling, J. L. (2009). *Budgetary politics in American governments,* 5th ed. New York, NY: Routledge.
- Joyce, P. (2011). *The Congressional Budget Office: Honest numbers, power and policymaking.* Washington, DC: Georgetown University Press.
- Konigsberg, C. (2007). *America's priorities: How the U.S. government raises and spends $3,000,000,000,000 (trillion) per year.* Bloomington, IN: AuthorHouse.
- Koven, S. G. (1999). *Public budgeting in the United States.* Washington, DC: Georgetown University Press.
- Lu, Y., & Willoughby, K. (2018). *Public performance budgeting: Principles and practice.* New York, NY: Routledge.
- McCaffery, J. L., & Jones, L. R. (2001). *Budgeting and financial management in the federal government.* Greenwich, CT: Information Age.
- Michel, R. G. (2002). *Organization and design of an effective budget function.* Chicago, IL: Government Finance Officers Association.
- Mikesell, J. L. (2018). *Fiscal administration,* 10th ed. Boston, MA: Cengage.
- Nice, D. C. (2002). *Public budgeting.* Belmont, CA: Wadsworth.
- Office of the United Nations High Commissioner on Human Rights, & the International Budget Partnership. (2017). *Realizing human rights through government budgets.* New York, NY: United Nations.
- Reed, B. J., & Swain, J. W. (1996). *Public finance administration,* 2nd ed. Thousand Oaks, CA: Sage.
- Rubin, I. (2003). *Balancing the federal budget.* New York, NY: Chatham House.
- Rubin, R. (2010). *The politics of public budgeting: Getting and spending, borrowing and balancing,* 6th ed. Washington, DC: CQ Press.
- Savage, J. (2013). *Reconstructing Iraq's budgetary institutions: Coalition state building after Saddam.* New York, NY: Cambridge University Press.
- Schick, A. (2007). *The federal budget: Politics, policy, process,* 3rd ed. Washington, DC: Brookings Institution Press.
- Smith, R. W., & Lynch, T. D. (2003). *Public budgeting in America,* 5th ed. Upper Saddle River, NJ: Pearson Prentice Hall.
- Steiss, A. W., & Cyprian Nwagwu, E. O. (2001). *Financial planning and management in public organizations.* New York, NY: Marcel Dekker.
- Thurmaier, K. M., & Willoughby, K. G. (2001). *Policy and politics in state budgeting.* Armonk, NY: M. E. Sharpe.
- Vogt, A. J. (2004). *Capital budgeting and finance: A guide for local governments.* Washington, DC: International City/County Management Association.
- Wildavsky, A. (2001). *Budgeting and governing.* New Brunswick, NJ: Transaction.
- Wildavsky, A., & Caiden, N. (2001). *The new politics of the budgetary process,* 5th ed. New York, NY: Longman.
- Willoughby, K. (2014). *Public budgeting in context.* San Francisco, NY: Jossey Bass.

Edited volumes provide reprints of journal articles and originally prepared pieces. Many are more likely to be interesting for historical perspective:

- Aronson, J. R., & Schwartz, E. (Eds.) (2004). *Management policies in local government finance*, 5th ed. Washington, DC: International City/County Management Association.

- Banovetz, J. M. (Ed.) (1996). *Managing local government finance: Cases in decision making*. Washington, DC: International City/County Management Association.
- Bartle, J. R. (Ed.) (2001). *Evolving theories of public budgeting*. New York, NY: Emerald Group.
- Golembiewski, R. T., & Rabin, J. (Eds.) (1997). *Public budgeting and finance*, 4th ed. New York, NY: Marcel Dekker.
- Ho, A., deJong, M., & Zhao, Z. (2019). *Performance budgeting reform: theories and international practices*. Milton Park, Abingdon-on-Thames, Oxfordshire, United Kingdom: Taylor and Francis.
- Hyde, A. C. (Ed.) (2001). *Government budgeting: Theory, process, and politics*, 3rd ed. Fort Worth, TX: Harcourt College.
- Khan, A., & Hildreth, W. B. (Eds.) (2003). *Case studies in public budgeting and financial management*, 2nd ed. New York, NY: Marcel Dekker.
- Menifield, C. (Ed.) (2011). *Comparative budgeting: A global perspective*. Sudbury, MA: Jones & Bartlett Learning.
- Meyers, R. T. (Ed.) (1999). *Handbook of government budgeting*. San Francisco, CA: Jossey-Bass.
- Rabin, J., Hildreth, W. B., & Miller, G. J. (Eds.) (1996). *Budgeting formulation and execution*. Athens, GA: Carl Vinson Institute of Government, University of Georgia.

A variety of simulations are available to assist students in appreciating the dynamics of budget decision making. A web search for budget simulations will produce many possibilities for the student to explore. There are also simulations on reducing federal debt. The Committee for a Responsible Budget's simulation, called The Debt Fixer (http://www.crfb.org/debtfixer/), is a good place to start. Another good one is *Principles and Priorities*, sponsored by the Concord Coalition (https://www.concordcoalition.org/principles-and-priorities); there is also an online version, *Federal Budget Challenge,* of this exercise.

For literature on decision making, program budgeting, zero-base budgeting, accounting, economic policy, program evaluation, and the like, the reader is encouraged to turn to the notes for each chapter.

Happy reading.

Index

A

Ability to pay principle, 121
Accenture, 347
Accountability for results, concept of, 11
Account groups, 349–350
Accounting. *see also* Auditing, government; Governmental accounting
  accrual, 355–356
  allowable costs, 359
  approaches to the basis, 360
  blue book, 346–347
  cash, 355
  Chief Financial Officers Act, 1990, 345, 355, 380
  Circular A-134, 346
  classification of receipts and expenditures, 352–355
  cost, 356–358
  cost finding, 359
  double-entry, 351
  encumbrance, 355, 360
  fraud, identifying, 347–348
  of funds, 348–352
  generational, 360
  organizational responsibilities and standards, 344–348
  organizations, 345–346
  private sector reforms, 361–365
  project-based, 358
  purpose, 344–345
  risk and credit, 359–360
  standards and principles, 347
  state and local accounting systems, 346–347
  structure and rules of, 350–352
Accounting and Auditing Act (1950), 345
Accounting formula, 350–351
Accounting organizations, professional, 346
Accrual accounting, 355–356
Activity-based costing, 357

Activity-based management, 357
Adjusted gross income (AGI), 124, 127
Administrators, 10, 186, 230, 308, 311, 382, 501, 512
Adopt budget reforms, 199–200
Ad valorem taxes, 150, 156
Advance funding, 363
Advisory Commission on Intergovernmental Relations (ACIR), 478–479
Affirmative action, 327
Affordable Care Act (ACA), 482
Afghanistan war, 24
Age Discrimination in Employment Act, 499
Agency for International Development, 194, 233, 325, 352
Agency funds, 349
Aid for Dependent Children (AFDC), 495
Aid to Families with Dependent Children (AFDC), 275
Air emissions, 474
Airport passenger facility charges, 434–435
Alcohol, taxes on, 123, 155
Allison, Graham, 16
Allotments, 110, 298–299
Allowable costs, 359
Alternative minimum tax (AMT), 85, 128, 435
American Association of Motor Vehicle Administrators, 512
American Economic Association, 50
American Institute of Certified Public Accountants (AICPA), 347, 381
American Recovery and Reinvestment Act (ARRA) of 2009, 74, 85, 89, 217
American Society of Civil Engineers (ASCE), 417
Americans with Disabilities Act (ADA), 499, 510

Amusement taxes, 165–166
Analytical Perspectives (Office of Management and Budget), 226, 227, 310
Annual budgets, 115–116, 333, 455
Anti-Deficiency Act (1950), 274
Apportionment process
  and allotments, 110, 298–299
  apportionment plans, 301, 312
  budget execution subsystems, 110
  and budget revision, 301
  congressional passage of an appropriation bill, 109
  impoundment, role in, 109, 274
  influence on spending patterns, 74, 79
  legislative, 245–246
  preaudit, 110
  and sequestration, 275
Appropriations
  budget cycle and, 108–109
  lump-sum, 258
  subcommittees, 79, 272, 273, 282–283
Appropriations Committees, 289
  jurisdiction of, 283
  reconciliation process, 282
Approval of budget. *see* Budget approval
Army Corps of Engineers, 256
Arthur Andersen, 346
Articles of Confederation, 8
Asian Development Bank notes, 314
Asian financial crisis 1997, 42
Assessment ratio, 138
Asset decline in countries, 417–418
Asset management
  international asset decline and, 418
  overview of, 416–417
  reporting requirements and, 419
  spending on infrastructure and, 418–419
  U.S. asset decline and, 417–418
Audit committees, 382

E